Fouchard, Gaillard, Goldman
On
International Commercial Arbitration

Fouchard, Gaillard, Goldman

On

International Commercial Arbitration

Edited by
Emmanuel Gaillard
and
John Savage

KLUWER LAW
INTERNATIONAL
THE HAGUE / BOSTON / LONDON

Library of Congress Cataloging-in-Publication Data

ISBN 90-411-1025-9

Published by Kluwer Law International,
P.O. Box 85889, 2508 CN The Hague, The Netherlands.

Sold and distributed in North, Central and South America
by Kluwer Law International,
675 Massachusetts Avenue, Cambridge, MA 02139, U.S.A.

In all other countries, sold and distributed
by Kluwer Law International, Distribution Centre,
P.O. Box 322, 3300 AH Dordrecht, The Netherlands.

Printed on acid-free paper

TABLE OF CONTENTS

PART II
THE ARBITRATION AGREEMENT

CHAPTER I
THE AUTONOMY OF THE ARBITRATION AGREEMENT
(388 to 451)

CHAPTER II
FORMATION OF THE ARBITRATION AGREEMENT
(452 to 623)

CHAPTER III
EFFECTS OF THE ARBITRATION AGREEMENT
(624 to 688)

CHAPTER IV
ASSIGNMENT AND EXPIRATION OF THE ARBITRATION AGREEMENT
(689 to 741)

PART III
THE ARBITRAL TRIBUNAL

CHAPTER I
THE CONSTITUTION OF THE ARBITRAL TRIBUNAL
(745 to 1008)

CHAPTER II
THE STATUS OF THE ARBITRATORS
(1009 to 1168)

PART IV
THE ARBITRAL PROCEDURE

CHAPTER I
THE LAW GOVERNING THE PROCEDURE
(1171 to 1208)

CHAPTER II
THE ARBITRAL PROCEEDINGS
(1209 to 1301)

CHAPTER III
PROVISIONAL AND CONSERVATORY MEASURES IN THE COURSE OF THE ARBITRATION PROCEEDINGS
(1302 to 1345)

CHAPTER IV
THE ARBITRAL AWARD
(1346 to 1419)

PART V
THE LAW APPLICABLE TO THE MERITS OF THE DISPUTE

CHAPTER I
APPLICABLE LAW CHOSEN BY THE PARTIES
(1421 to 1536)

CHAPTER II
APPLICABLE LAW CHOSEN BY THE ARBITRATORS
(1537 to 1557)

PART VI
COURT REVIEW OF ARBITRAL AWARDS

CHAPTER I
FRENCH LAW
(1560 to 1662)

CHAPTER III
INTERNATIONAL CONVENTIONS
(1663 to 1716)

ANNEXES

TABLE OF ABBREVIATIONS

AAA	American Arbitration Association
AFDI	Annuaire français de droit international
AJDA	Actualité juridique – Droit administratif
AIA	Italian Arbitration Association
Alb. L. Rev.	Albany Law Review
All E.R.	All England Law Reports
Am. J. Int'l L.	American Journal of International Law
Am. Rev. Int'l Arb.	The American Review of International Arbitration
Ann. Inst. Dr. Int.	Annuaire de l'Institut de droit international
Ann. suisse dr. intern.	Annuaire suisse de droit international
App. Cas.	Appeal Cases
Arb. & Disp. Resol. L.J.	The Arbitration and Resolution Dispute Law Journal
Arb. Int'l	Arbitration International
Arb. J.	The Arbitration Journal
Arb. Mat.	Arbitration Materials
ATF	Arrêts du Tribunal Fédéral Suisse
Arbitration	Arbitration: The Journal of the Chartered Institute of Arbitrators
[Belg] Journ. Trib.	[Belgian] Journal des Tribunaux
BGB	Bürgerlisches Gesetzbuch
BGBl.	Bundesgesetzblatt
BGH	Bundesgerichtshof
Brit. Y.B. Int'l L.	British Yearbook of International Law
Bull. ASA	Bulletin de l'Association Suisse d'Arbitrage
Bull. Civ.	Bulletin des arrêts de la Cour de cassation (chambres civiles)
Bull. Joly	Bulletin Joly
Brit. Y.B. Int'l L.	British Yearbook of International Law
Cah. Jur. Fisc. Exp.	Cahiers juridiques et fiscaux de l'exportation
CACNIQ	Quebec National and International Commercial Arbitration Centre
Cal. W. Int'l L.J.	California Western International Law Journal
Can. Bus. L.J.	Canadian Business Law Journal
C.A.	Recueil de jurisprudence du Québec, Cour d'appel

CEPANI	Belgian Centre for Arbitration and Mediation
Chron.	Chroniques (Dalloz)
Colum. J. Transnat'l L.	Columbia Journal of Transnational Law
Comp. L. Y.B. Int'l Bus.	Comparative Law Yearbook of International Business
Dalloz Aff.	Dalloz Affaires
Dep't St. Bull.	Department of State Bulletin
DIS	Deutsche Institution für Schiedsgerichtsbarkeit
Disp. Resol. J.	Dispute Resolution Journal
D.L.R.	Dominion Law Reports
Doct.	Doctrine (Gazette du Palais)
D.P.	Recueil périodique et critique Dalloz
DPCI	Droit et pratique du commerce international
Dr. mar. fr.	Droit maritime français
E.C.R.	Report of Cases before the Court of Justice of the European Communities
Ed. C.I.	Edition Commerce et Industrie (JCP)
Ed. G.	Edition Générale (JCP)
E.T.S.	European Treaty Series
F. 2d	Federal Reporter 2d Series
F. 3d	Federal Reporter 3d Series
F. Supp.	Federal Supplement
FIDIC	Fédération Internationale des Ingénieurs-Conseils
Fin. Times	The Financial Times
F.R.D.	Federal Rules Decisions
GATT	General Agreement on Tariffs and Trade
Gaz. Pal.	Gazette du Palais
IBA	International Bar Association
ICC	International Chamber of Commerce
ICCA	International Council for Commercial Arbitration
ICC Bulletin	The ICC International Court of Arbitration Bulletin
Int'l & Comp. L.Q.	International and Comparative Law Quarterly
ICSID	International Centre for the Settlement of Investment Disputes
ICSID Rep.	ICSID Reports
ICSID Rev. – Foreign Inv. L.J.	ICSID Review – Foreign Investment Law Journal
I.L.M.	International Legal Materials
I.R.	Informations Rapides (Recueil Dalloz)
Int'l Arb. Rep.	International Arbitration Report
Int'l Bus. Law.	International Business Lawyer
Int'l Bus. L.J.	International Business Law Journal

Int'l Constr. L. Rev.	International Construction Law Review
Int'l Fin. L. Rev.	International Financial Law Review
Int'l Law.	International Lawyer
Int'l L. Rep.	International Law Reports
IPrax	Praxis des internationalen Privat- und Verfahrens- rechts
Iran-U.S. Cl. Trib. Rep.	Iran-United States Claims Tribunal Reports
J. Bus. L.	Journal of Business Law
JCP	Juris-Classeur Périodique (La Semaine Juridique)
J.-Cl. Comm.	Juris-Classeur Commercial
J.-Cl. Proc. Civ.	Juris-Classeur (Procédure civile)
J.-Cl. Dr. Int.	Juris-Classeur (Droit international)
J.D.I.	Journal du droit international
J. Int'l Arb.	Journal of International Arbitration
J.O.	Journal officiel
Journ. not. av.	Journal des notaires et des avocats
Jur.	Jurisprudence (Recueil Dalloz)
Law & Pol'y Int'l Bus.	Law and Policy in International Business
LCIA	London Court of International Arbitration
Leb. Rev. Arb.	The Lebanese Review of Arab and International Arbitration
Lég.	Législation (Dalloz)
Lloyd's Rep.	Lloyd's Law Reports
LMAA	London Maritime Arbitrators Association
L.N.T.S.	League of Nations Treaty Series
L.Q. Rev.	The Law Quarterly Review
McGill L.J.	McGill Law Journal
Mich. Y.B. Int'l Stud.	Michigan Yearbook of International Studies
NAI	Nederlands Arbitrage Instituut
NCPC	Nouveau Code de Procédure Civile
NJW	Neue Juristische Wochenschrift
Nw. J. Int'l L. & Bus.	Northwestern Journal of International Law and Business
N.Y.A.D.	New York Appelate Division
N.Y.L.J.	New York Law Journal
O.J.	Official Journal of the European Communities
O.A.S.T.S.	Organization of American States Treaty Series
Pas.	Pasycrisie
Rass. dell'arb.	Rassegna dell'Arbitrato
Rec. Penant	Recueil Penant

Rev. arb.	Revue de l'arbitrage
Rev. Barreau	Revue du Barreau
Rev. belge dr. int.	Revue belge de droit international
Rev. Cor. Esp. Arb.	Revista de la Corte Española de Arbitraje
Rev. crit. DIP	Revue critique de droit international privé
Rev. der. Mercosur	Revista de Derecho del Mercosur
Rev. dr. com. belge	Revue de droit commercial belge
Rev. int. dr. éco.	Revue internationale de droit économique
Rev. dr. int. dr. comp.	Revue de droit international et de droit comparé
Rev. dr. int. pr. et dr. pén. int.	Revue de droit international privé et de droit pénal international
Rev. suisse dr. int. et dr. eur.	Revue suisse de droit international et droit européen
Riv. dell'arb.	Rivista dell'arbitrato
Riv. dir. int. e proc.	Rivista di diritto internazionale e processuale
RD McGill	Revue de droit McGill
RGDIP	Revu générale de droit international public
RID comp.	Revue internationale de droit comparé
RID éco	Revue internationale de droit économique
RIW	Recht der Internationalen Wirtschaft
R.S.O.	Revised Statutes of Ontario
RTD civ.	Revue trimestrielle de droit civil
RTD com.	Revue trimestrielle de droit commercial et de droit économique
S.C. L. Rev.	South Carolina Law Review
S.C.R.	Supreme Court Reports
S. Ct.	Supreme Court Reporter
Sem. Jud.	La Semaine Judiciaire
Somm.	Sommaires (Gazette du Palais)
St. John's L. Rev.	St. John's Law Review
S.C.J.	Supreme Court Journal
[Sw.] Journ. Trib.	[Swiss] Journal des Tribunaux
Sw. Rev. Int'l Antitrust L.	Swiss Review of International Antitrust Law
SZ	Sammlung zivilrechtlicher Entscheidungen
Texas Int'l L.J.	Texas International Law Journal
Tex. Rev. Civ. Stat. Ann.	Texas Revised Civil Statutes Annotated
TGI	Tribunal de Grande Instance
T.I.A.S.	Treaties and other International Acts Series
Tul. L. Rev.	Tulane Law Review
Tul. Eur. & Civ. L.F.	Tulane European & Civil Law Forum

U. Miami Y.B. Int'l L.	University of Miami Yearbook of International Law
UNCITRAL	United Nations Commission on International Trade Law
UNIDROIT	International Institute for the Unification of Private Law
Uniform L. Rev.	Uniform Law Review
U.N.T.S.	United Nations Treaty Series
U.S.T.	United States Treaties and Other International Agreements
Virg. J. Int'l L.	Virginia Journal of International Law
WL	Westlaw
W.L.R.	Weekly Law Reports
World Arb. & Med. Rep.	World Arbitration & Mediation Report
Y.B. Com. Arb.	Yearbook Commercial Arbitration
ZPO	Zivilprozeßordnung

FOREWORD

This treatise is based on the authors' *Traité de l'Arbitrage Commercial International*, published in 1996 in the French language by Litec, Paris. However, this is not simply an English version. It is more in the nature of a second and revised edition, particularly given the rapid evolution of the law of international arbitration over the past three years. Several new arbitration statutes have come into force (notably in England in 1997, in Germany and Belgium in 1998, and in Sweden in 1999); major institutional arbitration rules were revised (including the International Arbitration Rules of the AAA in 1997 and the Arbitration Rules of both the ICC and LCIA in 1998); there have also been important decisions of both the courts and arbitral tribunals. These recent developments are of course fully considered throughout this book.

The original French language text, although a collective work, was divided between the authors as follows:

Part I	Definition and Sources	Philippe Fouchard
Part II	The Arbitration Agreement	Emmanuel Gaillard
	(on the basis of an early draft by Berthold Goldman)	
Part III	The Arbitral Tribunal	Philippe Fouchard
Part IV	The Arbitral Procedure	Emmanuel Gaillard
Part V	The Law Applicable to the Merits of the Dispute . . .	Emmanuel Gaillard
Part VI	Court Review of Arbitral Awards	Emmanuel Gaillard

This English version has been prepared and edited by Emmanuel Gaillard and John Savage, both of Shearman & Sterling, with Philippe Fouchard contributing to its updating. It would not have been possible without the contribution of a team of lawyers and legal assistants from Shearman & Sterling's international arbitration group. The team was headed by Nanou Leleu-Knobil, who also researched and edited all references. We are also very grateful to Andrew Butler for his translation work.

About the authors

Philippe Fouchard is the General Editor of the *Revue de l'arbitrage*, the leading French-language arbitration journal. He is Professor of Law at the University of Paris II, where he teaches international business and arbitration law.

Emmanuel Gaillard is a partner in the Paris office of Shearman & Sterling, and heads the firm's international arbitration practice group. He is also Professor of Law at the University of Paris XII and was Visiting Professor at Harvard Law School in 1984.

The late **Berthold Goldman** was President of the University of Paris II, where he was also Professor of Law. He edited two major French international law publications, the *Juris-Classeur de droit international* and the *Journal du droit international*.

* * * * * * * * * * * * * * * *

John Savage, co-editor of this book with Emmanuel Gaillard, is an English solicitor and a member of the Paris Bar. He is a member of Shearman & Sterling's international arbitration practice group, and is based in the firm's Paris office.

INTRODUCTION

1. — International commercial arbitration has witnessed dramatic growth over the last twenty years.[1] Although this reflects to a certain degree the underlying development of international commerce, international arbitration has flourished for a number of other reasons: arbitration is often perceived, rightly or wrongly, as being cheaper and less time-consuming than court proceedings, and is unquestionably more confidential; the resulting award is generally easier to enforce than a court decision, largely thanks to the New York Convention; more importantly, international arbitration is now acknowledged—because its international character reflects the nature of the disputes being resolved—to be a neutral method of settling commercial disputes between parties from different nations, allowing each of the parties to avoid the "home" courts of its co-contractors; finally, international arbitration gives the parties substantial liberty to design their own dispute resolution mechanism, largely free of the constraints of national law. This party autonomy is found at every stage of the arbitral process and, although not often fully exploited (with parties frequently preferring the plain application of institutional rules),[2] is perhaps the most fundamental difference between international commercial arbitration and the courts. Indeed, it will generally be when parties make effective use of their entitlement to tailor their own arbitration proceedings to their needs that international arbitration will provide cheaper and more satisfactory justice than any national court system.

It is for all these reasons that international arbitration has become the normal method of resolving disputes in international transactions. By contrast, in many legal systems domestic arbitration continues to be seen as an exception to the jurisdiction of local courts, even if the influence of international arbitration is now causing this perception to diminish.

2. — Over the same twenty-year period, there has been tremendous change in the law and practice of international arbitration. In the early 1980s, there was a marked contrast between a small number of arbitration-friendly jurisdictions with sound legislation and a developed body of case law, and a majority of legal systems which had yet to modernize their international arbitration regime or which were intentionally hostile to arbitration. Today, primarily through the influence of international instruments such as the 1985 UNCITRAL Model Law, there is much less to distinguish—at least at first glance—those legal systems which have traditionally favored arbitration from those which have only recently modernized their legislation. Likewise, the major institutional arbitration rules previously diverged on a number of key issues, but have now been revised and contain few significant differences.

---

[1] See, for example, with respect to ICC arbitration, *infra* para. 349.

[2] *See infra* para. 306.

In particular, the 1997 AAA International Arbitration Rules, the 1998 ICC Arbitration Rules and the 1998 LCIA Rules are strikingly similar.[3]

This trend towards harmonization is nonetheless tempered in three respects. First, an identical rule found in different legal systems or arbitration rules may give rise to contrasting solutions in practice. One telling example is the extent to which document discovery is ordered by arbitrators sitting in different venues but applying the same rule granting them virtually unfettered discretion to determine how evidence is to be taken. In practice, although they now generally agree to hear live witness testimony, arbitrators with a civil law background will prove far more reluctant to order extensive discovery than common law arbitrators.[4] Likewise, courts in different jurisdictions may adopt inconsistent interpretations of similar provisions of arbitration legislation. Second, despite the narrowing of the divergences as to the appropriate degree of liberalism to be afforded to international arbitration, recent legislation shows that significant differences remain. For example, although the principle of competence-competence is commonly perceived as being recognized worldwide, this is only really true of its positive effect (whereby arbitrators can decide their own jurisdiction when the validity of the arbitration agreement is challenged) and not of its negative effect (whereby the courts cannot rule on the existence of a valid arbitration agreement before an award has been issued by the arbitrators deciding their own jurisdiction).[5] Similarly, while most legal systems now allow parties to choose to have the merits of their disputes governed by "rules of law" (including transnational rules, rules common to certain legal systems and *lex mercatoria*), where the choice of governing law falls to the arbitrators there is no consensus as to whether they are entitled to apply anything other than the laws of one identified jurisdiction.[6] Other examples of subsisting divergence include the methodology to be followed by arbitrators examining the existence and validity of an arbitration agreement,[7] the appointment of arbitrators where one of the parties defaults,[8] and the grounds available to challenge an award before the courts.[9] Third, beyond traditional differences which have not—or not yet—been bridged, new ideas emerge which, at the outset, naturally find acceptance in only a minority of legal systems, thus creating fresh areas of divergence. This is the case of the recent Swiss, Tunisian, Belgian and Swedish statutes, which allow parties with no connection with those jurisdictions to waive actions to set aside before the courts of the seat of arbitration.[10] In the same way, the fact that parties are able to enforce in France and, possibly, in the United States awards which have been set aside at the seat of arbitration is a radical departure from the traditional position that awards annulled in their country of origin are unenforceable in other jurisdictions.[11]

---

[3] *See infra* paras. 321 *et seq.*

[4] *See infra* paras. 1272 and 1277 *et seq.*

[5] *See infra* paras. 671 *et seq.*

[6] *See infra* para. 1554.

[7] *See infra* paras. 422 *et seq.*

[8] *See infra* para. 792.

[9] *See infra* para. 1594.

[10] *See infra* para. 1594.

[11] *See infra* para. 1595.

3. — In fact, many of these examples of divergence find their source in a more fundamental debate: that surrounding the role of the seat in international arbitration or, in more abstract terms, that surrounding the source of the binding effect of international arbitral awards. As such awards are made by private adjudicators on the basis of a contract—the private expression of the parties' intentions—their binding force must be sanctioned by national legal orders. For some, this legal order can only be that of the seat of the arbitration. Following this reasoning, arbitrators derive their powers from the law of the place where they perform their duties, in the same way as judges serving in local courts. For others, however, the binding effect of an award—and hence the source of the arbitrators' powers—derives from the community of legal orders which, under certain conditions, are prepared to recognize and enforce that award in their respective jurisdictions.

This fundamental difference of philosophy explains many of the specific controversies regarding a number of very practical issues: according to the first theory, the arbitral procedure should be governed, failing agreement of the parties, by the law of the seat; the choice of law rules of the seat should be used in determining the law applicable to the merits of the dispute; the mandatory rules to be applied by the arbitrators should be those of the seat; no waiver of an action to set aside can be tolerated without jeopardizing the whole arbitral process; and, lastly, when set aside, an award ceases to exist and cannot be enforced in any jurisdiction. In contrast, under the second theory the arbitrators enjoy extensive freedom to determine the applicable procedural rules; they are also free to select the rules applicable to the merits, which, in keeping with the source of their powers, may be transnational rules; the only overriding requirements to be applied by international arbitrators are those of truly international public policy; a waiver of any action to set aside the award in its country of origin is conceivable; and, conversely, an award set aside in the country of origin may still be enforced elsewhere.

As will be seen throughout this book, of these two fundamentally different conceptions of international commercial arbitration, it is the second which is gaining ground and which represents, in our view, the better approach. This movement towards international arbitration as a transnational institution reflects the needs and expectations of the "consumers" of international arbitration, as international business itself becomes increasingly global and less country-specific. In this context, a uniform, transnational mechanism for resolving disputes is clearly the way forward.

4. — We shall examine hereafter both the broader trends prevailing in international arbitration and the more specific issues arising in national legislation and arbitral practice. In order to do so, we will follow the chronology of a typical arbitration. Thus, after considering the definition of international commercial arbitration and the sources of international arbitration law (Part I), we will address in turn the arbitration agreement (Part II), the constitution of the arbitral tribunal (Part III), the arbitral procedure (Part IV), the law applicable to the merits of the dispute (Part V) and the court review of arbitral awards (Part VI).

PART ONE

DEFINITION AND SOURCES

5. — Before examining the substantive aspects of international arbitration law, two preliminary questions need to be addressed.

First, international commercial arbitration must be defined as precisely as possible. The definition of international commercial arbitration is therefore considered in Chapter I.

Second, in light of the growing independence of international commercial arbitration from national laws, and especially from that of the seat of the arbitration, it is essential to analyze the various legal systems, international conventions and rules introduced by international practice which together contribute to the legal regime governing this method of dispute resolution. This analysis is set forth in Chapter II.

CHAPTER I
DEFINITION OF INTERNATIONAL COMMERCIAL ARBITRATION

6. — The expression "international commercial arbitration" is found in the European Convention signed in Geneva on April 21, 1961[1] and in the Model Law adopted by the United Nations Commission on International Trade Law (UNCITRAL) on June 21, 1985.[2] It also forms part of the full title of both of these important international instruments. To properly understand the meaning of the expression, it is necessary to define what is meant by each of the words "arbitration" (Section I),"commercial" (Section II) and "international" (Section III).

SECTION I
DEFINITION OF ARBITRATION

7. — In France, arbitration is traditionally defined along the following lines:

> Arbitration is a device whereby the settlement of a question, which is of interest for two or more persons, is entrusted to one or more other persons—the arbitrator or arbitrators—who derive their powers from a private agreement, not from the authorities of a State, and who are to proceed and decide the case on the basis of such an agreement.[3]

At first glance, there does not appear to be a serious divergence between French law and other legal systems as to the concept of arbitration. In Switzerland, for example, arbitration has been defined as:

---

[1] On this Convention, see *infra* para. 274.

[2] *See infra* para. 203.

[3] RENÉ DAVID, ARBITRATION IN INTERNATIONAL TRADE 5 (1985). *See also* PHILIPPE FOUCHARD, L'ARBITRAGE COMMERCIAL INTERNATIONAL ¶ 11 (1965); Eric Loquin, *Arbitrage – Définition – Nature juridique – Distinction avec d'autres institutions – Avantages et inconvénients*, J.-CL. PROC. CIV., Fasc. 1005, ¶ 1 (1997); CHARLES JARROSSON, LA NOTION D'ARBITRAGE ¶ 785 (1987).

a private method of settling disputes, based on the agreement between the parties. Its main characteristic is that it involves submitting the dispute to individuals chosen, directly or indirectly, by the parties. In international arbitration, this definition is preferable to the negative definition found in domestic law, according to which the principal characteristic of arbitration is the fact that the dispute is removed from the jurisdiction of the courts.[4]

Common law authors have defined arbitration similarly, as involving:

> two or more parties faced with a dispute which they cannot resolve themselves, agreeing that some private individual will resolve it for them and if the arbitration runs its full course . . . it will not be settled by a compromise, but by a decision.[5]

8. — Nevertheless, the difficulties encountered in certain domestic legal systems when defining arbitration and distinguishing it from similar institutions or mechanisms[6] are further complicated in international arbitration, for two reasons. First, there are differences between national legal systems as to their respective definitions of arbitration. Second, there is an ever increasing tendency in international rather than domestic trade to find new methods of preventing or settling disputes.

9. — In private international law, issues of characterization are generally resolved by reference to the *lex fori* (the law of the forum). However, that approach is unsatisfactory in the case of arbitration. In most countries, the courts will only rarely intervene in international arbitration, and then generally only after the arbitration has taken place and a party seeks to have the arbitral award enforced or set aside. Even if the courts of just one country were to review an award after it was made—which will not necessarily be the case—by that stage it would be too late for the courts to query whether they really were dealing with an arbitral award. Yet they would only be able to apply their national laws governing the review of arbitral awards if they were convinced that the decision submitted to them was indeed an arbitral award, and they would of course look to their own law for an answer to that question.

However, the issue must first be resolved by the arbitrators. Which law should apply? Given the contractual basis of arbitration, one may take the view that it should be the law

---

[4] BERNARD DUTOIT, FRANÇOIS KNOEPFLER, PIERRE LALIVE, PIERRE MERCIER, RÉPERTOIRE DE DROIT INTERNATIONAL PRIVÉ SUISSE – VOL. 1 – LE CONTRAT INTERNATIONAL – L'ARBITRAGE INTERNATIONAL 241 (1982).

[5] ALAN REDFERN AND MARTIN M. HUNTER, LAW AND PRACTICE OF INTERNATIONAL COMMERCIAL ARBITRATION 3 (2d ed. 1991).

[6] For all of these distinctions, see JARROSSON, *supra* note 3. On the concept of arbitration, its function as a dispute resolution mechanism and its attachment to a national or anational legal order, see BRUNO OPPETIT, THÉORIE DE L'ARBITRAGE (1998).

applicable to the agreement from which the arbitrators derive their powers.[7] In France, private international law traditionally favors this analysis, but it also recognizes the judicial nature of the arbitrator's role, which could conceivably cause the law of the seat of the arbitration to apply. The law of the seat is favored by those who traditionally think of arbitration as a judicial process to be assimilated with court litigation.[8] The weakness of such a position is that it is somewhat circular, but the law of the seat of the arbitration nevertheless has the advantage, in some cases, of being more predictable than the law governing the arbitration agreement.

10. — There are further differences between national legal systems concerning the arbitrators' powers to add to or modify contracts.[9] During the 1970s, this was a contentious issue among international arbitration practitioners,[10] and when, in 1978, the International Chamber of Commerce adopted special rules concerning the adaptation of contracts, it provided for recourse to a "third person," without being more specific, rather than to an arbitrator as such.[11]

11. — In our view, arbitration should be defined by reference to two constituent elements which commentators[12] and the courts almost unanimously recognize. First, the arbitrators' task is to resolve a dispute. Second, the source of this judicial role is a contract: the arbitrators' power to decide a dispute originates in the common intention of the parties. Thus, arbitration comprises both a judicial (§ 1) and a contractual element (§ 2).

---

[7]   For the determination of this law, see *infra* para. 422.

[8]   *See* F.A. Mann, *Lex Facit Arbitrum, in* INTERNATIONAL ARBITRATION – LIBER AMICORUM FOR MARTIN DOMKE 157 (P. Sanders ed., 1967), *reprinted in* 2 ARB. INT'L 241 (1986) .

[9]   *See* René David, *Le concept d'arbitrage privé et les conventions internationales, in* ETUDES JURIDIQUES OFFERTES À LÉON JULLIOT DE LA MORANDIÈRE PAR SES ÉLÈVES ET AMIS 147 (1964).

[10] See, in particular, the communications by the Fourth Working Party of the Fifth International Arbitration Congress, held in New Delhi, on January 7–10, 1975, on the "Techniques for resolving problems in forming and performing long-term contracts", *in* FIFTH INTERNATIONAL ARBITRATION CONGRESS – NEW DELHI, 1975 – PROCEEDINGS, C. IV and D. 239 (1975); for a summary, see N. Krishnamurthi, *Fifth International Arbitration Congress – New Delhi – January 1975*, I Y.B. COM. ARB. 227 (1976); 1975 REV. ARB. 3–140.

[11] ADAPTATION OF CONTRACTS – RULES – STANDARD CLAUSES – APPLICATION TO STANDING COMMITTEE (ICC Publication No. 326, 1978). Concerning these rules, which were withdrawn in 1994, see *infra* para. 40.

[12] In French law, see JACQUELINE RUBELLIN-DEVICHI, L'ARBITRAGE – NATURE JURIDIQUE – DROIT INTERNE ET DROIT INTERNATIONAL PRIVÉ (1965); FOUCHARD, *supra* note 3, ¶¶ 11 *et seq.*; HENRI MOTULSKY, ECRITS – VOL. 2 – ETUDES ET NOTES SUR L'ARBITRAGE 5 *et seq.* (1974); Gérard Cornu, *Le décret du 14 mai 1980 relatif à l'arbitrage – Présentation de la réforme*, 1980 REV. ARB. 583, especially at 584 *et seq.* Without seeking to give a definition of arbitration that is too abstract and summary, common law authors also highlight certain significant features of the process of international commercial arbitration: the consent of the parties, and the binding nature of the arbitrators' award, which can be rendered enforceable by the courts; *see* REDFERN AND HUNTER, *supra* note 5, at 3; MICHAEL J. MUSTILL, STEWART C. BOYD, COMMERCIAL ARBITRATION 41 *et seq.* (2d ed. 1989).

§ 1. – The Arbitrators' Judicial Role

12. — Arbitrators perform their judicial role by making an award. Thus, for example, Article 1496 of the French New Code of Civil Procedure, which states that "the arbitrator shall resolve the dispute," provides one indication that French law gives preference to this judicial aspect of the arbitrators' role. Other indications include references in the Code to the "arbitral tribunal" (Art. 1502) and, at Article 1476, to the fact that "[o]nce it is made, the arbitral award is *res judicata* in relation to the dispute it resolves." This domestic law provision applies to international arbitration, as is clear from Article 1500 of the same Code. Consequently, any arbitral award, whether made in France or not, is immediately deemed to be *res judicata* in France.[13]

13. — The judicial character of arbitration allows it to be distinguished from similar mechanisms, such as conciliation, mediation, settlement and expert proceedings.[14]

14. — There are two aspects to the arbitrators' judicial role: their decisions must be binding on the parties (A) and must resolve a dispute (B). These simple principles determine whether or not the proceedings in question in fact constitute an arbitration.

A. – ARBITRATORS' DECISIONS ARE BINDING

15. — An arbitral award will bind the parties to the arbitration. Arbitration can therefore be easily distinguished from other procedures where the intervention of a third party does not culminate in a binding decision.[15]

1° Arbitration, Conciliation and Mediation

16. — From a theoretical standpoint, the distinction between arbitration, conciliation and mediation is straightforward. The conciliator and the mediator endeavor to bring together the parties to a dispute but, unlike the arbitrator, they do not have the power to impose a solution on the parties. A solution in the case of conciliation or mediation can only result from an agreement reached by the parties, which generally takes the form of a settlement.

---

[13] On the consequences of this rule, see *infra* para. 1419.

[14] *See* Loquin, *supra* note 3, ¶¶ 56 *et seq.*; JARROSSON, *supra* note 3, at 111 *et seq.*; Bruno Oppetit, *Arbitrage, médiation et conciliation*, 1984 REV. ARB. 307; Bruno Oppetit, *Sur le concept d'arbitrage*, *in* LE DROIT DES RELATIONS ÉCONOMIQUES INTERNATIONALES – ETUDES OFFERTES À BERTHOLD GOLDMAN 229 (1982).

[15] *See* CHRISTIAN BÜHRING-UHLE, ARBITRATION AND MEDIATION IN INTERNATIONAL BUSINESS – DESIGNING PROCEDURES FOR EFFECTIVE CONFLICT MANAGEMENT (1998).

Although the search for a settlement by direct negotiation between the parties is a common means of settling disputes in international trade, it is only where a third party (the conciliator or mediator)[16] is involved that there is some likeness to arbitration.

17. — Over the past few years, conciliation and mediation have attracted a high level of attention in many legal systems.[17] This has been the case in France,[18] where various recent initiatives,[19] such as encouraging settlements in public law disputes[20] and allowing the courts to appoint mediators,[21] will doubtless have an impact on international disputes. It has been suggested that this revival of interest may be due in part to the growing role of Far Eastern countries in international trade, as they are traditionally considered to prefer conciliation to litigation.[22] More importantly, disillusion with the cumbersome, lengthy and costly nature of court and, to a certain extent, arbitral proceedings, particularly in the United States, have also contributed to this new-found enthusiasm for more flexible and less expensive methods of resolving disputes.

---

[16] There is no difference in nature between conciliation and mediation. Some commentators consider that "the mediator is a particularly active conciliator" (JARROSSON, *supra* note 3, ¶ 348).

[17] *See* BÜHRING-UHLE, *supra* note 15.

[18] Gérard Blanc, *La conciliation comme mode de règlement des différends dans les contrats internationaux*, 1987 RTD COM. 173; Robert Guillaumond, *Sur la conciliation interne et internationale*, JCP, Ed. C.I., Pt. I, No. 14,021 (1983); MICHÈLE GUILLAUME-HOFNUNG, LA MÉDIATION (1995); Gerold Herrmann, *Conciliation as a new method of dispute settlement*, *in* ICCA CONGRESS SERIES NO. 1, NEW TRENDS IN THE DEVELOPMENT OF INTERNATIONAL COMMERCIAL ARBITRATION AND THE ROLE OF ARBITRAL AND OTHER INSTITUTIONS 145 (P. Sanders ed., 1983), and, for the French version, *La conciliation, nouvelle méthode de règlement des différends*, 1985 REV. ARB. 343.

[19] These initiatives led one author to refer to the "blossoming of conciliators and other mediators" (Loïc Cadiet, *Chronique de droit judiciaire privé*, JCP, Ed. G., Pt. I, No. 3723, at 522 (1993)).

[20] *See* CONSEIL D'ETAT, SECTION DU RAPPORT ET DES ÉTUDES, RÉGLER AUTREMENT LES CONFLITS: CONCILIATION, TRANSACTION, ARBITRAGE EN MATIÈRE ADMINISTRATIVE (Work adopted by the General Assembly of the *Conseil d'Etat* on February 4, 1993, published by La documentation française (1993)); *see also* Yves Gaudemet, *Le "précontentieux" – Le règlement non juridictionnel des conflits dans les marchés publics*, *in* AJDA NUMÉRO SPÉCIAL, ACTUALITÉ DES MARCHÉS PUBLICS – TRANSPARENCE, FINANCEMENT, EXÉCUTION: UNITÉ ET DIVERSITÉ D'UN DROIT EN MUTATION 84 (July 20 /Aug 20, 1994); the French Prime Minister's circular of February 6, 1995 "regarding the development of recourse to settlement as a means of amicably resolving disputes," J.O., Feb. 15, 1995, p. 2518; Dalloz, Lég. 196 (1995).

[21] Following a law of February 8, 1995 (Art. 21), the French courts are now expressly authorized, with the parties' agreement, to appoint a third party as mediator, at all stages of the proceedings (*see* Charles Jarrosson, *Les dispositions sur la conciliation et la médiation judiciaires de la loi du 8 février 1995*, 1995 REV. ARB. 219; Richard H. Kreindler, *A New Impetus for ADR in France?: The New French Law on Mediation and Conciliation*, 7 WORLD ARB. & MED. REP. 59 (1996)). This law was implemented by Decree No. 96-652 of July 22, 1996 regarding conciliation and judicial mediation, J.O., July 23, 1996, p. 11,125; JCP, Ed. G., Pt. III, No. 68,072 (1996). Generally, see Gérard Pluyette, *Principes et applications récentes des décrets des 22 juillet et 13 décembre 1996 sur la conciliation et la médiation juidiciaires*, 1997 REV. ARB. 505.

[22] On conciliation in Japan and in Asia, see, for example, Noboru Koyama and Ichiro Kitamura, *La conciliation en matière civile et commerciale au Japon*, *in* RID COMP., SPECIAL ISSUE, VOL. 10, JOURNÉES DE LA SOCIÉTÉ DE LÉGISLATION COMPARÉE – ANNÉE 1988, at 255 (1989); Kazuo Iwasaki, *ADR: Japanese Experience with Conciliation*, 10 ARB. INT'L 91 (1994); Neil Kaplan, *Mediation in Hong Kong*, INSTITUTE OF INTERNATIONAL BUSINESS LAW AND PRACTICE NEWSLETTER NO. 14, at 59 (1995).

18. — A significant development is the promotion, in American and English business and legal circles,[23] of Alternative Dispute Resolution (ADR) methods and "mini-trials" in particular.[24] These techniques are not really new, but their proponents are attempting to revive and remodel them, to the point that some commentators also consider arbitration to be a method of ADR.[25] Yet, despite the exchange of written pleadings, the hearing of the parties and the presence of a "neutral advisor," a mini-trial is merely a conciliation (or mediation) procedure which will only bring about the end of a dispute if, following the hearing, the parties negotiate and sign a settlement agreement.[26] Whatever the name given to them (mini-trial, mediation or conciliation), these ADR procedures are found increasingly frequently in international trade.[27] However, they complement arbitration rather than compete with it.[28]

19. — There are certainly strong links between arbitration and conciliation. Because the role of any arbitrator involves attempting to reconcile the parties,[29] it is not uncommon in international arbitration for the proceedings to be suspended and subsequently brought to an end as a result of a settlement agreement reached by the parties and promoted or

---

[23] In the United States, the CPR Institute for Dispute Resolution (formerly the Center for Public Resources) is one of the many organizations successfully seeking to develop ADR; in England, the Centre for Dispute Resolution (CEDR) is active in this field.

[24] See Bruno Oppetit, *Les modes alternatifs de règlement des différends de la vie économique*, 1995 JUSTICES 53; the report of the *Rencontres internationales de droit comparé*, held in Damascus on October 5–8, 1996, on alternative dispute resolution methods, 49 RID COMP. 311–438 (1997); see especially the introductory report by Charles Jarrosson and the Canadian report by Nabil N. Antaki, published in LEB. REV. ARB., No. 2, at 10 and 20 (1996); H.J. BROWN AND ARTHUR L. MARRIOTT, ADR: PRINCIPLES AND PRACTICE (1993); Matthieu de Boisséson, *Réflexions sur l'avenir des solutions alternatives de règlement des différends (A.D.R.) en Europe*, INSTITUTE OF INTERNATIONAL BUSINESS LAW AND PRACTICE NEWSLETTER NO. 15, at 45 (1995); Hans van Houtte, *A.D.R. Discussed – A summary of an ICC Seminar on the Settlement of International Commercial Disputes – Brussels, 24-25 October 1995*, ICC BULLETIN, Vol. 7, No. 1, at 76 (1996). For a comprehensive overview of these alternative dispute resolution methods (ADR), see Jean-Claude Goldsmith, *Les modes de règlement amiable des différends (RAD)/Means of Alternative Dispute Resolution (ADR)*, 1996 INT'L BUS. L.J. 221.

[25] For this broad view, and for the sociological environment surrounding ADR methods, see THOMAS E. CARBONNEAU, ALTERNATIVE DISPUTE RESOLUTION – MELTING THE LANCES AND DISMOUNTING THE STEEDS (1989).

[26] For a description of the concept of a mini-trial, and numerous references, see Douglas A. Henderson, *Avoiding Litigation With the Mini-Trial: The Corporate Bottom Line as Dispute Resolution Technique*, 46 S.C. L. REV. 237 (1995); Jean-Claude Najar, *Le mini-trial: chimère ou panacée?*, 1988 DPCI 451.

[27] Robert Coulson, *Will the Growth of Alternative Dispute Resolution (ADR) in America be Replicated in Europe?*, 9 J. INT'L ARB. 39 (Sept. 1992).

[28] CLAUDE SAMSON AND JEREMY MCBRIDE, SOLUTIONS DE RECHANGE AU RÈGLEMENT DES CONFLITS – ALTERNATIVE DISPUTE RESOLUTION (1993); Bernard Hanotiau, *Arbitrage, médiation, conciliation: approches d'Europe contintentale et de common law/Arbitration, Mediation, Conciliation: Continental and Common Law Approaches*, 1996 INT'L BUS. L.J. 203.

[29] According to the French New Code of Civil Procedure (Art. 21), the courts also share this role as conciliator.

facilitated by the arbitrator.[30] The International Chamber of Commerce's Arbitration Rules[31] have long allowed for this possibility in a provision covering "awards by consent." Article 26 of the ICC Rules (Art. 17 of the previous Rules) provides as follows:

> [i]f the parties reach a settlement after the file has been transmitted to the Arbitral Tribunal in accordance with Article 13, the settlement shall be recorded in the form of an Award made by consent of the parties if so requested by the parties and if the Arbitral Tribunal agrees to do so.

The concept of an "award by consent" has also been adopted in the UNCITRAL Rules and Model Law.[32] It is primarily a settlement agreement "recorded" by a third party, but it also constitutes a genuine arbitral award. As such, it must satisfy the rules concerning the form of the award and, in the case of ICC arbitration, will also be reviewed by the Court of Arbitration before being notified to the parties.[33] It will then be subject to the same enforcement rules as an arbitral award made without consent, rendering it more effective than an ordinary settlement agreement should further disputes arise between the parties.

20. — However, the trend at an international level is to draw a clear distinction between conciliation and arbitration. For example, UNCITRAL adopted arbitration rules in 1976, and only then began to draft conciliation rules, which were completed in 1980.[34]

Likewise, several international arbitral institutions decided to offer a conciliation procedure entirely separate from their existing arbitration rules. This is the case, in particular, with:

– the International Centre for Settlement of Investment Disputes (ICSID), set up by the Washington Convention of March 18, 1965,[35] Articles 28 to 35 of which deal specifically with conciliation; in 1967, ICSID adopted Rules of Procedure for Conciliation Proceedings, which were revised on September 26, 1984;[36]

– the Euro-Arab Chambers of Commerce, whose Rules of Conciliation, Arbitration and Expertise, which came into force on December 17, 1994,[37] contain a special chapter (Arts. 12 to 18) on conciliation proceedings;

---

[30] However, the arbitral tribunal will—rightly, in our view—be entitled to refuse to perform the role of arbitrator-conciliator if it disapproves of the content of the settlement agreement.

[31] On these Rules, see *infra* para. 350.

[32] Art. 34 of the Arbitration Rules and Art. 30 of the Model Law.

[33] W. LAURENCE CRAIG, WILLIAM W. PARK, JAN PAULSSON, INTERNATIONAL CHAMBER OF COMMERCE ARBITRATION, Part II, ¶ 19.02, at 320 (1990).

[34] *See* UNCITRAL Conciliation Rules, VI Y.B. COM. ARB. 165 (1981), and the commentary by Gerold Herrmann, *id.* at 170.

[35] On this Convention, see *infra* para. 43.

[36] *See* ICSID BASIC DOCUMENTS 91 (1985).

[37] On these Rules, see *infra* para. 348; for the 1982 text, to which no changes were made concerning conciliation, see XI Y.B. COM. ARB. 228 (1986); 1983 REV. ARB. 217.

– the ICC which, on January 1, 1988, introduced fully revised conciliation rules, as a result of which conciliation proceedings, which remain optional, are now overseen by the Secretariat of the International Court of Arbitration of the ICC (and not, as was previously the case, by the ICC General Secretariat) and involve the appointment of a sole conciliator (rather than a conciliation commission);[38]

– the World Intellectual Property Organization (WIPO), whose Arbitration Center now offers Mediation Rules distinct from its Arbitration Rules.[39]

21. — The various conciliation rules referred to above all contain a number of principles fundamental to all international conciliation or mediation proceedings.[40]

Conciliation and mediation share some characteristics of arbitration. They can only be initiated by agreement of both parties, either in the main contract between those parties or later in a conciliation agreement. Above all, in spite of the non-judicial nature of conciliation and mediation, the procedure is set out in rules modeled on arbitration: there will be exchanges of written pleadings, hearings, and some rules even address issues such as the conciliators' jurisdiction and challenges.

On the other hand, a clear distinction is maintained between the "personnel" involved in arbitration on the one hand and mediation or conciliation on the other. The administrative bodies are often separate and, in principle, a conciliator may not subsequently be appointed as an arbitrator in a case where the conciliation process has failed.[41]

The role of the conciliator or mediator is simply to "[c]larify the issues in dispute between the parties and to endeavor to bring about agreement between them upon mutually acceptable terms."[42] The proposals or recommendations made to the parties after an initial investigation into the case are not binding. They will only become binding if and when the parties accept them by entering into a settlement agreement.[43]

---

[38] *See* ICC RULES OF CONCILIATION AND ARBITRATION 8 (ICC Publication No. 447, 1987); see also the commentary of these Rules, by Christophe Imhoos, *Le Règlement de Conciliation Facultative de la Chambre de Commerce Internationale: un autre mode de résolution des litiges commerciaux internationaux*, 12 CAH. JUR. FISC. EXP. 1279 (1991). The Rules of Optional Conciliation were not amended in 1997, but in the new ICC brochure (ICC Publication No. 581, 1997) they now appear after the Arbitration Rules and its annexes (at 46).

[39] These Rules are effective from October 1, 1994. *See* XX Y.B. COM. ARB. 331 (1995). Regarding the creation of this new Arbitration Center, see *infra* para. 336.

[40] *See* Marc Van Der Haegen, *Les procédures de conciliation et de médiation organisées par les principaux instituts d'arbitrage et de médiation en Europe/The Conciliation and Mediation Procedures Organized by the Main Arbitration and Mediation Institutes of Europe*, 1996 INT'L BUS. L.J. 255.

[41] There are, however, procedures referred to as "Med-Arb" proceedings, where the mediator, having failed to secure an agreement between the parties, is then required to decide the case as an arbitrator. Another similar procedure is known as "MEDALOA" (mediation and last-offer arbitration), in which the arbitrator must choose from the parties' final settlement offers; *see* Robert Coulson, *MEDALOA: A Practical Technique for Resolving International Business Disputes*, 11 J. INT'L ARB. 111 (June 1994); see also the "MEDALOA" model clause suggested by Marc Blessing, *Drafting an Arbitration Clause*, in ASA SPECIAL SERIES No. 8, THE ARBITRATION AGREEMENT – ITS MULTIFOLD CRITICAL ASPECTS 32, 76 (1994).

[42] Washington Convention, Art. 34.

[43] *See, e.g.*, Arts. 7 and 13 of the UNCITRAL Conciliation Rules; Arts. 7 and 8 of the ICC Rules of Optional Conciliation.

Finally, the confidentiality of mediation or conciliation proceedings is extremely important. All of the major international rules prohibit the parties from referring to proposals or evidence put forward during the conciliation in the course of subsequent court or arbitral proceedings.

2° Arbitration and the Role of the Engineer in FIDIC Contracts

22. — The *Fédération Internationale des Ingénieurs-Conseils* (FIDIC) authors the "Conditions of Contract for Works of Civil Engineering Construction" (often known as the "Red Book"), the fourth and latest edition of which was adopted in 1987.[44] This is a standard contract widely used in international construction and civil engineering projects and is based on the English Institution of Civil Engineers (ICE) Standard Contract.[45] The FIDIC contract involves three parties: the owner or employer, the contractor, and the engineer. The latter will generally be the firm of consultants, engineers or architects engaged by the owner under a separate contract to assist the owner and to act on its behalf during the performance of the works.

23. — Article 67 of the FIDIC Conditions provides for a fairly complex two-tier procedure for settling disputes arising between the owner and the contractor.[46] Any such dispute is to be submitted first to the engineer, who informs the parties of its "decision" within 84 days of the date on which the dispute was submitted. This "decision" must be complied with immediately by the parties, even if one of them disagrees with it. If there is disagreement, the dissatisfied party may challenge the engineer's decision within 70 days of notification, by informing the engineer and the owner of its decision to resort to ICC arbitration.[47] The arbitral tribunal then has full powers to amend, uphold or overrule the

---

[44] Regarding these new Conditions, see 5 INT'L CONSTR. L. REV. Part 1 (1988); E.C. CORBETT, FIDIC 4TH – A PRACTICAL LEGAL GUIDE – A COMMENTARY ON THE INTERNATIONAL CONSTRUCTION CONTRACT (1991); NAEL G. BUNNI, THE FIDIC FORM OF CONTRACT – THE FOURTH EDITION OF THE RED BOOK (1991).

[45] *See also* FIDIC CONDITIONS OF CONTRACT FOR ELECTRICAL AND MECHANICAL WORKS (3d ed. 1987), and the commentary by Dan Graham, *The F.I.D.I.C. Conditions of Contract for Electrical and Mechanical Works (Including Erection on Site) 3rd Edition*, 4 INT'L CONSTR. L. REV. 283 (1987).

[46] Georges Flécheux, *Le cahier des charges "FIDIC" et l'arbitrage*, 1984 REV. ARB. 451; Christopher R. Seppala, *Les principaux "claims" de l'entrepreneur aux termes des Conditions FIDIC/Principal Contractor's Claims under the FIDIC International Civil Engineering Contract*, 1985 INT'L BUS. L.J. 171; for a commentary on the version of Article 67 found in the 4th edition, see Christopher R. Seppala, *La procédure pré-arbitrale de règlement des litiges selon les conditions du contrat-type de génie civil de la FIDIC/The Pre-Arbitral Procedure for the Settlement of Disputes in the FIDIC (Civil Engineering) Conditions of Contract*, 1987 INT'L BUS. L.J. 579; Isabelle Hautot and Georges Flécheux, *La clause de règlement des différends dans les Conditions F.I.D.I.C. génie civil de 1987*, 1989 REV. ARB. 609; Hubert André-Dumont, *The F.I.D.I.C. Conditions and Civil Law*, 5 INT'L CONSTR. L. REV. 43 (1988); Christopher R. Seppala, *International Construction Contract Disputes: Commentary on ICC Awards Dealing with the FIDIC International Conditions of Contract*, ICC BULLETIN, Vol. 9, No. 2, at 32 (1998).

[47] Many ICC awards have been made following a decision of an engineer, and some are published in INT'L CONSTR. L. REV., or in ICC BULLETIN (Vol. 2, No. 1, at 15 (1991) and Vol. 9, No. 1, at 74 (1998)); *see also*

(continued...)

engineer's decision. However, the arbitration cannot begin unless the parties have first attempted to resolve their dispute amicably. In the absence of a stipulation to the contrary, this pre-condition is deemed satisfied simply upon the expiration of a period of 56 days.

24. — In disputes arising from FIDIC contracts there is thus a compulsory pre-arbitral stage, which takes place before the engineer. However, in addition to the fact that it is appointed and remunerated exclusively by the owner, the engineer itself is often at the heart of the dispute. For instance, the dispute may concern the involvement of the engineer in the performance of the contract, often in matters of certification of works for payment. For these reasons, the powers attributed to the engineer have often been criticized.[48] As a result, in a supplement to the Red Book published in 1996, FIDIC proposed the submission of disputes to a Dispute Adjudication Board (DAB) rather than to the engineer.[49]

The engineer's intervention can hardly be described as arbitration[50] or even quasi-arbitration. The engineer is not required to follow a pre-determined procedure before reaching a decision, and any decision is provisional. Although the engineer's decision must be carried out immediately in order to ensure continuation of the works, it will only become final if it remains unchallenged or if it is upheld by an arbitral award. The compulsory nature of the decision stems, in the former case, from the common intention of the parties and, in the latter, from the fact that the award is *res judicata*.

3° Arbitration and Expert Proceedings

25. — The role of a court-appointed expert is strictly limited to giving an opinion to enlighten the court on specific technical issues.[51] The expert's opinion binds neither the parties nor the court. The same is true, in principle, where an expert is appointed by an

---

[47](...continued)
ICC Award No. 6535 (1992), 120 J.D.I. 1024 (1993), and observations by D. Hascher; regarding compliance with the condition that the engineer be seized first, see CA Paris, Mar. 10, 1988, Crocodile Tourist Project Co. (Egypte) v. Aubert, 1989 REV. ARB. 269, and P. Fouchard's note; on the result of a failure to respond to an engineer's decision, which raises the question of admissibility and not the jurisdiction of the arbitrator, see CA Paris, Dec. 1, 1995, Ministère de l'Agriculture d'Irak v. Hochtief, 1996 REV. ARB. 456, and J.-M. Talau's note.

[48] See the articles by Flécheux and Seppala, *supra* note 46.

[49] On the nature and role of these Dispute Adjudication Boards, see *infra* para. 28.

[50] *See* ICC Award No. 3790 (1983), French contractor v. Libyan owner, 110 J.D.I. 910 (1983), and observations by S. Jarvin; for an English translation, see XI Y.B. COM. ARB. 119 (1986); Flécheux, *supra* note 46; JARROSSON, *supra* note 3, ¶ 712; André-Dumont, *supra* note 46; *comp. with* Fritz Nicklisch, *The Role of the Engineer as Contract Administrator and Quasi-Arbitrator in International Construction and Civil Engineering Projects*, 7 INT'L CONSTR. L. REV. 322 (1990).

[51] See, for example, in France, Article 232 of the French New Code of Civil Procedure.

international arbitral tribunal.[52] Even if the expert is required to give all parties a fair hearing, in no way does his or her report constitute an arbitral award.

26. — This fairly simple distinction between arbitration and expert proceedings is sometimes blurred by the terminology used and the diversity of situations encountered in international practice. If the parties confer a power of decision (to decide a technical dispute, or to evaluate an item of property or loss) on a third party to whom they refer as an expert, that third party is in fact either an arbitrator[53] or, in the absence of a dispute, an agent appointed by both parties.[54] This form of binding expert proceedings is often referred to as expertise-arbitration (*Schiedsgutachten* in German, *arbitraggio* in Italian, *bindend advies* in Dutch).[55]

27. — In practice, arbitrations where the dispute relates solely to the quality of goods delivered, or "quality arbitrations," are very common. In such cases, the goods are examined by technical experts acting as arbitrators, and are compared with the contractual specifications and the samples provided. The arbitrators then decide whether the goods meet the specifications and may order payment by the seller of the difference in price resulting from the actual quality (or quantity) of the goods delivered. As the binding nature of these decisions is not in doubt, they will constitute arbitral awards if they resolve a dispute between the parties.[56]

28. — In the engineering and construction fields, many of the difficulties which arise between the parties are of a purely technical nature. When these difficulties lead to a genuine dispute, the parties may consider the appointment of arbitrators, all or some of whom are themselves technically qualified. Alternatively, the parties may appoint non-technical arbitrators who in turn may find that they need to seek expert advice.

In practice, efforts are often made to prevent these international construction disputes reaching arbitration by appointing independent experts as soon as the first incident arises.

---

[52] In practice, alongside this neutral expert, to whom a technical brief is given by the arbitrators themselves, there may also be expert witnesses, who provide technical advice for the arbitrators on the initiative and generally in favor of the party which appointed and paid them to do so. The confrontation of expert witnesses is favored in common law systems, whereas civil law systems usually prefer neutral experts appointed by the arbitrator. On this issue, see ARBITRATION AND EXPERTISE (ICC Publication No. 480/7, 1994), and, in particular, the introductory report by Isabelle Hautot (at 11) and the summary by Jean-François Poudret (at 119).

[53] To avoid any difficulties of characterization, the 1986 Netherlands Arbitration Act allows the parties in any event to "submit . . . to arbitration: (a) the determination only of the quality or condition of goods; (b) the determination only of the quantum of damages or a monetary debt" (Code of Civil Procedure, Art. 1020(4)).

[54] On the power of the arbitrator to construe an "irrevocable" expert report, see CA Paris, Apr. 6, 1995, Thyssen Stahlunion v. Maaden, 1995 REV. ARB. 448, 5th decision; 122 J.D.I. 971 (1995), and E. Loquin's note; 1996 RTD COM. 447, and observations by J.-C. Dubarry and E. Loquin.

[55] *See* KLAUS PETER BERGER, INTERNATIONAL ECONOMIC ARBITRATION 73 *et seq.* (1993).

[56] *See infra* paras. 30 *et seq.*

In such cases, the technical expertise is moved upstream of the arbitration proceedings and may enable them to be avoided entirely.[57]

Since experts or panels of experts are assumed to be totally independent, their involvement in arbitration proceedings does not give rise to the same reservations as that of the FIDIC engineer. In large contracts, it is not uncommon for the parties to confer the same decision-making power on an expert as is conferred upon a FIDIC engineer, so that the decision made by the expert binds the parties unless they challenge it within a fixed period before an arbitral tribunal. This is the case with the standard contract for factory construction adopted in 1992 by the Engineering Advancement Association of Japan (ENAA),[58] and likewise with the Channel Tunnel construction contract, Article 67 of which provided for the involvement of a panel of three individuals acting as experts.[59] More recently, FIDIC opted for this system in its 1995 Conditions of Contract for Design-Build and Turnkey (known as the "Orange Book"). From the outset of the contract, the parties together appoint a Dispute Adjudication Board (DAB), all members of which are independent of the parties and impartial. The Board's decision is binding unless challenged before an arbitrator.[60] Similarly, in its 1996 Supplement to the Red Book, FIDIC now offers, as an "acceptable alternative" to the submission of disputes to the engineer, the constitution of a DAB, consisting of either one or three independent persons.[61] A party that is dissatisfied with the decision of the DAB may then refer the dispute to arbitration.[62] Dispute Review Boards are also often found in international engineering contracts. They are set up for the duration of the project and can only make recommendations.[63] The same is true of the Adjudicator

---

[57] See Lazare Kopelmanas, *Le rôle de l'expertise dans l'arbitrage commercial international*, 1979 REV. ARB. 205.

[58] Article 6.2, published with a commentary by Jean-François Bourque, *L'expérience du Centre international d'expertise de la CCI et le développement de l'expertise internationale*, 1995 REV. ARB. 231, 241.

[59] Article 67 provided for an initial panel of three individuals acting as "independent experts but not as arbitrators," making rapid and immediately binding decisions which could be challenged within a fixed time period before an arbitral tribunal (*see* Channel Tunnel Group Ltd. v. Balfour Beatty Construction Ltd., [1993] A.C. 334; [1993] 1 All E.R. 664; [1993] 2 W.L.R. 262; [1993] 1 Lloyd's Rep. 291; XIX Y.B. COM. ARB. 736 (1994); 1993 BULL. ASA 97, especially at 102 *et seq.* (H.L. 1993)).

[60] See Part I, General conditions, Art. 20.3 (1st ed. 1995), *reprinted in* DICTIONNAIRE JOLY – PRATIQUE DES CONTRATS INTERNATIONAUX, Book XXIV, Doc. 9-1; *see also* Gordon L. Jaynes, *The New Colour in FIDIC's Rainbow: The Trial Edition of the "Orange Book"*, 12 INT'L CONSTR. L. REV. 367 (1995). Bruno de Cazalet and Rupert Reece, *Conditions applicables aux contrats de conception-construction et clés en main/Conditions of Contract for Design-Build and Turnkey*, 1996 INT'L BUS. L.J. 279.

[61] See *supra* paras. 22 *et seq.*

[62] For the full text of the amendments made to Clause 67, see 1997 INT'L BUS. L.J. 986; for a commentary, see Christopher R. Seppala, *The New FIDIC Provision for a Dispute Adjudication Board/ Les nouvelles dispositions FIDIC pour un Comité de règlement des différends*, 1997 INT'L BUS. L.J. 967; Pierre M. Genton, *Le DRB/DAB, un véritable complément à l'arbitrage*, 1997 BULL. ASA 416; Pierre M. Genton and François Vermeille, *Soft and Hard Dispute Resolution – Quelques réflexions et expériences pratiques dans le cadre de grands projets/Soft and Hard Dispute Resolution – Some Remarks and Practical Experiences Regarding Mega-projects*, 1998 INT'L BUS. L.J. 131.

[63] These Dispute Review Boards, which were first set up by the American Society of Civil Engineers, have been used in a variety of major international projects; *see* Bourque, *supra* note 58.

provided for in the standard engineering contract drawn up by the Institution of Civil Engineers in England.[64]

Thus, in international engineering contracts, there is a tendency to provide for a package of different contractual mechanisms geared to the resolution of disputes: first, negotiations and/or mediation; then a decision by an engineer and/or adjudicator or Dispute Review Board; and, finally, arbitration.[65]

29. — In 1976, the ICC created an International Centre for Technical Expertise and put forward both a model clause and a set of rules. These have proved relatively successful.[66] According to the Centre's new rules, which took effect on January 1, 1993,[67] the Centre "has for its function the appointment or the proposal of experts in connection with international business transactions."[68] Any person or entity, including an arbitral tribunal, may ask the President of the Centre's Standing Committee to "propose the name(s) of one or more experts" (Art. 4), whose brief is not determined by the Centre.[69] An "appointment," on the other hand, requires a contractual clause providing for recourse to the Centre, together with a request to that effect by one of the parties (Art. 5).

Article 8, paragraph 1 of the Rules states that the expert appointed under those circumstances, who must be independent,

> a) . . . is empowered to make findings within the limits set by the request for expertise, after giving the parties an opportunity to make submissions.

---

[64] "The New Engineering Contract" (1st ed. 1993) moves away from the FIDIC engineering system, as the adjudicator is appointed by the owner and the contractor jointly; *see* Bourque, *supra* note 58, at 245.

[65] James J. Myers, *Developing Methods for Resolving Disputes in World-Wide Infrastructure Projects*, 13 J. INT'L ARB. 101 (Dec. 1996); Richard A. Shadbolt, *Resolution of Construction Disputes by Disputes Review Boards*, 16 INT'L CONSTR. L. REV. 101 (1999). An example of the extreme diversity of these methods of dispute resolution within the same project can be seen in the project for the construction of Hong Kong's new airport; *see* Dean Lewis, *Dispute Resolution in the New Hong Kong International Airport Core Programme Projects* (pts. 1–3), 10 INT'L CONSTR. L. REV. 76 (1993), 11 INT'L CONSTR. L. REV. 25 (1994), 12 INT'L CONSTR. L. REV. 131 (1995). See also the recommendations of the World Bank requesting the parties to include in FIDIC contracts an additional clause providing for recourse to a dispute review board or an adjudicator (*see* Andrew Pike, *Disputes Review Boards and Adjudicators*, 10 INT'L CONSTR. L. REV. 157 (1993)).

[66] *See* THE INTERNATIONAL CENTRE FOR TECHNICAL EXPERTISE (ICC Publication No. 307, 1977); *see also* Yves Derains, *Expertise technique et référé arbitral*, 1982 REV. ARB. 239, 242. By 1995, the Centre had dealt with 115 applications from parties of 50 different nationalities (*see* Bourque, *supra* note 58, at 236). It received 15 requests in 1995, 19 requests in 1996 and 33 requests in 1997 (*see 1995 Statistical Report*, ICC BULLETIN, Vol. 7, No. 1, at 3, 6 (1996); *1996 Statistical Report*, ICC BULLETIN, Vol. 8, No. 1, at 6, 12 (1997); *1997 Statistical Report*, ICC BULLETIN, Vol. 9, No. 1, at 4, 9 (1998)).

[67] For a commentary on the new Rules and a description of the Centre's practice, see ICC BULLETIN, Vol. 4, No. 1, at 57 (1993); Bourque, *supra* note 58; Hervé Charrin, *The ICC International Centre for Expertise – Realities and Prospects*, ICC BULLETIN, Vol. 6, No. 2, at 33 (1995).

[68] *See* Art. 1 of the ICC Rules for Expertise, *in* THE ICC INTERNATIONAL CENTRE FOR EXPERTISE (ICC Publication No. 520, 1992).

[69] This function, aimed only at assisting the parties, results in notification of the proposal. In practice, this is the most frequently used of the Centre's services.

b) The expert may also be empowered, by express agreement between the parties, either in a prior agreement or in their request for the appointment of an expert, to:
– recommend, as needed, those measures which he deems most appropriate for the performance of the contract and/or those which would be necessary in order to safeguard the subject matter;
– supervise the carrying out of the contractual operations.

While this procedure may lead to the resolution of disagreements between the parties, or even to the settlement of their disputes, experts are nevertheless not arbitrators, as their decisions do not bind the parties. Paragraph 3 of Article 8 states that "[u]nless otherwise agreed the findings or recommendations of the expert shall not be binding upon the parties."

Any such stipulation to the contrary would render the expert's findings binding and would have the effect of transforming the expert proceedings into an arbitration, even if the parties had not expressly employed such terminology. The expert's decision would therefore take on the authority of an arbitral award.

The ICC International Centre for Technical Expertise has recently extended its jurisdiction: following an agreement with the ICC Commission on Banking Technique and Practice, which has drawn up Uniform Customs and Practice for Documentary Credits and oversees their interpretation internationally, a set of rules for expert proceedings in the field of documentary credit (DOCDEX) came into force on October 1, 1997. This is intended to facilitate the settlement of difficulties that arise between banks when a letter of credit contains irregularities.[70] The parties may choose whether the decision of the expert panel is to be binding or not.

B. – ARBITRATORS' DECISIONS RESOLVE DISPUTES

30. — One of the main characteristics illustrating the judicial nature of the role of arbitrators is that, in their award, they resolve a dispute between two or more parties. This is universally recognized in national legal systems and in international conventions. For example, in the New York Convention of June 10, 1958,[71] the parties submit their "differences" to arbitration, and signatory states recognize arbitral awards as "binding."[72] Article 1496 of the French New Code of Civil Procedure is even more explicit, stating that "[t]he arbitrator shall resolve the dispute."

On whatever grounds they base their decision, *amiables compositeurs* are still arbitrators. Likewise, the subject-matter of the arbitrators' decision is of little consequence: assessing the quality of goods sold, however technical the task may be, still amounts to the resolution

---

[70] *Rules for Documentary Credit Dispute Resolution Expertise – Presentation and Full Text of DOCDEX*, ICC BULLETIN, Vol. 8, No. 2, at 51 (1997); *see also* Jean-François Bourque, *New System to Resolve L/C Disputes Through Expertise*, ICC BULLETIN, Vol. 7, No. 1, at 12 (1996).

[71] On this Convention, see *infra* para. 247.

[72] Arts. II(1) and III of the New York Convention.

of a dispute. A legitimate question arises, however, as to whether the same is true where a third party is asked to add to or modify a contract.

1° *Amiable Composition*

31. — *Amiable composition* is widely accepted in national legal systems and in international commercial law,[73] although the exact powers of an *amiable compositeur* are sometimes unclear.[74] In all statutes and international conventions which allow the parties to empower the arbitrator to rule as an *amiable compositeur* (which is sometimes referred to as ruling either *ex aequo et bono* or in equity), the *amiable compositeur* is still considered to be an arbitrator who decides the dispute. Thus, the European Convention of April 21, 1961 provides that "arbitrators shall act as '*amiable compositeurs*' if . . . ."[75]

In acting as *amiables compositeurs*, the arbitrators must give all parties a fair hearing, and their decision will be a genuine arbitral award. Any obligation to state the grounds for the award therefore applies as it does to an award made by an arbitrator not acting as *amiable compositeur*.[76]

2° **Quality Arbitrations**

32. — The importance in international arbitration practice of disputes relating solely to the quality of goods delivered has been discussed earlier, as has the fact that the decisions reached in such cases are binding.[77] But does this mean that those decisions are genuine arbitral awards? There is some doubt on this point, because a number of legal systems draw a distinction between the purely technical task of evaluation and the resolution of actual disputes.[78]

However, whether or not a dispute exists should be clear in practice, and its nature and the technical means used to resolve it are of little consequence. For the "experts" officiating in quality disputes to be genuine arbitrators, all that is required is that their decision (which we have seen to be binding) draw all the appropriate legal conclusions from their technical evaluation. In other terms, it should order a price reduction or fix appropriate compensation.

---

[73] *See* ERIC LOQUIN, L'AMIABLE COMPOSITION EN DROIT COMPARÉ ET INTERNATIONAL ¶¶ 22 *et seq.* (1980).

[74] On *amiable composition* generally, see *infra* paras. 1500 *et seq.*

[75] Art. VII(2). On this Convention, see *infra* para. 274.

[76] *See infra* para. 1508.

[77] *See supra* para. 26.

[78] *See* Walther J. Habscheid, *L'expertise-arbitrage – Etude de droit comparé, in* INTERNATIONAL ARBITRATION – LIBER AMICORUM FOR MARTIN DOMKE 103 (P. Sanders ed., 1967); René David, *L'arbitrage en droit civil, technique de régulation des contrats, in* MÉLANGES DÉDIÉS À GABRIEL MARTY 383 (1978); Eric Loquin, *Normalisation agricole et arbitrage de qualité, in* UNIVERSITÉ DE DIJON, INSTITUT DE RELATIONS INTERNATIONALES, TRAVAUX DU CENTRE DE RECHERCHE SUR LE DROIT DES MARCHÉS ET DES INVESTISSEMENTS INTERNATIONAUX (CREDIMI), LA GESTION DES RESSOURCES NATURELLES D'ORIGINE AGRICOLE 397 (P. Kahn and J.-C. Fritz eds., 1983).

Experts will only be acting as the parties' agents where they confine themselves to making comments and leave the parties or arbitrators to review the contract or to resolve the dispute themselves.

3° The Completion or Adaptation of Contracts

33. — When signing an international contract, parties are sometimes unable to agree upon all of its terms. They may therefore postpone the inclusion of a particular provision and appoint a third party to complete their agreement at a later stage. This may arise, for example, where the parties lack information required to determine a price or the exact scope of a particular undertaking. The task entrusted to the third party is strictly contractual, whatever name may be given to it.[79] An example in French law is the determination of the sale price, as provided for in Article 1592 of the Civil Code.[80] Other examples are where a third party is instructed to evaluate stocks in the mutual interest of both debtor and creditors, where an architect is instructed to calculate the amount of work carried out by a contractor so as to provide an estimate of the payment due, and where an accountant is instructed to ascertain the value of shares to be sold by the holder. The Canadian Supreme Court (in the first of these cases) and the English House of Lords (in the second and third cases) both considered that the third parties were not arbitrators and were therefore not entitled to the immunity enjoyed by arbitrators by virtue of their judicial role.[81]

Long-term international contracts sometimes contain a clause providing for modification of the contract in the event that, following a change of economic, technical or other circumstances, there is a serious imbalance in the parties' reciprocal undertakings. The existence of such hardship will then lead to renegotiation of the contract and, if this renegotiation fails, a third party will be required to determine whether the contractual conditions triggering modification of the contract have been satisfied and, if they have, to carry out that modification.[82] International contracts may also contain mechanisms which, in cases of frustration (in the common law sense of the word) or *force majeure* (construed more broadly than in civil law systems), suspend, modify or terminate the contract, and which may require the intervention of a third party to do so.[83]

---

[79]   On the terminology used in comparative law, see *supra* para. 26.

[80]   This states that the sale price may be "left to the arbitration of a third party," who is in fact merely a joint agent of the parties.

[81]   Canadian Supreme Court, Sport Maska Inc. v. Zittrer, [1988] 1 S.C.R. 564; Sutcliffe v. Thackrah, [1974] A.C. 727; [1974] 1 All E.R. 859; [1974] 1 Lloyd's Rep. 319 (H.L. 1974); Arenson v. Arenson, [1977] A.C. 405 (H.L. 1975). On the immunity of arbitrators, see *infra* paras. 1076 *et seq.*

[82]   On these clauses and the role of the "third party," see Bruno Oppetit, *L'adaptation des contrats internationaux aux changements de circonstances: la clause de "hardship"*, 101 J.D.I. 794 (1974); MARCEL FONTAINE, DROIT DES CONTRATS INTERNATIONAUX – ANALYSE ET RÉDACTION DE CLAUSES 249 (1989) ("Les clauses de hardship"); Harold Ullmann, *Droit et pratique des clauses de hardship dans le système juridique américain/Law and Practice of Hardship Clauses in the American Legal System*, 1988 INT'L BUS. L.J. 889.

[83]   Pierre Van Ommeslaghe, *Les clauses de force majeure et d'imprévision (hardship) dans les contrats internationaux*, 57 REV. DR. INT. DR. COMP. 7 (1980); Philippe Kahn, *Force majeure et contrats internationaux*

(continued...)

34. — Strictly speaking, "the fixing of a price by third parties does not, in principle, constitute a judicial act:"[84] there is no "dispute" or, more precisely, there is neither a prior "claim" by one party, nor an assessment of that claim by a third party. Such factors would be characteristic of a judicial act and therefore also of the role of an arbitrator. The latter could not, in that capacity, be required to extend or modify a contract.

However, this narrow interpretation of the arbitrator's role does not reflect the practice or indeed the current needs of international trade. The issue has been debated extensively by practitioners[85] and has been the subject of numerous arbitral awards over the past thirty years. In fact, there are two aspects to the question, depending on whether or not the contract submitted to the arbitrator contains a specific hardship clause.

a) In the Absence of a Hardship Clause

35. — Most of the controversy surrounding this issue centers on arbitrators' powers to add to a contract, or to adapt it to a change in circumstances, in the absence of a clause expressly allowing them to do so. The position varies according to the attachment of the applicable law to the *pacta sunt servanda* principle, and to whether or not that law grants the courts the power to substitute themselves for the agreement between the parties.[86] As this is primarily a matter of contract law, the solutions found in each national legal system need not be examined further here.[87]

36. — The trend in international arbitral case law[88] is in favor of a fairly narrow, conservative conception of the arbitrator's powers. Arbitrators will generally be reluctant to accept the doctrine of change in circumstances even in long-term, non-speculative contracts. Instead, they will often consider that parties to international contracts are, generally speaking, experienced professionals well able to protect themselves in their agreements from changes in circumstances.[89]

---

[83](...continued)
de longue durée, 102 J.D.I. 467 (1975); Henry Lesguillons, *Frustration, Force majeure, Imprévision, Wegfall der Geschäftsgrundläge,* 1979 DPCI 507; A.H. Puelinckx, *Frustration, Hardship, Force majeure, Imprévision, Wegfall der Geschäftsgrundlage, Unmöglichkeit, Changed Circumstances – A Comparative Study in English, French, German and Japanese Law,* 3 J. INT'L ARB. 47 (June 1986); regarding the drafting of these clauses, see FORCE MAJEURE AND HARDSHIP (ICC Publication No. 421, 1985).

[84] MOTULSKY, *supra* note 12, at 47.

[85] See the communications and reports presented at the New Delhi arbitration congress, *supra* note 10.

[86] On this issue, generally, see Stefan Kröll, *Contractual Gap-Filling by Arbitration Tribunals,* 2 INT'L ARB. L. REV. 9 (1999); see also, in French domestic law, see Loquin, *supra* note 3, ¶¶ 12–23 and 90–96; JARROSSON, *supra* note 3, ¶¶ 633 *et seq.*

[87] For an in-depth comparative study of the main European legal systems, see DENIS M. PHILIPPE, CHANGEMENT DE CIRCONSTANCES ET BOULEVERSEMENT DE L'ÉCONOMIE CONTRACTUELLE (1986).

[88] Regarding the possibility of discerning trends in international arbitral awards, see *infra* paras. 383 *et seq.*

[89] On this issue, generally, see Philippe Fouchard, *L'adaptation des contrats à la conjoncture économique,* 1979 REV. ARB. 67; Jan A.S. Paulsson, *L'adaptation du contrat,* 1984 REV. ARB. 249; Denis Philippe, *"Pacta sunt*
(continued...)

37. — Even when acting as *amiables compositeurs*, arbitrators are generally reluctant to interpret clauses giving them powers to rule in equity as enabling them to fill gaps left in the contract[90] or to adapt the contract to future circumstances.[91] Some arbitrators do, however, consider that their *amiable compositeur* status allows them to attenuate the overly harsh consequences of a strict application of the contract,[92] and recent French case law has accepted this practice.[93]

b) Where the Contract Contains a Hardship Clause

38. — The situation is different where the parties have agreed that the contract may be supplemented or adapted to reflect changes in circumstances, and have also inserted an arbitration clause. Are the arbitrators entitled to make such alterations if the parties fail to reach a consensus?

---

[89](...continued)

servanda" et "Rebus sic stantibus", *in* L'APPORT DE LA JURISPRUDENCE ARBITRALE, SÉMINAIRE DES 7 ET 8 AVRIL 1986, at 181 (ICC Publication No. 440/1, 1986); Jean-Louis Delvolvé, *L'imprévision dans les contrats internationaux*, *in* TRAVAUX DU COMITÉ FRANÇAIS DE DROIT INTERNATIONAL PRIVÉ 1988–1990, at 147 (1991); among a number of ICC awards, see, for example, ICC Awards No. 1512 (1971), Indian cement company v. Pakistani bank, I Y.B. COM. ARB. 128 (1976); for a French translation, see 101 J.D.I. 904 (1974), and observations by Y. Derains; No. 2216 (1974), State-owned company, seller v. Norwegian purchaser, 102 J.D.I. 917 (1975), and observations by Y. Derains; No. 2291 (1975), French transporter v. English company, 103 J.D.I. 989 (1976), and observations by Y. Derains; No. 2404 (1975), Belgian seller v. Romanian purchaser, 103 J.D.I. 995 (1976), and observations by Y. Derains; No. 2708 (1976), Japanese buyer v. Belgian seller, 104 J.D.I. 943 (1977), and observations by Y. Derains; for an opposing view, see the *ad hoc* award in Société Européenne d'Etudes et d'Entreprises v. République fédérale de Yougoslavie, delivered on July 2, 1956 by Messrs. Ripert and Panchaud (86 J.D.I. 1074 (1959)), which is now enforceable—although as yet unenforced—in France. For an overview of arbitral case law, *lex mercatoria* and comparative law on this issue, see Hans van Houtte, *Changed circumstances and pacta sunt servanda*, *in* TRANSNATIONAL RULES IN INTERNATIONAL COMMERCIAL ARBITRATION 105 (E. Gaillard ed., ICC Publication No. 480/4, 1993). *See also infra* para. 1482.

[90] For example, by substituting a new index for an index which has disappeared, so as to enable the contract to continue (*see* ICC Award No. 3938 (1982), French purchaser v. Dutch seller, 111 J.D.I. 926 (1984), and observations by S. Jarvin).

[91] *See* ICC Award No. 3267 (1979), Mexican construction company v. Belgian company (member of a consortium), VII Y.B. COM. ARB. 96 (1982); for a French translation, see 107 J.D.I. 961 (1980), and observations by Y. Derains; No. 3327 (1981), French company v. African state, 109 J.D.I. 971 (1982), and observations by Y. Derains.

[92] In favor of such measures, see the award rendered in Geneva on May 20, 1983 by Messrs. Van Ommeslaghe, president, Hirsch and Martineau, arbitrators, subsequently discussed by the Paris Court of Appeals in its decision of March 12, 1985, which granted enforcement of the Geneva award in France (Intrafor Cofor v. Gagnant, 1985 REV. ARB. 299; Dalloz, I.R. 467 (1985), and observations by P. Julien; *see also* ICC Award No. 4972 (1989), X & Y v. Z & Mr. W, 116 J.D.I. 1100 (1989), and observations by G. Aguilar Alvarez; Eric Loquin, *Pouvoirs et devoirs de l'amiable compositeur. A propos de trois arrêts de la Cour d'appel de Paris*, 1985 REV. ARB. 199, and the references cited therein; *see also* Jean-Denis Bredin, *L'amiable composition et le contrat*, 1984 REV. ARB. 259; Nabil N. Antaki, *L'amiable composition*, *in* PROCEEDINGS OF THE 1ST INTERNATIONAL COMMERCIAL ARBITRATION CONFERENCE 151 (N. Antaki and A. Prujiner eds., 1985).

[93] In addition to the cases cited by Loquin, *supra* note 92, see Cass. 1e civ., Apr. 28, 1987, Krebs v. Milton Stern, 1987 Bull. Civ. I, No. 128; 1991 REV. ARB. 345, and observations by J.-H. Moitry and C. Vergne. On this issue, generally, see *infra* para. 1507.

On the theoretical grounds discussed above some commentators considered the answer to be in the negative, arguing that an arbitral award is a judicial act and that the role of an arbitrator, a private judge, does not include performance of an "exclusively creative act."[94]

39. — These reservations were mainly raised in France, and generally related to the initial determination by a third party of the price of goods, which Article 1592 of the French Civil Code inaccurately describes as an "arbitration."[95] Other legal systems, such as that of the United States, were more inclined to take a broad view of the arbitrators' powers, provided they originated in the common intention of the parties.[96]

40. — With these potential difficulties in mind, in 1978 the ICC produced rules specifically regarding the adaptation of contracts.[97] There were concerns that such a role might not be compatible, in some legal systems, with the definition of arbitration, and the rules therefore provided for the appointment of a "third party," who would make either a recommendation or a decision. In the latter case, the rules specified that the "decision is binding on the parties to the same extent as the contract in which it is deemed to be incorporated. The parties agree to give effect to such a decision as if it were the expression of their own will" (Art. 11). The ICC thus deliberately opted to confer contractual status on the decision of the third party, who acted as the parties' agent, instructed by the parties, jointly, to complete or adapt the contract as they could have done directly. However, the intervention of this third party was governed by procedural rules involving a contentious hearing,[98] and the third party's decision could assume a different status if a court hearing an application to enforce it considered that the third party had in fact resolved a dispute.

This issue will no longer arise, as the rules in question were withdrawn by the ICC in 1994 because, in more than fifteen years, they had never been used. The reasons for this lack of success[99] include a wariness among practitioners, who tended to favor the *pacta sunt*

[94] MOTULSKY, *supra* note 12, at 47; see also the somewhat more reserved views of David, *supra* note 78, at 383; Bruno Oppetit, *L'arbitrage et les contrats commerciaux à long terme*, 1976 REV. ARB. 91; Bruno Oppetit, *Arbitrage juridictionnel et arbitrage contractuel: à propos d'une jurisprudence récente*, 1977 REV. ARB. 315.

[95] See JARROSSON, *supra* note 3, at 158 *et seq.*, and the references cited therein.

[96] In addition to the reports on comparative law from the ICCA New Delhi Congress, *supra* note 10, see WOLFGANG PETER, ARBITRATION AND RENEGOTIATION OF INTERNATIONAL INVESTMENT AGREEMENTS (2d ed. 1995); Wolfgang Peter, *Arbitration and Renegotiation Clauses*, 3 J. INT'L ARB. 29 (June 1986); Heinz Strohbach, *Force Majeure and Hardship Clauses in International Commercial Contracts and Arbitration – The East-German Approach*, 1 J. INT'L ARB. 39 (Apr. 1984); Martin Bartels, *Contractual adaptation and conflict resolutions*, in 8 STUDIES IN TRANSNATIONAL LAW OF NATURAL RESOURCES (1985).

[97] See ADAPTATION OF CONTRACTS, *supra* note 11. This provided for recourse to a "Standing Committee," distinct from the ICC International Court of Arbitration, pursuant to model clauses which likewise differed from the ICC's model arbitration clause.

[98] These rules also concerned issues such as the option of challenging the third party (Art. 7), the right to a fair hearing (Art. 9), and the obligation to state the grounds of the recommendation or decision (Art. 12).

[99] Yves Derains, *A Report on the ICC Rules on the Regulation of Contractual Relations (ICC Publication N° 326)*, ICC BULLETIN, Vol. 5, No. 2, at 31 (1994).

servanda principle, competition from other methods of dispute resolution,[100] and the dangers of a contractual decision with no recourse.

There is another lesson to be learned from the failure of the rules: any distinction between so-called contractual arbitration and judicial arbitration is extremely tenuous. It is therefore preferable, both for theoretical and practical reasons, to define arbitration relatively broadly, at least as far as the adaptation of contracts is concerned.

41. — As a result, it may well be fair for a third party instructed to implement an adaptation mechanism to consider that there is a dispute between the parties, where those parties cannot agree either as to the principle that adaptation is required because of hardship, or as to the extent of such adaptation.

In practice, when the contract contains an arbitration clause and arbitrators are asked to give effect to a hardship clause, they consider there to be a dispute and they will therefore interpret or apply the disputed clause.[101] This is a common sense approach, and it reflects the solution generally favored by legal commentators.[102]

The only question which may arise is whether the parties did actually confer a power of adaptation on the arbitrators. This is a matter of interpretation of the parties' common intention. If such an intention does exist, one has to accept both that it is legitimate, and that there is nothing improper about calling the intended procedure arbitration. After all, in such cases the arbitrators will be required to determine which of the conflicting positions is well-founded, and therefore to resolve a dispute.

42. — These practical considerations led the 1986 Netherlands Arbitration Act to allow parties to agree to have their contracts adapted by arbitrators. According to Article 1020, paragraph 4 of the Code of Civil Procedure[103]

> [p]arties may also agree to submit the following matters to arbitration:
> . . .
> (c) the filling of gaps in, or modification of, the legal relationship between the parties.

---

[100] The ICC alone offers four more: arbitration, conciliation, technical expertise and pre-arbitral referee procedure.

[101] *See, e.g.*, ICC Award No. 1990 (1972), Italian company v. Spanish company, 101 J.D.I. 897 (1974), and observations by Y. Derains; No. 2291 (1975), *supra* note 89; No. 5754 (1988), unpublished; No. 5953 (1989), Primary Coal v. Compania Valenciana, 117 J.D.I. 1056 (1990), and observations by Y. Derains; *ad hoc* award rendered in Vancouver on May 28, 1990, Nippon Steel v. Quintette, analyzed by Pierre-Yves Gautier, *L'arbitrage Quintette devant les juges de Colombie Britannique: la clause de hardship, invitation à l'ultra petita*, 1991 REV. ARB. 611.

[102] Werner Melis, *Force Majeure and Hardship Clauses in International Commercial Contracts in View of the Practice of the ICC Court of Arbitration*, 1 J. INT'L ARB. 213 (Oct. 1984); *see also* Alain Prujiner, *L'adaptation forcée du contrat par arbitrage*, 37 MCGILL L.J. 428 (1992), and the numerous references therein; MATTHIEU DE BOISSÉSON, LE DROIT FRANÇAIS DE L'ARBITRAGE INTERNE ET INTERNATIONAL 185 (2d ed. 1990).

[103] The text appears *supra* para. 26.

43. — The position of French law in this respect has become less restrictive, as can be seen from an important decision concerning an "escape clause" in contracts for the supply of fuel-oil which provided that the parties would meet to adapt the price to new circumstances. The Paris Court of Appeals referred the parties to an "observer" so that they might reach agreement on the basis of principles determined by the observer, failing which the Court reserved the right to fix the new price.[104] Whatever a court, bound by the principle of the intangibility of contracts,[105] can do to give full effect to the parties' intentions, can also be done by international arbitrators.[106] The Paris Court of Appeals had already implicitly adopted this view by not querying the arbitral status of an award submitted to it for review, where the arbitrators held that the conditions triggering the operation of a hardship clause and permitting the adaptation of the contract were satisfied.[107] Nowadays, commentators are largely in favor of arbitrators being empowered, in French law, to adapt a contract.[108]

§ 2. – The Contractual Basis of Arbitration

44. — The fact that the basis of arbitration is contractual is not disputed: an arbitrator's power to resolve a dispute is founded upon the common intention of the parties to that dispute.[109]

Recent developments concerning the arbitration of disputes arising out of state contracts[110] do not directly affect this principle. However, they do qualify the requirement that there be a true contract containing the parties' consent to have their dispute resolved by arbitration.[111] Increasing numbers of international treaties allow a private entity (usually an investor) to commence arbitration proceedings against a state that has signed a treaty (or against a public entity of that state) where the private party alleges that its rights guaranteed under the treaty have been infringed by the state or public entity.[112] Although there is no

---

[104] CA Paris, Sept. 28, 1976, EDF v. Shell Française, 1977 REV. ARB. 341, and the commentary by Bruno Oppetit, *Arbitrage juridictionnel et arbitrage contractuel: à propos d'une jurisprudence récente, id.* at 315; JCP, Ed. G., Pt. II, No. 18,810 (1978), and J. Robert's note.

[105] However, recent French case law reveals a tendency to "bend contract law" (Jacques Mestre, *Obligations et contrats spéciaux – Obligations en général*, 1989 RTD CIV. 71), by referring to concepts recognized in Articles 1134 and 1135 of the Civil Code, such as equity, usages and good faith.

[106] See, for example, Delvolvé, *supra* note 89, and the contributions of other participants reported in that volume.

[107] CA Paris, Jan. 13, 1971, Entreprise de Recherches et d'Activités Pétrolières (E.R.A.P.) v. Société pour la Recherche et l'Exploitation des Pétroles en Algérie (S.O.F.R.E.P.A.L.), 1973 REV. ARB. 68, and P. Fouchard's note.

[108] See JARROSSON, *supra* note 3, at 304 *et seq.*, and the references cited therein.

[109] See *supra* para. 11. See also Cass. req., July 27, 1937, Roses v. Moller et Cie., D.P., Pt. I, at 25 (1938), and the report by Judge Castets; JCP, Ed. G., Pt. II, No. 449 (1937); Sirey, Pt. I, at 25 (1938); 65 J.D.I. 86 (1938).

[110] On such arbitrations between private companies or individuals and foreign states, see *infra* paras. 69 *et seq.*

[111] On the requirement of consent to arbitration, see *infra* paras. 471 *et seq.*

[112] See Geneviève Burdeau, *Nouvelles perspectives pour l'arbitrage dans le contentieux économique intéressant les Etats*, 1995 REV. ARB. 3; Jacques Werner, *The Trade Explosion and Some Likely Effects on International*

(continued...)

arbitration agreement in its traditional form, the arbitrators' jurisdiction results from the initial consent of the state or public entity—expressed prior to the arbitration in abstract terms in the treaty or in the state's own legislation—and the subsequent consent of the plaintiff, who accepts the arbitrators' jurisdiction by beginning the arbitration.

This unilateral commencement of proceedings is provided for:
- in the 1965 ICSID Convention,[113] as well as certain bilateral treaties and national investment laws;
- the 1992 North American Free Trade Agreement (NAFTA);[114]
- the Energy Charter Treaty signed in Lisbon on December 17, 1994.[115]

As stated by one commentator: "[w]e enter the era of arbitration without contractual relationships."[116] However, the resolution of a dispute by private judges without the parties' consent is not arbitration. This is why the Claims Resolution Tribunal for Dormant Accounts in Switzerland can be characterized as an arbitral tribunal, its jurisdiction being based on the consent given during its establishment by all Swiss banks and by each claimant presenting an application to it against an identified bank.[117]

---

[112](...continued)
Arbitration, 14 J. INT'L ARB. 5 (June 1997).

[113] On this Convention, see *infra* paras. 301 *et seq.* See, for example, the June 27, 1990 Award by A.S. El-Kosheri, president, S.K.B. Asante and B. Goldman, arbitrators (S.K.B. Asante dissenting), in ICSID Case No. ARB/87/3, Asian Agricultural Products (AAPL) v. Republic of Sri Lanka, 30 I.L.M. 577 (1991); 6 ICSID REV. – FOREIGN INV. L.J. 526 (1991); 6 INT'L ARB. REP. A1 (May 1991); XVII Y.B. COM. ARB. 106 (1992); for a French translation, see 119 J.D.I. 215 (1992), and observations by E. Gaillard; the Feb. 21, 1997 Award in ICSID Case No. ARB/93/1, American Manufacturing & Trading, Inc. v. Republic of Zaire, 125 J.D.I. 243 (1998), and observations by E. Gaillard; for an English translation, see XXII Y.B. COM. ARB. 60 (1997); 36 I.L.M. 1531 (1997); 12 INT'L ARB. REP. A1 (Apr. 1997); the July 11, 1997 Decision of the Tribunal on Objections to Jurisdiction in ICSID Case No. ARB/96/3, Fedax N.V. v. The Republic of Venezuela; for a French translation, see 126 J.D.I. 278 (1999), and observations by E. Gaillard.

[114] This treaty was ratified by Canada, the United States and Mexico. Its Chapter 11B allows an investor from one contracting state to submit disputes against another contracting state to arbitration if the investor considers that that state has violated its rights under NAFTA; *see* Gary N. Horlick and Alicia L. Marti, *NAFTA Chapter 11B – A Private Right of Action to Enforce Market Access through Investments*, 14 J. INT'L ARB. 43 (Mar. 1997).

[115] This Treaty has been signed by over 40 states; see *infra* para. 239. Article 26 allows the private investor to submit the dispute, at its discretion, either to the International Centre for Settlement of Investment Disputes (on the basis of the 1965 Washington Convention or of the Additional Facility Rules), or to an *ad hoc* tribunal applying the UNCITRAL Rules, or to the Arbitration Institute of the Stockholm Chamber of Commerce. On this Treaty, see Thomas W. Wälde, *Investment Arbitration Under the Energy Charter Treaty – From Dispute Settlement to Treaty Implementation*, 12 ARB. INT'L 429 (1996); THOMAS WÄLDE, THE ENERGY CHARTER TREATY (1996); Florence Poirat, *L'article 26 du Traité relatif à la Charte de l'Energie: procédures de règlement des différends et statut des personnes privées*, 1998 RGDIP 45. The text of the Treaty is reprinted in 34 I.L.M. 381 (1995).

[116] Werner, *supra* note 112.

[117] See THE CLAIMS RESOLUTION TRIBUNAL FOR DORMANT ACCOUNTS IN SWITZERLAND, a brochure published by this body which is headquartered in Zurich (Löwenstrasse, 17, PO Box 7589, CH – 8023 Zurich), including the Rules of Procedure for the Claims Resolution Process, adopted on October 15, 1997; *see also* 1998 BULL. ASA 258; Hans Michael Riemer, Georg von Segesser, and Brigitte von der Crone, *Das "Schiedsgericht für Nachrichtenlose Konten in der Schweiz"*, 1998 BULL. ASA 253; Amance Dourthe-Perrot, *Le Tribunal arbitral*
(continued...)

45. — The contractual basis of arbitration has been constantly reaffirmed in legislation and case law. Among the most important consequences is that, in very general terms, international arbitration depends solely on the parties' intentions, and not on the procedural rules of the law of the seat of the arbitration.[118] In other words, the judicial nature of international arbitration in no way weakens the equally firm principle of party autonomy (A).

However, the importance of party autonomy has diminished in practice, because international arbitration owes its success to the development of permanent arbitral institutions, and the involvement of these institutions has in fact reduced the role played by the parties. The phenomenon of the institutionalization of international arbitration (B) should therefore also be examined, and in particular the extent to which it has affected the contractual nature of arbitration.

A. – PARTY AUTONOMY IN INTERNATIONAL ARBITRATION

46. — The contract between the parties is the fundamental constituent of international arbitration. It is the parties' common intention which confers powers upon the arbitrators. The consequences of that common intention shall be discussed later.[119] At this stage we shall simply examine the role of the contract in determining the rules governing international arbitration.

1° The Choice of a National Law to Govern the Procedure or the Merits of a Dispute

47. — Although the choice of law method and the application of a particular national law retain some relevance in international arbitration, the principle of party autonomy is of more importance given the contractual basis of arbitration.

48. — In so far as a national law must be applied, and subject to the determination of its scope, it is the law or laws, if any, chosen by the parties which will govern the arbitration agreement itself, the arbitration proceedings and the merits of the dispute. These are the choice of law rules favored by the New York Convention (Art. V(1)(a) and (d)) and the European Convention (Arts. VI(2) and VII).

---

[117](...continued)
pour les comptes en déshérence en Suisse, 1999 REV. ARB. 21.

[118] *See, e.g.,* Court of Justice of the European Communities, Mar. 23, 1982, Case 102/81, "Nordsee" Deutsche Hochseefischerei GmbH v. Reederei Mond Hochseefischerei Nordstern AG, 1982 E.C.R. 1095; VIII Y.B. COM. ARB. 183 (1983); 1982 REV. ARB. 473, and the commentary by Xavier de Mello, *Arbitrage et droit communautaire, id.* at 349; Dalloz, Jur. 633 (1983), and J. Robert's note; Court of Justice of the European Communities, Apr. 27, 1994, Case C–393/92, Gemeente Almelo e.a. v. Energiebedrijf Ijsselmij NV, 1994 E.C.R. I–1477; XX Y.B. COM. ARB. 187 (1995); 1995 REV. ARB. 503, and P. Fouchard's note; *see also* Patrick Hetsch, *Arbitration in Community Law,* ICC BULLETIN, Vol. 6, No. 2, at 47 (1995).

[119] *See infra* paras. 624 *et seq.*

49. — The French New Code of Civil Procedure, on the other hand, does not require that international arbitration be governed by a law or laws selected by applying choice of law rules. Nevertheless, the emphasis it places on the freedom of the parties is such that the Code leaves open the possibility of applying the law chosen by the parties, if need be, not only to the arbitration agreement, but also to the arbitration proceedings (Art. 1494) and to the merits of the case (Art. 1496).

50. — The same trend can be found in comparative private international law. In Switzerland, for example, the contractual nature of international arbitration justified, from a constitutional standpoint, the enactment of the 1987 Federal Private International Law Statute and most of its liberal provisions.[120]

With respect to choice of law rules—to the extent that the choice of law method is still used[121]—the fact that arbitration is primarily a contractual institution leads, as we have seen, to the application of the law chosen by the parties. In contrast, the application of the *lex fori*, favored by those who place more emphasis on arbitration's judicial side and argue that arbitration should form part of a national legal order, has lost much of its appeal.[122]

2° The Choice of Substantive Transnational Rules to Govern the Procedure or the Merits of a Dispute

51. — In international arbitration, party autonomy extends beyond the choice of a national law to govern the procedure or merits of a case.

The parties themselves determine the procedure to be followed, directly or by reference to arbitration rules.[123] This was implicitly recognized in the 1958 New York Convention (Art. V(1)(d)) and expressly set out in the 1961 European Convention (Art. IV). In French law, for example, the traditional leaning of the courts towards "substantive" party autonomy was given the clearest possible endorsement in Article 1494 of the New Code of Civil Procedure, which states that "[t]he arbitration agreement may, directly or by reference to arbitration rules, determine the procedure to be followed in the arbitral proceedings."

Likewise, in most legal systems the parties now have total freedom to determine the "rules of law" to be applied to the merits of the dispute. Modern arbitration statutes do not oblige the arbitrators to choose a particular national law and instead allows them to give preference to all or some of the components of *lex mercatoria*.[124]

52. — This emphasis on party autonomy, which thus frees the parties from all strictly national constraints, is certainly the most important of recent developments in international commercial arbitration. From a theoretical standpoint, this development was only possible

---

[120] On this statute, see *infra* para. 162.

[121] See *infra* paras. 1171 *et seq.*

[122] See *infra* paras. 1178 *et seq.*

[123] On this issue, generally, see *infra* paras. 1171 *et seq.*

[124] On this issue, generally, see *infra* paras. 1444 *et seq.*

because arbitration is contractual. It remains to be seen whether the contractual basis of arbitration is under threat.

B. – THE INSTITUTIONALIZATION OF INTERNATIONAL COMMERCIAL ARBITRATION

53. — International practice has witnessed a trend which is not entirely in keeping with the principle of the primacy of the parties' intentions.

It is becoming increasingly rare for the parties to choose their arbitrators and organize their procedure directly. Instead, permanent arbitral institutions have been set up throughout the world and now handle the vast majority of international commercial arbitrations.[125] The existence of an institution and the application of its procedural rules may lead to greater efficiency, but will also entail a corresponding reduction of the role of the parties in selecting the arbitrators and in the conduct of the proceedings. The advantages of *ad hoc* arbitration, principally the confidence the parties have in arbitrators whom they have selected directly and the flexibility of a procedure suited to each particular case, are sometimes lost in institutional arbitration. Instead, there is the risk of an anonymous, cumbersome administration, and a "judicialization" of arbitration, albeit in a private setting.[126]

54. — The French New Code of Civil Procedure (Art. 1455) therefore sought to limit the role of arbitral institutions in French domestic law, by prohibiting the appointment of an entity or organization as an arbitrator and by favoring the direct appointment of arbitrators by the parties, even in institutional arbitration.[127]

Such restrictions were never imposed in French international arbitration law. In fact, the role of arbitral institutions in international arbitration was expressly recognized in French law[128] as well as in the 1958 New York Convention.(Art. I(2)) and in the 1961 European Convention (Art. I(2)(b)).[129] These conventions thus acknowledged the realities of international arbitration, officially endorsing the essential functions performed by arbitral institutions in both the appointment of the arbitral tribunal and the administration and supervision of the arbitral proceedings.

There can therefore be no doubt that an institutional arbitration is a true arbitration. The institution may even act as the arbitral tribunal or appoint one or more of the arbitrators,

---

[125] For a description of the most important of these institutions, see *infra* paras. 323 *et seq.* Regarding the development of this phenomenon in France, see 1990 REV. ARB. 225–545.

[126] On this debate, see Pierre Lalive, *Avantages et inconvénients de l'arbitrage "ad hoc"*, in ETUDES OFFERTES À PIERRE BELLET 301 (1991); Bruno Oppetit, *Philosophie de l'arbitrage commercial international*, 120 J.D.I. 811, 819 (1993).

[127] *See* Jacqueline Rubellin-Devichi and Eric Loquin, *Arbitrage – Compromis et clause compromissoire*, J.-CL. PROC. CIV., Fasc. 1020, ¶¶ 23 *et seq.* (1995).

[128] *See* Art. 1493 of the New Code of Civil Procedure.

[129] On these conventions, see *infra* paras. 247 and 274.

although of course natural persons would in fact carry out such roles in the institution's name.

55. — However, not all problems surrounding institutional arbitration have been resolved. In particular, the intention of the parties to submit their disputes to institutional arbitration is not always evident. For example, an arbitral institution specialized in a particular trade may administer the arbitration proceedings solely because the general conditions used in that trade refer to the institution, even if this reference is not a direct result of the parties' contract. There is no reason to deny the validity of an arbitration clause incorporated by reference in this way in international arbitration.[130] However, the existence of consent given in these circumstances by a party that is not a member of the relevant professional association, and has no knowledge of the association or of the rules of its arbitral institution, will sometimes be in doubt.

For other reasons, the arbitral institutions created alongside foreign trade chambers in formerly socialist countries have been considered by some commentators to be more akin to specialized courts than to arbitral institutions. However, the requirement that, for each of these institutions to have jurisdiction, there be a common intention of the parties to submit their disputes to it, has enabled those bodies to retain the status of arbitral institutions.

Finally, there have been doubts regarding the Iran-United States Claims Tribunal, established by the Algiers Accords of January 19, 1981. The fact that it was created by an international treaty and that its jurisdiction is compulsory for disputes between parties from Iran and America again weakens the contractual basis of arbitration.[131]

This contractual basis has almost entirely disappeared in the case of the United Nations Compensation Commission, established pursuant to a 1991 Resolution of the United Nations Security Council in order to determine the compensation due by Iraq to the different categories of victims of the invasion of Kuwait.[132]

---

[130] *See infra* paras. 491 *et seq.*

[131] On this institution, see *infra* para. 238.

[132] *See* the United Nations Security Council Resolution 687 of April 3, 1991, paras. 16–19, 30 I.L.M. 846, 852 (1991). See also the reports and decisions published in I.L.M. since 1991; Brigitte Stern, *Un système hybride: la procédure de règlement pour la réparation des dommages résultants de l'occupation illicite du Koweit par l'Iraq*, 37 MCGILL L.J 625 (1992); Bachir Georges Affaki, *The United Nations Compensation Commission – A New Era in Claims Settlements?*, 10 J. INT'L ARB. 21 (Sept. 1993); Carlos Alzamora, *Reflections on the UN Compensation Commission*, 9 ARB. INT'L 349 (1993); Jacques-Michel Grossen, *Un quasi-arbitrage? A propos de la Commission de compensation des Nations Unies et de sa procédure*, *in* ETUDES DE DROIT INTERNATIONAL EN L'HONNEUR DE PIERRE LALIVE 509 (1993); Nicolas C. Ulmer, *Claimant's Expectations from the United Nations Compensation Commission*, 15 J. INT'L ARB. 7 (Mar. 1998); Michael E. Schneider, *How Fair and Efficient is the United Nations Compensation Commission System? – A Model to Emulate?*, 15 J. INT'L ARB. 15 (Mar. 1998).

56. — By contrast, it is because of the importance it places on the intention of the parties that international arbitration law is more willing than domestic law to recognize the binding character of the arbitration rules of the institution chosen by the parties.[133]

57. — Thus, the role of institutions in the organization of arbitrations, especially in appointing the arbitral tribunal and deciding challenges of arbitrators, increases the efficiency of arbitral proceedings but brings with it a number of problems leading to uncertainty as to the nature of the institutions' involvement.[134]

This phenomenon of the institutionalization of arbitration should be considered in conjunction with other trends which bring arbitration closer to both the courts and other methods of alternative dispute resolution. Although arbitration has thus diversified and has become a less original form of dispute resolution,[135] these developments testify to its richness and vitality.

SECTION II
THE MEANING OF "COMMERCIAL"

58. — The fact that this treatise is confined to international arbitration of a commercial nature calls for an explanation. It has nothing to do with an extension to international arbitration of the concept of commerciality found in certain civil law countries. That concept is outdated and of increasingly little relevance, even in domestic law. The French New Code of Civil Procedure, for instance, does not refer to commerciality, and in its rules specifically governing arbitration the Code merely refers to "international arbitration." Although the Code features the word "trade" in Article 1492, this is in the expression "the interests of international trade" which is used to define the concept of internationality. We shall see that, in this context, international commerce means all economic exchanges across national boundaries, rather than the narrow, technical definition found in French domestic law.[136]

59. — In international arbitration, a broad interpretation of commerciality should therefore be adopted: any international arbitration between companies where the dispute is economic in character will be considered to be commercial.

This is the only universally accepted approach and is found, for example, in the UNCITRAL Model Law on international commercial arbitration.[137] However, two points should be explored further: first, the fact that this definition causes the disappearance of the

---

[133] *See infra* paras. 359 *et seq.*; on the importance of these rules as sources of arbitration law, see *infra* paras. 323 *et seq.*, and regarding international arbitration procedure, see *infra* paras. 1209 *et seq.*

[134] On the issues raised by institutional arbitration, see *infra* paras. 233 *et seq.*

[135] On these developments, see Laurent Gouiffès, *L'arbitrage international propose-t-il un modèle original de justice?, in* RECHERCHE SUR L'ARBITRAGE EN DROIT INTERNATIONAL ET COMPARÉ 1 (1997).

[136] *See infra* paras. 102 *et seq.*

[137] On the Model Law, see *infra* para. 203.

rigid distinction between civil and commercial arbitration found, for example, in French domestic law (§ 1); second, the fact that this broad interpretation gives rise to a different distinction, between commercial arbitration and public law arbitration (§ 2).

§ 1. – Civil and Commercial Arbitration

60. — The latest universal international instrument on arbitration, namely the 1985 UNCITRAL Model Law, makes no distinction between civil and commercial arbitration, favoring a wide definition of commerciality (A). We therefore need to consider what remains of the distinction in modern arbitration laws (B) and in international conventions on arbitration (C).

A. – THE UNCITRAL MODEL LAW

61. — Although its title contains the words "international commercial arbitration," it is rather striking that the Model Law does not define the term "commercial" in the main body of its provisions, but only in a footnote, which states as follows:

> (**) The term "commercial" should be given a wide interpretation so as to cover matters arising from all relationships of a commercial nature, whether contractual or not. Relationships of a commercial nature include, but are not limited to, the following transactions: any trade transaction for the supply or exchange of goods or services; distribution agreement; commercial representation or agency; factoring; leasing; construction of works; consulting; engineering; licensing; investment; financing; banking; insurance; exploitation agreement or concession; joint venture and other forms of industrial or business co-operation; carriage of goods or passengers by air, sea, rail or road.

62. — The fact that this wording is contained in a footnote, suggesting that it is merely a guide to interpretation,[138] is of little consequence because legislators of countries wishing to adopt the Model Law are at liberty to implement the Model Law as they see fit. Thus, for example, in the 1986 arbitration statute enacted by the Canadian province of British

---

[138] *See, e.g., Analytical Commentary on Draft Text of a Model Law on International Commercial Arbitration, Report of the Secretary-General,* UN Doc. A/CN.9/264, Mar. 25, 1985, ¶¶ 16 *et seq.,* reprinted in UNCITRAL MODEL LAW OF INTERNATIONAL COMMERCIAL ARBITRATION: A DOCUMENTARY HISTORY, Vol. I, Annex 35.0; *Report of the United Nations Commission on International Trade Law on the work of its eighteenth session – 3–21 June 1985,* Official Records of the General Assembly, Fortieth Session, Supplement No. 17 (A/40/17), ¶¶ 19 *et seq., reprinted in* UNCITRAL MODEL LAW OF INTERNATIONAL COMMERCIAL ARBITRATION: A DOCUMENTARY HISTORY, Vol. II, Annex 66.0.

Columbia, which is almost identical to the Model Law, Article 1, paragraph 6 contains and reclassifies most of the examples listed in the footnote to the Model Law.[139]

63. — If one ignores its tautologies and redundancies, this footnote clearly conveys the idea that all exchanges of property, services or assets will be commercial. In other words, the definition includes all economic relations the object of which is the production, transformation or circulation of goods, or services associated with those goods, or financial and banking activities. The status of the parties is not taken into consideration, although the list does make it fairly clear that the Model Law does not apply to consumer or labor law disputes.[140] On the other hand, there is no reference to whether or not the parties are merchants ("*commerçants*"), as the Model Law is aimed at legal systems which draw no distinction between merchants and non-merchants as well as those which maintain that distinction. Finally, this wide definition of the term "commercial" only applies to the scope of the Model Law, without prejudice to that of the arbitration itself, which is a matter to be determined by the arbitrators or the courts, as the case may be.[141]

B. – MODERN LEGISLATION

64. — Historically, French domestic law was noted for its hostility towards the arbitration of non-commercial disputes. This hostility resulted, in particular, in a prohibition on arbitration clauses for disputes other than those within the jurisdiction of the commercial courts. The courts generally held void an arbitration clause which failed to comply with this prohibition.[142]

Fortunately, the French courts soon decided that the prohibition did not to apply to international arbitration, and consequently there is no need to refer in this context to the French domestic law concepts of "merchants" ("*commerçants*") and "acts of commerce" ("*actes de commerce*"). The distinction between civil arbitration and commercial arbitration became redundant in French international arbitration law as a result of the 1972 *Hecht* decision.[143] As the validity of the arbitration clause is recognized pursuant to a specific substantive rule of international arbitration, regardless of whether the arbitration be commercial, civil or a combination of the two, the concept of commerciality has lost much of its relevance in international arbitration. At the very most, some doubt remains as to the

---

[139] *See* International Commercial Arbitration Act, R.S.B.C. 1996, c. 233.

[140] See the commentary *supra* note 138, ¶ 18.

[141] On this issue, see *infra* paras. 559 *et seq.*

[142] On all these points, see Charles Jarrosson, *La clause compromissoire (art. 2061 C. civ.)*, 1992 REV. ARB. 259.

[143] Cass. 1e civ., July 4, 1972, Hecht v. Buisman's, 99 J.D.I. 843 (1972), and B. Oppetit's note; 1974 REV. CRIT. DIP 82, and P. Level's note; *see also infra* para. 418. In a January 5, 1999 decision, the *Cour de cassation* unequivocally referred to "the principle of validity of the international arbitration agreement without any condition of commerciality" (*see* Cass. 1e civ., Zanzi v. de Coninck, 1999 DALLOZ AFF. 474).

validity of arbitration clauses in employment contracts.[144] In consumer contracts, the French courts have held, in their *V2000 (Jaguar)* decisions,[145] that the international character of the purchase of consumer goods was sufficient for an arbitration clause to be effective. Of course, the arbitrability of the dispute will be assessed by the arbitrators in the light of international public policy, and their decision will be subject to review by the courts. Thus international arbitration has not entirely abandoned the protection of the consumer. However, these decisions clearly allow the notion of international commerce to prevail over the distinction between civil and commercial transactions.

65. — European law and other legal systems still show that the arbitration of consumer disputes, even where they are international, are subject to specific rules. Thus the April 5, 1993 EC Directive on unfair terms in consumer contracts states that "a contractual term which has not been individually negotiated shall be regarded as unfair if . . . it causes significant imbalance in the parties' rights and obligations arising under the contract, to the detriment of the consumer" (Art. 3). In an Annex entitled "Terms Referred to in Article 3(3)," the Directive lists among clauses which states should hold ineffective "[t]erms which have the object or effect of . . . (9) excluding or hindering the consumer's right to take legal action or exercise any other legal remedy, particularly by requiring the consumer to take disputes exclusively to arbitration not covered by legal provisions."[146]

This Directive, which has now been implemented in member states of the European Union, significantly restricts the effectiveness of arbitration clauses in consumer contracts.

C. – INTERNATIONAL CONVENTIONS ON ARBITRATION

66. — The 1958 New York Convention enabled its signatories to maintain a distinction between the rules applicable to commercial arbitration and non-commercial arbitration. Article I, paragraph 3 contains what is known as the commercial reservation:

> When signing, ratifying or acceding to this Convention . . . , any State may . . . declare that it will apply the Convention only to differences arising out of legal

---

[144] *See* CA Grenoble, Sept. 13, 1993, Compagnie Française d'Etanchéité (C.F.T.E.) v. Dechavanne, 1994 REV. ARB. 337, and M.-A. Moreau's note; for an English translation, see XX Y.B. COM. ARB. 656 (1995); CA Paris, Mar. 24, 1995, Bin Saud Bin Abdel Aziz v. Crédit Industriel et Commercial de Paris, 1996 REV. ARB. 259, and J.-M. Talau's note.

[145] CA Paris, Dec. 7, 1994, V 2000 (formerly Jaguar France) v. Renault, 1996 REV. ARB. 245, and C. Jarrosson's note; 1995 RTD COM. 401, and observations by J.-C. Dubarry and E. Loquin; 1996 JUSTICES 435, and observations by M.-C. Rivier, *aff'd,* Cass. 1e civ., May 21, 1997, Renault v. V 2000 (formerly Jaguar France), 1997 REV. ARB. 537, and E. Gaillard's note; 1998 REV. CRIT. DIP 87, and V. Heuzé's note; 125 J.D.I. 969 (1998), and S. Poillot-Peruzzetto's note. On this issue, see *infra* para. 579.

[146] Council Directive 93-13 of April 5, 1993, on unfair terms in consumer contracts, 1993 O.J. (L 95) 29; Dalloz, Lég. 360 (1993).

relationships, whether contractual or not, which are considered as commercial under the national law of the State making such declaration.

Of the 121 countries that have ratified the Convention,[147] roughly one-third have made the commercial reservation. Accordingly, in those countries the New York Convention applies solely to arbitration agreements and awards relating to commercial disputes.

Each country that has made the commercial reservation applies its own law to determine whether or not a dispute is commercial. This obviously leads to a risk of divergence as to the concept of commerciality, but this could not be overcome in 1958 as a result of the considerable reluctance in certain jurisdictions to allow arbitration of civil disputes.[148] Case law on the interpretation of the New York Convention commercial reservation is divided. The more liberal approach, found mainly in the United States, considers that the commerciality requirement only excludes from the ambit of the Convention matrimonial, personal and employment matters. Indian law reflects a more restrictive trend: it holds neither a factory construction contract entailing a transfer of technology nor a contract for the provision of technical know-how to be commercial.[149] Similarly, the Tunisian *Cour de cassation* refused to consider as commercial a contract entrusting a town-planning program to an architect.[150]

67. — In 1989, with one of its objectives being to ensure that its courts would not have to address the same difficulties of interpretation, France decided to withdraw the commercial reservation initially made upon ratification of the New York Convention. In so doing, it clearly came out in favor of abolishing all distinctions between international civil and commercial arbitration.[151]

68. — The 1961 European Convention did not contain a commercial reservation. According to its official title, the Convention concerns only "international commercial arbitration," but it contains no reference to a concept of commerciality such as might result

---

[147] On March 31, 1999. For the list of Contracting States, see Annex IV. The list can also be found on the UNCITRAL Web site, where it is updated as soon as any new information becomes available (<http://www.un.or.at/uncitral>).

[148] However, the same reservation already contained in the 1923 Geneva Protocol had not given rise to serious difficulties of interpretation. On this Protocol, see *infra* para. 241.

[149] On these cases, see ALBERT JAN VAN DEN BERG, THE NEW YORK ARBITRATION CONVENTION OF 1958, at 51 *et seq.* (1981); *see also* Albert Jan van den Berg, *New York Convention of 1958 – Commentary Cases*, XII Y.B. COM. ARB. 419 *et seq.* (1987), XIII Y.B. COM. ARB. 497 *et seq.* (1988), XIX Y.B. COM. ARB. 495 *et seq.* (1994). This broad interpretation of the notion of commerciality is also found in the United States, where the courts have gone as far as to hold that an international employment contract must be considered commercial with the meaning of the Convention de New York: *see* Prograph Int'l, Inc. v. Barhydt, 928 F. Supp. 983 (N.D. Cal. 1996); XXIII Y.B. COM. ARB. 901 (1998). *But see* Supreme Court of India, Feb. 10, 1994, RM Investment & Trading Co. Pvt. v. Boeing Co., XXII Y.B. COM. ARB. 710 (1997).

[150] Nov. 10, 1993, Haddad v. Société d'Investissement Kal, XXIII Y.B. COM. ARB. 770 (1998).

[151] Philippe Fouchard, *La levée par la France de sa réserve de commercialité pour l'application de la Convention de New York*, 1990 REV. ARB. 571.

from a national law. On the contrary, the term "commercial" is intended to have a purely economic meaning, although no specific definition is given; Article I provides as follows:

> This Convention shall apply:
> (*a*) to arbitration agreements concluded for the purpose of settling disputes arising from international trade . . . .

This provision is comparable to that employed in the French New Code of Civil Procedure, which refers to "interests of international trade." Like the French expression, it should be given a broad interpretation.[152] Without confining themselves to the international circulation of goods, the authors of the Convention undoubtedly wished to cover all activities or undertakings with an economic purpose, based on a relationship which would generally be contractual and which would involve more than one country. The Convention therefore applies not only to exchanges of goods, but also to their manufacture and to all services.

§ 2. – Public Law Arbitration and Commercial Arbitration

69. — The parties to an international arbitration often include states, other public law entities, or public international law bodies such as international organizations. Can the arbitration still be considered commercial in such cases? To answer this difficult question, we do not propose to enter into a discussion of the extent of state sovereignty or the pluralism of legal orders. We will instead restrict our analysis to defining the limits of the subject-matter of this treatise.

The arbitration of a dispute arising in the course of an international economic transaction involving one or more public entities will be considered to be commercial, particularly where the arbitration takes place between a state, or a state-owned entity, and a foreign private undertaking. The arbitration of disputes arising in such state contracts[153] (A) is based on arbitration agreements, usually in the form of arbitration clauses, concluded directly between the state (or state-owned entity) and the foreign party. For the same reasons, arbitrations between international organizations and private parties are also considered to be commercial. On the other hand, arbitrations concerning only public international law issues (B) (generally, arbitrations between two states regarding the exercise of their sovereignty, or between a state and an international organization) are not commercial arbitrations.

---

[152] *See, e.g.*, Jean Robert, *La convention européenne sur l'arbitrage commercial international signée à Genève le 21 avril 1961*, Dalloz, Chron. 173 (1961).

[153] On terminology, see *infra* para. 72.

A. – The Arbitration of State Contracts

70. — Based on the understanding of "commerciality" discussed above,[154] disputes involving public entities and arising from their international trade transactions should be included in the definition of international commercial arbitration. Whether it is the states themselves or their various offshoots that are actually involved, it is sufficient for them to participate in such transactions for the resolution of any resulting disputes to fall within the definition of international commercial arbitration. Disputes arising from state contracts, where such contracts contain an arbitration clause, are therefore within the scope of the present study.

71. — We believe this approach to be correct for two reasons. First, because public law bodies are increasingly frequently involved in international trade. Second, because their public law status (of which the other contracting parties may be unaware) does not always affect the rules governing the contract and any international arbitration in which they participate. Where that status does give rise to a special regime,[155] it is important to reconcile the application of that regime with the requirements of international trade, particularly the need for ensuring the respect of agreements freely entered into by the parties.[156]

72. — In light of the complexity of these cases, some authors prefer to describe them as "transnational arbitrations."[157] However, the disputes at issue are resolved by applying the statutes, case law and practice of international commercial arbitration.

Thus, the prohibition imposed in France and in other legal systems on public law entities submitting disputes to arbitration has been held, at the very least, to be inapplicable where such entities are participating in an international commercial transaction. As the French *Cour de cassation* held in its 1966 *Galakis* decision,

---

[154] *See supra* paras. 58 *et seq.*

[155] Because, for example, of the incidence of domestic public law rules governing the entity in question, or because that entity is exercising state prerogatives or sovereignty.

[156] *See* PHILIPPE LEBOULANGER, LES CONTRATS ENTRE ETATS ET ENTREPRISES ÉTRANGÈRES (1985); Jean-Flavien Lalive, *Contrats entre Etats ou entreprises étatiques et personnes privées – Développements récents, in* COLLECTED COURSES OF THE HAGUE ACADEMY OF INTERNATIONAL LAW, Vol. 181, Year 1983, Part III, at 9.

[157] *See* Bernard Audit, *Transnational Arbitration and State Contracts: Findings and Prospects, in* HAGUE ACADEMY OF INTERNATIONAL LAW, CENTRE FOR STUDIES AND RESEARCH IN INTERNATIONAL LAW AND INTERNATIONAL RELATIONS, TRANSNATIONAL ARBITRATION AND STATE CONTRACTS (in the French version, at 23 and in an English translation, at 77 (1988)); François Rigaux, *Souveraineté des Etats et arbitrage transnational, in* LE DROIT DES RELATIONS ÉCONOMIQUES INTERNATIONALES – ETUDES OFFERTES À BERTHOLD GOLDMAN 261 (1982).

this rule, which is intended to apply to domestic contracts . . . cannot apply to an international contract entered into for the purposes of the shipping trade under conditions complying with the usages thereof.[158]

A 1996 decision of the Paris Court of Appeals is more explicit still. It clearly affirms that the commercial nature of arbitration is not affected by the participation in the proceedings of a state or a state entity, nor by the fact that the dispute concerns public works (in this case the construction of an embassy).[159] A new concept of "international commerciality" is thus emerging, which goes far beyond the inappropriate concepts found in French domestic law.

As international arbitration agreements entered into by public entities are now universally considered to be valid,[160] the specific impact of the involvement of a public entity will be primarily in the determination of the rules governing the merits of the dispute and in the enforcement of the award, rather than in the arbitral proceedings. For example, the arbitrators may be required to apply rules of public international law, or a party may claim sovereign immunity, if not to challenge the arbitrator's jurisdiction, then at least to attempt to prevent enforcement of the award. Nevertheless, even in these areas, the arbitration of disputes arising from state contracts will not lead to the wholesale inapplicability of the principles of international commercial arbitration.[161]

73. — ICSID arbitration, as provided for in the 1965 Washington Convention,[162] was designed to resolve investment-related disputes between states and nationals of other states. It is unique in that ICSID was established by an international treaty and ICSID awards are not subject to the ordinary rules of international arbitration. Nonetheless, ICSID arbitrations usually involve economic disputes arising from an international contract between a state (or state-owned entity) and a foreign private undertaking. These arbitrations are therefore properly considered as "international commercial arbitrations." This is not to say that ICSID does not retain certain specific features, especially as regards questions of jurisdiction and procedure. On substantive issues, however, ICSID has not led to the creation of a body of international development law distinct from that arising from ordinary international

---

[158] Cass. 1e civ., May 2, 1966, Trésor Public v. Galakis, JCP, Ed. G., Pt. II, No. 14,798 (1966), and P. Ligneau's note; 93 J.D.I. 648 (1966), and P. Level's note; 1967 REV. CRIT. DIP 553, and B. Goldman's note; Dalloz, Jur. 575 (1966), and J. Robert's note. *See also infra* para. 543.

[159] CA Paris, June 13, 1996, KFTCIC v. Icori Estero, 124 J.D.I. 151 (1997), and E. Loquin's note; 1997 REV. ARB. 251, and E. Gaillard's note.

[160] On this issue, generally, see *infra* paras. 534 *et seq.*

[161] *See* KARL-HEINZ BÖCKSTIEGEL, ARBITRATION AND STATE ENTERPRISES – SURVEY ON THE NATIONAL AND INTERNATIONAL STATE OF LAW AND PRACTICE (1984); for the impact of recent awards on international commercial arbitration law as defined above, see Bruno Oppetit, *Arbitrage et contrats d'Etat – L'arbitrage Framatome et autres c/ Atomic Energy Organization of Iran*, 111 J.D.I. 37 (1984); Philippe Fouchard, *L'arbitrage Elf Aquitaine Iran c/ National Iranian Oil Company – Une nouvelle contribution au droit international de l'arbitrage*, 1984 REV. ARB. 333.

[162] On this Convention, see *infra* para. 301.

arbitration.[163] The same will most likely be true, in the future, of arbitrations regarding state contracts and organized under other international treaties, which will generally be between a private investor (the claimant) and a defendant state.[164]

74. — For the same reasons, cases heard by the Iran-United States Claims Tribunal, which primarily consisted of international economic disputes between United States companies and the Iranian state or state-owned organizations, also fall within the definition of international commercial arbitration.[165]

B. – PUBLIC INTERNATIONAL LAW ARBITRATIONS

75. — The scope of the present work therefore only excludes international arbitrations strictly confined to issues of public international law. In such cases, the parties are either sovereign states or international organizations.[166] Arbitration is traditionally one of the means of settling disputes between such parties, and is sometimes referred to simply as "international arbitration." Although this description is not incorrect, in the same way as the expression "international law" is sometimes used to mean public international law, it is clearly a little ambiguous.[167]

This ambiguity is purely a matter of terminology, as the involvement of states or international organizations in international trade can only cause public international law to apply to their disputes if their contracting partners are also states or international organizations. Although of course arbitrations between states or international organizations concern, broadly speaking, international or transnational law, they are essentially governed by the rules of international commercial arbitration.

76. — It is of little consequence that some state contracts stipulate that any arbitrators hearing disputes arising from such contracts shall apply rules of public international law. If one of the parties is not a state or international organization, that is enough to prevent the rules of public international law from applying to the arbitration itself. This will also be true where both parties are states or international organizations, provided that they entered into their agreement merely in their capacity as parties to strictly commercial contracts.

---

[163] *See* Philippe Leboulanger, *L'arbitrage international Nord-Sud, in* ETUDES OFFERTES À PIERRE BELLET 323 (1991).

[164] On these new treaties, see *supra* para. 44 and *infra* para. 239-3.

[165] On this Tribunal and the rules it applies, see *infra* para. 238.

[166] *See, e.g.,* Emmanuel Decaux, *Arbitrage entre sujets du droit international: Etats et organisations internationales,* J.-CL. DR. INT., Fascs. 245 to 248 (1990–1996). On arbitration of international tax disputes, see also Jean-Pierre Le Gall, *Fiscalité et arbitrage,* 1994 REV. ARB. 3, especially at 24 *et seq.*

[167] *See supra* paras. 6 and 58.

77. — We therefore do not propose to cover arbitration between states exercising their sovereignty, particularly in the context of the performance or interpretation of a treaty containing an arbitration clause.

Inter-state arbitration of economic disputes has been growing in recent years,[168] as a result of radical changes in the methods of resolving inter-state disputes of that kind. Under the auspices of the GATT, economic disputes between states had chiefly been settled by negotiation and conciliation, even if the procedures of the panels had gradually become more like those of the courts.[169] The three Inter-American free trade agreements also illustrate this evolution: in the 1988 Canada-United States Free Trade Agreement the system of consensus is partially replaced by a more judicial procedure.[170] In the 1992 North American Free Trade Agreement (NAFTA), all disputes arising, including trade disputes concerning anti-dumping and countervailing duty investigations, are settled in proceedings that lead to binding decisions.[171] The Argentina–Brazil–Paraguay–Uruguay Treaty Establishing a Common Market (MERCOSUR) has set up a fully-fledged arbitration procedure for the resolution of disputes between member states.[172]

The Marrakesh Agreement establishing the World Trade Organization (WTO)[173] also illustrates how inter-state dispute resolution procedures are becoming increasingly similar to those of the courts: a Dispute Settlement Body is created to administer all contentious matters. The reports made by the panels established by the Dispute Settlement Body can be challenged before the Standing Appellate Body.[174]

---

[168] *See* Burdeau, *supra* note 112, at 27 *et seq.*

[169] Pierre Pescatore, *The GATT Dispute Settlement Mechanism – Its Present Situation and its Prospects*, 10 J. INT'L ARB. 27 (Mar. 1993); PIERRE PESCATORE, WILLIAM J. DAVEY, ANDREAS F. LOWENFELD, HANDBOOK OF WTO/GATT DISPUTE SETTLEMENT (1991).

[170] William C. Graham, *Dispute Resolution in the Canada-United States Free Trade Agreement: One Element of a Complex Relationship*, 37 MCGILL L.J. 544 (1992); Gary N. Horlick and F. Amanda DeBusk, *Dispute Resolution Panels of the U.S.-Canada Free Trade Agreement: The First Two and One-Half Years*, 37 MCGILL L.J. 574 (1992); Andreas F. Lowenfeld, *The Free Trade Agreement Meets its First Challenge: Dispute Settlement and the Pork Case*, 37 MCGILL L.J. 597 (1992).

[171] On this Agreement, see *supra* para. 44. *See* Gary N. Horlick and F. Amanda DeBusk, *Dispute Resolution under NAFTA – Building on the U.S.–Canada FTA, GATT and ICSID*, 10 J. INT'L ARB. 51 (Mar. 1993). Also, the settlement of commercial disputes arising in the context of the NAFTA can be submitted to the Commercial Arbitration and Mediation Center for the Americas, established in December 1995 (*see infra* paras. 239 and 336).

[172] The Mercosur Treaty was done at Asunción on March 26, 1991 (30 I.L.M. 1041 (1991)). See also the Protocol of Brasilia dated November 29, 1991 (34 I.L.M. 691 (1997)) between the same countries. *See* Jaime Greif, *El arbitraje como mecanismo de solución de controversias en el Protocolo de Brasilia*, 1994 RIV. DELL'ARB. 403.

[173] *See* Final Act Embodying the Results of the Uruguay Round of Multilateral Trade Negotiations, signed in Marrakesh on April 15, 1994, 33 I.L.M. 1143 (1994); see especially the Understanding on Rules and Procedures Governing the Settlement of Disputes, 33 I.L.M. 1226 (1994).

[174] On these various procedures, see Burdeau, *supra* note 112; Norio Komuro, *The WTO Dispute Settlement Mechanism – Coverage and Procedures of the WTO Understanding*, 12 J. INT'L ARB. 81 (Sept. 1995). *See also* LA RÉORGANISATION MONDIALE DES ÉCHANGES (PROBLÈMES JURIDIQUES) (Colloquium organized in Nice (France) by the Société Française pour le Droit International, 1996), with the reports by Eric Canal-Forgues, *Le système de règlement des différends de l'OMC*, at 281, and Frieder Roessler, *Evolution du système de règlement des différends du GATT/de l'OMC*, at 309.

We have seen that certain international economic treaties allow private parties to commence arbitral proceedings directly against states which fail to comply with their obligations regarding the protection of investments or the free movement of goods and services. Those disputes are arbitrations of a commercial nature, even if the state seeks to exercise its sovereign prerogatives. However, if the dispute is exclusively between two states, it is a matter of public international law and therefore falls outside the scope of this treatise.

SECTION III
THE MEANING OF "INTERNATIONAL"

78. — It is essential to know what is meant by the international nature of arbitration, as that is central to the private international law regime governing arbitration and to the associated methodological ambiguity and controversy.

79. — In private international law, the international nature of a relationship or institution is generally examined with a view to establishing a connection with a particular national legal system. Without internationality, there can be no conflict of laws. The existence of a conflict of laws also naturally arises in the context of arbitration. However, that is neither the only nor the most important consequence of the international nature of an arbitration. Instead, it is increasingly frequent for the main consequence of the international nature of an arbitration to be whether or not a set of specific substantive rules applies to it.

80. — In view of their very different effects, these two aspects of the international nature of arbitration must be carefully distinguished, not least because the definition of what is meant by the word "international" differs in each case.[175] In order to determine whether or not an arbitration is connected to a specific legal order, its international nature will be defined on the basis of certain legal criteria (§ 1). However, where the international nature of arbitration is a condition governing the application of specific substantive rules, it will be established using economic criteria drawn from the substance of the dispute (§ 2).

§ 1. – The International Nature of Arbitration and the Connection of an Arbitration to a Specific Legal Order

81. — Where a question arises as to the connection of an arbitration to a particular legal order, the legal order which naturally comes to mind is that of a particular country. For those who believe that a legal relationship—including an arbitration—can only be governed by

---

[175] On the origins of this distinction, see Philippe Fouchard, *Quand un arbitrage est-il international?*, 1970 REV. ARB. 59.

rules found in national law,[176] this is the only possible connection. In such a case, from the viewpoint of a particular legal system there would be only national arbitrations and foreign arbitrations (A).

82. — However, international arbitral practice is becoming increasingly independent of national law, and national legislators and international conventions are accepting that independence. This raises the question of whether, as well as national arbitrations, there can be arbitrations entirely detached from all national legal orders, so as to be connected—if need be—to an "a-national" or truly international legal order (B).

A. – NATIONAL ARBITRATION AND FOREIGN ARBITRATION

83. — The distinction between national and foreign arbitration serves to determine to which national legal order a particular arbitration is connected. The method used involves examining a situation or relationship and seeking to establish a connection with one or more legal systems.

84. — Any foreign elements found in this examination will provide possible connections with other countries. According to their importance, the situation or relationship will be governed either by a foreign legal system or by the national legal system.[177]

For the purposes of this method, an arbitration involving elements which are foreign vis-à-vis a particular country would be considered to be international. This is a "minimalist" interpretation of the word international. The only effect of the diversity of the connecting factors is that it causes a conflict of laws and leads to a search for the governing law. Once the connection has been established, the arbitration will be "re-nationalized."

85. — The factors which may connect an arbitration to a particular jurisdiction are fairly numerous, as there are several facets to arbitration itself: it is based on an agreement (or several agreements); it establishes a procedure, but it also deals with the substance of a legal relationship; most importantly, it is a relatively complex mechanism involving several participants and a number of different stages.

86. — The possible connecting factors are therefore the following:
- the nationality and domicile of the arbitrator or arbitrators;
- the nationality of the parties;
- the domicile, residence or company headquarters of the parties;
- other connecting factors related to the substance of the dispute (such as the place where the contract was signed, the place where it was performed, the location of any property involved and the place where any loss was suffered).

---

[176] For a striking example of this view, see Mann, *supra* note 8.

[177] *See* Berthold Goldman, *Arbitrage (droit international privé), in* ENCYCLOPÉDIE DALLOZ – DROIT INTERNATIONAL ¶¶ 1 *et seq.* (1968).

- the nationality or headquarters of the arbitral institution;
- the seat of the arbitration;
- the place where the award will be enforced;
- the law chosen to govern the arbitral proceedings;
- the law chosen to govern the merits of the dispute.

87. — Clearly, if all of these connecting factors lead to a single country, then the arbitration in question will be a national arbitration, governed by the domestic law of that country. For example, if two French nationals, both residing in France, submit a dispute concerning a contract which they signed and performed entirely in France to a French arbitrator, and if the entire arbitral procedure takes place in France, with the arbitrator applying French law, there is no doubt that this will be a "French" arbitration. More specifically, it will be a French domestic arbitration.

88. — Let us suppose, on the other hand, that one or more of these connecting factors leads to one or several other countries. For the purpose of connecting the arbitration to a particular national law, the connecting factors listed above vary in importance, and the choice of law method therefore involves weighing them up.

In the course of this study, we will examine each of the issues raised in the course of an arbitration involving more than one country, and at that stage we will assess the importance of these various connecting factors in order to establish which law or laws should govern the arbitration agreement, the arbitral procedure, the award, and the merits of the dispute. However, we should first consider the principles generally applied when determining the particular legal system to which an international arbitration is connected.

89. — First of all, do such principles exist?

The uncertainty on this point is not simply the result of each legal system having its own choice of law mechanisms: in private international law that is accepted as being the ordinary course of things. The various choice of law rules converge in some areas, and this convergence is reinforced by the approach adopted in international conventions and by arbitral case law. However, determining connections is rarely going to be simple, chiefly because the diversity of the connecting factors reflects that of an arbitration's constituent parts: an agreement, a procedure, a dispute and an award.

90. — There are essentially two kinds of connection: one is the law chosen by the parties and is based on the contractual nature of arbitration; the other is procedural and results from the seat of the arbitration.

91. — The 1958 New York Convention[178] clearly reflects the existence of these two different tendencies. The arbitration agreement is governed by the law chosen by the parties (Art. V(1)(a)), as is the procedure (Art. V(1)(d)). However, the law of the seat of the arbitration applies in both cases in the absence of agreement between the parties. More

---

[178] On this Convention, see *infra* para. 247.

importantly, the place where the arbitration takes place, and where the award is made, is taken into account in determining whether the award is binding (Art. V(1)(e)) and whether the rules of the New York Convention will apply to it for the purpose of enforcement in other countries. Although, in principle, the Convention governs awards made "in the territory of a State other than the State where the recognition and enforcement of such awards are sought," if the host country has adopted the reciprocity reservation, the award must have been made in a country bound by the New York Convention for the rules of the Convention to apply to it.

There is, however, an exception to this rule: the Convention also applies "to arbitral awards not considered as domestic awards in the State where their recognition and enforcement are sought" (Art. I(1)).

This provision effectively authorizes countries to allow any connecting factor other than that of the place where the arbitration takes place, or even to completely detach the arbitration from any legal system.[179]

92. — Comparative law also reveals the importance and the limitations of the place of arbitration as a connecting factor.

For example, certain statutes provide, implicitly or explicitly, that a country's procedural rules automatically apply to arbitrations held on its territory, without distinguishing between domestic and international arbitration. This is true, for instance, of the 1969 Swiss *Concordat*, the 1986 Netherlands Arbitration Act, the 1996 English Arbitration Act and the 1997 German Arbitration Act.[180]

Other laws share this "territorialist" attitude, but enact separate provisions for international arbitration.[181] For example, the UNCITRAL Model Law states that its provisions only concern arbitrations held in the territory of the jurisdiction adopting it (Art. 1(2)). Likewise, the 1987 Swiss Private International Law Statute[182] contains specific rules on international arbitration which apply "if the seat of the arbitral tribunal is in Switzerland" (Art. 176).

93. — However, this territorialist approach cannot be absolute. The legal systems which adopt it must have at least some special rules concerning the recognition of foreign awards.[183] As for the Model Law, several of its articles (Arts. 8, 9, 35 and 36) apply irrespective of the place of arbitration.

There are other limits to this localization of international arbitration. First, no localization can cover all aspects of arbitration. To take the Netherlands as an example, an arbitration may be governed by a law specified in the arbitration agreement (Art. 1074 of the Code of Civil Procedure). Likewise, the rules of law applicable to the merits of the dispute are those

---

[179] *See infra* paras. 95 *et seq.*

[180] On these statutes, see *infra* paras. 157, 159, 162 and 160.

[181] These provisions must then be defined as such; *see infra* paras. 98 *et seq.*

[182] On this law, see *infra* para. 162.

[183] *See, e.g.*, Arts. 1075 and 1076 of the Netherlands Code of Civil Procedure.

chosen by the parties or, in the absence of such a choice, those chosen by arbitral tribunal (Art. 1054).

Second, in modern legislation this localization is generally no longer mandatory. The procedural rules enacted for arbitrations taking place on national territory will usually apply only in the absence of an agreement between the parties, and more particularly in the absence of a reference by the parties to a set of procedural rules. This absence of localization will be accentuated with the growth of electronic arbitration. Arbitration on the Internet is necessarily totally delocalized: "virtual arbitrators" and "cybertribunals" have no real seat, and any attachment to one national legal system would be arbitrary and lead to unpredictability. The adoption of specific substantive rules seems the only appropriate solution.[184]

94. — In the light of this liberalization of international arbitration, in 1981 the French legislature considered the localization of international arbitration to be superfluous. Enacting rules specific to international arbitration, it decided against defining their territorial sphere of application and therefore also refrained from connecting an arbitration with foreign aspects to a particular country's legal system. The French courts will still sometimes examine which law should govern an arbitration of that kind. However, they now do so only in exceptional cases, encouraged to abandon the choice of law method by the French New Code of Civil Procedure, which contains no choice of law rules. In other words, under French law international arbitration does not need to be characterized, *prima facie*, as being national or foreign.

Nevertheless, French law does not entirely disregard the place of arbitration. In particular, it draws a number of consequences from the fact that an award has been made outside France. In France, an award made outside France will be governed by the same enforcement rules as an award made in an international arbitration taking place in France, although only awards made in France can be set aside by the French courts (Arts. 1502 and 1504 of the New Code of Civil Procedure). Aside from this enforcement issue, international arbitration is thus largely "denationalized" in France.

---

[184] On the initiatives of the American Arbitration Association (Virtual Magistrate), the University of Montreal (Cybertribunal), and the World International Property Organization (for disputes related to trade mark infringement by Internet domain names), see, for example, Michael E. Schneider and Christopher Kuner, *Dispute Resolution in International Electronic Commerce*, 14 J. INT'L ARB. 5 (Sept. 1997); Jasna Arsić, *International Commercial Arbitration on the Internet – Has the Future Come Too Early?*, 14 J. INT'L ARB. 209 (Sept. 1997); Richard Hill, *The Internet, Electronic Commerce and Dispute Resolution: Comments*, 14 J. INT'L ARB. 103 (Dec. 1997); M. Scott Donahey, *Dispute Resolution in Cyberspace*, 15 J. INT'L ARB. 127 (Dec. 1998) and the contributions of Paul A. Gélinas, Richard Hill, Nabil N. Antaki, Richard Allan Horning and Michael E. Schneider, *Electronic means for dispute resolution: extending the use of modern information technologies, in* IMPROVING INTERNATIONAL ARBITRATION – THE NEED FOR SPEED AND TRUST – LIBER AMICORUM MICHEL GAUDET 51 (ICC Publication No. 598, 1998); Gabrielle Kaufmann-Kohler, *Le lieu de l'arbitrage à l'aune de la mondialisation – Réflexions à propos de deux formes récentes d'arbitrage*, 1998 REV. ARB. 517; Catherine Kessedjian and Sandrine Cahn, *Dispute Resolution On-Line*, 32 INT'L LAW. 977 (1998).

B. – NATIONAL ARBITRATION AND A-NATIONAL ARBITRATION

95. — Despite their diversity,[185] all modern sources of international arbitration law recognize or express the increasing independence of international arbitration from national laws.

This trend leads some to take what might be described as the "maximalist" view of international arbitration, comprising only arbitrations which are not subject to national laws. These would include arbitrations governed by public international law, as well as those organized pursuant to international treaties (such as ICSID arbitrations or Iran-United States disputes).[186] These may also encompass all arbitrations entirely detached from national laws and governed solely by autonomous rules constituting a genuine international legal order.

96. — We do not share this "maximalist" view, although not on the grounds on which the gradual development of this kind of *lex mercatoria* is sometimes criticized.[187] That criticism seems somewhat futile in the face of an objectively identifiable phenomenon and the cautious interpretation for which it calls.[188] As it indirectly recognizes the concept of a "non-national" award, the New York Convention is not opposed to the idea of an arbitration being totally detached from national legal systems. This is true with respect to the arbitration agreement, the arbitral procedure and to the rules applicable to the substance of the dispute. However, the idea of an arbitration detached from national legal systems will remain of limited relevance so long as the ultimate remedy—the enforcement of the arbitral award—is controlled by national courts.[189] This will be the case as long as national authorities have sole power over the police and other bodies responsible for ensuring the enforcement of awards. Proposals have been made to create a genuinely international court whose decisions on the setting aside and enforcement of arbitral awards would bind all national courts.[190] It is unlikely that many countries would be ready to agree to this extension of the concept of truly international arbitration to the post-arbitral stage of proceedings.

97. — Accordingly, it is impossible to determine whether an arbitration is "international" solely on the basis of its legal regime. In fact, an arbitration's legal regime is often the

---

[185] *See infra* paras. 127 *et seq.*

[186] *See supra* paras. 73 *et seq.*

[187] *See infra* paras. 1449 *et seq.*

[188] *See* Berthold Goldman, *La Lex Mercatoria dans les contrats et l'arbitrage internationaux: réalité et perspectives*, 106 J.D.I. 475 (1979); Berthold Goldman, *Nouvelles réflexions sur la Lex Mercatoria, in* ETUDES DE DROIT INTERNATIONAL EN L'HONNEUR DE PIERRE LALIVE 241 (1993); Emmanuel Gaillard, *Thirty Years of Lex Mercatoria: Towards the Selective Application of Transnational Rules,* 10 ICSID REV. – FOREIGN INV. L.J. 208 (1995), and, for the French version, *Trente ans de Lex Mercatoria – Pour une application sélective de la méthode des principes généraux du droit,* 122 J.D.I. 5 (1995); on this issue, generally, in relation to the substance of the dispute, see *infra* paras. 1443 *et seq.*

[189] On the review by the courts, see *infra* paras. 1558 *et seq.*

[190] Howard M. Holtzmann, *A Task for the 21st Century: Creating a New International Court for Resolving Disputes on the Enforceability of Arbitral Awards, in* THE INTERNATIONALISATION OF INTERNATIONAL ARBITRATION – THE LCIA CENTENARY CONFERENCE 109 (M. Hunter, A. Marriott and V.V. Veeder eds., 1995).

consequence of the fact that the arbitration is international. It is thus necessary to ascertain exactly which arbitrations qualify as international and therefore should be governed by specific substantive rules.

§ 2. – The International Nature of Arbitration and the Application of Specific Substantive Rules

98. — The substantive rules found in national laws, in international conventions and in non-national sources such as arbitration rules and arbitral awards, concern all the various aspects of arbitration. They deal with the arbitration agreement, the arbitral procedure and the merits of the dispute.

99. — For present purposes, we need only establish to which situations they apply. This is determined on the basis of a criterion of "internationality" which, unlike that used to connect an arbitration to a particular legal system, does not take all foreign elements into account. It does not depend on the circumstances of the conduct of the arbitration which will necessarily vary from one case to another. For example, the nationality or nationalities of the arbitrator or arbitrators, the place of arbitration or the choice of law are not sufficiently significant to allow an arbitration to benefit from substantive rules which would doubtless be more liberal than those applicable to domestic arbitration. Instead, account should be taken of more objective factors of "internationality," based on the international nature of the dispute itself. It is necessary and sufficient for the dispute to be intrinsically international.

100. — This approach has been adopted in French law, which takes an exclusively economic view of "internationality." Article 1492 of the New Code of Civil Procedure provides that "[a]n arbitration is international when it involves the interests of international trade."

This is symptomatic of a general trend which is based essentially on economic factors and certainly places more emphasis on the disputed relationship than on the means of resolving it. It has led to some interesting developments in comparative and treaty law (A), although they are generally more conservative than French law on this point (B).

A. – TREATY AND COMPARATIVE LAW

101. — By confining its application to "foreign" or "non-domestic" awards, the 1958 New York Convention made no attempt to provide a direct definition of international arbitration. As a result, the scope of the Convention's few substantive rules (such as Article II, on the arbitration agreement) is uncertain.[191]

---

[191] *See infra* paras. 255 *et seq.*

102. — On the other hand, the 1961 European Convention, which expressly concerns "international commercial arbitration" and aims to provide special substantive rules in that field, does provide a direct definition. The Convention applies to arbitration agreements, as well as the resulting arbitral proceedings and awards (Art. I(1)(b)), entered into:

> for the purpose of settling disputes arising from international trade between physical or legal persons having . . . their habitual place of residence or their seat in different Contracting States (Art. I(1)(a)).

As "international trade" is not defined, it must be considered as meaning all exchanges of property, services or assets involving the economies of at least two countries.

Unfortunately, the second criterion—which requires the parties to be residents of different countries—will prevent some arbitrations which are genuinely international from falling within the scope of the Convention. This will be the case of a dispute between two companies from the same jurisdiction which relates to a contract performed abroad, such as an international freight contract, or a sub-contract for a foreign construction project.

103. — This criticism cannot be leveled at the UNCITRAL Model Law.[192] Its definition of international arbitration consists of a series of alternative criteria, some of which are probably too broad. Under Article 1, paragraph 3 of the Model Law:

> [a]n arbitration is international if:
> (a) the parties to an arbitration agreement have, at the time of the conclusion of that agreement, their places of business in different States; or
> (b) one of the following places is situated outside the State in which the parties have their places of business:
> > (i)   the place of arbitration if determined in, or pursuant to, the arbitration agreement;
> > (ii)   any place where a substantial part of the obligations of the commercial relationship is to be performed or the place with which the subject-matter of the dispute is most closely connected; or
> (c) the parties have expressly agreed that the subject-matter of the arbitration agreement relates to more than one country.

The first criterion, identical to that adopted in the European Convention, is relatively strict. However, it is then significantly qualified where the parties are from the same country. It is perfectly justifiable to consider an arbitration as being international if a substantial part of the disputed contract is to be performed in another country. On the other hand, it is not clear why the fact that the place of arbitration is located abroad—a choice made exclusively by the parties—should suffice to render the arbitration international. The same criticism applies to the last part of the definition of "internationality," whereby an arbitration is

---

[192] On the Model Law, see *infra* para. 203.

international if the parties expressly agree that the subject-matter of the arbitration agreement relates to more than one country. This, again, is entirely within the control of the parties and may therefore prove to be fictitious. It is not up to the parties to agree that their arbitration "relates to more than one country," so as to ensure that it will be governed by rules that are more liberal than those governing domestic arbitration. Even if this does not constitute a fraud against the law ordinarily applicable, it does at least allow the parties to avoid its application without being objectively justified to do so by the requirements of international trade.

When adopting the Model Law, some legislators took these considerations into account and excluded this last case of "internationality."[193] On the other hand, the Tunisian Arbitration Code of 1993 retained all the criteria found in the Model Law and even added another, directly inspired by the French law notion of "internationality:" "[a]n arbitration is international . . . generally, if the arbitration concerns international trade."[194]

However, the substantive provisions of the Model Law are not excessively liberal in their treatment of international arbitration. They differ little from those enacted in modern statutes applicable to all arbitration, both international and domestic. This has led several countries to apply the Model Law to both international and domestic arbitration.[195] A broader interpretation of "internationality," based on subjective criteria, therefore does not lead to a very different international arbitration regime.

104. — Other statutes which create a special regime for international arbitration also define international arbitration by reference to circumstances guaranteeing that the dispute is intrinsically international, and not to the existence of a wide range of foreign elements.

105. — In England, the 1979 Arbitration Act allowed for the exclusion of various forms of appeal to the High Court if so provided for in a "non-domestic" arbitration agreement, which was defined as an arbitration agreement to which none of the parties was either a national of or resident in, or a company incorporated or managed in, England.[196] Sections 85 through 87 of the 1996 Arbitration Act provide for more extensive court intervention in proceedings resulting from domestic arbitration agreements within the meaning of Section 85, paragraph 2, than in international arbitrations.[197] However, these provisions have not entered into force and probably never will, as the government is concerned that they would

---

[193] *See, e.g.*, Sec. 2(3) of the Ontario International Commercial Arbitration Act, R.S.O. 1990, c. I.9; *see also* Louis Kos-Rabcewicz-Zubkowski, *L'adaptation de la loi-type de la C.N.U.D.C.I. dans les provinces de common law au Canada*, 1989 REV. ARB. 37; Sec. 47 of Hungarian Act LXXI of 1994 on Arbitration; Art. 819-27 of the Senegalese Code of Civil Procedure (Decree No. 98-492 of June 5, 1998; on this statute, see *infra* para. 173).

[194] *See* Art. 48 of the Tunisian Arbitration Code (Law of April 26, 1993). For a commentary, see Kalthoum Meziou and Ali Mezghani, *Le code tunisien de l'arbitrage*, 1993 REV. ARB. 521, 525.

[195] *See infra* paras. 203 *et seq.*

[196] Sections 3 and 4; on this Act, see *infra* para. 157.

[197] RUSSELL ON ARBITRATION ¶ 2–022 at 41 (D. Sutton, J. Kendall, J. Gill eds., 21st ed. 1997), quoting the press release issued by the Department of Trade and Industry on January 30, 1997. On this Act, *see infra* para. 157.

violate the principles of non-discrimination and freedom of movement of goods and services set forth in Articles 6 and 59 of the Treaty of Rome.[198]

The 1985 Belgian arbitration law was more direct and prohibited actions to set aside arbitral awards made in Belgium where none of the parties was either a Belgian national, a Belgian resident, or a company incorporated or established in Belgium. However, in 1998, the Belgian legislature amended this rule to apply only where the parties expressly so agreed.[199]

In Switzerland, Chapter 12 of the 1987 Private International Law Statute, entitled "International Arbitration," provides rules specifically applicable to international arbitrations taking place in Switzerland.[200] Article 176 of the Swiss statute indirectly defines international arbitration by stipulating that these rules shall apply only if "at the time when the arbitration agreement was concluded, at least one of the parties had neither its domicile nor its habitual residence in Switzerland."

The 1994 Italian arbitration law contains special provisions governing international arbitration which, under the new Article 832 of the Italian Code of Civil Procedure, apply where "at least one of the parties is resident or has its *de facto* headquarters abroad, or where a substantial part of the relationship from which the dispute has arisen must be performed abroad."[201]

The legislation in these countries, without explicitly requiring that the dispute should be intrinsically international from an economic standpoint, attributes greater independence to an arbitration taking place on national territory, provided either that no national interests are at stake (Belgium and Switzerland), or that at least one of the parties is not resident in the country (Switzerland and Italy). It is of course conceivable that this would include a dispute which, from an economic point of view, concerns only one foreign country (that of the residence or headquarters of both parties). However, it is more likely that it will cover only international commercial arbitrations in which companies from different countries seek arbitration in a "neutral" location—in this case Belgium, Switzerland or Italy.

In the case of Italy, where a dispute arising between two Italian companies performing a substantial part of their contract abroad will constitute an international arbitration, the "international" aspect is clearly determined using economic criteria which require a movement of goods, services or assets across national boundaries.[202]

Meanwhile, the new Algerian law imposes a cumulative requirement:

---

[198] DEPARTMENTAL ADVISORY COMMITTEE ON ARBITRATION LAW (DAC), 1997 SUPPLEMENTARY REPORT ON THE ARBITRATION ACT 1996; reproduced in 13 ARB. INT'L 317, 326 (1997). On the reform of English arbitration law, see *infra* para. 157. The position taken by the English legislature is not wholly satisfactory, as the more favorable rules applicable to international arbitrations under many arbitration statutes do not lead to discrimination based on a party's nationality; *see* Jean-François Poudret, *Critères d'extranéité de l'arbitrage international et droit communautaire*, 1998 BULL. ASA 22.

[199] Law of March 27, 1985 Relating to the Setting Aside of Arbitral Awards, amended by the May 19, 1998 statute. On these statutes, see *infra* para. 158.

[200] On this statute, see *infra* para. 162.

[201] Law No. 25 of January 5, 1994. On this law, see *infra* para. 164.

[202] For French decisions applying the same solutions in such cases, see *infra* para. 126.

an arbitration is international if it relates to a dispute involving the interests of international trade, in which at least one of the parties has its headquarters or its domicile abroad.[203]

In contrast, the Chinese law of August 31, 1994,[204] which sets forth specific rules governing arbitrations "involving a foreign element," does not define that expression. Commentators suggest that it has a fairly broad economic meaning, so as to include disputes involving companies incorporated in China but at least partially under foreign control.[205]

106. — There is thus a distinct tendency in legislation worldwide to select criteria leading an arbitration to be classified as international if the dispute itself is international in an economic sense. However, these instruments rarely provide that it is sufficient for the dispute to relate to an international commercial transaction. Instead, most also prefer to adopt a stricter criterion, namely the place where the parties are resident.

Only the arbitration statutes of Lebanon,[206] Portugal[207] and the Côte d'Ivoire[208] contain an exclusively economic definition of international arbitration, closely modeled on French law.

B. – FRENCH LAW

107. — Article 1492 of the French New Code of Civil Procedure, which has its origins in pre-1981 case law, opts clearly and exclusively for an economic definition of internationality: "[a]n arbitration is international when it involves the interests of international trade."

---

[203] Art. 458 bis of the Algerian Code of Civil Procedure (Legislative Decree No. 93–09 of April 25, 1993); *see* Mohand Issad, *Le décret législatif algérien du 25 avril 1993 relatif à l'arbitrage international*, 1993 REV. ARB. 377.

[204] On this law, see *infra* para. 174.

[205] Sally A. Harpole, *International Arbitration in the People's Republic of China under the New Arbitration Law*, ICC BULLETIN, Vol. 6, No. 1, at 19 (1995); Didier Nedjar, *L'arbitrage international en Chine après la loi du 31 août 1994*, 1995 REV. ARB. 411.

[206] *See* Art. 809, para. 1 of the New Code of Civil Procedure of September 16, 1983; *see also* Marie Sfeir-Slim, *Le nouveau droit libanais de l'arbitrage a dix ans*, 1993 REV. ARB. 543; Abdul Hamid El-Ahdab, *The Lebanese Arbitration Act*, 13 J. INT'L ARB. 39, 41 (Sept. 1996).

[207] Art. 32 of Law No. 31/86 on Voluntary Arbitration, dated August 29, 1986; for a commentary, see Dário Moura Vicente, *L'évolution récente du droit de l'arbitrage au Portugal*, id. at 419, 433.

[208] Art. 50 of Law No. 93-671 of August 9, 1993 on Arbitration, Official Journal of the Republic of Côte d'Ivoire, Sept. 16, 1993, and the commentary by Laurence Idot, *Loi ivoirienne No. 93–671 du 9 août 1993 relative à l'arbitrage*, 1994 REV. ARB. 783.

108. — The leading French case prior to the 1981 reform was the *Matter* decision of 1927.[209] This held that a transaction will be international where it produces a movement across borders with reciprocal consequences in more than one country.

109. — This economic definition of international transactions was extended by the *Cour de cassation* to contracts, and specifically to the validity of arbitration clauses.[210] The court addressed the question in two cases concerning commercial contracts with arbitration clauses providing for arbitration in London under the auspices of the London Corn Trade Association. Justifying the application to those clauses of English law (which validated the clauses whereas French law would have held them void at the time), the court did not take into account the fact that the two parties were French; it simply held that the transaction from which the dispute arose "involved the interests of international trade."

110–113. — More recently, a number of decisions[211] have confirmed the marked preference of the French courts for an economic definition of the international character of an arbitration. These cases are discussed later in the context of the substantive rules which they have helped to develop in favor of arbitration agreements.[212]

We shall now examine Article 1492 (1°), as well as its application by the French courts (2°).

---

[209] Cass. civ., May 17, 1927, Pélissier du Besset v. The Algiers Land and Warehouse Co. Ltd., D.P., Pt. I, at 25 (1928), with the conclusions by Matter and H. Capitant's note.

[210] Cass. civ., Feb. 19, 1930, Mardelé v. Muller, and Cass. civ., Jan. 27, 1931, Dambricourt v. Rossard, 1931 REV. CRIT. DIP 514; Sirey, Pt. I, at 41 (1933), and J.-P. Niboyet's note.

[211] *See* Cass. 1e civ., May 2, 1966, *Galakis, supra* note 158; CA Colmar, Nov. 29, 1968, Impex v. P.A.Z., 1968 REV. ARB. 149; JCP, Ed. G., Pt. II, No. 16,246 (1970), and B. Oppetit and P. Level's note; CA Paris, June 20, 1969, Impex v. Malteria Adriatica, 1969 REV. ARB. 95; 1969 REV. CRIT. DIP 738, and E. Mezger's note; 98 J.D.I. 118 (1971), and B. Oppetit's note (both decisions were affirmed); Cass. 1e civ., May 18, 1971, Impex v. P.A.Z. Produzione Lavorazione, 1972 REV. ARB. 2, 2 decisions, and P. Kahn's note; Dalloz, Jur. 37 (1972), 2 decisions, and D. Alexandre's note; 1972 REV. CRIT. DIP 124, 2 decisions, and E. Mezger's note; 99 J.D.I. 62 (1972), 3 decisions, and B. Oppetit's note; CA Paris, Feb. 21, 1980, General National Maritime Transport Co. v. Götaverken Arendal A.B., 107 J.D.I. 660 (1980), and P. Fouchard's note; 1980 REV. ARB. 524, and F.C. Jeantet's note; Dalloz, Jur. 568 (1980), and J. Robert's note; 1980 REV. CRIT. DIP 763, and E. Mezger's note; for an English translation, see VI Y.B. COM. ARB. 221 (1981); 20 I.L.M. 883 (1981), with an introductory note by F.C. Jeantet; CA Paris, Dec. 9, 1980, Aksa v. Norsolor, 1981 REV. ARB. 306, and F.C. Jeantet's note; 1981 REV. CRIT. DIP 545, and E. Mezger's note; Cass. 1e civ., Oct. 7, 1980, Tardieu v. S.A. Bourdon, JCP, Ed. G., Pt. II, No. 19,480 (1980), with conclusions by Gulphe; 1981 REV. CRIT. DIP 313, and J. Mestre's note; 1982 REV. ARB. 36 , and P. Level's note; CA Toulouse, Oct. 26, 1982, Sieur Behar v. Monoceram, 111 J.D.I. 603 (1984), and H. Synvet's note; CA Paris, Jan. 18, 1983, Sporprom Service B.V. v. Polyfrance Immo, 1984 REV. ARB. 87, and P. Mayer's note; CA Paris, Nov. 9, 1984, Berlaty v. Esselte Map Service, 113 J.D.I. 1039 (1986), and E. Loquin's note. For further details, see PHILIPPE FOUCHARD, EMMANUEL GAILLARD, BERTHOLD GOLDMAN, TRAITÉ DE L'ARBITRAGE COMMERCIAL INTERNATIONAL ¶¶110–13 (1996).

[212] *See infra* paras. 435 *et seq.*

1° Article 1492 of the New Code of Civil Procedure

114. — Article 1492 is the first provision of Book IV, Title V of the New Code of Civil Procedure. Title V, which concerns "international arbitration," contains only six articles (1492 to 1497). The first aims to define the scope of the rules that follow. These are all substantive rules which apply where the arbitration is international, dealing in turn with the composition of the arbitral tribunal, the arbitral procedure and the law applicable to the merits of the dispute. These very liberal rules are supplemented by the provisions of Title VI, concerning the enforcement and review by the French courts of awards made "abroad or in international arbitration." Review by the French courts of such awards is more flexible than for awards made in France in domestic arbitration.

The advantages enjoyed by international arbitration in French law are thus considerable. In fact, French law has two completely distinct legal regimes governing domestic and international arbitration.

115. — Under French law, an arbitration derives its international character solely from the transaction that gives rise to the dispute. The extraneous elements discussed earlier[213] (and in particular the nationality of the parties, that of the arbitrators, their residence, the place where the contract was signed and the place of the arbitration) are all irrelevant in determining whether an arbitration is international. All of these legal criteria are rejected in favor of a purely economic definition of "internationality."

Any transaction involving a movement of goods, services or funds across national boundaries, or concerning the economies or currencies of at least two countries, necessarily involves the interests of international trade. The same is true of any dispute to which that transaction may give rise.

116–118. — The definition found in Article 1492 is therefore not tautologous: an arbitration cannot be international in the abstract; it must result from a dispute involving the economies of more than one country.

The definition has been criticized for being too general, and even for being "elastic and likely to cause uncertainty."[214] Indeed, the fact that the UNCITRAL Model Law did not follow the French approach is probably a result of the problems of interpretation to which that approach can give rise. Nevertheless, we have seen that other national legislators have adopted the criterion of the interests of international trade, cumulatively,[215] alternatively[216] or exclusively.[217]

---

[213] *See supra* paras. 84 *et seq.*

[214] Pierre Bellet and Ernst Mezger, *L'arbitrage international dans le nouveau code de procédure civile*, 1981 REV. CRIT. DIP 611.

[215] In the case of Algeria.

[216] In the case of Tunisia.

[217] In the case of Lebanon, Portugal and the Côte d'Ivoire.

2° The Application of Article 1492 by the French Courts

119. — On the whole, the interpretation by the courts of Article 1492 has been consistent with the spirit of the text. They have never conferred international status on an arbitration the subject-matter of which did not affect the interests of international trade.

120-121. — Rather than describing the French case law in detail,[218] we will confine ourselves to a brief discussion of the interpretation by the Paris Court of Appeals of the words "involve the interests of international trade." The view of the Court is that

> the international nature of an arbitration must be determined according to the economic reality of the process during which it arises. In this respect, all that is required is that the economic transaction should entail a transfer of goods, services or funds across national boundaries, while the nationality of the parties, the law applicable to the contract or to the arbitration, and the place of arbitration are irrelevant.[219]

The *Cour de cassation* approved this interpretation in the *V 2000 (Jaguar)* case.[220]

---

[218] *See, e.g.,* CA Paris, Jan. 17, 1984, Bloc'h et Fils v. Delatrae Mockfjaerd, 1984 REV. ARB. 498, and P. Fouchard's note; TGI Paris, réf., June 3, 1985, Europe Etudes Gecti v. E.T.P.O., 1987 REV. ARB. 179, 1st decision, and P. Fouchard's note; CA Paris, Jan. 28, 1988, C.C.C. Filmkunst v. E.D.I.F., 1988 REV. ARB. 565; 116 J.D.I. 1021 (1989), and E. Loquin's note.

[219] CA Paris, Mar. 14, 1989, Murgue Seigle v. Coflexip, 1991 REV. ARB. 355, and observations by J.-H. Moitry and C. Vergne; 1991 RTD COM. 575, and observations by J.-C. Dubarry and E. Loquin; for identical or comparable reasoning, see CA Paris, Apr. 26, 1985, Aranella v. Italo-Ecuadoriana, 1985 REV. ARB. 311, and E. Mezger's note; 113 J.D.I. 175 (1986), and J.-M. Jacquet's note; CA Paris, Dec. 8, 1988, Chantiers Modernes v. C.M.G.C., 1989 REV. ARB. 111, 2d decision, and observations by J. Pellerin; CA Paris, Apr. 5, 1990, Courrèges Design v. André Courrèges, 1991 REV. CRIT. DIP 580, and C. Kessedjian's note; 1992 REV. ARB. 110, and H. Synvet's note; TGI Paris, réf., Apr. 10, 1990, European Country Hotels Ltd. v. Consorts Legrand, and CA Paris, Nov. 14, 1991, Consorts Legrand v. European Country Hotels Ltd., 1994 REV. ARB. 545, 2d decision, and observations by P. Fouchard; CA Paris, Apr. 4, 1991, Icart v. Quillery, 1991 REV. ARB. 659, 2d decision, and observations by J. Pellerin; CA Paris, Apr. 24, 1992, Sermi v. Hennion, Dalloz, I.R. 197 (1992); 1992 REV. ARB. 598, and C. Jarrosson's note and the two decisions cited therein; CA Paris, July 10, 1992, International Contractors Group v. X, Dalloz, Jur. 459 (1992), and C. Jarrosson's note; 1992 REV. ARB. 609, and P. Leboulanger's note; CA Paris, Mar. 23, 1993, Ets. Marcel Sebin v. Irridelco International Corp., 1998 REV. ARB. 541, and P. Fouchard's note; CA Paris, Nov. 25, 1993, Paco Rabanne Parfums v. Les Maisons Paco Rabanne, 1994 REV. ARB. 730, and observations by D. Bureau; CA Paris, Feb. 24, 1994, Ministère tunisien de l'équipement v. Bec Frères, 1995 REV. ARB. 275, and Y. Gaudemet's note; for an English translation, see XXII Y.B. COM. ARB. 682 (1997); CA Paris, Mar. 24, 1994, Deko v. Dingler, 1994 REV ARB. 515, and C. Jarrosson's note; CA Paris, Dec. 7, 1994, *V. 2000, supra* note 145; CA Paris, June 20, 1996, PARIS v. Razel, 1996 REV. ARB. 657, and observations by D. Bureau; CA Paris, July 1, 1997, Agence Transcongolaise des Communications-Chemins de fer Congo Océan (ATC-CFCO) v. Compagnie minière de l'Ogooué (Comilog), 1998 REV. ARB. 131, and D. Hascher's note; CA Paris, Oct. 8, 1997, Solna International AB v. SA Destouche, Dalloz, I.R. 233 (1997).

[220] Cass. 1e civ., May 21, 1997, *Renault, supra* note 145.

122. — Any international factors of a purely voluntary or legal nature are thus considered to be irrelevant, and unless the transaction is international in an economic sense, the arbitration will remain domestic. This will be so where, for instance, the only non-French element is the fact that one party is not a French national,[221] or that the parties to the dispute are French companies controlled by non-French entities,[222] or that the arbitration is before an international arbitral institution such as the ICC.[223]

123. — The most common scenario, and the most straightforward, is that of a contract for the movement of goods,[224] services[225] or funds[226] across national boundaries. In most cases, the parties are resident or have their headquarters in different countries, although this is not always noted by the courts and is not considered to be necessary for a dispute to be international.[227]

---

[221] CA Paris, May 26, 1992, Guyapêche v. Abba Import Aktiebolag, 1993 REV. ARB. 624, and L. Aynès' note.

[222] CA Paris, Nov. 28, 1996, CN France v. Minhal France, 1997 REV. ARB. 380, and E. Loquin's note. This decision held that control of a French company by non-French persons did not lead there to be a cross-border movement of goods, services or funds, as the dispute concerned only the management and lease of a hotel located in Paris.

[223] CA Paris, Apr. 11, 1996, OIP v. Pyramide, 1996 REV. ARB. 467, and D. Bureau's note.

[224] CA Paris, Feb. 19, 1988, Firme Peter Biegi v. Brittania, 1990 REV. ARB. 657 (exportation of turkey meat from France to Germany); CA Paris, June 15, 1989, Granomar v. Compagnie Interagra, 1992 REV. ARB. 80, and J.-J. Arnaldez' note (sale by a Swiss company to a French company of wheat intended for the Soviet Union); CA Paris, Apr. 19, 1991, Parfums Stern France v. CFFD, 1991 REV. ARB. 673, and observations by J. Pellerin (distribution, in France and outside, of products imported from the United States); CA Paris, Feb. 27, 1992, Sohm v. Simex, 1992 REV. ARB. 590, and P. Ancel's note (dispute concerning payment of the price of a Franco-Belgian sale); CA Paris, Oct. 27, 1994, de Diseno v. Mendes, 1995 REV. ARB. 263, 2d decision, and P. Level's note (distribution of French products in Spain); CA Paris, Dec. 7, 1994, *V 2000, supra* note 145, 3 decisions (purchase by French collectors, via a company incorporated in France, of cars manufactured in the United Kingdom); CA Paris, Mar. 22, 1995, SMABTP v. Statinor, 1997 REV. ARB. 550, and the commentary by Daniel Cohen, *Arbitrage et groupes de contrats, id.* at 471, especially at 496 *et seq.*; 1996 RTD COM. 247, and observations by J.-C. Dubarry and E. Loquin (distribution in France of products manufactured in Germany); Cass. 1e civ., May 21, 1997, *Renault, supra* note 145.

[225] CA Paris, Jan. 28, 1988, *C.C.C. Filmkunst, supra* note 218 (broadcasting of a film throughout the world); 116 J.D.I. 1021 (1989), and the extended note by E. Loquin; CA Paris, Apr. 5, 1990, Damon v. Abu Nasser, 1990 REV. ARB. 875, and P. Fouchard's note (payment of commission to an intermediary working outside France in a transaction involving the sale of real estate in Paris); CA Paris, July 10, 1992, *International Contractors Group, supra* note 219 (civil engineering works carried out in Kuwait by an Italian company, and incidental agreements for transferring funds); CA Paris, Mar. 24, 1994, *Deko, supra* note 219 (license contract entitling a French company to use a French patent owned by a German company).

[226] CA Paris, June 9, 1983, Iro-Holding v. Sétilex, 1983 REV. ARB. 497, and M. Vasseur's note (financing of companies involving transfers of capital across national boundaries); CA Paris, June 10, 1993, Compagnie Aeroflot v. AGF, 1995 REV. ARB. 448, 3d decision (payment by a non-French airline company of rent for a lease in France).

[227] For example, in the *Aranella* case the disputed contract (for the construction and sale of ships) had been concluded between two Italian companies but, in order to treat the arbitration as international, the court noted that the purchaser was under foreign control and could not have financed the disputed acquisitions without the capital contributions made by its parent company (CA Paris, Apr. 26, 1985, *supra* note 219).

124. — It is of little consequence whether the contract was actually performed, or whether the movement of goods, services or funds across national boundaries in fact took place. All that matters is that the disputed transaction "involved" a transfer of that kind.[228]

125. — Likewise, it was immaterial that a share acquisition leading to a corporate take-over concerned a French company and was governed by French law. All that was required was that the investment originate abroad for it to lead to a movement of funds from a foreign country into France.[229]

126. — Difficulties most commonly arise where the dispute concerns two French companies, based in France, who enter into an agreement (generally a sub-contract) to carry out a project abroad. Will any dispute arising from their contract be international? One case decided prior to the 1981 reform of French international arbitration law held that it would not.[230] A post-1981 decision did not decide the issue.[231] More recently, however, the courts have taken a consistent approach: the fact that a dispute exclusively concerns two French companies does not prevent it from being treated as an international dispute, provided that it involves interests of international trade. This will be the case where, for the French parties, performance of the contract involves an international transfer of goods, services or technology.[232] Where both delivery and payment are to take place in France, there is some

---

[228] CA Paris, Nov. 25, 1993, *Paco Rabanne, supra* note 219.

[229] *See* CA Paris, Nov. 9, 1983, Wasteels v. Ampafrance, 1985 REV. ARB. 81, 11th decision, and, in the same case, CA Paris, May 13, 1986, and Cass. 1e civ., May 10, 1988, 1989 REV. ARB. 51, and J.-L. Goutal's note; CA Paris, Apr. 5, 1990, *Courrèges Design, supra* note 219; TGI Paris, Apr. 10, 1990 and CA Paris, Nov. 14, 1991, *European Country Hotels, supra* note 219; CA Paris, Nov. 29, 1990, Payart v. Morgan Crucible Co., 1991 REV. ARB. 659, 1st decision, and observations by J. Pellerin; 118 J.D.I. 414 (1991), and P. Kahn's note; CA Paris, Jan. 24, 1991, Salice v. Haas, 1992 REV. ARB. 158, and observations by D. Cohen; in favor of the characterization of arbitration as domestic, CA Paris, Feb. 21, 1984, Andree und Wilkerling Komanditgesellschaft v. Leboeuf, 1986 REV. ARB. 65, and P. Fouchard's disapproving note.

[230] This decision concerned a joint venture involving companies headquartered in France, see CA Paris, Nov. 30, 1972, S.A. Eau et Assainissement SOCEA v. S.A. CAPAG-CETRA, 100 J.D.I. 390 (1973), and B. Oppetit's note; 1973 REV. ARB. 91, and E. Mezger's note.

[231] CA Paris, July 9, 1986, Alexandre Giuliani v. Colas, 1987 REV. ARB. 179, 5th decision, and P. Fouchard's note.

[232] CA Paris, May 23, 1986, Worthington Turbodyne v. Heurtey Industries, Gaz. Pal., Somm. 12 (1987) (delivery of goods to Morocco); Cass. 1e civ., Mar. 8, 1988, Thinet v. Labrely, 1988 Bull. Civ. I, No. 65; Dalloz, Jur. 577 (1989), and J. Robert's note; 1989 REV. ARB. 473, and P. Ancel's note (sub-contract between French parties for the execution of a construction contract in Saudi Arabia); CA Paris, Dec. 8, 1988, *Chantiers Modernes, supra* note 219 (sub-contract in Algeria); CA Paris, Mar. 14, 1989, *Murgue Seigle, supra* note 219 (sub-contract); CA Paris, Jan. 26, 1990, Boccard v. S.A.R.L. Stapem, 1991 REV. ARB. 125, 2d decision, and observations by J.-H. Moitry and C. Vergne; 1991 RTD COM. 575, and observations by J.-C. Dubarry and E. Loquin (two French companies in a joint venture to introduce their technology into Angola and to develop their activities there); CA Paris, Apr. 4, 1991, *Icart, supra* note 219 (sub-contract for the construction of a real estate complex abroad); CA Paris, Apr. 24, 1992, *Sermi, supra* note 219 (sub-contract for the construction of industrial plant abroad); CA Paris, Oct. 2, 1992, Colas routière v. Tracet, 1992 REV. ARB. 625, 5th decision, and observations by J. Pellerin; CA Paris, June 20, 1996, *PARIS, supra* note 219 (guarantee given by a French insurance group to a French company, relating to the transfer into France of the consideration for the sale of

(continued...)

doubt as to whether any international transfer actually occurs. In such cases, the courts may still treat the arbitration as international on other grounds, including the close connection between the sub-contract and the main contract, and the fact that the dispute results from technical requirements laid down by the foreign contractor.[233] However, they will not confer international status on an arbitration if the part of the contract which is performed outside France is insignificant and therefore does not involve the interests of international trade.[234]

One of the most important features of the French conception of internationality is thus that it disregards the fact that the parties may share the same nationality or be resident in the same country. In a dispute that is genuinely international in economic terms, the arbitration will be international even where both parties are French[235] or share another nationality.[236]

---

[232](...continued)
   a shareholding in Algeria).

[233] CA Paris, Mar. 14, 1989, *Murgue Seigle, supra* note 219.

[234] CA Paris, Nov. 12, 1993, Alexandre Films v. Partners Production, 1995 REV. ARB. 68.

[235] This applies to most of the cases cited above.

[236] CA Paris, Apr. 26, 1985, *Aranella, supra* note 219; CA Paris, Jan. 19, 1990, Immoplan v. Mercure, 1991 REV. ARB. 125, and observations by J.-H. Moitry and C. Vergne (dispute involving two Italian companies concerning the ownership of real estate located in France, and the payment of sums denominated in Swiss Francs).

CHAPTER II
SOURCES OF INTERNATIONAL COMMERCIAL ARBITRATION

127-128. — The sources of international arbitration law are of both public (Section I) and private origin (Section II).

SECTION I
PUBLIC SOURCES

129. — The public sources of international arbitration law consist, for the most part, of rules enacted or simply proposed by competent national authorities acting in a domestic or international context (§ 1). In addition, however, the growth over the past thirty years of international arbitration as a means of settling disputes has led to a proliferation of inter-governmental conventions and instruments drawn up by international organizations (§ 2).

§ 1. – National Sources

130. — The national sources of international arbitration law are of course found within the legal systems of each country. In recent years, there have been numerous legislative reforms worldwide, with each jurisdiction seeking to make international arbitration on its own territory more attractive. This is certainly the case with French law (A). However, the competition between the traditional international arbitration locations and the ambitions of a number of other countries can be clearly seen from an examination of other legal systems (B).

A. – FRENCH LAW

131-135. — France was one of the first countries to modernize its arbitration legislation. French law is considered by many to be, if not a model, then at least an essential point of reference. Although the foundations were laid by the courts beforehand,[1] the major reform of arbitration law in France took place in the early 1980s (1°). It was a two-stage process: first, in 1980, domestic arbitration law was brought up to date; then, a year later, specific rules were enacted governing international arbitration. This affirmation of the specific nature of international arbitration is one of the most significant features of French law. Following these statutory reforms, the more liberal regime applicable to international arbitration was maintained and reinforced by the French courts (2°).

1° The 1980-1981 Reforms

136. — A decree dated May 14, 1980[2] laid down new rules for French domestic arbitration. This reform was part of the overhaul of the Code of Civil Procedure.

At that time, the legislature considered that international arbitration should continue to be governed either by case law (which was viewed as the best way to resolve issues of private international law) or by the international instruments ratified by France.

The dangers resulting from this diversity of sources soon became clear: the new domestic law provisions, which were more detailed and inherently less flexible than the old Code, seemed overly restrictive for certain aspects of international arbitration. In addition, the review of arbitral awards by the courts was limited to domestic awards made in France. This was clearly not suitable for foreign awards or for awards resolving international disputes.[3]

---

[1] Before 1981, there were no statutory rules relating to international arbitration alone. The courts thus laid the foundations of French international arbitration law without the support of any legislation. *See, e.g.*, Cass. 1e civ., May 7, 1963, Ets. Raymond Gosset v. Carapelli, JCP, Ed. G., Pt. II, No. 13,405 (1963), and B. Goldman's note; 91 J.D.I. 82 (1964), and J.-D. Bredin's note; 1963 REV. CRIT. DIP 615, and H. Motulsky's note; Dalloz, Jur. 545 (1963), and J. Robert's note (confirming the autonomy of the arbitration agreement from the main contract in international arbitration); Cass. 1e civ., May 2, 1966, Trésor Public v. Galakis, JCP, Ed. G., Pt. II, No. 14,798 (1966), and P. Ligneau's note; 93 J.D.I. 648 (1966), and P. Level's note; 1967 REV. CRIT. DIP 553, and B. Goldman's note; Dalloz, Jur. 575 (1966), and J. Robert's note (confirming the validity of the arbitration agreement in an international contract involving a state or a state-controlled entity); Cass. 1e civ., July 4, 1972, Hecht v. Buisman's, 99 J.D.I. 843 (1972), and B. Oppetit's note; 1974 REV. CRIT. DIP 82, and P. Level's note (acknowledging the principle of the validity of the arbitration clause in international arbitration). On the nature and scope of the rules laid down by the courts, see, for example, Berthold Goldman, *Règles de conflit, règles d'application immédiate et règles matérielles dans l'arbitrage commercial international*, in TRAVAUX DU COMITÉ FRANÇAIS DE DROIT INTERNATIONAL PRIVÉ 1966–1969, at 119 (1971). For an illustration of the impact of these rules on the subsequent legislative reforms, see the report by the *Garde des Sceaux* to the Prime Minister, JCP, Ed. G., No. 23, Supp. June 3, 1981 (for a translation, see JEAN-LOUIS DELVOLVÉ, ARBITRATION IN FRANCE – THE FRENCH LAW OF NATIONAL AND INTERNATIONAL ARBITRATION 93 (1982)); *see also* Philippe Fouchard, *L'arbitrage international en France après le décret du 12 mai 1981*, 109 J.D.I. 374, 381 (1982)). For more details on pre-1981 French law, see PHILIPPE FOUCHARD, EMMANUEL GAILLARD, BERTHOLD GOLDMAN, TRAITÉ DE L'ARBITRAGE COMMERCIAL INTERNATIONAL ¶¶ 131–35 (1996).

[2] Decree No. 80-354 of May 14, 1980, concerning arbitration and intended for inclusion in the New Code of Civil Procedure, J.O., May 18, 1980, p. 1238; 1980 REV. ARB. 725.

[3] On this issue, see Philippe Fouchard, *La réforme de l'arbitrage international en France – Introduction: spécificité de l'arbitrage international*, 1981 REV. ARB. 449.

137. — The French Ministry of Justice set about addressing the problem, and a second decree was enacted on May 12, 1981.[4] Book IV, entitled "arbitration," now forms the last part of the New Code of Civil Procedure. The first four titles of Book IV incorporate the provisions of the 1980 Decree into the Code as Articles 1442 to 1491. Then come the rules of private international law covering "international arbitration," found at Title V (Arts. 1492 to 1497), and "recognition of, enforcement of, and recourse against arbitral awards made abroad or in international arbitration," at Title VI (Arts. 1498 to 1507).

138. — In spite of their brevity, these articles constituted a major step forward, as all commentators recognized.[5]

139. — In many respects the new provisions confirm the previous case law. This is true of the definition of international arbitration,[6] as well as its legal regime. The detachment of international arbitration from national legal systems had, on the whole, already been accepted by the *Cour de cassation*, with respect to both arbitral procedure[7] and the merits

---

[4] Decree No. 81-500 of May 12, 1981 enacting the provisions of Books III and IV of the New Code of Civil Procedure and modifying various provisions of that Code, J.O., May 14, 1981, p. 1380; 1981 REV. ARB. 317.

[5] *See* Jacques Béguin, *Les grands traits du Décret français du 12 mai 1981 sur l'arbitrage international*, *in* RID COMP., SPECIAL ISSUE, VOL. 5, JOURNÉES DE LA SOCIÉTÉ DE LÉGISLATION COMPARÉE – ANNÉE 1983, at 359 (1983); Pierre Bellet and Ernst Mezger, *L'arbitrage international dans le nouveau code de procédure civile*, 1981 REV. CRIT. DIP 611; W. Laurence Craig, William W. Park, Jan A.S. Paulsson, *French Codification of a Legal Framework for International Commercial Arbitration: the Decree of May 12, 1981*, 13 LAW & POL'Y INT'L BUS. 727 (1981); VII Y.B. COM. ARB. 407 (1982); Georges R. Delaume, *International Arbitration under French Law*, 37 ARB. J. 38, first paragraph (Mar. 1982); Fouchard, *supra* note 3; Fouchard, *supra* note 1; Philippe Fouchard, *Le nouveau droit français de l'arbitrage*, 59 REV. DR. INT. DR. COMP. 29 (1982); Berthold Goldman, *La réforme de l'arbitrage international en France – La volonté des parties et le rôle de l'arbitre dans l'arbitrage international*, 1981 REV. ARB. 469; Berthold Goldman, *La nouvelle réglementation française de l'arbitrage international*, *in* THE ART OF ARBITRATION – ESSAYS ON INTERNATIONAL ARBITRATION – LIBER AMICORUM PIETER SANDERS 153 (J. Schultz and A.J. van den Berg eds., 1982); Fernand Charles Jeantet, *La réforme de l'arbitrage international en France – L'accueil des sentences étrangères ou internationales dans l'ordre juridique français*, 1981 REV. ARB. 503; Patrice Level, *La réforme de l'arbitrage international (D. n° 81-500, 12 mai 1981, Nouveau Code de procédure civile, art. 1492 à 1507)*, JCP, Ed. C.I., Pt. I, No. 9899 (1981); R. Perrot, *Sur la réforme de l'arbitrage international*, *in* TRAVAUX DU COMITÉ FRANÇAIS DE DROIT INTERNATIONAL PRIVÉ 1981–1982, at 53 (1985); Jean Robert, *L'arbitrage en matière internationale – Commentaire du décret n° 81-500 du 12 mai 1981 (art. 1492 à 1507 nouv. c. pr. civ.)*, Dalloz, Chron. 209 (1981); Bernard Audit, *A National Codification of International Commercial Arbitration: The French Decree of May 12, 1981*, *in* RESOLVING TRANSNATIONAL DISPUTES THROUGH ARBITRATION 117 (T. Carbonneau ed., 1984); Yves Derains and Rosabel E. Goodman-Everard, *France*, *in* ICCA INTERNATIONAL HANDBOOK ON COMMERCIAL ARBITRATION (1998).

[6] *See supra* paras. 107 *et seq.*

[7] *See, e.g.*, Cass. 1e civ., June 16, 1976, Krebs v. Milton Stern, 104 J.D.I. 671 (1977), and P. Fouchard's note; 1977 REV. ARB. 269, and E. Mezger's note; 1978 REV. CRIT. DIP 767; Cass. 1e civ., June 30, 1976, Bruynzeel Deurenfabrik N.V. v. Ministre d'Etat aux Affaires Etrangères de la République Malgache, 104 J.D.I. 114 (1977), and B. Oppetit's note; 1977 REV. ARB. 137, and J. Rubellin-Devichi's note; Gaz. Pal., Jur. 70 (1977), and J. Viatte's note.

of disputes.[8] In these two areas, the new provisions endorsed that approach. The constitution of the arbitral tribunal (Art. 1493) and the arbitral procedure (Art. 1494) are governed primarily by the parties' intentions alone. The parties or, in the absence of a choice by the parties, the arbitrators, may make reference to arbitration rules alone.[9] National laws only apply where the parties or, subsidiarily, the arbitrators choose to apply them. French domestic law only applies on a subsidiary basis and in a non-mandatory way (Art. 1495). As to the merits of the dispute, the arbitrators apply the rules of law chosen by the parties or, in the absence of such a choice, those which they consider to be most appropriate. In all cases these rules are to be applied in conjunction with trade usages (Art. 1496). The new provisions thus acknowledge not only the principle of party autonomy in international trade, but also the existence or development of rules of law other than those contained within the narrow framework of a single national legal system.

140. — Perhaps the most interesting aspect of Title V, which applies to all international arbitrations, is the methodology adopted. It sets forth only substantive rules as opposed to choice of law rules. For an institution as complex and diverse as arbitration, with its several different stages and facets (contractual for the arbitration agreement, judicial for the proceedings and the award), it would have been extremely laborious to have developed an exhaustive list of connecting factors. For the fairly rare cases, generally concerning the arbitration agreement, where French courts were required to establish which rules govern an international arbitration, it was considered preferable to give them total discretion to make such a determination, without confining them within certain more or less artificial criteria. The chief consideration was to allow the parties (or subsidiarily the arbitrators) the greatest possible freedom, either in choosing the applicable law, or in fixing the rules governing the constitution of the arbitral tribunal, the arbitral procedure and the merits of the dispute.

These substantive rules apply, as far as the French legal order is concerned, to all international arbitrations without requiring a particular connection between the arbitration and France. Their territorial scope thus appears to be unlimited. However, it would be going too far to interpret this as legal imperialism on the part of the French legislature,[10] for at least two reasons. First, these rules, far from unilaterally imposing any particular style of international arbitration, are remarkably liberal in content. Second, and more importantly, for these rules to be relevant to a given international arbitration in practice, the dispute must have some connection with France (either the fact that the arbitration is held in France or that the enforcement of the award made outside France is sought in France).[11]

---

[8] *See, e.g.,* CA Paris, June 12, 1980, Banque du Proche-Orient v. Fougerolle, 1981 REV. ARB. 292, 2d decision, and G. Couchez' note; 109 J.D.I. 931 (1982), 2d decision, and B. Oppetit's note , *aff'd,* Cass. 2e civ., Dec. 9, 1981, Fougerolle v. Banque du Proche-Orient, 1982 REV. ARB. 183, and G. Couchez' note; 109 J.D.I. 931 (1982), 3d decision, and observations by B. Oppetit.

[9] On these private sources of international arbitration law, see *infra* para. 366.

[10] *See* A. Hirsch, 1981 REV. ARB. 490.

[11] On these possible links between an international arbitration and French law, see, for example, *infra* paras. 502 *et seq.* (application to the French courts in connection with the constitution of the arbitral tribunal), 1199 *et seq.* (selection by the parties or the arbitrators of French law to govern the arbitral procedure), 1564 *et seq.*

(continued...)

141. — The French courts are thus able to intervene to resolve difficulties concerning the constitution of the tribunal where the arbitration takes place in France or is governed by French procedural law (Art. 1493, para. 2). They will also have jurisdiction where a party seeks enforcement or recognition in France of an award made outside France. Prior to the 1981 reform, the French system for recognition of foreign awards was extremely complex. New statutory provisions were needed to eliminate certain forms of recourse and simplify the others. This was the underlying aim of Title VI. Enforcement of such awards is now a simple matter (Arts. 1498 *et seq.*), and the grounds for their review by the courts, limited to the short list found at Article 1502, are fewer in number than those available in domestic arbitration, and must be brought directly before the Courts of Appeals. As to the distinction between the treatment of awards made in France and those made outside France, the former may be challenged directly in an action to set aside, whereas the latter can be reviewed only on appeal against an enforcement order. Nevertheless, the same grounds apply in an action to set aside as in an action to contest enforcement of the award. If the award was made in France, it may be set aside in France. If an award with the same flaws was made outside France, the Court of Appeals will simply refuse enforcement on the same grounds (Arts. 1502 to 1505). The place where the award is made thus does not affect the scope of the review by the courts; it merely conditions which form of recourse is available (an action to set aside or an appeal against the enforcement order). This straightforward system was adopted in preference to any attempt to connect the award to a particular legal system, and it is no coincidence that the concept of a "foreign award" has not been used in French legislation.

142–147. — The point in time at which these new international arbitration provisions became applicable was determined at Articles 55 and 56 of the Decree of May 12, 1981. Article 55 stipulates that:

> the provisions of Book IV, Title V of the New Code of Civil Procedure shall only apply to arbitration agreements concluded on or after the date on which the present decree is published.

As a result, Articles 1492 to 1497 did not immediately apply on enactment of the 1981 Decree. However, as these provisions essentially codified pre-existing case law, their deferred application created no great difficulty in practice.

Article 56 of the 1981 Decree states that "[t]he provisions of Book IV, Title VI of the New Code of Civil Procedure shall only apply if the arbitral award was rendered after the date on which the present decree is published."

Unlike the rules contained in Title V, those of Title VI concerning recourse against non-French arbitral awards considerably modified existing law.[12] Awards made before

---

[11](...continued)
(application to the French courts to enforce or set aside an award).

[12] *See supra* para. 141.

October 1, 1980 remained subject to pre-reform law.[13] Awards made according to French procedural law between October 1, 1980 and May 14, 1981 (when the new legislation came into force) were subject to the new domestic arbitration law.[14] All other awards made during the same period (considered as foreign) were not subject to the new legislation. For enforcement of such awards in France, the Paris Court of Appeals applied principles governing the enforcement of foreign court judgments.[15]

2° Developments Since the 1981 Reform

148. — No further upheavals have occurred in French arbitration law since the enactment of the New Code of Civil Procedure.

149. — On the whole, the courts have encountered no particular difficulties in applying the new provisions. All the major cases since the reform show that the courts have properly understood and implemented the spirit of the new law.

The President of the Paris Tribunal of First Instance has carefully exercised the powers aimed at facilitating international arbitration conferred on him by Article 1493, paragraph 2 of the New Code.[16] When reviewing awards, the Paris Court of Appeals has maintained and even developed its liberal stance towards arbitration agreements, arbitral procedure, the substance of awards made abroad, and towards the removal of international arbitrations from the effects of choice of law rules and national legal systems, within the limits of international public policy.[17]

Generally speaking, the *Cour de cassation* has endorsed this liberal attitude, particularly by confirming that the list of grounds on which an award can be set aside under Article 1502 of the New Code is to be interpreted restrictively.

150. — The legislature has only intervened twice since the 1981 reform, on specific issues on both occasions. The Law of August 19, 1986, in its Article 9, stated that:

> notwithstanding Article 2060 of the Civil Code, the State, local authorities and public establishments are entitled, in contracts which they conclude with foreign companies for the purpose of carrying out transactions in the national

---

[13] *See* JEAN ROBERT, ARBITRAGE CIVIL ET COMMERCIAL ¶¶ 460 *et seq.* (4th ed. 1967); P. Fouchard, note following CA Paris, Feb. 21, 1980, General National Maritime Transport Co. v. Götaverken Arendal A.B., 107 J.D.I. 660, 674 (1980).

[14] *See* Cass. 1e civ., May 25, 1983, Maatschappij voor Industriele Research en Ontwikkeling v. Lievremont, 1985 REV. ARB. 415, 1st decision, and H. Synvet's note; 1983 Bull. Civ. I, No. 156; for an English translation, see XII Y.B. COM. ARB. 480 (1987).

[15] *See* CA Paris, July 6, 1982, Omrane les 5 étoiles v. Portman Ltd., 1982 REV. ARB. 321, and E. Mezger's note.

[16] *See infra* paras. 834 *et seq.*

[17] *See* SOPHIE CRÉPIN, LES SENTENCES ARBITRALES DEVANT LE JUGE FRANÇAIS – PRATIQUE DE L'EXÉCUTION ET DU CONTRÔLE JUDICIAIRE DEPUIS LES RÉFORMES DE 1980–1981 (1995).

interest, to enter into arbitration agreements with a view to resolving, definitively if appropriate, disputes connected with the application and interpretation of such contracts.[18]

This provision, referred to as the "Eurodisney law," was of no utility in practice, and could have had the damaging effect of limiting the scope of the *Galakis* decision[19] and that of international instruments authorizing the government and public law entities to enter into international arbitration agreements.[20] Fortunately, the courts maintained their very liberal approach to the arbitrability of disputes involving states and state-owned entities after the enactment of the 1986 statute.

In addition, Law No. 91-650 of July 9, 1991, reforming civil enforcement procedures, stated that "applications for recognition and enforcement . . . of French or foreign arbitral awards" are to be heard by a single judge of the relevant Tribunal of First Instance.[21]

151. — French international arbitration law is thus currently drawn from two sources: a brief, liberal Code of Civil Procedure, and well-established case law that is generally able to overcome the Code's shortcomings—by declaring, for example, that certain domestic law rules, such as Articles 1458 and 1466 of the New Code of Civil Procedure, are applicable to international arbitration[22]—and to deal with difficulties of interpretation which may yet arise.

However, in the interest of greater clarity, it would perhaps be useful to set forth the substantive rules applicable to international arbitration in more explicit terms, as the rather general principles of party autonomy found in Articles 1494 and 1495 may be confusing for non-specialists. It might also be helpful to update Articles 2060 and 2061 of the Civil Code, which are frequently criticized as being archaic and are in any event completely superseded

---

[18] Law No. 86-972 of August 19, 1986, J.O., Aug. 22, 1986, p. 10,190. For a commentary, see Matthieu de Boisséson, *Interrogations et doutes sur une évolution législative: l'article 9 de la loi du 19 août 1986*, 1987 REV. ARB. 3; on this issue, generally, see APOSTOLOS PATRIKIOS, L'ARBITRAGE EN MATIÈRE ADMINISTRATIVE (1997).

[19] Cass. 1e civ., May 2, 1966, *supra* note 1.

[20] On this issue, generally, see *infra* paras. 542 *et seq.*

[21] Article 6 of Law No. 91-650 of July 9, 1991 reforming civil enforcement procedures, modifying Article L. 311-11 of the Code of Judicial Organization (J.O., July 14, 1991, p. 9228) and Article 305 of the implementation Decree No. 92-755 of July 31, 1992, which modified Article 1477 of the New Code of Civil Procedure (J.O., Aug. 5, 1992, p. 10,530, and erratum, J.O., Oct. 31, 1992, p. 15,104). See Philippe Théry, *Quelques observations à propos de la loi du 9 juillet 1991 portant réforme des procédures civiles d'exécution*, 1991 REV. ARB. 727; Philippe Théry, *Les procédures civiles d'exécution et le droit de l'arbitrage*, 1993 REV. ARB. 159.

[22] *See* Cass. 1e civ., June 28, 1989, Eurodif v. République Islamique d'Iran, 1989 Bull. Civ. I, No. 255; 1989 REV. ARB. 653, 2d decision, and P. Fouchard's note; 117 J.D.I. 1004 (1990), 2d decision, and P. Ouakrat's note; CA Paris, Sept. 10, 1997, Chambon v. Thomson CSF, 1997 DALLOZ AFF. 1253; 1999 REV. ARB. 121, and observations by D. Bureau; Cass. 1e civ., Jan. 5, 1999, Zanzi v. de Coninck, 1999 DALLOZ AFF. 474.

by case law.[23] Subject to these two reservations, French law appears to be settled and it is unlikely that any major changes are imminent.

B. – OTHER LEGAL SYSTEMS

152. — Although some new arbitration legislation was passed in the late 1960s and 1970s—in Switzerland, Belgium and England, for example—it was not particularly forward-looking. The modernization movement began in earnest with the French reforms of 1980 and 1981 followed, in Western Europe, by new legislation in the Netherlands in 1986, in Switzerland in 1987, and most recently in England in 1996, Germany in 1997, Belgium in 1998, and Sweden in 1999.

153. — The causes of this modernizing trend include long-term factors such as the growth of international trade and the resulting increase in the number of associated disputes. As discussed earlier, arbitration is now considered to be the normal means of resolving such disputes.[24] To conform with international trends, jurisdictions formerly opposed to arbitration (such as Spain), or which confined domestic arbitration within a strict statutory and judicial framework (such as England), had to take a more liberal position, if only in order not to overly disadvantage their legal communities.

More recently, a number of more short-term economic and legal factors also contributed to the impetus for reform. First came the influence of the major multilateral instruments, which governments felt compelled to ratify. The most significant of these instruments were the 1958 New York Convention[25] and the 1985 UNCITRAL Model Law,[26] the latter of which provides both an opportunity to modernize international arbitration legislation and a means of doing so, by harmonizing the laws of countries adopting or adapting the Model Law. In addition, there is now a great deal of competition between the various arbitration locations. The direct and indirect economic return encourages the legal communities in those locations to make significant efforts to retain or attract international arbitration. A simple, liberal and modern international arbitration law is a strong selling point. This accounts for the pressure to reform exerted on national legislatures (as was the case in Italy, England, Germany and Sweden, and is now the case in Japan and, to a certain extent, in the United States).

154. — It is of course not feasible to discuss here the international arbitration law of every jurisdiction worldwide, and we shall therefore restrict ourselves to a brief analysis of some of the more important legal systems. We shall then attempt to summarize both the

---

[23] On these Articles, see *supra* paras. 560 *et seq.* On a rather cautious proposal for reform, see the reports and interventions at the colloquium organized by the Comité français de l'arbitrage on January 27, 1992, *Perspectives d'évolution du droit français de l'arbitrage*, 1992 REV. ARB. 193–412.

[24] *See supra* para. 1.

[25] On this Convention, see *infra* para. 247.

[26] On this instrument, see *infra* para. 203.

worldwide legislative trends and, on the basis of our analysis of those trends, the characteristics of a typical national law on international arbitration.

1° Analysis

155. — The legal systems discussed hereafter have been selected on account of the originality and extent of the reforms which they have implemented or will soon implement.[27] We shall first discuss a number of European legal systems, then certain others from outside Europe.

a) Europe

156. — The most profound reform of international arbitration law has taken place in Europe. It is far from comprehensive, either because in some countries the reforms implemented to date are incomplete, or because in other countries, such as the former socialist states of Central and Eastern Europe, the institutions and rules of international commercial law are still undergoing substantial change.

i)   United Kingdom

157. — The long tradition of arbitration in England was founded on legislation that gave the English courts broad powers to intervene in the conduct of arbitration proceedings and the revision of arbitral awards. The reform of the 1950 Arbitration Act in 1979 removed the statement of case procedure and the power of the courts to annul any arbitral award for a manifest error of fact or law. However, the 1979 Arbitration Act did create a right of appeal before the High Court on "any question of law arising out of an award" and allowed the parties to put a "preliminary point of law" arising during the arbitration before the courts. Further, the legislature did not make it easy for the parties to agree to exclude these statutory rights of recourse in international disputes.

Despite the efforts of the English courts to liberalize the English regime of international arbitration,[28] a more far-reaching reform was needed. In 1989, the Departmental Advisory Committee on Arbitration Law of the Department of Trade and Industry, chaired by Lord Justice Mustill, concluded that England, Wales and Northern Ireland should not adopt the

---

[27] For English translations of the main arbitration statutes and commentaries, see ICCA INTERNATIONAL HANDBOOK ON COMMERCIAL ARBITRATION (A.J. van den Berg ed.); PARKER SCHOOL OF FOREIGN AND COMPARATIVE LAW, THE WORLD ARBITRATION REPORTER (H. Smit and V. Pechota eds.). For French translations, see RÉPERTOIRE PRATIQUE DE L'ARBITRAGE COMMERCIAL INTERNATIONAL (1997).

[28] On court control before and after 1979, see, for example, MICHAEL J. MUSTILL, STEWART C. BOYD, COMMERCIAL ARBITRATION 431 *et seq.* and 583 *et seq.* (2d ed. 1989); Stewart C. Boyd and V.V. Veeder, *Le développement du droit anglais de l'arbitrage depuis la loi de 1979*, 1991 REV. ARB. 209.

UNCITRAL Model Law, and recommended passing a new statute codifying the whole of English arbitration law.[29]

By contrast, following the recommendations of the Scottish Advisory Committee, set up shortly afterwards, it was considered that the UNCITRAL Model Law was compatible with Scotland's interests and that it should therefore be adopted: in 1990 the Model Law was therefore introduced in Scotland with only minor changes, and has been in force since January 1, 1991.[30]

On the basis of a draft prepared and circulated in February 1994,[31] the wholesale reform of English arbitration law[32] was organized by the Departmental Advisory Committee, chaired successively by Lord Justice Steyn and Lord Justice Saville.[33] The result was the 1996 Arbitration Act, which entered into force on January 31, 1997.

The Act is very long, comprising 110 sections and 4 schedules. It has already been the subject of much commentary.[34] In its Section 1, it sets forth the general principles underlying the reform: the fair resolution of disputes without unnecessary delay or expense, the freedom of parties to agree how their disputes are to be resolved, and restricted powers of intervention of the courts. It was initially thought that those powers would be broader in

---

[29] DEPARTMENT OF TRADE AND INDUSTRY, A NEW ARBITRATION ACT – THE RESPONSE OF THE DEPARTMENTAL ADVISORY COMMITTEE TO THE UNCITRAL MODEL LAW ON INTERNATIONAL COMMERCIAL ARBITRATION (1989), *reprinted in* 6 ARB. INT'L 3 (1990). *See also* Michael J. Mustill, *Vers une nouvelle loi anglaise sur l'arbitrage*, 1991 REV. ARB. 383; Johan Steyn, *Towards a New English Arbitration Act*, 7 ARB. INT'L 17 (1991); Roy Goode, *The Adaptation of English Law to International Commercial Arbitration*, 8 ARB. INT'L 1 (1992).

[30] The Law Reform (Miscellaneous Provisions) (Scotland) Act 1990, Sec. 66 and Sched. 7; XVII Y.B. COM. ARB. 460 (1992); *see also* John Murray, *The UNCITRAL Model Law and Judicial Control of Arbitration in Scotland,* 9 ARB. INT'L 97 (1993).

[31] DEPARTMENT OF TRADE AND INDUSTRY, A CONSULTATION PAPER ON DRAFT CLAUSES AND SCHEDULES OF AN ARBITRATION BILL (Feb. 1994), *reprinted in* 10 ARB. INT'L 189 (1994); *see also* Johan Steyn, *England's Response to the UNCITRAL Model Law of Arbitration*, 10 ARB. INT'L 1 (1994); Brian Davenport, *The New English Draft Arbitration Bill: The DTI Consultation Document*, 10 ARB. INT'L 163 (1994); John Uff and Donald Keating, *Should England Reconsider the UNCITRAL Model Law or Not?*, 10 ARB. INT'L 179 (1994); A.H. Hermann, *The Draft English Bill: Pulling the Wrong Punches*, 10 ARB. INT'L 185 (1994).

[32] By English law, we mean here the law in force in England, Wales and Northern Ireland.

[33] *See* DEPARTMENTAL ADVISORY COMMITTEE ON ARBITRATION LAW, 1996 REPORT ON THE ARBITRATION BILL (Feb. 1996), *reprinted in* 13 ARB. INT'L 275 (1997).

[34] See, in particular, 13 ARB. INT'L 331 *et seq.* (1997); Mark Saville, *The Origin of the New English Arbitration Act 1996: Reconciling Speed with Justice in the Decision-making Process*, 13 ARB. INT'L 237 (1997); Martin Hunter, *The Procedural Powers of Arbitrators Under the English 1996 Act*, 13 ARB. INT'L 345 (1997); Stewart R. Shackleton, *The Applicable Law in International Arbitration Under the New English Arbitration Act 1996*, 13 ARB. INT'L 375 (1997); V.V. Veeder, *England, in* ICCA INTERNATIONAL HANDBOOK ON COMMERCIAL ARBITRATION 67 (1997); Vincenzo Vigoriti, *Riflessioni comparative sull'Arbitration Act 1996*, 1997 RIV. DELL'ARB. 37; V.V. Veeder, *La nouvelle loi anglaise sur l'arbitrage de 1996: la naissance d'un magnifique éléphant*, 1997 REV. ARB. 3; Lord Mustill, *La nouvelle loi anglaise sur l'arbitrage de 1996: philosophie, inspiration, aspiration*, 1997 REV. ARB. 29; Claude Reymond, *L'arbitration Act, 1996 – Convergence et originalité*, 1997 REV. ARB. 45; Eric Robine, *La nouvelle loi anglaise sur l'arbitrage*, 1997 INT'L BUS. L.J. 608; RUSSELL ON ARBITRATION (D. Sutton, J. Kendall, J. Gill eds., 21st ed. 1997); MARTIN HUNTER AND TOBY LANDAU, THE ENGLISH ARBITRATION ACT 1996: TEXT AND NOTES (1998); William W. Park, *The Interaction of Courts and Arbitrators in England: the 1996 Act as a Model for the United States?*, 1 INT'L ARB. L. REV. 54 (1998).

domestic arbitration but, when the Act was due to come into force, the distinction was removed.[35] As a result, there is no longer any difference in treatment of domestic and international arbitration.

The new Act contains a number of important differences from previous law. These generally extend the freedom of the parties and the arbitrators. Thus, the autonomy of the arbitration agreement is provided for at Section 7, the competence-competence principle at Section 30, and the requirement that the grounds for the award be given, unless the parties agree otherwise, is found at Section 52. However, idiosyncratic English tradition subsists in certain respects: the powers of intervention of the courts remain substantial; there are numerous mandatory provisions (Sched. 1); the powers of the court to determine a preliminary point of law and to hear an appeal of a point of law are maintained where English law is applicable to the merits, even if they can be excluded by agreement of the parties (Secs. 45 and 69). Finally, there remains an impressive list of "serious irregularities" affecting the tribunal, the proceedings or the award" which allow a party to challenge the award (Sec. 68).

ii)   Belgium

158. — By a law dated July 4, 1972, Belgium incorporated into its Judicial Code the provisions of the European Convention on Arbitration, signed at Strasbourg on January 20, 1966, which set forth a Uniform Law.[36] These provisions form Part 6 of the Code (Arts. 1676–1723). This is therefore a modern text, but given its origins and the conditions in which it was conceived, it is also relatively complex.[37]

A further law, dated March 27, 1985, introduced an important reform, aimed at enhancing the appeal of international arbitration in Belgium. The goals of the reform were limited, however. The new law restricted access to the Belgian courts for applications to set aside international arbitral awards made in Belgium. The new Article 1717, paragraph 4 of the Judicial Code provided that an action to set aside was not available where none of the parties was a Belgian national, or was resident in Belgium, or was an entity "constituted in Belgium or having a branch or any form of business headquarters in Belgium." In other words, the Belgian courts would no longer intervene where the arbitration involved no Belgian interests

---

[35] Arbitration Act 1996, Part II, Domestic Arbitration Agreements, Secs. 85–88. *See also* DEPARTMENTAL ADVISORY COMMITTEE ON ARBITRATION LAW, SUPPLEMENTARY REPORT ON THE ARBITRATION ACT 1996, Nos. 47 to 50 (Jan. 1997), *reprinted in* 13 ARB. INT'L 317 (1997); Reymond, *supra* note 34, at 49 *et seq.* Following a decision of the Court of Appeal dated July 12, 1996, the English legislature decided not to enact rules specific to domestic arbitration. Its concern was that to do so would violate the principle of the free movement of services within the Common Market, and discriminate between European Union nationals on the basis of their nationality (Phillip Alexander Securities and Futures Ltd. v. Bamberger, THE TIMES, July 22, 1996; XXII Y.B. COM. ARB. 872 (1997); for a French translation, see 1999 REV. ARB. 167, and V.V. Veeder's note). For a discussion of this position, see Jean-François Poudret, *Critères d'extranéité de l'arbitrage international et droit communautaire*, 1998 BULL. ASA 22.

[36] On this Convention, see *infra* para. 290.

[37] MARCEL HUYS, GUY KEUTGEN, L'ARBITRAGE EN DROIT BELGE ET INTERNATIONAL (1981); JACQUELINE LINSMEAU, L'ARBITRAGE VOLONTAIRE EN DROIT PRIVÉ BELGE (1991).

and where Belgium had been chosen as the seat of an international arbitration purely on account of its neutrality.[38]

This bold reform does not seem to have been overwhelmingly successful. In fact, it was repealed by a new statute, dated May 19,1998.[39] This, in the same way as the 1987 Private International Law Statute in Switzerland, simply allows the parties to agree to waive recourse in Belgium where there is no connection with Belgium other than the location of the seat of arbitration, rather than prohibiting recourse in those circumstances. The new statute makes a number of other changes to the Judicial Code: it reinforces the contractual character of arbitration and the powers of the arbitrators, promotes *amiable composition* and permits arbitration involving public law entities.[40]

iii)   The Netherlands

159. — On July 2, 1986, the Netherlands legislature carried out a total overhaul of its arbitration law, with the new legislation taking effect on December 1, 1986. The new law appears in Book IV of the Code of Civil Procedure,[41] which is divided into two Titles, the first of which covers arbitrations held in the Netherlands (Arts. 1020 to 1073), and the second arbitrations held abroad (Arts. 1074 to 1076).

This reform, rather than organizing a specific, more liberal regime for international arbitration, is instead a model of pragmatism, designed to promote efficient arbitration. In particular, it consistently emphasizes the fact that a party will be barred from seeking to set aside an award unless the ground on which such action is based was raised during the course of the arbitration, and as soon as the party became aware of it. This is a very effective means of discouraging frivolous actions to set aside. Subject to compliance with due process and the principle of equal treatment of the parties (Art. 1039), the parties or, subsidiarily, the

---

[38] *See* Guy Horsmans, *Actualité et évolution du droit belge de l'arbitrage (Titre III. – L'étranger)*, 1992 REV. ARB. 417, especially at 437 *et seq.*; H. van Houtte, *La loi belge du 27 mars 1985 sur l'arbitrage international*, 1986 REV. ARB. 29; Alain Vanderelst, *Increasing the Appeal of Belgium as an International Arbitration Forum? – The Belgian Law of March 27, 1985 Concerning the Annulment of Arbitral Awards*, 3 J. INT'L ARB. 77 (June 1986); Lambert Matray, *La loi belge du 27 mars 1985 et ses répercussions sur l'arbitrage commercial international*, 64 REV. DR. INT. DR. COMP. 243 (1987); Bernard Hanotiau, *International Commercial Arbitration in Belgium*, 1 AM. REV. INT'L ARB. 1 (1990); Bernard Hanotiau, *L'arbitrage international en Belgique*, in L'ARBITRAGE – TRAVAUX OFFERTS AU PROFESSEUR ALBERT FETTWEIS 143 (L. Matray and G. de Leval eds., 1989).

[39] Law modifying the dispositions of the Judicial Code concerning arbitration, *Moniteur belge*, Aug. 7, 1998, p. 25,353. For an English translation, see 1998 BULL. ASA 540.

[40] On the 1998 statute, see Guy Keutgen, *La nouvelle loi sur l'arbitrage*, 1998 [BELG.] JOURN. TRIB. 761; Herman Verbist, *Reform of the Belgian Arbitration Law (Law of May 19, 1998)/Réforme du droit de l'arbitrage en Belgique (la loi du 19 mai 1998)*, 1998 INT'L BUS. L.J. 842; Bernard Hanotiau and Guy Block, *The Law of 19 May 1998 Amending Belgian Arbitration Legislation*, 15 ARB. INT'L 97 (1999).

[41] For English, French and German translations of this statute, see PIETER SANDERS AND ALBERT JAN VAN DEN BERG, THE NETHERLANDS ARBITRATION ACT 1986 (1987); *see also* Pieter Sanders, *The New Dutch Arbitration Act*, 3 ARB. INT'L 194 (1987); Pieter Sanders, *The New Dutch Arbitration Act/La nouvelle loi néerlandaise sur l'arbitrage*, 1987 INT'L BUS. L.J. 539; Jan C. Schultsz, *Les nouvelles dispositions de la législation néerlandaise en matière d'arbitrage*, 1988 REV. ARB. 209; A.J. VAN DEN BERG, R. VAN DELDEN, H.J. SNIJDERS, NETHERLANDS ARBITRATION LAW (1993).

arbitrators, are free to organize the arbitral procedure (Art. 1036). In addition, the parties may grant the arbitrators the power to complete or modify a contract (Art. 1020(4)(c)), and it is possible for a Dutch court to decide that distinct but connected arbitral proceedings should be consolidated (Art. 1046). As regards awards made abroad, Dutch law provides a system of court review and enforcement inspired by the French model, which is more liberal than that contained in the New York Convention. The application of the new law in practice has shown the reform to be satisfactory.[42]

iv) Germany

160. — Until 1997, the German legislature had made only a few alterations to the 1879 Code of Civil Procedure (ZPO), which covered arbitration in Articles 1025 to 1048. A law dated July 25, 1986, which reformed German private international law, eliminated a number of overly restrictive rules concerning international arbitration.

This "mini-reform"[43] disappointed many German arbitration practitioners. They were frustrated that their country played only a very modest role as an international arbitration situs and had therefore sought a more spectacular reform designed to make Germany an attractive place for arbitration. To meet their concerns, a draft statute was prepared in 1994.[44] In 1996, a slightly modified draft was put before the *Bundestag* and it was enacted on December 22, 1997.[45] The new statute modifies a number of provisions of the Code of Civil Procedure and completely revises its Book X (Arts. 1025 to 1066). It is essentially based on the UNCITRAL Model Law and does not distinguish, in principle, between domestic and international arbitration.

---

[42] *See* Pieter Sanders, *First Lustrum of the New Dutch Arbitration Act/Le premier quinquennat de la nouvelle loi néerlandaise sur l'arbitrage*, 1992 INT'L BUS. L.J. 37.

[43] This expression was used by Peter Schlosser, *Quelques nouvelles de l'arbitrage outre-Rhin*, 1987 REV. ARB. 293; *see also* KLAUS PETER BERGER, INTERNATIONAL ECONOMIC ARBITRATION 44 *et seq.* (1993).

[44] KOMMISSION ZUR NEUORDNUNG DES SCHIEDSVERFAHRENSRECHTS, BERICHT, MIT EINEM DISKUSSIONENTWURF ZUR NEUFASSUNG DES ZEHNTEN BUCHS DER ZPO. For an English translation of this draft, see *The German Arbitration Draft (for Discussion) of a Reform of the 10th Book of the Code of Civil Procedure*, 11 ARB. INT'L 415 (1995).

[45] *Gesetz zur Neuregelung des Schiedsverfahrensrechts*, v.30.12.1997 (BGBl. I S.3224). *See* Claudia Kälin-Nauer, *Das neue Schiedsverfahrensgesetz in Deutschland – Das neue 10. Buch der ZPO*, 1997 BULL. ASA 432; Karl-Heinz Böckstiegel, *An Introduction to the New German Arbitration Act Based on the UNCITRAL Model Law*, 14 ARB. INT'L 19 (1998); Otto Sandrock, *Procedural Aspects of the New German Arbitration Act*, *id.* at 33; Klaus Lionnet, *The New German Arbitration Act – A User's Perspective*, *id.* at 57; Richard H. Kreindler and Thomas Mahlich, *A Foreign Perspective on the New German Arbitration Act*, *id.* at 65; Peter Schlosser, *La nouvelle législation allemande sur l'arbitrage*, 1998 REV. ARB. 291; Walther J. Habscheid, *Il nuovo diritto dell'arbitrato in Germania*, 1998 RIV. DELL'ARB. 175; Gino Lörcher, *La nouvelle loi allemande sur l'arbitrage*, 1998 BULL. ASA 275; Gino Lörcher, *The New German Arbitration Act*, 15 J. INT'L ARB. 85 (June 1998).

Meanwhile, the reunification of Germany led to the introduction of the West German legal system, and hence, for arbitration, the rules of the Code of Civil Procedure, in the *Länder* which were formerly part of East Germany.[46]

v) Portugal

161. — A new law on "voluntary arbitration" was enacted in Portugal in 1986,[47] followed by a legislative decree later in the same year regulating the creation of arbitral institutions.[48] This law includes a number of special provisions concerning international arbitration (Arts. 32 to 35), which were strongly influenced by the French reforms. This is the case, for instance, of the definition of the international nature of arbitration and the determination of the law applicable to the merits of the dispute.[49]

vi) Switzerland

162. — The Swiss Constitution gives legislative jurisdiction over civil procedure to the Cantons. As Switzerland considers arbitration to be of a procedural rather than a contractual nature, for many years the country had as many arbitration laws as there are cantons. In a bid to unify the law, an inter-cantonal *Concordat*—a treaty between the Cantons—was enacted in 1969.[50] However, this uniform law proved to be ill-suited to the needs of international arbitration. In particular, the number of mandatory provisions (Art. 1, para. 3) formed a serious obstacle to the application of institutional arbitration rules, such as those of the ICC. The litigation that resulted was exacerbated both by the strict control over international arbitrations taking place in Switzerland exercised by the cantonal courts and the Federal Court, and by the *Concordat*'s numerous (and sometimes excessively broad) grounds for actions to set awards aside.[51]

The situation underwent dramatic change with the federal Private International Law Statute of December 18, 1987, which contained a chapter devoted to "international arbitration" and entered into force on January 1, 1989. Even if some commentators have

---

[46] *See* Claude Witz and Ralf-Charley Schultze, *La réunification de l'Allemagne et ses conséquences sur le droit de l'arbitrage*, 1991 REV. ARB. 599.

[47] Law No. 31/86 of August 29, 1986, published in *Diário da República*, Ser. I, No. 198, Aug. 29, 1986, pp. 2259–64, and entered into force on November 29, 1986.

[48] Decree Law No. 425/86 of December 27, 1986, published in *Diário da República*, Ser. I, No. 297, Dec. 27, 1986, pp. 3832–33; for a French translation, see 1991 REV. ARB. 498.

[49] *See* Dário Moura Vicente, *L'évolution récente du droit de l'arbitrage au Portugal*, 1991 REV. ARB. 419; ISABEL DE MAGALHAES COLLAÇO, L'ARBITRAGE INTERNATIONAL DANS LA RÉCENTE LOI PORTUGAISE SUR L'ARBITRAGE VOLONTAIRE (L. NO 31/86 DU 29 AOÛT 1986) – QUELQUES RÉFLEXIONS: DROIT INTERNATIONAL ET DROIT COMMUNAUTAIRE 55 (1991); Dário Moura Vicente, *Applicable Law in Voluntary Arbitrations in Portugal*, 44 INT'L & COMP. L.Q. 179 (1995).

[50] PIERRE JOLIDON, COMMENTAIRE DU CONCORDAT SUISSE SUR L'ARBITRAGE (1984).

[51] Article 36 which, in particular, allows an award to be challenged on the grounds that it is "arbitrary."

expressed doubts on this point,[52] the rules governing international arbitration taking place in Switzerland contained in the new act are significantly different[53] from the *Concordat*, although the parties are still entitled to opt for the application of the latter (Art. 176, para. 2).

Perhaps even more so than in France, the specificity of international arbitration is very much in evidence in Switzerland.[54] The new act contains liberal substantive rules governing international arbitration, particularly with respect to the arbitration agreement.[55] Likewise, the arbitral procedure is determined primarily by the intentions of the parties or the arbitration rules to which they refer (Art. 182). Choice of law rules are generally used only on a subsidiary basis, with very flexible connecting factors (Arts. 178 and 182). The courts intervene only to assist the parties or the arbitrators (Arts. 179, 180 and 183 *et seq.*) and actions to set awards aside have been restricted in two respects: the number of admissible grounds has been reduced (Art. 190), and an action may only be brought before the Federal Tribunal, except where the parties together prefer the cantonal jurisdictions, in which case the decisions of those courts will also be final (Art. 191). Furthermore, if both parties are neither domiciled, nor resident, nor established in Switzerland, they may exclude in advance all procedures for setting the award aside in Switzerland (Art. 192). In this respect, the Swiss legislature followed the lead set by Belgium in 1985,[56] albeit more cautiously. This more cautious position served, in turn, as a model for the Tunisian legislature in 1993, the Belgian legislature in 1998 and for the Swedish legislature in 1999.[57]

The new Swiss law on international arbitration generated a great deal of interest, not only in Switzerland.[58] The application and interpretation of the new rules understandably gave rise to a considerable body of Federal Tribunal case law.[59] On the whole, the Federal Tribunal respected the liberal spirit of the law, by broadly construing the questions of

---

[52] *See* Jean-François Poudret, *Quelles sont les innovations réelles apportées par la L.D.I.P. à l'arbitrage international en Suisse?*, 1991 DPCI 151.

[53] Arts. 176 to 199.

[54] On the definition of international arbitration, see *supra* para. 105.

[55] On the form and the autonomy of the arbitration agreement, see Article 178; on whether a state can enter into such agreements, see Article 177.

[56] *See supra* para. 158.

[57] *See supra* para. 158 and *infra* paras. 164-1 and 173.

[58] PIERRE LALIVE, JEAN-FRANÇOIS POUDRET, CLAUDE REYMOND, LE DROIT DE L'ARBITRAGE INTERNE ET INTERNATIONAL EN SUISSE (1989); ANDREAS BUCHER AND PIERRE-YVES TSCHANZ, INTERNATIONAL ARBITRATION IN SWITZERLAND (1988); 1989 INT'L BUS. L.J. 739–810, a special issue entirely dedicated to the then new Swiss Private International Law Statute; Claude Reymond, *La nouvelle loi suisse et le droit de l'arbitrage international – Réflexions de droit comparé*, 1989 REV. ARB. 385; Marc Blessing, *The New International Arbitration Law in Switzerland – A Significant Step Towards Liberalism*, 5 J. INT'L ARB. 9 (June 1988); Pierre Lalive and Emmanuel Gaillard, *Le nouveau droit de l'arbitrage international en Suisse*, 116 J.D.I. 905 (1989); Robert Briner, *Switzerland*, *in* ICCA INTERNATIONAL HANDBOOK ON COMMERCIAL ARBITRATION (1998).

[59] *See Droit transitoire de la LDIP en ce qui concerne l'arbitrage*, 1989 BULL. ASA 132, and Jean-Emmanuel Rossel, *Observations sur les arrêts récemment rendus à propos du droit transitoire relatif à l'arbitrage international*, *id.* at 134.

arbitrability and competence-competence, for example, and narrowly construing the concept of public policy as a ground on which awards can be set aside.[60]

vii)   Spain

163. — The Spanish statute of December 5, 1988[61] replaced the old 1953 Act, of which the least that can be said is that it was hardly favorable to arbitration. Political developments allied to economic growth made it possible to adopt the liberal measures introduced in 1988. Nevertheless, Spain was not yet prepared to venture as far as France, the Netherlands, or Switzerland. One is therefore left with the impression of unfinished reforms, and various areas of ambiguity remain as to the scope and the content of a number of provisions. The freedom of the parties to choose the arbitral procedure is certainly affirmed (Art. 9), and the role of institutional arbitration recognized (Art. 10), but the statute does contain a number of mandatory rules. The provisions covering international arbitration are also rather unsatisfactory. As Spain has ratified the New York Convention without making the reciprocity reservation, the Convention is in principle applicable to the enforcement of all awards made outside Spain. However, the Convention's rules are supplemented (or contradicted) by the provisions of Title IX of the 1988 statute (Arts. 56 *et seq.*). In addition, the private international law rules found at Title X are essentially choice of law rules. The Spanish courts, which had already done much to facilitate arbitration under the 1953 Act, will certainly be called upon again to clarify the meaning of the 1988 statute.[62]

viii)   Italy

164. — The Italian Code of Civil Procedure of 1942 provided Italy with legislation which was so unfavorable to arbitration that, alongside statutory or "*rituale*" arbitration, authors and the courts developed and introduced the concept of "*irrituale*" or "*libero*" arbitration, based solely on the parties' intentions and culminating in an award which was essentially a contract. This second form of arbitration was used extensively in international disputes, and the Italian Supreme Court held it to be within the scope of the New York Convention. However, the situation was not really satisfactory.

---

[60]   For an initial assessment, see 1992 BULL. ASA No. 1, a special issue entitled, *"Le chapitre 12 de la LDIP: Trois ans après."*

[61]   Law No. 36/1988 of December 5, 1988, published in *Boletin Oficial del Estado,* Dec. 7, 1988.

[62]   Bernardo M. Cremades, *L'Espagne étrenne une nouvelle loi sur l'arbitrage,* 1989 REV. ARB. 189; Jean-Marie Vulliemin, *La nouvelle loi espagnole sur l'arbitrage,* 1989 BULL. ASA 194; ARBITRATION IN SPAIN (B. Cremades ed., 1991); Bernardo M. Cremades, *The New Spanish Law of Arbitration,* 6 J. INT'L ARB. 35 (June 1991).

It was improved by an initial legislative revision in 1983,[63] but the major reforms were contained in a statute dated January 5, 1994, which at last gave Italy the modern arbitration regime it badly needed.[64] The rules on domestic arbitration, which appear in Articles 806 to 831 of the Code of Civil Procedure, finally provide the consistency and efficiency which was lacking at all stages of such proceedings. The new provisions relating to international arbitration (Arts. 832 to 838) and to foreign awards (Arts. 839 and 840) make it easier to enforce the latter and underline the autonomy of the former. As in French law, international arbitration[65] is governed by only a few liberal substantive rules concerning, in particular, the form of the arbitration agreement (which no longer requires specific approval if it appears in general conditions) (Art. 833), and the rules of law applicable to the merits of the dispute (Art. 834). As a result, *irrituale* arbitration should lose its relevance, particularly in international disputes.[66] More recently, however, certain doubts have been raised as to the impact of Law No. 218 of May 31, 1995, which reformed Italian private international law.[67]

ix)   Sweden

164-1. — Sweden has always had an important role in international arbitration, largely because the country's political neutrality made Stockholm an acceptable place of arbitration for the former socialist states and for China. This tradition has survived to an extent, and

---

[63] Law No. 28 of Feb. 9, 1983, published in the *Gazzetta Officiale della Repubblica Italiana* No. 44, dated February 15, 1983; *see* Giorgio Recchia, *La nouvelle loi italienne sur l'arbitrage*, 1984 REV. ARB. 65; Giorgio Bernini, *Domestic and International Arbitration in Italy after the Legislative Reform*, 5 PACE L. REV. 543 (1985); the essential features of this first reform were its lifting of the prohibition on foreigners acting as arbitrators in Italy, and its recognition of the *res judicata* effect of an award on its signature by the arbitrator (rather than requiring it to be filed with the court).

[64] Law No. 25 of January 5, 1994, published in the *Gazzetta Officiale della Repubblica Italiana* No. 12, dated January 17, 1994; *see* Piero Bernardini, *L'arbitrage en Italie après la récente réforme*, 1994 REV. ARB. 479; Renzo Morera, *The New Italian Law on Domestic and International Arbitration*, in ICC BULLETIN, SPECIAL SUPPLEMENT, INTERNATIONAL COMMERCIAL ARBITRATION IN EUROPE 69 (1994); Elio Fazzalari, *La riforma dell'arbitrato*, 1994 RIV. DELL'ARB. 1; Giorgio Recchia, *La nuova legge sull'arbitrato e le esperienze straniere*, *id.* at 23; Andrea Giardina, *La legge n. 25 del 1994 e l'arbitrato internazionale*, *id.* at 257; Mauro Rubino-Sammartano, *New International Arbitration Legislation in Italy*, 11 J. INT'L ARB. 77 (Sept. 1994); A. RENATO BRIGUGLIO, E. FAZZALARI AND R. MARENGO, LA NUOVA DISCIPLINA DELL'ARBITRATO – COMMENTARIO (1994); SERGIO LA CHINA, L'ARBITRATO – IL SISTEMA E L'ESPERIENZA (1995); Gabriele Mecarelli, *La spécificité de la réforme italienne de l'arbitrage international*, in RECHERCHE SUR L'ARBITRAGE EN DROIT INTERNATIONAL ET COMPARÉ 201 (1997); Fabrizio Marella, *International business law and international commercial arbitration: the Italian approach*, 1997 ARB. & DISP. RESOL. L.J. 25; PIERO BERNARDINI, IL DIRITTO DELL'ARBITRATO (1998); Piero Bernardini, *Italy*, in ICCA INTERNATIONAL HANDBOOK ON COMMERCIAL ARBITRATION (forthcoming in 1999).

[65] On the definition of the international character of arbitration (Art. 832 of the Italian Code of Civil Procedure), see *supra* para. 105.

[66] *But see* Luciana Laudisa, *Arbitrato rituale e libero: ragioni del distinguere*, 1998 RIV. DELL'ARB. 211.

[67] In particular, this law laid down new private international law rules on the form of arbitration clauses providing for arbitration outside Italy (Art. 4) and on the law applicable to international contracts (Art. 57); *see* Sergio La China, *L'arbitrato e la riforma del sistema italiano di diritto internazionale privato*, 1995 RIV. DELL'ARB. 629; Giorgio Gaja, *L'arbitrato in materia internazionale tra la legge n. 25/1994 e la riforma del diritto internazionale privato*, 1996 RIV. DELL'ARB. 487.

Chinese state-owned entities still favor Stockholm as a venue, second only to arbitration in China under the CIETAC Rules. Sweden's two 1929 statutes, respectively entitled the Arbitration Act and the Act concerning Foreign Arbitration Agreements and Awards were revised in 1971, 1976 and in 1981. They contained a number of interesting provisions, in particular on the prevention of delaying tactics.

This legislation was replaced by a new Arbitration Act, which came into force on April 1, 1999,[68] repealing the 1929 statutes.[69] The new Act applies to both domestic and international arbitration (Sec. 46). However, certain provisions relate specifically to "international matters" (Secs. 47–51) and to the recognition and enforcement of foreign awards (Secs. 52–60). One of the most important new provisions is that allowing parties with no links to Sweden to waive their right to bring an action before the Swedish courts to set aside an award made in Sweden (Sec. 51). This was inspired by Swiss law,[70] but a liberal line of Swedish cases concerning international arbitration had already paved the way.[71]

x)   Other countries of the European Union

165. — Recent reforms in several other European Union countries also demonstrate the extent to which arbitration law is being constantly modernized.

Although the Greek Code of Civil Procedure has not been modified since 1971, that is because the major reform occurred in 1967[72] and has so far proved to be satisfactory, especially for international arbitration.[73]

In 1983, Austria made a few welcome changes to its Code of Civil Procedure (Arts. 577–99) concerning, in particular, the form of the arbitration agreement, as well as the signing of and recourse against the award. Above all, the review by the courts of the

---

[68] *Lag om skiljeförfarande*, dated March 4, 1999, SFS 1999:116. For a commentary, see the special issue of the STOCKHOLM ARBITRATION REPORT entirely dedicated to the new Act (forthcoming in 1999). For the text of the draft law and commentaries, see THE DRAFT NEW SWEDISH ARBITRATION ACT – A PRESENTATION (June 1994), *reprinted in* 10 ARB. INT'L 407 (1994); *see also* 1994 BULL. ASA 261 and Frank-Bernd Weigand, *The UNCITRAL Model Law: New Draft Arbitration Acts in Germany and Sweden*, 11 ARB. INT'L 397 (1995); *Sweden*, XXI Y.B. COM. ARB. 382 (1996).

[69] On Swedish arbitration law prior to the 1999 Act, see STOCKHOLM CHAMBER OF COMMERCE, ARBITRATION IN SWEDEN (2d ed. 1984); Nils Mangard and Patrik Schöldström, *The Enforcement of Arbitral Awards in Sweden*, 1997 RIV. DELL'ARB. 251.

[70] *See supra* para. 162.

[71] Jan Paulsson, *Arbitrage international et voies de recours. La Cour suprême de Suède dans le sillage des solutions belge et helvétique*, 117 J.D.I. 589 (1990).

[72] Arts. 867–903 of the Code of Civil Procedure; *see* ANGHELOS C. FOUSTOUCOS, L'ARBITRAGE INTERNE ET INTERNATIONAL EN DROIT PRIVÉ HELLÉNIQUE (1976); Anghelos C. Foustoucos, *Greece*, *in* ICCA INTERNATIONAL HANDBOOK ON COMMERCIAL ARBITRATION (1985).

[73] Anghelos C. Foustoucos, *L'arbitrage international en Grèce*, 1987 REV. ARB. 23; Konstantinos D. Kerameus, *Arbitrage international et ordre juridique hellénique*, 1987 REV. ARB. 35; Anghelos C. Foustoucos, *Sentences arbitrales nationales et étrangères: exécution et voies de recours en Grèce/Domestic and Foreign Arbitral Awards: How They Are Enforced and Challenged in Greece*, 1991 INT'L BUS. L.J. 285.

substance of an international arbitral award is now confined to the issue of compliance with Austrian public policy, as understood in private international law.[74]

Finland totally reformed its arbitration law in 1992, closely following the UNCITRAL Model Law.[75]

On May 20, 1998, a new statute on international arbitration was adopted in the Republic of Ireland. It too reproduces in substance the UNCITRAL Model Law.[76]

xi) Central and East European countries

166. — The political and economic turmoil in the countries of Central and Eastern Europe since 1989 has led to far-reaching and ongoing changes in their arbitration law and practice,[77] not all of which can be discussed here.[78] The privatization of companies made the methods of settling disputes used by socialist economic organizations obsolete. This led to the reintroduction of the old Codes of Civil Procedure, which contained rules on domestic arbitration, in countries such as Hungary, Poland and Romania, and to the enactment of new arbitration statutes. This occurred first in Bulgaria, where a law dated August 5, 1988 concerning international commercial arbitration introduced the 1985 UNCITRAL Model Law.[79] This law was amended on November 2, 1993, as a result of which most of its provisions also apply to domestic arbitration.[80] The Bulgarian example has been or will soon

---

[74] *See* Article 595(1)(6) of the Code of Civil Procedure (as amended by the Federal Law of February 2, 1983); *see also* Werner Melis, *La réforme autrichienne de l'arbitrage (Loi du 2 février 1983)*, 1987 REV. ARB. 451; WERNER MELIS, A GUIDE TO COMMERCIAL ARBITRATION IN AUSTRIA (1983). On the role of Austria as a "neutral" place of international arbitration, see F. Schwank, *Arbitrage commercial international en Autriche*, 1990 CAH. JUR. FISC. EXP. 593.

[75] Law of October 23, 1992 (967/92). *See* Bengt Broms, *The New Law on Arbitration in Finland*, ICC BULLETIN, Vol. 4, No. 2, at 59 (1993); Risto Kurki-Suonio, *L'influence sur la nouvelle loi finlandaise de la loi-type CNUDCI*, 1994 REV. ARB. 499; Petri Taivalkoski, *Le nouveau droit finlandais de l'arbitrage international*, *in* RECHERCHE SUR L'ARBITRAGE EN DROIT INTERNATIONAL ET COMPARÉ 127 (1997), with a French translation of the arbitration law of October 23, 1992 annexed at 183.

[76] Law No. 14/1998. *See* LCIA ARBITRATION INTERNATIONAL NEWSLETTER, Vol. 3, No. 3, at 6 (1998); Christopher Koch, *The New Irish Arbitration Act of 1998*, 1999 BULL. ASA 51.

[77] For an overview, see Heinz Strohbach, *Commercial Arbitration in Eastern Europe Today*, 1993 RIV. DELL'ARB. 141; Eva Horváth, *Arbitration in Central and Eastern Europe*, 11 J. INT'L ARB. 5 (June 1994); Werner Melis, *Continuation et succession en matière d'arbitrage commercial international/Continuation and Succession in the Field of International Commercial Arbitration*, *in* DISSOLUTION, CONTINUATION ET SUCCESSION EN EUROPE DE L'EST 353 (G. Burdeau and B. Stern eds., 1994); LITIGATION AND ARBITRATION IN CENTRAL AND EASTERN EUROPE (D. Rivkin and C. Platto eds., 1998).

[78] On the May 26, 1972 Moscow Convention, of which these countries, in particular, were signatories, see *infra* para. 293; on the reform of the arbitration courts of their foreign trade chambers, see *infra* para. 333.

[79] Law on International Commercial Arbitration, published in State Gazette (*Durzhaven Vestnik*) No. 60 of August 5, 1988; for an English translation, see BULGARIAN CHAMBER OF COMMERCE AND INDUSTRY, INTERNATIONAL COMMERCIAL ARBITRATION IN BULGARIA 11 (1989), with an introduction by Professor Zhivko Stalev at 5; Vratislav Pechota, *A New Law on International Commercial Arbitration in Bulgaria*, 1 AM. REV. INT'L ARB. 310 (1990).

[80] Law amending the Law on International Commercial Arbitration, published in State Gazette No. 93 of November 2, 1993. On the other principal modifications made in 1993, see Zhivko Stalev, *Bulgaria*, XIX Y.B.

(continued...)

be followed in other formerly socialist states, eager to equip themselves with legislation allowing private law arbitration, while affirming, in countries such as Slovenia[81] and Croatia,[82] their new international status. In Poland, the legislature has so far confined itself to amending, in 1989, the 1964 Code of Civil Procedure, opening up arbitration to all individuals and entities in Poland, but a draft law aims to introduce the UNCITRAL Model Law.[83] In 1992, Romania enacted a Private International Law Statute concerning the absence of court jurisdiction where the parties had agreed to arbitrate, as well as the conditions for enforcement of foreign arbitral awards in Romania.[84] This was followed by a law dated July 23, 1993, which modified the Code of Civil Procedure so as to promote both *ad hoc* arbitration[85] and institutional arbitration.[86] This law was partly inspired by the UNCITRAL Model Law.[87]

In the Czech Republic, Law No. 216 of November 1, 1994 concerns arbitration and the enforcement of arbitral awards. It came into force on January 1, 1995 and covers both domestic and international arbitration, with several provisions specifically applicable to the latter.[88]

Finally, on November 8, 1994, Hungary enacted a law based on the UNCITRAL Model Law.[89]

---

[80](...continued)
COM. ARB. 449 (1994); on the content of the new Bulgarian legislation, see Sevdalin Staikov, *International Commercial Arbitration in Bulgaria*, in ICC BULLETIN, SPECIAL SUPPLEMENT, INTERNATIONAL COMMERCIAL ARBITRATION IN EUROPE 76 (1994); Emile Gueorguiev, *La loi bulgare sur l'arbitrage commercial international*, 1996 REV. ARB. 39.

[81] Mirko Ilesic, *International Arbitration in Slovenia*, in ICC BULLETIN, SPECIAL SUPPLEMENT, INTERNATIONAL COMMERCIAL ARBITRATION IN EUROPE 122 (1994).

[82] Kresimir Sajko, *International Commercial Arbitration in Croatia – Present Status and Future Development*, in ICC BULLETIN, SPECIAL SUPPLEMENT, INTERNATIONAL COMMERCIAL ARBITRATION IN EUROPE 81 (1994); a preliminary draft of a statute containing distinct rules for domestic and international disputes was prepared in April 1997; *see* Petar Šarcevic, *Brief Introduction to the "First Draft Proposal of the Law on Arbitration of the Republic of Croatia"*, 1997 BULL. ASA 58, and an English translation of the Draft at 61.

[83] Tadeusz Szurski, *Arbitration in Poland*, in ICC BULLETIN, SPECIAL SUPPLEMENT, INTERNATIONAL COMMERCIAL ARBITRATION IN EUROPE 102 (1994).

[84] Law No. 105 of September 22, 1992 on the Settlement of Private International Law Relations, Articles 167, 168, 180 and 81.

[85] Law No. 59 of July 23, 1993, published in the Official Gazette on July 26, 1963; *see* Grigore Florescu, *The Evolution of Commercial Arbitration in Romania*, 10 J. INT'L ARB. 95 (Mar. 1993).

[86] On the reform of the arbitration courts of the foreign trade chambers of Eastern European countries since 1989, see *infra* para. 333.

[87] Victor Babiuc and Octavian Capatina, *International Commercial Arbitration in Romania*, in ICC BULLETIN, SPECIAL SUPPLEMENT, INTERNATIONAL COMMERCIAL ARBITRATION IN EUROPE 109 (1994); *Romania*, XX Y.B. COM. ARB. 592 (1995).

[88] Act on Arbitral Proceedings and Enforcement of Arbitral Awards, Part Five, Relations to Foreign Countries; *see* Svetozar Hanak, *Arbitration in the Czech Republic*, in ICC BULLETIN, SPECIAL SUPPLEMENT, INTERNATIONAL COMMERCIAL ARBITRATION IN EUROPE 88 (1994).

[89] Act LXXI of 1994 on Arbitration, published in the Hungarian Official Journal of November 28, 1994, and entered into force on December 13, 1994. *See* Eva Horváth, *Arbitration in Hungary*, in ICC BULLETIN, SPECIAL SUPPLEMENT, INTERNATIONAL COMMERCIAL ARBITRATION IN EUROPE 95 (1994); Miklos Bauer, *La nouvelle*
(continued...)

xii)   States of the former USSR

167. — Within the Commonwealth of Independent States, the situation is even more fluid. Once the international and constitutional problems of each of the new countries have been resolved,[90] and once their legislatures are in a position to consider enacting international arbitration legislation, many will no doubt seek to adopt or adapt the UNCITRAL Model Law. The Russian Federation has already moved in that direction: on July 7, 1993, it passed a law on international commercial arbitration reproducing the provisions of the Model Law almost in their entirety.[91] The law also specifies that any assistance required in constituting the arbitral tribunal is to be provided by the President of the Federal Chamber of Commerce and Industry, and that review of arbitral awards will be carried out—more traditionally—by the federal Supreme Courts or by the local courts (Art. 6). Ukraine has likewise followed the example of the Model Law[92] although, a few months later, Moldova chose not to do so.[93]

b) Other Continents

168. — The same legislative enthusiasm can be seen outside Europe. A few brief, selective examples are provided below.

i)   United States of America

169. — As early as 1925, the United States adopted a modern federal law, known as the Federal Arbitration Act (FAA) or United States Arbitration Act (USAA), which draws no distinction between domestic and international arbitration. Chapter 2 of the Act, which was added on July 31, 1970, introduced the New York Convention into federal law and thus

---

[89](...continued)
loi hongroise sur l'arbitrage, 1995 BULL. ASA 44; Eva Horváth, *The New Arbitration Act in Hungary,* 12 J. INT'L ARB. 53 (Sept. 1995).

[90] On the resulting difficulties affecting the enforcement of foreign awards, see Kaj Hobér, *Enforcing Foreign Arbitral Awards Against Russian Entities,* 10 ARB. INT'L 17 (1994).

[91] Law on International Commercial Arbitration, published in *Rossiiskaia Gazeta* of August 14, 1993. *See* Daniel Guyot, *Fédération de Russie: La loi du 7 juillet 1993 sur l'arbitrage commercial international,* 1993 CAH. JUR. FISC. EXP. 1079; Sergei Lebedev, *Russia: New Laws on International Arbitration,* 1993 RIV. DELL'ARB. 589; Alexander S. Komarov, *Russian Federation Legislation on International Commercial Arbitration, in* ICC BULLETIN, SPECIAL SUPPLEMENT, INTERNATIONAL COMMERCIAL ARBITRATION IN EUROPE 117 (1994).

[92] Law of February 24, 1994 on International Commercial Arbitration, published in State Gazette (*Golos Ukrainy*), No. 73 (823), April 20, 1994. *See* Igor G. Pobirchenko, *International Commercial Arbitration in Ukraine, in* ICC BULLETIN, SPECIAL SUPPLEMENT, INTERNATIONAL COMMERCIAL ARBITRATION IN EUROPE 126 (1994).

[93] Law No. 129-XIII of May 31, 1994 on Arbitration; *see* Bernd Lindemeyer, *Moldavia: The Arbitration Law of 31 May 1994, in* ICC BULLETIN, SPECIAL SUPPLEMENT, INTERNATIONAL COMMERCIAL ARBITRATION IN EUROPE 99 (1994).

deals with international arbitration and non-US awards.[94] Since the enactment of this legislation, the United States federal courts have proved to be substantially in favor of arbitration, seeking to give it full autonomy and a very wide scope. The liberal policy underlying this approach (on grounds including the easing of the courts' caseload) has not always met with unanimous approval.[95] In international arbitration, after confirming the principle of the autonomy of arbitration agreements,[96] the United States Supreme Court took a broad view of the arbitrability of disputes,[97] despite the existence of compulsory legislation concerning securities law[98] and antitrust issues in particular.[99] In domestic arbitration, the Supreme Court now accepts not only that an action for securities fraud is arbitrable, in spite of the applicability of mandatory rules,[100] but also that arbitrators are empowered to award punitive damages.[101]

---

[94] 9 U.S.C.A. §§ 1–302 (West 1999). For Chapter 2, see 9 U.S.C.A. §§ 201–08. On the legal framework and court control of such awards in the United States, see Laurent A. Niddam, *L'exécution des sentences arbitrales internationales aux Etats-Unis*, 1993 REV. ARB. 13; Gerald Aksen, Wendy S. Dorman, *Application of the New York Convention by United States Courts: A Twenty-Year Review (1970-1990)*, 2 AM. REV. INT'L ARB. 65 (1991); Joseph T. McLaughlin and Laurie Genevro, *Enforcement of Arbitral Awards Under the New York Convention – Practice in U.S. Courts*, 3 INT'L TAX & BUS. LAW. 249 (1986). On case law applying the New York Convention to awards made in the United States but considered to be international, see *infra* para. 257.

[95] See the reservations expressed by Thomas E. Carbonneau, *L'arbitrage devant les cours américaines*, in RID COMP., SPECIAL ISSUE, VOL. 10, JOURNÉES DE LA SOCIÉTÉ DE LÉGISLATION COMPARÉE – ANNÉE 1988, at 653 (1989); on this issue, see also TOM CARBONNEAU, CASES AND MATERIALS ON COMMERCIAL ARBITRATION (1997); GARY B. BORN, INTERNATIONAL COMMERCIAL ARBITRATION IN THE UNITED STATES 186 *et seq.* (1994).

[96] Prima Paint Corp. v. Flood & Conklin Mfg. Co., 388 U.S. 395 (1967); *see* Gerald Aksen, *Prima Paint v. Flood & Conklin – What Does It Mean?*, 43 ST. JOHN'S L. REV. 1 (1968); for a French translation, see 1968 REV. CRIT. DIP 91, and the commentary by Ernst Mezger, *Vers la consécration aux Etats-Unis de l'autonomie de la clause compromissoire dans l'arbitrage international, id.* at 25; *see infra* para. 402.

[97] For a general overview, see Joseph T. McLaughlin, *Arbitrability: Current Trends in the United States*, 59 ALB. L. REV. 905 (1996); 12 ARB. INT'L 113 (1996).

[98] Scherk v. Alberto-Culver Co., 417 U.S. 506 (1974); for a French translation, see 1975 REV. CRIT. DIP 643, and H. Gaudemet-Tallon and D. Tallon's note; 1975 REV. ARB. 213, and observations by P. Courteault; *see* BORN, *supra* note 95, at 341 *et seq.*

[99] Mitsubishi Motors Corp. v. Soler Chrysler-Plymouth, Inc., 473 U.S. 614 (1985); for a French translation, see 1986 REV. ARB. 273; among the numerous commentaries of this important case, see, for example, Sigvard Jarvin, *Arbitrability of Anti-Trust Disputes: The Mitsubishi v. Soler Case*, 2 J. INT'L ARB. 69 (Sept. 1985); Thomas E. Carbonneau, *Mitsubishi: the folly of quixotic internationalism*, 2 ARB. INT'L 116 (1986); Andreas F. Lowenfeld, *The Mitsubishi case: another view*, 2 ARB. INT'L 178 (1986); Jean Robert, *Une date dans l'extension de l'arbitrage international: l'arrêt Mitsubishi c/ Soler – Cour Suprême des Etats-Unis – 2 juillet 1985*, 1986 REV. ARB. 173; Hans Smit, *Mitsubishi: It is Not What it Seems to Be*, 4 J. INT'L ARB. 7 (Sept. 1987); *see infra* para. 575.

[100] Racketeer Influenced and Corrupt Organizations Act (RICO), 18 U.S.C.A. §§ 1961–68 (West Supp. 1999); the Securities Exchange Act of 1934, 15 U.S.C.A. § 78 (West 1997); *see* Shearson/American Express, Inc. v. McMahon, 482 U.S. 220 (1987); XIII Y.B. COM. ARB. 165 (1988); *see also* Michael Hoellering, *Shearson/American Express v. McMahon: Broadened Domain of Arbitration in U.S.A.*, 4 J. INT'L ARB. 153 (Sept. 1987); lastly, Rodriguez de Quijas v. Shearson/American Express, Inc., 490 U.S. 477 (1989); for a French translation, see 1989 REV. ARB. 735, and T. Carbonneau's note; *see infra* para. 579.

[101] Mastrobuono v. Shearson Lehman Hutton, Inc., 514 U.S. 52 (1995); 6 WORLD ARB. & MED. REP. 82 (1995); 10 INT'L ARB. REP. 3 (Mar. 1995); for a French translation, see 1995 REV. ARB. 295, and L. Niddam's note; *see also* the references cited *infra* para. 579, note 471.

However, the liberalism of federal case law[102] does not go far enough, in particular as regards the recognition in the United States of international arbitral awards. In addition, the jurisdiction of arbitrators to determine their own jurisdiction has still not been fully accepted.[103] The desire to serve as a competitive international arbitration venue is leading some U.S. states to enact new laws on international commercial arbitration. Some states reproduce the UNCITRAL Model Law in full,[104] or adapt it slightly,[105] while others merely draw inspiration from it[106] or make altogether less ambitious reforms.[107]

ii)   Canada

170. — Until 1986, Canada remained isolated from the worldwide development of international arbitration. The common law provinces and territories had enacted statutes inspired by the English 1889 Arbitration Act, without providing for recognition of foreign arbitral awards. Quebec was equally hostile to foreign awards in its Code of Civil Procedure, which provided that such awards had to go through an "exemplification" process, consisting of a rehearing of the merits of the case which could result in a wholesale revision of the award.[108] In addition, almost all arbitration fell within the legislative and judicial jurisdiction

---

[102] *See, e.g.*, Howard M. McCormack, *Recent U.S. Legal Decisions on Arbitration Law*, 11 J. INT'L ARB. 73 (Dec. 1994); Georgios Zekos, *Courts' Intervention in Commercial and Maritime Arbitration Under U.S. Law*, 14 J. INT'L ARB. 99 (June 1997).

[103] William W. Park, *The Arbitrability Dicta in First Options v. Kaplan: What Sort of Kompetenz-Kompetenz Has Crossed the Atlantic?*, 12 ARB. INT'L 137 (1996); Tom Carbonneau, *A Comment Upon Professor Park's Analysis Of The Dicta In First Options v. Kaplan*, 11 INT'L ARB. REP. 18 (Nov. 1996); Lawrence W. Newman and Charles M. Davidson, *Arbitrability of Timeliness Defenses – Who Decides?*, 14 J. INT'L ARB. 137 (June 1997).

[104] Connecticut in 1989 (UNCITRAL Model Law on International Commercial Arbitration, CONN. GEN. STAT. ANN. § 50a–100 (West 1999)).

[105] California in 1988 (Arbitration and Conciliation of International Disputes Act, CAL. CIV. PROC. CODE Tit. 9.3 (West 1999)); Texas in 1989 (Arbitration and Conciliation of International Disputes Act, TEX. REV. CIV. PRAC. & REM. CODE ANN. Arts. 249-1 to 249-43, redesignated as TEX. CIV. PRAC. & REM. CODE ANN. §§ 172.101 to 172.106 (West 1999)); North Carolina in 1991 (International Commercial Arbitration and Conciliation Act, N.C. GEN. STAT. § 1-567.30 (Lexis 1999)); Oregon in 1991 (Oregon International Commercial Arbitration and Conciliation Act, OR. REV. STAT. § 36.450–36.558 (1998)); Ohio in 1991 (OHIO REV. CODE ANN. § 2711.01 (Banks-Baldwin 1991)).

[106] Florida in 1986 (Florida International Arbitration Act, FLA. STAT. ANN. § 684.01 (West 1999)); Georgia in 1988 (GA. CODE ANN. § 9-9-30 (1998)); Hawaii in 1988 (Hawaii International Arbitration, Mediation and Conciliation Act, HAW. REV. STAT. ANN. § 658D-1 (Lexis 1998)).

[107] This is the case with the arbitration statute enacted in Maryland in 1990 (Maryland International Commercial Arbitration Act, MD. CODE ANN., CTS. & JUD. PROC. §§ 3-2B-01 to 3-2B-09 (1998)). For commentaries on these legislative trends, see Christine Lécuyer-Thieffry, *Les nouvelles lois des Etats américains sur l'arbitrage international*, 1989 REV. ARB. 43; Stewart J. McClendon, *State International Arbitration Laws: Are They Needed or Desirable?*, 1 AM. REV. INT'L ARB. 245 (1990); Xavier E. Romeu-Matta, *New Developments in International Commercial Arbitration: A Comparative Survey of New State Statutes and the UNCITRAL Model Law*, 1 AM. REV. INT'L ARB. 140 (1990). For an overview, see BORN, *supra* note 95.

[108] Manon Pomerleau, *L'arbitrage interprovincial et international au Canada: aspects constitutionnel et législatif*, 1985 REV. ARB. 373.

of the provinces, leading to difficulties in harmonizing and modernizing arbitration statutes and in ratifying the New York Convention.

On the initiative of the federal government, an agreement was reached between it, the provinces and the territories to simultaneously ratify the New York Convention and introduce new rules on international commercial arbitration into their legal systems by adopting the UNCITRAL Model Law. This program was implemented between 1986 and 1988 through the enactment of some twenty similar statutes. A majority of the provinces and territories enacted only one statute, to which they appended the New York Convention and, with minor alterations, the UNCITRAL Model Law. Others, including the federal legislature, preferred to enact two separate instruments, while British Columbia enacted three, the first of which implemented the New York Convention, the second, the Model Law on international arbitration,[109] with a third statute covering domestic commercial arbitration. In contrast, Ontario, where the 1986 Foreign Arbitral Awards Act implemented the New York Convention,[110] adopted the Model Law through the International Commercial Arbitration Act of June 8, 1988, which applies to international commercial arbitration and to all awards made outside Canada. The International Commercial Arbitration Act thus repeals the 1986 Foreign Arbitral Awards Act. Quebec likewise introduced a single statute,[111] which implemented the New York Convention and drew inspiration from the Model Law for its new provincial law.

This substantial legislative program[112] is inadequate in some areas. Most provinces (although not Quebec) ultimately treat arbitral awards from other provinces less favorably than those from outside Canada. Their modernization and harmonization efforts were confined to international arbitration and, in most cases, intra-provincial and inter-provincial

---

[109] 1986 International Commercial Arbitration Act, R.S.B.C. 1996, c. 233.

[110] 1986 Act to implement the United Nations Convention on the Recognition and Enforcement of Foreign Arbitral Awards, S.O. 1986, c. 25.

[111] An Act to Amend the Civil Code and the Code of Civil Procedure in Respect of Arbitration, assented to and entered in force on November 11, 1986, S.Q. 1986, ch. 73 (inserting Arts. 1926.1–1926.6 of the Civil Code and amending Arts. 940–951.2 of the Code of Civil Procedure). For a commentary, see Alain Prujiner, *Les nouvelles règles de l'arbitrage au Québec*, 1987 REV. ARB. 425; John E.C. Brierley, *Quebec's New (1986) Arbitration Law*, 13 CAN. BUS. L.J. 58 (July 1987); Louis Marquis, *La notion d'arbitrage commercial international en droit québécois*, 37 MCGILL L.J./R.D. MCGILL 448 (1992); Louis Marquis, *L'influence du modèle juridique français sur le droit québécois de l'arbitrage conventionnel*, 1993 RID COMP. 577.

[112] *See* Henri Alvarez, *La nouvelle législation canadienne sur l'arbitrage commercial international*, 1986 REV. ARB. 529; John E.C. Brierley, *Une loi nouvelle pour le Québec en matière d'arbitrage*, 47 REV. BARREAU 259 (1987); Marc Lalonde, *The New Environment for Commercial Arbitration in Canada*, 1988 INT'L BUS. L.J. 963; Ludwig Kos-Rabcewicz-Zubkowski, *International Commercial Arbitration Laws in Canada – Adaptation of UNCITRAL Model Law on International Commercial Arbitration*, 5 J. INT'L ARB. 43 (Sept. 1988); Ludwig Kos-Rabcewicz-Zubkowski, *International Commercial Arbitration Laws in Canada: Recent Legislation (Ontario and Saskatchewan)*, 5 J. INT'L ARB. 165 (Dec. 1988); Louis Kos-Rabcewicz-Zubkowski, *L'adaptation de la loi-type de la C.N.U.D.C.I. dans les provinces de common law au Canada*, 1989 REV. ARB. 37; Robert K. Paterson, *Implementing the UNCITRAL Model Law – The Canadian Experience*, 10 J. INT'L ARB. 29 (June 1993); Serge Gravel, *Arbitration Within the NAFTA Area (Canada, Mexico, U.S.A.): Current Difficulties and Future Trends*, ICC BULLETIN, Vol. 4, No. 2, at 22 (1993).

arbitrations are still governed by the previous legal regime[113] and by choice of law rules which hamper the growth of arbitration. It is too early to say whether this dichotomy is viable and, in particular, whether the desired development of international arbitration in Canada will materialize in the absence of solid support in domestic law and practice. Judging by the number of Canadian court decisions concerning the application of the UNCITRAL Model Law to international cases, there does seem to be a significant increase in international arbitration in Canada.[114]

iii)   Latin America

171. — Latin American countries, traditionally hostile to arbitration, are now embarking on a process of legislative modernization.[115] There have been reforms in Colombia,[116]

---

[113]   With the exception, however, of at least two provinces: Quebec (see above) and Ontario, where a new law on domestic arbitration entered into force on January 1, 1992 (Arbitration Act 1991, S.O. 1991, c. 17).

[114]   *See* UNCITRAL, Case Law on UNCITRAL Texts (CLOUT), Cases relating to the UNCITRAL Model Arbitration Law (MAL), UN Docs. A/CN.9/SER.C/ABSTRACTS/1 *et seq.*; the full text of CLOUT is also available on UNCITRAL's Web site (<http://www.un.or.at/uncitral>); from 1987 to 1999, more than forty decisions were handed down. *See also* Alain Prujiner, *Chronique de jurisprudence canadienne et québécoise – La force obligatoire des clauses d'arbitrage (Article 8 de la Loi-type de la CNUDCI)*, 1994 REV. ARB. 569.

[115]   For a general overview, see Albert J. van den Berg, *L'arbitrage commercial en Amérique latine*, 1979 REV. ARB. 123; COMMERCIAL AND LABOR ARBITRATION IN CENTRAL AMERICA (A.M. Garro ed., 1991); Robert Layton, *Changing Attitudes Toward Dispute Resolution in Latin America*, 10 J. INT'L ARB. 123 (June 1993); ICC BULLETIN, SPECIAL SUPPLEMENT, INTERNATIONAL COMMERCIAL ARBITRATION IN LATIN AMERICA (ICC Publication No. 580E, 1997); CLAUDIA FRUTOS-PETERSON, L'ÉMERGENCE D'UN DROIT EFFECTIF DE L'ARBITRAGE COMMERCIAL INTERNATIONAL EN AMÉRIQUE LATINE (Thesis, University of Paris I (France), 1998).

[116]   Decree No. 2279, signed and published on October 7, 1989. The decree was amended by Law No. 23 of 1991, published on March 21, 1991. *See* Fernando Mantilla-Serrano, *La nouvelle législation colombienne sur l'arbitrage*, 1992 REV. ARB. 41; *Colombia*, XIX Y.B. COM. ARB. 451 (1994).

Peru,[117] Mexico,[118] Brazil,[119] Bolivia,[120] Ecuador[121] and Venezuela.[122] It is likely that through ratification of the New York Convention,[123] the Panama Convention,[124] and the MERCOSUR Treaty,[125] and through the influence of the UNCITRAL Model Law[126] in particular, the modernization process will continue.

172. — In other parts of the world, the same diversity is to be found. Most African, Asian and Pacific countries remain attached either to having their disputes heard by the courts, or to methods of dispute resolution which are closer to conciliation and mediation. Nevertheless, the movement to reform and modernize arbitration, especially for international disputes, is gaining a foothold, and there is a growing tendency to enact new legislation based on the UNCITRAL Model Law.

iv)   Africa

173. — In Africa, the situation is one of strong contrasts. Many African countries, even when reforming their codes or legislation governing civil procedure, have not really

---

[117] Legislative Decree No. 25935 of November 7, 1992, entered into force on December 11, 1992, with provisions specific to international arbitration, inspired by the UNCITRAL Model Law; *see Peru*, XIX Y.B. COM. ARB. 460 (1994).

[118] Law of July 22, 1993, very closely modeled on the UNCITRAL Model Law, amending and supplementing the Code of Commerce and the Federal Code of Civil Procedure, published in *Diario Official de la Federación* of July 22, 1993. *See* Isabel Zivy, *La nouvelle loi sur l'arbitrage au Mexique*, 1994 REV. ARB. 295; Julio C. Treviño, *The New Mexican Legislation on Commercial Arbitration*, 11 J. INT'L ARB. 5 (Dec. 1994); Gravel, *supra* note 112; Michael Tenenbaum, *International Arbitration of Trade Disputes in Mexico – The Arrival of the NAFTA and New Reforms to the Commercial Code*, 12 J. INT'L ARB. 53 (Mar. 1995); José Luis Siqueiros and Alexander C. Hoagland, *Mexico, in* ICCA INTERNATIONAL HANDBOOK ON COMMERCIAL ARBITRATION (1995).

[119] Law No. 9.307-96 of September 23, 1996 on arbitration, *Diario Official*, Sept. 24, 1996, pp. 18,897–18,900; on the new law, inspired by the UNCITRAL Model Law, see João Bosco Lee, *Le nouveau régime de l'arbitrage au Brésil*, 1997 REV. ARB. 199; José Carlos Barbosa Moreira, *La nuova legge brasiliana sull'arbitrato*, 1997 RIV. DELL'ARB. 1; Maruska Guerreiro Lopes, *La nouvelle loi brésilienne sur l'arbitrage*, 1997 DALLOZ AFF. 1205 (and erratum at 1347); Welber Barral and Frederico Cardoso, *Arbitration in Brazil: The 1996 Act*, 13 INT'L ARB. REP. 16 (Aug. 1998).

[120] Law No. 1770 of Mar. 10, 1997, *Gaceta Oficial de Bolivia*, Mar. 10, 1997, *reprinted in* 1998 RIV. DELL'ARB. 149.

[121] Law of August 26, 1997 on Arbitration and Mediation, Official Register No. 145 dated September 4, 1997, repealing the Law of October 23, 1963. On this new law, see FRUTOS-PETERSON, *supra* note 115, at 302–04; Isabel Zivy, *La nouvelle loi relative à l'arbitrage en Equateur*, 126 J.D.I. 115 (1999).

[122] Law of Commercial Arbitration, Official Gazette No. 36,430 of April 7, 1998; *see* 1 INT'L ARB. L. REV. N–104 (1998).

[123] By countries such as Argentina; *see* Horacio A. Grigera Naon, *The Enforcement of Arbitral Awards in Argentina*, 1996 RIV. DELL'ARB. 411.

[124] On this Convention, see *infra* para. 294.

[125] On this Treaty, see *supra* para. 77.

[126] On the Model Law, see *infra* para. 203.

attempted to promote arbitration, whether domestic or international.[127] Togo, however, has set up an Arbitration Court with jurisdiction over both domestic and international disputes.[128] In 1993, the Côte d'Ivoire enacted a law reproducing almost word-for-word Articles 1442 to 1507 of the French New Code of Civil Procedure.[129] Mali did likewise by a decree dated June 28, 1994: Articles 879 to 942 of its New Code of Civil Procedure reproduce Articles 1442 to 1506 of the French New Code of Civil Procedure.[130] Finally, Senegal has just carried out a far-reaching reform of its arbitration law by a statute enacted on April 14, 1998 and a decree dated June 5, 1998.[131] Domestic arbitration law now essentially follows French law, with the provisions on international arbitration inspired by the UNCITRAL Model Law.

The theme underlying the modernization of arbitration laws in French-speaking Africa today is regional harmonization. This can be seen in the projected establishment of the arbitral institutions provided for in the October 17, 1993 Treaty creating the "Organization for the Harmonization of business law in Africa" (OHADA),[132] and in both the enactment of a uniform law[133] and the promulgation of arbitration rules of the Joint Court of Justice and Arbitration on March 11, 1999.[134]

In English-speaking Africa, Nigeria enacted new arbitration legislation in 1988.[135] Strongly influenced by the UNCITRAL Model Law, this statute put an end to court revision of domestic awards, which can now only be set aside in a limited number of situations. The

---

[127] For an overview, see ROLAND AMOUSSOU-GUENOU, LE DROIT ET LA PRATIQUE DE L'ARBITRAGE COMMERCIAL INTERNATIONAL EN AFRIQUE SUBSAHARIENNE 29–144 (Thesis, University of Paris II (France), 1995); Roland Amoussou-Guenou, *Redécouvrir l'arbitrage commercial international en Afrique francophone*, 1995 CAH. JUR. FISC. EXP. 799; Roland Amoussou-Guenou, *International Commercial Arbitration in Subsaharan Africa: Law and Practice*, ICC BULLETIN, Vol. 7, No. 1, at 59 (1996); ARBITRATION IN AFRICA (E. Cotram and A. Amissah eds., 1996); for a presentation and the text of a number of arbitration laws of French-speaking African countries (Cameroon, Côte d'Ivoire, Gabon, Madagascar, Mali, Togo), see JUSTICE ET DÉVELOPPEMENT – LE RÔLE DE L'ARBITRAGE COMMERCIAL INTERNATIONAL (1997); on enforcement issues, see Amazu A. Asouzu, *African States and the Enforcement of Arbitral Awards: Some Key Issues*, 15 ARB. INT'L 1 (1999).

[128] Law No. 89-31 of November 28, 1989, Official Journal of the Republic of Togo, Jan. 10, 1990. *See* ARBITRATION IN AFRICA, *supra* note 127, at 276.

[129] Law No. 93-671 of August 9, 1993, Official Journal of the Republic of Côte d'Ivoire, Sept. 16, 1993; *see* Laurence Idot, *Loi ivoirienne N° 93-671 du 9 août 1993 relative à l'arbitrage*, 1994 REV. ARB. 783; ARBITRATION IN AFRICA, *supra* note 127, at 276. On the situation beforehand, see L. Idot, note following Supreme Court of Côte d'Ivoire, Apr. 29, 1986, Talal Massih v. Omais, 1989 REV. ARB. 530.

[130] Decree No. 94-226 of June 28, 1994, Official Journal of the Republic of Mali, July 15, 1994; *see* ARBITRATION IN AFRICA, *supra* note 127, at 269.

[131] Law No. 98-30 of April 14, 1998 on arbitration, Official Journal of the Republic of Senegal, Apr. 24, 1998, p. 249; Decree No. 98-492 of June 5, 1998 on domestic and international arbitration, Official Journal of the Republic of Senegal, July 25, 1998, p. 486; *see* Fatou Camara, *Le nouveau droit de l'arbitrage au Sénégal: du libéral et de l'éphémère*, 1999 REV. ARB. 45.

[132] On the OHADA Treaty, see *infra* para. 300.

[133] This uniform law will apply if at least one of the parties to an arbitration is from a state that has signed the OHADA treaty, or if the seat of the arbitration is in such a country.

[134] On the Joint Court of Justice and Arbitration, see *infra* para. 300.

[135] Arbitration and Conciliation Decree No. 11 of 1988, Official Gazette, Vol. 75, No. 18 of Mar. 14, 1988, Pt. A (Supplement), at A503. This decree was transformed in 1990 into The Arbitration and Conciliation Act 1990 (Cap. 19, Laws of Federation of Nigeria 1990).

provisions covering international arbitration (Arts. 43 to 54) allow for considerable autonomy, and the New York Convention now governs the enforcement in Nigeria of all foreign awards.[136] Kenya also adopted a slightly modified version of the UNCITRAL Model Law in its 1995 Arbitration Act.[137] That statute governs both domestic and international arbitration. The influence of the UNCITRAL Model Law in English-speaking Africa can also be seen in legislation passed in Zimbabwe in 1996, and expected soon in South Africa.[138]

The Republic of Djibouti adopted an international arbitration code on February 13, 1984, adhering fairly closely to the French substantive rules of 1981, and aiming to provide facilities for international arbitration in Djibouti.[139] This could prove to be an attractive arbitration situs, given its geopolitical situation and the establishment of an international "Commission for Arbitration Appeals" which, in certain limited circumstances, has exclusive jurisdiction to review the validity of international awards made in Djibouti.

Egypt, at one stage noted for its hostility towards international arbitration[140] implemented important legislation in 1994, strongly influenced by the UNCITRAL Model Law.[141]

In North Africa, both Algeria and Tunisia have recently legislated to introduce specific rules governing international arbitration. In Algeria, a legislative decree of April 25, 1993 liberalized the regime governing international arbitration, drawing inspiration from the

---

[136] For a commentary, see Roland Amoussou-Guénou, *La réforme de l'arbitrage en République fédérale du Nigéria*, 1989 REV. ARB. 445; Edward Atanda, *The Nigerian Arbitration and Conciliation Decree of 1988*, 1 AM. REV. INT'L ARB. 452 (1990); Amazu A. Asouzu, *The Legal Framework for Commercial Arbitration and Conciliation in Nigeria*, 9 ICSID REV. – FOREIGN INV. L.J. 214 (1994); Andrew I. Okekeifere, *The Enforcement and Challenge of Foreign Arbitral Awards in Nigeria*, 14 J. INT'L ARB. 223 (Sept. 1997); EPHRAIM AKPATA, THE NIGERIAN ARBITRATION LAW IN FOCUS (1997); CHUMA UWECHIA, NIGERIAN ARBITRATION AND CONCILIATION LAW IN PRACTICE (1997); Dakas Clement James Dakas, *The Legal Framework for the Recognition and Enforcement of International Commercial Arbitral Awards in Nigeria – Dilemmas and Agenda for Action*, 15 J. INT'L ARB. 95 (June 1998).

[137] Arbitration Act 1995, enacted on August 10, 1995, and entered into force on January 2, 1996. On the changes from the Model Law, see Amos Wako, *Kenya*, XXI Y.B. COM. ARB. 379 (1996).

[138] *See* Roland Amoussou-Guenou and Rosabel E. Goodman-Everard, *Compte rendu du Congrès de Johannesburg (5-8 mars 1997)*, 1997 REV. ARB. 451.

[139] 1984 REV. ARB. 533, and the commentary by Yves Derains, *Le Code djiboutien de l'arbitrage international*, *id.* at 465; *see also* S.K. Chatterjee, *The Djibouti Code of International Arbitration*, 4 J. INT'L ARB. 57 (Mar. 1987).

[140] *See* Y. Derains, observations following ICC Award No. 5721 (1990), European company v. American and Egyptian parties, 117 J.D.I. 1020 (1990), and the references cited therein; Egyptian *Cour de cassation*, Dec. 23, 1991, Société d'assurances Misr v. Agence de navigation Amon, 1994 REV. ARB. 757, and observations by A.H. El-Ahdab.

[141] Law No. 27 for 1994 Promulgating the Law Concerning Arbitration in Civil and Commercial Matters; for a commentary, see Bernard Fillion-Dufouleur and Philippe Leboulanger, *Le nouveau droit égyptien de l'arbitrage*, 1994 REV. ARB. 665; Yehia El Gamal, *Some Remarks on Egyptian Law No. 27/1994 Concerning Arbitration*, ICC BULLETIN, Vol. 5, No. 2, at 38 (1994); M.I.M. Aboul-Enein, *Reflections on the New Egyptian Law on Arbitration*, 11 ARB. INT'L 75 (1995); Abdul Hamid El-Ahdab, *The New Egyptian Arbitration Act in Civil and Commercial Matters*, 12 J. INT'L ARB. 65 (June 1995). A law of May 13, 1997 provides that Egyptian administrative contracts are arbitrable, if the relevant Minister has approved (*see* 12 INT'L ARB. REP. 18 (Sept. 1997)); *see also* P. Leboulanger, note following Court of Appeals of Cairo, Mar. 19, 1997, Organisme des Antiquités v. G. Silver Night Company, 1997 REV. ARB. 283, 293.

French New Code of Civil Procedure and the Swiss Private International Law Statute.[142] On April 26, 1993, Tunisia enacted a statute creating an arbitration code, with rules specific to both domestic and international arbitration, the latter being largely based on the UNCITRAL Model Law.[143]

v)   The Middle East

173-1. — Lebanon was the first of the Arab countries[144] to modernize its arbitration legislation. The 1983 Lebanese Code of Civil Procedure draws a distinction between domestic arbitration (Arts. 762 to 808) and international arbitration (Arts. 809 to 821), and closely models its rules on the French New Code of Civil Procedure.[145]

---

[142] Decree No. 93-09 of April 25, 1993 amending and completing Order No. 66-54 of June 8, 1966 on the Code of Civil Procedure, Official Journal No. 27, Apr. 27, 1993, pp. 42–46; for a commentary, see Mohand Issad, *Le décret législatif algérien du 25 avril 1993 relatif à l'arbitrage international*, 1993 REV. ARB. 377; Mohammed Bedjaoui and Ali Mebroukine, *Le nouveau droit de l'arbitrage international en Algérie*, 120 J.D.I. 873 (1993); Mohammed Bedjaoui, *Remarkable Turning Point in the Algerian Law Relating to International Commercial Arbitration*, ICC BULLETIN, Vol. 4, No. 2, at 53 (1993); Ali Mebroukine, *Actualité du droit algérien de l'arbitrage international/Current Situation of the Algerian Law on International Arbitration*, 1994 INT'L BUS. L.J. 321; Dahmane Ben Abderrahmane, *Le nouveau droit algérien de l'arbitrage international*, 1993 CAH. JUR. FISC. EXP. 1007. On the situation pre-reform, see the Minutes of the seminar on commercial arbitration organized by the National Chamber of Commerce of Algiers on December 14 and 15, 1992, CHAMBRE NATIONALE DE COMMERCE, ACTES DU SÉMINAIRE SUR L'ARBITRAGE COMMERCIAL (1993).

[143] Arbitration Code promulgated by Law No. 93-42 of 26 April 1993, Official Journal of the Republic of Tunisia, May 4, 1993, p. 580; for a commentary, see Sami Kallel, *The Tunisian Law on International Arbitration: Introductory Note*, 5 ARB. MATERIALS 369 (Sept. & Dec. 1993), with an English translation of the statute at 376; Kalthoum Meziou and Ali Mezghani, *Le Code tunisien de l'arbitrage*, 1993 REV. ARB. 521; Habib Malouche, *A Brief Survey of the Tunisian Arbitration Code*, ICC BULLETIN, Vol. 4, No. 2, at 63 (1993); Mohamed Larbi Hachem, *L'arbitrage international dans le nouveau Code de l'arbitrage tunisien*, 1994 RIV. DELL'ARB. 599; *see also* CENTRE D'ETUDES JURIDIQUES ET JUDICIAIRES, L'ARBITRAGE INTERNATIONAL DANS LE NOUVEAU CODE TUNISIEN, ACTES DU COLLOQUE ORGANISÉ À TUNIS LES 26 - 27 NOVEMBRE 1993 (1995) (in Arabic and in French).

[144] For an analysis of the national laws of the Arab states, with English translations of the legislation in force in the various countries, see ABDUL HAMID EL-AHDAB, ARBITRATION WITH THE ARAB COUNTRIES (2d ed. 1999). For a more synthetic study, see EURO-ARAB CHAMBERS OF COMMERCE, EURO-ARAB ARBITRATION – ARBITRAGE EURO-ARABE (Proceedings of the First Euro-Arab Arbitration Conference) (F. Kemicha ed., 1987); EURO-ARAB CHAMBERS OF COMMERCE, EURO-ARAB ARBITRATION II – ARBITRAGE EURO-ARABE II (Proceedings of the Second Euro-Arab Arbitration Congress, Bahrain) (F. Kemicha ed., 1989); EURO-ARAB CHAMBERS OF COMMERCE, EURO-ARAB ARBITRATION III – ARBITRAGE EURO-ARABE III (Proceedings of the Third Euro-Arab Arbitration Congress, Amman) (F. Kemicha ed., 1991); *see also* ICC BULLETIN, SPECIAL SUPPLEMENT, INTERNATIONAL COMMERCIAL ARBITRATION IN THE ARAB COUNTRIES (1992); Samir Saleh, *La perception de l'arbitrage au Machrek et dans les pays du Golfe*, 1992 REV. ARB. 537.

[145] Legislative Decree No. 90/83 of September 16, 1983, which came into force on January 1, 1985 (slightly amended by Legislative Decree No. 20/85, dated March 23, 1985); the full Arabic text is published in the Lebanese Official Gazette No. 40 of October 6, 1983; for a commentary, see Nassib G. Ziadé, *Introductory Note to the International Arbitration Provisions of the Code of Civil Procedure*, 27 I.L.M. 1022 (1988); Marie Sfeir-Slim, *Le nouveau droit libanais de l'arbitrage a dix ans*, 1993 REV. ARB. 543; Nasri Antoine Diab, *L'arbitrage international en droit libanais*, 1994 DPCI 163; Abdul Hamid El-Ahdab, *The Lebanese Arbitration Act*, 13 J. INT'L ARB. 39 (Sept. 1996).

This is not the case in Saudi Arabia where, although the 1983 and 1985 reforms clarify and simplify the previous traditional system, many restrictions based on grounds of religion and nationality remain in place.[146] Over the past few years, other Gulf countries, such as Qatar, the United Arab Emirates, and Yemen, have enacted modern arbitration legislation, although they do not provide a specific regime for international arbitration.[147] Bahrain, meanwhile, simply adopted the UNCITRAL Model Law to govern international commercial arbitration.[148] More recently, the Sultanate of Oman passed an arbitration statute dated July 27, 1997,[149] which reproduces almost word for word the 1994 Egyptian arbitration statute which, as we have seen, is itself closely modeled on the UNCITRAL Model Law.

On the other side of the Gulf, Iran adopted a new statute on international commercial arbitration in 1997, again heavily influenced by the UNCITRAL Model Law.[150]

vi)   Asia and the Pacific Rim

174. — A number of countries from Asia and the Pacific Rim are enacting new legislation governing international arbitration.[151]

---

[146] Arbitration Act Promulgated by Royal Decree No. M/46 dated July 12, 1403 H (April 25, 1983 AD); Implementation Rules No. 7/2021/M dated 8/9/1405 H (May 27, 1985 AD). *See* Abdul Hamid El-Ahdab, *Arbitration in Saudi Arabia under the New Arbitration Act, 1983 and Its Implementation Rules of 1985* (Pts. 1 & 2), 3 J. INT'L ARB. 27 (Sept. 1986), 3 J. INT'L ARB. 23 (Dec. 1986); Nancy B. Turk, *Arbitration in Saudi Arabia*, 6 ARB. INT'L 281 (1990).

[147] Qatari Law No. 13/1990, published in the Official Gazette No. 13 of September 1, 1990; *see* Abdul Hamid El-Ahdab, *The Qatari Arbitration Act – A Study*, 10 J. INT'L ARB. 143 (June 1993). United Arab Emirates Act on Civil Procedure containing a chapter on arbitration, Act No. 11/1992, published in the Official Gazette No. 235 of March 8, 1992; *see* Abdul Hamid El-Ahdab, *La nouvelle loi sur l'arbitrage de l'Etat des Emirats Arabes Unis*, 1993 REV. ARB. 229; Abdul Hamid El-Ahdab, *The New Arbitration Act of the State of The United Arab Emirates*, 11 INT'L ARB. REP. 32 (Aug. 1996).Yemenite Presidential Decree No. 22-1992 issuing the Arbitration Act, dated March 29, 1992, published in the Official Gazette No. 6 of March 31, 1992; *see* Abdul Hamid El-Ahdab, *The New Yemeni Arbitration Act*, 11 J. INT'L ARB. 51 (June 1994).

[148] Decree Law No. 9 of 1994 with respect to Promulgation of the Law on International Commercial Arbitration, adopted on August 16, 1994; *see Bahrain*, XX Y.B. COM. ARB. 583 (1995); 1994 REV. ARB. 790.

[149] Act on Arbitration in Civil and Commercial Matters, published in the Omani Official Gazette No. 602; for a commentary, see Abdul Hamid El-Ahdab, *La nouvelle loi sur l'arbitrage du Sultanat d'Oman*, 1997 REV. ARB. 527; Abdul Hamid El-Ahdab, *The New Omani Arbitration Act in Civil and Commercial Matters*, 14 J. INT'L ARB. 59 (Dec. 1997).

[150] International Commercial Arbitration Law, enacted and approved by the the Majlis and the Guardian Council on October 2, 1997, published in the Iranian Official Gazette, No. 15335, Oct. 20, 1997, pp. 1–4; *see* Shirin O. Entezari, *Iranian Arbitration Proceedings*, 14 J. INT'L ARB. 53 (Dec. 1997); Shirin O. Entezari, *Iran Adopts International Commercial Arbitration Law*, 13 INT'L ARB. REP. 15 (Feb. 1998); Jamal Seifi, *The New International Commercial Arbitration Act of Iran — Towards Harmony with the UNCITRAL Model Law*, 15 J. INT'L ARB. 5 (June 1998); Mansour Jafarian and Mehrdad Rezaeian, *The New Law on International Commercial Arbitration in Iran*, 15 J. INT'L ARB. 31 (Sept. 1998); Hamid G. Gharavi, *The 1997 Iranian International Commercial Arbitration Law; the UNCITRAL Model Law à l'Iranienne*, 15 ARB. INT'L 85 (1999); Hamid Gharavi, *Le nouveau droit iranien de l'arbitrage commercial international*, 1999 REV. ARB. 35.

[151] Michael J. Moser, *The ICC Arbitral Process – Part VII: The Recognition and Enforcement of Foreign Arbitral Awards: A Survey of the Asia-Pacific Region*, ICC BULLETIN, Vol. 5, No. 2, at 20 (1994); KENNETH R.

(continued...)

174-1. — In Hong Kong, the 1982 Arbitration Ordinance, based on the 1979 English Arbitration Act,[152] removed the special case procedure and promoted exclusion agreements, under which the parties agree not to appeal arbitral awards before the courts. The ordinance also allowed the arbitral tribunal to consolidate connected arbitrations (Art. 6B). An ordinance enacted in 1989 introduced the UNCITRAL Model Law to govern international arbitration.[153] This ordinance was amended in 1996.[154] The handover of Hong Kong to China on June 30, 1997 raises, among other issues, the question of whether arbitral awards made in China will continue to be considered foreign awards in Hong Kong and will thus be governed by the New York Convention and, conversely, whether awards made in Hong Kong will still be characterized as foreign awards in China.[155]

174-2. — China plays a very important role in international arbitration. Several Chinese laws regulating international trade[156] provide for international arbitration as the method of dispute resolution. China has also ratified the New York and Washington Conventions and

---

[151](...continued)
SIMMONDS, BRIAN H.W. HILL, SIGVARD JARVIN, COMMERCIAL ARBITRATION LAW IN ASIA AND THE PACIFIC (1987); DISPUTE RESOLUTION IN ASIA (M. Pryles ed., 1997); ICC BULLETIN, SPECIAL SUPPLEMENT, INTERNATIONAL COMMERCIAL ARBITRATION IN ASIA (1998).

[152] *See supra* para. 157.

[153] Arbitration (Amendment) (No. 2) Ordinance 1989 (No. 64 of 1989). *See* Neil Kaplan, *The Hong Kong Arbitration Ordinance, Some Features and Recent Amendments*, 1 AM. REV. INT'L ARB. 25 (1990); David St. John Sutton, *Hong Kong Enacts the UNCITRAL Model Law*, 6 ARB. INT'L 358 (1990); NEIL KAPLAN, JILL SPRUCE, MICHAEL J. MOSER, HONG KONG AND CHINA ARBITRATION CASES AND MATERIALS (1994); Neil Kaplan, *The Model Law in Hong Kong – Two Years On*, 8 ARB. INT'L 223 (1992); Stephen D. Mau, *Enforceability of Arbitral Awards – Hong Kong*, 1994 BULL. ASA 345. For court decisions applying the Model Law, see UNCITRAL, Case Law on UNCITRAL Texts (CLOUT), *supra* note 114.

[154] Hong Kong Arbitration (Amendment) Ordinance 1996 (No. 75 of 1996), Legal Supplement No. 1 to the Hong Kong Government Gazette, No. 52, Vol. CXXXVIII (Dec. 27, 1996), which was signed on December 24, 1996 and came into force on June 27, 1997; *see* Robert Morgan, *The English Arbitration Act 1996 And Reform Of Arbitration Law In Hong Kong and Singapore: A Brave New World?*, 11 INT'L ARB. REP. 20 (Dec. 1996); on the other modifications contained in this amendment, see XXII Y.B. COM. ARB. 570 (1997).

[155] Guiguo Wang, *One Country, Two Arbitration Systems – Recognition and Enforcement of Arbitral Awards in Hong Kong and China*, 14 J. INT'L ARB. 5 (Mar. 1997); *see also* Michael J. Moser, *Hong Kong, in* DISPUTE RESOLUTION IN ASIA, *supra* note 151, at 95.

[156] These include the Law of the People's Republic of China on Chinese-Foreign Equity Joint-Ventures adopted at the Second Session of the Fifth National People's Congress on July 1, 1979 (Art. 14), and the Foreign Economic Contract Law of the People's Republic of China, adopted at the 10th Session of the Standing Committee of the Sixth National People's Congress, March 21, 1985, effective July 1, 1985; *see* CHENG DEJUN, MICHAEL J. MOSER, WANG SHENGCHANG, INTERNATIONAL ARBITRATION IN THE PEOPLE'S REPUBLIC OF CHINA 607 and 596 (1995).

its arbitration legislation[157] and institutions[158] have been gradually internationalized. A 1994 statute contains rules specific to international arbitration, and lays the foundations for a private law domestic arbitration system.[159]

In Taiwan, the 1961 Commercial Arbitration Act, which had already been amended in 1982 and 1986, was more radically revised by the 1998 Arbitration Act, which came into force on December 24, 1998. This new, more liberal statute draws inspiration from the UNCITRAL Model Law.[160]

174-3. — In Japan, there is more of a tradition of international arbitration, and there have, as a result, been fewer recent developments. Nevertheless, a draft arbitration law was prepared by a working group and published in 1989. Very similar to the UNCITRAL Model Law, this draft statute is intended to apply to both domestic and international arbitration, although the latter would also be governed by a number of special rules.[161] The more urgent reform was that of the Foreign Lawyers Law which, since 1996, allows non-Japanese lawyers to represent parties in international arbitration taking place in Japan.[162]

---

[157] For example, provisions specific to international arbitration were included in 1991 in the Code of Civil Procedure (Arts. 257 to 261) (Law of the People's Republic of China on Civil Procedure adopted at the Fourth Session of the Seventh National People's Congress on April 9, 1991, promulgated by Order No. 44 of the President of the People's Republic of China on April 9, 1991, and effective as of the same day); *see* DEJUN, MOSER, SHENGCHANG, *supra* note 156, at 498; Jacques Sagot and Hanqi Xie, *Le régime chinois d'arbitrage pour le commerce international*, 1993 REV. ARB. 63.

[158] On the different reforms of the rules of China's arbitral institutions (international and maritime), see *infra* para. 333.

[159] Law of August 31, 1994, adopted at the 9th Session of the Standing Committee of the 8th National People's Congress of the People's Republic of China, and promulgated by the President on August 31, 1994, effective from September 1, 1995. For a commentary, see Sally A. Harpole, *International Arbitration in the People's Republic of China Under the New Arbitration Law*, ICC BULLETIN, Vol. 6, No. 1, at 19 (1995); Chen Min, *The Arbitration Act of the People's Republic of China – A Great Leap Forward*, 12 J. INT'L ARB. 29 (Dec. 1995); Didier Nedjar, *L'arbitrage international en Chine après la loi du 31 aôut 1994*, 1995 REV. ARB. 411; Guiguo Wang, *The Unification of the Dispute Resolution System in China – Cultural, Economic and Legal Contributions*, 13 J. INT'L ARB. 5 (June 1996); Luming Chen, *Some Reflections on International Commercial Arbitration in China*, 13 J. INT'L ARB. 121 (June 1996); Jacques Sagot, *Règlement des différends – Les derniers développements de l'arbitrage chinois après la loi de 1994*, Gaz. Pal., Doct. 1668 (1997); Herman Verbist, *Recognition of Foreign Arbitral Awards in China*, 1997 INT'L BUS. L.J. 375; Andrew Shields, *China's Two-Pronged Approach to International Arbitration*, 15 J. INT'L ARB. 67 (June 1998); Michael J. Moser, *People's Republic of China*, in DISPUTE RESOLUTION IN ASIA, *supra* note 151, at 73.

[160] *See* Hong-lin Yu, *The Taiwanese Arbitration Act 1998*, 15 J. INT'L ARB. 107 (Dec. 1998).

[161] For the text of the draft, see 10 J. INT'L ARB. 110 (June 1993); *see also* Kuniko Oyama, *Recent Developments in Japanese Arbitration Law – An Introduction to the Draft Arbitration Law of Japan*, 10 J. INT'L ARB. 55 (June 1993).

[162] Charles Russell Stevens, *Foreign Lawyer Advocacy in International Arbitrations in Japan*, 13 ARB. INT'L 103 (1997).

174-4. — India, whose 1940 Arbitration Act aged badly, particularly as a result of a number of court decisions hostile to international arbitration,[163] adopted new legislation, based on the UNCITRAL Model Law, in its 1996 Arbitration and Conciliation Ordinance (No. 8/1996).[164] This governs domestic and international arbitration, limits interference by the courts and allows arbitrators to rule on their own jurisdiction. In line with the spirit of this legislation, the Indian Supreme Court, when applying it for the first time, clearly opted for an interpretation in favor of arbitration.[165]

174-5. — Singapore is another South-East Asian country to have adopted new arbitration legislation. It amended its 1953 Act in 1980 to reflect the English 1979 Arbitration Act, and ratified the New York Convention in 1986, simultaneously adopting a number of specific provisions governing international arbitration.[166] Then, in 1994, it adopted the UNCITRAL Model Law.[167]

In 1987, Thailand, which traditionally favored conciliation and mediation to arbitration, enacted a fairly simple law specifically covering arbitration, without distinguishing between domestic and international disputes.[168]

---

[163] The Arbitration Act 1940 (No. 10 of 1940). *See* F.S. Nariman, *Finality in India: the Impossible Dream*, 10 ARB. INT'L 373 (1994); Fali S. Nariman, *A Comment on Two Recent Important Decisions of the Supreme Court of India*, ICC BULLETIN, Vol. 5, No. 2, at 35 (1994); Tony Khindria, *Enforcement of Arbitration Awards in India/Exequatur des sentences arbitrales en Inde*, 1995 INT'L BUS. L.J. 256.

[164] The Arbitration and Conciliation Ordinance, 1996 (No. 8/1996), 8 WORLD TRADE & ARB. MATERIALS 87 (Mar. 1996); Vikram Raghavan, *New Horizons for Alternative Dispute Resolution in India – The New Arbitration Law of 1996*, 13 J. INT'L ARB. 5 (Dec. 1996); Jan Paulsson, *La réforme de l'arbitrage en Inde*, 1996 REV. ARB. 597; Anita Thomas Anand and John R. Dingess, *Update On Indian Arbitration: The Arbitration And Conciliation Ordinance, 1996*, 11 INT'L ARB. REP. 24 (Nov. 1996); Fali S. Nariman, *India's New Arbitration Law*, ICC BULLETIN, Vol. 8, No. 1, at 37 (1998); D.P. MITTAL, NEW LAW OF ARBITRATION, ADR AND CONTRACT LAW IN INDIA (1997); for an analysis of the changes brought about by this statute, see G.K. KWATRA, NEW LEGAL DIRECTIONS FOR ARBITRATION AND CONCILIATION IN INDIA (Publication of the Indian Council of Arbitration, 1998).

[165] Supreme Court of India, Nov. 18, 1996, MMTC Ltd. v. Sterlite Industries (India) Ltd., Judgments Today [1996] 10 S.C. 390; 12 INT'L ARB. REP. G1 (May 1997); 1997 BULL. ASA 136; ICC BULLETIN, Vol. 8, No. 1, at 39 (1997). On this decision, *see infra* para. 771.

[166] Arbitration Act 1953, as amended in 1969 and 1980, Singapore Statutes, Chapter 16; The Arbitration (Foreign Awards) Act 1986, No. 24 of 1986, Singapore Statutes, Chapter 25. See these statutes in SIMMONDS, HILL, JARVIN, *supra* note 151; *see also Singapore*, XII Y.B. COM. ARB. 388 (1987); Philip R. Kimbrough, *Viabilité générale de l'arbitrage à Singapour: l'accession à la Convention de New York comble la dernière lacune/General Viability of Arbitration in Singapore: Singapore's Accession to the New York Convention Fills the Last Gap*, 1986 INT'L BUS. L.J. 783.

[167] The International Arbitration Act 1994 (No. 23 of 1994), adopted by Parliament on October 31, 1994, published in the Government Gazette of December 9, 1994, and in force since January 27, 1995, 7 WORLD TRADE & ARB. MATERIALS 2 (Mar. 1995) (the UNCITRAL Model Law and the 1958 New York Convention are included as Schedules 1 and 2 of the Act); *see* Benny S. Tabalujan, *Singapore's Adoption of the UNCITRAL Model Law on International Commercial Arbitration – Some Preliminary Observations*, 12 J. INT'L ARB. 51 (June 1995); Lawrence Boo and Charles Lim, *Overview of the International Arbitration Act and Subsidiary Legislation in Singapore*, 12 J. INT'L ARB. 75 (Dec. 1995); *Singapore*, XX Y.B. COM. ARB. 594 (1995).

[168] Arbitration Act BE 2530 (1987); *see* Hideki Ogawa, *The New Thai Arbitration Act of 1987*, 6 J. INT'L ARB. 97 (Sept. 1989); Thawatchai Suvanpanich, *Thailand*, in DISPUTE RESOLUTION IN ASIA, *supra* note 151, at 261.

174-6. — There has also been intense legislative activity in the Antipodean countries.

Australia, whose eight states and territories adopted very similar Commercial Arbitration Acts[169] between 1984 and 1990, amended its 1974 Arbitration (Foreign Awards and Agreements) Act on May 15, 1989. The 1989 International Arbitration Amendment Act allows parties to choose to have the UNCITRAL Model Law apply to their international disputes.[170]

New Zealand adopted a slightly modified version of the UNCITRAL Model Law in its 1996 Arbitration Act, which applies to all arbitrations taking place on its territory. However, there remains the possibility of relatively extensive court interference, inspired by English law prior to the entry into force of the 1996 English Arbitration Act, although rules allowing court interference only apply to international arbitration if the parties so expressly agree.[171]

2° Trends

175. — We will attempt to identify the trends reflected in the worldwide legislative movement described above by briefly examining the variety of legislative techniques used, the content of the reforms[172] and, in particular, the convergence of their objectives.

a) Diversity of Legislative Techniques

176. — The diversity of methods used by legislators worldwide to reform their arbitration laws allows those reforms to be classified according to their scale, but also, and more importantly, according to the extent to which they create a specific regime for international arbitration.

177. — We have seen that some reforms have only led to limited changes. In certain cases, the reforms that took place were only the beginning of the wider process of the

---

[169] John Goldring and A.G. Christie, *Australia*, XIII Y.B. Com. Arb. 381 (1988).

[170] *See* Clyde Croft, *Australia Adopts the UNCITRAL Model Law*, 5 Arb. Int'l 189 (1989), with the text of the Act at 194; Michael Pryles, *Current Issues in International Arbitration in Australia*, 9 J. Int'l Arb. 57 (Dec. 1992); Marcus S. Jacobs, *Recognition and enforcement of arbitral awards in Australia*, 1997 Riv. dell'arb. 167; Michael Pryles, *Australia, in* Dispute Resolution in Asia, *supra* note 151, at 25.

[171] Arbitration Act. 1996, No. 99 (NZ), s. 1(2), enacted on September 2, 1996, in force since July 1, 1997; *see* Megan Richardson, *Arbitration Law Reform: The New Zealand Experience*, 12 Arb. Int'l 57 (1996); Megan Richardson, *Arbitration Law Reform: The New Zealand Experience – An Update*, 13 Arb. Int'l 229 (1997).

[172] Bruno Oppetit, *Philosophie de l'arbitrage commercial international*, 120 J.D.I. 811 (1993); *comp. with* W. Laurence Craig, *Some Trends and Developments in the Laws and Practice of International Commercial Arbitration*, 30 Tex. Int'l L.J. 1 (1995); Philippe Fouchard, *Les tendances actuelles en matière d'arbitrage*, RID Comp., Special Issue, Vol. 17, Journées de la Société de Législation Comparée – Année 1995, at 383 (1996); Peter Gottwald, *International Arbitration – Current Positions and Comparative Trends*, 1996 Riv. dell'arb. 211. For a more detailed comparison between a number of national arbitration laws, see especially Pieter Sanders, *Chapter 12 – Arbitration, in* International Encyclopedia of Comparative Law, Vol. XVI – Civil Procedure (1996).

modernization of the law of the country in question. This was true in England in 1979 and Germany in 1986. In other cases, limited reform was sufficient where it involved the modification of legislation which, on the whole, had proved to be satisfactory (as in Austria).

It is now far more usual for legislative reforms to be of a more far-reaching nature. A complete overhaul, apart from being the best means of marketing a country as a venue for arbitration, also guarantees simplicity and consistency. This tendency has increased under the influence of the UNCITRAL Model Law.[173]

178. — However, one of the most important features of recent arbitration legislation is the extent to which it accords international arbitration specific treatment. In this respect, three different categories of rules need to be distinguished.

179. — The first category includes rules relating to the recognition and enforcement of foreign arbitral awards. Nearly all countries apply specific rules to the determination of the conditions under which a foreign arbitral award can be recognized, enforced, or contested on national territory.[174]

Some countries (such as Lebanon until May 29, 1998 and Brazil) have done so without ratifying the New York Convention. Others have instead ratified the Convention without making the reciprocity reservation.[175] In those countries, the Convention will effectively constitute the law on the recognition and enforcement of foreign arbitral awards, together with a few national rules on procedure and jurisdiction.[176]

A larger group of countries have made the reciprocity reservation. This means that, alongside the New York Convention system, they have a general set of rules governing the recognition of awards made in non-signatory countries. Paradoxically, this general regime is sometimes more favorable to foreign awards than the regime provided for in the New York Convention—this is the case, for instance, in France, Lebanon, the Netherlands, Quebec and the Côte d'Ivoire. The two regimes are equivalent in countries which, without withdrawing the reciprocity reservation, have reproduced the rules of the New York Convention in their domestic law—this is the case of all countries which have adopted the UNCITRAL Model Law, as Articles 35 and 36 of the Model Law are identical to Articles IV and V of the New York Convention.

180. — A growing number of countries combine their regime governing the recognition of foreign awards with a second category of rules specific to international arbitrations held on their territory.

---

[173] On the Model Law, see *infra* para. 203.

[174] Iran is a notable exception. Its 1997 law on international commercial arbitration contains no provisions concerning the enforcement of arbitral awards made outside Iran. Until Iran accedes to the New York Convention it appears that, under Iranian law, the rules of enforcement of foreign court judgments will apply to foreign arbitral awards.

[175] Fifty-seven as of March 31, 1999.

[176] See *infra* para. 247; for the text of the Convention and the List of Contracting States, see *infra* Annex IV.

This territorialist approach is intended to promote compliance with the rules of other legal systems. Nevertheless, it has a number of disadvantages, both theoretical (through the arguably excessive emphasis on the seat of the arbitration) and practical (as it fails to satisfactorily address international arbitrations where the seat is undetermined). Here again, certain distinctions need to be made according to the scope of the specific rules adopted.

181. — Some countries simply enact a limited number of specific rules containing exceptions to the principle that the same regime applies to all arbitrations (whether domestic or international) held on their territory. We have seen that this approach finds favor in the many countries, such as England, Austria and the Netherlands, which consider that what is satisfactory for domestic arbitration is satisfactory for international arbitration, and vice-versa. This position is perfectly legitimate where domestic arbitration practice is based on a strong tradition and on simple, proven rules. On the other hand, it is not tenable where domestic law, rightly or wrongly, appears to foreign users to be overly complex or restrictive: this was the case with the Swiss *Concordat* and English law prior to the 1996 Act.

Nonetheless, the specificity of international arbitration can never be entirely eliminated. Appropriate legislative measures therefore include:

– broadening the jurisdiction of the courts to provide assistance with international arbitrations taking place on national territory, if there is no other jurisdictional basis for them to intervene. This is the objective of the 1993 reform of Austrian law;[177]

– determining which rules of law are to be applied by arbitrators to the merits of an international dispute. Portuguese legislation has done so expressly,[178] while legislation in the Netherlands, Quebec, and England does so implicitly. By providing that arbitrators shall apply the rules of law they consider to be appropriate,[179] this legislation necessarily concerns international arbitration alone;[180]

– seeking to reduce the extent of court review of international arbitral awards made on national territory. This is done either by limiting the grounds for bringing an action to set aside,[181] or by allowing the parties to exclude actions to set aside,[182] or by prohibiting actions to set aside altogether.[183]

182. — Switzerland allows parties to waive all actions to set aside an international award made in Switzerland and where none of the parties has its domicile, habitual residence or

---

[177] *See supra* para. 165.

[178] *See supra* para. 161.

[179] Art. 1054(2) of the Netherlands Code of Civil Procedure; Art. 944.10 of the Quebec Code of Civil Procedure.

[180] *Comp. with* Art. 2 of the 1996 Brazilian Law.

[181] *See, e.g.*, Art. 595(1)(6) of the 1983 Austrian Code of Civil Procedure.

[182] Art. 78, para. 6 of the 1993 Tunisian Code of Arbitration; Sec. 51 of the 1999 Swedish Arbitration Act.

[183] This was the case in Belgium, in certain circumstances, between the entry into force of the Law of March 27, 1985 and its modification by the law of May 19, 1998. *See supra* para. 158.

business establishment in Switzerland.[184] However, Switzerland has gone much further in its recognition of the specificity of international arbitrations held on its territory, with such arbitrations governed by a separate statute, entirely distinct from the rules applicable to domestic arbitrations. This is also the case in Algeria and a number of other countries.

A similar system is also found in the UNCITRAL Model Law, which is intended to apply only to international arbitrations[185] held in jurisdictions that decide to adopt it. Most of the countries that have adopted the Model Law apply it to international arbitration alone, although some also apply it to domestic arbitration (including Quebec, the Canadian Federation, Kenya and India) or allow the parties to choose to have it govern their domestic arbitrations (Scotland and New Zealand, for example).[186]

183. — A third category of rules is found in countries where it is considered appropriate to legislate for any international arbitration, irrespective of where it is held. Although, in theory, there is no territorial limit to the scope of such rules, which leads to criticism on the grounds of perceived legal imperialism,[187] their application will always be subject to the existence of a minimum of contact between the legislating country and the international arbitration which it purports to regulate.

In most cases, that contact will be the fact that an application has been made before a court of that country. This will be the case where a foreign award is submitted to a local court for enforcement, despite the fact that the arbitration may have no connection with that jurisdiction and that the beneficiary of the award may simply be seeking to attach goods or debts belonging to the losing party and located in that country. In such cases, there is no doubt as to the existence of the country's legislative jurisdiction, and it is universally exercised.[188] However, an action may be heard by a court concerning the merits of a dispute covered by an arbitration agreement, or on other questions arising from that arbitration (such as applications for an arbitration agreement to be declared void, for an arbitrator to be appointed or challenged, or for provisional or protective measures), despite the fact that the arbitration may not be taking place, or be required to take place in the country of that court. In such circumstances, it is not unusual for the court to apply the *lex fori* to determine a choice of law rule or a specific substantive rule.

Another non-territorial connection is possible—and equally legitimate—between a legal system and an international arbitration. It is the connection resulting from the choice by the parties or the arbitrators of the law of that country to govern the arbitration agreement or the arbitral procedure.

---

[184] Art. 192 of the Swiss Private International Law Statute. The same rule is now found in Tunisia, Belgium and Sweden; *see supra* para. 162.

[185] On the definition of international arbitration provided by the Model Law, see *supra* para. 103.

[186] For a comparison of the different ways of adopting the UNCITRAL Model Law, see Pieter Sanders, *Unity and Diversity in the Adoption of the Model Law*, 11 ARB. INT'L 1 (1995).

[187] On criticism of this kind directed at Articles 1493 to 1497 of the French New Code of Civil Procedure, see *supra* para. 140.

[188] *See supra* para. 179.

In any event, a rule found in one legal system intended to apply to international arbitrations taking place abroad will not necessarily be considered applicable under the laws or by the courts of the country where the arbitration is held or where the award is to be enforced. Those countries will retain their sovereignty, thus creating a genuine conflict of laws.

In fact, whether the extra-territorial application of such rules is appropriate or effective will depend on their content and scope. Again, two sets of rules must be distinguished.

184. — The most common extra-territorial rules applicable in international arbitration are of a specific nature. These will very occasionally be choice of law rules. For example, the 1999 Swedish Arbitration Act provides that an arbitration agreement which has an "international connection" shall be governed by the law agreed upon by the parties or, in the absence of such agreement, by the law of the seat of the arbitration (Sec. 48). If that law is foreign, the Act co-ordinates its application and that of certain provisions of Swedish law (Sec. 49).

The goal of more modern legislation is often to determine the jurisdiction of the courts of one country, where a contractual clause provides that any disputes are to be resolved by international arbitration in another country. If an application is brought before a court concerning the merits of the dispute and the defendant promptly argues that there is an arbitration agreement, then the court must decline jurisdiction.[189] This rule is found in the Dutch and Swiss arbitration statutes, for example,[190] as well as in the UNCITRAL Model Law, Article 8, paragraph 1 of which applies even if the seat of the arbitration is located abroad.[191] Likewise, Article II, paragraph 3 of the New York Convention makes no distinction according to the country where the arbitration is to be held, as is the case, indirectly, of all legal systems which have adopted these provisions of the Model Law[192] or of the New York Convention.

If, on the other hand, the sole purpose of the action before the court is to obtain provisional or protective measures, the court may declare that it has jurisdiction, even where the arbitration agreement stipulates that the arbitration is to be held in another country. This is expressly provided for in the UNCITRAL Model Law (Art. 9) and in Title II of the Dutch Code of Civil Procedure, entitled "Arbitration Outside the Netherlands" (Art. 1074(2)).

The Dutch Code also contains a rule whereby the Dutch courts will have jurisdiction where the place of arbitration is unknown when the arbitrators are to be appointed. In such cases, Article 1073, paragraph 2 provides that the appointment or challenge of an arbitrator may take place before a Dutch court "if at least one of the parties is domiciled or has his

---

[189] On this rule in international conventions and French law, see *infra* paras. 662 *et seq.*

[190] Art. 1074(1) of the Netherlands Code of Civil Procedure; Art. 7 of the Swiss Private International Law Statute; *see* BUCHER AND TSCHANZ, *supra* note 58, ¶ 144 at 78.

[191] Art. 1(2); *see* Philippe Fouchard, *La Loi-type de la C.N.U.D.C.I. sur l'arbitrage commercial international*, 114 J.D.I. 861, 869 (1987). For additional references on the Model Law, see *infra* para. 203.

[192] *See, e.g.*, Art. 47(2) of Tunisian Law No. 93-42 of April 26, 1993.

actual residence in the Netherlands." This rule might be useful in certain circumstances,[193] but it does reflect a certain degree of interference by the Dutch legislature in the organization of international arbitrations outside the Netherlands.

185. — The proliferation of these specific extraterritorial rules is perfectly justifiable where there is a link between the arbitration in question and the legal system in which they appear.

Thus, the Egyptian arbitration law of April 21, 1994 applies not only to arbitrations held in Egypt, but also to arbitrations taking place abroad where the parties have agree that Egyptian law shall govern the arbitration (Art. 1). Likewise, in the Tunisian arbitration law of April 26, 1993, the provisions specifically applicable to international arbitration (which are based on the UNCITRAL Model Law) will apply if they have been chosen either by the parties or by the arbitral tribunal (Art. 47(2)). The contractual nature of international arbitration and the principle of party autonomy are thus clearly acknowledged.[194]

The same position is taken in France, Lebanon, Djibouti, the Côte d'Ivoire, Mali and Algeria.[195] There is, for example, no territorial limit to the substantive rules contained in Articles 1493 to 1497 of the French New Code of Civil Procedure. The parties to an international arbitration may adopt these rules, if only to obtain confirmation from a national legal system that they are entirely free (directly or indirectly) to choose the rules governing the arbitral procedure or the merits of the dispute. The consequence of the rule of party autonomy in arbitration is that the parties' choice will generally be accepted by other national legal systems. However, this may lead to a genuinely extraterritorial phenomenon: a French court, hearing an action concerning the enforcement of an international arbitral award made outside France, may apply French substantive rules to exclude the more restrictive provisions of the law of the seat of the arbitration, even where the latter are intended to be of mandatory application.[196]

However, the extent of this conflict should not be overestimated, for at least three reasons. First, the application of such substantive rules, although theoretically unlimited, is only possible in practice where a connection exists between the international arbitration at issue and the country enacting the rules. Second, as demonstrated by the Swiss reform, it is increasingly rare for a country to impose its own rules on an international arbitration taking place on its territory. Finally, for a conflict to arise, the content of the laws in question must differ. The current trend is instead towards the convergence of legislative objectives.

---

[193] On this issue of the international jurisdiction of a judge with respect to the constitution of an arbitral tribunal, see *infra* paras. 837 *et seq.* and 917.

[194] See *supra* paras. 44 *et seq.*

[195] See *supra* paras. 140, 173, and 173-1.

[196] See, in relation to the inter-cantonal *Concordat* prior to the 1987 reform of Swiss international arbitration law, Frédéric-Edouard Klein, *La nouvelle réglementation française de l'arbitrage international et les lois suisses*, in RECUEIL DE TRAVAUX SUISSES SUR L'ARBITRAGE INTERNATIONAL 57 (1984).

b) Convergence of Legislative Objectives

186. — As the foregoing analysis suggests, the various reforms of recent years share very similar objectives. The results of the reforms certainly differ according to the state of the previous law and to the lengths to which each legislature was prepared to go, but the underlying trends are the same. Without seeking to describe them in detail, or even to illustrate them by specific reference to each of the legal systems we have considered, we shall briefly introduce three such trends, each of which will be further discussed throughout this book.

187. — The primary objective of all the recent reforms is to ensure or reinforce the effectiveness of arbitration agreements. This involves the recognition of both the validity of arbitration agreements and their autonomy, as well as the relaxation of previous requirements regarding form and evidence. The parties are also left entirely free to appoint their arbitrators, to refer to a particular set of rules or to an arbitral institution, and the class of arbitrable disputes is becoming ever broader. The courts, rather than discouraging parties seeking to use a private form of justice, are required to promote arbitration as a method of dispute resolution. This may involve assisting in the setting up or progress of the arbitration, even if this may sometimes lead the courts to go further than the parties might have actually agreed, as where a court orders related arbitrations to be consolidated. It may, of course, also involve the court declining jurisdiction when an arbitration agreement exists.

188. — The second common legislative objective is more directly related to our present discussion, as it concerns the various sources of international arbitration. There is a distinct global movement towards an increased independence of international arbitration from national legal systems. In particular, by leaving the parties free to choose the rules governing the arbitral procedure and the merits of the dispute, national legal systems acknowledge that arbitrators and arbitral institutions share that independence. This leads to the growing importance of private sources of international arbitration.[197] However, even the most liberal reforms do have certain limits. Indeed, the requirement that parties adhere to certain fundamental principles is another constant feature of the reforms: during the arbitral proceedings, each party's right to a fair hearing is guaranteed under all circumstances; arbitral institutions and arbitrators must likewise ensure that all parties receive equal treatment; lastly, in deciding the merits of a dispute, the arbitral award must, at the very least, comply with international public policy.

189. — The third common legislative objective is to limit court intervention. In order to discourage delaying tactics, the courts tend to intervene—except, of course, to assist in the setting up of the arbitral tribunal—only after the arbitration has ended. The number of grounds on which an award can be set aside has been reduced. In spite of the apparent

---

[197] *See infra* paras. 303 *et seq.* On this double trend of liberalization and globalization, see Philippe Fouchard, *L'arbitrage et la mondialisation de l'économie, in* PHILOSOPHIE DU DROIT ET DROIT ÉCONOMIQUE – QUEL DIALOGUE? MÉLANGES EN L'HONNEUR DE GÉRARD FARJAT 377 (1999).

diversity found in different legal systems, the international validity of the award ultimately depends on two fundamental conditions: the validity of the arbitrators' powers and the acceptability of their decision, although control by the courts can never go as far as revising the decision as to fact or law. The available means of recourse have also been limited. The tendency is to leave just one possible action: an application to set the award aside. Even this is denied under certain circumstances in some jurisdictions. Of course, there will always remain the option of resisting enforcement of the award.

§ 2. – International Sources

190. — The international sources of international commercial arbitration law are invariably of public origin. They largely consist of international conventions but also include international custom, general principles of law and judicial decisions, as listed in Article 38 of the Statute of the International Court of Justice.

191. — In international commercial arbitration, however, only general principles of law play an important role. They are frequently applied by arbitrators, particularly, though not exclusively, when dealing with international state contracts.[198] In such cases, there is some doubt as to the exact nature of the principles applied. Do they still form part of "traditional" public international law? Do they constitute a new law, sometimes described as transnational rules[199] or *lex mercatoria*?[200] Alternatively, are they informal sources of law?[201]

192. — There is also a form of international law which can be described, without any derogatory connotation, as "soft law." This consists of instruments drawn up by international organizations, but which are simply recommended to, rather than imposed upon, potential

---

[198] *See infra* paras. 1443 *et seq.*

[199] Prosper Weil, *Principes généraux du droit et contrats d'Etat, in* LE DROIT DES RELATIONS ÉCONOMIQUES INTERNATIONALES – ETUDES OFFERTES À BERTHOLD GOLDMAN 387 (1982); Michel Virally, *Un tiers droit? Réflexions théoriques, in* LE DROIT DES RELATIONS ÉCONOMIQUES INTERNATIONALES – ETUDES OFFERTES À BERTHOLD GOLDMAN 373 (1982); *see also* TRANSNATIONAL RULES IN INTERNATIONAL COMMERCIAL ARBITRATION (E. Gaillard ed., ICC Publication No. 480/4, 1993).

[200] Berthold Goldman, *La lex mercatoria dans les contrats et l'arbitrage internationaux: réalité et perspectives,* 106 J.D.I. 475 (1979); Ole Lando, *The Lex Mercatoria in International Commercial Arbitration,* 34 INT'L & COMP. L.Q. 747 (1985); Michael J. Mustill, *The New Lex Mercatoria: The First Twenty-five Years,* 4 ARB. INT'L 86 (1988); Philippe Kahn, *Les principes généraux du droit devant les arbitres du commerce international,* 116 J.D.I. 305 (1989); Andreas F. Lowenfeld, *Lex Mercatoria: An Arbitrator's View,* 6 ARB. INT'L 133 (1990); Emmanuel Gaillard, *La distinction des principes généraux du droit et des usages du commerce international, in* ETUDES OFFERTES À PIERRE BELLET 203 (1991); Berthold Goldman, *Nouvelles réflexions sur la Lex Mercatoria, in* ETUDES DE DROIT INTERNATIONAL EN L'HONNEUR DE PIERRE LALIVE 241 (1993); Emmanuel Gaillard, *Thirty Years of Lex Mercatoria: Towards the Selective Application of Transnational Rules,* 10 ICSID REV. – FOREIGN INV. L.J. 208 (1995) and, for a French version, *Trente ans de Lex Mercatoria – Pour une application sélective de la méthode des principes généraux du droit,* 122 J.D.I. 5 (1995).

[201] *See* DOMINIQUE BUREAU, LES SOURCES INFORMELLES DU DROIT DANS LES RELATIONS PRIVÉES INTERNATIONALES (Thesis, University of Paris II (France), 1992).

users. These optional instruments (A) play a significant role in international arbitration, alongside the more traditional bilateral treaties (B) and, most importantly, multilateral conventions (C).

A. – OPTIONAL INSTRUMENTS

193. — The most important optional instruments[202] have been drawn up by specialized commissions of the United Nations.

194. — We shall not, at this stage, consider instruments which have in fact led to the signature of international conventions,[203] but rather those with the more modest aim of providing recommended texts to be used if parties see fit. These include various rules of arbitral procedure (1°) and, more significantly, the UNCITRAL Model Law (2°).

1° Arbitration Rules

195–199. — The earliest arbitration rules contained in optional instruments of the United Nations were drafted by two United Nations regional economic commissions. The first of these were the Arbitration Rules of the United Nations Economic Commission for Europe, adopted in 1963,[204] together with an annex containing a List of Chambers of Commerce and other institutions which may be required to act as "appointing authority." These Rules were officially published in 1966.[205]

The second set of rules was that prepared by the United Nations Economic Commission for Asia and the Far East, through its Centre for Commercial Arbitration, also published in 1966.[206]

200. — Of far more importance, however, are the Arbitration Rules produced by the United Nations Commission on International Trade Law (UNCITRAL), which were approved on April 28, 1976, and recommended by the United Nations General Assembly

---

[202] *See* UNITED NATIONS, REGISTER OF TEXTS OF CONVENTIONS AND OTHER INSTRUMENTS CONCERNING INTERNATIONAL TRADE LAW (Vol. I, 1971 and Vol. II, 1973).

[203] *See infra* paras. 247 *et seq.*

[204] On this text, see UNION INTERNATIONALE DES AVOCATS, INTERNATIONAL COMMERCIAL ARBITRATION, Vol. III, at 361 (P. Sanders ed., 1965).

[205] UN Doc. E/ECE/625/Rev.1, *reprinted in* REGISTER OF TEXTS, *supra* note 202, Vol II, at 100. For a commentary, see Peter Benjamin, *New Arbitration Rules for Use in International Trade, in* UNION INTERNATIONALE DES AVOCATS, *supra* note 204, at 323; PHILIPPE FOUCHARD, L'ARBITRAGE COMMERCIAL INTERNATIONAL ¶¶ 69 *et seq.* (1965).

[206] Rules for International Commercial Arbitration, *reprinted in* REGISTER OF TEXTS, *supra* note 202, Vol. II, at 95; for a commentary, see Pieter Sanders, *ECAFE Rules for International Commercial Arbitration, in* INTERNATIONAL ARBITRATION – LIBER AMICORUM MARTIN DOMKE 252 (P. Sanders ed., 1967). For more details on these early arbitration rules, see FOUCHARD, GAILLARD, GOLDMAN, *supra* note 1, at 195–99.

in its resolution of December 15, 1976.[207] The conditions under which the Rules were prepared (with the participation of representatives from all political, legal and economic systems), as well as the quality of the provisions adopted, account for their success.

At its first session, in January 1968, UNCITRAL had already decided to treat international commercial arbitration as a priority. The Commission decided against the drafting of a new international convention, or the revision of the New York Convention, in spite of its flaws.[208] It also considered that it was unrealistic to attempt to unify national arbitration laws. From 1973 onwards, having considered harmonizing the existing rules of the main arbitral institutions, the Commission focused on drafting a set of arbitration rules to be used on an optional basis in *ad hoc* arbitration. The draft, prepared in collaboration with the International Council for Commercial Arbitration (ICCA) and after consultation with numerous arbitral institutions, was adopted in 1976.

201. — The UNCITRAL Arbitration Rules are optional: they apply only if the parties to an arbitration agreement have referred to them in writing (Art. 1). However, the Rules do not prevail over the mandatory rules of the law applicable to an arbitration. This goes against the trend found in national laws and international conventions, which are in favor of more autonomy of international arbitral procedure from national law. Naturally, however, it was not for arbitration rules to provide for such a principle.[209]

The UNCITRAL Rules are intended for *ad hoc* arbitrations, which the parties set up independently of any arbitral institution. As discussed earlier, the main disadvantage of *ad hoc* arbitration is that the constitution of the arbitral tribunal may be obstructed if the parties refuse to accept or disagree as to the appointment of an arbitrator. As a result, it is important to provide for a third party, designated in advance, to be responsible for making the necessary appointments in such cases. The authors of the Rules could not choose such an "appointing authority," because of the universal reach of the Rules. The Rules therefore simply provide a mechanism for appointing the arbitrator or arbitrators. To overcome any obstacles which may arise, they provide for the intervention of the appointing authority chosen by the parties in their arbitration agreement. Where that authority has not been chosen by the parties, it will be designated by the Secretary General of the Permanent Court of Arbitration in The Hague.[210]

The rules of procedure themselves are precise enough to preclude the need for any subsidiary recourse to national laws, and are flexible enough to be compatible with most such laws.

---

[207] For a commentary, see Pieter Sanders, *Commentary on UNCITRAL Arbitration Rules*, II Y.B. COM. ARB. 172 (1977); Pieter Sanders, *Règlement d'arbitrage de la CNUDCI*, 1978 DPCI 269; P. Jenard, *Le Règlement d'arbitrage de la Commission des Nations Unies pour le droit commercial international*, 54 REV. DR. INT. DR. COMP. 201 (1977); Philippe Fouchard, *Les travaux de la C.N.U.D.C.I. – Le règlement d'arbitrage*, 106 J.D.I. 816 (1979); STEWART ABERCROMBIE BAKER, MARK DAVID DAVIS, THE UNCITRAL ARBITRATION RULES IN PRACTICE – THE EXPERIENCE OF THE IRAN-UNITED STATES CLAIMS TRIBUNAL (1992).

[208] *See infra* para. 272.

[209] *See infra* para. 1171.

[210] Arts. 6 and 7. On this system, see *infra* para. 964.

202. — The autonomy and universality of the UNCITRAL Rules have undoubtedly played a major role in their success. They have provided developing nations and socialist states with a means of competing with established arbitral institutions, which are generally located in Western industrialized nations. Many companies, wherever they are headquartered, consider that this "semi-organized" system of arbitration can be equally effective, less costly[211] and "politically" easier to negotiate than an institutional arbitration. Moreover, the arbitral institutions themselves, which might have felt threatened by the advent of the UNCITRAL Rules, in fact welcomed them. More than twenty institutions, including some of the most prestigious centres, have agreed to act as an appointing authority for the purposes of the Rules.[212] A number of institutions even apply the Rules to the arbitrations they supervise. This is the case of the Kuala Lumpur Regional Centre for Arbitration, the Cairo Regional Centre for International Commercial Arbitration (CRCICA), Hong Kong International Arbitration Centre, the British Columbia International Commercial Arbitration Centre, the Arbitration Institute of the Stockholm Chamber of Commerce, the Spanish Court of Arbitration, the Inter-American Commercial Arbitration Commission, and, on an optional basis, the Japan Commercial Arbitration Association.[213] Other institutions refer to the UNCITRAL Rules in the co-operation agreements which they sign among themselves.[214] The Rules have thus proved an effective means of harmonizing institutional arbitration. In addition, arbitrations under the auspices of the Iran-United States Claims Tribunal in The Hague are governed, with certain minor changes,[215] by the UNCITRAL Rules, and it is in that setting that the Rules demonstrated their effectiveness in practice.[216]

More recently, the UNCITRAL Rules were the inspiration for the Procedural Rules on Conciliation and Arbitration of Contracts Financed by the European Development Fund, developed during the 1989 Fourth Lomé Convention between EEC member states and African, Caribbean and Pacific (ACP) countries.[217] These Rules, adopted in 1990, provide a mechanism for *ad hoc* arbitration of disputes arising out of contracts financed by the European Development Fund where the foreign supplier (or contractor) and the government of the ACP country adopt no other dispute resolution mechanism. The Rules only deviate from the UNCITRAL Rules on a few issues, including the identity of the authority

---

[211] This perceived advantage is somewhat illusory due to the fact that, in *ad hoc* arbitration, arbitrators themselves determine their fees and the parties are hardly in a position to challenge that determination. On this issue, see *infra* paras. 1160 and 1253.

[212] Such as the ICC, AAA and LCIA, for example; *see infra* para. 971.

[213] *See* Hiroshi Hattori, XVII Y.B. COM. ARB. 352 (1992).

[214] On these inter-institutional agreements, *see infra* para. 317.

[215] *See* JACOMIJN J. VAN HOF, COMMENTARY ON THE UNCITRAL ARBITRATION RULES – THE APPLICATION BY THE IRAN–U.S. CLAIMS TRIBUNAL (1991).

[216] *See* Karl-Heinz Böckstiegel, *Experiences as an Arbitrator Using the UNCITRAL Arbitration Rules, in* ETUDES DE DROIT INTERNATIONAL EN L'HONNEUR DE PIERRE LALIVE 423 (1993); on the Iran-United States Claims Tribunal, see *infra* para. 238.

[217] *See* Art. 307 of the Fourth ACP-EEC Convention signed in Lomé on December 15, 1989, 29 I.L.M. 749, 874 (1990).

appointing the arbitrators, the place of arbitration and the law applicable to the substance of the dispute.[218]

The success of the UNCITRAL Rules convinced UNCITRAL to continue working in the field of arbitration. Between 1993 and 1996, the Commission prepared a document entitled the "UNCITRAL Notes on Organizing Arbitral Proceedings."[219] This is not a set of rules of arbitral procedure, but only a set of "notes" (in the English version) or an *aide-mémoire* (in the French version). The goal of the document is only to "assist arbitration practitioners by listing and briefly describing questions on which appropriately timed decisions on organizing arbitral proceedings may be useful." This list and accompanying remarks may be helpful to inexperienced arbitrators,[220] although there is a risk that they might complicate matters by giving rise to preliminary argument on a number of issues that would not otherwise arise in many cases. Further, certain of the procedural options proposed (particularly concerning evidence) are too complex to be satisfactory in most arbitration proceedings.[221]

A more successful initiative, aimed at harmonizing international arbitration legislation, was UNCITRAL's 1985 Model Law. As we shall see, the Model Law is still an optional instrument, but one that is intended for use not by practitioners, but by legislators.

2° The UNCITRAL Model Law

203. — Although the idea of providing legislators with a model law on arbitration had been suggested to UNCITRAL as early as 1972, work on the project did not begin until 1979. In 1984, a draft model law produced by a working group was submitted to members

---

[218] Procedural Rules on Conciliation and Arbitration of Contracts Financed by the European Development Fund (EDF), in force since June 1, 1991 (Annex V to the Decision No. 3/90 of the ACP-EEC Council of Ministers of March 29, 1990, adopting the general regulation, general conditions and procedural rules on conciliation and arbitration for works, supply and service contracts financed by the European Development Fund (EDF) and concerning their application, 1990 O.J. (L 382) 95; for the English version, see also XVII Y.B. COM. ARB. 323 (1992); for the French version, see DICTIONNAIRE JOLY, PRATIQUE DES CONTRATS INTERNATIONAUX, Vol. 4, Book XIX, Annex 9, at 109; *see* Austin Amissah, *The ACP/EEC Conciliation and Arbitration Rules*, 8 ARB. INT'L 167 (1992).

[219] UNCITRAL NOTES ON ORGANIZING ARBITRAL PROCEEDINGS, U.N. Doc. V. 96–84935, U.N. Sales No. E.97.V.11 (1996). *See* XXII Y.B. COM. ARB. 448 (1997), with background remarks by J. Sekolec; 1998 REV. ARB. 273, and observations by P. Fouchard. *See infra* para. 1226.

[220] *See* Olivier Tell, *L'aide-mémoire de la CNUDCI sur l'organisation des procédures arbitrales*, 1997 INT'L BUS. L.J. 744; Roberto Ceccon, *UNCITRAL Notes on Organizing Arbitral Proceedings and the Conduct of Evidence – A New Approach to International Arbitration*, 14 J. INT'L ARB. 67 (June 1997).

[221] See, for criticism of the draft, Pierre Lalive, *De la fureur réglementaire*, 1994 BULL. ASA 213; Philippe Fouchard, *Une initiative contestable de la CNUDCI – A propos du projet de "Directives pour les conférences préparatoires dans le cadre des procédures arbitrales"*, 1994 REV. ARB. 461. For other commentary, prior to the adoption of the Notes, see Jernej Sekolec, *UNCITRAL Project for Improving Methods of Planning Arbitral Proceedings, in* ICCA CONGRESS SERIES No. 7, PLANNING EFFICIENT ARBITRATION PROCEEDINGS/THE LAW APPLICABLE IN INTERNATIONAL ARBITRATION 100 (A.J. van den Berg ed., 1996); Howard M. Holtzmann, *Questions Concerning the Desirability and Text of the UNCITRAL Project to Improve Planning of Arbitral Proceedings, id.* at 173.

of the UN and to interested international organizations. It was examined at an interim meeting of the ICCA in Lausanne[222] and, following final revisions,[223] the Model Law was adopted by UNCITRAL on June 21, 1985.[224] By a resolution dated December 11, 1985, the United Nations General Assembly recommended

> that all States give due consideration to the Model Law on International Commercial Arbitration, in view of the desirability of uniformity of the law of arbitral procedures and the specific needs of international commercial arbitration practice.[225]

204. — The model proposed by UNCITRAL (a set of 36 articles) is intended to govern all international commercial arbitrations[226] taking place in the territory of countries adopting it.[227] To ensure its acceptance in jurisdictions with widely differing legal and political systems, as well as diverse conceptions of arbitration, the model was necessarily a compromise to a certain extent, and that is indeed the impression it gives. The need to reconcile divergent ideas may have led to certain omissions and complications but, on the whole, the harmonization achieved is satisfactory. In addition, prior developments in comparative law are confirmed in the model.[228] Further, the parties are given considerable freedom to organize the arbitration, and the effectiveness of the arbitration agreement and the award is secured.

205. — The quality of the efforts to achieve harmonization has been one of the keys to the success of the Model Law. The use of a model law as opposed to a treaty has in no sense

---

[222] *See* ICCA CONGRESS SERIES NO. 2, UNCITRAL'S PROJECT FOR A MODEL LAW ON INTERNATIONAL COMMERCIAL ARBITRATION (P. Sanders ed., 1984).

[223] *See Analytical Commentary on Draft Text of a Model Law on International Commercial Arbitration, Report of the Secretary-General*, UN Doc. A/CN. 9/264, Mar. 25, 1985, *reprinted in* UNCITRAL MODEL LAW OF INTERNATIONAL COMMERCIAL ARBITRATION: A DOCUMENTARY HISTORY, Vol. I, Annex 35.0; *Report of the United Nations Commission on International Trade Law on the work of its eighteenth session – 3–21 June 1985*, Official Records of the General Assembly, Fortieth Session, Supplement No. 17 (A/40/17), Chap. II, ¶¶ 11–333, *reprinted in* UNCITRAL MODEL LAW OF INTERNATIONAL COMMERCIAL ARBITRATION: A DOCUMENTARY HISTORY, Vol. II, Annex 66.0.

[224] *See* Sigvard Jarvin, *La loi-type de la C.N.U.D.C.I. sur l'arbitrage commercial international*, 1986 REV. ARB. 509; Gerold Herrmann, *The UNCITRAL Model Law – its background, salient features and purposes*, 1 ARB. INT'L 6 (1985); Gerold Herrmann, *UNCITRAL adopts Model Law on International Commercial Arbitration*, 2 ARB. INT'L 2 (1986); PROCEEDINGS OF THE 1ST INTERNATIONAL COMMERCIAL ARBITRATION CONFERENCE (N. Antaki and A. Prujiner eds., 1986), with the report by Gerold Herrmann, (at 351), and commentaries by Jean Thieffry (at 379), Laurie Slade (at 385), Stephen M. Boyd (at 393), and Manon Pomerleau (at 419); Fouchard, *supra* note 191; *see also* HOWARD M. HOLTZMANN AND JOSEPH E. NEUHAUS, GUIDE TO THE UNCITRAL MODEL LAW ON INTERNATIONAL COMMERCIAL ARBITRATION (1989); ARON BROCHES, COMMENTARY ON THE UNCITRAL MODEL LAW ON INTERNATIONAL COMMERCIAL ARBITRATION (1990).

[225] General Assembly Resolution 40/72, UN Doc. A/40/935 (Dec. 11, 1985), *reprinted in* UNCITRAL MODEL LAW OF INTERNATIONAL COMMERCIAL ARBITRATION: A DOCUMENTARY HISTORY, Vol. II, Annex 68.0.

[226] On the definition of "international" and "commercial" in the Model Law, see *supra* paras. 61 and 103.

[227] On this territorial application, and the exceptions found in the Model Law, see *supra* paras. 178 to 185.

[228] *See supra* paras. 186 *et seq.*

been an obstacle to that success. On the contrary, it has ultimately proved to be at least as effective, if not more so, than traditional public international law techniques. Although the Model Law does not take the form of a treaty, legislators who have decided to review their arbitration legislation since 1985 have all "given due consideration" to the UNCITRAL Model Law, as recommended by the United Nations General Assembly.

Some countries adopted certain of the provisions of the Model Law, but considered that they could extend, simplify or liberalize it. Examples include the Netherlands in 1986 and Switzerland in 1987. Because of the specificity of their respective legal systems, Italy and England decided not to follow the Model Law closely. Also, as described earlier,[229] the Model Law has been introduced into a number of legal systems, and that trend is continuing. On March 31, 1999, a total of 29 countries had adopted legislation based to a certain extent on the Model Law,[230] along with Hong Kong, 8 American states and all 12 Canadian provinces and territories.[231] The 1999 Swedish Arbitration Act, which entered into force on April 1, 1999, is also based to a large extent on the Model Law. All continents and all legal traditions are represented, reflecting the universality of the text. Another important feature is the Model Law's flexibility,[232] each country being free to determine:

– the extent to which it chooses to adopt the Model Law;
– its scope (whether or not it will apply only to international arbitration); and
– whether or not it is to be binding.

In the near future, countries such as Japan[233] will reform their arbitration laws on the basis of the Model Law.

The importance of this gradual process of harmonization is such that court decisions applying the Model Law, from all the countries that have adopted or adapted it, have been published since 1992. There is thus a growing body of case law concerning the interpretation of the Model Law.[234]

B. – BILATERAL AGREEMENTS

206. — Despite the large number of bilateral agreements in the field of international arbitration, their practical importance has declined as a result of the proliferation of

---

[229] *See supra* paras. 157 and 165 *et seq.*

[230] These countries are: Australia, Bahrain, Bermuda, Bulgaria, Canada, Cyprus, Egypt, Finland, Germany, Guatemala, Hungary, India, Iran, Ireland, Kenya, Lithuania, Malta, Mexico, New Zealand, Nigeria, Oman, Peru, the Russian Federation, Scotland, Singapore, Sri Lanka, Tunisia, Ukraine, Zimbabwe. The list of these countries can be found on the UNCITRAL Web site, where it is regularly updated (<http://www.un.or.at/uncitral>).

[231] *See supra* paras. 169 and 170.

[232] *See* Sanders, *supra* note 186.

[233] *See supra* para. 174-3.

[234] *See* UNCITRAL, Case Law on UNCITRAL Texts (CLOUT), *supra* note 114; see also the first cumulative "Index of Articles" of the UNCITRAL Model Law Reported in CLOUT, XXII Y.B. COM. ARB. 297–300 (1997), which shows that the greatest number of court decisions regarding the Model Law have been made in Canada, followed by Hong Kong, the Russian Federation and Bermuda.

multilateral conventions.[235] However, bilateral agreements played a significant role in the initial recognition and expansion of international arbitration as a method of dispute resolution.[236]

207. — Unlike multilateral conventions, most bilateral agreements covering arbitration do so only incidentally and their main objective lies elsewhere. Arbitration is simply treated as one of the aspects or means of increased bilateral co-operation and, to that end, the two signatories consider it appropriate to improve the enforceability of arbitration agreements and awards (1°). Bilateral agreements which primarily concern arbitration are less common (2°).

1° Bilateral Agreements Concerning Arbitration Incidentally

208. — Most bilateral treaties deal with arbitration only incidentally. Their principal purpose is usually to govern economic relations or judicial assistance.[237]

a) Bilateral Treaties Governing Economic Relations

209. — Economic treaties take a number of forms, and have both a variety of goals and a variety of provisions concerning arbitration. The only point they have in common is that they consider arbitration to be the most appropriate method of resolving disputes arising from the economic relations that they aim to promote. As a result, they promote arbitration itself.

Of particular interest, given the specificity of the subject matter, is the Treaty of Canterbury of February 12, 1986 between the United Kingdom and France, concerning the construction and exploitation by private concession-holders of the Channel Tunnel. The treaty provides that disputes between the governments and the concession-holders will be settled by arbitration, under an *ad hoc* procedure and rules set forth in Article 19 of the treaty and in the annex to an exchange of letters between the two governments signed in Paris on July 29, 1987.[238]

---

[235] *See infra* paras. 239 *et seq.*

[236] See, for a global but doubtless incomplete overview of these bilateral treaties in 1957, see UNITED NATIONS, ECONOMIC COMMISSION FOR EUROPE, TABLE OF BILATERAL CONVENTIONS RELATING TO THE ENFORCEMENT OF ARBITRAL AWARDS AND THE ORGANIZATION OF COMMERCIAL ARBITRATION PROCEDURE, U.N. Sales No. 1957.IIE/Mim.18 (1957).

[237] For the list and text of these treaties to which France is a signatory as of July 1, 1990, see LOUIS CHATIN AND BRUNO STURLÈSE, RECUEIL PRATIQUE DE CONVENTIONS SUR L'ENTRAIDE JUDICIAIRE INTERNATIONALE (1990). For information on treaties to which the United States is a signatory, see BRUNO A. RISTAU, INTERNATIONAL JUDICIAL ASSISTANCE – CIVIL AND COMMERCIAL (2 vols.).

[238] Treaty between the United Kingdom of Great Britain and Northern Ireland and the French Republic concerning the construction and operation by private concessionaires of a channel fixed link with exchange of notes, signed at Canterbury on 12th of February 1986, HMSO Treaty Series No. 15 (1992), Cmnd. 1872; published in France

(continued...)

210–212. — The earliest economic treaties were treaties on trade and navigation or conventions of establishment, which generally contained provisions on the validity of arbitration agreements and the enforcement of arbitral awards.[239] Some also included rules governing the appointment of arbitrators and arbitral procedure, or simply referred to arbitration rules.[240]

213. — Reference is also made to arbitration in many of the numerous bilateral treaties designed to promote and protect investments. Over thirteen hundred such conventions are in force today, most of them between industrialized countries and developing countries.[241] Among the different forms of protection offered by host states to foreign investors, those concerning dispute resolution seem to be of particular importance to the investing parties. Investors consider that their entitlement to submit disputes to an international arbitral tribunal will encourage the host state to respect its undertakings regarding the investment. These often include tax and legislative stabilization obligations, the commitment to treat the foreign investor equitably, the duty to indemnify the investor if its investment is nationalized and, more generally, the commitment to protect foreign investment.

214. — If the two contracting states are parties to the 1965 Washington Convention, their bilateral treaty will often give investors the right to bring ICSID arbitration proceedings

---

[238](...continued)
by Decree No. 87-757 dated Sept. 9, 1987, J.O., Sept. 16, 1987, p. 10,769; 115 J.D.I. 207 (1988), and Decree No. 87-870 dated Oct. 23, 1987, J.O., Oct. 29, 1987, p. 12,572; 115 J.D.I. 217 (1988).

[239] *See, e.g.*, Treaty of Friendship, Commerce and Navigation, Aug. 3, 1951, U.S.-Greece, 224 U.N.T.S. 279; Treaty of Commerce and Navigation, Dec. 11, 1948, U.S.S.R.-Italy, 217 U.N.T.S. 202; Treaty of Trade and Navigation (with annex), Oct. 17, 1955, U.S.S.R.-Aus., 240 U.N.T.S. 304; Treaty of Establishment, Nov. 25, 1959 (Art. III), Fr.-U.S., 401 U.N.T.S. 75.

[240] Agreement on the Exchange of Goods and Payments, U.S.S.R.-Swed., Sept. 7, 1940, SVERIGES ÖVERENSKOMMELSER MED FRÄMMANDE MAKTER 1941–1946, at 259 (1947); Treaty of Commerce and Navigation, U.S.S.R.-Den., Aug. 17, 1946, 8 U.N.T.S. 218. On these conventions, see FOUCHARD, *supra* note 205, ¶¶ 61 *et seq.*; Agreement Between the Government of the United States of America and the Government of the Union of Soviet Socialist Republics Regarding Trade, signed at Washington on October 18, 1972, DEP'T ST. BULL., Nov. 20, 1972, at 595; on this agreement, see Donald B. Straus, *Interim Observations on Arbitration Arrangements in Soviet-American Trade*, 28 ARB. J. 105 (1973); Giorgio Gaja, *Notiziario di legislazione e convenzioni*, 1972 RASS. DELL'ARB. 236. On these earlier treaties, see FOUCHARD, GAILLARD, GOLDMAN, *supra* note 1.

[241] The UNCTAD counted 1310 of them as of January 17, 1997; see UNCTAD Note to correspondents No. 22 dated May 28, 1997, *BIT by BIT: Understanding the Development Implications of Bilateral Investment Treaties*, and Annex 1 thereto, which lists "Countries and Territories that have concluded bilateral investment treaties as of 1 January 1997" <http://www.unctad.org/en/press/nc9722.htm>; *see also* BILATERAL INVESTMENT TREATIES 1959–1996 (Doc. ICSID/17 (May 30, 1997)); RUDOLF DOLZER AND MARGRETE STEVENS, BILATERAL INVESTMENT TREATIES (1995); Giorgio Sacerdoti, *Bilateral Treaties and Multilateral Instruments on Investment Protection*, *in* COLLECTED COURSES OF THE HAGUE ACADEMY OF INTERNATIONAL LAW, Vol. 269, Year 1997, at 251, especially at 412–54.

against the host state. A general commitment of that nature is considered sufficient to allow investors to bring ICSID proceedings unilaterally.[242]

215. — If one of the states party to a bilateral treaty has not ratified the Washington Convention, the treaty will generally provide for *ad hoc* arbitration, often under the UNCITRAL Rules.[243]

b) Conventions on Judicial Assistance

216. — Bilateral conventions concerning judicial assistance are very common. A number of countries have signed dozens of such treaties. They principally govern cooperation between courts and the enforcement in one country of court decisions made in the other. For a long period, they also addressed the recognition and enforcement in one country of arbitral awards made in the second. That is less frequently the case today, with the success of multilateral treaties on the recognition and enforcement of arbitral awards such as the New York Convention.[244] However, parties still do sign bilateral treaties on judicial assistance containing provisions on arbitration, although many of these are limited to a reference to the New York Convention.

217. — The number of international treaties concerning arbitration (whether as their principal subject matter or only incidentally) create a risk of conflicts between conventions. What will be the solution where two conventions do conflict, assuming of course that the earlier convention has not been superseded by the later instrument?

---

[242] Award of June 27, 1990 by A.S. El-Kosheri, president, S.K.B. Asante and B. Goldman, arbitrators (S.K.B. Asante dissenting), in ICSID Case No. ARB/87/3, Asian Agricultural Products Ltd. v. Republic of Sri Lanka, 6 ICSID REV. – FOREIGN INV. L.J. 526 (1991); 30 I.L.M. 577 (1991); 6 INT'L ARB. REP. A1 (May 1991); XVII Y.B. COM. ARB. 106 (1992); for a French translation, see 119 J.D.I. 216 (1992), and observations by E. Gaillard; Award of February 21, 1997 in ICSID Case No. ARB/93/1, American Manufacturing & Trading Inc. v. Republic of Zaire, 125 J.D.I. 243 (1998), and observations by E. Gaillard; for an English translation, see XXII Y.B. COM. ARB. 60 (1997); 36 I.L.M. 1531 (1997); 12 INT'L ARB. REP. A1 (Apr. 1997); Decision of the Tribunal on Objections to Jurisdiction of July 11, 1997 in ICSID Case No. ARB/96/3, Fedax N.V. v. The Republic of Venezuela; for a French translation, see 126 J.D.I. 298 (1999), and observations by E. Gaillard; on this issue, see Georges R. Delaume, *How to Draft an ICSID Arbitration Clause*, 7 ICSID REV. – FOREIGN INV. L.J. 168 (1992); Emmanuel Gaillard, *Centre International pour le Règlement des Différends Relatifs aux Investissements (C.I.R.D.I.) – Chronique des sentences arbitrales*, 126 J.D.I. 273 (1999), and the references cited therein; Geneviève Burdeau, *Nouvelles perspectives pour l'arbitrage dans le contentieux économique intéressant les Etats*, 1995 REV. ARB. 3, 10; Jan Paulsson, *Arbitration Without Privity*, 10 ICSID REV. – FOREIGN INV. L.J. 232 (1995); Antonio R. Parra, *Provisions on the Settlement of Investment Disputes in Modern Investment Laws, Bilateral Investment Treaties and Multilateral Instruments on Investment*, 12 ICSID REV. – FOREIGN INV. L.J. 287 (1997).

[243] See, for example, the May 26, 1992 agreement between France and Vietnam (Art. 8), published in France by decree dated November 8, 1994, J.O., Nov. 16, 1994, p. 16,222; 122 J.D.I. 218 (1995).

[244] *See infra* para. 248.

218. — The principles usually applied to resolve such a conflict are that either the later or the more specific convention prevails. There exists another principle which should apply to both international arbitration and, generally speaking, conventions for judicial assistance: it is the rule of "maximum effectiveness," whereby the treaty that is most favorable to the validity of the arbitration and the enforcement of the arbitral award will be preferred.[245]

219. — Often, however, the treaties themselves resolve any conflicts that may arise through what is known as a "compatibility clause." The most significant illustrations of such provisions can be found in multilateral conventions on the recognition and enforcement of foreign awards. They generally provide that they do not affect the application of earlier treaties that are more favorable to arbitration: examples can be seen in the 1927 Geneva Convention[246] and the 1958 New York Convention.[247] These provisions often lead bilateral treaties on judicial assistance to be superseded, as the rules they contain governing the enforcement of foreign awards—often modeled on rules governing the enforcement of court decisions—are generally more restrictive than those found in multilateral conventions specifically concerning arbitration.

220–223. — Nonetheless, the procedural and substantive advantages of certain bilateral conventions on judicial assistance have led them to be applied in relations between countries which have ratified more recent multilateral conventions on arbitrations.[248]

224–232. — Certain of these bilateral conventions contain specific provisions regarding the recognition and enforcement in one contracting state of arbitral awards made in the second. These frequently only go as far as stating that such awards must comply with the

---

[245] *See* P. Mayer, note following Cass. 1e civ., June 2, 1987, Vogeleer v. Guide de l'Automobiliste européen, 1988 REV. ARB. 283; ALBERT JAN VAN DEN BERG, THE NEW YORK ARBITRATION CONVENTION OF 1958, at 90–91(1981); Bernard Dutoit and Ferenc Majoros, *Le lacis des conflits de conventions en droit privé et leurs solutions possibles*, 1984 REV. CRIT. DIP 565; FERENC MAJOROS, LES CONVENTIONS INTERNATIONALES EN MATIÈRE DE DROIT PRIVÉ – ABRÉGÉ THÉORIQUE ET TRAITÉ PRATIQUE, VOL. II, PARTIE SPÉCIALE I, LE DROIT DES CONFLITS DE CONVENTIONS (1980); Paul Lagarde, 1982 REV. CRIT. DIP 231 (reviewing FERENC MAJOROS, *supra*); E. Mezger, note following CA Paris, June 20, 1980, Clair v. Berardi, 1981 REV. ARB. 424.

[246] Art. 5; see *infra* para. 244.

[247] Art. VII; see *infra* para. 267.

[248] See, for example, in France, TGI Paris, réf., May 12, 1975, Banque de Financement Industriel v. Roudy, 1977 REV ARB. 175, 1st decision, and E. Mezger's note and TGI Paris, Oct. 24, 1975, Roudy v. Banque de Financement Industriel, 1976 REV. ARB. 210, and E. Mezger's note; 1976 REV. CRIT. DIP 538, and Y. Derains' note (The Franco-Swiss Convention of June 15, 1869; the Franco-Monegasque Convention of September 21, 1949, and the 1958 New York Convention); Cass 1e civ., June 2, 1987, Vogeleer v. Guide de l'Automobiliste européen, 1987 Bull. Civ. I, No. 174; 1988 REV. ARB. 283, and P. Mayer's note (The Franco-Belgian Convention of July 8, 1899, and the 1958 New York Convention). For a fuller presentation of bilateral judicial assistance treaties of which France is a signatory, see FOUCHARD, GAILLARD, GOLDMAN, *supra* note 1, ¶¶ 216–35.

equivalent conditions concerning court decisions, "to the extent that such conditions are applicable;"[249] it is less usual to find specific conditions applicable only to arbitral awards.[250]

233–234. — A larger category of bilateral treaties on judicial assistance simply declare that the 1958 New York Convention will apply as between the two contracting states.[251]

235. — Such a reference serves little purpose where the two parties to the bilateral treaty have already ratified the New York Convention. The aim of such a provision is perhaps to increase the awareness of the parties and, more importantly, of the courts of both countries of the applicability of the New York Convention. However, a reference of this kind has no substantive impact on the application of the New York Convention. It even may confuse issues, as happened in the *Chromalloy* case, where Egypt claimed that Article VII of the New York Convention was not included in the reference made to the New York Convention in the Franco-Egyptian bilateral treaty. It argued that, as a result, French courts could not rely on ordinary French rules of enforcement of international awards where the award was made in the territory of the other party to the bilateral treaty. The French courts rightly dismissed this argument.[252]

On the other hand, a reference to the New York Convention is extremely effective where one of the countries signing the bilateral treaty has not ratified the New York Convention, particularly if it does not intend to do so in the future. Of course, the selective "ratification" by that country of the New York Convention only benefits awards made in the other state party to the bilateral treaty.[253]

2° Conventions Primarily Concerning Arbitration

236. — Certain developing countries have been reluctant to agree to certain forms of arbitration proceedings, such as those under the auspices of the ICC. At the same time, however, they recognize that having disputes resolved by arbitration helps promote trade

---

[249] See, for example, the Convention between France and Brazil, dated January 30, 1981, published in France by Decree No. 85-394 dated March 28, 1985, J.O., Apr. 3, 1985, p. 3883 (Article 25 referring to Article 20); JCP, Ed. G., Pt. III, No. 57,073 (1985).

[250] See the Convention between France and the United Arab Emirates, dated September 9, 1991, published in France by Decree No. 93-419 dated March 15, 1993, J.O., Mar. 24, 1993, p. 4547 (Art. 17); 1993 REV. CRIT. DIP 333.

[251] Of the bilateral conventions of which France is a signatory, fifteen contain such a reference. For the list of such conventions, see FOUCHARD, GAILLARD, GOLDMAN, *supra* note 1, ¶ 234, to which must be added the Convention between France and Argentina, dated July 2, 1991, published in France by Decree No. 92-1213 dated November 12, 1992, J.O., Nov. 18, 1992, p. 15,816; 120 J.D.I. 212 (1993).

[252] CA Paris, Jan. 14, 1997, République arabe d'Egypte v. Chromalloy Aero Services, 1997 REV. ARB. 395, and P. Fouchard's note; 125 J.D.I. 750 (1998), and E. Gaillard's note; for an English translation, see 12 INT'L ARB. REP. B1 (Apr. 1997); XXII Y.B. COM. ARB. 691 (1997); on the content and application of Article VII of the New York Convention, see *infra* paras. 267 *et seq.*

[253] See, for example, the Convention between France and Gabon dated July 23, 1963, published in France by Decree No. 65-159 dated February 25, 1965, J.O., Mar. 2, 1965, p. 1723 (Art. 40).

with developed countries. They have therefore concluded bilateral treaties with those developed countries, establishing specific arbitration systems to which parties from each country may refer in their contracts.[254]

237. — Arbitration rules were also adopted in an exchange of letters between France and Algeria dated March 27, 1983.[255] The signatories agreed that parties from their respective countries could use the arbitration rules if their contracts referred to them. The rules are thus optional, although their source is an inter-state agreement. As to their content, they reflect modern international practice with respect to arbitral procedure, although the provisions concerning the constitution of the arbitral tribunal are somewhat less conventional.[256]

238. — The most important bilateral treaty primarily concerning arbitration is that known as the "Algiers Accords" of January 19, 1981, which takes the form of a set of agreements and declarations by the Algerian government.[257] The Accords provide for the creation of an "International Arbitral Tribunal" to decide certain economic disputes between Iran and the United States.[258]

---

[254] For an example, see the Arbitration and Conciliation Rules for Contracts signed between French and Iranian parties, drawn up on the basis of the principles laid down in the Protocol of the Third Session of the French-Iranian Ministerial Joint Commission for Economic Co-operation held in Paris on May 12-14, 1976, unpublished.

[255] *See* 111 J.D.I. 989 (1984); 1986 REV. ARB. 311; for a commentary, see Ali Mebroukine, *Le Règlement d'arbitrage algéro-français du 27 mars 1983*, 1986 REV. ARB. 191. On the application of these rules in two Franco-Algerian arbitrations, see Nour-Eddine Terki, *L'arbitrage international et l'entreprise publique économique en Algérie*, 1990 REV. ARB. 585, especially 597 *et seq.*

[256] If the defendant fails to appoint an arbitrator, the court will do so (in France or Algeria, as the case may be) and if the court fails to do so, the Secretary-General of the Permanent Court of Arbitration in The Hague will make the appointment. The third arbitrator is chosen by the first two arbitrators by drawing lots from a list of ten names agreed upon by the two parties and attached to the contract.

[257] These Accords include: the Declaration of the Government of the Democratic and Popular Republic of Algeria Relating to the Commitments Made by Iran and the United States; the Undertakings of the Government of the United States of America and the Government of the Islamic Republic of Iran with Respect to the Declaration of the Government of the Democratic and Popular Republic of Algeria; the Declaration of the Government of the Democratic and Popular Republic of Algeria Concerning the Settlement of Claims by the Government of the United States of America and the Government of the Islamic Republic of Iran; and the Escrow Agreement. They are reproduced in 20 I.L.M. 223–40 (1981).

[258] On these Accords and the Iran-U.S. Claims Tribunal, see, for example, Bernard Audit, *Les "Accords" d'Alger du 19 janvier 1981 tendant au règlement des différends entre les Etats-Unis et l'Iran*, 108 J.D.I. 713 (1981), with an unofficial French translation of the Algiers accords; Ignaz Seidl-Hohenveldern, *Le règlement du contentieux irano-américain par les accords d'Alger du 19 janvier 1981*, *in* LE DROIT DES RELATIONS ÉCONOMIQUES INTERNATIONALES – ETUDES OFFERTES À BERTHOLD GOLDMAN 343 (1982); CAHIERS DU CEDIN, LE TRIBUNAL DES DIFFÉRENDS IRANO-AMÉRICAINS – JOURNÉE D'ACTUALITÉ INTERNATIONALE, 19 AVRIL 1984 (B. Stern ed. 1985); Bernard Audit, *Le Tribunal des Différends Irano-Américains (1981-1984)*, 112 J.D.I. 791 (1985); the survey of awards, decisions and orders issued by the Tribunal, published in the YEARBOOK COMMERCIAL ARBITRATION since 1982 (Part III – B. Iran-U.S. Claims Tribunal); RAHMATULLAH KHAN, THE IRAN-UNITED STATES CLAIMS TRIBUNAL – CONTROVERSIES, CASES AND CONTRIBUTION (1990); Jamal Seifi, *Procedural Remedies against Awards of Iran-United States Claims Tribunal*, 8 ARB. INT'L 41 (1992); Charles N. Brower, *Lessons to be Drawn from the Iran–U.S. Claims Tribunal*, 9 J. INT'L ARB. 51 (Mar. 1992);

(continued...)

Based in The Hague, this international arbitral tribunal has heard over four thousand claims since 1981. Most have been brought by United States companies against the Iranian state or state-owned entities, although some claims have been filed by Iranian entities against the United States or United States companies, or by one State against the other. The rules governing the constitution and jurisdiction of the Tribunal are set out in the Algiers Accords, and the procedure is governed by a slightly modified version of the UNCITRAL Rules.[259] However, a number of factors have led to doubts as to the arbitral nature of the institution. These factors include the role of the two States, the political origins of the disputes, and the extreme difficulties facing any non-state parties who might prefer to submit their disputes to a judicial authority other than to the Tribunal imposed upon them. Comparisons thus have been drawn between the Tribunal and certain similar bodies created under public international law to address reparation claims arising from military conflicts. The courts seem hesitant in this respect. For example, in 1985 the absence of an arbitration agreement led the English High Court to refuse to apply the New York Convention to the recognition in England of an arbitral award made by the Tribunal.[260] On the other hand, United States courts hearing applications by Iran for the enforcement of decisions of the Tribunal have applied the New York Convention, both to grant and to refuse enforcement.[261] The question thus remains unsettled.[262]

C. – MULTILATERAL CONVENTIONS

239. — There are also a large number of multilateral conventions on arbitration. But, unlike bilateral conventions, the most important conventions concern exclusively arbitration.[263] We will nevertheless briefly examine those multilateral conventions which may have an incidental impact on arbitration or which contain ancillary provisions concerning arbitration.

---

[258](...continued)
GEORGES H. ALDRICH, THE JURISPRUDENCE OF THE IRAN-UNITED STATES CLAIMS TRIBUNAL (1996); CHARLES N. BROWER, JASON D. BRUESCHKE, THE IRAN-UNITED STATES CLAIMS TRIBUNAL (1998); for a bibliography up to 1987, see Nassib G. Ziadé, *Selective Bibliography on the Iran–United States Claims Tribunal*, 2 ICSID REV. – FOREIGN INV. L.J. 534 (1987).

[259] *See supra* para. 202.

[260] Mark Dallal v. Bank Mellat, [1986] 1 Q.B. 441; [1986] 1 All E.R. 239; [1986] 2 W.L.R. 745 (High Ct., Q.B. (Com. Ct.) 1985); excerpts in XI Y.B. COM. ARB. 547 (1986), and the commentary *id.* at 412.

[261] Iran v. Gould Marketing, Inc., 887 F.2d 1357 (9th Cir. 1989); XV Y.B. COM. ARB. 605 (1990); Iran Aircraft Indus. v. Avco Corp., 980 F.2d 141 (2d Cir. 1992); XVIII Y.B. COM. ARB. 596 (1993); *see* Lawrence W. Newman and Michael Burrows, *Enforceability of Hague Tribunal Awards*, N.Y.L.J., Mar. 18, 1993, at 3.

[262] See also, the respective viewpoints of Philippe Fouchard, Michel Virally, Berthold Goldman, *La nature juridique de l'arbitrage du Tribunal des Différends Irano-Américains*, in CAHIERS DU CEDIN, *supra* note 258, at 27, 49 and 60; Aida B. Avanessian, *The New York Convention and Denationalised Arbitral Awards (With Emphasis on the Iran–United States Claims Tribunal)*, 8 J. INT'L ARB. 5 (Mar. 1991); Seifi, *supra* note 258.

[263] For an overview and an explanation of the situation regarding conventions in Europe, see Jean-François Bourque, *The Legal Framework of Arbitration in the European Union*, in ICC BULLETIN, SPECIAL SUPPLEMENT, INTERNATIONAL COMMERCIAL ARBITRATION IN EUROPE 8 (1994).

239-1. — In the field of judicial co-operation, the Brussels Convention of September 27, 1968 on Jurisdiction and Enforcement of Judgments in Civil and Commercial Matters, which applies in the European Union, and later the Lugano Convention of September 16, 1988, which extended the Brussels Convention to the Member States of the European Free Trade Association, expressly excluded arbitration from their scope (Art. 1, paragraph 2(4)). The Court of Justice of the European Communities has interpreted this exclusion broadly:

> [it] extends to litigation pending before a national court concerning the appointment of an arbitrator, even if the existence or validity of an arbitration agreement is a preliminary issue in that litigation.[264]

The Court of Justice thus rightly considered that arbitration as a whole, and therefore any dispute concerning arbitration, fell outside the scope of the Brussels Convention. In so doing, it left the way clear for other treaties dealing specifically with arbitration, thereby avoiding the difficult conflicts between conventions which would otherwise have arisen.

There remains, however, some scope for conflict: the Brussels and Lugano Conventions do not of course apply to the recognition and enforcement of arbitral awards, but some courts have considered applying the Brussels Convention to awards incorporated in court judgments, decisions reviewing awards on appeal, decisions setting awards aside,[265] and decisions on the merits of cases where a court rejects a claim, based on the existence of an arbitration agreement, that it lacks jurisdiction.[266] In its recent *Van Uden* decision, the Court of Justice of the European Communities held that, despite the existence of an arbitration agreement and pending arbitration proceedings, Article 24 of the Brussels Convention was applicable to a request to the courts for provisional measures, and could justify the jurisdiction of those courts.[267] This decision is unsatisfactory because it unnecessarily infringes upon both the letter and the spirit of Article 1(2)(4) of the Convention. The best

---

[264] Court of Justice of the European Communities, July 25, 1991, Case C–190/89, Marc Rich and Co. AG v. Società Italiana Impianti PA, 1991 E.C.R. I–3894, with the opinion of the advocate general, Mr. Darmon; 1991 REV. ARB. 677, and D. Hascher's note; 119 J.D.I. 488 (1992), and observations by A. Huet; 1993 REV. CRIT. DIP 310, and P. Mayer's note. *See also* Bernard Audit, *Arbitration and the Brussels Convention*, 9 ARB. INT'L 1 (1993); 7 ARB. INT'L 179–298 (1991), an issue entirely devoted to the Arbitration Exception to the Brussels Convention; Riccardo Monaco, *Compétence arbitrale et compétence selon la Convention communautaire de 1968*, in ETUDES DE DROIT INTERNATIONAL EN L'HONNEUR DE PIERRE LALIVE 587 (1993); Bernard Audit, *L'arbitre, le juge et la Convention de Bruxelles*, in L'INTERNATIONALISATION DU DROIT – MÉLANGES EN L'HONNEUR DE YVON LOUSSOUARN 15 (1994).

[265] Dominique T. Hascher, *Recognition and Enforcement of Arbitration Awards and the Brussels Convention*, 12 ARB. INT'L 233 (1996).

[266] Audit, *Arbitration and the Brussels Convention*, *supra* note 264; Dominique T. Hascher, *Recognition and Enforcement of Judgments on the Existence and Validity of an Arbitration Clause under the Brussels Convention*, 13 ARB. INT'L 33 (1997); Hans van Houtte, *May Court Judgments that Disregard Arbitration Clauses and Awards be Enforced under the Brussels and Lugano Conventions?*, 13 ARB. INT'L 85 (1997).

[267] Court of Justice of the European Communities, Nov. 17, 1998, Case C–391/95, Van Uden Maritime BV, trading as Van Uden Africa Line v. Kommanditgesellschaft in Firma Deco-Line e.a., 1998 E.C.R. I–7122; 14 INT'L ARB. REP. C1 (Jan. 1999); 1998 ECJ CELEX LEXIS 3138; 1999 REV. ARB. 143, and H. Gaudemet-Tallon's note; 1999 BULL. ASA 68, and the commentary by M. Scherer at 83; see also the opinion of the advocate general, Mr. Léger, presented on June 10, 1997, 1998 BULL. ASA 166.

approach is to give the broadest possible effect to the exclusion of arbitration from the two Conventions. Allowing these Conventions to interfere in arbitration would be dangerous and serve no purpose. Conflicts between conventions would result, with the risk of upsetting the delicate balance struck between the autonomy of arbitration and the review of arbitral awards by the courts.

239-2. — The 1950 European Convention for Protection of Human Rights and Fundamental Freedoms[268] (and to a lesser extent the International Covenant on Civil and Political Rights, signed in New York on December 19, 1966) are often relied upon by parties contesting the conduct of certain arbitrations. Article 6 of the European Convention on Human Rights provides that "everyone is entitled to a fair and public hearing within a reasonable time by an independent and impartial tribunal established by law." The Convention only creates obligations for signatory governments and for the courts, and is therefore not directly applicable as such to arbitration or to arbitrators. However, when hearing cases connected with an arbitration (whether in assisting the arbitration, or reviewing or enforcing an award), the courts must comply with the Convention's fundamental procedural guarantees.[269] Although such guarantees are in fact found in most arbitration laws, it is nevertheless useful for them to be formally set out in the Convention. As a result, arbitrators and arbitral institutions are invited to take them into account in all cases, and the courts must apply them in the absence of sufficiently stringent national legislation. The provisions of the Convention have already been relied upon before the European Commission of Human Rights and the European Court of Human Rights in Strasbourg, as well as before a number of national courts, particularly in France and Switzerland.[270]

239-3. — There are also a number of recent multilateral conventions in which states, seeking to minimize the potential for political differences, encourage their nationals to settle their international disputes, particularly in trade and investment matters, by arbitration.

An example is the North American Free Trade Agreement (NAFTA), signed in 1992. As we have seen, each of the three signatory States (Canada, Mexico and the United States)

---

[268] Signed in Rome on November 4, 1950, E.T.S. No. 5.

[269] On the question of whether a state may, by the subsequent enactment of legislation, oppose the enforcement of an arbitral award against it, see European Court of Human Rights, Stran Greek Refineries and Stratis Andreadis v. Greece, Dec. 9, 1994, Series A, No. 301-B; 1996 REV. ARB. 283, and the commentary by Ali Bencheneb, *La contrariété à la Convention européenne des droits de l'homme d'une loi anéantissant une sentence arbitrale, id.* at 181; *see also infra* para. 406-1.

[270] *See* Charles Jarrosson, *L'arbitrage et la Convention européenne des droits de l'homme,* 1989 REV. ARB. 573; Jean-François Flauss, *L'application de l'art. 6 de la Convention européenne des droits de l'Homme aux procédures arbitrales,* Gaz. Pal., Doct. 407 (1986); Jean-Hubert Moitry, *Right to a Fair Trial and the European Convention on Human Rights – Some Remarks on the République de Guinée Case,* 6 J. INT'L ARB. 115 (June 1989); Giorgio Recchia, *Arbitrato e Convenzione europea dei diritti dell'uomo (prospettive metodologiche),* 1993 RIV. DELL'ARB. 381; Bourque, *supra* note 263, at 10 *et seq. See also* the decisions of the European Commission on Human Rights, March 4, 1987, 1990 BULL. ASA 251, and July 11, 1989, 1990 BULL. ASA 262, which examine the position of the Swiss courts in their review of the duration of the arbitral proceedings. On the Convention, generally, see A.H. ROBERTSON AND J.G. MERRILLS, HUMAN RIGHTS IN EUROPE: A STUDY OF THE EUROPEAN CONVENTION ON HUMAN RIGHTS (3d ed. 1993).

consented to the submission to arbitration of claims against it brought by investors from the two other States concerning rights protected by the Treaty.[271] Furthermore, Article 2022 provides that each of the three signatory States must also encourage and facilitate the submission to arbitration of international commercial disputes between private parties in the free trade area. To that end, the same article established an Advisory Committee on Private Commercial Disputes.[272] Four disputes had been brought before the International Centre for Settlement of Investment Disputes (ICSID), on the basis of NAFTA, as of January 1, 1999.

Similar in certain respects is the Energy Charter Treaty, which was signed by more than 40 countries in Lisbon on December 17, 1994, and entered into force on April 16, 1998.[273] The initial purpose of the Treaty was to promote investment in the countries of the former Soviet Union, although its scope has been subsequently broadened. To achieve this, the Treaty allows foreign investors to submit disputes with a state that is party to the Treaty to one of four systems of arbitration, chosen by the claimant in its discretion.[274]

Another multilateral convention in the field of international investments relating only incidentally to arbitration is the Convention Establishing the Multilateral Investment Guarantee Agency (MIGA), signed in Seoul on October 11, 1985. It entered into force on April 12, 1988[275] and counts 150 member states.[276] It provides for disputes between the Agency and member states (Art. 57), or between the Agency and holders of a guarantee or reinsurance (Art. 58),[277] to be resolved by arbitration.

---

[271] Chapter 11 of the Agreement; *see supra* para. 44 and the references cited therein. *See also* Cheri D. Eklund, *A Primer on the Arbitration of NAFTA Chapter Eleven Investor-State Disputes*, 11 J. INT'L ARB. 135 (Dec. 1994).

[272] For the text of Article 2022 of NAFTA and its implementation through the establishment of a regional arbitration center, see Michael F. Hoellering, *Commercial Arbitration and Mediation Center for the Americas*, 13 J. INT'L ARB. 117 (June 1996); *see also infra* para. 336.

[273] *See* NEWS FROM ICSID, Vol. 15, No. 2, at 1 (1998).

[274] Article 26 of the Treaty: the private investor has the choice between submitting its claim to either the International Centre for Settlement of Investment Disputes (ICSID) (on the basis of the 1965 Washington Convention or of the Additional Facility Rules), an *ad hoc* arbitral tribunal applying the UNCITRAL Arbitration Rules, or the Arbitration Institute of the Stockholm Chamber of Commerce (Art. 26(4)). Irrespective of the type of arbitration chosen, the dispute must be decided "in accordance with [the] Treaty and applicable rules and principles of international law" (Art. 26(6)). *See* Nigel Rawding, *Protecting Investments Under State Contracts: Some Legal and Ethical Issues*, 11 ARB. INT'L 341, 367 (1995); Thomas W. Wälde, *Investment Arbitration Under the Energy Charter Treaty – From Dispute Settlement to Treaty Implementation*, 12 ARB. INT'L 429 (1996); Bernd-Roland Killman, *The Access of Individuals to International Trade Dispute Settlement*, 13 J. INT'L ARB. 143 (Sept. 1996); Jan Linehan, *Investment, Trade and Transit: Dispute Settlement under the Energy Charter Treaty*, NEWS FROM ICSID, Vol. 15, No. 2, at 4 (1998); Florence Poirat, *L'article 26 du Traité relatif à la Charte de l'Energie: procédures de règlement des différends et statut des personnes privées*, 1998 RGDIP 45. For the text of the Treaty, see 34 I.L.M. 381 (1995).

[275] *See* 24 I.L.M. 1605 (1985), and for the French version, 117 J.D.I. 770 (1990). For further information, consult the MIGA Web site (<http://www.miga.org>).

[276] As of March 31, 1999; another 13 countries were in the process of fulfilling membership requirements. *See* MIGA Web site, *supra* note 275.

[277] The proposed arbitration mechanisms are listed in Annex II of the Convention for disputes between the Agency and member states and, for disputes between the Agency and holders of a guarantee or reinsurance, in the Rules of Arbitration for Disputes Under Contracts of Guarantee of the Multilateral Investment Guarantee Agency,

(continued...)

We shall now consider in more detail those multilateral conventions relating exclusively to arbitration. These include the conventions signed in Geneva in the 1920s (1°), the 1958 New York Convention (2°), certain regional conventions (3°), and the 1965 Washington Convention establishing the International Centre for Settlement of Investment Disputes (4°).

1° The Early Conventions

240. — Two multilateral conventions were drawn up under the auspices of the League of Nations in Geneva following World War I. They removed a number of obstacles then facing international arbitration.[278] However, the progress made by those instruments has been confirmed and extended by the New York Convention, and its two forerunners are no longer relevant, except in relations between countries which are not bound by the New York Convention. Article VII, paragraph 2 of the New York Convention provides that:

> [t]he Geneva Protocol on Arbitration Clauses of 1923 and the Geneva Convention on the Execution of Foreign Arbitral Awards of 1927 shall cease to have effect between Contracting States on their becoming bound and to the extent that they become bound, by this Convention.

a) The Geneva Protocol of September 24, 1923

241. — This protocol "on Arbitration Clauses in Commercial Matters"[279] entered into force on July 28, 1924. Thirty-three countries ratified or acceded to the Protocol, but it also applied to those former dependent territories to which it had been extended. Of all these states, only Albania, Brazil, The Democratic Republic of Congo, The Gambia, Guyana, Iraq, Jamaica, Malta, Myanmar (formerly Burma), Pakistan and Zambia have yet to accede to the New York Convention. In their relations with each other and with other countries bound by both the Protocol and the New York Convention, they remain bound by the terms of the Protocol (New York Convention, Art. VII(2)).

---

[277](...continued)
adopted in January 1990 (*see* XVI Y.B. COM. ARB. 248 (1991)). *See* Ibrahim F.I. Shihata, *Towards a Greater Depoliticization of Investment Disputes: The Roles of ICSID and MIGA*, 1 ICSID REV. – FOREIGN INV. L.J. 1 (1986); for the text of the Convention and the Commentary, see *id.* at 145 and 193; *see also* Jean Touscoz, *Le règlement des différends dans la Convention instituant l'Agence Multilatérale de Garantie des Investissements (A.M.G.I.): un développement de l'arbitrage international et du droit des investissements internationaux*, 1988 REV. ARB. 629.

[278] *See* Giorgio Balladore Pallieri, *L'arbitrage privé dans les rapports internationaux*, *in* COLLECTED COURSES OF THE HAGUE ACADEMY OF INTERNATIONAL LAW, Vol. 51, Year 1935, Part I, at 291.

[279] 27 L.N.T.S. 158 (1924); see the text and the List of the Contracting States, including the dates of ratification or accession, and any reservations made, in REGISTER OF TEXTS, *supra* note 202, Vol. II, at 8.

242. — Although the Protocol is brief, containing only four articles covering the validity and effect of arbitration clauses, it nevertheless had a decisive impact on the future of arbitration throughout the world. In France, the signing of the Protocol, even prior to ratification, prompted the legislature to make arbitration clauses valid in commercial transactions.[280] The Protocol also laid a foundation for the worldwide development of international arbitration, which is obviously dependent on the effectiveness of arbitration agreements in international contracts. It also left the parties free to determine the arbitral procedure (Art. 2) and obliged states and national courts to ensure that arbitration agreements (Art. 4) and the resulting awards (Art. 3) could be enforced.

243. — The Geneva Protocol is intended to apply to submission agreements and arbitration clauses concluded "between parties subject respectively to the jurisdiction of different contracting states," whether by their nationality, domicile, registered office or principal place of business, and hence to proceedings and awards resulting from such agreements. On ratifying or acceding to the Protocol, many countries implemented the "commercial reservation" provided for in Article 1, paragraph 2, whereby "[e]ach contracting state reserves the right to limit the obligation mentioned above to contracts which are considered as commercial under its national law."

b) The Geneva Convention of September 26, 1927

244. — The Geneva Convention of September 26, 1927, on the "Execution of Foreign Arbitral Awards," came into force on July 25, 1929.[281] It has been ratified or acceded to by twenty-seven countries, and also applied to countries to which, as former dependent territories, the Convention had been extended. Of all these countries, only The Democratic Republic of Congo, Guyana, Jamaica, Malta, Myanmar (formerly Burma), Pakistan, and Zambia have yet to accede to the New York Convention. Thus, in their relations with each other, and in their relations with other countries bound by both the 1927 Geneva Convention and the 1958 New York Convention, those countries remain bound by the 1927 Convention (New York Convention, Art. VII(2)).[282]

245. — The 1927 Convention contains uniform conditions for the recognition and enforcement of "foreign" arbitral awards. Unfortunately, these conditions are expressed in obscure, restrictive terms (Arts. 1 to 4). Assessing the validity of the various stages of the arbitration involves reference to a number of national legal systems, and the courts in the

---

[280] Article 631, last paragraph, of the Commercial Code (Law of Dec. 31, 1925).

[281] 92 L.N.T.S. 302 (1929–30); see the text and the List of Contracting States, including the dates of ratification or accession, and any reservations made, in REGISTER OF TEXTS, *supra* note 202, Vol. II, at 13.

[282] On the refusal to apply, other than on a subsidiary basis, the 1927 Convention to the enforcement in France of an award made in Switzerland in 1956, see CA Rouen, Nov. 13, 1984, Société Européenne d'Etudes et d'Entreprises (S.E.E.E.) v. République de Yougoslavie, 1985 REV. ARB. 115, and J.-L. Delvolvé's note; 112 J.D.I. 473 (1985), and B. Oppetit's note; for an English translation, see XI Y.B. COM. ARB. 491 (1986); 24 I.L.M. 345, 349 (1985).

host country can only grant enforcement if it has been established that the award is "final" in its country of origin. In practice, this amounts to requiring two enforcement orders ("double *exequatur*"). However, the Geneva Convention usefully excludes any review of the merits of the award, and some of its terms are presented in the form of substantive rules which constitute universal conditions governing the international validity of awards. These include the parties' right to a fair hearing and the respect of the limits of the arbitrator's brief.

246. — The scope of the 1927 Geneva Convention is determined on the basis of that of the 1923 Protocol, with certain unsatisfactory restrictions. The Convention applies only to awards made "in the territories of any high contracting party . . . between persons who are subject to the jurisdiction of one of the high contracting parties."

Although this wording need not be interpreted to the letter—that would be tantamount to requiring that both parties share the same nationality—it nevertheless has the disadvantage of confining the scope of the Convention to awards made in a contracting state and, in particular, to awards between parties both of which are subjects of contracting states. These conditions of location and nationality hardly represent a realistic approach to international commercial arbitration.[283]

2° The 1958 New York Convention

247. — Following World War II and the subsequent growth of international trade, the weaknesses of the 1927 Geneva Convention, which neither the United States nor the Soviet Union had ratified, became very apparent. It needed to be revised if arbitration was to become an efficient means of resolving international disputes. The International Chamber of Commerce was aware of this and began work on a new instrument, and in 1953 it submitted a "Draft Convention" on the enforcement of international arbitral awards[284] to the United Nations. Although the UN Economic and Social Committee (ECOSOC) endorsed this draft, in 1955 its panel of experts produced a second draft[285] which was much more conservative than the ICC text. An international conference was then held in New York beginning May 20, 1958 under the UN banner. The text which it adopted on June 10, 1958 was considerably more liberal than that put forward by the panel of experts and came closer to the ideas, if not to the wording, of the ICC draft.[286]

---

[283] *See supra* paras. 78 *et seq.*

[284] INTERNATIONAL CHAMBER OF COMMERCE, ENFORCEMENT OF INTERNATIONAL ARBITRAL AWARDS – REPORT AND PRELIMINARY DRAFT CONVENTION (ICC Publication No. 174, 1953), *reprinted in* ICC BULLETIN, Vol. 9, No. 1, at 32 (1998).

[285] *Reprinted in* INTERNATIONAL TRADE ARBITRATION 288 (M. Domke ed., 1958).

[286] On the legislative history of the Convention, see United Nations Economic and Social Council (ECOSOC), Docs. E/Conf.26/2 to E/Conf.26/7 and E/CONF.26/SR.1 to E/CONF.26/SR.24, *reprinted in* INTERNATIONAL COMMERCIAL ARBITRATION – NEW YORK CONVENTION – PART III – PREPARATORY WORKS (G. Gaja ed., 1978).

248. — The "Convention on the Recognition and Enforcement of Foreign Arbitral Awards" was open for signature in New York from June 10, 1958 until December 31, 1958. It was signed by twenty-five countries. On March 31, 1999, among those signatories only Pakistan had yet to ratify the Convention. It entered into force on June 7, 1959.

On March 31, 1999, a total of 121 countries were bound by the Convention, through ratification, accession or succession.[287] This constitutes a resounding success, and the Convention has become the universal instrument that its proponents intended it to be. Success came gradually, though, because it was not until the 1970s and 1980s that a number of important countries ratified it: the United States in 1970, the United Kingdom in 1975, Canada in 1986, China in 1987, Algeria and Argentina in 1989, Saudi Arabia in 1994, both Venezuela and Vietnam in 1995, and Lebanon in 1998. The cases of Argentina, Saudi Arabia, Venezuela and Vietnam are particularly significant, as those signatory countries have traditionally, for various political or legal reasons, been hostile towards international arbitration.[288] The number of members states is so great that it is now easier to point out a few "conspicuous absences." There are no longer any in Europe, but a few can be found in the Middle East (including Iran, Iraq and the United Arab Emirates) and Asia (including Pakistan), in Latin America (including Brazil) and in Africa (including The Democratic Republic of Congo (formerly Zaire)).

249. — The New York Convention, and its application and interpretation by courts worldwide, have been the subject of numerous commentaries.[289] The Convention's various

---

[287] For the text of the Convention and the List of Contracting States, including the dates of ratification or accession, see *infra* Annex IV. The updated list of Contracting States is regularly published in the YEARBOOK COMMERCIAL ARBITRATION, Part V – A. It can also be found on the UNCITRAL Web site, where the list is updated as soon as new information becomes available (<http://www.un.or.at/uncitral>).

[288] On the position taken in Arab countries, see Abdul Hamid El-Ahdab, *Enforcement of Arbitral Awards in the Arab Countries*, 11 ARB. INT'L 169 (1995); EL-AHDAB, *supra* note 144.

[289] *See* Jean Robert, *La Convention de New York du 10 juin 1958 pour la reconnaissance et l'exécution des sentences arbitrales étrangères*, Dalloz, Chron. 223 (1958); Martin Domke, *The United Nations Conference on International Commercial Arbitration*, 53 AM. J. INT'L L. 414 (1959); Jean-Denis Bredin, *La Convention de New-York du 10 juin 1958 pour la reconnaissance et l'exécution des sentences arbitrales étrangères/The New York Convention of June 10th 1958 for the Recognition and Enforcement of Foreign Arbitral Awards*, 87 J.D.I. 1002 (1960); Henri Motulsky, *L'évolution récente en matière d'arbitrage international*, 1959 REV. ARB. 3; Frédéric-Edouard Klein, *Autonomie de la volonté et arbitrage*, 1958 REV. CRIT. DIP 479; Pieter Sanders, *The New York Convention*, *in* UNION INTERNATIONALE DES AVOCATS, ARBITRAGE INTERNATIONAL COMMERCIAL – INTERNATIONAL COMMERCIAL ARBITRATION, Vol. II, at 293 (P. Sanders ed., 1960). *See also* INTERNATIONAL COMMERCIAL ARBITRATION, *supra* note 286; ALBERT JAN VAN DEN BERG, THE NEW YORK ARBITRATION CONVENTION OF 1958 (1981); McLaughlin and Genevro, *supra* note 94; Andrea Giardina, *Court Decisions in Italy Interpreting and Implementing the New York Convention*, 7 J. INT'L ARB. 77 (June 1990); ASA SPECIAL SERIES NO. 9, THE NEW YORK CONVENTION OF 1958 (1996) (collection of reports and materials delivered at the ASA Conference held in Zurich on February 2, 1996). For commentaries on New York Convention case law, see Pieter Sanders, *A Twenty Years' Review of the Convention on the Recognition and Enforcement of Foreign Arbitral Awards*, 13 INT'L LAW. 269 (1979), and the references cited therein, and for a French version, 1979 DPCI 359; see also, starting in 1976, the chronicle in the YEARBOOK COMMERCIAL ARBITRATION, Part. V – A, where Pieter Sanders and then Albert Jan van den Berg have carefully collected and analyzed a considerable number of court decisions; the various reports in ICCA CONGRESS SERIES NO. 9, IMPROVING THE EFFICIENCY OF ARBITRATION AGREEMENTS AND AWARDS: 40 YEARS OF APPLICATION OF THE

(continued...)

strengths and weaknesses have become clearer as a result. Given its important contribution to the effectiveness of international arbitration, we will discuss the Convention in detail when examining each of the various stages of arbitration.[290] For present purposes, we shall simply make a few general observations as to the principal characteristics of the Convention and, in particular, as to its scope.

a) Principal Characteristics

250. — The title of the Convention suggests that it relates only to "the recognition and enforcement of foreign arbitral awards." That, indeed, is its essential purpose and the subject of most of its rules (Arts. III to VI), which are intended to replace those of the 1927 Geneva Convention. However, the initial idea of a separate protocol, intended to replace the 1923 Geneva Protocol, was abandoned at the last minute. As a result, Article II also covers arbitration agreements. Furthermore, the underlying theme of the New York Convention as a whole is clearly the autonomy of international arbitration.

251. — As regards the conditions for recognition and enforcement of awards, the New York Convention makes significant progress in two areas as compared to the 1927 Geneva Convention. First, the burden of proof is reversed: once the award and arbitration agreement have been submitted by the party applying for recognition and enforcement of the award (Art. IV), the party opposing enforcement must prove why the award should not be enforced against it (Art. V). Second, there are fewer grounds on which an application resisting enforcement will be admissible, and these are defined in more restrictive terms. For example, it is no longer necessary that the award should be "final" in its country of origin; the award must simply be "binding." Although that term may create difficulties of interpretation in some countries, the existence of an action to set aside no longer prevents enforcement abroad, and a "double *exequatur*," in the country of origin as well as in the country of enforcement, is no longer necessary. The procedure governing recognition and enforcement (Arts. III and IV) is still determined by each contracting state, although contracting states agree not to impose on the recognition and enforcement of foreign awards substantially more onerous conditions than those imposed on the recognition and enforcement of domestic awards.

252. — As far as arbitration agreements are concerned, Article II of the New York Convention usefully sets forth a general principle of their recognition. It also determines the conditions of form and the effects of all arbitration agreements, again by means of a substantive rule.

---

[289](...continued)
NEW YORK CONVENTION (A.J. van den Berg ed., 1999).

[290] See the following parts of this book and particularly that concerning the enforcement of the award, paras. 1666 *et seq.*

253. — Another feature of the New York Convention, which is not set out in detail but is highly significant, is its recognition of the parties' freedom in the constitution of the arbitral tribunal and the determination of arbitral procedure. These two aspects of the arbitration need only be "in accordance with the agreement of the parties, or, failing such agreement, . . . in accordance with the law of the country where the arbitration took place" (Art. V(1)(d)).

This reflects the primacy of the Convention and the purely subsidiary role of national law which, unless the parties have stipulated otherwise, will be that of the seat of the arbitration.[291] As a result, the influence of the seat of the arbitration and, more generally, that of national laws on arbitral procedure, is substantially reduced. As the New York Convention also confirms the existence and legitimacy of institutional arbitration (Art. I(2)), it follows that, in the absence of a specific agreement between the parties as to procedure, the rules of arbitral institutions are considered to be the principal source of rules governing arbitral proceedings.[292]

254. — A comparison of the final text of the Convention with the ECOSOC draft of 1955[293] shows the extent to which ties between international arbitration and national laws were reduced. Nevertheless, the representatives gathered at the New York conference did not go as far as to give their full endorsement to the concept of an "international" arbitral award, as had been proposed by the ICC. The central principle remains that an arbitration should be localized and the idea of denationalized arbitration is barely addressed. This caution is apparent not only in the list of admissible grounds of recourse against awards and in the terms used to express them, but also in the definition of the scope of the Convention.

b) The Scope of the Convention

255. — The scope of the New York Convention is not limited by reference to the nationality of the parties to the arbitration agreement or the award. This constitutes significant progress as compared to the 1927 Convention, which applied only where the parties were "subject to the jurisdiction of one of the high contracting parties."[294] Thus, in France, the Rouen Court of Appeals had no hesitation in applying the New York Convention to an award made in Switzerland, in the context of an application for enforcement, as both Switzerland and France had ratified the Convention. It was irrelevant that Yugoslavia, which was a party to the arbitration, had only ratified the Convention on condition that it would not

---

[291] See, for example, the commentaries cited above by Sanders, *The New York Convention, supra* note 289; Robert, *supra* note 289, at 226; Motulsky, *supra* note 289, at 11; Bredin, *supra* note 289, at 1022. *But see* Arthur Bülow, *La convention des parties relative à la procédure d'arbitrage visée à l'Art. V, par. 1, litt. d) de la Convention de New York, in* COMMERCIAL ARBITRATION – ESSAYS IN MEMORIAM EUGENIO MINOLI 81 (1974).

[292] On these private sources, see *infra* paras. 323 *et seq.* On this issue, generally, see *infra* paras. 1171 *et seq.*

[293] *See supra* note 285.

[294] *See supra* para. 246.

apply to awards made prior to such ratification, because "the parties' nationality does not affect the application of the Convention."[295]

Likewise, in another French case, the Paris Court of Appeals and the *Cour de cassation* applied the New York Convention to the enforcement in France of an arbitral award made in Vienna, rightly disregarding the fact that the award was in favor of a Turkish company and that, at that time, Turkey was not bound by the Convention.[296]

256. — The application of the New York Convention is not restricted to international arbitration. The text contains no "internationality" requirement. The concept of a "foreign" award, as mentioned in the title of the Convention, still suggests a national connection. Article I of the Convention provides that, in principle, a "foreign" award is an award made in a country other than that in which its recognition and enforcement are sought. Whether the dispute involves the interests of international trade is irrelevant. So too is whether the arbitration has one or more foreign components.[297] In order for the Convention to apply in a contracting state, all that is necessary, in principle,[298] is that the award in question be made in another country. The award may have been made in a purely domestic dispute following an arbitration in which all elements were connected to that one country. The arbitration would then be national, but the award becomes foreign when enforcement is sought outside the country where it was made.

Despite its apparent simplicity, this criterion governing the application of the Convention has raised a number of difficulties. Some are the result of courts in the host jurisdiction taking into account other factors connecting the arbitration with that jurisdiction, leading them to exclude the Convention and to exercise their power to set aside an award which they consider to be "national." Published case law contains very few examples of this kind of confusion: one is a much criticized decision of the Indian Supreme Court, which, in 1992, held that the substance of the dispute before it was governed by Indian law and, on that basis, allowed an ICC award made in London to be set aside in India.[299] Another difficulty

---

[295] CA Rouen, Nov. 13, 1984, *S.E.E.E.*, *supra* note 282.

[296] CA Paris, Nov. 19, 1982, Norsolor v. Pabalk Ticaret Sirketi, 1983 REV. ARB. 465, 3d decision, and the commentary by Berthold Goldman, *Une bataille judiciaire autour de la lex mercatoria – L'affaire Norsolor*, *id.* at 379; for an English translation, see XI Y.B. COM. ARB. 484 (1986); Cass. 1e civ., Oct. 9, 1984, Pabalk Ticaret Sirketi v. Norsolor, 1985 REV. ARB. 431, and B. Goldman's note; 112 J.D.I. 679 (1985), and P. Kahn's note; 1985 REV. CRIT. DIP 551, 2d decision, and B. Dutoit's note; Dalloz, Jur. 101 (1985), and J. Robert's note; *see also* Jean Robert, *Retour sur l'arrêt Pabalk-Norsolor (Civ. 1re, 9 oct. 1984, D. 1985.101)*, Dalloz, Chron. 83 (1985); for an English translation, see 2 J. INT'L ARB. 67 (June 1985), with comments by D. Thompson; XI Y.B. COM. ARB. 484 (1986); 24 I.L.M. 360 (1985), with an introductory note by E. Gaillard; see also the decisions cited by Albert Jan van den Berg in his Commentary on Court Decisions on the New York Conventions appearing in the YEARBOOK COMMERCIAL ARBITRATION, Part V-A.– ¶ 103 (Nationality of the Parties no Criterion); lastly, Luxembourg Court of Appeals, Nov. 24, 1993, Kersa Holding Co. Luxembourg v. Infancourtage, XXI Y.B. COM. ARB. 617, ¶ 5 (1996).

[297] On the international nature of an arbitration, see *supra* paras. 78 *et seq.*

[298] That is, except where the reciprocity reservation has been made; *see infra* para. 261.

[299] National Thermal Power Corp. v. The Singer Corp., May 7, 1992, [1992] 2 S.C.J. 431; 7 INT'L ARB. REP. C1 (June 1992); XVIII Y.B. COM. ARB. 403 (1993); Jan Paulsson, *The New York Convention's Misadventures in India*, 7 INT'L ARB. REP. 18 (June 1992); *comp.* V.S. Deshpande, *"Foreign award" in the 1958 New York*
(continued...)

stems from how the country where the award is made is defined. For example, prior to the 1996 English Arbitration Act, the mere fact that an award was signed by a sole arbitrator in Paris, whereas the arbitration had been held in London, prompted the English courts to exercise their power to review the award under the New York Convention.[300] Happily, Section 3 of the 1996 Act ensures that such a decision cannot recur.[301]

257. — However, Article I, paragraph 1 of the Convention extends the Convention's scope beyond strictly "foreign" awards: the Convention also governs awards which are not considered as domestic awards in the country where their recognition and enforcement are sought. Such awards are, of course, made in the same country as that in which their enforcement is subsequently sought. The Convention allows them to be governed by rules other than the law of that country, either where they are governed by another national law, or where they are "denationalized." They will then be governed by the New York Convention, which is presumed to be more liberal than the local law.[302]

Thus, on June 17, 1983, a United States Federal Court of Appeals held that an arbitral award made in New York involving two foreign entities was not a domestic award and its enforcement in the United States was therefore governed by the New York Convention. The Court considered that such awards are governed by the Convention

> not because [they are] made abroad, but because [they are] made within the legal framework of another country, e.g., pronounced in accordance with a foreign law or involving parties domiciled or having their principal place of business outside the enforcing jurisdiction . . . . We prefer this broader construction because it is more in line with the intended purpose of the Treaty, which was entered into to encourage the recognition and enforcement of international arbitration awards.[303]

---

[299] (...continued)
Convention, 9 J. INT'L ARB. 51 (Dec. 1992); the 1996 Indian Arbitration and Conciliation Ordinance, which uses the definition of foreign awards contained in the New York Convention, should prevent any further difficulties; *see* Jan Paulsson, *La réforme de l'arbitrage en Inde,* 1996 REV. ARB. 597, 601. On this issue, see *infra* paras. 1593 and 1668.

[300] Hiscox v. Outhwaite, (No. 1) [1992] 1 A.C. 562; [1991] 3 All E.R. 641; [1991] 3 W.L.R. 297; [1991] 2 Lloyd's Rep. 435; XVII Y.B. COM. ARB. 599 (1992) (H.L. 1991); Claude Reymond, *Where is an Arbitral Award Made?,* 108 L.Q. REV. 1 (1992); Michael E. Schneider, *L'arrêt de la Chambre des Lords dans l'affaire Hiscox v. Outhwaite,* 1991 BULL. ASA 279.

[301] In this provision, the English legislature adopts a definition of arbitration based on legal rather than purely geographical criteria.

[302] On this notion of "non domestic" awards, see VAN DEN BERG, *supra* note 289, ¶ I–1.5 at 22; Albert Jan van den Berg, *Non-domestic arbitral awards under the 1958 New York Convention,* 2 ARB. INT'L 191 (1986); Albert Jan van den Berg, *The New York Convention: Summary of Court Decisions, in* ASA SPECIAL SERIES NO. 9, THE NEW YORK CONVENTION OF 1958, at 46, especially ¶ 109 at 57 (1996), and the references cited therein.

[303] Bergesen v. Joseph Muller Corp., 710 F.2d 928, 932 (2d Cir. 1983); for a French translation, see 1984 REV. ARB. 393, and P. Courteault's note.

Although the general spirit of this decision was unanimously welcomed,[304] two reservations should be made as to its content: first, it is by no means certain that the fact that both parties are foreign suffices to render such awards "non-national;" second, an award may be foreign as regards the country where it was made without necessarily being governed by another national law. This was the solution reached in two decisions of the Paris Court of Appeals declining jurisdiction, on the ground that an award was "non French," over an action to set aside the award made in France and governed by the ICC Arbitration Rules rather than by a national procedural law. Although this solution was repealed by the 1981 decree on international arbitration, its rationale continues to reflect the position taken in French law: an award made at the outcome of proceedings "which are not those of French law cannot be considered to be French."[305]

Likewise, the Netherlands Supreme Court reversed a decision in which the application of the New York Convention to a foreign award had been made subject to the requirement that the award should be "made in accordance with the law of a particular jurisdiction." The Court held that such an interpretation "had no basis in the Convention."[306] The United States courts have, on at least three occasions, followed the *Bergesen* decision,[307] applying the New York Convention to awards made in the United States, in a case between foreign parties,[308] between an American party and a foreign party,[309] and even in cases between two American parties, where the dispute arose from a contract to be performed outside the United States.[310]

258. — The provisions of Article II of the Convention extend the Convention's scope further still. These provisions are substantive rules directly applicable to arbitration agreements. They are independent of any subsequent procedure for recognition or

---

[304] *See* van den Berg, *Non-domestic arbitral awards under the 1958 New York Convention, supra* note 302, and the references cited therein.

[305] CA Paris, Feb. 21, 1980, General National Maritime Transport Co. v. Götaverken Arendal A.B., 107 J.D.I. 660 (1980), and P. Fouchard's note; 1980 REV. ARB. 524, and F.C. Jeantet's note; Dalloz, Jur. 568 (1980), and J. Robert's note; 1980 REV. CRIT. DIP 763, and E. Mezger's note; for an English translation, see VI Y.B. COM. ARB. 221 (1981); 20 I.L.M. 883 (1981), with an introductory note by F.C. Jeantet. But see *infra* paras. 261 and 265, the two grounds—unsatisfactory in our view—which led the Paris Court of Appeals to reject the application in that case of the New York Convention; CA Paris, Dec. 9, 1980, Aksa v. Norsolor, 1981 REV. ARB. 306, and F.C. Jeantet's note; 1981 REV. CRIT. DIP 545, and E. Mezger's note; for an English translation, see 20 I.L.M. 887 (1981).

[306] Netherlands Supreme Court, Oct. 26, 1973, Société Européene d'Etudes et d'Entreprises v. République Socialiste Fédérative de Yougoslavie, 1974 REV. ARB. 311, 2d decision, and H. Batiffol's note; summary in I Y.B. COM. ARB. 197 (1976).

[307] *Supra* note 303.

[308] *See* Trans Chemical Ltd. v. China Nat'l Mach. Import and Export Corp., 978 F. Supp. 266 (S.D. Tex. 1997); XXIII Y.B. COM. ARB. 995 (1998).

[309] Productos Mercantiles e Industriales, S.A. v. Fabergé USA, Inc., 23 F.3d 41 (2d Cir. 1994); XX Y.B. COM. ARB. 955 (1995); for a French translation, see 1996 REV. ARB. 553, and J.B. Lee's note.

[310] Lander Co. v. MMP Inv., Inc., 107 F.3d 476 (7th Cir. 1997); *see* Georges R. Delaume, *Non-domestic US Awards Qualify for Recognition Under the New York Convention*, 1998 INT'L BUS. L.J. 102.

enforcement of an award, and there is no territorial limitation based on the localization of such agreements or of the arbitration for which they provide.[311]

259. — The New York Convention makes no attempt to define an "arbitral award." However, at the request of the representatives of certain Eastern European countries, who wanted official recognition of their arbitral institutions, the Convention does make it clear that awards can be made not only by "arbitrators appointed for each case," but also by "permanent arbitral bodies to which the parties have submitted."[312]

All other problems of characterization are to be resolved by the courts of each contracting state applying their own law. One such problem concerned *arbitrato irrituale* under Italian law.[313] This form of arbitration, which was designed to avoid the overly restrictive rules of the Italian Code of Civil Procedure, is founded solely on the parties' common intentions, and the arbitrators' decision carries no more legal weight than a contract. The German Federal Court considered that such decisions could neither be recognized nor enforced outside Italy under the New York Convention,[314] but the Italian Supreme Court took the contrary view.[315]

260. — Article I, paragraph 3 of the Convention provides for two reservations which, to the extent they are implemented when signing, ratifying or acceding to the Convention, restrict the Convention's territorial and substantive scope.

261. — The first of these is known as the "reciprocity" reservation. Any signatory may "on the basis of reciprocity declare that it will apply the Convention to the recognition and enforcement of awards made only in the territory of another Contracting State."

This reservation had been made, as of March 31, 1999, by sixty-five of the contracting states. Although it complicates the implementation of the Convention, and despite the fact that its effectiveness is sometimes questionable, it proved impossible to require contracting states to be more open at the time the Convention was adopted. If the influence of the UNCITRAL Model Law continues to grow, and if national legislative reforms continue to relax the conditions governing the international enforcement of arbitral awards, the progress made in the New York Convention will eventually lose its importance. That is why

---

[311] On this point, see *infra* para. 264. See, implicitly, Cass. 1e civ, Oct. 11, 1989, Bomar Oil N.V. v. Entreprise Tunisienne d'Activités Pétrolières (E.T.A.P.), 1989 Bull Civ. I, No. 314, at 209; 1990 REV. ARB. 134, and C. Kessedjian's note; 117 J.D.I. 633 (1990), and E. Loquin's note; for an English translation, see XV Y.B. COM. ARB. 447 (1990); 4 INT'L ARB. REP. A1 (Dec. 1989); *see also* VAN DEN BERG, *supra* note 289, Part I–2, at 56 *et seq.*; Jean-François Poudret and Gabriel Cottier, *Remarques sur l'application de l'article II de la Convention de New York (Arrêt du Tribunal fédéral du 16 janvier 1995)*, 1995 BULL. ASA 383.

[312] *See infra* paras. 810 *et seq.*

[313] *See supra* para. 164.

[314] *Bundesgerichtshof*, Oct. 8, 1981, Compania Italiana di Assicurazioni (COMITAS) S.p.A. v. Schwartzmeer und Ostsee Versicherungsaktien-gesellschaft, VIII Y.B. COM. ARB. 366 (1983).

[315] Italian *Corte di Cassazione*, Sept. 18, 1978, Butera v. Pagnan, IV Y.B. COM. ARB. 296 (1979).

Switzerland chose to withdraw its reciprocity reservation in 1993.[316] Other countries are likely to follow suit. France is an example of a country where the national legislation governing the review of foreign awards (found at Article 1502 of the New Code of Civil Procedure) is more liberal than the equivalent provisions of the New York Convention.[317] As a result, the reciprocity reservation made by France is of no significance.

Further, the reciprocity reservation can only apply to the conditions for recognition and enforcement of foreign awards. It cannot be extended to Article II of the Convention, as the substantive rules contained therein are applicable independently of any recognition or enforcement procedure.

262. — A second reservation is also provided for in Article I, paragraph 3:

> [any State] may also declare that it will apply the Convention only to differences arising out of legal relationships, whether contractual or not, which are considered as commercial under the national law of the State making such declaration.

This is known as the "commercial" reservation. Forty member states had made this reservation as of March 31, 1999. They draw a distinction between commercial and civil relationships and consider that disputes arising from the latter should not be entrusted to private judges to the same extent as the former. As the scope of this reservation is determined by the law of each jurisdiction adopting it, a new area of uncertainty would have arisen, were it not for the fact that the rare court decisions on this point have shown that the courts generally interpret the concept of commerciality fairly broadly.[318] Furthermore, some courts do not apply the commercial reservation so as to exclude the application of the Convention unless one of the parties raises the issue.[319] The same reservation, adopted under the 1923 Geneva Protocol, likewise raised no major difficulties in practice.[320] However, China's Supreme People's Court considers that, as a result of the commercial reservation, "arbitration between a foreign investor and the host country is not included" in the scope of the New York Convention.[321]

As with the reciprocity reservation,[322] some countries have withdrawn the commercial reservation after ratifying the Convention. For instance, by letter dated November 17, 1989

---

[316] Withdrawal by the Federal Council of the reciprocity reservation, which took effect on April 23, 1993, ROLF 1993 III 2439, cited by Poudret and Cottier, *supra* note 311, at 384.

[317] On the existence and consequences of such differences, see *infra* paras. 269 *et seq.*

[318] *See supra* paras. 58 *et seq.* and 72; see, for example, on the position of Indian case law, Supreme Court of India, Feb. 10, 1994, RM Investment & Trading Co. Pvt. Ltd. v. Boeing Co., XXII Y.B. Com. Arb. 710 (1997).

[319] See, for instance, in France, when this reservation was still applicable, CA Paris, June 20, 1980, Clair v. Berardi, 1981 Rev. Arb. 424, and E. Mezger's note.

[320] Van den Berg, *supra* note 289, ¶ I–1.8 at 51.

[321] Circular of 1967, cited by Gerold Herrmann, *Implementing Legislation – The IBA/UNCITRAL Project, in* ASA Special Series No. 9, The New York Convention of 1958, at 140 (1996).

[322] *See supra* para. 261 and note 316.

to the Secretary General of the United Nations,[323] the French government withdrew the commercial reservation which it had made on ratifying the New York Convention in 1959.[324] That decision reflected an intention to give the Convention the widest possible scope and to confirm the rejection made by the French courts of the archaic prohibition on arbitration agreements in civil matters.[325]

263. — There is another, more controversial limitation to the scope of the New York Convention, which is both territorial and substantive. Under Article I, paragraph 1 of the Convention,

> [t]his Convention shall apply to the recognition and enforcement of arbitral awards made in the territory of a State other than the State where the recognition and enforcement of such awards are sought . . . .

Does this mean, as some authors have suggested, that the Convention can never apply in the country where the award was made,[326] and that it can apply only in recognition and enforcement proceedings initiated in another country?

264. — Such a general exclusion seems contrary to the letter and spirit of the Convention.

It is contrary to the letter, because other provisions of the Convention are plainly incompatible with such a restriction. For instance, the same article goes on to introduce an exception covering awards which are not considered as domestic awards in the country where they were made. These awards (the awards themselves, and not only their recognition and enforcement) are governed directly by the New York Convention in the country where they were made, as that country does not consider them to be domestic awards.

Likewise, the application of Article II, which sets out substantive rules for arbitration clauses and submission agreements, does not depend on the existence of a subsequent award, nor on any condition that the award be made in a different country, nor on the issue arising in proceedings to recognize or enforce the award.[327]

Such an exclusion is contrary to the spirit of the Convention because the Convention's aim is to facilitate the international recognition of awards and hence the efficiency of international arbitration. The principles laid down in the Convention as to the conditions for enforcement of foreign awards can therefore be transposed and applied, with the authority inherent in a universal convention, to other scenarios. Thus, the validity of the arbitration

---

[323] Published by Decree No. 90-170 dated Feb. 16, 1990, J.O., Feb. 23, 1990, p. 2344.

[324] *See* Philippe Fouchard, *Convention de New York de 1958 – La France retire sa réserve de commercialité*, 1990 REV. ARB. 210.

[325] On both the short-term and long-term consequences of this measure, see Philippe Fouchard, *La levée par la France de sa réserve de commercialité pour l'application de la Convention de New York*, 1990 REV. ARB. 571.

[326] *See* VAN DEN BERG, *supra* note 289, ¶ I–1.4 at 19.

[327] *See* CA Paris, Jan. 20, 1987, Bomar Oil N.V. v. Entreprise Tunisienne d'Activités Pétrolières (E.T.A.P.), 1987 REV. ARB. 482, and C. Kessedjian's note; 114 J.D.I. 934 (1987), and E. Loquin's note; for an English translation, see XIII Y.B. COM. ARB. 466 (1988), *overturned on other grounds*, Cass. 1e civ., Oct. 11, 1989, *supra* note 311, which, however, also applies Article II of the New York Convention.

agreement (Art. II) or the procedural freedom enjoyed by the parties to an arbitration or by arbitral institutions (Art. V(1)(d)) can be taken into account by the arbitrators in making their award,[328] or by the courts before the award is made. For example, in ruling on an action to set aside an award, a court might observe that the New York Convention rejects the review by the courts of the merits of an award.

265. — Nevertheless, the Paris Court of Appeals, in a 1980 decision concerning an action to set aside an international arbitral award made in Paris, refused to apply the New York Convention to the issue of whether or not the award should be governed by French law. The Court held that:

> the provisions of the New York Convention, destined to facilitate the recognition and enforcement of arbitral awards, are not applicable where the action in Court does not seek the enforcement of an award rendered in an international arbitration.[329]

The same reasoning was reiterated word for word, on two occasions, by the *Cour de cassation*, also with a view to excluding the application of the New York Convention in the context of an action to set aside an award.[330]

266. — We believe the position taken in these cases to be too restrictive. It reflects the current state of French law, although it was implicitly challenged by a 1989 decision of the *Cour de cassation*, which applied Article II of the New York Convention to an action to set aside an award made in France.[331] At any rate, the practical consequences of this position are not unduly harmful. The three actions to set aside described above were all brought prior to the 1981 reform, and the New York Convention was relied on to support the admissibility of those actions, which was an unsettled area at the time. The question no longer arises today because, under the rules introduced by the 1981 decree, an action to set aside is now

---

[328] For an example of the taking into consideration or even the application by arbitrators of the New York Convention, see the 1988 Partial Award in ICC Case No. 5730, Société de lubrifiants Elf Aquitaine v. A.R. Orri, 1992 REV. ARB. 125; 117 J.D.I. 1029 (1990), and observations by Y. Derains; ICC Award No. 6149 (1990), Seller (Korea) v. Buyer (Jordan), XX Y.B. COM. ARB. 41 (1995); *see also* Albert Jan van den Berg, *Should an international arbitrator apply the New York Arbitration Convention of 1958?*, *in* THE ART OF ARBITRATION – ESSAYS ON INTERNATIONAL ARBITRATION – LIBER AMICORUM PIETER SANDERS 39 (J. Schultz and A.J. van den Berg eds., 1982).

[329] CA Paris, Feb. 21, 1980, *Götaverken, supra* note 305, VI Y.B. COM. ARB. 224 (1981).

[330] Cass. 1e civ., May 25, 1983, *Lievremont, supra* note 14; see also, rejecting a petition to overturn CA Paris, Dec. 20, 1984, Commandement des Forces Aériennes de la République Islamique d'Iran v. Bendone Derossi International Ltd., 1985 REV. ARB. 415, 2d decision, and H. Synvet's note (for an English translation, see XII Y.B. COM. ARB. 482 (1987)) and, using the same terms, Cass. 1e civ., May 5, 1987, Commandement des Forces Aériennes de la République Islamique d'Iran v. Bendone Derossi International Ltd., 114 J.D.I. 964 (1987), and B. Oppetit's approving note; 1988 REV. ARB. 137, and H. Synvet's note (for an English translation, see XIV Y.B. COM. ARB. 627 (1989)).

[331] Cass. 1e civ., Oct. 11, 1989, *Bomar Oil, supra* note 311.

available in respect of any award made in France.[332] The situations in which such an action may be commenced are well defined, as is the applicable procedure. As a result, the New York Convention now serves little purpose in France. Its provisions are more restrictive than those of French law and, in light of its Article VII, they have become irrelevant.

267. — Article VII, paragraph 1 contains the final limitation of the scope of the New York Convention:

> The provisions of the present Convention shall not affect the validity of multilateral or bilateral agreements concerning the recognition and enforcement of arbitral awards entered into by the Contracting States nor deprive any interested party of any right he may have to avail himself of an arbitral award in the manner and to the extent allowed by the law or the treaties of the country where such award is sought to be relied upon.

This rule, which is also contained in Article 5 of the 1927 Geneva Convention, is referred to by one commentator as the "more-favourable-right (mfr) provision."[333] It ensures that whenever the New York Convention proves to be less favorable to the recognition and enforcement of a foreign award than the treatment provided for in another treaty, or in the law of the host country, the more favorable treatment shall prevail over the rules of the New York Convention.

This "more-favourable-right provision" provides an innovative solution to two kinds of conflicts.

268. — First, it resolves conflicts between international conventions:[334] the convention which prevails is neither the most recent, nor the most specific, but instead that which is most favorable to enforcement of the award. This ties in with the idea of the "maximum effectiveness" of each treaty. The Swiss Federal Tribunal has applied this principle in order to exclude the provisions of the Franco-Swiss Convention of 1869[335] and thereby give precedence to the New York Convention.[336] Having compared the respective requirements of the two conventions as to the evidence to be submitted by a party seeking enforcement in Switzerland of an award made in France,[337] the Tribunal observed that the New York Convention was more favorable, in so far as it did not require the submission of a certificate issued by the clerk of the court in the country in which the award was made confirming that

---

[332] *See infra* para. 1589.

[333] VAN DEN BERG, *supra* note 289, ¶ 1–4.2 at 82.

[334] On these conflicts, see *supra* paras. 217 *et seq.*

[335] This Convention was terminated by an exchange of letters dated November 6 and 14, 1991 (*see* 119 J.D.I. 509 (1992)).

[336] Swiss Fed. Trib., Mar. 14, 1984, Denysiana v. Jassica, ATF 110 Ib 191; 1984 BULL. ASA 206; 1985 REV. CRIT. DIP 551, 1st decision, and B. Dutoit's note; for an English translation, see XI Y.B. COM. ARB. 536 (1986).

[337] Art. 16 of the Franco-Swiss Convention; Art. IV of the New York Convention.

no objection, appeal or other action had been brought against the award. The Court then referred to Article VII of the New York Convention and stated that:

> It can, therefore, be assumed that France and Switzerland intended to grant the parties, also in the bilateral relations between the two countries, the benefits of the more favorable conditions of the New York Convention concerning recognition and enforcement of awards when the case arises. This solution corresponds to the so-called rule of maximum effectiveness, as was correctly referred to by the lower court. According to this rule, in case of discrepancies between provisions in international conventions regarding the recognition and enforcement of arbitral awards, preference will be given to the provision allowing or making easier such recognition and enforcement, either because of more liberal substantive conditions or because of a simpler procedure. This rule is in conformity with the aim of bilateral or multilateral conventions in this matter, which is to facilitate, as far as possible, recognition and enforcement of arbitral awards.

269. — The second type of conflict avoided through the application of the "more-favourable-right provision" is that between the rules of the New York Convention and those of the law of the contracting state in which the award is to be enforced. The traditional solution to such a conflict, whereby international treaties prevail over national laws, is thus rejected.[338] The contracting states clearly intended that the Convention provide only the minimum level of protection for the beneficiary of the award.

270. — That intention was clearly acknowledged by the French *Cour de cassation* in the *Norsolor* case. Relying on Article V, paragraph 1(e) of the New York Convention, the Paris Court of Appeals had refused to grant enforcement in France of an arbitral award made in Austria, because the award had been set aside by the Vienna Court of Appeals. The *Cour de cassation* reversed this decision, relying instead on Article VII of the Convention and Article 12 of the French New Code of Civil Procedure. The Court held that as a result of the first of these provisions,

> the judge cannot refuse enforcement when his own national legal system permits it and, by virtue of Article 12 of the New Code of Civil Procedure he should, even *sua sponte*, research the matter if such is the case.[339]

Thus, because the ground for setting aside the award in the country where it was made does not appear in the limited list of admissible grounds found in French law (Article 1502

---

[338] For a classic application of this principle, which led the arbitrator to give preference to the New York Convention over the restrictive rules of Egyptian law regarding the conditions of validity of the arbitration clause, see ICC Award No. 4406, rendered in Cairo by Mr. Abdul Hamid El-Ahdab, sole arbitrator, on April 5, 1984, X v. Y, 1986 REV. ARB. 469, and H. Synvet's note; for a commentary, see also ABDUL HAMID EL-AHDAB, L'ARBITRAGE DANS LES PAYS ARABES 984 (1988).

[339] Cass. 1e civ., Oct. 9, 1984, *supra* note 296, 24 I.L.M. 360 (1985).

of the New Code of Civil Procedure), the French courts cannot rely on that setting aside to reject the award. The court must verify itself, on its own initiative if need be, whether the objection allowed by the foreign court as a ground on which to set aside the award would also be accepted by the French courts. The only aspect of the award which had been censured in Vienna was its reference to *lex mercatoria* (although that was ultimately allowed by the Austrian Supreme Court). However, that objection was held unfounded under French law.[340]

This was followed by two further decisions of the *Cour de cassation*. The first was the *Polish Ocean Line* case of 1993.[341] The second was the *Hilmarton* case, where the Court again confirmed that:

> applying Art. VII of the [1958 New York Convention], OTV could rely upon the French law on international arbitration concerning the recognition and enforcement of international arbitration awards rendered abroad, and especially upon Art.1502 NCCP, which does not list the ground provided for in Art. V of the 1958 Convention among the grounds for refusal of recognition and enforcement.[342]

More recently, in the *Chromalloy* case, the United States Federal District Court for the District of Columbia reached a similar conclusion, holding an award set aside in Egypt (where it had been made) to be enforceable in the United States.[343] The same award was also

---

[340] On this issue, generally, see Goldman, *supra* note 296, and the references contained therein to various prior French and Austrian decisions.

[341] Cass. 1e civ., Mar. 10, 1993, Polish Ocean Line v. Jolasry, 1993 REV. ARB. 255, 2d decision, and D. Hascher's note; 120 J.D.I. 360 (1993), 1st decision, and P. Kahn's note; for an English translation, see XIX Y.B. COM. ARB. 662 (1994).

[342] Cass. 1e civ., Mar. 23, 1994, Hilmarton v. OTV, 1994 Bull. Civ. I, No. 104; 1994 REV. ARB. 327, and C. Jarrosson's note; 121 J.D.I. 701 (1994), and E. Gaillard's note; 1994 RTD COM. 702, and observations by J.-C. Dubarry and E. Loquin; 1995 REV. CRIT. DIP 356, and B. Oppetit's note; for an English translation, see XX Y.B. COM. ARB. 663, 665 (1995); 9 INT'L ARB. REP. E1 (May 1994), rejecting the application to overturn CA Paris, Dec. 19, 1991, Hilmarton v. OTV, 1993 REV. ARB. 300; for an English translation, see XIX Y.B. COM. ARB. 655 (1994). After these decisions, the extraordinary resistance put up by the Versailles Court of Appeals (June 29, 1995, OTV v. Hilmarton, 2 decisions, 1995 REV. ARB. 639, and C. Jarrosson's note; 123 J.D.I. 120 (1996), and E. Gaillard's note) was rightly condemned by the *Cour de cassation* (Cass. 1e civ., June 10, 1997, 1997 REV. ARB. 376, and P. Fouchard's note; 124 J.D.I. 1033, and E. Gaillard's note; for an English translation, see XXII Y.B. COM. ARB. 696 (1997); 12 INT'L ARB. REP. 11 (July 1997)). See also, in favor of Article 1502 of the French New Code of Civil Procedure generally having priority over Article V of the New York Convention, CA Paris, Feb. 24, 1994, Ministère tunisien de l'équipement v. Bec Frères, 1995 REV. ARB. 275, and Y. Gaudemet's note; for an English translation, see XXII Y.B. COM. ARB. 682 (1997).

[343] *In re* Arbitration of Certain Controversies between Chromalloy Aeroservices v. the Arab Republic of Egypt, 939 F. Supp. 907 (D.D.C. 1996); 11 INT'L ARB. REP. C64 (Aug. 1996); XXII Y.B. COM. ARB. 1001 (1997); 35 I.L.M. 1359 (1996); for a French translation, see 1997 REV. ARB. 439. For favorable commentary, see Gary H. Sampliner, *Enforcement Of Foreign Arbitral Awards After Annulment In Their Country Of Origin*, 11 INT'L ARB. REP. 22 (Sept. 1996); Jan Paulsson, *Rediscovering The N.Y. Convention: Further Reflections On Chromalloy*, 12 INT'L ARB. REP. 20 (Apr. 1997); for critical commentary, see Hamid G. Gharavi, *Chromalloy: Another View*, 12 INT'L ARB. REP. 21 (Jan. 1997), and *The Legal Inconsistencies of Chromalloy*, 12 INT'L ARB.

(continued...)

held to be enforceable in France.[344] The 1961 European Convention had already opened the way for this development.[345]

The international co-ordination of judicial control over arbitral awards, which the New York Convention sought to achieve, is impaired as a consequence of this case law, as an award set aside in the country where it was made may be declared enforceable in another country.[346] However, given the existence of differing views on the grounds for setting aside or refusing enforcement of an award, there is no reason why the conceptions of the seat of the arbitration should prevail over those of the place of enforcement of the award. This situation also begs the question of whether it is worth having an action to set aside awards in countries where they were made.[347]

Article VII of the New York Convention has also been applied in France and other countries to allow more favorable provisions of national law to prevail over the Convention itself.[348] It will undoubtedly apply increasingly often in the future, as the New York Convention becomes more outdated and recent arbitration legislation becomes more favorable to the recognition and enforcement of foreign awards.[349]

---

[343](...continued)
REP. 21 (May 1997); Eric A. Schwartz, *A Comment on Chromalloy – Hilmarton, à l'américaine*, 14 J. INT'L ARB. 125 (June 1997); Jean-François Poudret, *Quelle solution pour en finir avec l'affaire Hilmarton? Réponse à Philippe Fouchard*, 1998 REV. ARB. 7.

[344] CA Paris, Jan. 14, 1997, *République arabe d'Egypte*, *supra* note 252.

[345] On this Convention and its Article IX, see *infra* paras. 274, 285 and 1714 *et seq.*

[346] *See* B. Oppetit, note following Cass. 1e civ., Mar. 23, 1994, Hilmarton v. OTV, 1995 REV. CRIT. DIP 356; Bruno Leurent, *Reflections on the International Effectiveness of Arbitration Awards*, 12 ARB. INT'L 269 (1996).

[347] On this issue, generally, see Philippe Fouchard, *La portée internationale de l'annulation de la sentence arbitrale dans son pays d'origine*, 1997 REV. ARB. 329; Emmanuel Gaillard, *Enforcement of Awards Set Aside in the Country of Origin: The French Experience*, *in* ICCA CONGRESS SERIES NO. 9, IMPROVING THE EFFICIENCY OF ARBITRATION AGREEMENTS AND AWARDS: 40 YEARS OF APPLICATION OF THE NEW YORK CONVENTION 505 (A.J. van den Berg ed., 1999); Emmanuel Gaillard, *L'exécution des sentences annulées dans leur pays d'origine*, 125 J.D.I. 645 (1998); Mohamed Salah, *Faut-il réviser la Convention de New York pour la reconnaissance et l'exécution des sentences arbitrales?*, 1997 DALLOZ AFF. 1237; Sébastien Besson and Luc Pittet, *La reconnaissance à l'étranger d'une sentence annulée dans son Etat d'origine – Réflexions à la suite de l'affaire Hilmarton*, 1998 BULL. ASA 498; Jan Paulsson, *Enforcing Arbitral Awards Notwithstanding a Local Standard Annulment (LSA)*, ICC BULLETIN, Vol. 9, No. 1, at 14 (1998); Jan Paulsson, *L'exécution des sentences arbitrales dans le monde de demain*, 1998 REV. ARB. 637; Philippe Fouchard, *Suggestions pour accroître l'efficacité internationale des sentences arbitrales*, 1998 REV. ARB. 653.

[348] In Germany, prior to the 1997 reform, see *Oberlandesgericht* of Hamm, Nov. 2, 1983, X v. Y, XIV Y.B. COM. ARB. 629 (1989). For a commentary by A.J. van den Berg, see XIV Y.B. COM. ARB. 609 (1989). See also, on the application of a more favorable provision of German law, *Bundesgerichtshof*, Mar. 26, 1987, Swiss and German buyer v. German seller, XIII Y.B. COM. ARB. 471 (1988). For other examples by German and Dutch courts, see XXI Y.B. COM. ARB. 514 (1996); in France, see also CA Paris, Oct. 23, 1997, Inter-Arab Investment Guarantee Corp. (IAIGC) v. Banque arabe et internationale d'investissements SA (BAII), 1998 REV. ARB. 143, and P. Fouchard's note.

[349] For a more exhaustive analysis of the relationship between the New York Convention and French law, see Jacques Béguin, *Le droit français de l'arbitrage international et la Convention de New York du 10 juin 1958*, *in* PROCEEDINGS OF THE 1ST INTERNATIONAL COMMERCIAL ARBITRATION CONFERENCE, *supra* note 224, at 217.

271. — The rule laid down in Article VII, paragraph 1 of the Convention, has raised another difficulty in practice. One author argues that if a party applying for enforcement chooses, on the basis of that provision, to rely on domestic law or on another treaty, it can no longer rely on any provisions of the New York Convention.[350] However, in support of this view, he refers only to an ambiguous decision of the Düsseldorf Court of Appeals from 1971. More recently, a German court of appeals had no hesitation about simultaneously applying the provisions of both the German New Code of Civil Procedure and the New York Convention to the enforcement of a foreign award.[351] Similarly, we saw above that where the Swiss Federal Tribunal held that, in the case of competing treaty provisions concerning the recognition and enforcement of arbitral awards, precedence should be given to "the provision allowing or making easier such recognition and enforcement," it implicitly accepted a fragmented application of two competing systems.[352]

In fact, there seems to be little justification for this suggested "all-or-nothing" condition. It is not provided for in Article VII, which imposes no restrictions on the application of the most favorable rule. Admittedly, one could argue that Article II, because it applies directly to arbitration agreements independently of any recognition or enforcement proceedings, is not covered by the provisions of Article VII. However, no justification of this restrictive view can be found in the intentions of the authors of the Convention, whose sole aim was to facilitate the international enforcement of arbitral awards. There is no reason why this should not be achieved with the support of national laws, even on a partial basis, if those laws are more favorable in some respects than the Convention itself. In the future, the combination of national laws and the Convention will become increasingly important, with national laws becoming more liberal.[353] The New York Convention will itself come to represent only the minimum, universally acceptable standard of harmonization. To prevent the Convention from playing such a role would be to deprive it of its most vital function.

This co-ordination between the New York Convention and national law is both necessary and entirely feasible.[354] The only limitation is the more important requirement of consistency, which we have already seen in the context of conflicts of conventions.[355] In France, for instance, there is total compatibility between French law on arbitration and the New York Convention: in 1981, the principle that an award can be set aside in the country in which it was made was retained. As enforcement procedures are governed by the national law of each country, and as the admissible grounds for actions against the award under Article 1502 of the French New Code of Civil Procedure and Article V of the Convention are perfectly compatible, there is no risk of inconsistency. Because the control exercised by the French courts over an award is more liberal than that provided for in the New York Convention,

---

[350] VAN DEN BERG, *supra* note 289, ¶ 1–4.2.3 at 85 and note 172, at 180.

[351] *Oberlandesgericht* of Hamm, Nov. 2, 1983, *supra* note 348.

[352] Swiss Fed. Trib., Mar. 14, 1984, *Denysiana*, *supra* note 336, XI Y.B. COM. ARB. 538 (1986); *see supra* para. 268.

[353] *See supra* paras. 26 *et seq.*

[354] As regards French law, see Béguin, *supra* note 349.

[355] *See supra* para. 223.

French law will be substituted for the Convention increasingly frequently, without causing the slightest difficulty.

272. — The authors of the New York Convention thus clearly sensed that the rules they were drafting would eventually be considered too restrictive in some areas. Forty years after the adoption of the Convention, its weaknesses have certainly become apparent. In fact, serious consideration was given to revising the Convention during the first UNCITRAL projects on arbitration.[356] It was instead decided to seek to have the Convention ratified by the greatest possible number of states. Patient efforts to promote the Convention have paid off, with it now binding more than one hundred and twenty countries and more continuing to ratify it. The ecumenical nature of the Convention is clear. However, its application in practice does give rise to a number of difficulties, usually resulting from either the specific characteristics of national procedure or the courts' lack of experience in the field of arbitration. Improved international coordination is thus essential and, in 1995, UNCITRAL began taking steps to achieve this.[357] UNCITRAL no longer, however, rules out the drafting of a new convention.[358]

The New York Convention thus remains, for the time being, an instrument permitting cautious harmonization through being acceptable to the largest possible number of countries. Those who wish to reinforce the autonomy and efficiency of international arbitration can move onwards, and they often do so, either unilaterally or by entering into regional conventions.

3° Regional Conventions

273. — There are a number of regional conventions on international arbitration, many of which were established after the introduction of the New York Convention. However, only certain of these regional conventions have made significant progress when compared to that achieved by the New York Convention.

a) The European Convention of April 21, 1961

274. — Signed in Geneva on April 21, 1961, the European Convention is one of the few regional conventions to have sought to go further than the New York Convention, and to have succeeded in doing so. Its proponents recognized that international commercial

---

[356] *See supra* para. 200.

[357] *Report of the United Nations Commission on International Trade Law on the work of its thirtieth session – 12-30 May 1997*, GAOR, 52d Sess., Supp. No. 17, Chapter VI, "Monitoring implementation of the 1958 New York Convention", ¶¶ 257 *et seq.* at 55, U.N. Doc. A/52/17 (1997).

[358] *Id.*, ¶ 259. On this issue, see Salah, *supra* note 347; Jan Paulsson, *Towards Minimum Standards of Enforcement: Feasibility of a Model Law, in* ICCA CONGRESS SERIES NO. 9, IMPROVING THE EFFICIENCY OF ARBITRATION AGREEMENTS AND AWARDS: 40 YEARS OF APPLICATION OF THE NEW YORK CONVENTION (A.J. van den Berg ed., 1999).

arbitration was obstructed, in the stages prior to enforcement of the award, in a number of ways. They provided original solutions to those problems, often based on specific substantive rules and underlining the independence of international arbitration from national laws.

275. — The origins of the European Convention in fact pre-dated the New York Conference. For several years, the Economic Commission for Europe of the United Nations had assigned a number of experts to draft general conditions of sale which covered a variety of products and were specifically intended for East-West trade within Europe. In 1954, a special working group on arbitration was set up to investigate the archaic and divergent aspects of national laws which were compromising the efficiency of international arbitration in Europe. A list was compiled, empirical solutions were devised, and it was eventually decided that these solutions should be published, not in a set of optional arbitration rules,[359] but in a full international convention. The first draft was prepared in 1959.[360] Following a ministerial meeting which opened on April 10, 1961 in Geneva, involving representatives of twenty-two countries, the Convention was adopted and signed on April 21, 1961 by the representatives of sixteen countries. Two more countries also signed it before December 31, 1961.

The Convention entered into force on January 7, 1964. Its provisions on arbitration are contained in nine articles and an annex.[361]

By March 31, 1999, twenty-eight countries were bound by the Convention.[362] Only one signatory country (Finland) had not ratified it. All of the former European socialist states (except Albania) are bound. In Western Europe, however, countries such as the United Kingdom and the Netherlands are missing. Two non-European states (Burkina Faso and Cuba) are also parties. Bearing in mind the regional context in which it was prepared and the fact that the New York Convention stole the limelight three years earlier, the European Convention has been successful on the whole. Since 1990, it has been the subject of regular reports in the Yearbook Commercial Arbitration, which analyze the interpretation and application of the Convention by the countries bound by it.[363]

---

[359] On these rules, which were subsequently adopted, see *supra* para. 196.

[360] On this legislative history, see FOUCHARD, *supra* note 205, ¶ 69, and the references cited therein.

[361] For the text and the List of Contracting States, including the dates of ratification, accession or succession, see *infra* Annex V.

[362] The updated list of Contracting States has been published yearly since 1988 in the YEARBOOK COMMERCIAL ARBITRATION, Part V – B.

[363] Dominique T. Hascher, *European Convention on International Commercial Arbitration of 1961 – Commentary*, XX Y.B. COM. ARB. 1006 (1995); for the most recent decision, see *Oberlandesgericht* Hamburg, Nov. 15, 1995, German party v. Austrian GmbH, XXI Y.B. COM. ARB. 845 (1996).

276. — Commentators of the European Convention[364] are unanimous in the view that it has made an important contribution to the development of international commercial arbitration law, through both its method and its content.

277. — As far as its method is concerned, the European Convention was the first international instrument to treat international commercial arbitration as a whole, and consequently to provide it with rules directly governing all of its various stages.

278. — In order to do so, it was necessary to define international commercial arbitration and to determine the scope of the Convention. Article I thus provides as follows:

> This Convention shall apply:
> (*a*) to arbitration agreements concluded for the purpose of settling disputes arising from international trade between physical or legal persons having, when concluding the agreement, their habitual place of residence or their seat in different Contracting States;
> (*b*) to arbitral procedures and awards based on agreements referred to in paragraph 1(*a*) above.

This provision defines the international nature of the arbitration by reference to the dispute and in economic terms, combined with the legal criterion of the seat or residence of the parties.[365] This is the most appropriate method for providing international arbitration with specific rules adapted to its needs.[366] "International trade" should not be confined by a narrow notion of "trade." It is characterized by "a movement of goods, services and currencies across borders," to quote an *ad hoc* award. In that award, the Convention was applied to a protocol entered into by a German company, which was taking a shareholding in a Belgian company and participating in its restructuring, management and marketing. The arbitral tribunal considered that this joint venture was an international trade transaction, despite the involvement of the Belgian government and the political motivation for the deal (helping to restructure the Belgian iron and steel industry).[367] An even wider interpretation

---

[364] *See, e.g.*, Jean Robert, *La convention européenne sur l'arbitrage commercial international signée à Genève le 21 avril 1961*, Dalloz, Chron. 173 (1961); Lazare Kopelmanas, *La place de la Convention européenne sur l'arbitrage commercial international du 21 avril 1961 dans l'évolution du droit international de l'arbitrage*, 1961 AFDI 331; P.I. Benjamin, *The European Convention on International Commercial Arbitration*, 37 BRIT. Y.B. INT'L L. 478 (1961); Peter Benjamin, *The Work of the Economic Commission for Europe in the Field of International Commercial Arbitration*, 7 INT'L & COMP. L.Q. 22 (1958); David A. Godwin Sarre, *European Commercial Arbitration*, 1961 J. BUS. L. 352; Frédéric-Edouard Klein, *La Convention européenne sur l'arbitrage commercial international*, 1962 REV. CRIT. DIP 621; Pierre Jean Pointet, *The Geneva Convention on International Commercial Arbitration*, *in* UNION INTERNATIONALE DES AVOCATS, INTERNATIONAL COMMERCIAL ARBITRATION, Vol. III, at 263 (P. Sanders ed., 1965); FOUCHARD, *supra* note 205.

[365] *See infra* para. 279.

[366] *See supra* paras. 98 *et seq.*

[367] Rendered in Lausanne on November 18, 1983, Claude Reymond presiding, Benteler v. Etat belge, 1984 [BELG.] JOURN. TRIB. 230; 1989 REV. ARB. 339, and D. Hascher's note; *see also* Hascher, *supra* note 363, at 1012.

of "international trade" is possible[368]—and was used in an earlier award[369]—where the 1961 Convention was applied to a lease of office premises granted in France to an international organization.

279. — The Convention will only apply where the parties are located in different contracting states. This significant geographical limitation is a result of the geo-political context in which the Convention was prepared, and of the important concessions made to East-West arbitration or, at least, to intra-European arbitration. A few national courts and arbitral tribunals have not interpreted this requirement strictly[370] by applying, for instance, the Convention where only one party was a resident of or had its headquarters in a contracting state,[371] or where both parties were located in the same contracting state,[372] or by wrongly deciding that "the only relevant criterion is the parties' nationality."[373] However, a majority of decisions have given the Convention an orthodox interpretation, either by applying it between parties having their headquarters in different contracting states,[374] or by refusing to apply it where that condition was not satisfied.[375]

It is understandable that the European Convention should have been construed broadly by the courts and arbitrators.[376] Provided that they do not transgress a clearly contradictory rule of national law, they are generally at liberty to consider the Convention as setting forth new rules adapted to the needs of international arbitration, and to apply them on that basis.

280. — Unlike the New York Convention, the seat of the arbitration is not a factor in the determination of whether the European Convention should apply. In other words, it is immaterial whether the arbitration is to be held, or has been held, in the territory of a contracting state.[377] This novel approach reflects a wider view of international arbitration, no longer confined to—and in fact largely ignoring— the enforcement of an award in a country other than that where it was made.

---

[368] *See, e.g.,* D. Hascher, note following the Nov. 18, 1983 award in *Benteler, supra* note 367.

[369] ICC Award No. 2091 (May 14, 1972), International organization A v. Company B, 1975 REV. ARB. 252, and P. Fouchard's note.

[370] *See* Hascher, *supra* note 363, at 1010.

[371] Spanish *Tribunal Supremo,* Oct. 8, 1981, X S.A. v. Y, VIII Y.B. COM. ARB. 406 (1983); *Tribunal Supremo,* Oct. 7, 1986, T.H. v. Dominguez, XIV Y.B. COM. ARB. 708 (1989).

[372] Italian *Corte di Cassazione,* May 18, 1978, Società Atlas General Timbers S.p.A. v. Agenzia Concordia Line S.p.A., V Y.B. COM. ARB. 267 (1980); ICC Award No. 2091 (May 14, 1972), *supra* note 369.

[373] CA Rouen, Nov. 13, 1984, *S.E.E.E., supra* note 282.

[374] Nov. 18, 1983 award in *Benteler, supra* note 367.

[375] *Oberlandesgericht* Düsseldorf, Nov. 8, 1971, Dutch seller v. German (F.R.) buyer, II Y.B. COM. ARB. 237 (1977); *Corte di Appello* of Venice, May 21, 1976, S.A. Pando Compania Naviera v. S.a.S. Filmo, III Y.B. COM. ARB. 277 (1978); *Corte di Appello* of Trieste, July 2, 1982, Jassica S.A. v. Ditta Polojaz, X Y.B. COM. ARB. 462 (1985); CA Paris, Nov. 19, 1982, *Norsolor, supra* note 296.

[376] For an analysis of awards referring to it, see Hascher, *supra* note 363, at 1013.

[377] *See* Italian *Corte di Cassazione,* Feb. 8, 1982, Fratellli Damiano s.n.c. v. August Tropfer & Co., IX Y.B. COM. ARB. 418 (1984).

281. — The Convention is intended to provide specific rules for all stages of international arbitration, from the arbitration agreement (Art. II) to the award (Arts. VII, VIII and IX), and including the composition of the arbitral tribunal and the arbitral procedure (Arts. III, IV and Annex). Thus, the recognition and enforcement of the award by the courts, on which the New York Convention was heavily focused, is considered only very indirectly. Although the involvement of the courts is not overlooked, the main goal is to limit that involvement, with emphasis placed on the jurisdiction of the arbitrators (Arts. V and VI) and on the autonomy of the parties and arbitral institutions in organizing the arbitration (Art. IV and Annex). Finally, the choice of law method is used only to the extent required to avoid contradicting the New York Convention and to provide the courts, when their intervention is required, with acceptable, unified choice of law rules (Arts. VI, VII and IX). The European Convention relies far more on specific substantive rules in promoting the independence of international arbitration from national legal systems and in removing the influence of obstacles found in some national laws.

282. — The content of the Convention is quite varied, and its empiricism and novelty are striking. However, it does focus on arbitration in Europe, and above all on East-West arbitration.

283. — A number of national rules were rejected as being inappropriate. This was the case with the rule prohibiting governments or public entities (Art. II) from concluding arbitration agreements (which at the time, applied in countries such as France and Belgium), and with the rule, then found in Italy, preventing foreigners from acting as arbitrators (Art. III). Other national rules, such as the obligation to state the grounds on which an award was made, were found to be too rigid, and they were therefore qualified (Art. VIII).

284. — In the context of East-West trade at the time of the Convention, arbitration was the only dispute resolution method acceptable to both sides. It was therefore simplified, and thus removed as far as possible from the influence of national legal systems. This is apparent from Article VII, for example, which provides that the parties or, subsidiarily, the arbitrators are free to choose the law applicable to the substance of the dispute, and that such choice may include trade usages.

The general principle is that the parties are free to organize the arbitration (Art. IV). They control the composition of the arbitral tribunal and the arbitral procedure. They may opt for institutional arbitration, or an *ad hoc* arbitration with the intervention of a pre-appointed third party in the event that the procedure comes to a standstill. That third party will be the President of the chamber of commerce of the seat of the arbitration or of the defendant's jurisdiction, or a "Special Committee" in which East and West are equally represented (Art. IV and Annex). This is a complex system, designed chiefly to encourage the parties to reach an agreement directly. For political reasons, it was decided that the role of providing assistance would not be given to the courts. In this respect, it is clear that the European

Convention is somewhat outdated[378] and the Economic Commission for Europe is taking steps to revise it.[379] UNCITRAL has suggested that when the Convention is revised, its most successful features might be made available to a universal membership, those features including provisions missing from the New York Convention.[380]

285. — The intervention of the courts in the course of the arbitration or after the award has been made is also addressed with some caution. The courts are required to respect the arbitrators' jurisdiction to determine their own jurisdiction (Arts. V and VI), and the effects of any setting aside of the award are limited by Article IX, which constitutes an express derogation from the New York Convention.[381] These various rules enhance the efficiency and autonomy of international arbitration as compared to the regime contained in the New York Convention.

286. — The negotiators of the European Convention were convinced that they could and should go further than their New York counterparts, but without harming the effectiveness of the New York Convention. They therefore decided that the provisions of the European Convention would not affect the validity of existing or future multilateral or bilateral agreements (Art. X(7)). In fact, all the European countries bound by the European Convention are also bound by the New York Convention. As a result, their courts treat the two conventions as complementary instruments,[382] which are "simultaneously" applicable.[383]

287. — However, the scope of the European Convention has been somewhat restricted by the subsequent impact of two other European regional conventions, one applicable in Western Europe,[384] the other in Eastern Europe.[385]

b) The Paris Agreement of December 17, 1962

288. — The reference in the European Convention to the President of a national chamber of commerce and a Special Committee with East-West parity as a subsidiary mechanism for

---

[378] *See infra* para. 931.

[379] *United Nations, Economic and Social Council, Economic Commission for Europe, Committee for Trade, Industry and Enterprise Development, Working Party on International Contract Practices in Industry (Forty-sixth, 29 September – 1 October 1997)*, Report of the Forty-sixth Session, at paragraph 14, U.N. Doc. TRADE/WP.5/62 (Oct. 24, 1997).

[380] UNCITRAL Report, *supra* note 357, ¶ 259.

[381] On the application of this provision, see Austrian Supreme Court (*Oberster Gerichtshof*), Oct. 20, 1993, Radenska v. Kajo; for an English translation, see XX Y.B. Com. Arb. 1051 (1995); for a French translation, see 1998 Rev. Arb. 419, and P. Lastenouse and P. Senkovic's note; 125 J.D.I. 1003 (1998); *see infra* paras. 1714 *et seq.*

[382] On the relationship between the two Conventions, see Van den Berg, *supra* note 289, ¶ I–4.4.2 at 92.

[383] *See* CA Rouen, Nov. 13, 1984, *S.E.E.E.*, *supra* note 282.

[384] The 1962 Paris Agreement; *see infra* para. 288.

[385] The 1972 Moscow Convention; *see infra* para. 292.

organizing arbitration proceedings was initially designed with East-West arbitration in mind. It therefore did not meet the specific needs of arbitrations between parties from Western European countries alone. Several of these countries, under the aegis of the Council of Europe, sought to benefit from the freedom which they enjoyed under Article X, paragraph 7 of the European Convention, so as to create an exception to the European Convention for disputes between parties located in their territories.[386]

That was the purpose of the "Agreement Relating to Application of the European Convention on International Commercial Arbitration," done in Paris on December 17, 1962. It entered into force on January 25, 1965 and, as of March 31, 1999, had been ratified by eight European countries.[387] If the European Convention is eventually revised, Central and Eastern European countries could then be invited to accede to the Paris Agreement.

289. — The Paris Agreement provides that paragraphs 2 to 7 of Article IV of the European Convention shall not apply in relations between parties established in contracting states. It also stipulates that, in the event that the parties encounter any difficulty with regard to the composition or operation of the arbitral tribunal, the most diligent party shall apply to the "competent authority," with no further indication as to what this might be. The French text is hardly more explicit: it refers to "the competent judicial authority."[388]

The vagueness of this provision, and the involvement of the Council of Europe in the field of arbitration, are explained by the fact that the Council was then working on the draft of what was to become the 1966 Strasbourg Convention.

c) The Strasbourg Convention of January 20, 1966

290. — In preparing the Strasbourg Convention, the Council of Europe had a different perspective from that of the drafters of the 1961 European Convention. The aim was to produce a genuine uniform law, intended to govern both domestic and international arbitration in countries incorporating it into their legislation.[389] This culminated in the adoption of the "European Convention Providing a Uniform Law on Arbitration"[390] in Strasbourg on January 20, 1966. The uniform law consists of 31 articles forming annex I of the introductory Convention which, in eight of its articles and in two further annexes, extended the reservations available to signatory states and the issues left within their jurisdiction. To bring the project to a close, the Convention's authors ultimately had to make a number of concessions to national idiosyncrasies.

---

[386] *See* FOUCHARD, *supra* note 205, ¶ 454 at 286.

[387] For the text and the List of Contracting States, see *infra* Annex V.

[388] On these issues concerning the constitution of the arbitral tribunal, see *infra* paras. 828 *et seq.*

[389] On this draft, see P. Jenard, *Draft European Convention Providing a Uniform Law on Arbitration,* in UNION INTERNATIONALE DES AVOCATS, *supra* note 204, Vol. III, at 371.

[390] E.T.S. No. 56; the text of the Convention is reprinted in REGISTER OF TEXTS, *supra* note 202, Vol. II, at 65; MULTILATERAL CONVENTIONS AND OTHER INSTRUMENTS ON ARBITRATION 161 (Ass. Italiana per l'Arbitrato ed., 1974).

291. — However, the Convention has not entered into force and is unlikely to do so. It was signed by only two countries: Austria and Belgium, and Belgium was the only country to ratify it. Belgium thus resigned itself to introducing the Convention unilaterally into its own legislation. The Convention now forms Part VI of the Belgian Judicial Code.[391] Belgium subsequently amended its arbitration legislation in 1985[392] and in 1998.[393]

d) The Moscow Convention of May 26, 1972

292. — Under the auspices of a different regional organization, namely the Council for Mutual Economic Assistance (CMEA), the "Convention on the Settlement by Arbitration of Civil Law Disputes Resulting from Economic, Scientific and Technical Co-operation" was prepared and then signed in Moscow on May 26, 1972. It entered into force on August 13, 1973. Until 1992, most of its members remained bound by it.[394]

293. — The aim of the Convention was to allocate jurisdiction between the Arbitration Courts attached to the Chambers of Commerce of each socialist country over disputes between the economic organizations of those countries.[395] However, the Moscow Convention has not survived the dismantling of the CMEA. Beginning in 1994, most of the countries bound by the Convention repealed it, and the new states of the former Soviet Union have generally refused to recognize it.[396] In theory, countries such as Cuba and Mongolia may still be bound by the Convention, although most commentators consider that it is no longer in effect.[397]

---

[391] Law of July 4, 1972, see *supra* para. 158. *See also* HUYS AND KEUTGEN, *supra* note 37, and the text of Part VI, at 656.

[392] *See supra* para. 158.

[393] *See supra* para. 158.

[394] These members were Bulgaria, Cuba, Hungary, Mongolia, Poland, Romania, the successor states to Czechoslovakia and the Commonwealth of Independent States, the latter by decision of their Heads of State in Kiev of March 20, 1992; *see* Strohbach, *supra* note 77; Eva Horváth, *Arbitration in Hungary – The Problematics of the Moscow Convention*, 10 J. INT'L ARB. 17 (Mar. 1993).

[395] For an English translation by UNCITRAL, see 13 I.L.M. 5 (1974); for an unofficial French translation, see 1973 REV. ARB. 111; for a commentary, see Jerzy Jakubowski, *La Convention de Moscou du 29 mai 1972 sur le règlement des litiges par voie d'arbitrage*, 1973 REV. ARB. 59; Octave Capatina, *L'arbitrage du commerce extérieur selon la Convention de Moscou de 1972*, 102 J.D.I. 503 (1975); Henrik Trammer, *La Convention de Moscou sur l'arbitrage du 26 mai 1972, in* COMMERCIAL ARBITRATION – ESSAYS IN MEMORIAM EUGENIO MINOLI 517 (1974); Heinz Strohbach, *National Reports – General Introduction*, I Y.B. COM. ARB. 4 (1976); Sergei N. Lebedev, *International Commercial Arbitration in the Socialist Countries Members of the CMEA, in* COLLECTED COURSES OF THE HAGUE ACADEMY OF INTERNATIONAL LAW, Vol. 158, Year 1977, Part V, at 87.

[396] *See* Strohbach, *supra* note 77 and, more recently, the very exhaustive and well-informed article by Tadeusz Szurski, *The Problems and Future of the Moscow Convention, in* ICC BULLETIN, SPECIAL SUPPLEMENT, INTERNATIONAL COMMERCIAL ARBITRATION IN EUROPE 131 (1994); *see also* Staikov, *supra* note 80; Horváth, *Arbitration in Hungary*, *supra* note 89.

[397] Peter Schlosser, *Chronique de jurisprudence allemande*, 1995 REV. ARB. 663, 665.

e) Inter-American Conventions

294. — Latin America is a region which had both a number of important international treaties on the private international law of judicial co-operation, and a traditional hostility towards international arbitration.

The most important of these treaties are the two Montevideo treaties on procedure, dated January 11, 1889, and March 19, 1940 (the latter concerning the enforcement of arbitral awards),[398] the Convention on Private International Law of February 20, 1928, concerning submission agreements and the enforcement of foreign arbitral awards,[399] and the Inter-American Convention on Extraterritorial Validity of Foreign Judgments and Arbitral Awards, signed in Montevideo on May 8, 1979.[400] For the purposes of recognition and enforcement, these four texts assimilate awards made in a contracting state with court judgments delivered in that country.

295. — Until recently, Latin American countries showed little interest in the global conventions: only one, Brazil, ratified the Geneva Protocol of 1923, and none ratified the Geneva Convention of 1927. Although the majority of them are now bound by the New York Convention, only four were bound in 1975. It was then that, under the aegis of the Organization of American States (OAS), they adopted the "Inter-American Convention on International Commercial Arbitration." This Convention was signed on January 30, 1975, in Panama, and is now in force in fifteen Latin American countries (Argentina, Brazil, Chile, Colombia, Costa Rica, Ecuador, El Salvador, Guatemala, Honduras, Mexico, Panama, Paraguay, Peru, Uruguay and Venezuela) and, since October 27, 1990, in the United States.[401]

---

[398] Treaty Concerning the Union of South American States in Respect of Procedural Law, signed at Montevideo at the First South American Congress on Private International Law, on January 11, 1889, REGISTER OF TEXTS, *supra* note 202, Vol. II, at 5. Treaty on International Procedural Law, signed at Montevideo at the Second South American Congress on Private International Law, on March 19, 1940, 37 AM. J. INT'L L. 116 (1943); REGISTER OF TEXTS, *supra* note 202, Vol. II, at 21.

[399] Commonly known as the Code Bustamante, 86 L.N.T.S. 246 (1929); REGISTER OF TEXTS, *supra* note 202, Vol. II, at 18.

[400] *See* ICC BULLETIN, SPECIAL SUPPLEMENT, INTERNATIONAL COMMERCIAL ARBITRATION IN LATIN AMERICA 122 (ICC Publication No. 580E, 1997). For an analysis, see Dominique Hascher, *Enforcement of Arbitral Awards – The New York, Panama and Montevideo Conventions, id.* at 107.

[401] *See infra* Annex VI; *see* Philippe Fouchard, *La Convention interaméricaine sur l'arbitrage commercial international (Panama, 30 janvier 1975)*, 1977 REV. ARB. 203; Charles Robert Norberg, *General Introduction to Inter-American Commercial Arbitration*, III Y.B. COM. ARB. 1 (1978); Hugo Caminos, *The Inter-American Convention on International Commercial Arbitration*, 3 ICSID REV. – FOREIGN INV. L.J. 107 (1988); van den Berg, *supra* note 115; RUBEN B. SANTOS BELANDRO, ARBITRAJE COMERCIAL INTERNACIONAL – TENDENCIAS Y PERSPECTIVAS (1988); Joseph Jackson, Jr., *The 1975 Inter-American Convention on International Commercial Arbitration: Scope, Application and Problems*, 8 J. INT'L ARB. 91 (Sept. 1991); Fernando Mantilla Serrano, *Nouvelles de l'arbitrage en Amérique latine*, 1995 REV. ARB. 552.

296. — The Panama Convention is a fairly faithful reproduction of the New York Convention (Arts. 1, 4, 5 and 6), although it is applicable only regionally.[402] International arbitration is liberalized, but only as far as Latin American disputes are concerned. Within that regional context, the Convention makes significant progress as compared to the 1958 Convention, adding substantive rules concerning the organization of the arbitration (Arts. 2 and 3), in the same way as the 1961 European Convention. The substantive rules are simpler and less radical than those of the European Convention. The most important such rule stipulates that:

> [i]n the absence of an express agreement between the parties, the arbitration shall be conducted in accordance with the rules of procedure of the Inter-American Commercial Arbitration Commission.

On January 1, 1978, that Commission adopted the UNCITRAL Rules,[403] with a few alterations (notably with regard to the appointment of the arbitrators, for which the Commission is directly responsible.)[404] The Rules were amended in 1988 and in 1996.[405] The UNCITRAL Rules will thus apply on a subsidiary basis to all inter-American arbitrations governed by the Panama Convention.

The Panama Convention is thus both innovative and of some importance,[406] and its application by the courts of signatory states is now the subject of regular commentary.[407]

More recently, the four MERCOSUR member states (Argentina, Brazil, Paraguay and Uruguay) signed a *"Acuerdo sobre arbitraje comercial internacional del MERCOSUR"* in Buenos Aires. This Agreement, dated July 27, 1998, will enter into force when two member states have ratified it. It will apply to any arbitration which has an economic or legal link with one of the MERCOSUR countries, or even sometimes a link created by the intentions of the parties alone. The Agreement's rules concern the whole of the arbitral process, from the arbitration agreement to court control of the award.

---

[402] On the application of the Inter-American Convention to an award rendered in New York between parties from Guatemala, the United States and Salvador, see *Productos Mercantiles, supra* note 309; *see also* Neil E. McDonnell, *Obtaining Arbitral Awards Under the Inter-American Convention*, DISP. RESOL. J., Vol. 50, No. 1, at 19 (Jan. 1995).

[403] Rules of Procedure of the Inter-American Commercial Arbitration Commission, as amended and in effect January 1, 1978, III Y.B. COM. ARB. 231 (1978). *See supra* para. 202.

[404] *See* LAMY – CONTRATS INTERNATIONAUX, Vol. 7, Division XI, *"Prévention et Règlement des litiges"*, by Sigvard Jarvin, Arts. 343 *et seq.*

[405] On these amendments, see FRUTOS-PETERSON, *supra* note 115, at 257 *et seq.* The 1996 Amendment will enter into force upon acceptance by the U.S. Department of State.

[406] *See* Albert Jan van den Berg, *The New York Convention 1958 and Panama Convention 1975: Redundancy or Compatibility?*, 5 ARB. INT'L 214 (1989).

[407] In 1997, the YEARBOOK COMMERCIAL ARBITRATION created a new section devoted to Court Decisions on the Panama Convention 1975 (Part V – D, XXII Y.B. COM. ARB. 1073 (1997)).

f) Inter-Arab Conventions

297. — The Arab world previously displayed much the same hostility towards international arbitration as that found in Latin America, although the legal and political reasons underlying that hostility were quite different. For many years, very few Arab countries had ratified the New York Convention.[408] They instead focused their efforts on inter-Arab arbitration.

298. — The development of arbitration in the Arab world can be divided into three different stages. First, Arab regional conventions dealt with arbitration in the context of judicial co-operation, allowing for the enforcement in each member country of arbitral awards made in other member countries. Under the aegis of the Arab League, and following an initial Convention dated September 14, 1952,[409] there is now a Convention on Judicial Co-operation, signed in Riyadh on April 6, 1983.[410] Second, the desire to foster inter-Arab investment led to the promotion of arbitration as a means of resolving disputes in that field. This resulted in the Convention of June 10, 1974,[411] modeled on the Washington Convention, and two other treaties—signed in Kuwait in 1971 and Amman in 1980—which promote investment and provide for the resolution of disputes by arbitration.[412]

299. — The third stage of this process is perhaps the most important. The Amman Arab Convention on Commercial Arbitration, signed by fourteen Arab countries on April 14, 1987, established an Arab Center for Commercial Arbitration in Rabat, Morocco. The Center will handle a dispute if an arbitration clause or submission agreement refers disputes to it. The only applicable objective condition is that one of the parties must be a subject of a country bound by the Convention. The Convention governs the constitution of the arbitral tribunal and the arbitral procedure, and it stipulates that the only available means of setting aside an award is by an action before the Center itself. Enforcement of the award in member

---

[408] *See infra* Annex IV.

[409] Convention on the Enforcement of Judgments. *See* Ezzedine Abdallah, *La Convention de la Ligue arabe sur l'exécution des jugements – Etude comparative du droit conventionnel comparé avec le droit interne, in* COLLECTED COURSES OF THE HAGUE ACADEMY OF INTERNATIONAL LAW, Vol. 138, Year 1973, Part I, at 503. See, generally, Nassib G. Ziadé, *Selective Bibliography on Arbitration and Arab Countries*, 3 ICSID REV. – FOREIGN INV. L.J. 423 (1988).

[410] This entered into force on October 30, 1985.

[411] Convention on the Settlement of Investment Disputes Between Host States of Arab Investments and Nationals of Other Arab States, in force since August 20, 1976. For a French translation, see 1981 REV. ARB. 348, and the commentary by Jean-François Rycx, *L'accord sur le règlement des litiges entre Etats hôtes d'investissements arabes et ressortissants des autres Etats arabes et ses perspectives*, 1981 REV. ARB. 259.

[412] Convention Establishing the Inter-Arab Investment Guarantee Corporation, in force since April 1, 1974. The Unified Agreement for the Investment of Arab Capital in Arab Countries (signed in Amman on November 27, 1980, and entered into force on September 7, 1981); for an English translation, see 3 ICSID REV. – FOREIGN INV. L.J. 191 (1988); *see* Ahmed Sharaf Eldin, *Legislative Stability and the Investment Climate: A Comment on the Unified Agreement for the Investment of Arab Capital in the Arab Countries*, 3 ICSID REV. – FOREIGN INV. L.J. 147 (1988); FERHAT HORCHANI, L'INVESTISSEMENT INTER-ARABE – RECHERCHE SUR LA CONTRIBUTION DES CONVENTIONS MULTILATÉRALES ARABES À LA FORMATION D'UN DROIT RÉGIONAL DES INVESTISSEMENTS (1992).

states is a matter for the Supreme Court of each state, which may only refuse enforcement on the ground that public policy has been violated.[413] The Amman Convention has been ratified by six countries: Iraq, Jordan, Mauritania, Tunisia, Libya and Yemen.[414] Ratification by seven countries is needed for the Convention to enter into force. Also, the Rabat Arbitration Center has not yet actually been set up; by a decision of the Council of Arab Justice Ministers dated November 28, 1994, it was decided that cases would be provisionally administered by the Cairo Regional Centre for Commercial Arbitration.[415]

g) The OHADA Treaty of October 17, 1993

300. — The Organization for the harmonization of business law in Africa (OHADA) was established by a treaty signed by fourteen African countries in Port-Louis, Mauritius, on October 17, 1993. Those signatory countries are Benin, Burkina-Faso, Cameroon, the Central African Republic, Chad, the Comoros, the Democratic Republic of Congo, the Côte d'Ivoire, Gabon, Equatorial Guinea, Mali, Niger, Senegal, and Togo. Two other countries (Guinea and Guinea-Bissau) later joined the organization. Under this Treaty, which entered into force on September 18, 1995,[416] several uniform laws have been adopted. A uniform law on arbitration, repealing all contrary provisions in national legislation, was adopted by the OHADA Council of Ministers on March 11, 1999. The Convention also established a "Joint Court of Justice and Arbitration," which plays the dual role of an arbitral institution and a court empowered to review awards.[417] The regime thus devised, which applies to both domestic and international arbitration, remains voluntary, but the Court administering the arbitration and approving the draft award is a true international jurisdiction, which subsequently orders enforcement of the award.[418]

---

[413] For an English translation, see EL-AHDAB, *supra* note 144, at 971. For a French translation of this Convention, see 1989 REV. ARB. 743, and the commentary by Abdul Hamid El-Ahdab, *Le Centre arabe d'arbitrage commercial à Rabat – Convention arabe d'Amman sur l'arbitrage commercial (1987)*, *id.* at 631. *See also* Hamzeh A. Haddad, *Inter-Arab Conventions on Commercial Arbitration, in* EURO-ARAB ARBITRATION III, *supra* note 144, at 48; Hamzeh Haddad, *The 1987 Amman Convention on Commercial Arbitration,* 1 AM. REV. INT'L ARB. 132 (1990).

[414] For a table of the multilateral treaties signed or ratified by Arab countries, see ICC BULLETIN, SPECIAL SUPPLEMENT, INTERNATIONAL COMMERCIAL ARBITRATION IN THE ARAB COUNTRIES 72–73 (1992); *see also* El-Ahdab, *supra* note 288, at 180.

[415] On this Centre, see *infra* para. 336 and note 521.

[416] *See* Martin Kirsch, *Historique de l'organisation pour l'harmonisation de droit des affaires en Afrique (OHADA),* 108 REC. PENANT 129 (1998).

[417] Title IV: Arbitration, Arts. 21 to 26.

[418] See the Rules of Arbitration of the Joint Court of Justice and Arbitration adopted by the Council of Ministers on March 11, 1999. *See* Roland Amoussou-Guenou, *L'arbitrage dans le Traité relatif à l'harmonisation du droit des affaires en Afrique (OHADA)/Arbitration Pursuant to the Treaty for the Harmonization for African Business Law (OHADA),* 1996 INT'L BUS. L.J. 321. For additional information on the OHADA Treaty, see the OHADA Web site at <http://www.refer.org/camer_ct /eco/ecoohada /ohada.htm>.

4° The 1965 Washington Convention

301. — Under the auspices of the International Bank for Reconstruction and Development (the World Bank), the "Convention on the Settlement of Investment Disputes Between States and Nationals of other States," opened for signature in Washington, D.C. on March 18, 1965. It created an institutional arbitration mechanism specially adapted to foreign investment disputes: the International Centre for Settlement of Investment Disputes (ICSID).

The Convention aroused considerable interest among authors and practitioners and has been successful in establishing a system of international arbitration offering foreign investors and host countries impressive guarantees of impartiality. By January 1, 1999, it had been signed by 146 countries, 131 of which have ratified it.[419] In addition, over nine hundred bilateral investment treaties and four major multilateral treaties (NAFTA, MERCOSUR, the Cartagena Free Trade Agreement, and the Energy Charter Treaty) have selected ICSID as an arbitral institution to which disputes may be submitted. For many years, ICSID cases were few and far between. It is only over the past fifteen years that new cases have been submitted to it on an annual basis.[420] In 1997, the Centre witnessed an unprecedented increase in demands for arbitration: the Secretary-General registered ten new cases. More than half of these cases were based on investment treaties as opposed to arbitration agreements signed by both parties. Eleven new cases were registered in 1998, only three of which were based on a traditional arbitration agreement. Given the number of international

---

[419] The text of the Convention, the Centre's different sets of rules (Doc. ICSID/15 (1985)) and model clauses (Doc. ICSID/5/Rev. 2 (Feb. 1993)), a comprehensive bibliography concerning ICSID (Doc. ICSID/13/Rev. 4 (Apr. 1997)), and the list of ICSID cases (Doc. ICSID/16/Rev. 5 (Nov. 1996)) are available free of charge from the Centre, at 1818 H Street N.W., Washington, DC 20433, U.S.A. See also ICSID REVIEW – FOREIGN INV. L.J., which is published twice a year. The *travaux préparatoires* are found in CONVENTION ON THE SETTLEMENT OF INVESTMENT DISPUTES BETWEEN STATES AND NATIONALS OF OTHER STATES – ANALYSIS OF DOCUMENTS CONCERNING THE ORIGIN AND THE FORMULATION OF THE CONVENTION (4 volumes, 1968–1970).

[420] On the Washington Convention and ICSID, see the extensive bibliography contained in the ICSID brochure *supra* note 419 and, in particular Georges R. Delaume, *Convention on the Settlement of Investment Disputes Between States and Nationals of Other States,* 1 INT'L LAW. 64 (1966); MARIO AMADIO, LE CONTENTIEUX INTERNATIONAL DE L'INVESTISSEMENT PRIVÉ ET LA CONVENTION DE LA BANQUE MONDIALE DU 18 MARS 1965 (1967); Aron Broches, *The Convention on the Settlement of Investment Disputes Between States and Nationals of Other States, in* COLLECTED COURSES OF THE HAGUE ACADEMY OF INTERNATIONAL LAW, Vol. 136, Year 1972, Part II, at 331; Georges R. Delaume, *Le Centre International pour le Règlement des Différends Relatifs aux Investissements (CIRDI),* 109 J.D.I. 775 (1982); Christoph Schreuer, *Commentary on the ICSID Convention,* 11 ICSID REV. – FOREIGN INV. L.J. 318 (1996), 12 ICSID REV. – FOREIGN INV. L.J. 59 and 365 (1997), 13 ICSID REV. – FOREIGN INV. L.J. 150 (1998); ARON BROCHES, SELECTED ESSAYS – WORLD BANK, ICSID, AND OTHER SUBJECTS OF PUBLIC AND PRIVATE INTERNATIONAL LAW (1995); SÉBASTIEN MANCIAUX, INVESTISSEMENTS ÉTRANGERS ET ARBITRAGE ENTRE ÉTATS ET RESSORTISSANTS D'AUTRES ÉTATS: 25 ANNÉES D'ACTIVITÉ DU CENTRE INTERNATIONAL POUR LE RÈGLEMENT DES DIFFÉRENDS RELATIFS AUX INVESTISSEMENNTS (Thesis, University of Dijon (France), 1998) and on ICSID awards, see the systematic commentary of all published cases by Emmanuel Gaillard, *Centre International pour le Règlement des Différends Relatifs aux Investissements (C.I.R.D.I.) – Chronique des sentences arbitrales,* published yearly since 1986 in the JOURNAL DU DROIT INTERNATIONAL.

instruments which choose ICSID as a mechanism for resolving disputes, this trend is likely to continue.[421]

302. — ICSID arbitration is specific in a number of respects: it was created by international treaty and is used only to resolve investment-related disputes; it also has specific rules governing jurisdiction,[422] arbitral procedure and the authority of awards. In particular, although awards can be set aside by *ad hoc* committees—which have sometimes construed their powers of review very broadly—there can be no action to set aside before national courts.[423] In addition, pursuant to the Treaty, an ICSID award has to be treated in each member state "as if it were a final judgment of the courts" of that state (Art. 54(1)). The awards made, which are almost always published, are particularly helpful in the creation of a body of international investment law.[424]

The importance of ICSID arbitration is such that we address its different aspects throughout this work.

SECTION II
Private Sources

303. — Despite the abundance of public sources of international commercial arbitration law, international companies, professional organizations and their lawyers need other rules to supplement national or international laws or to exclude—where possible—aspects of those laws which they consider to be inappropriate. To achieve the resolution of their disputes in a manner adapted to their needs, they opt for international arbitration. Naturally, they want to be able to determine the rules governing that arbitration as freely as possible.

In this respect, the diversity of international arbitration is an important factor. Rules suitable for an arbitration relating to the quality of perishable goods will not be suited to the resolution of a dispute concerning the delivery of an industrial plant. An arbitration organized by a professional body for all disputes arising from contracts relating to a

---

[421] On this issue, see, for example, Emmanuel Gaillard, *The International Centre for Settlement of Investment Disputes*, N.Y.L.J., Apr. 2, 1998, at 3. On January 1, 1999, twenty-four cases were pending before the Centre, more than ever in the past. *See* Emmanuel Gaillard, *Centre International pour le Règlement des Différends Relatifs aux Investissements – Chronique des sentences arbitrales*, 126 J.D.I. 273 (1999).

[422] In particular, on the conditions regarding consent, the nature of the dispute, and the parties' nationality, see Schreuer, *supra* note 420, 11 ICSID REV. – FOREIGN INV. L.J. 318 (1996); 12 ICSID REV. – FOREIGN INV. L.J. 59 (1997); Broches, *supra* note 420; Burdeau, *supra* note 242; Gaillard, *supra* note 242, at 175; Aron Broches, *Denying ICSID's Jurisdiction – The ICSID Award in Vacuum Salt Products Limited*, 13 J. INT'L ARB. 21 (Sept. 1996).

[423] Cass. 1e civ., June 11, 1991, Société ouest-africaine de bétons industriels (SOABI) v. Sénégal, 118 J.D.I. 1005 (1991), and E. Gaillard's note; 1991 REV. ARB. 637, and A. Broches' note; 1992 REV. CRIT. DIP 331, and P.L.'s note; for an English translation, see 30 I.L.M. 1167 (1991), with an introductory note by G. Delaume; XVII Y.B. COM. ARB. 754 (1992); *see also* Okezie Chukwumerije, *International Law and Article 42 of the ICSID Convention*, 14 J. INT'L ARB. 79 (Sept. 1997).

[424] Gaillard, *supra* note 420.

particular commodity (such as wheat or cocoa) will have little in common with an ICC arbitration relating to an international distribution agreement, or an ICSID arbitration concerning foreign investment. In order to satisfy the varying requirements inherent in such a diverse institution, international arbitration requires extreme flexibility. This cannot be found to the extent necessary in national laws. It is instead achieved through party autonomy.

304. — With the agreement or at least the tolerance of national authorities, arbitration practitioners have been able to enjoy such rule-making autonomy. Most modern national laws and multilateral conventions now leave the parties free to determine, in their arbitration agreement, the procedural and substantive rules to be applied to their dispute. This is particularly true of most recent arbitration laws,[425] as well as the New York Convention[426] and later regional conventions.[427]

305. — We shall not, however, directly examine the agreement between the parties at this stage. That agreement, which is generally negotiated on a case-by-case basis in the form of an arbitration clause or submission agreement, cannot be considered to be a "source" of international arbitration law, for at least two reasons.

First, from a theoretical standpoint, a degree of repetition and generality is required for a rule of contractual origin to govern situations for which it was not expressly intended and thus contribute to the creation of a non-national body of legal rules.[428]

Second, from a more practical point of view, *ad hoc* clauses agreed between parties to a contract clearly do not have the same authority and relevance as instruments intended for use in—and actually used in—an indefinite number of cases.

306. — Further, in practice parties do not use all of the autonomy available to them. They have neither the means nor the desire to do so. In their agreements, they will usually confine themselves to referring to existing instruments, particularly those which have been drafted by professional organizations or by arbitral institutions. They often incorporate existing model clauses or arbitration rules into their agreement or delegate their powers to determine the rules governing the procedure or the merits of the dispute to third parties, namely arbitral institutions or arbitrators.

---

[425] *See supra* paras. 139 and 188.

[426] *See supra* para. 253.

[427] *See supra* paras. 284 and 296.

[428] On this part of the debate surrounding *lex mercatoria*, see the convergence, on this point at least, of Berthold Goldman, *La lex mercatoria dans les contrats et l'arbitrage internationaux: réalité et perspectives*, 106 J.D.I. 475 (1979) and Paul Lagarde, *Approche critique de la lex mercatoria*, *in* LE DROIT DES RELATIONS ÉCONOMIQUES INTERNATIONALES – ETUDES OFFERTES À BERTHOLD GOLDMAN 125 (1982). On this issue, generally, see *infra* paras. 1443 *et seq.*

The private sources of international arbitration are thus model arbitration agreements (§ 1), arbitration rules (§ 2) and arbitral awards (§ 3).[429]

§ 1. – Model Arbitration Agreements

307. — There are two types of model arbitration agreements found in international commerce. The first and larger category consists of agreements drawn up by organizations—generally arbitral institutions or professional associations—which offer their model clauses to potential arbitration users or include them in general contractual conditions. Alongside these clauses drafted unilaterally by a single institution (A), there is another category of clauses resulting from agreements between two or more such institutions from more than one country (B). All of these model agreements provide for an arbitration mechanism which is generally institutional and which the parties are invited to adopt either in their contracts or when a dispute arises.

A. – MODEL ARBITRATION AGREEMENTS PREPARED BY INDIVIDUAL INSTITUTIONS

308. — Every arbitral institution invites potential arbitration users to incorporate into their contracts an arbitration agreement whereby arbitrators acting under the auspices of that institution will be granted jurisdiction to resolve any dispute arising under those contracts.

309. — Thus, the International Chamber of Commerce proposes a very simple "standard ICC arbitration clause." It warns that certain additions may be required and draws the user's attention to the requirements of form found in some national laws.[430]   Since January 1, 1998, the clause reads:

> All disputes arising out of or in connection with the present contract shall be finally settled under the Rules of Arbitration of the International Chamber of Commerce by one or more arbitrators appointed in accordance with the said Rules.

310. — A very similar model clause has been proposed by the LCIA since 1985:

---

[429] On the issue of whether the understanding of the law involves the consideration of all its various sources, see the subtle but convincing analysis of Bruno Oppetit, *La notion de source du droit et le droit du commerce international*, *in* ARCHIVES DE PHILOSOPHIE DU DROIT – TOME 27 – "SOURCES" DU DROIT 43 (1982); Jean-Louis Sourioux, *"Source du droit" en droit privé*, *id.* at 33; see also, for an overview, concerning contracts more than arbitration, DOMINIQUE BUREAU, LES SOURCES INFORMELLES DU DROIT DANS LES RELATIONS PRIVÉES INTERNATIONALES (Thesis, University of Paris II (France), 1992).

[430] *See* ICC RULES OF ARBITRATION IN FORCE AS FROM JANUARY 1, 1998 – ICC RULES OF CONCILIATION IN FORCE AS FROM JANUARY 1, 1988, at 8 (ICC Publication No. 581, 1997); and, previously, the ICC RULES OF CONCILIATION AND ARBITRATION IN FORCE AS FROM JANUARY 1, 1988, at 6, 7 (ICC Publication No. 447, 1987).

> Any dispute arising out of or in connection with this contract, including any
> question regarding its existence, validity or termination, shall be referred to and
> finally resolved by arbitration under the LCIA Rules, which Rules are deemed
> to be incorporated by reference into this clause.[431]

As with the ICC, the LCIA then warns the parties that they may avoid difficulties and
additional expenditure by specifying the law governing their contract and, if they so wish,
the number of arbitrators, as well as the place and the language of the arbitration. Standard
text is then suggested for making those choices.

310-1. — Similarly, the International Arbitration Rules of the American Arbitration
Association, effective April 1, 1997, contain the following recommended clause, and
provide a few additional guidelines:

> Any controversy or claim arising out of or relating to this contract shall be
> determined by arbitration in accordance with the International Arbitration Rules
> of the American Arbitration Association.[432]

311. — All other arbitral institutions likewise recommend a model arbitration clause,
generally drafted in similar terms, except for ICSID given its strong specificity.[433]

312. — The UNCITRAL Arbitration Rules[434] also contain a model arbitration clause,
drafted in broad terms with respect to the disputes it may cover.[435] As the clause provides
for *ad hoc* arbitration, UNCITRAL includes the determination of the appointing authority
(an individual or an institution) in the list of additional provisions which it recommends that
users draw up. It is particularly important to identify that authority in advance.

313. — These model clauses, recommended for non-specialized institutional or *ad hoc*
arbitrations, share a number of characteristics. They are the fruit of many years of invaluable
experience of international arbitration, and they provide models which can be adapted to any
other form of arbitration. An international arbitration clause should be drafted in the most
general terms possible, and it should include, in particular, a comprehensive definition of
the disputes which it is intended to cover. The clause should also be simple and confined to

---

[431] *See* LCIA RULES – EFFECTIVE 1 JANUARY 1998, at 24.

[432] *See* AAA INTERNATIONAL ARBITRATION RULES – AS AMENDED AND EFFECTIVE APRIL 1, 1997, at 1.

[433] See, for example, the model clauses of the Grain and Feed Trade Association (GAFTA) (No. 2205), the
Federation of Oils, Seeds and Fats Associations Limited (FOSFA) (No. 2206), the Inter-American Commercial
Arbitration Commission (IACAC) (No. 2212), and the Arbitration Institute of the Stockholm Chamber of
Commerce (No. 2214), *in* ERIC LEE, ENCYCLOPEDIA OF INTERNATIONAL COMMERCIAL ARBITRATION (1986).
On ICSID arbitration clauses, see ICSID MODEL CLAUSES (Doc. ICSID/5/Rev. 2); Emmanuel Gaillard, *Some
Notes on the Drafting of ICSID Arbitration Clauses*, 3 ICSID REV. – FOREIGN INV. L.J. 136 (1988); Georges
R. Delaume, *How to Draft an ICSID Arbitration Clause*, 7 ICSID REV. – FOREIGN INV. L.J. 168 (1992).

[434] *See supra* para. 200.

[435] The model clause and the UNCITRAL Arbitration Rules are reproduced *infra* Annex X.

the essentials. In other words, it should provide for an effective mechanism for setting up the arbitration which is not dependent on any further agreement between the parties.[436] In institutional arbitration, that effectiveness is guaranteed by the intervention of the institution, which explains the concise nature of the corresponding clauses. However, the institutions do give indications to the parties as to how they might add to the agreement (by specifying the number of arbitrators, the place and language of the arbitration, and the law applicable to the merits of the dispute).

314. — In the standard contracts produced by professional bodies, particularly those concerning international sales of commodities, the arbitration clause will often be more detailed. It may reproduce a substantial part of the arbitration rules of the professional body (in cases such as the international cereal trade, where that body has set up an arbitration center of its own). Alternatively, the clause will provide for a specific *ad hoc* arbitration mechanism (as in the case of the international timber trade).

315. — In the construction industry, the *Fédération Internationale des Ingénieurs-Conseils* (FIDIC) has produced general conditions for civil engineering works which it revises periodically. In this widely used contract, Article 67 organizes a rather complicated system for resolving disputes, whereby the dispute must be submitted to either the engineer or a dispute adjudication board prior to any request for arbitration, and only thereafter may the decision of the engineer or the board (or the absence thereof) be challenged before an ICC arbitral tribunal.[437]

316. — How important are these model arbitration clauses? As they are prepared by professional bodies or arbitral institutions and offered to potential users, they amount to a contract, provided of course that they are actually accepted by the parties.[438] Where they contain detailed provisions as to the mechanism for appointing the arbitrators, the arbitral procedure and the powers of the arbitral tribunal, they come closer to being arbitration rules. The fact that they are incorporated into general contractual conditions does not affect their authority. The instrument remains private in character and external to the parties, and is capable of applying in an indefinite number of situations. Therefore, as with arbitration rules, model arbitration clauses incorporating procedural rules constitute private sources of international arbitration law.[439]

---

[436] On pathological clauses, see *infra* paras. 484 *et seq.*

[437] On the nature of the role of the "engineer" or the dispute adjudication board, and on the evolution of the drafting of the FIDIC Conditions in the area of dispute resolution, see *supra* paras. 22 *et seq.*

[438] On the form of the arbitration agreement, the applicable conditions of proof and arbitration clauses incorporated by reference, see *infra* paras. 491 *et seq.*

[439] On this issue, see *infra* paras. 357 *et seq.*

B. – INTER-INSTITUTIONAL AGREEMENTS

317. — Many arbitral institutions retain an essentially national character, through their location, their staff and the rules they apply.[440] As a result, when negotiating its contract and selecting the institution to which any disputes are submitted, a party might object to a particular choice of arbitral institution because it considers the institution to be too closely linked to another party to the contract.

Aware of this problem, arbitral institutions sought to offer more balanced arbitration clauses. They did so by concluding numerous inter-institutional agreements, often on the initiative of the AAA, the Japanese Arbitration Association, the Italian Arbitration Association and the arbitration courts of the chambers of commerce of Central and East European countries.

318. — These inter-institutional agreements provide for co-operation between the signatory institutions and recommend that parties insert an arbitration clause into their contracts enabling the place of arbitration to be determined, the arbitrators appointed and the institution and/or the applicable arbitration rules designated.[441] During the 1970s and 1980s, the arbitration clause recommended in these agreements generally attributed jurisdiction to the arbitral institution located in the defendant's country, which would apply a set of international arbitration rules. The Rules of the United Nations Economic Commission for Europe were used until 1976.[442] More recently, as we have seen,[443] most arbitral institutions prefer the UNCITRAL Arbitration Rules.[444]

319. — Another recent practice—of the AAA at least—involves the intervention of a third institution. This can be seen in agreements concluded by the AAA with the chambers of commerce of Russia (formerly the USSR), Hungary,[445] Bulgaria,[446] Poland[447] and the

---

[440] On institutional arbitration generally, see *infra* paras. 330 *et seq.*

[441] On these agreements at the beginning of the 1960s, see FOUCHARD, *supra* note 205, ¶¶ 372 *et seq.*

[442] On these Rules, see *supra* para. 195–99.

[443] *See supra* para. 202.

[444] See, for example, the January 20, 1998 Cooperation Agreement Between the Federal Economic Chamber, Vienna and the Czechoslovak Chamber of Commerce and Industry, Prague, in the Field of Commercial Arbitration; *see* XV Y.B. COM. ARB. 151 (1990).

[445] Agreement between the American Arbitration Association, the Hungarian Chamber of Commerce and the Austrian Federal Economic Chamber concerning the optional arbitration clause for use in contracts in USA–Hungarian Trade–1984, dated September 7, 1984, *reprinted in* AMERICAN ARBITRATION ASSOCIATION, THE INTERNATIONAL ARBITRATION KIT 321 (4th ed. 1993); X Y.B. COM. ARB. 141 (1985).

[446] Agreement between the American Arbitration Association, the Bulgarian Chamber of Commerce and Industry and the Austrian Federal Economic Chamber concerning the optional arbitration clause for use in contracts in USA–Bulgarian Trade–1985, dated October 22, 1985, *reprinted in* THE INTERNATIONAL ARBITRATION KIT, *supra* note 445, at 326; XII Y.B. COM. ARB. 197 (1987).

[447] Agreement between the American Arbitration Association, the Polish Chamber of Foreign Trade and the Austrian Federal Economic Chamber concerning the optional arbitration clause for use in contracts in USA–Polish Trade–1988, dated March 15, 1988, *reprinted in* THE INTERNATIONAL ARBITRATION KIT, *supra*

(continued...)

former Czechoslovakia.[448] For example, the 1992 agreement between the AAA and the Chamber of Commerce and Industry of the Russian Federation invites American and Russian companies to include in their contracts an "Optional Arbitration Clause for Use in Contracts in USA-Russian Trade and Investment."[449] This clause provides for arbitration in Stockholm under the UNCITRAL Rules, with the Stockholm Chamber of Commerce acting as the appointing authority, subject to special stipulations concerning the appointment of arbitrators and certain procedural issues.

320. — The exact content of these inter-institutional agreements and arbitration clauses need not be analyzed in detail here. For the most part, they seek to internationalize arbitration, at least as far as the arbitral procedure and the constitution of the arbitral tribunal are concerned.

Inter-institutional agreements were essentially prompted by the existence, in the formerly socialist countries of Eastern Europe, of commissions or arbitration courts for external trade. These often bore strong national characteristics, and the aim of the agreements was to lessen the impact of those national characteristics and to internationalize institutional arbitration between East and West. However, the political and economic changes in Eastern Europe have transformed those arbitral institutions. As a result, the usefulness of the agreements—many of which are now doubtless void—is uncertain. In any case, they can only be effective if the parties adopt the arbitration clauses which they recommend.

§ 2. – Arbitration Rules

321. — The somewhat ambiguous expression "arbitration rules" denotes a set of provisions intended to govern arbitral procedure and drafted by an arbitral institution or other organization. Arbitration rules constitute a private source of international arbitration law because their binding nature is not derived from the acts of one or more public authorities.

Of course, we must go beyond this initial, negative definition and establish the legal value of these instruments and, more generally, their role in the creation and development of international arbitration law (B). First, however, we need to describe the various sets of rules, underlining their diversity (A).

---

[447](...continued)
   note 445, at 335; XIV Y.B. COM. ARB. 284 (1989).

[448] Agreement between the American Arbitration Association, the Czechoslovak Chamber of Commerce and Industry and the Austrian Federal Economic Chamber concerning the optional arbitration clause for use in contracts in USA–Czechoslovak Trade–1989, dated March 29, 1989, *reprinted in* THE INTERNATIONAL ARBITRATION KIT, *supra* note 445, at 342; XV Y.B. COM. ARB. 186 (1990).

[449] Agreement between the American Arbitration Association, the Chamber of Commerce and Industry of the Russian Federation and the Stockholm Chamber of Commerce concerning the optional arbitration clause for use in contracts in USA–Russian trade and investment–1992, dated December 15, 1992, *reprinted in* THE INTERNATIONAL ARBITRATION KIT, *supra* note 445, at 378; XIX Y.B. COM. ARB. 279 (1994).

A. – THE DIVERSITY OF ARBITRATION RULES

322. — The organizations which draft and publish arbitration rules are chiefly arbitral institutions (1°), although they are not alone in doing so (2°).

1° Rules Prepared by Arbitral Institutions

323. — Institutional arbitration plays a dominant role in international arbitral practice. Given that *ad hoc* arbitration inevitably remains confidential, a statistical assessment of the respective importance of these two forms of arbitration is impossible. Nevertheless, it is clear that over the past twenty years, the well-established arbitral institutions have witnessed a significant growth in their activity, and a number of new arbitral institutions have opened for business.[450] It is true that many of the new institutions have yet to have a substantial impact on the international commercial arbitration "market," and that many may never do so.[451] However, not all of them will fail and, often located in countries which have yet to develop a strong practice or tradition of international arbitration, they bear witness to the rise of international arbitration, especially in its institutional form.

324. — Under these circumstances, there is little point in drawing up a list of arbitral institutions and their arbitration rules. The list would not be exhaustive and it would inevitably include institutions which exist only on paper. Similar surveys have been performed in the past, often with unsatisfactory results.

325. — In 1958, for instance, a detailed study by the United Nations Economic Commission for Europe listed 127 permanent arbitral institutions. Their respective rules were the subject of a comparative analysis, the scale and scientific accuracy of which were

---

[450] By way of illustration, the following institutions have been recently established: the Centre de conciliation et d'arbitrage de Tunis (8, rue du Nigeria, 1002 Tunis, Tunisia); the St. Petersburg International Commercial Arbitration Court (Admiralteisky pr., 12, St. Petersburg, 19000 Russia); the Corte arbitrale nazionale ed internazionale di Venezia (for an English version of the Rules, see 1998 BULL. ASA 328, and for the Italian original, 1998 BULL. ASA 545); the Centre d'arbitrage de la Chambre de commerce, d'industrie et d'agriculture de Dakar (Senegal).

[451] To take just one example, albeit an important one, the Arbitration and Mediation Center of the World Intellectual Property Organization (WIPO) in Geneva has so far only administered one mediation; *see WIPO Arbitration And Mediation Center Poised To Accept Cases*, 12 INT'L ARB. REP. 17 (June 1997); on this Center, created in 1994, see *infra* para. 336.

exceptional.[452] In 1965, the study was updated.[453] In 1970, lists were again drawn up by the Italian Arbitration Association and by the French Arbitration Committee.[454]

In 1981, a list of "generalist" arbitration institutions[455] was compiled, and this was updated until 1988.[456] By then, the list contained sixty-five institutions, and although all of these institutions are well-known, it is by no means certain that all are genuinely active, especially in the field of international arbitration. Furthermore, many new institutions have appeared since then.

In addition, an International Federation of Commercial Arbitration Institutions was created in 1985, aiming to bring arbitral institutions together so as to promote exchanges of information, international cooperation, and institutional arbitration in general. In 1986, the Federation published its first guide,[457] listing seven international institutions and ninety-eight national institutions located in forty-seven countries around the globe.[458] Unfortunately, this list was not complete and included certain organizations that were not active. The list has been substantially revised recently. In 1998, one publication listed about 70 arbitral institutions from 44 countries.[459]

326. — Without carrying out research on an entirely different scale, it is impossible to give an economically and sociologically accurate picture, at any given moment, of the world's arbitral institutions. Some, but not all, benefit from an active professional community, or are located in a country or region of the world that encourages international arbitration. Only in those circumstances can an arbitral institution prosper.

There is also the question of how to identify all the specialized arbitration centers backed by or incorporated into a variety of national or international professional organizations. The

---

[452] *See* UNITED NATIONS, ECONOMIC COMMISSION FOR EUROPE, COMMITTEE ON THE DEVELOPMENT OF TRADE, HANDBOOK OF NATIONAL AND INTERNATIONAL INSTITUTIONS ACTIVE IN THE FIELD OF INTERNATIONAL COMMERCIAL ARBITRATION, TRADE/WP1/15/Rev. 1, Vols. I–V (1958). This research was used by its principal author in two more condensed works, one devoted to institutions in Eastern Europe, the other to all the institutions of Western Europe and the United States (*see* Peter Benjamin, *Aperçu des institutions arbitrales de l'Europe de l'Est qui exercent une activité dans le domaine de l'arbitrage commercial international* (pts. 1 & 2), 1957 REV. ARB. 114, 1958 REV. ARB. 2; Peter Benjamin, *A Comparative Study of International Commercial Institutional Arbitration in Europe and in the United States of America, in* UNION INTERNATIONALE DES AVOCATS, INTERNATIONAL COMMERCIAL ARBITRATION, Vol. II, at 351 (P. Sanders ed., 1960)).

[453] FOUCHARD, *supra* note 205, ¶¶ 274–371, and the table of permanent arbitral institutions, at 582.

[454] See the list of those centers and their addresses at the time in 1970 REV. ARB. 44.

[455] List compiled by Rosabel E. Everard, then of the T.M.C. Asser Instituut in The Hague. *See* VI Y.B. COM. ARB. 264 (1981).

[456] XIII Y.B. COM. ARB. 713 (1988).

[457] COMMERCIAL ARBITRATION INSTITUTIONS: AN INTERNATIONAL DIRECTORY AND GUIDE.

[458] *See* the information provided by Ludwick Kos-Rabcewicz-Zubkowski, *Fédération internationale des nstitutions d'arbitrage commercial*, 1987 REV. ARB. 408; Paul J. Davidson, *The International Federation of Commercial Arbitration Institutions*, 5 J. INT'L ARB. 131 (June 1988).

[459] *See* MARTINDALE-HUBBELL INTERNATIONAL ARBITRATION AND DISPUTE RESOLUTION DIRECTORY 1998, at 337.

task is not an easy one. In particular, do they organize true arbitrations, or only expertise procedures and the examination of goods?

327. — We shall not attempt to describe the content of institutional rules here either. That will be covered later, particularly by considering the most important institutions, such as the ICC, the LCIA and the AAA, the rules of which feature in the annexes of this book. The role of these institutions is especially significant in the composition of the arbitral tribunal, where the distinction between institutional and *ad hoc* arbitration is fundamental,[460] and in the conduct of the arbitral proceedings.[461]

328. — Unfortunately, the available bibliographies, including that contained in the Yearbook Commercial Arbitration,[462] do not list the specialized or trade institutions (despite the fact that they are often very active). Instead, they publish and analyze only the rules of "generalist" institutions.[463] Nonetheless, a fairly representative picture emerges from that analysis and from that of arbitration rules annexed to recent arbitration treatises.[464]

329. — There are more than one hundred institutions which are truly active in the field of international arbitration. That figure would certainly double if one were to take into account other organizations which aspire to reach those levels of activity. However, our general presentation of this private source of international arbitration law will be confined to a classification of the various institutions and their rules (a), with a more detailed discussion of the most prominent institution, the ICC International Court of Arbitration (b).

a) Classification of Arbitral Institutions

330. — Several distinctions need to be drawn between different categories of arbitral institution.

331. — An initial distinction must be made between national and international institutions. Even if we consider only those which handle international arbitrations, there are many more national than international institutions.

---

[460] *See infra* paras. 952 *et seq.*

[461] *See infra* paras. 1209 *et seq.*

[462] This publication lists all the major centers and gives their precise contact details.

[463] *See, e.g.,* HANDBOOK OF INSTITUTIONAL ARBITRATION IN INTERNATIONAL TRADE – FACTS, FIGURES AND RULES (E. Cohn, M. Domke, F. Eisemann eds., 1977); LEE, *supra* note 433, Part. II; LAMY, *supra* note 404; DICTIONNAIRE JOLY, PRATIQUE DES CONTRATS INTERNATIONAUX, Vol. 2, Livre X, Annex 3; PARKER SCHOOL OF FOREIGN AND COMPARATIVE LAW – COLUMBIA UNIVERSITY, GUIDE TO INTERNATIONAL ARBITRATION AND ARBITRATORS (2d ed. 1992).

[464] *See, e.g.,* MATTHIEU DE BOISSÉSON, LE DROIT FRANÇAIS DE L'ARBITRAGE INTERNE ET INTERNATIONAL (2d ed. 1990); ALAN REDFERN AND MARTIN M. HUNTER, LAW AND PRACTICE OF INTERNATIONAL COMMERCIAL ARBITRATION (2d ed. 1991); WILLIAM W. PARK, INTERNATIONAL FORUM SELECTION (1995).

332. — A national institution is one which is located in a single country with employees (administrative staff and arbitrators) drawn primarily from that country. Any links with the chamber of commerce of a town, region or country will reinforce the national character of the institution, as will the law (including choice of law and procedural rules) selected by that institution in its arbitration rules.

333. — Included in the category of national institutions are the arbitration courts and commissions established alongside the chambers of commerce of the former socialist countries. Until 1989, these arbitral institutions shared the same profile: they were closely linked to the organization responsible for the country's foreign trade and usually had a *de facto* monopoly over international arbitrations held in the countries concerned. The combination of this monopoly, the Rules of the Council for Mutual Economic Assistance (CMEA) General Conditions and the 1972 Moscow Convention led these institutions to be fairly active, although this depended to an extent on the economic importance of each country and on the appeal of the institution to foreign companies and economic organizations. Each institution originally had its own arbitration rules, but from 1974 onwards they all adopted the "Uniform Rules of Procedure for Arbitration Courts in the Chambers of Commerce of the CMEA Countries," with the exception of the Chinese and Yugoslavian institutions (those states being outside the CMEA).[465] Despite their title, these Rules do not harmonize all the rules of the various institutions, although they do draw them together to a certain extent and are fairly heavily influenced by the UNCITRAL Rules. Of course, many of the institutions have been or are now being substantially transformed[466] as a result of the privatization of the economies of the Eastern European countries and accompanying political upheavals. Consequently, the number of institutions, their status and their rules are subject to reform. Most of these reforms seek to liberalize the institutions' procedures and to internationalize their structure. The most important examples are now examined in turn:
– The "Court of Arbitration attached to the Chamber for Foreign Trade of the GDR"[467] became the Berlin Court of Arbitration (*Schiedsgericht Berlin*) following the reunification of Germany and the dissolution of the Chamber on August 31, 1990. It was established as a private association and adopted the UNCITRAL Arbitration Rules.[468] An interesting debate arose in Germany between those who believed that arbitration agreements submitting disputes to the socialist institution were void, and those who considered that the Berlin Court of Arbitration automatically succeeded its socialist predecessor unless the parties provided

---

[465] For the text of the Rules and a commentary by Heinz Strohbach, see I Y.B. COM. ARB. 147 and 10 (1976); see also Strohbach, *supra* note 77.

[466] *See* Strohbach, *supra* note 77; see also ICC BULLETIN, SPECIAL SUPPLEMENT, INTERNATIONAL COMMERCIAL ARBITRATION IN EUROPE (1994), which describes the changes affecting the arbitral institutions of these countries.

[467] Feb. 24, 1982 Rules; *see* Heinz Strohbach, *German Democratic Republic: the Arbitration Court attached to the Chamber of Foreign Trade*, in HANDBOOK OF INSTITUTIONAL ARBITRATION, *supra* note 463, at 59.

[468] Heinz Strohbach, *Arbitration in Berlin*, 8 ARB. INT'L 185 (1992).

otherwise.[469] The *Bundesgerichtshof* eventually decided that such agreements were void.[470] At the same time, the Berlin Court of Arbitration merged with the German Institution for Arbitration.[471]

– The Court of Arbitration at the Bulgarian Chamber of Commerce and Industry repealed its rules of April 24, 1979, but its new rules, adopted on January 17, 1989,[472] were themselves replaced on July 1, 1993.[473] A different set of rules governs *ad hoc* arbitration, which is simply assisted by the Arbitration Court.

– The Court of Arbitration attached to the Hungarian Chamber of Commerce and Industry likewise abandoned its old rules of May 29, 1975, adopting new rules in 1989 closely based on the UNCITRAL Rules.[474] These were in turn replaced by new provisions with effect from March 15, 1993.[475]

– In 1990, the Court of Arbitration at the Polish Chamber of Foreign Trade[476] came under the control of the new Polish Chamber of Commerce. In 1985, it began to administer international *ad hoc* arbitrations governed by special rules and, unless the parties agreed otherwise, by the UNCITRAL Rules.[477]

– The Arbitration Court of the Romanian Chamber of Commerce and Industry also underwent profound transformation in 1990 and 1991.[478] On March 30, 1993, it became the Court of International Commercial Arbitration at the Chamber of Commerce and Industry of Romania, and on November 17, 1993 it adopted new international arbitration rules, applicable with effect from January 1, 1994.[479]

---

[469] On this debate and the position of the courts, see Otto Sandrock, *The German-German Merger: Changes in Arbitration Law and Practice*, 1 AM. REV. INT'L ARB. 272 (1990); Jörg Kirchner and Arthur L. Marriott, *International Arbitration in the Aftermath of Socialism – The Example of the Berlin Court of Arbitration*, 10 J. INT'L ARB. 5 (Mar. 1993); Walter J. Habscheid and Edgar Habscheid, *The End of East–West Commercial Arbitration—Arbitration between the Former Two Germanies*, 9 ARB. INT'L 203 (1993).

[470] *Bundesgerichtshof*, Jan. 20, 1994, NJW 94, 1008–1012 (*see* 1994 BULL. ASA 433; the observations by H.J. Schroth, Les Petites Affiches, Feb. 1, 1995, No. 14, at 7; 1995 REV. ARB. 663, 664); *Bundesgerichtshof*, Feb. 9, 1995, Iprax 95, 387–391 (*see* Hans-Jürgen Schroth, *L'invalidité des clauses compromissoires sous le régime de l'ancienne R.D.A. – A propos d'un arrêt de la Cour fédérale d'Allemagne du 9 février 1995*, Les Petites Affiches, Mar. 1, 1996, No. 27, at 14); *see also* Peter Schlosser, *Chronique de jurisprudence allemande*, 1995 REV. ARB. 663, 664.

[471] Ottoarndt Glossner, *Federal Republic of Germany*, XIX Y.B. COM. ARB. 452 (1994).

[472] *See* BULGARIAN CHAMBER OF COMMERCE AND INDUSTRY, *supra* note 79, which provides the text of the Rules.

[473] Staikov, *supra* note 80, at 77.

[474] Rules of Procedure for the Court of Arbitration Attached to the Hungarian Chamber of Commerce, XVI Y.B. COM. ARB. 209 (1991), *see also* Horváth, *supra* note 394; Horváth, *Arbitration in Hungary*, *supra* note 89.

[475] *See* XX Y.B. COM. ARB. 295 (1995).

[476] Jan. 22, 1984 Rules; *see* Jerzy Jakubowski and Andrzej W. Wisniewski, *Poland: the Court of Arbitration at the Polish Chamber of Foreign Trade*, *in* HANDBOOK OF INSTITUTIONAL ARBITRATION, *supra* note 463, at 147.

[477] Rules for *ad hoc* Arbitrations, XII Y.B. COM. ARB. 224 (1987); *see* Szurski, *supra* note 83, at 105.

[478] Octavian Capatina, *L'arbitrage commercial international en Roumanie/International Commercial Arbitration in Romania*, 1990 INT'L BUS. L.J. 591; Florescu, *supra* note 85.

[479] Babiuc and Capatina, *supra* note 87.

– The Arbitration Court attached to the Czechoslovak Chamber of Commerce and Industry[480] was of course affected by the division of that country. On January 1, 1993, the Slovak Chamber of Commerce and Industry set up a new Arbitration Court, while the old court continues to sit in Prague and now belongs to the Czech Republic, and has changed its name to the Arbitration Court attached to the Economic Chamber of the Czech Republic and Agricultural Chamber of the Czech Republic. Its rules were subsequently relaxed on November 1, 1994, particularly by allowing the appointment of foreign arbitrators (a change which also applies to most other formerly socialist institutions).

– The Arbitration Court at the USSR Chamber of Commerce and Industry adopted new rules in 1987.[481] However, the break-up of the USSR and the uncertain future of the Commonwealth of Independent States prompted several of the new countries to set up arbitration centers to handle international disputes. The Moscow Court has become the International Commercial Arbitration Court at the Chamber of Commerce and Industry of the Russian Federation, with a new statute since 1993[482] and new rules since May 1, 1995.[483] The Maritime Arbitration Commission of the USSR Chamber of Commerce and Industry[484] has likewise become an arbitral institution belonging to the Russian Federation with a new statute adopted on July 7, 1993.[485] In the other formerly Soviet republics, political instability and economic uncertainty are slowing the restructuring process.

– In Estonia, a Permanent Arbitration Court was established in 1991, attached to the Chamber of Commerce and Industry. Its rules were adopted on March 3, 1992.[486]

– Ukraine has already set up a Court of International Commercial Arbitration and a Maritime Arbitration Commission.[487]

– In Cuba, following the dissolution of the CMEA, the former Arbitration Court for External Trade at the Cuban Chamber of Commerce is now called the "Court of Arbitration

---

[480] Rules of January 1, 1982.

[481] Rules of the Arbitration Court at the USSR Chamber of Commerce and Industry, approved by the Decision of the Presidium of the USSR Chamber of Commerce and Industry of 11 March 1988, XIV Y.B. COM. ARB. 290 (1989); *see also* Dominique Hascher, *Actualité de l'arbitrage international en U.R.S.S.*, 1988 REV. ARB. 237; Dominique Hascher, *Règles de procédure de la Cour d'arbitrage de la Chambre de commerce et d'industrie de l'U.R.S.S.*, *id.* at 753.

[482] The new Statute was published as an Annex I to the Law of the Russian Federation on International Commercial Arbitration of 7 July 1993 No. 5338-1; *see* XXI Y.B. COM. ARB. 286 (1996).

[483] *See* 11 ARB. INT'L 198 (1995), with an introductory note by V.V. Veeder at 187; XXI Y.B. COM. ARB. 265 (1996); 7 WORLD TRADE AND ARB. MATERIALS 161 (Nov. 1995); *see also* Komarov, *supra* note 91; Philipp A. Habegger, *The 1995 Rules of the International Commercial Arbitration Court at the Chamber of Commerce and Industry of the Russian Federation*, 12 J. INT'L ARB. 65 (Dec. 1995).

[484] For the Commission's Rules of Procedure, see VIII Y.B. COM. ARB. 219 (1983).

[485] Annex II to the Law of the Russian Federation on International Commercial Arbitration of 7 July 1993 No. 5338-1; *see* 8 INT'L ARB. REP. E1, E10 (Sept. 1993); *Russian Federation* (Annex I, App. II), *in* ICCA INTERNATIONAL HANDBOOK ON COMMERCIAL ARBITRATION (Jan. 1994); XXI Y.B. COM. ARB. 265 (1996).

[486] *See* Andres Hallmägi, *Estonia: The First Steps in Arbitration*, *in* ICC BULLETIN, SPECIAL SUPPLEMENT, INTERNATIONAL COMMERCIAL ARBITRATION IN EUROPE 93 (1994).

[487] Pobirchenko, *supra* note 92.

of Foreign Trade of the Republic of Cuba" and is no longer "attached" to the Chamber of Commerce.[488]

– As a result of the break-up of the Yugoslavian Federation, the Foreign Trade Arbitration Court of the Yugoslavian Federal Economic Chamber[489] has become attached to Serbia, with national institutions being created in other former Yugoslavian countries. A Permanent Court of Arbitration was set up in Slovenia in 1991, attached to the Chamber of Economy of Slovenia.[490] In Croatia, the Permanent Arbitration Court attached to the Croatian Chamber of Commerce adopted Rules of International Arbitration on April 15, 1992.[491]

– In China, the Foreign Trade Arbitration Commission (later renamed the Foreign Economic and Trade Arbitration Commission (on February 26, 1980)) has been known as the China International Economic and Trade Arbitration Commission (CIETAC) since 1988. It was created in 1954 and is affiliated to the China Council for the Promotion of International Trade. It adopted new rules in 1988.[492] As a result of the development of international trade with China, this institution is very active,[493] and is seeking to internationalize and liberalize its organs and rules, with the aim of overcoming the continuing reluctance of Western companies to use its services.[494] New rules were adopted on March 17, 1994 and came into force on June 1, 1994.[495] These were in turn amended on

---

[488] The Rules of May 26, 1976 remain in force.

[489] Its Rules were adopted December 25, 1981. See the text of these rules and commentary by Tibor Varady, *Notes sur le nouveau règlement de la Cour d'arbitrage auprès de la Chambre économique de Yougoslavie*, 1984 REV. ARB. 171.

[490] New Rules of Procedure are in force since August 5, 1993; *see* Ilesic, *supra* note 81.

[491] The Rules of International Arbitration of the Permanent Arbitration Court attached to the Croatian Chamber of Commerce were published in the Croatian Official Gazette No. 25/92 of April 29, 1992; *see* Sajko, *supra* note 82. For an English translation, see 1993 RIV. DELL'ARB. 737.

[492] For the original Chinese text and an official English translation, see CHUNG DEJUN, MICHAEL J. MOSER, WANG SHENGCHANG, INTERNATIONAL ARBITRATION IN THE PEOPLE'S REPUBLIC OF CHINA – COMMENTARY, CASES AND MATERIALS 332 (1995); for a French translation, see 1993 REV. ARB. 147, and the commentary by Sagot and Xie, *supra* note 157.

[493] Since 1994, around 800 disputes are submitted to it every year (statistics provided by Professor Tang Houzhi, Vice-President of the CIETAC). On the previous figures and this increase, see Wang, *supra* note 159, at 27; Chen, *supra* note 159.

[494] The High Court of the Supreme Court of Hong Kong has declared the vast majority of arbitral awards made under the auspices of CIETAC since 1989 to be enforceable, in application of the New York Convention. Only two of around 80 awards have been denied enforceability for a violation of due process; *see* Judith O'Hare, *The Denial of Due Process and the Enforceability of CIETAC Awards under the New York Convention – The Hong Kong Experience*, 13 J. INT'L ARB. 179 (Dec. 1996); see also the interesting experience related by Justin Hughes, *Foreign lis alibi pendens, Non-Chinese Majority Tribunals and Other Problems of Neutrality in CIETAC Arbitration*, 13 ARB. INT'L 63 (1997).

[495] *See* XXI Y.B. COM. ARB. 213 (1996); 6 WORLD TRADE AND ARB. MATERIALS 227 (Sept. 1994); for the Rules in French, see 1995 REV. ARB. 535, and the commentaries by Zhao-Hua Wang, *Arbitrage international en Chine: le nouveau règlement de la Commission d'arbitrage économique et commercial international*, 1994 REV. ARB. 597; Jacques Sagot and Hanqi Xie, *Principales nouveautés dans le règlement d'arbitrage 1994 de la CIETAC*, 1995 REV. ARB. 427; Zhang Yulin, *Towards the UNCITRAL Model Law – A Chinese Perspective*, 11 J. INT'L ARB. 87 (Mar. 1994); Michael J. Moser, *China's New International Arbitration Rules*, 11 J. INT'L ARB. 5 (Sept. 1994); Huang Yanming, *Some Remarks about the 1994 Rules of CIETAC and "China's New*

(continued...)

September 4, 1995, and the amended rules entered into force on October 1, 1995.[496] They were again revised in 1998. The new rules apply to cases filed after May 10, 1998, and both expand the jurisdiction of the CIETAC, to domestic disputes in particular, and give more freedom to the parties and the arbitrators in procedural matters.[497] The Maritime Arbitration Commission, set up in 1958 and also attached to the China Council for the Promotion of International Trade, has developed along similar lines.[498]

– The Arbitration Commission for External Commerce of the Socialist Republic of Vietnam was created in 1963 and absorbed the Maritime Arbitration Commission to become the Vietnam International Arbitration Centre in 1993. This Centre then adopted new rules with a more international emphasis.[499]

334. — Elsewhere in the world, there has been no systematic restructuring of the kind seen in the formerly socialist countries. National arbitral institutions are more diversified. Distinctions can be drawn between the following categories:

---

[495](...continued)
International Arbitration Rules", 11 J. INT'L ARB. 105 (Dec. 1994); Rong R. Yan and Christopher Kuner, *The New Arbitration Rules of the China International Economic Trade and Arbitration Commission*, 11 ARB. INT'L 183 (1995); on the review by the Japanese courts of arbitration in China, see Tokyo High Court, Jan. 27, 1994, Buyer v. Seller, XX Y.B. COM. ARB. 742 (1995); in France, see CA Paris, 1e Ch., Sec. C, Feb. 3, 1998, Metimex v. Zhuji Foreign Trade Corp. of Zhejiang, No. 96/83718, unpublished; in Switzerland, see Geneva Court of Justice, Dec. 11, 1997, G. S.A. v. C. Import and Export Company, 1997 BULL. ASA 667; in the United States, see Polytek Eng'g Co. v. Jacobson Companies, 984 F. Supp. 1238 (D. Minn. 1997); XXIII Y.B. COM. ARB. 1103 (1998). *See* David E. Wagoner, *U.S Court Demonstrates Pro-enforcement Bias in a Comprehensive Review of a CIETAC Award Under the New York Convention*, 1998 BULL. ASA 289.

[496] *See* CIETAC Arbitration Rules (Revised and Adopted by China Chamber of International Commerce on September 4, 1995. Effective as from October 1, 1995), 8 WORLD TRADE & ARB. MATERIALS 117 (Mar. 1996); for a commentary on the 1995 amendment, see Michael J. Moser and Zhang Yulin, *The New Arbitration Rules of the China International Economic and Trade Arbitration Commission*, 13 J. INT'L ARB. 15 (Mar. 1996); Sagot, *supra* note 159; for an early assessment, see Michael J. Moser, *CIETAC Arbitration: A Success Story?*, 15 J. INT'L ARB. 27 (Mar. 1998).

[497] *See* 13 INT'L ARB. REP. B1 (July 1998); *CIETAC Arbitration Rules Amended*, 13 INT'L ARB. REP. 14, 16 (June 1998); Jingzhou Tao, *Modifications des règles d'arbitrage de la CIETAC*, 1998 REV. ARB. 597.

[498] Its rules were first adopted on January 8, 1959, and were replaced on September 12, 1988, and then on October 1, 1995. *See* Moser, *supra* note 159.

[499] Decision of the Prime Minister, By-laws of the Center and Arbitration Rules of April 28, 1993, in force since August 20, 1993; *see* XXI Y.B. COM. ARB. 288 (1996); *see also* Kazuo Iwasaki, *Arbitration Of Foreign Investment Disputes In The Vietnam Arbitration Centre*, 11 INT'L ARB. REP. 29 (July 1996); Liem Chinh Pham, *Vietnam: Textes sur l'exécution des sentences arbitrales étrangères*, 1996 REV. ARB. 293; Tran Hun Huynh, *Le Centre d'arbitrage international du Vietnam (CAIV)*, 1997 RID COMP. 913; CHINH PHAM LIEM, L'ARBITRAGE COMMERCIAL INTERNATIONAL AU VIETNAM (Thesis, University of Paris II (France), 1999).

– arbitration centers attached to chambers of commerce of towns and cities. Numerous examples can be found in countries such as Austria,[500] Brazil,[501] Colombia,[502] Italy,[503] Sweden,[504] and Switzerland;[505]

– autonomous institutions created at a national level, as in Belgium,[506] England,[507] Germany,[508] India,[509] Italy,[510] Japan,[511] the Netherlands,[512] the United States,[513] and, more

---

[500] International Arbitration Centre of the Austrian Federal Economic Chamber, old rules of June 17, 1983, XI Y.B. COM. ARB. 221 (1986). *See also* LAMY, *supra* note 404, Arts. 541 *et seq.* Rules of Arbitration and Conciliation in force since September 1, 1991, XVIII Y.B. COM. ARB. 207 (1993).

[501] Camara de Mediaçao e Arbitragem de Sao Paulo (Centro das Industrias do Estado de Sao Paulo, Regulamento e Normas de Funcionamento).

[502] Bogota Chamber of Commerce Commercial Arbitration and Conciliation Center.

[503] Chamber of National and International Arbitration of Milan, established in 1986. In 1987, this institution brought in two distinct sets of arbitration rules, one for domestic arbitration, the other for international arbitration. They were revised in 1996. For the text of the International Arbitration Rules in force since May 1, 1996, see XXI Y.B. COM. ARB. 247 (1996).

[504] Arbitration Institute of the Stockholm Chamber of Commerce; Arbitration Rules, in force from January 1, 1988; *see* XIV Y.B. COM. ARB. 251 (1989); LAMY, *supra* note 404, Annex 11-060/5, Arts. 491 *et seq.* These Rules were modified with effect from April 1, 1999, when the 1999 Swedish Arbitration Act entered into force.

[505] These include the Chamber of Commerce in Zurich (with International Arbitration Rules effective since January 1, 1989); the Chamber of Commerce and Industry in Geneva (with Rules in force since January 1, 1992 (*see* XVIII Y.B. COM. ARB. 195 (1993); 1993 CAH. JUR. FISC. EXP. 242, and the commentary by Christophe Imhoos, *Le nouveau Règlement d'arbitrage de la Chambre de commerce et d'industrie de Genève, id.* at 193; Gabrielle Kaufmann, *The Geneva Chamber of Commerce and Industry Adopts Revised Arbitration Rules,* 9 J. INT'L ARB. 71 (June 1992); Pierre-Yves Tschanz, *Le règlement d'arbitrage de la Chambre de commerce et d'industrie de Genève,* 1992 REV. ARB. 690)); the Camera commercio, industria e artigianato cantone Ticino in Lugano (with Arbitration and Conciliation Rules in force since March 1997).

[506] Centre Belge d'arbitrage et de médiation/Belgisch Centrum voor arbitrage en mediatie (CEPANI); *see infra* para. 344.

[507] The London Court of International Arbitration; on this institution, see *infra* para. 345.

[508] The German Institution of Arbitration (*Deutsche Institution für Schiedsgerichtsbarkeit* (DIS)), established on January 1, 1992 following the merger of the German Arbitration Committee (*Deutscher Ausschuss für Shiedsgerichtswesen* (DAS)) and the German Arbitration Institute (*Deutsches Institut für Schiedsgerichtswesen* (DIS)) which itself merged with the Berlin Court of Arbitration. The 1988 rules were then adapted to meet the requirements of this new structure. Further amendments were made in 1998: DIS Arbitration Rules 1998, in force as from July 1, 1998, 13 INT'L ARB. REP. A1 (July 1998); 1998 RIV. DELL'ARB. 831; *see* Joachim A. Kuckenburg and Stewart R. Shackleton, *The German Institution of Arbitration Issues New Arbitration Rules,* 13 INT'L ARB. REP. 37 (July 1998).

[509] The Indian Council of Arbitration, with Rules dated April 24, 1990, amended in 1998 (Publication of the Indian Council of Arbitration). *See* XXIII Y.B. COM. ARB. 310 (1998), with an introductory note by G.K. Kwatra at 307.

[510] The Italian Arbitration Association (Associazione Italiana per l'Arbitrato); *see infra* para. 344.

[511] The Japanese Commercial Arbitration Association; *see infra* para. 344.

[512] The Netherlands Arbitration Institute (Rules in force since December 1, 1986, XIII Y.B. COM. ARB. 205 (1988), last amended on January 1, 1998, XXIII Y.B. COM. ARB. 394 (1998)).

[513] The American Arbitration Association; *see infra* para. 344.

recently, Lebanon[514] and Mauritius.[515] These bring together arbitration specialists from both legal and business circles;

– institutions established by and attached to commodity markets or trade organizations. These institutions can be found in most countries which have a large volume of international trade.[516]

Over the past few years, new arbitral institutions have been set up, sometimes at the initiative of the government, as in Bahrain,[517] and often dedicated to international arbitration, as in Singapore.[518]

There is a marked contrast between the largest of these institutions, such as the AAA, which has offices throughout the United States, and others which operate on a much smaller scale. Networks have also been created comprising institutions set up in neighboring countries.[519]

335. — The genuinely international institutions are as diverse as the national institutions described above. Their international nature owes more to their structure than to their location, which may have fairly strong national connections. However, the founders and members of these institutions—whether individuals or organizations—invariably come from different countries. The institutions are also international by virtue of the fact that the arbitrators acting in the cases they supervise are of many different nationalities, and as a result of their rules, which are not governed by a particular national law.

336. — Some international institutions are bilateral: an example is the Arbitration Center of the Franco-German Chamber of Commerce and Industry, which was created in 1985.[520]

---

[514] The Lebanese Center of Arbitration (1996 Rules, adapted from the UNCITRAL Arbitration Rules; see 1996 REV. ARB. 673. These Rules are currently being revised).

[515] The Mauritius Chamber of Commerce and Industry (MCCI), Permanent Arbitration Court, Rules of Arbitration of January 1996, inspired by the ICC Arbitration Rules; see Gaston Kenfack Douajni, *La Cour Permanente d'Arbitrage de la Chambre de Commerce et d'Industrie de Maurice (CCIM)*, 1996 REV. ARB. 671; Barlem Pillay, *Setting up of an International Arbitration Center in Mauritius*, 1996 BULL. ASA 431.

[516] *See infra* paras. 340 *et seq.*

[517] Bahrain International Commercial Arbitration Center, established by Law No. 9 of May 20, 1993, and later amended by Legislative Decree No. 17 of 1996, effective June 12, 1996 (*see* 19 No. 10 MIDDLE E. EXECUTIVE REP. 10 (Oct. 1996)); for a French translation of the Law of May 20, 1993, see 1994 REV. ARB. 790.

[518] Singapore International Arbitration Centre, established in July 1991; Arbitration Rules effective as of October 22, 1997, XXIII Y.B. COM. ARB. 424 (1998); *see* Tabalujan, *supra* note 167.

[519] One example is the European Network for Dispute Resolution, set up in 1997 to cooperate in the settlement of small disputes (of a maximum of 100,000 euros). It currently groups together five French institutions (the Chambre Arbitrale de Paris, the Centre d'arbitrage Bordeaux Aquitaine (CABA), the Cour d'arbitrage et de médiation de l'Europe du Nord (CAREN, Lille), the Centre d'arbitrage Rhône Alpes (CARA, Lyon) and the Chambre de Conciliation et d'Arbitrage de Toulouse), two Spanish institutions (the Tribunal Arbitral de Comercio de Bilbao and the Corte de Arbitraje de Murcia), one English institution (the Centre for Dispute Resolution (CEDR) in London), and one Italian institution (the Camera Arbitrale del Piemonte, Torino).

[520] For the rules, see 1986 REV. ARB. 293, with an introductory note by F. Chartier at 291; Thomas Groos, *L'arbitrage de la Chambre officielle franco-allemande de commerce et d'industrie*, 1986 INT'L BUS. L.J. 205; *see also* 1986 CAH. JUR. FISC. EXP. 297; for the text of the new rules dated January 1993, see DICTIONNAIRE
(continued...)

Others have a broader base, such as the two regional arbitration centers founded in 1978, at the initiative of the Asian-African Legal Consultative Committee, in Cairo[521] and Kuala-Lumpur.[522] These institutions apply the UNCITRAL Rules and are intended to redress the imbalance in the location of international arbitrations by having more arbitrations take place in Asia and Africa rather than in Western Europe and the United States. Other examples include the Inter-American Commercial Arbitration Commission[523] (IACAC), the Euro-Arab Chambers of Commerce Arbitration System[524] and, more recently, the Commercial Arbitration and Mediation Center for the Americas (CAMCA), set up pursuant to the NAFTA Treaty[525] for the settlement of private international disputes between companies from Canada, the United States and Mexico.[526]

Finally, of the truly international organizations, several are public bodies: the most important of these is ICSID,[527] but other examples include the Permanent Court of Arbitration in The Hague, which has recently adopted two sets of arbitration rules for certain transnational disputes,[528] and the World Intellectual Property Organization (WIPO)

---

[520](...continued)
   JOLY, *supra* note 463, Vol. 2, Livre X, Annex 3–6.

[521] *See* 1986 REV. ARB. 487; *see also* M.I.M. Aboul Enein, *Arbitration Under the Auspices of the Cairo Regional Centre for Commercial Arbitration (An AALCC Centre)*, 2 J. INT'L ARB. 23 (Dec. 1985); LAMY, *supra* note 404, Arts. 298 *et seq.* The Centre adopted New Arbitration Rules, which became effective as of January 1, 1998. *See* XXIII Y.B. COM. ARB. 241 (1998).

[522] *See* LEE, *supra* note 433, ¶ 1230; *see also* P.G. Lim, *The Kuala Lumpur Regional Arbitration Centre*, 3 ICSID REV. – FOREIGN INV. L.J. 118 (1988); P.G. Lim, *The Regional Centre for Arbitration at Kuala Lumpur, Malaysia*, 5 INT'L CONSTR. L. REV. 53 (1988); Homayoon Arfazadeh, *New Perspectives in South East Asia and Delocalised Arbitration in Kuala Lumpur*, 8 J. INT'L ARB. 103 (Dec. 1991); LAMY, *supra* note 404, Arts. 451 *et seq.*; Jan Paulsson, *Contrats en Asie: Kuala Lumpur comme lieu d'arbitrage*, 1994 INT'L BUS. L.J. 248.

[523] L. Kos-Rabcewicz-Zubkowski, *L'arbitrage de la Commission interaméricaine d'arbitrage commercial*, *in* PROCEEDINGS OF THE 1ST INTERNATIONAL COMMERCIAL ARBITRATION CONFERENCE, *supra* note 224, at 87; LAMY, *supra* note 404, Arts. 341 *et seq.*; on this institution, the rules of which are of subsidiary application under the 1975 Panama Convention and the 1998 MERCOSUR Agreement, see FRUTOS-PETERSON, *supra* note 115, at 257 *et seq.*; Horacio Zapiola Perez, *Comission Interamerican de Arbitraje Comercial. CIAC–OEA. Seccion Argentina*, REV. DER. MERCOSUR, Year 2, No. 1, at 170 (Feb. 1998); Charles Norberg, *General Introduction to Inter-American Commercial Arbitration*, *in* ICCA INTERNATIONAL HANDBOOK ON COMMERCIAL ARBITRATION (Feb. 1998). On the IACAC Rules, see *supra* para. 296.

[524] *See infra* para. 348.

[525] Article 2022 of the NAFTA Treaty; on this Treaty, see *supra* paras. 77 and 239.

[526] For the English text of the Arbitration Rules of the CAMCA, which are derived from the UNCITRAL Rules, see XXII Y.B. COM. ARB. 320 (1997); for the Spanish text, see XIII REV. COR. ESP. ARB. 501 (1997); on the CAMCA, established on December 4, 1995 by the American Arbitration Association, the British Columbia International Commercial Arbitration Centre, the Camara Nacional de Comercio de la Ciudad de México and the Quebec Centre for National and International Commercial Arbitration, see Michael F. Hoellering, *Commercial Arbitration and Mediation Center for the Americas*, 13 J. INT'L ARB. 117 (June 1996); Edward C. Chiasson, *The Commercial Arbitration and Mediation Centre for the Americas: NAFTA's Mandate for the Private Sector*, 13 ARB. INT'L 93 (1997).

[527] *See supra* para. 301.

[528] Optional Rules for Arbitrating Disputes Between Two Parties of Which Only One Is a State, in force since July 6, 1993, XIX Y.B. COM. ARB. 338 (1994), with a foreword by P.J.H. Jonkman at 309; Optional Rules for Arbitration between International Organizations and Private Parties, effective July 1, 1996, XXII Y.B. COM.

(continued...)

Arbitration Center, which was set up in 1994 in Geneva.[529] Today, the only private institution with a genuinely universal reach is the ICC Court of Arbitration[530] although it now has strong competition from the LCIA and the AAA.

337. — In addition to this first distinction drawn between national and international arbitration institutions, there is a second distinction between generalist and specialist centers. The former will agree to organize the resolution of any form of dispute, while the latter specialize in arbitrations relating to particular products or activities.

338. — The generalist category contains the most well-known arbitral institutions. Some are attached to a Chamber of Commerce (as in Stockholm, Geneva or Zurich), while others are autonomous. They may be locally based (as is often the case in France) or established nationally (as with the AAA and the Japanese Commercial Arbitration Association). Most of the international centers are generalist institutions.

The disputes submitted to these institutions are usually of a legal nature, and the arbitration rules take this into account.[531]

339. — The specialist category is considerably larger. It comprises arbitral institutions set up by professional organizations with a view to resolving disputes relating to particular types of activity or trade.

340. — There are various arbitration centers specializing in maritime disputes, located in China, England,[532] France,[533] Germany, India,[534] Japan,[535] Poland, Russia[536] and the United States.[537]

---

[528](...continued)
ARB. 409 (1997).

[529] World Intellectual Property Organization (WIPO) Arbitration Rules, effective from October 1, 1994, XX Y.B. COM. ARB. 340 (1995).

[530] *See infra* para. 349.

[531] This is particularly the case with respect to the choice of arbitrators and the conduct of the arbitral procedure.

[532] London Maritime Arbitrators Association (*see* LEE, *supra* note 433, ¶ 550); LMAA Terms (1987), *in* MUSTILL AND BOYD, *supra* note 28, at 780. See also the London Maritime Arbitrators Association Terms (1987) as amended by the 1991 Revisions, 9 ARB. INT'L 289 (1993); Bruce Harris, Michael Summerskill and Sara Cockerill, *London Maritime Arbitration*, 9 ARB. INT'L 275 (1993).

[533] Paris Maritime Arbitration Chamber; for the Rules, see Eric Loquin, *Arbitrage – Institutions d'arbitrage, Annexes*, J.-CL. PROC. CIV., Fasc. 1003 or J.-CL. COMM., Fasc. 252, at 15 (1997).

[534] Indian Council of Arbitration; for the 1991 Rules, see XVII Y.B. COM. ARB. 345 (1992).

[535] Japan Shipping Exchange, Tokyo Maritime Arbitration Commission (TOMAC); for the TOMAC Arbitration Rules, as amended on September 1, 1996, see XXII Y.B. COM. ARB. 371 (1997); on the previous rules, see Hironori Tanimoto, *Sources of Law Relating to Maritime Arbitration in Japan*, 12 J. INT'L ARB. 101 (Mar. 1995).

[536] *See supra* para. 333.

[537] Society of Maritime Arbitrators, Inc. *See* Maritime Arbitration Rules, effective as of May 10, 1994, XX Y.B. COM. ARB. 321 (1995); 7 WORLD TRADE & ARB. MATERIALS 227 (Jan. 1995); *see also* Lucienne Carasso
(continued...)

There are also a number of institutions specialized in construction and civil engineering disputes, especially in Canada and France.[538]

341. — The international trade in commodities and foodstuffs has witnessed significant growth of specialized arbitration centers established by and operating under the control of national or international professional organizations. Among the most active centers on the international stage are, in England, those of the Grain and Feed Trade Association (GAFTA), which took over from the London Corn Trade Association in 1971,[539] and the Federation of Oils, Seeds and Fats Associations Limited (FOSFA).[540] In France,[541] important examples include the French Association pour le Commerce des Cacaos, which handles disputes relating to the cocoa trade, and the Paris Chamber of Arbitration, which principally deals with disputes relating to the domestic or international trade in agricultural products such as cereals, fruit and vegetables and animal feed.[542]

These specialized institutions have jurisdiction over disputes as a result of the application of model arbitration clauses contained in the general conditions or codes of practice incorporated in contracts for the sale of the goods in question. Most disputes concern the quality of goods, where the arbitrators take on the role of experts, except that their decision will be binding. The arbitrators may also deal with disputes concerning the interpretation or performance of the contract, although they will generally be professionals of the trade, familiar with both the goods and trade practices. Trade arbitration of this kind is generally very quick and therefore inexpensive. On the other hand, the rules of these institutions will very often provide for an appeal stage (again before arbitrators who belong to the same profession).

342. — The third distinction is between institutions handling both international and domestic arbitrations and those dealing exclusively with international arbitration.

343. — The former are more numerous and reflect the policy usually adopted by arbitral institutions: irrespective of whether their jurisdiction is generalist or specialist, institutions will not, in theory, discriminate on the basis of the international or domestic nature of the dispute, or the nationality or location of the parties. They are equally willing to deal with domestic and international arbitrations. To be in a position to do so they may have two

---

[537](...continued)
   Bulow, *The Revised Arbitration Rules of the Society of Maritime Arbitrators*, 12 J. INT'L ARB. 87 (Mar. 1995).

[538] Comité d'arbitrage de la Fédération nationale des travaux publics; for the Rules, see J.-CL. PROC. CIV., Fasc. 1003 or J.-CL. COMM., Fasc. 252, at 17 (1997).

[539] *See* LEE, *supra* note 433, ¶ 340.

[540] *See* LEE, *supra* note 433, ¶ 300.

[541] *See* 1990 REV. ARB. 227 *et seq.* (a special issue entirely dedicated to arbitral institutions in France).

[542] For the Rules, see J.-CL. PROC. CIV., Fasc. 1003 or J.-CL. COMM., Fasc. 252, at 9 (1997); 1981 REV. ARB. 336, and the commentary by Jean Petit, *Le Règlement de la Chambre arbitrale de Paris et le décret du 14 mai 1980 N° 80-354 relatif à l'arbitrage, id.* at 251.

different sets of rules, one for domestic arbitration, the other for international arbitration.[543] More usually, however, one set of rules will suffice, provided that those rules are not overly influenced by a particular national legal system.

344. — In America, Asia and Western Europe, most of the arbitral institutions attached to a chamber of commerce or operating at a national level handle both domestic and international arbitrations, although the latter generally represent a smaller proportion of their work. This is the case, for example, of the Quebec National and International Commercial Arbitration Centre (CACNIQ),[544] the Japanese Commercial Arbitration Association (JCAA),[545] the Italian Arbitration Association[546] and the Belgian Centre for Arbitration and Mediation (CEPANI).[547]

A few newer institutions have names suggesting that they deal only with international arbitration, despite the fact that their by-laws or rules do not exclude domestic arbitration. These include the Channel Islands International Arbitration Centre in Guernsey, which applies a variety of English, American and international rules depending on the choice made by the parties and the domestic or international nature of the dispute;[548] the Australian Centre for International Commercial Arbitration;[549] the British Columbia International Commercial

---

[543] This is the case, for example, of the Italian Arbitration Association (*see infra* para. 344), the Chamber of National and International Arbitration of Milan (*see supra* para. 334), the American Arbitration Association (*see infra* para. 344), and the Zurich Chamber of Commerce (*see supra* para. 334).

[544] For an English translation of the Rules, see PIERO BERNARDINI, ANDREA GIARDINA, CODICE DELL'ARBITRATO – AGGIORNAMENTO 482 (1994); for the French version, see 1994 REV. ARB. 201, and the commentary by Joëlle Thibault, *Le Centre d'arbitrage commercial national et international du Québec et son Règlement général d'arbitrage commercial, id.* at 69.

[545] Commercial Arbitration Rules, effective as of October 1, 1992; see XIX Y.B. COM. ARB. 285 (1994), with an introductory note by H. Hattori at 283; Charles R. Stevens, *Japan Commercial Arbitration Rules Revisited*, 9 ARB. INT'L 317 (1993).

[546] Following the new Italian law of January 5, 1994, the Association adopted two new sets of rules, effective as of September 30, 1994, one for domestic arbitration (1994 RIV. DELL'ARB. 609), and the other for international arbitration (1994 RIV. DELL'ARB. 815; for an English translation, see XXI Y.B. COM. ARB. 230 (1996)).

[547] See the institution's Rules, in force as of April 1, 1988, 1988 REV. ARB. 397; for a commentary, see G. Keutgen, *Le Centre belge pour l'étude et la pratique de l'arbitrage national et international – Une approche de l'arbitrage institutionnel en Belgique*, 68 REV. DR. INT. DR. COMP. 314 (1991). The new edition of these Rules, applicable as of January 1, 1997, simply adds provisions concerning arbitrations where the amount at stake is limited (Sec. V, Arts. 34 to 49), i.e., where each claim or counterclaim is for less than 500,000 Belgian francs (*see Nouvelles du CEPANI*, 1997 REV. ARB. 157; for an English translation, see XXIII Y.B. COM. ARB. 271 (1998)). On CEPANI case law, see Guy Keutgen, *Le règlement des incidents de procédure par les arbitres*, *in* JURA VIGILANTIBUS: ANTOINE BRAUN, LES DROITS INTELLECTUELS, LE BARREAU 205 (1994).

[548] *See* P.W.D. Redmond, *Arbitration in the Channel Islands*, 2 J. INT'L ARB. 45 (Dec. 1985).

[549] This is located in Melbourne.

Arbitration Centre;[550] and the Hong Kong International Arbitration Centre.[551] The French Arbitration Association (AFA) seldom handles international disputes.[552]

Finally, although the AAA primarily organizes the resolution of domestic disputes under its Commercial Dispute Resolution Procedures (formerly Commercial Arbitration Rules),[553] in 1982 it introduced Supplementary Procedures for International Commercial Arbitration.[554] This was followed in 1991 by the International Arbitration Rules, which were amended in 1992,[555] 1993 and 1997,[556] and seek to remove the aspects of the AAA's Commercial Arbitration Rules perceived as being too influenced by judicial procedure in the United States, in order to provide more flexibility (concerning, for example, the nationality of the arbitrators, written submissions and exchanges of evidence, hearings, the language of proceedings and the grounds for the award). In 1996, the AAA set up the International Center for Dispute Resolution in New York, to administer all AAA international arbitrations.[557] The latest reform of the rules has added a number of technical improvements.[558]

345. — Despite its name, the London Court of International Arbitration (LCIA) does not deal exclusively with international arbitration. However, its 1985 rules emphasized the independence of the LCIA's procedure from the rules of English law, under the influence of the draft version of the UNCITRAL Model Law.[559] Formerly known as the London Court of Arbitration, in 1975 it merged with several other equally well-established organizations,

---

[550] This is located in Vancouver.

[551] The Center has its own domestic arbitration rules and recommends the UNCITRAL Rules for international arbitrations; *see* LAMY, *supra* note 404, Arts. 441 *et seq.*

[552] For the Rules, see 1989 REV. ARB. 117, with an introductory note by Jean Robert.

[553] *See* LEE, *supra* note 433, ¶¶ 816 and 800; *see* Robert Coulson, *L'avenir de l'arbitrage international (formule américaine)*, 1990 CAH. JUR. FISC. EXP 631.

[554] *See* VIII Y.B. COM. ARB. 195 (1983); for the 1986 amendment, see XII Y.B. COM. ARB. 195 (1987).

[555] This amendment was effective as of May 1, 1992; for a commentary, see Françoise Joly, *Le Règlement d'arbitrage international de l'Association Américaine d'Arbitrage*, 1993 REV. ARB. 401.

[556] American Arbitration Association, International Arbitration Rules as amended and effective April 1, 1997, *reprinted in* 12 INT'L ARB. REP. C1 (June 1997); 9 WORLD TRADE AND ARB. MATERIALS 249 (July 1997); XXII Y.B. COM. ARB. 303 (1997).

[557] *See Commentary on the Proposed Revisions to the International Arbitration Rules of the American Arbitration Association*, ADR CURRENTS 6 (Winter 1996/1997). The Center's international caseload grew from 320 in 1997 to 430 in 1998, involving parties from 50 different countries (DISPUTE RESOLUTION TIMES, Apr. 199, at 1).

[558] According to the AAA Task Force on the International Rules, "[a]mong others, they shorten various time periods in order to accelerate the arbitration process; they clarify the scope of impartiality and independence of party-appointed arbitrators, while also providing a new rule for appointment of arbitrators in multi-party situations; and they clarify the ability and the duty of arbitrators to conduct arbitration proceedings by the most effective and efficient method possible" (*see Commentary*, *supra* note 556, at 7).

[559] 2 ARB. INT'L 47 (1986); *see* J. Martin H. Hunter and Jan Paulsson, *A Commentary on the 1985 Rules of the London Court of International Arbitration*, X Y.B. COM. ARB. 167 (1985); Carl F. Salans, *The 1985 Rules of the London Court of International Arbitration*, 2 ARB. INT'L 40 (1986); Jean de Hauteclocque, *Renouveau et croissance de la London Court of International Arbitration*, 1991 DPCI 170; Jean-Louis Delvolvé, *Le centenaire de la LCIA (London Court of International Arbitration)*, 1993 REV. ARB. 599.

including the Chartered Institute of Arbitrators, and celebrated its centenary in 1992.[560] In 1996, the LCIA began amending its rules, a process which was completed by the end of 1997. The new rules, which entered into force on January 1, 1998, are much longer than the previous rules. They now comprise 32 (instead of 20) articles, including a number of perhaps excessively detailed provisions taken from the WIPO Rules.[561] However, the new LCIA Rules do not yet take full advantage of the 1996 English Arbitration Act, which considerably expanded the autonomy of arbitral procedure. They were also influenced by the new ICC Arbitration Rules, which were completed a few months earlier.[562] The reform of the LCIA Rules, together with that of the rules of the AAA and the ICC, all contribute to the gradual harmonization of the rules governing international arbitral procedure.

346. — Other institutions, both national and international, deal exclusively with international arbitration.

347. — National institutions of this kind include the arbitration courts or commissions attached to the national chambers of commerce of the formerly socialist countries.[563] Even where these institutions have been "privatized," they have generally maintained their international specialization. This is also the case of the Center for International Commercial Arbitration in Los Angeles, which was created in 1986 solely for international commercial arbitration and has rules incorporating many of the provisions of the UNCITRAL Rules.[564] Another example is the Singapore International Arbitration Centre, established in 1991.[565]

348. — Of course, institutions with an international structure deal primarily, if not exclusively, with international arbitration.[566]

The Arbitration System of the Euro-Arab Chambers of Commerce, which was initially located in Paris but which transferred to London in 1994, broadened the scope of the arbitration mechanism which had originally been set up by the Franco-Arab Chamber of Commerce.[567] In 1982, all the Euro-Arab chambers of commerce in Western Europe adopted Rules of Conciliation, Arbitration and Expertise for disputes arising between European

---

[560] *See* 8 ARB. INT'L 313 (1992), a LCIA Centenary Special Issue. In 1999, the LCIA announced that, in 1998, it had received 70 new matters (*see Registrar's Review of 1998*, LCIA NEWSLETTER (Feb. 1999)).

[561] The 1998 Rules are reprinted in 37 I.L.M. 669 (1998); XXIII Y.B. COM. ARB. 369 (1998), with an introductory note by V.V. Veeder at 366; on the WIPO Rules, see *supra* paras. 323 and 336.

[562] On the updating of the ICC Rules, see *infra* para. 350.

[563] *See supra* para. 333.

[564] *See* 5 J. INT'L ARB. 150 (June 1988).

[565] Lawrence Boo, *SIAC Provides Mechanism for Resolving Disputes in Singapore*, 2 WORLD ARB. & MED. REP. 245 (1991). On arbitration in Singapore, see *supra* note 167.

[566] *See supra* para. 336. However, the 1998 ICC Rules of Arbitration now expressly allow the ICC, "[i]f so empowered by an arbitration agreement," to administer arbitrations resolving "business disputes not of an international character" (Art. 1(1)).

[567] See the text of these first rules at 1976 REV. ARB. 130, and the commentary by Philippe Fouchard, *Les nouvelles procédures de conciliation, d'arbitrage et d'expertise de la Chambre de commerce franco-arabe, id.* at 143.

companies and Arab companies.[568] The Rules came into force on January 1, 1983, and their administrative framework was revised on December 17, 1994. The specificity of this arbitration system is that the institution is composed of Arab and non-Arab members in equal numbers and that the applicable procedural and substantive rules are completely transnational, with particularities of neither Arab nor European legislation.

b) The International Court of Arbitration of the International Chamber of Commerce

349. — The ICC International Court of Arbitration was established in 1923 by the International Chamber of Commerce. It is based in Paris but organizes international arbitrations in many countries, and is undoubtedly the most important, most active and most "ecumenical" of the international arbitration institutions.[569] Admittedly, the ICC itself represents the business communities of countries with free market economies, and it does not yet have national committees[570] in a number of developing countries or in some of the existing or former socialist states.[571] However, in 1998 it fixed or confirmed a seat of arbitration in forty-one different countries.[572] Its remarkable development is demonstrated by the following figures: its 10,000th case was filed on June 8, 1998; of the 7,778 international disputes submitted to it between its founding in 1923 and December 31, 1992, 3,193 were submitted to it during the ten year period between 1982 and 1992, which amounts to more than 40% of the total volume, giving an annual average of 319 requests for arbitration over those ten years. Recently, its activity has grown again: it received 352 new cases in 1993, 384 in 1994, 427 in 1995, 433 in 1996, 452 in 1997, and 466 in 1998.[573] The International Court of Arbitration, for the period from April 8, 1997 to December 31, 1999, has 65 members representing 56 different countries, half of whom come from developing nations.[574] The universality of ICC arbitration can also be seen from the nationalities of the parties to ICC proceedings. In 1996, for the first time in the institution's history, less than half the parties involved in ICC arbitration were from Western Europe. In particular, in

---

[568] *See* XI Y.B. COM. ARB. 228 (1986); 1983 REV. ARB. 217, and the commentary by Michel Habib-Deloncle, *Le Règlement de conciliation, d'arbitrage et d'expertise des Chambres de commerce euro-arabes, id.* at 239; Richard Beaumont, *The Rules of Conciliation, Arbitration and Expertise of the Euro-Arab Chambers of Commerce,* 2 INT'L CONSTR. L. REV. 392 (1985); *see* BUSINESSMAN'S GUIDE TO THE EURO-ARAB ARBITRATION SYSTEM (1988).

[569] See the various reports and commentaries marking the 60th anniversary of the ICC Court of Arbitration, *in* INTERNATIONAL ARBITRATION – 60 YEARS OF ARBITRATION – A LOOK AT THE FUTURE (ICC Publication No. 412, 1984) and the articles on its history, by Frédéric Eisemann, *The Court of Arbitration: Outline of its Changes from Inception to the Present Day,* at 391, and its influence, by Ottoarndt Glossner, *The Influence of the International Chamber of Commerce upon Modern Arbitration,* at 399.

[570] These numbered 65 in 1998.

[571] In countries where there is no national committee, there is direct membership: this was the case in 130 countries in 1998.

[572] *1998 Statistical Report,* ICC BULLETIN, Vol. 10, No. 1 (1999).

[573] *1996 Statistical Report – A Historical Breakthrough,* ICC BULLETIN, Vol. 8, No. 1, at 6 (1997), and *1997 Statistical Report,* ICC BULLETIN, Vol. 9, No. 1, at 4 (1998); *1998 Statistical Report,* supra note 572.

[574] For its exact composition, see ICC BULLETIN, Vol. 8, No. 1, at 13 (1997).

recent years, there has been a significant increase in the number of parties from Latin America and the countries of the former Soviet Union. In total, the 1,151 parties to new ICC cases in 1998 came from 104 different countries.[575] The establishment in January 1997 of an ICC regional office in Hong Kong (ICC Asia) has led to an increase in the number of parties from South and South-East Asia from the figure of 15.1% of the 1997 total to 19.5% of the 1998 total.[576]

350. — The ICC Arbitration Rules have been revised on several occasions,[577] and the most recent reform is one of the most important. The revision process began in 1995 and involved two years of discussion within the ICC's International Arbitration Committee.[578] The new rules were adopted in April 1997 by the ICC Council and entered into force on January 1, 1998.[579] The ICC International Court of Arbitration will apply the new rules to all arbitrations beginning on or after that date unless otherwise agreed by the parties.[580]

The ICC Rules are the result of very extensive experience of international arbitration. They are therefore particularly representative of the private sources of international arbitration law and have had considerable influence on the rules and practice of other institutions. They are notable for the flexibility of their procedural provisions, for the powers

---

[575] ICC BULLETIN, Vol. 9, No. 1, at 5 (1998). For more detailed statistics on the origins of the parties, the nature of the disputes and the amounts at stake, see the various statistical reports published in ICC BULLETIN since 1991.

[576] ICC BULLETIN, Vol. 9, No. 1, at 4–5 (1998).

[577] The rules were revised in 1955, 1975, 1988 and, most recently, in 1998; for the 1988 Rules, see GUIDE TO ICC ARBITRATION (ICC Publication No. 448, 1994).

[578] *See* Richard H. Kreindler, *Impending Revision of the ICC Arbitration Rules – Opportunities and Hazards for Experienced and Inexperienced Users Alike*, 13 J. INT'L ARB. 45 (June 1996); Yves Derains, *The Revision of the ICC Rules of Arbitration – Method and Objectives*, ICC BULLETIN, Vol. 8, No. 2, at 10 (1997).

[579] ICC RULES OF ARBITRATION, *supra* note 430, *reprinted in* 12 INT'L ARB. REP. E1 (May 1997); XXII Y.B. COM. ARB. 347 (1997), with a foreword by H. Grigera Naon at 345. For a commentary, see YVES DERAINS AND ERIC A. SCHWARTZ, A GUIDE TO THE NEW ICC RULES OF ARBITRATION (1998); W. LAURENCE CRAIG, WILLIAM W. PARK, JAN PAULSSON, ANNOTATED GUIDE TO THE 1998 ICC ARBITRATION RULES WITH COMMENTARY (1998); ICC BULLETIN, SPECIAL SUPPLEMENT, THE NEW 1998 ICC RULES OF ARBITRATION – PROCEEDINGS OF THE ICC CONFERENCE PRESENTING THE RULES (ICC Publication No. 586, 1997); Stephen R. Bond and Christopher R. Seppala, *The New (1998) Rules Of Arbitration Of The International Chamber Of Commerce*, 12 INT'L ARB. REP. 33 (May 1997); Herman Verbist and Christophe Imhoos, *The New 1998 ICC Rules of Arbitration/Le nouveau Règlement d'arbitrage de la Chambre de Commerce Internationale de 1998*, 1997 INT'L BUS. L.J. 989; Michel A. Calvo, *The New ICC Rules of Arbitration – Substantial and Procedural Changes*, 14 J. INT'L ARB. 41 (Dec. 1997); Marc Blessing, *The ICC Arbitral Procedure Under the 1998 ICC Rules – What Has Changed?*, ICC BULLETIN, Vol. 8, No. 2, at 16 (1997); Horacio A. Grigera Naon, *The Appendices to the 1998 ICC Arbitration Rules*, ICC BULLETIN, Vol. 8, No. 2, at 37 (1997); Andreas Reiner, *Le Règlement d'arbitrage de la CCI, version 1998*, 1998 REV. ARB. 25; Walther J. Habscheid, *La giuridizione arbitrale della Camera di Commercio Internazionale – Osservazioni sul nuovo Regolamento del 1998*, 1998 RIV. DELL'ARB. 643.

[580] According to Article 6 of the new Rules, the parties, unless they otherwise agree, "shall be deemed to have submitted *ipso facto* to the Rules in effect on the date of commencement of the arbitration proceedings." On this issue, see Robert Briner, *The Implementation of the 1998 ICC Rules of Arbitration*, ICC BULLETIN, Vol. 8, No. 2, at 7 (1997).

conferred on the parties, the arbitrators and the Court itself, and for their complete independence, since 1975, from the procedural law of the seat of arbitration.[581]

In common with most arbitral institutions, the ICC International Court of Arbitration does not actually resolve the disputes submitted to it. It appoints or confirms the nomination of the arbitrators, oversees the progress of the arbitration, and approves the draft award.[582] The main provisions of its Rules and the role of the Court of Arbitration will be examined later in this book, in the context of the various stages of the arbitral process. The influence of ICC arbitration can also be seen in its awards, which, along with ICSID awards, are among the best known and most frequently invoked for their precedential value.[583]

The ICC is also responsible for other initiatives in the field of arbitration. One example is the publication in February 1990 of the ICC Rules for Pre-arbitral Referee Procedure, whereby the president of the International Court of Arbitration nominates a third party responsible for making provisional orders regarding any urgent measures which may be required.[584] A second example is the International Arbitration Rules for Airline Passenger Liability Claims, which should enter into force in 1999. As stated in Article 1 of the Draft dated October 8, 1997, the Rules are intended

> to be used for the conduct of arbitrations concerning recoverable compensatory damages sought in case of death or personal injury of a passenger arising out of or in connection with international air transportation.[585]

---

[581] *See, e.g.,* W. LAURENCE CRAIG, WILLIAM W. PARK, JAN PAULSSON, INTERNATIONAL CHAMBER OF COMMERCE ARBITRATION (2d ed. 1990); see also *ICC Arbitral Process,* published in ICC BULLETIN, since November 1991; Jean-Jacques Arnaldez, *Réflexions sur l'autonomie et le caractère international du Règlement d'arbitrage de la CCI,* 120 J.D.I. 857 (1993); DOMINIQUE HASCHER, COLLECTION OF PROCEDURAL DECISIONS IN ICC ARBITRATION – RECUEIL DES DÉCISIONS DE PROCÉDURE DANS L'ARBITRAGE CCI – 1993–1996 (1997).

[582] *See* Alain Prujiner, *La gestion des arbitrages commerciaux internationaux: l'exemple de la Cour d'arbitrage de la CCI,* 115 J.D.I. 663 (1988). See also the criticisms of ANTOINE KASSIS, RÉFLEXIONS SUR LE RÈGLEMENT D'ARBITRAGE DE LA CHAMBRE DE COMMERCE INTERNATIONALE (1988), and the response of Jan Paulsson, *Vicarious Hypochondria and Institutional Arbitration,* 6 ARB. INT'L 226 (1990); Robert H. Smit, *An Inside View of the ICC Court,* 10 ARB. INT'L 53 (1994); on the application of the ICC Rules by the ICC International Court of Arbitration, see the articles by members of the Court in ICC BULLETIN, Vol. 7, No. 2, at 6–91 (1996). On the principal modifications made in 1997, see the commentaries cited *supra* note 579.

[583] *See infra* para. 384.

[584] *See* ICC PRE-ARBITRAL REFEREE PROCEDURE – RULES IN FORCE AS OF JANUARY 1, 1990 (ICC Publication No. 482, 1990); 1990 REV. ARB. 937, and the commentary by Jean-Jacques Arnaldez and Erik Schafer, *Le Règlement de référé pré-arbitral de la Chambre de commerce internationale (en vigueur depuis le 1er janvier 1990), id.* at 835.

[585] Commission on International Arbitration, ICC International Court of Arbitration, Docs. No. 420/365 (Oct. 8, 1997) and 420/371 (July 15, 1998).

2° Rules of Other Organizations

351. — We shall not discuss here the arbitration rules prepared by organizations attached to the United Nations as, although they are optional *ad hoc* rules, they are of public origin.[586]

Other sets of rules with a more limited purpose have recently been adopted and published at the initiative of professional legal organizations and, in particular, bar associations and institutes specializing in the study of arbitration. These rules cover two of the more sensitive issues raised in everyday arbitration practice: evidence (a) and arbitrators' ethics (b).

a) Rules of Evidence

352. — The Anglo-American method of presenting evidence (including document production and the examination of witnesses) is often very different from that found in countries with a civil law tradition, which generally favor the unsupervised exchange of written evidence. In order to bridge the gap between the two systems and the resulting problems that often arise in international arbitration, in 1983 the International Bar Association (IBA) adopted "Supplementary Rules Governing the Presentation and Reception of Evidence in International Commercial Arbitration."[587] These rules have been revised and new "IBA Rules on the Taking of Evidence in International Commercial Arbitration" should be adopted by the IBA Council at its June 1, 1999 meeting in Boston. The IBA succeeded in retaining the most useful common law rules, while adapting them to be more flexible and less disconcerting for civil lawyers. It also maintained the two essential principles of compliance with due process and the arbitrator's discretion to make the ultimate decision as to the approach best suited to the case at hand.

353. — The same goal was pursued by the Mediterranean and Middle East Institute of Arbitration. Founded in Athens in 1987 with the aim of promoting international arbitration through conferences and academic analysis, it offers Standard Rules of Evidence[588] for use in international arbitration.

---

[586] *See supra* paras. 195 *et seq.*

[587] *See* 1 ARB. INT'L 125 (1985), and the commentary by D.W. Shenton, *An Introduction to the IBA Rules of Evidence, id.* at 118; X Y.B. COM. ARB. 152 (1985), with an explanatory note by D.W. Shenton at 145.

[588] 4 J. INT'L ARB. 157 (Sept. 1987).

b) Rules Governing Arbitrators' Ethics

354. — The issue of arbitrators' ethical standards is extremely important.[589] What degree of independence and impartiality should be required of arbitrators and, in practice, how can such standards be enforced without having to wait for a court to set an award aside? Lawyers and their professional associations have made useful contributions in this area. However, on some issues, and especially with regard to the degree of independence required of party-appointed arbitrators, they have yet to reach full consensus.[590]

355. — In the United States, the American Bar Association and the AAA jointly adopted a Code of Ethics for Arbitrators in Commercial Disputes in 1977, comprising seven canons.[591] The two organizations took a pragmatic approach, bringing their rules into line with practice. In many respects, they reduced the obligations of independence and impartiality borne by party-appointed arbitrators, considering them to be non-neutral arbitrators.

Practitioners in Europe, on the other hand, are hostile to the idea of non-neutral arbitrators. It was opposed first by the Governing Council of the Paris Bar,[592] then by the Council of the bars and law societies of the European Community and, most importantly, by the International Bar Association. The IBA's Rules of Ethics for International Arbitrators, adopted in 1987,[593] reflect the views of European lawyers, requiring all arbitrators, including those appointed by the parties, to be entirely neutral. To guarantee this, the Rules impose on all arbitrators the obligation to fully disclose their relations with the parties.

356. — This more demanding conception of arbitrators' ethical standards is beginning to prevail internationally, as a result of the support of arbitral institutions. It is important to note in this regard that the AAA no longer provides for non-neutral arbitrators in its 1997 International Arbitration Rules, Article 7 of which insists on the impartiality and independence of the arbitrators.[594] Certain other institutions, such as the Chamber of

---

[589] It should not, however, be confused with the ethical issues encountered by bar associations seeking to harmonize the conduct of counsel in international arbitrations. *See, e.g.*, François Dessemontet, *Les Usages du Barreau et l'arbitrage international*, *in* L'AVOCAT MODERNE – REGARDS SUR UNE PROFESSION DANS UN MONDE QUI CHANGE – MÉLANGES PUBLIÉS PAR L'ORDRE DES AVOCATS VAUDOIS À L'OCCASION DE SON CENTENAIRE 177 (F. Chaudet & O. Rodondi eds., 1998).

[590] On these issues, see *infra* paras. 1041 *et seq.*

[591] *See* X Y.B. COM. ARB. 131 (1985), with an introductory note by Howard Holtzmann.

[592] Decision of the Conseil de l'Ordre des Avocats au Barreau de Paris dated December 20, 1983; *see* 1984 REV. ARB. 438, with an introductory note by Jean-Louis Delvolvé, *Devoirs et responsabilités de l'avocat exerçant la fonction d'arbitre*, at 435.

[593] *See* XII Y.B. COM. ARB. 199 (1987); 3 ARB. INT'L 74 (1987), and the commentary by David J. Branson, *Ethics for International Arbitrators, id.* at 72; compare with the critical commentary by Robert Coulson, *An American Critique of the IBA's Ethics for International Arbitrators*, 4 J. INT'L ARB. 103 (June 1987); for a French translation, see 1988 REV. ARB. 333, and the commentary by Xavier de Mello, *Réflexions sur les règles déontologiques élaborées par l'International Bar Association pour les arbitres internationaux, id.* at 339.

[594] On this issue, see *infra* paras. 1041 *et seq.*

National and International Arbitration of Milan[595] and the Belgian Centre for Arbitration and Mediation (CEPANI)[596] have also produced ethical rules or codes. Similarly, in its publication entitled "Defining a status for international arbitrators: Elementary principles," the Commission on International Arbitration of the ICC also focused on arbitrators' rights and obligations.[597]

These ethical instruments have a significant influence over the performance by arbitrators of their brief. Admittedly, the IBA Rules stipulate that they apply only where the parties have expressly adopted them. However, the mere fact that these rules exist will lead the parties, the arbitrators and the courts to take them into account when examining arbitrators' conduct and liability. In spite of both their presentation as a code of ethics and the requirement for the express agreement of the parties, they constitute new rules, and therefore a new private source of arbitration law with a certain degree of authority.

B. – THE AUTHORITY OF PRIVATE ARBITRATION RULES

357. — In order to assess the authority of private arbitration rules, two issues must be addressed: what is the basis of that authority (1°), and what is the status of such rules in international arbitration law (2°)?

1° Basis of the Authority of Arbitration Rules

358. — Private arbitration rules apply for two reasons. At the very least, they have contractual value (a). They also, under certain conditions, illustrate usages or general principles of international arbitration (b).

a) The Contractual Value of Arbitration Rules

359. — The French courts have consistently held that if the parties refer to private arbitration rules in their arbitration agreements, those rules will apply.[598] Further, where an arbitration agreement specifies that a dispute is to be submitted to an arbitral institution, that means the rules of that institution will apply.[599]

---

[595] *Norme di comportamento dell'arbitrato*, 1997 RIV. DELL'ARB. 463.

[596] *Règles de bonne conduite pour les arbitrages CEPANI*, 1997 REV. ARB. 157.

[597] *See* ICC BULLETIN, Vol. 7, No. 1, at 29 (1996). *See also infra* para. 1010.

[598] For example, concerning the UNCITRAL Rules, see Cass. 1e civ., June 15, 1994, Sonidep v. Sigmoil, 1995 REV. ARB. 88, 1st decision, and E. Gaillard's note.

[599] Cass. civ., Feb. 26, 1941, Compagnie continentale d'importation du Sud-Ouest v. Passerieux, Sirey, Pt. I, at 53 (1941); FOUCHARD, *supra* note 205, ¶ 472, and the references cited in n. 3; CA Paris, Feb. 21, 1980, *Götaverken, supra* note 305; CA Paris, Dec. 9, 1980, *Aksa, supra* note 305; CA Paris, Jan. 22, 1982, Appareils

(continued...)

360. — The binding character of the procedural rules of the institution chosen by the parties is also recognized in all modern arbitration legislation. The 1961 European Convention, in its Article IV, is particularly clear on this issue. Under the heading "Organization of the Arbitration," it provides that "[t]he parties to an arbitration agreement shall be free to submit their disputes: (*a*) to a permanent arbitral institution; in this case the arbitration proceedings shall be held in conformity with the rules of the said institution."

361. — An arbitral institution can therefore provide in its rules that they will apply in principle if a dispute is submitted to arbitration under that institution's auspices. This is the case, for instance, of the ICC (Art. 6(1); Art. 8(1) of the previous Rules), and the LCIA (preamble of the 1998 Rules).

b) Arbitration Rules as Usages or Principles of International Arbitration

362. — On the whole, the content of arbitration rules is nowadays very similar.[600] In pursuing their common goal of organizing simple and effective proceedings, they include comparable provisions governing issues such as the commencement of proceedings, the preliminary examination of each party's case, and the powers of the arbitrators to examine questions of fact and law. If those rules are "widely known and regularly observed" (to quote the definition used in Article 9 of the United Nations Convention on Contracts for the International Sale of Goods (Vienna, April 11, 1980) to describe a usage in the field of international sales of goods), they may be considered usages, and can be applied as such, without the need for an express provision to that effect. At any rate, the abundance of, and similarities between, these private sources should certainly promote their recognition as usages. The importance of the organization that endorsed the rules will also contribute to

---

[599](...continued)
Dragon v. Construimport, 1982 REV. ARB. 91, 2d decision, and E. Mezger's note; *see also* Cass. 2e civ., June 8, 1983, Appareils Dragon v. Empresa central de abastecimientas y vantas de equipos, and CA Paris, May 17, 1983, Techni Import Professionnel (T.I.P.) v. Electro Scientific Industries (E.S.I.), 1987 REV. ARB.309; CA Paris, Nov. 18, 1983, Intercontinental Hotels NV v. Istanbul Turizm Ve Otelcilik, 1987 REV. ARB. 77, and observations by T. Bernard; CA Paris, Jan. 15, 1985, Opinter France v. Dacomex, 1986 REV. ARB. 87, and E. Mezger's note; CA Paris, Apr. 26, 1985, Abess Bros. and Sons Ltd. v. Société des Grands Moulins de Pantin, 1986 REV. ARB. 98, and observations by T. Bernard; CA Paris, Nov. 29, 1985, Société commerciale de produits agricoles (S.C.P.A.) v. Société coopérative de la Roche Clermault, 1987 REV. ARB. 335; Cass. com., May 19, 1987, Caille v. Peter Cremer France, 1987 Bull. Civ. IV, No. 117; 1988 REV. ARB. 142, and P. Ancel's note; CA Paris, July 7, 1987, Pia Investments Ltd. v. Cassia, 1988 REV. ARB. 649, and E. Mezger's note; CA Paris, Nov. 18, 1987 and May 4, 1988, Chambre arbitrale de Paris v. République de Guinée, 1988 REV. ARB. 657, 1st and 2d decisions, and P. Fouchard's note; TGI Paris, réf., June 23, 1988, République de Guinée v. MM. R... et O..., 1988 REV. ARB. 657, 3d decision, and P. Fouchard's note; TGI Paris, réf., Oct. 28, 1988, Drexel Burnham Lambert Ltd. v. Philipp Brothers, 1990 REV. ARB. 497, 1st decision; CA Paris, Jan. 17, 1992, Guangzhou Ocean Shipping Co. v. Société Générale des Farines, 1992 REV. ARB. 656, and observations by D. Bureau; TGI Paris, May 21, 1997, Cubic Defense Systems Inc. v. Chambre de commerce internationale, 1997 REV. ARB. 417, *aff'd*, CA Paris, Sept. 15, 1998, 126 J.D.I. 162 (1999), and E. Loquin's note; 1999 REV. ARB. 103, and P. Lalive's note.

[600] The reforms of the rules of the AAA, the ICC and the LCIA in 1997 are of great significance in this respect; *see supra* para. 345.

their general acceptance. Thus, the IBA's Code of Ethics, or the ICC Rules of Arbitration, will carry more weight than rules drawn up by a new institution or one that has no real activity.

363. — The courts and international organizations can also further this process. This will be so, for example, where a court applies usages created by arbitral institutions. In France, a number of substantive rules specific to international arbitration have been derived by the courts on the basis of institutional rules and the needs of international practice.[601] In the same vein, the French *Cour de cassation*, when reviewing a decision of the Court of Appeals regarding the recognition, enforcement, or setting aside of awards, will sometimes refer to "the principles of international arbitration" as opposed to a specific rule found in the New Code of Civil Procedure.[602] The attitude of international organizations such as the United Nations has a similar impact. The active participation of arbitral institutions in the drafting of instruments such as the UNCITRAL Rules of Arbitration and the UNCITRAL Model Law has helped to produce rules based on the practice of those institutions.

The importance of private arbitration rules is increased by the status granted to them in national legal systems.

2° The Status of Private Arbitration Rules in International Arbitration Law

364. — Public sources such as national laws and international conventions acknowledge the significant role played by private arbitration rules. Despite the essentially contractual nature of such rules, they will, in principle, take priority over other sources of arbitration law (a), and they generally prove to be sufficient on their own to regulate an arbitration (b).

a) Arbitration Rules Take Priority over Other Sources

365. — The principle that the agreement between the parties as to the arbitral procedure or, in practice, the parties' chosen arbitration rules, takes priority is contained in the New York Convention.[603] It is expressed in stronger terms in the 1961 European Convention, which makes no reference to national procedural laws even in a subsidiary capacity, and expressly declares that the arbitration rules of the chosen institution will govern.[604]

The priority of the arbitration rules chosen by the parties has been recognized in turn in national legislation. In Swiss law, for example, the mandatory provisions of the inter-cantonal *Concordat*, which formerly prevailed over arbitration rules according to its Article

---

[601] *See supra* paras. 132 *et seq.*

[602] Cass. 1e civ., Oct. 13, 1981, Société Européenne d'Etudes et d'Entreprises (S.E.E.E.) v. République socialiste fédérale de Yougoslavie, 109 J.D.I. 931 (1982), 1st decision, and B. Oppetit's note; 1983 REV. ARB. 63, and J.-L. Delvolvé's note.

[603] Art. V(1)(d); *see supra* para. 253.

[604] *See supra* paras. 284 and 360.

1, paragraph 2, no longer apply. Instead, under Article 182 of the Swiss Private International Law Statute, national law plays only a subsidiary role behind arbitration rules.[605] As for the 1996 English Arbitration Act, although it contains a fairly large number of mandatory provisions,[606] it contains, for the first time in an English arbitration statute, the principle that "the parties may make [their own] arrangements by agreeing to the application of institutional rules."[607]

366. — The liberal approach adopted in French international arbitration law as early as 1981 is equally clear. Under Article 1494 of the New Code of Civil Procedure, the arbitral procedure is determined in the arbitration agreement or, in the absence of any such determination, by the arbitrators. In either case, the incorporation of arbitration rules will suffice, with the selection of a procedural law simply optional. Article 1495 provides that if French law has been chosen, the agreement of the parties (and therefore the arbitration rules they choose) will always take precedence.[608]

Since 1981, the French courts have simply confirmed the position they had already taken before the reform of French law: international arbitration should not be restricted by having national law, including French law, govern the arbitral procedure. This has been the constant approach of the Paris Court of Appeals:[609]

> the provisions of the Rules of the [ICC] Court of Arbitration, which constitute the law between the parties, must be applied to the exclusion of all other rules.[610]

The *Cour de cassation* is equally firm: arbitration rules chosen in an arbitration agreement "serve as the parties' procedural law."[611]

367. — Most arbitral institutions have taken this development into account in order to avoid any legal uncertainty which might arise in the determination of the applicable national law. For example, Article 15, paragraph 1 of the 1998 ICC Arbitration Rules provides as follows:

---

[605] *See supra* para. 162.

[606] Sec. 4 and Sched. 1.

[607] Sec. 4(3); *see* Toby Landau, *The Effect of the New English Arbitration Act on Institutional Arbitration*, 13 J. INT'L ARB. 113 (Dec. 1996).

[608] *See supra* para. 139.

[609] *See, e.g.*, CA Paris, Apr. 26, 1985, *Abess Bros. and Sons*, and CA Paris, Nov. 29, 1985, *Société commerciale de produits agricoles, supra* note 599.

[610] CA Paris, May 15, 1985, Raffineries de pétrole d'Homs et de Banias v. Chambre de Commerce Internationale, 1985 REV. ARB. 141, 2d decision; JCP, Ed. G., Pt. II, No. 20,755 (1987), and P. Level's note.

[611] Cass. 1e civ., June 17, 1997, Thomson CSF v. Groupement Sanitec Megco (Beyrouth), 1998 REV. ARB. 414, and L. Kiffer's note.

The proceedings before the Arbitral Tribunal shall be governed by these Rules, and, where these Rules are silent, by any rules which the parties or, failing them, the Arbitral Tribunal may settle on, whether or not reference is thereby made to the rules of procedure of a national law to be applied to the arbitration.[612]

368. — Private sources of international arbitration law thus take precedence over public sources subject to two conditions. The first is that the rules comply with the fundamental principles of due process and equality of the parties. The second is that the rules be exhaustive.

b) Arbitration Rules Are Generally Sufficient to Regulate the Arbitration

369. — Private arbitration rules take the form of short codes of arbitral procedure. They are drafted and amended to reflect practical experience of litigation and the needs of potential users, and they regulate all aspects of the proceedings, from the constitution of the arbitral tribunal to the delivery of the award.

370. — If the content of arbitration rules is compared to that of the most recent national laws, it becomes clear that, in most cases, national legislators have not only abstained from providing a precise legal framework for international arbitration, but do not even suggest an appropriate model. National legislation is deliberately incomplete, thereby avoiding conflicts of rules and, as a result, increasing certainty. This legislative approach encourages arbitral institutions to draft exhaustive rules, and they have duly done so. In addition, by empowering the arbitrators to decide unresolved issues, arbitration rules reinforce the autonomy of international arbitration.[613]

§ 3. – Arbitral Awards

371. — Arbitrators in international trade are in effect private judges. However, in reaching their decisions, can they, like public judges, create law? This is not a problem of authority: all legal systems recognize the powers of arbitrators to identify and to apply rules of law to the extent necessary to resolve a dispute.[614] The question is whether there is such a thing as arbitral precedent.

Even in the context of court decisions, the concept of precedent and the extent of the court's ability to make law remains a controversial issue in civil law jurisdictions, and

---

[612] This replaces Article 11 of the previous Rules, which contained a similar provision. *See also* Art. 23-1 of the Rules of the Euro-Arab Chambers of Commerce.

[613] On the confirmation of this power of the arbitrators in procedural matters, see, in France, Cass. 1e civ., Mar. 8, 1988, Sofidif v. O.I.A.E.T.I., 1988 Bull. Civ. I, No. 64; 1989 REV. ARB. 481, and C. Jarrosson's note.

[614] Charles Jarrosson, *Arbitrage et juridiction*, DROITS, Vol. 9, at 107 (Apr. 1989).

particularly in France.[615] That debate will not be covered here, and the following observations regarding the notion of arbitral precedent are largely empirical.

372-373. — The decisions reached in arbitral awards naturally concern two bodies of rules: the law of arbitration itself, as a means of resolving disputes, and the law governing the merits of the dispute. Arbitral case law therefore exists in both of these areas: it helps to determine the substantive rules governing each stage of an international arbitration; it also confirms or creates usages, general principles of law and other rules of law specific to international commerce. Arbitral awards will sometimes, although not always, involve the determination of the applicable national law, especially with respect to the merits of a dispute. However, the way in which a choice of law is made by an arbitrator will be significantly different from the approach taken by a court, as the latter is obliged to follow its national choice of law rules.[616]

374. — Three conditions must be satisfied or, rather, three obstacles surmounted, for arbitral awards to have the same sort of influence as court decisions. First, the substance of the decisions reached in the awards must not have been reviewed by the courts, as that would cause them to be dependent on national legal systems. Second, the various decisions reached on a particular issue should display some degree of homogeneity. Third, the decisions should be accessible to the public. The value of arbitral awards as a source of law thus depends on their autonomy (A), consistency (B) and publication (C).

A. – AUTONOMY OF ARBITRAL AWARDS

375. — If a court hearing an action to enforce or set aside an arbitral award were to have a general power to review the substance of that award, it would be impossible for arbitral awards to have any precedential value. Any arbitral award which a court could confirm or reject as it pleased would ultimately be no more than one element of a given legal order, and its content would simply be that authorized by the supreme court, the body at the top of the judicial hierarchy.

376. — However, neither the New York Convention nor most national legal systems confer on the courts the power to review the merits of an award. Appeals aimed at reversing an arbitral award are generally excluded in international arbitration. For an award to be set aside, or for enforcement to be refused, it must be established that the award is so seriously

---

[615] *See* in particular, ARCHIVES DE PHILOSOPHIE DU DROIT, TOME 30, LA JURISPRUDENCE (1985); EVELYNE SERVERIN, DE LA JURISPRUDENCE EN DROIT PRIVÉ – THÉORIE D'UNE PRATIQUE (1985); Philippe Jestaz, *La jurisprudence, ombre portée du contentieux*, Dalloz, Chron. 149 (1989), and the references cited therein.

[616] On the content of the rules constituting *lex mercatoria* and the methods of determining the law applicable to the merits of the dispute, see *infra* paras. 1459 *et seq.* and 1538 *et seq.*

flawed that its international validity is affected. Such grounds for setting aside or refusing to enforce an award are very limited.[617]

When a court exercises its powers of review within that defined framework, the arbitrator's findings are not generally considered binding on the court.[618] Accordingly, an arbitral tribunal deciding upon the validity of an arbitration agreement or of its own appointment may well lack the autonomy necessary to create "arbitral case law."

377. — However, at least where an arbitral tribunal rules on the merits of a dispute, the situation is different. The merits of its award can only be reviewed by the courts to assess whether or not that award contravenes international public policy. This is an essential principle of international arbitration, which is constantly reaffirmed by the courts. The soundness of an arbitrator's judgment, in fact or in law, cannot therefore be reviewed.[619]

In the *Valenciana* case, the French courts provided a good example of the extent of the autonomy of the arbitrators in determining the applicable law. The *Cour de cassation*, reviewing a Court of Appeals' decision rejecting an action to set aside an award in which the arbitrator, when deciding the merits of the dispute, had applied *lex mercatoria*, held that the arbitrator had made a ruling in law, and continued that:

> it was not for the Court of Appeals, instructed for violations covered by articles 1504 and 1502 3° of the New Code of Civil Procedure, to examine the conditions of the arbitrators' determination and implementation of the selected rule of law.[620]

This type of reasoning unquestionably contributes to the creation of a climate that promotes the development of arbitral case law distinct from court precedent.[621]

378. — In order to develop autonomous case law of this kind, arbitrators need to apply rules of law which differ from those applied by the courts. It is a firmly established principle of modern international arbitration law that arbitrators are in an entirely different position to that of courts. They have no forum and therefore do not have to apply a national law or a particular choice of law system—even that of the seat of the arbitration. These principles are widely recognized in comparative and treaty law, but views differ as to the exact nature and hierarchy of the relevant rules. The application of trade usages is unanimously

---

[617] See *infra* paras. 1601 *et seq.*

[618] On this issue, see *infra* para. 1605.

[619] See *infra* para. 1603.

[620] See, for example, in France, Cass. 1e civ., Oct. 22, 1991, Compania Valenciana de Cementos Portland v. Primary Coal Inc., 1991 Bull. Civ. I, No. 275; 119 J.D.I. 177 (1992), and B. Goldman's note; 1992 REV. ARB. 457, and P. Lagarde's note; 1992 REV. CRIT. DIP 113, and B. Oppetit's note; 1992 RTD COM. 171, and observations by J.-C. Dubarry and E. Loquin; for an English translation, see 6 INT'L ARB. REP. B1, B4 (Dec. 1991).

[621] On the arbitrators' freedom to determine the rules applicable to the merits of the dispute in the absence of an agreement of the parties, see *infra* paras. 1537 *et seq.*

accepted,[622] as is the principle that, when deciding the merits of a dispute, arbitrators must apply the law chosen by the parties or, in the absence of such a choice, will enjoy a certain freedom in determining the applicable law.[623] French law has led the way in this respect: Article 1496 of the New Code of Civil Procedure makes no reference to the use of the choice of law method. Instead, it refers to the "rules of law" selected by the parties or chosen by the arbitrators, thus authorizing the arbitrators to look beyond the application of a particular national law and to consider general principles of law and *lex mercatoria* in establishing the legal basis for their decision.[624] This also prepares the way for the autonomy of arbitral case law.

The same trend can be seen in other jurisdictions. Certain modern arbitration statutes, borrowing from Article 1496 of the French Code, have in turn decided that arbitrators need only apply "rules of law," and not a particular national law. This is the case, in particular, in the Netherlands (Art. 1054 of the Code of Civil Procedure) and Switzerland[625] This approach allows arbitrators to apply rules of law of various types and origins, and in particular those now often referred to collectively as *lex mercatoria*, if they so decide, in the absence of a choice of law made by the parties themselves.

Although it remains disputed whether general principles of law and trade usages constitute a complete, autonomous legal order, the legal value of its rules is being confirmed with increasing frequency.[626] Moreover, even commentators who oppose *lex mercatoria* recognize that it is essentially a phenomenon linked to arbitration, and that its rules, which arbitrators consider to be specific to international trade, are principally found in arbitral awards.[627]

---

[622] Art. 7 of the 1961 European Convention; Art. 28(4) of the UNCITRAL Model Law; Art. 1496 of the French New Code of Civil Procedure; Art. 17(2) of the ICC Rules of Arbitration (Art. 13(5) of the previous Rules). On this issue, see Gaillard, *La distinction des principes généraux du droit et des usages du commerce international*, *supra* note 200.

[623] See the texts cited *supra*.

[624] On the use of these powers in arbitral awards, see *infra* paras. 1459 *et seq.*

[625] Art. 187 of the Swiss Private International Law Statute; *see* Reymond, *supra* note 58, at 407. In Algeria, see also Art. 458 bis 14 of the Code of Civil Procedure; *see* Mohand Issad, *Le décret législatif algérien du 25 avril 1993 relatif à l'arbitrage international*, 1993 REV. ARB. 377; in Lebanon, see Article 776 of the New Code of Civil Procedure.

[626] See the notes following Cass. 1e civ., Oct. 22, 1991, *Valenciana*, *supra* note 620; BUREAU, *supra* note 201; Andreas F. Lowenfeld, *Lex Mercatoria: An Arbitrator's View*, 6 ARB. INT'L 133 (1990); Gaillard, *La distinction des principes généraux du droit et des usages du commerce international*, *supra* note 200; TRANSNATIONAL RULES IN INTERNATIONAL COMMERCIAL ARBITRATION (ICC Publication No. 480/4, E. Gaillard ed., 1993); Fali S. Nariman, *International Commercial Arbitration and the Rule of Law*, ICC BULLETIN, Vol. 2, No. 2, at 7 (1991); Goldman, *Nouvelles réflexions sur la Lex Mercatoria*, *supra* note 200.

[627] On this issue, generally, see *infra* paras. 1443 *et seq.*

B. – CONSISTENCY OF ARBITRAL CASE LAW

379. — In order for arbitral awards to be sources of law, they must display a sufficient degree of consistency. However, does this consistency depend on the existence of a hierarchical judicial system lacking in the context of arbitration?

380. — The answer is less clear-cut than one might expect. Admittedly, there is no hierarchy in international arbitration comparable to that found in national court systems, with lower courts, appellate courts, and a supreme court responsible for ensuring the consistency of case law. Each arbitral tribunal is totally isolated, particularly in *ad hoc* arbitration, and is accountable only to the parties, subject at the very most to limited review by the courts.[628]

381. — However, most arbitrations are organized by institutions. When selecting the arbitrators, administering and overseeing the procedure, and in some cases reviewing the draft award (in the case of the ICC International Court of Arbitration) the institutions are able to give advice to arbitrators with a view to guaranteeing a minimum level of consistency in the awards made under their auspices.

Where an arbitral institution is specialized or where it is attached to a chamber of commerce, commodity market or professional organization, the arbitrators themselves are often professionals in that field. The resulting case law will be all the more consistent because the questions which arise will often be presented in similar terms, and because the arbitrators are responsible for applying the usages of the trade, which they help to create or adapt.

382. — Even where the arbitral institution is not specialized, it is possible for its awards to display a significant degree of consistency. A particularly important example is the ICC. It is true, of course, that its awards are made not by the Court of Arbitration, but by the members of each arbitral tribunal who are not bound by precedent. However, the ICC performs a vital regulatory function in codifying the usages of international commerce (in their collection of Incoterms, for example). The arbitrators acting under its auspices are naturally inclined to take this into account, and will generally consider that an arbitration agreement submitting disputes to ICC arbitration justifies the application of rules promoted by the ICC. Furthermore, for more general (and more complex) questions of international commercial law, the well-informed, specialized lawyers who act as arbitrators will tend to look to the same sources and to reason in the same way, based on a sound knowledge of new contractual practices and the same general principles. In any event, there is clearly an increasing tendency for arbitrators to refer to earlier arbitral awards and to recognize their

---

[628] *See supra* para. 376.

value as precedent.[629] However, achieving consistent solutions requires a knowledge of earlier decisions, as we shall now discuss.

C. – PUBLICATION OF ARBITRAL AWARDS

383. — Traditionally, the very idea of arbitral precedent is considered to be contrary to the confidential nature of both arbitration and the resulting arbitral awards.

This is a powerful objection, but it is not conclusive. It is true that if awards were known only to the parties, they could not constitute genuine sources of law.

384. — Of course, confidentiality will never be absolute: a small circle of people will be aware of the award, and that circle will grow if the award gives rise to litigation before the courts and thereby becomes public.[630] In addition, the principle of confidentiality is not universally applied and there is some discussion as to its legal basis. The primary purpose of the principle is the protection of business secrets.[631] In any event, it is important to underline that confidentiality is not breached by the publication of the reasons for an award on an anonymous basis. Such publication satisfies the general interests of business and legal practice, as it is legitimate that arbitration users and practitioners have access to the rules applied and the decisions reached by arbitrators. However, there are many other ways in which the effect of the principle of confidentiality[632] is diminished, to the extent that it has ever been strictly observed in practice. First, there has never been a general tradition of confidentiality. In many areas, arbitral awards are published, in most cases without disclosing the names of the parties. This is the case in maritime arbitration,[633] in institutional arbitration in the formerly socialist countries of Eastern Europe and in some trade

---

[629] This is clear from COLLECTION OF ICC ARBITRAL AWARDS, cited *infra* note 637. On the role of precedent in arbitral awards, see Klaus Peter Berger, *The International Arbitrators' Application of Precedents*, 9 J. INT'L ARB. 5 (Dec. 1992); Rolf A. Schütze, *The Precedential Effect of Arbitration Decisions*, 11 J. INT'L ARB. 69 (Sept. 1994); Vincenzo Vigoriti, *La decisione arbitrale come precedente*, 1996 RIV. DELL'ARB 33.

[630] For the censure by French courts of a breach of confidentiality resulting from recourse being brought before a court that clearly had no jurisdiction, see CA Paris, Feb. 18, 1986, Aïta v. Ojjeh, 1986 REV. ARB. 583, and G. Flécheux's note; Dalloz, Jur. 339 (1987). On this issue, generally, see Emmanuel Gaillard, *Le principe de confidentialité de l'arbitrage commercial international*, Dalloz, Chron. 153 (1987).

[631] *See* François Dessemontet, *Arbitration and confidentiality*, 7 AM. REV. INT'L ARB. 299 (1996), and, for a French version, *in* LE DROIT EN ACTION 61 (Publication of the Lausanne Law Faculty, 1996). On the issue, generally, see *infra* para. 1412.

[632] *See* Jan Paulsson and Nigel Rawding, *The Trouble with Confidentiality*, ICC BULLETIN, Vol. 5, No. 1, at 48 (1994); see also the special issue concerning confidentiality in arbitration, 11 ARB. INT'L 231–340 (1995); *see infra* para. 1412; Jean-Louis Delvolvé, *Vraies et fausses confidences, ou les petits et les grands secrets de l'arbitrage*, 1996 REV. ARB. 373; Edouard Bertrand, *Confidentialité de l'arbitrage: évolution ou mutation après l'affaire Esso/BHP v. Plowman/The Confidentiality of Arbitration: Evolution or Mutation Following Esso/BHP v. Plowman*, 1996 INT'L BUS.L.J. 169; Patrick Neill, *Confidentiality in Arbitration*, 12 ARB. INT'L 287 (1996); Andrew Rogers and Duncan Miller, *Non-Confidential Arbitration Proceedings*, 12 ARB. INT'L 319 (1996).

[633] For example, in France, the DROIT MARITIME FRANÇAIS review publishes numerous arbitral awards made in the shipping field.

arbitrations. The disclosure of awards is universally considered to contribute to the predictability of results, and the codification of usages by a professional organization will very often be the result of the publication of such decisions.

Second, in the field of state contracts, ICSID awards, *ad hoc* awards concerning disputes arising out of state contracts, and awards made in important and well-known cases are often published with commentaries, and will naturally serve as precedents. More generally, a broad movement has developed in favor of publishing awards: in France, the *Journal du droit international* has had an annual review of ICC arbitral awards since 1974[634] and ICSID awards since 1986.[635] The Yearbook Commercial Arbitration, among a number of other publications,[636] has also contributed to the "lifting of the veil." On reading the ICC awards and their commentaries,[637] one significant phenomenon becomes clear: the more recent awards are based on earlier decisions, and the decisions reached are generally consistent. The publication of awards thus enhances their homogeneity. In both arbitration law and international commercial law, arbitral awards have now become a private source carrying considerable weight and have undoubtedly helped to create the arbitral component of *lex mercatoria*.[638]

---

[634] With commentary by Y. Derains, S. Jarvin, J.-J. Arnaldez, D. Hascher.

[635] With commentary by E. Gaillard.

[636] For example, the REVUE DE L'ARBITRAGE, the ICC BULLETIN, the JOURNAL OF INTERNATIONAL ARBITRATION, the BULLETIN DE L'ASA, the RIVISTA DELL'ARBITRATO, and the INTERNATIONAL CONSTRUCTION LAW REVIEW.

[637] *See* COLLECTION OF ICC AWARDS (1974–1985), by Sigvard Jarvin and Yves Derains, 1986–1990, by Sigvard Jarvin, Yves Derains and Jean-Jacques Arnaldez, and 1991–1995 by Jean-Jacques Arnaldez, Yves Derains, and Dominique Hascher (respectively published in 1990, 1994, and 1997). On the methodology of these publications, see Kenji Tashiro, *Quest for a Rational and Proper Method for the Publication of Arbitral Awards*, 9 J. INT'L ARB. 97 (June 1992); *see also* L'APPORT DE LA JURISPRUDENCE ARBITRALE (ICC Publication No. 440, 1986); Philippe Kahn, *Les principes généraux du droit devant les arbitres du commerce international*, 116 J.D.I. 305 (1989); E. Loquin, *La réalité des usages du commerce international*, 1989 RID ÉCO. 163; Jan Paulsson, *La lex mercatoria dans l'arbitrage C.C.I.*, 1990 REV. ARB. 55; Filali Osman, *Les principes généraux de la "lex mercatoria"*, *in* CONTRIBUTION À L'ÉTUDE D'UN ORDRE JURIDIQUE ANATIONAL (1992); Yves Derains, *Les tendances de la jurisprudence arbitrale internationale*, 120 J.D.I. 829 (1993). On this issue, generally, see *infra* paras. 1458 *et seq.*

[638] *See infra* para. 1458.

PART TWO

THE ARBITRATION AGREEMENT

385. — An international arbitration agreement is an agreement in which two or more[1] parties agree that a dispute which has arisen or which may arise between them, and which has an international character,[2] shall be resolved by one or more arbitrators.[3]

386. — This definition covers two types of arbitration agreement: the arbitration clause, defined as an agreement by which the parties to a contract undertake to submit to arbitration the disputes which may arise in relation to that contract; and the submission agreement, which is an agreement by which the parties to a dispute that has arisen submit that dispute to arbitration.[4]

The distinction between arbitration clauses and submission agreements was of paramount importance when submission agreements alone were valid and enforceable, and when arbitration clauses were only enforceable if followed by a submission agreement.[5] This has never been the case in international arbitration in France. However, such a rule did exist

---

[1]   On multi-party arbitration, see JEAN-FRANÇOIS BOURQUE, LE RÈGLEMENT DES LITIGES MULTIPARTITES DANS L'ARBITRAGE COMMERCIAL INTERNATIONAL (Thesis, University of Poitiers (France), 1989) and *infra* para. 521 and in ICC arbitration, Eric A. Schwartz, *Multi-Party Arbitration and the ICC*, 10 J. INT'L ARB. 5 (Sept. 1993); Jean-Louis Delvolvé, *Final Report on Multi-party Arbitrations*, ICC BULLETIN, Vol. 6, No. 1, at 26 (1995) (approved by the ICC International Arbitration Committee), which contains several examples of clauses; Patrice Level, *Joinder of Proceedings, Intervention of Third Parties, and Additional Claims and Counterclaims*, ICC BULLETIN, Vol. 7, No. 2, at 36 (1996); Bernard Hanotiau, *Complex – Multicontract-Multiparty – Arbitrations*, 14 ARB. INT'L 369 (1998); YVES DERAINS AND ERIC A. SCHWARTZ, A GUIDE TO THE NEW ICC RULES OF ARBITRATION 62 *et seq.* (1998).

[2]   On the notion of internationality, see *supra* paras. 78 *et seq.*

[3]   On the drafting of an arbitration agreement from a practical standpoint, see especially ROGER P. BUDIN, LES CLAUSES ARBITRALES INTERNATIONALES (1993); THE FRESHFIELDS GUIDE TO ARBITRATION AND ADR (1993); Stephen Bond, *How to Draft an Arbitration Clause*, 6 J. INT'L ARB. 65 (June 1989); Marc Blessing, *Drafting an Arbitration Clause, in* ASA SPECIAL SERIES No. 8, THE ARBITRATION AGREEMENT – ITS MULTIFOLD CRITICAL ASPECTS 32 (1994); Arthur Rovine and Lawrence W. Newman, *Drafting Effective Dispute Resolution Clauses* (pts. I–II), 6 WORLD ARB. & MED. REP. 148 and 174 (1995); Markham Ball, *Just Do it – Drafting the Arbitration Clause in an International Agreement*, 10 J. INT'L ARB. 29 (Dec. 1993); Paul-A. Gelinas, *Arbitration Clauses: Achieving Effectiveness, in* ICCA CONGRESS SERIES No. 9, IMPROVING THE EFFICIENCY OF ARBITRATION AGREEMENTS AND AWARDS: 40 YEARS OF APPLICATION OF THE NEW YORK CONVENTION 47 (A.J. van den Berg ed., 1999); Charles Spragge and Neil Aitken, *Drafting the Arbitration Agreement*, 1 INT'L ARB. L. REV. 145 (1998); in ICSID arbitration, see Emmanuel Gaillard, *Some Notes on the Drafting of ICSID Arbitration Clauses*, 3 ICSID REV. – FOREIGN INV. L.J. 136 (1988); Georges R. Delaume, *How to Draft an ICSID Arbitation Clause*, 7 ICSID REV. – FOREIGN INV. L.J. 168 (1992).

[4]   See, for example, in French domestic arbitration law, the definitions given in Articles 1442 and 1447 of the New Code of Civil Procedure.

[5]   On this issue, see *infra* paras. 631 *et seq.*

until 1925 in French domestic arbitration, where the courts sought to protect weaker parties from arbitration clauses contained in standard form agreements. A law dated December 31, 1925 put an end to this situation and made arbitration clauses enforceable even in domestic cases.[6] A similar requirement that consent to arbitration be renewed after the emergence of the dispute has been repealed in most other jurisdictions.[7] Thus, today, the distinction between arbitration clauses and submission agreements has lost most of its significance,[8] even in domestic arbitration.[9]

As a result, although the distinction can be found in early treaties,[10] more recent instruments group the two concepts together, describing both as arbitration agreements.[11] This terminology is now widely accepted,[12] to the point that some recent statutes on arbitration no longer feel the need to specify that an arbitration agreement may take the form of either a submission agreement or an arbitration clause. This has been the case in Belgium since the law of July 4, 1972[13] and in Switzerland since the December 18, 1987 Private International Law Statute, Article 178(3) of which explicitly rejects the distinction, stating that "[t]he validity of an arbitration agreement cannot be contested on the ground that . . . the arbitration agreement concerns disputes which have not yet arisen." Likewise, the 1965

---

[6]   For a description of the evolution of the rules of French law governing the arbitration clause, see Matthieu De Boisséson, Le droit français de l'arbitrage interne et international 19 et seq. (2d ed. 1990).

[7]   See, for example, Article 2 of the Colombian Decree No. 2279 of October 7, 1989, as amended by Law No. 23 of March 21, 1991, which states that both arbitration clauses and submission agreements are valid; Art. 1416 of the Mexican Code of Commerce, as amended on July 22, 1993. On this issue, see Horacio Grigera Naon, *Arbitration in Latin America: Recent Developments in Mexico and Colombia*, in Jahrbuch für die Schiedsgerichtsbarkeit 263 (1990); Alexander C. Hoagland, *Modification of Mexican Arbitration Law*, 7 J. Int'l Arb. 91 (Mar. 1990); Isabel Zivy, *La nouvelle loi sur l'arbitrage au Mexique*, 1994 Rev. Arb. 295; Julio C. Treviño, *The New Mexican Legislation on Commercial Arbitration*, 11 J. Int'l Arb. 5 (Dec. 1994). The Brazilian arbitration statute dated September 23, 1996 maintains a clear distinction between arbitration clauses and submission agreements, but does not allow the implementation of the arbitration clause to be at the discretion of the defendant. See Articles 3 et seq. and the commentary by João Bosco Lee, *Le nouveau régime de l'arbitrage au Brésil*, 1997 Rev. Arb. 199; the introductory note by Paulo Borba Casella and Eduardo Lorenzetti Marques, 34 I.L.M. 1562 (1997); Carlos Nehring Netto, *Brazil* (at 5), in ICCA International Handbook on Commercial Arbitration (1998).

[8]   But see *infra* paras. 738 et seq. for the rules governing their expiration.

[9]   For a concurring view in French law, see Jean Robert, L'arbitrage – Droit interne – Droit International Privé ¶ 57 at 46 (6th ed. 1993); *comp. with* Jacqueline Rubellin-Devichi and Eric Loquin, *Arbitrage – Compromis et clause compromissoire*, J.-Cl. Proc. Civ., Fasc. 1020, ¶¶ 1 et seq. (1995); De Boisséson, *supra* note 6, at 111.

[10]   *See* Art. 1 of the Geneva Protocol of September 24, 1923 on Arbitration Clauses in Commercial Matters; Art. 1 of the Geneva Convention of September 26, 1927 on the Execution of Foreign Arbitral Awards.

[11]   *See* Art. II(2) of the 1958 New York Convention; Art. I(2)(a) of the 1961 European Convention.

[12]   *See, e.g.*, Art. 7(1) of the UNCITRAL Model Law of 1985.

[13]   Article 1677 of the Belgian Judicial Code. See also Article 1020(2) of the Netherlands Code of Civil Procedure, which, in its definition of the arbitration agreement, includes both submission agreements and arbitration clauses. The impact of this distinction is, however, limited to the manner in which the arbitral proceedings are commenced (Arts. 1024 and 1025). Compare with Articles 806 and 808 of the Italian Code of Civil Procedure, as amended by Law No. 25 of January 5, 1994, which continue to distinguish between submission agreements and arbitration clauses in domestic arbitration; Piero Bernardini, *Italy*, in ICCA International Handbook on Commercial Arbitration (forthcoming in 1999).

ICSID Convention simply refers to the concept of "consent" to arbitration (Art. 25(1)) in order to convey the additional idea that a state may, in a treaty or law on investments, agree to arbitration prior to the existence of a dispute.[14] The UNCITRAL Model Law only mentions the distinction to ensure that national legislation does not differentiate between the validity of each form of arbitration agreement.[15] Similarly, the 1996 English Arbitration Act states, in its Section 6(1), that "an arbitration agreement means an agreement to submit to arbitration present or future disputes."

In France, the courts have been using generic terms for some time. At first, they referred to "compromissory agreements" (*"accords compromissoires"*), as in the 1963 *Gosset* decision which set forth for the first time the principle of the autonomy of the arbitration agreement.[16] This terminology was also used in subsequent cases,[17] but the expression "arbitration agreement"[18] (*"convention d'arbitrage"*) was eventually preferred.[19] The

---

[14] On this issue, see especially Geneviève Burdeau, *Nouvelles perspectives pour l'arbitrage dans le contentieux économique intéressant les Etats*, 1995 REV. ARB. 3; Emmanuel Gaillard, *Centre International pour le Règlement des Différends Relatifs aux Investissements (C.I.R.D.I.) – Chronique des sentences arbitrales*, 126 J.D.I. 273 (1999); Christoph Schreuer, *Commentary on the ICSID Convention — Article 25*, 12 ICSID REV. – FOREIGN INV. L.J. 60 (1997). Regarding disputes concerning the interpretation of the consent requirement, see for example the Decision on Jurisdiction rendered on November 27, 1985 by E. Jimenez de Arechaga, president, M. El Mahdi and R. Pietrowski, Jr., in ICSID Case No. ARB/84/3, Southern Pacific Properties (Middle East) Ltd. v. Arab Republic of Egypt, XVI Y.B. COM. ARB. 16 (1991); 3 ICSID REP. 112 (1995); for a French translation, see 121 J.D.I. 218 (1994), together with E. Gaillard's note and the references cited therein.

[15] Article 7(1), and for an example of its implementation, Article 1029 of the German ZPO in force as of January 1, 1998.

[16] Cass. 1e civ., May 7, 1963, Ets. Raymond Gosset v. Carapelli, JCP, Ed. G., Pt. II, No. 13,405 (1963), and B. Goldman's note; 91 J.D.I. 82 (1964), and J.-D. Bredin's note; 1963 REV. CRIT. DIP 615, and H. Motulsky's note; Dalloz, Jur. 545 (1963), and J. Robert's note.

[17] Cass. 1e civ., May 18, 1971, Impex v. P.A.Z. Produzione Lavorazione, 99 J.D.I. 62 (1972), 3 decisions, and B. Oppetit's note; 1972 REV. CRIT. DIP 124, 2 decisions, and E. Mezger's note; 1972 REV. ARB. 2, 2 decisions, and P. Kahn's note; Dalloz, Jur. 37 (1972), 2 decisions, and D. Alexandre's note; Cass. 1e civ., July 4, 1972, Hecht v. Buisman's, 99 J.D.I. 843 (1972), and B. Oppetit's note; 1974 REV. CRIT. DIP 82, and P. Level's note; CA Paris, Feb. 21, 1964, Meulemans et Cie. v. Robert, 92 J.D.I. 113 (1965), and B. Goldman's note; 1964 REV. ARB. 55; 1964 REV. CRIT. DIP 543, and E. Mezger's note; *aff'd*, Cass. com., June 15, 1967, Cts. Robert v. Meulmans et Cie., 95 J.D.I. 929 (1968), and B. Goldman's note; CA Orléans, Feb. 15, 1966, Jean Tardits v. Wynmouth Lehr, Dalloz, Jur. 340 (1966); CA Colmar, Nov. 29, 1968, Impex v. P.A.Z., 1968 REV. ARB. 149; JCP, Ed. G., Pt. II, No. 16,246 (1970), and B. Oppetit and P. Level's note; CA Paris, June 19, 1970, Hecht v. Buisman's, JCP, Ed. G., Pt. II, No. 16,927 (1971), and B. Goldman's note; 98 J.D.I. 833 (1971), and B. Oppetit's note; 1971 REV. CRIT. DIP 692, and P. Level's note; 1972 REV. ARB. 67, and P. Fouchard's note; CA Paris, Dec. 13, 1975, Menicucci v. Mahieux, 104 J.D.I. 106 (1977), and E. Loquin's note; 1977 REV. ARB. 147, and P. Fouchard's note; 1976 REV. CRIT. DIP 506, and B. Oppetit's note.

[18] See for example, before the expression was used in the 1980 and 1981 Decrees, Cass. 1e civ., June 6, 1978, British Leyland International Services v. Société d'Exploitation des Etablissements Richard, 1979 REV. ARB. 230, and P. Level's note.

[19] Even where French law has been chosen by the parties to govern the proceedings, the fact that French domestic law still uses different terms to describe the two forms of arbitration agreement is of no consequence.

expression "arbitration agreement" also prevails in the leading institutional arbitration rules.[20]

387. — Against that background, we will consider in turn the autonomy of the arbitration agreement (Chapter I), its formation (Chapter II), its effects (Chapter III) and, lastly, its assignment and expiry (Chapter IV).

---

[20] *See* Art. 6 of the ICC 1998 Arbitration Rules (Art. 8 of the previous Rules); Art. 23 of the LCIA 1998 Arbitration Rules and Art. 15(1) of the 1997 AAA International Arbitration Rules. Compare with Article 3(3)(c) of the UNCITRAL Rules, adopted in 1976, which still refers to "the arbitration clause" and "the separate arbitration agreement that is invoked."

CHAPTER I
THE AUTONOMY OF THE ARBITRATION AGREEMENT

388. — The fundamental legal principle governing international arbitration agreements is that of their autonomy.[1] However, it should be emphasized at the outset that the term "autonomy" has a dual meaning. It is sometimes used in its traditional sense, which is to refer to the autonomy or separability of the arbitration agreement from the main contract to which it relates. Sometimes though, the courts, especially in France, refer to the autonomy of the arbitration agreement from "all national laws," which is an entirely different concept, related to the issue of the selection of the rules on the basis of which the existence and validity of an arbitration agreement must be assessed.[2]

We shall therefore examine each form of autonomy in turn.

---

[1] On the autonomy of the arbitration agreement, generally, see Frédéric-Edouard Klein, *Du caractère autonome de la clause compromissoire, notamment en matière d'arbitrage international (Dissociation de la nullité de cette clause de celle du contrat principal)*, 1961 REV. CRIT. DIP 499 and 1961 REV. ARB. 48; Pieter Sanders, *L'autonomie de la clause compromissoire, in* HOMMAGE À FRÉDÉRIC EISEMANN 31 (ICC Publication No. 321, 1978); STEPHEN SCHWEBEL, INTERNATIONAL ARBITRATION: THREE SALIENT PROBLEMS 1–60 (1987) ("The Severability of the Arbitration Agreement"); Pierre Mayer, *L'autonomie de l'arbitre international dans l'appréciation de sa propre compétence, in* COLLECTED COURSES OF THE HAGUE ACADEMY OF INTERNATIONAL LAW, Vol. 217, Year 1989, Part V, ¶ 110; Jean-Pierre Ancel, *L'actualité de l'autonomie de la clause compromissoire, in* TRAVAUX DU COMITÉ FRANÇAIS DE DROIT INTERNATIONAL PRIVÉ 1991–1993, at 75 (1994); CATHERINE BLANCHIN, L'AUTONOMIE DE LA CLAUSE COMPROMISSOIRE: UN MODÈLE POUR LA CLAUSE ATTRIBUTIVE DE JURIDICTION (with a preface by Hélène Gaudemet-Tallon (1995)); Antonias Dimolitsa, *Separability and Kompetenz-Kompetenz, in* ICCA CONGRESS SERIES NO. 9, IMPROVING THE EFFICIENCY OF ARBITRATION AGREEMENTS AND AWARDS: 40 YEARS OF APPLICATION OF THE NEW YORK CONVENTION 217 (A.J. van den Berg ed., 1999), and, for the French version, *Autonomie et "Kompetenz-Kompetenz"*, 1998 REV. ARB. 305; Pierre Mayer, *The Limits of Severability of the Arbitration Clause, in* ICCA CONGRESS SERIES NO. 9, IMPROVING THE EFFICIENCY OF ARBITRATION AGREEMENTS AND AWARDS: 40 YEARS OF APPLICATION OF THE NEW YORK CONVENTION 261 (A.J. van den Berg ed., 1999), and, for the French version, *Les limites de la séparabilité de la clause compromissoire*, 1998 REV. ARB. 359.

[2] On the dual meaning of the term, see Eric Loquin's excellent observations in his note following Cass. 1e civ., July 10, 1990, Cassia v. Pia Investments Ltd., 1990 REV. ARB. 851, 2d decision, and J.-H. Moitry and C. Vergne's note; 119 J.D.I. 168 (1992), and E. Loquin's note. The decision of the *Cour de cassation* in the *Comité populaire de la municipalité de Khoms El Mergeb v. Dalico Contractors* case on December 20, 1993 also clearly distinguishes between the two forms of autonomy of the arbitration agreement (121 J.D.I. 432 (1994), and E. Gaillard's note; 121 J.D.I. 690 (1994), and E. Loquin's note; 1994 REV. ARB. 116, and H. Gaudemet-Tallon's note; 1994 REV. CRIT. DIP 663, and P. Mayer's note).

SECTION I
AUTONOMY OF THE ARBITRATION AGREEMENT FROM THE MAIN CONTRACT

389. — What is traditionally meant by the autonomy of the arbitration agreement is its autonomy from the main contract in which it is found or to which it relates. Common law authors, long reluctant to accept the principle of autonomy,[3] tend to refer to it as the principle of "severability" or "separability." Some authors with a civil law background have also suggested that common law terminology such as the "separability,"[4] "independence"[5] or "detachment"[6] of the arbitration agreement should be preferred when referring to the traditional meaning of autonomy, so as to avoid any confusion with its second, more recent and more controversial meaning.[7] However, at least in continental Europe, the practice of referring to the principle of autonomy to denote the rule whereby the fate of the arbitration agreement is dissociated from that of the main contract is so firmly established that it would be unhelpful to change the accepted terminology merely for the purposes of avoiding the risk of such confusion.

390. — We will now examine in turn the nature (§ 1) and the consequences (§ 2) of the rule that the arbitration agreement is autonomous from the main contract.

§ 1. – Nature of the Rule

391. — The principle that the arbitration agreement is separable from the main contract has long been established in French law.[8] In its 1963 *Gosset* decision,[9] the *Cour de cassation* held that:

---

[3]   *See infra* para. 404.

[4]   *See* Mayer, *L'autonomie de l'arbitre international dans l'appréciation de sa propre compétence, supra* note 1; Mayer, *The Limits of Severability of the Arbitration Clause, supra* note 1.

[5]   *See* P. Mayer, note following CA Paris, Mar. 8, 1990, Coumet et Ducler v. Polar-Rakennusos a Keythio, 1990 REV. ARB. 675, 685, and P. Mayer's note.

[6]   *See* JEAN ROBERT, L'ARBITRAGE DROIT INTERNE – DROIT INTERNATIONAL PRIVÉ ¶283 at 249 (6th ed. 1993).

[7]   *See infra* para. 420.

[8]   On this issue, generally, see Phocion Francescakis, *Le principe jurisprudentiel de l'autonomie de l'accord compromissoire après l'arrêt Hecht de la Cour de Cassation,* 1974 REV. ARB. 67; HENRI MOTULSKY, ECRITS – VOL. 2 – ETUDES ET NOTES SUR L'ARBITRAGE 335 *et seq.* (1974); Mayer, *L'autonomie de l'arbitre international dans l'appréciation de sa propre compétence, supra* note 1; Ancel, *supra* note 1.

[9]   Cass. 1e civ., May 7, 1963, Ets. Raymond Gosset v. Carapelli, JCP, Ed. G., Pt. II, No. 13,405 (1963), and B. Goldman's note; 91 J.D.I. 82 (1964), and J.-D. Bredin's note; 1963 REV. CRIT. DIP 615, and H. Motulsky's note; Dalloz, Jur. 545 (1963), and J. Robert's note.

[i]n international arbitration, the arbitration agreement, whether concluded separately or included in the contract to which it relates, shall, save in exceptional circumstances . . . , have full legal autonomy and shall not be affected by the fact that the aforementioned contract may be invalid.

The principle was reiterated in almost identical terms in subsequent decisions of various courts of appeals,[10] and has been consistently reaffirmed by the *Cour de cassation*.[11] The courts have, however, abandoned the reservation regarding "exceptional circumstances," which had never been applied in practice.

The principle that the arbitration agreement is autonomous of the main contract is without doubt a substantive rule of French international arbitration law. In other words, the French courts will consider an international arbitration agreement to be independent of the main contract regardless of both the position of any foreign law applicable to the contract and that of the rules governing the arbitration agreement itself.[12]

392. — Today, the autonomy of the arbitration agreement is so widely recognized that it has become one of the general principles of arbitration upon which international arbitrators rely, irrespective of their seat and of the law governing the proceedings.

This results from the recognition of the principle in the leading institutional arbitration rules (A) and, more importantly, from the fact that the principle has been almost unanimously accepted in arbitration statutes (B) and arbitral case law (C). Its acceptance can also be seen in recent decisions of international courts (D).

A. – RECOGNITION OF THE PRINCIPLE IN LEADING ARBITRATION RULES

393. — Arbitration rules derive their authority from the intentions of the parties who refer to them in their arbitration agreements. Consequently, where parties have referred to arbitration rules which enshrine the principle of the autonomy of the arbitration agreement,

---

[10] CA Paris, Feb. 21, 1964, Meulemans et Cie. v. Robert, 92 J.D.I. 113 (1965), and B. Goldman's note; 1964 REV. ARB. 55; 1964 REV. CRIT. DIP 543, and E. Mezger's note, *aff'd*, Cass. com., June 15, 1967, Cts. Robert v. Meulemans et Cie., 95 J.D.I. 929 (1968), and B. Goldman's note; CA Orléans, Feb. 15, 1966, Jean Tardits v. Wynmouth Lehr, Dalloz, Jur. 340 (1966), and J. Robert's note; CA Paris, June 19, 1970, Hecht v. Buisman's, JCP, Ed. G., Pt. II, No. 16,927 (1971), and B. Goldman's note; 98 J.D.I. 833 (1971), and B. Oppetit's note; 1971 REV. CRIT. DIP 692, and P. Level's note; 1972 REV. ARB. 67, and P. Fouchard's note. More recently, see CA Toulouse, Oct. 26, 1982, Sieur Behar v. Monoceram, 111 J.D.I. 603 (1984), and H. Synvet's note.

[11] *See* Cass. le civ., May 18, 1971, Impex v. P.A.Z. Produzione Lavorazione, 99 J.D.I. 62 (1972), 3 decisions, and B. Oppetit's note; 1972 REV. CRIT. DIP 124, 2 decisions, and E. Mezger's note; 1972 REV. ARB. 2, 2 decisions, and P. Kahn's note; Dalloz, Jur. 37 (1972), 2 decisions, and D. Alexandre's note; Cass. le civ., July 4, 1972, Hecht v. Buisman's, 99 J.D.I. 843 (1972), and B. Oppetit's note; 1974 REV. CRIT. DIP 82, and P. Level's note; CA Paris, Dec. 13, 1975, Menicucci v. Mahieux, 104 J.D.I. 106 (1977), and E. Loquin's note; 1977 REV. ARB. 147, and P. Fouchard's note; 1976 REV. CRIT. DIP 506, and B. Oppetit's note; Cass. le civ., Dec. 14, 1983, Epoux Convert v. Droga, 1984 REV. ARB. 483, and M.-C. Rondeau-Rivier's note; JCP, Ed. G., Pt. IV, at 60 (1984).

[12] *See infra* paras. 420 *et seq.*

those parties are presumed to have intended that the arbitration agreement be treated separately from the main contract. This is only a rebuttable presumption, of course, as the parties can always depart from the provisions of the arbitration rules they adopt. Nevertheless, the presumption may prove useful in the increasingly rare cases where the law governing the arbitration agreement does not recognize the principle of autonomy. In such a case the arbitrators or the courts can dissociate the treatment of the arbitration agreement from that of the main contract simply by basing their decision on the intentions of the parties, provided only that the law in question, although it may not expressly recognize the principle, does not expressly oppose it.

394. — The first leading arbitral institution to recognize the principle of the autonomy of arbitration agreements was the ICC in 1955.[13] Article 6, paragraph 4 of that institution's 1998 Rules (the same in substance as Article 8, paragraph 4 of the previous Rules) provides that:

> [u]nless otherwise agreed, the Arbitral Tribunal shall not cease to have jurisdiction by reason of any claim that the contract is null and void or allegation that it is non-existent provided that the Arbitral Tribunal upholds the validity of the arbitration agreement. The Arbitral Tribunal shall continue to have jurisdiction to determine the respective rights of the parties and to adjudicate their claims and pleas even though the contract itself may be non-existent or null and void.

The ICC Rules thus clearly confirm the autonomy of the arbitration agreement, both where it is alleged that the main contract is void and where it is alleged to be non-existent. As a result, there is no doubt that if the arbitrators hold the main contract to be void or even non-existent, they must rule accordingly without jeopardizing their jurisdiction by the same token. The arbitrators should only decline jurisdiction if they find that the arbitration agreement itself is either void or non-existent.

The ICC Rules are less explicit on the issue of whether the International Court of Arbitration must apply the same principle of severability when reviewing the existence and *prima facie* validity of the arbitration agreement, pursuant to Article 6, paragraph 2 of the ICC Rules (Article 8, paragraph 3 of the previous Rules). It is reasonable to assume that, as this *prima facie* review will be a scaled-down version of the examination carried out subsequently by the arbitrators, the principle of autonomy applicable by the arbitrators must necessarily be applied by the International Court of Arbitration. This is particularly so because when the source of the principle of autonomy is a set of arbitration rules, the parties are presumed to have intended that the arbitration agreement be treated as distinct from the main contract.[14] The International Court of Arbitration is therefore only asked to examine the existence and *prima facie* validity of the arbitration agreement, and not of the main

---

[13] On the history of this provision, see YVES DERAINS AND ERIC A. SCHWARTZ, A GUIDE TO THE NEW ICC RULES OF ARBITRATION 104 *et seq.* (1998).

[14] *See supra* para. 393.

contract. Thus, the two decisions of the International Court of Arbitration which have so far given rise to proceedings before the French courts, one upholding and one denying the existence of an ICC arbitration clause, were both reached after deliberations regarding the arbitration agreements alone.[15] The revision of the ICC Rules in 1998 reinforces this approach, the goal of the Court's *prima facie* review being now only to establish whether "an arbitration agreement under the Rules may exist."[16]

395. — The UNCITRAL Arbitration Rules adopted in 1976 also explicitly address the autonomy of the arbitration agreement. Article 21, paragraph 2 provides that:

> [f]or the purposes of article 21 [i.e., the determination by the arbitral tribunal on its jurisdiction], an arbitration clause which forms part of a contract and which provides for arbitration under these Rules shall be treated as an agreement independent of the other terms of the contract. A decision by the arbitral tribunal that the contract is null and void shall not entail *ipso jure* the invalidity of the arbitration clause.

Contrary to what has sometimes been suggested,[17] this text does not distinguish between the various kinds of jurisdictional challenges which can be put forward as a consequence of the flaws affecting the main contract. In particular, no distinction is to be made between situations where the action is based on the purported absence or non-existence of the main contract, and those where it is based on the allegation that such contract is void. Furthermore, the provision that a decision holding the contract to be null and void shall not entail "*ipso jure*" the invalidity of the arbitration clause should not be understood as some sort of limitation of the principle of separability. It simply means that:

> if the event causing the main contract to be void also affects the arbitration clause (invalid consent, for example), both must be declared void by the arbitrators who, as a result, will be unable to rule on the other aspects of the dispute.[18]

396. — More recently, institutional arbitration rules originating in common law countries have also adopted the principle of the autonomy of arbitration agreements. Article 14.1 of

---

[15] *See* CA Paris, 1e Ch. supp., July 11, 1980, Japan Time v. Kienzle France, No. H 2827, unpublished, discussed by Philippe Fouchard in *Les institutions permanentes d'arbitrage devant le juge étatique (A propos d'une jurisprudence récente)*, 1987 REV. ARB. 225, 232–33; TGI Paris, Oct. 8, 1986, Ceskoslovenska Obchodni Banka A.S. (Cekobanka) v. Chambre de Commerce Internationale (CCI), 1987 REV. ARB. 367, and comments by Fouchard, *supra*, at 233 *et seq.*

[16] On this issue, see Andreas Reiner, *Le Règlement d'arbitrage de la CCI, version 1998*, 1998 REV. ARB. 25, especially at 30 *et seq.*; DERAINS AND SCHWARTZ, *supra* note 13, at 89.

[17] *See infra* para. 411.

[18] Philippe Fouchard, *Les travaux de la C.N.U.D.C.I. – Le règlement d'arbitrage*, 106 J.D.I. 816, 837 (1979). *See also* Berthold Goldman, *Arbitrage (droit international privé)*, *in* ENCYCLOPÉDIE DALLOZ – DROIT INTERNATIONAL ¶ 57 (1968).

the 1985 LCIA Rules used terms almost identical to those of Article 21, paragraph 2 of the UNCITRAL Rules, as does its replacement, Article 23 of the 1998 Rules. Article 15, paragraph 2 of the 1991 AAA International Arbitration Rules was again very similar to Article 21, paragraph 2 of the UNCITRAL Rules. In the new Rules, which entered into force on April 1, 1997, it was clarified that the principle applies to cases where it is the scope of the arbitration agreement that is challenged. After stating that "an arbitration clause shall be treated as an agreement independent of the other terms of the contract," the previous text did not go on to mention that "a decision by the arbitral tribunal that the contract is null and void shall not for that reason alone render invalid the arbitration clause." This omission, which simply reflected the idea that the first sentence was self-explanatory, was addressed by having the new Rules add the above language in Article 15, paragraph 2. The decisions to incorporate the above provisions in the LCIA and AAA Rules are particularly significant in light of the historical reluctance of a number of common law countries to recognize the principle of the separability of the arbitration agreement.[19]

397. — Several other institutional arbitration rules have also recognized the principle of the separability of the arbitration agreement.[20] The same is true of a number of national arbitration laws.

B. – RECOGNITION OF THE PRINCIPLE IN ARBITRATION STATUTES

398. — The principle of the autonomy of the arbitration agreement has taken on a new dimension with its recognition in national legal systems, rather than simply by norms of private origin such as arbitration rules. As a result of this wider recognition, the principle has acquired a greater legitimacy and can now be considered a true transnational rule of international commercial arbitration.

399. — Admittedly, the recognition of the principle of autonomy is not clearly expressed in the major international arbitration treaties. The adoption of the principle by national legal systems therefore involved more than merely ratifying those treaties.

The 1958 New York Convention makes no direct reference to the principle of separability. It simply states that recognition and enforcement of the award may be refused if the party against whom such measures are sought can establish that the arbitration agreement "is not valid under the law to which the parties have subjected it or, failing any indication thereon, under the law of the country where the award was made" (Art. V(1)(a)). One author, noting that this provision could have the effect of subjecting the arbitration agreement to a law other than that governing the main contract, has suggested that the New York Convention is therefore implicitly in favor of the autonomy of the arbitration

---

[19] On this issue in England, see *infra* para. 404. But see, for the United States, *infra* para. 402.

[20] *See, e.g.*, Art. 19(4) of the 1997 Belgian CEPANI Rules and Art. 9(5) of the 1998 Netherlands Arbitration Institute Arbitration Rules.

agreement.[21] However, it is more likely that the drafters of the Convention in fact left the issue of separability to be decided by the relevant national legal systems.[22] The 1961 European Convention only deals explicitly with the question of whether arbitrators are competent to rule on the issue of their own jurisdiction (Art. V(3)). This question is of course closely related to that of the autonomy of the arbitration agreement,[23] but recognition of the principle of autonomy in the European Convention remains implicit nonetheless. The 1965 Washington Convention establishing the ICSID also confines itself to stating, at Article 41, paragraph 1, that "[t]he tribunal shall be the judge of its own competence."

400. — The principle of autonomy has been, however, expressly recognized in the statutes or case law of a large number of countries.

401. — Most modern arbitration laws contain an express provision setting forth the principle of the separability of the arbitration agreement. This is the case of Article 1697, paragraphs 1 and 2 of the Belgian Judicial Code (Law of July 4, 1972). Similarly, the 1986 version of Article 1053 of the Netherlands Code of Civil Procedure provides that "[a]n arbitration agreement shall be considered and decided upon as a separate agreement," and that "[t]he arbitral tribunal shall have the power to decide on the validity of the contract of which the arbitration agreement forms part or to which the arbitration agreement is related." Likewise, Article 178, paragraph 3 of the 1987 Swiss Private International Law Statute provides that "[t]he validity of an arbitration agreement cannot be contested on the ground that the main contract may not be valid."[24] Article 8 of the 1988 Spanish Arbitration Statute provides that the fact that a contract is void, non-existent or has expired does not necessarily invalidate the arbitration agreement relating to it.[25] The new Algerian,[26] Tunisian[27] and Egyptian[28] arbitration laws also clearly endorse the same approach, and recent statutes

---

[21] PETER SCHLOSSER, DAS RECHT DER INTERNATIONALEN PRIVATEN SCHIEDSGERICHTSBARKEIT ¶ 316 (1975).

[22] *See* ALBERT JAN VAN DEN BERG, THE NEW YORK ARBITRATION CONVENTION OF 1958, at 146 (1981).

[23] *See infra* para. 416.

[24] For similar case law under the Swiss *Concordat*, see PIERRE JOLIDON, COMMENTAIRE DU CONCORDAT SUISSE SUR L'ARBITRAGE 137–39 (1984). For case law based on Article 178 of the 1987 statute, see, for example, Swiss Fed. Trib., Oct. 13, 1992, State X v. Companies Y & Z, 1993 BULL. ASA 68; 1994 REV. SUISSE DR. INT. ET DR. EUR. 131, and observations by F. Knoepfler; Swiss Fed. Trib., Sept. 2, 1993, National Power Corp. v. Westinghouse, 1994 BULL. ASA 244, 246; 1994 REV. SUISSE DR. INT. ET DR. EUR. 159, and observations by F. Knoepfler.

[25] For a commentary, see Paz García Rubio's observations in ARBITRATION IN SPAIN 49–50 (B. Cremades ed., 1991).

[26] Art. 458 *bis* 1, para. 4 of the Algerian Code of Civil Procedure (Legislative Decree No. 93-09 of Apr. 25, 1993).

[27] Art. 61(1) of the Tunisian Arbitration Code promulgated by Law No. 93-42 of Apr. 26, 1993.

[28] Art. 23 of Egyptian Law No. 27 for 1994 Promulgating the Law Concerning Arbitration in Civil and Commercial Matters.

adopted in Latin America have followed the same path.[29] The same rule is found in the 1999 Swedish Arbitration Act (Sec. 3).

402. — In other legal systems, the courts have been responsible for the adoption of the principle of autonomy. This was the case in France in 1963[30] and in the United States where, in the 1967 *Prima Paint v. Flood & Conklin* decision, the Supreme Court declared that "arbitration clauses as a matter of federal law are 'separable' from the contracts in which they are embedded."[31] The Japanese courts have taken the same position,[32] as did the German[33] and Italian[34] courts prior to the adoption of the rule in their recently enacted statutes on arbitration.

403. — The most significant development in the area of the autonomy of the arbitration agreement came in 1985, with the introduction of the UNCITRAL Model Law on International Commercial Arbitration. Article 16, paragraph 1 of the Model Law reproduces the terms of Article 21, paragraph 2 of the UNCITRAL Arbitration Rules, and provides that:

> an arbitration clause which forms part of a contract shall be treated as an agreement independent of the other terms of the contract. A decision by the arbitral tribunal that the contract is null and void shall not entail *ipso jure* the invalidity of the arbitration clause.[35]

---

[29] *See, e.g.,* Art. 8 of the Brazilian arbitration statute of September 23, 1996; for a commentary, see João Bosco Lee, *Le nouveau régime de l'arbitrage au Brésil,* 1997 REV. ARB. 199; see also the introductory note by Paulo Borba Casella and Eduardo Lorenzetti Marques, 36 I.L.M. 1562 (1997); Carlos Nehring Netto, *Brazil* (at 8), *in* ICCA INTERNATIONAL HANDBOOK ON COMMERCIAL ARBITRATION (1998).

[30] *See supra* para. 391.

[31] Prima Paint Corp. v. Flood & Conklin Mfg. Co., 388 U.S. 395, 402 (1967); for a French translation, see 1968 REV. CRIT. DIP 91, and the commentary by Ernst Mezger, *Vers la consécration aux Etats-Unis de l'autonomie de la clause compromissoire dans l'arbitrage international, id.* at 25; *see also In re* Arbitration between Belship Navigation, Inc. v. Sealift, Inc., No. 95 CIV. 2748 (RPP), 1995 WL 447656 (S.D.N.Y. July 28, 1995); 1996 A.M.C. 209; 6 WORLD ARB. & MED. REP. 226 (1995); 10 INT'L ARB. REP. A1 (Aug. 1995); JACK J. COE, JR., INTERNATIONAL COMMERCIAL ARBITRATION: AMERICAN PRINCIPLES AND PRACTICE IN A GLOBAL CONTEXT 57 (1997).

[32] Kokusan Kinzoku Kōgyō K. K. v. Guard-Life Corp., 29 MINSHŪ 1061 (Sup. Ct., July 15, 1975); IV Y.B. COM. ARB. 122 (1979).

[33] *Landgericht* Hamburg, Mar. 16, 1977, Italian company v. German (F.R.) firm, III Y.B. COM. ARB. 274 (1978). With the introduction of a statute based on the UNCITRAL Model Law as of January 1, 1998, the rule is now found in Article 1040, paragraph 1 of the ZPO.

[34] *Corte di Appello* of Venice, Apr. 26, 1980, S.p.A. Carapelli v. Ditta Otello Mantovani, VII Y.B. COM. ARB. 340 (1982); *Corte di Appello* of Bologna, Dec. 21, 1991, SpA Coveme v. Compagnie Française des Isolants S.A., XVIII Y.B. COM. ARB. 422, ¶ 10 at 425 (1993). Since the entry into force of the January 5, 1994 law on international arbitration, the rule is found in Article 808, paragraph 3 of the Italian Code of Civil Procedure.

[35] For a commentary, see HOWARD M. HOLTZMANN AND JOSEPH E. NEUHAUS, A GUIDE TO THE UNCITRAL MODEL LAW ON INTERNATIONAL COMMERCIAL ARBITRATION – LEGISLATIVE HISTORY AND COMMENTARY 478 *et seq.* (1989).

A variety of countries, including many with a common law tradition, have implemented legislation based on the Model Law. As a result, the recognition of the principle of autonomy has become widespread.[36]

404. — This trend undoubtedly inspired the recent acceptance of the principle in English law.[37] English law's longstanding hostility to the rule, perhaps because it was viewed as paving the way for the even more unpalatable principle of "competence-competence,"[38] was clearly leaving the country increasingly isolated.

In particular, it was only recently that English law acknowledged the autonomy of the arbitration agreement where the main contract is void *ab initio*. Previously that was only the case where the arbitration agreement was contained in a separate document.[39] After some indications that things were beginning to change,[40] the English courts re-examined the principle in *Harbour v. Kansa*. The plaintiffs argued that a reinsurance contract containing an arbitration clause was illegal and therefore void on the grounds that the defendants had failed to observe regulations governing insurance businesses. The High Court in 1991,[41] followed by the Court of Appeal in 1993,[42] held the arbitration agreement to be valid and therefore declined jurisdiction. English law thus fell into line with a principle long admitted

---

[36] On this trend in common law countries, see, for example, Court of Appeal of Bermuda, July 7, 1989, Sojuznefteexport (SNE) v. Joc Oil Ltd., XV Y.B. COM. ARB. 384 (1990); 4 INT'L ARB. REP. B1 (July 1989); in Australia, Court of Appeal of New South Wales, Aug. 17, 1994, Ferris & Anor v. Plaister & Anor, 9 INT'L ARB. REP. D1 (Aug. 1994); Andrew Rogers and Rachel Launders, *Separability – The Indestructible Arbitration Clause*, 10 ARB. INT'L 77 (1994); in Canada, British Columbia Supreme Court, Vancouver, Sept. 13, 1991, Brian Harper v. Kvaerner Fjellstrand Shipping A.S., XVIII Y.B. COM. ARB. 358 (1993); in Hong Kong, Supreme Court, High Court, Oct. 29, 1991, Fung Sang Trading Ltd. v. Kai Sun Sea Products & Food Co. Ltd., XVII Y.B. COM. ARB. 289 (1992).

[37] Adam Samuel, *Separability in English Law—Should an Arbitration Clause Be Regarded as an Agreement Separate and Collateral to a Contract in Which It Is Contained?*, 3 J. INT'L ARB. 95 (Sept. 1986); Johan Steyn and V.V. Veeder, *England, in* ICCA INTERNATIONAL HANDBOOK ON COMMERCIAL ARBITRATION (1988), who stated at page 14 that "[t]he concept of the separability of the arbitration clause has not yet been fully worked out by the English courts." Compare with ALAN REDFERN AND MARTIN HUNTER, THE LAW AND PRACTICE OF INTERNATIONAL COMMERCIAL ARBITRATION (2d ed. 1991), where the authors, with a certain degree of optimism, presented the autonomy of the arbitration agreement as being a "relatively new but widely recognized" concept (at 174 *et seq.*, especially at 176). *See also* Carl M. Svernlöv, *The Evolution of the Doctrine of Separability in England: Now Virtually Complete?*, 9 J. INT'L ARB. 115 (Sept. 1992); RUSSELL ON ARBITRATION (D. Sutton, J. Kendall, J. Gill eds., 21st ed. 1997).

[38] *See infra* para. 416.

[39] *See, e.g.*, V.V. Veeder, *England*, XVII Y.B. COM. ARB. 456 (1992).

[40] Paul Smith Ltd. v. H & S International Holding Inc., [1991] 2 Lloyd's Rep. 127; XIX Y.B. COM. ARB. 725 (1994) (High Ct, Q.B. (Com. Ct.) 1991), where it is suggested that English law could accept the principle of autonomy even when it is argued that the contract is void *ab initio* (¶ 11 at 728).

[41] Harbour Assurance Co. (U.K.) Ltd. v. Kansa General International Insurance Co. Ltd., [1992] 1 Lloyd's Rep. 81 (Q.B. (Com. Ct.) 1991).

[42] Harbour Assurance Co. (U.K.) Ltd. v. Kansa General International Insurance Co. Ltd., [1993] Q.B. 701; [1993] 3 W.L.R. 42; [1993] 3 All E.R. 897; [1993] 1 Lloyd's Rep. 455; XX Y.B. COM. ARB. 771 (1995). For a commentary, see Peter Gross, *Separability Comes of Age in England: Harbour v. Kansa and Clause 3 of the Draft Bill*, 11 ARB. INT'L 85 (1995).

in most contemporary international arbitration laws. This case law was very clearly confirmed by Section 7 of the 1996 Arbitration Act, which provides that:

> [u]nless otherwise agreed by the parties, an arbitration agreement which forms or was intended to form part of another agreement (whether or not in writing) shall not be regarded as invalid, non-existent or ineffective because that other agreement is invalid, or did not come into existence or has become ineffective, and it shall for that purpose be treated as a distinct agreement.

405. — Given this overwhelming movement in national legal systems towards the recognition of the principle of autonomy, arbitrators now feel able to treat the rule as a general principle of international commercial law, and felt so even before the change in position of English law.[43]

C. – RECOGNITION OF THE PRINCIPLE IN INTERNATIONAL ARBITRAL CASE LAW

406. — Many arbitral awards have recognized the separability of the arbitration agreement as a general principle of international commercial arbitration, without considering it necessary to justify such recognition by reference to a particular national law.[44]

In the 1970s, the principle was applied in three arbitral awards made in the Libyan oil concession disputes. In all three cases, the arbitrators held that the arbitration agreements survived the termination, through nationalization, of the concession contracts, and that those arbitration agreements could therefore confer jurisdiction on the arbitrators. In *BP v. Libya* the plaintiff claimed that the nationalization law and subsequent legislation could not terminate the concession agreement, which remained valid and in force. In an award dated October 10, 1973, the sole arbitrator implicitly referred to the principle of autonomy, holding that "[the] BP Nationalisation Law was effective to terminate the BP concession, except in the sense that the BP concession forms the basis of the jurisdiction of the Tribunal and of

---

[43] In his course at the Hague Academy of International Law, *supra* note 1, Pierre Mayer argued that, even though England was isolated in its hostility towards the autonomy (or separability) of the arbitration agreement, the fact that it has one of the world's most sophisticated legal systems sufficed to show that the principle of autonomy did not constitute one of the general principles of international arbitration. We disagree with that view. To acknowledge the existence of a general principle only where the rule is unanimously accepted would be to deprive the notion of general principles of its effectiveness. The recognition of the principle in both national legal systems and international instruments was so wide even before English law fell in line that the principle was already, in our view, a general principle of international commercial law (*see supra* para. 404). The fact that England subsequently changed its law provides further evidence of the merits of the general principles approach.

[44] On this issue, see Yves Derains, *Les tendances de la jurisprudence arbitrale internationale*, 120 J.D.I. 829 (1993), especially at 832 *et seq.*

the rights of the Claimant to claim damages from the Respondent before the Tribunal."[45] In *Texaco v. Libya*, the sole arbitrator was more explicit in his recognition of the principle. In his preliminary award on jurisdiction dated November 27, 1975, he referred expressly to the principle in rejecting the Libyan government's argument that nationalization had rendered the concession contracts void and that the same necessarily applied to the arbitration clauses contained in those contracts.[46] Likewise, the sole arbitrator in *LIAMCO v. Libya* stated in his award of April 12, 1977 that "it is widely accepted in international law and practice that an arbitration clause survives the unilateral termination by the State of the contract in which it is inserted and continues in force even after that termination."[47] That survival is, of course, the major consequence of the autonomy of the arbitration agreement from the main contract.

The principle was developed further in the *Elf v. NIOC* preliminary award made in Copenhagen on January 14, 1982.[48] The sole arbitrator was presiding over a dispute arising from a contract which provided that:

> in arriving at the award, the Arbitration Board or the sole arbitrator shall in no way be restricted by any specific rule of law, but shall have the power to base his award on considerations of equity and on generally recognized principles of law and in particular international law.[49]

The contract also stipulated that in the absence of the agreement of the parties, the seat of the arbitration and the rules governing the arbitral procedure would be determined by the

---

[45] BP Exploration Co. (Libya) Ltd. v. Government of the Libyan Arab Republic, 53 INT'L L. REP. 297 (1979); V Y.B. COM. ARB. 143 (1980); see excerpts in French reproduced in 1980 REV. ARB. 117; for a commentary, see Brigitte Stern, *Trois arbitrages, un même problème, trois solutions – Les nationalisations pétrolières libyennes devant l'arbitrage international, id.* at 3; Robert B. von Mehren and P. Nicholas Kourides, *International Arbitrations Between States and Foreign Private Parties: The Libyan Nationalization Cases*, 75 AM. J. INT'L L. 476 (1981).

[46] Texaco Overseas Petroleum Co./California Asiatic Oil Co. v. Government of the Libyan Arab Republic; see summary of the preliminary award contained in IV Y.B. COM. ARB. 177, 179 (1980); the commentary by Stern, *supra* note 45. For the award on the merits, see extracts of the French original text in 104 J.D.I. 350 (1977), with a commentary by Jean-Flavien Lalive, *Un grand arbitrage pétrolier entre un Gouvernement et deux sociétés privées étrangères (Arbitrage Texaco/Calasiatic c/ Gouvernement Libyen), id.* at 319; for an English translation, see 17 I.L.M. 1 (1978), and extracts in IV Y.B. COM. ARB. 177 (1980); *see also* Gérard Cohen Jonathan, *L'arbitrage Texaco-Calasiatic contre Gouvernement libyen (Sentence au fond du 19 janvier 1977),* 1977 AFDI 452; François Rigaux, *Des dieux et des héros – Réflexions sur une sentence arbitrale,* 1978 REV. CRIT. DIP 435; Joe Verhoeven, *Droit international des contrats et droit des gens (A propos de la sentence rendue le 19 janvier 1977 en l'affaire California Asiatic Oil Company et Texaco Overseas Oil Company c. Etat libyen),* REVUE BELGE DE DROIT INTERNATIONAL 209 (1978–1979); von Mehren and Kourides, *supra* note 45.

[47] Libyan American Oil Co. (LIAMCO) v. Government of the Libyan Arab Republic, 20 I.L.M. 1 (1981); VI Y.B. COM. ARB. 89, 96 (1981); for a French translation, see 1980 REV. ARB. 132, and the commentary by Stern, *supra* note 45; *see also* von Mehren and Kourides, *supra* note 45.

[48] Elf Aquitaine Iran v National Iranian Oil Co. (NIOC), XI Y.B. COM. ARB. 97 (1986); for a French translation, see 1984 REV. ARB. 401, at 413 *et seq.*, and the commentary by Philippe Fouchard, *L'arbitrage Elf Aquitaine Iran c. National Iranian Oil Company – Une nouvelle contribution au droit international de l'arbitrage, id.* at 333 *et seq.*

[49] XI Y.B. COM. ARB. 97, 99 (1986).

arbitrator. The arbitrator decided upon Copenhagen as the seat of the arbitration and Danish law as that governing the arbitral procedure. However, he also ruled that the issues of "competence-competence" and the autonomy of the arbitration agreement would be governed by the *lex contractus*, as defined in the clause set out above. On that basis, the arbitrator held that:

> [t]he autonomy of an arbitration clause is a principle of international law that has been consistently applied in decisions rendered in international arbitrations, in the writings of the most qualified publicists on international arbitration, in arbitration regulations adopted by international organizations and in treaties. Also, in many countries, the principle forms part of national arbitration law.[50]

The arbitrator concluded that:

> the arbitration clause binds the parties and is operative unimpaired by the allegation by NIOC that the Agreement, as a whole, is null and void *ab initio*.[51]

Many other awards have recognized the principle of the autonomy of the arbitration agreement in similar terms.[52] This confirms the broad acceptance of a principle that is now applied in arbitral practice as a general principle of international arbitration law.

---

[50] *Id.* at 102–03.

[51] *Id.* at 103.

[52] *See, e.g.,* ICC Award No. 1507 (1970), German company v. South Eastern Asian state, 101 J.D.I. 913 (1974); ICC Award No. 1526 (1968), Belgian parties v. African state, 101 J.D.I. 915 (1974), and observations by Y. Derains, which reproduces word for word the reasoning used in the *Gosset* decision (*supra* note 9); ICC Award No. 2476 (1976), which relies on Article 13(4) of the ICC Rules of June 1, 1955 (corresponding to Article 6(2) of the current Rules) and which makes numerous references to Swiss law as that of the seat of arbitration (Swiss company v. Italian company, 104 J.D.I. 936 (1977), and observations by Y. Derains); ICC Award No. 2694 (1977), which, after having referred to the *Gosset* and *Hecht* decisions (*supra* notes 9 and 11), states that the principle of the autonomy of the arbitration agreement appears to be a substantive rule of international commercial law (French company v. Swiss, French and Luxembourg companies, 105 J.D.I. 985 (1978), and observations by Y. Derains); the interim award in ICC Case No. 4131 (Sept. 23, 1982), Dow Chemical v. Isover-Saint-Gobain, which holds, relying on the autonomy of the arbitration agreement, that "the sources of law applicable to determine the scope and the effects of an arbitration clause providing for international arbitration do not necessarily coincide with the law applicable to the merits of a dispute submitted to such arbitration" (IX Y.B. COM. ARB. 131, 133 (1984); for the original French text, see 110 J.D.I. 899 (1983), and observations by Y. Derains; 1984 REV. ARB. 137); interim awards in ICC Case No. 4504 (1985 and 1986), which infer from the principle of autonomy that the arbitration agreement is subject to a law other than the law of the main contract (Petroleum producer v. Two companies, 113 J.D.I. 1118 (1986), and observations by S. Jarvin); ICC Award No. 4381 (1986), which analyzes separately the validity of the arbitration agreement and that of the main contract (French company v. Iranian company, 113 J.D.I. 1102 (1986) and observations by Y. Derains); the September 10, 1975 award of the Arbitral Tribunal of the Netherlands Oils, Fats and Oilseeds Trade Association, Dutch private company v. German merchant, II Y.B. COM. ARB. 156 (1977); the June 23, 1973 award of the Court of Arbitration at the Bulgarian Chamber of Commerce and Industry, German (F.R.) enterprise v. Two Bulgarian State enterprises, IV Y.B. COM. ARB. 189 (1979); the July 9, 1984 award of the Foreign Trade Arbitration Commission at the USSR Chamber of Commerce and Industry in Case No. 109/1980, Sojuznefteexport v. Joc Oil Ltd., XVIII Y.B. COM. ARB. 92 (1993).

D. – RECOGNITION OF THE PRINCIPLE BY INTERNATIONAL COURTS

406–1. — The European Court of Human Rights has also made a contribution to the recognition of the principle of the autonomy of the arbitration agreement. In a case where the Greek Government claimed that it had terminated by statute both a construction contract and the arbitration clause contained in it, despite an award having already been made on the basis of the arbitration clause, the Court held that:

> the unilateral termination of a contract does not take effect in relation to certain essential clauses of the contract, such as the arbitration clause. To alter the machinery set up by enacting an authoritative amendment to such a clause would make it possible for one of the parties to evade jurisdiction in a dispute in respect of which specific provision was made for arbitration.[53]

407. — We will now examine how a similar consensus has emerged with respect to the consequences of the principle of autonomy.

§ 2. – Consequences of the Autonomy of the Arbitration Agreement

408. — The autonomy of the arbitration agreement from the main contract is a legal concept, not a factual determination. Thus, it does not mean that acceptance of the arbitration agreement must be separate from that of the main contract.[54] Neither does it mean that the arbitration agreement cannot follow the main contract where the latter is assigned to a third party.[55]

The consequences of the principle of autonomy are of some importance. They are either direct (A) or indirect (B).

A. – DIRECT CONSEQUENCES OF THE PRINCIPLE OF AUTONOMY

409. — The autonomy of the arbitration agreement from the main contract gives rise to at least two direct consequences: first, the arbitration agreement is unaffected by the status of the main contract (1°) and, second, it may be governed by a law different from that governing the main contract (2°).

---

[53] European Court of Human Rights, Stran Greek Refineries and Stratis Andreadis v. Greece, Dec. 9, 1994, Series A, No. 301-B; 1996 REV. ARB. 283, 292, and the commentary by Ali Bencheneb, *La contrariété à la Convention européenne des droits de l'homme d'une loi anéantissant une sentence arbitrale, id.* at 181; see also the references given *infra* para. 1169.

[54] *See infra* para. 492.

[55] *See infra* para. 712. *See* Mayer, *The Limits of Severability of the Arbitration Clause, supra* note 1.

1° The Status of the Main Contract Does Not Affect the Arbitration Agreement

410. — The fundamental consequence of the principle of autonomy is that the arbitration agreement is unaffected by events affecting the main contract.

As a result, the validity of the arbitration agreement does not depend on that of the main contract. The arbitration agreement will remain effective despite allegations that the main contract never came into existence,[56] was avoided,[57] was discharged[58] or was repudiated.[59] In the same way, the novation of obligations contained in the main contract will not deprive the arbitration agreement of effect,[60] and a settlement relating to the main contract will not necessarily terminate the arbitration agreement.[61]

411. — The extent of the rule that the arbitration agreement is unaffected by the status of the main contract has been the subject of some debate. Some authors have suggested that although an arbitration agreement would not be affected by the nullity of the main contract, it would be affected by the main contract's non-existence.[62] This distinction, which is

---

[56] See, for a case where a contract containing an arbitration agreement was signed but never came into force, Cass. 1e civ., Dec. 6, 1988, Navimpex Centrala Navala v. Wiking Trader Shiffahrtsgesellschaft MbH, 1989 REV. ARB. 641, and B. Goldman's note. *See also* Decision No. 30 of the Bucharest Court of Arbitration dated July 11, 1994, German seller v. Romanian buyer, 122 J.D.I. 670 (1995). For a case where a party alleged that a contract was "never applied," see Swiss Fed. Trib., June 9, 1998, C. S.r.l. (Italy) v. L.S. S.A. (Switzerland), 1998 BULL. ASA 653, 657.

[57] *See* Cass. 1e civ., May 7, 1963, *Gosset, supra* note 9; Cass. 1e civ., May 18, 1971, *Impex, supra* note 11; CA Orléans, Feb. 15, 1966, *Jean Tardits, supra* note 10; CA Colmar, Nov. 29, 1968, Impex v. P.A.Z., 1968 REV. ARB. 149; JCP, Ed. G., Pt. II, No. 16,246 (1970), and B. Oppetit and P. Level's note. In French domestic arbitration, see CA Paris, Mar. 9, 1972, Lefrère René v. Les Pétroles Pursan, 1972 RTD COM. 344, and observations by M. Boitard and J.-C. Dubarry and also the clumsy formulation used in CA Paris, July 6, 1995, Pigadis v. Prodim, 1997 REV. ARB. 85, and disapproving observations by Y. Derains; *see also* ICC Award No. 6503 (1990), French company v. Spanish company, 122 J.D.I. 1022 (1995), and observations by Y. Derains; ICC Award No. 5943 (1990), 123 J.D.I. 1014 (1996), and observations by D. Hascher.

[58] CA Paris, Feb. 21, 1964, *Meulemans, supra* note 10; Cass. com., Nov. 12, 1968, S.A. Minoteries Lochoises v. Langelands Korn Foderstof Og Cogningsforretning A.S., 1969 REV. ARB. 59.

[59] In French domestic arbitration, see Cass. 2e civ., Nov. 25, 1966, Société des mines d'Orbagnoux v. Fly Tox, Dalloz, Jur. 359 (1967), 2d decision, and J. Robert's note; 1967 RTD CIV. 680, and observations by P. Hébraud; in international arbitration, see the April 12, 1977 *LIAMCO* award, *supra* note 47; the award on jurisdiction made under the auspices of the Geneva Chamber of Commerce and Industry in the Kis v. TAG Markets case on June 1, 1989, which was upheld by the Swiss Federal Tribunal on November 15, 1989 (unpublished); Swiss Fed. Trib., Mar. 15, 1990, Sonatrach v. K.C.A. Drilling Ltd., 1990 REV. ARB. 921, and P.-Y. Tschanz' note. *See also* European Court of Human Rights, Dec. 9, 1994, *Stran Greek Refineries, supra* note 53.

[60] CA Paris, Mar. 4, 1986, Cosiac v. Consorts Luchetti, 1987 REV. ARB. 167, *aff'd*, Cass. 1e civ., May 10, 1988, 1988 REV. ARB. 639 , which holds that "the novation—should it be proven—cannot deprive the arbitration agreement inserted in the main contract of effect," without, however, relying expressly on the autonomy of the arbitration agreement. Both decisions are commented by C. Jarrosson. For other examples, see *infra* paras. 727 *et seq.*

[61] CA Paris, Mar. 4, 1986, *Cosiac, aff'd*, Cass. 1e civ., May 10, 1988, *supra* note 60; *see also* Swiss Fed. Trib., Sept. 6, 1996, X. v. Y., 1997 BULL. ASA 291, 300.

[62] *See* Sanders, *supra* note 1, and JOLIDON, *supra* note 24.

reminiscent of that found in English case law prior to the 1993 *Harbour v. Kansa* decision,[63] appears unfounded. To reject the autonomy of the arbitration agreement on the ground that one of the parties has claimed that the main contract never came into existence would be to run the risk of facilitating the delaying tactics which the principle of autonomy aims to prevent. This is because it is difficult to distinguish between a contract which is void and one which never came into existence. Further, the concept of a contract which never existed is both hard to define and rarely encountered. A mere allegation that a main contract never existed should not therefore suffice for an arbitrator's jurisdiction to be denied. The arbitrators must examine the allegation, and if they indeed decide that the main contract never existed—as in the case of a total absence of consent, for example—then they must apply the consequences of that finding to the merits of the dispute. If the arbitrators consider that the allegation that the contract never existed also applies to the arbitration agreement—not simply because the main contract never existed, but because the cause of that non-existence also affects the arbitration agreement—then they must likewise apply the consequences of that finding by declining jurisdiction.

The distinction between void and non-existent contracts is thus seldom found in court decisions concerning the validity of the arbitration agreement.[64] The distinction is also emphatically rejected in the 1961 European Convention, which provides that the arbitral tribunal is "entitled . . . to decide upon the existence or the validity . . . of the contract of which the [arbitration] agreement forms part" (Art. V(3)). It is also rejected in the UNCITRAL Arbitration Rules,[65] the 1997 AAA International Arbitration Rules (Art. 15(1)), and the 1998 LCIA Rules (Art. 23.1). The ICC Arbitration Rules, which state that "the Arbitral Tribunal shall not cease to have jurisdiction by reason of any claim that the contract is null and void or allegation that it is non-existent" (Art. 6(4) of the current Rules; Art. 8(4) of the previous Rules), also clearly oppose the distinction.[66] Likewise, the 1996 English Arbitration Act provides that an arbitration agreement is not affected by the contract of which it forms part being "invalid, non-existent or ineffective."[67]

---

[63] This decision was codified at Section 7 of the 1996 Arbitration Act. *See supra* para. 404 and notes 41 and 42.

[64] Examples from France are listed at para. 386 above. See also, on the formal validity of the arbitration agreement, the unsatisfactory decisions of Cass. 1e civ., July 10, 1990, *Cassia, supra* note 2; CA Paris, Nov. 14, 1996, Gefimex v. Transgrain, 1997 REV. ARB. 434, and observations by Y. Derains; CA Paris, Sept. 11, 1997, Alfalfas v. Comexol, 1998 REV. ARB. 564, and the commentary by Xavier Boucobza, *La clause compromissoire par référence en matière d'arbitrage commercial international, id.* at 495; CA Paris, 1e Ch., Sec. C, Jan. 19, 1999, CIC International Ltd. v. Ministre de la Défense de la République Fédérale d'Allemagne, No. 1998/03375, unpublished.

[65] Art. 21(2). See above at para. 395. Compare with Article 16(1) of the UNCITRAL Model Law which provides that "[a] decision by the arbitral tribunal that the contract is null and void shall not entail *ipso jure* the invalidity of the arbitration clause."

[66] For a commentary, see, for example, DERAINS AND SCHWARTZ, *supra* note 13, at 104 *et seq.*

[67] Section 7. Compare with Article 23.1 of the LCIA Rules which allows an arbitral tribunal to declare the main contract "non-existent, invalid or ineffective." *See supra* para. 396.

2° The Arbitration Agreement May Be Governed by a Law Different from that Governing the Main Contract

412. — The autonomy of the arbitration agreement also means that such agreements will not necessarily be governed by rules of the same nature and origin as those governing the main contract. This is true if the arbitration agreement is subject to a particular national law, following the application of traditional choice of law rules. It is equally true if, as in recent French cases, the existence and validity of the arbitration agreement are held to be governed by substantive rules adapted to the international nature of arbitration.

413. — Even if one considers that the existence and validity of an arbitration agreement should be determined by reference to a particular national law,[68] such law will not necessarily be that governing the main contract, as a result of the autonomy of the arbitration agreement. If one were to use the language of the Rome Convention of June 19, 1980 on the Law Applicable to Contractual Obligations, the arbitration agreement would be considered a "severable part," which the parties or even the courts may subject to a law other than that governing the rest of the contract.[69]

French case law, which at one stage adopted this choice of law approach,[70] provides many illustrations of this distinction. In a 1972 decision, the Paris Court of Appeals declared that "performance [of the arbitration clause] is not necessarily governed by the law governing [the contract containing the said clause]."[71] Likewise, in 1983 the Paris Court of Appeals rejected an action to set aside an award where the grounds for such action were that the arbitral tribunal had failed to apply the law governing the main contract when confirming its own jurisdiction. The Court based its decision on the fact that in the terms of reference the law governing the merits of the dispute had been distinguished, implicitly at least, from the rules governing jurisdiction.[72] Similarly, in another 1983 decision, the *Cour de cassation* upheld a ruling in which the court of appeals had refused to apply the law governing the main contract when interpreting its arbitration clause.[73] Finally, in the 1992 *Sonetex* decision, the *Cour de cassation* endorsed a decision of the Paris Court of Appeals which confirmed the existence of disputed arbitration agreements without examining the law governing the main contract. The Court of Appeals had held that "as far as the form and proof of these

---

[68] On this issue, see *infra* paras. 420 *et seq.* and, for a detailed discussion of the question, see Klein, *supra* note 1.

[69] *See* Arts. 3(1) and 4; for a commentary, see Paul Lagarde, *Le nouveau droit international privé des contrats après l'entrée en vigueur de la Convention de Rome du 19 juin 1980,* 1991 REV. CRIT. DIP 287. Arbitration agreements are of course excluded from the scope of the Convention (Art. 1(2)(d); IAN FLETCHER, CONFLICT OF LAWS AND EUROPEAN COMMUNITY LAW – WITH SPECIAL REFERENCE TO THE COMMUNITY CONVENTIONS ON PRIVATE INTERNATIONAL LAW 147 (1982).

[70] For an examination of French law, see *infra* para. 437.

[71] CA Paris, Jan. 25, 1972, Quijano Aguero v. Marcel Laporte, 1973 REV. ARB. 158, and P. Fouchard's note.

[72] CA Paris, Oct. 21, 1983, Isover-Saint-Gobain v. Dow Chemical France, 1984 REV. ARB. 98, and A. Chapelle's note.

[73] Cass. 1e civ., Dec. 14, 1983, *Epoux Convert, supra* note 11.

clauses is concerned, the Court need not refer to a law which, in light of the autonomy of such clauses in international arbitration, might not apply to them."[74]

Arbitral case law also recognizes that the law applicable to an arbitration agreement may, as a result of the principle of autonomy, differ from that governing the main contract.[75]

414. — The French courts now consider that the existence and validity of the arbitration agreement should be determined by reference to substantive rules, independently of any applicable national law.[76] Here again, as a result of the principle of autonomy these substantive rules may not be those of the legal system governing the main contract.[77]

B. – INDIRECT CONSEQUENCES OF THE PRINCIPLE OF AUTONOMY

415. — As with any firmly established rule that is well formulated, the principle of the autonomy of arbitration agreements has often been relied upon as the basis for developments which go far beyond its initial *raison d'être*.[78] These developments include the "competence-competence" rule (1°), and the combination of the "principle of validity" of arbitration agreements and the rejection of the choice of law method (2°).

1° The Principle of Autonomy and "Competence-Competence"

416. — One of the fundamental principles of arbitration law is that arbitrators have the power to rule on their own jurisdiction.[79] That principle is often presented as the corollary of the principle of the autonomy of the arbitration agreement. It is true that at one time tactical concerns prompted certain litigants to assimilate the somewhat contentious principle of "competence-competence" with the more firmly established principle of autonomy. Leaving those concerns aside, it is clear that while the two principles are closely linked and have a similar objective, they only partially overlap.

---

[74] Cass. 1e civ., Mar. 3, 1992, Sonetex v. Charphil, 1993 REV. ARB. 273, and P. Mayer's note; 120 J.D.I. 140 (1993), and B. Audit's note.

[75] *See, e.g.,* interim awards in ICC Case No. 4504 (1985 and 1986), *supra* note 52; 1988 Partial Award in ICC Case No. 5730, Société de lubrifiants Elf Aquitaine v. A.R. Orri, 117 J.D.I. 1029, 1032 (1990), and observations by Y. Derains; 1992 REV. ARB. 125.

[76] *See infra* paras. 435 *et seq.*

[77] See also, in arbitral case law, interim award in ICC Case No. 4131 (Sept. 23, 1982), *Dow Chemical, supra* note 52; interim award of November 1984, by Messrs. Jimenez de Arechaga, chairman, K.-H. Böckstiegel and J.H. Pickering, arbitrators, in ICC Case No. 4695, Parties from Brazil, Panama and U.S.A. v. Party from Brazil, XI Y.B. COM. ARB. 149 (1986); ICC Award No. 5065 (1986), Lebanese party v. Two Pakistani companies, 114 J.D.I. 1039, 1041 (1987), and observations by Y. Derains.

[78] For other examples, see Emmanuel Gaillard, *La distinction des principes généraux du droit et des usages du commerce international, in* ETUDES OFFERTES À PIERRE BELLET 203 (1991).

[79] On this issue generally, see *infra* paras. 650 *et seq.*

The principle of autonomy is of course the first stage of the process which results in the arbitrators being able to determine their own jurisdiction. It is thanks to the autonomy of the arbitration agreement that any claim that the main contract is in some way void or voidable will have no direct impact on the arbitration agreement and hence on the jurisdiction of the arbitrators. That autonomy thus allows the examination by the arbitrators of jurisdictional challenges based on the alleged ineffectiveness of the disputed contract. In such a situation, the autonomy of the arbitration agreement and the "competence-competence" rule do overlap and are mutually supportive.

In some respects, however, the principle of autonomy extends beyond the "competence-competence" rule. The "competence-competence" rule allows arbitrators to examine their own jurisdiction. If they find the main contract to be ineffective, with only the principle of competence-competence they would have no option but to decline jurisdiction. However, the principle of autonomy enables arbitrators to declare the main contract ineffective, without necessarily concluding that the arbitration agreement is likewise ineffective and therefore declining jurisdiction. In other words, the decision of an arbitrator to retain jurisdiction and then declare a disputed contract ineffective must be founded on the principle of autonomy, and not solely on the "competence-competence" rule.[80]

In other respects, the "competence-competence" rule goes much further than the principle of autonomy. The principle of autonomy cannot serve as the basis for the arbitrator's jurisdiction over any direct challenge of the arbitration agreement rather than the main contract. In this area, the advantages of the "competence-competence" rule become clear, and we shall consider these in greater detail when examining the effects of the arbitration agreement.[81]

Thus, in spite of the tendency to consider the two as intertwined, the "competence-competence" rule must be carefully distinguished from the principle of autonomy of the arbitration agreement.[82]

417. — The inclination to capitalize on the strength of the principle of the autonomy of the arbitration agreement has also led the French courts to go as far as to derive from it a principle known as that of the "validity" and "effectiveness" of the arbitration agreement.

2° The Principle of Autonomy, the Principle of Validity and the Rejection of the Choice of Law Method

418. — Although the principle of autonomy was initially intended as a means of isolating the arbitration agreement from flaws affecting the main contract, it has gradually acquired

---

[80] *See* W. LAURENCE CRAIG, WILLIAM W. PARK, JAN PAULSSON, INTERNATIONAL CHAMBER OF COMMERCE ARBITRATION ¶ 5.04 at 65 (2d ed. 1990).

[81] *See infra* para. 660.

[82] In favor of such a distinction, see also RENÉ DAVID, ARBITRATION IN INTERNATIONAL TRADE ¶ 209 (1985); Mayer, *L'autonomie de l'arbitre international dans l'appréciation de sa propre compétence, supra* note 1, at 430.

a new purpose which complements, rather than replaces, its original objective. The French courts, in particular, now use the principle of autonomy as the source for the principle of the validity of international arbitration agreements, under which such agreements are not subject to the traditional choice of law method.

The French courts first referred to this "principle of validity" in the *Hecht* case, decided by the *Cour de cassation* in 1972. The dispute concerned the validity of an arbitration clause contained in an international commercial agency contract which was expressly made subject to the French 1958 Decree on commercial agency. The defendant claimed that the arbitration agreement was invalid on the grounds that French law, as chosen by the parties, prohibited arbitration agreements between merchants (*commerçants*) and non-merchants (*non-commerçants*). In a 1970 decision, the Paris Court of Appeals rejected this argument, emphasizing that notwithstanding the reference to French statute the contracting parties were entitled to conclude an arbitration agreement in situations not authorized by French domestic law. The Court based this solution on the principle of the autonomy of the arbitration agreement, to which it referred in terms identical to those used in the *Gosset* case.[83] However, the Court in fact went far beyond the logical consequences of the autonomy of the arbitration agreement.[84] The decision did not apply any national law to the arbitration agreement, and the validity of the agreement was instead inferred from the parties' intentions alone. The principle of autonomy thus began to evolve into a substantive rule imposing the validity of international arbitration agreements, subject to two exceptions—concerning French mandatory rules and public policy—which were discussed by the Court but held to be inapplicable.[85] The action against this ruling was rejected by the *Cour de cassation*. The Court simply declared[86] that:

> having drawn attention to the international nature of the contract between the parties and to the total autonomy of arbitration agreements in the field of international arbitration, the Court of Appeals rightly held the disputed clause to be applicable in the present case.[87]

As observed by one commentator, in so doing,

> the *Cour de cassation* . . . concludes . . . that the arbitration agreement is valid, purely on the basis of the principle of autonomy, without any reference to the law governing that agreement: the concept of linking the agreement to a particular law disappears entirely.[88]

---

[83] Cass. 1e civ., May 7, 1963, *Gosset, supra* para. 391 and note 9.

[84] *See supra* paras. 409 *et seq.*

[85] CA Paris, June 19, 1970, *Hecht, supra* note 10.

[86] B. Oppetit, note following Cass. 1e civ., July 4, 1972, *Hecht*, 99 J.D.I. 843, 845 (1972).

[87] Cass. 1e civ., July 4, 1972, *Hecht, supra* note 11.

[88] Oppetit, *supra* note 86, at 845.

The fact that the arbitration agreement is autonomous from the main contract explains not only its autonomy from the law governing that contract, but also, albeit less obviously, its autonomy from any law which may result from the application of a choice of law rule.

Even prior to the decision of the *Cour de cassation* in the *Hecht* case, the Paris Court of Appeals had ruled, in a 1972 decision, that the arbitration agreement was not necessarily governed by the law governing the main contract. To hold the arbitration agreement to be valid, the Court relied exclusively upon the intention of the parties and their choice of institutional arbitration rules, without referring to any national law.[89] This principle of validity was later formally established by the same court in its 1975 *Menicucci* decision. In that case, the Court overruled a judgment at first instance which had declared void an arbitration agreement contained in a contract signed in France by two French nationals for the sale of French-made items in Canada and the United States. At first instance, the court had based its decision on two factors: the fact that the contract in question was between a merchant and a non-merchant and the finding that it was not international in nature. The Paris Court of Appeals did not dispute the fact that the contract was between a merchant and a non-merchant, in which circumstances arbitration agreements are prohibited under French domestic law. However, the Court did hold the contract to be international in nature and declared that the prohibition at French law did not apply, given the full autonomy of the arbitration agreement. The Court stated that:

> in order to admit a plea of lack of jurisdiction [which the first instance court had rejected on the basis that the arbitration agreement was void], it is not necessary to determine the law governing the contract . . . or indeed the arbitral proceedings and the award . . . . It need only be established that, in light of the principle of the autonomy of the arbitration agreement providing for arbitration in an international contract, the latter is valid independently of any reference to a national law.[90]

A similar solution was reached by the Toulouse Court of Appeals in 1982 when considering the validity of an arbitration clause in an international commercial agency contract to be performed in France. The Court found that in order to exclude the application of the French rule whereby arbitration agreements are prohibited in contracts between merchants and non-merchants, it was sufficient to

> rely upon the uncontested principle of the autonomy of the arbitration agreement, given that recent case law considers that this autonomy applies not only with respect to the remainder of the contract, but also with respect to any national law.[91]

---

[89] CA Paris, Jan. 25, 1972, *Quijano Aguero, supra* note 71.

[90] CA Paris, Dec. 13, 1975, *Menicucci, supra* note 11.

[91] CA Toulouse, Oct. 26, 1982, *Sieur Behar, supra* note 10; *see also* CA Paris, Mar. 4, 1986, *Cosiac, supra* note 60; Cass. com., Nov. 12, 1968, *Minoteries Lochoises, supra* note 58.

419. — Significant though it may be, this decision is less radical than the terms in which it is expressed.

In international arbitration, the substantive rule referred to as the "principle of validity" is merely the reverse of Article 2061 of the French Civil Code, pursuant to which "an arbitration clause shall be void unless the law provides otherwise." French law previously allowed arbitration agreements only in cases falling within the jurisdiction of the French *Tribunal de Commerce.*[92] It was therefore vital for the development of international arbitration that this rule be reversed.[93]

On the other hand, as a result of the Court's reference to the autonomy of the arbitration agreement from any national law, the principle took on an entirely new meaning. Although traditionally "the principle of autonomy" denoted autonomy from the main contract, here it refers to autonomy from all national laws. This accounts for the fact that a French court, when determining the existence or validity of an international arbitration agreement, can confine itself to reasoning in terms of substantive rules.[94] Even if one accepts that the two types of autonomy are linked—and that autonomy from the main contract, which may of course be governed by a national law, is the necessary precondition of autonomy from any national law—one can see that there has been a definite evolution. However, this evolution does not mean that the principle of validity or that of autonomy from any national law are unsatisfactory. It simply demonstrates that we must now accept that two distinct principles exist, each of which needs to be examined separately.

---

[92] Art. 631, para. 2 of the French Commercial Code. On the current status of French domestic law on arbitration, see MATTHIEU DE BOISSÉSON, LE DROIT FRANÇAIS DE L'ARBITRAGE INTERNE ET INTERNATIONAL 43 *et seq.* (2d ed. 1990); Jacqueline Rubellin-Devichi and Eric Loquin, *Arbitrage – Compromis et clause compromissoire,* J-CL. PROC. CIV., Fasc. 1020, ¶¶ 74 *et seq.* (1995).

[93] *See also* CA Paris, Mar. 8, 1990, Coumet et Ducler v. Polar – Rakennusos a Keythio, 1990 REV. ARB. 675, and P. Mayer's note; CA Grenoble, Sept. 13, 1993, Compagnie Française Technique d'Etanchéité (C.F.T.E.) v. Dechavanne, 1994 REV. ARB. 337, and M.-A. Moreau's note; for an English translation, see XX Y.B. COM. ARB. 656 (1995); but see the isolated and unanimously criticized decision of Cass. soc., Feb. 12, 1985, Ceramiche Ragno v. Chauzy, 1986 REV. ARB. 47, and M.-A. Moreau's note; 1986 REV. CRIT. DIP 469, and M.-L. Niboyet-Hoegy's note; André Ponsard, *La jurisprudence de la Cour de cassation et le droit commercial international, in* LE DROIT DES RELATIONS ÉCONOMIQUES INTERNATIONALES – ETUDES OFFERTES À BERTHOLD GOLDMAN 241 (1982). On the reversal of this case law of the section of the *Cour de cassation* specializing in labor law matters following the withdrawal by France of the New York Convention commercial reservation, see Philippe Fouchard, *La levée par la France de sa réserve de commercialité pour l'application de la Convention de New York,* 1990 REV. ARB. 571; Charles Jarrosson, *La clause compromissoire (art. 2061 C. civ.),* 1992 REV. ARB. 259, 268–69. For an unequivocal statement that Article 2061 of the Civil Code is not applicable in international arbitration, see Cass. 1e civ., Jan. 5, 1999, Zanzi v. de Coninck, 1999 DALLOZ AFF. 474.

[94] For case law confirming this understanding of the principle of autonomy, see the decisions cited *infra* paras 436 *et seq.*

SECTION II
AUTONOMY OF THE ARBITRATION AGREEMENT FROM ALL NATIONAL LAWS

420. — The concept of the autonomy of the arbitration agreement is sometimes used, especially in France, to describe that agreement's autonomy from the various national laws which may apply to it, rather than its autonomy from the main contract. In other words, it means that the arbitration agreement remains independent of the various national laws liable to govern it under the choice of law method.[95] One might be tempted to conclude that the arbitration agreement is therefore self-sufficient, relying on no particular legal system for its effectiveness. However, understood in such a way, the principle would in fact amount to a new form of *contrat sans loi*, or contract without a governing law. In fact, this is not what the French courts mean when they refer to the autonomy of the arbitration agreement from any national law. That simply denotes a method of determining the rules applicable to the arbitration agreement.

421. — This substantive rules method (§ 2), will be examined alongside the other available means of determining the existence and validity of the arbitration agreement, namely, the choice of law method (§ 1), and the method which consists in combining, *in favorem*, choice of law rules and substantive rules (§ 3).

§ 1. – The Choice of Law Method

422. — The application of choice of law rules is both the oldest method of determining the law governing an arbitration agreement and that most commonly encountered in comparative law.[96] The principal conventions on arbitration refer to the choice of law

---

[95] On this issue, generally, see Ancel, *supra* note 1.

[96] *See, e.g.*, Art. 1074 of the Netherlands Code of Civil Procedure, which addresses the validity of an arbitration agreement "under the law applicable thereto," and PIETER SANDERS, ALBERT JAN VAN DEN BERG, THE NETHERLANDS ARBITRATION ACT 1986, at 99 (1987); for an example of a decision based on the criterion of the closest connection, see Court of Appeals of The Hague, Aug. 4, 1993, Owerri Commercial Inc. v. Dielle S.r.l., XIX Y.B. COM. ARB. 703 (1994); Art. 61 of the Spanish Law 36/1988 on Arbitration of December 5, 1988 which requires that the law designated by the parties to govern the arbitration agreement "have some connection with the . . . dispute," and the commentary by Santiago Alvarez González and Carlos Esplugues Mota, in ARBITRATION IN SPAIN 117 *et seq.* (B. Cremades ed , 1991). *See also* Sec. 48 of the 1999 Swedish Arbitration Act according to which the arbitration agreement is governed by the law chosen by the parties or, absent such choice, by the law of the place of arbitration; for English law, see Channel Tunnel Group Ltd. v. Balfour Beatty Construction Ltd., [1992] 1 Q.B. 656; [1992] 2 All E.R. 609; [1992] 2 W.L.R. 741; [1992] 2 Lloyd's Rep. 291; XVIII Y.B. COM. ARB. 446, ¶ 20 at 455 (1993) (C.A. 1992), and, after the 1996 Arbitration Act, RUSSELL, *supra* note 37, at 71 *et seq.* On this issue, generally, see KLAUS PETER BERGER, INTERNATIONAL ECONOMIC ARBITRATION 156 *et seq.* (1993); Jean-François Poudret, *Le droit applicable à la convention d'arbitrage*, in ASA SPECIAL SERIES No. 8, THE ARBITRATION AGREEMENT – ITS MULTIFOLD CRITICAL ASPECTS 23 (1994); Julian D. M. Lew, *The Law Applicable to the Form and Substance of the Arbitration*
(continued...)

method. For example, Article V(1)(a) of the 1958 New York Convention provides that recognition or enforcement of an award may be refused if the arbitration agreement is "not valid under the law to which the parties have subjected it or, failing any indication thereon, under the law of the country where the award was made." The 1961 European Convention employs similar language at Article IX(1).[97] In France, prior to the *Cour de cassation* decision of December 20, 1993 in the *Dalico* case,[98] most authors considered that the choice of law method still played a residual role.[99] It even appeared to be generating renewed interest among certain authors.[100]

However, the Paris Court of Appeals, whose approach was unequivocally approved by the *Cour de cassation* in 1993,[101] has now clearly moved away from the choice of law method.[102] It is true that the 1980 Rome Convention on the Law Applicable to Contractual Obligations helped to marginalize the choice of law method by expressly excluding the arbitration agreement from its sphere of application (Art. 1(2)(d)). Nevertheless, the choice of law method requires a detailed examination, not only because arbitrators themselves are often tempted to resort to it, but also because it allows the comparative assessment of the merits of the substantive rules method now adopted in French law and of the combined method which prevails in Swiss law.

We shall see that, when applied to an arbitration agreement, the traditional choice of law method raises a number of difficulties: first, when choosing the relevant legal category or categories which may be subject to different laws (A) and, second, when deciding which connecting factor or factors should be used to identify those laws (B).

A. – LEGAL CATEGORIES

423. — A number of questions arise when selecting the legal category or categories used to determine the law or laws that apply to the arbitration agreement. As always in private

---

[96](...continued)
Clause, in ICCA CONGRESS SERIES NO. 9, IMPROVING THE EFFICIENCY OF ARBITRATION AGREEMENTS AND AWARDS: 40 YEARS OF APPLICATION OF THE NEW YORK CONVENTION 114 (A.J. van den Berg ed., 1999).

[97] *See infra* para. 431.

[98] *See supra* note 2 and *infra* para. 437.

[99] ROBERT, *supra* note 6, ¶¶ 267 *et seq.*; DE BOISSÉSON, *supra* note 92, ¶¶ 582 *et seq.* (2d ed. 1990); DAVID, *supra* note 82, ¶¶ 239 *et seq.*; Pierre Bellet and Ernst Mezger, *L'arbitrage international dans le nouveau code de procédure civile,* 1981 REV. CRIT. DIP 611, 622 (regarding questions of capacity and powers of attorney, not the form of the arbitration agreement); André Huet, *Les procédures de reconnaissance et d'exécution des jugements étrangers et des sentences arbitrales, en droit international privé français,* 115 J.D.I. 5, 19 (1988). *Comp. with* Philippe Fouchard, *L'arbitrage international en France après le décret du 12 mai 1981,* 109 J.D.I. 374, especially at 382 *et seq.* (1982).

[100] *See* H. Gaudemet-Tallon, note following CA Paris, Mar. 26, 1991, Comité populaire de la municipalité de Khoms El Mergeb v. Dalico Contractors, 1991 REV. ARB. 456; H. Synvet, note following CA Paris, Dec. 17, 1991, Gatoil v. National Iranian Oil Co., 1993 REV. ARB. 281.

[101] *See infra* para. 437.

[102] *See infra* para. 436. See, however, the very isolated decisions discussed *infra* para. 1610.

international law, it may be preferable not to create too many legal categories, although this may make the choice of a connecting factor more difficult. On the other hand, it is sometimes appropriate to distinguish between a number of legal categories: this facilitates the selection of the most appropriate connecting factors, but also leads to the fragmentation of the laws applicable to the various different aspects of a single institution. Such a fragmentation would occur if there were a straightforward application of the rules of private international law to the arbitration agreement.[103] This is because the process entails distinguishing between the law or laws applicable to a party's capacity to contract, to a signatory's power to contract, to the form of the arbitration agreement and to its substance.[104] Moreover, the arbitration agreement is almost invariably torn between two possible characterizations, one connecting it to the arbitral procedure (1°), the other connecting it to the main contract to which it relates (2°).

1° The Arbitration Agreement and Procedure

424. — One of the problems which arises from applying the choice of law approach to the arbitration agreement is whether that agreement should be characterized as substantive or procedural. In the former case, the arbitration agreement will be characterized as a contract, whereas in the latter the law governing the arbitral procedure will also govern the arbitration agreement.

In the past, the characterization of the arbitration agreement as procedural was promoted by authors influenced by English law, which traditionally had a much broader conception of procedure than continental legal systems. Initially it met with a degree of acceptance. For instance, in 1957 and 1959, the Institute of International Law adopted a resolution that the validity of the arbitration agreement would be governed by the law of the seat of the arbitration.[105] The Institute thus implicitly characterized the arbitration agreement as procedural and applied a supposed principle that the arbitral procedure was necessarily

---

[103] For an example of the unsatisfactory consequences to which this method may give rise, see CA Paris, Feb. 26, 1988, Pia Investments Ltd. v. Cassia, which distinguishes between the burden and the subject matter of the proof, which were held to be connected to the law governing the formation of the contract, and the methods of establishing the proof, which were held to be connected to the law of the seat, without prejudice to the parties' rights to rely on the rules of evidence of the law of the place where the contract was concluded (1990 REV. ARB. 851, and J.-H. Moitry and C. Vergne's note, *aff'd*, Cass. 1e civ., July 10, 1990, *supra* note 64, which, happily, did not endorse the Court of Appeals' analysis on this issue). On the equally subtle distinction between the form of the arbitration agreement and the form of the capacity to conclude an arbitration agreement, see ICC Award No. 5832 (1988), Liechtenstein company v. Austrian company, rendered in Zürich before the 1987 Swiss arbitration law came into force (115 J.D.I. 1198 (1988), and observations by G. Aguilar Alvarez). See also, on the importance which English law has traditionally given to the seat of arbitration, Naviera Amazonica Peruana S.A. v. Compania Internacional De Seguros Del Peru, [1988] 1 Lloyd's Rep. 116; XIII Y.B. COM. ARB. 156 (1988) (C.A. 1987).

[104] For further discussion of each of these issues, see *infra* at, respectively, paras. 456 *et seq.*, 461 *et seq.*, 600 *et seq.*, and 472 *et seq.*

[105] Resolutions on Arbitration in Private International Law, ANNUAIRE DE L'INSTITUT DE DROIT INTERNATIONAL, Vol. II, at 479 (1957) and Vol. II, at 372, especially at 374, Art. 5 (1959); for an English translation, see INSTITUT DE DROIT INTERNATIONAL, TABLEAU DES RÉSOLUTIONS ADOPTÉES (1957–1991), at 237 and 251.

governed by the law of the country where the arbitration was held. This approach was followed to a certain extent in arbitral case law.[106] However, it must be firmly rejected, for several reasons.[107] First, it is no longer correct to say that arbitral procedure will necessarily be governed by the law of the seat of the arbitration. The parties may subject it to the law or rules of law of their choice,[108] and even the arbitrators, in the absence of a choice by the parties, are not bound to apply the procedural rules of the law of the seat of arbitration.[109]

Furthermore, connecting the arbitration agreement to the law governing procedure would create practical difficulties. The parties, as well as the arbitrators, may prefer not to determine in advance which law is to govern the arbitral procedure, so as to leave open the possibility for the arbitral tribunal to rule on an issue-by-issue basis.[110] To characterize the arbitration agreement as procedural would thus only complicate the matter without providing a clear solution.

Finally, there is no theoretical justification for the assimilation of the arbitration agreement and the arbitral procedure. The arbitration agreement is essentially a contract, even if its object is to set up a procedure. It comes before the procedure and does not constitute a part of it.

Accordingly, if one does decide to use the choice of law method, it is at the very least necessary to characterize the arbitration agreement as an autonomous contract. This was the characterization adopted by the French courts when they reasoned in choice of law terms.[111]

---

[106] *See, e.g.*, ICC Award No. 5832 (1988), *supra* note 103.

[107] *See* PHILIPPE FOUCHARD, L'ARBITRAGE COMMERCIAL INTERNATIONAL ¶¶ 115 *et seq.* (1965).

[108] *See infra* para. 1197.

[109] *See infra* para. 1178.

[110] *See infra* para. 1198.

[111] *See, e.g.*, Cass. civ., Feb. 19, 1930, Mardelé v. Muller, 1931 REV. CRIT. DIP 514; Sirey, Pt. I, at 41, 1st decision (1933), and J.-P. Niboyet's note; 58 J.D.I. 90 (1931); Cass. civ., Jan. 27, 1931, Dambricourt v. Rossard, Sirey, Pt. I, at 41, 2d decision (1933), and J.-P. Niboyet's note; 59 J.D.I. 93 (1932); Cass. 1e civ., Apr. 14, 1964, O.N.I.C. v. Capitaine du S. S. San Carlo, JCP, Ed. G., Pt. II, No. 14,406 (1965), and P. Level's note; 92 J.D.I. 646 (1965), and B. Goldman's note; 1966 REV. CRIT. DIP 68, and H. Batiffol's note; Dalloz, Jur. 637 (1964), and J. Robert's note; 1964 REV. ARB. 82; CA Paris, Dec. 9, 1955, Goldschmidt v. Vis et Zoon, Dalloz, Jur. 217 (1956), and J. Robert's note; 1956 REV. CRIT. DIP 253, and H. Motulsky's note; 1955 REV. ARB. 101; CA Paris, Apr. 10, 1957, Myrtoon Steam Ship v. Agent judiciaire du Trésor, JCP, Ed. G., Pt. II, No. 10,078 (1957), and H. Motulsky's note; 85 J.D.I. 1002 (1958), and B. Goldman's note; 1958 REV. CRIT. DIP 120, and Y. Loussouarn's note; Dalloz, Jur. 699 (1958), and observations by J. Robert; French *Tribunal des conflits*, May 19, 1958, Myrtoon Steamship v. France, Dalloz, Jur. 699 (1958), and J. Robert's note; 1958 REV. PRAT. DR. ADM. 118; CA Monaco, June 17, 1957, Audibert v. Hanssen et Soofus Eltvedt, Gaz. Pal. 2, Jur. 294 (1957); CA Paris, Feb. 21, 1961, Galakis v. Trésor Public, 90 J.D.I. 156 (1963), and observations by J.-B. Sialelli; 1961 RTD COM. 351, and observations by M. Boitard; CA Paris, Mar. 27, 1962, Compagnie Marchande de Tunisie v. Costa de Marfil, JCP, Ed. G., Pt. II, No. 13,036 (1963), and P. Level's note; 1962 REV. CRIT. DIP 512, and E. Mezger's note; 90 J.D.I. 468 (1963), and observations by J.-B. Sialelli. For a decision holding that French "procedural" law governs the form and the proof of the arbitration agreement (when it would have sufficed to have referred to Articles 1502 and 1504 of the French New Code of Civil Procedure), see CA Paris, Jan. 20, 1987, Bomar Oil N.V. v. Entreprise Tunisienne d'Activités Pétrolières (E.T.A.P.), 1987 REV. ARB. 482, and C. Kessedjian's note; 114 J.D.I. 934 (1987), and E. Loquin's note; for an English translation, see XIII Y.B. COM. ARB. 466 (1988), *rev'd.*, Cass. 1e civ., Oct. 11, 1989, 1989 Bull. Civ. I, No. 314; 1990 REV. ARB. 134, and C. Kessedjian's note; 117 J.D.I. 633 (1990), and E. Loquin's note; for an English translation, see XV Y.B.

(continued...)

In other legal systems, the extent to which the characterization of the arbitration agreement as procedural has lost ground can be seen in the fact that, even in England, most authors now clearly characterize the arbitration agreement as a contract.[112]

2° The Arbitration Agreement and the Main Contract

425. — When the traditional choice of law method is used, the principle of the autonomy of the arbitration agreement from the main contract requires each to be treated separately when determining the applicable law.[113] However, there has often been confusion between the law applicable to the arbitration agreement and the law applicable to the main contract. This can be seen in the few French judgments which persisted in adopting the choice of law approach when examining the validity or other aspects of the arbitration agreement.[114]

In practice, this confusion commonly occurs where the arbitration agreement takes the form of an arbitration clause. It is easy to understand how this confusion arises, whether or not the parties have chosen a law to govern the main contract.

Where the main contract does contain a choice of law clause, it is perfectly legitimate to query whether that choice, which is usually expressed in broad terms ("the present contract shall be governed by the law of Country A," for example), applies only to the main contract, or whether it also applies to the arbitration agreement. The parties will of course only very rarely have given thought to the law applicable to the arbitration agreement. In our opinion, it would therefore be going too far to interpret such clauses as containing an express choice as to the law governing the arbitration agreement.

Where, however, the parties have not chosen a law to govern the main contract, it is generally considered that the disputed agreement should be governed by the legal system with which it has the closest connection. Here, the confusion may stem from whether it is the arbitration agreement or the main contract which needs to be closely connected to a particular law for that law to be applicable to the arbitration agreement. Identifying the law

---

[111](...continued)
COM. ARB. 447 (1990); 4 INT'L ARB. REP. A1 (Dec. 1989). It should be noted, however, that the second Court of Appeals' decision in this case did not characterize the issue in this way and based itself largely on the New York Convention (CA Versailles, Jan. 23, 1991, 1991 REV. ARB. 291, and C. Kessedjian's note; for an English translation, see XVII Y.B. COM. ARB. 488 (1992)). In addition, in its second decision in this matter, dated November 9, 1993, the *Cour de cassation* applied substantive rules, which is the better approach (1994 REV. ARB. 108, and C. Kessedjian's note; 121 J.D.I. 690 (1994), and E. Loquin's note; for an English translation, see XX Y.B. COM. ARB. 660 (1995); *see also infra* para. 610).

[112] *See* MICHAEL J. MUSTILL, STEWART C. BOYD, COMMERCIAL ARBITRATION 62 (2d ed. 1989); REDFERN AND HUNTER, *supra* note 37, at 149. RUSSELL, *supra* note 37, at 72 *et seq.*

[113] *See supra* para. 412.

[114] See, for example, on the application to the question of the existence of the arbitration agreement of the law governing the form of the main contract, CA Paris, Feb. 26, 1988, *Pia Investments, supra* note 103, *aff'd*, Cass. 1e civ., July 10, 1990, *supra* note 64, and our discussion of these decisions, *infra* para. 595. Approving this approach, which was later subject to various adjustments, see Bernard Hanotiau, *L'arbitrabilité et la favor arbitrandum: un réexamen*, 121 J.D.I. 899, ¶ 15 at 909 (1994).

most closely connected to the arbitration agreement itself [115] means giving priority to connecting factors which apply specifically to that agreement (for example, the chosen arbitration rules and the seat or the language of the arbitration). By contrast, the selection of the law most closely connected to the main contract will involve using very different connecting factors, some of which may be found in applicable international conventions[116] (for example, the place of performance of the contract or the domicile of one of the parties). Without disregarding the principle of autonomy quite as much as some decisions have done,[117] it has been suggested that the law governing the main contract provides an indication as to the law applicable to the arbitration agreement.[118] However, the fact remains that, if the choice of law method is used, such a connecting factor will often be defeated by that constituted by the seat of the arbitration. One situation that may arise will be where the parties have not only subjected their main contract to the law of a particular country, but have also chosen that country as the seat of the arbitration. In such a case, it would be possible to subject the arbitration agreement to the law of that country, either by giving effect to the parties' presumed intentions, or by making an objective assessment that the connecting factors provided by the law governing the main contract and the seat of the arbitration are the same. However, where these two connecting factors diverge, particularly where the chosen seat of the arbitration is neutral with respect to the parties, it is more difficult to accept that the law governing the arbitration agreement should always be determined by reference to the law governing the main contract, and not that of the seat of the arbitration. This is because the law governing the main contract will generally have been chosen for reasons other than those on which the choice of the law governing the arbitration agreement is based.[119] That is not to say that the connecting factor consisting of the seat of

---

[115] To which the Rome Convention of June 19, 1980 on the Law Applicable to Contractual Obligations is inapplicable (Art. 1(2)(d)).

[116] These include the Rome Convention of June 19, 1980 on the Law Applicable to Contractual Obligations or the Hague Convention of June 15, 1955 on the Law Applicable to International Sales of Goods .

[117] *See* CA Paris, Feb. 26, 1988, *Pia Investments*, *supra* note 103, *aff'd*, Cass. 1e civ., July 10, 1990, *supra* note 64.

[118] In favor of employing this criterion, described as "in the absence of particular circumstances, the safest and most often used, even if only implicitly," see Goldman, *supra* note 18, ¶ 59; DE BOISSÉSON, *supra* note 92, ¶ 585. For a similar view with respect to arbitration clauses inserted in the body of the main contract, see REDFERN AND HUNTER, *supra* note 37, at 149. For an example of the application of the law governing the main contract to the arbitration agreement see, in German case law prior to the 1998 reform (which does not address the issue), *Oberlandesgericht* of Hamburg, Sept. 22, 1978, Italian company v. German (F.R.) firm, V Y.B. COM. ARB. 262 (1980) and, in arbitral case law, the September 5, 1977 award of the Arbitral Tribunal of the Netherlands Oils, Fats and Oilseeds Trade Association, Dutch private company v. Iranian private company, IV Y.B. COM. ARB. 218 (1979); ICC Award No. 2626 (1977), German company v. Italian company, 105 J.D.I. 980 (1978), and observations by Y. Derains; ICC Award No. 6840 (1991), Egyptian seller v. Senegalese buyer, where the sole arbitrator, sitting in Paris, found it "reasonable and natural, absent [any indication by the parties as to the law applicable to the arbitration agreement, as well as to the main contract] to subject the arbitration clause to the same law as that applicable to the main contract" (119 J.D.I. 1030 (1992), and observations by Y. Derains). *But see* 1988 Partial Award in ICC Case No. 5730, *supra* note 75, 117 J.D.I. 1034 (1990); see also, for a different methodology, CA Paris, Mar. 26, 1991, Comité populaire de la municipalité de Khoms El Mergeb v. Dalico Contractors, 1991 REV. ARB. 456, and H. Gaudemet-Tallon's note; for an English translation, see 6 INT'L ARB. REP. B1 (Sept. 1991), *aff'd*, Cass. 1e civ., Dec. 20, 1993, *supra* note 2.

[119] On this issue, generally, see *infra* paras. 1421 *et seq.*

the arbitration alone is to be automatically preferred,[120] but only that, in such circumstances, it will certainly counterbalance the law governing the merits of the dispute.

Thus, where the choice of law method is used, the law governing the arbitration agreement cannot be determined solely on the basis of a presumption that the law governing the merits of the dispute will be the same as that governing the arbitration agreement.

B. – CONNECTING FACTORS

426. — If the choice of law method is to be applied to the arbitration agreement, no one obvious connecting factor emerges from which the applicable law can be established.

The only case presenting no difficulty is that where the parties themselves have chosen the law governing the arbitration agreement: it is widely accepted that their choice must be followed.[121] However, where the choice of law approach is used and the parties have made no express choice, there is little evidence of agreement, either among authors or in arbitral case law, as to the relative importance of each of the various connecting factors from which the applicable law might be determined. The view according to which the law governing the arbitration agreement should be selected by considering all of the connecting factors (or by determining the law with the closest connection to the case, which amounts to the same thing) is not very helpful. The real issue is what weight should be given to each of the connecting factors that may be taken into account when selecting the law governing the arbitration agreement.

We shall therefore now examine the weight of the following possible connecting factors: the place where the arbitration agreement was concluded (1°), factors specific to the arbitration agreement (2°) and the seat of the arbitration (3°).

1° The Place Where the Arbitration Agreement Was Concluded

427. — Neither the substantive conditions governing the validity of the arbitration agreement nor the conditions governing its form should automatically be subjected to the law of the place where the contract was concluded, despite a traditional leaning in favor of applying that law to conditions of form. The place where the contract was concluded is not only difficult to establish in some cases,[122] but is also usually chosen completely by chance. Its importance as a factor "localizing" the arbitration agreement is therefore "extremely minor."[123]

---

[120] *See infra* para. 429.

[121] See *infra* para. 449 and, for a criticism of the mandatory application of the law of the seat of arbitration, *supra* para. 424.

[122] For an example of such difficulties, in a case regarding the form of arbitration agreements, see E. Loquin, note following CA Paris, Jan. 20, 1987, *Bomar Oil, supra* note 111, 114 J.D.I. 934, 950 (1987).

[123] *See* 1998 Partial Award in ICC Case No. 5730 (1988), *supra* note 75, 117 J.D.I. 1033 (1990).

2° Factors Specific to Certain Arbitration Agreements

428. — Some elements specific to a given arbitration agreement may carry more weight than the place where that agreement was concluded. This will be the case where the parties have used an arbitration clause taken from a standard contract which is drafted by a professional organization in a particular country and is closely linked to that country's legal system. An example is found in shipping contracts modeled on English charter parties.[124] By choosing such a contract, the parties might well be considered to have intended the arbitration clause to be subject to the laws of that jurisdiction.[125] However, the choice of a truly international arbitration institution, such as the ICC's International Court of Arbitration, cannot be interpreted in the same way. The geographical location of the institution arises from the need for it to be based somewhere, but its links with the country in which it is located are not strong enough to dictate that the law of that country should necessarily govern an arbitration agreement referring to the institution. That result is only possible where the parties have referred to an arbitration institution created and operating in an essentially national context, which is the case, for example, of a number of purely national arbitration institutions[126] and of certain national or quasi-public institutions in Eastern Europe and the Far East.[127] Only in such circumstances can it legitimately be assumed that the parties intended the arbitration agreement to be governed by the law of the country in which the institution has its headquarters.

3° The Seat of Arbitration

429. — Where the parties have not chosen a law governing the arbitration, the seat of the arbitration is undoubtedly considered to be the most significant factor in the determination of the applicable law. That, after all, is the place where the arbitration agreement is to be

---

[124] See also, regarding arbitration agreements contained in the London Corn Trade Association's standard contracts, Cass. civ., Jan. 27, 1931, *Dambricourt, supra* note 111; CA Paris, Dec. 9, 1955, *Goldschmidt, supra* note 111.

[125] *See, e.g.*, CA Paris, Apr. 10, 1957, *Myrtoon Steam Ship, supra* note 111; CA Paris, Feb. 21, 1961, *Galakis, supra* note 111; CA Paris, Mar. 27, 1962, *Compagnie marchande de Tunisie, supra* note 111.

[126] See, for example, The London Bar Arbitration Scheme, administered by The London Common Law Bar Association, *in* RONALD BERNSTEIN, HANDBOOK OF ARBITRATION PRACTICE, Appendix M, at 555 (1987) (which no longer appears in the subsequent editions).

[127] The same would not be true, in light of their more international nature, of arbitral institutions such as the LCIA or the AAA (at least, in the case of the AAA, when the parties have not specifically referred to that institution's domestic arbitration rules).

performed.[128] However, the weight given to the seat of the arbitration still gives rise to criticism, especially where the seat was not chosen by the parties themselves.[129]

430. — In earlier decisions, some courts considered that where the parties had chosen the seat of the arbitration, it could be inferred that they intended to subject the arbitration agreement to the law of that place.[130]

431. — Without adopting that presentation, the major international conventions also treated the seat of the arbitration as the main connecting factor in the determination of the law governing the arbitration agreement.

The 1923 Geneva Protocol on Arbitration Clauses in Commercial Matters makes no reference to the law governing the arbitration agreement, and the 1927 Geneva Convention on the Execution of Foreign Arbitral Awards merely states that "the award [must have] been made in pursuance of a submission to arbitration which is valid under the law applicable thereto," without specifying how that law is to be identified (Art. 1(a)). However, the 1958 New York Convention provides that recognition and enforcement of an arbitral award may be refused if the arbitration agreement "is not valid under the law to which the parties have subjected it or, failing any indication thereon, under the law of the country where the award was made" (Art. V(1)(a)). Thus, where the parties themselves have not subjected the arbitration agreement to a particular law, the applicable law will be the law of the country where the award was made or, in other words, the law of the seat.[131]

Article VI, paragraph 2 of the 1961 European Convention provides that, when required to rule on the existence or validity of an arbitration agreement,

---

[128] On the importance of the place of performance in determining the law applicable to the main contract before the 1980 Rome Convention came into force, see, in France, HENRI BATIFFOL, PAUL LAGARDE, DROIT INTERNATIONAL PRIVÉ, Vol. 2, ¶ 581 (7th ed. 1983); PIERRE MAYER, DROIT INTERNATIONAL PRIVÉ ¶ 723 at 469 (6th ed. 1998); BERNARD AUDIT, DROIT INTERNATIONAL PRIVÉ ¶ 164 (2d ed. 1997); in England, DICEY & MORRIS, THE CONFLICT OF LAWS, Vol. 2, at 1233 (12th ed. 1993 and 4th cumulative supp. 1997).

[129] See infra para. 433.

[130] See, e.g., CA Monaco, June 17, 1957, Audibert, supra note 111; CA Paris, Dec. 9, 1955, Goldschmidt, supra note 111; Rotterdam Court of First Instance, Sept. 28, 1995, Petrasol BV v. Stolt Spur Inc., XXII Y.B. COM. ARB. 762 (1997).

[131] Differences exist among authors as to whether the "indication" should be an explicit reference (see FOUCHARD, supra note 107, ¶ 126; VAN DEN BERG, supra note 22, at 292–93) or any other element in the contract reflecting a common intention of the parties (see Jean-Denis Bredin, La Convention de New- York du 10 juin 1958 pour la reconnaissance et l'exécution des sentences arbitrales étrangères/The New York Convention of June 10th 1958 for the Recognition and Enforcement of Foreign Arbitral Awards, 87 J.D.I. 1002, 1020 (1960)). The former approach seems to be more in keeping with the intentions of the Convention's drafters. For the unconvincing argument that Article V(2)(a) of the New York Convention contains only a rebuttable presumption in favor of the law of the seat of the arbitration, see MUSTILL AND BOYD, supra note 112, at 63 and n. 15. In situations where the seat is not necessarily known (for example where a party brings the matter before the courts and the validity of the arbitration agreement is called into question), in favor of applying the same rule and taking into account the law of the place where the award "will be made," see VAN DEN BERG, supra note 22, at 127 and the cases cited therein; see also the USSR Maritime Arbitration Commission Award No. 24/1984 of April 16, 1985, Soviet insurance company v. Panamanian shipowner, XIV Y.B. COM. ARB. 209 (1989). But see MUSTILL AND BOYD, supra note 112, at 63, who see a vicious circle in this situation.

courts of Contracting States shall examine the validity of such agreement . . . [for issues other than that of their own jurisdiction]

(*a*) under the law to which the parties have subjected their arbitration agreement;

(*b*) failing any indication thereon, under the law of the country in which the award is to be made;

(*c*) failing any indication as to the law to which the parties have subjected the agreement, and where at the time when the question is raised in court the country in which the award is to be made cannot be determined, under the competent law by virtue of the rules of conflict of the court seized of the dispute.

As with the New York Convention, this provision gives priority to the law chosen by the parties, treats the seat as a subsidiary connecting factor, and refers to the choice of law rules of the *lex fori* only as a last resort.[132]

432. — It is not unusual for the same thinking to appear in arbitral awards which subject the arbitration agreement to the law of the seat.[133] This approach was adopted, for example, by an arbitral tribunal sitting in Paris in ICC Case No. 5730, in an award which gives a particularly comprehensive explanation of the arbitral tribunal's reasoning.[134]

433. — However, the use of this connecting factor in the absence of a choice by the parties is based on a philosophy which differs considerably from that of the resolutions of the Institute of International Law in 1957 and 1959, which treated the seat of the arbitration as a mandatory connecting factor.[135] Here, the seat of the arbitration is used for its value as a connecting factor, and not because it reflects the characterization of the arbitration agreement as procedural. However, the value of the seat as a connecting factor is still relatively low, as it is often chosen for reasons of geographical convenience or neutrality in relation to the parties. Further, where the choice has been made by the parties themselves, the legal considerations on which it is based are often somewhat superficial. Where, in the absence of a choice by the parties, the choice is made by the arbitral institution or by the

---

[132] Here again, "indications" other than an express designation should not be taken into account when determining the law chosen by the parties. *See, e.g.*, CA Brussels, Oct. 15, 1992, B.V. Haegens Bouw v. N.V. Theuma Deurenindustrie, XVIII Y.B. COM. ARB. 612 (1993).

[133] *See, e.g.*, ICC Award No. 1803 (1972), Société des Grands Travaux de Marseille v. East Pakistan Indus. Dev. Corp., V Y.B. COM. ARB. 177, 200 (1980), *set aside by* Swiss Fed. Trib., May 5, 1976, Société des Grands Travaux de Marseille v. Peoples' Republic of Bangladesh, V Y.B. COM. ARB. 217 (1980); ICC Award No. 4392 (1983), Yugoslavian company v. German company, 110 J.D.I. 907 (1983), and observations by Y. Derains; ICC Award No. 4472 (1984), German party v. German party, 111 J.D.I. 946 (1984), and observations by S. Jarvin; award on jurisdiction in ICC Case No. 4604 (1984), Italian company v. U.S. company, 112 J.D.I. 973 (1985), and observations by Y. Derains; ICC Award No. 5832 (1988), *supra* note 103.

[134] *See supra* note 75.

[135] *See supra* note 105.

arbitrators themselves, the seat's value as a connecting factor is even weaker, if the goal is to identify the legal system to which the parties intended to subject their agreement.

434. — This analysis of the various possible connecting factors which may apply when the choice of law method is used illustrates the great uncertainty to which the method gives rise. A thorough comparative law analysis led one author to the same conclusion. After studying a number of laws in force at the time, in Germany, Belgium, Italy and Switzerland in particular, he observed with regard to the choice of law rules applicable to arbitration agreements that:

> [it is not] possible to deduce principles of much certainty from the cases. The occasional pronouncements of the courts in this respect cannot be interpreted as an adhesion to a given doctrine and are only meant in general to explain in a convenient manner how the court has arrived at a solution in a particular case.[136]

That is undoubtedly one of the reasons why, in France, the substantive rules method has replaced the traditional choice of law method.

§ 2. – The Substantive Rules Method

435. — In recent years, an entirely new method of assessing the existence and validity of the arbitration agreement has been used in France. This method consists in the exclusive application of substantive rules, independently of any applicable law. However, its formulation has been so radical at times (A) that it prompted reservations among certain authors (B). However, a careful examination of the substantive rules method shows it to be, in our opinion, entirely justified (C).

A. – FRENCH CASE LAW ESTABLISHING THE SUBSTANTIVE RULES METHOD

436. — The line of French cases which, during the early 1970s, extended the principle of the autonomy of the arbitration agreement to include "the principle of [its] validity"[137] culminated, during the late 1980s and early 1990s, in two series of decisions by the Paris Court of Appeals.

---

[136] DAVID, *supra* note 82, ¶ 242 at 219.

[137] *See supra* para. 418.

The first series unequivocally affirmed that, in an international context, "the arbitration agreement has a validity and effectiveness of its own".[138] That is simply another way of saying that the arbitration agreement is autonomous of any national law. However, it is important to emphasize that the Court generally does not use this expression in decisions on the validity of arbitration agreements. It does so primarily in reaching various conclusions regarding the scope of the arbitration agreement, particularly as regards parties who were not signatories.[139]

The second series of decisions expressed the more qualified view that:

> in the field of international arbitration, the principle of the autonomy of the arbitration agreement is of general application, as an international substantive rule upholding the legality of the arbitration agreement, quite apart from any reference to a system of choice of law, because the validity of the agreement must be judged solely in the light of the requirements of international public policy.[140]

---

[138] CA Paris, Apr. 20, 1988, Clark International Finance v. Sud Matériel Service, 1988 REV. ARB. 570; CA Paris, Nov. 30, 1988, Korsnas Marma v. Durand-Auzias, and Feb. 14, 1989, Ofer Brothers v. The Tokyo Marine and Fire Insurance Co. Ltd., 1989 REV. ARB. 691, and P.-Y. Tschanz' note, aff'd, Cass. com., Mar. 3, 1992, 1992 REV. ARB. 560, and P. Delebecque's note; CA Paris, Nov. 28, 1989, Compagnie tunisienne de navigation (Cotunav) v. Comptoir commercial André, 1990 REV. ARB. 675, and P. Mayer's disapproving note (affirmed, but on a different ground, Cass. 1e civ., June 25, 1991, 1991 REV. ARB. 453, and P. Mayer's approving note); CA Paris, Jan. 11, 1990, Orri v. Société des Lubrifiants Elf Aquitaine, 1992 REV. ARB. 95, and D. Cohen's note; 118 J.D.I. 141 (1991), and B. Audit's note; 1992 RTD COM. 596, and observations by J.-C. Dubarry and E. Loquin, aff'd, Cass. 1e civ., June 11, 1991, 1992 REV. ARB. 73, and D. Cohen's note; CA Paris, Mar. 22, 1995, SMABTP v. Statinor, 1997 REV. ARB. 550, and the commentary by Daniel Cohen, Arbitrage et groupes de contrats, id. at 471; 1996 RTD COM. 247, and observations by J.-C. Dubarry and E. Loquin; CA Paris, Oct. 8, 1997, Solna International AB v. S.A. Destouche, Dalloz, I.R. 233 (1997). For an analysis of this case law, see also XIAO-YING LI, LA TRANSMISSION ET L'EXTINCTION DE LA CLAUSE COMPROMISSOIRE DANS L'ARBITRAGE INTERNATIONAL ¶¶ 419 et seq. (Thesis, University of Dijon (France), 1993).

[139] On these cases, see infra para. 505. But see CA Paris, Jan. 19, 1999, CIC International, supra note 64.

[140] CA Paris, Dec. 17, 1991, Gatoil v. National Iranian Oil Co., 1993 REV. ARB. 281; for an English translation, see 7 INT'L ARB. REP. B1 (July 1992); CA Paris, Dec. 7, 1994, V 2000 (formerly Jaguar France) v. Renault, 1996 REV ARB. 245, and C. Jarrosson's note; 1995 RTD COM. 401, and observations by J.-C. Dubarry and E. Loquin; 1996 JUSTICES 435, and observations by M.-C. Rivier; aff'd, Cass. 1e civ., May 21, 1997, Renault v. V 2000 (formerly Jaguar France), 1997 REV. ARB. 537, and E. Gaillard's note; 1998 REV. CRIT. DIP 87, and V. Heuzé's note; 125 J.D.I. 969 (1998), 1st decision, and S. Poillot-Peruzzetto's note; CA Paris, Sept. 10, 1997, Chambon v. Thomson CSF, 1997 DALLOZ AFF. 1253; 1999 REV. ARB. 121, and observations by D. Bureau; for earlier cases, see CA Paris, Mar. 8, 1990, Coumet et Ducler, supra note 93, which holds that "in international arbitration, the arbitration clause enjoys full autonomy from both the main contract—the inexistence and validity of which have no impact on the arbitration clause—and the law applicable to the main contract, other than provisions of international public policy;" CA Paris, Mar. 26, 1991, Dalico, supra note 118, which holds that "in international arbitration, the principle of the autonomy of the arbitration clause—intended to ensure that the parties' intentions take full effect—causes the arbitration agreement to be independent of both the main contract and the national law governing that contract, subject only to the provisions of international public policy—particularly those concerning the arbitrability of the dispute" (aff'd, Cass. 1e civ., Dec. 20, 1993, supra note 2).

This more accurately reflects the views of the Paris Court of Appeals on the issue: the arbitration agreement is governed not by national laws, but only by the requirements—which are, by definition, very limited—of international public policy.

437. — In the seminal 1993 *Dalico* decision, the *Cour de cassation* endorsed the substantive rules method promoted by the Paris Court of Appeals in its second series of decisions. Rejecting an action against the Paris Court of Appeals' decision, which was expressed in similar terms,[141] the *Cour de cassation* held that:

> by virtue of a substantive rule of international arbitration, the arbitration agreement is legally independent of the main contract containing or referring to it, and the existence and effectiveness of the arbitration agreement are to be assessed, subject to the mandatory rules of French law and international public policy, on the basis of the parties' common intention, there being no need to refer to any national law.

The *Cour de cassation* concluded, in a case arising from a relationship between Danish and Libyan entities, that the Paris Court of Appeals had rightly rejected arguments based on Libyan law when examining the existence and validity of the arbitration agreement.[142]

B. – CRITICISM OF THE SUBSTANTIVE RULES METHOD

438. — Several commentators have expressed reservations regarding the decisions of the Paris Court of Appeals confirming, in one way or another, the autonomy of the arbitration agreement from national law. They have observed that in reality the arbitration agreement cannot be entirely independent of national law, and that the intention of the Court cannot have been to confer absolute validity on the arbitration agreement:

> [d]oes this mean that an arbitration agreement cannot be void for lack of capacity, for lack of consent, for being non-arbitrable, etc.? Such a suggestion can hardly be serious.[143]

The example of the absence of the requisite power to contract has also been used by critics of the substantive rules method. They argue that the courts cannot have intended that

---

[141] *See supra* note 118.

[142] Cass. 1e civ., Dec. 20, 1993, *Dalico, supra* note 2.

[143] Mayer, *L'autonomie de l'arbitre international dans l'appréciation de sa propre compétence, supra* note 1, ¶ 112. *See also* B. Oppetit, note following CA Paris, Dec. 13, 1975, *Menicucci, supra* note 11. *Comp. with* E. Loquin, note following CA Paris, Dec. 13, 1975, *Menicucci, supra* note 11.

a party be unable to establish that it was not be bound by the actions of an unauthorized representative.[144]

The concept of the autonomy of the arbitration agreement and that of its "own effectiveness" have also been the subject of criticism on a theoretical level. One author commented that:

> a contract cannot be 'valid in principle.' It is only valid if it satisfies the relevant conditions as to its form and substance under a law which governs that contract; such conditions may be liberal, but they cannot be non-existent.[145]

These commentators conclude that the choice of law method is better suited to determining the law applicable to the arbitration agreement than the substantive rules method. They argue that to resolve the issue of the existence and validity of an arbitration agreement between Libyans and Danes, as in the *Dalico* case, solely on the basis of French legal concepts, albeit limited to those which are important enough to be characterized as requirements of international public policy, is to show unwarranted legal imperialism.[146]

C. – SCOPE AND MERIT OF THE SUBSTANTIVE RULES METHOD

439. — In order to discuss the merit of the French case law whereby the existence and validity of the arbitration agreement are examined solely by reference to French substantive rules, a distinction must be drawn between certain expressions used on occasions by the Paris Court of Appeals and the substantive position adopted first by the Paris Court of Appeals and later by the *Cour de cassation*.

440. — It is true that somewhat unfortunate terminology has been used in decisions concerning certain aspects of the autonomy of the arbitration agreement from "any national law." The same is especially true of those decisions which refer to the arbitration agreement's "own effectiveness." In particular, the Paris Court of Appeals was ill-advised in resorting to terms such as "the principle of validity" and the arbitration agreement's "own effectiveness" when ruling on whether an arbitration agreement bound parties who were not formally signatories, but were involved in the negotiation or the performance of the agreement containing the arbitration clause. In addition to the pertinent criticism that a contract can only be valid by reference to a law that recognizes such validity,[147] the Court's affirmation appears to be circular. Where the disputed issue is whether a party agreed to be bound by an arbitration agreement, it is unhelpful to refer to the "validity" and

---

[144] *See* Synvet, *supra* note 100, at 295.

[145] Gaudemet-Tallon, *supra* note 100, at 469.

[146] *See* H. Gaudemet-Tallon, *supra* note 100 and note following Cass. 1e civ., Dec. 20, 1993, *Dalico*, 1994 REV. ARB. 116, 121; V. Heuzé, note following Cass. 1e civ., May 21, 1997, Renault v. V 2000 (formerly Jaguar France), 1998 REV. CRIT. DIP 87. *Comp. with* Synvet, *supra* note 100, at 296.

[147] *See supra* para. 438.

"effectiveness" of an agreement which may not even have been concluded in the first place. Here, the debate is unconnected with both the principle of autonomy and that of the effectiveness of the arbitration agreement. The only relevant issue in such cases is the proof of the existence and the extent of the parties' consent to the arbitration agreement, which is an entirely different question.[148] Happily, in rejecting the actions against these decisions of the Paris Court of Appeals, the *Cour de cassation* carefully refrained from endorsing the dicta contained in those decisions concerning the scope of the arbitration agreement.[149]

441. — However, the foregoing should not detract from the true significance of the decisions of the Paris Court of Appeals and, later, the *Cour de cassation*. As the validity of the arbitration agreement is examined solely by reference to the French conception of international public policy, it simply means that the agreement is no longer affected by the idiosyncrasies of local law. As has been rightly pointed out,[150] this understanding of the expression "public policy" is not one which leads to the exclusion of the law normally applicable, but instead consists of the French legal system's view of the fundamental requirements of justice in an international context. As such, it is particularly suited to international arbitration. This is true both where the question of the validity of an arbitration agreement arises before the courts reviewing an award (1°), and where it arises before the arbitrators themselves by virtue of the "competence-competence" principle (2°).

1° Application of the Substantive Rules Method by Courts Reviewing Arbitral Awards

442. — Generally speaking, the circumstances in which the French courts will examine the validity of an arbitration agreement are fairly limited,[151] as a result of the "competence-competence" principle[152] and the limited grounds on which an award can be set aside or refused enforcement. The issue will arise where a party has petitioned for an award to be set aside or enforced, and where it is alleged either that the award was made "in the absence of an arbitration agreement or on the basis of an arbitration agreement that was void or had expired,"[153] or that the arbitral tribunal declined jurisdiction after wrongly deciding that an arbitration agreement was non-existent or invalid.[154] It was in this context that the courts held that the existence and effectiveness of the arbitration agreement "should only be scrutinized

---

[148] *See infra* paras. 472 *et seq.*

[149] Cass. 1e civ., June 11, 1991, *Orri, supra* note 138; Cass. 1e civ., June 25, 1991, *Cotunav, supra* note 138.

[150] *Synvet, supra* note 100, at 294.

[151] On the *prima facie* control on the existence and the validity of the arbitration agreement, see *infra* para. 851.

[152] On this issue, see *infra* para. 650.

[153] *See* Arts. 1502 1° and 1504 of the French New Code of Civil Procedure and, on this issue, *infra* paras. 1608 *et seq.*

[154] *See* Arts. 1502 3° and 1504 of the French New Code of Civil Procedure, and *infra* para. 1629.

in the light of the requirements of international public policy,"[155] to use the expression coined by the Paris Court of Appeals.

We have seen that the criticism leveled at these decisions was prompted by the Court's use of unfortunate terminology regarding the arbitration agreement's own effectiveness,[156] and was particularly concerned with the practical and theoretical impossibility of basing the validity of a contract on no law at all.[157] This criticism is unfounded, however. In French case law, the intention is not to remove the arbitration agreement from all forms of control. It is, instead, to restrict such control to a review of the arbitration agreement in the light of the French conception of the fundamental requirements of justice in international commerce, referred to by the French courts as international public policy. Although the goal is not to avoid the application of the law otherwise competent,[158] the expression "international public policy" is well chosen where the decision to be taken is whether or not a dispute is arbitrable, an issue falling within the scope of Article 1502 5° of the French New Code of Civil Procedure, which ensures compliance with the requirements of international public policy.[159] The courts' approach is more innovative, however, where they are examining the existence and validity of the arbitration agreement, as that ground for setting aside an award (Art. 1502 1°) is distinct from a violation of international public policy (Art. 1502 5°). Nevertheless, the idea remains clear: all aspects of the arbitration agreement should be examined solely by reference to the fundamental notions generally recognized in civilized legal systems. Reduced to its simplest procedural form, the rule laid down in the *Dalico* case is that the concept of an "arbitration agreement," and that of "an agreement that was void or had expired" within the meaning of Article 1502 1° of the New Code of Civil Procedure, have a meaning of their own and are not subject to any choice of law rule which may point to the application of national laws. The arbitration agreement is not a contract without a governing law, but a contract without a choice of law. In other words, these cases cannot be interpreted as laying down a principle that the arbitration agreement is immune to any sort of challenge. It is perfectly possible to derive the validity of the arbitration agreement not from the agreement itself—which would be autonomy in the purest sense—but from the principles considered by French law to be fundamental in an international context. For that reason, the convenient term "autonomy" goes too far. What is meant here by international public policy is merely the limited body of rules which must, in the French conception of international arbitration, be observed for an arbitration agreement to be effective.[160]

Equally unfounded is the accusation of legal imperialism directed at the substantive rules method. Certain commentators question why, in a dispute which has only tenuous links with

---

[155] CA Paris, Dec. 17, 1991, *Gatoil*, *supra* note 140, 7 INT'L ARB. REP. B3 (July 1992). *Comp. with* Cass. 1e civ., Dec. 20, 1993, *Dalico*, *supra* note 2.

[156] *See supra* paras. 436 and 440.

[157] *See supra* para. 438.

[158] *See supra* para. 441.

[159] *See infra* para. 1617.

[160] On the position that the reference to "the mandatory rules of French law" contained in the *Dalico* decision is a reference to the "French *lois de police*," which does little to explain the nature of such rules, see CA Paris, Mar. 24, 1995, Bin Saud Bin Abdel Aziz v. Crédit Industriel et Commercial de Paris, 1996 REV. ARB. 259, and J.-M. Talau's note. On this issue, see *infra* paras. 1515 *et seq.*

the French legal system, rules of French origin are given precedence over rules designated by the choice of law method.[161] They believe the latter method to pay greater respect to local laws. However, when a French court hears an application to set aside or enforce an award, it must decide whether it is appropriate for the award made on the basis of the arbitration agreement to be enforced in France. To that end, it is hardly surprising that the court should examine the validity of the agreement on which the award is based by reference to concepts of French law applicable in an international context.[162]

As for the unpredictability of the resulting decisions, it is clear that this more internationalist method leaves less to chance than the choice of law method. The substantive rules method derives rules specific to international arbitration from comparative law and from the legitimate requirements of international commerce. With the choice of law method, the status of the arbitration agreement depends on the application of a national law determined by French choice of law rules. Those choice of law rules apply solely by virtue of the existence of an action to set aside or enforce an award in France, and may well not correspond to what the parties would have intended.[163]

The approach adopted by the French courts whereby the existence and validity of the arbitration agreement are examined exclusively by reference to the conception held by French law of the needs of international commerce, subject, of course, to international conventions applicable to arbitration,[164] should therefore, in our opinion, be approved.

2° Application of the Substantive Rules Method by Arbitrators

443. — Where arbitrators are required to examine the existence and validity of the arbitration agreement on which their jurisdiction is founded, it is even more important that transnational rules apply, rather than those designated by a choice of law rule.

Since arbitrators belong to no national legal order, they have no institutional reason to give precedence to the choice of law rules or substantive provisions of any of the legal systems connected to the dispute. In the absence of any indication by the parties on the point, the approach most consistent with the role of the arbitrators is to apply what they consider to be the fundamental requirements of justice. These can be determined on the basis of comparative law and international arbitral case law, leaving aside the idiosyncrasies of domestic laws.

From a practical standpoint, the use of transnational substantive rules undoubtedly leads to more predictable results than having the validity of the arbitration agreement depend on

---

[161] *See supra* para. 438.

[162] The objection that such an approach leads to the eviction of the entire body of choice of law rules in favor of French law (*see, e.g.,* Heuzé, *supra* note 146) does not take into account the fact that the goal here is the recognition of an award and not the determination of the law to be applied to the merits of a dispute by a French court. The approach is no more objectionable than that whereby a French court hearing an action to enforce a judgment of a foreign court applies a French law jurisdictional test to assess the jurisdiction of the foreign court.

[163] On the unpredictability of the choice of law method with regard to the arbitration agreement, see *supra* para. 434.

[164] *See infra* para. 449.

the applicability of the law of one of the parties. Again taking the example of a contract between Libyan and Danish parties containing a clause providing for arbitration in Paris, it seems less arbitrary for the arbitrators to apply transnational rules to the arbitration agreement than to have the law of the country of one of the parties govern the arbitration agreement as a result of factors with only a weak connecting value.[165]

Another way of limiting the effect of the idiosyncrasies of local law is to subject the validity of the arbitration agreement to the law of the seat of the arbitration. This is of course the solution found in the major international conventions.[166] As the seat of the arbitration is often located in a country which is neutral for both parties, the validity of the arbitration agreement and thus the jurisdiction of the arbitral tribunal will not be dependent on one or other of the laws of the parties' home countries. However, the seat may have been chosen for reasons of convenience alone, or may not have been chosen by the parties at all, and its connecting value in such cases would be weak.[167] For that reason, it seems preferable to pursue the reasoning based on the transnational nature of the arbitrators' powers to its logical conclusion. This would allow the arbitrators to examine the existence and validity of the arbitration agreement solely by reference to genuinely transnational concepts, referred to by the French *Cour de cassation* as international public policy.

An alternative would be a purely utilitarian approach, based on the idea of giving full efficacy to the award, as embodied in particular in Article 35 of the ICC Arbitration Rules (Art. 26 of the previous Rules). This would involve the arbitrators attempting to satisfy both the requirements of the law of the seat—where the award may be subject to an action to set aside—and the requirements of the laws of the countries where the award is likely to be enforced. Such laws might themselves impose substantive conditions, just as they might use a choice of law method to designate the laws applicable to the arbitration agreement. However, the disadvantage with this "cumulative method" is that if the award were to be enforced in a country which is unfavorable to arbitration (which, in practice, will arise where the law of one of the parties' home countries is not "arbitration-friendly"), the more restrictive rules would prevail over those of other legal systems. That would hardly be an appropriate way to select the law applicable to the arbitration agreement.[168]

444. — There is consequently a strong tendency in arbitral case law to examine the existence and validity of the arbitration agreement exclusively by reference to transnational substantive rules, in keeping with the transnational nature of the source of the arbitrators'

---

[165] *See supra* paras. 412 and 426.

[166] *See supra* para. 431.

[167] *See supra* para. 433.

[168] On this issue, see the very pertinent observations in the November 1984 award on jurisdiction in ICC Case No. 4695, *supra* note 77, at 158. Compare with the arbitral tribunal's statement in ICC Award No. 2476 (1976), *supra* note 52, that "the question of the enforceability of the award is not within the arbitral tribunal's jurisdiction;" on the limitations inherent in this approach based on the effectiveness of the award, see also the observations by Y. Derains following the award on jurisdiction in ICC Case No. 4604 (1984), *supra* note 133.

powers. This tendency is apparent in both disputes between private entities[169] and disputes arising from state contracts.[170]

As one author has commented, this solution "has the merit of emphasizing the independence of international arbitration from the shackles of national laws, too few of which are equipped to address anything but domestic issues."[171]

This approach also appears to be most consistent with the provisions of the ICC Rules (Arts. 6(2) and 6(4); Arts. 8(3) and 8(4) of the previous Rules). As stated in a number of awards, Article 6 of the Rules (Art. 8 of the previous Rules) "confer[s] on the arbitrator the power to take any decision as to his own jurisdiction . . . without obliging him to apply any national law whatever in order to do so."[172]

445. — Several recent arbitration statutes have gone even further in their attempts to ensure the validity of arbitration agreements, by allowing choice of law rules to be combined with substantive rules.

§ 3. – Combining *In Favorem Validitatis* Choice of Law Rules and Substantive Rules

446. — A number of legal systems shared the same concern as French law that, in international arbitration, the validity of the arbitration agreement should not depend on considerations specific to any of the laws that might be connected to the case. As a result,

---

[169] See, for example, the January 14, 1970 second preliminary award by P. Lalive, sole arbitrator, in ICC Case No. 1512, Indian cement company v. Pakistani bank, V Y.B. COM. ARB. 174 (1980); the September 23, 1982 interim award in ICC Case No. 4131, *Dow Chemical, supra* note 52 (on the rejection of the action to set aside this award, see CA Paris, Oct. 21, 1983, *Isover-Saint-Gobain, supra* note 72); the November 1984 interim award in ICC Case No. 4695, *supra* note 77, which bases the existence and validity of an arbitration agreement on the ICC Arbitration Rules to which the parties have referred; ICC Award No. 4381 (1986), *supra* note 52, which, while ruling that the capacity to enter into an arbitration agreement is subject to a specific national law, holds that "it is for the Arbitral Tribunal to choose the [sources of applicable law] for the purposes of determining the validity of the arbitration agreement. The Tribunal need not establish the applicable choice of law rules, provided that such law be compatible with Iranian and French arbitration law [the parties being of Iranian and French origin];" ICC Award No. 5065 (1986), *supra* note 77, which carefully refrains from addressing the issue of capacity as it was not raised. On this issue, see also Derains, *supra* note 44, at 835 *et seq.*

[170] See, for example, the April 12, 1977 *LIAMCO* award, *supra* note 47, which bases the binding nature of an arbitration agreement entered into by a state on "international practice . . . confirmed in many international conventions and resolutions" (20 I.L.M. 40 (1981)); the January 14, 1982 *Elf* award, *supra* note 48, and the April 30, 1982 Award on Jurisdiction in ICC Case No. 3896, Framatome S.A. v. Atomic Energy Organization of Iran (AEOI), regarding the rule prohibiting states from relying on their national law to renege on arbitration agreements (111 J.D.I. 58 (1984)); Bruno Oppetit, *Arbitrage et contrats d'Etat – L'arbitrage Framatome et autres c/ Atomic Energy Organization of Iran,* 111 J.D.I. 37 (1984).

[171] Y. Derains, observations following ICC Award No. 6840 (1991), *supra* note 118, at 1035.

[172] Interim award in ICC Case No. 4131 (1982), *Dow Chemical, supra* note 52. *See also* ICC Award No. 4381 (1986), *supra* note 52. The same should also be the case with the *prima facie* examination of the existence and validity of the arbitration agreements by the ICC Court of Arbitration under Article 6(2) of the ICC Rules (Art. 8(3) of the previous Rules).

several recent statutes have adopted substantive rules governing the validity of the arbitration agreement, which they have combined with the traditional choice of law method so as to increase the chances of the arbitration agreement being held valid.

We shall begin by examining the laws which use, *in favorem*, this combination of substantive rules and choice of law rules (A), before considering whether a similar combination might not, in fact, be invoked under French law (B).

A. – THE SWISS MODEL

447. — Switzerland was the first country to combine, *in favorem validitatis*, substantive rules and choice of law rules regarding the arbitration agreement.[173]

Article 178, paragraph 2 of the Swiss Private International Law Statute provides that an arbitration agreement shall be valid, as to its substance, "if it conforms either to the law chosen by the parties, or to the law governing the subject-matter of the dispute, in particular the law governing the main contract, or if it conforms to Swiss law."[174]

This provision is framed as a choice of law rule, but it in fact also allows Swiss courts to apply the substantive rules of Swiss law.[175] As in the *Dalico* decision,[176] the only connection with the seat of the arbitration is the fact that recognition or enforcement of the award may be sought in that country. The Swiss legislature considered, in the same way as the French courts, that in an international case the fact that the award was to produce effects within the Swiss legal system was enough to justify having the validity of the arbitration agreement governed by Swiss rules. Thus, in practice, to ensure that the award will be valid, parties concluding an arbitration agreement providing for arbitration in Switzerland need only meet the very liberal conditions imposed by Swiss law on the validity of the arbitration agreement.

---

[173] See also the Resolution on Arbitration Between States, State Enterprises or State Entities and Foreign Enterprises adopted by the Institute of International Law on September 12, 1989 at its Santiago de Compostela Session, Article 4 of which provides that: "[w]here the validity of the agreement to arbitrate is challenged, the tribunal shall resolve the issue by applying one or more of the following: the law chosen by the parties, the law indicated by the system of private international law stipulated by the parties, general principles of public or private international law, general principles of international arbitration, or the law that would be applied by the courts of the territory in which the tribunal has its seat. In making this selection, the tribunal shall be guided in every case by the principle *in favorem validitatis*" (XVI Y.B. COM. ARB. 233, 238 (1991), with an explanatory note by A.T. von Mehren; for the French text, see 1990 REV. ARB. 931, and observations by P. Fouchard. See also the commentaries cited *infra* para. 1446).

[174] For a commentary, see PIERRE LALIVE, JEAN-FRANÇOIS POUDRET, CLAUDE REYMOND, LE DROIT DE L'ARBITRAGE INTERNE ET INTERNATIONAL EN SUISSE 312 *et seq.* (1989); ANDREAS BUCHER, PIERRE-YVES TSCHANZ, INTERNATIONAL ARBITRATION IN SWITZERLAND ¶¶ 78 *et seq.* (1988); Marc Blessing, *The New International Arbitration Law in Switzerland – A Significant Step Towards Liberalism*, 5 J. INT'L ARB. 9, 29 *et seq.* (June 1988).

[175] On the fact that the arbitrability of a dispute is determined by reference to substantive rules, not choice of law rules, see the unambiguous position adopted by the Swiss Federal Tribunal on June 23, 1992, Fincantieri-Cantieri Navali Italiani S.p.A. v. M., 1993 BULL. ASA 58; 1993 REV. ARB. 691, and F. Knoepfler's note; 1994 REV. SUISSE DR. INT. ET DR. EUR. 111, and observations by F. Knoepfler; for an English translation, see XX Y.B. COM. ARB. 766 (1995).

[176] *See supra* para. 437.

Swiss law differs from French law in that the substantive validity of the arbitration agreement may also result from the law chosen by the parties, or from the law governing the merits of the dispute (which in most cases will be the law governing the main contract). The first of these alternatives is the traditional application of the principle of autonomy. The second is more unusual in that it places particular emphasis on the connecting factor provided by the law governing the substance of the dispute, as had been suggested by some commentators.[177]

The fact that these various solutions are considered as alternatives, provided that they lead to validation of the arbitration agreement, is the clearest possible indication of the strong pro-arbitration bias of the 1987 Swiss Private International Law Statute.

448. — The Swiss approach was followed in the Algerian legislative decree of April 25, 1993. The new Article 458 *bis* 1, paragraph 3 of the Code of Civil Procedure contains a provision identical to that of Article 178, paragraph 2 of the Swiss Private International Law Statute.[178]

It is also worth considering whether, in the absence of a similar statute, the same approach is valid in France.

B. – THE POSITION IN FRANCE

449. — If it were impossible for an arbitration agreement to be held valid under the applicable French substantive rules, could a French court not hold it valid by applying a different law?

It would be possible if one were to combine French law with the conventions on international arbitration applicable in France, and if the arbitration agreement were valid under the law chosen by the parties or, if not, under the law of the seat of the arbitration. Even if, as will seldom be the case, the substantive rules applied pursuant to the *Dalico* decision[179] did not validate an arbitration agreement, the French courts could not refuse to recognize or enforce an award based on that arbitration agreement if such agreement complied with the law chosen by the parties or, in the absence of such a choice, with the law of the seat of the arbitration. That results from Article V, paragraph 1(a) of the 1958 New York Convention.[180] A more liberal French regime could, of course, take precedence over the New York Convention, Article VII of which permits such a derogation, but the French courts could not adopt a more restrictive stance without violating the Convention. Likewise, where no award has been made, French courts are prohibited, under Article VI, paragraphs 2(a) and (2)(b) of the 1961 European Convention, where applicable, from refusing to give

---

[177] *See* Goldman, *supra* note 18, ¶ 59; *see also supra* para. 425.

[178] For a commentary, see Mohand Issad, *Le décret législatif algérien du 25 avril 1993 relatif à l'arbitrage international*, 1993 REV. ARB. 377, 384 *et seq.*; Mohammed Bedjaoui and Ali Mebroukine, *Le nouveau droit de l'arbitrage international en Algérie*, 120 J.D.I. 873, 883 *et seq.* (1993).

[179] *See supra* para. 437.

[180] *See supra* para. 431.

effect to an arbitration agreement which is valid under the law chosen by the parties or, in the absence of such a choice, under the law of the seat of the arbitration.[181]

Thus, French law could currently be interpreted as following Swiss law, in that it recognizes the validity of arbitration agreements which comply either with the law chosen by the parties, or with the law of the seat of the arbitration, or with the substantive provisions of French law on international arbitration.

450. — Realistically, however, there is every reason to believe that the question will not arise in practice. For it to do so, the arbitration agreement would have to be invalid under French law, despite its extremely liberal stance, and valid under the law of another country, such as that chosen by the parties. Although it is conceivable that such a situation might arise, it is more than likely that the law of the other country would, in such a case, be deemed too permissive by the French courts, which would then hold that law inapplicable on the grounds that it violates international public policy in its traditional sense. Indeed, the 1958 New York Convention expressly allows recognition and enforcement of an award to be refused in circumstances which contravene public policy (Art. V(2)(b)). The position is less clear as regards the 1961 European Convention, where the only express exception to the application of the law designated by the Convention concerns cases which are not arbitrable under the *lex fori* (Art. VI(2), para. 2). However, it is reasonable to assume that the traditional public policy exception is implicit in Article VI of that Convention.

In practice, then, French law is so liberal with regard to international arbitration agreements that it is hard to imagine that such an agreement could be valid under a foreign law, but invalid under French law, without the French courts considering the non-French law to be overly liberal. For instance, an arbitration agreement obtained through the corruption of the representative of one of the parties would undoubtedly be void under French substantive rules of international arbitration.[182] For the purposes of this example we should assume that either the law chosen by the parties or the law of the seat of the arbitration treats such a situation as one which does not cause the arbitration agreement to be void. Alternatively, we could assume that such laws fail to address the issue, or that the parties specifically excluded any actions to set aside (for example, on the basis of Article 192 of the Swiss Private International Law Statute). In all such cases, enforcement of the award could nevertheless be refused in France on the grounds of the invalidity of the arbitration agreement. The reasoning would be that even if it were accepted that a foreign law applicable pursuant to an international treaty could displace the substantive rules of French law, the content of that foreign law would be immediately rejected on the basis of its non-conformity with international public policy.

Thus, "international public policy," as referred to in the *Dalico* case to denote the substantive rules applicable under French law to the existence and validity of an international arbitration agreement, may well have precisely the same meaning as the expression used in a traditional choice of law context. In other words, the substantive rules governing the existence and validity of an international arbitration agreement under French

---

[181] *See supra* para. 431.

[182] On the impact of corruption on the validity of the main contract, see *infra* para. 1468.

law constitute both the minimum and the maximum standard of liberalism acceptable in that legal system.

451. — We shall now examine the content of these substantive French law rules and of those found in other legal systems by considering, in turn, the formation of the arbitration agreement (Chapter II) and its effects (Chapter III), before discussing its assignment and expiry (Chapter IV).

CHAPTER II
FORMATION OF THE ARBITRATION AGREEMENT

452. — In the same way as every other contract, an arbitration agreement must satisfy a number of conditions in order to be valid. To assess whether or not these conditions are met, in international trade one should consider not the requirements of a particular legal system, but rather those found over a broader spectrum, including international treaties, comparative law and arbitral precedents. This substantive rules approach was adopted as early as 1981 by one leading author, who examined the conditions of the validity of an arbitration agreement only in the light of comparative and international law requirements.[1] Since the 1993 decision of the French *Cour de cassation* in the *Dalico* case,[2] the French courts have followed the same approach when reviewing the existence, validity and scope of an arbitration agreement in an action to set aside or enforce an arbitral award. More importantly, arbitrators having to decide these issues often use similar reasoning, either as the basis, or at least the background, for their decision. We will therefore follow the same substantive rules methodology, with limited excursions into more traditional choice of law territory, when addressing in turn the issues of capacity and power (Section I), the existence and validity of the parties' consent (Section II), the arbitrability of the dispute (Section III), and the form and proof of the arbitration agreement (Section IV). All of these concepts are so widely accepted in comparative law that each needs to be studied in detail when considering the formation of the arbitration agreement.[3]

---

[1] RENÉ DAVID, ARBITRATION IN INTERNATIONAL TRADE 169 *et seq.* (1985); L'ARBITRAGE DANS LE COMMERCE INTERNATIONAL 231 *et seq.* (1981).

[2] Cass. 1e civ., Dec. 20, 1993, Comité populaire de la municipalité de Khoms El Mergeb v. Dalico Contractors, 121 J.D.I. 432 (1994), and E. Gaillard's note; 121 J.D.I. 690 (1994), and E. Loquin's note; 1994 REV. ARB. 116, and H. Gaudemet-Tallon's note; 1994 REV. CRIT. DIP 663, and P. Mayer's note.

[3] The concept of consideration, on the other hand, is not one that is universally accepted and it has no particular relevance with respect to the arbitration agreement. Compare, in French domestic arbitration law, Pascal Ancel, *Arbitrage – Conventions d'arbitrage – Conditions de fond – Consentement. Capacité. Pouvoir. Objet. Cause,* J.-CL. PROC. CIV., Fasc. 1022, ¶ 92–94 (1996). We shall therefore not discuss consideration further.

SECTION I
CAPACITY AND POWER

453. — The issues of a party's capacity and power to contract are often confused in everyday legal language, although here, as in other areas, they must be carefully distinguished. The issue of capacity arises where an agreement is entered into in a person's own name and on that person's own account. The issue of power arises where an agreement is entered into other than in the signatory's sole interest, be it in the interest of another individual, in that of a juridical person, or in that of an entity having no autonomous legal existence.[4]

454. — It is in the areas of a party's capacity and power to contract that there is generally the most reluctance to abandon the choice of law method. Capacity is always cited as an example in support of criticism of French court decisions which reject the choice of law method when ruling on the recognition or enforcement of international arbitral awards.[5] Indeed, the 1958 New York Convention provides that recognition and enforcement of an award may be refused where the parties to an arbitration agreement (or in practice, one of those parties) "were, under the law applicable to them, under some incapacity" (Art. V(1)(a)). This provision does not stipulate which law is to govern the question of capacity, but it is generally considered to require the application of the choice of law method.[6] However, the Convention could be interpreted differently. There is nothing to prevent courts from construing "the law applicable to them" as meaning the substantive rules they deem applicable in an international context, the aim being to determine whether the parties have the required capacity to enter into an arbitration agreement which is liable to produce effects in the country in which those courts are located.[7] The 1961 European Convention follows the example of the New York Convention, providing, in its Article VI(2), that "[i]n taking a decision concerning . . . the validity of an arbitration agreement, courts of Contracting States shall examine the validity of such agreement with reference to the capacity of the parties, under the law applicable to them." The European Convention thus shares the limitations of the New York Convention, in that it too fails to give any further indication as to how to determine the "law applicable to [the parties]." In addition, it is not conclusive as to the need to use choice of law rules in the first place, as discussed above with regard to the New York Convention.

---

[4]   EMMANUEL GAILLARD, LE POUVOIR EN DROIT PRIVÉ ¶¶ 64 *et seq.* (1985); PHILIPPE FOUCHARD, L'ARBITRAGE COMMERCIAL INTERNATIONAL ¶ 151 (1965); DAVID, *supra* note 1, ¶ 189. On the issue sometimes presented as that of the capacity of states and state-owned entities to enter into an arbitration agreement, but which is in fact a question of arbitrability, see *infra* paras. 534 *et seq.*

[5]   *See supra* para. 438.

[6]   *See, e.g.,* MATTHIEU DE BOISSÉSON, LE DROIT FRANÇAIS DE L'ARBITRAGE INTERNE ET INTERNATIONAL ¶ 583 at 498 (2d ed. 1990); ALAN REDFERN AND MARTIN HUNTER, LAW AND PRACTICE OF INTERNATIONAL COMMERCIAL ARBITRATION 147 (2d ed. 1991).

[7]   *See supra* para. 442.

This traditional position, still favored by some arbitral tribunals,[8] calls for an analysis of the application of the choice of law method to the capacity and power to enter into a valid arbitration agreement (§ 1). We shall then consider the role that substantive rules have played and could play in the future in this area (§ 2).

§ 1. – The Choice of Law Method

455. — Under the choice of law method, the laws applicable to a party's capacity and to its powers will not necessarily be the same. This is because it is generally accepted that the capacity to contract is governed by the personal law of the party in question, while the power to contract is governed by the law of the source of such power. We shall therefore consider each in turn.

A. – THE LAW GOVERNING THE CAPACITY TO ENTER INTO AN ARBITRATION AGREEMENT

456. — The law governing the capacity to enter into an arbitration agreement is determined differently according to whether one is dealing with a natural or a juridical person.[9]

1° Natural Persons

457. — Under the traditional continental choice of law rule, the legal capacity of natural persons, and in particular their capacity to contract, is governed by their national law or, if they are stateless or have refugee status, by the law of their domicile or residence. This is

---

[8] *See, e.g.*, ICC Award No. 2694 (1977), French company v. Swiss, French and Luxembourg companies, 105 J.D.I. 985 (1978), and observations by Y. Derains.

[9] It has sometimes been suggested, in order to limit the number of connecting factors and thus laws that may govern the various aspects of the validity of an arbitration agreement, that instead of being subject to a traditional choice of law rule, a party's capacity to enter into an arbitration agreement should be assimilated to the conditions of substantive validity of the agreement, and thus governed by the law applicable to that agreement. *See* Berthold Goldman, *Les conflits de lois dans l'arbitrage international de droit privé*, in COLLECTED COURSES OF THE HAGUE ACADEMY OF INTERNATIONAL LAW, Vol. 109, Year 1963, Part II, at 351, ¶ 39; Berthold Goldman, *Arbitrage (droit international privé)*, in ENCYCLOPÉDIE DALLOZ – DROIT INTERNATIONAL ¶ 64 (1968). This solution is inspired by that in force in some common law jurisdictions. Its purpose is to reduce the risk of having different approaches taken in different legal systems, as there is less divergence arising from the choice of law rule concerning the substance of the contract than arising from that concerning capacity. Nevertheless, this proposal can only be effective if widely followed in all legal systems, which has not been the case.

the choice of law rule that a French[10] or German[11]court, for instance, might consider applying to the question of the capacity of a natural person who is a party to an arbitration agreement, a scenario which rarely occurs in practice. Common law countries, on the other hand, generally favor the domicile or habitual residence of the party as their connecting factor, and some jurisdictions (for example, a number of U.S. states) apply the law governing the substance of the contract.[12]

458. — For arbitrators, the issue is more delicate. Having no forum,[13] arbitrators cannot resort to the choice of law rules "of the forum" when determining the validity of an arbitration agreement entered into by a natural person who, for example, claims to be a minor. Neither can they refer to a universally recognized choice of law rule, as national legal systems are divided on the issue.

Reliance on the choice of law rules of the seat—a prudent approach given the risk of actions to set aside before the courts of the seat, and one which has found favor in a number of somewhat dated instruments[14]—may lead to inappropriate results. As the seat is chosen by the parties, they might locate the seat in a country whose choice of law rules lead to the application of a law recognizing the capacity of one of those parties. However, issues of capacity ought not to depend on the skill of the parties—one of whom may in fact require the protection of rules on capacity—in choosing the seat.[15]

Another equally unsatisfactory approach is to apply the choice of law rules of the country where the arbitrators consider that the award may have to be enforced. In ICC arbitrations, this may be founded upon Article 35 of the ICC Rules (Art. 26 of the previous Rules) and, more generally, on the arbitrators' legitimate concern to avoid compromising the validity of

---

[10] *See* Trib. civ. Seine, July 31, 1894, Del Drago v. Czartoryski, 112 J.D.I. 1079 (1985); *see also* TGI Seine, June 25, 1959, Agent judiciaire du Trésor public v. Galakis, Gaz. Pal. 2, Jur. 294 (1959); 1960 REV. ARB. 30; 87 J.D.I. 488 (1960), and observations by J.-B. Sialelli (this case concerned the capacity of a state to enter into an arbitration agreement but confirms, in general terms, the principle that a party's national law should apply to its capacity to enter into an arbitration agreement); *see also* JEAN ROBERT, L'ARBITRAGE – DROIT INTERNE – DROIT INTERNATIONAL PRIVÉ ¶ 268 (6th ed. 1993); DE BOISSÉSON, *supra* note 6, ¶ 583 at 497; René Bourdin, *La convention d'arbitrage international en droit français depuis le décret du 12 mai 1981*, *in* FONDATION POUR L'ETUDE DU DROIT ET DES USAGES DU COMMERCE INTERNATIONAL, DROIT ET PRATIQUE DE L'ARBITRAGE INTERNATIONAL EN FRANCE 11, especially at 18 *et seq.* (Y. Derains ed., 1984).

[11] Art. 7 of the Introductory Law to the Civil Code (EGBGB).

[12] *See* RESTATEMENT (SECOND) OF CONFLICT OF LAWS § 198 (1971). *See also* ALBERT JAN VAN DEN BERG, THE NEW YORK ARBITRATION CONVENTION OF 1958, at 276–77 (1981) and, on the use of the law of the place where the contract was made, ROBERT A. LEFLAR, LUTHER L. MCDOUGAL, III, ROBERT L. FELIX, AMERICAN CONFLICTS OF LAW 408 (4th ed. 1986).

[13] *See infra* para. 1181.

[14] *See* Art. 4 of the September 26, 1957 Resolution of the Institute of International Law relating to the conflicts of laws to which private arbitration may give rise, "[c]apacity to submit to arbitration shall be regulated by the law indicated according to the rules of choice of law in force at the seat of the arbitral tribunal." (*reprinted in* INSTITUT DE DROIT INTERNATIONAL, TABLEAU DES RÉSOLUTIONS ADOPTÉES (1957–1991), at 253 (1992)). *See also* REDFERN AND HUNTER, *supra* note 6, at 148 and n. 84.

[15] For a criticism of this method, see also DE BOISSÉSON, *supra* note 6, at 498.

their award. However, it can lead to bizarre results, as the capacity of natural persons might thus vary according to the location of their assets.

In practice, the risk is that arbitrators using the choice of law method may, when faced with the difficulties described above, simply apply the choice of law rule with which, as a result of their own background, they are most familiar, and which they therefore instinctively consider to be the appropriate choice.[16]

2° Juridical Persons

459. — In the private international law of most civil law countries, the capacity of a juridical person is governed by the law of the country where its headquarters (*siège social réel*) are located. If a French court, for instance, applies the choice of law method, it will, in principle, apply the law of a juridical person's headquarters when considering the capacity of such a person to enter into an arbitration agreement.[17]

Other legal systems, especially those of common law countries, subject companies to the law of the country of incorporation. The country of incorporation is that where the formal requirements of registration and publication were carried out.

460. — This divergence of choice of law rules regarding the capacity of a juridical person to enter into an arbitration agreement could again, depending on the legal systems selected, lead to differing results. Arbitrators deciding issues concerning the capacity of a juridical person to enter into an arbitration agreement face the same difficulty as encountered in the case of natural persons. Under the choice of law process, the arbitrators are required to choose between choice of law rules which are widely divergent and which are equally well represented in major legal systems. To prefer the choice of law rules of the seat of the arbitration, as recommended by the Institute of International Law in 1959, gives, in our view, too much weight to the seat, which may have been chosen by an arbitral institution or by the arbitrators themselves. It is also open to various forms of manipulation as, in choosing carefully, the parties can ensure that a law recognizing the capacity of the juridical person in question will apply. This is hardly appropriate given that the goal of rules governing a party's capacity is to provide protection for those parties that need it. An equally artificial approach is to apply the choice of law rules of the country or countries in which it is assumed the award will be enforced.[18]

As a result, arbitrators again often apply the rules closest to their own preferences. This amply demonstrates the disadvantages of using the choice of law method in this area.[19]

---

[16] *See* FOUCHARD, *supra* note 4, ¶¶ 152 *et seq.*

[17] On the power of a company's representatives, see *infra* para. 461.

[18] See *supra* para. 458 for similar reasoning concerning the capacity of natural persons.

[19] See, for example, the ICC Award cited in FOUCHARD, *supra* note 4, ¶ 154, n. 9, stating that "according to a generally recognized principle of international private law, a company's capacity to undertake binding
(continued...)

B. – THE LAW GOVERNING POWERS

461. — As a general rule, powers are governed by the law of their source.[20]

For example, the powers of spouses over their marital assets are governed by the law under which they were married, subject to specific mandatory rules, and the powers of the legal representative of a minor are determined by the law governing the protection of that minor.

Under the Hague Convention of March 14, 1978 on the law applicable to Agency,[21] the powers of an agent are governed by the law chosen by the parties (Art. 5). In the absence of such a choice, an agent's powers will be governed by the law of its business headquarters or habitual residence, except where the principal's own business headquarters or habitual residence are situated in the country where the agent is to exercise the bulk of its functions, in which case the law of that country governs (Art. 6). These rules only apply, however, to relations between the principal and the agent.

In private international law, the powers of a juridical person are generally governed by the law under which that juridical person operates.[22] Yet, this law will not necessarily be the same in every choice of law system. The French choice of law rule, for example, is found in Article 1837, paragraph 1 of the Civil Code, which provides that "any company whose headquarters are located on French territory is subject to the provisions of French law."[23] Paragraph 2 of the same article adds that "third parties may rely on the location of the company's registered office, but the company may not do so vis-à-vis third parties where the company's actual headquarters are located elsewhere."[24] Thus, when using the choice of law method to decide whether a corporation was validly represented when entering into an arbitration agreement, a French court will apply the law of the corporation's *de facto* headquarters (in other words, the law of the country where its central management is located and operates). The only exception will be where the third party elects to have the question governed by the law of the registered office because that law will allow the party's claim

---

[19](...continued)
obligations is governed by its national law" without explaining how, for a company, "its national law" is to be determined. *Comp. with* the June 25, 1992 order in ICC Case No. 6848, 122 J.D.I. 1047 (1995), and observations by D. Hascher.

[20]   *See* GAILLARD, *supra* note 4, ¶ 338. Compare, in the United States, EUGENE F. SCOLES, PETER HAY, CONFLICT OF LAWS §§21.8 *et seq.* (2d ed. 1992).

[21]   In force in four countries: Argentina, France, the Netherlands and Portugal (see 1998 REV. CRIT. DIP 169).

[22]   See, with regard to the application of French law to a French limited liability company's power to enter into an arbitration agreement, CA Douai, July 8, 1954, Van Hullebusch v. Danubia, 1955 REV. CRIT. DIP 165, and E. Mezger's note; Gaz. Pal. 2, Jur. 157 (1954). *See also* ICC Award No. 2694 (1977), *supra* note 8, which applies the law of the company to the powers of the company's representatives.

[23]   See also, for commercial companies, Article 3, paragraph 1, of Law No. 66-537 of July 24, 1966 on commercial companies, J.O., July 26, 1966, and J.O., Oct. 19, 1966.

[24]   The same reservation is found in Article 3, paragraph 2 of Law No. 66-537 of July 24, 1966, *supra* note 23.

regarding the power or lack of power of the person representing the corporation.[25] In England, however, the primary criterion used to determine the law applicable to a corporation is the place of incorporation.[26]

462. — As we have seen in the context of the capacity to contract, the choice of law method has a clear disadvantage in that it is liable to produce different outcomes depending on the forum. Some countries apply the law of the corporation's headquarters (*de jure* or *de facto*), while others prefer the law of the country in which the company was incorporated.

The difficulties facing arbitrators having to decide on these issues in choice of law terms are aggravated by the fact that, strictly speaking, arbitrators have no forum. As with the question of capacity, the Institute of International Law suggested in its 1959 resolution that the seat of the arbitration should be considered to be the arbitrators' forum, and the choice of law rules of the seat should therefore apply. However, this solution has the same flaws as those discussed above in relation to the issue of capacity.[27]

The results produced by the choice of law method are thus not sufficiently convincing or predictable to deflate the appeal of substantive transnational rules.[28]

§ 2. – The Substantive Rules Method

463. — The difficulties encountered, particularly by international arbitrators, when applying the choice of law method to issues of capacity and power to enter into an arbitration agreement naturally lead them to apply the substantive rules method. For the courts reviewing an award, the question is to establish the conditions under which an arbitration agreement can be effective within their legal system. In that case, it seems appropriate to apply substantive concepts of that law limited to those considered essential in an international context.[29] For arbitrators, the divergence of choice of law rules in this area is so great that it would be artificial, where different systems are involved, to give precedence to one system over another. The interests of justice and predictability would probably be better served if the arbitrators were able to adopt substantive solutions which

---

[25] This distinction will not apply to a company incorporated under the law of a member state of the European Union with its registered office in such country, even if its actual headquarters are in another member state. The company will be considered to be connected to the country of its incorporation and will be governed by its law. This results implicitly from the first paragraph of Article 58 of the Treaty of Rome founding the EEC. On this issue, generally, see BERTHOLD GOLDMAN, ANTOINE LYON-CAEN, LOUIS VOGEL, DROIT COMMERCIAL EUROPÉEN ¶¶ 110-1 *et seq.* (5th ed. 1994).

[26] *See* DICEY & MORRIS, THE CONFLICT OF LAWS 1103 *et seq.* (12th ed. 1993 and 4th cumulative supp. 1997).

[27] *See supra* para. 458.

[28] On the substantive rules method more generally, see *supra* paras. 435 *et seq.*

[29] *See supra* para. 442.

they judge appropriate given the international character of the disputes, without compromising the enforceability of their award.[30]

The substantive rules method can be used either exclusively (A) or as a corrective measure complementing the choice of law method (B).

A. – THE EXCLUSIVE USE OF SUBSTANTIVE RULES

464. — The substantive rules method applies differently to the issues of capacity (1°) and power (2°).

1° Capacity

465. — The one area where issues of capacity are easily resolved by the use of substantive rules is the capacity of a juridical person to enter into an arbitration agreement. In all likelihood, neither the courts nor international arbitrators would have difficulty in admitting the substantive rule that all juridical persons engaging in commercial activities are capable of entering into an arbitration agreement relating to those activities. The rule has yet to be expressly established in arbitral case law. The reason is probably that, in practice, this aspect of the capacity issue has never been contested, as the only real difficulty arising as regards juridical persons is that of the powers of their representatives.[31]

466. — The position is less clear as regards natural persons, be they minors or protected adults, as most authors are particularly reluctant to admit the application of substantive rules in situations involving different nationalities.[32]

Nevertheless, several substantive rules could easily be derived from the fundamental requirements of justice, following the methodology suggested in the *Dalico* decision.[33] The first of these rules would undoubtedly be that any natural person carrying on an economic activity on a professional basis is at least presumed to have the capacity to enter into arbitration agreements relating to that activity. This rule should be easy to accept in France, given that even in a purely domestic context "a minor carrying on a trade may not obtain restitution in respect of undertakings made in the exercise of that trade."[34] This should apply *a fortiori* in an international context. However, some commentators have expressed the concern that the substantive law of international arbitration would have considerable

---

[30] *See supra* para. 443.

[31] *See infra* para. 468.

[32] See the authors cited *supra* para. 438.

[33] CA Paris, Mar. 26, 1991, Comité populaire de la municipalité de Khoms El Mergeb v. Dalico Contractors, 1991 REV. ARB. 456, and H. Gaudemet-Tallon's note; for an English translation, see 6 INT'L ARB. REP. B1 (Sept. 1991), *aff'd*, Cass. 1e civ., Dec. 20, 1993, *supra* note 2. *See supra* para. 437.

[34] *See, e.g.*, Art. 1308 of the French Civil Code.

difficulty in addressing issues as technical as the age of majority or the circumstances in which an adult should require protection in international trade.[35] This is not necessarily an insurmountable obstacle, as cases involving arbitration agreements entered into by a minor or by a protected adult are likely to remain hypothetical for some time hence. Also, to take the example of French law, the remedy available to natural persons considered by French domestic law to be minors or protected adults is usually rescission of the contract. However, this will only be the case where the transaction in question constitutes an unfair bargain (*lésion*), which shows that the person lacking capacity was indeed unable to act in his or her own interests. This will apply to agreements entered into by non-emancipated minors[36] and by legally-protected adults.[37] Allowing the rescission of transactions entered into by those who are in need of protection has the advantage of enabling the court to examine, *in concreto*, the risks which actually existed for the individual claiming protection. For that reason, we believe the rule could be transposed to the international context and applied more generally. If such a rule were to be applied in practice, it would no doubt become clear that an arbitration agreement could not in itself be considered to be unfair, given the procedural guarantees of the arbitral process, save in exceptional circumstances.[38]

467. — The substantive rules method can also be used to decide an issue on which legal systems are divided,[39] namely whether the capacity to enter into an arbitration agreement presupposes the capacity to contract or the capacity to commence legal proceedings. Article 2059 of the French Civil Code stipulates that "all persons may submit to arbitration those rights which they are free to dispose of,"[40] and it is generally inferred from this provision that the capacity to contract will suffice.[41] Belgian law on this issue, which the statute of May 19, 1998 left untouched, requires the capacity to enter into a settlement ("*la capacité ou le pouvoir de transiger*").[42] Italian law requires the capacity to enter into a contract which goes beyond administration in the ordinary course of business, at least for the purposes of entering into a submission agreement.[43] Other legal systems require the capacity to dispose

---

[35] *See, e.g.*, H. Synvet, note following CA Paris, Dec. 17, 1991, Gatoil v. National Iranian Oil Co., 1993 REV. ARB. 281, 295.

[36] Art. 1305 of the French Civil Code.

[37] Art. 491-2 of the French Civil Code.

[38] *See infra* paras. 1209 *et seq.* Such exceptional circumstances might include cases where the low amount in dispute makes recourse to international arbitration a denial of justice in itself.

[39] *See* DAVID, *supra* note 1, ¶ 189.

[40] On the meaning of this provision in the context of the arbitrability of disputes, see *infra* para. 560.

[41] *See* Ancel, *supra* note 3, ¶¶ 15–17. *But see* ROBERT, *supra* note 10, ¶ 268.

[42] Art. 1676(2) of the Judicial Code, the drafting of which, not the substance, results from the May 19, 1998 statute.

[43] Art. 807 of the Code of Civil Procedure regarding submission agreements, but which was generally considered to apply to arbitration clauses as well (*see* Giorgio Bernini, *Italy* (at 13 *et seq.*), *in* ICCA INTERNATIONAL HANDBOOK OF COMMERCIAL ARBITRATION (1985)). Law No. 25 of 1994 relaxed that position for arbitration clauses by providing that "the capacity to enter into [a] contract includes the capacity to agree to the arbitration

(continued...)

of assets. This is the case, for instance, of Egyptian law,[44] which departs on this point from the UNCITRAL Model Law, which remains silent on this issue. As recourse to arbitration is a day-to-day management decision, at least as far as commercial business is concerned, it would be legitimate to infer that in international trade the required capacity is the capacity to enter into day-to-day business contracts,[45] rather than the capacity to dispose of assets.

2° Powers

468. — Two methods are used by arbitrators when considering the powers of the signatory of an arbitration agreement. The traditional choice of law method[46] co-exists with another approach, under which the signatory's powers are governed by substantive rules deemed suited to the international nature of the case.

For example, a sole arbitrator from England, sitting in Paris, confronted with "the classic problem of an existing entity contracting on behalf of a future entity," concluded that "in accordance with the general principles of international commercial law, usages, and [the principle] of good faith, . . . the existing entity is personally bound," adding that this was the current solution in English law and, generally speaking, in European Community law.[47]

The same reasoning might also be applied to three other issues of considerable practical importance.

The first is whether the validity of an arbitration agreement entered into by an agent is conditional upon the existence of a specific authorization given by the principal, which then raises the question of how specific that authorization must be. Will a general authorization to enter into arbitration agreements suffice, or does the agent need a specific authorization

---

[43](...continued)
clause" (*see* Piero Bernardini, *Italy*, *in* ICCA INTERNATIONAL HANDBOOK ON COMMERCIAL ARBITRATION (forthcoming in 1999)).

[44] *See, e.g.*, Art. 11 of Egyptian Law No. 27 for 1994 Promulgating the Law Concerning Arbitration in Civil and Commercial Matters.

[45] CA Paris, Jan. 4, 1980, Intercast v. Ets. Peschaud et Cie. International, 1981 REV. ARB. 160, and P. Level's note. Earlier cases include Cass. com., May 25, 1959, Francinalp Films v. Dame Manson, Sirey, Pt. I, at 7 (1960); Cass. com., Jan. 30, 1963, Société industrielle des Abattoirs parisiens v. Vormus, 1963 REV. ARB. 91; CA Paris, Feb. 12, 1963, Société des Ets. Bailly v. Comptoir Régional du Bourbonnais, JCP, Ed. G., Pt. II, No. 13,281, 1st decision (1963), and P. Level's note; CA Paris, May 7, 1963, Société Coopérative l'Union v. Aux Ouvriers Réunis, 1963 REV. ARB. 138. These decisions concern the power rather than the capacity to enter into an arbitration agreement but the analysis of the arbitration agreement which they provide is of general application.

[46] For an example of the traditional approach, see ICC Award No. 2694 (1977), *supra* note 8, or the preliminary award on jurisdiction rendered in 1992 in Geneva by Mr. Recordon, chairman, Ms. de Senarclens and Mr. Reichert, arbitrators, in *ad hoc* arbitration No. 27, Alpha Inc. v. Beta Corp., 1994 BULL. ASA 481, 487.

[47] ICC Award No. 5065 (1986), Lebanese party v. two Pakistani companies, 114 J.D.I. 1039, 1043 (1987), and observations by Y. Derains. Compare, on the questionable submission to the law applicable to the merits of the issue of whether the signatory of a contract in the name of a company to be formed is personally bound by the arbitration clause embodied in the contract, ICC Award No. 6850 (1992), Manufacturer Y SA v. Distribution X GmbH, XXIII Y.B. COM. ARB. 37 (1998).

to sign a particular arbitration clause or submission agreement, or an authorization to enter into an arbitration agreement relating to a particular dispute or to any dispute concerning the principal? Under Article 1989 of the French Civil Code, "an agent may act only within the scope of its mandate, and the power to settle disputes does not confer a power to enter into arbitration agreements." Similarly, Article 1008 of the Austrian Civil Code requires a specific power to enter into an arbitration agreement.[48] So did Italian law until the rule was reversed by the January 5, 1994 reform.[49] This restrictive philosophy is not well-suited to international commerce. One can therefore only hope that a substantive rule will be adopted whereby a general authorization to contract will suffice for the purpose of entering into a valid international arbitration agreement.[50]

The second issue of practical importance concerns the powers of corporate officers and directors. A satisfactory approach would be to recognize a principle whereby corporate representatives responsible for management are empowered to enter into arbitration agreements which are enforceable against the corporation, notwithstanding any restrictive provisions in its by-laws or in the law governing those by-laws. The European law approach to this problem could contribute to the acceptance of such a rule.[51]

The third important issue arising in practice concerns the form of the power to enter into an arbitration agreement. In international trade, we believe no particular conditions of form should be imposed provided that the parties' consent is certain.[52]

469. — Arbitrators sometimes find that, as far as powers are concerned, it is difficult to completely exclude the choice of law method. They may feel that certain disciplines display too many of the idiosyncrasies of each legal system for an international substantive rule to apply, and that certain issues do not arise with sufficient frequency to allow arbitrators to rely on significant arbitral case law when seeking to identify such substantive rules. This

---

[48] On the application of this provision, see ICC Award No. 5832 (1988), Liechtenstein company v. Austrian company, 115 J.D.I. 1198 (1988), and observations by G. Aguilar Alvarez.

[49] *See* Art. 808, para. 3, *in fine*, of the Italian Code of Civil Procedure, as amended by Law No. 25 of January 5, 1994; *see also* Piero Bernardini, *L'arbitrage en Italie après la récente réforme*, 1994 REV. ARB. 479, 486; Bernardini, *supra* note 43.

[50] For an illustration of a liberal approach to the question of powers in the case of the ratification of the underlying agreement, see the February 28, 1994 award in ICC Case No. 7047, Corporation W. v. State agency F., 1995 BULL. ASA 301, 319.

[51] *See* Directive 68/151/EEC of March 9, 1968 on co-ordination of safeguards which, for the protection of the interests of members and others, are imposed by Member States on companies within the meaning of the second paragraph of Article 58 of the Treaty, with a view to making such safeguards the same throughout the Community, 1968 O.J. (L 065) 8, Art. 9, para. 2: "[t]he limits on the powers of the organs of the company, arising under the statutes or from a decision of the competent organs, may never be relied on as against third parties, even if they have been disclosed."

[52] See the concurring view of Andreas Reiner, based on Article II(2) of the New York Convention interpreted as a uniform rule, in *The form of the agent's power to sign an arbitration agreement and article II(2) of the New York Convention, in* ICCA CONGRESS SERIES NO. 9, IMPROVING THE EFFICIENCY OF ARBITRATION AGREEMENTS AND AWARDS: 40 YEARS OF APPLICATION OF THE NEW YORK CONVENTION 82 (A.J. van den Berg ed., 1999).

may be the case of the powers of representatives of minors, of spouses under their matrimonial regime, of co-owners, or those of entities in bankruptcy.

Accordingly, the use of substantive rules as a corrective measure applied to the choice of law method may provide an appropriate compromise, especially for arbitrators reluctant to stray from the choice of law method.

B. – THE CORRECTIVE USE OF SUBSTANTIVE RULES

470. — One of the oldest substantive rules of French private international law—and one which has now been adopted in European law—is the rule that a party cannot rely on its lack of capacity or on the absence of power of its apparent representative, where the other party could legitimately have been unaware of that incapacity or absence of power. This rule was first established in connection with a party's capacity, in a 1861 decision of the French *Cour de cassation* in the *Lizardi* case.[53] The rule was later extended to a party's absence of power.[54] With respect to capacity, the rule now appears in Article 11 of the 1980 Rome Convention on the Law Applicable to Contractual Obligations. The justification for the rule is the necessity to protect third parties who rely on apparent authority, a concern which exists in one form or another in most legal systems.[55]

The application of this substantive rule to arbitration agreements, whether by the courts[56] or by international arbitrators, should not therefore present any particular difficulty. A judge or an arbitrator could overlook the lack of capacity of one of the parties (determined by reference to specific substantive rules or to the party's personal law) or the absence of power of a party's representative (determined by reference to substantive rules or to the law of the source of that power) if it were established that the other party entered into the contract in circumstances in which it could legitimately have been unaware of the lack of capacity or absence of power. However, some commentators have expressed reservations on this point, observing that a party entering into an arbitration agreement should at least be required to inform itself as to the capacity of the other party.[57] This objection is not fatal, as the rule established in the *Lizardi* case allows the arbitrators, and subsequently the court reviewing the award, to decide whether the other party could legitimately have believed in the capacity or power of the signatory of the arbitration agreement.

---

[53] Cass. req., Jan. 16, 1861, Lizardi v. Chaize, D.P., Pt. I, at 193 (1861); Sirey, Pt. I, at 305 (1861); JEAN-PIERRE ANCEL AND YVES LEQUETTE, GRANDS ARRÊTS DE LA JURISPRUDENCE FRANÇAISE DE DROIT INTERNATIONAL PRIVÉ 34 (1998).

[54] *See, e.g.,* Trib. civ. Seine, June 12, 1963, Harielle v. Sadek, 91 J.D.I. 285 (1964), and A. Ponsard's note; 1964 REV. CRIT. DIP 689, and H. Batiffol's note.

[55] On this issue, generally, see MARIE-NOËLLE JOBARD-BACHELLIER, L'APPARENCE EN DROIT INTERNATIONAL PRIVÉ (1984).

[56] See, in the case of France, *supra* paras. 435 *et seq.*

[57] JEAN ROBERT, L'ARBITRAGE – DROIT INTERNE – DROIT INTERNATIONAL PRIVÉ ¶ 268 (5th ed. 1983). These reservations no longer appear in the sixth edition published in 1993.

For arbitrators unwilling to apply substantive rules alone, this method, applied in conjunction with the party's personal law in the case of capacity or, in the case of powers, with the law of their source, could provide a less radical alternative. It also offers a further advantage where a natural person has the necessary capacity to contract under his or her personal law and that law is more liberal than the generally accepted rule: subject only to the compliance of that personal law with international public policy, arbitration agreements entered into by that natural person could not be challenged for lack of capacity. At the same time, to apply substantive rules in this way would prevent a party from successfully contesting the validity of an arbitration agreement on the basis of a law which is clearly out of step with what might reasonably be expected in international commerce. This is the major achievement of the substantive rules method.[58]

In 1980, the Paris Court of Appeals had an opportunity to apply the doctrine of apparent authority to an international arbitration agreement. Having noted that "arbitration is one of the normal means of settling disputes between merchants," and that "the signature of an arbitration agreement is therefore, in commercial matters, an act of day-to-day management," the Court held that one of the parties had legitimately believed that the mandate held by a company director entitled him to enter into arbitration agreements. The Court went on to conclude that "even though it may not have given a formal authorization to its director, [the] company . . . was therefore bound by the actions of its apparent agent."[59] This solution is, in our view, the correct one.

Similarly, where a party ratifies an agreement entered into by a representative whose powers are disputed, it manifests its consent to the arbitration agreement and is therefore bound by it.[60]

SECTION II
CONSENT

471. — Consent to an arbitration agreement lies in the parties' common intention to submit disputes which have arisen or which may arise between them to one or more private adjudicators.

---

[58] On the combination, *in favorem validitatis*, of the choice of law method and substantive rules, see *supra* para. 446.

[59] CA Paris, Jan. 4, 1980, *Intercast, supra* note 45. For a decision rejecting a claim as to the absence of the necessary powers on the grounds that the party making that allegation had failed to prove that the other party's powers were limited, see Italian *Corte di Cassazione*, Jan. 15, 1992, Privilegiata Fabbrica Maraschino Excelsior Girolamo Luxardo SpA v. Agrarcommerz AG, XVIII Y.B. COM. ARB. 427 (1993); *see also* the March 12, 1984 award of the Arbitral Tribunal of the Hamburg Commodity Exchange, FR German buyer v. Thai seller, XVI Y.B. COM. ARB. 11 (1991).

[60] *See, e.g.*, CA Paris, Mar. 24, 1995, Bin Saud Bin Abdel Aziz v. Crédit Industriel et Commercial de Paris, 1996 REV. ARB. 259, and J.-M. Talau's note.

Arbitrators, as well as courts called upon to review an award, are often required to rule on the existence of consent to the arbitration agreement (Subsection I). However, before giving effect to that consent, they must also establish its validity (Subsection II).

SUBSECTION I
THE EXISTENCE OF CONSENT

472. — When determining whether or not the parties actually agreed to submit their disputes to arbitration, arbitrators and the courts apply various principles of interpretation (§ 1). In the light of these principles, they establish the degree of certainty required for the parties' consent to be effective (§ 2) as well as the scope of that consent (§ 3).

§ 1. – Interpreting the Parties' Consent

473. — Under the "competence-competence" principle,[61] an arbitral tribunal has jurisdiction to interpret the arbitration agreement on the basis of which it has been seized. However, the arbitral tribunal's decision on the meaning of the arbitration agreement will not be final. The courts of the situs of the arbitration will have jurisdiction to hear an application to set an award aside,[62] and the courts of the place or places of enforcement will also exercise a certain control over the award. In both cases, the courts will consider the existence and scope of the arbitration agreement on the basis of which the award was made (or the lack of such basis when the arbitrators declined jurisdiction for want of a valid arbitration agreement).[63] An important issue here will be to know whether the court performing this review will necessarily follow the arbitrators' interpretation of the facts in dispute and, in particular, of the arbitration agreement, or whether they will make a determination of their own. Although the question is still controversial in certain jurisdictions,[64] we believe that the review of the existence and the scope of the arbitration agreement by the courts with jurisdiction over the validity and enforceability of the award should be independent and not based on the findings of the arbitrators. This is the position in France, where the courts have made clear that, when reviewing the award, they are not

---

[61] *See infra* para. 650.

[62] Unless, in the case of Switzerland, Belgium or Sweden, this possibility has been specifically excluded. *See infra* para. 1594.

[63] *See, e.g.,* Art. 1502 1° of the French New Code of Civil Procedure; Art. 190, para. 2(b) of the Swiss Private International Law Statute; Art. 1065(1)(a) of the Netherlands Code of Civil Procedure; Art. 1704, para. 2(c) of the Belgian Judicial Code, which was left untouched by the May 19, 1998 reform or Art. 36(1)(a)(i) of the UNCITRAL Model Law, and, as far as enforcement is concerned, Art. V(1)(a) of the 1958 New York Convention. *Comp. with* Sec. 67 of the 1996 English Arbitration Act. On this issue, see *infra* paras. 1608 *et seq.*

[64] *See infra* para. 1605.

bound by the arbitrators' findings of fact or law. Thus, the *Cour de cassation* in the *Pyramids* case held that:

> whereas, if the role of the Court of Appeals, seized by virtue of Articles 1502 and 1504 of the New Code of Civil Procedure, is limited to the examination of the grounds listed in these provisions, there is no restriction upon the power of the court to examine, as a matter of law and in consideration of the circumstances of the case, elements pertinent to the grounds in question; and that in particular, it is for the court to construe the contract in order to determine itself whether the arbitrator ruled in the absence of an arbitration clause.[65]

474. — On the other hand, when the courts, at an earlier stage, are called upon to appoint an arbitrator where the implementation of an arbitration agreement gives rise to difficulties,[66] they have, at least in France, no jurisdiction to interpret the arbitration agreement.[67]

475. — The application of the choice of law method to the interpretation of the arbitration agreement would lead to the conclusion that the rules of law governing the interpretation of the agreement are those which govern its existence and validity.[68]

However, it is often held in arbitral awards that the scope of the arbitration agreement need only be examined by reference to transnational rules and trade usages,[69] and this

---

[65] Cass. 1e civ., Jan. 6, 1987, Southern Pacific Properties Ltd. v. République Arabe d'Egypte, 114 J.D.I. 638 (1987), and B. Goldman's note; 1987 REV. ARB. 469, and P. Leboulanger's note; 1988 RTD CIV. 126, and J. Mestre's note; for an English translation, see 26 I.L.M. 1004, 1006 (1987); XIII Y.B. COM. ARB. 152 (1988); 2 INT'L ARB. REP. 17 (Jan. 1987) (commonly known as the "Pyramids" case because the dispute arose out of a contract for the construction of a tourist complex near the Pyramids). On the subsequent turn of events in this case, which was brought before ICSID on the basis of Egyptian investment laws, see the Award dated May 20, 1992 by E. Jimenez de Arechaga, president, R. Pietrowski, Jr. and M. El Madhi, arbitrators (M. El Madhi dissenting), in ICSID Case No. ARB/84/3, Southern Pacific Properties (Middle East) Ltd. v. Arab Republic of Egypt, 8 ICSID REV. – FOREIGN INV. L.J. 328 (1993); 32 I.L.M. 933 (1993), with correction at 32 I.L.M. 1470 (1993); XIX Y.B. COM. ARB. 51 (1994); 8 INT'L ARB. REP. A1 (Aug. 1993); 3 ICSID REP. 189 (1995); for a French translation, see 121 J.D.I. 229 (1994), and observations by E. Gaillard; *see also* CA Paris, June 16, 1988, Swiss Oil v. Petrogab, 1989 REV. ARB. 309, and C. Jarrosson's note; for an English translation, see XVI Y.B. COM. ARB. 133 (1991). On this issue, generally, see *infra* para. 1605.

[66] On the extent of the review of the arbitration agreement by the courts at this stage of the arbitral process, see *supra* paras. 1608 *et seq.*

[67] See, before the 1981 reform of French international arbitration law, Cass. 2e civ., Nov. 19, 1980, Société immobilière du 8, rue de Penthièvre v. Union Générale Cinématographique, 1981 REV. ARB. 411, and P. Fouchard's note. On the point that, after the 1981 reform, the French courts should appoint an arbitrator without considering the interpretation of the disputed clauses—which has to be carried out first by the arbitral tribunal—see Fouchard's note, *supra*, and *infra* paras. 832 *et seq.*

[68] For the determination of such rules, see *supra* paras. 422 *et seq.*

[69] *See, e.g.,* ICC Award No. 5721 (1990), European company v. American and Egyptian parties, 117 J.D.I. 1020 (1990), and observations by Y. Derains (regarding the interpretation of the clause *ratione personae*).

method was adopted by the French courts even prior to the 1993 *Dalico* decision.[70] As early as 1983 the *Cour de cassation* rejected the argument that:

> in the field of international arbitration, arbitration agreements should be interpreted by applying the law of the contract, in accordance with French choice of law rules, and the decision now contested has no legal basis as it failed to observe that procedure.

In support of its decision, the *Cour de cassation* referred to the principle of the autonomy of the arbitration agreement and declared that the court of appeals had given a proper legal basis for its ruling by rightly interpreting the arbitration agreement, which conferred jurisdiction on the "Belgrade Chamber of Commerce," as referring to the "Foreign Trade Arbitration Court at the Economic Chamber of Yugoslavia," the latter being the only Yugoslavian institution which then resolved disputes relating to international trade.[71] At first glance, this decision appears to be an ordinary application of the principle of the autonomy of the arbitration agreement from the main contract. In fact, the *Cour de cassation* went further by not criticizing the lower court for failing to interpret the arbitration agreement under the law which, following the traditional choice of law method, would have been applicable. Although it refers to the autonomy of the arbitration agreement "from the contract," the *Cour de cassation* actually applied the principle of autonomy "from any national law" other than the French rule defining the arbitration agreement by reference to the parties' common intention.[72] Indeed, autonomy from the main contract was irrelevant here, as the validity of the arbitration agreement was not challenged on the basis of an alleged flaw in the main contract. The only issue brought before the lower court was that of the interpretation of the arbitration agreement, and the *Cour de cassation* accepted that the lower court could perform that task without determining the law applicable to that agreement.[73]

476. — The principles of interpretation applied to arbitration agreements are the same as the general principles frequently adopted with respect to all contracts.[74] They include the principle of interpretation in good faith (A), the principle of effective interpretation (B) and the principle of interpretation *contra proferentem* (C). However, the principles of strict

---

[70] Cass. 1e civ., Dec. 20, 1993, *supra* note 2.

[71] Cass. 1e civ., Dec. 14, 1983, Epoux Convert v. Droga, 1984 REV. ARB. 483, and M.-C. Rondeau-Rivier's note; JCP, Ed. G., Pt. IV, at 60 (1984).

[72] On the evolution of these two ideas in French case law, see *supra* para. 418.

[73] On pathological arbitration agreements such as the one which gave rise to the dispute at hand, see *infra* para. 485.

[74] On these principles of interpretation, see *infra* paras. 1469 *et seq.*, and, on principles of interpretation applied to arbitration agreements, see Emmanuel Gaillard, *Centre International pour le Règlement des Différends Relatifs aux Investissements (C.I.R.D.I.) – Chronique des sentences arbitrales*, 113 J.D.I. 197, 226–33 (1986), and the references cited therein.

interpretation (D) and of interpretation *in favorem validitatis* (E) should not, in our view, apply.

A. – THE PRINCIPLE OF INTERPRETATION IN GOOD FAITH

477. — The first and most widely accepted principle of interpretation applied to arbitration agreements is the principle of interpretation in good faith. This principle does not of course mean, as is sometimes suggested, that to challenge the existence or validity of an arbitration is necessarily an act of bad faith. In order for there to be bad faith, the existence and validity of the agreement on which a party seeks to renege must have been previously established.[75] In fact, this rule of interpretation means that a party's true intention should always prevail over its declared intention, where the two are not the same. An example of bad faith will be the conduct of a party relying on an argument of pure form, which is wholly out of context or plainly contrary to the structure or the purpose of the agreement, in a bid to evade obligations which it had clearly undertaken to perform but which were expressed in ambiguous terms. Here, "interpretation in good faith" is simply a less technical way of saying that "when interpreting a contract, one must look for the parties' common intention, rather than simply restricting oneself to examining the literal meaning of the terms used."[76] However, the moral connotation of the expression "interpretation in good faith" is more in keeping with the tenor of general principles of law.

From this broad rule that contracts must be interpreted in good faith, more specific rules of interpretation can be derived, all of which stem from the need to establish the actual intention of the parties.[77] First, the intention of the parties must be examined in context, that is to say, by taking into account the consequences which the parties reasonably and

---

[75] On the dangers arising from the vague nature of the principle of good faith—particularly from the all too frequent abuse of the principle in practice—see Pierre Mayer, *Le principe de bonne foi devant les arbitres du commerce international, in* ETUDES DE DROIT INTERNATIONAL EN L'HONNEUR DE PIERRE LALIVE 543 (1993); *see also infra* paras. 1452 *et seq.*

[76] Art. 1156 of the French Civil Code. *Comp. with* Art. 133 of the German BGB. On this issue see Gaillard, *supra* note 74, at 231. *See also* the September 25, 1983 Jurisdictional Decision by B. Goldman, president, I. Foigel and W. Rubin, arbitrators, in ICSID Case No. ARB/81/1, Amco Asia Corp. v. Republic of Indonesia, which provides that "any convention, including conventions to arbitrate, should be construed in good faith, that is to say by taking into account the consequences of their commitments the parties may be considered as having reasonably and legitimately envisaged" (23 I.L.M. 351, ¶ 14 at 359 (1984); X Y.B. COM. ARB. 61 (1985); 1 ICSID REP. 389 (1993); for a French translation, see 1985 REV. ARB. 259; 113 J.D.I. 200, 207 (1986), and observations by E. Gaillard); the award was annulled on other grounds by a decision of an *ad hoc* committee dated May 16, 1986, by I. Seidl-Hohenveldern, president, F. Feliciano and A. Giardina, arbitrators, 25 I.L.M. 1439 (1986); XII Y.B. COM. ARB. 129 (1987); 1 INT'L ARB. REP. 649 (1986); 1 ICSID REP. 509 (1993); for a French translation, see 114 J.D.I. 175 (1987), and observations by E. Gaillard; ICC Award No. 1434 (1975), Multinational group A v. State B, 103 J.D.I. 978, 979–80 (1976), and observations by Y. Derains.

[77] On the increasing specialization of general principles of international trade law, see *infra* para. 1450.

legitimately envisaged.[78] Second, the attitude of the parties after the signature of the contract and up until the time when the dispute arose should be taken into account, as that attitude will indicate how the parties themselves actually perceived the agreements in dispute. This rule is sometimes referred to as "practical and quasi-authentic interpretation" or "contemporary practical interpretation" and is commonly applied in arbitral case law.[79] In particular, recognition of the existence of an arbitration agreement will often result from a party initially relying on the existence of that agreement to avoid the jurisdiction of the courts, but subsequently denying its existence or validity before an arbitral tribunal.[80] Third and finally, the agreement must be interpreted as a whole.[81] This need for an interpretation of the agreement or of its various constituent parts as a whole, bound together by the true intention of the parties, is one of the factors to be taken into account in disputes involving the construction of arbitration agreements contained in related contracts.[82]

B. – THE PRINCIPLE OF EFFECTIVE INTERPRETATION

478. — The second principle of interpretation of arbitration agreements is the principle of effective interpretation. This principle is inspired by provisions such as Article 1157 of the French Civil Code, according to which "where a clause can be interpreted in two different ways, the interpretation enabling the clause to be effective should be adopted in preference to that which prevents the clause from being effective."[83] This common-sense rule whereby, if in doubt, one should "prefer the interpretation which gives meaning to the

---

[78] *See* the Sept. 25, 1983 *Amco* Jurisdictional Decision, *supra* note 76.

[79] *See, e.g.,* the Aug. 23, 1958 *ad hoc* award by Messrs. Sauser-Hall, referee, Hassan and Habachy, arbitrators, in Saudi Arabia v. Arabian American Oil Co. (ARAMCO), 27 INT'L L. REP. 117, 198 (1963); for a French translation, see 1963 REV. CRIT. DIP. 272, 338.

[80] For an example of the censure of such conduct (which was held to constitute the recognition of the arbitration agreement), see, in the United States, *In re* Petition of Transrol Navegacao S.A. v. Redirekommanditselskaber Merc Scandia XXIX, 782 F. Supp. 848 (S.D.N.Y. 1991); XVIII Y.B. COM. ARB. 499 (1993). See also the 1995 award on jurisdiction in ICC Cases No. 7604 and 7610, Moroccan company v. Algerian company, 125 J.D.I. 1027 (1998), and observations by D. Hascher and 125 J.D.I. 1053 (1998), and observations by J.-J. Arnaldez. In this case, the arbitral tribunal held that it had jurisdiction over the parent of a company that had signed an agreement containing an arbitration clause because the parent had claimed that the national courts of its co-contractor had no jurisdiction due to the existence of the same arbitration clause. On the general principle of international trade whereby one party cannot contradict itself to the detriment of another, known in common law countries as estoppel, see *infra* para. 1462.

[81] Sept. 25, 1983 *Amco* Jurisdictional Decision, *supra* note 76, ¶ 18; ICC Award No. 8694 (1996), American company v. Belgian company, 124 J.D.I. 1056 (1997), and observations by Y. Derains.

[82] On this issue, see *infra* para. 518.

[83] This provision has been contained in the French Civil Code since its initial publication in 1804. Since then it has been adopted in a large number of jurisdictions. It was recently adopted in a transnational context in the UNIDROIT Principle 4.5 (UNIDROIT, PRINCIPLES OF INTERNATIONAL COMMERCIAL CONTRACTS 96 (1994)).

words, rather than that which renders them useless or nonsensical,"[84] is widely accepted not only by the courts but also by arbitrators who readily acknowledge it to be a "universally recognized rule of interpretation."[85] To give just one example of the application of this principle, an arbitral tribunal interpreting a pathological clause held that:

> when inserting an arbitration clause in their contract the intention of the parties must be presumed to have been willing to establish an effective machinery for the settlement of disputes covered by the arbitration clause.[86]

C. – THE PRINCIPLE OF INTERPRETATION *CONTRA PROFERENTEM*

479. — The third major principle of interpretation, less frequently encountered in arbitral case law but widely recognized in comparative law, is the principle that the agreement should be interpreted *contra proferentem*, or against the party that drafted the clause in dispute.[87] This rule is not to be confused with the rule that "in case of doubt, the agreement should be interpreted against the party who has stipulated and in favor of the party who has contracted the obligation."[88] The latter rule is meaningless in the context of an arbitration agreement, where both parties are under an equal obligation to submit disputes to arbitrators. On the other hand, it is not unusual to find that one party has simply signed contractual

---

[84] *See* ICC Award No. 1434 (1975), *supra* note 76, at 982.

[85] *See, e.g.,* ICC Award No. 1434 (1975), *supra* note 76; ICC Award No. 3380 (1980), Italian enterprise v. Syrian enterprise, 108 J.D.I. 927 (1981), and observations by Y. Derains; for an English translation, see VII Y.B. COM. ARB. 116 (1982); ICC Award No. 3460 (1980), French company v. Ministry of an Arab country, 108 J.D.I. 939 (1981), and observations by Y. Derains; the March 24, 1982 *ad hoc* award by P. Reuter, president, H. Sultan and G. Fitzmaurice, arbitrators, The Government of the State of Kuwait v. The American Independent Oil Co. (AMINOIL), 21 I.L.M. 976 (1982); IX Y.B. COM. ARB. 71 (1984); for a French translation, see 109 J.D.I. 869, ¶ 89 at 892 (1982), and the commentary by Philippe Kahn, *Contrats d'Etat et nationalisation, id.* at 844; *see* Pierre-Yves Tschanz, *The Contributions of the Aminoil Award to the Law of State Contracts,* 18 INT'L LAW. 245 (1984). In ICSID arbitration, the argument was raised in Case No. ARB/72/1, Holiday Inns S.A. v. Government of Morocco; *see* Pierre Lalive, *The First 'World Bank' Arbitration (Holiday Inns v. Morocco)—Some Legal Problems,* 51 BRIT. Y.B. INT'L L. 1980, at 123 (1982). See also, in French case law regarding the constitution of the arbitral tribunal, CA Paris, May 5, 1989, B.K.M.I. Industrieanlagen GmbH v. Dutco Construction Co. Ltd., 1989 REV. ARB. 723, and P. Bellet's note; 119 J.D.I. 707 (1992), 1st decision, and C. Jarrosson's note; for an English translation, see XV Y.B. COM. ARB. 124 (1990); 4 INT'L ARB. REP. A1 (July 1989); TGI Paris, Jan. 31, 1986, Fillold C. M. v. Jacksor Enterprise, 1987 REV. ARB. 179, and P. Fouchard's note; CA Paris, Mar. 22, 1991, Mavian v. Mavian, 1992 REV. ARB. 652, and observations by D. Cohen. On the application of this principle to certain pathological clauses, see *infra* paras. 485 and 490.

[86] Preliminary award in ICC Case No. 2321 (1974), Two Israeli companies v. Government of an African state, I Y.B. COM. ARB. 133 (1976); for a French translation, see 102 J.D.I. 938 (1975), and observations by Y. Derains. On this issue, generally, see *infra* paras. 484 *et seq.*

[87] *See also* UNIDROIT Principle 4.6, *supra* note 83.

[88] Art. 1162 of the French Civil Code. On this distinction, see Jacques Dupichot, *Pour un retour aux textes: défense et illustration du « petit guide-âne » des articles 1156 à 1164 du Code civil, in* ETUDES OFFERTES À JACQUES FLOUR 179 (1979).

documents drafted by the other party, and that a question has subsequently arisen as to whether various provisions of that contract constitute an arbitration agreement or, more commonly, as to the scope of that arbitration agreement. In such cases, it is perfectly reasonable that the party responsible for drafting the ambiguous or obscure text should not be entitled to rely on that ambiguity or obscurity (in claiming, for example, that a particular disputed matter is not covered) and that, consequently, the agreement should be interpreted *contra proferentem*.[89]

D. – REJECTION OF THE PRINCIPLE OF STRICT INTERPRETATION

480. — Some decisions are still based on the idea that an arbitration agreement should be interpreted "restrictively."[90] Even if one were to accept this principle, it would be preferable to say that the agreement should be interpreted "strictly," in the sense that the task conferred on the arbitrators should be confined to following the clearly expressed intentions of the parties.[91]

However, this principle is generally rejected in international arbitration. It is based on the idea that an arbitration agreement constitutes an exception to the principle of the jurisdiction of the courts, and that, as laws of exception are strictly interpreted, the same should apply to arbitration agreements.[92] This view is not consistent with the fact that arbitration is now unanimously considered to be a normal means of settling international disputes.[93]

This has been frequently confirmed in arbitral case law. For example, the Decision on Jurisdiction rendered in the *Amco* arbitration sets out the principle in general terms:

---

[89] For a case where this principle was implicitly applied, see the April 3, 1987 award in ICC Case No. 4727, Swiss Oil v. Petrogab, enforced by CA Paris, June 16, 1988, *supra* note 65, 1989 REV. ARB. 325. *See also* TGI Paris, Feb. 1, 1979, Techniques de l'Ingénieur v. Sofel, 1980 REV. ARB. 97.

[90] *See, e.g.*, ICC Award No. 4392 (1983), Yugoslavian company v. German company, 110 J.D.I. 907 (1983), and observations by Y. Derains.

[91] See, in French domestic arbitration, CA Paris, Mar. 11, 1986, Compagnie d'assurance La Zurich v. Bureau central français: "the arbitration clause must be strictly interpreted as it departs from the norm—and in particular from the usual rules as to the jurisdiction of the courts" (Gaz. Pal., Jur. 298, 2d decision (1986), and J. Ripoll's note). In international arbitration, see ICC Award No. 2138 (1974), 102 J.D.I. 934 (1975), and observations by Y. Derains. Compare, for the recognition obiter of the principle of strict interpretation, the preliminary award in ICC Case No. 2321 (1974), *supra* note 86. Authors in favor of the principle of strict interpretation include Yves Derains and Sylvie Schaf, *Clauses d'arbitrage et groupes de sociétés*, 1985 INT'L BUS. L.J. 231.

[92] On the rejection of the analogy between the principles of interpretation of laws and treaties and the principles of interpretation of arbitration agreements, see Gaillard, *supra* note 74, at 228.

[93] See, for example, André Chapelle, *L'arbitrage et les tiers: II. – Le droit des personnes morales (Groupes de sociétés; Interventions d'Etat)*, 1988 REV. ARB. 475, 480, which describes the "purported principle of strict interpretation of arbitration agreements" as archaic; Ibrahim Fadlallah, *Clause d'arbitrage et groupes de sociétés*, in TRAVAUX DU COMITÉ FRANÇAIS DE DROIT INTERNATIONAL PRIVÉ 1984–85, at 105, especially at 105 (1987); Bruno Oppetit, *La clause arbitrale par référence*, 1990 REV. ARB. 551, 557.

like any other convention, a convention to arbitrate is not to be construed restrictively, nor, as a matter of fact, broadly or liberally. It is to be construed in a way which leads to find out and to respect the common will of the parties: such a method of interpretation is but the application of the fundamental principle *pacta sunt servanda*, a principle common, indeed, to all systems of internal law and to international law.[94]

The interpretation of arbitration agreements by the French courts has, likewise, never been strict nor restrictive. For example, in a case concerning an international arbitration, the *Cour de cassation* held that an arbitration clause conferring jurisdiction on the International Chamber of Commerce "for all disputes arising during *performance* [of the contract]"[95] encompassed disputes arising from the *termination* of the contract. The least that can be said is that this was hardly a restrictive interpretation.

E. – REJECTION OF THE PRINCIPLE OF INTERPRETATION *IN FAVOREM VALIDITATIS*

481. — It is equally inappropriate to resort to a general principle of interpretation *in favorem validitatis* or *in favorem jurisdictionis*, whereby arbitration agreements are to be interpreted extensively.[96] Although it is true that arbitration is now a normal means of resolving disputes in international trade, and that arbitration agreements should therefore not be interpreted "restrictively" or "strictly,"[97] it remains perfectly legitimate to choose to have one's international disputes settled by the courts. Consequently, and in contrast to statutory interpretation, there is no place here for the logic of principle and exception. All that matters is the parties' common intention, established on the basis of the principles of interpretation

---

[94] Sept. 25, 1983, *supra* note 76, 23 I.L.M. 359. See also, with regard to the interpretation of consent given by a state in its investment legislation, the April 14, 1988 Decision on Jurisdiction by E. Jimenez de Arechaga, president, R. Pietrowski, Jr. and M. El Mahdi, arbitrators, in ICSID Case No. ARB/84/3, Southern Pacific Properties (Middle East) Ltd. v. Arab Republic of Egypt, 3 ICSID REP. 131, 143 (1995); XVI Y.B. COM. ARB. 28 (1991); for a French translation, see 121 J.D.I. 218 (1994), especially ¶ 63 at 221, and observations by E. Gaillard.

[95] Cass. com., Mar. 13, 1978, Hertzian v. Electronska Industrija, 1979 REV. ARB. 339, and P. Fouchard's note. On this issue, generally, see *infra* para. 514.

[96] In favor of this principle, see, for example, in ICSID arbitration, C.F. Amerasinghe, *Jurisdiction Ratione Personae Under the Convention on the Settlement of Investment Disputes Between States and Nationals of Other States*, 47 BRIT. Y.B. INT'L L. 1974–1975, at 227, 267 (1977); in the United States, for a ruling that any ambiguity in the arbitration clause should be interpreted in favor of arbitration, see CGB Marine Services Co. v. M/S Stolt Entente, Civ. A. No. 86-3877, 1990 WL 134664 (E.D. La. Sept. 12, 1990); XVII Y.B. COM. ARB. 653, ¶ 25 at 660 (1992); Remy Amerique, Inc. v. Touzet Distribution, S.A.R.L., 816 F. Supp. 213 (S.D.N.Y. 1993); XIX Y.B. COM. ARB. 820, ¶ 7 at 823 (1994), and the references cited therein. *See also* Pierre A. Karrer and Claudia Kälin-Nauer, *Is there a Favor Iurisdictionis Arbitri? – Standards of Review of Arbitral Jurisdiction Decisions in Switzerland*, 13 J. INT'L ARB. 31 (Sept. 1996).

[97] *See supra* para. 480.

described earlier. A mere allegation that an arbitration agreement exists will not raise a presumption that the allegation is well-founded by virtue of a supposed principle of *favorem validitatis*. This in no way contradicts the idea that when determining the law governing the validity of the arbitration agreement, one option is to consider, *in favorem validitatis*, the application of a number of different laws.[98] The aim in that context is to choose a legal regime to govern the arbitration agreement. The interpretation of the parties' consent is entirely different: the question is whether parties in fact intended to resort to arbitration and, if so, which parties and for which types of dispute. For the same reasons, the terminology employed by the Paris Court of Appeals when examining the scope of an arbitration agreement, suggesting that as a matter of principle the agreement is valid and enjoys its own effectiveness, is unsatisfactory. Indeed, the French *Cour de cassation* has wisely chosen not to adopt the terminology used by the Court of Appeals.[99]

482. — Case law shows that the primary concern shared by both arbitrators and the courts is to give full effect to the parties' intention to refer their disputes to arbitration. This is true of both the degree of certainty required of the consent given by the parties and its scope.

§ 2. – The Degree of Certainty Required of the Parties' Consent

483. — The efforts of arbitrators and the courts to give full effect to the parties' intention to refer their disputes to arbitration appear clearly from an examination of pathological clauses (A), combined clauses (B) and arbitration agreements incorporated by reference (C).

A. – PATHOLOGICAL CLAUSES

484. — The expression "pathological clause" was first used in 1974 by Frédéric Eisemann, then honorary Secretary General of the ICC. It denotes arbitration agreements, and particularly arbitration clauses, which contain a defect or defects liable to disrupt the smooth progress of the arbitration.[100] Arbitration agreements can be pathological for a variety of reasons.[101] The reference to an arbitration institution may be inaccurate or totally

---

[98] *See supra* paras. 446 *et seq.*

[99] On this issue, see *supra* para. 440.

[100] Frédéric Eisemann, *La clause d'arbitrage pathologique, in* COMMERCIAL ARBITRATION – ESSAYS IN MEMORIAM EUGENIO MINOLI 129 (1974).

[101] For a "chamber of horrors" of pathological clauses, see, besides Eisemann, *supra* note 100, Hugues Scalbert and Laurent Marville, *Les clauses compromissoires pathologiques*, 1988 REV. ARB. 117; Benjamin G. Davis, *Pathological Clauses – Frederic Eisemann's Still Vital Criteria*, 7 ARB. INT'L 365 (1991); W. LAURENCE CRAIG, WILLIAM W. PARK, JAN PAULSSON, INTERNATIONAL CHAMBER OF COMMERCE ARBITRATION 157 *et seq.* (2d ed. 1990); Lazare Kopelmanas, *La rédaction des clauses d'arbitrage et le choix des arbitres, in* HOMMAGE À FRÉDÉRIC EISEMANN 23 (ICC Publication No. 321, 1978); see also, on how to draft an arbitration clause that
(continued...)

incorrect;[102] the agreement may appear to allow submission of disputes to arbitration to be optional;[103] it may contain a defective mechanism for appointing arbitrators in that, for example, the chosen appointing authority refuses to perform that function;[104] alternatively, the agreement might itself appoint arbitrators who have died by the time the dispute arises.[105] The agreement may stipulate that the tribunal is to comprise three arbitrators where the dispute involves three or more parties whose interests differ;[106] it may impose impracticable conditions for the arbitral proceedings (such as unworkable deadlines),[107] or provide that certain issues (such as the validity of the contract) are not to be dealt with by the arbitrators, despite the fact that such issues are closely related to the dispute which the arbitrators are called upon to decide.[108] Another example is an agreement that permits an appeal from the award before national courts in cases where the subject-matter is international.[109] At best, these defects will give rise to associated litigation, fueling the arguments of the party attempting to avoid arbitration and making the overall process more time-consuming and expensive. At worst, the defect will prevent the arbitration from taking place at all. This will be the case where it is impossible to infer an intention which is sufficiently coherent and effective to enable the arbitration to function.

These clauses will need to be interpreted by the arbitrators, and by the courts reviewing the existence of an arbitration agreement and ensuring that the arbitrators remained within the bounds of their jurisdiction. In most cases, the arbitrators or the courts—relying on the principle of effective interpretation more than on any rule *in favorem validitatis*[110]—will salvage the arbitration clause by restoring the true intention of the parties, which was previously distorted by the parties' ignorance of the mechanics of arbitration. We shall consider two examples: error by the parties in designating the arbitral institution, and "blank clauses."

---

[101](...continued)
is not pathological, the references cited *supra* para. 385.

[102] *See infra* para. 485.

[103] For example: "The parties may refer their disputes to arbitration." On this issue, see Davis, *supra* note 101, at 367; Cass. 1e civ., Oct. 15, 1996, Calberson Int'l v. Schenker, 1998 REV. ARB. 409, and C. Malinvaud's note. Compare, in the United States, for the difficulties resulting from a clause providing that an arbitrator should be "chosen by mutual agreement" of the parties, Cargill Rice, Inc. v. Empresa Nicaraguense de Alimentos Basicos, 25 F.3d 223 (4th Cir. 1994); 5 WORLD ARB. & MED. REP. 164 (1994); 9 INT'L ARB. REP. D1 (June 1994).

[104] On the validation by Swiss courts of the appointment of an arbitrator by the ICC in the place of the director general of the World Health Organization (who was chosen by the parties but refused to carry out the task), see Swiss Fed. Trib., Apr. 16, 1984, Y. v. X., 1986 REV. ARB. 596, and observations by R. Budin.

[105] On this issue, see *infra* paras. 879 *et seq.*

[106] *See infra* para. 485.

[107] *See infra* para. 1385.

[108] *See infra* para. 514.

[109] On the issue of the validity of such clauses, see *infra* para. 1597.

[110] *See supra* paras. 478 and 481.

1° Selecting an Institution Which Does Not Exist or Which Is Inadequately Defined

485. — Through the ignorance of the parties, or as a result of a clerical error, some arbitration clauses refer to an arbitration institution which is inadequately identified, or to one which does not exist at all.[111] If interpreted literally, these clauses would be ruled ineffective. However, if the institution can be identified with a significant degree of certainty, such clauses will remain effective.

In international arbitration, a relatively common mistake is to refer to the International Chamber of Commerce "in Geneva," "in Zurich" or "in Vienna,"[112] although the ICC's headquarters are in fact located in Paris. A number of arbitral awards have held arbitration agreements containing that kind of error to be valid, as they adequately reflected the parties' intention to refer their disputes to arbitration under the ICC Rules in the specified city.[113] Likewise, in ICC Case No. 5103, it was held that a clause referring to the non-existent "International Section of the Paris Chamber of Commerce" should be interpreted as a valid reference to the International Chamber of Commerce.[114] Similarly, the Arbitration Court of

---

[111] The winding up of the organization chosen by the parties gives rise to similar difficulties. See, for example, on the nullity of clauses referring to the Arbitration Court at the Chamber of Foreign Trade of the German Democratic Republic, which has ceased to exist, *Bundesgerichtshof*, Jan. 20, 1994, NJW 94, 1008–1012; *see* 1994 BULL. ASA 433; the observations by H.J. Schroth, Les Petites Affiches, Feb. 1, 1995, No. 14, at 7; Peter Schlosser, *Chronique de jurisprudence allemande*, 1995 REV. ARB. 663, 664; *see supra* para. 333. On the fact that the Court of Arbitration at the Chamber of Commerce and Industry of the Russian Federation is the legal successor of the Court of Arbitration of the Chamber of Commerce and Industry of the USSR, see Austrian *Oberster Gerichtshof*, Nov. 30, 1994, XXII Y.B. COM. ARB. 628 (1997). For another decision in favor of redeeming the arbitration clause, which referred to an institution that had ceased to exist, see Austrian *Oberster Gerichtshof*, July 24, 1997, XXIII Y.B. COM. ARB. 163 (1998).

[112] *Oberlandesgericht* Dresden, Dec. 5, 1994, Distributor v. Manufacturer, XXII Y.B. COM. ARB. 266 (1997).

[113] See, for example, for a clause designating "the International Chamber of Commerce in Geneva," ICC Award No. 3460 (1980), *supra* note 85; ICC Award No. 2626 (1977), German company v. Italian company, 105 J.D.I. 980 (1978), and observations by Y. Derains; ICC Award No. 4023 (1984), French company v. Ministry of an Arab country, 111 J.D.I. 950 (1984), and observations by S. Jarvin; ICC Award No. 5983 of October 31, 1989, by Messrs J.-F. Poudret, chairman, G. Flécheux and L. Simont, arbitrators, 1993 BULL. ASA 507; for a clause designating "the International Chamber of Commerce of Zurich," see interim award in ICC Case No. 4472 (1984), German party v. German party, 111 J.D.I. 946 (1984), and observations by S. Jarvin; ICC Award No. 5294 (1988), Danish company v. Egyptian company, XIV Y.B. COM. ARB. 137 (1989) or "the International Chamber of Commerce of Geneva," ICC Award No. 7920 (1993), Distributor v. Manufacturer, XXIII Y.B. COM. ARB. 80 (1998). See, however, for a decision that "ICC of Paris" or "ICC in Paris" is not sufficient for the seat to be fixed in Paris, the order of the President of the Paris Tribunal of First Instance dated January 10, 1996, National Iranian Oil Co. v. Israel, 1996 BULL. ASA 319; for an English translation, see 11 INT'L ARB. REP. B1 (Feb. 1996). This seems unduly harsh. On the fact that the words used refer to the ICC in any event, see the award in Case No. 7895 (1994), ICC BULLETIN, Vol. 8, No. 2, at 67 (1997). *See also* Jean Denglin, *Inaccurate Reference to the ICC*, ICC BULLETIN, Vol. 7, No. 2, at 11 (1996); YVES DERAINS AND ERIC A. SCHWARTZ, A GUIDE TO THE NEW ICC RULES OF ARBITRATION 89 *et seq.* (1998).

[114] ICC Award No. 5103 (1988), Three European companies v. Four Tunisian companies, 115 J.D.I. 1206 (1988), and observations by G. Aguilar Alvarez. See also, for an interpretation of a clause designating "the Paris Chamber of Commerce" as meaning the ICC, the 1991 partial award in ICC Case No. 6709, German licensor

(continued...)

the German Coffee Association upheld its own jurisdiction on the basis of a clause which merely stipulated "arbitration: Hamburg, West Germany." The Court's grounds were that it was the only organization in Hamburg which handled disputes concerning the quality of coffee, and that the standard-form contract to which the parties referred also stipulated that disputes were to be resolved under the auspices of the arbitration institution of the place provided for in the contract.[115] In addition, a tribunal sitting under the auspices of the Italian Arbitration Association held it had jurisdiction over a dispute relating to a contract referring to "The Italy Commercial Arbitration Association."[116]

French case law has followed a similar course. Thus, for example, the Paris Court of Appeals held in 1985 that an arbitration agreement referring to an arbitration institution described as "the Tribunal of the Paris Chamber of Commerce" was valid and conferred jurisdiction on the "Arbitration Chamber of Paris." This latter institution was the only arbitral body empowered by the Paris Chamber of Commerce, and was therefore necessarily the organization to which the parties had inaccurately referred.[117] Likewise, in 1983 the *Cour de cassation* upheld a Court of Appeals finding that the parties to an arbitration agreement referring to the "Yugoslavian Chamber of Commerce in Belgrade" in fact intended to refer to the "Foreign Trade Arbitration Court at the the Economic Chamber of Yugoslavia," which had its headquarters in Belgrade.[118] Similarly, the Paris Court of Appeals held in 1994 that "the fact that the arbitration agreement refers to the Paris Chamber of Commerce rather than to the ICC is merely a clerical error."[119]

---

[114](...continued)
v. French licensee, 119 J.D.I. 998 (1992), and observations by D. Hascher.

[115] Award of September 28, 1992, Panamanian buyer v. Papua New Guinean seller, XIX Y.B. COM. ARB. 48 (1994). See also, validating a clause despite an inaccurate reference to the Court of Arbitration of the Bulgarian Chamber of Commerce and Industry, the December 3, 1984 award in Case No. 151/1984, Bulgarian sport organization v. Greek sport organization, XV Y.B. COM. ARB. 63 (1990). Likewise, the "International Trade Arbitration Organization in Zurich" was interpreted as meaning the Zurich Chamber of Commerce (Preliminary Award on Jurisdiction of November 25, 1994, European party v. Canadian affiliate of a Chinese group, 1996 BULL. ASA 303), and the "Arbitration Court in Genf working beside the Swiss Chamber of Commerce" was interpreted as meaning the Geneva Chamber of Commerce and Industry (Interlocutory Award on Jurisdiction dated June 30, 1987, 1997 BULL. ASA 122). *See also* the November 29, 1996 Interlocutory Award on Jurisdiction of the Geneva Chamber of Commerce and Industry in Matter No. 117, Agent v. Principal, 1997 BULL. ASA 534. In contrast, by an award dated March 25, 1996, an arbitrator sitting under the auspices of the Zurich Chamber of Commerce held that a clause referring to the non-existent "Arbitration Commission in Switzerland" could not be salvaged (Zurich Chamber of Commerce Award in Case No. 287/95, dated March 25, 1996, 1996 BULL. ASA 290).

[116] Award in Case No. 41/92 of 1993, Manufacturer v. Distributor, XXII Y.B. COM. ARB. 178 (1997).

[117] CA Paris, Feb. 14, 1985, Tuvomon v. Amaltex, 1987 REV. ARB. 325, and P. Level's note. See also, for a clause providing for "arbitration before the official Chamber of Commerce of Paris, France," TGI Paris, réf., Dec. 13, 1988, Asland v. European Energy Corp., 1990 REV. ARB. 521.

[118] Cass. 1e civ., Dec. 14, 1983, *Epoux Convert, supra* para. 475 and note 71.

[119] CA Paris, Mar. 24, 1994, Deko v. Dingler, 1994 REV. ARB. 515, and C. Jarrosson's note.

The approach of the French courts is thus invariably to interpret pathological arbitration clauses so as to render them effective if at all possible.[120] The same trend can be found in other jurisdictions. For example, in the United States, a clause designating "the New York Commercial Arbitration Association" was interpreted as meaning the American Arbitration Association in New York.[121] In another case, a clause referring to "[the] Arbitration Court of [the] Chamber of Commerce in Venice (Italy)" was understood as a reference to the ICC.[122] Nevertheless, occasional court decisions are rendered which seize upon defects in arbitration agreements as a basis for disregarding them altogether, even in cases where more sophisticated courts would have held such agreements to be sufficiently clear and therefore valid and enforceable.[123]

2° "Blank Clauses"

486. — A "blank clause" (*clause blanche*) is one which contains no indication, whether directly or by reference to arbitration rules or to an arbitral institution, as to how the arbitrators are to be appointed. This is the case where, for example, the clause merely states "Resolution of disputes: arbitration, Paris."

---

[120] For an example of a clause so vague that the courts were unable to give effect to it (where the reference was to the "London Arbitral Chamber"), see CA Versailles, Oct. 3, 1991, Ltd. Capital Rice v. SARL Michel Come, 1992 REV. ARB. 654, and observations by D. Bureau. For a clause designating two arbitral institutions, see Lebanese *Cour de cassation*, Apr. 27, 1987, Romanian company v. Lebanese company, 1988 REV. ARB. 723, and S. Jahel's note. For clauses designating both an arbitral institution and the courts, see *infra* para. 490.

[121] *See* Warnes, S.A. v. Harvic Int'l, Ltd., No. 92 Civ. 5515, 1993 WL 228028 (S.D.N.Y. June 22, 1993); 4 WORLD ARB. & MED. REP. 229 (1993).

[122] *See* Tennessee Imports, Inc. v. Pier Paulo Filippi, 745 F. Supp. 1314 (M.D. Tenn. 1990); XVII Y.B. COM. ARB. 620 (1992), especially ¶ 24 at 632; and for the validation by the English courts, in a less controversial case, of a clause which merely provides for "arbitration, if any, by ICC rules in London," Mangistaumunaigaz Oil Production Association v. United World Trading Inc., [1995] 1 Lloyd's Rep. 617; 10 INT'L ARB. REP. 10 (June 1995) (High Ct., Q.B. (Com. Ct.) 1995). See also, in favor of holding an arbitration in London where the arbitration clause left room for hesitation over whether the parties intended to hold the arbitration in London or Lima, Naviera Amazonica Peruana SA v. Compania Internacional De Seguros Del Peru, [1988] 1 Lloyd's Rep. 116; XIII Y.B. COM. ARB. 156 (1988) (C.A. 1987).

[123] For an example of such an unfortunate decision, see Vaud Cantonal Court, Mar. 30, 1993, Nokia-Maillefer SA v. Mazzer, which did not validate a clause in a telex which referred to the "International Chamber of Commerce in Paris." The grounds given were that the replacement by that text of the word "Milan" under the heading "forum," which appeared in earlier contracts, did not resolve the question of the competent jurisdiction "in a clear and indisputable manner" (1995 BULL. ASA 64, and J.-F. Poudret's disapproving note). In the same vein, see the very surprising decision that the expression "arbitral tribunal of the International Chamber of Commerce in Paris, seat in Zurich" was ambiguous and therefore void, *Oberlandesgericht* Hamm, Nov. 15, 1994, Slovenian company, formerly Yugoslav state enterprise v. Agent, XXII Y.B. COM. ARB. 707 (1997). See also CA Grenoble, Jan. 24, 1996, Harper Robinson v. Société internationale de maintenance et de réalisation industrielles, which, just as unsatisfactorily, did not interpret the parties' clause which read "International Court of Arbitration of The Hague" as meaning "The Permanent Court of Arbitration in The Hague" (1997 REV. ARB. 87, and observations by Y. Derains; 124 J.D.I. 115 (1997), and P. Kahn's note).

In French domestic arbitration law, such clauses will be held ineffective. Article 1443, paragraph 2 of the New Code of Civil Procedure provides that the arbitration agreement must "either appoint the arbitrator or arbitrators or provide for a mechanism for their appointment," failing which the clause is void.[124]

However, such clauses are valid in French international arbitration law. There is no French statutory provision requiring the parties to an international arbitration agreement to themselves specify a mechanism for appointing the arbitrators. Further, French case law has consistently confirmed that Article 1443 of the New Code of Civil Procedure "does not apply to international arbitration."[125] In practice, the French courts will interpret such clauses as providing for *ad hoc* arbitration in which any difficulties with the composition of the arbitral tribunal will be resolved by the President of the Paris *Tribunal de grande instance*, under Article 1493 of the New Code of Civil Procedure.[126] Similar case law is found in Italy[127] and the United States.[128] That is not to say, however, that blank clauses are to be recommended.[129]

The pathological element of a blank clause really only emerges where the arbitration agreement contains no detail linking the blank clause, by the choice of a seat or a procedural law, to a country whose courts are able to appoint the arbitrators. An example will be a clause stipulating that "any disputes arising from the interpretation of the present contract will be settled by an arbitral tribunal sitting in a country other than that of each of the parties."[130] It is not clear whether the French courts, for instance, would agree to rule on a request to appoint arbitrators if confronted with an arbitration agreement of that kind between two non-French parties, one of which sought to commence arbitration in France.

---

[124] For an example of the invalidity, in French domestic law, of a blank clause, see Cass. com., Jan. 18, 1994, Nègre v. Aux délices de Bourgogne, 1994 REV. ARB. 536, and observations by P. Fouchard.

[125] *See* CA Paris, Nov. 14, 1991, Consorts Legrand v. European Country Hotels Ltd., 1994 REV. ARB. 545, 2d decision, and observations by P. Fouchard; CA Paris, Dec. 7, 1994, V 2000 (formerly Jaguar France) v. Renault, 1996 REV. ARB. 245, and C. Jarrosson's note; 1995 RTD COM. 401, and observations by J.-C. Dubarry and E. Loquin; 1996 JUSTICES 435, and observations by M.-C. Rivier; *aff'd*, Cass. 1e civ., May 21, 1997, Renault v. V 2000 (formerly Jaguar France), 1997 REV. ARB. 537, and E. Gaillard's note; 1998 REV. CRIT. DIP 87, and V. Heuzé's note; 125 J.D.I. 969 (1998), 1st decision, and S. Poillot-Peruzzetto's note.

[126] *See* Philippe Fouchard, *L'arbitrage international en France après le décret du 12 mai 1981*, 109 J.D.I. 374, 386 (1982); Bourdin, *supra* note 10, at 21. See also the mechanisms created by Article IV(6) of the 1961 European Convention to validate such clauses.

[127] For the validation of a clause providing for "General average/arbitration, if any, in London in the usual manner," see *Corte di Appello* of Genoa, Feb. 3, 1990, Della Sanara Kustvaart-Bevrachting & Overslagbedrijf BV v. Fallimento Cap. Giovanni Coppola Srl, XVII Y.B. COM. ARB. 542 (1992).

[128] For the validation of a clause between a French party and an Indian party, providing that the disputes would be resolved by an "arbitral committee", without mentioning any seat, see Jain v. Courier de Mere, 51 F.3d 686 (7th Cir. 1995); 7 WORLD ARB. & MED. REP. 109 (1995); 10 INT'L ARB. REP. A1 (Apr. 1995).

[129] *See* Pierre Bellet and Ernst Mezger, *L'arbitrage international dans le nouveau code de procédure civile*, 1981 REV. CRIT. DIP 611, 627. See also the doubts expressed by Scalbert and Marville, *supra* note 101, at 127, and, for an example of the ineffectiveness of such a clause, Hoogovens Ijmuiden Verkoopkantoor B.V. v. M.V. Sea Cattleya, 852 F. Supp. 6 (S.D.N.Y. 1994); XXII Y.B. COM. ARB. 881 (1997).

[130] Clause cited by Davis, *supra* note 101, at 385. On the defect consisting in failing to include in the scope of the clause disputes concerning the validity and the performance of the contract, see *infra* para. 517.

In order for the courts to agree to carry out such an appointment, the clause would have to be interpreted as containing an agreement between the parties whereby, in the event of a dispute, the plaintiff would be entitled to choose the seat of arbitration. If France were the chosen seat, the courts would then be able to apply Article 1493 of the New Code of Civil Procedure,[131] which empowers the President of the Paris Tribunal of First Instance to rule on any difficulty encountered in the constitution of the arbitral tribunal. In the above example, this result could be obtained by an *a contrario* interpretation of the arbitration agreement, the parties having excluded the jurisdiction of the courts of each of their home countries. However, the courts' response to this line of reasoning remains uncertain.[132]

B. – COMBINED CLAUSES

487. — In some cases, parties combine in a single clause the submission of their disputes to arbitration and the designation of a state court. At first glance, this combination may appear to be contradictory, with the inevitable outcome that the whole agreement will be held invalid. However, the courts have not systematically adopted such an approach. There are three situations to be distinguished: that where one or more of the parties is granted an option to choose between arbitration and the courts; that where the parties specify that the courts are to serve as an appeal jurisdiction; and that where the contradiction appears more evident.

1° Option to Choose Between Arbitration and the Courts

488. — Certain dispute resolution clauses purport to give one party the option to choose between having disputes resolved by arbitration or by the courts. This clause is not uncommon in banking contracts, for example. The resulting lack of equality between the parties raises the issue of the validity of such an arrangement.[133] French law has held such agreements to be valid. In 1972, the Angers Court of Appeals refused to hold void a clause in a contract between several Dutch corporations and a French corporation, in which the Dutch corporations reserved the right to choose between arbitration and the courts (in both cases in the Netherlands). The French corporation had brought proceedings before the French court on the basis of Article 14 of the French Civil Code. However, the Angers Court of Appeals rejected the French party's argument that by leaving this option open to one of the parties "the arbitration agreement . . . shows that there was no intention to submit the dispute to an arbitrator." On the contrary, the Court considered that "the fact that the foreign

---

[131] *See infra* paras. 750 *et seq.*

[132] On a restrictive approach to the implicit choice of arbitral fora, see TGI Paris, réf., Jan. 10, 1996, *National Iranian Oil Co., supra* note 113.

[133] When the option is given to both parties, the clause is unquestionably pathological since one party may opt for arbitration and the other for the courts thus creating inextricable conflicts.

companies reserved this option does not alter the fact that the [French] company waived its right to rely on the jurisdiction of French courts on the basis of its nationality."[134] The *Cour de cassation* rejected the French party's action against this decision.[135] Admittedly in a purely domestic context, and prior to the 1998 reform (which remains silent on this issue), the German courts were not always as liberal. On October 10, 1991, the *Bundesgerichtshof*, applying German law rules on general conditions, held void a clause giving the party that drafted the disputed conditions the choice between the courts and arbitration.[136]

2° The Courts as an Appeal Jurisdiction

489. — Where the parties have agreed to submit their disputes first to arbitration and then to the courts, the extent of the arbitral tribunal's jurisdiction ought, in principle, to be determined by the arbitral tribunal itself.[137] Nevertheless, the Paris Court of Appeals recently held that in international arbitration a clause providing for the possibility of an appeal before the courts was void because of the mandatory nature of the organization of the judicial system. Consequently, given the essential nature of that provision for the parties, the arbitration agreement allowing for the possibility of an appeal was itself void.[138] This decision is, in our view, unduly restrictive. In the United States, the Court of Appeal for the Ninth Circuit enforced an agreement which provided for an ICC arbitration in San Francisco but also that "the United States District Court for the Northern District of California may enter judgment upon any award, either by confirming the award or by vacating, modifying or correcting the award" in particular "where the arbitrators' findings of fact are not supported by substantial evidence or . . . where the arbitrators' conclusions of law are erroneous." The District Court had taken the same position as the Paris Court of Appeals in the *de Diseno* decision, holding that "the parties may not by agreement alter by expansion the provisions for judicial review contained in the Federal Arbitration Act."[139] The Court of Appeals for the Ninth Circuit reversed the decision and held the agreement valid. Although the clause drafted by the parties in the *Lapine Technology* matter is far from satisfactory, it

---

[134] CA Angers, Sept. 25, 1972, S.A. Sicaly v. Grasso Stacon Koninklijke Machine Fabrieken NV, 1973 REV. ARB. 164, and J. Rubellin-Devichi's note; Gaz. Pal., Jur. 210 (1973).

[135] Cass. 1e civ., May 15, 1974, S.A. Sicaly v. Grasso Stacon Koninklijke Machine Fabrieken NV, 1974 Bull. Civ. I, No. 143.

[136] *Bundesgerichtshof*, Oct. 10, 1991, Seller v. Buyer, XIX Y.B. COM. ARB. 200 (1994).

[137] TGI Paris, réf., Oct. 25, 1983, AA Mutual Ins. Ltd. Automutual House v. Groupe Sprinks, 1984 REV. ARB. 372. See also, in French domestic arbitration, Cass. 2e civ., July 7, 1971, Aurorga v. Laboratoires Gerda, JCP, Ed. G., Pt. II, No. 16,898 (1971), and P. Level's note; 1972 REV. ARB. 12; CA Nancy, Dec. 12, 1985, Langlais v. Bruneau, 1986 REV. ARB. 255, and C. Jarrosson's note, which held that "preliminary arbitration" is no more than a mandatory conciliation requirement.

[138] CA Paris, Oct. 27, 1994, de Diseno v. Mendes, 1995 REV. ARB. 263, 2d decision, and P. Level's note. On this issue, generally, see *infra* para. 1597.

[139] Lapine Tech. Corp. v. Kyocera Corp., 909 F. Supp. 697, 705 (N.D. Cal. 1995).

is still preferable, in our view, to respect the parties' intentions to the greatest extent possible.[140]

3° Conflict Between Arbitration and the Courts

490. — The situation is even more delicate where the parties refer both to the jurisdiction of the arbitrators and to that of the courts, without giving further detail. Such a clause could be interpreted as granting the parties an option to choose between the two, or as providing for recourse to arbitration followed by an appeal to a court, or as submitting certain questions to arbitration and others to the courts.[141] When the contradiction is flagrant, however, the courts may have no alternative but to hold the clause or clauses void. To assess whether or not there is such a contradiction, the arbitral tribunal, subject of course to review by the courts, must establish the parties' true intention. In so doing, the arbitrators will often salvage the arbitration agreement. An example is a 1992 award made in ICC Case No. 6866. The contract provided in one clause that an ICC arbitral tribunal sitting in Algiers would resolve disputes "in first and last instance," and in a second clause that "in last instance only the Algerian courts will have jurisdiction." The arbitral tribunal decided that the latter provision referred only to the recourse available under Algerian law against awards made in Algeria,[142] thus giving full effect to the arbitration clause. Another illustration can be seen in an award made in 1993 in ICC Case No. 5488.[143] In somewhat cryptic terms which rendered the arbitration clause pathological for want of clarity,[144] the parties had referred, in two successive articles of a construction contract, to the jurisdiction of the ICC and to that of the courts of the country party to the dispute. Relying on the principle of effective interpretation,[145] the arbitral tribunal ruled that the parties had intended to confer general jurisdiction on the arbitral tribunal to hear actions which might arise once the works had been completed, and specific jurisdiction on the courts over issues to be decided during the performance of the works. In the same way, when faced with an apparent contradiction between an arbitration clause and a clause providing for the jurisdiction of courts, the French courts have systematically attempted to ensure that the former prevails over the latter. As the Paris Tribunal of First Instance held in 1979

---

[140] Lapine Tech. Corp. v. Kyocera Corp., 130 F.3d 884 (9th Cir. 1997). For a discussion of the case, see Eric A. Schwartz, *Choosing Between Broad Clauses and Detailed Blueprints, in* ICCA CONGRESS SERIES, No. 9, IMPROVING THE EFFICIENCY OF ARBITRATION AGREEMENTS AND AWARDS: 40 YEARS OF APPLICATION OF THE NEW YORK CONVENTION 105 (A.J. van den Berg ed., 1999).

[141] For an example of the difficulties of interpretation to which this gives rise, see the 1989 award rendered in Zurich in ICC Case No. 5759, Sub-Contractor v. Contractor, XVIII Y.B. COM. ARB. 34 (1993), especially ¶¶ 1 *et seq.* at 35. See also the examples cited *infra* para. 521.

[142] ICC BULLETIN, Vol. 8, No. 2, at 73 (1997).

[143] Unpublished.

[144] *See supra* para. 484.

[145] *See supra* para. 478.

an ambiguous arbitration clause should be interpreted by considering that if the parties had not wished to submit their disputes to arbitration, they would simply have refrained from mentioning the possibility of doing so; . . . by including an arbitration clause in their contract, they demonstrated that it would be necessary to submit any disputes arising from their contract to [the arbitral tribunal to which they referred].[146]

In 1991, the Paris Court of Appeals reached a similar conclusion in a case arising from contracts containing a clause attributing jurisdiction "in the event of a dispute" to "the Paris courts" and a clause conferring "jurisdiction on arbitrators in the event of a dispute concerning the interpretation or performance of the present contracts." The Court held that the first of these clauses "can only be interpreted as an attribution of territorial jurisdiction, subordinate to the arbitration agreement, to cover the eventuality that the arbitral tribunal is unable to rule."[147] In a decision of November 26, 1997, in a case concerning a French domestic arbitration, the *Cour de cassation* upheld a decision of a Court of Appeals which, when faced with a contract containing both an arbitration clause and a clause providing for the jurisdiction of the courts, had held that the latter clause played only a subsidiary role and had therefore declined jurisdiction in favor of the arbitral tribunal.[148] Courts in other jurisdictions often display the same tendency to salvage the arbitration clause whenever possible. In a case where the parties had incorporated, in two successive articles of their contract, an ICC arbitration clause and a clause providing for the exclusive jurisdiction of the English courts, the High Court saved the arbitration clause by ruling that the reference to English courts applied only to incidents arising during the conduct of the arbitration.[149] A similar approach has been adopted by United States courts.[150]

All the cases described above show that in order for the parties to be bound by the arbitration agreement, it is essential that they should have wanted their disputes to be

---

[146] TGI Paris, Feb. 1, 1979, *Techniques de l'Ingénieur, supra* note 89, *aff'd,* on this issue, by CA Paris, Oct. 16, 1979, 1980 REV. ARB. 101, and J. Robert's note. For a case where apparently contradictory general and special conditions were more easy to reconcile, see CA Paris, Dec. 1, 1995, Ministère de l'Agriculture d'Irak v. Hochtief, 1996 REV. ARB. 456, and J.-M. Talau's note.

[147] CA Paris, Nov. 29, 1991, Distribution Chardonnet v. Fiat Auto France, 1993 REV. ARB. 617, and L. Aynès' note. *See also* TGI Paris, Nov. 20, 1969, Ets. Didier Jour v. Ets. Marcel Satiat, Dalloz, Jur. 199 (1970); CA Paris, Nov. 26, 1981, Société Internationale du siège v. Bocuir, 1982 REV. ARB. 439, and E. Mezger's note.

[148] Brigif v. ITM-Entreprises, 1997 REV. ARB. 544, and the commentary by Daniel Cohen, *Arbitrage et groupes de contrats, id.* at 471.

[149] Paul Smith Ltd. v. H & S International Holding Inc., [1991] 2 Lloyd's Rep. 127; XIX Y.B. COM. ARB. 725 (1994) (High Ct., Q.B. (Com. Ct.) 1991).

[150] For a clause submitting disputes to United States courts co-existing with an arbitration clause, the former of which was interpreted as only concerning enforcement of any award, see *In re* Montauk Oil Transportation Corp. v. Steamship Mutual Underwriting Ass'n, No. 90 Civ. 3801 (JFK), 1991 U.S Dist. LEXIS 1364 (S.D.N.Y. Feb. 5, 1991); No. 90 Civ. 3801 (JFK), 1991 U.S. Dist. LEXIS 2972 (S.D.N.Y. Mar. 13, 1991); No. 90 Civ. 3792 (DNE), 1991 U.S. Dist. LEXIS 3452 (S.D.N.Y. Mar. 20, 1991); XVIII Y.B. COM. ARB. 463 (1993). *See also* Ryobi North American, Inc. v. Singer Co., CV No. 8:96-1615-21 (D.S.C. Aug. 30, 1996); 11 INT'L ARB. REP. B1 (Sept. 1996); XXII Y.B. COM. ARB. 1020 (1997).

resolved by that means, whether or not in combination with another dispute resolution mechanism. The same thinking prevails in the context of arbitration clauses incorporated by reference.

C. – ARBITRATION CLAUSES INCORPORATED BY REFERENCE

491. — In international trade, parties often decide not to set out the terms of their contract in detail, referring instead to pre-existing documents, such as previous contracts between the parties or standard-form agreements produced by professional bodies. Where the document referred to contains an arbitration clause, a question arises as to whether the reference to that document is sufficient for the parties to be bound by the arbitration agreement.[151]

Before addressing the real issues at the heart of this debate (3°), there are two potential obstacles to the validity of such clauses which should be addressed at the outset: these result from a misunderstanding of the principle of the autonomy of the arbitration agreement (1°) and from a questionable interpretation of the requirements of form laid down in certain arbitration statutes (2°).

1° Arbitration Clauses Incorporated by Reference and the Autonomy of the Arbitration Agreement

492. — The principle of the autonomy of the arbitration agreement from the main contract raises no obstacle to the validity of an arbitration agreement incorporated by reference. The principle of autonomy does not require the arbitration agreement to be contained in a separate document in order to be valid. This would place excessive emphasis on requirements of form—an approach which is alien to the law of international arbitration. This is true of any self-contained contract. It is equally true of the reference made in a contract to another document. This is why a general reference to a document, such as general conditions, which contains, *inter alia*, an arbitration clause, can be held to constitute valid consent to arbitration, regardless of the principle of the autonomy of the arbitration agreement, which is irrelevant to this issue. Any other understanding of the principle of autonomy would resuscitate the anachronistic distinction between arbitration clauses and submission agreements, thus creating new obstacles to the validity of the arbitration

---

[151] On this issue, generally, see Oppetit, *supra* note 93; Claude Reymond, *La clause arbitrale par référence, in* RECUEIL DE TRAVAUX SUISSES SUR L'ARBITRAGE INTERNATIONAL 85 (1984); Jean-François Poudret, *La clause arbitrale par référence selon la Convention de New York et l'art. 6 du Concordat sur l'arbitrage, in* RECUEIL DE TRAVAUX OFFERTS À M. GUY FLATTET 523 (1985); Lucius Huber, *Arbitration Clause "by Reference," in* ASA SPECIAL SERIES No. 8, THE ARBITRATION AGREEMENT – ITS MULTIFOLD CRITICAL ASPECTS 78 (1994) (in German); KLAUS PETER BERGER, INTERNATIONAL ECONOMIC ARBITRATION 149 *et seq.* (1993); Xavier Boucobza, *La clause compromissoire par référence en matière d'arbitrage commercial international,* 1998 REV. ARB. 495.

agreement, despite the fact that the principle of autonomy was precisely intended to promote that validity.[152]

2° Arbitration Clauses Incorporated by Reference and Requirements of Form

493. — The second potential obstacle to the validity of an arbitration agreement incorporated by reference stems from the requirement set forth in a number of arbitration statutes that the arbitration agreement be in writing.[153] Where the written form is a condition of the validity of the arbitration agreement, is it sufficient simply to refer, in writing, to a document such as a standard-form contract?

494. — This question has arisen in connection with the application of the 1958 New York Convention. Although the Convention contains no provision dealing specifically with arbitration clauses incorporated by reference, it does require "an arbitral clause in a contract . . . signed by the parties or contained in an exchange of letters or telegrams" (Art. II(2)). Some commentators consider this condition to be satisfied only where the parties have specifically referred to the arbitration agreement contained in the appended document.[154]

---

[152] *See also* M.-L. Niboyet-Hoegy, note following Cass. 1e civ., Dec. 6, 1988, Navimpex Centrala Navala v. Wiking Trader Shiffahrtsgesellschaft MbH, 117 J.D.I. 134, 140 (1990); Oppetit, *supra* note 93, at 558; PIERRE LALIVE, JEAN-FRANÇOIS POUDRET, CLAUDE REYMOND, LE DROIT DE L'ARBITRAGE INTERNE ET INTERNATIONAL EN SUISSE 315 (1989); ICC Award No. 4381 (1986), French company v. Iranian company, 113 J.D.I. 1102, 1108 (1986), and observations by Y. Derains; *Corte di Appello* of Milan, Oct. 4, 1991, Black Sea Shipping Co. v. Italturist SpA, XVIII Y.B. COM. ARB. 415 (1993).

[153] On the liberal position taken in French law, see *infra* paras. 592 *et seq.*, especially para. 608.

[154] VAN DEN BERG, *supra* note 12, at 217 *et seq.*; Pieter Sanders, *A Twenty Years' Review of the Convention on the Recognition and Enforcement of Foreign Arbitral Awards*, 13 INT'L LAW. 269 (1979) and, for a French version, 1979 DPCI 359, 379; Poudret, *supra* note 151, at 534.

Although some decisions concerning this clause have allowed a reference expressed in general terms,[155] others have taken a more restrictive position.[156]

495. — In France, this issue gave rise to a great deal of controversy in the *Bomar Oil* case. ETAP, a Tunisian oil company, sold crude oil to Bomar Oil, a company incorporated in the Netherlands Antilles. The sale was concluded by an exchange of telexes referring to the general conditions of ETAP's standard contract, which contained an ICC arbitration clause. A disagreement arose between the parties concerning a contractual clause providing for the re-negotiation of the price in the event of a significant change in market conditions, and ETAP commenced arbitration proceedings. Following the procedure set forth in the standard contract, ETAP requested that the President of the ICC appoint an arbitrator, as the defendant had refused to make such appointment on the grounds that it had not agreed to the arbitration agreement incorporated by reference. In its award, the arbitral tribunal[157] rejected the defendant's challenge to its jurisdiction. An action to set aside the award was brought before the Paris Court of Appeals, which held that:

---

[155] *See* Swiss Fed. Trib., Feb. 7, 1984, Tradax Export S.A. v. Amoco Iran Oil Co., 1986 REV. ARB. 589, and R. Budin and D. Henchoz' note; XI Y.B. COM. ARB. 532 (1986), with a critical commentary by Poudret, *supra* note 151, at 534; Rotterdam *Rechtbank*, June 26, 1970, Israel Chemicals & Phosphates Ltd. v. N.V. Algemene Oliehandel, I Y.B. COM. ARB. 195 (1976); Supreme Court of Hong Kong, High Court, Aug. 23, 1991, Guangdong New Technology Import & Export Corp. Jiangmen Branch v. Chiu Shing trading as B.C. Property & Trading Co., XVIII Y.B. COM. ARB. 385 (1993); *Corte di Appello* of Milan, Oct. 4, 1991, *Black Sea Shipping*, *supra* note 152; and, in a scenario where two successive documents incorporated a clause by reference, Zurich *Handelsgericht*, Dec. 14, 1989, Assignee of Singapore seller v. Swiss buyer, XVIII Y.B. COM. ARB. 442 (1993). See also, in the United States, the very liberal decision in Kahn Lucas Lancaster, Inc. v. Lark Int'l Ltd., No. 95 Civ. 10506 (DLC), 1997 U.S. Dist. LEXIS 11916 (S.D.N.Y. Aug. 6, 1997); 1997 BULL. ASA 516, and observations by R. Hill; 12 INT'L ARB. REP. F1 (Aug. 1997). In arbitral case law, see, on the basis of the Swiss Private International Law Statute, ICC Award No. 9160 (1998), Panamanian company v. French companies, unpublished: Swiss law "does not require for the text of the arbitration clause itself to be quoted in a document if it clearly results from a text that the concerned party accepted it."

[156] See, for example, before the reform of German and Italian law, which now expressly allow for the possibility of an arbitration clause by reference (*see* Art. 1031(2) of the German ZPO (in force as of Jan. 1, 1998) and Art. 833, para. 2 of the Italian Code of Civil Procedure (Law No. 25 of Jan. 5, 1994)), *Bundesgerichtshof*, Feb. 12, 1976, Romanian firm v. German (F.R.) firm, II Y.B. COM. ARB. 242 (1977) (which noted that the general conditions of sale and delivery containing the arbitration agreement were annexed to the contract executed by the parties); Italian *Corte di Cassazione*, Sept. 18, 1978, Butera v. Pagnan, IV Y.B. COM. ARB. 296 (1979) (which appeared to allow reference to general conditions only for the purposes of giving details of how the arbitration provided for in the contract itself was to be conducted). It should be noted, however, that both decisions held the arbitration agreement to be valid in light of the specific circumstances of the cases. *But see* Italian *Corte di Cassazione*, Oct. 28, 1993, Robobar Ltd. v. Finncold sas, XX Y.B. COM. ARB. 739 (1995) (which held invalid as to its form an arbitration agreement contained in a purchase confirmation, even though the contract had been partially performed). *Comp. with* Italian *Corte di Cassazione*, Mar. 2, 1996, Molini Lo Presti S.p.A. v. Continentale Italiana S.p.A., XXII Y.B. COM. ARB. 734 (1997).

[157] Award of Jan. 25, 1985, by Messrs. Oppetit, chairman, and Malouche and Craig, arbitrators, in Entreprise Tunisienne d'Activités Pétrolières (E.T.A.P.) v. Bomar Oil., unpublished.

[b]y reason of the general nature of the wording . . . of Art. II of the New York Convention, it must be admitted that this text expresses a substantive rule which must be applied in all cases. This is true whether the arbitration agreement is invoked in support of an objection for lack of competence before a State court or is contested before an arbitral tribunal so that the case will be remitted to the ordinary court . . . . [T]he said Convention admits the adoption of an arbitration agreement by reference only to the extent that the agreement of the parties does not involve any ambiguity.

The Court considered that there was no ambiguity, noting that the buyer had considerable oil industry experience and therefore could not "assert to have not been aware of the usual clauses in contracts concluded in this sector of activity."[158]

In a widely criticized decision, the *Cour de cassation* reversed the ruling of the Paris Court of Appeals on the grounds that, although the New York Convention does not exclude the adoption of an arbitration agreement incorporated by reference, Article II of the Convention required

that the existence of the clause be mentioned in the main contract, unless there exists between the parties a longstanding business relationship which insures that they are properly aware of the written conditions normally governing their commercial relationships.[159]

However, when the case was sent back to the Versailles Court of Appeals, that Court refused to set aside the disputed award. It held that, although the New York Convention and French law do not bar an arbitration agreement by reference to a document containing an arbitration clause,

[i]f the existence of such clause, however, is not mentioned in the main agreement, the principle of consensualism requires the party invoking the arbitration agreement to prove that the other party knew about the arbitral clause at the time it entered into the main agreement. As both parties in this case are merchants, all types of evidence are allowed.

---

[158] CA Paris, Jan. 20, 1987, Bomar Oil N.V. v. Entreprise Tunisienne d'Activités Pétrolières (E.T.A.P.), 1987 REV. ARB. 482, and C. Kessedjian's note; 114 J.D.I. 934 (1987), and E. Loquin's note; for an English translation, see XIII Y.B. COM. ARB. 466, 469–70 (1988).

[159] Cass. 1e civ., Oct. 11, 1989, Bomar Oil N.V. v. Entreprise Tunisienne d'Activités Pétrolières (E.T.A.P.), 1989 Bull. Civ. I, No. 314; 1990 REV. ARB. 134, and C. Kessedjian's disapproving note; 117 J.D.I. 633 (1990), and E. Loquin's disapproving note; for an English translation, see XV Y.B. COM. ARB. 447 (1990); 4 INT'L ARB. REP. A1 (Dec. 1989).

The Court considered that the required awareness was demonstrated by the exchange of telexes between the parties.[160] This approach is preferable to that of the *Cour de cassation*. The test is that of the actual consent of the parties, rather than that of formal requirements not even imposed by the New York Convention.[161]

Perhaps the initial error lay in the fact that the Paris Court of Appeals, and subsequently the *Cour de cassation* and the Versailles Court of Appeals, applied the New York Convention in the first place,[162] overlooking the fact that the French courts can always recognize an award under the more liberal conditions of French law.[163]

In fact, even prior to the Versailles Court of Appeals' ruling in the *Bomar Oil* case, the *Cour de cassation* had reached another decision which was much more favorable to arbitration clauses incorporated by reference, based on French arbitration law rather than the New York Convention. A foreign supplier to a French corporation had referred, in a telex, to an arbitration clause contained in UN general conditions No. 188 prior to carrying out repairs requested by its French client. The Nancy Court of Appeals held this arbitration clause to be inapplicable. Its ruling was, however, quashed by the *Cour de cassation* on the grounds that the appeal court had ruled "without establishing whether the [French] corporation was familiar with the content of the UN general conditions containing the arbitration clause and, if so, whether by remaining silent it had tacitly agreed to incorporate those conditions into the contract."[164]

When the *Bomar Oil* case returned to the *Cour de cassation*, the Court in its second decision clearly came down in favor of a consensualist approach. The Court set forth a substantive rule of international arbitration law, without any reference to the New York Convention:

---

[160] CA Versailles, Jan. 23, 1991, Bomar Oil N.V. v. Entreprise Tunisienne d'Activités Pétrolières (E.T.A.P.), 1991 REV. ARB. 291, and C. Kessedjian's approving note; for an English translation, see XVII Y.B. COM. ARB. 488 (1992).

[161] For such a view, see E. Loquin, note following Cass. 1e civ., Oct. 11, 1989, *supra* note 159, at 639; Oppetit, *supra* note 93, at 562; Jean Robert, *La Convention de New York du 10 juin 1958 pour la reconnaissance et l'exécution des sentences arbitrales étrangères*, Dalloz, Chron. 223 (1958). On the reference, supporting the contrary view, to the *travaux préparatoires* of the 1958 New York Convention, see FOUCHARD, *supra* note 4, ¶ 140.

[162] On whether the Convention applies to situations other than where enforcement of an award rendered abroad is sought, see C. Kessedjian, notes following CA Paris, Jan. 20, 1987, Cass. 1e civ., Oct. 11, 1989, and CA Versailles, Jan. 23, 1991, *supra* notes 158, 159 and 160, especially 1991 REV. ARB. 291, 301.

[163] *See infra* para. 1664.

[164] Cass. 1e civ., June 26, 1990, Dreistern Werk v. Crouzier, 1991 REV. ARB. 291, and C. Kessedjian's note. *See also* CA Paris, Apr. 18, 1991, Afric Viande v. Brittania, 1994 REV. ARB. 95, 2d decision, and Y. Paclot's note; in French domestic arbitration, see Cass. 2e civ., June 30, 1993, Ferruzzi France v. Roquette Frères, and CA Paris, May 30, 1991, SARL Diva Fruits v. Simfruits, 1994 REV. ARB. 95, 1st and 3d decisions, and Y. Paclot's note; CA Paris, Mar. 22, 1991, Caval Coopérative Anjou Val de Loire v. Laraison, 1993 REV. ARB. 680, and observations by D. Cohen; CA Paris, Nov. 14, 1996, Gefimex v. Transgrain, 1997 REV. ARB. 434, and observations by Y. Derains.

in the field of international arbitration, an arbitration clause, if not mentioned in the main contract, may be validly stipulated by written reference to a document which contains it, for instance general conditions or a standard contract, when the party against which the clause invoked was aware of the contents of this document at the moment of concluding the contract and when it has, albeit tacitly, accepted the incorporation of the document in the contract.[165]

495-1. — The UNCITRAL Model Law underlines that it is outdated to construe the New York Convention as requiring a specific reference to the arbitration clause itself. In terms which, admittedly, are not as clear as they might be, the UNCITRAL Model Law, while in principle requiring a document in writing, nevertheless allows an arbitration agreement incorporated by reference. The language of the Model Law is somewhat obscure in that it not only requires the reference to be in writing but also that "the reference is such as to make that clause part of the contract" (Art. 7(2)). The same language is found in Section 6 of the 1996 English Arbitration Act and in the new Article 1031(3) of the German ZPO.[166] The provision found, since the 1986 reform, in Article 1021 of the Netherlands Code of Civil Procedure is much clearer. It provides that

"[t]he arbitration agreement shall be proven by an instrument in writing. For this purpose an instrument in writing which provides for arbitration or which refers to standard conditions providing for arbitration is sufficient, provided that this instrument is expressly or impliedly accepted by or on behalf of the other party."

Ultimately, what matters is the parties' true intentions. There is therefore no reason to take a hostile position towards arbitration clauses incorporated by reference.

---

[165] Cass. le civ., Nov. 9, 1993, Bomar Oil N.V. v. Entreprise Tunisienne d'Activités Pétrolières (E.T.A.P.), 1994 REV. ARB. 108, and C. Kessedjian's note; 121 J.D.I. 690 (1994), and E. Loquin's note; for an English translation, see XX Y.B. COM. ARB. 660 (1995). *See also* CA Paris, May 17, 1995, Trafidi v. International Spice and Food, 123 J.D.I. 110 (1996), and E. Loquin's note; 1997 REV. ARB. 90, and observations by Y. Derains; Cass. le civ., June 3, 1997, Prodexport v. FMT Productions, 1998 REV. ARB. 537, with the commentary by Boucobza, *supra* note 151.

[166] For express legislative confirmation of the validity of arbitration clauses incorporated by reference, see also, for example, Article 833, paragraph 2 of the Italian Code of Civil Procedure (Law No. 25 of Jan. 5, 1994); Art. 10(3) of Egyptian Law No. 27 for 1994 Promulgating the Law Concerning Arbitration in Civil and Commercial Matters; Art. 1423 of the Mexican Commercial Code (Decree of July 22, 1993).

3° Arbitration Clauses Incorporated by Reference and the Interpretation of the Consent of the Parties

496. — Arbitration agreements incorporated by reference must therefore be analyzed in terms of the existence and extent of the parties' consent to have their disputes resolved by arbitration. The existence and extent of that consent should be interpreted using the general principles of interpretation of arbitration agreements, that is, neither extensively nor restrictively.[167]

The French courts have traditionally followed that approach, with the unfortunate exception of the *Cour de cassation*'s first *Bomar Oil* decision.[168] In 1980, the Paris Court of Appeals upheld an award made on the basis of an arbitration agreement contained in a standard-form contract to which the foreign party had referred in a document sent to the French party confirming its order.[169] In 1988, the same court held valid an arbitration agreement between a main contractor and sub-contractor, where the clause was contained in the main contract and was incorporated by reference in the sub-contract.[170] In 1990, it upheld an arbitration agreement contained in documents attached to correspondence sent by one party to the other. The latter party claimed not to have received the attached documents, an argument which the Court of Appeals rejected on the grounds that:

> the principle of good faith governing contractual relations prior to any dispute leads to the conclusion that a document which was mentioned as being attached to a letter was indeed so attached. The party receiving the letter announcing that the document was attached was obliged to verify whether the document was in fact attached, failing which it ought to have asked for it. As the document was necessarily of a contractual nature, the recipient could not ignore it without running the risk of it subsequently being used against such party, in which case such party would be bound by it.[171]

In 1991, in the *Dalico* case, which concerned a works contract, the Paris Court of Appeals considered that given the facts of the case

> the Annex to the Standard Conditions of Contract, in stipulating the arbitration agreement through reference to tender offer documents which are themselves

---

[167] *See supra* para. 480.

[168] Cass. 1e civ., Oct. 11, 1989, *supra* note 159 and para. 495.

[169] CA Paris, Nov. 13, 1980, Coopérative de déshydratation de la région de Soulaines v. Hindrichs, 1982 REV. ARB. 283, and P. Lepoittevin's note.

[170] "All disputes will be settled according to clause [X] of the contract between [A] and [B]," CA Paris, Jan. 20, 1988, V.S.K. Electronics v. Sainrapt et Brice International, 116 J.D.I. 1032 (1989), and E. Loquin's note; 1990 REV. ARB. 651, and the commentary by Oppetit, *supra* note 93, at 551.

[171] CA Paris, Nov. 30, 1990, Jongerius Hanco BV v. Poilâne, 1992 REV. ARB. 645, and J. Pellerin's note.

part of the contract, was integrated into the contract group binding upon the parties, by the parties' common desire, although the document does not contain a signature . . . .

This decision was upheld by the *Cour de cassation* on December 20, 1993.[172]
On February 18, 1992, the *Cour de cassation* confirmed a decision of the Paris Court of Appeals, which had decided that:

> since an intermediary had simultaneously sent a note to both vendor and purchaser setting out the general conditions of sale, and since those conditions had been accepted by the parties, the arbitration clause contained in the general conditions is effective, to the exclusion of the contradictory clauses appearing in the documentation relating to the acceptance of the goods.[173]

On March 3, 1992, the commercial chamber of the *Cour de cassation* upheld a judgment at first instance which refused to set aside an award made on the basis of an arbitration clause contained in a charter-party, which was referred to but not reproduced in a bill of lading.[174] In another decision made on the same day, the first civil chamber of the *Cour de cassation* held that:

> as a court of appeals, which has exclusive jurisdiction to examine the facts of the case, has established that the text of the arbitration agreements had been attached to confirmation slips sent by the vendor and accepted by the purchaser, the arbitration agreements were therefore accepted at the same time as the main contract.[175]

The only case in which a French court has refused to recognize the existence of an arbitration clause incorporated by reference was where the factual circumstances left genuine doubt as to the existence of the consent. In that case, a bill of lading signed by the captain of a ship "referred, in general terms and without reproducing or annexing them" to the general conditions of a charter-party to which the shipowner was not a party but which contained an arbitration clause. The Court of Appeals of Saint-Denis-de-la-Réunion noted that "in view of the changes made unilaterally by the shipowner," it had not been established that the arbitration clause "had been firmly accepted by the other parties to the initial

---

[172] CA Paris, Mar. 26, 1991, *Dalico, supra* note 33, 6 INT'L ARB. REP. B8 (Sept. 1991), *aff'd*, Cass. 1e civ., Dec. 20, 1993, *supra* note 2.

[173] Cass. 1e civ., Feb. 18, 1992, Firme Peter Biegi v. Brittania, 1993 REV. ARB. 103, and observations by J.-H. Moitry, *affirming* CA Paris, Feb. 19, 1988, 1990 REV. ARB. 657, and commentary by Oppetit, *supra* note 93.

[174] Cass. com., Mar. 3, 1992, OFER Brothers v. The Tokyo Marine and Fire Insurance Co. Ltd., 1992 REV. ARB. 560, and P. Delebecque's note.

[175] Cass. 1e civ., Mar. 3, 1992, Sonetex v. Charphil, upholding, on this ground only, a decision of the Paris Court of Appeals of May 15, 1990 (1993 REV. ARB. 273, and P. Mayer's note; 120 J.D.I. 140 (1993), and B. Audit's note).

charter-party." The Court therefore held that the arbitration clause was not incorporated into the contractual relationship between the shipowner and the parties to the initial charter-party.[176] This decision was upheld by the *Cour de cassation*. This case thus turned on a question of fact which, necessarily, was not reviewed by the *Cour de cassation*, except in order to verify that the first instance judges had sought to determine the intentions of the parties. This decision therefore in no way contradicts the previous cases affirming the validity of arbitration clauses incorporated by reference.

§ 3. – Scope of the Parties' Consent

497. — In the complex situations which frequently arise in international trade, arbitrators and the courts often have to rule on differences of interpretation as to which parties are bound by the consent to arbitrate (A), and as to the subject-matter covered by such consent (B).

A. – WHICH PARTIES ARE BOUND BY THE CONSENT TO ARBITRATE?

498. — The arbitration agreement binds only those parties that have entered into it. However, a party need not be physically present in order to be bound—an arbitration agreement can be entered into by an agent[177] or, more generally, by any form of representation.[178] In such cases, the principal is bound, and not its representative. In contrast, a stipulation in favor of a third party does not entail representation, and the beneficiary of that provision will therefore only be bound if it subsequently agrees to the specified method

---

[176] Cass. com., Jan. 7, 1992, Psichikon Compania Naviera Panama v. SIER, 1992 REV. ARB. 553, and P. Delebecque's note.

[177] See, for example, in France, Cass. 2e civ., Oct. 14, 1987, Ampafrance v. Wasteels, 1988 REV. ARB. 288, and J.-L. Goutal's note. On the rules applicable to the powers to enter into an arbitration agreement, see *supra* para. 468. For an example of a case in which the principal, not the agent, was held to be bound by the arbitration clause, see the award in ICC Case No. 7883, rendered in Geneva on September 10, 1997, unpublished.

[178] See, in the case of parties which have agreed to be jointly and severally liable, in France, Cass. com., Nov. 13, 1967, SOIFAM v. S.A. Junker-Ruh, 1967 REV. ARB. 116. For a case where the liability of a guarantor could not be pleaded before an arbitral tribunal as the guarantor had not accepted the arbitration clause, even tacitly, see Cass. com., Nov. 22, 1977, Buy Van Tuyen v. Merrill Lynch Pierce Fenner, 1978 REV. ARB. 461, and P. Fouchard's note. Compare, in French domestic arbitration, with CA Versailles, Apr. 29, 1981, Sté. civ. immobilière Le Clos Mariette v. P.A. Leymarie, which can probably be explained by the fact that the arbitrators reached their decision *ultra petita* (1983 REV. ARB. 207, and observations by T. Bernard). On this issue, generally, see Eric Loquin, *Arbitrage et cautionnement*, 1994 REV. ARB. 235, who correctly argues that as a guarantor is not represented by the principal debtor, it must personally accept to be bound by the arbitration agreement in order to be bound by or to benefit from it. On the different issue of a party subrogated in the rights of another party, see *infra* para. 719.

of dispute resolution.[179] This explains why the French *Cour de cassation* held in one case that a consignee was not bound by an arbitration clause contained in a bill of lading which had been accepted by the shipper but not by the consignee.[180] Similarly, a party guaranteeing an obligation arising from a contract containing an arbitration clause will not be bound by that clause,[181] unless it can be established from other circumstances that the parties' true intentions in drawing up the guarantee were that the guarantor—often the parent company—would be party to the arbitration agreement.[182]

499. — Aside from any representation mechanism, difficulties may arise in determining the exact scope of an arbitration agreement whenever a contract has been entirely or partially negotiated or performed by a party that did not actually sign the contract.[183] In such cases, arbitrators,[184] as well as the French courts,[185] have developed the approach that such involvement can raise the presumption that the contracting parties' true intention was that the non-signatory party would be bound by the arbitration agreement. Thus, a long line of similar decisions[186] led to the ruling of the Paris Court of Appeals, in the 1994 *V 2000* case, that:

---

[179] On this issue, see, in French domestic arbitration, Cass. 1e civ., Oct. 20, 1987, Delaroche v. S.E.R.P., 1988 REV. ARB. 559, and the commentary by Jean-Louis Goutal, *L'arbitrage et les tiers: I. – Le droit des contrats*, *id.* at 439, 448; Cass. 1e civ., July 16, 1992, Tareau v. Martin, 1993 REV. ARB. 611, and P. Delebecque's note; 1993 RTD COM. 295, and observations by E. Loquin. On the interpretation of the intentions of the beneficiary of a promise made in favor of a third party, see Cargill Int'l S.A. v. M/T Pavel Dybenko, 991 F.2d 1012 (2d Cir. 1993); XIX Y.B. COM. ARB. 835 (1994), especially ¶ 18 at 842. On this issue, generally, see XIAO-YING LI, LA TRANSMISSION ET L'EXTINCTION DE LA CLAUSE COMPROMISSOIRE DANS L'ARBITRAGE INTERNATIONAL ¶¶ 79 *et seq.* (Thesis, University of Dijon (France), 1993); Jean-François Poudret, *L'extension de la clause d'arbitrage: approches française et suisse*, 122 J.D.I. 893 (1995).

[180] Cass. com., June 20, 1995, Mediterranean Shipping Co. v. GAFL Assurance, 1995 REV. ARB. 622, and J.-L. Goutal's note. *See also* Jean-Louis Goutal, *La clause compromissoire dans les connaissements: la Cour de Cassation française et la Cour Suprême des Etats-Unis adoptent des solutions opposées*, 1996 REV. ARB. 605. See also, on the fact that a consignee will not be bound by an arbitration clause contained in a charter-party unless there is proof of explicit acceptance of the arbitration agreement on delivery at the latest, see CA Rouen, Oct. 14, 1997, Lorico v. Italgrani, 1998 REV. ARB. 569, and the commentary by Boucobza, *supra* note 151.

[181] *See, e.g.*, CA Paris, July 7, 1994, Uzinexportimport Romanian Co. v. Attock Cement Co., 1995 REV. ARB. 107, and S. Jarvin's note; for an English translation, see 10 INT'L ARB. REP. D1 (Feb. 1995).

[182] On groups of companies, see *infra* paras. 500 *et seq.*

[183] For a typology, see Marc Blessing, *Extension of the Arbitration Clause to Non-Signatories*, *in* ASA SPECIAL SERIES No. 8, THE ARBITRATION AGREEMENT – ITS MULTIFOLD CRITICAL ASPECTS 151 (1994); Otto Sandrock, *Extending the Scope of Arbitration Agreements to Non-Signatories*, *id.* at 165. See also the observations by Emmanuel Stauffer, *L'extension de la portée de la clause arbitrale à des non signataires*, *id.* at 229 and by Yves Derains, *L'extension de la clause d'arbitrage aux non signataires – La doctrine des groupes de sociétés*, *id.* at 241.

[184] See, for example, the awards cited *infra* para. 501.

[185] See, for example, the decisions cited *infra* paras. 502 *et seq.*

[186] On the fact that some of these cases are expressed in terms which go too far, see *supra* para. 440.

in international arbitration law, the effects of the arbitration clause extend to parties directly involved in the performance of the contract, provided that their respective situations and activities raise the presumption that they were aware of the existence and scope of the arbitration clause, so that the arbitrator can consider all economic and legal aspects of the dispute.[187]

In that case, this reasoning enabled the Court to decline jurisdiction, accepting the arguments put forward by a French distributor being sued in the French courts by the purchaser of a vintage car. The purchaser had signed a contract containing an arbitration clause with an English company, but in fact, both before and after signing the contract, had dealt with the French distributor, which had acted as an intermediary in the transaction. The distributor was therefore allowed to rely on the arbitration clause.

Typically, however, this problem arises in two types of situation: the first concerns groups of companies (1°); the second concerns arbitration agreements entered into by states or state-owned entities (2°).

1° Groups of Companies

500. — A question with which both arbitrators and the courts are often confronted is whether an arbitration agreement signed by a company belonging to a group of companies can be extended to include another company of the same group which has not signed the agreement.[188] This question can only arise where each entity has a separate legal personality.

---

[187] CA Paris, Dec. 7, 1994, *V 2000, aff'd*, Cass. 1e civ., May 21, 1997, *supra* note 125. See also, in a case where the supplier of the main contractor had signed the contract, CA Paris, Oct. 26, 1995, SNCFT v. Voith, 1997 REV. ARB. 553, and the commentary by Cohen, *supra* note 148; Cass. 1e civ., June 25, 1991, Compagnie tunisienne de navigation (Cotunav) v. Comptoir commercial André, which holds, in less excessive terms than the decision it confirms (CA Paris, Nov. 28, 1989, 1990 REV. ARB. 675, and P. Mayer's note), that informed involvement by a company in the performance of a contract constitutes the ratification of the arbitration agreement (1991 REV. ARB. 453, and P. Mayer's note). Compare, in the United States, with the idea that a party that accepted the benefits of a contract that it has not signed cannot challenge the arbitration agreement contained in that contract (Deloitte Noraudit A/S v. Deloitte Haskins & Sells, 9 F.3d 1060, 1064 (2d Cir. 1993); 4 WORLD ARB. & MED. REP. 306 (1993)).

[188] On this issue, generally, see Fadlallah, *supra* note 93, at 105 *et seq.*; Derains and Schaf, *supra* note 91; Charles Jarrosson, *Conventions d'arbitrage et groupes de sociétés, in* GROUPES DE SOCIÉTÉS: CONTRATS ET RESPONSABILITÉS 53 (1994) and ASA SPECIAL SERIES No. 8, THE ARBITRATION AGREEMENT – ITS MULTIFOLD CRITICAL ASPECTS 209 (1994); Otto Sandrock, *Arbitration Agreements and Groups of Companies, in* ETUDES DE DROIT INTERNATIONAL EN L'HONNEUR DE PIERRE LALIVE 625 (1993); Sigvard Jarvin, *The Group of Companies Doctrine, in* ASA SPECIAL SERIES No. 8, THE ARBITRATION AGREEMENT – ITS MULTIFOLD CRITICAL ASPECTS 181 (1994); Jean-François Poudret, *Trois remarques au sujet de la théorie des groupes de sociétés*, 1995 BULL. ASA 145; XIAO-YING Li, *supra* note 179, ¶¶ 107 *et seq.*; observations by S. Jarvin following the two interim awards made in 1985 and 1986 in ICC Case No. 4504, Petroleum producer v. Two companies, 113 J.D.I. 1118 (1986); André Chapelle, note following CA Paris, Oct. 21, 1983, Isover-Saint-Gobain v. Dow Chemical France, 1984 REV. ARB. 98, and note following CA Pau, Nov. 26, 1986, Sponsor A.B. v. Lestrade, 1988 REV. ARB. 153; Chapelle, *supra* note 93; Xavier Giocanti, observations on the arbitrators'

(continued...)

If one of the entities is merely a branch of another entity, any arbitration agreement the former signs will be extended to the latter simply because together both entities comprise a single juridical person.[189]

In the case of a genuine group of companies, consisting of entities each having its own legal personality, arbitrators and the courts will sometimes extend the agreement. The thinking is that one can go beyond a strict view of a group divided into separate legal entities to extend an arbitration agreement signed by one company of the group to encompass other companies of the same group when certain conditions are satisfied.[190] Clearly, however, it is not so much the existence of a group that results in the various companies of the group being bound by the agreement signed by only one of them, but rather the fact that such was the true intention of the parties.[191]

---

[188](...continued)
symposium held in Paris on October 5, 1982 at the ICC's Institute of International Business Law and Practice of the ICC, 1982 REV. ARB. 495.

[189] For an illustration, see ICC Award No. 5721 (1990), *supra* note 69, at 1022. On a similar issue regarding states, see *infra* para. 507.

[190] The question also arises, although much less frequently, where a company is wholly controlled by one individual. On the jurisdiction of the arbitral tribunal over the individual in such a case, on the basis of an arbitration clause signed by the controlled company and the *alter ego* doctrine, see, in the United States, National Dev. Co. v. Adnan M. Khashoggi, 781 F. Supp. 959 (S.D.N.Y. 1992); XVIII Y.B. COM. ARB. 506 (1993); Carte Blanche (Singapore) PTE, Ltd. v. Diners Club Int'l, Inc., 2 F.3d 24 (2d Cir. 1993); 8 INT'L ARB. REP. 3 (Sept. 1993); 4 WORLD ARB. & MED. REP. 228 (1993). *But see* Nordell Int'l Resources, Ltd. v. Triton Indon. Inc., No. CV 90-06894-ER (C.D. Cal., May 31, 1994); 5 WORLD ARB. & MED. REP. 243 (1994); 9 INT'L ARB. REP. E1 (June 1994), *aff'd*, No. 94-56110, 1996 U.S. App. LEXIS 11594 (9th Cir. May 3, 1996). Compare, in French law, on the basis of the existence of fraud, Cass 1e civ., June 11, 1991, Orri v. Société des Lubrifiants Elf Aquitaine, 1992 REV. ARB. 73, and D. Cohen's note and *infra* para. 505.

[191] On the conditions of form that may constitute a further obstacle, in certain legal systems, to the extension of the arbitration agreement *ratione personae*, see *infra* paras. 590 *et seq.* For reasoning based on conditions of form to defeat the extension of the arbitration agreement within a group of companies, see the 1985 and 1986 interim awards in ICC Case No. 4504 (*supra* note 188): applying Swiss law, the arbitral tribunal founded its decisions on the requirement in the *Concordat* that an arbitration agreement be in writing. As this was before the reform of Swiss international arbitration law, the restrictive position taken by the Swiss Federal Tribunal in the *Cartier* decision (October 10, 1979, unpublished) clearly influenced the arbitral tribunal. On the current position of the Swiss courts, which is consistent with the principle discussed above, see, for example, Fed. Trib., Jan. 29, 1996, Saudi Butec Ltd. v. Saudi Arabian Saipem Ltd., 1996 BULL. ASA 496; 1996 REV. SUISSE DR. INT. ET DR. EUR. 581, and observations by F. Knoepfler.

a) Arbitral Case Law

501. — Arbitral case law in this area[192] is neatly summarized by the award made in Geneva, in 1990, in ICC Case No. 5721. The tribunal stated that:

> the mere fact that two companies belong to the same group, or that they are dominated by a single shareholder, will not automatically justify lifting the corporate veil. However, where a company or individual appears to be the pivot of the contractual relations in a particular matter, one should carefully examine whether the parties' legal independence ought not, exceptionally, be disregarded in the interests of making a global decision. This exception is acceptable in the case of confusion deliberately maintained by the group or by the majority shareholder.

It was rightly emphasized in the same award that because of the contractual basis of arbitration, the scope of the arbitration agreement should not be extended

> to punish the behavior of a third party. Such measures should only be taken by the courts, before which a party will always be able to argue that the corporate veil should be lifted.

On the basis of these principles, the tribunal considered that the plaintiff, who claimed that the arbitration agreement extended to the person controlling the company which signed the disputed agreements, had not established that it "intended to deal with" that person, or indeed that such person "intended personally to be a party to the arbitration agreement."[193] The existence of the parties' consent is thus clearly the key issue.[194]

Arbitral case law has also allowed an arbitration clause to be extended to a group company where it could be assumed from the latter's involvement in the negotiation or

---

[192] For ICC case law, see excerpts of Awards No. 5103 (1988), Three European companies v. Four Tunisian companies, No. 5891 (1988), French company v. French company, No. 5894 (1989), French bank v. French company, No. 5920 (1989), Contractor v. Yugoslavian enterprise, No. 6000 (1988), French textile company v. U.S. distributor, and No. 6519 (1991), French shareholder v. English company, ICC BULLETIN, Vol. 2, No. 2, at 20 *et seq.* (1991); ICC Awards No. 7604 and 7610 (1995), *supra* note 80. On the practice of the ICC International Court of Arbitration, see DERAINS AND SCHWARTZ, *supra* note 113, at 92.

[193] ICC Case No. 5721 (1990), *supra* note 69, at 1024. *See also* ICC Award No. 4972 (1989), X & Y v. Z & Mr. W, 116 J.D.I. 1100, 1103 (1989), and observations by G. Aguilar Alvarez; ICC Award No. 2138 (1974), *supra* note 91, which rejects the extension of an arbitration clause to a company which had "negotiated the transaction, and signed the main provisions," but which had not signed the contract containing the arbitration agreement. The tribunal ruled that "there is no proof that if the company had signed the latter contract it would have agreed to the arbitration clause;" ICC Award No. 6610 (1991), Owner v. Contractor, XIX Y.B. COM. ARB. 162 (1994).

[194] *See also* Jarrosson, *supra* note 188.

performance of the contract that it tacitly agreed to be bound by the clause.[195] This may be the case where the contract directly concerns the group company,[196] or where it is clear from both the spirit of the disputed agreement and the conduct of the parties involved that the group itself is considered to be a party to the contract, particularly where circumstances might lead third parties to confuse the different companies of the group.[197] Other awards have extended the arbitration clause to a non-signatory company of the same group as the signatory in cases where the facts were particularly favorable to such a decision.[198]

A minority of awards underline the moral aspect of the requirement that a company should not be able to avoid its responsibilities by exploiting the fact that the group to which it belongs comprises distinct companies. Thus an ICC arbitral tribunal sitting in New York held a parent company to be bound by an arbitration clause signed by its subsidiary on the following grounds:

> Whether the corporate veil may be pierced very much depends on the circumstances of the particular case. Certain elements are almost invariably deemed necessary. They include a significant measure of direct control of the subsidiary's activities by the parent or shareholder and the insolvency of the subsidiary. But this is generally not sufficient. The cessation of meaningful activities by the subsidiary and its own management is also a factor that further

---

[195] Compare, on the merits, with regard to companies within the same group: "The three claimant companies appear to have been at the time of the conclusion, execution, non-execution and re-negotiation of their contractual links with [the defendant companies], genuine partners to all these contracts, by the common will of all the parties to the proceedings" (ICC Award No. 5103 (1988), Three European companies v. Four Tunisian companies, 115 J.D.I. 1206 (1988); ICC BULLETIN, Vol. 2, No. 2, at 20, 22 (1991)). This finding was used as the basis for holding the companies to be jointly and severally liable. For a case where the relevant conditions were not fulfilled, see ICC Award No. 7155 (1993), Norwegian company v. Three French companies, 123 J.D.I. 1037 (1996), and observations by J.-J. Arnaldez.

[196] See ICC Award No. 6519 (1991), French shareholder v. English company, 118 J.D.I. 1065 (1991), and observations by Y. Derains; for excerpts translated into English, see ICC BULLETIN, Vol. 2, No. 2, at 34 (1991). Compare with ICC Award No. 6673 (1992), which rejects the extension of the arbitration agreement (Licensor v. Licensee, 119 J.D.I. 992 (1992), and observations by D. Hascher).

[197] See, e.g., interim award in ICC Case No. 4131 (1982), Dow Chemical v. Isover-Saint-Gobain, 1984 REV. ARB. 137; 110 J.D.I. 899 (1983), and observations by Y. Derains; for excerpts translated into English, see IX Y.B. COM. ARB. 131 (1984), and on the subsequent court proceedings, see infra para. 503.

[198] See, for example, ICC Award No. 1434 (1975), supra note 76, in a case where the signatory of the contract containing the arbitration clause explicitly stated that it was acting on behalf of the group; ICC Award No. 2375 (1975), French company v. Two Spanish companies, 103 J.D.I. 973 (1976), where it was held that a contract signed by two parent companies bound both them and their subsidiaries; 1988 Partial Award in ICC Case No. 5730, which allowed the extension of the consequences of an arbitration agreement to the director of a group of companies on the basis that the clause had been signed "in his name, on his instructions and in his presence" by his employee "who simply carried out his wishes and had no other involvement" (Société de lubrifiants Elf Aquitaine v. A.R. Orri, 117 J.D.I. 1029, 1036 (1990), and observations by Y. Derains; 1992 REV. ARB. 125).

facilitates piercing the veil. And if the actual control and management of the subsidiary by the parent has contributed to making illusory recourse against the subsidiary, the case for piercing the corporate veil becomes even more compelling. Wrongful conduct by the subsidiary at the direction of the parent towards the person seeking to pierce the corporate veil is a further element that facilitates piercing the veil. In the end, the question is whether and to what extent the legal fiction of corporate personality must give way to the realities of human conduct and should no longer protect those who hide behind the corporate veil in order to promote their own interests at the expense of those who have dealt with the corporation.[199]

b) French Case Law

502. — The French courts have generally proved to be in favor of extending the arbitration clause to group companies where that extension is justifiable on the basis of the parties' express or implied intention.[200]

503. — One of the first cases in which this issue was directly addressed arose in the early 1980's between various companies of the Dow Chemical group and the French company Isover-Saint-Gobain. In that case, two subsidiaries of the Dow Chemical Company had entered into contracts for the distribution of thermal insulation products with a number of companies whose rights were subsequently assumed by Isover-Saint-Gobain. Each contract contained an arbitration clause. Problems arose concerning the quality of the goods, and arbitral proceedings were initiated by the two Dow group companies that had signed the contracts, together with their parent company and another subsidiary, neither of which had signed the contracts. The defendant claimed that the arbitral tribunal had no jurisdiction to hear the claims raised by the non-signatory companies, as they were not parties to the contracts containing the arbitration clauses.

By an interim award made on September 23, 1982, the arbitral tribunal[201] rejected the arguments of the defendant, Isover-Saint-Gobain. Having decided in favor of applying substantive rules of international commerce to this issue, the arbitral tribunal carefully analyzed the circumstances surrounding the signing, performance and termination of the disputed contracts. The tribunal concluded, having regard to the "undivided economic

---

[199] ICC Award No. 8385 (1995), U.S. company v. Belgian company, 124 J.D.I. 1061 (1997), and observations by Y. Derains.

[200] No distinction should be drawn between the situation where it is a non-signatory company that seeks to benefit from the arbitration clause, and that where a signatory attempts to enforce the arbitration clause against a non-signatory. On this issue, see the discussion which followed Ibrahim Fadlallah's presentation before the Comité français de droit international privé on April 24, 1985, *supra* note 93, and particularly the observations made by Paul Lagarde and Berthold Goldman at 129.

[201] Composed of P. Sanders, chairman, B. Goldman and M. Vasseur, arbitrators.

reality" of a group of companies and "irrespective of the distinct juridical identity of each of its members"

> that the arbitration clause expressly accepted by certain of the companies of the group should bind the other companies which, by virtue of their role in the conclusion, performance, or termination of the contracts containing said clauses, and in accordance with the mutual intention of all parties to the proceedings, appear to have been veritable parties to these contracts or to have been principally concerned by them and the disputes to which they may give rise.[202]

In 1983, the Paris Court of Appeals rejected an action to set aside that award on the grounds that:

> the arbitrators, who are exclusively empowered to interpret the contracts . . . and the documents exchanged when negotiating and terminating them, decided on good, consistent grounds that the common intention of all companies involved was that Dow Chemical France and Dow Chemical Company were parties to the contracts, despite the fact that they had not signed them, and that the arbitration clause was therefore applicable to them.

The Court added that the arbitrators

> also referred, in passing, to the concept of a 'group of companies,' and the claimant [in the action to set aside the award] has not seriously contested the existence of this concept as a usage of international commerce.[203]

Once again, the decision was based not so much on the existence of a group of companies as on the intentions of the parties, the interpretation of which was left in this case, wrongly in our view, to the arbitrators alone.[204]

504. — Similarly, in 1986, the Pau Court of Appeals held in the *Sponsor A.B.* case that an arbitration clause signed by a subsidiary was binding on the parent company, despite the fact that the latter had not signed it. Two of the grounds given in the *Dow Chemical* decision were reproduced word for word (the role played by the parent company in signing, performing and terminating the contracts, and the undivided economic reality of a group of

---

[202] ICC Case No. 4131, *supra* note 197, IX Y.B. COM. ARB. 131, 136 (1984).

[203] CA Paris, Oct. 21, 1983, Isover-Saint-Gobain v. Dow Chemical France, 1984 REV. ARB. 98, and A. Chapelle's note.

[204] But see, on the extent of the review carried out by the court of appeals of facts establishing the existence or not of an arbitration agreement, Cass. 1e civ., Jan. 6, 1987, *Southern Pacific Properties*, *supra* note 65 and, on this issue, generally, *infra* para. 1605.

companies). The Court prefaced these grounds with the phrase "it is accepted in law that," thus suggesting the existence of a genuine principle to that effect.[205] In so doing, the Court undoubtedly went too far. There can be no general rule that an arbitration agreement signed by one or more group companies can be extended to other companies within the group. The extension of each arbitration agreement instead depends on the intentions of the parties, which can only be deduced from all the circumstances of the case.[206]

505. — We are therefore of the view that the Paris Court of Appeals wrongly based the extension of the arbitration agreement in a number of cases, concerning groups of companies in particular, on the purported principle of the arbitration agreement's "own effectiveness and validity." The Paris Court of Appeals held in 1988 that:

> an arbitration clause in an international contract has a validity and an effectiveness of its own, such that the clause must be extended to parties directly implicated in the performance of the contract and in any disputes arising out of the contract, provided that it has been established that their respective situations and activities raise the presumption that they were aware of the existence and scope of the arbitration clause, and irrespective of the fact that they did not sign the contract containing the arbitration agreement.[207]

The same reasoning was used in the *Orri* decision of January 11, 1990. The Paris Court of Appeals allowed the extension of an arbitration agreement signed by a company to the individual controlling the company, relying on the existence of "a group of companies . . . bound together as an economic unit under the same authority" and on the fact that a fraud had been committed by having a straw man sign the contract.[208] An action against this decision was rejected by the *Cour de cassation*, which carefully based its own decision on the "subterfuge, amounting to fraud, aimed at concealing the identity of the actual contractor."[209] This decision illustrates the *Cour de cassation*'s reservations—in our view entirely justified—with respect to the "principle of the arbitration agreement's own effectiveness and validity,"[210] but is also consistent with the earlier decisions on groups of companies founded on the parties' expressed or implied intentions.

506. — In the *Kis France v. Société Générale* case, the Paris Court of Appeals provided a further example of the circumstances in which an arbitration agreement can be extended

---

[205] CA Pau, Nov. 26, 1986, Sponsor A.B. v. Lestrade, 1988 REV. ARB. 153, and A. Chapelle's note.

[206] On this issue, see also Jarrosson, *supra* note 188.

[207] CA Paris, Nov. 30, 1988, Korsnas Marma v. Durand-Auzias, 1989 REV. ARB. 691, and P.-Y. Tschanz' note.

[208] CA Paris, Jan. 11, 1990, Orri v. Société des Lubrifiants Elf Aquitaine, 1992 REV. ARB. 95, and D. Cohen's note; 118 J.D.I. 141 (1991), and B. Audit's note; 1992 RTD COM. 596, and observations by J.-C. Dubarry and E. Loquin.

[209] Cass. 1e civ., June 11, 1991, *Orri, supra* note 190.

[210] *See supra* para. 440.

within a group. In that case, a group's parent company and its co-contractor had signed a "framework contract" in which the parent company declared that it was acting on behalf of its subsidiaries. Pursuant to that contract, the subsidiaries themselves dealt with the co-contractor and its subsidiaries in specific contracts referring to the framework contract. The arbitral tribunal[211] held that the co-contractor and its subsidiaries could commence arbitration proceedings based on the framework contract against both the parent company and its subsidiaries. The grounds for this decision lay primarily in the contracts between the parties. An action to set the award aside was brought before the Paris Court of Appeals, which agreed with the approach taken by the arbitral tribunal:

> the arbitrators examined the agreements between the parties and held that the parties' mutual obligations were inexorably linked and that the parent companies played a dominant role vis-à-vis their subsidiaries, which were bound to abide by the former's commercial and financial decisions.

The arbitral tribunal had deduced from those facts that:

> there was a common intention of the parties to consider Kis France and Kis Photo liable for any amounts owed by them or their subsidiary Kis Corporation. Hence, the arbitrators deemed that the claim filed by Société Générale and its subsidiaries was admissible.[212]

Again, it was not so much the existence of a group, but instead the intention of the parties—revealed in this case by the interrelated contracts—which justified the extension of the arbitration agreement.[213]

The same principles apply to arbitration agreements entered into by states and state-owned entities.

---

[211] ICC Partial award of Jan. 27, 1989, unpublished.

[212] CA Paris, Oct. 31, 1989, Kis France v. Société Générale, 1992 REV. ARB. 90, and D. Cohen and L. Aynès' notes, respectively at 74 and 70; for excerpts translated into English, see XVI Y.B. COM. ARB. 145, 147 (1991).

[213] Compare the approach of the English courts, founded in part on the proper administration of justice, in Roussel-Uclaf v. G.D. Searle & Co. Ltd., [1978] 1 Lloyd's Rep. 225; IV Y.B. COM. ARB. 317 (1979) (High Ct., Chancery Div. 1977). It was held that a 100% subsidiary of a U.S. company, which was defending a claim of breach of an exclusivity contract signed by its parent, was entitled to the benefit of an arbitration clause contained in the exclusive license contract signed by the parent. See also, for the additional justification that the arbitral tribunal "should be able to address all the commercial and legal aspects of the dispute." CA Paris, Dec. 7, 1994, V 2000, supra note 125. On the question of the scope of an arbitration agreement in a group of contracts, see infra paras. 518 et seq.

2° States and State-Owned Entities

507. — The determination of which state or state-owned parties[214] are bound by an arbitration agreement can be problematic in state contracts.[215] For example, the question may arise as to whether a state is bound by an arbitration agreement signed by a public entity that it owns. It may even be the case that several states contract using another entity as a vehicle, a scenario which will often give rise to difficulties in identifying which entities should be party to the arbitration.

By analogy with groups of companies, some authors have presented these issues under the heading "groups of states," thereby covering not only "the vertical relationship" between a state and the entities it owns, but also "the horizontal relationship" between several states.[216] However, the terminology "groups of states" is only relevant in the rare situations where several states are involved. The question of whether a state is bound by an arbitration agreement signed by one of the entities it owns is the same, irrespective of whether that entity is owned by one or several states. We shall therefore confine our discussion to the two difficult issues: first, whether and under which conditions a state can be bound by an arbitration agreement concluded by one of the entities it owns; and, second, whether a state-owned entity can be bound by an arbitration agreement which only the state itself has actually signed.

In both cases, difficulties will only arise if the entity concerned has its own legal personality. In the absence of its own legal personality, the entity is assimilated with the state, so that a clause signed by the state will bind the entity and vice-versa.[217] This is illustrated by the *Westland* case.[218] A dispute arose between the English company Westland

---

[214] "State, State enterprises or State entities," to use the terminology of the resolution adopted by the Institute of International Law on September 12, 1989 at its Santiago de Compostela session (XVI Y.B. COM. ARB. 233 (1991), with an explanatory note by A.T. von Mehren; for the French text, see 1990 REV. ARB. 931, and observations by P. Fouchard). See also the references cited *supra* para. 447.

[215] On ICC practice in such circumstances, see DERAINS AND SCHWARTZ, *supra* note 113, at 94 *et seq.*

[216] Philippe Leboulanger, *Groupes d'Etat(s) et arbitrage*, 1989 REV. ARB. 415. The author concludes, however, that one cannot assimilate the rules governing groups of companies and those governing "groups of states." *See also* C. Jarrosson, note following CA Paris, June 16, 1988, *Swiss Oil, supra* note 65, at 323; XIAO-YING LI, *supra* note 179, at 126 *et seq.*; BERTHOLD GOLDMAN, COURS DE DROIT DU COMMERCE INTERNATIONAL. LES COURS DE DROIT, 1970–71, at 186.

[217] On the question of what constitutes the state in this context, see Paul Lagarde, *Une notion ambivalente: l'« émanation » de l'État nationalisant, in* DROITS ET LIBERTÉS À LA FIN DU XXᴱ SIÈCLE – INFLUENCE DES DONNÉES ÉCONOMIQUES ET TECHNOLOGIQUES – ETUDES OFFERTES À ALBERT COLLIARD 539 (1984); Pierre Mayer, *La neutralisation du pouvoir normatif de l'Etat en matière de contrats d'Etat*, 113 J.D.I. 5, 7 (1986).

[218] Interim Award in ICC Case No. 3879 (Mar. 5, 1984), by E. Bucher, chairman, P. Bellet and N. Mangård, arbitrators (E. Bucher dissenting), Westland Helicopters Ltd. v. Arab Organization for Industrialization, 112 J.D.I. 232 (1985); 1989 REV. ARB. 547, and the commentary by Philippe Leboulanger, *Groupes d'Etat(s) et arbitrage, id.* at 415; for an English translation, see 23 I.L.M. 1071 (1984); XI Y.B. COM. ARB. 127 (1986); the award, governed by the regime applicable prior to the 1987 reform of Swiss international arbitration law (see *supra* para. 162), was set aside by the Court of Justice of the Geneva Canton in November 3, 1987 (Arab Organization for Industrialization v. Westland Helicopters Ltd., *aff'd*, Swiss Fed. Trib., July 19, 1988, 1989

(continued...)

Helicopters Limited and the Arab Organization for Industrialization (AOI), which was set up in 1975 by Egypt, Saudi Arabia, the United Arab Emirates and Qatar to promote the defense industry interests of those countries. AOI signed a contract with Westland creating a joint venture—The Arab British Helicopter Company (ABH)—70% of which was owned by AOI and 30% by Westland, with a view to manufacturing and selling a particular type of helicopter designed by Westland. Westland signed a series of contracts with ABH to enable the latter to fulfil its corporate objectives. A dispute arose between the parties, and the arbitral tribunal was required to decide whether the ICC arbitration clause in the contract between AOI and Westland bound AOI alone, or whether it also bound the governments which established AOI. The arbitral tribunal examined certain elements relevant to determining whether or not AOI had its own legal personality and ultimately held that the governments were bound by the arbitration agreement, together with AOI and not in lieu of AOI. The tribunal considered the documents founding the organization and noted their similarity to the concepts of partnership recognized under French, Swiss, German, English and American law, in which the partners are jointly liable for the group's obligations. However, the tribunal simply concluded from this that:

> the legal status of such a joint inter-state enterprise ['*entreprise commune interétatique*']—to the extent that it can exist at all—cannot be relied upon in order to eliminate the liability of the States which are partners therein.[219]

In deciding that the four states were bound by the arbitration agreement, the tribunal, which noted that "Westland would not have entered into the transaction" without the "guarantees" of the states,[220] thus did not clearly distinguish the issue of separate legal personality from that of the scope of the arbitration agreement concluded by that person. It would certainly have been preferable to have begun by considering the existence of a distinct legal personality, leaving aside the issue of the scope of the clause. The existence of a separate legal personality does not depend upon the intention of the parties to the arbitration agreement, except perhaps in order to determine the point in time at which the existence of a separate legal person should be assessed. The relevant time can only be that of the signature of the arbitration agreement, as any subsequent attribution of legal personality cannot affect the rights of the party which contracted with an entity with no legal personality.[221]

---

[218](...continued)
REV. ARB. 514, and the commentary by Leboulanger, *supra* note 216, at 415; for excerpts translated into English, see 28 I.L.M. 688 (1989); XVI Y.B. COM. ARB. 174 (1991); for subsequent events, see *infra* para. 509).

[219] 112 J.D.I. 232, 240 (1985); 23 I.L.M. 1071, 1085 (1984); XI Y.B. COM. ARB. 127, 132 (1986).

[220] 112 J.D.I. 232, 241 (1985); 23 I.L.M. 1071, 1085 (1984); XI Y.B. COM. ARB. 127, 132 (1986).

[221] In the *Westland* case, after the default of the three other countries, Egypt passed a decree which provided that the AOI "was still in existence as a legal person" (112 J.D.I. 232, 233 (1985); 23 I.L.M. 1071, 1074 (1984); XI Y.B. COM. ARB. 127, 128 (1986)). This should not have had any impact on the effectiveness of the earlier
(continued...)

When deciding the action to set aside the initial award, the Swiss courts took a more direct approach to the issue of separate legal personality. They established the existence of AOI's separate personality from its by-laws and its legal, financial and procedural autonomy, particularly the fact that it was authorized to sign arbitration clauses and submission agreements. The court considered these elements to "show plainly and unequivocally the total juridical independence of that organization from the founding States."[222] This enabled the Swiss courts to go on to address the issue of the scope of the arbitration agreement.[223]

This demonstrates that it is only where the state-controlled entity has its own legal personality that difficulties can arise as to which parties are bound by the clause signed by the state or state-owned entity. We have seen that this is also the case with groups of companies, where the question of the extension of the arbitration agreement will only arise where each of the group companies is a distinct legal entity.[224] In the case of states, the scope of a clause signed by a legally independent state-owned entity has sometimes been extended to the state, and vice versa. We shall examine each of these situations in turn.

a) Extension of an Arbitration Agreement Signed by a State-Owned Entity to the State

508. — One of the most important decisions to date addressing the issue of whether an arbitration agreement signed by a legally independent state-owned entity can be extended to the state was made in the *Pyramids* case.[225] A company incorporated in Hong Kong (SPP) had signed a contract (the Supplemental Agreement) with an Egyptian state-owned entity responsible for tourism (EGOTH). This contract referred to a pre-existing framework contract (the Heads of Agreement) between the same parties and the Egyptian government, concerning the construction of two tourist centers, one of which was located near the Pyramids. Unlike the Heads of Agreement, the Supplemental Agreement contained an ICC arbitration clause with Paris as the seat, and the last page of that agreement contained the words "approved, agreed and ratified," followed by the signature of the Egyptian minister for tourism.

The Egyptian authorities subsequently canceled the project, whereupon SPP initiated arbitration proceedings against both EGOTH and the Arab Republic of Egypt. The Egyptian state contested the jurisdiction of the arbitral tribunal, principally on the grounds that it had

---

[221](...continued)
arbitration clause.

[222] Court of Justice of the Geneva Canton, Nov. 3, 1987, The Arab Organization for Industrialization v. Westland Helicopters Ltd.,and Swiss Fed. Trib., July 19, 1988, République arabe d'Egypte v. Westland Helicopters, 1989 REV. ARB. 514, 526; for an English translation, see 28 I.L.M. 688, 691 (1989).

[223] *See infra* para. 509.

[224] *See supra* para. 500.

[225] On this issue, generally, see Philippe Leboulanger, *Etat, politique et arbitrage – L'affaire du Plateau des Pyramides*, 1986 REV. ARB. 3; Bruno Oppetit, *Les Etats et l'arbitrage international: esquisse de systématisation*, 1985 REV. ARB. 493; Georges R. Delaume, *The Pyramids Stand – The Pharaohs Can Rest in Peace*, 8 ICSID REV. – FOREIGN INV. L.J. 231 (1993).

not agreed to be personally bound by the arbitration agreement. The arbitral tribunal nevertheless ruled that it had jurisdiction over the Egyptian state. The tribunal's grounds were that, although there is a principle whereby "acceptance of an arbitration clause should be clear and unequivocal," there was no ambiguity in that case as "[t]he Government, in becoming a party to that agreement, could not have reasonably doubted that it would be bound by the arbitration clause contained in it."[226]

The Egyptian government then brought an action to set the award aside, relying in particular on Article 1502 1° of the French New Code of Civil Procedure (which concerns the absence of an arbitration agreement).[227] The Paris Court of Appeals allowed the government's claim, refusing to consider that the "approval, agreement and ratification" of the arbitration clause implied an intention to become a party thereto. However, in reaching its decision, the Court stated that the words "approved, agreed and ratified" should be interpreted in the light of Egyptian legislation, which empowered the minister for tourism to approve the construction, operation and management of tourist centers and hotels, and in the light of a declaration by EGOTH and SPP that the obligations assumed by EGOTH under the Supplemental Agreement would be subject to approval by the relevant government authorities.[228] The Court's ruling was thus based on the particular facts of the case, rather than on a literal interpretation of the terminology used. When the case came before the *Cour de cassation*, it simply declared that:

> the ambiguity of the terms preceding the signature of the Minister called for an interpretation [which the *Cour de cassation* understandably considered as being within the discretion of the Court of Appeals], which the Court of Appeals gave in ruling that it only involved the intervention of a supervisory authority.[229]

Consequently, it may be that under different circumstances the same terms (especially the word "agreed") could be interpreted as indicating that a person not signing the arbitration agreement did in fact intend to be bound by that agreement. However, in a 1995 award in an ICC case involving Libya, the arbitral tribunal followed the precedent set in the *Pyramids* case. It held, in the context of a contract between a state-owned company and a foreign company, that the terms "approved and endorsed" followed by a signature given on behalf of a state did not necessarily constitute consent by the state to be bound by the obligations contained in the contract, including, in particular, the arbitration clause. The wording was

---

[226] ICC Award No. 3493 (1983), S.P.P. (Middle East) Ltd. v. Arab Republic of Egypt, rendered by G. Bernini, chairman, M. Littman and A. El Ghatit, arbitrators, 22 I.L.M. 752, ¶ 46 at 767 (1983); IX Y.B. COM. ARB. 111 (1984); for a French translation, see 1986 REV. ARB. 105, 112, and the commentary by Leboulanger, *supra* note 225.

[227] On this issue, see *infra* paras. 1608 *et seq.*

[228] CA Paris, July 12, 1984, République Arabe d'Egypte v. Southern Pacific Properties Ltd., 112 J.D.I. 129 (1985), and B. Goldman's note; 1986 REV. ARB. 75, and commentary by Leboulanger, *supra* note 225; for an English translation, see 23 I.L.M. 1048 (1984).

[229] Cass. 1e civ., Jan. 6, 1987, *Southern Pacific Properties, supra* note 65.

again construed as an authorization given by the company's supervising body.[230] Thus, to avoid any difficulty, the intention that a state be bound by an arbitration agreement signed primarily by a state-owned entity should be expressed in unequivocal terms.[231]

509. — The *Westland* case—an ICC arbitration held in Switzerland—raised similar problems. The arbitral tribunal ought, as we have seen, to have distinguished more clearly between the existence of separate legal personality and the effect on the states involved of the signing of the arbitration agreement by an entity under their control.[232] Having decided that AOI was an entity with a legal personality separate from that of the four states, the tribunal should have ruled on the issue of whether the arbitration clause in the shareholders' agreement between Westland and AOI revealed an intention on the part of the four states to be bound by the arbitration agreement. The first arbitral tribunal seemed to favor that result. It held that the provisions of the shareholders' agreement, as well as the guarantees given by the states to the British government that the companies controlled by AOI would fulfil their obligations towards the English companies involved in the project, were evidence of "Westland's desire to be protected by the States' guarantees and the latter could not help but be aware of the implications of their actions."[233]

As with the French courts in the *Pyramids* case, the Swiss courts, initially at least, were not convinced that the facts set forth in the tribunal's award were sufficient to establish an intention on the part of the four states to be bound by the arbitration agreement. In particular, the Swiss Federal Tribunal, referring to the decision of the French *Cour de cassation* in the *Pyramids* case, reiterated the principles applicable to the issue, observing that:

> [t]he strict control of a legal entity by the State, or the close relationship between that entity and the State is not sufficiently pertinent to overcome the presumption that, when the State has not signed the arbitration clause, the entity which signed it should be regarded as the sole party to the arbitration.

The Federal Tribunal also held that:

---

[230] ICC Award No. 8035 (1995), Party to an oil concession agreement v. State, 124 J.D.I. 1040 (1997), and observations by D. Hascher.

[231] For another case where it was held that the signature by a third party of a contract containing an arbitration clause did not mean that such party was bound by the arbitration clause, see ICC Award No. 6769 (1991), African company v. Eastern European company, 119 J.D.I. 1019 (1992), and observations by Y. Derains (where a subcontractor signed the main contract).

[232] *See supra* para. 507.

[233] Interim Award in ICC Case No. 3879 (Mar. 5, 1984), *Westland Helicopters, supra* note 218, 112 J.D.I. 241; 23 I.L.M. 1085; XI Y.B. COM. ARB. 132. On this case, see also Oppetit, *supra* note 225, at 507; Chapelle, *supra* note 93, at 490 *et seq.*

if the State is not a party to the instrument containing the arbitration agreement, the approval of that instrument by a Minister—i.e. a representative of the State—is not sufficient to imply the intention of the State to be a party to that instrument and to waive its immunity from suit.

It then concluded that:

by letting the AOI alone subscribe the 'Shareholders Agreement' with [Westland], the founding States (which furthermore have expressly conferred upon AOI authority to sue and to determine with its partners the means to settle disputes) have manifestly shown that they did not want to be bound by the arbitration agreement.[234]

However, in 1993, the second arbitral tribunal constituted in the case made an award against AOI primarily, but also against Egypt, Qatar and Saudi Arabia.[235] In 1994, the Swiss Federal Tribunal rejected an action to set the award aside on the grounds that:

the idea that economic interdependence can create legal ties, or that economic reality makes legal independence a relative matter, is not contrary to any fundamental legal principle. It follows that the theory of the emanation of the state whereby the state can be liable for obligations contracted by companies which are legally independent of it but entirely under its control (cf. Chapelle, *loc. cit.*, with numerous references),[236] complies with negative public policy. This conclusion applies *a fortiori* where the legally independent economic entity created by the state is not subject to national regulations which are familiar, or at least available, to its co-contractor, but instead takes the form of an international corporation, unattached to any one national legal system.[237]

The Federal Tribunal added that:

---

[234] Swiss Fed. Trib., July 19, 1988, *République arabe d'Egypte*, *supra* note 218, 1989 REV. ARB. 526 and 527; 28 I.L.M. 691 and 692.

[235] ICC Award No. 3879 (June 28, 1993), Westland Helicopters Ltd. v. Arab Organization for Industrialization, unpublished, cited in 1994 BULL. ASA 404.

[236] *Supra* note 93.

[237] Apr. 19, 1994, Les Emirats Arabes Unis v. Westland Helicopters Ltd., 1994 BULL. ASA 404, 422; 1995 BULL. ASA 186, and P. Schweizer's note; 1995 REV. SUISSE DR. INT. ET DR. EUR. 564, and P. Schweizer's note.

> it is . . . not contrary to fundamental principles of international law to recognize that contractual ties can arise in situations where that is not the intention of a party internally, if that party displays an attitude such that the other party may legitimately believe, in good faith, that such intention does exist.[238]

The Federal Tribunal's 1994 ruling goes considerably further than the French decision in the *Pyramids* case. Economic interdependence is presented as being the basis on which the arbitration agreement is extended. That basis is simply reinforced by the subjective factor consisting of the parties' legitimate expectations.

However far-reaching this terminology may appear, the mere control exercised by the state (or states in this case) over the legally independent public entity was not sufficient to justify extending the effects of the arbitration agreement signed by the state-owned entity. That control is evidence of the fact that the party exercising it has an interest in the performance of the contract concluded by its signatory. It provides the backdrop against which the true intentions of the parties, whether implied or express, can be understood. Contrary to what has been suggested by some commentators, the rules applicable to states and state-owned entities are thus no different to those applicable to groups of companies,[239] where the mere existence of a group is not sufficient for the entire group to be bound.[240] In both cases, the intention of the parties is the essential criterion determining the existence and scope of the arbitration agreement.

510. — The same principle applies to the issue of whether an arbitration agreement signed by a state can be extended to a company under its control.

b) Extension of an Arbitration Agreement Signed by a State to a State-Owned Entity

511. — The question of the extension to a state-owned company of an arbitration agreement signed by a state alone arose in ICC Case No. 4727, between the Swiss Oil Corporation, Petrogab and the Republic of Gabon. Swiss Oil, a company incorporated in the Cayman Islands, had signed an oil purchasing agreement with the Republic of Gabon containing an arbitration clause providing for dispute resolution by ICC arbitration in Paris. The Deputy General Manager of Petrogab—a company owned by the Gabonese government—had signed at the bottom of an amendment to the agreement, indicating his position in the company and adding the words "on behalf of the Republic of Gabon." When a dispute arose, Swiss Oil attempted to include Petrogab in the arbitration, arguing that Petrogab had become a party to the agreement by having one of its directors sign the

---

[238] *Id.* On the subsequent settlement of this dispute, see 5 WORLD ARB. & MED. REP. 258 (1994). On another aspect of the case, see Frédéric-Edouard Klein, *De la forclusion en matière d'arbitrage international – Réflexions sur un récent arrêt*, 1995 BULL. ASA 132.

[239] *Comp.* Leboulanger, *supra* note 216, at 420; XIAO-YING LI, *supra* note 179, ¶¶ 140 *et seq.*

[240] *See supra* paras. 500 *et seq.*

amendment. The arbitral tribunal rejected this claim. It held instead that the facts that the words "on behalf of the Republic of Gabon" accompanied the signature of Petrogab's director, and that the amendment did not refer to Petrogab as a party, demonstrated that the amendment had been entered into not in the name of Petrogab, but in the name of the Republic. The arbitral tribunal also rejected the argument that the mere fact that the contract contained a stipulation in favor of Petrogab was sufficient to make the latter a party to the arbitration agreement.[241] The Paris Court of Appeals rejected an action to set aside the award on the grounds that:

> Petrogab's intervention in the negotiations for a new oil price, following a worldwide decrease in oil prices, did not result in the common intention of Petrogab and SOC to conclude a contract between them, and in the substitution of Gabon by Petrogab. According to the uncontested parts of the award, SOC always meant to deal with Gabon and refused to sign a standard contract presented in November 1981 by Petrogab.

> The Addendum of 1982, which amended and supplemented the contract of 1979, was signed by Mr. Bangolé, Deputy General Manager of Petrogab, only in his capacity as the representative of Gabon.

> . . .

> The arbitrators correctly assessed the relations between SOC and Petrogab on the one hand, and Gabon and Petrogab on the other, and legitimately held that Petrogab was not bound by the arbitration clause contained in the contract of 15 November 1979.[242]

Once again, the decision aims to establish the parties' true intention despite the lack of clarity of the terms used.

B. – WHAT SUBJECT-MATTER IS COVERED BY THE PARTIES' CONSENT?

512. — Determining the exact scope of an arbitration agreement will often entail considering not only the parties thereto but also the subject-matter that those parties agreed to refer to arbitration. The parties to a submission agreement are under no obligation to have all aspects of their dispute resolved by arbitration, just as the parties to a contract containing an arbitration clause need not agree to submit all disputes which might arise between them

---

[241] April 3, 1987 Award by C. Reymond, chairman, B. Goldman and J.-D. Bredin, arbitrators, unpublished.

[242] CA Paris, June 16, 1988, *Swiss Oil, supra* note 65.

to arbitration. Because the basis for arbitration is the will of the parties, arbitrators can only hear disputes over issues which the parties have agreed to put before them.

In some cases, the parties specify that particular questions are not to be submitted to arbitration. More commonly, however, they provide for separate dispute resolution methods for different aspects of their relationship. For example, disputes concerning protective measures may be excluded from the arbitrators' jurisdiction and put exclusively before the courts. In ICSID arbitration, this is now the only way in which the courts have any jurisdiction. In other forms of arbitration, such clauses merely prevent the concurrent jurisdiction of arbitrators and the courts.[243] Similarly, in a series of contracts, or even in a single contract, the parties can choose to resort to various different forms of arbitration, or to submit some issues to arbitration and others to the courts.[244] In view of the delicate questions to which they often give rise in the event of a dispute, such exclusions or distinctions are not to be recommended.[245] However, they are generally permitted by law and in such cases the arbitrators, and subsequently the courts, must determine the parties' true intention.

These questions of interpretation usually arise in three situations: where it appears that the parties have not agreed to submit all disputes arising out of a particular contract to arbitration (1°); where the parties have signed several contracts so closely linked that they constitute a group of contracts (2°); and where the dispute which a party intends to submit to arbitration is not contractual in nature (3°).

1° Diversity of Disputes Arising from a Single Contract

513. — A well-drafted arbitration clause will be wide enough to embrace all disputes which could conceivably arise from the main contract between the parties.[246] That is the aim

---

[243] On this issue, generally, see *infra* paras. 1306 *et seq.*

[244] See also, on combined clauses and associated difficulties, *supra* paras. 487 *et seq.*

[245] For an unfortunate example of the drafting of an arbitration clause see, in a case arising from a French domestic arbitration, Cass. com., Mar. 5, 1980, where the fact that the arbitration clause in a company's by-laws covered only disputes "between two or more shareholders" led the court to conclude that the clause did not cover disputes also involving the company (Duparchy v. Duparchy, 1983 REV. ARB. 59, and B. Moreau's note).

[246] On the questionable view that a "dispute" or "difference" supposes the existence of a real controversy, in the absence of which the matter can be brought before the courts, see MICHAEL J. MUSTILL, STEWART C. BOYD, COMMERCIAL ARBITRATION 123 (2d ed. 1989) and the references cited therein and, even after the UNCITRAL Model Law was adopted, Supreme Court of Hong Kong, Sept. 24, 1992, Guangdong Agriculture Co. Ltd. v. Conagra Int'l Ltd., XVIII Y.B. COM. ARB. 187 (1993). The 1996 English Arbitration Act removed this "confusing and unnecessary" nuance (*see* DEPARTMENTAL ADVISORY COMMITTEE ON ARBITRATION LAW, 1996 REPORT ON THE ARBITRATION BILL ¶ 55 (Feb. 1996), *reprinted in* 13 ARB. INT'L 275, 286 (1997)). As a result, English courts can no longer refuse to grant a stay of the proceedings where there is an arbitration agreement, even where it can be said that "there is not in fact any dispute before the parties." *See, e.g.*, Halki Shipping Corp. v. Sopex Oils Ltd., [1998] 2 All E.R. 23; [1998] 1 Lloyd's Rep. 465; [1998] 1 W.L.R. 726; XXIII Y.B. COM. ARB. 802 (1998) (C.A. 1997). On the issue, see Jonathan Rawlings, *A Mandatory Stay*, 13 ARB. INT'L 421 (1997).

of the model clauses contained in the major institutional arbitration rules. The clause recommended by the UNCITRAL Rules covers "[a]ny dispute, controversy or claim arising out of or relating to this contract, or the breach, termination or invalidity thereof." Similarly, since the revision of its Arbitration Rules on January 1, 1998, the ICC's standard clause covers "all disputes arising out of or in connection with the present contract," whereas the previous standard clause referred to "any disputes arising in connection with the present contract." Most arbitral institutions now favor the broadest possible model clauses.[247] When interpreting such clauses, no distinction should be drawn between the terms "dispute" and "difference," which are used interchangeably in arbitration agreements.[248]

Where the parties elect to specify the types of dispute they intend to submit to arbitration, it is always preferable for them to do so only by way of illustration. In that way they will avoid excluding any aspect of the differences which may arise between them. Thus, having submitted "all disputes arising out of or in connection with the present contract" to arbitration, the parties sometimes add the phrase "including those disputes concerning the validity, interpretation and performance thereof." This clarification raises no particular difficulties. However, clauses of this type will often be pathological[249] where there is no general "catch-all" language and where the clause omits various types of issues liable to arise in a contractual dispute. For instance, some such clauses do not refer to disputes concerning the validity or the interpretation of the contract (a). More rarely, certain clauses cover only disputes concerning a contract's interpretation (b).

a) Omission of Disputes Concerning the Validity or Interpretation of the Contract

514. — All too frequently parties only refer "disputes concerning the interpretation and performance of the present contract" to arbitration. The parties clearly have in mind that these two aspects of the contract may give rise to litigation, but never imagine that the contract they are about to sign might, for some reason, be void or voidable or that one party may allege that to be so. Consequently, when a dispute arises, a party may attempt to delay the arbitration proceedings by claiming that the contract is in some way invalid and that the arbitrators therefore have no jurisdiction to rule on the issue. If such an argument were to

---

[247] See, for example, the model clauses of the Arbitration Institute of the Stockholm Chamber of Commerce, the Euro-Arab Chambers of Commerce, the AAA and the LCIA. For ICSID model clauses, see Emmanuel Gaillard, *Some Notes on the Drafting of ICSID Arbitration Clauses*, 3 ICSID REV. – FOREIGN INV. L.J. 136 (1988); Georges R. Delaume, *How to Draft an ICSID Arbitration Clause*, 7 ICSID REV. – FOREIGN INV. L.J. 168 (1992).

[248] See also, in English legal thinking, despite the tendency to favor a strict interpretation of arbitration clauses, MUSTILL AND BOYD, *supra* note 246, at 128. The 1996 Arbitration Act has endorsed a broad approach by defining the word "dispute" as including "any difference" (Sec. 82(1); *see also* V.V. Veeder, *La nouvelle loi anglaise sur l'arbitrage de 1996: la naissance d'un magnifique éléphant*, 1997 REV. ARB. 3, 11; RUSSELL ON ARBITRATION 62 (D. Sutton, J. Kendall, J. Gill eds., 21st ed. 1997)). On the broad interpretation of the word "dispute" by the French courts, see CA Paris, Apr. 11, 1996, OIP v. Pyramide, 1996 REV. ARB. 467, and D. Bureau's note.

[249] On pathological clauses, generally, see *supra* paras. 484 *et seq.*

prevail, it would seriously impair the conduct of the arbitration, even where the arbitrators are in fact dealing with a question of interpretation or performance, because the party making that claim will naturally argue that the validity of the contract is a preliminary issue which can only be decided by the competent courts. This can often lead to a side-debate before the arbitrators and before courts asked to rule on the issue and, later, before courts reviewing the award. Such clauses should therefore be carefully avoided.

Fortunately, however, arbitrators and courts in sophisticated jurisdictions consistently interpret such clauses as implicitly extending to disputes concerning the validity of the disputed contract. Indeed, it is not difficult to accept that such an omission was caused by carelessness rather than by the parties' deliberate intention to restrict the jurisdiction of the arbitral tribunal.[250]

515. — Similarly, where an arbitration agreement contains no reference to disputes concerning the interpretation of the contract, an arbitral tribunal expressly instructed by the parties to resolve disputes regarding the performance of the contract may hold that in order to do so it must necessarily interpret the contract, and that the parties implicitly empowered it to do so.

516. — The issue is more delicate where the parties have only expressly empowered the arbitrators to decide disputes concerning the interpretation of the contract.

b) Submission to Arbitration of Disputes Concerning only Interpretation

517. — This situation where parties omit to refer to arbitration disputes concerning validity and performance occurs much less frequently than the omission of disputes concerning the validity of the contract alone. However, parties sometimes do draft arbitration clauses covering only the interpretation of the main contract rather than its interpretation and validity. In such cases, there will generally be a presumption that the wording chosen by the parties reflects their deliberate intention to confine the arbitrators' jurisdiction to that issue. Indeed, unless there are special circumstances clarifying the situation, it is hard to imagine that the parties did not first consider, and then discard, the idea of covering in their arbitration clause disputes concerning the performance of their contract. This explains why in one case the Paris Court of Appeals held that an arbitration clause giving the arbitrators

---

[250] See, for example, in French domestic arbitration, CA Paris, Mar. 9, 1972, Lefrère René v. Les Pétroles Pursan, 1972 RTD COM. 344, and observations by M. Boitard and J.-C. Dubarry; for a clause referring to "all disputes arising during [the] performance [of the contract]," see Cass. com., Mar. 13, 1978, *Hertzian, supra* note 95; CA Paris, Mar. 10, 1995, Tardivel v. Cejibe, 1996 REV. ARB. 143, and observations by Y. Derains; 1996 RTD COM. 659, and observations by J.-C. Dubarry and E. Loquin. But see, also in French domestic arbitration, the difficulties caused by a clause that covered only "the interpretation and performance of the contract" (Trib. com. Poitiers, réf., Feb. 1, 1993, UC2 v. Poupard, 1994 REV. ARB. 564, and observations by P. Fouchard).

the task of interpreting the contract did not empower them to censure a party's breach of contract by declaring the contract terminated and awarding damages.[251]

2° Groups of Contracts

518. — The second major area where difficulties arise with the subject-matter covered by the arbitration agreement is that of groups of contracts.[252]

Where several contracts appear to be connected, but only some contain an arbitration clause, it may well be unclear whether the parties intended to refer to arbitration disputes arising out of the whole contractual scheme. This problem occurs where the contracts forming the group have the same purpose (a), as well as where the group consists of successive contracts between the same parties (b).

a) Contracts with the Same Purpose

519. — Most major international transactions involve not just one contract between two parties, but a number of contracts involving more than two parties. For example, there may be heads of agreement followed by contracts for the performance of various aspects of the project. Alternatively, there may be a contract setting up a joint-venture, accompanied by various agreements concerning the activity of the resulting corporation and its contractual relations with certain or all members of the joint venture. For present purposes, we shall leave aside the specific problems raised by the number of parties to a particular arbitration agreement[253] and the question of which parties are bound by that agreement.[254] We shall instead focus on the contracts covered by the arbitration agreement. A distinction should be drawn between three different situations.

520. — The first is where only the heads of agreement, or framework agreement, contains an arbitration clause to which the other related contracts refer. This case presents no difficulty. The parties' intention is clear: they sought to refer all disputes arising out of the whole set of contracts to arbitration, before a single arbitral tribunal constituted in accordance with the heads of agreement.

---

[251] CA Paris, Jan. 25, 1972, Quijano Aguero v. Laporte, 1973 REV. ARB. 158, and P. Fouchard's note. For another example of a clause with the same defect, see *supra* para. 486.

[252] On this issue, generally, see Cohen, *supra* note 148; Philippe Leboulanger, *Multi-Contract Arbitration*, 13 J. INT'L ARB. 43 (Dec. 1996); Bernard Hanotiau, *Complex – Multicontract-Multiparty – Arbitrations*, 14 ARB. INT'L 369 (1998).

[253] *See infra* para. 792.

[254] *See supra* paras. 498 *et seq.*

521. — The second case is where each of the contracts with the same objective contains its own arbitration clause. Even where the parties have simply reiterated the same arbitration clause in each contract, there may be a difficulty. Should a single tribunal be constituted to resolve all disputes arising from the contractual ensemble, or should there instead be a different arbitral tribunal for each contract? Once a dispute has arisen, and in the absence of an agreement between the parties on the point, the answer depends on the interpretation of the parties' intention at the outset. However, it is generally legitimate to presume that by including identical arbitration clauses in the various related contracts, the parties intended to submit the entire operation to a single arbitral tribunal.[255] In ICC arbitration, this situation is addressed by Article 4(6) of the 1998 Rules, which enables the International Court of Arbitration to consolidate arbitrations between the same parties which are in connection with the same "legal relationship."

The problem is aggravated where the arbitration clause differs from one contract to another. This occurs quite often in practice, in spite of the resulting difficulties.[256] For example, in a group of contracts which clearly had the same overall purpose, disputes arising from one of the contracts were submitted to ICC arbitration in Geneva, while disputes arising from another were referred to ICC arbitration in Paris.[257] Another example is where one contract contains an ICSID arbitration clause, and a second an ICC arbitration clause.[258] In order to avoid two or more tribunals reaching conflicting decisions, one might be tempted to conclude that the better solution would be to appoint a single arbitral tribunal, or to consolidate the two or more arbitrations. The difficulties liable to occur in the event of two parallel arbitrations are illustrated in the situation where one party refuses to fulfil its

---

[255] See, for example, the award rendered in Geneva in ICC Case No. 5989 (1989), Contractor v. Employers A & B, XV Y.B. COM. ARB. 74 (1990); 124 J.D.I. 1046 (1997), and observations by D. Hascher; see also the award made in Paris in ICC Case No. 7184 (1994), ICC BULLETIN, Vol. 8, No. 2, at 63 (1997). On the other hand, where parallel contracts are entered into by one party and a series of other parties, the claims brought by the latter between themselves cannot be considered as being covered by an arbitration clause, absent specific circumstances showing that to be the true intention of the parties. *See* Chamber of National and International Arbitration in Milan award of February 2, 1996, Pharmaceutical company v. Pharmaceutical company, XXII Y.B. COM. ARB. 191 (1997).

[256] On pathological clauses, see *supra* paras. 484 *et seq.*

[257] *See, e.g.,* Cass. 1e civ., Mar. 8, 1988, Sofidif v. O.I.A.E.T.I., 1988 Bull. Civ. I, No. 64; 1989 REV. ARB. 481, and C. Jarrosson's note, *reversing* CA Paris, Dec. 19, 1986, O.I.A.E.T.I. v. SOFIDIF, 1987 REV. ARB. 359, and the commentary by Emmanuel Gaillard, *L'affaire SOFIDIF ou les difficultés de l'arbitrage multipartite (à propos de l'arrêt rendu par la Cour d'appel de Paris le 19 décembre 1986), id.* at 275; CA Versailles, Mar. 7, 1990, O.I.A.E.T.I. v. COGEMA, 1991 REV. ARB. 326, and E. Loquin's note; for an English translation, see 5 INT'L ARB. REP. A1 (June 1990). *Comp. with* ICC Award No. 5971, Swedish company v. Two entities from former Yugoslavia, 1995 BULL. ASA 728. Compare, for a case where an ICC arbitration clause replaced a clause referring to the Franco-Swiss Chamber of Commerce after the liquidation of one of the initial parties, CA Paris, 1e Ch., Sec. C, Ferring AB v. SA Debliopharm, No. 97/18134, unpublished, which upheld the award made by Messrs. de Boisséson, chairman, Karrer and Recordon, arbitrators, on June 25, 1997.

[258] See, for example, the October 21, 1983 Award by E. Jimenez de Arechaga, president, W.D. Rogers, and D. Schmidt, arbitrators (D. Schmidt dissenting), in ICSID Case No. ARB/81/2, Klöckner Industrie-Anlagen GmbH v. United Republic of Cameroon, 111 J.D.I. 409 (1984), and observations by E. Gaillard, 114 J.D.I. 137 (1987); for an English translation, see 1 J. INT'L ARB. 145 (1984); X Y.B. COM. ARB. 71 (1985); 2 ICSID REP. 9 (1994).

obligations under one contract on the grounds that its co-contractor failed to fulfil its obligations under a second contract. In the absence of an agreement between the parties, neither the arbitral institution, nor the arbitral tribunal constituted on the basis of one or other of the arbitration clauses, will be entitled to resolve the whole dispute. Only where both arbitrations take place in a jurisdiction in which the courts are entitled to consolidate related actions, such as the Netherlands[259] or where two proceedings refer to the same arbitration rules allowing consolidation,[260] will it be possible to avoid the difficulties associated with having separate arbitral tribunals without further exploring the true intentions of the parties.[261] Otherwise, if an award were made on the basis of the arbitration clause contained in one contract, but concerned issues found in another contract, the decision of the arbitral tribunal could be challenged on the basis that the tribunal ruled, at

---

[259] Art. 1046 of the Code of Civil Procedure (Arbitration Act of December 1, 1986). On the practical application of this provision, see Jacomijn J. van Haersolte-van Hof, *Consolidation Under the English Arbitration Act 1996: A View from the Netherlands*, 13 ARB. INT'L 427 (1997).

[260] See, for example, the possibility of consolidation afforded in cases between the same parties by Article 4(6) of the 1998 ICC Rules, prior to the signature or approval by the International Court of Arbitration of the Terms of Reference. On the position under the previous ICC Rules, see the partial award in Case No. 6719 (Geneva, 1994), Syrian party v. Two Italian companies, 121 J.D.I. 1071 (1994), and observations by J.-J. Arnaldez and, on the issue generally, DERAINS AND SCHWARTZ, *supra* note 113, at 62 *et seq*. On the consent given in advance, by adopting the LCIA Rules, to allow one party to the arbitration to join one or more third parties in the proceedings with the consent of such third parties but not with the renewed consent of the other parties to the proceedings, see Article 22.1(h) of the 1998 LCIA Rules.

[261] On the consolidation of related arbitrations in comparative law, see JEAN-FRANÇOIS BOURQUE, LE RÈGLEMENT DES LITIGES MULTIPARTITES DANS L'ARBITRAGE COMMERCIAL INTERNATIONAL 508 *et seq.* (Thesis, University of Poitiers (France), 1989); ISAAK DORE, THEORY AND PRACTICE OF MULTIPARTY COMMERCIAL ARBITRATION (1990); Patrice Level, *Joinder of Proceedings, Intervention of Third Parties, and Additional Claims and Counterclaims*, ICC BULLETIN, Vol. 7, No. 2, at 36 (1996). Other than in Dutch law, consolidation is also recognized in the 1982 Hong Kong Arbitration Ordinance (*see* Sec. 6B(1)) which, after the adoption in 1996 of the UNCITRAL Model Law for international arbitration, now applies only to domestic arbitration, and in certain American states where the case law has long been founded on considerations of the proper administration of justice, and not only on the intentions of the parties. For a while, this was the position of the U.S. Court of Appeals for the Second Circuit (*see* Compania Espanola de Petroleos, S.A. v. Nereus Shipping, S.A., 527 F.2d 966 (2d Cir. 1975)). On this case law, see Gerald Aksen, *Les arbitrages multipartites aux Etats-Unis*, 1981 REV. ARB. 98; Dominique Hascher, *Consolidation of Arbitration by American Courts: Fostering or Hampering International Arbitration?*, 1 J. INT'L ARB. 127 (July 1984); William M. Barron, *Court-Ordered Consolidation of Arbitration Proceedings in the United States*, 4 J. INT'L ARB. 81 (Mar. 1987); David J. Branson and Richard E. Wallace Jr., *Court-Ordered Consolidated Arbitrations in the United States: Recent Authority Assures Parties the Choice*, 5 J. INT'L ARB. 89 (Mar. 1988); Emmanuel Gaillard, *L'arbitrage multipartite et la consolidation des procédures arbitrales connexes, in* INTERNATIONAL LAW ASSOCIATION, REPORT OF THE SIXTY-THIRD CONFERENCE – WARSAW 478 (1988). However, awards made in cases consolidated under the law of the place of arbitration without reference to the intentions of the parties may not be enforced in other jurisdictions, as Article V(1)(d) of the New York Convention requires that the arbitral tribunal be constituted in accordance with the intentions of the parties. More recently, the U.S. Court of Appeals for the Second Circuit changed position and is now against the consolidation of related arbitrations: *see* United Kingdom v. Boeing Co., 998 F.2d 68 (2d Cir. 1993); 8 INT'L ARB. REP. 3 (July 1993); *see also* North River Ins. Co. v. Philadelphia Reinsurance Corp., 856 F. Supp. 850 (S.D.N.Y. 1994). For a commentary, see Richard E. Wallace, Jr., *Consolidated Arbitration in the United States – Recent Authority Requires Consent of the Parties*, 10 J. INT'L ARB. 5 (Dec. 1993). For ICC arbitration, see the references cited *supra* para. 385.

least in part, in the absence of an arbitration agreement.[262] For the same reasons, where a contract containing a clause attributing jurisdiction to the courts is related to another contract containing an arbitration clause, there can be no extension of the arbitration clause to the first contract. Thus, an award made in 1983, in ICC Case No. 4392, rightly refused to extend the scope of an arbitration clause contained in heads of agreement to a related agreement, on the grounds that the related contract referred to general conditions of sale which included a clause attributing jurisdiction to the courts. The arbitral tribunal considered that, irrespective of any implied acceptance of the conditions by the purchaser, the buyer's intention was clearly incompatible with the extension of the arbitration agreement and had to be complied with.[263] The reverse is also true: the court with jurisdiction under the second contract would not be able to rule on the obligations arising out of the first contract without violating the arbitration clause contained in that first contract.

522. — The third situation to be considered with respect to groups of contracts with the same purpose is that where one or more of those contracts contains an arbitration clause, but others do not provide for any dispute resolution method. This raises the question of whether the arbitral tribunal constituted pursuant to one of the contracts can resolve disputes arising from the other contracts. Once again, the problem should be addressed by interpreting the parties' intentions. Provided that the circumstances reveal that the parties intended, at least implicitly, to empower the arbitral tribunal to resolve all disputes arising out of a single group of contracts, then the tribunal shall have jurisdiction to do so. The Paris Court of Appeals reached this conclusion in the case of an employment contract annexed to a protocol which had been signed during the sale of a company and which contained an arbitration clause.[264] The French *Cour de cassation* also allowed an arbitration clause to be extended from one contract to a second aimed at formalizing the existing agreement between the parties.[265] Similarly, United States courts have held that litigation regarding a construction contract aimed at facilitating the performance of a charter agreement containing an

---

[262] See the *Sofidif* case, *supra* note 257.

[263] *See supra* note 90; *see also* ICC Award No. 6829 (1992), Shipping company (Panama) v. Shipping company (Liberia), XIX Y.B. COM. ARB. 167 (1994), especially ¶¶ 5 *et seq.* at 170 *et seq.* But see, in French domestic arbitration, CA Paris, Nov. 29, 1991, *Distribution Chardonnet, supra* note 147.

[264] CA Paris, Feb. 28, 1992, Freyssinet International v. Renardet, 1992 REV. ARB. 649, 650, and observations by D. Cohen.

[265] Cass. com., Mar. 5, 1991, Pepratx v. Fichou, 1992 REV. ARB. 66, 1st decision, and L. Aynès' note; 1992 RTD COM. 591, and observations by J.-C. Dubarry and E. Loquin. *See also* Trib. com. Bobigny, Mar. 29, 1990, Sofremines v. Samin, 1992 REV. ARB. 66, and L. Aynès' note; 1992 RTD COM. 592, and observations by J.-C. Dubarry and E. Loquin; Cass. com., June 9, 1970, Sté. des Transports de Pétrole de l'est saharien TRAPES v. Mobil Producing Sahara Inc., extending the effects of an arbitration clause in a contract to a dispute concerning the commercial paper issued under that contract as a means of payment (1970 Bull. Civ. IV, No. 190). See also, in French domestic arbitration, Cass. 1e civ., May 14, 1996, Sigma Corp. v. Tecni-Ciné-Phot, 1997 REV. ARB. 535, and the commentary by Cohen, *supra* note 148.

arbitration clause should be referred to arbitration on the basis of that clause.[266] In the same way, in an award rendered on May 31, 1996, an arbitral tribunal retained its jurisdiction to rule on a group of five related contracts, three of which contained an express arbitration clause.[267]

b) Successive Contracts Between the Same Parties

523. — Parties enjoying an ongoing business relationship will often sign a succession of more or less identical contracts. On occasions, one of those contracts may contain no arbitration clause, while the other contracts in the series do provide for arbitration. Consider, for example, a relationship between a supplier and its client. The client can place orders by means of a brief telex or facsimile. But what if one of those orders does not refer to the usual arbitration clause? If the parties' prior practice leads to the presumption that they implicitly agreed that the latest contract was to contain an arbitration clause, then disputes arising from that contract can also be submitted to arbitration.

Thus, the Paris Court of Appeals held in one decision that since there was a significant and regular business relationship between the parties, and as all the parties' invoices contained an arbitration clause, it could be inferred that the parties considered that clause to form part of their usual agreements. They were therefore held to have tacitly incorporated it into an earlier disputed contract, which they had concluded solely by an exchange of telexes.[268] Arbitral case law takes the same position. For example, in a 1986 award in ICC Case No. 5117, the arbitrators allowed the extension of an arbitration clause contained in a works contract to cover disputes relating to subsequent orders or modifications made pursuant to a variation clause in the initial contract.[269]

In order for an arbitration clause to be extended in this way, it is essential to establish that a genuine prior practice exists between the parties.[270] However, where despite the prior practice of the parties a subsequent contract contains either a clause conferring jurisdiction

---

[266] *See* Mississippi Phosphates Corp. v. Unitramp Ltd., Civ. No. 5:95 CV49-Br-N (S.D. Miss. Jan. 16, 1996); 11 INT'L ARB. REP. E1 (Feb. 1996); XXII Y.B. COM. ARB. 923 (1997).

[267] See the May 31, 1996 Award made under the aegis of the Zurich Chamber of Commerce by P.A. Karrer, chairman, C. Kälin-Nauer and B.F. Meyer-Hauser, arbitrators, in Case No. 273/95, Raw material processor v. Processing group, XXIII Y.B. COM.. ARB. 128, 132 (1998).

[268] CA Paris, Mar. 18, 1983, Quemener et Fils v. Van Dijk France, 1983 REV. ARB. 491, and J. Robert's note. *See also* CA Paris, Mar. 25, 1983, Sorvia v. Weinstein International Disc Corp., 1984 REV. ARB. 363, and J. Robert's note.

[269] Mexican and French companies v. Mexican and French companies, 113 J.D.I. 1113 (1986), and observations by Y. Derains.

[270] See, for example, for a refusal to extend the arbitration clause contained in three contracts to a fourth contract of a similar nature in the absence of prior practice, ICC Award No. 7154 (1993), Algerian shipowner v. French shipyard, 121 J.D.I. 1059 (1994), and observations by Y. Derains; ICC Award No. 7375 (June 5, 1996), Ministry of Defence and Support for Armed Forces of the Islamic Republic of Iran v. Westinghouse Electric Corp., by M. Blessing, chairman, P. Bernardini and A. Movahed, arbitrators (A. Movahed dissenting), 11 INT'L ARB. REP. A1 (Dec. 1996), especially ¶¶ 61 *et seq.*

on the courts or an arbitration clause that differs from the previous clauses, the parties' later choice constitutes sufficient grounds on which to reject any suggestion that the earlier clause has been tacitly renewed.[271] Where a more recent contract concerns the same subject-matter as earlier contracts, but contains a different arbitration clause, it can usually be inferred that the parties agreed to amend the arbitration clause.[272]

3° Extra-Contractual Disputes

524. — There is nothing to prevent the referral of extra-contractual issues to arbitration.[273] There is no doubt that disputes of a tortious nature are arbitrable. The same is true of actions based on unjust enrichment and other quasi-contractual claims. Even where a claim of unlawful conduct is filed on the basis of a breach of public policy, the courts are likely to consider the dispute to be arbitrable, subject, of course, to the possibility of subsequent recourse against the award to ensure the proper application by the arbitrators of the relevant public policy rules.[274]

Where extra-contractual disputes are submitted to arbitration by means of a submission agreement, that agreement will generally be sufficiently precise to avoid any doubt as to the scope of the arbitrators' jurisdiction. By contrast, where the basis of that jurisdiction is an arbitration clause, it may be more difficult to determine the limits of the arbitrators' powers.

This question is of some importance in practice because certain legal systems are more willing than others to allow a claim based on both contractual and tortious grounds. Thus, on the merits, the law governing a disputed contract will be applied to resolve the contractual issues but will presumably also govern the issue of whether the parties can at the same time bring claims in tort, in order to obtain redress in respect of tortious conduct committed

---

[271] See, for example, CA Paris, Dec. 9, 1987, G.I.E. Acadi v. Thomson-Answare, which rejected the extension of the arbitration clause in one contract to subsequent contracts between the same parties on the grounds that the second contract expressly attributed jurisdiction to the courts (1988 REV. ARB. 573, 2d decision, and the observations made by G. Pluyette at 530). See also, for the refusal to extend an arbitration clause in an exclusive distribution contract to cover a maintenance contract entered into by the same parties "independently of the distribution contract, for occasional acts outside the scope of, and without reference to, the distribution contract," CA Paris, June 21, 1990, Compagnie Honeywell Bull S.A. v. Computacion Bull de Venezuela C.A., 1991 REV. ARB. 96, and J.-L. Delvolvé's note.

[272] See, for example, regarding the successive conclusion of two sales contracts concerning the same goods and submitting disputes to two different arbitral institutions, one in Hong Kong, one in Beijing, Supreme Court of Hong Kong, High Court, Mar. 2, 1991, Shenzhen Nan Da Industrial and Trade United Co. Ltd. v. FM International Ltd., XVIII Y.B. COM. ARB. 377 (1993); for a case where the most recent clause prevailed, see CA Aix, Oct. 9, 1997, SA Grupo Acciona v. Bellot, 1998 REV. ARB. 383, and J.-L. Delvolvé's note.

[273] On this issue, generally, see Claude Reymond, *Conflits de lois en matière de responsabilité délictuelle devant l'arbitre international*, TRAVAUX DU COMITÉ FRANÇAIS DE DROIT INTERNATIONAL PRIVÉ 1988–1989, 1989–1990, at 97 (1991).

[274] For French case law on this matter, see *infra* para. 567, and for the solutions reached in other legal systems, paras. 568 and 575 *et seq.*

during performance of the contract, for example.[275] Likewise, it is not unusual for arbitrators to encounter claims based on allegations of unjust enrichment of one of the parties in the context of the performance or non-performance of a contract. Once again, on the merits, the law governing the contract will determine the availability of an action of that kind when a contract has been entered into by the parties. Such claims often arise in nationalization disputes, which come before arbitrators as a result of arbitration clauses contained in investment contracts.

From a purely procedural standpoint, the arbitrators will have jurisdiction over claims in tort and for quasi-contract provided that the terms of the arbitration agreement are wide enough for it to be to established that the parties intended such claims to be resolved through arbitration. That will be the case, for instance, where the clause refers to all disputes arising "during the performance of the present contract" or "in connection with the present contract."[276]

SUBSECTION 2
VALIDITY OF THE PARTIES' CONSENT

525. — It is uncommon for a party to seek to have an arbitration agreement declared ineffective on the basis of a defect (such as duress, misrepresentation or mistake) vitiating that party's consent to arbitration. In ICC Case No. 4381, which was decided in 1986, an allegation of duress was raised.[277] Misrepresentation was alleged in ICC Case No. 3327, decided in 1981.[278] However, in both these cases the allegations were found to be unsubstantiated. On the other hand, there have been several cases where one of the

---

[275] See, for example, in English law, the well-known *Re Polemis and Furness, Withy & Co.* case, [1921] 3 K.B. 560 (C.A. 1921); Section 6(1) of the 1996 English Arbitration Act specifies that the dispute referred to arbitration may be contractual or not; in Canadian law, the January 16, 1992 decision of the Court of Appeals of Alberta, Kaverit Steel and Crane Ltd. v. Kone Corp. (87 D.L.R. 4th 129; XIX Y.B. COM. ARB. 643 (1994), especially ¶ 12 at 647) and, on the fact that a non-contractual claim may be "commercial" within the meaning of the New York Convention, see Ontario Court of Justice, October 1, 1992, Canada Packers Inc. v. Terra Nova Tankers Inc. (XXII Y.B. COM. ARB. 669 (1997)); in the United States, Difwind Farms Ltd. v. Ventilatoren Stork Hengelo BV, No. CV 88-5038 MRP (C.D. Cal. Jan. 23, 1989); XV Y.B. COM. ARB. 611 (1990).

[276] *See, e.g.,* ICC Award No. 5779 (1988), quoted in 115 J.D.I. 1206 (1988), and observations by G. Aguilar Alvarez; the Sept. 25, 1983 Jurisdictional Decision in *Amco, supra* para. 480 and note 76. *Comp. with* ICC Award No. 5477 (1988), Italian company v. U.S. company, 115 J.D.I. 1204 (1988), and observations by G. Aguilar Alvarez. In French case law, see Cass. com., June 21, 1965, Supra-Penn v. Swan Finch Oil Corp., 1966 REV. CRIT. DIP 477, and E. Mezger's note; CA Paris, Dec. 11, 1981, Bureau de recherches géologiques et minières v. Patino International N.V., Dalloz, Jur. 387 (1982), and the opinion of the advocate general J.-C. Lecante.

[277] *Supra* note 152.

[278] French company v. African state, 109 J.D.I. 971 (1982), and observations by Y. Derains.

contracting parties has alleged that it was mistaken as to the neutrality or suitability of the chosen arbitrators or arbitral institution.[279]

526. — Where a party challenges the validity of its consent to arbitration on the grounds that it was in some way vitiated, the first question to arise is procedural: should the allegedly vitiated consent be examined, initially at least, by the arbitrators or by the courts? The answer is that, under the "competence-competence" principle, the matter must initially be decided by the arbitrators. Otherwise, a mere allegation of defective consent, probably leading to factual inquiries going beyond a *prima facie* examination, would suffice to delay the constitution of the arbitral tribunal. That is precisely what the "competence-competence" rule seeks to avoid.[280] The Paris *Tribunal de grande instance*, confronted with an allegation of mistake as to the nature of an arbitration institution, therefore rightly decided that:

> the consideration of claims based on the existence of a flaw in a party's consent to the choice of an arbitration institution, which, in accordance with the parties' common intention, is responsible for organizing the arbitral proceedings and participating in the constitution of the arbitral tribunal, forms part of the examination of the validity of the arbitration agreement; consequently, those claims are to be examined by the arbitral tribunal to which the dispute is submitted.[281]

The Paris Court of Appeals confirmed that aspect of the ruling, declaring that:

> since the task [of the arbitrators] is governed by the principle of the autonomy of the arbitration agreement, the arbitrator must exercise his entire jurisdiction over all aspects of the dispute before him, subject to any subsequent action to set his award aside.[282]

That is not to say that the arbitral tribunal will have the last word on the matter, as the existence of a valid arbitration agreement will be reviewed, in fact and law, by the courts in the course of any enforcement procedure or action to set aside.[283]

527. — The second issue raised by allegations of vitiated consent to international arbitration concerns the rules to be applied to such claims, first by the arbitrators, and then

---

[279] On the qualities required of the arbitrators, see *infra* paras. 1019 *et seq.*

[280] *See infra* para. 650.

[281] TGI Paris, Jan. 28, 1987, République de Guinée v. Chambre arbitrale de Paris, 1987 REV. ARB. 371, 3d decision, and the commentary by Philippe Fouchard, *Les institutions permanentes d'arbitrage devant le juge étatique (A propos d'une jurisprudence récente)*, at 225.

[282] CA Paris, May 4, 1988, Chambre arbitrale de Paris v. République de Guinée, 1988 REV. ARB. 657, 2d decision, and P. Fouchard's note.

[283] *See supra* para. 473 and *infra* para. 1605.

by the courts reviewing the award. If the choice of law method is adopted, as some authors suggest,[284] the issue will be governed by the law chosen by the parties or, in the absence of such choice, by the law with the closest connection to the arbitration agreement. As we have seen earlier, the results achieved when using the choice of law method are unpredictable in practice. It is therefore preferable for arbitrators to apply generally accepted principles, and for courts to employ the rules which they deem best suited to assess the validity of an international arbitration agreement.[285] In this area, arbitrators would have few problems identifying the relevant general principles, given that there is little divergence among legal systems as to the invalidating effect on a party's consent of misrepresentation, mistake or duress.[286] Admittedly, however, this means that the distinction between the choice of law and substantive rules methods is of less significance in this context.

In practice, arbitral tribunals and courts called upon to resolve these issues have rarely needed to resort to a particular law to reach their decisions.[287] In fact, some awards have held that these issues should be examined in the light of

> the common intention of the parties, as evidenced by the circumstances surrounding the creation, performance and the termination of the parties' contractual relations, also having regard to the usages of international commerce.[288]

528. — Arbitrators and the courts have applied those principles in cases where the issues of duress (§ 1), misrepresentation (§ 2) and mistake (§ 3) have arisen in connection with the entry into the arbitration agreement.

§ 1. – Duress

529. — Allegations of duress in connection with the entry into an arbitration agreement have never found favor with arbitrators in the factual circumstances in which they have been

---

[284] *See* DE BOISSÉSON, *supra* note 6, at 500.

[285] *See supra* paras. 435 *et seq.*

[286] See, for example, in common law countries, ANTHONY G. GUEST, ANSON'S LAW OF CONTRACT ("Misrepresentation," at 209, and "Mistake," at 252) (6th ed. 1984); E. ALLAN FARNSWORTH, CONTRACTS §§ 4.9 *et seq.* (1990); on the arbitration agreement, specifically, in English law prior to the 1996 Arbitration Act, see MUSTILL AND BOYD, *supra* note 246, at 113.

[287] On French law's rejection of the choice of law method in the context of arbitration agreements, see *supra* para. 437. In the United States, see, for example, Technetronics, Inc. v. Leybold-Geaeus GMBH, which restricts the court's involvement to a review of internationally recognized principles such as duress, mistake, fraud or waiver (No. Civ. A. 93-1254, 1993 WL 197028 (E.D. Pa. June 9, 1993); 8 INT'L ARB. REP. F1; XIX Y.B. COM. ARB. 843 (1994), especially ¶ 18 at 848, and the references cited therein).

[288] See the 1986 award rendered in Stockholm in ICC Case No. 4381, *supra* note 152; the 1981 award rendered in Geneva in ICC Case No. 3327, *supra* note 278.

raised.[289] In ICC Case No. 4381, a party claimed that a letter referring to an agreement containing the arbitration agreement had been "written under duress." This claim was rejected by the arbitral tribunal on the grounds that the defendant's allegations "had not been proven and, in any case, would not have sufficed to deprive the said letter of its contractual value."[290] It has been pointed out that while the first part of the tribunal's statement provides sufficient justification for the decision reached, the second part is rather unusual and may be best understood as relating to the different issue of the powers of the signatory which the award goes on to discuss.[291]

§ 2. – Misrepresentation

530. — In ICC Case No. 3327, which involved an allegation of misrepresentation in the conclusion of an arbitration agreement, the arbitral tribunal again held the allegation to be unsubstantiated, as the claimant voluntarily performed the agreement and thus demonstrated the validity of its consent.[292] There is a paucity of case law on misrepresentation, but this may be due to the fact that one party's mistake, even if not the result of the other party's deliberate conduct, can provide sufficient grounds for the arbitration agreement to be held void.

§ 3. – Mistake

531. — A party's mistake as to an arbitrator or to the arbitration institution responsible for organizing the proceedings has given rise to more serious challenges of the validity of arbitration agreements.

In French domestic arbitration, a consistent and "unanimously approved"[293] line of cases has held that where a party to the arbitration agreement is unaware of links between an arbitrator and the other party, that absence of awareness constitutes mistake. Further, if that mistake is the result of deliberate concealment, it may amount to misrepresentation which

---

[289] But see, in U.S. domestic arbitration, for a refusal to enforce an award on the grounds that the arbitration clause, part of the renegotiation of a loan, was signed under economic duress, ITT Commercial Finance Corp. v. Tyler, No. 917660, 1994 WL 879497 (Mass. Super. Aug. 10, 1994); 5 WORLD ARB. & MED. REP. 285 (1994).

[290] ICC Award No. 4381, *supra* note 152, at 1105.

[291] *See* Y. Derains, observations following ICC Award No. 4381, *supra* note 152, at 1113. *Comp. with* Pierre Mayer, *L'autonomie de l'arbitre international dans l'appréciation de sa propre compétence*, *in* COLLECTED COURSES OF THE HAGUE ACADEMY OF INTERNATIONAL LAW, Vol. 217, Year 1989, Part V, at 378.

[292] ICC Award No. 3327 (1981), *supra* note 278.

[293] *See* P. Fouchard, note following Cass. 2e civ., Mar. 31, 1978, Métal Profil v. Intercraft, 1979 REV. ARB. 457, 460.

also vitiates the mistaken party's consent to the arbitration agreement, thus rendering that agreement void.[294]

Summarizing that case law, the *Cour de cassation* observed

> that independence is indispensable for the exercise of judicial power, whatever the source of that power may be and that it is one of the essential qualities of arbitrators. Where one of the parties is unaware of a fact which is liable to affect that independence, that party's consent to the arbitration agreement will be invalid, and the arbitration agreement will be void under Article 1110 of the Civil Code.[295]

Although it referred to a provision of French law, the *Cour de cassation*, and the Paris Court of Appeals before it, based their decision on grounds which are of general application. It is therefore unlikely that a French court would rule differently even if the arbitration agreement were also connected to other legal systems that differ from French law with regard to mistake as to the determining qualities of an individual entering into a contract. The validity of an arbitration agreement affected by mistake will therefore be assessed by reference to a substantive rule of international arbitration.[296]

In a case concerning an international arbitration agreement, a party sought to bring an action directly before the Paris Court of Appeals on the basis that the arbitration agreement it had signed, which provided for ICC arbitration, was void for mistake or misrepresentation. The claimant alleged that it was unaware of the fact that the vice-president of the ICC Court of Arbitration had been the other party's lawyer. This claim was rejected by the Paris Court of Appeals, which sent the case back to the arbitral tribunal. An action against this decision before the *Cour de cassation* was rejected on the grounds that the judges at first instance, exercising their discretion to examine the facts, had decided that it had "not been established that, at the time when the contracts containing the arbitration clause were signed, the vice-president of the Court of Arbitration had already acted as the defendant company's lawyer." Consequently, the claimant failed to prove the alleged mistake or misrepresentation.[297]

Although in that case the parties' consent was not considered invalid, there is no reason why an arbitration agreement could not be held void for mistake as to the neutrality of the arbitration institution or the arbitrators when the factual circumstances so require. The arbitration institution is not the arbitral tribunal and does not resolve the dispute, but the role it plays in appointing the arbitrators and in organizing the proceedings is sufficient for there to be grounds for mistake as to its neutrality. In both international and domestic arbitration,

---

[294] *See* Cass. com., July 16, 1964, Georges et Cie. v. X, 1964 REV. ARB. 125.

[295] Cass. 2e civ., Apr. 13, 1972, Consorts Ury v. S.A. des Galeries Lafayette, JCP, Ed. G., Pt. II, No. 17,189 (1972), and P. Level's note; Dalloz, Jur. 2 (1973), and J. Robert's note; 1975 REV. ARB. 235, and E. Loquin's note, *affirming* CA Paris, May 8, 1970, 1970 REV. ARB. 80, and the opinion of the advocate general Mr. Granjon.

[296] In the United States, see *supra* note 287.

[297] Cass. 2e civ., Mar. 31, 1978, *Métal Profil, supra* note 293.

this approach should apply *a fortiori* where the mistake, whether or not caused by deliberate misrepresentation, concerns the independence and neutrality of an arbitrator.[298] However, it has been held that the use of the non-existent title "ICC arbitrator" by an arbitrator who had been involved in several ICC arbitrations was not enough to give rise to a substantive mistake as to his personal qualities such as might invalidate the arbitration agreement.[299]

Where a party is unaware of ties between an arbitrator and the other party which would have entitled it to challenge the arbitrator had it been aware of such ties, that party can seek to have the arbitral award set aside or refused enforcement on that ground alone, without necessarily having to contest the validity of the arbitration agreement.[300]

SECTION III
ARBITRABILITY

532. — We have seen that for an arbitration agreement to be effective, it must be the result of the valid consent of the parties. However, it must also be lawful. This means, first, that the agreement must relate to subject-matter which is capable of being resolved by arbitration and, second, that the agreement must have been entered into by parties entitled to submit their disputes to arbitration. These considerations are referred to under the heading of arbitrability, and are founded upon the protection of the general interest. This is as opposed to the requirement of valid consent, which is intended to protect the private interests of the parties to the arbitration agreement. The term "arbitrability" is sometimes given a broader meaning, covering the existence and validity of the parties' consent to arbitration, as is the case with the terminology used by the United States Supreme Court.[301] However, that meaning is liable to generate confusion, and is not widely used in international practice.[302] This is why we will use the term arbitrability exclusively in its narrow sense, to cover disputes capable of being resolved through arbitration.

533. — The question of the arbitrability of a dispute arises in two situations. The first is where certain individuals or entities are considered unable to submit their disputes to

---

[298] *See also* CA Paris, Apr. 9, 1992, Annahold BV v. L'Oréal, 1996 REV. ARB. 483, 2d decision, and the commentary by Philippe Fouchard, *Le statut de l'arbitre dans la jurisprudence française, id.* at 325; 1993 REV. CRIT. DIP, Som. 760; for an English translation, see 7 INT'L ARB. REP. A1 (July 1992).

[299] TGI Paris, réf., Jan. 15, 1988, Société des Equipements industriels Stolz S.A. v. Ets. Letierce, 1988 REV. ARB. 316, and J. Robert's note.

[300] *See, e.g.,* CA Paris, Dec. 4, 1979, Cornu v. Comptoir Commercial André, 1981 REV. ARB. 146; CA Paris, Mar. 13, 1981, Ets. Cornet et Fils v. Union Nationale des Coopératives Agricoles (U.N.C.A.C.), 1983 REV. ARB. 83, and B. Moreau's note. On this issue, see *infra* paras. 1019 *et seq.*

[301] *See, e.g.,* First Options of Chicago, Inc. v. Kaplan, 514 U.S. 938 (1995); 10 INT'L ARB. REP. 4 (June 1995); 6 WORLD ARB. & MED. REP. 128 (1995); XXII Y.B. COM. ARB. 278 (1997).

[302] See, for example, in the context of the negotiation of the UNCITRAL Model Law, HOWARD M. HOLTZMANN AND JOSEPH E. NEUHAUS, A GUIDE TO THE UNCITRAL MODEL LAW ON INTERNATIONAL COMMERCIAL ARBITRATION – LEGISLATIVE HISTORY AND COMMENTARY 135 *et seq.* (1989).

arbitration because of their status or function. This essentially concerns states, local authorities and other public entities. This is known as "subjective arbitrability" or "arbitrability *ratione personae*." Although it has met with criticism from some authors,[303] the concept of subjective arbitrability is now widely accepted.[304]

In fact, the main benefit of bringing the issue of whether public entities can submit their disputes to arbitration within the concept of arbitrability, as opposed to that of capacity, was that the uncertainties of the choice of law method in this area were thereby avoided. Initially, in French law, a party's capacity to enter into arbitration agreements was governed by its personal law, whereas the issue of arbitrability was governed by the substantive rules of the jurisdiction in which the award was to be enforced.[305] The *Dalico* case,[306] however, applied the substantive rules method to all aspects of the existence and validity of the arbitration agreement. As a result, the characterization of the question as one of capacity or arbitrability has become irrelevant in French international arbitration law, except as a matter of terminology. This may not be the case in jurisdictions which still resort to choice of law rules to determine a party's capacity.

The second situation where the question of the arbitrability of a dispute arises is where the subject-matter of the dispute submitted to arbitration is not one which can be resolved by arbitration. This is known as "objective arbitrability," or "arbitrability *ratione materiae*."

We shall examine subjective and objective arbitrability in turn.

§ 1. – Subjective Arbitrability

534. — Subjective arbitrability, or arbitrability *ratione personae*, concerns in particular the entitlement of states and public entities to submit their disputes to arbitration.

In some legal systems, public entities remain prohibited from submitting their disputes, or at least their domestic disputes, to arbitration. For example, French domestic law has

---

[303] *See* FOUCHARD, *supra* note 4, ¶ 184.

[304] To our knowledge, the notion of subjective arbitrability was first conceived by Berthold Goldman. *See, e.g.,* J.-CL. DR. INT., Fasc. 586-3, ¶ 7 (1989). On the issue of arbitrability in general, see especially Karl-Heinz Böckstiegel, *Public Policy and Arbitrability, in* ICCA CONGRESS SERIES NO. 3, COMPARATIVE ARBITRATION PRACTICE AND PUBLIC POLICY IN ARBITRATION 177, 181 (P. Sanders ed., 1987); Pierre Lalive, *Transnational (or Truly International) Public Policy and International Arbitration, id.* at 257, 296 *et seq.* and, for the French version, 1986 REV. ARB. 329; Bernard Hanotiau, *L'arbitrabilité et la favor arbitrandum: un réexamen,* 121 J.D.I. 899 (1994); Bernard Hanotiau, *The Law Applicable to Arbitrability, in* ICCA CONGRESS SERIES NO. 9, IMPROVING THE EFFICIENCY OF ARBITRATION AGREEMENTS AND AWARDS: 40 YEARS OF APPLICATION OF THE NEW YORK CONVENTION 146 (A.J. van den Berg ed., 1999); Antoine Kirry, *Arbitrability: Current Trends in Europe,* 12 ARB. INT'L 373 (1996); JEAN-BAPTISTE RACINE, L'ARBITRAGE COMMERCIAL INTERNATIONAL ET L'ORDRE PUBLIC (1999). All of these authors except for RACINE (¶ 347) make the distinction between objective and subjective arbitrability. See also, on the use of this terminology in Swiss law, Article 177, paragraph 2 of the Private International Law Statute and *infra* para. 549.

[305] *See infra* para. 559.

[306] CA Paris, Mar. 26, 1991, *supra* note 33, *aff'd,* Cass. 1e civ., Dec. 20, 1993, *supra* note 2 and para. 437.

always been restrictive in this respect.[307] Article 1004 of the 1806 version of the French Code of Civil Procedure provided that "disputes subject to notification to the *Ministère Public* [the public prosecutor's office] cannot be referred to arbitration." Article 83 of the same Code stipulated that "actions . . . concerning . . . the state, the public domain, local authorities and public entities [must be] referred to the public prosecutor." These two provisions were interpreted by the courts as meaning that the state and local authorities could not validly enter into arbitration agreements with respect to domestic disputes. These articles were repealed with the introduction of the New Code of Civil Procedure, but in the meantime the prohibition they imposed had been reiterated by Article 2060 of the Civil Code. Article 2060 states, in particular, that "disputes concerning public collectivities and public establishments" cannot be referred to arbitration. The prohibition thus subsists in French domestic arbitration law.[308] Belgian law contained a similar rule. Initially, Article 1676, paragraph 2 of the Judicial Code provided that "anyone, except public law entities, with the power to enter into a settlement, may enter into an arbitration agreement. The state may enter into an arbitration agreement when authorized by treaty." This provision was amended by the law of May 19, 1998 so that, in the absence of a statutory provision to the contrary, public law entities may "enter into an arbitration agreement only where the purpose of that agreement is to settle disputes arising out of the preparation or performance of a contract." The same Article also stipulates that the conclusion of the arbitration agreement is subject to the same conditions as the formation of the main contract, the performance of which will be the subject-matter of any arbitration. However, the new Article 1700 of the Judicial Code specifies that "where a public law entity is party to the arbitration agreement, the arbitrators always apply the rules of law . . ." as opposed to equitable principles.[309]

In other legal systems, arbitration agreements entered into by the government or by various public bodies may be valid on condition that certain prior authorizations are obtained. This is the case with Iranian law, for instance, where the question has given rise to a considerable amount of litigation. Article 139 of the Iranian Constitution of 1979 provides that:

---

[307] This provision was introduced by the Law of July 5, 1972. On this issue, see Charles Jarrosson, *L'arbitrage en droit public*, AJDA, Jan. 20, 1997, at 16; in international arbitration, see Gérard Teboul, *Arbitrage international et personnes morales de droit public*, AJDA, Jan. 20, 1997, at 25.

[308] For examples of similar prohibitions in other legal systems, especially in jurisdictions influenced by French law, see Claude Reymond, *Souveraineté de l'Etat et participation à l'arbitrage*, 1985 REV. ARB. 517, 527.

[309] For a commentary on the May 19, 1998 reform, see Bernard Hanotiau and Guy Block, *La loi du 19 mai 1998 modifiant la législation belge relative à l'arbitrage*, 1998 BULL. ASA 528; Guy Keutgen, *La nouvelle loi sur l'arbitrage*, 1998 [BELG.] JOURN. TRIB. 761; Bernard Hanotiau and Guy Block, *The Law of 19 May 1998 Amending Belgian Arbitration Legislation*, 15 ARB. INT'L 97 (1999).

the resolution of disputes concerning state property, or the submission of such disputes to arbitration, shall in each case be subject to approval by the Council of Ministers and must be notified to Parliament. Cases in which one party to the dispute is foreign, as well as important domestic disputes, must also be approved by Parliament.[310]

This is also the case in Syrian law, which requires that state-owned companies obtain administrative approval to submit disputes to arbitration.[311]

Having signed an arbitration agreement, it is not uncommon for governments or public entities to rely on legislation of this kind in an attempt to avoid having their disputes resolved by arbitration.

535. — As a result of the various correcting devices which apply in any event,[312] the practical answer to the question of the arbitrability of state contracts should be the same regardless of whether one applies the traditional choice of law method, as some arbitral tribunals may still do, or substantive rules, the approach preferred in French law and—on this issue—in most other sources of international arbitration law. However, the choice of law method raises a number of difficulties which should be considered (A) before we examine the substantive rules method (B).

A. – THE CHOICE OF LAW METHOD

536. — Where a party to a state contract—usually the state or state-owned entity, but sometimes a private party[313]—relies on the law of the state in question to challenge the validity of the arbitration agreement, the choice of law method gives rise to a particularly delicate question from the outset. Is this a matter of the party's capacity or power to enter into an arbitration agreement, or is it a matter of arbitrability?

537. — The debate stems from the fact that this issue is often presented as "the capacity of states and state-owned entities to submit their disputes to arbitration." Article II, paragraph 1 of the European Convention of 1961, which provides that states or state-owned entities "have the right to conclude valid arbitration agreements" is entitled "Right of Legal Persons of Public Law to Resort to Arbitration." However, the official French language

---

[310] This provision was left untouched by the 1997 Iranian International Commercial Arbitration Law. *See* Mansour Jafarian and Mehrdad Rezaeian, *The New Law on International Commercial Arbitration in Iran*, 15 J. INT'L ARB. 31 (Sept. 1998); Hamid G. Gharavi, *The 1997 Iranian International Commercial Arbitration Law: The UNCITRAL Model Law à L'Iranienne*, 15 ARB. INT'L 85 (1999).

[311] Sami Sarkis, *L'autorisation d'arbitrage, obstacle au recours à l'arbitrage des entreprises du secteur public en Syrie*, 1998 REV. ARB. 97.

[312] See, for example, for reasoning based on the ground of international public policy, *infra* para. 555.

[313] See, for example, in the *Gatoil* case, *infra* para. 545.

version uses the word "capacity" (*capacité des personnes morales de droit public de se soumettre à l'arbitrage*). Some commentators consider this latter terminology to be appropriate and that a state's right to enter into an arbitration agreement is indeed an issue of capacity to be determined "by reference to its personal law."[314] The question could even be seen as related to a party's powers to enter into an arbitration agreement.[315] This is especially so where reference to arbitration is permitted but is conditional upon certain authorizations, because in such cases the main difficulty lies in the authority of the entity entering into the contract.[316]

538. — Under the choice of law method, the consequences of each of these characterizations differ. If the issue is considered to be one of capacity, the tendency will be, in civil law countries, to apply the national law of the party in question and, in common law countries, to apply the law of its domicile.[317] Generally, this will give effect to the prohibition on states or state-owned entities referring disputes to arbitration, unless the relevant provision is either interpreted as applying solely to domestic disputes[318] or disregarded as being contrary to the traditional conception of international public policy.[319] The effect of the prohibition may also be limited by the doctrine of apparent authority or on grounds of estoppel.[320] Likewise, if the issue is characterized as one of a party's powers,

---

[314] See, for example, as contrasted with the law of the contract, H. Motulsky, note following CA Paris, Apr. 10, 1957, Myrtoon Steam Ship v. Agent judiciaire du Trésor, JCP, Ed. G., Pt. II, No. 10,078 (1957), and H. Motulsky's note; 85 J.D.I. 1002 (1958), and B. Goldman's note; 1958 REV. CRIT. DIP 120, and Y. Loussouarn's note; Dalloz, Jur. 699 (1958), and observations by J. Robert; *reprinted in* HENRI MOTULSKY, ECRITS – VOL. 2 – ETUDES ET NOTES SUR L'ARBITRAGE 355 *et seq.*, especially at 367 (1974); or, as contrasted with a matter of arbitrability, FOUCHARD, *supra* note 4, ¶ 173. See also, regarding state-owned corporations and not the state itself, Mayer, *supra* note 291, ¶ 125 at 449. English-speaking authors also generally use the term "capacity;" *see, e.g.*, MUSTILL AND BOYD, *supra* note 246, at 151; REDFERN AND HUNTER, *supra* note 6, at 73.

[315] *See* DE BOISSÉSON, *supra* note 6, at 583.

[316] *See* French *Tribunal des conflits*, May 19, 1958, Myrtoon Steamship v. France, Dalloz, Jur. 699 (1958), and J. Robert's note; 1958 REV. PRAT. DR. ADM. 118. Compare, on the notion of "jurisdiction" in French public law, Georges Vedel, *Le problème de l'arbitrage entre gouvernements ou personnes de droit public et personnes de droit privé*, 1961 REV. ARB. 116, 124.

[317] This will be the case unless capacity is connected, as has sometimes been suggested, to the law applicable to the substance of the arbitration agreement (see *supra* para. 456). The same result could be achieved by characterizing the authorizations required for some arbitration agreements to be effective as conditions precedent to be fulfilled for the agreement in question to be perfected.

[318] *See infra* paras. 543, 551 and 553.

[319] *See infra* para. 553.

[320] See, for example, the November 18, 1983 *ad hoc* award by C. Reymond, president, K.-H. Böckstiegel and M. Franchimont, arbitrators, in Benteler v. Etat belge, 1989 REV. ARB. 339, and D. Hascher's note; 1984 [BELG.] JOURN. TRIB. 230; see also the commentary by Jan Paulsson, *May a state invoke its internal law to repudiate consent to international commercial arbitration? – Reflections on the Benteler v. Belgium Preliminary Award*, 2 ARB. INT'L 90 (1986).

under the traditional choice of law method the law under which the public entity is organized will apply,[321] subject to the same corrective factors.[322]

539. — However, it is questionable whether the issue should in fact be characterized as one of a party's capacity or power to enter into an arbitration agreement. Where a public entity is prohibited from entering into arbitration agreements, that prohibition cannot be explained in terms of capacity on the basis that the entity is incapable of judging where its own interests lie. In particular, it is unclear how one could reconcile such an explanation with a state's extensive powers to manage a country's interests. In international arbitration, the French *Cour de cassation* long considered that "the prohibition [formerly] imposed by Articles 83 and 1004 of the Code of Civil Procedure is not a matter of capacity within the meaning of Article 3, paragraph 3 of the Civil Code."[323] That prohibition was in fact based on public interest considerations, entirely unconnected with the rationale behind the law on capacity, which is the need to protect those unable to defend their own interests. Laws preventing states and state-owned entities from validly entering into arbitration agreements are thus true examples of the non-arbitrability of disputes, founded on public policy. That basis should not be overlooked, even by those who consider that not all aspects of the existence and validity of the arbitration agreement should be determined by reference to substantive rules.[324] The question of arbitrability should therefore be treated like any other international public policy issue: courts reviewing an arbitral award should apply the concepts of international public policy recognized in their own legal system, while arbitrators should determine themselves the requirements of truly international public policy.[325]

540. — The question is more delicate where there is a requirement for prior state authorization of the kind found in Article 139 of the 1979 Iranian Constitution.[326] Again, however, the characterization cannot be one of capacity, where capacity is defined as a party's ability to act in its own interest.[327] Neither can it be one of a party's power to enter into an arbitration agreement. This is because any claim raised contesting the validity of the

---

[321] On the law applicable to powers, under the traditional choice of law method, see *supra* para. 461.

[322] *See, e.g., infra* para. 556.

[323] Cass. 1e civ., Apr. 14, 1964, O.N.I.C. v. Capitaine du S. S. San Carlo, JCP, Ed. G., Pt. II, No. 14,406 (1965), and P. Level's note; 92 J.D.I. 646 (1965), and B. Goldman's note; 1966 REV. CRIT. DIP 68, and H. Batiffol's note; Dalloz, Jur. 637 (1964), and J. Robert's note; 1964 REV. ARB. 82; Cass. 1e civ., May 2, 1966, Trésor Public v. Galakis, JCP, Ed. G., Pt. II, No. 14,798 (1966), and P. Ligneau's note; 93 J.D.I. 648 (1966), and P. Level's note; 1967 REV. CRIT. DIP 553, and B. Goldman's note; Dalloz, Jur. 575 (1966), and J. Robert's note; ANCEL AND LEQUETTE, *supra* note 53, at 341.

[324] *See supra* paras. 435 *et seq.*

[325] *See infra* para. 1534.

[326] *See supra* para. 534.

[327] On this issue, see GAILLARD, *supra* note 4, ¶¶ 64 *et seq.*

arbitration agreement[328] will be founded upon restrictions relating not to the inability of certain state-owned entities to bind the state in general, but specifically to the ability of those entities to enter into a valid arbitration agreement. In such cases, the restrictions imposed (such as the requirement for prior authorization or ratification by Parliament) are the manifestation of hostility towards arbitration agreements and are merely a more moderate form, based on public policy considerations, of a straightforward prohibition from entering into arbitration agreements. Consequently, this is indeed a question of arbitrability. The courts will therefore resolve the issue by applying the conception of international arbitrability accepted in their jurisdiction, while arbitrators will rely on their own universal conception of the requirements of justice.[329] French law, as well as arbitral practice, shows that this is a well-defined, substantive approach, and is not, as is sometimes suggested,[330] merely another way of leaving the issue to the subjective assessment of the arbitrators.

B. – SUBSTANTIVE RULES

541. — The French courts have developed particularly important substantive rules concerning arbitrability (1°). These have been so often adopted in international conventions, in comparative law and in international arbitral practice that they now also constitute general principles of international arbitration law regularly applied by arbitrators, irrespective of the seat of the arbitration and the applicable law (2°).

1° French Law

542. — The restrictions imposed in French domestic law[331] on the arbitrability of disputes involving the government and government-owned entities have long been held inapplicable in international arbitration. This principle was first established by the Paris Court of Appeals' decision in the 1957 *Myrtoon Steamship* case.[332] The Court held that "the prohibition [preventing the government from submitting its disputes to arbitration] is confined to domestic contracts and does not apply to contracts which are international in

---

[328] We would underline that, in traditional choice of law thinking, it is the claim made by the party challenging the validity of the arbitration agreement which is to be characterized. This characterization should be made according to the law of the forum, at a point in time in the reasoning when it remains to be seen whether the law containing the restriction is applicable (*see* Bertrand Ancel, *L'objet de la qualification*, 107 J.D.I. 227 (1980)). For arbitrators, who have no forum, characterizing any concept under the law of the forum necessarily means a characterization under general principles drawn from comparative law and international arbitral practice.

[329] *See infra* para. 1534.

[330] Pierre Mayer, *La règle morale dans l'arbitrage international, in* ETUDES OFFERTES À PIERRE BELLET 379 (1991); on this issue, see *infra* para. 1535.

[331] *See supra* para. 534.

[332] CA Paris, Apr. 10, 1957, *supra* note 314.

nature." The Court also stated that "the prohibition [formerly] imposed by Article 1004 of the Code of Civil Procedure is not a matter of international public policy," no doubt implying that a French court should not refuse to apply a foreign law containing no such prohibition. The same conclusions were reached in subsequent decisions, but the courts no longer considered it necessary to discuss the nature of the prohibition nor indeed the basis for not applying it in international arbitration.[333]

543. — In the 1964 *O.N.I.C. v. San Carlo* case, the *Cour de cassation* held that the prohibition resulting from Articles 1004 and 83 of the old Code of Civil Procedure, preventing public bodies from submitting disputes to arbitration, did not apply in international arbitration. The Court referred to the specific demands of international commerce, and held that:

> the Court of Appeals was only required to consider whether this general prohibition applicable to domestic contracts should also apply to a private international law contract entered into for the purposes and in accordance with the usages of maritime commerce.

However, the *Cour de cassation* still expressed its decision in terms of choice of law rules, confirming the Court of Appeals' finding that "this was an issue governed by the law of the contract and not by the personal law of the contracting parties."[334] The Court's reference to the law of the contract is unsatisfactory in that it leads to different results in different cases. Fortunately, the *Cour de cassation* abandoned the choice of law method in its 1966 *Galakis* decision. The Court rejected the characterization of the issue as one of capacity, but reasoned solely in terms of substantive rules, confirming the Court of Appeals' decision that the prohibition did not apply "to an international contract entered into for the purposes and in accordance with the usages of maritime commerce."[335]

544. — The French governmental decree of May 12, 1981, which brought about the reform of French international arbitration law, was not intended to modify the position taken by the French courts on arbitrability. Neither, however, could it confirm the position of the courts, as a decree cannot formally repeal or amend a law. As a result, two questions remained unresolved until recently.

First, in an unfortunate decision, the *Conseil d'Etat* (the highest French administrative court which also acts as an advisory body to the Government) refused to allow an arbitration

---

[333] CA Aix, May 5, 1959, Capitaine S/S San Carlo v. Office national interprofessionnel des céréales, 87 J.D.I. 1076 (1960), and observations by J.-B. Sialelli; 1959 RTD COM. 875, and observations by M. Boitard; 1961 RTD COM. 218, and observations by Y. Loussouarn; TGI Seine, June 25, 1959, *Galakis, supra* note 10; CA Paris, Feb. 21, 1961, Galakis v. Trésor Public, 90 J.D.I. 156 (1963), and observations by J.-B. Sialelli; 1961 RTD COM. 351, and observations by M. Boitard.

[334] Cass. 1e civ., Apr. 14, 1964, *O.N.I.C., supra* note 323.

[335] Cass. 1e civ., May 2, 1966, *supra* note 323.

clause to be included in a contract between Walt Disney Productions, the French government and two local authorities for the construction of a leisure park outside Paris. The grounds given by the *Conseil d'Etat* were that the contract was governed by French domestic law, despite the fact that one of the parties to the contract was a foreign corporation. Further confusion resulted from the fact that a dedicated statute was required in order to allow such a clause to be incorporated into the contract. The new statute was, however, drafted in very restrictive terms, and seemed to allow arbitration only on condition that "the subject-matter of the contract be in the national interest."[336] The *Conseil d'Etat* has taken the same position in its most recent working papers.[337]

That position may change, however, with the withdrawal by the French government of the New York Convention commercial reservation,[338] especially since the *Conseil d'Etat* is now clearly in favor of giving precedence to international conventions over domestic law.[339]

The second remaining question with respect to French law on subjective arbitrability was whether the *Galakis* case concerned only the rights of French public entities to refer their disputes to arbitration, or whether the rule also applied to foreign public entities.[340]

545. — The decision of the Paris Court of Appeals in the 1991 *Gatoil* case dispelled all remaining doubt on both questions. The case involved an action to set aside an award made in Paris in an arbitration between an Iranian government-owned company, NIOC, and a privately-owned Panamanian company, Gatoil. Gatoil claimed that under Article 139 of the

---

[336] Law No. 86-972 of August 19, 1986, J.O., Aug. 22, 1986, p. 10,190, Article 9 of which provides that "notwithstanding Article 2060 of the Civil Code, the State, local authorities and public establishments are entitled, in contracts which they conclude with foreign companies for the purpose of carrying out transactions in the national interest, to enter into arbitration agreements with a view to resolving, definitively if appropriate, disputes connected with the application and interpretation of such contracts". This provision is pathological in that it does not include disputes concerning the validity of contracts, an omission sometimes made by contracting parties (*see supra* para. 514). For a commentary, see Matthieu de Boisséson, *Interrogations et doutes sur une évolution législative: l'article 9 de la loi du 19 août 1986*, 1987 REV. ARB. 3. The Belgian law of May 19, 1998 is pathological in the same way on the same issue. *See supra* para. 534.

[337] CONSEIL D'ETAT, SECTION DU RAPPORT ET DES ÉTUDES, RÉGLER AUTREMENT LES CONFLITS: CONCILIATION, TRANSACTION, ARBITRAGE EN MATIÈRE ADMINISTRATIVE, Title III, *L'arbitrage*, at 83 *et seq.* (adopted by the General Assembly of the *Conseil d'Etat* on February 4, 1993, published by La documentation française (1993)).

[338] *See* Philippe Fouchard, *La levée par la France de sa réserve de commercialité pour l'application de la Convention de New York*, 1990 REV. ARB. 571. *See supra* para. 262.

[339] Conseil d'Etat, Oct. 20, 1989, Nicolo, 1989 Lebon 190; Conseil d'Etat, Sept. 24, 1990, Boisdet, 1990 Lebon 250.

[340] *See* E. Loquin, note following CA Paris, Jan. 20, 1987, *Bomar Oil, supra* note 158, 114 J.D.I. 963 *et seq.* (1987). According to the author of the note, the rule in the *Galakis* case (Cass. 1e civ., May 2, 1966, *supra* note 323) can only apply to the French state, as the French legal system cannot intervene in the organization of another legal system. He also doubts whether the usages of international trade, which are sometimes considered to be the basis of the *Galakis* rule, could so clearly contradict the principle of state sovereignty (*see* Mayer, *supra* note 217). This argument is unconvincing as each state is capable of addressing the consequences, in its own legal system, of contracts seeking to restrict the scope of international agreements freely entered into by another state.

1979 Iranian Constitution[341] it was not bound by an arbitration agreement concluded with NIOC in 1980. Gatoil argued that under Iranian law, which governed the parties' "capacity and power to submit disputes to arbitration,"[342] the arbitration agreement was void as the requisite parliamentary authorizations had not been obtained. This argument was rejected by the Paris Court of Appeals on the grounds that:

> international public policy . . . [prohibited] NIOC from availing itself of restrictive dispositions in its national law to withdraw a posteriori from the arbitration to which the parties agreed; . . . similarly, neither can Gatoil base its objections to the capacity and powers[343] of NIOC upon the dispositions of Iranian law since international public policy is not concerned by conditions set in this domain in the internal legal order.[344]

The *Gatoil* decision thus confirms that, as far as French courts are concerned, the *Galakis* decision is still good law, that it is general in scope and that it applies to all public entities, French or foreign. This was confirmed by the Paris Court of Appeals in its 1994 decision in a case arising from a construction contract between the Tunisian Ministry of Industry and the French company, Bec Frères. The Paris Court of Appeals held that:

> the prohibition excluding governments from referring their disputes to arbitration is confined to domestic contracts. Consequently, the prohibition is not a matter of international public policy. In order for an arbitration agreement in a contract to be valid, it must simply be established that the contract is international and that it was concluded for the purposes and in accordance with the usages of international commerce.[345]

Further confirmation is provided by the *KFTCIC* decision of the Paris Court of Appeals dated June 13, 1996.[346]

546. — As with the *Galakis* decision, the *Gatoil* and *Bec Frères* decisions did not address the issue of whether the substantive rule which they endorse is specific to French law, or whether it instead reflects the incorporation into French law of a general principle of

---

[341] *See supra* para. 534.

[342] On the issue of characterization, see *supra* para. 540.

[343] On the terminology used, see *supra* para. 540.

[344] CA Paris, Dec. 17, 1991, Gatoil v. National Iranian Oil Co., 1993 REV. ARB. 281, and H. Synvet's note; for an English translation, see 7 INT'L ARB. REP. B1, B3 (July 1992).

[345] CA Paris, Feb. 24, 1994, Ministère tunisien de l'équipement v. Bec Frères, 1995 REV. ARB. 275, and Y. Gaudemet's note; for an English translation, see XXII Y.B. COM. ARB. 682 (1997).

[346] CA Paris, June 13, 1996, KFTCIC v. Icori Estero, 1997 REV. ARB. 251, and E. Gaillard's note; 1997 RTD COM. 236, and observations by J.-C. Dubarry and E. Loquin; for an English translation, see 11 INT'L ARB. REP. D1 (July 1996).

international arbitration. The fact remains that the rule prohibiting a state—and, *a fortiori*, its co-contractors—from relying on the provisions of that state's national law to challenge the validity of an arbitration agreement into which they freely entered is now so widely accepted that, in our view, it undoubtedly constitutes a general principle of international arbitration.

2° General Principles of International Arbitration

547. — The rule that states and state-owned entities cannot rely on restrictive provisions of their own law to challenge the validity of an arbitration agreement into which they unreservedly entered is now firmly established. It is found in international conventions (a), in comparative law (b), in international arbitral case law (c) and in non-binding texts expressing the consensus of the international legal community (d).

a) International Conventions

548. — Under the heading "Right of Legal Persons of Public Law to Resort to Arbitration,"[347] Article II, paragraph 1 of the 1961 European Convention provides that:

> [i]n the cases referred to in Article I, paragraph 1, of this Convention [i.e. arbitration agreements and awards within the scope of the Convention], legal persons considered by the law which is applicable to them as "legal persons of public law" have the right to conclude valid arbitration agreements.

Thus, after having paid lip service to the law under which public entities are organized, the Convention lays down a substantive rule establishing the subjective arbitrability of disputes involving such entities. However, the Convention does allow parties to make a reservation limiting the effects of this provision.[348] Only Belgium has made that reservation, confining the impact of the rule to the state. Article II of the European Convention was applied in the 1983 *Benteler* case, in which the Belgian state sought to rely on the old Article 1676, paragraph 2 of the Belgian Judicial Code[349] in challenging the validity of an arbitration agreement contained in a contract with two German companies.[350] An arbitral tribunal sitting in Switzerland rejected the Belgian claim, relying primarily on the European Convention. However, the tribunal, having discussed the French *Galakis* case and other means of achieving the same result (such as the principle that a state cannot contradict itself to the

---

[347] In the official French version, "*Capacité des personnes morales de droit public de se soumettre à l'arbitrage.*" On the terminology used, see *supra* paras. 537 *et seq.*

[348] *See* Art. II(2).

[349] *See supra* para. 534.

[350] The Law of May 19, 1998 replaced this provision by a more liberal rule. *See supra* para. 534.

detriment of others)[351] observed that international arbitration law in its then current state merely confirmed the position of the European Convention.[352]

In addition, the fact that the 1965 Washington Convention, establishing the ICSID, has been signed by 146 countries and ratified by 131 of them[353] shows that most states do consider disputes in which they are involved to be arbitrable.[354]

b) Comparative Law

549. — The position of French law, as illustrated by the *Galakis*, *Gatoil* and *Bec Frères* decisions, has been followed in many other jurisdictions.

This is the case in Greece,[355] and is largely so in both England[356] and Italy.[357] Similarly, the Tunisian courts have held that Tunisian state-owned corporations cannot rely on Tunisian law to avoid the application of arbitration agreements to which they are parties. In particular, the Tunis Tribunal of First Instance held, in a dispute arising from a public works contract between a French company and the Tunisian state, that it was entitled to appoint an arbitrator in place of the state, which had refused to do so. The Court ruled that the provisions of Tunisian law restricting the right of the government and of public entities to submit their disputes to arbitration did not apply where the contract was international. Instead, the applicable rules were "those of international commerce, and the customs and usages of the sector, which alone govern the relationship between the parties."[358] This decision is important in that the rule applied by the Court appears to be one of international

---

[351] On this principle, see *infra* para. 1462 and the references cited therein.

[352] Nov. 18, 1983 *ad hoc* award, *supra* note 320.

[353] These figures were correct as of October 27, 1998. *See supra* para. 301.

[354] On the impact of the lifting by France of the 1958 New York Convention commercial reservation, see *supra* para. 544.

[355] *See* ANGHELOS C. FOUSTOUCOS, L'ARBITRAGE INTERNE ET INTERNATIONAL EN DROIT PRIVÉ HELLÉNIQUE 259–65 (1976).

[356] Gatoil International Inc. v. National Iranian Oil Co., XVII Y.B. COM. ARB. 587 (1992), especially ¶ 10 (High Ct., Q.B. 1988), according to which, if Article 139 of the Iranian Constitution were applicable, it would be incumbent on the Iranian party to satisfy its requirements. The decision was affirmed by the Court of Appeal in 1990.

[357] *Corte di Cassazione*, May 9, 1996, Société Arabe des Engrais Phosphates et Azotes – SAEPA v. Société Industrielle d'Acide Phosphorique et d'Engrais – SIAPE, XXII Y.B. COM. ARB. 737 (1997).

[358] Oct. 17, 1987, BEC-GTAF v. Etat tunisien, 1988 REV. ARB. 732, and F. Mechri's note, *aff'd*, CA Tunis, Feb. 1, 1988, Etat tunisien v. BEC-GTAF, *id.*

origin.[359] The position taken by the Court[360] was later adopted in the Tunisian Arbitration Code of April 26, 1993.[361]

As part of the 1993 reform of its arbitration laws, the Algerian legislature likewise accepted that public entities can enter into arbitration agreements "in international commercial relations."[362] The same rule had already been adopted by the Lebanese legislature in 1983[363] and was also, albeit less explicitly, enacted in Egyptian law in 1994.[364] The Cairo Court of Appeals confirmed the application of the rule in clear terms in a decision dated March 19, 1997:

> the legislature has authorized the parties to refer disputes to arbitration even where one such party is a public law entity, and irrespective of the nature of the legal relationship with which the arbitration is concerned."[365]

In a provision dealing specifically with the "arbitrability" of disputes,[366] the Swiss Private International Law Statute of 1987 also implemented a particularly forceful substantive rule whereby

> [i]f a party to the arbitration agreement is a state or an enterprise or organisation controlled by it, it cannot rely on its own law in order to contest

---

[359] See, for a similar decision concerning Tunisian state-owned corporations, ICC Award No. 5103 (1988), *supra* note 114.

[360] But see, on the invalidation of the arbitration clause by the Tunisian administrative courts, the discussion in CA Paris, Feb. 24, 1994, *Bec Frères, supra* para. 545 and note 345.

[361] Article 7 of the new Tunisian Code on Arbitration provides that although "disputes concerning the State, State administrative agencies and local communities" are not arbitrable, there is an exception for "disputes arising in international relations of an economic, commercial or financial nature" (Law No. 93-42 of Apr. 26, 1993).

[362] Art. 442 of the Algerian Code of Civil Procedure (Art. 1 of Legislative Decree No. 93-09 of April 25, 1993); for a commentary see Mohand Issad, *Le décret législatif algérien du 25 avril 1993 relatif à l'arbitrage international*, 1993 REV. ARB. 377; Mohammed Bedjaoui and Ali Mebroukine, *Le nouveau droit de l'arbitrage international en Algérie*, 120 J.D.I. 873 (1993).

[363] Art. 809 of the Lebanese New Code of Civil Procedure (Decree-Law of Sept. 16, 1983).

[364] Art. 1 of Law No. 27 for Promulgating the Law Concerning Arbitration in Civil and Commercial Matters; *see* Bernard Fillion-Dufouleur and Philippe Leboulanger, *Le nouveau droit égyptien de l'arbitrage*, 1994 REV. ARB. 665, 671.

[365] CA Cairo, Mar. 19, 1997, Organisme des Antiquités v. G. Silver Night Company, 1997 REV. ARB. 283, and P. Leboulanger's note.

[366] On the terminology used, see *supra* paras. 539 and 548.

its capacity to be a party to an arbitration or the arbitrability of a dispute covered by the arbitration agreement.[367]

Formulating this principle as a substantive rule prevents its exclusion in cases where the private party is aware of the restrictions of the law of the public entity.[368] This is not simply an application of the rule that parties to a contract must act in good faith. It is also the election of a method resulting in the issue of subjective arbitrability no longer being considered in traditional choice of law terms, but instead depending solely on the substantive rules of the jurisdiction in which the validity of the arbitration agreement is examined by the courts. The case law of the Swiss Federal Tribunal has clearly confirmed that in Swiss law the arbitrability of the dispute is to be resolved by applying a Swiss substantive rule.[369]

The fact that, unlike the UNCITRAL Model Law that it otherwise generally followed, the German law of December 22, 1997 on arbitration adopted the same criterion for arbitrability as the Swiss legislature (the existence of claims involving an economic interest)[370] has led authors to conclude that it implicitly recognized "the general principle of arbitration law" that "a state-controlled entity may not deny the subjective arbitrability with reference to its own internal laws and negotiations."[371]

c) International Arbitral Case Law

550. — International arbitral tribunals have consistently taken the view that a state cannot rely on restrictions in its own law to avoid being subject to an arbitration agreement to which it freely consented. The reasoning behind these decisions sometimes varies as a function of differences in the facts of the cases, in the arguments raised by the parties and in the legal

---

[367] Art. 177, para. 2 of the 1987 Swiss Private International Law Statute. This approach is not entirely new in Switzerland. In the court proceedings which followed ICC Case No. 3526 (1982), State of Iran v. Cementation International Ltd., the Court of Justice of the Geneva Canton upheld, in a decision dated December 21, 1983, the February 17, 1982 award made in spite of Article 139 of the Iranian Constitution. The Court held that Article 139 did not apply to the case before it, although the arbitration agreement was governed "in all respects" by Iranian law, on the grounds that to have Article 139 apply would make the parties' choice of the ICC Rules a nonsense: "to admit the principle of the approval of recourse to arbitration by the government or legislature of a country that is party to the arbitration agreement is to allow that party to unilaterally avoid the obligations that it freely undertook" (unpublished). For an application of Article 177, paragraph 2 of the Swiss Private International Law Statute, see Swiss Fed. Trib., Oct. 13, 1992, State X v. Companies Y & Z, 1993 BULL. ASA 68; 1994 REV. SUISSE DR. INT. ET DR. EUR. 131, and observations by F. Knoepfler.

[368] *See* LALIVE, POUDRET, REYMOND, *supra* note 152, at 311. *But see* ANDREAS BUCHER, PIERRE-YVES TSCHANZ, INTERNATIONAL ARBITRATION LAW IN SWITZERLAND ¶ 87 (1988).

[369] *See* Swiss Fed. Trib., June 23, 1992, Fincantieri-Cantieri Navali Italiani S.p.A. v. M., 1993 BULL. ASA 58; 1993 REV. ARB. 691, and F. Knoepfler's note; 1994 REV. SUISSE DR. INT. ET DR. EUR. 111, and observations by F. Knoepfler; for an English translation, see XX Y.B. COM. ARB. 766 (1995). On the similar approach in French law, see *supra* para. 545.

[370] *See infra* para. 568.

[371] *See* Klaus Peter Berger, *Germany adopts the UNCITRAL Model Law*, 1 INT'L ARB. L. REV. 121, 124 (1998), and the reference made by this author to the *travaux préparatoires* of the law.

background of the arbitrators. The consistency of the resulting awards is therefore all the more remarkable.

551. — A particularly telling example can be found in the 1971 award made in ICC Case No. 1939. The arbitrator was required to rule on the validity of an arbitration agreement entered into by a state. The state argued that the arbitration agreement was invalid on the grounds that its own Code of Civil Procedure stipulated that state contracts could not be referred to arbitration. The arbitrator rejected this argument, holding in particular that:

> although a number of legal systems inspired by French law . . . prohibit the state and other public entities from entering into arbitration agreements, it is established that such prohibitions do not apply to international contracts. Thus, if this rule is one of public policy, it can only be one of domestic public policy. That is the undisputed view now accepted in French case law . . . . There is no reason to give any other interpretation to Article [X] of the Code of Civil Procedure [of the country in question].

Going beyond this interpretation of the legislative provision relied on by the government, the arbitrator added that:

> international public policy would be strongly opposed to the idea that a public entity, when dealing with a foreign party, could openly, knowingly and willingly enter into an arbitration agreement, on which its co-contractor would
>
> rely, only to claim subsequently, whether during the arbitral proceedings or on enforcement of the award, that its own undertaking was void.[372]

552. — Many other awards, in both ICC and *ad hoc* arbitration, have come to the same conclusion.

553. — For example, in the 1968 award in ICC Case No. 1526, it was held that the law of the state in question should be interpreted as recognizing the state's right to enter into arbitration agreements. However, the award also made it clear that:

> even if one were to apply to [the state] the same prohibition banning the French or Belgian states from referring their disputes to arbitration, one would have to

---

[372] Italian company v. African state-owned entity, cited by Yves Derains, *Le statut des usages du commerce international devant les juridictions arbitrales*, 1973 REV. ARB. 122, 145, and 109 J.D.I. 971, 977 (1982) (observations following ICC Award No. 3327 (1981), where the government unsuccessfully argued that the arbitration agreement was included in a contract which it characterized as a treaty subject to a ratification procedure).

make an exception, in the same way as the French *Cour de cassation* [in the *Galakis* case],[373] for arbitration agreements in international commercial contracts, such as that in the present case.[374]

Similarly, in the 1975 award in ICC Case No. 2521, the tribunal noted that the national law of the public entity in question did not expressly prohibit it from entering into arbitration agreements, and added that

> if the [public entity] were prohibited from entering into arbitration agreements, such prohibition would have to be considered as ineffective on the grounds that it would contravene international public policy, the provisions of which cannot be excluded by applying the law of [the country in question].[375]

This reasoning was reiterated word for word in the 1986 award in ICC Case No. 4381:

> [the foreign co-contractor of a state-owned corporation] acted in . . . good faith in agreeing to the arbitration clause. Consequently, [the state-owned corporation's inability to enter into arbitration agreements] must be considered

ineffective on the grounds that it contravenes international public policy, the provisions of which cannot be excluded by applying the law [of the country of the corporation in question].[376]

Likewise, the 1982 award in the *Framatome v. Atomic Energy Organization of Iran* case rejected the Iranian company's claim that Article 139 of the Iranian Constitution[377] rendered the arbitration agreement void. The tribunal held, in particular, that:

> a general principle exists which is now universally recognized in relationships between states as well as in international relations between private entities (whether the principle be considered a rule of international public policy, an international trade usage, or a principle recognized by public international law,

---

[373] *See* Cass. 1e civ., May 2, 1966, *supra* note 323.

[374] Belgian parties v. African state, 101 J.D.I. 915 (1974), and observations by Y. Derains.

[375] French construction company v. African state-owned entity, 103 J.D.I. 997 (1976), and observations by Y. Derains.

[376] *See supra* note 152.

[377] *See supra* para. 534.

international arbitration law or *lex mercatoria*), whereby the Iranian state would in any event—even if it had intended to do so, which is not the case—be prohibited from reneging on an arbitration agreement entered into by itself or, previously, by a public entity such as AEOI.[378]

The 1988 award in ICC Case No. 5103 established that the provisions of Tunisian law restricting the capacity of public entities to conclude arbitration agreements did not apply to international contracts,[379] and then added that "arbitral practice and legal authors" would be "almost unanimous" in condemning the application of Tunisian law "to deny the validity of an agreement . . . entered into with full knowledge of the facts."[380]

554. — In *ad hoc* arbitration, further illustrations are found in the 1983 award in the *Benteler v. Belgium* case[381] and the 1982 award in the *Elf Aquitaine Iran v. NIOC* case. In the latter, the arbitrator held that:

> it is a recognized principle of international law that a State is bound by an arbitration clause contained in an agreement entered into by the State itself or by a company owned by the State and cannot thereafter unilaterally set aside the access of the other party to the system envisaged by the parties in their agreement for the settlement of disputes.[382]

555. — This arbitral case law confirms that the subjective arbitrability of international disputes involving a state or state-owned entity is a principle of truly international public policy in international arbitration law, and that the position of that entity's domestic law is irrelevant.[383]

It matters little whether the legislative or constitutional provision relied upon by the public law entity in its attempt to avoid the application of the arbitration agreement comes into effect before or, as in the *Framatome* and *Elf Aquitaine Iran* cases, after the signing of

---

[378] Apr. 30, 1982 Award on Jurisdiction in ICC Case No. 3896, 111 J.D.I. 58 (1984); *see also* Bruno Oppetit, *Arbitrage et contrats d'Etat – L'arbitrage Framatome et autres c/ Atomic Energy Organization of Iran*, 111 J.D.I. 37 (1984).

[379] *See supra* para. 534.

[380] *See supra* note 114. See also the award upheld by CA Paris, Feb. 24, 1994, *Bec Frères, supra* note 345.

[381] *See* Nov. 18, 1983 award, *supra* note 320.

[382] Jan. 14, 1982 *Ad hoc* preliminary Award by B. Gomard, sole arbitrator, XI Y.B. COM. ARB 97, ¶ 24 at 104 (1986); for a French translation, see 1984 REV. ARB. 401, 418.

[383] It has been argued, on the basis of numerous international arbitral and court decisions, that the refusal of a state to participate in an arbitration where it has previously signed an arbitration agreement constitutes a denial of justice under public international law; *see* STEPHEN SCHWEBEL, INTERNATIONAL ARBITRATION: THREE SALIENT PROBLEMS 61 (1987) ("Denial of justice by governmental negation of arbitration").

the arbitration agreement. The introduction of such legislation after the signature of the arbitration agreement is merely an additional ground on which to reject it.[384]

556. — In some instances the public entity also claims that the agreement was signed by an agent without the requisite powers. In the *Framatome* case, this argument was rejected on the grounds that:

> in any event, the party challenging the tribunal's jurisdiction cannot rely on irregularities attributable to itself when contesting the validity of an arbitration agreement which, moreover, was quite clearly entered into with the full knowledge and approval of the highest levels of the Iranian government.[385]

One commentator observed that:

> for reasons similar to those encountered in relation to a party's lack of capacity,[386] a party cannot successfully rely on a failure to comply with provisions [concerning the extent and the powers of the governmental bodies on the technicalities of the implementation of such process].[387]

d) Resolution of the Institute of International Law

557. — Following its session held at Santiago di Compostela in September 1989, the Institute of International Law adopted a resolution that "a State, a state enterprise, or a state entity cannot invoke incapacity to arbitrate in order to resist arbitration to which it has agreed."[388] The Institute's resolutions reflect a certain consensus in the international community, and this resolution was intended to confirm the principle established in the French *Galakis* case and now followed in many other jurisdictions.

558. — The sources considered above show a remarkable convergence, and there is no significant difference between the position taken in French law, which on this point has often led the way, and the ideas now generally accepted in the international community.

---

[384] *See* the *Framatome* and *Elf Aquitaine Iran* awards, *supra* notes 378 and 382.

[385] *See* Apr. 30, 1982 award on jurisdiction, *supra* note 378, at 72 *et seq.*

[386] On the issue of characterization, see *supra* para. 539.

[387] Bernard Audit, *Transnational Arbitration and State Contracts: Findings and Prospects, in* HAGUE ACADEMY OF INTERNATIONAL LAW, CENTRE FOR STUDIES AND RESEARCH IN INTERNATIONAL LAW AND INTERNATIONAL RELATIONS, TRANSNATIONAL ARBITRATION AND STATE CONTRACTS (in the French version at 23 and in an English translation at 77 (1988)).

[388] Art. 5 of the Resolution on Arbitration between States, State enterprises or State Entities and Foreign Enterprises, *supra* note 214, at 238. See also the references cited *infra* para. 1446.

§ 2. – Objective Arbitrability

559. — When examining the objective arbitrability of an international dispute, a court must apply its conception of international public policy.[389] As they are not the organs of a particular legal order, arbitrators dealing with the same issue will generally apply the requirements of genuinely international public policy, subject to considerations regarding the enforceability of their award.[390] We shall therefore discuss both the position of the courts with respect to the objective arbitrability of disputes, concentrating on the example of French law[391] (A), and that of international arbitral case law (B). Once again, we shall see that there is no substantial difference between the two.

A. – French Law

560. — Article 2059 of the French Civil Code states that "[a]ll persons may submit to arbitration those rights which they are free to dispose of," and Article 2060, paragraph 1 of the same code provides that "[o]ne may not submit to arbitration questions of personal status and capacity, or those relating to divorce or to judicial separation or disputes . . . and more generally in all areas which concern public policy." These provisions were enacted by statute dated July 5, 1972, which in substance retained the provisions of Articles 1004 and 83 of the 1806 Code of Civil Procedure.

The provisions of Article 2060 concerning the non-arbitrability of "disputes concerning public collectivities and public establishments," and those of Article 2061, stating that "[a]n arbitration clause shall be void unless the law provides otherwise" were the first to be held by the courts to be inapplicable in international arbitration.[392] The other provisions of Article 2060, as well as those of Article 2059, were to share the same fate. In one of the three *Impex* cases which came before the *Cour de cassation* on May 18, 1971, the Court was called upon to review a decision of the Paris Court of Appeals[393] holding that the provisions of Articles 2059 and 2060 did not apply to international arbitration. The *Cour de cassation* took a cautious approach, confirming the decision of the Court of Appeals while declaring that "all

---

[389] *See supra* para. 452.

[390] *See supra* para. 443. For an example of arbitrability being decided under the law of the place of the arbitration, see ICC Award No. 4604 (1984), Italian company v. U.S. company, 112 J.D.I. 973 (1985), and observations by Y. Derains.

[391] For other legal systems, see especially *infra* paras. 568 and 573, and the footnotes *infra* paras. 574 *et seq.*

[392] *See supra* para. 419.

[393] CA Paris, June 20, 1969, Impex v. Malteria Adriatica, 1969 Rev. arb. 95; 1969 Rev. crit. DIP 738, and E. Mezger's note; 98 J.D.I. 118 (1971), and B. Oppetit's note.

other grounds for the decision," including the argument that the provisions of Articles 2059 and 2060 only applied to domestic arbitration,[394] were superfluous.[395]

However, in another of the three *Impex* decisions handed down the same day, the *Cour de cassation* affirmed a decision by the Colmar Court of Appeals which, having determined that the arbitration agreement was international in nature, had rightly held that:

> arbitral tribunals have exclusive jurisdiction to rule on disputes falling within the terms of the brief conferred upon them, subject to review by the courts hearing the application for an enforcement order [or to set the award aside...] if . . . a party claims that public policy has been contravened.[396]

Thus, the stage had been set for a more liberal approach to arbitrability. It can now safely be said that, although the French courts have not confirmed the reversal of the principle contained in Article 2060 regarding objective arbitrability as explicitly as they have for subjective arbitrability, they have on this issue managed to free themselves from the shackles of statutory provisions clearly unsuited to international arbitration, and to establish principles only loosely derived from those texts. We shall now examine the methodology followed (1°), and its application in practice (2°).

1° Methodology

561. — In any society, it is quite understandable that the legislature should consider that certain types of dispute should not be left to a private dispute resolution mechanism such as arbitration. Even in an international context this is a legitimate concern. For example, it is not appropriate for arbitrators to pronounce a divorce or hear a paternity dispute. The difficulty thus lies not in the principle that certain issues are non-arbitrable, but in determining the limits of that non-arbitrability, and in the rules governing that determination.

a) Scope of Objective Non-Arbitrability

562. — The scope of objective non-arbitrability largely depends on the confidence placed in arbitration as a dispute resolution mechanism. Arbitration was once viewed with a degree of suspicion, but has now become the normal method of resolving disputes, at least in the

---

[394] *See* Cass. 1e civ., May 18, 1971, Impex v. P.A.Z. Produzione Lavorazione, 99 J.D.I. 62 (1972), 3 decisions, and B. Oppetit's note; 1972 REV. CRIT. DIP 124, 2 decisions, and E. Mezger's note; 1972 REV. ARB. 2, 2 decisions, and P. Kahn's note; Dalloz, Jur. 37 (1972), 2 decisions, and D. Alexandre's note.

[395] This cautious approach has led certain authors to question the exact impact of the three *Impex* decisions. See, in particular, B. Oppetit, note following Cass. 1e civ., May 18, 1971, *Impex*, *supra* note 394.

[396] Cass. 1e civ. May 18, 1971, Impex v. P.A.Z. Produzione Lavorazione, 1972 REV. ARB. 2, 3.

international arena.[397] This accounts for the fact that French case law has significantly evolved in this area.

563. — When a legal system wishes to ensure that certain matters considered to be sensitive should be decided in accordance with the interests of society, there are three possible methods of achieving that aim.

The first simply consists in excluding from resolution by arbitration disputes which are perceived as involving questions of public policy. There are two possible justifications for this solution. First, it may be considered inappropriate for private judges to rule on certain issues, such as those arising in divorce proceedings, even where there is an international element. The second justification is of an entirely different nature and betrays more of a wariness towards arbitration: it is founded upon the idea that the chances of arbitrators reaching decisions that are socially acceptable are too uncertain to allow recourse to arbitration in sensitive areas. On this basis arbitrators might be prohibited from resolving disputes involving questions of antitrust law, for example.

The second method, which is a wholly unsatisfactory hybrid, entails excluding from resolution by arbitration all disputes where one of the parties has violated a rule of public policy. Again taking the example of antitrust law, the exclusion would apply to disputes in which the main contract containing the arbitration agreement contravenes antitrust rules. Thus, for example, disputes arising from a contract partitioning markets could not be submitted to arbitration. The aim here is to avoid the risk that arbitrators—whose seat may be located in a country which does not condemn such practices or whose background may be in legal systems which are less sensitive to such issues—attach insufficient importance to the enforcement of such rules and that the parties subsequently agree to comply with the resulting award. This view reveals a mistrust of arbitration and, above all, is hardly practicable.[398] Aside from a few extreme examples, assessing whether there has been a violation of public policy involves an often complex factual and legal analysis. It is therefore hardly appropriate to have the arbitrability of a dispute—a criterion on which jurisdiction is based—dependent upon an examination of the merits of the case. For the sake of efficiency, the criterion of non-arbitrability must be simple, and should be capable of being the subject of a *prima facie* review.

For these reasons, a third method of ensuring that the interests of society are protected in sensitive areas has developed. It consists of allowing the arbitrators to hear disputes relating to matters of public policy, whether or not the main contract containing the arbitration agreement actually contravenes public policy. The courts will then be able to review the public policy issue if an action is subsequently brought to enforce or set aside the resulting

---

[397] However, see the unflattering remarks regarding arbitration made by certain French parliamentarians in debates leading to the adoption of the Law of July 5, 1972 reported in Charles Jarrosson, *La clause compromissoire (art. 2061 C. civ.)*, 1992 REV. ARB. 259, 265.

[398] On this issue, generally, see Pierre Mayer, *Le contrat illicite*, 1984 REV. ARB. 205.

award.[399] This approach shows far more respect for international arbitration than the first two methods, as there is no basis for the presumption that arbitrators will not consider it essential to uphold the requirements of international public policy.[400] Further, although there is no doubt that international arbitrators will be more ready than the courts to apply what they conceive to be the requirements of truly international public policy, it is unreasonable to suggest that this will necessarily differ from the local conception of international public policy. Moreover, even if that proved to be the case, it would always be possible for a court to impose its conception of international public policy on hearing an action to enforce or set aside the award. The only credible argument put forward in support of the non-arbitrability from the outset of contracts that violate public policy is that there is a risk that the parties might voluntarily comply with an award in which the requirements of public policy have been disregarded. However, even that argument is ultimately unsatisfactory as none of the suggested mechanisms of control can really protect society in such circumstances. In order for the illegal aspects of an agreement to be uncovered, it must be in the interest of one of the parties to reveal them, by arguing, for instance, that it is void. Yet, the benefit for a party of denouncing the illegal aspects of an agreement remain the same whether the party chooses to plead the nullity of the arbitration agreement directly before the courts or before an arbitral tribunal, subject to subsequent review by the courts.

564. — French case law concerning the objective arbitrability of international disputes has progressed from the first method of control discussed above, passing by the second method, to the third. An exception is made for disputes concerning family law issues, which are rightly considered inappropriate for resolution by arbitration, and to which the immediate prohibition comprised in the first method still applies.[401]

565. — This process of evolution began in domestic arbitration, when the first method described above was abandoned in favor of the second. The view that all disputes "implicating public policy" were not arbitrable prevailed in 19th and early 20th century case law.[402] As late as 1954, the Paris Court of Appeals held that an arbitral tribunal could not validly hear disputes relating to the direct or indirect performance of a contract concerning taxable goods, on the grounds that "the legal or regulatory provisions relating to the taxation of goods are a matter of public policy." As a result "no dispute concerning the interpretation

---

[399] On this issue, see *infra* paras. 1645 *et seq.*

[400] See *infra* para. 1534.

[401] On the expansion of the category of arbitrable disputes in French domestic arbitration law, see Pascal Ancel, *Arbitrage – Conventions d'arbitrage – Conditions de fond – Litiges arbitrables*, J.-CL. PROC. CIV., Fasc. 1024, ¶¶ 10 *et seq.* (1986).

[402] *See, e.g.,* Cass. civ., Jan. 9, 1854, Williams v. Laporte, D.P., Pt. I, at 69 (1854); Cass. req., Nov. 7, 1865, Desmaze v. Authié-Bellerose, D.P., Pt. I, at 204 (1866); Cass. civ., July 6, 1899, Vermeersch v. Chambre des notaires de Boulogne, D.P., Pt. I, at 500 (1899); Sirey, Pt. I, at 357 (1901).

or application of such provisions [could] be resolved by arbitration as to do so would constitute a violation of Article 1004 of the Code of Civil Procedure."[403]

The second approach, whereby the non-arbitrability of a dispute could only result from the illegality of the contract in question, seems to have originated in a 1950 decision of the *Cour de cassation* in the *Tissot* case. The Court overturned a decision confirming an order enforcing an award in a dispute arising from a contract for the sale of barley, the price of which was regulated. The grounds for the Court's decision were that the Court of Appeals had omitted "to establish whether the price at which the barley was sold was higher than the rate published on September 1, 1939, which would render the sale contrary to public policy and hence non-arbitrable."[404] The Paris Court of Appeals subsequently followed this approach in two decisions dated June 15, 1956, holding that:

> although it is forbidden in principle to submit any dispute implicating public policy to arbitration, this rule does not mean, and has never meant, that every dispute relating to a transaction which is governed in some respects by regulations based on public policy should be excluded for that reason from arbitration in general; the rule is much more limited in scope and will only invalidate the arbitration agreement where the disputed transaction or contract to which that agreement relates is found to be illegal and void for having indeed contravened public policy; in short . . . , the arbitration agreement will be void not because the dispute touches on issues of public policy, but solely because public policy has been violated.[405]

Other more recent decisions confirmed this position.[406] For example, a dispute involving "the indemnification of a loss caused by a breach of a corporation's by-laws" was held to be arbitrable on the grounds that "the criterion on which the arbitrators' jurisdictional powers are determined lies in the subject-matter of the dispute, and not in the nature of the rules governing its resolution."[407] Likewise, it was held that arbitrators were able

---

[403] CA Paris, Feb. 9, 1954, Société anonyme agricole v. Torris, Dalloz, Jur. 192 (1954).

[404] Cass. com., Nov. 29, 1950, Tissot v. Neff, Dalloz, Jur. 170 (1951); Sirey, Pt. I, at 120 (1951), and J. Robert's note.

[405] Sigma v. Bezard, and Totaliment v. Comptoir agricole du Pays Bas normand, Dalloz, Jur. 587, 588 (1957), and J. Robert's note. Compare, concerning another French award, regarding exports, with Cass 2e civ., Dec. 2, 1964, S.A.R.L. Douillet et Fils v. Four et Cie., JCP, Ed. G., Pt. II, No. 14,277 bis (1965), and P.L.'s note, *affirming* CA Paris, June 14, 1962, Ets. Douillet et Cie. v. Comptoirs d'Approvisionnement Pierre Four et Cie., 1962 REV. ARB. 107.

[406] *See* CA Paris, May 22, 1980, J. C. Decaux Paris Publicité Abribus v. Avenir Publicité, and Cass. com., Oct. 21, 1981, Dauphin O.T.A. v. Decaux Paris Publicité Abribus, 1982 REV. ARB. 264, and J.-B. Blaise's note.

[407] CA Rennes, Sept. 26, 1984, Auvinet S.A. v. S.A. Sacomi et Poirier, 1986 REV. ARB. 442, and P. Ancel's note.

to hear contractual or tortious disputes involving mandatory [antitrust] rules, in so far as the arbitrators confine themselves to examining the implications of public policy on their mission, without ordering any measures of redress in respect of any violations they may find.[408]

566. — A similar development can be seen in international arbitration. The Orléans Court of Appeals, in two decisions dated May 15, 1961, adopted the first method of review and applied to the letter the principle of non-arbitrability of matters "concerning public policy." The Court held that "this dispute concerns public policy, and the arbitration agreement is void whenever the resolution of the arbitration entails interpreting and applying a rule of public policy." As a result, in one of the cases the Court held that the issue of the liability of a French grain exporter could not be submitted to arbitration in London because that issue "could only be resolved by interpreting and applying rules of French economic public policy, which governed the performance of the contract."[409] In other words, it was irrelevant that the subject-matter of the dispute was not in itself contrary to public policy; what mattered was that in order to resolve the dispute, it was necessary to interpret and apply rules of public policy.

The second method, under which the dispute is not arbitrable if the main contract breaches public policy, was subsequently applied on several occasions by the Paris Court of Appeals.[410] In the *Meulemans* case, the Court clearly stated that:

> although it is forbidden to enter into arbitration agreements concerning disputes implicating public policy, that rule does not mean that every case which in some respects depends on regulations based on public policy will be held non-arbitrable on those grounds.[411]

The *Cour de cassation* also ruled that a dispute was arbitrable where, although it concerned public policy, it did not concern the legality or illegality of the transaction in question. Thus, in the three *Impex* decisions of May 18, 1971, the Court accepted that arbitrators could resolve disputes regarding the non-performance of contracts alleged to be

---

[408] CA Paris, Jan. 20, 1989, Phocéenne de Dépôt v. Depôts pétroliers de Fos, 1989 REV. ARB. 280, 2d decision, and L. Idot's note.

[409] Jean Tardits et Cie. v. Jydsk Andels Foderstof Forretning, and Jean Tardits et Cie. v. Korn og Foderstof Kompagniet, 1961 REV. CRIT. DIP 778, and E. Mezger's note; 89 J.D.I. 140 (1962), and B. Goldman's note.

[410] *See* CA Paris, Jan. 22, 1954, Rafidex v. Société Ch. de Vries, JCP, Ed. G., Pt. II, No. 8566 (1955), and observations by H. Motulsky; Dalloz, Jur. 335 (1955), and J. Robert's note; CA Paris, Jan. 9, 1962, Varimex v. Pathé-Marconi, JCP, Ed. G., Pt. II, No. 12,478 (1962), with the opinion of the advocate general M. Desangles; 1962 REV. ARB. 12.

[411] CA Paris, Feb. 21, 1964, Meulemans et Cie. v. Robert, 92 J.D.I. 113 (1965), and B. Goldman's note; 1964 REV. ARB. 55; 1964 REV CRIT. DIP, and E. Mezger's note; *aff'd*, Cass. com., June 15, 1967, Cts. Robert v. Meulemans et Cie., 95 J.D.I. 929 (1968), and B. Goldman's note. The dispute related to an export of barley which was subject to a license that was not obtained. The importer did not seek specific performance from the arbitral tribunal, but instead sought damages for breach by the exporter of its obligation to obtain a license, which was still possible when the sale was concluded.

illegal and any resulting entitlement to damages, but that they could not determine the validity of the contracts.[412] However, in its third *Impex* decision, the Court affirmed a decision of the Colmar Court of Appeals declining jurisdiction over the issue of whether the contract was void. The Court of Appeals had sent the matter back to the arbitral tribunal, highlighting three aspects: the fact that the contract was international, the autonomy of the arbitration agreement, and the exclusive jurisdiction of the arbitral tribunal subject to the subsequent review of its award by the courts if it were later claimed that the award contravened public policy.[413]

The third *Impex* decision heralded the third decisive stage of the evolution of the French courts' attitude towards objective non-arbitrability, which began in earnest with the decision of the Paris Court of Appeals in the 1991 *Ganz* case. With the exception of a few subjects considered to be non-arbitrable as a matter of principle, the Court accepted that arbitrators were entitled, initially at least, to rule on both the non-performance and the validity of contracts contravening public policy and in general on the legality of the parties' conduct. The Court held that:

> in international arbitration, an arbitrator . . . is entitled to apply the principles and rules of [international] public policy and to grant redress in the event that those principles and rules have been disregarded, subject to review by the courts hearing an application to set aside the award . . . . as a result, except in cases where the non-arbitrability is a consequence of the subject-matter—in that it implicates international public policy and absolutely excludes the jurisdiction of the arbitrators because the arbitration agreement is void—an international arbitrator, whose functions include ensuring that international public policy is complied with, is entitled to sanction conduct which is contrary to the good faith required in relations between partners in international trade.[414]

In the *Ganz* case, the Hungarian company Ganz Mavaz had been divided into seven separate companies, and a dispute arose as to which of those seven companies succeeded to the rights of the former Ganz Mavaz with respect to its contracts with the Tunisian company SNCFT. The arbitral tribunal had determined that the seven companies were jointly bound by the contracts entered into by their predecessor, and an action to set aside was brought on the grounds that the arbitral tribunal had wrongly agreed to decide the Tunisian company's

---

[412] *See supra* note 394.

[413] Impex v. P.A.Z. Produzione Lavorazione, 99 J.D.I. 62 (1972), 1st decision, and B. Oppetit's note.

[414] CA Paris, Mar. 29, 1991, Ganz v. Société Nationale des Chemins de Fer Tunisiens (SNCFT), 1991 REV. ARB. 478, and L. Idot's note. This important decision followed a case decided by the Paris Court of Appeals on February 16, 1989, Almira Films v. Pierrel, where it was held that "the impact of public policy on the arbitrability of a dispute does not cause arbitrators to be prohibited from applying rules of an imperative nature, but only from hearing cases which can be heard by the courts alone, because of their subject-matter, and from allowing a violation of public policy" (1989 REV. ARB. 711, and L. Idot's note, *aff'd*, Cass. 1e civ., Feb. 5, 1991, 1991 REV. ARB. 625, and L. Idot's note). Compare, in French domestic arbitration, with CA Paris, Jan. 20, 1989, *Phocéenne de Dépôt*, *supra* note 408.

allegations of fraud which, it was claimed, rendered the case non-arbitrable. On the strength of the general principles discussed above, the Court of Appeals held that "the allegation of fraud or expropriation [was] not in itself such as to exclude the jurisdiction of the arbitral tribunal."[415]

The same principles, expressed in the same terms, were applied by the Paris Court of Appeals in the 1993 *Beyrard*[416] and *Labinal* cases. In the latter case, the arbitral tribunal was asked to apply EC antitrust law. The Court of Appeals allowed this, rightly stating that:

> if the character of the law of economic policy of the Community rule in competition law prohibits arbitrators from pronouncing injunctions or levying fines, they may nonetheless draw the civil conclusions of behavior judged to be illicit with respect to public order rules that can be directly applied to the relations of the parties in the action, even if these are not all drawn together to the arbitration proceedings.[417]

567. — French law thus draws a distinction between two types of situations: those where the subject-matter in itself suffices to render the dispute non-arbitrable (such as divorce and legitimation), and those (such as fraud and antitrust cases) where the review of compliance with the fundamental requirements of French public policy will only be exercised in the context of an action to set aside or to enforce the award. One author has suggested that the first situation should be referred to as non-arbitrability *per se*.[418] However, there is no longer really any other form of non-arbitrability, since all other sensitive questions have in fact become arbitrable.

This solution considerably clarifies a subject where simplification was long overdue. It entails no sacrifice of the requirement that the court review the activities of the parties and the arbitrators, and it reflects a modern conception of the role of international arbitration.

568. — The tendency to expand the category of arbitrable disputes is not specific to France, but rather reflects a widespread movement in comparative law. This trend is found in the case law of common law jurisdictions.[419] In civil law jurisdictions, objective

---

[415] 1991 REV. ARB. 478, 480.

[416] CA Paris, Jan. 12, 1993, République de Côte d'Ivoire v. Norbert Beyrard, 1994 REV. ARB. 685, and the commentary by Pierre Mayer, *La sentence contraire à l'ordre public au fond, id.* at 615.

[417] CA Paris, May 19, 1993, Labinal v. Mors, 1993 REV. ARB. 645, and C. Jarrosson's note; 120 J.D.I. 957 (1993), and L. Idot's note; 1993 RTD COM. 494, and observations by E. Loquin; for an English translation, see 8 INT'L ARB. REP. E1, E18 (July 1993). *See also* CA Paris, Oct. 14, 1993, Aplix v. Velcro, 1994 REV. ARB. 164, and C. Jarrosson's note.

[418] *See* L. Idot, note following CA Paris, Apr. 28, 1988, Matra v. Alkan, and CA Paris, Jan. 20, 1989, *Phocéenne de Dépôt, supra* note 408, 1989 REV. ARB. ¶ 10 at 299; L. Idot, note following CA Paris, Mar. 29, 1991, *Ganz, supra* note 414, ¶ 16 at 485.

[419] See especially, in the United States, the Supreme Court decisions which successively recognized the arbitrability, subject to review of the award by the courts, of questions of antitrust law (*infra* para. 575), of

(continued...)

arbitrability is often governed by a broad statutory provision. This is the case in Switzerland in particular, where the 1987 Private International Law Statute states that any dispute that involves an economic interest will be arbitrable.[420] Article 1030 of the German ZPO, in force as of January 1, 1998, is similar. It is one of the provisions of the new law on international arbitration that departs from the UNCITRAL Model Law, which is silent on this issue. Article 1030 provides that in the absence of statutory provisions to the contrary, any claim involving an economic interest will be arbitrable.[421] These general provisions will very probably be used as a model both by countries adopting new laws on arbitration and by courts in other countries. In France, for example, it is to be expected that the courts will gradually reduce the number of disputes which are presently non-arbitrable by virtue of being "closely connected with international public policy" within the meaning of the *Ganz* decision,[422] leaving only those subjects which do not involve an economic interest, as in Switzerland or Germany, where the general rule coexists with specific exclusions for areas such as residential leases and labor law.[423]

b) Establishing Non-Arbitrability

569. — The *Ganz* and *Labinal* cases[424] also simplify the procedural aspects of the arbitrability issue, as the two situations which they distinguish are treated in different ways.

Disputes concerning matters that remain non-arbitrable (such as divorce) can be brought directly before the courts, even where they are the subject of an existing arbitration agreement. In that case, the court will establish its jurisdiction by carrying out a *prima facie*

---

[419](...continued)
securities law (*infra* para. 579) and of the RICO Act (*infra* para. 579). On this issue, generally, see Joseph T. McLaughlin, *Arbitrability: Currents Trends in the United States*, 59 ALB. L. REV. 905 (1996). For a more general overview of the common law approach, see Andrew Rogers, *Arbitrability*, 10 ARB. INT'L 263 (1994). For a comparative law analysis, see Eric A. Schwartz, *The Domain of Arbitration and Issues of Arbitrability: The View from the ICC*, 9 ICSID REV.– FOREIGN INV. L.J. 17 (1994); Hanotiau, *L'arbitrabilité et la favor arbitrandum: un réexamen*, *supra* note 304. See also the decisions cited *infra* paras. 574 *et seq.*

[420] Art. 177, para. 1 of the Private International Law Statute states, in its semi-official translation, that "[a]ny dispute involving property" is arbitrable. The word "property" is a translation of the expression "*de nature patrimoniale*." It includes contractual rights and any right that can be assessed in monetary terms. This concept may also be translated as meaning "disputes which involve an economic interest."

[421] Peter Schlosser, *La nouvelle legislation allemande sur l'arbitrage*, 1998 REV. ARB. 291, 293–95; Berger, *supra* note 371, at 123–24.

[422] CA Paris, Mar. 29, 1991, *supra* para. 566 and note 414.

[423] Art. 1030 of the ZPO. For a commentary, see Schlosser, *supra* note 421, at 293; Berger, *supra* note 371, who also includes in the list of non-arbitrable disputes issues related to the granting or withdrawal of patents (at 124). In Italy, the principle set forth in Article 806 of the Code of Civil Procedure is based on the ability to settle a dispute, also with specific exclusions, including with respect to labor law, personal status and matrimonial issues. On this issue, see Luigi Fumagalli, *Mandatory Rules and International Arbitration: an Italian Perspective*, 1998 BULL. ASA 43; Bernardini, *supra* note 43. *See infra* paras. 573 *et seq.*, especially para. 579.

[424] CA Paris, Mar. 29, 1991, *Ganz*, *supra* note 414, and CA Paris, May 19, 1993, *Labinal*, *supra* note 417.

review of the arbitration agreement and determining that it is patently void.[425] Under the previous approach, where the criterion was a breach of public policy in the disputed contract, determining the arbitrability of the dispute entailed examining often complex aspects of the merits of the case.[426] By contrast, using a criterion based on the subject-matter of the dispute enables the courts to determine the arbitrability or non-arbitrability of a dispute with ease. French law has thus returned to the simple technique of "non-arbitrable blocks"[427] used in Article 2060 of the Civil Code, although these categories are now extremely limited.

In contrast, disputes which, although relating to sensitive subjects such as antitrust or securities law, are not considered non-arbitrable as a matter of principle, must initially be submitted to the arbitrators. The arbitrators can rule on the merits of the dispute and, if need be, declare a contract contravening the requirements of public policy to be void, without necessarily holding the arbitration agreement—which is autonomous—to be invalid.[428] They can also examine the validity of the arbitration agreement, even if fraud or any other breach of public policy is alleged, pursuant to the "competence-competence" principle.[429] It was therefore perfectly consistent for the Paris Court of Appeals to rule in its 1991 *Ganz* decision, that "in international arbitration, arbitrators are entitled to determine their own jurisdiction with regard to the arbitrability of the dispute in the light of international public policy."[430]

570. — We shall now describe how this method of examining the question of arbitrability applies to each particular category of dispute.

2° **Specific Applications**

571. — Although not every legal system has stated in general terms that all disputes involving an economic interest are arbitrable,[431] it is clear that matters which do not involve an economic interest are non-arbitrable (a). However, we also need to consider the arbitrability of disputes concerning inalienable rights (b), and that of disputes which raise other sensitive issues (c).

---

[425] On this issue, see *infra* para. 672.

[426] *See supra* para. 565.

[427] In French "*blocs d'incompétence*." The expression was first used by Patrice Level (*L'arbitrabilité*, 1992 REV. ARB. 213, 234).

[428] *See supra* para. 410.

[429] *See infra* para. 650 and, for the distinction between the principle of autonomy of the arbitration agreement and "competence-competence," see *supra* para. 416.

[430] CA Paris, Mar. 29, 1991, *supra* note 414, at 480.

[431] *See* Art. 177, para. 1 of the Swiss Private International Law Statute; Art. 1030 of the German ZPO and *supra* para. 568 and note 420.

a) Matters Which Do Not Involve an Economic Interest

572. — Even the most "arbitration-friendly" legal systems recognize that disputes which do not involve an economic interest cannot be submitted to arbitration. For example, the 1987 Swiss Private International Law Statute provides that any dispute which can be assessed in monetary terms (*de nature patrimoniale*) may be the subject-matter of an arbitration.[432] In its negative form, the principle also applies in French law where matters which do not involve an economic interest are undoubtedly "closely related to international public policy" and "are absolutely excluded from the jurisdiction of arbitrators" within the meaning of the *Ganz* decision. Even in international arbitration, it is inconceivable that arbitrators could, for instance, grant a divorce, hear an action contesting the validity of a marriage, an application to establish paternity, or a case relating to human rights. Article 2060 of the French Civil Code, which limits the arbitrability of disputes, refers specifically to "questions of personal status and capacity" and to "those relating to divorce or to judicial separation." Although this text does not apply in international arbitration,[433] it nevertheless reveals the importance the French legislature attaches to such questions. We believe that the only valid exception to the principle of the non-arbitrability of disputes not involving an economic interest would be a situation that is purely internal to a jurisdiction which takes a more liberal view than France of the arbitrability of a dispute.[434] This situation could only arise if the sole connection between the dispute and France were the existence of property located in France.

b) Inalienable Rights

573. — Although rights which do not involve an economic interest are considered to be inalienable, the reverse is not true, as a number of rights which do involve an economic interest are still deemed, in certain legal systems such as French domestic law, to be inalienable.[435] Some authors have therefore suggested that French law should use the inalienability criterion set forth in Article 2059 of the Civil Code to determine the boundaries of arbitrability.[436] Domestic disputes concerning commercial leases, rural

---

[432] *See supra* para. 568 and note 420.

[433] *See supra* para. 560.

[434] See the cases cited *infra* para. 573, note 443.

[435] On this issue, generally, see Ancel, *supra* note 401, ¶¶ 71 *et seq.*

[436] See, in favor of using this criterion rather than that found in Article 2060, even in international cases, Level, *supra* note 427, at 216 and 219 *et seq.*; Bruno Oppetit, *L'arbitrage en matière de brevets d'invention après la loi du 13 juillet 1978*, 1979 REV. ARB. 83, 88. *But see* BÉNÉDICTE FAUVARQUE-COSSON, LIBRE DISPONIBILITÉ DES DROITS ET CONFLITS DE LOIS ¶¶ 153 *et seq.*, especially ¶ 165 (1996).

tenancies or labor law,[437] for example, would thus be considered non-arbitrable. Similarly, despite the May 19, 1998 reform of the provisions regarding subjective arbitrability,[438] the Belgian legislature retained the notion of rights "which can give rise to a settlement" (*droit . . . sur lequel il est permis de transiger*) as a general criterion of objective arbitrability (Art. 1676, para. 1 of the Judicial Code). This is another way of referring to inalienable rights. Several recent arbitration statutes in other jurisdictions have also favored this approach.[439]

However, the notion of inalienability is in fact somewhat elusive, and it would therefore perhaps be preferable to adopt more direct criteria.[440] This is the reason why in its December 22, 1997 arbitration statute, the German legislature favored the establishment of a specific list of non-arbitrable disputes. This list includes disputes concerning residential leases in Germany, despite the fact that they fall within the general category of disputes involving an economic interest.[441] The inalienability criterion is also unsuitable in that its origins lie in the outdated idea that the law as a whole can be understood in terms of subjective rights.[442] In addition, provided that the award is carefully reviewed in subsequent court proceedings regarding its validity or enforceability, there is no reason why parties should not be allowed to submit their international disputes concerning commercial leases or even individual employment contracts to arbitration.[443] The withdrawal by France of the New York Convention commercial reservation[444] provided a Court of Appeals with an additional ground on which to validate an international arbitration agreement contained in a contract

---

[437] On these issues, see, in French domestic arbitration, Ancel, *supra* note 401, ¶¶ 80 *et seq.* On the confirmation, in French domestic arbitration law, that "parties to an employment contract may only resort to arbitration after termination of the contract," see CA Paris, June 4, 1992, Wattelet v. Geteba, 1993 REV. ARB. 449. The same solution applies in an international context; *see* Cass. soc., Feb. 16, 1999, Château Tour Saint Christophe v. Aström, No. K 96-40.643, unpublished.

[438] *See supra* para. 534.

[439] *See, e.g.,* Art. 1020(3) of the Netherlands Code of Civil Procedure (Law of December 1, 1986); Art. 1.1 of Portuguese Law No. 31/86 of August 29, 1986 on Voluntary Arbitration; Art. 1 of Spanish Law No. 36/1988 of December 5, 1988 on Arbitration; Art. 1 of Algerian Legislative Decree No. 93-09 of April 25, 1993 (amending Art. 442 of the Code of Civil Procedure); Art. 7, para. 4 of Tunisian Law No. 93-42 of April 26, 1993, which provides that "matters on which a settlement cannot be made" may not be subject to arbitration; Sec. 1 of the 1999 Swedish Arbitration Act.

[440] See the observations by Ancel, *supra* note 401, ¶ 72.

[441] Art. 1030 of the ZPO.

[442] See the observations by Ancel, *supra* note 401, ¶ 72.

[443] On the arbitrability, in French domestic law, of financial aspects of family law, see Ancel, *supra* note 401, ¶ 29. The arguments in favor of liberalizing French domestic law on this subject are developed by Pierre Catala in *Arbitrage et patrimoine familial*, 1994 REV. ARB. 279. Compare, in the United States, with the arbitrability of alimony issues in certain states: *see* Kelm v. Kelm, 623 N.E. 2d 39 (Ohio 1993); 5 WORLD ARB. & MED. REP. 85 (1994); for the arbitrability of child custody issues, see Dick v. Dick, 534 N.W.2d 185 (Mich. Ct. App. 1995); 6 WORLD ARB. & MED. REP. 131 (1995).

[444] 1990 REV. ARB. 210, and commentary by P. Fouchard, *supra* note 338.

which included employment terms.[445] The same approach can be seen in decisions recognizing the arbitrability of consumer law issues.[446]

The outdated notion of inalienable rights should thus be abandoned in international arbitration, except where the rights in question do not involve an economic interest. A list of exceptions is also acceptable as it ensures sufficient predictability.

c) Other Sensitive Areas

574. — Except as discussed above with regard to inalienable rights, the French courts now accept that arbitrators can hear disputes regarding, in particular, antitrust, intellectual property, bankruptcy and corporate law issues, despite the fact that these subjects are considered sensitive from a public policy standpoint.

575. — A great deal has been written about the arbitrability of disputes involving the application of domestic or EC antitrust law.[447] In France, the arbitrability of such disputes

---

[445] CA Grenoble, Sept. 13, 1993, Compagnie Française Technique d'Etanchéité (C.F.T.E.) v. Dechavanne, 1994 REV. ARB. 337, and M.-A. Moreau's note; for an English translation, see XX Y.B. COM. ARB. 656 (1995). *See also* Pierre Mayer, *Les clauses relatives à la compétence internationale insérées dans des contrats de travail,* in MÉLANGES DÉDIÉS À DOMINIQUE HOLLEAUX 262 (1990). *But see* Cass. soc., Feb. 16, 1999, Château Tour Saint Christophe v. Aström, No. K 96-40.643, unpublished.

[446] See the references cited *infra* para. 579.

[447] *See* COMPETITION AND ARBITRATION LAW (ICC Publication No. 480-3, 1993), especially, in French law, the reports by Berthold Goldman, *La situation en France,* at 109, and Laurence Idot, *Rapport introductif sur le contrôle judiciaire de la sentence arbitrale,* at 273. *See also* Mayer, *supra* note 398; Jean-Hubert Moitry, *Arbitrage international et droit de la concurrence,* 1989 REV. ARB. 3; Robert Kovar, *Droit communautaire de la concurrence et arbitrage, in* LE DROIT DES RELATIONS ÉCONOMIQUES INTERNATIONALES – ETUDES OFFERTES À BERTHOLD GOLDMAN 109 (1982); Yves Derains, *Arbitrage et droit de la concurrence,* SW. REV. OF INT'L ANTITRUST L., No. 14, at 39 (1982); DOMINIQUE HAHN, L'ARBITRAGE INTERNATIONAL EN SUISSE FACE AUX RÈGLES DE CONCURRENCE DE LA CEE (1983); L. Goffin, *L'arbitrage et le droit européen,* 1990 REV. DR. INT. DR. COMP. 315; Charles Jarrosson and Laurence Idot, *Arbitrage, in* ENCYCLOPÉDIE DALLOZ – RÉPERTOIRE DE DROIT COMMUNAUTAIRE, Vol. I, ¶¶ 11–21 (1992); Berthold Goldman, *L'arbitrage international et le droit de la concurrence,* 1989 BULL. ASA 260; Böckstiegel, *supra* note 304, at 190 *et seq.*; Pierre Jolidon, *A propos de l'arbitrabilité (objective) en matière de brevets d'invention et de concurrence, in* ASSOCIATION SUISSE D'ÉTUDE DE LA CONCURRENCE, ETUDES DE DROIT SUISSE ET DE DROIT COMPARÉ DE LA CONCURRENCE 117 (1986); Jacques-Michel Grossen, *Arbitrage et droit de la concurrence. Aperçu de droit comparé, in* RECUEIL DE TRAVAUX SUISSES SUR L'ARBITRAGE INTERNATIONAL 35 (1984); William J.T. Brown and Stephen D. Houck, *Arbitrating International Antitrust Disputes,* 7 J. INT'L ARB. 77 (Mar. 1990); Frank-Bernd Weigand, *Evading EC Competition Law by Resorting to Arbitration?,* 9 ARB. INT'L 249 (1993); Hanotiau, *L'arbitrabilité et la favor arbitrandum: un réexamen, supra* note 304, ¶¶ 51–75; Herman Verbist, *The Application of European Community Law in ICC Arbitrations – Presentation of Arbitral Awards, in* ICC BULLETIN, SPECIAL SUPPLEMENT, INTERNATIONAL COMMERCIAL ARBITRATION IN EUROPE 33 (1994); ASA SPECIAL SERIES NO. 6, OBJECTIVE ARBITRABILITY – ANTITRUST DISPUTES – INTELLECTUAL PROPERTY DISPUTES (1994); Jacques Werner, *Application of Competition Laws by Arbitrators – The Step Too Far,* 12 J. INT'L ARB. 21 (Mar. 1995); J.H. Dalhuissen, *The Arbitrability of Competition Issues,* 11 ARB. INT'L 151 (1995); Patrick Hetsch, *Arbitration in Community Law,* ICC BULLETIN, Vol. 6, No. 2, at 47 (1995); Hamid G. Gharavi, *The Proper Scope of*

(continued...)

was expressly recognized by the Paris Court of Appeals in the 1993 *Labinal*[448] and *Aplix*[449] cases. The arbitrability of EC antitrust law issues has also been recognized in Switzerland[450] and Italy.[451] The 1999 Swedish Arbitration Act expressly recognizes that "arbitrators may rule on the civil law effects of competition law as between the parties" (Sec. 1, para. 3). Likewise, in the United States, the courts now consistently confirm the arbitrability of disputes involving issues of American antitrust law.[452]

---

[447](...continued)

Arbitration in European Community Competition Law, 11 TUL. EUR. & CIV. L.F. 185 (1996); John Beechey, *Arbitrability of Anti-Trust/Competition Law Issues – Common Law*, 12 ARB. INT'L 179 (1996); see also the presentations by Bernard Hanotiau, *L'arbitrage et le droit européen de la concurrence, in* L'ARBITRAGE ET LE DROIT EUROPÉEN 31 (1997); Yves Derains, *L'application du droit européen par les arbitres – Analyse de la jurisprudence, id.* at 65; Peter F. Schlosser, *Arbitration and the European Public Policy, id.* at 81.

[448] CA Paris, May 19, 1993, *supra* note 417.

[449] CA Paris, Oct. 14, 1993, *supra* note 417. *See also* Cass. 2e civ., Apr. 5, 1994, S.a.r.l. Hostin Armes Blanches v. Prieur Sports, 1995 REV. ARB. 85, and C. Jarroson's note; Dalloz, Jur. 363 (1994), and Y. Chartier's note; 1994 RTD COM. 477, and observations by J.-C. Dubarry and E. Loquin, which addresses the issue only from the perspective of the binding nature of the award in question.

[450] *See* Fed. Trib. Apr. 28, 1992, V S.p.A. v. G. S.A., 1992 BULL. ASA 368; 1993 REV. ARB. 124, and L. Idot's note; 1994 REV. SUISSE DR. INT. ET DR. EUR. 108, and observations by F. Knoepfler; XVIII Y.B. COM. ARB. 143 (1993) and, on subsequent proceedings, the *ad hoc* award rendered on June 30, 1994 by P. Lalive, chairman, and M. Bonnant and E. Verbrüggen arbitrators, S. S.p.A. v. G. S.A., 1995 BULL. ASA 269.

[451] *See Corte di Appello* of Bologna, Dec. 21, 1991, SpA Coveme v. Compagnie Française des Isolants S.A., XVIII Y.B. COM. ARB. 422 (1993).

[452] *See* Mitsubishi Motors Corp. v. Soler Chrysler-Plymouth, Inc., 473 U.S. 614 (1985); for a French translation, see 1986 REV. ARB. 273, and the commentary by Jean Robert, *Une date dans l'extension de l'arbitrage international: L'arrêt Mitsubishi c/ Soler – Cour Suprême des Etats-Unis – 2 juillet 1985*, at 173; XI Y.B. COM. ARB. 555 (1986); *see also* Sigvard Jarvin, *Arbitrability of Anti-Trust Disputes: The Mitsubishi v. Soler Case*, 2 J. INT'L ARB. 69 (Sept. 1985); Thomas E. Carbonneau, *Mitsubishi: the folly of quixotic internationalism*, 2 ARB. INT'L 116 (1986); Andreas F. Lowenfeld, *The Mitsubishi case: another view*, 2 ARB. INT'L 178 (1986); Hans Smit, *Mitsubishi: It is Not What it Seems To Be*, 4 J. INT'L ARB. 7 (Sept. 1987); Gilmer v. Interstate/Johnson Lane Corp., 500 U.S. 20 (1991); Nghiem v. NEC Elec., Inc., 25 F.3d 1437 (9th Cir. 1994); 5 WORLD ARB. & MED. REP. 184 (1994); Coors Brewing Co. v. Molson Breweries, 51 F.3d 1511 (10th Cir. 1995); 6 WORLD ARB. & MED. REP. 110 (1995); George Fisher Foundry Systems, Inc. v. Adolph H. Hottinger Maschinenbau GmbH, 55 F.3d 1206 (6th Cir. 1995); 10 INT'L ARB. REP. 11 (June 1995); 6 WORLD ARB. & MED. REP. 156 (1995).

576. — Similar questions arise in the area of intellectual property law.[453] Given that the granting of a patent or a trademark affects third parties, no arbitration agreement can validly empower arbitrators to decide such issues.[454] However, following the logic of the *Ganz* precedent, there is no reason why arbitrators should not, for example, determine the validity of the assignment,[455] performance or termination of a contract granting a licence in respect of intellectual property rights.[456] The Paris Court of Appeals held in 1994 that "disputes concerning the interpretation or performance of contracts for the licensing of patents are arbitrable."[457]

577. — As bankruptcy procedures also affect third parties, the courts alone are in a position to open, supervise and close such procedures, decide the admissibility of receivables, distribute the debtor's property and so on. However, this does not prevent arbitrators from ruling on disputes involving bankruptcy law issues. In France, this principle was established by the Paris Court of Appeals in the 1989 *Almira Films v. Pierrel*[458] case,

---

[453] On this issue, see Oppetit, *supra* note 436; Georges Bonet and Charles Jarrosson, *L'arbitrabilité des litiges de propriété industrielle, in* INSTITUT DE RECHERCHE EN PROPRIÉTÉ INTELLECTUELLE HENRI-DESBOIS (IRPI), ARBITRAGE ET PROPRIÉTÉ INTELLECTUELLE 61 (1994). See also the contributions by Jean Robert, Albert Chavanne, Briseno Sierra, G. Sebestyen, Yves Derains, Pierre Lalive, Philippe Fouchard, Bernardo Cremades, Giovanni de Berti, Giorgio Recchia and Jen Tsien-Hsin, *in* 1977 REV. ARB. 5–103; Jacques Guyet, *La propriété industrielle et l'arbitrage en Suisse, in* RECUEIL DE TRAVAUX SUISSES SUR L'ARBITRAGE INTERNATIONAL 45 (1984); Albert Chavanne, *Arbitrage, propriété industrielle et ordre public, in* MÉLANGES DÉDIÉS À JEAN VINCENT 51 (1981); David W. Plant, *Binding Arbitration of U.S. Patents*, 10 J. INT'L ARB. 79 (Sept. 1993); Hanotiau, *L'arbitrabilité et la favor arbitrandum: un réexamen, supra* note 304, ¶¶ 76–77; Pierre Véron, *Arbitration of Intellectual Property Disputes in France*, 23 INT'L BUS. LAW. 132 (Mar. 1995); Marc Blessing, *Arbitrability of Intellectual Property Disputes*, 12 ARB. INT'L 191 (1996); the contributions by Marc Blessing, Bernard Hanotiau, Julian D.M. Lew, François Dessemontet, Jens Drolshammer, Francis Gurry, David Plant, Kamen Troller, Cornelis Canenbley, and Bharat Dube in ASA SPECIAL SERIES No. 6, OBJECTIVE ARBITRABILITY – ANTITRUST DISPUTES – INTELLECTUAL PROPERTY DISPUTES (1994); the presentations by B. Hanotiau, Y. Derains and P. Schlosser *in* ARBITRATION AND EUROPEAN LAW (1997). See also, on the creation of a center for arbitration under the auspices of the World Intellectual Property Organization, 1993 REV. ARB. 782, and the WIPO Arbitration Rules (effective as of Oct. 1, 1994).

[454] *See* CA Paris, Mar. 24, 1994, *Deko, supra* note 119.

[455] Level, *supra* note 427, at 228.

[456] CA Paris, June 15, 1981, Aplix v. Velcro (arbitrability of a dispute concerning patent royalties) and TGI Paris, Mar. 17, 1981, Velcro v. Aplix (arbitrability of the termination of a contract following trademark infringement), 1983 REV. ARB. 89, and A. Françon's note; TGI Paris, réf., June 30, 1988, Cordons et Equipements v. Bretegnier (arbitrability in French domestic law of a dispute concerning the use of a patent), 1994 REV. ARB. 542, and observations by P. Fouchard. In the United States, American Diagnostica of Conn. Inc. v. Centerchem, Inc., No. 94 Civ. 7047 (DC), 1996 U.S. Dist. LEXIS 1722 (S.D.N.Y. Feb. 15, 1996); 11 INT'L ARB. REP. E1 (Apr. 1996).

[457] CA Paris, Mar. 24, 1994, *Deko, supra* note 119. In German law, see the reservations expressed by Berger regarding the arbitrability of the granting or withdrawal of a patent as opposed to disputes arising out of licensing agreements, *supra* note 371.

[458] CA Paris, Feb. 16, 1989, *aff'd*, Cass. 1e civ., Feb. 5, 1991, *supra* note 414. *See also* Hanotiau, *L'arbitrabilité et la favor arbitrandum: un réexamen, supra* note 304, ¶ 79.

and confirmed in more explicit terms in the 1991 *Ganz* decision.[459] Similarly, the Paris Court of Appeals held in 1995 that arbitrators had jurisdiction to apply the public policy provisions of French bankruptcy law which provide that shares held by *de jure* or *de facto* directors of a company in receivership are non-transferrable as of the date on which the receivership procedure is opened.[460] The arbitrators' award could only be set aside if they had disregarded the "domestic and international public policy" rules of French bankruptcy law. This will be the case where, for example, by failing to suspend the arbitral proceedings, the arbitrators disregard the "principle that all proceedings against persons in bankruptcy shall be stayed . . . [which] concerns both domestic and international public policy."[461] Such a suspension is in fact favorable to arbitration in that it has the effect of extending the deadline before which the arbitral award must be made.[462] Similarly, an award will be set aside if it violates the principle of the equality of creditors, which is "a matter of both domestic and international public policy," by ordering a party to pay a sum of money in respect of a breach of a contract existing prior to the court bankruptcy order, which "as such, . . . should have been subject to the law governing the bankruptcy arrangement."[463]

The limits of this case law can be seen in a dispute where a state-controlled company had been put into receivership under the bankruptcy law of the state controlling it. The company sought to rely on the receivership order to avoid performing its contractual obligation to cover the losses of another company which had been taken over by a foreign investor. The arbitrators did not give effect to the receivership order, and it was held that their decision complied with the principle of international public policy that contracts should be executed in good faith. The state-controlled company's claim that the arbitrators' decision contravened the public policy aspects of its bankruptcy law was rejected on the grounds that arbitrators are entitled, subject to review by the courts, to examine the international legality of a bankruptcy order.[464]

578. — The operation of companies set up by parties of different nationalities often gives rise to agreements, incorporated in the company by-laws or appearing in separate documents,

---

[459] CA Paris, Mar. 29, 1991, *supra* note 414.

[460] CA Paris, Sept. 20, 1995, Matra Hachette v. Reteitalia, 1996 REV. ARB. 87, and D. Cohen's note.

[461] Cass. 1e civ., Mar. 8, 1988, Thinet v. Labrely, 1988 Bull. Civ. I, No. 65; 1989 REV. ARB. 473, and P. Ancel's note; Dalloz, Jur. 577 (1989), and J. Robert's note.

[462] CA Paris, Feb. 16, 1989, *Almira Films*, *supra* note 414. The arbitrators had extended the deadline for the conclusion of the arbitration in view of the stay of all proceedings. The Court held this position to be justified on the basis that "the principle of the stay of proceedings . . . is a rule of both domestic and international public policy which takes precedence even where an arbitration taking place in France is not subject to French law."

[463] Cass. com., Feb. 4, 1992, Saret v. SBBM, Dalloz, Jur. 181 (1992), and G. Cas' note; 1992 REV. ARB. 663, and observations by J.-H. Moitry (*reversing* CA Paris, Jan. 26, 1990, Dalloz, Jur. 201 (1991), and G. Cas' note; 1991 REV. ARB. 127, and observations by J.-H. Moitry and C. Vergne). See also CA Paris, Feb. 27, 1992, which set aside an award of damages against an insolvent company before the liquidator had determined the nature of the insolvent company's debts (Sohm v. Simex, 1992 REV. ARB. 590, and P. Ancel's note).

[464] CA Paris, Jan. 12, 1993, *Beyrard*, *supra* note 416. On the issue, generally, see Philippe Fouchard, *Arbitrage et faillite*, 1998 REV. ARB. 471.

to submit any disputes between the shareholders to arbitration. For the reasons set forth in the *Ganz* decision, such agreements are undoubtedly valid, without prejudice to the arbitrators' duty to uphold the requirements of international public policy which possibly include the equality of shareholders.[465]

---

[465] On this issue, generally, see DANIEL COHEN, ARBITRAGE ET SOCIÉTÉ (1993); XAVIER BOUCOBZA, L'ACQUISITION INTERNATIONALE DE SOCIÉTÉ ¶¶ 376 *et seq.* (1998); Paule Gauthier, *La clause d'arbitrage dans le contexte des conventions entre actionnaires, in* JAHRBUCH FÜR DIE PRAXIS DER SCHIEDSGERICHTSBARKEIT 42 (1990). In favor of the arbitrability of a dispute arising from the takeover of a company between the new shareholder and the chairman of the company acquired, see CA Paris, Feb. 28, 1992, *Freyssinet International, supra* note 264; on the arbitrability of the winding up of a company, even in French domestic law, CA Colmar, Sept. 21, 1993, Morin v. Morin, 1994 REV. ARB. 348, and D. Cohen's note; 1994 REV. JUR. COM. 154, and C. Jarrosson's note; on the arbitrability of a dispute regarding the transfer of a company's stock, CA Paris, May 19, 1998, Torno SpA v. Kumagai Gumi Co. Ltd., 13 INT'L ARB. REP. E1 (July 1998), which rejects the very artificial argument made by the losing party that the arbitrators had no imperium and therefore should not have required a party to comply with its obligation to transfer stock. On the fact that an AAA arbitration clause in a contract between two lawyers concerning a law firm located in France is not necessarily void, and therefore requires the courts to hold that they lack jurisdiction and allow the arbitrators to rule first on their own jurisdiction, see CA Paris, Dec. 1, 1993, Rawlings v. Kevorkian & Partners, 1994 REV. ARB. 695, and D. Cohen's note; 1994 BULL. JOLY 310, ¶ 82, and E. Loquin's note. See also, for a decision holding that an action to invalidate a shareholder's resolution is arbitrable, the award (in German) at 1993 BULL. ASA 520. For the position in German law prior to the December 22, 1997 arbitration statute, see Oleg de Lousanoff, *Schiedsklauseln in Gesellschaftsverträgen* (with a summary in English) and, for the position in Swiss law, see Stephen V. Berti, *Some Thoughts on the Validity of Arbitration Clauses in the Articles of Association of Corporations Under Swiss Law, in* ASA SPECIAL SERIES No. 8, THE ARBITRATION AGREEMENT – ITS MULTIFOLD CRITICAL ASPECTS 89 and 120 (1994). In Italy, see the September 23, 1997 award under the aegis of the Chamber of National and International Arbitration of Milan, Shareholders in Company X srl v. Company X srl, XXIII Y.B. COM. ARB. 93 (1998).

579. — The same approach has been adopted with respect to laws governing the carriage of goods by sea,[466] boycotts,[467] embargoes,[468] foreign investments,[469] exchange control,[470] securities,[471] EC agricultural subsidies,[472] the termination of exclusive sales concessions,[473] subcontracts of works,[474] product liability[475] and consumer rights in general.[476] It also applies

---

[466] See, in the United States, the acknowledgment by the Supreme Court that the Carriage of Goods by Sea Act (COGSA) (46 App. U.S.C.A. §§1300–15 (West 1999)) does not invalidate an arbitration clause with a foreign situs contained in a bill of lading, Vimar Seguros y Reaseguros, S.A. v. M/V Sky Reefer, 515 U.S. 528 (1995); 34 I.L.M. 1615 (1995); 10 INT'L ARB. REP. 5 (June 1995); for a French translation, see 1996 REV. ARB. 665, and the commentary by Goutal, *supra* note 180.

[467] On this issue, see Jean-Hubert Moitry, *L'arbitre international et l'obligation de boycottage imposée par un Etat*, 118 J.D.I. 349 (1991).

[468] *See, e.g.*, Swiss Fed. Trib., June 23, 1992, *Fincantieri-Cantieri Navali Italiani, supra* note 369; on the U.S. embargo of Cuba, see *In re* Arbitration between Belship Navigation, Inc. v. Sealift, Inc., No. 95 CIV. 2748 (RPP), 1995 WL 447656 (S.D.N.Y. July 28, 1995); 1996 A.M.C. 209; 6 WORLD ARB. & MED. REP. 226 (1995); 10 INT'L ARB. REP. A1 (Aug. 1995). See also the arbitral case law cited *infra* para. 586.

[469] CA Paris, Apr. 5, 1990, Courrèges Design v. André Courrèges, 1991 REV. CRIT. DIP 580, and C. Kessedjian's note; 1992 REV. ARB. 110, and H. Synvet's note. Prior to the December 22, 1997 reform of German arbitration law, a decision to the contrary was reached by a German court where the circumstances of the case led to the inference that if the dispute were found to be arbitrable, mandatory provisions of German law would not be applied (*Bundesgerichtshof*, June 15, 1987, German individual v. New York corporation, XIX Y.B. COM. ARB. 653 (1994)). On the new regime, see *supra* para. 573.

[470] On the issue see Klaus Peter Berger, *Acts of State and Arbitration: Exchange Control Regulations, in* ACTS OF STATE AND ARBITRATION 99 (K.-H. Böckstiegel ed., 1997).

[471] In the United States, see Scherk v. Alberto-Culver Co., 417 U.S. 506 (1974); Shearson/American Express, Inc. v. McMahon, 482 U.S. 220 (1987); XIII Y.B. COM. ARB. 165 (1988); Rodriguez de Quijas v. Shearson American Express, Inc., 490 U.S. 477 (1989); for a French translation, see 1989 REV. ARB. 735, and T. Carbonneau's note; Riley v. Kingsley Underwriting Agencies, Ltd., 969 F.2d 953 (10th Cir. 1992); XIX Y.B. COM. ARB. 775 (1994); and, on the scope for arbitrators to award punitive damages (an issue which is particularly relevant in this area), see Mastrobuono v. Shearson Lehman Hutton, Inc., 514 U.S. 52 (1995); 6 WORLD ARB. & MED. REP. 82 (1995); 10 INT'L ARB. REP. 3 (Mar. 1995); for a French translation, see 1995 REV. ARB. 295, and L. Niddam's note; *see also* Hans van Houtte, *Arbitration Involving Securities Transactions*, 12 ARB. INT'L 405 (1996); John J. Kerr, Jr., *Arbitrability of Securities Law Claims in Common Law Nations*, 12 ARB. INT'L 171 (1996).

[472] In France, see Cass. 1e civ., Nov. 19, 1991, Société des Grands Moulins de Strasbourg v. Compagnie continentale France, 1992 REV. ARB. 76, and L. Idot's note.

[473] On this question, which raises a difficulty under Belgian law, see the arbitral awards cited *infra* para. 588.

[474] CA Paris, Sept. 10, 1997, Chambon v. Thomson CSF, 1997 DALLOZ AFF. 1253; 1999 REV. ARB. 121, and observations by D. Bureau.

[475] *See* Richard H. Kreindler, *The Arbitration Clause: The Validity of an Arbitration Clause in Matters of Product Liability, in* ASA SPECIAL SERIES No. 8, THE ARBITRATION AGREEMENT – ITS MULTIFOLD CRITICAL ASPECTS 123 (1994).

[476] CA Paris, Dec. 7, 1994, *V 2000* ("the fact that consumer protection legislation may apply to the dispute is not in itself sufficient to exclude arbitral jurisdiction,") *aff'd*, Cass. 1e civ., May 21, 1997, *supra* note 125. See also the May 6, 1994 European Parliament Resolution on Encouraging Recourse to Arbitration to Settle Legal Disputes, 1994 O.J. (C 205) 519; 1995 BULL. ASA 42. But see, in France, the February 1, 1995 statute concerning abusive clauses (Art. L 132-1 of the Consumer Code), implementing EC Council Directive 93/13/EEC of April 5, 1993 on unfair terms in consumer contracts (1993 O.J. (L 95) 29) which considers that

(continued...)

where fraud is alleged.[477] Even issues of taxation, the perfect example of a government prerogative, are not necessarily non-arbitrable.[478]

B. – INTERNATIONAL ARBITRAL CASE LAW

580. — The position in arbitral practice is that a tribunal resolving a dispute that involves issues of public policy is responsible for enforcing the requirements of public policy itself.[479] As arbitrators have no forum, they will generally apply what they consider to be the requirements of truly international public policy. We shall consider examples of this in awards concerning questions of antitrust law (1°), intellectual property law (2°), corruption (3°), bankruptcy law (4°), exclusive sales concessions (5°) and embargoes (6°).

---

[476](...continued)
"in contracts between a seller or supplier and a consumer," clauses the purpose or the effect of which is to oblige the consumer "to bring disputes to arbitration that is not covered by provisions of law" will be abusive, 1995 REV. ARB. 147, and observations by P. Fouchard; and in England, Phillip Alexander Securities and Futures Ltd. v. Bamberger, THE TIMES, July 22, 1996; XXII Y.B. COM. ARB. 872 (1997) (C.A. 1996); for a French translation, see 1999 REV. ARB. 167, and V.V. Veeder's note. Compare with CA Paris, Mar. 24, 1995, *Bin Saud Bin Abdel Aziz, supra* note 60, which held arbitrable a dispute concerning a loan intended to facilitate the construction of a hotel on the grounds that such a loan did not fall within Book 1 of the Consumer Code. In the United States, for a decision in favor of the arbitrability of consumer disputes, in this case arising from mail-order sales, see Hill v. Gateway 2000, Inc., 105 F.3d 1147 (7th Cir. 1997), *cert. denied*, 118 S. Ct. 47 (1997); 1997 BULL. ASA 138; but for a decision that a clause providing for ICC arbitration before a sole arbitrator in Chicago is excessive in such a matter and, as such, not enforceable, see Brower v. Gateway 2000, Inc., No. 750, 1998 WL 481066 (N.Y. App. Div. Aug. 13, 1998). *See* Emmanuel Gaillard, *Resolution of Consumer Disputes: A New Trend?*, N.Y.L.J., Dec. 4, 1997, at 3. On the question of the arbitrability of consumer law disputes, see also Matthieu de Boisséson and Thomas Clay, *Recent Developments in Arbitration in Civil Law Countries*, 1 INT'L ARB. L. REV. 150 (1998).

[477] See, for example, CA Paris, Dec. 7, 1994, *V 2000, aff'd*, Cass. 1e civ., May 21, 1997, *supra* note 125, and, in the United States, Meadows Indemnity Co. v. Boccala & Shoop Ins. Services, Inc., 760 F. Supp. 1036 (E.D.N.Y. 1991); XVII Y.B. COM. ARB. 686 (1992). For decisions in favor of the arbitrability of cases concerning the Racketeer Influenced and Corrupt Organizations Act (the RICO Act), see the awards rendered on Mar. 28, 1990 (Award No. 2642, Triumph Tankers Ltd. v. Kerr McGee Refining Corp.) and Aug. 23, 1990 (No. 2699, Trade & Transport Inc. v. Valero Refining Co., Inc.) under the aegis of the Society of Maritime Arbitrators, Inc., New York, XVIII Y.B. COM. ARB. 112 and 124 (1993), the first of which was enforced by Kerr-McGee Ref. Corp. v. M/T Triumph, 924 F.2d 467 (2d Cir. 1991); XVIII Y.B. COM. ARB. 150 (1993); *see also* ICC Award No. 6320 (1992), Owner v. U.S. Contractor, ICC BULLETIN, Vol. 6, No. 1, 59 (1995); XX Y.B. COM. ARB. 62 (1995); 122 J.D.I. 986 (1995), and observations by D. Hascher; ICC Award No. 8385 (1995), *supra* note 199. *See also* Wolfgang Kuhn, *RICO Claims in International Arbitration and their Recognition in Germany*, 11 J. INT'L ARB. 37 (June 1994).

[478] On this issue, generally, see Jean-Pierre Le Gall, *Fiscalité et arbitrage*, 1994 REV. ARB. 3; Ibrahim Fadlallah, *L'ordre public dans les sentences arbitrales, in* COLLECTED COURSES OF THE HAGUE ACADEMY OF INTERNATIONAL LAW, Vol. 249, Year 1994, Part V, at 369, ¶¶ 54 *et seq.* at 410; see also the awards cited *infra* para. 589-1.

[479] *See supra* para. 566.

1° Antitrust Law

581. — A large number of arbitral awards have recognized the arbitrability of disputes involving issues of antitrust law.[480] As early as 1966, the award made in ICC Case No. 1397 rejected the argument that a contract granting an exclusive know-how licence was non-arbitrable because it allegedly contravened Article 85 of the Treaty of Rome. The arbitrators, admittedly using reasoning that is now somewhat outdated,[481] held that:

> a dispute relating essentially to the validity or nullity of a contract under Article 85 of the Treaty of Rome would be beyond the jurisdiction of an arbitrator, and no arbitration agreement could substitute a private judge for a public judge to resolve a dispute concerning public policy *in se* and *per se*. However, if in the context of a private law dispute a defendant claims that the contract on which the other party relies is void on the grounds of public policy and in particular for breach of Article 85 of the Treaty of Rome, the arbitrator has a duty to establish whether the disputed contract satisfies the substantive and legal conditions leading to the application of the said article. Having made such enquiry, the arbitrator must consider whether the nullity of any contractual clauses under Article 85 renders the entire contract void. The arbitrator can neither accept the performance of an obligation contravening public policy nor, conversely, admit a claim for a stay of proceedings without examining the basis of that claim, nor indeed extend to an entire complex agreement the nullity which may affect a part thereof.

The arbitrators then considered the substance of the dispute and held that the contract did not contravene Article 85 of the Treaty of Rome. They therefore went on to rule on the merits.[482]

In an award made in 1979 in ICC Case No. 2811, the arbitral tribunal held that it had jurisdiction to resolve a dispute which likewise involved the application of Article 85 of the Treaty of Rome and, specifically, the application of an EC regulation providing for a block exemption with respect to Exclusive Dealing Agreements.[483]

In a 1984 award rendered in ICC Case No. 4604, the arbitral tribunal decided in favor of the arbitrability of a dispute concerning an exclusive licence containing a non-competition

---

[480] On this issue, in addition to the authorities cited *supra*, para. 575, see Berthold Goldman, *The Commplementary Roles of Judges and Arbitrators in Ensuring that International Commercial Arbitration is Effective, in* INTERNATIONAL ARBITRATION – 60 YEARS OF ICC ARBITRATION – A LOOK AT THE FUTURE 257, especially at 269 *et seq.* (ICC Publication No. 412, 1984).

[481] *See supra* para. 566.

[482] French company v. Italian company, 101 J.D.I. 878 (1974), and observations by Y. Derains; *see also* Yves Derains, *L'expérience de la Cour d'arbitrage de la Chambre de commerce internationale en matière de propriété industrielle*, 1977 REV. ARB. 40, especially at 50 *et seq.*

[483] Italian company v. French company, 106 J.D.I. 984 (1979), and observations by Y. Derains. On this issue, see Goldman, *supra* note 480, at 271.

clause. The plaintiff sought to enforce the clause, but the defendant claimed that it was incompatible with Italian and EC antitrust law. The arbitral tribunal based its decision to retain jurisdiction not only on Swiss law, the law of the seat, but also on Italian law, the law governing the contract in dispute.[484] Likewise, in a 1990 interim award in ICC Case No. 6106, also concerning a non-competition clause, the tribunal recognized the arbitrability of the issue of compliance with Articles 85 and 86 of the Treaty of Rome.[485] Again, in 1993, the arbitral tribunal sitting in Lausanne in ICC Case No. 7673 upheld the arbitrability of a claim of abuse of a dominant position, where one party had allegedly attempted to exclude a competitor from certain markets.[486] Arbitral case law now consistently confirms the arbitrability of disputes involving the application of EC antitrust law.[487]

582. — In our view, these awards rightly recognize the arbitrability of such disputes, although there is no need to distinguish, as did the 1966 award in ICC Case No. 1397, between cases where the alleged nullity of the contract for breach of antitrust rules is relied on in support of a plaintiff's claim, or as a defense against a claim to enforce the contract. In each of these cases, the arbitrator must consider the applicable economic public policy rules. Far from having to refrain from resolving such issues, international arbitrators are perfectly qualified to do so.

These disputes should only be non-arbitrable where the arbitrator is asked to make a decision over which the public authorities have sole jurisdiction under the applicable rules. This will be the case, for instance, with decisions under Article 85, paragraph 3, of the Treaty of Rome to exempt anti-competitive agreements that would otherwise fall within the prohibition set forth in paragraph 1 of the same Article. Under Article 9, paragraph 1 of EEC Regulation No. 17/62, the European Commission "shall have sole power to declare Article 85(1) inapplicable pursuant to Article 85(3) of the Treaty."[488] The Commission's

---

[484] *See supra* note 390. See also the award issued in Rotterdam on July 22, 1964, ARBITRALE RECHTSPRAAK, No. 524, at 240 (1964); 1965 REV. ARB. 28.

[485] U.S. buyer of shares v. Italian seller of shares, discussed and quoted by Verbist, *supra* note 417, at 33. See also, for a contract organizing a cartel, ICC Award No. 7097 (1993), ICC BULLETIN, SPECIAL SUPPLEMENT, INTERNATIONAL COMMERCIAL ARBITRATION IN EUROPE 38 (1994).

[486] French licensor v. Finnish licensee, *id.* at 35.

[487] See the awards on various issues of EC law rendered under the ICC Rules in cases No. 6106 (1988 and 1991), U.S. company v. Italian company, No. 6709 (1992), German licensor v. French licensee, No. 7081 (1992), European company v. African organization, No. 7319 (1992), French supplier v. Irish distributor (ICC BULLETIN, Vol. 5, No. 2, at 44 *et seq.* (1994)) and in cases No. 6475 (1994), U.S. licensor v. French licensee, No. 6614 (1991), American company v. French company, No. 7181 (1992), Parties to a joint venture agreement for the development of software packages, No. 7673 (1993), French licensor v. Finnish licensee, ICC BULLETIN, Vol. 6, No. 1, at 51 *et seq.* (1995); ICC Award No. 7539 (1995), French company v. Greek company, 123 J.D.I. 1030 (1996), and observations by Y. Derains. For a refusal to apply U.S. antitrust law extraterritorially, see ICC Award No. 6773 (1992), Belgian and U.S. companies v. Luxembourg and Italian companies, ICC BULLETIN, Vol. 6, No. 1, at 66 (1995). See also the *ad hoc* award rendered in Geneva on June 30, 1994, *supra*, note 450, in which there is a long discussion of the arbitrability of EC antitrust law and the respective positions of the Commission and the arbitrators.

[488] 1962 O.J. (13) 204.

jurisdiction, which excludes that of the courts of member states, also excludes the jurisdiction of arbitral tribunals.

However, the application of the rules of EC antitrust law by arbitrators is somewhat hampered by the position taken by the EC Court of Justice according to which arbitrators are not entitled to request a preliminary ruling from the Court, under Article 177 of the Treaty of Rome, as to the interpretation of the Treaty. This is because an arbitral tribunal having its situs in a member state is not considered by the Court of Justice to be "a court or tribunal of a Member State" within the meaning of Article 177 of the Treaty. Arbitrators could however ask the courts, in the performance of their supervising role, to themselves request such an interpretation.[489] In such circumstances, the Court of Justice would entertain the court's request.[490]

However, whether that option is available to them or not, if arbitrators decline to rule on a claim that a contract is void for the breach of EC antitrust law, their award is liable to be set aside on the grounds that they ruled *infra petita*.[491] That was the view rightly taken by the Swiss Federal Tribunal on April 28, 1992, in a case involving a Belgian company and a Spanish company. The arbitral tribunal, sitting in Geneva, was asked to declare that a "specialization and participation agreement" was invalid. The tribunal held that it was not in a position to determine the compatibility of the agreement with EC law. The Swiss Federal Tribunal set aside the award on the basis of Article 190 of the Swiss Private International Law Statute, holding that "arbitrators must verify that contracts submitted to them comply with EC legislation, to avoid making awards contravening the requirements thereof."[492]

---

[489] *See* Court of Justice of the European Communities, Mar. 23, 1982, Case 102/81, "Nordsee" Deutsche Hochseefischerei GmbH v. Reederei Mond Hochseefischerei Nordstern AG, 1982 E.C.R. 1095; VIII Y.B. COM. ARB 183 (1983); 1982 REV. ARB. 473, and the commentary by Xavier de Mello, *Arbitrage et droit communautaire*, *id.* at 349; Dalloz, Jur. 633 (1983), and J. Robert's note; Court of Justice of the European Communities, Apr. 27, 1994, Case C–393/92, Gemeente Almelo e.a. v. Energiebedrijf Ijsselmij NV, 1994 E.C.R. I–1477; XX Y.B. COM. ARB. 187 (1995); 1995 REV. ARB. 503, and P. Fouchard's note; on this issue generally, see Robert Kovar, *Cour de Justice – Recours préjudiciel en interprétation et en appréciation de validité – Mise en oeuvre du renvoi préjudiciel par les juridictions nationales*, J.-CL. EUROPE, Fasc. 360, ¶ 29 (1991); Jean-François Bourque, *The Legal Framework of Arbitration in the European Union, in* ICC BULLETIN, SPECIAL SUPPLEMENT, INTERNATIONAL COMMERCIAL ARBITRATION IN EUROPE 8, especially at 18 *et seq.* (1994); Johan Erauw, *Reference by Arbitrators to the European Court of Justice for Preliminary Rulings, in* ARBITRATION AND EUROPEAN LAW 101 (1997), and the doubts of L. Idot on the chances for a reversal of this case law, 1998 REV. ARB. 459, 460 (reviewing ARBITRATION AND EUROPEAN LAW (1997)).

[490] *See supra* note 489.

[491] On this ground for setting an award aside in French law, see *infra* para. 1628.

[492] *See* Fed. Trib., Apr. 28, 1992, *supra* note 450. *See also* Laurence Idot, *Les conflits de lois en droit de la concurrence*, 122 J.D.I. 321, 335 (1995). For an example of the annulment by arbitrators of a provision contravening European antitrust law, see CA Paris, Mar. 30, 1995, Fabre v. Espitalier, 1996 REV. ARB. 131.

2° Intellectual Property

583. — Given that intellectual property rights are granted by states in the exercise of their sovereignty, it might be legitimate to conclude that disputes concerning such rights are not arbitrable. This is clearly the case insofar as they concern third parties. However, arbitrators can hear disputes between parties contesting the performance or even the validity of contracts relating to such rights.[493]

Certain arbitral awards have drawn a distinction between disputes concerning the existence or validity of intellectual property rights, which are not arbitrable, and disputes concerning the performance of contracts, particularly licensing agreements, relating to patents or trade marks, which are arbitrable.[494]

For example, in a partial award made in 1991 in ICC Case No. 6709, where the dispute concerned a licensing contract for the manufacture and sale of a product protected by two French patents owned by a German party and licensed to a French company, the arbitral tribunal held that although Article 68 of the French statute of January 2, 1968

> gives the national courts exclusive jurisdiction over disputes involving public policy, i.e. the issuance, cancellation or validity of patents . . . ; yet it is nevertheless clear that disputes relating to the exploitation of a patent remain beyond doubt arbitrable.[495]

International disputes concerning the validity, performance or termination of contracts relating to intellectual property rights involving third parties are thus clearly arbitrable, provided that the existence or validity of the rights themselves are not at issue. However, given that such rights are granted by a public authority or are created by filing documents with a public body, a dispute regarding the existence or validity of such rights vis-à-vis third parties could not be effectively arbitrable because the decisions reached by the arbitral

---

[493] On this issue, generally, see Derains, *supra* note 482. For statistics on ICC case law on this issue, see Julian D.M. Lew, *Final Report on Intellectual Property Disputes and Arbitration*, ICC BULLETIN, Vol. 9, No. 1, at 37 (1998).

[494] See, for the arbitrability of a dispute concerning the assignment of a trademark or patent, ICC Award No. 2048 (1972), cited in Derains, *supra* note 482, at 45; but see, for the refusal by an arbitral tribunal to hear a dispute concerning the validity of a French patent, ICC Award No. 1912 (1974), cited in Derains, *supra* note 482, at 46. More recently, in ICC Case No. 4491 (1984), Finnish licensor v. Australian licensee, an arbitral tribunal ruled that it had jurisdiction over a claim concerning royalties due under a trademark license agreement, but not over a claim relating to the unauthorized use of the trademark. The arbitral tribunal did, however, interpret the arbitration clause as excluding the second claim (112 J.D.I. 966 (1985), and observations by S. Jarvin). Compare, on the question of the conformity of a trademark or patent license agreement with EC antitrust law, ICC Award No. 6709 (1992) (*supra* note 487, at 49) and ICC Award No. 4604 (1984) (*supra* note 390 and para. 576).

[495] *See supra* note 114; for excerpts translated into English, see ICC BULLETIN, Vol. 5, No. 1, at 69 (1994). *See also* CA Paris, Mar. 24, 1994, *Deko*, *supra* note 119.

tribunal cannot bind such third parties.[496] With the exception of this inherent limitation of the arbitrators' jurisdiction, there is no reason why, between the parties, disputes regarding the validity of a patent or a trademark cannot be resolved through arbitration.

3° Corruption

584. — A question has arisen in arbitral case law as to whether arbitrators dealing with claims of corruption should retain jurisdiction and, if appropriate, declare the contract to be void, or whether cases where corruption is alleged are non-arbitrable.[497]

585. — In his famous 1963 award in ICC Case No. 1110, Gunnar Lagergren chose not to rule on the merits of the case as a result of his findings of corruption. The case concerned a contract under which a British company had engaged an Argentine intermediary to obtain a public works contract in Argentina, in return for which the intermediary was to receive a commission of 10% of the value of the contract. When the British company refused to pay the commission, the dispute was referred to Mr Lagergren, as sole arbitrator. He considered that it had been clearly established that "the agreement between the parties contemplated the bribing of Argentine officials" and, referring to "the general principles denying arbitrators the power to entertain disputes of this nature rather than . . . any national rules on arbitrability," he declined jurisdiction on the grounds that:

> [p]arties who ally themselves in an enterprise of the present nature must realize that they have forfeited any right to ask for assistance of the machinery of justice (national courts or arbitral tribunals) in settling their disputes.[498]

It has been noted that this decision was in fact based not so much on a finding of non-arbitrability, but rather on the inadmissibility of the claim founded on a rule similar to

---

[496] See excerpts of various arbitral awards on intellectual property rights in ICC BULLETIN, Vol. 4, No. 2, at 70 *et seq.* (1993), and ICC BULLETIN, Vol. 5, No. 1, at 65 *et seq.* (1994). *See also* ICC Award No. 8694 (1996), *supra* note 81.

[497] On this issue, see Bruno Oppetit, *Le paradoxe de la corruption à l'épreuve du droit du commerce international*, 114 J.D.I. 5 (1987); Ahmed S. El Kosheri and Philippe Leboulanger, *L'arbitrage face à la corruption et aux trafics d'influence*, 1984 REV. ARB. 3; François Knoepfler, *Corruption et arbitrage international*, *in* LES CONTRATS DE DISTRIBUTION – CONTRIBUTIONS OFFERTES AU PROFESSEUR FRANÇOIS DESSEMONTET À L'OCCASION DE SES 50 ANS 357 (1998); Jacques Malherbe, Yann François, Jean-Charles Papeians de Morchoven, *Les Commissions illicites et l'arbitrage*, *in* ACTS OF STATE AND ARBITRATION 127 (K.-H. Böckstiegel ed., 1997); EXTORTION AND BRIBERY IN BUSINESS TRANSACTIONS (ICC Publication No. 315, 1977); Vincent Heuzé, *La morale, l'arbitre et le juge*, 1993 REV. ARB. 179.

[498] Mr. X, Buenos Aires v. Company A, 10 ARB. INT'L 282 (1994). See also the analysis provided by El Kosheri and Leboulanger, as well as Oppetit, *supra* note 497. For a defense of this award, see J. Gillis Wetter, *Issues of Corruption before International Arbitral Tribunals: The Authentic Text and True Meaning of Judge Gunnar Lagergren's 1963 Award in ICC Case No. 1110*, 10 ARB. INT'L 277 (1994); *see also* Fadlallah, *supra* note 478, ¶¶ 38 *et seq.*

that reflected by the adage *nemo auditur propriam turpitudinem allegans.*[499] In any event, this award has long been construed as holding disputes involving allegations of corruption to be non-arbitrable.

586. — Subsequent awards rightly rejected that approach. In those cases, the arbitrators ruled on the merits of the dispute, and they either rejected the defense that the contract was void for corruption on the grounds that the defendant had failed to substantiate its claims,[500] or held the contract to be void either under the applicable law or under international public policy.[501]

The 1988 award made in Geneva in the *Hilmarton* case (ICC No. 5622) concerned a contract governed by Swiss law under which a company agreed to pay a 4% commission in respect of various advisory services aimed at obtaining a works contract in Algeria. The tribunal held that the subject-matter was arbitrable and decided on the merits that the request for payment of the balance of the commission should be rejected on the grounds that the contract providing for such payment violated mandatory rules of Algerian law which prevailed over the *lex contractus.*[502] This award was set aside by the Court of Justice of the Canton of Geneva, in a decision subsequently upheld by the Swiss Federal Tribunal, on grounds unconnected with the arbitrability of the dispute. The Court considered that, with regard to the requirements of Swiss public policy,

---

[499] This rule prevents parties from successfully relying on arguments based on their own illegal conduct. *See* Goldman, *supra* note 480, at 272; *comp. with* Oppetit, *supra* note 497, at 7; Böckstiegel, *supra* note 304, at 201–02.

[500] *See, e.g.,* ICC Award No. 4145 (1984), Establishment of Middle East country v. South Asian construction company, XII Y.B. COM. ARB. 97 (1987); for a French translation, see 112 J.D.I. 985 (1985), and observations by Y. Derains; ICC Award No. 6286 (1991), U.S. partner v. German and Canadian partners, XIX Y.B. COM. ARB. 141, ¶ 22 (1994). *See also* Swiss Fed. Trib., Sept. 2, 1993, National Power Corp. v. Westinghouse, which describes as outdated the idea that disputes concerning questions of corruption are not arbitrable and which refused to set aside the award dated December 19, 1991, Mr. Claude Reymond presiding, which found that the allegations of corruption had not been proven (1994 BULL. ASA 244, 247; 1994 REV. SUISSE DR. INT. ET DR. EUR. 159, and observations by F. Knoepfler).

[501] *See, e.g.,* ICC Award No. 3916 (1981), referred to in Y. Derains, observations following ICC Award No. 4145 (1984), *supra* note 500, at 988; ICC Award No. 3916 (1982), Iranian party v. Greek party, 111 J.D.I. 930 (1984), and observations by Y. Derains. On the general principles of law applicable to corruption, see *infra* para. 1468, and, on the fact that these principles amount to requirements of international public policy, see *infra* para. 1535.

[502] Aug. 19, 1988 award, Hilmarton v. OTV, 1993 REV. ARB. 327, and the commentary by Heuzé, *supra* note 497; for an English translation, see XIX Y.B. COM. ARB. 105 (1994). On the question of the applicability of mandatory rules by arbitrators, see *infra* para. 1515.

in the absence of fraudulent conduct, the negotiation by an intermediary of a contract with the government is an activity which normally, and by definition, forms part of the activities of a broker, on the same basis as the negotiation of a contract between private entities.[503]

Regardless of the requirements of Swiss public policy on this matter, it would appear that arbitral tribunals now generally admit the arbitrability of disputes involving allegations of corruption, and that where corruption is proved, they will hold the relevant contracts to be void. This approach protects the interests of the government or company that suffers the effects of improper influence, and it seeks to ensure that international commerce retains a certain degree of morality.[504]

4° Bankruptcy Proceedings

587. — In the *Casa v. Cambior* case, the ICC arbitral tribunal was required to decide whether it had jurisdiction to hear a claim brought by Casa, a company incorporated in Luxembourg, which was subject to a bankruptcy procedure in Luxembourg known as "controlled administration with a view to re-organizing its business." After filing its request for arbitration against Cambior, a company incorporated under the laws of Quebec, Casa was placed under a regime of "controlled administration with a view to liquidating its business." For that reason, it requested the arbitral tribunal to decline jurisdiction over Cambior's counter-claim for provisional measures. The tribunal rejected this request, pointing out in particular that:

> [the tribunal] should examine whether Cambior's request for provisional measures falls within the exclusive jurisdiction of the courts of Luxembourg, as claimed by Casa, which argues that the public policy provisions adopted in the context of administration proceedings have a substantial influence on the dispute, to the extent that they render it non-arbitrable . . . . [T]he fact that one of the parties is subject to bankruptcy proceedings is not in itself sufficient to

---

[503] Court of Justice of the Geneva Canton, Nov. 17, 1989, Hilmarton v. OTV, 1993 REV. ARB. 315, and the commentary by Heuzé, *supra* note 497; for an English translation, see XIX Y.B. COM. ARB. 214 (1994). On these decisions, see also Ali Mebroukine, *Le choix de la Suisse comme siège de l'arbitrage dans les clauses d'arbitrage conclues entre entreprises algériennes et entreprises étrangères*, 1994 BULL. ASA 4; on the enforcement in France of the award set aside in Switzerland, see Cass. 1e civ., Mar. 23, 1994, Hilmarton v. OTV, 1994 Bull. Civ. I, No. 104; 1994 REV. ARB. 327, and C. Jarrosson's note; 121 J.D.I. 701 (1994), and E. Gaillard's note; 1994 RTD COM. 702, and observations by J.-C. Dubarry and E. Loquin; 1995 REV. CRIT. DIP 356, and B. Oppetit's note; or an English translation, see XX Y.B. COM. ARB. 663 (1995); 9 INT'L ARB. REP. E1 (May 1994).

[504] On the substantive requirements of international public policy in this area, see *infra* para. 1535.

render a dispute non-arbitrable per se. The best proof of this is that, despite the fact that it was placed under administration, Casa did not hesitate to request arbitration on the basis of the arbitration clause appearing in the contract which it had signed with Cambior many years prior to being placed under administration. The only disputes which are excluded are those which have a direct link with the bankruptcy proceedings, namely those disputes arising from the application of rules specific to those proceedings. Since Cambior's claim does not have that direct link, the arbitral tribunal has jurisdiction to hear it.[505]

Similarly, in a 1993 interim award in ICC Case No. 6632, an arbitral tribunal sitting in Brussels considered that the bankruptcy proceedings to which the Italian defendant was subject did not prevent the tribunal from hearing the parties' claims for security for costs.[506]

By contrast, the 1993 award in ICC Case No. 7563 applied the principle that individual proceedings should be suspended in the event of bankruptcy, as laid down in France in the 1988 *Thinet* decision.[507] The dispute was between a Belgian bank and a French company on the one hand, and an insurance group on the other, and the arbitral tribunal held that it could not award costs against the French company, which was in receivership. The tribunal therefore confined itself to discussing the principle of liability.[508]

5° Exclusive Sales Concessions

588. — The issue of the arbitrability of disputes concerning the termination of exclusive sales concessions raises a difficulty under Belgian law. The Belgian law of July 27, 1961, as amended by the law of April 13, 1971, states that whenever an exclusive sales concession "produces its effects in all or part of the Belgian territory," resulting disputes fall within the jurisdiction of the Belgian courts, and are subject to "Belgian law exclusively."[509]

---

[505] Partial Award in ICC Case No. 6697 (Dec. 26, 1990), Casa v. Cambior, 1992 REV. ARB. 135, and P. Ancel's note (award by E. Robine, chairman, N. Decker and A. Mayrand, arbitrators); *comp. with* ICC Award No. 6057 (1991), Syrian company v. French company, 120 J.D.I. 1016 (1993), and observations by Y. Derains. On this issue, generally, see Fernando Mantilla-Serrano, *International Arbitration and Insolvency Proceedings*, 11 ARB. INT'L 51 (1995).

[506] Award of Jan. 27, 1993, unpublished. *See also* ICC Award No. 7205 (1993), French company v. Owner of Saudi company, 122 J.D.I. 1031 (1995), and observations by J.-J. Arnaldez.

[507] Cass. 1e civ., Mar. 8, 1988, *supra* note 461.

[508] Belgian bank v. International pool of insurance companies, 121 J.D.I. 1054 (1994), and observations by Y. Derains.

[509] Belgian case law on these statutes is sometimes interpreted as meaning that, according to Article II of the 1958 New York Convention, when a case is being heard by the Belgian courts, the arbitrability of the dispute should be determined by reference to the law applicable to the substance of the contract (CA Brussels, Oct. 4, 1985, Company M. v. M. S.A., 1986 [BELG.] JOURN. TRIB. 93, and A. Kohl's note; XIV Y.B. COM. ARB. 618 (1989)). On the violation of the principle of the autonomy of the arbitration agreement that this approach entails, see *supra* para. 412. By contrast, according to Article V, paragraph 2(a) of the New York Convention, the argument
(continued...)

In ICC Award No. 6379 of 1991, an arbitral tribunal sitting in Cologne had to examine the arbitrability of a dispute between an Italian manufacturer and a Belgian company with an exclusive concession covering Belgium, Luxembourg and Zaire. The distribution contract had been terminated, and the distributor relied on Belgian law in claiming the dispute to be non-arbitrable.[510] Rejecting this argument, the arbitral tribunal based its reasoning essentially on Article II of the New York Convention, and Article VI(2)(a) of the European Convention, whereby the validity of the arbitration agreement should be examined by reference to the law chosen by the parties. As a result, Italian law applied, as it governed the merits of the dispute, and under Italian law the dispute was held to be arbitrable.[511]

Although the outcome seems perfectly justified, the reasoning is unsatisfactory in many respects. Assuming that the New York Convention can be applied in a context other than the recognition and enforcement of awards,[512] it does not follow that the issue of arbitrability should be determined by the law governing the arbitration agreement. On the contrary, arbitrability is conceived in Article V, paragraph 2 of the Convention as forming part of the international public policy of the country where the award is to be enforced.[513] In addition, to resolve the question by reference to the law governing the merits of the dispute is both contrary to the principle of the autonomy of the arbitration agreement in its traditional sense,[514] and leads to unjustified discrimination in practice. Thus, on the same facts, the parties' choice of Italian law, Belgian law or the law of a third country to govern their contract would have determined whether or not the dispute was arbitrable.[515] The arbitrability of a dispute is a matter which concerns the fundamental convictions of each jurisdiction, and it would undoubtedly be inappropriate to abandon that issue to the skill or good fortune of parties in choosing the law governing their contracts. The approach taken by the arbitral tribunal in this case is thus reminiscent of that of the French courts in the

---

[509](...continued)
continues, the arbitrability of the dispute should be determined, at the enforcement stage, by reference to Belgian law. This would give rise to problems with recognition of the award in Belgium if the arbitration agreement were entered into prior to the existence of the dispute and was intended to and did in fact cause a foreign law to apply (Belgian *Cour de cassation*, June 28, 1979, Audi-NSU Auto Union A.G. v. S.A. Adelin Petit et Cie., Pas. I 1260; V Y.B. COM. ARB. 257 (1980)). See also, in favor of this distinction, Brussels Commercial Court, Oct. 5, 1994, Van Hoplynus v. Coherent Inc., 1995 REV. ARB. 311, and B. Hanotiau's note; for an English translation, see XXII Y.B. COM. ARB. 643 (1997). On this issue, see Hanotiau, *L'arbitrabilité et la favor arbitrandum: un réexamen*, *supra* note 304, ¶¶ 67 *et seq*. We do not find this interpretation convincing. On this issue, generally, see ARNAUD NUYTS, LA CONCESSION DE VENTE EXCLUSIVE, L'AGENCE COMMERCIALE ET L'ARBITRAGE (1996).

[510] On the arguments raised by the distributor on the merits regarding the mandatory nature of the Belgian law rules, see *infra* para. 1527.

[511] Italian principal v. Belgian distributor, XVII Y.B. COM. ARB. 212 (1992); 1993 REV. DR. COM. BELGE 1146, and B. Hanotiau's note.

[512] On this issue, see *supra* paras. 263 *et seq*.

[513] *See* Albert Jan van den Berg, *New York Convention of 1958 – Consolidated Commentary – Cases Reported in Volumes XVII (1992) – XIX (1994)*, XIX Y.B. COM. ARB. 475, 597 (1994), and *supra* para. 532.

[514] *See supra* para. 412.

[515] See also on the questions of interpretation of the exact requirements of Belgian law, *supra* note 509.

1964 *O.N.I.C. v. San Carlo* decision, where the court, relying on the foreign law governing the merits of the dispute, held an arbitration agreement entered into by a state-owned entity to be valid. This was before the French *Cour de cassation* reached the same conclusion in 1966 by applying substantive rules to the exclusion of the law chosen by the parties.[516] It is to be hoped that arbitral tribunals determining the arbitrability of the termination of exclusive sales concessions in Belgium will follow the same path and hold such disputes to be arbitrable solely by reference to generally accepted principles of international trade, as befits the international basis of their jurisdiction.[517]

6° Embargoes

589. — Parties have sometimes argued, on the basis of the outdated view that matters implicating public policy are non-arbitrable, that international arbitrators cannot hear disputes concerning an embargo imposed by the international community on a particular country.[518] In ICC Case No. 6719, in which a partial award was made in Geneva in 1994, arbitral proceedings were initiated by a Syrian individual against two Italian companies in connection with the payment of commissions on sales of military equipment to the government of Iraq. The defendants claimed that the dispute was non-arbitrable because of the United Nations sanctions in force against Iraq. Using somewhat questionable reasoning, the tribunal subjected the arbitrability issue to the law governing the arbitration agreement and hence to the principle of party autonomy.[519] Nonetheless, the tribunal rightly held the dispute to be arbitrable under Article 177 of the Swiss Private International Law Statute:

> the Tribunal is convinced that in so far as they may apply to the dispute, the international and legislative provisions [organizing the sanctions against Iraq] are matters of international public policy. However, the Tribunal is also convinced, in common with legal authors and recent case law, that one should not confuse the application by international arbitrators of public policy provisions, on the one hand, and the non-arbitrability of a dispute on the other.

---

[516] Cass. 1e civ., Apr. 14, 1964, *O.N.I.C.*, and Cass. 1e civ., May 2, 1966, *Galakis*, *supra* note 323.

[517] *See supra* para. 443. *See also* ICC Award No. 6752 (1991), Grantor of exclusive distributorship v. (former) exclusive distributors, XVIII Y.B. COM. ARB. 54 (1993).

[518] For court decisions on this subject, see *supra* para. 579.

[519] *See supra* para. 532.

The mere fact that the nature of the dispute may lead the arbitrator to apply various rules of law implicating public policy does not mean that the dispute becomes non-arbitrable as a result. The arbitrator must comply with the rules of international public policy, but he need not decline jurisdiction.[520]

On the basis of that distinction, the arbitral tribunal held the dispute to be arbitrable. In so doing, it clearly endorsed the modern conception of arbitrability.[521]

7° Taxation Disputes

589-1. — Several awards, most of which are currently unpublished, show that arbitral tribunals do agree to rule on taxation disputes. In fact, the question of the arbitrability of tax law issues does not raise any serious difficulty when the decision to be made is one sharing a tax burden between parties according to the terms of their contract.[522] However, while indicating that it did not seek to replace tax courts, an arbitral tribunal did, at the request of the parties to a dispute and fully aware of the fiscal consequences of its decision, agree to characterize its earlier award of an indemnity for rescission of a contract as a loss and loss of profit, rather than as profit accruing in the course of business.[523] Even more clearly, in disputes arising from petroleum concession agreements signed in parallel between a state and two private companies and containing tax stabilization provisions, two *ad hoc* arbitral tribunals, by awards dated November 30, 1996 and December 9, 1996, expressly rejected the claims of non-arbitrability raised by the state and went on to decide that arbitration was mandatory in the presence of an arbitration clause covering the type of dispute before them. According to these awards, the scope of the arbitration clause would be artificially reduced by a state party if it were allowed to successfully argue that the disputed matter was outside the jurisdiction of the arbitrators.[524]

---

[520] Partial Award in ICC Case No. 6719 (1994), Syrian party v. two Italian companies, 121 J.D.I. 1071 (1994), and observations by J.-J. Arnaldez. On the *force majeure* impact of national and international sanctions against Iraq on the relationship between an Italian company and its Italian subcontractor, see the award rendered by Professor Riccardo Luzzatto, sole arbitrator, on July 20, 1992, under the rules of the Chamber of National and International Arbitration of Milan, Subcontractor v. Contractor, 1993 INT'L CONSTR. L. REV. 201; XVIII Y.B. COM. ARB. 80 (1993). On the issue, generally, see Lambert Matray, *Embargo and Prohibition of Performance*, *in* ACTS OF STATE AND ARBITRATION 69 (K.-H. Böckstiegel ed., 1997).

[521] *See supra* para. 566.

[522] *See, e.g.*, ICC Award No. 6515 (1994), cited by Fadlallah, *supra* note 478, ¶ 54.

[523] Award cited by Fadlallah, *supra* note 478, ¶ 55.

[524] Unpublished awards. *See* Emmanuel Gaillard, *Tax Disputes Between States and Foreign Investors*, N.Y.L.J., Apr. 3, 1997, at 3.

SECTION IV
FORM AND PROOF

590. — Proving the existence and validity of an arbitration agreement raises no difficulty in principle. It is widely accepted that the burden of proving the existence of a valid arbitration agreement lies with the party seeking to rely on it in order to challenge the jurisdiction of the courts or to refer disputes to arbitration. In legal systems where the principle of "competence-competence" is fully accepted, only *prima facie* proof of the existence of an arbitration agreement must be adduced before a court hearing argument on the issue.[525] The existence of the arbitration agreement must then be fully evidenced before the arbitrators, and likewise before the courts in a subsequent action to set aside or enforce the award.[526]

The methods of establishing the existence of an arbitration agreement are those generally admissible before the relevant jurisdiction, be it an arbitral tribunal or the courts of a particular country.[527] In practice, arbitrators and the courts generally do not seek to identify the law governing the proof of the existence of an arbitration agreement. In France, the choice of law approach adopted by the Paris Court of Appeals in the 1988 *Cassia* case[528] has been rejected since the 1993 *Dalico* decision, in which the *Cour de cassation* ruled in the clearest possible terms that the existence and validity of an international arbitration agreement should be examined exclusively by reference to substantive rules accepted in international trade.[529]

The only issue left open is that of form. Is a written instrument required?[530] Clearly, a document establishing the existence and validity of the arbitration agreement is always helpful as evidence.[531] However, the real question is whether or not evidence in writing is essential to the validity of the agreement. Are the parties simply required to establish, with documentary support if need be, their common intention to submit their existing or future

---

[525] *See infra* paras. 662 *et seq.*

[526] *See infra* para. 1605.

[527] On the hesitations in private international law as to whether to resolve questions of proof by applying the law of the contract, the law of the place where the contract was signed, or the law of the forum, see HENRI BATIFFOL, PAUL LAGARDE, DROIT INTERNATIONAL PRIVÉ, Vol. 2, ¶ 707 (7th ed. 1983). On the application *in favorem* of either the law of the forum or the law governing the form of the contract, see Article 14 of the June 19, 1980 Rome Convention on the Law Applicable to Contractual Obligations.

[528] CA Paris, Feb. 26, 1988, Pia Investments Ltd. v. Cassia, 1990 REV. ARB. 851, 1st decision, and J.-H. Moitry and C. Vergne's note, *aff'd*, Cass. 1e civ., July 10, 1990, 1990 REV. ARB. 851, 2d decision, and J.-H. Moitry and C. Vergne's note; 119 J.D.I. 168 (1992), and E. Loquin's note.

[529] Cass. 1e civ., Dec. 20, 1993, *supra* note 2.

[530] On the relationship between the form and the proof of the arbitration agreement, see FOUCHARD, *supra* note 4, ¶ 134.

[531] On the practice of the ICC International Court of Arbitration on this issue, and the fact that the ICC Rules do not require a written instrument, see DERAINS AND SCHWARTZ, *supra* note 113, at 87 *et seq.*

disputes to arbitration, or is it necessary for that intention to have been expressed in writing for the arbitration agreement to be valid?

591. — This is the debate between consensualism and formalism. Contrary to what is sometimes suggested, consensualism should not be confused with the principle of party autonomy. Under the latter principle, the effectiveness of the arbitration agreement is founded upon the common intention of the parties without prejudice to whether a particular form is required or not. The principle of consensualism, on the other hand, is the reverse of formalism in that it holds that the common intention of the parties suffices to render the agreement perfect. Thus, the concept of consensualism should apply only with respect to questions of form.

In this section, we shall examine whether, under both French arbitration law (§1) and the main international conventions on arbitration (§2), an arbitration agreement follows the rule of consensualism or instead must be in a particular form to be valid.

§ 1. – French Law

592. — The rules applicable to the form of an arbitration agreement (B) cannot be determined without returning to the distinction between the rules of law governing the main contract and those governing the arbitration agreement itself. This distinction is of course based on the principle of the autonomy of the arbitration agreement from the main contract (A).

A. – FORMAL VALIDITY AND AUTONOMY OF THE ARBITRATION AGREEMENT

593. — The principle that the arbitration agreement is autonomous of the main contract is among the most firmly established rules of international arbitration.[532] However, one French case seemed to imply that this principle did not apply to the form of the arbitration agreement (1°). Fortunately, most subsequent decisions have reverted to a more orthodox approach (2°).

1° The *Cassia* Decision

594. — In the *Cassia* case, one of the parties contested the formal validity of the arbitration agreement, but the Paris Court of Appeals, and subsequently the *Cour de cassation*, failed to draw the appropriate consequences from the principle of the autonomy

---

[532] On this issue, generally, see *supra* paras. 389 *et seq.*

or separability of the arbitration agreement.[533] The dispute was between two plaintiffs, a Lebanese company (Cassia) and a Pakistani company, and a defendant company incorporated in Sharjah (Pia). It concerned the performance of a contract for the design of an extension to a stadium in Karachi. The contract stated that it had been signed in Karachi, but it was not dated and the parties had simply initialed the document at the bottom of each page. Cassia sought to rely on the ICC arbitration clause appearing in the contract. In a preliminary award dated September 25, 1986, the arbitral tribunal held that it had jurisdiction, finding that the parties had agreed to refer their disputes to arbitration. However, in a decision dated February 26, 1988, the Paris Court of Appeals set aside the award on the grounds that:

> although in international arbitration the arbitration agreement is fully autonomous of the contract containing it, its validity must be examined by reference to the choice of law rule determining the applicable law, where it is alleged, as in the present case, that the arbitration agreement is non-existent because the main contract was not validly signed.

The Court held that the place where the contract was performed and that where it was signed both implied that "Pakistan was the center of gravity for the relations between the parties, despite the fact that the fees were paid in Lebanon, where the architects were domiciled." Having heard evidence as to the content of Pakistani law the Court concluded that:

> the fact that the parties, who were fully aware of the formalities required of a valid contract in Pakistan (stamp, date, signature, and the authority of those who initial the document), did not comply with those requirements, demonstrates that they did not intend the document in question to form a binding contract between the parties; consequently, there can be no valid agreement to submit disputes arising out of the said contract to arbitration.[534]

On July 10, 1990, the *Cour de cassation* affirmed that decision on the grounds that:

> in international arbitration, the autonomy of the arbitration clause pre-supposes the formal existence of the main contract containing it; that existence is necessarily established by reference to the law which, under the principles of

---

[533] CA Paris, Feb. 26, 1988, *aff'd*, Cass. 1e civ., July 10, 1990, *supra* note 528.
[534] 1990 REV. ARB. 855.

private international law, governs the form of the contract. The Court of Appeals, having referred to the principle of autonomy, rightly examined the existence of the arbitration clause by reference to the law resulting from the choice of law rule [and the appellant is wrong in suggesting that the conditions governing the formation of an arbitration agreement should be considered in isolation from those governing the formation of the main contract and solely by reference to the usages of international trade].[535]

595. — This decision is most unfortunate in that it fails to apply the principle of the autonomy of the arbitration agreement where the main contract to which the arbitration agreement relates is non-existent. It is widely accepted in comparative law and in international arbitral case law[536] that the purpose of the principle of autonomy is to ensure that the arbitration agreement remains unaffected by flaws in the main contract. That is not to say that the arbitration agreement can never be held to be void or non-existent; the arbitration agreement will be non-existent or void if directly affected, but not simply as a function of the existence or validity of the main contract. In the *Cassia* case, the correct approach would have been to establish whether the arbitration agreement had actually been signed, and whether it was subject to any particular conditions of form. If, in the light of rules which remained to be determined,[537] the arbitration agreement had not been signed, the decision could have been set aside on the basis of Article 1502 1° of the New Code of Civil Procedure. Conversely, if the court were to establish that the arbitration agreement did exist and was valid as to its form, the arbitrators would then be responsible for examining the existence and formal validity of the main contract, subject to review by the courts confined to the issue of compliance with international public policy. In failing to adopt this approach, both the Paris Court of Appeals and the *Cour de cassation* compromised the effectiveness of the principle of the autonomy of the arbitration agreement.[538]

2° The Prevailing Position in French Law

596. — Decisions subsequent to that in the *Cassia* case have reached a different conclusion.[539] In particular, in its 1992 *Sonetex* decision, the *Cour de cassation* rejected an action challenging a Court of Appeals decision which upheld the existence and validity of an arbitration clause incorporated by reference without determining "the law applicable to

---

[535] 1990 REV. ARB. 859; 119 J.D.I. 170 (1992).

[536] *See supra* paras. 392 *et seq.*

[537] *See supra* paras. 420 *et seq.*

[538] For a criticism of these decisions, see E. Loquin, note following Cass. 1e civ., July 10, 1990, *supra* note 528.

[539] However, the Paris Court of Appeals did follow the *Cassia* approach in its decision of September 11, 1997 in the *Alfalfas v. Comexol* case, 1998 REV. ARB. 564, and the commentary by Boucobza, *supra* note 151. *See also* CA Paris, 1e Ch., Sec. C, Jan. 19, 1999, CIC International Ltd. v. Ministre de la Défense de la République Fédérale d'Allemagne, No. 1998/03375, unpublished.

the contract with regard to the form and proof of the arbitration clause." The *Cour de cassation* held that "[the Court of Appeals] had to establish that the [disputed] arbitration clauses had been accepted, and it was not required to apply a law which, as a result of the autonomy of the arbitration agreement in international arbitration, may not have been applicable."[540]

597. — The *Cour de cassation's* decision in the 1993 *Dalico* case is equally clear.[541] The dispute concerned a works contract between a Libyan local authority and a Danish company (Dalico). The main contract was subject to Libyan law and stipulated that standard terms and conditions, amplified or amended by an annex, formed part of the contract. These standard terms and conditions conferred jurisdiction on the Libyan courts, but the annex amended them by providing for international arbitration. On the basis of the arbitration clause in the annex Dalico had referred the dispute to arbitration and had obtained an award against the Libyan local authority. An action to set aside the award was brought before the Paris Court of Appeals, based on the formal requirements of Libyan law. The Court rejected the action to set aside, citing in particular the fact that the principle of the autonomy of the arbitration agreement "confirms the independence of the arbitration clause, not only from the substantive provisions of the contract to which it relates, but also from the domestic law applicable to that contract." The Court then held that the wording of the disputed documents revealed the parties' intention to submit their disputes to arbitration. The *Cour de cassation* dismissed an action against the decision of the Court of Appeals, emphasizing that "the Court of Appeals justified its decision in law by establishing the existence of the arbitration agreement without referring to Libyan law, which governed the contract." The *Cour de cassation* thus went back to a perfectly orthodox application of the principle of the autonomy of the arbitration agreement.[542]

598. — It is therefore clear that the *Cassia* decision should no longer be considered to reflect the position of French law on this issue.[543]

B. – RULES GOVERNING THE FORMAL VALIDITY OF AN ARBITRATION AGREEMENT

599. — As with other aspects of the validity of the arbitration agreement, several approaches have been used to determine whether an arbitration agreement is valid as to its

---

[540] Cass. 1e civ., Mar. 3, 1992, *Sonetex, supra* note 175. On the validity of arbitration agreements by reference, which often generate discussion over requirements of form, see *supra* paras. 493 *et seq.*

[541] On the consequences of the *Dalico* decision with regard to questions of methodology, see *supra* para. 437.

[542] CA Paris, Mar. 26, 1991, *supra* note 33, *aff'd*, Cass. 1e civ., Dec. 20, 1993, *supra* note 2. *See also* CA Paris, May 17, 1995, *Trafidi, supra* note 165.

[543] *See* E. Loquin, note following Cass. 1e civ., July 10, 1990, *supra* note 528, at 176. *But see supra* note 539.

form.[544] The first involves applying the choice of law method and thus the requirements of the legal system designated by the choice of law rule governing the formal aspects of arbitration agreements. In contrast, the second approach entails determining and applying substantive rules which are considered appropriate in an international context. In other words, for a French court reviewing whether an arbitral award has been made on the basis of an arbitration agreement, the second approach involves referring solely to the requirements of French international arbitration law on the question.

Since the *Cour de cassation*'s 1993 *Dalico* decision, the French courts have favored the second approach when examining the existence and validity of an arbitration agreement, and in particular where a question arises as to that agreement's formal validity.[545] However, since arbitrators sometimes adopt a different approach, and as courts in some jurisdictions may still resort to the choice of law method, we shall discuss in turn the application to this issue of both the choice of law method (1°) and the substantive rules method (2°).

1° The Choice of Law Method

600. — When reasoning in choice of law terms, the search for rules governing the formal validity of an arbitration agreement gives rise to a number of possible connecting factors.

601. — First, the formal validity of the arbitration agreement might be subject to the law of the seat of the arbitration. Thus, in a 1983 award made in Zurich in ICC Case No. 4392, it was held that Swiss law governed the formal validity of an arbitration agreement in a dispute between a Yugoslavian company and a German company.[546] This approach is, in our view, unsatisfactory. The seat of arbitration is a weak connecting factor, especially where it has not been chosen by the parties themselves. In Switzerland, the issue is now governed by the substantive rule found at Article 178, paragraph 1, of the Private International Law Statute.[547] In France, the position taken in ICC Case No. 4392 has been rejected by the courts. In the 1987 *Bomar Oil* case, for instance, the Paris Court of Appeals specifically denied the existence of any presumption connecting the arbitration agreement with the law of the seat of the arbitration.[548]

602. — A second possibility would be to have the formal aspects of the arbitration agreement governed by the law chosen by the parties. Thus, the parties might provide that the formal aspects of the arbitration agreement are to be determined by the law governing its substance. In practice, the French courts have, on several occasions, relied on the

---

[544] For a general discussion of these different approaches and their justification, see *supra* paras. 435 *et seq.*

[545] *See supra* para. 597.

[546] *See supra* note 90.

[547] *See infra* para. 606.

[548] CA Paris, Jan. 20, 1987, *supra* note 158, *rev'd*, on different grounds, Cass. 1e civ., Oct. 11, 1989, *supra* note 159. On subsequent developments in the case, see *infra* para. 610.

"contractual nature of arbitration" to uphold the formal validity of an arbitration agreement which complies with the law governing its substance.[549]

However, this outdated case law is ambiguous in a number of respects. First, is the relevant law that chosen by the parties to govern the arbitration agreement, or that chosen to govern the main contract? Although most decisions specifically refer to the law chosen by the parties to govern the arbitration agreement,[550] a minority validate the arbitration agreement by applying the law governing the main contract. This reveals a degree of uncertainty as to the precise scope of the principle of the autonomy of the arbitration agreement,[551] although it is true that the choice of the law governing the main contract can sometimes be interpreted as extending to the arbitration agreement. The principle of autonomy in fact requires the application of the law governing the arbitration agreement, which may differ from that governing the main contract.[552] Of course, it will often be difficult to establish the parties' true intentions where a contract containing an arbitration clause refers in general terms to a particular law.

The second ambiguity found in this case law concerns the way in which the courts interpreted the recourse to the principle of party autonomy. Earlier decisions confirming the formal validity of the arbitration agreement by reference to the law governing the substance of the contract did not exclude the possibility of validating the agreement by applying the law of the place where the agreement was concluded. The explanation for these decisions lies in the optional nature of the *locus regit actum* rule in French private international law.[553] More recently, however, the courts appeared to have taken a different view, holding that the formal aspects of the arbitration agreement were necessarily governed by the law applicable to the substance of that agreement. For example, in the 1987 *Bomar Oil* case, the Paris Court of Appeals ruled that "the arbitration agreement, in common with the main contract, is subject to the principle of party autonomy."[554] This position is more restrictive than its

---

[549] *See* CA Aix, Sept. 29, 1959, Goldschmidt v. Cottaropoulos, 88 J.D.I. 168 (1961), and observations by J.-B. Sialelli; TGI Seine, Feb. 23, 1961, Costa de Marfil Naviera v. Compagnie Marchande de Tunisie, 1961 REV. ARB. 25; CA Paris, Mar. 27, 1962, Compagnie Marchande de Tunisie v. Costa de Marfil, JCP, Ed. G., Pt. II, No. 13,036 (1963), and P. Level's note; 1962 REV. CRIT. DIP 512, and E. Mezger's note; 90 J.D.I. 468 (1963), and observations by J.-B. Sialelli; CA Paris, May 30, 1963, Gerstlé v. Merry Hull et Cie., 91 J.D.I. 82 (1964), and J.-D. Bredin's note; JCP, Ed. G., Pt. II, No. 13,338 (1963), and observations by H. Motulsky.

[550] But *see* the decisions cited *supra* note 549.

[551] See, in a case where the French decree of May 12, 1981 did not apply, CA Paris, Mar. 25, 1983, *Sorvia*, *supra* note 268. The Court held an arbitration clause contained in a confirmation of sale tacitly accepted by the buyer to be valid as to its form. The Court applied the law governing the substance of the contract, on the grounds of both the parties' tacit agreement and Articles 2 and 3 of The Hague Convention of June 15, 1955 on the Law Applicable to International Sales of Goods. *See also supra* para. 594.

[552] *See supra* para. 412.

[553] *See* Cass. 1e civ., May 28, 1963, Les Films Roger Richebé v. Roy export Co. and Charlie Chaplin, 90 J.D.I. 1004 (1963), and B. Goldman's note; JCP, Ed. G., Pt. II, No. 13,347 (1963), and P. Malaurie's note; 1964 REV. CRIT. DIP 513, and Y. Loussouarn's note. On the adoption of the rule in the 1980 Rome Convention on the Law Applicable to Contractual Obligations, see *infra* para. 603.

[554] CA Paris, Jan. 20, 1987, *supra* note 158.

predecessor in that it appears to exclude the possibility of validating an arbitration agreement which complies with the formal requirements of the jurisdiction in which it was concluded.

The third ambiguity, and one which becomes particularly serious if the alternative of resorting to the *lex locus contractus* is excluded, arises where the parties have not chosen a law to govern the substance of the arbitration agreement. If one accepts that the formal aspects of the arbitration agreement should be subject to the law governing its substance, one must then identify that law by objectively localizing the agreement. If there are a number of relevant connecting factors, which is particularly likely where the arbitration agreement is between parties of different nationalities and fixes the seat of the arbitration in a neutral country, unsatisfactory and unpredictable consequences may result. The dangers inherent in this approach are clearly demonstrated by the 1990 *Cour de cassation* decision in the *Cassia* case, even ignoring the Court's misguided reasoning in referring to the main contract rather than to the arbitration agreement alone.[555] As we have seen, the Court confirmed a decision of the Paris Court of Appeals which ruled that an arbitration agreement, which it localized in Pakistan (by confusing the arbitration agreement with the main contract, the latter of which was to be performed in Pakistan), was invalid as it breached the formal requirements of Pakistani law which "governed both the formal and the substantive conditions."[556] This decision is based on reasoning which has been abandoned in other areas.[557] It is also liable to produce results which, depending on the localization of the arbitration agreement (or worse still, of the main contract),[558] will vary according to local idiosyncrasies, or according to the degree of confidence of the relevant countries in international arbitration. This represented a clear departure from the previous case law recognizing that arbitration agreements could be validated by applying the law chosen by the parties.[559]

If the courts, and particularly arbitral tribunals, were to continue to reason in choice of law terms when determining the law governing the formal validity of an arbitration agreement, they should at least have had a sounder understanding of the choice of law rule applicable to the question.[560]

603. — The third possible connecting factor applicable to the form of the arbitration agreement derives from the rule "*locus regit actum*" which, in French and now European Community private international law, applies to contracts.[561] For many years, French courts held that a contract was valid as to its form if the parties complied with the law of the

---

[555] *See supra* para. 594.

[556] Cass. 1e civ., July 10, 1990, *supra* note 528.

[557] *See supra* paras. 541 *et seq.*

[558] *See supra* para. 412.

[559] *See supra* note 549.

[560] On the prevailing trend in French law, see *infra* para. 608.

[561] BATIFFOL AND LAGARDE, *supra* note 527, at 257; PIERRE MAYER, DROIT INTERNATIONAL PRIVÉ ¶ 753 at 487 (6th ed. 1998); BERNARD AUDIT, DROIT INTERNATIONAL PRIVÉ 155 (2d ed. 1997); IAN F. FLETCHER, CONFLICT OF LAWS AND EUROPEAN COMMUNITY LAW 147 *et seq.* (1982).

jurisdiction where it was signed.[562] However, in contract the rule was never mandatory. The parties were therefore free to depart from it, choosing instead to comply with the formal requirements of the law governing the substance of the agreement,[563] or those of their common national law.[564] These rules have now been replaced by the provisions of the 1980 Rome Convention on the Law Applicable to Contractual Obligations, which codifies the private international law of contracts in the European Union. Article 9 of that Convention provides for only two possible governing laws for the validation of the formal aspects of a contract: that of the place where the contract was concluded (*lex locus contractus*) and that governing the substance of the contract (the "proper law" of the contract). Nevertheless, the Convention is more liberal than earlier case law in that it validates agreements which comply with the proper law of the contract or with the *lex locus contractus*, without requiring proof that the parties intended to depart from the *locus regit actum* rule.[565] The Convention does not apply directly to arbitration agreements, which are specifically excluded from its scope (Art. 1(2)(d)). However, its Article 9 is a modern expression of the choice of law rules governing the form of contracts in Europe, and could easily serve as a model for the purposes of identifying the law governing the arbitration agreement if one were to elect to apply the choice of law approach. In fact, arbitral tribunals have already applied the *locus regit actum* rule as an alternative to the law governing the arbitration agreement itself. For example, in a 1988 award a tribunal rightly considered that "in an international case, the form [of the arbitration agreement] may also be in accordance with the law at the place of the conclusion of the agreement according to the principle that *locus regit formam actus*."[566]

604. — This solution is by no means incompatible with that validating an arbitration agreement which complies with the formal requirements of the law chosen by the parties.[567] Reasoning in choice of law terms, one should be able to conclude that an arbitration agreement is valid as to its form if it complies either with the requirements of the law chosen by the parties to govern the substance of the arbitration agreement, or with those of the place where that agreement was concluded.[568]

However, the growing preference in favor of substantive rules of international commercial arbitration is likely to deprive that choice of law rule of any application.

---

[562] *See* Cass. req., Apr. 18, 1865, Stiepowitch v. Alléon, D.P., Pt. I, at 342 (1865).

[563] Cass. 1e civ., May 28, 1963, *Chaplin, supra* note 553.

[564] Cass. 1e civ., Dec. 10, 1974, Pierrucci v. Harnay, 102 J.D.I. 542 (1975), and P. Kahn's note; 1975 REV. CRIT. DIP 474, and A.P.'s note.

[565] On this issue, see Paul Lagarde, *Le nouveau droit international privé des contrats après l'entrée en vigueur de la convention de Rome du 19 juin 1980*, 1991 REV. CRIT. DIP 287, 329; FLETCHER, *supra* note 561, at 158.

[566] ICC Award No. 5832 (Zurich, 1988), Liechtenstein company v. Austrian company, 115 J.D.I. 1198 (1988), and observations by G. Aguilar Alvarez; 7 INT'L CONSTR. L. REV. 421, 428 (1990).

[567] *See supra* para. 602.

[568] *See* ROBERT, *supra* note 10, ¶ 270; DE BOISSÉSON, *supra* note 6, ¶ 575 at 483.

2° Substantive Rules

605. — Applying the choice of law method to the form of an arbitration agreement is unsatisfactory because the outcome will often be artificial, especially where the parties have made no express choice as to the law applicable to the arbitration agreement. More so than in any other field, it must be accepted that when a court is called upon to review an award, it should apply the substantive rules of its jurisdiction to determine whether to apply principles of consensualism or formalism to international arbitration agreements.[569]

606. — All recent international arbitration statutes favor having the form of the arbitration agreement governed by substantive rules. However, they differ as to the solution actually adopted. Some, such as the new Algerian[570] and Egyptian[571] arbitration laws, require a written document *ad validitatem*. In such a case, the agreement is not valid if the formal requirements are not met. Other laws either expressly state, or can be interpreted as stating, that a written document is merely required *ad probationem*,[572] that is, in order to evidence the existence of the agreement which, in itself, is valid independently of the form in which it is expressed.[573] Most of these laws take a broad view of what constitutes a written

---

[569] *See supra* para. 442.

[570] Article 458 bis 1, paragraph 2, of the Algerian Code of Civil Procedure, as amended on April 25, 1993 which provides that unless the arbitration agreement is in writing it will be void; *see also* Issad, *supra* note 362, at 385; Bedjaoui and Mebroukine, *supra* note 362, at 882.

[571] Art. 12 of Law No. 27 for 1994 Promulgating the Law Concerning Arbitration in Civil and Commercial Matters.

[572] See Article 178, paragraph 1 of the Swiss Private International Law Statute, and Article 1021 of the Dutch Code of Civil Procedure which, under the heading "Form of arbitration agreement," requires the arbitration agreement to be evidenced in writing. Before the 1986 reform, the arbitration agreement could be verbal; see PIETER SANDERS, ALBERT JAN VAN DEN BERG, THE NETHERLANDS ARBITRATION ACT 1986, at 12 (1987).

[573] *See* Art. 1677 of the Belgian Judicial Code, as amended on July 4, 1972 (*see* MARCEL HUYS, GUY KEUTGEN, L'ARBITRAGE EN DROIT BELGE ET INTERNATIONAL ¶ 127 (1981)); Art. 6(1) of the Spanish law of December 5, 1988, and Paz Garcia Rubio's observations in ARBITRATION IN SPAIN 46 (B. Cremades ed., 1991). *See also* Article 7, paragraph 2, of the UNCITRAL Model Law which provides that "[t]he arbitration agreement shall be in writing" but which allows arbitration agreements by reference "provided that the contract [containing the reference to the document containing the arbitration clause] is in writing and the reference is such as to make that clause part of the contract" (for a commentary on these rather ambiguous provisions, see Philippe Fouchard, *La Loi-type de la C.N.U.D.C.I. sur l'arbitrage commercial international*, 114 J.D.I. 861, 884 (1987)); on the equivalent provisions in German law, see Article 1031 of the ZPO, in force as of January 1, 1998 which added to the provisions of the Model Law a paragraph (1031, para. 2) according to which an arbitration agreement is formally valid if contained in a document transmitted by one party to another and if the content of this document is considered part of the contract according to trade usages, provided that no objection was made in good time (see Schlosser, *supra* note 421, at 295; Berger, *supra* note 371, at 124). For the liberal case law prior to that statute, *Bundesgerichtshof*, Dec. 3, 1992, Buyer v. Seller, XX Y.B. COM. ARB. 666 (1995); Art. 6, para. 2, of the Tunisian Code of Arbitration of April 26, 1993 which follows the UNCITRAL Model Law, and the commentary by Kalthoum Meziou and Ali Mezghani, *Le code tunisien de l'arbitrage*, 1993 REV. ARB. 521. In England, see Section 5 of the Arbitration Act 1996. An arbitration agreement not in writing (within the very broad meaning given to the word 'writing' in the Act) is not necessarily void, but is merely outside the scope of the Act (*see* Sec. 81(1)(b)).

document, encompassing telexes, telegrams, facsimiles and all other means of communication which generate a record.[574] Likewise, Article 7, paragraph 2 of the UNCITRAL Model Law provides that:

> [a]n agreement is in writing if it is contained in a document signed by the parties or in an exchange of letters, telex, telegrams or other means of telecommunication which provide a record of the agreement, or in an exchange of statements of claim and defense in which the existence of an agreement is alleged by one party and not denied by another.

The 1987 Swiss arbitration statute takes the same position, requiring a document "in writing, by telegram, telex, telecopier or any other means of communication which permits it to be evidenced by a text" (Art. 178, para. 1). The provisions of the 1996 English Arbitration Act are broader still. The 'writing' need not be signed by the parties, and may result from a recording by one of the parties or by a third party if authorized by the parties to the agreement (Sec. 5).

Other legal systems, however, such as French law, do not require an international arbitration agreement to be in writing.

607. — French law does stipulate that a domestic arbitration agreement must be in writing. Article 1443 of the New Code of Civil Procedure provides that "[a]n arbitration clause is void unless it is set forth in writing in the main agreement or in a document to which that agreement refers." In addition, Article 1449 of the same Code, which can be interpreted as being only a rule of evidence as opposed to a rule of formal validity,[575] states that "a submission agreement shall be evidenced in writing."

608. — In contrast, Title V of Book IV of the French New Code of Civil Procedure—which concerns international arbitration—contains no similar provision covering either the form or the proof of the arbitration agreement. Article 1499 indirectly addresses the issue of form by stipulating, in the context of the recognition and enforcement of awards, that the existence of an award shall be established by submitting the original document "together with the arbitration agreement." It has been observed that this article

---

[574] See the references cited *supra* note 573. For a comparative law analysis of the form of the arbitration agreement, see DAVID, *supra* note 1, ¶¶ 215 *et seq*. On the similar requirements of the New York Convention, see *infra* para. 618.

[575] *See* P. Fouchard, note following Cass. 2e civ., Nov. 17, 1993, Pfister v. Zugmeyer (which, in a rather unsatisfactory decision, holds that in French domestic arbitration, where an agreement in writing is required, minutes of a meeting signed by the arbitrator alone cannot constitute a submission agreement (1995 REV. ARB. 78)). *See also* Jacqueline Rubellin-Devichi and Eric Loquin, *Arbitrage – Compromis et clause compromissoire*, J.-CL. PROC. CIV., Fasc. 1020, ¶ 4 (1995).

does little to promote verbal arbitration agreements,[576] but it is unclear whether it is legitimate to infer that it requires a written arbitration agreement, or at least an arbitration agreement evidenced in writing.[577] The answer is probably in the negative, because this provision in fact merely requires that the plaintiff should put the court hearing the action for enforcement in a position to establish, *prima facie*, the existence of an arbitration agreement.[578]

For that reason, most commentators of the 1981 Decree on international arbitration have concluded that French international arbitration law contains no requirements of form. For instance, it has been argued that among the grounds on which an award can be set aside for want of a valid arbitration agreement, "one can immediately exclude nullity for breach of requirements of form," and that this is a substantive rule of French law of international arbitration, given that "in view of Article 1493, no particular form, nor any minimum content is required in international arbitration."[579]

609. — This rule, which is specific to international arbitration, applies even where the parties have expressly made the arbitration subject to French law. In that case, Article 1495 states that the provisions of Title I concerning domestic arbitration agreements "only apply in the absence of a specific agreement." Thus, in international arbitration, the formal requirements of Articles 1443 (for arbitration clauses) and 1449 (for submission agreements) are only of subsidiary application. This raises a question as to whether a verbal arbitration agreement constitutes an exception to the requirements of Articles 1443 and 1449, or whether such an agreement is invalid because the parties' intentions are not expressed in writing. Most authors consider a verbal arbitration agreement to be valid in such circumstances, which is in keeping with the liberal spirit of the 1981 reform of French international arbitration law.[580] One can therefore legitimately conclude that in international arbitration, even where the arbitration is subject to French law, the mere fact that an

---

[576] Fouchard, *supra* note 126, at 385. *Comp. with* Berthold Goldman, *La nouvelle réglementation française de l'arbitrage international, in* THE ART OF ARBITRATION – ESSAYS ON INTERNATIONAL ARBITRATION – LIBER AMICORUM PIETER SANDERS 153, 161 (J. Schultz and A.J. van den Berg eds., 1982).

[577] See the observations made by Pieter Sanders at the Colloquium organized by the Comité français de l'arbitrage on *La réforme de l'arbitrage international en France – Décret du 12 mai 1981*, 1981 REV. ARB. 521.

[578] On the documents required in the absence of a written agreement, see *infra* para. 1576.

[579] Bellet and Mezger, *supra* note 129, at 622. *See also* Bernard Audit, *A National Codification of International Commercial Arbitration: The French Decree of May 12, 1981, in* RESOLVING TRANSNATIONAL DISPUTES THROUGH ARBITRATION 117, 126 (T. Carbonneau ed., 1984), who argues that the silence of the legislature on this point is not merely coincidental; Bourdin, *supra* note 10, at 21; Yves Derains and Rosabel E. Goodman-Everard, *France* (at 11), *in* ICCA INTERNATIONAL HANDBOOK ON COMMERCIAL ARBITRATION (1998); DE BOISSÉSON, *supra* note 6, ¶ 572 at 477.

[580] *See* Bellet and Mezger, *supra* note 129, at 627; E. Loquin, note following Cass. 1e civ., Oct. 11, 1989, *Bomar Oil, supra* note 159, at 642; Derains and Goodman-Everard, *supra* note 579, at 11. Compare the more skeptical position taken by Fouchard, *supra* note 126, at 385. *See also* Daniel Cohen, *La soumission de l'arbitrage international à la loi française (commentaire de l'article 1495 NCPC)*, 1991 REV. ARB. 155, esp. at 185 *et seq.*

arbitration agreement is in a form other than that prescribed in Article 1443 is sufficient to establish the parties' intention to depart from the provisions of that Article.[581]

For that reason, the French *Cour de cassation*'s first *Bomar Oil* decision was rather surprising: it suggested that both French law and the New York Convention[582] required that an arbitration agreement incorporated by reference should be mentioned in the main contract, except where the parties had an ongoing business relationship.[583] Even prior to the 1980 and 1981 reforms of French arbitration law, the courts consistently held that French law favored the application of the principle of consensualism to arbitration agreements, especially in international cases.[584] That case law came to an end, as far as domestic arbitration was concerned, with Article 1443. In contrast, however, the legislature remained silent on the question when reforming the law on international arbitration in 1981, and thus clearly intended to maintain the earlier position of the courts.

A number of recent decisions have rightly confirmed that French law continues to favor the principle of consensualism in international arbitration.[585] In its second *Bomar Oil* decision, the *Cour de cassation* clearly did so by establishing a substantive rule of international arbitration law to that effect.[586] Similarly, in its two decisions in the 1994 *V 2000* case, the Paris Court of Appeals came out in favor of the principle of consensualism by instructing the arbitrators to "determine whether [the] initialing of a document which is not the actual agreement constitutes the consent required to empower the arbitrators."[587] In even clearer terms, the Paris Court of Appeals observed in 1995 that an arbitration agreement existed despite the fact that none of the parties had signed a written contract "which is common practice in the [grain] trade in question."[588]

---

[581] CA Paris, Feb. 19, 1988, *Firme Peter Biegi, aff'd*, Cass. 1e civ., Feb. 18, 1992, *supra* note 173.

[582] *See infra* para. 616.

[583] See the disapproving notes of C. Kessedjian and E. Loquin, following Cass 1e civ., Oct. 11, 1989, *supra* note 159. On arbitration agreements incorporated by reference, see *supra* paras. 493 *et seq.*

[584] *See, e.g.*, CA Paris, Mar. 27, 1962, *Compagnie Marchande de Tunisie*, *supra* note 549. See also, stating that in French domestic arbitration prior to 1980 the parties' consent was subject to no particular conditions of form, Cass. com., Mar. 23, 1981, Rousseau v. Cie. européenne de céréales, 1982 REV. ARB. 176, and P. Fouchard's note.

[585] *See, e.g.*, CA Versailles, Jan. 23, 1991, *Bomar Oil, supra* note 160, *aff'd*, Cass. 1e civ., Nov. 9, 1993, *supra* note 165. *Comp. with* CA Paris, Mar. 26, 1991, *Dalico, supra* note 33, *aff'd*, Cass. 1e civ., Dec. 20, 1993, *supra* note 2.

[586] Cass. 1e civ., Nov. 9, 1993, *supra* note 165. The terms used are cited *supra* para. 495.

[587] CA Paris, Dec. 7, 1994, *supra* note 125.

[588] CA Paris, June 8, 1995, SARL Centro Stoccaggio Grani v. SA Granit, 1997 REV. ARB. 89, and observations by Y. Derains.

610. — French international arbitration law thus rejects formalism, opting instead for a strict application to arbitration agreements of the principle of consensualism, whereby no particular form is required.[589]

§ 2. – International Conventions

611. — Two important international conventions contain provisions governing the form of arbitration agreements: the 1958 New York Convention (A) and the 1961 European Convention (B).

A.–THE NEW YORK CONVENTION

612. — Under Article II, paragraph 1 of the 1958 New York Convention, each contracting state is required to recognize "an agreement in writing" under which the parties agree to submit their disputes to arbitration. Paragraph 2 of the same article stipulates that "the term 'agreement in writing' shall include an arbitral clause in a contract or an arbitration agreement, signed by the parties or contained in an exchange of letters or telegrams." In addition, the Convention specifies that the party applying for recognition and enforcement of an arbitral award must supply "the duly authenticated original award or a duly certified copy thereof."[590]

We shall discuss the formal requirements of the New York Convention in further detail (2°), after having first examined how such provisions tie in with those of national arbitration laws (1°).

1° The Relationship Between the Requirements of Form of the New York Convention and Those of National Arbitration Laws

613. — The relationship between the New York Convention and national arbitration laws raises two questions: first, can the law in countries that have ratified the Convention be more liberal than the Convention itself with regard to the form of the arbitration agreement (a); and, second, when a party does rely on the more liberal provisions of a particular national law or of another international convention, can it still rely on the New York Convention with regard to issues other than the form of the arbitration agreement (b)?

---

[589] See also, on the anachronistic nature of imposing requirements of form in international trade, Mayer, *supra* note 291, ¶¶ 114 *et seq.*

[590] *See* Art. IV, para. 1(a).

a) Can National Laws Be More Liberal than the New York Convention?

614. — By way of a substantive rule of international arbitration, the French Decree of 1981 removed all requirements of form conditioning the validity of an international arbitration agreement.[591] By contrast, the 1958 New York Convention is more restrictive, in that it demands an agreement in writing. Must the courts of a contracting state such as France, where national law is thus more liberal than the New York Convention, nevertheless enforce the requirements of the Convention? If that were the case, the Convention would be considered a convention establishing uniform legislation, rather than one aiming to facilitate the recognition and enforcement of awards.[592]

In France, this issue arose in the *Bomar Oil* case. In its 1987 decision, the Paris Court of Appeals ruled that:

> [b]y reason of the general nature of the wording of paragraphs 1 and 2 of Art. II of the New York Convention, it must be admitted that this text expresses a substantive rule which must be applied in all cases. This is true whether the arbitration agreement is invoked in support of an objection for lack of competence before a State court or is contested before an arbitral tribunal so that the case will be remitted to the ordinary court.

That decision was subsequently reversed by the *Cour de cassation*, not because the New York Convention cannot apply where a national law is more liberal, but because the *Cour de cassation* had a different interpretation of the requirements of Article II of the New York Convention. Likewise, the Court of Appeals to which the case was remitted did not rule on the issue of whether the Convention can apply where national laws are more liberal. However, in its second decision in the same case, the *Cour de cassation* did not refer to the New York Convention and based itself entirely on a substantive rule of international arbitration law.[593]

Even disregarding the actual provisions of both the New York Convention[594] and French international arbitration law[595] governing the form of an arbitration agreement, the method employed by the Paris Court of Appeals in its 1987 *Bomar Oil* decision is somewhat unsatisfactory. The New York Convention carefully stipulates, in Article VII, paragraph 1 that it shall not "deprive any interested party of any right he may have to avail himself of an arbitral award in the manner and to the extent allowed by the law or the treaties of the country where such award is sought to be relied upon." In other words, the Convention

---

[591] *See supra* para. 608.

[592] On this issue, see VAN DEN BERG, *supra* note 12, at 178 *et seq.*

[593] CA Paris, Jan. 20, 1987, *supra* note 158, XIII Y.B. COM. ARB. 469 (1988), *rev'd*, Cass. 1e civ., Oct. 11, 1989, *supra* note 159; on remand, CA Versailles, Jan. 23 1991, *supra* note 160, *aff'd*, Cass. 1e civ., Nov. 9, 1993, *supra* note 165 and the commentary *supra* para. 609.

[594] *See infra* paras. 616 *et seq.*

[595] *See supra* para. 609.

imposes only a certain degree of liberalism in the recognition and enforcement of awards, and each country can always choose a less restrictive approach on the basis of its national law or other international instruments. Thus, in the *Bomar Oil* case, the New York Convention could have been excluded once it had been shown that French law offered the parties more freedom.[596]

Such an argument must, however, be pleaded by the parties before the lower courts, because a plaintiff cannot rely on the New York Convention before the court of first instance and court of appeals and then purport to rely solely on French national law before the *Cour de cassation*.[597] In addition, there is the question of whether the New York Convention can be relied on only in part, and whether, in order to rely on it at all, all of its requirements must be satisfied.

b) In Order to Rely on the New York Convention, Is It Necessary to Comply with All Its Terms?

615. — There is some debate as to whether a party can rely on the New York Convention with regard to certain issues while relying, for others, on more favorable provisions of a national law. In particular, where a party relies on national rules imposing no particular conditions as to the form of the arbitration agreement, does it not definitively lose the right to rely on the New York Convention? In practice, this question is not relevant to the relationship between the New York Convention and French law, as French law is more liberal than the New York Convention in every respect, not only as regards the form of the arbitration agreement.[598] The French courts are therefore unlikely to encounter a situation where a party could benefit from relying on both the New York Convention and French law. That situation could arise, however, in other legal systems.

---

[596] *See also* C. Kessedjian, note following Cass. 1e civ., Oct. 11, 1989, *Bomar Oil, supra* note 159, at 137. Compare, on the basis of Article VII of the New York Convention, E. Loquin, note following Cass. 1e civ., Oct. 11, 1989, *Bomar Oil, supra* note 159 at 637. See also, for a decision that the New York Convention only applies to procedures for the recognition and enforcement of an arbitral award, CA Paris, Feb. 21, 1980, General National Maritime Transport Co. v. Götaverken Arendal A.B., 107 J.D.I. 660 (1980), and P. Fouchard's note; 1980 Rev. Arb. 524, and F.C. Jeantet's note; Dalloz, Jur. 568 (1980), and J. Robert's note; 1980 Rev. Crit. DIP 763, and E. Mezger's note; JCP, Ed. G., Pt. II, No. 19,512 (1981), and P. Level's note; for an English translation, see VI Y.B. Com. Arb. 221 (1981); 20 I.L.M. 883 (1981), with an introductory note by F.C. Jeantet; Cass. 1e civ., May 25, 1983, Maatschappij voor Industriele Research en Ontwikkeling v. Lievremont, 1985 Rev. Arb. 415, 1st decision, and H. Synvet's note; 1983 Bull. Civ. I, No. 156; for an English translation, see XII Y.B. Com. Arb. 480 (1987); CA Paris, Dec. 20, 1984, Commandement des Forces Aériennes de la République Islamique d'Iran v. Bendone Derossi International Ltd., 1985 Rev. Arb. 415, and H. Synvet's note; for an English translation, see XII Y.B. Com. Arb. 482 (1987); *aff'd*, Cass. 1e civ., May 5, 1987, 114 J.D.I. 964 (1987), and B. Oppetit's note; 1988 Rev. Arb. 137, and H. Synvet's note; for an English translation, see XIV Y.B. Com. Arb. 627 (1989).

[597] Cass. com., Feb. 25, 1986, C.O.N.F.E.X. v. Dahan, 113 J.D.I. 735 (1986), and J.-M. Jacquet's note; 1990 Rev. Arb. 623, and the commentary by Oppetit, *supra* note 93.

[598] *See infra* paras. 1644 *et seq.*

Some authors argue that in specifying the conditions governing the recognition and enforcement of an award, the New York Convention defines the situations which are considered as deserving protection, without prejudice to the potential recognition under national laws of awards which do not satisfy its requirements. For example, on the question of the form of the arbitration agreement, the Convention only seeks to protect agreements in writing or awards made on the basis of such agreements. It would therefore be contrary to the intentions of the authors of the Convention if awards made on the basis of agreements not complying with its requirements were nevertheless to benefit from the regime set forth in the Convention.[599]

However, other authors consider that the New York Convention contains nothing to prevent the combination of its provisions with national law rules which may be more liberal in some respects.[600] Several decisions in jurisdictions where this issue is important in practice appear to support that view.[601]

2° Provisions of the New York Convention Regarding the Form of the Arbitration Agreement

616. — Article II, paragraph 2 of the New York Convention contains a substantive rule requiring that an arbitration agreement be "signed by the parties or contained in an exchange of letters or telegrams."

617. — The Convention does not stipulate that the arbitration agreement must be contained in a single document and hence does not, as such, exclude agreements incorporated by reference.[602]

618. — With regard to the material form taken by a valid arbitration agreement, the Convention lists only contracts formally signed by the parties, letters and telegrams. That merely reflects the fact that the Convention was open for signature in 1958, and it has been held that telexes should be assimilated with telegrams.[603] The same would certainly apply

---

[599] *See* VAN DEN BERG, *supra* note 12, at 180, and the references cited therein.

[600] See, for example, E. Loquin, note following Cass. 1e civ., Oct. 11, 1989, *Bomar Oil, supra* note 159, at 638, who considers that the annotated case supports such a view.

[601] On this issue, generally, see *supra* para. 271 and the decisions cited therein.

[602] On the application of Article II of the New York Convention to arbitration clauses incorporated by reference, see the case law cited *supra* para. 494.

[603] CA Paris, Jan 20, 1987, *Bomar Oil, supra* note 158; Swiss Fed. Trib., Jan. 12, 1989, G. S.A. v. T. Ltd., XV Y.B. COM. ARB. 509 (1990); Court of Savona (Italy), Mar. 26, 1981, Dimitrios Varverakis v. Compañia de Navigacion Artico S.A., X Y.B. COM. ARB. 455 (1985); Austrian Supreme Court (*Oberster Gerichtshof*), May 2, 1972, X Y.B. COM. ARB. 417 (1985). On the fact that a telex will not satisfy the conditions of Article II of the Convention in circumstances where the offer to have disputes resolved by arbitration has not actually been accepted, see Sen Mar, Inc. v. Tiger Petroleum Corp., 774 F. Supp. 879 (S.D.N.Y. 1991); XVIII Y.B.

(continued...)

to facsimiles. Nowadays, a court could usefully refer to the generic phrases adopted in Article 7, paragraph 2 of the UNCITRAL Model Law, or Article 178, paragraph 1 of the Swiss Private International Law Statute.[604]

619. — Is it necessary for letters, telegrams and other assimilated documents to bear the signature of the parties? Taken literally, Article II of the Convention does require the signature of both arbitration clauses contained in a contract (in other words, the signature of the contract itself) and arbitration agreements contained in a separate document. Obviously, a signature on a telegram, telex, or faxed letter will necessarily be either typed or a copy of the original manuscript signature. It can therefore be assumed that a signature, in the traditional sense of the word, is not required. On the other hand, the same will not usually be the case with an exchange of letters. However, since Article II does not expressly require a signature in that case, it is clear that an arbitration agreement consisting of an exchange of letters will be valid as to its form even where some or all of the letters are not signed, provided that it is possible to identify the author of the letter, using all available means of evidence (such as correspondence, affidavits, declarations before the arbitral tribunal, and the involvement of the relevant party in the arbitral proceedings).[605]

620. — On the other hand, difficulties with regard to the conditions of form laid down by the New York Convention are likely to arise in the case of verbal arbitration agreements, arbitration agreements resulting from the tacit acceptance of a contractual offer containing an arbitration clause, and arbitration agreements alleged to exist because the same parties have entered into previous contracts containing arbitration clauses to which a subsequent contract does not refer.[606] In such circumstances, a party might claim that there is no agreement in writing, although of course a verbal agreement subsequently evidenced in writing (in an exchange of correspondence, for example) would satisfy the conditions of the

---

[603](...continued)
COM. ARB. 493 (1993).

[604] *See supra* para. 606. *See* Swiss Fed. Trib., Jan. 16, 1995, Compagnie de Navigation et Transports S.A. v. MSC Mediterranean Shipping Co. S.A., 1995 BULL. ASA 503, 509, and the commentary by J.-F. Poudret and G. Cottier at 383; for a summary in English, see 1996 BULL. ASA 488, and observations by R. Hill and by C.U. Mayer at 361; 1996 REV. SUISSE DR. INT. ET DR. EUR. 561, and observations by F. Knoepfler.

[605] See, in the United States, Sphere Drake Ins. PLC v. Marine Towing, Inc., 16 F.3d 666 (5th Cir. 1994); 9 INT'L ARB. REP. 8 (May 1994); Earthtrade, Inc. v. General Brands Int'l Corp., No. 95 Civ. 8913 (LMM), 1996 U.S. Dist. LEXIS 1520 (S.D.N.Y. Feb. 7, 1996); 11 INT'L ARB. REP. 4 (Apr. 1996); Overseas Cosmos, Inc. v. NR Vessel Corp., No. 97 Civ. 5898 (DC), 1997 U.S. Dist. LEXIS 19390 (S.D.N.Y. Dec. 8, 1997), *appeal dismissed*, 148 F.3d 51 (2d Cir. 1998); 13 INT'L ARB. REP. 11 (May 1998), and the commentary by Paul D. Friedland, *U.S. Courts' Misapplication of the 'Agreement In Writing' Requirement For Enforcement Of An Arbitration Agreement Under The New York Convention*, 13 INT'L ARB. REP. 21 (May 1998); *see also* Hong Kong Supreme Court, Apr. 6, 1995, Sulanser Co. Ltd. v. Jiangxi Provincial Metal and Minerals Import and Export Corp., 10 INT'L ARB. REP. B1 (June 1995).

[606] For a criticism of the requirement of the New York Convention in this respect, see Neil Kaplan, *Is the Need for Writing as Expressed in the New York Convention and the Model Law Out of Step with Commercial Practice?*, 12 ARB. INT'L 27 (1996).

Convention. Likewise, where a written offer containing an arbitration clause has been accepted verbally, the party seeking to rely on the New York Convention will be able to prove the existence of a written agreement, with the only remaining question concerning the existence of the other party's consent to arbitration.

B. – THE 1961 EUROPEAN CONVENTION

621. — Article I, paragraph 2 of the 1961 European Convention states that for the purpose of the Convention, the term "arbitration agreement" shall mean

> either an arbitral clause in a contract or an arbitration agreement, the contract or arbitration agreement being signed by the parties, or contained in an exchange of letters, telegrams, or in a communication by teleprinter and, in relations between States whose laws do not require that an arbitration agreement be made in writing, any arbitration agreement concluded in the form authorized by these laws.

622. — This provision contains a substantive rule similar to that in Article II of the New York Convention, although it is expressed in more precise terms. In addition to an exchange of letters and telegrams, it mentions teleprinters, but it still lacks the generic phrase later adopted in the UNCITRAL Model Law.[607] Given that the two instruments are similar in spirit, the European Convention should be interpreted as broadly as the New York Convention.[608]

623. — The same provision also contains a rule permitting verbal arbitration agreements in relations between countries whose laws require no written form.

This provision raises two problems of interpretation. The first concerns the definition of "States whose laws do not require that an arbitration agreement be made in writing:" does this refer to countries where, at the time the arbitration agreement was signed, the parties had their headquarters or habitual residence? Or should one also consider the country or countries where the arbitration agreement or award is to be enforced? The second interpretation appears to coincide with the position expressed, albeit in rather confused terms, at a special meeting of the plenipotentiaries.[609] However, we believe the first interpretation to be the correct one. Article I, paragraph 1(a) of the Convention states that the Convention applies to arbitration agreements entered into "between physical or legal

---

[607] *See supra* para. 606.

[608] *See supra* paras. 616 *et seq.* For the validation of an arbitration agreement concluded by telex, see Italian *Corte di Cassazione*, Oct. 15, 1992, Agrò di Reolfi Piera snc v. Ro Koproduct oour Produktiva, XX Y.B. COM. ARB. 1061 (1995).

[609] Dominique T. Hascher, *European Convention on International Commercial Arbitration of 1961 – Commentary*, XX Y.B. COM. ARB.1006, 1015 (1995). *See also* FOUCHARD, *supra* note 4, ¶ 144 at 83.

persons having, when concluding the agreement, their habitual place of residence or their seat in different Contracting States." Thus, when paragraph 2 of that same article refers to "relations between States whose laws do not require that the arbitration agreement be made in writing," it too seems to refer to the countries where the parties to the arbitration agreement have their habitual residence or their headquarters. Furthermore, the second interpretation would render paragraph 2 inoperative: if the law of the country where enforcement is sought does not require an arbitration agreement to be in writing, it can always recognize an award made on the basis of a verbal arbitration agreement under its own national law.[610] If, on the other hand, it is accepted that the terms "relations between States whose laws do not require that the arbitration agreement be made in writing" refer in fact to the countries of the parties, the provision is fully effective, in that the jurisdiction where enforcement is sought cannot be more restrictive than the "home" jurisdictions of the parties.[611] This interpretation is also in keeping with the reduced role of the seat of arbitration in contemporary international arbitration law.[612]

The second problem of interpretation is whether the Convention requires that the more liberal laws of the relevant countries which "do not require that the arbitration agreement be made in writing" be identical.[613] In fact, given the flexibility of the conditions provided for in the European Convention, the only more liberal form would be a verbal arbitration agreement, and it is hard to envisage how there could be different variants of the verbal form. Even if that were the case, the agreement would only be valid as to its form if it satisfied the requirements of the least liberal of the laws of the countries concerned, while still not requiring the agreement to be in writing.

---

[610] On the fact that although, unlike the New York Convention (Art. VII), it contains no express provision to that effect, the 1961 European Convention, the purpose of which "is only to facilitate the recognition of arbitration agreements" does not restrict the possibility of recognizing an award pursuant to more favorable rules of the country of recognition, see *Oberlandesgericht* of Hamburg, Sept. 22, 1978, Italian company v. German (F.R.) firm, V Y.B. COM. ARB. 262 (1980). *See also* Art. I, Scope of the Convention.

[611] For an example of the application of this Convention taking into account only the law of the habitual residence of a party, which was the same as the place where the contract was signed, see *Bundesgerichtshof*, May 25, 1970, Australian seller v. German F.R. buyer, II Y.B. COM. ARB. 237 (1977), and the disapproving observations by Hascher, *supra* note 609.

[612] See generally *infra* paras. 1178 *et seq.* and, for the European Convention, *supra* para. 280.

[613] *See* FOUCHARD, *supra* note 4, ¶ 144.

CHAPTER III
EFFECTS OF THE ARBITRATION AGREEMENT

624. — An arbitration agreement is a contract in which the parties agree to submit their existing or future disputes to arbitrators, and not to the courts.[1] Put positively, an arbitration agreement obliges the parties to honor this commitment and provides the basis for the jurisdiction of the arbitral tribunal; put negatively, the arbitration agreement prevents the parties from seeking the resolution by the courts of disputes covered by the arbitration agreement.[2]

We shall therefore consider in turn the positive (Section I) and the negative effects (Section II) of the arbitration agreement.

SECTION I
POSITIVE EFFECTS OF THE ARBITRATION AGREEMENT

625. — The arbitration agreement obliges the parties to submit disputes covered by it to arbitration (§ 1). It also provides the basis for the jurisdiction of the arbitral tribunal (§ 2).

§ 1. – The Parties' Obligation to Submit Disputes Covered by the Arbitration Agreement to Arbitration

626. — It is now firmly established that parties are obliged to submit disputes covered by an arbitration agreement to arbitration (A) and that this obligation is capable of specific performance (B). It is equally clear that this obligation prevails over any jurisdictional privilege or immunity enjoyed by the parties (C).

---

[1] *See supra* para. 385.

[2] On the distinction between positive and negative effects of the arbitration agreement, see RENÉ DAVID, ARBITRATION IN INTERNATIONAL TRADE ¶ 232 (1985).

A. – THE PRINCIPLE THAT PARTIES ARE OBLIGED TO SUBMIT DISPUTES COVERED BY THEIR ARBITRATION AGREEMENT TO ARBITRATION

627. — The obligation to submit disputes covered by an arbitration agreement to arbitration results from a straightforward application of the principle that parties are bound by their contracts. This principle, which is often expressed as the maxim *pacta sunt servanda*, is probably the most widely recognized rule of international contract law.[3] Consequently, the principle that arbitration agreements are binding has been readily accepted as a substantive rule of international commercial arbitration. The French courts, for instance, have therefore never sought to determine the applicable law when upholding the binding nature of an arbitration agreement.[4] Further, they would refuse to apply a law which fails to recognize the binding nature of arbitration agreements, even where the dispute is connected with that law, whether through the nationality of the parties, the subject-matter of the dispute or the law governing its merits.

628. — Thus, by applying a substantive rule of international arbitration law, the French courts will recognize an award made on the basis of an arbitration agreement considered to be ineffective by another legal system, even if that legal system has close connections with the dispute. This will be so regardless of the grounds on which the non-French legal system finds the arbitration agreement to be invalid.[5] For example, the 1989 Colombian decree on arbitration does not recognize the validity of an arbitration agreement between two parties where the dispute may concern a third party.[6] This is aimed at resolving problems arising from the fact that it is impossible to bring related disputes before the same judicial authority where the arbitration agreement has not been accepted by all the parties involved. It is, however, extremely unfavorable towards arbitration. For example, a dispute between a foreign contractor and a Colombian owner may involve construction works carried out in Colombia by local sub-contractors unwilling to have their disputes resolved by arbitration. In order to avoid being bound by the arbitration agreement contained in the main construction contract, a party to it—not necessarily the Colombian party—might argue that the award should be enforceable against the Colombian sub-contractors, and that, as the latter refuse to take part in the arbitral proceedings, the arbitration agreement is void. If the dispute were brought before the French courts—if the seat of arbitration were in France or

---

[3]   On the application of this principle to the merits of the contracts in dispute, see *infra* para. 1460.

[4]   *See, e.g.*, CA Paris, Apr. 20, 1988, Clark International Finance v. Sud Matériel Service, 1988 REV. ARB. 570, and the report by Jean-Louis Goutal, *L'arbitrage et les tiers: I. – Le droit des contrats, id.* at 439. On the generalization of this method as a result of the decision of the *Cour de cassation* in the *Dalico* case, see *supra* para. 437.

[5]   This will be the case, for example, where the non-French law only allows submission agreements. On the rejection of this position, even in French domestic arbitration law, by the French statute of December 31, 1925, see *supra* para. 386.

[6]   Art. 30 of Decree No. 2279 of October 7, 1989, as amended by Law No. 23 of March 21, 1991. See also the critical commentary of this provision by Fernando Mantilla-Serrano, *La nouvelle législation colombienne sur l'arbitrage*, 1992 REV. ARB. 41, 54.

the award were to be enforced there—those courts would not need to identify the law applicable to the arbitration agreement in order to determine whether, and under what conditions, that law validates the arbitration agreement. They would only need to apply the minimum requirements of French international arbitration law governing the validity of arbitration agreements.

629. — International conventions on arbitration soon recognized the binding nature of the obligation to refer to arbitration disputes covered by arbitration agreements. The 1923 Geneva Protocol on Arbitration Clauses in Commercial Matters implicitly did so by providing, in its Article 1, that:

> Each of the contracting states recognizes the validity of an agreement whether relating to existing or future differences between parties subject respectively to the jurisdiction of different contracting states by which the parties to a contract agree to submit to arbitration all or any differences that may arise in connection with such contract relating to commercial matters or to any other matter capable of settlement by arbitration, whether or not the arbitration is to take place in a country to whose jurisdiction none of the parties is subject.[7]

The 1958 New York Convention on the Recognition and Enforcement of Foreign Arbitral Awards also contains, at its Article II, paragraph 1, the principle that:

> Each Contracting State shall recognize an agreement in writing under which the parties undertake to submit to arbitration all or any differences which have arisen or which may arise between them in respect of a defined legal relationship, whether contractual or not, concerning a subject matter capable of settlement by arbitration.

Without explicitly restating the principle that parties to an arbitration agreement are bound to submit to arbitration disputes covered by it, the 1961 European Convention also endorses that principle by providing in great detail for the appointment of the arbitrator or arbitrators where the parties have failed to make such an appointment.[8] This clearly indicates that the parties are obliged to submit their disputes to arbitration if they want to have them resolved through a judicial process.

630. — However, the obligation to refer disputes covered by the arbitration agreement to arbitration would be of little use were it not capable of specific performance.

---

[7] Adopted in Geneva on September 24, 1923, this Protocol no longer applies to relationships between countries that are parties to the New York Convention; see *supra* para. 240.

[8] *See* Art. IV. On the indirect mechanisms set forth in this Convention for the appointment of the arbitral tribunal, see *infra* paras. 924 *et seq.*

B. – THE OBLIGATION TO SUBMIT TO ARBITRATION DISPUTES COVERED BY THE ARBITRATION AGREEMENT IS CAPABLE OF SPECIFIC PERFORMANCE

631. — If the only remedy for a party's refusal to perform an arbitration agreement were an award of damages, that arbitration agreement would be of little value. If a party were unable to bring its dispute before an international arbitral tribunal and the courts accepted jurisdiction to hear the case, it would be extremely difficult to assess the resulting loss in monetary terms. Clearly, a party unable to bring its claim before an arbitral tribunal will often suffer real damage. For example, if a court were to rule in its favor, a party might find it considerably more difficult to enforce the judgment of the court than an equivalent award made by an arbitral tribunal. This will generally be the case where the arbitral tribunal has its seat in a country which is a party to the 1958 New York Convention, because the Convention has been ratified by a large number of countries, greatly facilitating enforcement of the award.[9] On the other hand, the value of the loss of the opportunity to have a dispute resolved by arbitration is almost impossible to quantify. If a court has accepted jurisdiction over the dispute, any assessment of the loss in terms of equivalent reparation would involve an unfeasible—and in any case very unsatisfactory—comparison between the respective merits of arbitration and the relevant court system. It is therefore almost impossible to attribute a monetary value to the loss of the opportunity to have a dispute decided by arbitration, unless the lost opportunity results in a complete denial of justice.[10] Consequently, the only satisfactory outcome for the parties is for there to be specific performance of the arbitration agreement.

632. — However, that has not always been the case. In Roman law, arbitration agreements were not enforceable as such, and a party could avoid the application of an arbitration agreement, even after an award had been made, by paying the *poena* stipulated in the agreement itself.[11] Even today, a small number of legal systems remain hostile to arbitration and do not censure the failure to comply with an arbitration agreement by requiring specific performance. This was long the case with some Latin American countries, at least until the recent development of arbitration in that part of the world.[12] For example, before the Law of September 23, 1996 on Arbitration, the arbitration provisions of the Brazilian Civil Code and Code of Civil Procedure referred to submission agreements but not

---

[9] On this issue, see *infra* para. 1666.

[10] This is not so of the costs incurred by a party in having to put its case before a court that has no jurisdiction as a result of the existence of an arbitration agreement. The arbitral tribunal will have jurisdiction over disputes concerning the implementation of the arbitration agreement and could therefore require that those costs be paid by the party that failed to respect its obligation to submit disputes to arbitration, thus causing its co-contractor to incur costs. That would of course penalize the breach of the negative obligation not to submit disputes to the courts (*see infra* para. 661).

[11] *See* DAVID, *supra* note 2, ¶ 232 at 290.

[12] *See* Horacio A. Grigera Naón, *Latin America: Overcoming Traditional Hostility Towards Arbitration, in* PRACTISING LAW INSTITUTE, INTERNATIONAL COMMERCIAL ARBITRATION – RECENT DEVELOPMENTS, Vol. II, at 375 (1988); Horacio A. Grigera Naón, *Arbitration in Latin America: recent developments in Mexico and Colombia, in* JAHRBUCH FÜR DIE PRAXIS DER SCHIEDSGERICHTSBARKEIT 263 (1990); *see also supra* para. 171.

to arbitration clauses. For many years, both the courts and legal commentators considered that, even where an arbitration agreement existed, it was still necessary to enter into a submission agreement when the dispute arose. Further, if a party refused to enter into a submission agreement, it could not be compelled to do so. In other words, although an arbitration agreement was deemed to be a contract obliging the parties to enter into a further contract (the submission agreement), it was not capable of specific performance. At the very most, a refusal to enter into the submission agreement might render the party in question liable for the resulting loss, in so far as such loss could be established. [13] In 1990, however, the Brazilian Supreme Court abandoned that approach. Applying the 1923 Geneva Protocol, it held that an arbitration clause in an international contract was sufficient to allow an arbitration to proceed.[14] The Law of September 23, 1996 took the same position: it contains a complex mechanism which enables the party seeking arbitration to overcome another party's refusal to sign the submission agreement that is still required, at least for *ad hoc* arbitration.[15] Similarly, Mexico[16] and Colombia[17] now both recognize the fact that an arbitration agreement must be enforced. Jurisdictions which maintain the earlier position are thus becoming increasingly scarce.[18]

Most legal systems ensure that arbitration agreements are capable of specific performance. To that end, various mechanisms are set up to deal with situations where a party has entered into an arbitration agreement and, no longer wishing to take part in an arbitration, instead attempts to stall the proceedings. In such cases, the arbitration can go ahead, in spite of the refusal of a party to participate in the arbitral procedure, or in aspects of that procedure such as the appointment of the arbitral tribunal and the submission of pleadings and evidence. Almost all arbitration legislation provides a means of minimizing the adverse effects of such delaying tactics on the conduct of the arbitration.[19] For instance, a number of common law systems allow the arbitrator appointed by the claimant to act as

---

[13] *See* Vicente Marota Rangel, *Brazil* (at 4), *in* ICCA INTERNATIONAL HANDBOOK ON COMMERCIAL ARBITRATION (1988), and the exceptions mentioned therein.

[14] Brazilian *Superior Tribunal de Justiça*, Apr. 24, 1990, Companhia de Navegação Lloyd Brasileiro v. A.S. Ivarans Rederi, 1995 REV. ARB. 137, and J. Bosco Lee's note.

[15] Art. 7 of Law No. 9.307-96 of September 23, 1996 on arbitration, *Diario Official*, Sept. 24, 1996, pp. 18,897 to 18,900. *See also* João Bosco Lee, *Le nouveau régime de l'arbitrage au Brésil*, 1997 REV. ARB. 199; Carlos Nehring Netto, *Brazil* (at 5), *in* ICCA INTERNATIONAL HANDBOOK ON COMMERCIAL ARBITRATION.

[16] See the decree of January 4, 1989 which amended Article 1415 of the Mexican Commercial Code and, subsequently, the adoption of the UNCITRAL Model Law now found at Articles 1415 *et seq.* of the Mexican Commercial Code (Decree of July 22, 1993).

[17] Art. 2 of Decree No. 2279 of October 7, 1989. *See also* Mantilla-Serrano, *supra* note 6.

[18] See the various reports in ICCA INTERNATIONAL HANDBOOK ON COMMERCIAL ARBITRATION. *See also* YVES DERAINS AND ERIC A. SCHWARTZ, A GUIDE TO THE NEW ICC RULES OF ARBITRATION 229 (1998).

[19] On the question of delay and how to prevent it, see ICCA CONGRESS SERIES NO. 5, PREVENTING DELAY AND DISRUPTION OF ARBITRATION/EFFECTIVE PROCEEDINGS IN CONSTRUCTION CASES (A.J. van den Berg ed., 1991), with the contributions of Emmanuel Gaillard, *Law and Court Decisions in Civil Law Countries*, at 65 *et seq.*, and V.V. Veeder, *Laws and Court Decisions in Common Law Countries and the UNCITRAL Model Law*, at 169 *et seq.* On the different positions taken in comparative law regarding the constitution of the arbitral tribunal, see *infra* paras. 748 *et seq.*

sole arbitrator.[20] The 1996 English Arbitration Act maintained this dynamic solution in its Section 17.[21] In continental legal systems, a party's refusal to appoint an arbitrator is overcome by providing for a designating authority to replace the defaulting party or the defaulting arbitrators, as the case may be. In French law, if a party refuses to appoint an arbitrator, the President of the Paris Tribunal of First Instance will have the power to make that appointment instead.[22] Likewise, a subsequent refusal to participate in the proceedings will not paralyze the arbitration.[23] Whatever method is used, opposition by one party will not be allowed to obstruct the progress of the arbitration.

633. — Nonetheless, it will sometimes be impossible to constitute the arbitral tribunal in the first place, as a result of flaws in the arbitration agreement or obstacles found in the law or in the position of the authorities of the jurisdiction chosen by the parties as the seat of the arbitration. To address such situations, some legal systems provide that, in the absence of any other means of penalizing the defaulting party, the dispute should be referred to the courts. For example, Article 7 of the Swiss Private International Law Statute states that the Swiss courts will have jurisdiction notwithstanding the arbitration agreement if it is established that "the arbitral tribunal cannot be constituted for reasons which are manifestly attributable to the defendant." Both the French[24] and the United States[25] courts will hold that in those circumstances both parties have waived the arbitration agreement.

Similarly, Section 5 of the 1999 Swedish Arbitration Act provides that:

[a] party shall forfeit his right to invoke the arbitration agreement as a bar to court proceedings where the party:
1. has opposed a request for arbitration,
2. failed to appoint an arbitrator in due time, or
3. fails, within due time, to provide his share of the requested security for compensation to the arbitrators.[26]

These provisions, which are intended to prevent a denial of justice in cases where the arbitral tribunal genuinely cannot be constituted because of the obstructive attitude of one of the parties, give the other party the option of bringing its claim before the courts. That solution is obviously far from ideal, given the parties' initial intention to refer their disputes

---

[20] Veeder, *supra* note 19, at 77.

[21] *See* RUSSELL ON ARBITRATION 130 (D. Sutton, J. Kendall, J. Gill eds., 21st ed. 1997); Claude Reymond, *L'Arbitration Act, 1996 – Convergence et originalité,* 1997 REV. ARB. 45, 59.

[22] Art. 1493 of the New Code of Civil Procedure. On this issue, see *infra* paras. 750 *et seq.*

[23] *See infra* para. 1224.

[24] *See* Cass. 1e civ., June 6, 1978, British Leyland International Services v. Société d'Exploitation des Etablissements Richard, 105 J.D.I. 907 (1978), and B. Oppetit's note; 1979 REV. ARB. 230, and P. Level's note. *Comp. with* Sec. 9(3) *in fine* of the 1996 English Arbitration Act.

[25] *See* GARY B. BORN, INTERNATIONAL COMMERCIAL ARBITRATION IN THE UNITED STATES – COMMENTARY AND MATERIALS 279 *et seq.* (1994).

[26] A similar provision was already found in Section 3 of the 1929 Swedish Arbitration Act.

to arbitration. It may, however, be the only alternative where it really does prove impossible to constitute the arbitral tribunal. Nevertheless, such an alternative will only be used in exceptional circumstances and as the last resort, because in practice the subsidiary mechanisms provided by statute[27] or by the institutional arbitration rules initially chosen by the parties will ensure that a party will only very rarely be able to obstruct the arbitration simply by refusing to participate.[28]

634. — As with the obligation to submit disputes covered by the arbitration agreement to arbitration, the rule that that obligation is capable of specific performance must be considered a transnational rule of international arbitration. This means, in particular, that the courts reviewing the existence of a valid arbitration agreement, in an action to set aside an arbitral award or resisting enforcement, need not determine whether the law governing the arbitration agreement allows that agreement's specific performance.[29]

C. – THE OBLIGATION TO SUBMIT DISPUTES COVERED BY THE ARBITRATION AGREEMENT TO ARBITRATION PREVAILS OVER JURISDICTIONAL PRIVILEGES AND IMMUNITIES

635. — Although it has agreed to be bound by an arbitration agreement, a party may sometimes be tempted, once a dispute has arisen, to oppose the conduct of arbitral proceedings by relying on a jurisdictional privilege (1°) or immunity (2°). In both cases, a party is deemed to have waived such rights by entering into the arbitration agreement.

1° Jurisdictional Privileges

636. — Certain legal systems maintain jurisdictional privileges, which are not always excluded by international treaties. This is the case, for example, of Articles 14 and 15 of the French Civil Code.[30] Where the rules set forth in the 1968 Brussels Convention and the 1988 Lugano Convention on Jurisdiction and Enforcement of Judgments in Civil and Commercial Matters are not applicable, Article 14 enables a French national to sue any other person, regardless of their nationality, before the French courts. Article 15 allows anyone to sue a French national before the French courts and also enables a French national to resist enforcement of a foreign judgement obtained by a party who failed to sue the French national before French courts pursuant to that article. In addition, Articles 14 and 15, as

---

[27] See, e.g., Art. 1493 of the French New Code of Civil Procedure; Art. 179, para. 2 of the Swiss Private International Law Statute; Art. 1027 of the Netherlands Code of Civil Procedure as amended by the Arbitration Act of July 2, 1986; Art. 11 of the UNCITRAL Model Law and for its implementation in German law, Art. 1035 of the ZPO.

[28] On this issue, generally, see *infra* paras. 750 *et seq.* and 1224 *et seq.*

[29] See *supra* para. 631.

[30] In Belgium, see also Article 15 of the Belgian Civil Code.

extended by Article 4, paragraph 2 of the Brussels and Lugano Conventions, can also be used by anyone domiciled in France, within the scope of that Convention.[31] These jurisdictional privileges are not matters of public policy, in as much as the beneficiaries of the privileges are entitled to waive them.[32] There is no doubt that they waive them by entering into an arbitration agreement or submission agreement, even if the waiver is not expressly set forth in the agreement. This waiver results from the incompatibility of the purpose of the arbitration agreement, which is to ensure that disputes are submitted to arbitration, with that of Articles 14 and 15, which is to ensure that they are submitted to the French courts. This solution has long been accepted in French law.[33]

637. — However, the scope of this rule should be clarified in two respects.

638. — First, the waiver of Articles 14 and 15 is effective as regards both the arbitral proceedings themselves and ancillary actions before the courts.

In the course of an arbitration, it may be necessary to resort to proceedings before the courts in order to resolve any difficulties encountered when constituting the arbitral tribunal[34] and, once the award has been made, for the purposes of reviewing the validity or enforceability of the award.[35] When determining which court has jurisdiction to assist in constituting the arbitral tribunal, or later to hear an action to set aside the award or an application for enforcement, Articles 14 and 15 of the Civil Code play no role whatsoever, even where a French party is involved. By agreeing to submit their disputes to arbitration, the beneficiaries of those jurisdictional privileges necessarily accept the ordinary rules of jurisdiction concerning court proceedings associated with arbitration.[36] The French courts

---

[31] On the current extent of these privileges in light of the scope of the Brussels Convention, see, for example, BERNARD AUDIT, DROIT INTERNATIONAL PRIVÉ ¶ 505 (2d ed. 1997); PIERRE MAYER, DROIT INTERNATIONAL PRIVÉ ¶¶ 299 and 336 (6th ed. 1998); HÉLÈNE GAUDEMET-TALLON, LES CONVENTIONS DE BRUXELLES ET DE LUGANO ¶¶ 75 et seq. (1993); IAN F. FLETCHER, CONFLICT OF LAWS AND EUROPEAN COMMUNITY LAW—WITH SPECIAL REFERENCE TO THE COMMUNITY CONVENTIONS ON PRIVATE INTERNATIONAL LAW 103 et seq. (1982).

[32] See, for example, on Article 14, Cass. 1e civ., May 21, 1963, Compagnie marocaine de boissons v. Société vinicole du Languedoc, 1964 REV. CRIT. DIP 340, and Y. Loussouarn's note; 91 J.D.I. 113 (1964), and observations by J.-B. Sialelli; on Article 15, see Cass. com., Oct. 9, 1967, Oranit v. Meublacier, 95 J.D.I. 918 (1968), and J.-D. Bredin's note; Cass. 1e civ., May 18, 1994, Mme. X v. Y, Dalloz, Jur. 20 (1995), and P. Courbe's note.

[33] Cass. civ., Nov. 21, 1860, Couillard-Fautrel v. Boaden, Sirey, Pt. I, at 641 (1861), and, more recently, Cass. com., June 21, 1965, Supra-Penn v. Swan Finch Oil Corp., 1966 REV. CRIT. DIP 477, and E. Mezger's note; TGI Paris, réf., May 11, 1987, Les Silos du Sud-Ouest S.A. v. Société des Engrais du Bénin (S.E.B.), 1988 REV. ARB. 699, 1st decision, and P. Fouchard's note; CA Paris, Nov. 30, 1988, Korsnas Marma v. Durand-Auzias, 1989 REV. ARB. 691, and P.-Y. Tschanz' note. See also the cases referred to supra para. 490.

[34] See infra paras. 750 et seq.

[35] See infra paras. 1558 et seq.

[36] This should also be the case, in our opinion, where the action is based on the absence of a valid arbitration agreement. The claimant could argue that it has not waived Articles 14 and 15 for the reasons underlying its whole action. That argument should not succeed. Because of the specific and imperative nature of the rules governing actions challenging awards, the usual rules of jurisdiction should not apply. On the imperative nature of the rules governing the constitution of the arbitral tribunal where the arbitration takes place in France or

(continued...)

have confirmed that these ordinary rules apply in order to determine which court has jurisdiction to assist in the constitution of the arbitral tribunal. This enables the French courts to intervene in arbitrations which have their seat in France or which are subject to French procedural law.[37] However, they cannot intervene, through the application of Articles 14 and 15 of the Civil Code, where neither of those criteria is satisfied.[38] This will also be the case with an action to set an award aside. For instance, a French party cannot use Articles 14 and 15 of the Civil Code as the sole basis for an order from the French courts to set aside an award made outside France.[39] These rules are all intended to prevent interference with the system of recourse to the courts set up by the reform of French international arbitration law in 1981.

639. — The second situation where clarification of the scope of the waiver of Articles 14 and 15 is needed is where it has proved impossible to constitute the arbitral tribunal and it is necessary to bring the dispute to court despite the existence of an arbitration agreement. This may occur, for example, because the arbitration agreement is so pathological that it is simply not possible to appoint the arbitrators.[40] The question then arises as to whether the parties—particularly if they are French—regain the benefit of Articles 14 and 15, or whether their entry into the arbitration agreement amounts to a waiver of those jurisdictional privileges, despite the fact that the arbitration agreement is ineffective. The solution will depend on the way in which the parties' intentions are interpreted, although their intentions will of course be poorly expressed as the arbitration they sought to provide for is inoperative. In such cases it can often be argued that the parties only waived the benefit of Articles 14 and 15 on the understanding that they would be able to submit their disputes to arbitration, failing which there was no waiver of their jurisdictional privilege in favor of the ordinary rules of jurisdiction.[41]

640. — The immunity enjoyed by states and entities acting under the control or on behalf of states raises similar questions.

---

[36](...continued)
where the procedure is subject to French law, see TGI Paris, réf., May 11, 1987, *Les Silos du Sud-Ouest, supra* note 33, at 701. *See infra* paras. 837 *et seq.*

[37] Art. 1493, para. 2, of the New Code of Civil Procedure. *See infra* paras. 837 *et seq.*

[38] TGI Paris, réf., May 11, 1987, *Les Silos du Sud-Ouest, supra* note 33.

[39] On the jurisdiction of the French courts to hear actions to set aside awards made in France, see *infra* para. 1590.

[40] On this scenario, see *supra* para. 484.

[41] In a similar case, where the parties had agreed to submit their disputes only to an arbitrator chosen by mutual agreement, see CA Paris, Jan. 22, 1957, Carthian v. Wildenstein New-York, 1957 REV. CRIT. DIP 486, and E.M's note.

2° Jurisdictional Immunities

641. — Once it has entered into an arbitration agreement, can a state or state-owned entity rely on its immunity from jurisdiction to avoid being party to arbitration proceedings?[42] This issue must be considered with regard to both the jurisdiction of the arbitrators and the jurisdiction of courts handling litigation associated with arbitration.

642. — There is no doubt that arbitrators have jurisdiction to hear disputes that states or state-owned entities which otherwise enjoy immunity from jurisdiction agree to submit to arbitration. It is firmly established that immunity from jurisdiction can be waived.[43] An arbitration agreement is in direct contradiction with that immunity from jurisdiction, and must therefore be considered to be a waiver of that immunity by the state or public entity in question.[44] It has also been shown that the issue of the immunity of a foreign state does not arise in arbitration, because that immunity is intended to protect its beneficiary from being subject to the jurisdiction of the courts of other countries.[45]

643. — The same solution should apply to court proceedings associated with arbitration, such as requests for assistance in constituting the arbitral tribunal, or actions to set awards aside. This has been confirmed by the French courts in the context of litigation concerning

---

[42] On this issue generally, see ISABELLE PINGEL-LENUZZA, LES IMMUNITÉS DES ETATS EN DROIT INTERNATIONAL ¶¶ 269 *et seq.* (1998); MICHEL COSNARD, LA SOUMISSION DES ETATS AUX TRIBUNAUX INTERNES FACE À LA THÉORIE DES IMMUNITÉS DES ETATS 328 *et seq.* (1996); Pierre Bourel, *Arbitrage international et immunité des Etats étrangers – A propos d'une jurisprudence récente*, 1982 REV. ARB. 119; DICEY & MORRIS, THE CONFLICT OF LAWS, Vol. 1, at 241 *et seq.* (12th ed. 1993 and 4th cumulative supp. 1997). On the immunity of international organizations, see Christian Dominicé, *L'arbitrage et les immunités des organisations internationales, in* ETUDES DE DROIT INTERNATIONAL EN L'HONNEUR DE PIERRE LALIVE 483 (1993), and the decision cited *infra* para. 643.

[43] See, for an analysis of comparative law and public international law, PINGEL-LENUZZA, *supra* note 42, ¶¶ 135 *et seq.* On how such a waiver may come about, see also P. Kahn, observations following Cass. 1e civ., Mar. 19, 1980, Zavicha Blagojevic v. Etat japonais (Ministère des finances), 107 J.D.I. 896 (1980).

[44] *See* TGI Paris, réf., July 8, 1970, Société Européenne d'Etudes et d'Entreprises (S.E.E.E.) v. République socialiste fédérale de Yougoslavie, 98 J.D.I. 131 (1971), and P. Kahn's note; 1975 REV. ARB. 328, and J.-L. Delvolvé's note; JCP, Ed. G., Pt. II, No. 16,810 (1971), and observations by D. Ruzié. On subsequent events in that case, see *infra* para. 644. See also, in arbitral case law, the March 5, 1984 interim award in ICC Case No. 3879, Westland Helicopters Ltd. v. Arab Organization for Industrialization (112 J.D.I. 232, 243 (1985); 1989 REV. ARB. 547; for an English translation, see 23 I.L.M. 1071 (1984); XI Y.B. COM. ARB. 127 (1986)), which was set aside on other grounds by the Swiss courts (*see* Court of Justice of the Geneva Canton, Nov. 3, 1987, Arab Organization for Industrialization v. Westland Helicopters Ltd., *aff'd*, Swiss Fed. Trib., July 19, 1988, 1989 REV. ARB. 514; for excerpts translated into English, see 28 I.L.M. 688 (1989); XVI Y.B. COM. ARB. 174 (1991)) (on this case, see *supra* paras. 507 and 509); ICC Award No. 8035 (1995), Party to an oil concession agreement v. State, 124 J.D.I. 1040 (1997), and observations by D. Hascher.

[45] See the 1974 award rendered in Sweden in ICC Case No. 2321, Two Israeli companies v. Government of an African state, I Y.B. COM. ARB. 133 (1976); for a French translation, see 102 J.D.I. 938, 940 (1975), and observations by Y. Derains. *See also* P. Mayer, note following Cass. 1e civ., Nov. 18, 1986, Etat français v. Société Européenne d'Etudes et d'Entreprises (S.E.E.E.), 1987 REV. CRIT. DIP 786, 788, and P. Mayer's note; 114 J.D.I. 120 (1987), and B. Oppetit's note; 1987 REV. ARB. 149, and J.-L. Delvolvé's note; PINGEL-LENUZZA, *supra* note 42, ¶ 274.

enforcement of arbitral awards and, more recently, in decisions regarding the involvement of the courts in the constitution of the arbitral tribunal.[46]

644. — It would be absurd to conclude that a state could agree to submit disputes to arbitration despite its immunity from jurisdiction, but that it could subsequently prevent the award from becoming enforceable by simply relying on that immunity. For example, the Paris Tribunal of First Instance held in the 1970 *SEEE v. Yugoslavia* case that:

> by signing an arbitration agreement, the Yugoslavian State waived its immunity with regard to the arbitrators and their award, up until and including the *exequatur* procedure which is necessary for the award to be fully effective.[47]

That case then gave rise to a number of incidents concerning aspects of the law of immunity other than its impact on arbitration agreements.[48] The issue was then re-examined by the Rouen Court of Appeals—the second appeal court to which the case was remitted. The Court held, in 1984, that the Yugoslav government could not rely on its immunity because of the nature of the activity contemplated in the contract (the construction of a railway line) and the content of the agreement between the parties (there were no clauses which would not be found in normal commercial relationships). This was "corroborated by the inclusion of an arbitration clause demonstrating the wish of the Yugoslavian State to conduct itself for the performance of the contract as a simple private individual."[49] The Court thus used somewhat indirect reasoning to deprive the Yugoslav State of the benefit of its immunity. All that was required was to take full account of the effects of the arbitration agreement, as shown by the *Cour de cassation* in 1986 when it rejected an action against the decision of the Rouen Court of Appeals. The state claimed that "the mere fact that the contract contained an arbitration clause does not imply a waiver of jurisdictional immunity." The *Cour de cassation* rightly held that "by that clause, the foreign state, which had submitted its disputes to the jurisdiction of the arbitrators, thereby accepted that their award was capable of being rendered enforceable."[50] This was reiterated by the *Cour de cassation* in 1991 in another matter:

---

[46]   TGI Paris, réf., Jan. 10, 1996, National Iranian Oil Co. v. Israel, 1996 BULL. ASA 319; for an English translation, see 11 INT'L ARB. REP. B1 (Feb. 1996).

[47]   TGI Paris, réf., July 8, 1970, *S.E.E.E.*, *supra* note 44.

[48]   The July 8, 1970 order was withdrawn on other grounds. The withdrawal was confirmed by CA Paris, Jan. 29, 1975, République socialiste fédérale de Yougoslavie v. Société Européenne d'Etudes et d'Entreprises (S.E.E.E.), 103 J.D.I. 136 (1976), and B. Oppetit's note. The decision was reversed by Cass. 1e civ., June 14, 1977, République socialiste fédérale de Yougoslavie v. Société Européenne d'Etudes et d'Entreprises (S.E.E.E.) (104 J.D.I. 864 (1977), with a report by Justice A. Ponsard and a note by B. Oppetit), but on December 13, 1979 the Orléans Court of Appeals reaffirmed the withdrawal of the initial order (1983 REV. ARB. 63, and J.-L. Delvolvé's note). This last decision was reversed by Cass. 1e civ., Oct. 13, 1981, 1983 REV. ARB. 63, and J.-L. Delvolvé's note; 109 J.D.I. 931 (1982), 1st decision, and B. Oppetit's note.

[49]   CA Rouen, Nov. 13, 1984, Société Européenne d'Etudes et d'Entreprises (S.E.E.E.) v. République de Yougoslavie, 112 J.D.I. 473 (1985), and B. Oppetit's note; 1985 REV. ARB. 115, and J.-L. Delvolvé's note. For an English translation, see 24 I.L.M. 345, 349 (1985); XI Y.B. COM. ARB. 491 (1986).

[50]   Cass. 1e civ., Nov. 18, 1986, *S.E.E.E.*, *supra* note 45.

a foreign State which has consented to arbitration has thereby agreed that the award may be rendered enforceable which, as such, does not constitute a measure of execution that might raise issues pertaining to the immunity from execution of the State concerned.[51]

645. — The outcome should be the same where a party applies to the courts in order to resolve difficulties with the arbitral procedure, especially where that action is required to constitute the arbitral tribunal. The state or state-owned entity's agreement to submit disputes to arbitration would be meaningless if it could be circumvented by that party simply refusing to participate in the constitution of the arbitral tribunal and then relying on its immunity from jurisdiction to ensure that such refusal could not be overcome by action before the appropriate court. This was the solution reached by the Paris Tribunal of First Instance, and later by the Paris Court of Appeals, in a case concerning UNESCO. Faced with UNESCO's refusal to participate in the constitution of an arbitral tribunal, despite arbitration being provided for in the disputed contract, the President of the Paris Tribunal of First Instance rightly held that "in entering into an arbitration clause, UNESCO waived its immunity from jurisdiction and necessarily agreed to allow the implementation of the method of dispute resolution set forth in the contract."[52] This decision was upheld by the Paris Court of Appeals in very clear terms: "the immunity from jurisdiction on which UNESCO seeks to rely does not allow it to free itself from the *pacta sunt servanda* principle by refusing to nominate an arbitrator in compliance with the arbitration in the contract between it [and the claimant in the arbitration] on the grounds of the absence of a dispute as to the performance of the contract at issue, a question which is to be decided by the arbitrators alone; in addition, to allow [UNESCO's] objection would inevitably prevent [the claimant] from submitting the dispute to a judicial authority. This would be contrary to public policy in that it constitutes a denial of justice and a violation of the provisions of Article 6-1 of the European Convention for the Protection of Human Rights and Fundamental Freedoms, and should therefore lead the court—which is involved in this case only in support of the arbitration—to accept the claimant's request [to have the arbitral tribunal constituted with the assistance of the courts]."[53]

---

[51] Cass. 1e civ., June 11, 1991, Société ouest-africaine de bétons industriels (SOABI) v. Sénégal, 118 J.D.I. 1005 (1991), and E. Gaillard's note; 1991 REV. ARB. 637, and A. Broches' note; 1992 REV. CRIT. DIP 331, and P.L.'s note; for an English translation, see 30 I.L.M. 1167, 1169 (1991), with an introductory note by G. Delaume; XVII Y.B. COM. ARB. 754, 756 (1992); *reversing* CA Paris, Dec. 5, 1989, Etat du Sénégal v. Alain Seutin ès qualité de liquidateur amiable de la SOABI, 117 J.D.I. 141 (1990), and E. Gaillard's note; 1990 REV. ARB. 164, and A. Broches' note, 1991 REV. CRIT. DIP 121, and N. Ziadé's note; for an English translation, see 29 I.L.M. 1341 (1990). See also the criticisms made by Philippe Kahn, who considers that "the only thing that is certain with any arbitration clause is that . . . the State accepts to have the dispute resolved by arbitrators, and that is all" (note following TGI Paris, réf., July 8, 1970, *S.E.E.E.*, 98 J.D.I. 131, 136 (1971)). Approving this case law, see B. Goldman, note following CA Paris July 12, 1984, République Arabe d'Egypte v. Southern Pacific Properties Ltd., 112 J.D.I. 129, 145 (1985). *See also* PINGEL-LENUZZA, *supra* note 42, ¶ 332; COSNARD, *supra* note 42, at 333 *et seq.*

[52] TGI, Paris, réf., Oct. 20, 1997, Boulois v. UNESCO, 1997 REV. ARB. 575, and C. Jarrosson's note.

[53] CA Paris, 14e Ch., Sec. B, June 19, 1998, UNESCO v. Boulois, No. 97/26549, unpublished.

Regrettably, however, the Swiss Federal Tribunal did not reach the same conclusion with regard to CERN, the European organization for atomic research. The court denied a party access to the Swiss courts where that party sought to bring an action against an award made in an arbitration against CERN.[54]

646. — However, the act of entering into an arbitration agreement has no impact on a party's immunity from execution.[55] At the very most, some decisions have suggested that where a state agrees to submit a dispute to arbitration, that "necessarily entails a commitment to enforce the award," without drawing any further conclusions that could not be justified by the ordinary law of immunity.[56] However, in France, in a decision of the Rouen Court of Appeals dated June 20, 1996, it was held that by agreeing to an arbitration clause, a State accepts "the ordinary legal rules of international trade," and thus waives "its immunity from jurisdiction and, as agreements must be performed in good faith, its immunity from execution."[57] This decision is unsatisfactory. In most countries, immunity from execution is today acknowledged to be limited to assets used by a state to perform its sovereign activities as opposed to its commercial activities.[58] It is therefore perfectly consistent for a state to agree to refer disputes to arbitration on the basis that any award against it would be enforced against assets used for its commercial activities, rather than those used for traditional sovereign purposes. Only an express waiver of immunity from execution should allow a successful party to enforce its award against all state assets.

§ 2. – The Arbitral Tribunal Has Jurisdiction to Resolve Disputes Covered by the Arbitration Agreement

647. — The second positive consequence of the arbitration agreement is to confer jurisdiction on the arbitral tribunal to hear all disputes covered by the arbitration agreement. Of course, the relationship between the parties and the arbitrators, as well as the rights and obligations assumed by the latter, stem from a distinct agreement which results from the

---

[54] Swiss Fed. Trib., Dec. 21, 1992, Groupement Fougerolle v. CERN, 1994 REV. ARB. 175, and P. Glavinis' note; 123 J.D.I. 730 (1996).

[55] See, for example, in ICSID arbitration, Article 55 of the Washington Convention and, in French case law, CA Paris, Apr. 21, 1982, République Islamique d'Iran v. Eurodif, 1983 REV. CRIT. DIP 101, and P. Mayer's note; 110 J.D.I. 145 (1983), and B. Oppetit's note; 1982 REV. ARB. 204, and the commentary by Bourel, *supra* note 42, especially at 136. For the argument that an arbitration clause can, in certain circumstances, constitute a waiver of immunity from execution, see Bruno Oppetit, *La pratique française en matière d'immunité d'exécution, in* L'IMMUNITÉ D'EXÉCUTION DE L'ETAT ÉTRANGER 49, 56 (Report on the *4ème Journée d'actualité internationale* organized on April 22, 1988 by the Centre de droit international de Nanterre (1990)). On this issue, generally, see PINGEL-LENUZZA, *supra* note 42, ¶ 275.

[56] CA Paris, July 9, 1992, Norbert Beyrard France v. République de Côte d'Ivoire, 1994 REV. ARB. 133, and P. Théry's note.

[57] CA Rouen, June 20, 1996, Bec Frères v. Office des céréales de Tunisie, 1997 REV. ARB. 263, and E. Gaillard's note.

[58] For a broad comparative law survey, see PINGEL-LENUZZA *supra* note 42, ¶¶ 312 *et seq.*

acceptance by the arbitrators of their functions.[59] However, that agreement is itself a consequence of the arbitration agreement, and in the relations between the parties, it is the arbitration agreement that provides the basis for the arbitrators' jurisdiction.[60]

We shall consider in turn the extent of the jurisdiction of the arbitral tribunal (A) and its jurisdiction to rule on its own jurisdiction (B).

A. – THE EXTENT OF THE JURISDICTION OF THE ARBITRAL TRIBUNAL

648. — It has sometimes been suggested that a distinction should be drawn between the appointment (*l'investiture*) of arbitrators and their jurisdiction,[61] whereby their appointment is the act of conferring on the arbitral tribunal the power to resolve disputes, and their jurisdiction is the extent of that power.

The arbitration agreement empowers the arbitral tribunal to make a decision resolving a dispute which the parties are obliged to submit to it. That decision will be binding on the parties, and it may be rendered enforceable by the courts: that, it is suggested, results from the arbitrators' appointment.

The arbitration agreement also determines which issues can be examined and decided by the arbitral tribunal. For instance, if an arbitration agreement refers only to a principal claim—which could only be the case with a submission agreement and not an arbitration clause—the question would arise as to whether, in the course of the proceedings and without a further arbitration agreement, the arbitral tribunal could hear subsidiary claims or counterclaims. That would be a matter of jurisdiction.

However, the distinction between the arbitrators' appointment and their jurisdiction has been strongly criticized.[62] Even if one were to draw such a distinction, the appointment and jurisdiction of the arbitrator still both have the same source, namely the arbitration agreement. One commentator observed with respect to arbitration that:

> the granting of jurisdictional powers is carried out by mere private parties: the actual contractors. Those parties simultaneously confer upon the arbitral tribunal both its existence and its jurisdiction. As the arbitrator is only a judge

---

[59] *See infra* paras. 941 *et seq.*

[60] On the question of the jurisdiction of arbitrators, generally, see ADAM SAMUEL, JURISDICTIONAL PROBLEMS IN INTERNATIONAL COMMERCIAL ARBITRATION (1989).

[61] *See, e.g.*, Trib. civ. Seine, June 7, 1956, Constantine v. Buck, JCP, Ed. G., Pt. II, No. 9,460 (1956), and observations by H. Motulsky; CA Aix, Dec. 7, 1954, Ferrari v. Bresset, 1955 REV. ARB. 31. *See also* Ibrahim Fadlallah, *L'ordre public dans les sentences arbitrales*, *in* COLLECTED COURSES OF THE HAGUE ACADEMY OF INTERNATIONAL LAW, Vol. 249, Year 1994, Part V, at 369, 399.

[62] *See* Eric Loquin, *Arbitrage – Compétence arbitrale – Introduction générale*, J.-CL. PROC. CIV., Fasc. 1030, ¶¶ 6 *et seq.* (1994), and the references cited therein.

to the extent that the parties intend, to say that he has not been appointed is the same as saying that he lacks jurisdiction.[63]

Accordingly, the extent of the arbitrators' power to resolve disputes, and hence their jurisdiction, coincides exactly with the limits of the arbitration agreement. Where the arbitration agreement needs to be interpreted because it is ambiguous[64] or pathological,[65] the extent of the arbitrators' jurisdiction will depend on that interpretation. The question of which parties have agreed to arbitration, which often arises in the context of groups of companies or states and state-owned entities, invariably concerns the extent of the arbitrators' jurisdiction. The same is true of the question of which issues are covered by the parties' consent to arbitrate, which often arises where only certain disputes may have been submitted to arbitration. It therefore suffices to refer on this point to our discussion of the interpretation and extent of the arbitration agreement itself.[66]

649. — The arbitral tribunal's jurisdiction to decide its own jurisdiction, however, requires further analysis.

B. – The Arbitral Tribunal's Jurisdiction to Rule on Its Own Jurisdiction ("Competence-Competence")

650. — The fact that arbitrators have jurisdiction to determine their own jurisdiction—known as the "competence-competence" principle—is among the most important, and contentious, rules of international arbitration. It has given rise to much controversy and misunderstanding, and behind the appearance of unanimity—most laws now recognize the principle in some form—it continues to be the subject of considerable divergence between different legal systems.[67]

---

[63] HENRI MOTULSKY, ECRITS – VOL. 2 – ETUDES ET NOTES SUR L'ARBITRAGE 239 (1974).

[64] See supra paras. 473 et seq.

[65] See supra paras. 484 et seq.

[66] See supra paras. 472 et seq.

[67] On this issue, generally, see Emmanuel Gaillard, Les manœuvres dilatoires des parties et des arbitres dans l'arbitrage commercial international, 1990 REV. ARB. 759, especially at 769 et seq.; Emmanuel Gaillard, L'effet négatif de la compétence-compétence, in ETUDES DE PROCÉDURE ET D'ARBITRAGE EN L'HONNEUR DE JEAN-FRANÇOIS POUDRET (forthcoming in 1999); Ernest Mezger, Compétence-compétence des arbitres et indépendance de la convention d'arbitrage dans la Convention dite Européenne sur l'Arbitrage Commercial International de 1961, in COMMERCIAL ARBITRATION – ESSAYS IN MEMORIAM EUGENIO MINOLI 315 (1974); Antonias Dimolitsa, Separability and Kompetenz-Kompetenz, in ICCA CONGRESS SERIES NO. 9, IMPROVING THE EFFICIENCY OF ARBITRATION AGREEMENTS AND AWARDS: 40 YEARS OF APPLICATION OF THE NEW YORK CONVENTION 217 (A.J. van den Berg ed., 1999); and, for a much more restrictive position, see SAMUEL, supra note 60, at 177 et seq.; William W. Park, The Arbitrability Dicta in First Options v. Kaplan: What Sort of Kompetenz-Kompetenz Has Crossed the Atlantic?, 12 ARB. INT'L 137 (1996); William W. Park, Determining Arbitral Jurisdiction: Allocation of Tasks Between Courts and Arbitrators, 8 AM. REV. INT'L ARB. 133 (1997).

651. — Even the terminology used contains a paradox. Traditionally the rule that arbitrators have jurisdiction to decide their own jurisdiction was expressed by the German phrase "*Kompetenz-Kompetenz*." That expression has been used for many years by French[68] and other European legal authors.[69] The working papers[70] and commentaries[71] of the UNCITRAL Model Law also referred to the rule in those terms. Yet, the origin of the expression has never been very clear. Authors frequently refer to "the well-known principle of *Kompetenz-Kompetenz*," or describe the arbitrators' power to rule on their own jurisdiction as a principle "which is often referred to as *Kompetenz-Kompetenz*."[72]

This situation is paradoxical in that German legal terminology lends a meaning to the expression which differs substantially from that which the expression is intended to convey when used in international arbitration. If one were to follow the traditional meaning of the expression in Germany, "*Kompetenz-Kompetenz*" would imply that the arbitrators are empowered to make a final ruling as to their jurisdiction, with no subsequent review of the decision by any court. Understood in such a way, the concept is rejected in Germany,[73] just as it is elsewhere.[74] From a substantive viewpoint, the paradox is all the more marked for the fact that in Germany the question of whether the courts should refuse to examine the jurisdiction of an arbitral tribunal until such time as the arbitrators have been able to rule on the issue themselves (the negative effect of the "competence-competence" principle),[75] has

---

[68] *See, e.g.*, PHILIPPE FOUCHARD, L'ARBITRAGE COMMERCIAL INTERNATIONAL ¶ 203 (1965); Berthold Goldman, *Arbitrage (droit international privé), in* ENCYCLOPÉDIE DALLOZ – DROIT INTERNATIONAL ¶134 (1968); Pierre Mayer, *L'autonomie de l'arbitre international dans l'appréciation de sa propre compétence, in* COLLECTED COURSES OF THE HAGUE ACADEMY OF INTERNATIONAL LAW, Vol. 217, Year 1989, Part V, at 319, ¶ 9.

[69] *See, e.g.*, MAURO RUBINO-SAMMARTANO, INTERNATIONAL ARBITRATION LAW 329 (1990); Veeder, *supra* note 19, at 170; DEPARTMENT OF TRADE AND INDUSTRY, A CONSULTATION PAPER ON DRAFT CLAUSES AND SCHEDULES OF AN ARBITRATION BILL (Feb. 1994), *reprinted in* 10 ARB. INT'L 189 (1994) (which led to the enactment of the 1996 Arbitration Act); *see also* DEPARTMENTAL ADVISORY COMMITTEE ON ARBITRATION LAW, 1996 REPORT ON THE ARBITRATION BILL (Feb. 1996), *reprinted in* 13 ARB. INT'L 275 (1997); Dimolitsa, *supra* note 67.

[70] *See* HOWARD M. HOLTZMANN AND JOSEPH E. NEUHAUS, A GUIDE TO THE UNCITRAL MODEL LAW ON INTERNATIONAL COMMERCIAL ARBITRATION – LEGISLATIVE HISTORY AND COMMENTARY 508 (1989).

[71] *See* HOLTZMANN AND NEUHAUS, *supra* note 70, at 478 *et seq.*; ARON BROCHES, COMMENTARY ON THE UNCITRAL MODEL LAW ON INTERNATIONAL COMMERCIAL ARBITRATION 73 *et seq.* (1990).

[72] *See, e.g.*, HOLTZMANN AND NEUHAUS, *supra* note 70, at 478 and 508.

[73] See, before the January 1, 1998 reform, Ottoarndt Glossner, *Germany* (at 14), *in* ICCA INTERNATIONAL HANDBOOK ON COMMERCIAL ARBITRATION (1987); Günter Henn, *Gibt es eine bindende Kompetenz-Kompetenz der Schiedsgerichte?, in* JAHRBUCH FÜR DIE PRAXIS DER SCHIEDSGERICHTSBARKEIT 1990, at 50 (1991); since January 1, 1998, see Article 1040 of the ZPO and the commentary by Peter Schlosser, *La nouvelle legislation allemande sur l'arbitrage*, 1998 REV. ARB. 291, 297; Klaus Peter Berger, *Germany Adopts the UNCITRAL Model Law*, 1 INT'L ARB. L. REV. 121, 122 (1998).

[74] *See infra* para. 659. But see, in favor of allowing arbitrators exclusive jurisdiction to determine their own jurisdiction, except for review by the courts of the abusive exercise by the arbitrators of their powers, Clive M. Schmitthoff, *The jurisdiction of the arbitrator, in* THE ART OF ARBITRATION – ESSAYS ON INTERNATIONAL ARBITRATION – LIBER AMICORUM PIETER SANDERS 285 (J. Schultz and A.J. van den Berg eds., 1982). On the possibility for the parties to specifically agree to apply such a system, see Mayer, *supra* note 68, at 340.

[75] *See infra* para. 672.

never been accepted, neither before,[76] nor after the December 22, 1997 reform.[77] It therefore seems preferable to avoid the confusing German expression "*Kompetenz-Kompetenz*," in favor of "competence-competence," which is more in keeping with the origin of a principle which had been applied by the French courts as early as 1949.[78]

It should also be observed that Swiss authors, always sensitive to the finer distinctions of comparative law, were quick to point out that the expression "*Kompetenz-Kompetenz*" was inappropriate because of its traditional German meaning.[79]

652. — Having considered the terminology, we shall now examine how the principle of competence-competence was established (1°), its basis (2°) and its exact meaning (3°).

1° Recognition of the Principle

653. — The competence-competence principle is now recognized by the main international conventions on arbitration, by most modern arbitration statutes, and by the majority of institutional arbitration rules.

654. — As the 1958 New York Convention only deals with the conditions for recognition and enforcement of awards, it does not cover the competence-competence principle. By contrast, the 1961 European Convention provides very clearly, in Article V, paragraph 3 that:

> [s]ubject to any subsequent judicial control provided for under the *lex fori*, the arbitrator whose jurisdiction is called in question shall be entitled to proceed with the arbitration, to rule on his own jurisdiction and to decide upon the existence or the validity of the arbitration agreement or of the contract of which the agreement forms part.

The Washington Convention establishing ICSID contains a similar rule in its Article 41.

---

[76] *See* PETER SCHLOSSER, DAS RECHT DER INTERNATIONALEN PRIVATEN SCHIEDSGERICHTSBARKEIT 418, n. 546 (2d ed. 1989).

[77] See Article 1032(1) and (2) of the ZPO which, since January 1, 1998, allows parties to apply to the courts for a determination whether the arbitration is admissible "[p]rior to the constitution of the arbitral tribunal" without preventing the arbitral procedure from going forward. On the situation in comparative law, see *infra* para. 675 and Schlosser, *supra* note 73.

[78] *See infra* note 83.

[79] *See, e.g.*, PIERRE JOLIDON, COMMENTAIRE DU CONCORDAT SUISSE SUR L'ARBITRAGE 185 (1984), and the references cited therein. Swiss authors thus generally avoid using the expression "Kompetenz- Kompetenz;" *see, e.g.*, PIERRE LALIVE, JEAN-FRANÇOIS POUDRET, CLAUDE REYMOND, LE DROIT DE L'ARBITRAGE INTERNE ET INTERNATIONAL EN SUISSE 380 *et seq.* (1989); Robert Briner, *Switzerland* (at 26), *in* ICCA INTERNATIONAL HANDBOOK ON COMMERCIAL ARBITRATION (1998). *But see* Swiss Fed. Trib., Apr. 19, 1994, Les Emirats Arabes Unis v. Westland Helicopters Ltd., 1994 BULL. ASA 404, 412; 1995 BULL. ASA 186, and P. Schweizer's note; 1995 REV. SUISSE DR. INT. ET DR. EUR. 564, and P. Schweizer's note; ANDREAS BUCHER, PIERRE-YVES TSCHANZ, INTERNATIONAL ARBITRATION IN SWITZERLAND ¶¶ 139 *et seq.* (1988).

655. — Major international arbitration statutes also recognize the principle. The UNCITRAL Model Law provides in Article 16, paragraph 3 that "[t]he arbitral tribunal may rule on [a plea that the arbitral tribunal does not have jurisdiction] either as a preliminary question or in an award on the merits," and that, in the event of an action to set aside a partial award concerning jurisdiction, "the arbitral tribunal may continue the arbitral proceedings and make an award."[80] Most recent laws on arbitration contain similar provisions.[81]

In French domestic arbitration law, the principle is set forth at Article 1466 of the New Code of Civil Procedure. This provides that "[i]f, before the arbitrator, one of the parties challenges the principle or scope of the arbitrator's jurisdiction, the arbitrator shall rule on the validity or scope of his or her jurisdiction."[82] Where an international arbitration is subject to French law, the same rule applies by virtue of Article 1495 of the same Code. However, the rule in fact is of general application in French international arbitration law, as a result of case law predating the 1981 Decree.[83] Recent decisions have confirmed the principle, giving it a very broad scope.[84]

---

[80] For an example of the application of this provision, see Ontario Court of Justice, Mar. 1, 1991, Rio Algom Ltd. v. Sammi Steel Co. Ltd., XVIII Y.B. COM. ARB. 166 (1993).

[81] Art. 186 of the 1987 Swiss Private International Law Statute and Art. 8, para. 1, of the Swiss *Concordat*; Art. 1697(1) of the Belgian Judicial Code (Law of July 4, 1972); Art. 1052(1) of the Netherlands Code of Civil Procedure (Law of Dec. 1, 1986); Art. 23(3) of the Spanish Law 36/1988 of December 5, 1988 on Arbitration; Art. 21(1) of the Portuguese Law No. 31/86 of Aug. 29, 1986 on Voluntary Arbitration; Art. 61 of the Tunisian Arbitration Code promulgated by Law No. 93-42 of April 26, 1993; Art. 458 bis 7 of the Algerian Code of Civil Procedure (Legislative Decree No. 93-09 of April 25, 1993); Sec. 30 of the 1996 English Arbitration Act; Art. 1040 of the German ZPO (Law of Dec. 22, 1997).

[82] This provision, enacted by the Decree of May 14, 1980, brought to an end the controversial case law concerning French domestic arbitration whereby "any dispute regarding the validity of the arbitration clause . . . must be heard exclusively by the courts" (Cass. com., Oct. 6, 1953, Courtieu v. Blanchard, JCP, Ed. G., Pt. II, No. 8293 (1954); Dalloz, Jur. 25 (1954), and the commentary by MOTULSKY, *supra* note 63 ("*Menace sur l'arbitrage: la prétendue incompétence des arbitres en cas de contestation de l'existence ou de la validité d'une clause compromissoire*," at 189 *et seq.*)).

[83] Cass. com., Feb. 22, 1949, Caulliez-Tibergien v. Caulliez-Hannart, JCP, Ed. G., Pt. II, No. 4899 (1949), and observations by H. Motulsky. *See also* MOTULSKY, *supra* note 63, at 222 *et seq.*; Trib. civ. Seine, Oct. 17, 1956, Kohorn v. Dimitrov, JCP, Ed. G., Pt. II, No. 9647 (1956), and observations by H. Motulsky; CA Colmar, Nov. 29, 1968, Impex v. P.A.Z., JCP, Ed. G., Pt. II, No. 16,246 (1970), and observations by P. Level and B. Oppetit; 1968 REV. ARB. 149: "The principle is that the judge hearing a dispute has jurisdiction to determine his own jurisdiction. This necessarily implies that when that judge is an arbitrator, whose powers derive from the agreement of the parties, he has jurisdiction to examine the existence and validity of such agreement." On the subsequent developments in the case, see *supra* para. 560.

[84] *See* TGI Paris, réf., Apr. 10, 1990, European Country Hotels Ltd. v. Consorts Legrand, 1994 REV. ARB. 545, 1st decision, and observations by P. Fouchard; CA Paris, Mar. 29, 1991, Ganz v. Société Nationale des Chemins de Fer Tunisiens (SNCFT), 1991 REV. ARB. 478, and L. Idot's note; CA Paris, May 19, 1993, Labinal v. Mors, 1993 REV. ARB. 645, and C. Jarrosson's note; 120 J.D.I. 957 (1993), and L. Idot's note; 1993 RTD COM. 494, and observations by E. Loquin; for an English translation, see 8 INT'L ARB. REP. 7 (July 1993); TGI Paris, réf., Jan. 10, 1996, *National Iranian Oil Co.*, *supra* note 46.

656. — The fact that the main institutional arbitration rules also include the principle of competence-competence[85] is a further example of its widespread recognition. Of course, from a strictly technical viewpoint, the recognition of the principle by the arbitral institutions is not sufficient to ensure its effectiveness. Institutional arbitration rules, which derive their authority from the parties' agreement, cannot grant the arbitrators more rights than the applicable legal systems allow them to exercise. In other words, unlike national laws, arbitration rules are contractual in nature and therefore cannot resolve the apparent contradiction which allows arbitrators to determine whether or not they have jurisdiction.[86] The same is true of arbitral awards applying the competence-competence principle.[87]

2° Basis of the Principle

657. — We have already seen that because case law develops by building on well-established rules in order to create new ones, the competence-competence principle has often been presented as the corollary of the principle of the autonomy of the arbitration agreement from the main contract.[88] As we noted, these two rules in fact overlap only slightly and should be carefully distinguished.[89]

658. — More fundamentally, although the arbitrators' jurisdiction to rule on their own jurisdiction is indeed one of the effects of the arbitration agreement (or even of a *prima facie* arbitration agreement, since the question would not arise in the absence of a *prima facie* arbitration agreement), the basis of that power is neither the arbitration agreement itself, nor the principle of *pacta sunt servanda* under which the arbitration agreement is binding.[90]

The competence-competence principle enables the arbitral tribunal to continue with the proceedings even where the existence or validity of the arbitration agreement has been challenged by one of the parties for reasons directly affecting the arbitration agreement, and not simply on the basis of allegations that the main contract is void or otherwise ineffective. The principle that the arbitration agreement is autonomous of the main contract is sufficient to resist a claim that the arbitration agreement is void because the contract containing it is invalid, but it does not enable the arbitrators to proceed with the arbitration where the

---

[85] *See, e.g.,* Art. 21(1) of the UNCITRAL Arbitration Rules; Art. 6(2) of the ICC Arbitration Rules (Art. 8(3) of the previous Rules); DERAINS AND SCHWARTZ, *supra* note 18, at 99 *et seq.*; Art. 23.1 of the 1998 LCIA Arbitration Rules; Art. 15(1) of the 1997 AAA International Arbitration Rules.

[86] See, on the other hand, for national laws, *infra* para. 658.

[87] *See, e.g.,* ICC Awards No. 1526 (1968), Belgian parties v. African state, 101 J.D.I. 915 (1974), and observations by Y. Derains; No. 2476 (1976), Swiss company v. Italian company, 104 J.D.I. 936 (1977), and observations by Y. Derains; No. 2558 (1976), Y v. French company, 104 J.D.I. 951 (1977), and observations by Y. Derains; No. 3987 (1983), Austrian company v. Greek company, 111 J.D.I. 943 (1984), and observations by Y. Derains; No. 6437 (1990), ICC BULLETIN, Vol. 8, No. 1, at 63 (1997). *See also* Yves Derains, *Les tendances de la jurisprudence arbitrale internationale*, 121 J.D.I. 829, 838 (1994).

[88] *See, e.g.,* CA Colmar, Nov. 29, 1968, *Impex, supra* note 83.

[89] *See supra* para. 416.

[90] *See supra* para. 627.

alleged invalidity directly concerns the arbitration agreement.[91] That is a consequence of the competence-competence principle alone. The competence-competence principle also allows arbitrators to determine that an arbitration agreement is invalid and to make an award declaring that they lack jurisdiction without contradicting themselves.

Of course, neither of those effects results from the arbitration agreement. If that were the case, one would immediately be confronted with the "vicious circle" argument put forward by authors opposed to the competence-competence principle: how can an arbitrator, solely on the basis of an arbitration agreement, declare that agreement to be void or even hear a claim to that effect? The answer is simple: the basis for the competence-competence principle lies not in the arbitration agreement, but in the arbitration laws of the country where the arbitration is held and, more generally, in the laws of all countries liable to recognize an award made by arbitrators concerning their own jurisdiction. For example, an international arbitral tribunal sitting in France can properly make an award declaring that it lacks jurisdiction for want of a valid arbitration agreement, because it does so on the basis of French arbitration law, and not on the basis of the arbitration agreement held to be non-existent or invalid. Similarly, it is perfectly logical for the interested party to rely on that award in other jurisdictions, provided that those other jurisdictions also recognize the competence-competence principle. As we shall now see, the legal basis for the principle does not prejudice the subsequent review by the courts, in France or in the country where recognition is sought, of the arbitrators' finding that the arbitration agreement is non-existent or invalid.

3° Meaning of the Principle

659. — Even today, the competence-competence principle is all too often interpreted as empowering the arbitrators to be the sole judges of their jurisdiction.[92] That would be neither logical nor acceptable. In fact, the real purpose of the rule is in no way to leave the question of the arbitrators' jurisdiction in the hands of the arbitrators alone. Their jurisdiction must instead be reviewed by the courts if an action is brought to set aside or to enforce the award.[93] Nevertheless, the competence-competence rule ties in with the idea that there are no grounds for the *prima facie* suspicion that the arbitrators themselves will not be able to reach decisions which are fair and protect the interests of society as well as those of the parties to the dispute. This same philosophy is also found in the context of arbitrability, where it serves as the basis for the case law which entrusts arbitrators with the task of

---

[91] *See supra* para. 416.

[92] On the traditional meaning in German legal terminology of the expression "Kompetenz-Kompetenz," which gave rise to this confusion, see *supra* para. 651.

[93] *See infra* paras. 1608 and 1629. The English legislature felt it necessary to include a specific provision to this effect, at Section 30(2) of the 1996 Arbitration Act.

applying rules of public policy (in areas such as antitrust law and the prevention of corruption), subject to subsequent review by the courts.[94]

660. — However, it is important to recognize that the competence-competence rule has a dual function. Like the arbitration agreement,[95] it has or may have both positive and negative effects, even if the latter have not yet been fully accepted in a number of jurisdictions.[96] The positive effect of the competence-competence principle is to enable the arbitrators to rule on their own jurisdiction, as is widely recognized by international conventions and by recent statutes on international arbitration.[97] However, the negative effect is equally important. It is to allow the arbitrators to be not the sole judges, but the first judges of their jurisdiction. In other words, it is to allow them to come to a decision on their jurisdiction prior to any court or other judicial authority, and thereby to limit the role of the courts to the review of the award. The principle of competence-competence thus obliges any court hearing a claim concerning the jurisdiction of an arbitral tribunal—regarding, for example, the constitution of the tribunal or the validity of the arbitration agreement—to refrain from hearing substantive argument as to the arbitrators' jurisdiction until such time as the arbitrators themselves have had the opportunity to do so. In that sense, the competence-competence principle is a rule of chronological priority. Taking both of its facets into account, the competence-competence principle can be defined as the rule whereby arbitrators must have the first opportunity to hear challenges relating to their jurisdiction, subject to subsequent review by the courts.[98]

From a practical standpoint, the rule is intended to ensure that a party cannot succeed in delaying the arbitral proceedings by alleging that the arbitration agreement is invalid or non-existent. Such delay is avoided by allowing the arbitrators to rule on this issue themselves, subject to subsequent review by the courts, and by inviting the courts to refrain from intervening until the award has been made. Nevertheless, the interests of parties with legitimate claims concerning the invalidity of the arbitration agreement are not unduly prejudiced, because they will be able to bring those claims before the arbitrators themselves and, should the arbitrators choose to reject them, before the courts thereafter.

The competence-competence rule thus concerns not only the positive, but also the negative effects of the arbitration agreement.[99]

---

[94] *See supra* paras. 561 *et seq.*

[95] *See supra* para. 624.

[96] For a comparative law analysis, see *infra* para. 675.

[97] *See supra* paras. 653 *et seq.*

[98] For an illustration of this principle in common law jurisdictions which have adopted the UNCITRAL Model Law, see Ontario Court of Justice, Mar. 1, 1991, *Rio Algom, supra* note 80; Hong Kong Supreme Court, July 30, 1992, Pacific International Lines (Pte) Ltd. v. Tsinlien Metals and Minerals Co. Ltd., XVIII Y.B. COM. ARB. 180 (1993), which both accept the negative effect of the competence-competence principle.

[99] On the negative effects of the "competence-competence" rule, see *infra* paras. 671 *et seq.*

SECTION II
NEGATIVE EFFECTS OF THE ARBITRATION AGREEMENT

661. — To ensure that the arbitration agreement will be complied with, the positive effect of the arbitration agreement—the requirement that the parties honor their undertaking to submit to arbitration any disputes covered by their agreement—must be accompanied by a negative effect, namely that the courts are prohibited from hearing such disputes.

We shall consider in turn the principle that the courts have no jurisdiction (§ 1), its implementation (§ 2) and its limits (§ 3).

§ 1. – The Principle that the Courts Have No Jurisdiction

662. — The principle that the courts lack jurisdiction to hear disputes covered by an arbitration agreement can be found in the major international conventions on arbitration (A), as well as in national legislation (B).

A. – INTERNATIONAL CONVENTIONS

663. — Article 4, paragraph 1 of the 1923 Geneva Protocol on Arbitration Clauses in Commercial Matters provides that:

> [t]he tribunals of the contracting parties, on being seized of a dispute regarding a contract made between persons to whom Article 1 applies and including an arbitration agreement whether referring to present or future differences which is valid in virtue of the said article and capable of being carried into effect, shall refer the parties on the application of either of them to the decision of the arbitrators.[100]

The 1958 New York Convention contains the same rule in its Article II, paragraph 3:

> [t]he court of a Contracting State, when seized of an action in a matter in respect of which the parties have made an agreement within the meaning of this article, shall . . . refer the parties to arbitration."

Similarly, the 1961 European Convention indirectly recognizes the principle that courts have no jurisdiction where there is an arbitration agreement. Article VI, paragraph 3 states that:

---

[100] On the meaning of these provisions, see FOUCHARD, *supra* note 68, ¶ 233; Goldman, *supra* note 68, ¶¶ 155 *et seq.*

> [w]here either party to an arbitration agreement has initiated arbitration proceedings before any resort is had to a court, courts of Contracting States subsequently asked to deal with the same subject-matter between the same parties . . . shall stay their ruling on the arbitrator's jurisdiction until the arbitral award is made, unless they have good and substantial reasons to the contrary.

This provision is somewhat unsatisfactory, as it refers only to cases where arbitral proceedings have already been initiated. The same rule should apply simply where an arbitration agreement exists, in order to avoid turning the proceedings into a race to secure or avoid the jurisdiction of the courts.[101]

Of course, each of the above conventions allows for the review by the courts of the existence and validity of the arbitration agreement,[102] and the only real issue concerns the point in time at which that review should be exercised.[103]

B. – ARBITRATION LEGISLATION

664. — Most modern arbitration statutes recognize the principle that the courts have no jurisdiction to hear disputes covered by an arbitration agreement.

The UNCITRAL Model Law includes the principle in its Article 8. Under the heading "Arbitration agreement and substantive claim before court," paragraph 1 of the article provides that:

> [a] court before which an action is brought in a matter which is the subject of an arbitration agreement shall, if a party so requests not later than when submitting his first statement on the substance of the dispute, refer the parties to arbitration.

This provision is very similar to Article II, paragraph 3 of the New York Convention.

Leading arbitration statutes likewise recognize the principle that courts have no jurisdiction.[104]

665. — English law long considered that the effect of the arbitration agreement was to justify the grant of a stay of proceedings by the courts until the making of the arbitral award,

---

[101] On the similar distinction found in French law, see *infra* para. 680.

[102] *See* Art. 4, para. 1 of the Geneva Protocol; Art. II(3) of the 1958 New York Convention; Art. VI(3) of the 1961 European Convention.

[103] *See infra* para. 671.

[104] *See, e.g.*, Art. 7 of the 1987 Swiss Private International Law Statute; Art. 1022 of the Netherlands Code of Civil Procedure (Law of July 2, 1986); Art. 11 of the Spanish law 36/1988 on Arbitration of December 5, 1988; Art. 1679 of the Belgian Judicial Code (Law of July 4, 1972); Art. 458 bis 8 of the Algerian Code of Civil Procedure (Legislative Decree No. 93-09 of April 25, 1993); Art. 52 of the Tunisian Arbitration Code promulgated by Law No. 93-42 of April 26, 1993; Art. 1032 of the German ZPO and, before the December 22, 1997 reform, Art. 1027(a) of the ZPO.

rather than to exclude the jurisdiction of the courts altogether.[105] The 1996 Arbitration Act also takes this approach. Section 9, which is a mandatory provision, states that rather than asking a court to decline jurisdiction, "[a] party to an arbitration agreement against whom legal proceedings are brought . . . in respect of a matter which under the agreement is to be referred to arbitration may . . . apply to the court in which the proceedings have been brought to stay the proceedings so far as they concern that matter. . . ."[106] The English courts strictly apply the rule requiring a stay and will even enjoin parties bound by an arbitration agreement not to bring the dispute before courts outside England.[107] A similar rule is found in Section 3 of the United States Arbitration Act, according to which courts confronted with an arbitration agreement must stay the proceedings until the arbitration has taken place in accordance with the terms of the arbitration agreement.[108]

666. — In French domestic arbitration law, the principle is found in Article 1458 of the New Code of Civil Procedure, which provides that:

> [w]here a dispute submitted to an arbitral tribunal by virtue of an arbitration agreement is brought before a national court, such court shall decline jurisdiction.

The *Cour de cassation* has confirmed that this provision is "applicable to international arbitration."[109]

667. — Once again, all of the legislation discussed above recognizes that the courts are entitled to review the existence and validity of the arbitration agreement on which the arbitrators' jurisdiction is based,[110] although they differ as to when that review should take place.[111]

---

[105] *See* MICHAEL J. MUSTILL, STEWART C. BOYD, COMMERCIAL ARBITRATION 154 *et seq.* (2d ed. 1989); ALAN REDFERN AND MARTIN HUNTER, LAW AND PRACTICE OF INTERNATIONAL COMMERCIAL ARBITRATION 285 *et seq.* (2d ed. 1991).

[106] *See* RUSSELL ON ARBITRATION, *supra* note 21, at 324 *et seq.*

[107] Aggeliki Charis Compania Maritima SA v. Pagnan SpA (The "Angelic Grace"), [1995] 1 Lloyds Rep. 87; XXII Y.B. COM. ARB. 838 (1997) (C.A. 1994).

[108] *See also* Howard M. Holtzmann and Donald Francis Donovan, *United States* (at 23), *in* ICCA INTERNATIONAL HANDBOOK OF COMMERCIAL ARBITRATION (1999); JACK J. COE, JR., INTERNATIONAL COMMERCIAL ARBITRATION: AMERICAN PRINCIPLES AND PRACTICE IN A GLOBAL CONTEXT 154 *et seq.* (1997).

[109] Cass. 1e civ., June 28, 1989, Eurodif v. République Islamique d'Iran, 1989 Bull. Civ. I, No. 255; 1989 REV. ARB. 653, 2d decision, and P. Fouchard's note; 117 J.D.I. 1004 (1990), 2d decision, and P. Ouakrat's note. On the conditions governing challenges of the jurisdiction of the French courts, see CA Paris, June 23, 1993, Euro Disney v. Eremco, 1994 REV. ARB. 151, and L. Cadiet's note.

[110] See the references cited *supra* para. 664.

[111] On this issue, see *infra* para. 675.

§ 2. – Implementation of the Principle that the Courts Have No Jurisdiction

668. — Two aspects of the regime governing the courts' lack of jurisdiction require further examination: first, the fact that the courts cannot declare *ex officio* that they lack jurisdiction as a result of the existence of an arbitration agreement (A) and, second, the point in time at which the courts can hear actions concerning the existence or validity of an arbitration agreement (B).

A. – THE COURTS CANNOT DECLARE *EX OFFICIO* THAT THEY HAVE NO JURISDICTION AS A RESULT OF THE EXISTENCE OF AN ARBITRATION AGREEMENT

669. — Given that an arbitration is based, by definition, on the parties' agreement to have their disputes resolved by that means, it is always possible for the parties to agree to waive their obligation to submit disputes to arbitration and to go before the courts instead. Such a waiver may be either express or implied.[112]

For that reason, it is not for the court hearing a dispute covered by an arbitration agreement to declare *ex officio* that it has no jurisdiction. By bringing a court action on the merits, the plaintiff waives the benefit of the arbitration agreement.[113] By participating in the proceedings without challenging the court's jurisdiction, the defendant likewise accepts that jurisdiction.[114] The parties' intentions coincide and the court must give effect to those intentions, just as it would with an agreement in any other form.

670. — This approach is widely accepted. It is provided for in Article 4 of the 1923 Geneva Protocol,[115] Article II, paragraph 3 of the 1958 New York Convention[116] and in Article VI, paragraph 1 of the 1961 European Convention.[117] It also features in most

---

[112] *See infra* para. 736.

[113] This will not of course be the case where the claimant is seeking only provisional or protective measures compatible with the arbitration agreement. On this issue, see *infra* paras. 685 and 1302 *et seq.* For a counterclaim before the courts being deemed a waiver of the arbitration agreement, see Spanish *Tribunal Supremo*, Feb. 18, 1993, Black Sea Shipping Co. v. Novo Viaje, S.A., XXII Y.B. COM. ARB. 785, 788 (1997).

[114] See, for a late challenge of a court's jurisdiction on the basis of the existence of an arbitration agreement, Cass. 2e civ., Mar. 11, 1999, Project XJ 220 Ltd. v. de Dampierre, No. D 96-16.418, unpublished.

[115] Article 4 of this Protocol, set forth in part *supra* para. 663, makes the jurisdiction of the arbitrators conditional upon the request of one of the parties.

[116] *See supra* para. 663 (the courts will refer the parties back to the arbitrators "at the request of one of the parties").

[117] This provision reads as follows: "A plea as to the jurisdiction of the court made before the court seized by either party to the arbitration agreement, on the basis of the fact that an arbitration agreement exists shall, under penalty of estoppel, be presented by the respondent before or at the same time as the presentation of his substantial defence, depending upon whether the law of the court seized regards this plea as one of procedure

(continued...)

arbitration statutes.[118] In French law, Article 1458 of the New Code of Civil Procedure applies to both domestic and international arbitration[119] and expressly stipulates in paragraph 3 that if proceedings are pending before the arbitrators or if an arbitration agreement exists "the court cannot decline jurisdiction *ex officio*."[120] In the United States, the same rule has been developed by the courts.[121]

B. – WHEN CAN THE COURTS REVIEW THE EXISTENCE AND VALIDITY OF THE ARBITRATION AGREEMENT?

671. — The issue of when the courts are empowered to review the existence and validity of the arbitration agreement is more controversial. In most legal systems, the debate surrounding the competence-competence rule now focuses on this issue. We have seen that a vast majority of countries admit the positive effect of the competence-competence principle. Thus, challenging the existence or validity of the arbitration agreement will not prevent the arbitral tribunal from proceeding with the arbitration, ruling on its own jurisdiction and, if it retains jurisdiction, making an award on the substance of the dispute, all without waiting for the outcome of any court action aimed at setting aside the award deciding the jurisdiction issue.[122]

However, the negative effect of the competence-competence principle is more contentious. This negative effect is that the arbitrators are entitled to be the first to determine their jurisdiction (and not to be sole judges of the issue), so that the courts' review of the arbitral tribunal's jurisdiction occurs only where there is an action to enforce or set aside the arbitral award.

We shall examine the position adopted in comparative law in this respect (1°), before considering the underlying policy considerations which, in our view, justify postponing court intervention until after the award is made.

---

[117] (...continued)
or of substance."

[118] See, for example, Article 8(1) of the UNCITRAL Model Law and the statutes cited *supra* para. 664.

[119] Cass. 1e civ., June 28, 1989, *Eurodif, supra* note 109.

[120] See, before the 1980 and 1981 reforms, FOUCHARD, *supra* note 68, ¶ 225; Goldman, *supra* note 68, ¶ 148; CA Aix, Mar. 19, 1964, Unipol v. Capitaine du "Seacob," 1965 DR. MAR. FR. 220; Cass. 1e civ., June 6, 1978, *British Leyland, supra* note 24.

[121] BORN, *supra* note 25, at 279 *et seq.* (1994).

[122] *See supra* para. 655.

1° The Position Adopted in Comparative Law

672. — French law was quick to recognize the negative effect of the competence-competence principle.[123] Article 1458 of the New Code of Civil Procedure, which applies to both domestic and international arbitration,[124] obliges the courts to decline jurisdiction where an arbitration agreement exists, provided that the merits of the dispute have already been put before an arbitral tribunal. Even in domestic arbitration, the French courts have been very strict in applying this principle. For example, in the *Coprodag* case, the first instance court held that an arbitration agreement was void and that the arbitral tribunal should therefore not be constituted, although one party had already initiated the arbitral proceedings. That decision was confirmed by the Court of Appeals, but in 1995 the *Cour de cassation* reversed the Court of Appeal's decision, holding that:

> the President of the Tribunal of First Instance cannot declare that the arbitrators should not be appointed on the grounds that the arbitration agreement is patently void unless he is seized of a problem concerning the constitution of the arbitral tribunal; the arbitral tribunal alone has jurisdiction to rule on the validity or limits of its appointment, provided that question has been brought before it.[125]

Where the dispute is not before an arbitral tribunal, the courts must also decline jurisdiction unless the arbitration agreement is "patently void."[126] This amounts to a *prima facie* review of the existence and validity of the arbitration agreement. As the French *Cour de cassation* held in its *V 2000* decision, without even referring to the hypothesis of the arbitration clause being patently void, the arbitrators must "apply the arbitration clause subject to subsequent review by the courts in order to verify their own competence,

---

[123] See, for instance, prior to the 1980-81 reform, the clear recognition of the rule according to which the arbitral tribunal has to be the first to make a determination on its own jurisdiction, in CA Paris, Mar. 9, 1972, Lefrère v. SA Les Pétroles Pursan, 1972 RTD COM. 344, and observations by M. Boitard and J.-C. Dubarry. On the issue generally, see Gaillard, *L'effet négatif de la compétence-compétence, supra* note 67.

[124] Cass. 1e civ., June 28, 1989, *Eurodif, supra* note 109. *See also* Cass. 1e civ., June 7, 1989, Anhydro v. Caso Pillet, 1992 REV. ARB. 61, and Y. Derains' note; TGI Paris, réf., Apr. 10, 1990, *European Country Hotels, supra* note 84. *See also* Cass. 2e civ., June 18, 1986, Buzzichelli v. S.a.r.l. S.E.R.M.I., 1986 REV. ARB. 565, 1st decision, and G. Couchez' note; Cass. 1e civ., Mar. 20, 1989, The General Authority for Supply Commodities Cairo-Estram v. Ipitrade International, 116 J.D.I. 1045 (1989), and B. Oppetit's note; 1989 REV. ARB. 494, 3d decision, and G. Couchez' note.

[125] Cass. 2e civ., May 10, 1995, Coprodag v. Dame Bohin, 1995 REV. ARB. 617, and E. Gaillard's note; Dalloz, Jur. 79 (1996), and G. Bolard's note.

[126] *See, e.g.,* CA Paris, Dec. 7, 1994, V 2000 (formerly Jaguar France) v. Renault, 1996 REV. ARB. 245, and C. Jarrosson's note; 1995 RTD COM. 401, and observations by J.-C. Dubarry and E. Loquin; 1996 JUSTICES 435, and observations by M.-C. Rivier, *aff'd,* Cass. 1e civ., May 21, 1997, Renault v. V 2000 (formerly Jaguar France), 1997 REV. ARB. 537, and E. Gaillard's note; 1998 REV. CRIT. DIP 87 and V. Heuzé's note; 125 J.D.I. 969 (1998), and S. Poillot- Peruzzetto's note; CA Grenoble, Oct. 3, 1996, Logic groupe Concept v. Logi Concept, 1997 REV. ARB. 433, and observations by Y. Derains; Cass. 1e civ., Jan. 5, 1999, Zanzi v. de Coninck, 1999 DALLOZ AFF. 474.

particularly as regards the arbitrability of the dispute."[127] At the same time, when the French courts hear a request for the appointment of an arbitrator on the basis of an arbitration agreement the existence or validity of which is contested, they do not address the substance of the dispute and must, at the very most, make a *prima facie* assessment of the existence and validity of the agreement.[128]

673. — However, the major international conventions on arbitration and arbitration legislation in other legal systems do not always endorse this approach very clearly.

674. — Both the 1923 Geneva Protocol (Art. 4, para. 1) and the 1958 New York Convention (Art. II(3)), followed in this respect by the UNCITRAL Model Law (Art. 8), allow the courts to hear the merits of a dispute without referring it to arbitration, if they find that the arbitration agreement is "null and void, inoperative or incapable of being performed."[129] This provision is ambiguous in that it can be interpreted either as allowing a full trial of these issues before the courts or as requesting only their preliminary examination.[130] The 1961 European Convention (Art. VI(3)) goes further in prohibiting the courts from resolving the question of whether the arbitration agreement "was non-existent or null and void or had lapsed," unless they have "good and substantial reasons to the contrary." This language is intended to signal that only a *prima facie* assessment of the arbitration agreement's validity and scope may be performed by the courts at this stage, as opposed to the full review to be performed in the context of an enforcement action or action to set aside once an award has been made on the issue.

675. — The traditional approach is to allow a court which has been asked to rule on the merits of the case despite the existence of an arbitration agreement to fully review the existence and validity of such agreement without waiting for a decision from the arbitrators on those issues. That was the case in English law before the 1996 Arbitration Act[131] and

---

[127] Cass. 1e civ., May 21, 1997, *supra* note 126.

[128] On this issue, generally, see *infra* paras. 750 *et seq.*

[129] This formulation is that of the Model Law. The Geneva Protocol mentions the cases where "the agreement or the arbitration cannot proceed or becomes inoperative." The New York Convention refers to arbitration agreements that are "null and void." On the interpretation of these concepts by the courts of the countries bound by the New York Convention, see, every year, the YEARBOOK COMMERCIAL ARBITRATION, Part V – A, Court Decisions on the New York Convention 1958.

[130] In favor of the latter interpretation, see, for example, the Ontario and Hong Kong decisions cited *supra* notes 80 and 98 respectively. For a similar interpretation of the corresponding provisions of Swiss law, see *infra* note 136. The German legislature added to the provisions of the UNCITRAL Model Law a paragraph stating that "[p]rior to the constitution of the arbitral tribunal, an application may be made to the court to determine whether or not arbitration is admissible" (Art. 1032(2) of the ZPO (Law of Dec. 22, 1997)) This provision tracks the distinction made by the French law and the 1961 European Convention as regards the point in time when the court is entitled to intervene (*see supra* para. 672). However, very different consequences result from the suggestion that the court is not to limit its review to a *prima facie* examination of the matter (*see* Schlosser, *supra* note 73, at 300; Berger, *supra* note 73, at 122).

[131] Veeder, *supra* note 19, at 173. The author acknowledges, however, that the principle of the autonomy of the arbitration agreement and that of competence-competence are essential in international commercial arbitration

(continued...)

examples of this approach can still be found in the United States.[132] In other legal systems, the same position results from early cases which might be decided differently today. In Austria, for example, the Supreme Court held in 1935, that:

> it would entail duplication of effort if a party contesting the jurisdiction of an arbitral tribunal were obliged to pursue the proceedings before that tribunal before being able to bring a court action to annul the arbitral proceedings.[133]

The same position was taken more recently by the Swedish legislature in the 1999 Arbitration Act (Sec. 2, para. 1).

A number of recent statutes on arbitration have enacted provisions which, like the UNCITRAL Model Law,[134] are not completely determinative of the issue. For instance, Belgian law states that "a judge seized of a dispute which is covered by an arbitration agreement shall decline jurisdiction at the request of one of the parties, except where, with regard to the dispute in question, the arbitration agreement is invalid or has lapsed" (Art. 1679, para. 1 of the Judicial Code). Similarly, the 1986 Netherlands Arbitration Act provides that "[a] court seized of a dispute in respect of which an arbitration agreement has been concluded shall declare that it has no jurisdiction if a party invokes the existence of the said agreement before submitting a defense, unless the agreement is invalid" (Art. 1022(1) of the Code of Civil Procedure). The 1987 Swiss Private International Law Statute stipulates that "[i]f the parties have concluded an arbitration agreement covering an arbitrable dispute, a Swiss court seized of it shall decline jurisdiction unless: . . . b. the court finds that the arbitral agreement is null and void, inoperative or incapable of being performed" (Art. 7). These provisions could easily be read as implying that a court seized of the merits of a dispute in spite of the existence of an arbitration agreement would have to fully address the question of that agreement's effectiveness. However, after some hesitation,[135] the Swiss Federal Tribunal decided to interpret them as restricting the court's review at the outset of proceedings to a *prima facie* verification of the existence and effectiveness of the arbitration clause.[136] Swiss law thus now takes the same position as French law on this point.

The 1996 English Arbitration Act adopted a slightly different solution, whereby the courts may only rule on the issue of jurisdiction with the agreement of the parties or, if the parties do not agree, with the consent of the arbitral tribunal. In this latter case, the court must also

---

[131](...continued)

  (*id.* at 171). On these issues, see *supra* para. 416. *See also* Peter Gross, *Competence of Competence: An English View*, 8 Arb. Int'l 205 (1992).

[132] *See, e.g.,* Comptek Telecomm., Inc. v. IVD Corp., No. 94–CV–0827E(H), 1995 U.S. Dist. LEXIS 11876 (W.D.N.Y. Aug. 1, 1995); 10 Int'l Arb. Rep. A1 (Sept. 1995); XXII Y.B. Com. Arb. 905 (1997). See also the case discussed *infra* para. 680.

[133] *Oberster Gerichtshof*, Oct. 2, 1935, SZ17/131. On the situation in German law, see *supra* para. 651.

[134] *See supra* para. 674.

[135] See the discussion in Swiss Fed. Trib., Apr. 19, 1994, *Les Emirats Arabes Unis, supra* note 79, at 410.

[136] Swiss Fed. Trib., Apr. 29, 1996, Fondation M. v. Banque X., 1996 Bull. ASA 527, and the note by C.U. Mayer at 361; 1996 Rev. suisse dr. int. et dr. eur. 586, and observations by F. Knoepfler. For a similar interpretation of the language adopted by the UNCITRAL Model Law, see *supra* note 98.

find that its decision is liable to save substantial cost, that the application was made promptly, and that there is a valid reason for the claim to be heard by a court (Sec. 32). This is, needless to say, a significant step towards the full acceptance of the negative effect of the competence-competence rule.[137]

676. — As a result, and although it was at one time relatively isolated, the rule found in French law and in the 1961 European Convention has recently gained substantial acceptance. However, the fact that the issue remains controversial invites a more detailed study of the policy considerations that underlie each of the two different approaches.

2° Policy Considerations

677. — From a legislative standpoint, each of the two approaches to the question of when the courts should be entitled to rule on the existence and validity of the arbitration agreement has its own advantages and disadvantages.

678. — The approach whereby the courts seized of the merits of the case are entitled to rule immediately on the existence and validity of the arbitration agreement arguably leads to a certain degree of time and cost avoidance. It may prevent parties having to wait several months, or in some cases years, before knowing the final outcome of the dispute regarding jurisdiction—it will often take that long for the arbitrators and then the courts to reach their decisions.[138] However, that drawback is of less importance where the arbitrators are prepared to make a separate award on the issue of jurisdiction, which can generally be done relatively rapidly and will be subject to an immediate action to set aside. For that reason, Article 186, paragraph 3 of the Swiss Private International Law Statute suggests, without requiring it, that "[t]he arbitral tribunal shall, in general, decide on its jurisdiction by a preliminary decision."[139] In complex disputes, where the examination of the merits of the case is necessarily time-consuming, reaching a decision on jurisdiction by way of a preliminary award is certainly preferable.[140] The same considerations of cost and time explain the position taken in English law. Under Section 32(2) of the 1996 English Arbitration Act, the parties may agree (or, if the parties fail to agree, the arbitral tribunal may agree) that it would be more efficient to have the question resolved immediately by the courts.

---

[137] For an earlier discussion on the merits of each system, see the observations of Gaillard and Veeder, *supra* note 19, at 162 *et seq.* and 169 *et seq.* For an assessment of the current English rule, see *infra* para. 682.

[138] This consideration has sometimes been put forward as a basis for criticism of the position taken by French law in this respect; see Mayer, *supra* note 68, at 346.

[139] On the possibility of commencing an immediate action to set aside such awards, see *infra* para. 1357.

[140] On this issue, generally, see *infra* para. 1359.

679. — The approach adopted in the 1961 European Convention, in French law, and now in a number of other jurisdictions[141]—whereby courts asked to rule on the merits should restrict their investigation to a *prima facie* review of the arbitration agreement—is based on two considerations.

680. — The first is to ensure that parties seeking to obstruct the arbitration are not able to do so by exploiting court proceedings concerning the existence, scope and validity of the arbitration agreement. Although an immediate court action will not, in theory, prevent the arbitrators from continuing with the arbitration, the fact that a party contesting the existence or validity of the arbitration agreement can immediately bring such claims to court will necessarily interfere with the progress of the arbitration. Knowing that the courts have yet to rule on the issue will make neither the parties nor the arbitrators inclined to press ahead with the arbitration before the outcome of the court proceedings. For the French legislature and the drafters of the European Convention, the risk of having the arbitrators wrongly retain jurisdiction in some cases, and have that decision reversed by the courts several months, if not years, later, seemed less serious than the risk that parties acting in bad faith could disrupt arbitral proceedings by systematically challenging the jurisdiction of the arbitral tribunal not only before the arbitrators, but also before the courts.

That concern accounts for the distinction based on whether the arbitral tribunal has already been seized, found in Article 1458 of the French New Code of Civil Procedure[142] and in Article VI, paragraph 3 of the 1961 European Convention.[143] If the dispute is already before the arbitral tribunal, the courts have no jurisdiction, because of the risk of deliberate delay. On the other hand, the attitude of a plaintiff who brings its dispute directly before the courts is less likely to be in bad faith. Since the dispute has not yet gone before the arbitral tribunal, the idea of avoiding duplication of effort resurfaces: the court will retain jurisdiction to rule on the merits of the dispute only if it considers the arbitration agreement to be patently void.

The case law of jurisdictions which allow the courts to hear claims regarding the existence and validity of the arbitration agreement before the arbitrators are able to do so usefully illustrates the risks inherent in such an approach.

For example, an action was brought in 1991 before a United States federal court—the District Court for the Northern District of Illinois—by the exclusive distributor in the United States of a Swedish group, despite the existence of an ordinary ICC arbitration clause in the contract between the parties. This clause provided that the "agreement shall be governed in accordance with Swedish Law" and that "[t]he arbitration proceedings shall be conducted in the English Language and shall take place in London in accordance with the Rules of Conciliation and Arbitration of the International Chamber of Commerce." In deciding whether or not it should retain jurisdiction, the court observed that there are two types of arbitration agreement: one in which the parties may submit the dispute to arbitration, and one in which they must do so. The court then examined whether, under Swedish law—which it

---

[141] For Switzerland, see *supra* para. 675. On Hong Kong and Ontario, see *supra* notes 80 and 98 respectively.

[142] On the applicability of this provision in international arbitration, see *supra* para. 672.

[143] *See supra* para. 663. Compare, on the distinctions found in German law, *supra* para. 651, note 77.

considered as governing the arbitration agreement in spite of the principle of the autonomy of the arbitration agreement[144]—the arbitration clause in question was of the first or second variety. The court therefore reviewed the Swedish law opinions submitted by each of the parties, but found them to be poorly documented. It then requested further evidence as to the content of Swedish law, whereupon the parties submitted new opinions, which contradicted each other in every respect. On that evidence, the court concluded that the parties' submissions had shed little light on the interpretation of the clause under Swedish law and that, consequently, a hearing should be arranged, during which the parties were invited to provide proof of their true intentions as to the issue of jurisdiction.[145]

This case provides an extremely strong argument in favor of having the competence-competence principle apply to prevent the courts from intervening before the issue of the arbitrators' jurisdiction is heard by the arbitrators themselves. It also illustrates the benefits of the rejection of the use of the choice of law method in this area.[146]

681. — The negative effect of the competence-competence principle also satisfies another concern of the French legislature, the importance of which, although entirely procedural, should not be underestimated. It concerns the jurisdiction, both territorially and in terms of subject matter, of the courts responsible for reviewing the existence, validity and scope of the arbitration agreement. One of the major objectives of the French reform of international arbitration law in 1981 was to simplify the means of challenging arbitral awards before the courts and to direct such actions before the court of appeals of the place where those awards were made.[147] Similarly, the 1987 Swiss Private International Law Statute gives exclusive jurisdiction to the Federal Tribunal to hear actions to set aside awards made in Switzerland unless the parties specifically elect to give jurisdiction to the court which each Canton has designated for that purpose, or to have their arbitration governed by the rules of the *Concordat*.[148] The UNCITRAL Model Law itself has also attempted to centralize actions to set aside before certain courts in each country adopting it.[149] Without the negative effect of the competence-competence principle, this simplification exercise would be substantially undermined. The court which would normally have jurisdiction in the absence of an arbitration agreement would be any commercial or civil court, depending on the circumstances. To allow those courts to fully decide the validity and scope of such an arbitration agreement would clearly defeat the purpose of legislative provisions organizing the centralization of the court review of disputes associated with arbitration.

682. — The two policy reasons underlying the negative effect of the competence-competence principle, namely the prevention of delaying tactics and the centralization of

---

[144] *See supra* para. 412.

[145] SMG Swedish Machine Group v. Swedish Machine Group, Inc., No. 90 C 6081, 1991 U.S. Dist. LEXIS 780 (N.D. Ill. Jan. 4, 1991); XVIII Y.B. COM. ARB. 457 (1993).

[146] On this issue, see *supra* paras. 435 *et seq.*

[147] *See infra* paras. 1564 *et seq.*

[148] Art. 191 of the Swiss International Private Law Statute.

[149] Arts. 6 and 34(2).

litigation concerning the existence and validity of the arbitration agreement before certain courts, seemed more compelling to certain legal systems—and rightly so in our opinion—than the argument based on the desire to avoid duplication which led to the rejection of that approach in other legal systems. Thus, although it is not a rule which is yet universally accepted, we believe the approach adopted in French and Swiss law, as well as in the 1961 European Convention, to be sound.

It is, in our view, preferable to the intermediate position taken in 1996 English Arbitration Act.[150] Where the parties disagree, the decision by the arbitrators whether or not to authorize the immediate involvement of the courts can only properly be made after an examination—which will be superficial at least—of the jurisdictional issue in dispute. It might have been more efficient to have the arbitrators decide the question immediately by way of a preliminary award, and then to involve the courts in an action to set aside, rather than rely on the first instincts of the arbitrators themselves as to whether it is appropriate to ask the courts to resolve the question at the outset. On the other hand, enabling the parties to choose whether to have the courts dispose of the dispute immediately or not is an excellent idea, provided the parties can reach agreement. It remains to be seen how the fall-back position will be implemented by arbitrators.

§ 3. – The Limits of the Courts' Lack of Jurisdiction

683. — There is only one real exception to the principle that the courts have no jurisdiction to hear disputes covered by an arbitration agreement. That exception is the rare case where an arbitration agreement is ineffective to the extent that it is impossible to constitute the arbitral tribunal, whereupon it becomes necessary to revert to the courts in order to have the merits of the case resolved.[151] In contrast, where it is possible to constitute the arbitral tribunal and to give effect to the parties' initial intentions, the courts will intervene only on an incidental basis to ensure that the arbitration runs smoothly.

Such court intervention essentially occurs at three stages of the arbitral process: on constitution of the arbitral tribunal (A), where a party applies for provisional and conservatory measures (B) and on review of the award (C).

A. – THE CONSTITUTION OF THE ARBITRAL TRIBUNAL

684. — The intervention of the courts to assist, if need be, in constituting the arbitral tribunal is provided for in all modern arbitration laws. Such intervention is subsidiary in character: any means of constituting the arbitral tribunal chosen by the parties themselves, whether directly or by reference to institutional arbitration rules, will take precedence. Nevertheless, the possibility of court intervention is useful in cases where the mechanisms

---

[150] *See supra* para. 675 *in fine*.

[151] *See supra* para. 633.

agreed by the parties do not work satisfactorily or where no such mechanisms have been agreed upon in the first place. This is particularly true in *ad hoc* arbitration, where there is no arbitral institution to appoint an arbitrator where a party refuses to do so. However, the intervention of the courts does not compete with the arbitration in any way; on the contrary, it is designed to facilitate the progress of the arbitration in order to give effect to the intentions of the parties to enter into an arbitration agreement. It is therefore fully consistent with the principle that the courts have no jurisdiction to hear the merits of disputes covered by an arbitration agreement.

We shall examine this aspect of the intervention of the courts in more detail when considering the constitution of the arbitral tribunal.[152]

B. – PROVISIONAL AND CONSERVATORY MEASURES

685. — As the arbitration agreement can only bind the parties that entered into it, and as the arbitrators have no *imperium*, some measures can only be effectively taken by the courts.

First, even where they are purely conservatory, seizures can only be ordered by the courts. The same applies to a number of measures that facilitate the gathering of evidence. The privity of the arbitration agreement prevents the arbitrators from compelling third parties to submit documents. Likewise, since they lack *imperium*, arbitrators cannot compel a party to arbitration to submit documents against its wishes, although such a refusal may lead the arbitrators to make unfavorable inferences as to that party's case. In addition, it will generally be impossible for measures requiring urgent action, such as those intended to prevent the deterioration or disappearance of evidence, to be taken by arbitrators within the appropriate timeframe, especially where the arbitral tribunal has yet to be constituted.

In each of the above cases, the main purpose of the court's intervention is to promote efficiency. Once again, however, the intervention of the court is not so much an infringement of the jurisdiction of the arbitral tribunal as a means of assisting the tribunal so that its award will be as effective as possible. Whenever there appears to be a genuine violation of the jurisdiction of the arbitrators to hear the merits of the dispute, the jurisdiction of the courts will be rejected.[153]

The issue of provisional and conservatory measures will also be examined at a later stage, in the context of our analysis of the conduct of the arbitral proceedings.[154]

C. – REVIEW OF THE AWARD BY THE COURTS

686. — It is essential for the courts to exercise a minimum degree of control over the arbitral award. In order for the award to be enforceable in the same way as a court judgment,

---

[152] *See infra* paras. 742 *et seq.*

[153] See, however, on the issues raised by the French concept of *référé provision, infra* paras. 1339 *et seq.*

[154] *See infra* paras. 1302 *et seq.*

it must be the subject of an enforcement order, and it is hardly conceivable that an award could be rendered enforceable in a given country without some sort of review being exercised.[155]

687. — The only real policy question is whether the review of the award should take place in the jurisdiction where the arbitration has its seat, or in the jurisdictions where enforcement is sought, or in both.

As we shall see, not all legal systems deal with this question in the same way, with the general trend being to allow the courts to review arbitral awards in both the country of the seat of the arbitration and the country or countries where the award is to be enforced.[156]

688. — We shall discuss the review by the courts of arbitral awards in detail in Part Six below.[157] For present purposes, it is sufficient to note that the existence of such a review does not conflict with the jurisdiction of the arbitrators to hear the merits of disputes covered by the arbitration agreement. That would only be the case if the review of the award were to include a review of the merits. Most countries do not allow the courts reviewing the award to review the merits, as shown by the widespread ratification of the 1958 New York Convention, which specifically excludes such review by the courts.[158]

The existence of the review by the courts of arbitral awards, although limited in scope, is arguably one of the essential conditions for the development of arbitration. Indeed, review by the courts is the necessary counterpart of the inherently private nature of the arbitral process. In particular, it is the existence of subsequent court control which makes it acceptable for arbitrators to rule on their own jurisdiction[159] and for disputes involving matters of public policy to be arbitrable.[160] It is because the courts will review the arbitral award at a later stage that they can refrain from interfering with the conduct of the arbitration, no matter how serious the allegations may be as to irregularities affecting the proceedings.[161]

---

[155] On the specific position of ICSID arbitration, where the Contracting States of the 1965 Washington Convention undertook to recognize ICSID awards as decisions of their own courts subject only to the possible review by an *ad hoc* committee, see Articles 52 *et seq.* of the Washington Convention.

[156] *See infra* para. 1559.

[157] *See infra* paras. 1558 *et seq.*

[158] *See infra* paras. 1666 *et seq.*

[159] *See supra* para. 658.

[160] *See supra* paras. 532 *et seq.*

[161] See the examples cited *infra* para. 1169.

CHAPTER IV
ASSIGNMENT AND EXPIRATION OF THE ARBITRATION AGREEMENT

689. — Under normal circumstances, an arbitration agreement will have fulfilled its purpose when the arbitrators appointed under it have resolved all differences which may arise between the parties. However, as with any contract, the arbitration agreement may be assigned or may expire otherwise than by fulfilling its purpose. We shall therefore consider in turn both the assignment (Section I) and the expiration (Section II) of the arbitration agreement.

SECTION I
ASSIGNMENT OF THE ARBITRATION AGREEMENT

690. — The assignment of an arbitration agreement becomes relevant where a person who was not initially a party to it wishes to rely on the undertaking contained in it to have disputes resolved by arbitration, or where that undertaking is relied on against such party. This situation is not to be confused with that where one of the parties to the initial agreement undergoes a change in legal form. A change in legal form is more frequently encountered in practice, and will not affect the operation of the arbitration agreement unless it brings into question the continued existence of any legal entity that was party to the agreement.[1]

In spite of both its importance in practice and the particularly difficult issues it raises, the assignment of arbitration agreements was long ignored by authors and commentators. Recently, however, it has been the subject of several major studies.[2]

---

[1] *See, e.g.,* CA Paris, Mar. 11, 1993, Al-Kawthar Investment Co. Ltd. v. BNP, 1994 REV. ARB. 735, and observations by D. Cohen; for an English translation, see 8 INT'L ARB. REP. F1 (Apr. 1993); ICC Award No. 6754 (1993), Italian company v. Algerian State enterprise, 122 J.D.I. 1009 (1995), and observations by Y. Derains. Compare, in the context of the determination of the initial parties to the arbitration agreement, *supra* para. 507.

[2] *See* Jean-Louis Goutal, *L'arbitrage et les tiers: I. – Le droit des contrats,* 1988 REV. ARB. 439; Philippe Delebecque, *La transmission de la clause compromissoire (à propos de l'arrêt Cass. civ. Ire, 6 novembre 1990),* 1991 REV. ARB. 19; Daniel Girsberger and Christian Hausmaninger, *Assignment of Rights and Agreement to Arbitrate,* 8 ARB. INT'L 121 (1992); XIAO-YING LI, LA TRANSMISSION ET L'EXTENSION DE LA CLAUSE COMPROMISSOIRE DANS L'ARBITRAGE INTERNATIONAL (Thesis, University of Dijon (France), 1993); V.V. Veeder, *Towards a Possible Solution: Limitation, Interest and Assignment in London and Paris, in* ICCA CONGRESS SERIES NO. 7, PLANNING EFFICIENT ARBITRATION PROCEEDINGS/THE LAW APPLICABLE TO

(continued...)

691. — Before considering the rules of law relating to the assignment of an arbitration agreement, a preliminary question needs to be decided: should those rules be determined by applying the traditional choice of law method or by using substantive rules of international arbitration?

To resolve this issue, one needs to go beyond the *Dalico* decision, in which the French *Cour de cassation* held that the existence and validity of an arbitration agreement should be assessed exclusively by reference to substantive rules.[3] This is because the assignment of an arbitration agreement—except for the question of assignability[4]—is generally considered to be a mechanism external to the contract to which it relates. The rules of law governing assignment could therefore be determined by a method other than that employed to determine the rules applicable to the contract itself. For example, in the event of the death of a party, the consequences for the arbitration agreement and the identity of the succeeding parties might be determined by the law governing the estate of the deceased. To take an example more likely to occur in international trade, if a corporation were to be dissolved after signing an arbitration agreement, the consequences for the arbitration agreement and the identification of the assignees might be governed by the law to which the corporation is subject.

The latter example shows how the choice of law method would inevitably lead to the sort of problem which the substantive rules method seeks to avoid. Using choice of law rules creates the risk that the effectiveness of the arbitration agreement, once it is assigned to one or more parties genuinely capable of being considered as the economic successors of the initial contractor, may depend on peculiarities of the personal law of the initial parties to the agreement. This risk can be seen even more clearly in instances such as the voluntary assignment of the arbitration agreement, where the contract providing for the assignment of the arbitration agreement would be subject to the law chosen by the parties.[5] To avoid this danger, the French courts, for example, turn to concepts generally applicable in international arbitration in order to determine whether an arbitration agreement binds parties other than the initial signatories.[6] It is important to note that where the courts do resolve the question

---

[2] (...continued)
ARBITRATION 268 (A.J. van den Berg ed., 1996).

[3]   Cass. 1e civ., Dec. 20, 1993, Comité populaire de la municipalité de Khoms El Mergeb v. Dalico Contractors, 121 J.D.I. 432 (1994), and E. Gaillard's note; 121 J.D.I. 690 (1994), and E. Loquin's note; 1994 REV. ARB. 116, and H. Gaudemet-Tallon's note; 1994 REV. CRIT. DIP 663, and P. Mayer's note. *See also supra* para. 437.

[4]   *See infra* paras. 726 *et seq.*

[5]   *See infra* para. 696.

[6]   See, in the context of the demerger of a company, CA Paris, Mar. 29, 1991, Ganz v. Société Nationale des Chemins de Fer Tunisiens (SNCFT), which held, without determining the applicable law, that the companies resulting from the demerger were jointly bound by the arbitration clause signed by the company that subsequently demerged (1991 REV. ARB. 478, and L. Idot's note). In favor of the application of the substantive rules method to the transferability of arbitration clauses in chains of contracts, see Frédéric Leclerc, *Les chaînes de contrats en droit international privé*, 122 J.D.I. 267, 295 (1995). For another example, see CA Paris, Apr. 20, 1988, Clark International Finance v. Sud Matériel Service, 1988 REV. ARB. 570, and Goutal, *supra* note 2; see also the unequivocal position in favor of the substantive rules approach adopted by the Paris Court of Appeals on November 17, 1998 (1e Ch., Sec. C, S.A. CIMAT Burkinabe des Ciments et Matériaux v. S.A. (continued...)

by applying a choice of law approach, they do not always do so in the most orthodox manner.[7]

692. — This is therefore another area where it seems preferable to apply the substantive rules method (§ 2). However, since arbitrators are sometime reluctant to abandon the choice of law method entirely, it is worth considering in more detail the results to which its application leads (§ 1).

§ 1. – The Choice of Law Method

693. — The law governing the assignment of an arbitration agreement is determined differently according to whether the assignment is voluntary (A) or statutory (B).

A. – THE LAW GOVERNING VOLUNTARY ASSIGNMENTS

694. — We shall examine in turn the determination of the law governing the voluntary assignment of the arbitration agreement (1°), and the scope of that law (2°).

1° Determining the Applicable Law

695. — It is often assumed that voluntary assignments of an arbitration agreement only take the form of a contract (a). One should not, however, lose sight of the other ways of voluntarily assigning an obligation (b).

a) Contractual Assignment of the Arbitration Agreement

696. — The fundamental question raised by the assignment of a contract is whether it should be treated as the simultaneous assignment of a right and an obligation, where the respective conditions for each of the transactions must be satisfied, or as the assignment of

---

[6](...continued)
des Ciments d'Abidjan, No. 1997/02670, unpublished). In favor of adopting uniform rules in this area, see also Girsberger and Hausmaninger, *supra* note 2.

[7] See, for example, CA Paris, Feb. 6, 1997, Carter v. Alsthom, where the Court appears to apply French law to justify its decision to allow the subrogation of an insurer to the rights created by the arbitration clause entered into by the insured on the questionable ground that French law governed the substance of the contract (1997 REV. ARB. 556, and the note by Pierre Mayer, who approves of the choice of law approach but considers that the decision is wrong under French private international law principles).

an indivisible set of reciprocal obligations subject to an autonomous legal regime.[8] The assignment of an arbitration agreement can thus be seen either as the simultaneous assignment of a right (the right of each party to the arbitration agreement to submit to arbitration any dispute arising from the main contract) and an obligation (the obligation assumed by each party to accept to refer all such disputes to arbitration), or as the assignment of the agreement as a whole.

However, this continuing controversy as to the nature of a voluntary assignment of a contract appears to be irrelevant in determining the law applicable to the assignment of an arbitration agreement. Reasoning in terms of rights and obligations, the relationship between the assignee and the initial debtor (or creditor) will necessarily be governed by the law which originally governed the obligation, namely the law of the contract creating the obligation.[9] The application of that law is in keeping with the 1980 Rome Convention on the Law Governing Contractual Obligations which, although not directly applicable to arbitration agreements pursuant to its Article 1(2)(d), provides a useful analogy. The Convention states, at Article 12, paragraph 2, that:

> [t]he law governing the right to which the assignment relates shall determine its assignability, the relationship between the assignee and the debtor, the conditions under which the assignment can be invoked against the debtor and any question whether the debtor's obligations have been discharged.

In the absence of a clear indication to the contrary, the "law governing the right to which the assignment relates" will be the law of the contract creating the obligation. If, on the other hand, a contractual assignment of an arbitration agreement is viewed globally, and not as the simultaneous assignment of a right and an obligation, the contractual relations resulting from the assignment will again be governed in principle by the law applicable to the assigned agreement.[10] It would be hard to envisage that a different law could be imposed on the original co-contractor without its consent.[11]

---

[8] *See* Alfred Rieg, *Cession de contrat, in* ENCYCLOPÉDIE DALLOZ – RÉPERTOIRE DE DROIT CIVIL ¶ 39 (1987); LAURENT AYNÈS, LA CESSION DE CONTRAT ¶¶ 74 *et seq.* (1984); Jacques Ghestin, *La transmission des obligations en droit positif français, in* LA TRANSMISSION DES OBLIGATIONS, TRAVAUX DES IXES JOURNÉES D'ÉTUDES JURIDIQUES JEAN DABIN ORGANISÉES PAR LE CENTRE DE DROIT DES OBLIGATIONS, at 4 *et seq.* and 62 *et seq.* (1980).

[9] HENRI BATIFFOL AND PAUL LAGARDE, DROIT INTERNATIONAL PRIVÉ, Vol. 2, ¶ 611 at 339 (7th ed. 1983); PIERRE MAYER, DROIT INTERNATIONAL PRIVÉ ¶¶ 721 *et seq.*, especially ¶ 750 at 482 (6th ed. 1998); DICEY & MORRIS, THE CONFLICT OF LAWS, Vol. 2, at 1268–69 (12th ed. 1993 and 4th cumulative supp. 1997).

[10] Compare, for the application to the assignment of the arbitration agreement of the provisions of Article 178, paragraph 2 of the Swiss Private International Law Statute (pursuant to which an arbitration agreement will be valid as to its substance if it is valid under either the law chosen by the parties, the law of the main contract or Swiss law), Swiss Fed. Trib., Apr. 9, 1991, Clear Star Ltd. v. Centrala Morska Importowo-Eksportova "Centromor", 1991 REV. ARB. 709, and P.-Y. Tschanz' note.

[11] *See* BATIFFOL AND LAGARDE, *supra* note 9, ¶ 611; YVON LOUSSOUARN AND PIERRE BOUREL, DROIT INTERNATIONAL PRIVÉ ¶¶ 424 *et seq.* (5th ed. 1996); MAYER, *supra* note 9, ¶ 750; BERNARD AUDIT, DROIT INTERNATIONAL PRIVÉ ¶ 762 (2d ed. 1997); DICEY & MORRIS, *supra* note 9, at 1268–69.

b) Other Forms of Voluntary Assignment of the Arbitration Agreement

697. — The approach adopted for the contractual assignment of an arbitration agreement also applies to the impact on the arbitration agreement of voluntary subrogation,[12] delegation,[13] corporate mergers and stipulations in favor of third parties.

In these cases the relations between the party to the original contract who remains present in the newly-created relationship and the new partner will be governed by the law of the initial contract. Further, as Article 12 of the Rome Convention suggests, that law governs any conditions of form which may be needed in order to render the assignment enforceable against the assignor's initial co-contractor. Under the principle of the autonomy of the arbitration agreement,[14] the law in question will consist of the rules of law governing the assigned arbitration agreement, and not the law of the main contract to which the arbitration agreement relates. Thus, a French court, for example, will apply the substantive rules governing the existence and validity of the initial arbitration agreement.[15]

However, the relationship between the transferor and the transferee may be subject to the law chosen by those parties, distinct from that governing the original contract. This situation should not arise very often, because if the parties to the assignment have not specified that a different law will apply, there will be a presumption that they intended the assignment to be subject to the law governing the assigned contract.

2° Scope of the Applicable Law

698. — The law governing the arbitration agreement determines the assignability of the agreement, the conditions to which the assignment is subject, and the consequences of the assignment, at least as far as relations between the assignor and its initial co-contractor are concerned. This rule applies regardless of the form of voluntary assignment of the arbitration agreement (contractual subrogation, corporate merger, delegation or even a stipulation in favor of a third party).

By contrast, relations between assignor and assignee are governed by the law chosen by those parties for that purpose. In the absence of such choice, the law of the assigned agreement will be deemed to apply.

The scope of the law governing the assigned agreement may also be limited by the application of a different law to formalities aimed at ensuring that the assignment will be enforceable against the initial co-contractor (a), and by the effect of international mandatory rules (b).

---

[12] *See* MAYER, *supra* note 9, ¶ 721; LOUSSOUARN AND BOUREL, *supra* note 11, ¶ 383.

[13] For a discussion of the substantive concepts of delegation and the assignment of debts in comparative law, see, for example, ICC Award No. 6962 (1992), Seller v. Buyer, XIX Y.B. COM. ARB. 184 (1994).

[14] *See supra* paras. 389 *et seq.*

[15] *See supra* paras. 452 *et seq.*

a) The Law Governing Formalities Aimed at Ensuring Enforceability Against the Initial Co-Contractor

699. — An exception to the general applicability of the law governing the initial arbitration agreement may result from the application of a different law to any formalities required to ensure that the assignment of an obligation is enforceable against the initial co-contractor. For example, where rights are assigned, the French courts previously tended to apply the law of the domicile of the debtor to any formalities required to render the assignment enforceable against it.[16] However, that connecting factor was rejected by the Rome Convention, which stipulates in its Article 12, paragraph 2 that the conditions under which an assignment binds a debtor (i.e., the original contractor) are determined by the law governing the right to which the assignment relates, namely the law of the contract creating that right. Although the Rome Convention is not directly applicable to arbitration agreements, it is unlikely that such contracts would be subject to a choice of law rule other than that which applies to assignments in general. In addition, the mechanism ensuring that an arbitration agreement will be enforceable against the debtor has one peculiarity: if the assignee initiates arbitral proceedings against the initial co-contractor, the request for arbitration will be considered as satisfying the condition requiring notification of the transfer; if on the other hand the initial co-contractor commences arbitral proceedings against the assignee, that constitutes acceptance of the assignment.

b) International Mandatory Rules

700. — To the extent that they concern the protection of third parties, provisions governing the enforceability of an assignment might well be considered to be international mandatory rules (*lois de police*).[17] If that were the case, they would limit the scope of application of the law governing the assigned arbitration agreement.[18]

B. – THE LAW GOVERNING STATUTORY ASSIGNMENTS

701. — There are several ways in which a contract, including an arbitration agreement, can be assigned by law.[19] The first of these is assignment by succession. The heir or legatee succeeds to the rights and obligations of the deceased, including those resulting from

---

[16] CA Paris, Feb. 11, 1969, Marcille v. Firme Fritz, 96 J.D.I. 918 (1969), and P. Kahn's note; 1970 REV. CRIT. DIP 459, and R. Dayant's note; Dalloz, Jur. 522 (1970), and C. Larroumet's note; CA Paris, Sept. 27, 1984, Bitumina GmbH v. S.A. Lincoln, 112 J.D.I. 664 (1985), and P. Diener's note.

[17] *See* CA Paris, Sept. 27, 1984, *Bitumina, supra* note 16.

[18] On the controversy surrounding the application of international mandatory rules to the merits of disputes, see *infra* paras. 1515 *et seq.*

[19] *See* Rieg, *supra* note 8, ¶¶ 16 *et seq.*; Goutal, *supra* note 2, at 444 and 446; Delebecque, *supra* note 2, ¶¶ 10 *et seq.*

contracts to which the deceased was a party, some of which may contain an arbitration clause. There are also various other forms of statutory assignment, such as statutory subrogation,[20] the assignment of a lease to the purchaser of the leased property,[21] the statutory assignment of an employment contract where the employer's business changes hands,[22] or the statutory assignment of an insurance contract where the insured goods are assigned.[23] The various contracts thus assigned may contain an arbitration clause, or may be the subject of a separate arbitration agreement, both of which are capable of being assigned together with the main contract.

We shall examine in turn the determination of the law governing the statutory assignment of the arbitration agreement (1°), and the scope of application of that law (2°).

1° Determining the Applicable Law

702. — Being based on statute rather than on contract, the statutory assignment of a contract, and that of the arbitration agreement relating to it, are considered by the French courts to be governed by "the law of the institution for the operation of which it was created."[24] This somewhat obscure phrase has been understood as meaning

> the law governing the debtor's obligation to pay, if such an obligation exists, and if it does not exist, the law governing the legal relations between the debtor and the creditor which led the former to pay the latter.[25]

On the same basis, assignments by succession, as well as assignments of a lease or an employment contract, will be governed by the law applicable to the succession, lease, or employment contract, respectively, subject to the possibility of applying the *lex fori* where questions of international public policy arise.

2° Scope of the Applicable Law

703. — The law governing statutory assignments applies to both the conditions to which such assignments are subject and their consequences. The same law will determine the formalities required to make a statutory assignment enforceable against the assignor's initial

---

[20] See, for example, in France, Article 1251 of the French Civil Code.

[21] See, for example, in France, Article 1743 of the French Civil Code.

[22] See, for example, in France, Article L. 122-12, paragraph 2 of the French Labor Code.

[23] See, for example, in France, Article L. 121-10 of the French Insurance Code.

[24] Cass. 1e civ., Mar. 17, 1970, *Reyes v. Attorney général des Etats-Unis*, 97 J.D.I. 923 (1970), and G. de la Pradelle's note; 1970 REV. CRIT. DIP 688, 1st decision, and P. Lagarde's note. For statutory subrogation, see BATIFFOL AND LAGARDE, *supra* note 9, ¶ 611, n. 8.

[25] P. Lagarde, note following Cass. 1e civ., Mar. 17, 1970, *Reyes*, *supra* note 24, at 697. *See also* BATIFFOL AND LAGARDE, *supra* note 9, ¶ 611, n. 8, at 340.

co-contractor and third parties.[26] The law which provides for the assignment thus also determines the applicable formalities.

However, the assignability of an arbitration agreement depends on the law governing that agreement. For example, a French court will apply substantive rules of French international arbitration law to the issue,[27] and might therefore consider that the fact that the arbitration agreement was concluded in consideration of the person of the co-contractor (*intuitu personae*)[28] prevents any assignment of the agreement, even if the law governing the assignment does not so provide.

§ 2. – Substantive Rules

704. — Where the substantive rules method[29] is applied to issues arising on the assignment of an arbitration agreement, it is necessary to examine in turn the conditions governing that assignment (A) and its consequences (B).

A. – CONDITIONS GOVERNING THE ASSIGNMENT OF THE ARBITRATION AGREEMENT

705. — The assignment of an arbitration agreement seeks to change the status quo in two ways.[30] First, it places a new party—the assignee or, more generally, the beneficiary of the transfer—under an obligation to refer disputes to arbitration, and prohibits it from applying to the courts. Second, the initial co-contractor of the party assigning the arbitration agreement faces, whether as claimant or defendant, an adversary other than the party with which it initially contracted. The conditions governing the enforceability of the assignment must therefore be examined from the point of view of both the initial co-contractor and the beneficiary of the assignment.

---

[26] On the same issue in the context of voluntary assignments, see *supra* para. 699.

[27] *See supra* para. 437.

[28] *See infra* para. 720.

[29] On the justification of this method in general, see *supra* paras. 441 *et seq.*

[30] The assignment of the arbitration agreement must be distinguished from the situation where two companies, by accepting to perform a contract signed by other parties, "necessarily" subscribe to the arbitration clause contained in that contract; *see* CA Paris, Nov. 28, 1989, Compagnie tunisienne de navigation (Cotunav) v. Comptoir commercial André, 1990 REV. ARB. 675, and P. Mayer's note (affirmed, but on a different basis, Cass. 1e civ., June 25, 1991, 1991 REV. ARB. 453, and P. Mayer's note).

1° Enforceability Against the Assignee of the Assignment of an Arbitration Agreement

706. — The way in which the arbitration agreement is assigned necessarily affects whether the assignment will be enforceable against the new beneficiary. This can be seen from a comparative analysis of voluntary assignments, which require the consent of the assignee, and other means of assigning the arbitration agreement.

a) Voluntary Assignments

707. — In the case of voluntary assignment, two substantive rules tend to apply: first, the assignee must consent to the assignment of the arbitration agreement and, second, if the assignee has accepted the assignment of the main contract underlying the arbitration agreement, it is presumed to have accepted the assignment of the arbitration agreement.

1) The Assignee Must Consent to the Assignment

708. — As with any assignment of a contract, the assignment of an arbitration agreement requires the consent of the assignee. The latter will become a party to the arbitration agreement, and in the event of a dispute will be bound by that agreement. The assignee's consent to the assignment of the arbitration agreement must be proven in the same way as any other form of consent to an arbitration agreement.[31]

709. — Disputes over the existence of consent to the assignment of an arbitration agreement most often arise in the context of chains of successive contracts. The French *Cour de cassation* addressed the issue in the *Fraser* case, where various quantities of diesel fuel had been the subject of successive sales. The ultimate buyer considered that the fuel was unfit for the purpose for which it was intended, and sued its immediate seller, the intermediate sellers and the original seller. As the contract between one of the intermediate sellers and its buyer contained an arbitration clause, the intermediate seller sought to rely on that clause so as to be excluded from the court proceedings. On January 14, 1988, the Rouen Court of Appeals held that the intermediate seller could not rely on an arbitration clause which was "unenforceable against the parties other than the party with which the intermediate seller had concluded it." In 1990, the *Cour de cassation* was asked to rule on whether the Rouen decision could be immediately appealed. The Court held that it could not, on procedural grounds, but did add that the disputed arbitration clause was not enforceable against the initial plaintiff "because there was no contractual assignment."[32] In other words, "the arbitration clause remains subject to the principle of privity of contracts and can

---

[31] *See supra* paras. 472 *et seq.*

[32] Cass. 1e civ., Nov. 6, 1990, Fraser v. Compagnie européenne des Pétroles, 1991 REV. ARB. 73, and the commentary by Delebecque, *supra* note 2.

therefore not circulate in a chain of contracts, unless the parties have expressly provided otherwise."[33] Clearly, the parties to which this observation refers are those against whom the plaintiff was seeking to rely on the undertaking to submit disputes to arbitration, and not simply the parties to the contracts in the chain.

This analysis was confirmed by a 1995 decision of the Paris Court of Appeals. In a construction project, the main contractor sub-contracted various aspects of the works. The sub-contractors in turn sub-contracted the installation of the frame of the building to a French company which then acquired panels, manufactured by a German company, from an importer. The panels caused a number of problems, and the owner commenced proceedings against all parties to the contracts in the chain, including the importer and the German manufacturer. The latter sought to rely on an arbitration clause included in its contract with the importer. After referring to case law concerning the arbitration agreement's "own validity and effectiveness,"[34] the Court observed that the owner had simply acquired the disputed goods via sub-contractors and was not involved in the performance of the contract containing the arbitration clause. The Court concluded that:

> as [the owner] thus remained unconnected with the performance of a contract of which it was not aware and which it never ratified, the arbitration clause contained in that contract cannot be relied upon against it.[35]

In other words, in a chain of contracts the arbitration agreement will only circulate if the circumstances demonstrate that the assignee agreed, at least implicitly, to be bound by that agreement.

710. — The situation described above should not be confused with that where the same parties have signed a series of successive contracts of the same type, without always reiterating that they intend to resolve their disputes by arbitration. In such a case, it can generally be inferred from the parties' prior practice that they intended to submit all of their disputes to arbitration.[36] On the other hand, it is considerably more difficult to infer from the acquisition of goods that have been the subject of previous sales contracts containing arbitration agreements that a purchaser who has not expressly made a reference to arbitration has nonetheless implicitly agreed to it.

---

[33] Delebecque, *supra* note 2, at 21.

[34] *See supra* para. 436.

[35] CA Paris, Mar. 22, 1995, SMABTP v. Statinor, 1997 REV. ARB. 550, and the commentary by Daniel Cohen, *Arbitrage et groupes de contrats, id.* at 471; 1996 RTD COM. 247, and observations by J.-C. Dubarry and E. Loquin.

[36] *See supra* para. 523.

2) Acceptance of the Assignment of the Main Contract Raises a Presumption of Acceptance of the Arbitration Agreement

711. — It would be inconceivable for an arbitration agreement to be assigned without the assignment of the underlying contract. If it were otherwise, the assigned arbitration agreement would have no object.

However, the question frequently arises whether, by agreeing to assume rights and obligations under a contract containing an arbitration agreement, the assignee agrees, in the absence of any indication to the contrary, to submit disputes arising out of that contract to arbitration.[37]

712. — It has been suggested that the principle of the autonomy of the arbitration agreement[38] leaves no room for such a presumption, on the grounds that the arbitration agreement is legally autonomous and its assignment therefore requires separate acceptance in order to be valid.[39]

The French courts have consistently rejected that view.[40] For example, the Paris Court of Appeals held in 1988 that:

> an arbitration clause appearing in an international contract has a validity and effectiveness of its own, such that its application must be extended to a party succeeding—even partially—to the rights of one of the initial parties.

In other words, the assignee of a contract who enjoys the benefit of the rights assigned cannot avoid the application of the arbitration clause contained in that contract.[41] No specific acceptance is required from the assignee. Rather, an express provision is required to exclude the arbitration clause from the assignment of the main contract.[42] Leaving aside the Court's

---

[37] On the question of whether acceptance of an arbitration agreement gives rise to a presumption of acceptance of the underlying agreement, see ICC Award No. 7154 (1993), Algerian shipowner v. French shipyard, 121 J.D.I. 1059 (1994), and observations by Y. Derains.

[38] *See supra* paras. 391 *et seq.*

[39] See the reservations on this issue expressed by Philippe Fouchard and Eric Loquin in *L'arbitrage et les tiers*, 1988 REV. ARB. 469 and 472.

[40] *See, e.g.*, Cass. civ., July 12, 1950, Montané v. Compagnie des chemins de fer portugais, 77 J.D.I. 1206 (1950), and B. Goldman's note; 1952 REV. CRIT. DIP 509, and P. Francescakis' note; CA Paris, Mar. 15, 1966, Laboratoire de tirage cinématographique Franay v. Corona Films, 1966 REV. ARB. 100. *See also* Cass. com., Feb. 4, 1986, Soules v. Henry, 1988 REV. ARB. 718; CA Paris, Jan. 28, 1988, C.C.C. Filmkunst v. E.D.I.F., 1988 REV. ARB. 565; 116 J.D.I. 1021 (1989), and E. Loquin's note.

[41] *See* CA Aix, Jan. 9, 1997, SNTM Hyproc v. Banque Générale du Commerce, 1997 REV. ARB. 76, and D. Cohen's note.

[42] CA Paris, Apr. 20, 1988, *Clark International Finance*, *supra* note 6, and the report by Goutal, *supra* note 2. *See also* CA Rouen, Oct. 14, 1997, Lorico v. Italgrani, 1998 REV. ARB. 569, and the commentary by Xavier Boucobza, *La clause compromissoire par référence en matière d'arbitrage commercial international*, *id.* at 495.

remarks concerning the arbitration agreement's "validity" and "own effectiveness,"[43] we consider this approach to be the right one.[44] The autonomy of the arbitration agreement does not mean that upon entering into the initial contract the arbitration clause should necessarily be accepted separately—the signature of a contract containing an arbitration clause constitutes acceptance of both the main contract and the arbitration agreement.[45] Likewise, acceptance of the assignment of a contract which contains an arbitration clause—or which is the subject of a submission agreement of which the assignee is aware—must lead to the conclusion, in the absence of a clear indication to the contrary, that the assignee has accepted the contract as a whole, including the dispute resolution provisions. The principle of the autonomy of the arbitration agreement does not require proof that the parties had two distinct intentions—one regarding the main contract, one regarding the arbitration agreement—in the case of assignment any more than for the initial arbitration agreement.[46]

This approach was endorsed by the Supreme Court of Sweden in 1997. A Finnish engineering company, through its Swedish subsidiary, delivered machinery to a Dutch shipbuilder for installation in a ship under construction. The contract contained an ICC arbitration clause incorporated by reference to general conditions. The machinery proved to be faulty, and the purchaser of the ship had "all the rights" of the shipbuilder vis-à-vis the engineering company assigned to it, in order to recover damages from the engineering company. The purchaser sued before the Swedish courts, whereupon the engineering company argued that the arbitration clause prevented the courts from retaining jurisdiction. The lower courts and the Supreme Court all followed that argument, declining jurisdiction in favor of arbitration on the grounds that, *inter alia*:

> In support of the fact that the new party should be bound, it was argued that in the reverse case the remaining party would have its position substantially altered. It must be assumed that the remaining party—as well as the other original contractor—wanted their disputes to be resolved by arbitration. The original contractor should not therefore be able to unilaterally free itself from

---

[43] *See supra* para. 440.

[44] *See also* Leclerc, *supra* note 6, ¶¶ 35 *et seq.* at 292.

[45] *See supra* paras. 408 and 492.

[46] See the observations by Jean-Louis Delvolvé, 1988 REV. ARB. 470, and Pierre Mayer, *L'autonomie de l'arbitre international dans l'appréciation de sa propre compétence, in* COLLECTED COURSES OF THE HAGUE ACADEMY OF INTERNATIONAL LAW, Vol. 217, Year 1989, Part V, at 432. Swiss law had taken the same position prior to the enactment of the Private International Law Statute; *see* Swiss Fed. Trib., Jan. 25, 1977, Müller v. Bossard, 1979 REV. ARB. 511, and the commentary by Roger P. Budin, *Nature et cessibilité d'une convention d'arbitrage en droit suisse, id.* at 435. See also, in the U.S., Barsagin v. Shipowner's Mutual Protection and Indemnity Ass'n, No. A 94-474-CV (D. Alaska Feb. 16, 1995); XXII Y.B. COM. ARB. 894 (1997); XIAO-YING LI, *supra* note 2, ¶¶ 31 *et seq.*

the arbitration clause by a contract of assignment. If the purchaser does not agree to the arbitration clause, it can always refuse to acquire the assignor's right.[47]

Of course, the assignor and assignee of a contract containing an arbitration agreement can agree to exclude the arbitration agreement from the assignment of the main contract. Given that it is rather unusual to do so, such an exclusion must be expressly provided for. If the parties do so agree, disputes between the assignee and the initial co-contractor will be heard by the courts, although the initial co-contractor could always rely on the arbitration agreement so as to bring disputes with the assignor before arbitrators. The assignor, on the other hand, cannot submit its disputes with the initial co-contractor to arbitration, not because it no longer has the benefit of the arbitration agreement, but because, having assigned the main contract underlying the arbitration agreement, it no longer has *locus standi*, except as regards claims concerning the validity of the assignment.

b) Other Means of Assigning the Arbitration Agreement

713. — By definition, the requirement that the assignment of the arbitration agreement be accepted by the assignee does not apply to statutory assignments of the arbitration agreement. Instead the rule applicable to the main contract also applies to the arbitration agreement. This is the case with both statutory subrogation and universal succession.

1) Statutory Subrogation

714. — In cases where an insurer succeeds to the rights of an insured, the courts have consistently held that the insurer is bound by the arbitration agreement accepted by the insured from whom it derives its rights.[48] For example, the French *Cour de cassation* held that an insurance company which succeeded to the rights of an insured against a carrier could only initiate proceedings against the latter under the terms of the contract of carriage, which included the arbitration clause in the bill of lading.[49] Conversely, the United States Court of Appeals for the Sixth Circuit ruled on August 29, 1996 that third party claims against an insurance company which had insured the party alleged to be responsible should be settled in accordance with the arbitration clause contained in the insurance contract: the

---

[47] Supreme Court of Sweden, Oct. 15, 1997, MS Emja Braack Shiffahrts KG v. Wärtsilä Diesel Aktiebolag, 1998 REV. ARB. 431, and A.-C. Hansson Lecoanet and S. Jarvin's note.

[48] On whether the insured's co-contractor will be bound by the subrogation, see *infra* para. 719.

[49] Cass. com., May 13, 1966, Société d'approvisionnements textiles v. Compagnie de navigation "Fraissinet et Cyprien Fabre," 1967 REV. CRIT. DIP 355, and E. Mezger's note. On the impact of this case law, see Goutal, *supra* note 2, at 446.

insurance company "has both the right and the obligation to arbitrate disputes brought by parties claiming rights under the contract [containing an arbitration clause]."[50]

2) Universal Succession

715. — A 1977 award in ICC Case No. 2626 stated that:

> the dominant trend in case law holds that an arbitration agreement is not only valid between the parties, but can also be relied upon against their heirs, their legatees, their assignees and all those acquiring obligations. The only exceptions are cases where the arbitration agreement is drafted in such a way as to exclude successors and assignees.

In that award, the arbitrators concluded that the conversion of a limited liability company (*société à responsabilité limitée*), which had signed an arbitration agreement, into a joint stock corporation (*société par actions*) did not prevent the arbitration agreement from being relied upon against the company as it existed after the conversion.[51]

The award also touched on the separate question of the conditions governing the enforceability of an assignment against the initial co-contractor.

2° Conditions Governing the Enforceability of the Assignment of the Arbitration Agreement Against the Initial Co-Contractor

716. — As a result of the assignment of the arbitration agreement, the co-contractor of the party whose obligation is assigned will be dealing with a new contractual partner. The main question this raises is whether it can occur without the consent of the initial co-contractor who, having entered into an arbitration agreement with a particular person or entity, now finds itself in a different situation. If it accepts the new situation, either expressly or tacitly,[52] there is no difficulty and the only issue will be that of the arbitration agreement's

---

[50] Aasma v. American Steamship Owners Mutual Protection and Indemnity Ass'n, 95 F.3d 400 (6th Cir. 1996); XXII Y.B. COM. ARB. 1016 (1997).

[51] ICC Award No. 2626 (1977), German company v. Italian company, 105 J.D.I. 980 (1978), and observations by Y. Derains. Compare with ICC Award No. 3742 (1983), European contractor v. Three Middle Eastern state-owned entities, where the tribunal refused to rule on the consequences of the assignment to other entities of the assets of the state-owned entity that signed the arbitration agreement. The tribunal's grounds for so doing—the fact that the companies resulting from the reorganization were not included in the terms of reference—are unsatisfactory in our view (111 J.D.I. 910 (1984), and observations by Y. Derains).

[52] See, for example, the June 20, 1994 decision of an arbitral tribunal under the aegis of the Zurich Chamber of Commerce, where the debts of one company were assigned to another and both were sued by the initial co-contractor on the basis of an arbitration agreement in the assignment contract that was identical to the arbitration clause in the assigned contract (ABC v. XY and YZ, 1995 BULL. ASA 77). For an example of an express substitution provision, which was held to apply to the arbitration clause, see CA Lyon, May 15, 1997,

(continued...)

enforceability against the assignee.[53] If, on the other hand, the initial co-contractor refuses to be bound by the arbitration agreement vis-à-vis a party other than that with which it originally dealt, is its consent necessary to give effect to the assignment? Theoretically, the answer should be in the affirmative, given the contractual nature of the arbitration agreement—a party should not be obliged to go to arbitration against another party with which it has not agreed to arbitrate. However, this is subject to an important proviso: if the identity of the co-contractor was not a determining factor on signature of the initial arbitration agreement, there is a presumption that such agreement included the initial co-contractor's implicit acceptance of any assignment to a third party.

In any event, the "competence-competence" rule[54] dictates that it is for the arbitrators, initially at any rate, to determine whether the original arbitration agreement incorporates an express or implied acceptance of any assignment to a third party.

a) The Presumption that the Initial Co-Contractor Accepts the Assignability of the Arbitration Agreement

717. — In the absence of any indication to the contrary, there is a presumption, applicable to both contractual assignments and assignments by subrogation, that the signatory of an arbitration agreement accepts that the agreement may be assigned.

1) Contractual Assignments

718. — Civil law jurisdictions have not always accepted the idea that a bilateral contract can be assigned without the express consent of the initial co-contractor.[55] However, in the case of an assignment of an arbitration agreement together with the assignment of the underlying rights, there is no particular difficulty in enforcing that assignment against the initial co-contractor. For example, in a 1988 case, the Paris Court of Appeals rejected a claim by the initial signatory of an arbitration agreement that it was not bound by that agreement towards the assignee of film exploitation rights created by the contract containing the arbitration clause. In support of its decision, the Court noted that "the arbitration clause appearing in [the initial] contract is general, and it covers disputes arising not only during the production of the film but also during its exploitation."[56]

---

[52](...continued)
Parodi v. Annecy et France Boissons, 1997 REV. ARB. 402, and P. Ancel's note.

[53] *See supra* paras. 706 *et seq.*

[54] *See supra* para. 650.

[55] See, for example, in France, Cass. civ., Mar. 12, 1946, Commune de Carlencas v. Société des produits chimiques Alais, Froges et Camargue, Dalloz, Jur. 268 (1946).

[56] CA Paris, Jan. 28, 1988, *C.C.C. Filmkunst*, *supra* note 40, 1988 REV. ARB. 567, and the report by Goutal, *supra* note 2.

The Court thus interpreted the initial clause as presenting no bar to assignment. The Court added that the assignment "necessarily implies that the assignor transfers the benefit of the arbitration clause—which forms part of the economics [of the] contract—to the assignee,"[57] although this did not suffice in itself to justify a presumption of acceptance on the part of the initial co-contractor. Given the generality of the terms of the arbitration clause in dispute and the fact that arbitration has now become a normal method of resolving disputes in international trade, it was legitimate to assume that the initial co-contractor had accepted the possibility of an assignment of the arbitration agreement.[58] The French *Cour de cassation* has expressed the principle in very strong terms. In a 1999 decision, it held that:

> the international arbitration agreement, the validity of which is based exclusively on the will of the parties, is assigned together with the rights [to which it relates], in the same shape and form as those rights existed between the assignor and the original co-contractor.[59]

2) Assignment by Subrogation

719. — Both the courts and arbitral tribunals tend to admit that, in the absence of a provision to the contrary, by consenting to an arbitration agreement the initial co-contractor accepts any subrogation which may subsequently occur in favor of the other party's insurer. In a 1992 case before the Paris Court of Appeals, an insurer commenced arbitral proceedings after having been subrogated to the rights of the insured under a contract entered into by the insured and containing an arbitration clause. The Court held that "by virtue of the transferring effect of that subrogation, the arbitration agreement is assigned to the insurer together with the rights and obligations of the insured to which it relates."[60] The same court also held that where an insurer is subrogated to the rights of an insured, it is entitled to participate in the arbitral procedure even if it becomes involved only after the signature of the terms of reference.[61] In a 1997 decision concerning a case where the purchaser of the assets of a foreign corporation in bankruptcy had indicated its intention to carry on the company's activity, the Paris Court of Appeals held that the benefit of an arbitration clause signed by a French party with the company in bankruptcy extended to "the party taking over,

---

[57] CA Paris, Jan. 28, 1988, *C.C.C. Filmkunst, supra* note 40, 1988 REV. ARB. 568.

[58] For other examples, see the March 5, 1997 award made in Stockholm under the auspices of the Stockholm Chamber of Commerce, A.I. Trade Finance Inc. v. Bulgarian Foreign Trade Bank, Ltd., 12 INT'L ARB. REP. H1 (Mar. 1997); Supreme Court of Sweden, Oct. 15, 1997, *Emja Braack, supra* note 47; High Court of Kuala Lumpur, Malaysia, Dec. 10, 1993, Harris Adacom Corp. v. Perkom Sdn Bhd, XXII Y.B. COM. ARB. 753 (1997); for a case where the acceptance of a forthcoming assignment was given expressly, see CA Paris, May 26, 1992, Guyapêche v. Abba Import Aktiebolag, 1993 REV. ARB. 624, and L. Aynès' note. For a more restrictive approach, see, in Germany, before the December 22, 1997 reform, *Bundesgerichtshof,* Nov. 12, 1990, German assignee of a German shipping company v. Japanese shipyard, XVII Y.B. COM. ARB. 510 (1992).

[59] Cass. 1e civ., Jan. 5, 1999, Banque Worms v. Bellot, No. S 96-20.202, unpublished.

[60] CA Paris, Nov. 13, 1992, Casco Nobel France v. Sico, 1993 REV. ARB. 632, and J.-L. Goutal's note.

[61] CA Paris, Feb. 6, 1997, *Carter, supra* note 7.

even in part, the rights of one of the parties, on condition that the dispute is within the scope of the arbitration clause."[62]

Similarly, in a 1977 award in ICC Case No. 1704, it was held that a bank which had succeeded to the rights of the beneficiary of a bill of exchange endorsed in its favor was entitled to rely on the arbitration clause appearing in the contract between the subscriber of the bill of exchange and the beneficiary.[63] Likewise, in a 1978 award, an arbitral tribunal constituted under the aegis of the Netherlands Arbitration Institute held that an insurer assuming the rights of an owner could rely on the arbitration agreement entered into by the owner and the contractor. The Tribunal explained that the rights in question were covered by the arbitration agreement and that "nothing indicates that under the contract the parties have intended that the arbitral clause could not be applicable in case of a legal succession by means of a specific title of one of them."[64]

Of course, the beneficiary of the subrogated rights is not alone in being entitled to initiate proceedings against the debtor. The insured retains the right to commence arbitration against the party with which it concluded an arbitration agreement, and it will still have standing to take such action if the insurer requires it to do so, or if the action is wholly or partially for its benefit.[65]

We shall now see that there are only a very limited number of cases where the consent of the initial co-contractor is required for the assignment of the arbitration agreement.

b) Situations Where Express Acceptance by the Initial Co-Contractor Is Required for the Assignment of the Arbitration Agreement

720. — As with any contract, an arbitration agreement may be entered into *intuitu personae*, that is, in consideration of the identity of the co-contractor.[66] In such a situation, the assignment of the arbitration agreement will only bind the initial co-contractor if the initial co-contractor explicitly accepts to contract with the assignee. If it does not, the assignment will only have effect as between the party that sought to assign its rights and the party that sought to assume them. The practical effectiveness of an assignment in such circumstances is likely to be extremely limited. The only remedy available for a violation of the assignor's duty to render the arbitration clause effective would be damages for any loss

---

[62] CA Paris, Oct. 8, 1997, Solna International AB v. SA Destouche, Dalloz, I.R. 233 (1997).

[63] French bank v. Indian company, 105 J.D.I. 977 (1978), and observations by Y. Derains.

[64] August 31, 1978 Interim Award, English insurer v. Two Dutch contractors, V Y.B. COM. ARB. 194 (1980). On the fact that an arbitration clause in a contract between a creditor and debtor binds a guarantor subrogated to the debtor's rights, see Eric Loquin, *Arbitrage et Cautionnement*, 1994 REV. ARB. 235, 247.

[65] *See* ICC Award No. 6733 (1992), Bank v. Bank, 121 J.D.I. 1038 (1994), and observations by D. Hascher. *Comp. with* ICC Award No. 7563 (1993), Belgian bank v. International pool of insurance companies, 121 J.D.I. 1054 (1994), and observations by Y. Derains.

[66] On this issue, see Goutal, *supra* note 2; Delebecque, *supra* note 2.

suffered by the assignee in being unable to submit disputes with the initial co-contractor to arbitration. As we have seen, such a loss is extremely difficult to assess in monetary terms.[67]

1) *Intuitus Personae* Inferred from the Facts

721. — In some circumstances, the *intuitus personae* attached to the arbitration agreement can be inferred from the facts. In order to successfully avoid arbitration on the grounds of *intuitus personae*, the initial co-contractor must be able to establish that, although it was not expressly provided for, when it entered into the arbitration agreement the identity of the other party was a fundamental consideration. As a general rule, this will require the initial co-contractor to show that it viewed the assignor as possessing the good faith and procedural loyalty necessary for an arbitration to run smoothly, and that the assignee may not share those qualities. That will of course be very difficult to establish, given that arbitration is a common means of resolving international disputes. Nevertheless, the situation could conceivably arise in a narrow professional field, where it might be arguable that the decision to refer disputes to arbitration is based on mutual trust between companies pursuing similar activities, especially if those activities are carried on under the auspices of a body which is also responsible for organizing the arbitration.

2) *Intuitus Personae* Expressly Provided for by Contract

722. — The initial arbitration agreement may expressly stipulate that it has been entered into with a particular co-contractor in mind, or that it is not assignable, which amounts to the same thing. It is that type of provision which is contemplated when courts hold that, in the absence of a clause to the contrary, the arbitration agreement is assignable without the need for acceptance by the initial co-contractor.[68] Such provisions would undoubtedly be valid.[69]

B. – CONSEQUENCES OF THE ASSIGNMENT OF THE ARBITRATION AGREEMENT

723. — Where the conditions governing its assignment are fulfilled, the arbitration agreement gives rise to the same consequences, as between the initial co-contractor and the assignee, as any arbitration agreement. Each party to the new relationship is obliged to

---

[67] *See supra* para. 631.

[68] *See* CA Paris, Jan. 28, 1988, *C.C.C. Filmkunst, supra* note 40, 1988 REV. ARB. 568. See also ICC Award No. 2626 (1977), *supra* note 51, where an exception is made for "the case where the arbitration agreement is drafted in a way that excludes successors and assignees," and the August 31, 1978 interim award rendered under the aegis of the Netherlands Arbitration Institute, *supra* note 64.

[69] See, for example, in favor of upholding such a clause included in the main contract containing an arbitration clause, Swiss Fed. Trib., Apr. 9, 1991, *Clear Star, supra* note 10. But see, for a narrow interpretation of *intuitus personae* provisions, CA Paris, Nov. 17, 1998, *CIMAT, supra* note 6.

submit any disputes which may arise to arbitration, rather than to the courts (1°). However, if the assignment occurs after the arbitral tribunal has been constituted, a question arises as to whether new arbitrators should be appointed (2°).

1° The Obligation to Submit Disputes to Arbitration

724. — Once the assignment has taken place, the initial co-contractor and the assignee are obliged to submit any disputes arising between them to arbitration, in accordance with the provisions of the arbitration agreement, and not to the courts. That means, in particular, that neither party to the new relationship can rely on jurisdictional privileges which they may enjoy by virtue of their nationality.

Thus, in a 1950 decision, the French *Cour de cassation* held that the arbitration clause in a contract concluded outside France between two non-French companies was enforceable against the French company to which rights under the contract had been assigned. As a result, the French company could not rely on Article 14 of the French Civil Code against the initial foreign co-contractor in an attempt to have jurisdiction conferred on the French courts.[70] The Court based its decision on the interpretation of the disputed agreements by the court of first instance.[71] One commentator observed that:

> in law, in the absence of an express stipulation to the contrary, the assignor's rights are transferred to the assignee in the same form as in the relations between the assignor and the previous contractual partner. To the extent that this assignment implied that the French assignees waived their jurisdictional privilege under Article 14, such waiver was perfectly valid.[72]

In support of that view, another commentator remarked that:

> it would hardly be in keeping with the needs of international trade if one were entirely to dissociate the substantive aspects of the contract from the provisions concerning jurisdiction. To allow the assignee to avoid those provisions would be to disregard the parties' intentions, irrespective of whether one is dealing with a straightforward waiver of Articles 14 and 15, or a positive choice of jurisdiction, or even an arbitration clause.[73]

---

[70] On Articles 14 and 15 of the French Civil Code and their scope in light of the Brussels and Lugano Conventions, see *supra* para. 636.

[71] Cass. 1e civ., July 12, 1950, *Montané*, *supra* note 40.

[72] B. Goldman, note following Cass. 1e civ., July 12, 1950, *Montané*, 77 J.D.I. 1206 (1950).

[73] A. Ponsard, note following Cass. 1e civ., Mar. 21, 1966, La Métropole v. Muller, 1966 REV. CRIT. DIP 670, 677. *See also* Cass. 1e civ., Nov. 24, 1987, Europe Aéro Service v. Garrett Corp., 115 J.D.I. 793 (1988), and E. Loquin's note; 1988 REV. CRIT. DIP 364, and J.-L. Droz' note; JCP, Ed. G., Pt. II, No. 21,201 (1989), and P. Blondel and L. Cadiet's note: the French assignee of a debt was not entitled to the benefit of Article 14 of the Civil Code when the (foreign) assignor had agreed to the jurisdiction of a foreign court.

2° The Effect of an Assignment of the Arbitration Agreement on the Composition of the Arbitral Tribunal

725. — Where the arbitration agreement is assigned after the arbitral tribunal has been constituted, can the assignee rely on the fact that it was not involved in the appointment of the initial arbitral tribunal so as to obtain the constitution of a new tribunal?

The relations between each party and the arbitrator or arbitrators must be founded on trust. Consequently, where the assignee is not involved in the appointment of the tribunal, it is sometimes suggested that it should have the option of refusing to accept the existing arbitrators without having to give other grounds on which to challenge them. That is not to say that the assignee can avoid having the dispute resolved by arbitration. It would simply require the appointment of a new tribunal, either by agreement between the assignee and the initial co-contractor, or by resorting to the applicable procedure for resolving difficulties concerning the constitution of the arbitral tribunal. That approach seems to have been endorsed by an award made in 1977 in ICC Case No. 2626. In that case the arbitral tribunal upheld the validity of the assignment of an arbitration agreement to a joint stock corporation which had succeeded to the rights and obligations of the limited liability company which had initially signed the arbitration agreement. It did so on the basis that "the principle [of assignability] is all the more valid in this case for the fact that the arbitrator was not named in the contract, so that there was no relationship of trust between the contractual partners and an arbitrator of their choice."[74] However, that statement is ambiguous: does the existence of a "relationship of trust" constitute a bar to the assignment of the arbitration agreement,[75] or is it simply a feature of the assignment which led the tribunal to conclude that a new arbitral tribunal should be constituted?

The decision reached in Case No. 2626 places too much emphasis on the idea that each party has a right to participate in the constitution of the arbitral tribunal or, to use familiar but incorrect terminology, a right to appoint "its own" arbitrator.[76] Whether its basis be contractual or statutory, an assignment does not create a new arbitration agreement. Provided that the relevant conditions are fulfilled, it transfers an existing agreement which must continue to operate as it did before the assignment. Although there is a presumption that the initial co-contractor accepts that the arbitration agreement may be assigned under the normal conditions of international trade,[77] it would not be appropriate for the assignment, in which it has no involvement, to cause it delay through changes to the arbitral tribunal. In addition, it would not be appropriate for the assignee to effectively have the option—which the initial co-contractor does not have—of maintaining or replacing the existing tribunal in the course of the arbitration.

---

[74] *Supra* note 51.

[75] *See supra* para. 720.

[76] On this issue, see *infra* para. 792.

[77] *See supra* para. 717.

SECTION II
EXPIRATION OF THE ARBITRATION AGREEMENT

726. — The prevailing trend with respect to the expiration of international arbitration agreements is to treat the issue in terms of substantive rules without requiring the law governing the arbitration agreement to be identified.[78]

We shall first examine whether the arbitration agreement will necessarily expire as a result of the expiration of the main contract to which it relates (§ 1), before considering causes of expiration specific to the arbitration agreement (§ 2).

§ 1. – Expiration of the Arbitration Agreement as a Result of the Expiration of the Main Agreement?

727. — It is perhaps tempting to consider that because of the relationship between the arbitration agreement and the underlying contract, the former will necessarily expire with the latter, as the sole purpose of the former is to provide a means of resolving disputes arising from the latter. However, the arbitration agreement will continue to exist even when the rights created by the main contract have been extinguished, precisely where that extinguishment or its consequences are in dispute. As a result of the principle of the autonomy, or separability, of the arbitration agreement,[79] a party cannot avoid the consequences of an arbitration agreement simply by alleging that the main contract has expired, because the arbitration agreement can only be extinguished by a cause which specifically applies to it.

This can be demonstrated by examining each of the principal causes of expiration of the main contract.

A. – PERFORMANCE

728. — The most common reason for the expiration of the main contract is that all of the obligations it creates have been performed. However, the arbitration agreement will only expire if the performance of the contract has not given rise to a dispute, which may not be the case. Even if the arbitrators hearing such a dispute ultimately decide that all the obligations have been performed in full, and that consequently the object of the main contract has been exhausted, they will nevertheless have jurisdiction to rule on the issue because of the principle of the autonomy of the arbitration agreement.[80]

---

[78] On the justification for this method, see *supra* paras. 441 *et seq. See also* Veeder, *supra* note 2.

[79] On this issue, generally, see *supra* paras. 389 *et seq.*

[80] On the unsatisfactory finding, in a case concerning a French domestic arbitration, that an award which holds the main contract to be breached causes the arbitration clause contained in that contract to be ineffective

(continued...)

B. – STATUTE OF LIMITATIONS

729. — Similarly, the arbitration agreement will not be affected by an allegation that the rights generated by the main contract have been extinguished under a statute of limitations. Provided that the main contract contains an arbitration agreement, any dispute regarding limitation issues must itself be submitted to arbitration.[81]

C. – NOVATION

730. — The novation of the main contract is almost as straightforward. Novation causes existing rights to be extinguished and replaced by new rights. However, it will not extinguish an arbitration agreement contained in the initial contract. For example, the Paris Court of Appeals has held that:

> the arbitration agreement is fully autonomous. Consequently, a settlement or novation affecting the contract containing the arbitration agreement cannot have the effect of rendering that agreement inoperative.[82]

Some commentators have disputed the idea that the autonomy of the arbitration agreement could have such an effect, while conceding that not all the consequences of the principle have been explored as yet.[83] However, although the extinguishment of the obligations contained in the main contract deprives the arbitration agreement of its object, the principle of autonomy allows the arbitrators to rule on this issue without having to decide whether the cause of expiration of the main contract also affects the arbitration agreement. Of course, the arbitration agreement itself can be novated, which may lead to its expiration, not as a consequence of the expiration of the main contract, but for a reason specific to the arbitration agreement.[84]

---

[80](...continued)
    thereafter, see Cass. 2e civ., June 16, 1993, Fleury v. Bienaimé, 1994 REV. ARB. 321, and D. Cohen's note.

[81]   For an example of arbitrators resolving a question of limitation affecting the main contract, see ICC Award No. 4491 (1984), Finnish licensor v. Australian licensee, 112 J.D.I. 966 (1985), and observations by S. Jarvin.

[82]   CA Paris, Mar. 4, 1986, Cosiac v. Consorts Luchetti, 1987 REV. ARB. 167, and C. Jarrosson's note. The recourse against this decision was rejected in Cass. 1e civ., May 10, 1988, Cosiac v. Consorts Luchetti, 1988 REV. ARB. 639, and C. Jarrosson's note.

[83]   *See* C. Jarrosson, note following Cass. 1e civ., May 10, 1988, *Cosiac, supra* note 82, at 644.

[84]   See, for example, ICC Award No. 3383 (1979), in which it was held that an arbitration agreement that replaced an earlier one that had not given rise to an award within the prescribed time limit novated the first agreement. The first agreement could not be revived, although the second had been declared void (Belgian party v. Iranian party, 107 J.D.I. 978 (1980), and observations by Y. Derains; for an English translation, see VII Y.B. COM. ARB. 119 (1982)).

D. – SETTLEMENT

731. — In a 1986 decision, the Paris Court of Appeals held that an arbitration agreement does not expire as a result of a settlement.[85] In practice, this rule will apply where a dispute arises concerning the settlement, which might, for example, be alleged to be void or improperly implemented. That dispute would have to be submitted to arbitration, even if the actual settlement contains no arbitration clause, unless of course the settlement agreement itself contains an arbitration clause superseding that of the main contract.

Similarly, the Swiss Federal Tribunal held in a 1996 decision that:

> when parties settle claims arising from a contract containing an arbitration clause, this does not, as a general rule, lead to the nullity of the arbitration agreement. In fact, any disputes concerning the settlement also fall within the arbitration clause unless it is clear that the parties intended to make the arbitration clause void.[86]

E. – RESCISSION

732. — Likewise, rescission of the main contract will not render the associated arbitration agreement inoperative. In a 1966 decision, the French *Cour de cassation* held that:

> the effect of the rescission of a contract is merely to terminate, for the future, the parties' obligations. The Court of Appeals was thus right in considering that the parties, who had not waived the arbitration agreement, had "a vested right" to submit disputes concerning the contract to arbitration, even if those disputes had arisen after the rescission of the contract.[87]

Similarly, the Swiss Federal Tribunal has held that "the arbitration agreement does not necessarily share . . . the outcome of the main contract," adding that:

---

[85] CA Paris, Mar. 4, 1986, *Cosiac, supra* note 82.

[86] Fed. Trib., Sept. 6, 1996, X. v. Y., 1997 BULL. ASA 291. See also, in Swiss domestic arbitration, Vaud Cantonal Trib., Sept. 21, 1993, L & F v. P, 1995 BULL. ASA 68, and J.-F. Poudret's approving note.

[87] Cass. 2e civ., Nov. 25, 1966, Société des mines d'Orbagnoux v. Fly Tox, Dalloz, Jur. 359 (1967), 2d decision, and J. Robert's note; 1967 RTD CIV. 680, and observations by P. Hébraud.

this also applies where the parties terminate the principal contract by mutual agreement, but in that case, as a general rule, one should accept that in so far as the parties have not expressly provided otherwise, they also intend to retain their arbitration agreement for disputes concerning the consequences of the termination of the contract.[88]

The arbitration agreement thus obliges the parties to refer to arbitration disputes relating to the consequences of termination of the contract, as in the case which came before the Swiss Federal Tribunal, which concerned the repatriation by a construction contractor of materials stocked and equipment used on site.[89]

F. – Nullity

733. — The autonomy of the arbitration agreement also accounts for the fact that the alleged or established nullity of the main contract does not prevent the arbitral tribunal from ruling on the existence and consequences of that nullity. It is only where the cause of the nullity also directly affects the arbitration agreement that the arbitral tribunal must declare it to be void and decline jurisdiction accordingly. This the tribunal can do, under the "competence-competence" principle, without contradicting itself.[90]

§ 2. – Causes of Expiration Specific to the Arbitration Agreement

734. — Some events specific to the arbitration agreement will cause it to expire (A). Other events will extinguish submission agreements, but do not affect arbitration clauses in the same way (B).

A. – Events Extinguishing the Arbitration Agreement

735. — The arbitration agreement expires if waived by the parties (1°) or if directly affected by a defect leading it to be void (2°).

---

[88] Swiss Fed. Trib., Mar. 15, 1990, Sonatrach v. K.C.A. Drilling Ltd., 1990 REV. ARB. 921, and P.-Y. Tschanz' note.

[89] For another example, see ICC Award No. 2438 (1975), where the arbitral tribunal, while holding an action to rescind the main contract to be valid, also addressed the question of the mutual obligations performed prior to the rescission (Spanish company v. French company, 103 J.D.I. 969 (1976), and observations by Y. Derains). See also the examples referred to *supra* para. 410.

[90] *See supra* para. 410.

1° Waiver

736. — The parties can waive the arbitration agreement, expressly or implicitly, without necessarily waiving the main contract. An example of this can be found in a 1987 case decided by the Paris Court of Appeals. The dispute concerned a series of contracts, only one of which contained an arbitration clause. Given that the series of contracts was between the same parties, it was legitimate to consider that the arbitration agreement could be extended from one contract to all the others.[91] That was the view taken by the Paris Tribunal of First Instance, which held that it had no jurisdiction to rule on the claims for termination of all the contracts.[92] However, the decision at first instance was reversed by the Court of Appeals, on the grounds that:

> although the lower court rightly considered that it was dealing with one same contractual whole, in which the later contracts merely supplemented the initial contract . . . , it wrongly concluded that the arbitration agreement was applicable to the entire dispute. Given that the parties carefully specified, in the second contract, that the Paris Commercial Court would have jurisdiction in the event of a dispute and, in [another agreement], that any disputes would be submitted to the competent court [and given that] the parties adopted [such provisions] in a series of contracts, which was liable to generate complex disputes the various elements of which could scarcely be separated, those provisions can . . . only be interpreted as expressing the parties' intention to waive the arbitration agreement.[93]

In that case, the waiver had a two-fold effect: first, the arbitration agreement appearing in the first contract did not apply to the subsequent contracts (because of the provision attributing jurisdiction to a court) and, second, the parties implicitly waived the arbitration agreement with respect to the first contract because of the inseparable nature of the contractual whole.

The parties also implicitly waive the arbitration agreement where one of the parties submits a dispute to the courts and the other files a defense on the merits of the dispute without challenging the jurisdiction of the court.[94] In its 1994 decision in the

---

[91] On this issue, see *supra* para. 523.

[92] TGI Paris, May 20, 1987, G.I.E. Acadi v. Thomson-Answare, 1988 REV. ARB. 573, 1st decision, and the observations made by G. Pluyette at 534.

[93] CA Paris, Dec. 9, 1987, G.I.E. Acadi v. Thomson-Answare, 1988 REV. ARB. 573, 2d decision, and observations by G. Pluyette at 534.

[94] See, for example, in the United States, Khalid Bin Alwaleed Found. v. E.F. Hutton Inc., No. 88 C 5074, 1990 WL 17143 (N.D. Ill. Feb. 1, 1990); XVI Y.B. COM. ARB. 645 (1991); Menorah Ins. Co. v. INX Reinsurance Corp., 72 F.3d 218 (1st Cir. 1995); 11 INT'L ARB. REP. 5 (Jan. 1996); and, generally, GARY B. BORN, INTERNATIONAL COMMERCIAL ARBITRATION IN THE UNITED STATES 279 *et seq.* (1994); in France, Cass. le civ., June 6, 1978, British Leyland International Services v. Société d'Exploitation des Etablissements Richard, 105 J.D.I. 907 (1978), and B. Oppetit's note; 1979 REV. ARB. 230, and P. Level's note, where it was held that the waiver extended to the counterclaim raised by the other party. See also CA Paris, May 15, 1987,

(continued...)

Uzinexportimport case, the Paris Court of Appeals confirmed that a party's waiver of an arbitration agreement "can be inferred from the fact that [it] has applied to a court, provided that the claim in question concerns the merits of the dispute and thus ought to have been submitted to arbitration." In that case, one of the parties had requested an injunction to prevent the other party from repossessing a factory by force, and the Court therefore had to rule on the merits of the dispute.[95] However, there will be no waiver where the sole purpose of the court proceedings is to obtain provisional measures which do not prevent the performance of the arbitration agreement.[96] Similarly, a waiver cannot be inferred from the fact that a party has seized the courts of a claim falling outside the arbitrators' jurisdiction. This is irrespective of whether the claim is outside the arbitrators' jurisdiction because the subject-matter has been expressly excluded by the parties[97] or because the courts have exclusive jurisdiction over the issue in dispute.[98]

Finally, the fact that a party fails to nominate an arbitrator within the deadline stipulated in the arbitration agreement cannot be interpreted as a waiver of that agreement.[99] The same should be the case, in our opinion, if a claimant refuses to pay the defendant's share of the arbitration costs where the latter fails to do so. Depending on the arbitration rules applicable,[100] this may amount to a waiver of its arbitration request, but not of the arbitration agreement.[101]

---

[94](...continued)
Association E.S.C.P. v. G.I.E. Marquedit, which holds that where the parties enter into an arbitration agreement (in this case a submission agreement) without referring to an earlier arbitration clause, the latter is ineffective, as it is deemed to have been implicitly waived (1987 REV. ARB. 503, and L. Zollinger's note). Compare with the unsatisfactory *obiter dictum* of the Supreme Court of Hong Kong, High Court, Apr. 6, 1995, Sulanser Co. Ltd. v. Jiangxi Provincial Metal and Minerals Import and Export Corp., which inferred the waiver of the arbitration clause from the fact that a party defended its case on the merits before the national court after having its challenge of that court's jurisdiction refused (10 INT'L ARB. REP. B1 (June 1995)).

[95] CA Paris, July 7, 1994, Uzinexportimport Romanian Co. v. Attock Cement Co., 1995 REV. ARB. 107, and S. Jarvin's note; for an English translation, see 10 INT'L ARB. REP. D1 (Feb. 1995). On the unpublished decision rendered the same day between the same parties, see *infra* para. 1643.

[96] *See, e.g.,* ICC Award No. 4156 (1983), French company v. French company, 111 J.D.I. 937 (1984), and observations by S. Jarvin; on this issue, generally, see *infra* paras. 1302 *et seq.* See also, for a case where, somewhat curiously, a party claimed that the fact that it had not been subject to preliminary proceedings of *référé-provision* meant that the arbitration agreement had been waived, CA Aix, Oct. 9, 1997, SA Grupo Acciona v. Bellot, 1998 REV. ARB. 383, and J.-L. Delvolvé's note.

[97] *See supra* para. 490. For an example in French domestic arbitration, see Cass. 2e civ., Feb. 18, 1999, Igla v. Soulier, No. S 97-11.489, unpublished.

[98] On the example of a claim related to the insolvency of one party, see ICC Award No. 6840 (1991), Egyptian seller v. Senegalese buyer, 119 J.D.I. 1030, 1033 (1992), and observations by Y. Derains, especially at 1036.

[99] CA Paris, Nov. 14, 1991, Consorts Legrand v. European Country Hotels Ltd., 1994 REV. ARB. 545, 2d decision, and observations by P. Fouchard. See, however, Section 5 of the 1999 Swedish Arbitration Act, according to which "a party shall forfeit his right to invoke the arbitration agreement where the party . . . failed to appoint an arbitrator in due time."

[100] See, for example, in ICC arbitration, Articles 30 and 31 of the Rules and YVES DERAINS AND ERIC A. SCHWARTZ, A GUIDE TO THE NEW ICC RULES OF ARBITRATION 306 *et seq.* (1998).

[101] *But see* Sec. 5 of the 1999 Swedish Arbitration Act.

2° Avoidance

737. — The arbitration agreement is extinguished, independently of the main contract, where it is avoided because of a defect which does not concern the main contract. This will be the case, in particular, where the defect lies in the fact that the disputes capable of being resolved under it are non-arbitrable.[102] As we have seen, in such circumstances, the arbitrators can themselves declare the agreement to be void under the "competence-competence" principle.[103]

B. – EVENTS WHICH EXTINGUISH SUBMISSION AGREEMENTS BUT DO NOT AFFECT ARBITRATION CLAUSES

738. — The distinction between the two types of arbitration agreement—arbitration clauses and submission agreements[104]—has some practical relevance as far as the rules governing expiration are concerned. There are a number of events which will extinguish a submission agreement, but which will not, in theory, affect an arbitration clause on the basis of which an arbitration is commenced.[105] These events include the making of a final award (1°), the default of an arbitrator (2°), the expiration of the agreed deadline for making a final award (3°) and the setting aside of an award made on the basis of a submission agreement (4°).

The situation would be different were it established that, when they signed the submission agreement, the parties intended to novate the arbitration clause. However, there can be no presumption in favor of such novation.

1° The Making of a Final Award

738-1. — When the arbitral tribunal makes an award covering all points in dispute, the submission agreement on which the arbitration is based is extinguished and the arbitral proceedings come to an end.[106] In contrast, whether or not the main contract has been performed or terminated, an arbitration clause could still be operative if a new dispute were to arise from the underlying contractual relationship between the parties.

---

[102] *See supra* para. 532.

[103] *See supra* para. 650.

[104] On the distinction, see *supra* paras. 386 *et seq.*

[105] Cass. com., Jan. 11, 1983, Société libanaise Amine Aour v. Société des Etablissements Soules, 1984 REV. ARB. 132; this decision clearly distinguishes between the arbitration clause and the submission agreement. *See also* TGI Paris, réf., Feb. 12, 1991, Skako France v. SM Industrie, No. 231/91, unpublished.

[106] On the conclusion of the arbitral proceedings, see *infra* para. 1415.

2° The Default of an Arbitrator

739. — Under French domestic arbitration law, a submission agreement is void if one of the arbitrators appointed in it refuses to accept his or her brief.[107]

It has been argued that:

> an arbitration agreement will be extinguished as a result of the death, default or impediment of the arbitrators, or an arbitrator's refusal to act, unless the parties have agreed to overcome such problems or that the arbitrators would be replaced.[108]

In fact, even in French domestic arbitration law, the foregoing observation can only apply to submission agreements and not arbitration clauses. In practice, it is rare for arbitrators to be appointed in the arbitration clause and the question of the impact of their refusal to act, impediment or death will therefore seldom arise. Besides, even if the arbitration clause does appoint the arbitrators, it constitutes a general agreement providing for any disputes which might subsequently arise out of the main contract to be submitted to arbitration. The clause is thus not defeated by the default of an arbitrator, as that arbitrator can simply be replaced if and when a dispute arises, either by means of a new agreement or by using the procedure provided for that purpose by the parties or by the applicable arbitration law. The Paris Court of Appeals has endorsed this view, stating that:

> an alteration to the composition of the arbitral tribunal occurring after the appointment of the arbitrators does not affect the operation of the arbitration clause. In particular, the death, impediment, resignation or challenge of the arbitrators do not bring into question the jurisdiction of the arbitrators, but simply require a new arbitrator to be appointed.[109]

In international arbitration, the consequences of the default of an arbitrator depend solely on the parties' agreement. The parties are perfectly entitled to stipulate, directly or by reference to institutional arbitration rules, how the defaulting arbitrator is to be replaced, that the arbitral proceedings shall continue, and that the arbitral tribunal will decide whether any earlier procedural decisions should be reopened in the presence of the new arbitrator. Such rules are common in international practice,[110] and they help prevent manoeuvres such as the

---

[107] Art. 1448, para. 3 of the New Code of Civil Procedure.

[108] MATTHIEU DE BOISSÉSON, LE DROIT FRANÇAIS DE L'ARBITRAGE INTERNE ET INTERNATIONAL ¶ 130 (2d ed. 1990).

[109] CA Paris, July 7, 1992, Laiguède v. Ahsen Inox, 1994 REV. ARB. 728, *rev'd on other grounds*, Cass. 1e civ., May 10, 1995, 1995 REV. ARB. 605, and A. Hory's note.

[110] On the replacement of a defaulting arbitrator, see *infra* paras. 879 *et seq.*

resignation of a biased arbitrator at the point in the proceedings when it becomes clear that the party which appointed him or her is about to lose.[111]

3° Expiration of the Deadline for the Arbitrators' Award

740. — A deadline for making the award may be provided for either in an arbitration clause, whether directly or by reference to institutional arbitration rules, or by the law governing the arbitral procedure. If that deadline is reached before an award has been made, the arbitral proceedings come to an end. However, the parties remain bound by the arbitration clause, and they will therefore remain obliged to refer to arbitration or accept the referral to arbitration of the same dispute or other disputes arising out of the main contract containing the clause. This was confirmed in a 1992 decision of the Paris Court of Appeals, which held that "an award in which the arbitrator declines jurisdiction on the grounds that the deadline for the arbitral proceedings has passed" has no impact on the effectiveness of the arbitration clause.[112]

4° The Setting Aside of an Award

741. — The setting aside of an award made on the basis of an arbitration clause, whether or not the clause has been followed by a submission agreement, will not extinguish the arbitration clause with regard to different disputes covered by the clause. In the context of French domestic arbitration, Article 1485 of the New Code of Civil Procedure provides that "when a court seized of an action to set aside sets the arbitral award aside, it shall rule on the merits of the case within the limits of the arbitrator's mission, unless otherwise agreed by all the parties." However, precisely because it is confined to the dispute previously submitted to the arbitral tribunal, that power to decide the merits of the dispute leaves the arbitration clause intact. The clause remains applicable to all other disputes which may

---

[111] See, for example, in French domestic arbitration, Cass. 2e civ., Nov. 17, 1993, Pfister v. Zugmeyer, which is unsatisfactory in that it holds that after the resignation of an arbitrator the parties cannot agree to replace him or her and endorse the earlier procedure (1995 REV. ARB. 78, and P. Fouchard's disapproving note). *See also* Philippe Grandjean, *La durée de la mission des arbitres*, 1995 REV. ARB. 39, 45.

[112] CA Paris, July 7, 1992, *Laiguède, supra* note 109, and, in French domestic arbitration, CA Colmar, Sept. 21, 1993, Morin v. Morin, 1994 REV. ARB. 348, and D. Cohen's note; 1994 REV. JUR. COM. 154, and C. Jarrosson's note; Cass. 2e civ., Feb. 18, 1999, Igla v. Soulier, No. J 97-12.770, unpublished. *Comp. with* Cass. 2e civ., May 18, 1989, S.a.r.l. Hostin Armes Blanches v. Prieur Sports, 1990 REV. ARB. 903, and observations by B. Moreau. See, for a case also concerning French domestic arbitration where a submission agreement was held to have been extinguished following the expiration of the deadline by which the arbitral tribunal was to have rendered its award, CA Amiens, Oct. 20, 1959, S.A. Les Carrières de la Meilleraie v. Mercier, 1959 REV. ARB. 122.

subsequently arise and which are within its scope.[113] The same is true in French international arbitration law, where no such power to rule on the merits of the dispute exists.[114]

Of course, the situation will be different where the award is set aside on the grounds that the arbitration agreement is void. In that case, the arbitration agreement is extinguished.[115]

---

[113] *See* Cass. 2e civ., May 16, 1988, Paroutian v. Société de distribution de produits alimentaires et manufacturés Cedipam Cogedis, 1988 REV. ARB. 645, and M.-C. Rondeau-Rivier's note. On this issue, generally, see Bertrand Moreau, *Les effets de la nullité de la sentence arbitrale, in* ETUDES OFFERTES À PIERRE BELLET 403 (1991).

[114] Lebanese law takes the opposite position, allowing the courts to set aside an award and then resolve the merits of the case (Art. 801 of the New Code of Civil Procedure).

[115] *See supra* para. 737. On the continuation of the arbitral tribunal's mission once its award has been set aside, see, for example, in Switzerland, Geneva Tribunal of First Instance, 1993, 1993 BULL. ASA 79; 1994 REV. SUISSE DR. INT. ET DR. EUR. 170, and observations by F. Knoepfler.

PART THREE

THE ARBITRAL TRIBUNAL

742. — The function of the arbitral tribunal is to resolve disputes. It is therefore a judicial authority in its own right, despite the fact that it is a private body.[1] However, unlike the courts, the arbitral tribunal is not part of an established organization or public service. It has to be constituted, in each case, by the appointment of the arbitrator or arbitrators vested with the power to resolve the dispute. This process of constituting the arbitral tribunal is pivotal to the arbitration: it is both the immediate consequence of the arbitration agreement and the first stage of the proceedings themselves.[2]

The aim of this Part Three is to examine the rules governing the appointment and the status of the arbitrators. It is not concerned with the workings and decision-making of the arbitral tribunal, issues which are more directly related to the arbitral proceedings and the award.[3]

743. — The questions raised by the constitution of the arbitral tribunal are of substantial importance and complexity. For arbitration to be efficient, the arbitrators must be appointed rapidly and enjoy a certain stability. Equally, however, there is the need to protect the rights of the parties appointing the arbitrators, and the confidence the parties place in them. It is difficult to strike a balance between these conflicting interests. In addition, international arbitration tends today to give rise increasingly frequently to associated litigation concerning the constitution of the arbitral tribunal before arbitral institutions, the courts or both.

744. — Two areas need to be considered. The first is the constitution of the arbitral tribunal, a process which culminates in the acceptance by the arbitral tribunal of the brief conferred upon it (Chapter One). The second is the status of the arbitrator, a private individual who agrees to act as a judge (Chapter Two).

---

[1] *See supra* paras. 11 *et seq.*

[2] *See supra* paras. 631 *et seq.* and *infra* paras. 1209 *et seq.*

[3] *See infra* paras. 1346 *et seq.*

CHAPTER I
THE CONSTITUTION OF THE ARBITRAL TRIBUNAL

745. — Only certain of the rules governing the constitution of the arbitral tribunal are found in national legal systems. As a result, choice of law rules play a limited role in this area, with the intentions of the parties instead taking precedence. The parties are free to organize their justice as they wish, and thus to agree on the constitution of their arbitral tribunal. If it is necessary or useful to resort to a national law, that chosen by the parties will of course apply, just as it will apply to the arbitral proceedings themselves.[1] That is the most widely-accepted choice of law rule found in comparative law and in international conventions

746. — On a day-to-day basis, it is in fact international arbitral practice that governs the constitution of the arbitral tribunal. Here, a distinction must be drawn between *ad hoc* arbitration and institutional arbitration. In *ad hoc* arbitration, which is organized by the parties themselves, the parties alone choose the arbitrator or arbitrators for their particular dispute, directly or through a predetermined third party. This is in contrast with institutional arbitration, where the parties rely on an arbitral institution to determine the composition of the arbitral tribunal and organize the proceedings, although the parties are not necessarily excluded from the appointment process.

This distinction between *ad hoc* arbitration and institutional arbitration illustrates the importance of arbitral practice and private sources of international arbitration law. However, although national laws, international conventions and the courts allow the parties and arbitral institutions very substantial freedom to constitute their arbitral tribunals as they see fit, they do impose certain fundamental principles governing the constitution of the arbitral tribunal and the choice of arbitrators.

747. — We shall examine in turn the national and international rules governing the constitution of the arbitral tribunal (Section I), and the importance of international arbitral practice (Section II).

---

[1]   *See infra* para. 1200.

SECTION I
NATIONAL AND INTERNATIONAL RULES

748. — National laws and international conventions do not address in detail all the issues surrounding the constitution of the arbitral tribunal. For example, only one provision of the French New Code of Civil Procedure (Art. 1493) specifically deals with the question. French domestic law rules do not apply although, as we shall see, it is not unreasonable to extend certain of the principles contained therein to international arbitration.

749. — These national and international rules are mainly concerned with the appointment of the arbitrators (§1), but they also deal with difficulties in constituting the arbitral tribunal (§2) and with the acceptance by the tribunal of its brief (§3).

§ 1. – The Appointment of the Arbitrators

750. — In French law, Article 1493, paragraph 1 of the New Code of Civil Procedure provides that "the arbitration agreement may, directly or by reference to arbitration rules, appoint the arbitrator or arbitrators or provide for a mechanism for their appointment."

In spite of its brevity, this text—which is specific to international arbitration—is of considerable importance for at least three reasons. First, taken together with Articles 1494 and 1495 of the same Code, it means that the agreement of the parties governs the constitution of the arbitral tribunal, without it being necessary to refer to a national law. Second, it signifies that even if French law is chosen by the parties to govern the proceedings, it is not of mandatory application in international arbitration. Third, it emphasizes the role of arbitral institutions in appointing arbitrators.

751. — Although most modern legal systems and recent international conventions have adopted the first and third of these principles, only a minority of legal systems provide that their arbitration law shall not necessarily apply to international arbitration taking place on their territory.[2] It is against this background that these three principles will be considered.

A. – THE PRIMACY OF THE PARTIES' AGREEMENT

752. — In most modern international arbitration statutes, the primacy of the agreement of the parties is the fundamental principle underlying the whole of the arbitral proceedings, and especially the constitution of the arbitral tribunal. The same principle is also found in

---

[2]   Certain recent statutes have adopted provisions similar to Article 1493, paragraph 1 of the French New Code of Civil Procedure. These include the 1983 Lebanese Code of Civil Procedure (Art. 810, para. 1), the 1993 Algerian Code of Civil Procedure (Article 458 bis 2), and the August 9, 1993 statute of the Côte d'Ivoire (Art. 51).

international conventions. We shall examine in turn the meaning of this principle (1°), its consequences (2°), and its scope (3°).

1° The Meaning of the Primacy of the Parties' Agreement

753. — Article 1493, paragraph 1 of the French New Code of Civil Procedure clearly states that in their arbitration agreement the parties may appoint the arbitrators, or at least provide for the method of their appointment. There is no mention of the involvement of a national law, even that chosen by the parties. Of course, French law does not prevent the parties from choosing a law to govern the arbitral procedure and, by the same token, the constitution of the arbitral tribunal. Further, and although there is no specific wording to that effect, it is clear that if the law chosen to govern the arbitral procedure contains mandatory rules regulating the constitution of an international arbitral tribunal, those rules must be followed. That is simply a consequence of the intention of the parties.

However, although French international arbitration law does not prohibit the parties from subjecting themselves to such legal constraints, neither the letter nor the spirit of Article 1493 encourages them to do so. Rather, Article 1493 emphasizes that the arbitration agreement takes precedence, with the parties either directly choosing the arbitrators, or doing so indirectly by adopting pre-existing arbitration rules usually drawn up by an arbitral institution.[3]

Unlike Article 1494, which deals with "the procedure to be followed in the arbitral proceedings,"[4] Article 1493 does not allude to the possibility of referring to a national law. This is, in our view, the correct approach: if a minimum of trust is to be maintained between the parties and their judges in international arbitration, the appointment of the arbitrators must be left to the parties. It is up to them to exercise that right or, if they so choose, to delegate it to an arbitral institution. Only serious abuse of the process will be censured, and only where the parties are left powerless will the courts intervene.[5]

754. — In other legal systems, the same principle applies: the parties are free to appoint the arbitrators or to set forth a mechanism for their appointment. For instance, this is true of the 1985 UNCITRAL Model Law (Arts. 10(1) and 11(2)).[6] The same liberalism is found in the 1987 Swiss Private International Law Statute, Article 179 of which states that "the arbitrators shall be appointed . . . in accordance with the agreement of the parties." Similar provisions exist in particular in the Belgian Judicial Code (Art. 1682), the Netherlands Code of Civil Procedure (Art. 1027), the Italian Code of Civil Procedure (Art. 809), the 1996 English Arbitration Act (Secs. 15 and 16) and the 1997 German Arbitration Act (Art. 1035 of the ZPO).

---

[3]   *See infra* paras. 974 *et seq.*

[4]   *See infra* paras. 1200 *et seq.*

[5]   *See infra* paras. 832 *et seq.*

[6]   This is also true of all national laws adopting or adapting it. On the UNCITRAL Model Law and its worldwide influence, see *supra* paras. 203 *et seq.*

755. — This consensus is not surprising. As early as the 1920s, two major international conventions led the way. The Protocol on Arbitration Clauses in Commercial Matters, signed in Geneva on September 24, 1923,[7] states in its Article 2 that "the constitution of the arbitral tribunal shall be governed by the will of the parties." Likewise, Article 1, paragraph 2(c) of the Convention on the Execution of Foreign Arbitral Awards, signed in Geneva on September 26, 1927,[8] provides that for an award to be recognized or enforced it must have been "made by the arbitral tribunal provided in the submission to arbitration, or constituted in the manner agreed upon by the parties."

Although both conventions thus establish the principle of party autonomy, neither includes a substantive rule catering for the constitution of the arbitral tribunal where the agreement between the parties is inadequate. Both merely refer back to the applicable law, which will generally be that of the seat of the arbitration.

756. — The 1958 New York Convention takes a similar position.[9] Under Article V, paragraph 1(d), recognition and enforcement of an award may be refused if it is established that:

> [t]he composition of the arbitral authority . . . was not in accordance with the agreement of the parties, or, failing such agreement, was not in accordance with the law of the country where the arbitration took place.

Here again, there is no substantive rule governing the appointment of the arbitrators other than the parties' freedom of choice. There is, however, a noticeable improvement on the two earlier conventions, in that the New York Convention confirms the subsidiary role of national law.[10]

757. — In contrast, two more recent international conventions have adopted rules which either provide directly for the constitution of the arbitral tribunal or indicate how it is to be constituted.

758. — One of these, the 1965 Washington Convention, is unique in that it established the International Centre for Settlement of Investment Disputes (ICSID), an arbitral institution dealing with international investment disputes (Art. 1).[11] ICSID maintains a list of arbitrators nominated by each member state or by the Chairman of the Administrative Council.[12] The parties are not, however, obliged to choose their arbitrators from this list (Art. 40). Unless otherwise agreed by the parties, the arbitral tribunal will consist of three

---

[7] On this Convention, see *supra* para. 241.

[8] On this Convention, see *supra* para. 244.

[9] On this Convention, see *supra* paras. 247 *et seq.*

[10] *See infra* paras. 804 *et seq.*

[11] On this Convention, see *supra* para. 301.

[12] *See* Arts. 12 *et seq.* The list included 427 arbitrators in 1998; *see* ICSID 1998 Annual Report, at 12.

arbitrators, one nominated by each party and a third, the president, appointed by mutual agreement of the parties (Art. 37).

759. — The 1961 European Convention[13] is more general in scope. In its Article IV on the "organization of the arbitration," it directly regulates the constitution of the arbitral tribunal. To facilitate the setting up of the arbitral tribunal, the negotiators of the European Convention intentionally excluded any reference to national laws or courts. Instead, they adopted substantive rules which refer to private mechanisms. These substantive rules are based on the distinction between institutional and *ad hoc* arbitration which was outlined in the New York Convention but forms an integral part of the European Convention. Institutional arbitration is easier to organize than *ad hoc* arbitration, provided of course that the involvement of the chosen arbitral institution and the application of its rules are recognized as legitimate.[14] But the European Convention also acknowledges the legitimacy of *ad hoc* arbitration directly organized by the parties. Article IV, paragraph 1 of the Convention stipulates that the parties are free to

submit their disputes:

. . .

    (*b*) to an *ad hoc* arbitral procedure; in this case, they shall be free *inter alia*
        (i)   to appoint arbitrators or to establish means for their appointment in
            the event of an actual dispute;
       (ii) to determine the place of arbitration; and
      (iii) to lay down the procedure to be followed by the arbitrators.

The Convention thus authorizes, and even encourages, arbitration proceedings that are totally independent of national legal systems.[15] In particular, the parties are free to agree on every aspect of the constitution of the arbitral tribunal, including the number of arbitrators, their qualifications and how they are to be appointed.

760. — In its generality and flexibility, the European Convention is similar to many contemporary arbitration statutes. All give the parties a great degree of freedom as to the identity of the arbitrators (a), their number (b) and the method of their appointment (c).

---

[13] On this Convention, see *supra* para. 274.

[14] On this point, see *infra* paras. 815 *et seq.*

[15] *See, e.g.*, Lazare Kopelmanas, *La place de la Convention européenne sur l'arbitrage commercial international du 21 avril 1961 dans l'évolution du droit international de l'arbitrage*, 1961 AFDI 331; PHILIPPE FOUCHARD, L'ARBITRAGE COMMERCIAL INTERNATIONAL ¶¶ 513 *et seq.* (1965); Peter Benjamin, *The Work of the Economic Commission for Europe in the Field of International Commercial Arbitration*, 7 INT'L & COMP. L.Q. 22 (1958); P.I. Benjamin, *The European Convention on International Commercial Arbitration*, 37 BRIT. Y.B. INT'L L. 478 (1961); David A. Godwin Sarre, *European Commercial Arbitration*, 1961 J. BUS. L. 352.

a) Identity of the Arbitrators

761. — To ensure that the intentions of the parties prevail, all restrictions on their freedom of choice must either be limited or removed entirely.

762. — As regards the nationality of the arbitrators, some jurisdictions previously imposed restrictions on foreigners.[16] These were repealed in Italy in 1983[17] and in Ecuador in 1997,[18] and were eased in Colombia in 1989.[19] However, some legal systems still do prohibit certain individuals from acting as arbitrators on religious grounds.[20]

763. — Two international conventions have greatly contributed to the movement against prohibiting foreign nationals from acting as arbitrators. Article III of the 1961 European Convention[21] provides that "[i]n arbitration covered by this Convention, foreign nationals may be designated as arbitrators." Similarly, under Article 2 of the 1975 Inter-American Convention on International Commercial Arbitration,[22] "[a]rbitrators may be nationals or foreigners."

This liberal trend has been reinforced by the UNCITRAL Model Law, Article 11 of which provides that "[n]o person shall be precluded by reason of his nationality from acting as an arbitrator, unless otherwise agreed by the parties." The Model Law thus states that there can be no statutory discrimination on the basis of nationality. Although the parties are entitled to agree otherwise, that is principally in order to allow them to appoint arbitrators

---

[16] On the restrictions still imposed in Ecuador and Chile in 1978, see Albert Jan van den Berg, *L'arbitrage commercial en Amérique latine*, 1979 REV. ARB. 123, 153.

[17] *See* Giorgio Recchia, *La nouvelle loi italienne sur l'arbitrage*, 1984 REV. ARB. 65, 69; Giorgio Bernini, *Domestic and International Arbitration in Italy after the Legislative Reform*, 5 PACE L. REV. 543, 550 (1985).

[18] Law of August 29, 1997 on Arbitration and Mediation, Official Register No. 145 dated September 4, 1997, repealing the Law of October 23, 1963.

[19] Article 8 of Decree No. 2279 of October 7, 1989, which allowed foreign nationals to be arbitrators if the dispute had a foreign element, was held unconstitutional by the Supreme Court of Justice of Colombia on March 21, 1991 (for a French translation, see 1991 REV. ARB. 720, and F. Mantilla-Serrano's note); the text was amended by Law No. 23 of March 21, 1991, which provides that "[w]ithout prejudice to treaties in force containing provisions on international arbitration, the arbitrators shall be Colombian citizens;" *see* Fernando Mantilla-Serrano, *La nouvelle législation colombienne sur l'arbitrage*, 1992 REV. ARB. 41.

[20] See, for example in Saudi Arabia, where non-Muslims are prohibited from being arbitrators (*see* Art. 3 of the Rules for the Implementation of the Saudi Arabian Arbitration Regulation (Council of Ministers' Resolution 7/2021/M of May 27, 1985)); *see also* Abdul Hamid El-Ahdab, *Arbitration in Saudi Arabia under the New Arbitration Act, 1983 and Its Implementation Rules of 1985* (pts 1–2), 3 J. INT'L ARB. 27, 49 (Sept. 1986), 3 J. INT'L ARB. 23 (Dec. 1986). But these vestiges of traditionalist law often co-exist with modern legislation and the ratification of international conventions; *see* Samir Saleh, *La perception de l'arbitrage au Machrek et dans les pays du Golfe*, 1992 REV. ARB. 537.

[21] On this Convention, see *supra* para. 274.

[22] On this Convention, see *supra* para. 294.

who are not of the same nationality as the parties, which is often seen as a guarantee of their neutrality.[23]

764. — French law imposes no conditions regarding the nationality of arbitrators. In international arbitration, the arbitral tribunal may comprise French or foreign nationals, or both. In a case where it was required to assist with the constitution of an arbitral tribunal, the Paris Tribunal of First Instance refused to distinguish between an arbitrator nominated by a party and the third arbitrator,[24] and therefore appointed a third arbitrator of French nationality in a Franco-Mexican dispute.[25] The Court considered that the practice whereby under some arbitration rules the third arbitrator may not be of the same nationality as the parties "does not impose a duty on the President of the Tribunal of First Instance to exclude the possibility of appointing an arbitrator of the same nationality as one of the parties."

765. — Similarly, French law lays down no conditions as to the capacity of the arbitrators. This is because arbitrators must be legally capable in any event, as they enter into a contract to carry out their brief[26] and perform a judicial function. Their capacity will therefore be governed, in principle, by their personal law. In civil law countries this will be the arbitrators' national law or laws;[27] in common law jurisdictions it will be the law of their domicile or domiciles. Thus, if an arbitrator is French, the French courts may be inclined to apply the domestic arbitration rule found at Article 1451, paragraph 1 of the New Code of Civil Procedure, which provides that arbitrators must "have full capacity to exercise their civil rights."[28] The solution would only be different if the national law normally applicable to the capacity of the arbitrator were to unduly restrict a person's capacity to serve as an arbitrator: such restrictions might not apply in international arbitration on the grounds of good faith, estoppel, or excusable ignorance.

Certain other legal systems expressly require that arbitrators have the capacity to exercise their civil rights.[29]

766. — In contrast, the second condition imposed by Article 1451, namely that "the mission of arbitrator may only be entrusted to a natural person," does not mean that there is a general exclusion preventing "French" juridical persons from acting as arbitrators. Aside from the fact that it is difficult to define the nationality of a juridical person, this rule must

---

[23] On this practice, see *infra* para. 1037; on the requirement that arbitrators be independent and impartial, see *infra* paras. 1021 *et seq.*

[24] On this very real distinction in arbitral practice, see *infra* paras. 1041 *et seq.*

[25] TGI Paris, réf., May 22, 1987 and June 23, 1987, Transportacion Maritima Mexicana S.A. v. Alsthom, 1988 REV. ARB. 699, 2d and 3d decisions, and P. Fouchard's note.

[26] On the acceptance by arbitrators of their brief, see *infra* para. 941; on the resulting contract, see *infra* para. 1106.

[27] *See, e.g.*, Art. 3 of the French Civil Code.

[28] On the consequences of the setting aside of an award on the basis of the national law of the arbitrator, see *infra* para. 1625.

[29] *See, e.g.*, Art. 768, para. 2 of the Lebanese New Code of Civil Procedure.

be interpreted as applying only in French domestic arbitration.[30] It will not apply whenever the dispute is international, within the meaning of Article 1492 of the New Code of Civil Procedure, regardless of the location of the entity's headquarters, its nationality, the place where the arbitration is held, and, in our opinion, the parties' choice of French law to govern the arbitral procedure.

767. — Provided of course that the arbitrators appointed are independent and impartial,[31] the capacity in which they act, their profession and any other personal characteristics are of limited importance. The parties are free to choose anybody as their arbitrator, although they may agree to restrict that choice. For example, they may agree to nominate only people appearing on a list drawn up by themselves, by a third party, or by a chosen arbitral institution. If that is the case, both parties will be bound by their agreement.

768. — This was an important issue in the *Philipp Brothers* case. As a result of the embargo imposed by the government of the Côte d'Ivoire on cocoa exports, a British trading company, Philipp Brothers, was unable to fulfil a number of contracts for cocoa sales to other international cocoa traders. Those traders commenced arbitration proceedings against Philipp Brothers, as provided for in the contracts, under the Rules of the Chambre arbitrale de l'Association Française pour le Commerce des Cacaos (the AFCC). The Rules provided that the arbitrators were to be chosen from a list of prominent figures in the cocoa industry drawn up by the AFCC. Before the President of the Paris Tribunal of First Instance, Philipp Brothers claimed that this list was too short, given the number of disputes to be resolved (eighteen awards were eventually made on similar facts) and the fact that all or almost all of the individuals on the list had links of some sort with the plaintiffs. Philipp Brothers therefore refused to accept the appointment of any of the arbitrators appearing on the list, and instead nominated an arbitrator from outside the list and asked the judge to appoint a third arbitrator "chosen from among serving or retired French judges."

By two rulings, dated October 28, 1988, and June 29, 1989,[32] the President of the Paris Tribunal of First Instance refused to do so, holding in particular

> that in this instance, by agreeing to the arbitration clause in the disputed contracts, which designates the arbitration chamber of the AFCC as the institution in charge of the arbitration, Philipp Brothers accepted with full knowledge and without any reservation the application of the Rules of that Chamber.

---

[30] *See* MATTHIEU DE BOISSÉSON, LE DROIT FRANÇAIS DE L'ARBITRAGE INTERNE ET INTERNATIONAL ¶ 631 (2d ed. 1990); see also CA Grenoble, Apr. 26, 1995, Delattre v. Ascinter Otis, where, in a case concerning a domestic arbitration, it was rightly held that the appointment of a corporation as arbitrator did not cause the arbitration clause to be manifestly void, as a corporation has the power, under Article 1451, paragraph 2 of the New Code of Civil Procedure, to organize the arbitration (1996 REV. ARB. 452, and P. Fouchard's note).

[31] On these requirements, see *infra* paras. 784 and 1020 *et seq.*

[32] TGI Paris, réf., Oct. 28, 1988, Drexel Burnham Lambert Ltd. v. Philipp Brothers, and June 29, 1989, Philipp Brothers v. Drexel, 1990 REV. ARB. 497, lst and 3d decisions.

The Paris Court of Appeals subsequently heard the actions to set aside the awards made by the arbitrators chosen from the AFCC's list. The Court took the same position as the Tribunal of First Instance, holding that:

> by referring to the AFCC Arbitration Rules to resolve any disputes arising from their commercial relations, the parties fully agreed to all aspects of those Rules, including the existence of the lists of arbitrators and the regulations for appointing the arbitrators in each arbitration. The choice of a professional arbitral institution of this kind implies that the parties intended to submit their disputes to the judgment of those members of that profession chosen by the arbitral institution. As a result, the criticisms voiced by Philipp Brothers concerning the limitations of the system of lists of arbitrators are unfounded, because Philipp Brothers agreed to that procedure by adhering to the arbitration Rules in the first place.[33]

769. — The parties may also agree, for example, directly or by reference to institutional arbitration rules, that the arbitrators should have a particular professional qualification, that they should practice in a particular field, that they should be technicians, engineers or chartered accountants, or that they should have experience of a certain type of dispute or fluency in a certain language.[34] The parties may even agree to exclude lawyers, although to do so is forbidden by the Swiss *Concordat*.[35] The 1987 Swiss Private International Law Statute does not, however, contain such a prohibition.

The principle is thus firmly established: the choice of the arbitrators, the method by which that choice is made and any restrictions that apply are determined according to the intentions of the parties and the institutional arbitration rules they adopt.

b) Number of Arbitrators

770. — The number of arbitrators comprising the arbitral tribunal is also determined by agreement between the parties. Article 1493 of the French New Code of Civil Procedure refers to "the arbitrator or arbitrators," thus permitting the parties to provide for a sole arbitrator or for a tribunal of two or more arbitrators. It is possible, although less usual, for a tribunal to comprise more than three arbitrators (for example in a large dispute involving several parties with different interests).[36] In France, the requirement that an arbitral tribunal

---

[33] CA Paris, Apr. 6, 1990, Philipp Brothers v. Icco, 1990 REV. ARB. 880, and M. de Boisséson's note.

[34] For an illustration of similar requirements in the arbitration clauses used in the Eurodisney project and their interpretation, see TGI Paris, réf., Dec. 12 and 20, 1991, Campenon Bernard v. Eurodisneyland SCA, 1996 REV. ARB. 516, and P. Fouchard's note.

[35] *See* Art. 7; *see also* PIERRE LALIVE, JEAN-FRANÇOIS POUDRET, CLAUDE REYMOND, LE DROIT DE L'ARBITRAGE INTERNE ET INTERNATIONAL EN SUISSE 61 (1989).

[36] This would be one way of satisfying the requirement of equality laid down in the *Dutco* decision; *see infra* para. 792.

comprise an uneven number of arbitrators applies in domestic arbitration,[37] but not in international cases.

771. — Other jurisdictions display the same liberalism and do not impose any particular number of arbitrators,[38] although more commonly they will require that the tribunal comprise an uneven number of arbitrators.[39] The new Indian arbitration statute requires an odd number of arbitrators,[40] but the Supreme Court of India has interpreted this requirement very broadly. In order to ensure the effectiveness of the many arbitration clauses drafted prior to the enactment of that statute which provide for the appointment of two arbitrators, with an umpire appointed by those arbitrators if they disagree, the Court has held that such clauses should be interpreted as giving rise to a tribunal of three arbitrators, with the third acting as chairman.[41]

c) Method of Appointing Arbitrators

772. — Although national laws and international conventions set forth no particular procedure for the appointment of the arbitral tribunal, various methods of appointment do exist.

773. — In most cases, the arbitration agreement will take the form of an arbitration clause, rather than a submission agreement. It is rare (and not recommended) for the arbitrators to be appointed by name in the arbitration clause itself, as the dispute will not have arisen when the contract is signed. Instead, the arbitration clause will generally specify the mechanism for appointing the arbitrators, a mechanism which will be implemented after the dispute has arisen and the request for arbitration is filed. Arbitral practice, as well as institutional and *ad hoc* arbitration rules, illustrate the diversity of appointment mechanisms.[42] If there is only one arbitrator, the arbitration clause will usually provide that

---

[37] *See* Arts. 1453 and 1454 of the French New Code of Civil Procedure.

[38] See, for example, the 1987 Swiss Private International Law Statute (Art. 179) and the UNCITRAL Model Law, which only provide for three arbitrators in the absence of any other agreement between the parties (Art. 10); on the interpretation of a clause providing for a "tribunal of no less than two arbitrators" under the intercantonal *Concordat*, see Swiss Fed. Trib., Mar. 20, 1995, X Inc. v. S., 1995 BULL. ASA 511. Likewise, Section 15 of the 1996 English Arbitration Act states that, unless the parties agree otherwise, a clause providing for an even number of arbitrators requires a further arbitrator to be appointed by the chair of the arbitral tribunal.

[39] *See, e.g.*, Art. 1681(1) of the Belgian Judicial Code; Art. 1026 of the Netherlands Code of Civil Procedure, Art. 809 of the Italian Code of Civil Procedure.

[40] The Indian Arbitration and Conciliation Ordinance, 1996 (Sec. 10(1)). *See supra* para. 174.

[41] Supreme Court of India, Nov. 18, 1996, MMTC Ltd. v. Sterlite Industries (India) Ltd., Judgments Today [1996] 10 S.C. 390; 12 INT'L ARB. REP. G1 (May 1997); 1997 BULL. ASA 136; ICC BULLETIN, Vol. 8, No. 1, at 39 (1997).

[42] *See infra* paras. 951 *et seq.*

the parties are to make their appointment by mutual agreement,[43] failing which the arbitrator will be nominated by the arbitral institution or by a pre-determined third party. In most cases where three arbitrators are to be appointed, each party nominates one arbitrator, and the third arbitrator is chosen either by those two arbitrators,[44] by the arbitral institution, or by a pre-determined third party.

774. — The actual appointment of the arbitrator or arbitrators thus takes place after the signature of the contract containing the arbitration clause, and after a number of choices have been made, either unilaterally by each party or by a third party, or by mutual consent of the parties or the party-appointed arbitrators. In institutional arbitration, the appointment of the arbitrators may or may not be followed by confirmation of that appointment by the arbitral institution. The appointment of the tribunal may also result from a submission agreement, or it may be confirmed by a submission agreement or by the document often referred to in international practice as the terms of reference.[45]

2° Consequences of the Primacy of the Parties' Agreement

775. — Irrespective of the stage of the arbitral proceedings at which they have been required to intervene, and the grounds on which they do so, the French courts have repeatedly underlined the exclusively contractual nature of the appointment of the arbitrators.

776. — That would be the position taken, for example, if a party were to refer the substance of a dispute to the courts, arguing that the institutional arbitration mechanism provided for in the arbitration clause did not apply. The Lyon Tribunal of First Instance declined jurisdiction in a case where the plaintiff failed to establish that Orgalime, the institution chosen to organize the arbitration, had expressly refused to carry out its role.[46]

777. — Even before the reform of French arbitration law in 1980 and 1981, the French courts were already emphasizing that the appointment of the arbitral tribunal was a matter for the parties alone.[47] In its important decision in the *Ury v. Galeries Lafayette* case, the *Cour de cassation* held that:

---

[43] *See* Art. 11(3)(b) of the UNCITRAL Model Law.

[44] *See* Art. 11(3)(a) of the UNCITRAL Model Law.

[45] *See infra* paras. 1228 *et seq.*

[46] TGI Lyon, May 31, 1990, Castel Mac v. Pierre Pont, 1991 REV. ARB. 367, and observations by J.-H. Moitry and C. Vergne.

[47] *See* Jacqueline Rubellin-Devichi and Eric Loquin, *Arbitrage – Compromis et clause compromissoire*, J.-CL. PROC. CIV., Fasc. 1020, ¶¶ 16 *et seq.* (1995).

the appointment of each arbitrator is not a unilateral act, even when initiated by one party alone . . . . On the contrary, this appointment, which forms an important part of the arbitration agreement, results from the common intention of the parties.[48]

This principle was subsequently reiterated, after the enactment of the new laws, in both domestic[49] and international cases. In the case of *Raffineries de pétrole d'Homs et de Banias v. Chambre de Commerce Internationale*, the Paris Tribunal of First Instance held that:

> a chosen arbitrator—who is a judge, not a representative of the party which appointed him—must derive his judicial powers from a single, common manifestation of the intentions of the parties to the proceedings, even though his appointment may have been initiated by one party alone.[50]

In keeping with the contractual basis of arbitration, the French courts thus consider that every arbitrator is appointed by the mutual agreement of all parties to the arbitration.

778. — This has important repercussions. For example, an award may be set aside on grounds of mistake as to the identity of an arbitrator, and an arbitrator nominated by one party alone may be replaced if the other party was unaware or discovers that the relationship between arbitrator and party is such as to cast doubt on the arbitrator's independence or impartiality.[51] In other words, French law infers from the principle that the arbitrators are designated by the common intention of the parties that a "party-appointed" arbitrator is and must be as independent and impartial as a sole arbitrator or the chairman of an arbitral tribunal. The "party-appointed" arbitrator does not and cannot enjoy a special status of "non-neutral arbitrator," which law and practice in the United States have traditionally been more willing to accept.[52]

779. — When faced with a problem concerning the constitution of the arbitral tribunal,[53] the French courts will not override the common intention of the parties, provided it is clearly discernible. They will not substitute themselves for a third party charged with appointing an arbitrator,[54] and if they do eventually find themselves in the position of having to appoint an

---

[48] Cass. 2e civ., Apr. 13, 1972, Consorts Ury v. S.A. des Galeries Lafayette, JCP, Ed. G., Pt. II, No. 17,189 (1972), and P. Level's note; Dalloz, Jur. 2 (1973), and J. Robert's note; 1975 REV. ARB. 235, and E. Loquin's note.

[49] TGI Paris, réf., Mar. 22, 1983, V. and L. v. C., 1983 REV. ARB. 479, 2d decision, and B. Moreau's note; JCP, Ed. G., Pt. II, No. 20,004 (1983), and O. d'Antin and M. Lacorne's note.

[50] TGI Paris, Mar. 28, 1984, Raffineries de pétrole d'Homs et de Banias v. Chambre de Commerce Internationale, 1985 REV. ARB. 141, 1st decision.

[51] *See infra* paras. 1066 *et seq.*

[52] *See infra* paras. 1041 *et seq.*

[53] *See infra* paras. 832 *et seq.*

[54] See, for example, the decisions in the *Philipp Brothers* case, *supra* notes 32 and 33. *See also* TGI Paris, réf., Feb. 24 and Apr. 15, 1992, Icori Estero S.p.A. v. Kuwait Foreign Trading Contracting & Investment Co.
(continued...)

arbitrator, they will still take into account the intentions, or at least the wishes, of the parties.[55]

780. — The same preoccupation with respecting the intentions of the parties led the Paris Court of Appeals to criticize the "interventionism" of the first instance judge in the *République de Guinée* case. According to the Court of Appeals, provided that by the time the matter comes to court the institution organizing the arbitration has fulfilled its role, and the arbitrators have accepted to carry out theirs, the courts cannot suspend or hold void the agreement by which the parties had apparently designated that institution.[56] Relying on the autonomy of the arbitration agreement, the Court of Appeals added that the claims raised when the arbitral tribunal was being constituted could only be considered by the courts if and when the plaintiff subsequently brought an action to set the award aside.

Likewise, in Belgium the Brussels Tribunal of First Instance held it had no jurisdiction to order an arbitral institution to alter its decision concerning the constitution of the arbitral tribunal, because the only remedy available where the tribunal is alleged to have been irregularly constituted is an action to set the award aside.[57]

781. — Once an award has been made, the courts take care to ensure that the intentions of the parties are observed. They will not set aside an award if the constitution of the arbitral tribunal complies with the parties' agreement or with the chosen arbitration rules.[58]

782. — In contrast, the courts will not hesitate to set aside or refuse enforcement of an award made by an arbitral tribunal which was not constituted in accordance with the parties' agreement. That will be the case where the agreement of the parties is not complied with and where nothing in the subsequent attitude of the parties can be construed as a waiver of such non-compliance.[59] On the other hand, it matters little if the arbitration clause is complex, or

---

[54](...continued)
(KFTCIC), 1994 REV. ARB. 557, and observations by P. Fouchard.

[55] *See* Philippe Fouchard, *La coopération du Président du Tribunal de grande instance à l'arbitrage*, 1985 REV. ARB. 5, especially at 15 *et seq.*

[56] CA Paris, Nov. 18, 1987 and May 4, 1988, Chambre arbitrale de Paris v. République de Guinée, 1988 REV. ARB. 657, 1st and 2d decisions, and P. Fouchard's note.

[57] *See* Brussels Trib. of First Inst., réf., Dec. 24, 1993, Koninklijke Sphinx N.V. v. a.s.b.l. Centre belge pour l'étude et la pratique de l'arbitrage national et international, 1994 [BELG.] JOURN. TRIB. No. 5716.

[58] *See* CA Paris, Apr. 6, 1990, *Philipp Brothers, supra* note 33.

[59] *See* CA Paris, July 11, 1978, Compagnie d'Armement Maritime (CAM) v. Compagnie Tunisienne de Navigation (COTUNAV), 1979 REV. ARB. 258, and M. Boitard's note; CA Paris, June 24, 1997, Highlight Communications International AG v. Europex, 1997 REV. ARB. 588, and observations by D. Bureau; Supreme Court of Hong Kong, High Court, July 13, 1994, China Nanhai Oil Joint Serv. Corp. Shenzhen Branch v. Gee Tai Holdings Co. Ltd., which applied the doctrine of estoppel where a party belatedly sought to rely before the court hearing an action for enforcement on the fact that the award had been made under the aegis of the Shenzhen Sub-Commission of the China International Economic Trade Arbitration Commission (CIETAC), whereas the arbitration clause provided for the involvement of the Beijing Commission (10 INT'L ARB. REP. 10 (Aug. 1995); XX Y.B. COM. ARB. 671 (1995)).

even if it verges on the pathological: in the *Gas del Estado v. Ecofisa and E.T.P.M.* case,[60] the arbitration clause stated that each party would appoint an arbitrator, and that the two chosen arbitrators would agree on a third one; failing such agreement, the president of the International Court of Justice would choose the third arbitrator. However, the clause continued that the constitution of the arbitral tribunal was to be governed by the ICC Rules, and that the Argentine federal courts would be entitled to seek the constitution of the arbitral tribunal. At the plaintiffs' request, and despite the defendants' objections, the ICC Court of Arbitration appointed three arbitrators. An award was rendered by the arbitral tribunal thus constituted. On appeal against the order enforcing the award, the Paris Court of Appeals considered how the different provisions could be reconciled in order to determine the true intentions of the parties. It held that both the plaintiffs and the ICC had disregarded the derogations from the ICC Rules set forth in the arbitration clause. The constitution of the arbitral tribunal was therefore held to be irregular. The *Cour de cassation* upheld the Court of Appeals' decision on the basis that the latter had found, in the exercise of its discretion, that the different provisions of the arbitration clause could easily be reconciled and that the ICC's decision, confirmed by the arbitrators, did not reflect the intentions of the parties. Given that the ICC had failed to comply with the terms of the parties' agreement in appointing the arbitral tribunal, the Court of Appeals correctly ruled that "the arbitral tribunal was irregularly constituted" within the meaning of Article 1502 2° of the French New Code of Civil Procedure.

The penalty imposed by the French courts in cases of non-compliance with the intentions of the parties as to the constitution of the arbitral tribunal is thus clear: they will hold the arbitral tribunal to be irregularly constituted, and will either set aside or decline to enforce the award.[61]

3° Limits of the Primacy of the Parties' Agreement

783. — The primacy of the parties' agreement is not absolute. It is limited in some respects by the requirements of the proper administration of justice.

784. — Certain of these limits have already been outlined, and will be discussed later at greater length: they are the arbitrators' independence and impartiality.[62]

785. — Others result from the requirement that the parties' method of appointing the arbitrators, or the institutional rules chosen, comply with the fundamental principles of due

---

[60] CA Paris, Feb. 11, 1988, Gas del Estado v. Ecofisa and E.T.P.M., 1989 REV. ARB. 683, and L. Zollinger's note, *aff'd*, Cass. le civ., Dec. 4, 1990, E.T.P.M. and Ecofisa v. Gas del Estado, 1991 REV. ARB. 81, and P. Fouchard's note.

[61] On the review exercised by the courts on this ground, see *infra* para. 1620.

[62] *See infra* paras. 1021 *et seq.*

process. These principles include, in particular, the parties' right to a fair trial, and their right to equal treatment.[63]

786. — The latter principle is clearly expressed in the UNCITRAL Model Law, Article 18 of which states that "the parties shall be treated with equality." Dutch law is even more explicit: it allows a party to seek a court order departing from an arbitration agreement which "gives one of the parties a privileged position with regard to the appointment of the arbitrator or arbitrators."[64] The German arbitration statute of December 22, 1997, which differs on this issue from the UNCITRAL Model Law, has adopted the same rule. Article 1034, paragraph 2 of the ZPO states that:

> If the arbitration agreement grants preponderant rights to one party with regard to the composition of the arbitral tribunal which place the other party at a disadvantage, that other party may request the court to appoint the arbitrator or arbitrators in deviation from the nomination made, or from the agreed nomination procedure. The request must be submitted at the latest within two weeks of the party becoming aware of the constitution of the arbitral tribunal. Section 1032 subs. 3 applies mutatis mutandis.[65]

787. — Most other legal systems, as well as the relevant international conventions, do not contain such explicit provisions. Nevertheless, blatant violations of the parties' right to equal treatment can be censured by the courts if those violations are brought within areas where judicial scrutiny is admissible, such as the validity of the constitution of the arbitral tribunal, due process and, above all, compliance with international public policy. Thus, under the New York Convention, each party must be "given proper notice of the appointment of the arbitrator" (Art. V(1)(b)) and, more generally, "enforcement of the award [must not be] contrary to the public policy of [the country where such enforcement is sought]" (Art. V(2)(b)). Either of these provisions could be relied upon where, for example, the principle of equal treatment of the parties in the appointment of the arbitrators has not been observed, or where an arbitrator has concealed facts liable to affect his or her independence or impartiality. It was on the basis of Article V, paragraph 1(b) of the New York Convention that a German court refused the enforcement in Germany of an award made in Copenhagen by an Arbitration Committee for Grain and Feed Stuff Trade, as the Committee's Rules stipulated that the names of the arbitrators would not be revealed to the parties.[66] The German defendant was unable to ascertain whether the Committee members whom it had challenged had in fact been removed from the case, or whether the arbitrators who decided

---

[63] See DE BOISSÉSON, *supra* note 30, ¶¶ 717 *et seq.*

[64] See Art. 1028 of the Netherlands Code of Civil Procedure.

[65] See Peter Schlosser, *La nouvelle législation allemande sur l'arbitrage*, 1998 REV. ARB. 291; Gino Lörcher, *The New German Arbitration Act*, 15 J. INT'L ARB. 85 (June 1998); Klaus Peter Berger, *Germany adopts the UNCITRAL Model Law*, 1 INT'L ARB. L. REV. 121 (1998).

[66] *Oberlandesgericht* of Cologne, June 10, 1976, Danish buyer v. German (F.R.) seller, IV Y.B. COM. ARB. 258 (1979).

the dispute were actually drawn from the list of arbitrators which had been given to the parties.

788. — Likewise, in France, these principles of fairness and equality do not appear as such among the rules the application of which is reviewed by the Court of Appeals in actions to set aside or enforce international arbitral awards. The only grounds on which such actions are admissible under Article 1502 of the New Code of Civil Procedure are the breach of due process, which concerns primarily the conduct of the proceedings, and the violation of international public policy. The rules of international public policy may of course cover "procedural" issues and will include the protection of principles fundamental to the proper administration of justice.

789. — In addition, Article 6 of the 1950 European Convention for the Protection of Human Rights and Fundamental Freedoms, in common with Article 14 of the 1966 New York International Covenant on Civil and Political Rights, provides that "everyone is entitled to a fair and public hearing within a reasonable time by an independent and impartial tribunal." Clearly, an arbitral tribunal is not a court, and if its constitution contravenes the principles of the European Convention on Human Rights or the New York Covenant, the relevant government cannot be held directly responsible.[67] However, when reviewing arbitral awards, the courts must ensure that those principles have been observed.

790. — When examining the constitution of the arbitral tribunal in the *République de Guinée* case, the Paris Tribunal of First Instance and subsequently the Paris Court of Appeals both referred to the two international conventions described above, and to the overriding requirement which they impose, namely the right to a fair hearing. Various incidents led to a dispute between the defendant and the arbitral institution organizing the arbitration. The Tribunal of First Instance held, in a provisional ruling temporarily suspending the arbitral proceedings, that:

> in this case there is a serious risk that the parties will not be given a fair hearing, within the meaning of French domestic law and of the international agreements entered into by France, in particular Article 6 of the European Convention on Human Rights and Article 14 of the New York International Covenant on Civil and Political Rights.[68]

The Paris Tribunal of First Instance subsequently ruled on the claim that the contract binding the parties to the arbitral institution should be terminated. The Court considered the

---

[67] European Convention for the Protection of Human Rights and Fundamental Freedoms, signed at Rome on November 4, 1950, 213 U.N.T.S. 221; International Covenant on Civil and Political Rights, *opened for signature* in New York on December 19, 1966, 999 U.N.T.S. 171. *See* Charles Jarrosson, *L'arbitrage et la Convention européenne des droits de l'homme*, 1989 REV. ARB. 573.

[68] TGI Paris, réf., May 30, 1986, République de Guinée v. Chambre arbitrale de Paris, 1987 REV. ARB. 371, 1st decision.

decisions taken by the institution, held that a serious conflict had arisen, and allowed the claim for termination, concluding that:

> although the impartiality, neutrality and objectivity of all the appointed arbitrators have not been questioned, the objective circumstances described above make it impossible for the Paris Arbitration Chamber to reassure the plaintiff [before the court] that it is participating in arbitral proceedings which in every respect comply with the requirements of Article 6 of the European Convention on Human Rights, in particular its requirements of trust and serenity.[69]

The Paris Court of Appeals reversed both decisions, holding that since the arbitrators had been appointed, the arbitral proceedings could follow their normal course. It was the arbitrators themselves who were responsible for

> guaranteeing . . . the conditions for a 'fair hearing', in accordance with general, fundamental principles and, where appropriate, in accordance with Article 6 of the European Convention for the Protection of Human Rights and Fundamental Freedoms and Article 14 of the New York International Covenant on Civil and Political Rights.[70]

In other words, in keeping with the competence-competence principle,[71] the Court of Appeals considered that since the arbitral tribunal had been definitively constituted, the courts could no longer dispute the organizing role played by the arbitral institution. However, the Court of Appeals did not question the applicability to arbitration of the European Convention on Human Rights and the New York International Covenant on Civil and Political Rights. Nor did it question the duty of the court to guarantee the parties' rights to a fair hearing at all stages of the arbitral proceedings, including during the constitution of the arbitral tribunal. An inequitable system for appointing the arbitral tribunal would thus be rejected by the French courts, even if the parties had agreed to it.

791. — Furthermore, the French courts have held on several occasions that the principle of the equality of the parties must be observed in international arbitration "as a general principle of procedure founded in procedural public policy."[72] In the *Philipp Brothers* case, the Paris Tribunal of First Instance required that each party enjoy "equal treatment in the resolution of the dispute," emphasizing that this applied to, and with effect from, the

---

[69] TGI Paris, Jan. 28, 1987, République de Guinée v. Chambre arbitrale de Paris, 1987 REV. ARB. 371, 3d decision.

[70] CA Paris, Nov. 18, 1987 and May 4, 1988, *Chambre arbitrale de Paris, supra* note 56.

[71] *See supra* paras. 650 *et seq.*

[72] CA Paris, May 25, 1990, Fougerolle v. Procofrance, 1990 REV. CRIT. DIP 753, and B. Oppetit's note; 1990 REV. ARB. 892, and M. de Boisséson's note; *see also* Jean-Hubert Moitry, *Right to a Fair Trial and the European Convention on Human Rights – Some Remarks on the République de Guinée Case*, 6 J. INT'L ARB. 115 (June 1989).

constitution of the arbitral tribunal. However, as we saw earlier, the Tribunal of First Instance concluded that in this case the principle of equality had not been contravened by the system of appointing the arbitrators from lists drawn up in advance by the AFCC.[73]

792. — The application of the principle of equality to the constitution of the arbitral tribunal was examined more closely in the *Dutco* case, where three parties were involved. A consortium agreement between three companies—B.K.M.I., Siemens and Dutco—for the construction of a cement factory contained an arbitration clause stipulating that disputes arising out of the agreement would be submitted to an arbitral tribunal comprising three arbitrators appointed in accordance with the ICC Rules. Dutco initiated proceedings against its two partners and nominated an arbitrator. The ICC Court of Arbitration ordered B.K.M.I. and Siemens to jointly nominate one arbitrator, and it appointed the third arbitrator itself. However, B.K.M.I. and Siemens had differing interests at stake and they therefore contested the Court's order. The arbitral tribunal nevertheless considered itself to be validly constituted, and an application to set aside its award was brought before the Paris Court of Appeals. The two defendants argued, *inter alia*, that nothing in the agreements between the parties nor the ICC Rules indicated that the parties intended to agree to refer their disputes to multi-party arbitration, and that as a result of the principle of equality they could not be deprived of their right to each appoint one trusted arbitrator and thus to participate equally in the constitution of the arbitral tribunal. The Court of Appeals rejected their claim, holding that there had been no violation of the principle of equality in the constitution of the arbitral tribunal as the arbitration clause could have been construed as requiring two of the parties to choose a single arbitrator between them.[74]

The *Cour de cassation* disagreed. On January 7, 1992, in a decision intended to create a precedent, it held that "the principle of the equality of the parties in the designation of the arbitrators is a matter which concerns public policy, which can only be waived after the dispute has arisen."[75] The Court based its decision on Article 1502 2° of the French New Code of Civil Procedure (which provides that the arbitral tribunal must be validly constituted) and Article 6 of the French Civil Code (which concerns compliance with public policy).

This decision was not universally acclaimed. Although there has been no direct criticism of the affirmation of the principle of equality in the appointment of the arbitrators, there has been criticism of the application of the principle to the facts of the case and of the ruling that the parties could not waive it in their arbitration clause. The impact of this decision on the method of appointing arbitrators in institutional arbitration has also provoked an unfavorable

---

[73] TGI Paris, réf., June 29, 1989, *Philipp Brothers, supra* note 32.

[74] CA Paris, May 5, 1989, B.K.M.I. Industrieanlagen GmbH v. Dutco Construction Co. Ltd., 1989 REV. ARB. 723, and P. Bellet's note; 119 J.D.I. 707 (1992), 1st decision, and C. Jarrosson's note; for an English translation, see XV Y.B. COM. ARB. 124 (1990); 4 INT'L ARB. REP. A1 (July 1989).

[75] Cass. 1e civ., Jan. 7, 1992, B.K.M.I. v. Dutco, 1992 Bull. Civ. I, No. 2; 1992 REV. ARB. 470, and P. Bellet's note; 119 J.D.I. 707 (1992), 2d decision, and C. Jarrosson's note; 1992 RTD COM. 796, and observations by J.-C. Dubarry and E. Loquin; for an English translation, see XVIII Y.B. COM. ARB. 140 (1993); 7 INT'L ARB. REP. B1 (Feb. 1992).

reaction, sometimes excessively so, in certain quarters.[76] It is true that a more "liberal" solution could have been reached, based on the intentions of the parties: if three experienced, professional parties sign an arbitration agreement, knowing that between them they will be able to appoint only two arbitrators, does that not amount to a waiver which should take immediate effect? On the other hand, the plaintiff gained a definite and undeserved advantage by having placed its opponents in a delicate position when it would not have been to its disadvantage to sue each defendant separately.

The practical drawbacks of the *Dutco* case have, however, been exaggerated. Arbitral institutions can provide for and resolve situations in which more than two parties to the same contract are involved in the same arbitration, as illustrated by the new rules of the ICC,[77] the LCIA and the AAA.[78] The institutions can even dispense with specifically providing for such cases, as shown by the position taken by the ICC at the time of the *Dutco* case.[79]

In fact, the French *Cour de cassation* simply requires that all the parties should have the same rights with regard to the appointment of the arbitrators, not that they should all have a right to appoint "their" arbitrator. As far as we know, no other supreme court has ever been more "liberal." Since the principle laid down by the court is designed to protect the parties, it is legitimate that the parties should not be entitled to waive that protection before the right to appoint "their" arbitrator has vested. They will only be able to waive their protection once the dispute has arisen and, in practice, when the time comes to constitute the arbitral tribunal. Only then can a party waive its rights to equality of treatment by agreeing to appoint one arbitrator together with its co-defendant (or co-plaintiff).

Similarly, the principle of the equality of the parties in the appointment of the arbitrators, as set forth in the *Dutco* decision, should have no impact on the international validity of the English practice of having each party nominate an arbitrator but, if one party fails to do so before a specified deadline, having the arbitrator nominated by the other party serve as sole arbitrator. English law allows this practice, although the defaulting party may bring the question before the courts.[80] Although in some cases it may lead to difficulties with enforcing an English award abroad,[81] this has not proved to be the case in France and in Italy. The Paris Court of Appeals has ruled that the practice is not contrary to French public

---

[76] In addition to the notes and observations following Cass. le civ., Jan. 7, 1992, *Dutco*, *supra* note 75, see Jean-Louis Delvolvé, *L'arbitrage multipartite en 1992*, 1992 BULL. ASA 154; Jean-Louis Delvolvé, *Multipartism: The Dutco Decision of the French Cour de cassation*, 9 ARB. INT'L 197 (1993); Christopher R. Seppala, *French Supreme Court Nullifies ICC Practice for Appointment of Arbitrators in Multi-party Arbitration Cases*, 10 INT'L CONSTR. L. REV. 222 (1993); P. Bernardini, note following Cass. le civ., Jan. 7, 1992, *Dutco*, 1992 RIV. DELL'ARB. 99.

[77] Art. 10 ("Multiple parties") of the 1998 Arbitration Rules. On this new provision, see *infra* para. 988.

[78] Art. 6(5) of the 1997 AAA International Arbitration Rules; Art. 8 of the 1998 LCIA Rules: unless the parties agree otherwise, the institutions appoint all the arbitrators in such circumstances, irrespective of any nominations made by the parties.

[79] See *Note from the Secretariat of the ICC International Court of Arbitration on the Constitution of Arbitral Tribunals in Multi-Party Cases*, ICC BULLETIN, Vol. 4, No. 2, at 6 (1993). On proposed solutions, see *infra* para. 987. On the solutions reached in practice, see *infra* paras. 986 *et seq.*

[80] Section 17 of the 1996 English Arbitration Act, which replaces Section 7 of the 1950 Arbitration Act. *See* RUSSELL ON ARBITRATION 130 (D. Sutton, J. Kendall, J. Gill eds., 21st ed. 1997).

[81] *See* Claude Reymond, *L'Arbitration Act, 1996 – Convergence et originalité*, 1997 REV. ARB. 45.

policy.[82] This is because the inequality between the parties only emerges after the dispute has arisen, through the deliberate default of one of the parties. The President of the Paris Tribunal of First Instance has held that an arbitration clause containing this kind of mechanism allows the implementation of the arbitration despite the defendant's default, and therefore does not call for court intervention.[83] Likewise, the Italian Supreme Court approved the English approach because it involves a remedy exercisable only at the option of the non-defaulting party, with the arbitral institution (or the English courts) able to intervene if the impartiality of the arbitral tribunal is affected.[84]

793. — In any event, the *Dutco* case quite clearly revealed that the parties' discretion as to their choice of arbitrator is not without its limits, and that the French courts are determined to ensure that the agreement of the parties complies with the fundamental principles of fairness and equality.

B. - THE SUBSIDIARY ROLE OF NATIONAL LAWS

794. — While the position in French law is that the agreement of the parties as to the constitution of the tribunal should take precedence (1°), other legal systems and international conventions have chosen to place more emphasis on the subsidiary role of national law (2°).

1° French Law

795. — Article 1493, paragraph 1 of the French New Code of Civil Procedure leaves the parties to appoint the arbitral tribunal in their agreement. It does not refer to any other rule of French law on the subject, nor does it even suggest that French law might apply. Equally, no decision of the French courts on the constitution of the arbitral tribunal has ever referred to provisions of French law.

The reason for this is very straightforward. Neither the French international arbitration statute, enacted in 1981, nor French case law are founded on the choice of law method. They are instead based on specific substantive rules which grant the parties (and through them arbitral institutions and arbitrators) a great degree of freedom.[85] This can be very clearly seen in Articles 1494 and 1495 of the New Code of Civil Procedure. Under Article 1494, the arbitral proceedings are conducted principally in accordance with the arbitration agreement

---

[82] CA Paris, Jan. 20, 1972, Oromar v. Société Commerciale Matignon (SIMCOMA), 1974 REV. ARB. 105, and P. Fouchard's note.

[83] TGI Paris, Feb. 3, 1997, Delom v. Russanglia Ltd., No. 66545/97, unpublished.

[84] *Corte di Cassazione*, Mar. 14, 1995, SODIME v. Schuurmans & Van Ginnegen BV, XXI Y.B. COM. ARB. 602 (1996).

[85] *See* Berthold Goldman, *La volonté des parties et le rôle de l'arbitre dans l'arbitrage international*, 1981 REV. ARB. 469; E. Gaillard, note following Cass. 1e civ., Dec. 20, 1993, Comité populaire de la municipalité de Khoms El Mergeb v. Dalico Contractors, 121 J.D.I. 432 (1994); *see also supra* paras. 139 *et seq.*

or the arbitration rules, and subsidiarily in accordance with the rules laid down by the arbitrators, although the parties and the arbitrators may specify that the proceedings are to be governed by a procedural law. Article 1495 provides that:

> [w]here the international arbitration is governed by French law, the provisions of Titles I, II and III of the present Book shall only apply in the absence of a specific agreement, and subject to Articles 1493 and 1494.

It is thus possible for French law to apply in addition to the substantive provisions of Articles 1493 *et seq.*, particularly where the parties have chosen French law to govern the procedure. The rules relevant to the constitution of the arbitral tribunal are almost all found in Articles 1451 to 1457 of the New Code of Civil Procedure. These provisions are contained in Chapter III of Title I and all are mandatory, as Article 1459 states that "[a]ny provision or agreement contrary to the rules set forth in the present chapter shall be deemed not written."

796. — In contrast, and as set forth in Article 1495 of the New Code of Civil Procedure, in international arbitration these provisions "only apply in the absence of a specific agreement." They thus lose their mandatory character and become subsidiary to the intentions of the parties. This is consistent with the reference in Article 1495 to Article 1493: the latter provision of course confirms the precedence of the parties' agreement.[86] Their agreement will thus take precedence even where they have chosen French law to govern the procedure, and many of the mandatory requirements of French domestic law will not apply.

797. — These include the rule whereby, in French domestic law, only natural persons may act as arbitrators, and juridical persons are permitted only to organize arbitration proceedings (Art. 1451). As discussed earlier,[87] there is consequently no bar to the appointment of a juridical person as an arbitrator in international arbitration. Of course, the task of judging is necessarily carried out in practice by natural persons, but they will do so as the representatives of the institution in whose name the decision is made. Arbitral institutions, especially in Eastern Europe, may themselves act as arbitrators, although the ICC may not.[88] In any event, French international arbitration law is not opposed to such a practice.

Even before the reform of French international arbitration law in 1981, the French courts proved their liberalism on this issue in the context of *ad hoc* arbitration. A rather unusual arbitration clause stipulated that, where no other arbitrators were appointed, the arbitral tribunal "would comprise the Commercial Court of the Grand Duchy of

---

[86] *See* Daniel Cohen, *La soumission de l'arbitrage international à la loi française (Commentaire de l'article 1495 NCPC)*, 1991 REV. ARB. 155.

[87] *See supra* para. 766.

[88] Pursuant to its Rules, the International Court of Arbitration cannot itself serve as an arbitrator; *see infra* paras. 978 *et seq.*

Luxembourg . . . which would render a final decision."[89] The Paris Court of Appeals rejected the application for the enforcement of a Lebanese court decision in the matter. The Court thus did not question the validity of a clause which appoints a court as the "arbitral jurisdiction." The *Cour de cassation*,[90] dismissing an action against the Court of Appeals' decision, implicitly approved the Court's reasoning and held the clause to be valid. The fact that the chosen arbitral tribunal was a foreign court, rather than one or more natural persons, presented no difficulty under French international arbitration law.

798. — Similarly, in spite of the domestic law provisions to the contrary contained in Articles 1453 and 1454 of the New Code of Civil Procedure,[91] French law will allow an international arbitral tribunal to comprise an even number of arbitrators. The prohibition in domestic arbitration was principally intended to bring an end to the uncertainties and complexities of the old system of the "third arbitrator," whose function was to choose between the opinions of the two other arbitrators. In international arbitration, although arbitral tribunals of two (or four) arbitrators are uncommon, there seemed to be no reason to outlaw them. Any differences of opinion between the first two arbitrators would, in any event, be considered by the French courts to be a difficulty with the constitution of the arbitral tribunal, and would be resolved by appointing a third arbitrator so as to create a majority.[92]

799. — Finally, Article 1455 of the French New Code of Civil Procedure, which concerns cases where, in domestic arbitration, a person is entrusted with the task of organizing an arbitration, also becomes of subsidiary application in international arbitration. Article 1455 was the least well-received provision of the 1980 decree on domestic arbitration, as it reveals a pronounced distrust of institutional arbitration by requiring in principle that the arbitrators be "accepted by all the parties." Thus, even in minor disputes, it is impossible to appoint a sole arbitrator if one party is not in agreement. In practice, it also makes it impossible for an arbitral institution to organize a multiparty arbitration, because when more than two parties are involved the rule requiring the appointment of one arbitrator by each party leads to the constitution of tribunals with too many arbitrators. In such cases the better solution is for the institution to be able to appoint all the arbitrators itself.

In international arbitration, as Article 1455 is only of subsidiary application, its restrictions may be excluded by the rules of arbitral institutions.[93]

---

[89]   CA Paris, Nov. 14, 1975, Italiban v. Lux Air, 103 J.D.I. 429 (1976), and E. Loquin's note; 1976 REV. ARB. 250, and P. Fouchard's note; 1977 REV. CRIT. DIP 526, and D. Alexandre's note.

[90]   Cass. 1e civ., May 3, 1977, Italiban v. Lux Air, 1977 Bull. Civ. I, No. 199; 1978 REV. ARB. 28, and P. Fouchard's note; 1978 REV. CRIT. DIP 367, and D.A.'s note.

[91]   *See* Rubellin-Devichi and Loquin, *supra* note 47, ¶¶ 71 *et seq.*; *see also* CA Paris, May 15, 1987, Association E.S.C.P. v. G.I.E. Marquedit, 1987 REV. ARB. 503, and L. Zollinger's note; CA Paris, Apr. 18, 1989, S.N.C.-M.B.E. v. Fimotel, 1990 REV. ARB. 915, and observations by J.-H. Moitry and C. Vergne.

[92]   On difficulties relating to the constitution of the arbitral tribunal, see *infra* paras. 828 *et seq.*

[93]   On the content of certain of these rules and the practice followed, see *infra* paras. 951 *et seq.*

2° Other Legal Systems and International Conventions

800. — Certain countries whose laws are inspired by French law, such as Lebanon,[94] the Côte d'Ivoire,[95] and Mali,[96] have adopted the approach found in French law. Even when an international arbitration takes place on their territory, their laws apply only if the parties so agree. Algerian law is equally liberal, and does not require that it should be applied by arbitral tribunals sitting in Algeria. Moreover, probably because Algerian domestic law has not yet been modernized, Algerian international arbitration law does not even consider the possibility of applying it on a subsidiary basis.[97]

801. — A number of other modern laws, while recognizing the primacy of the agreement of the parties as to the appointment of the arbitrators, provide for their own application by arbitral tribunals sitting in their jurisdiction. They therefore necessarily play a subsidiary role in the constitution of an arbitral tribunal in that jurisdiction unless the parties agree otherwise. This is the case in Switzerland, the Netherlands, England, and in all legal systems which have adopted the UNCITRAL Model Law.

802. — The same distinctions can be found in international conventions on arbitration.

803. — The 1923 Geneva Protocol and the 1927 Geneva Convention both contain a number of ambiguities. Under the 1923 Protocol, the constitution of the arbitral tribunal is "governed by the will of the parties and by the law of the country in whose territory the arbitration takes place" (Art. 2), while the 1927 Convention requires that the arbitral tribunal be constituted "in the manner agreed upon by the parties and in conformity with the law governing the arbitration procedure" (Art. 1(2)(d)). The constitution of the arbitral tribunal thus depends not only on the intentions of the parties, but also on national law. What exactly is the effect of this combination? Does it mean that the agreement of the parties must comply with national law? Or does it mean that national law applies only on a subsidiary basis, where the parties' agreement fails to make sufficient provision for the appointment of the

---

[94] *See* Arts. 810–13 of the Lebanese Code of Civil Procedure.

[95] *See* Arts. 51–53 of the Law of August 9, 1993.

[96] *See* Arts. 929–31 of the Code of Civil Procedure (Official Journal of the Republic of Mali, July 15, 1994), *reprinted in* JUSTICE ET DÉVELOPPEMENT – LE RÔLE DE L'ARBITRAGE COMMERCIAL INTERNATIONAL – ACTES DU SÉMINAIRE DE PERFECTIONNEMENT, LE CAIRE, 14–21 DÉC. 1996, at 216 *et seq.* (1997).

[97] *See* Arts. 458 bis 2 and 458 bis 6 of Law Decree No. 93-09 of April 25, 1993.

arbitrators? Authors do not all agree,[98] but the courts, particularly in Italy,[99] Switzerland[100] and France,[101] have tended to hold that the intentions of the parties prevail, with the relevant law, particularly that of the seat of the arbitration, only applying on a subsidiary basis or where the parties have so elected.

804. — One of the most innovative provisions of the 1958 New York Convention stipulates that the agreement of the parties as to the constitution of the tribunal takes precedence, and that the national law of the country where the arbitration takes place applies only where the agreement of the parties does not allow the tribunal to be properly constituted. According to Article V, paragraph 1(d) of the Convention, recognition and enforcement of the award may be refused if it is established that:

> [t]he composition of the arbitral authority . . . was not in accordance with the agreement of the parties, or, failing such agreement, was not in accordance with the law of the country where the arbitration took place.

Almost all commentators have noted and approved the priority thus given not only to the arbitration agreement, but also to the rules and practice of arbitral institutions.[102] Although

---

[98] *See* JEAN ROBERT, ARBITRAGE CIVIL ET COMMERCIAL ¶¶ 293 and 341 (4th ed. 1967), and the references cited therein; Frédéric-Edouard Klein, *Autonomie de la volonté et arbitrage*, 1958 REV. CRIT. DIP 479, 484; Henri Motulsky and Rudolf Bruns, *Tendances et perspectives de l'arbitrage international (à propos de la réforme de la Convention de Genève de 1927)*, 1957 RID COMP. 717, at 724 *et seq.*; HENRI MOTULSKY, ECRITS – VOL. 2 – ETUDES ET NOTES SUR L'ARBITRAGE 493 *et seq.* (1974); FOUCHARD, *supra* note 15, ¶ 511, and the references cited therein.

[99] *Corte di Cassazione*, Mar. 27, 1954, Delfino et Cie. v. Compagnie du Niger français, 1955 REV. ARB. 107; 1956 REV. CRIT. DIP 511, and H. Motulsky and E. Barda's note; MOTULSKY, *supra* note 98, at 304.

[100] Vaud Cantonal Tribunal, Nov. 24, 1948, Omnium français des pétroles v. Gianotti, [SW.] JOURN. TRIB. 1949.III.112; CA of the Canton of Berne, May 12, 1954, P. B. Fr. L., v. D. W., 1955 REV. ARB. 27; Geneva Trib. of First Instance, July 2, 1959, Rhodiaceta S.A. v. Montecatini S.A., 1959 REV. ARB. 90.

[101] CA Paris, Dec. 9, 1955, Goldschmidt v. Vis et Zoon, 1955 REV. ARB. 101; 1956 REV. CRIT. DIP 523, and H. Motulsky's note; MOTULSKY, *supra* note 98, at 457; Dalloz, Jur. 217 (1956), and J. Robert's note; *see also* CA Nancy, Jan. 29, 1958, Elmassian v. Veuve Henri Broutchoux, 1958 REV. ARB. 122, and article by Yvon Loussouarn, *Remarque sur un récent arrêt, id.* at 114; 1958 REV. CRIT. DIP 148, and E. Mezger's note; 86 J.D.I. 128 (1959), and J. Robert's note; Cass. com, Mar. 17, 1964, Société Franco-Tunisienne d'Armement v. Goldschmidt, 1964 REV. ARB. 46; the December 22, 1954 Award, L. Python presiding, The Alsing Trading Co., Ltd. v. Etat Hellénique, 1955 REV. ARB. No. 2, at 27; for an English translation, see 23 INT'L L. REP. 633 (1956); *see also* Stephen M. Schwebel, *The Alsing Case*, 8 INT'L & COMP. L.Q. 320 (1959).

[102] *See* Jean Robert, *La Convention de New York du 10 juin 1958 pour la reconnaissance et l'exécution des sentences arbitrales étrangères*, Dalloz, Chron. 223, 226 (1958); Henri Motulsky, *L'évolution récente en matière d'arbitrage international*, 1959 REV. ARB. 2; MOTULSKY, *supra* note 98, at 295; Jean-Denis Bredin, *La Convention de New-York du 10 juin 1958 pour la reconnaissance et l'exécution des sentences arbitrales étrangères/The New York Convention of June 10th 1958 for the Recognition and Enforcement of Foreign Arbitral Awards*, 87 J.D.I. 1022 (1960); FOUCHARD, *supra* note 15, ¶ 52; Berthold Goldman, *Arbitrage (droit international privé)*, *in* ENCYCLOPÉDIE DALLOZ – DROIT INTERNATIONAL ¶ 208 (1968); Pieter Sanders, *A Twenty Years' Review of the Convention on the Recognition and Enforcement of Foreign Arbitral Awards*, 13 INT'L LAW. 269 (1979), and, for the French version, *Vingt années de la Convention de New York de 1958*, 1979 DPCI 359, 368; *comp. with* ALBERT JAN VAN DEN BERG, THE NEW YORK ARBITRATION CONVENTION OF

(continued...)

there is the occasional author who considers that neither the purpose nor the effect of the New York Convention is to allow the intentions of the parties to freely govern the constitution of the arbitral tribunal and the arbitral proceedings,[103] the Convention's *travaux préparatoires* squarely contradict that view.[104]

805. — Most court decisions interpreting and applying Article V, paragraph 1(d) have held that the agreement of the parties and institutional arbitration rules should take precedence. Thus, the Florence Court of Appeals, considering an arbitration clause providing for a tribunal of three arbitrators sitting in London, refused to enforce an award made by only two arbitrators in accordance with English law but contrary to the intentions of the parties.[105] The U.S. Court of Appeals for the Second Circuit[106] rejected a claim based on Article V, paragraph 1(d) of the Convention on the grounds that the appellant had agreed to the ICC appointing the sole arbitrator, and that the terms of reference had confirmed the jurisdiction of the arbitrator and Geneva as the place of arbitration.[107] A similar result was reached in an ICC award made in Cairo in 1984, which was also founded upon Article V, paragraph 1(d) of the New York Convention.[108] The tribunal held that the intentions of the parties, and therefore the ICC Rules regarding the appointment of the arbitral tribunal, prevailed over Article 502 of the Egyptian Code of Civil Procedure, which required the arbitration clause to specify the names of the arbitrators. Nonetheless, the law of the place

---

[102](...continued)
1958, at 325 (1981).

[103] Arthur Bülow, *La convention des parties relative à la procédure d'arbitrage visée à l'Art. V, par. 1, litt. d) de la Convention de New York, in* COMMERCIAL ARBITRATION – ESSAYS IN MEMORIAM EUGENIO MINOLI 81 (1974).

[104] See also the concurring view of Pieter Sanders, *The New York Convention, in* UNION INTERNATIONALE DES AVOCATS, ARBITRAGE INTERNATIONAL COMMERCIAL – INTERNATIONAL COMMERCIAL ARBITRATION, Vol. II, at 293, 317 (P. Sanders ed., 1960); FOUCHARD, *supra* note 15, ¶ 512, and the references cited therein; Albert Jan van den Berg, *New York Convention of 1958 – Consolidated Commentary – Cases Reported in Volumes XX (1995) – XXI (1996)*, XXI Y.B. COM. ARB. 394, ¶ 513 at 491 (1996).

[105] *Corte di Appello* of Florence, Apr. 13, 1978, Rederi Aktiebolaget Sally v. S.r.l. Termarea, IV Y.B. COM. ARB. 294, ¶ 32 (1979).

[106] Mechanised Constr. of Pak. Ltd. v. American Constr. Mach. and Equip. Corp. (ACME), 828 F.2d 117 (2d Cir. 1987); XV Y.B. COM. ARB. 539, para. 6 at 542 (1990).

[107] See also, confirming the primacy of the intentions of the parties under Art. V(1)(d), Geneva Tribunal of First Instance, Mar. 13, 1986, Maritime International Nominees Establishment (MINE) v. Republic of Guinea, XII Y.B. COM. ARB. 514, ¶ 13 at 522 (1987); 1 INT'L ARB. REP. 363 (May 1986); 1 ICSID REV. – FOREIGN INV. L.J. 383 (1986); Swiss Fed. Trib., Feb. 26, 1982, Joseph Müller A.G. v. Sigval Bergesen, ATF 108 Ib 85; 38 ANN. SUISSE DR. INTERN. 344 (1982); for an English translation, see IX Y.B. COM. ARB. 437, ¶¶ 2, 6 and 10 at 438–40 (1984); Spanish *Tribunal Supremo*, June 17, 1983, Ludmila C. Shipping Co. Ltd. v. Maderas G.L., S.A., XI Y.B. COM. ARB. 525, ¶ 4 at 526 (1986); Italian *Corte di Cassazione*, Jan. 20, 1995, Conceria G. De Maio & F. snc v. EMAG AG, XXI Y.B. COM. ARB. 602, ¶ 8 at 605–06 (1996).

[108] ICC Award No. 4406 (1984), X v. Y, 1986 REV. ARB. 469, and H. Synvet's note; for a commentary, see also ABDUL HAMID EL-AHDAB, L'ARBITRAGE DANS LES PAYS ARABES 984 (1988).

of arbitration will apply on a subsidiary basis, in particular to give effect to an arbitration clause that fails to indicate the number of arbitrators or the method of their appointment.[109]

806. — Commentators and the courts accept that the parties may choose a national law, in particular that of the country where the arbitration is to take place, to govern how the arbitral tribunal is to be constituted.[110] The application of the law of the place of arbitration either on a subsidiary basis or as a result of a choice made by the parties does not give rise to any of the drawbacks inherent in its mandatory application.[111]

807. — The 1961 European Convention went one step further: its authors deliberately refused to subject the constitution of the arbitral tribunal to national law, even on a subsidiary basis (Art. IV). Where the agreement of the parties fails to adequately provide for the appointment of the arbitral tribunal, the arbitrators are instead appointed by various professional bodies, with a distinction being made between *ad hoc* and institutional arbitration.[112]

C. – RECOGNITION OF THE ROLE OF ARBITRAL INSTITUTIONS

808. — The legitimacy of institutional arbitration was acknowledged earlier and more forcefully in international conventions on arbitration (1°) than in national legal systems (2°), and particularly French law (3°).

1° International Conventions

809. — We shall consider three conventions which, each in its own way, have made significant contributions to the international recognition of institutional arbitration: the New York Convention (a), the European Convention (b) and the Washington Convention (c).[113]

---

[109] *See Corte di Appelo* of Naples, Mar. 22, 1980, Federal Commerce & Navigation Co., Ltd. v. Giuseppe Rocco e Figli, 1981 RASS. DELL'ARB. 265; for an English translation, see VIII Y.B. COM. ARB. 380 (1983).

[110] *See* VAN DEN BERG, *supra* note 102, at 325 *et seq.*; Italian *Corte di Cassazione*, Feb. 8, 1982, Fratelli Damiano s.n.c. v. August Tropfer & Co., IX Y.B. COM. ARB. 418, ¶ 8 at 420–21 (1984); Associated Bulk Carriers of Berm. v. Mineral Import Export of Bucharest, No. 79 Civ. 5439, 1980 U.S. Dist. LEXIS 9005 (S.D.N.Y. Jan. 31, 1980); IX Y.B. COM. ARB. 462, ¶¶ 2 and 3 at 463–64 (1984).

[111] On the importance of this connection as regards the arbitration agreement, see *supra* para. 429, and as regards the arbitral procedure, see *infra* paras. 1178 *et seq.*; FOUCHARD, *supra* note 15, ¶¶ 114 *et seq.* and 498.

[112] On the system set up by the 1961 European Convention to resolve difficulties with the constitution of the arbitral tribunal, see *infra* para. 924.

[113] Regional conventions which have made relevant contributions include the 1975 Inter-American Convention on International Commercial Arbitration and the 1987 Amman Convention; *see supra* paras. 294 and 297.

a) The 1958 New York Convention

810. — Article I, paragraph 2 of the New York Convention provides that:

[t]he term 'arbitral awards' shall include not only awards made by arbitrators appointed for each case but also those made by permanent arbitral bodies to which the parties have submitted.[114]

811. — This endorsement of the role of permanent arbitral institutions was not merely an "indirect, superfluous, but legitimate tribute" to the efforts of the ICC in drafting the New York Convention,[115] nor simply the expression of an "important trend" in favor of the "formal integration of arbitral institutions in international arbitration law."[116] This provision in fact has its origins in a Czechoslovak amendment[117] which sought to combat the mistrust of certain courts, particularly Swiss, towards arbitral institutions of foreign trade chambers in socialist countries,[118] and more generally towards arbitral tribunals set up by professional associations or unions.[119] The position taken by those courts was rejected by the Convention, at least in principle, and that is how the Convention has been interpreted and applied.[120]

812. — The relevance of this provision has been called into question on the grounds that it is still necessary for the parties to stipulate that they wish to submit their dispute to institutional arbitration.[121] However, the importance of the role of those institutions in the organization of the arbitration should not be underestimated. As we shall see,[122] the involvement of arbitral institutions and the application of their rules give rise to arbitrations which are different, both in fact and law, from *ad hoc* arbitrations. The latter are of course directly and exclusively dependent, for each dispute, on the intentions of the parties and on the powers they confer on the arbitrators. In institutional arbitration, however, those

---

[114] On this Convention, see *supra* para. 247.

[115] Bredin, *supra* note 102, at 1014.

[116] Robert, *supra* note 102, at 223.

[117] *See* FOUCHARD, *supra* note 15, ¶ 336.

[118] *See* Sup. Trib. of the Zurich Canton, Mar. 15, 1957, Ligna v. Baumgartner et Cie. S.A., *overturned*, Swiss Fed. Trib., Feb. 12, 1958, 1958 REV. ARB. 59 and 1959 REV. ARB. 25; 1959 REV. CRIT. DIP 324, 2 decisions, and E. Mezger's note.

[119] *See* Swiss Fed. Trib., Oct. 13, 1954, Fédération suisse du Tabac v. Dame Ekimoff, 1956 REV. ARB. 106; Swiss Fed. Trib., Dec. 7, 1955, Lunesa Watch S.A. v. F.H., 1957 REV. ARB. 26.

[120] See, for example, among more recent decisions: concerning the Foreign Trade Arbitration Commission of the USSR Chamber of Commerce and Industry, Court of Appeal of Bermuda, July 7, 1989, Sojuznefteexport (SNE) v. Joc Oil Ltd., XV Y.B. COM. ARB. 384 (1990); 4 INT'L ARB. REP. B1 (July 1989); concerning the arbitration board of the Vienna Commodity Exchange, *Corte di Appello* of Florence, June 3, 1988, Holzindustrie Schweighofer GmbH v. Industria Legnami Trentina – ILET srl, 1989 RASS. DELL'ARB. 72; XV Y.B. COM. ARB. 498 (1990); see also, on this point, VAN DEN BERG, *supra* note 102, at 379–80, n. 405, which cites earlier decisions which applied this provision in Switzerland and Italy.

[121] VAN DEN BERG, *supra* note 102, at 379–80, n. 405; van den Berg, *supra* note 104, ¶ 111 at 447.

[122] *See infra* paras. 974 *et seq.*

intentions are less directly apparent as the parties' agreement will refer to an institution and its rules. It is therefore useful to have formal confirmation of the validity of institutional arbitration and thus of the fundamental distinction between it and *ad hoc* arbitration.

813. — Although the New York Convention is not innovative in this respect, the wording of its Article I, paragraph 2 clears up another ambiguity: it allows the arbitral institutions to make awards themselves. Of course, individuals are still involved within the arbitral tribunal, but the tribunal simply acts in the name of the institution and is not distinguished from it. In other words, the Convention allows a juridical person to be an arbitrator itself, a practice prohibited in French domestic law, for example.[123]

b) The 1961 European Convention

814. — Institutional arbitration is expressly recognized by the 1961 European Convention, Article I, paragraph 2(d) of which states that:

> the term 'arbitration' shall mean not only settlement by arbitrators appointed
> for each case (*ad hoc* arbitration) but also by permanent arbitral institutions.

This provision confirms the validity of institutional arbitration in the same way as the New York Convention.[124] However, the background to the European Convention, which was negotiated under the auspices of the Committee on the Development of Trade of the Economic Commission for Europe to promote economic relations between East and West, ensured that this confirmation had a specific political impact: socialist countries recognized the legitimacy of arbitration organized by professional associations and chambers of commerce in the West, and in particular the ICC; more importantly perhaps, there was a reciprocal recognition of the legitimacy of the arbitration commissions set up in each socialist country's foreign trade chamber and which in fact monopolized international arbitration in those countries.

815. — However, the most important provision in this connection appears in Article IV, paragraph 1 of the Convention, which reads as follows:

> The parties to an arbitration agreement shall be free to submit their disputes:

> (*a*) to a permanent arbitral institution; in this case, the arbitration proceedings
> shall be held in conformity with the rules of the said institution.

---

[123] *See* Arts. 1451 and 1455 of the French New Code of Civil Procedure; *see also supra* para. 766.

[124] On the application of these provisions, see Spanish *Tribunal Supremo*, July 13, 1982, Billerud Uddeholm Aktiebolag v. R. Cervigón Guerra, XIV Y.B. COM. ARB. 699 (1989).

The choice of an arbitral institution by the parties thus implies that the rules of that center automatically apply. That is the rule in French law,[125] but certain other legal systems are more circumspect and consider that a reference to an arbitral institution merely raises a presumption that the parties have agreed that their disputes are subject to the institution's procedural rules, and that they are familiar with those rules. This presumption is not necessarily irrebuttable, and the professional experience of the parties, the role of the chosen institution in the relevant business sector and the wording of the arbitration agreement are factors used to rebut or support it. The advantages for the efficiency of institutional arbitration of a rule as clear as that contained in the European Convention are thus apparent.

The efficiency of institutional arbitration is further bolstered by the total autonomy which the arbitral institutions enjoy under the Convention. The institutions' rules apply directly, with no need for authorization by, or compliance with, national law. Thus the autonomy of arbitral institutions does not result from choice of law rules, whether subsidiary or otherwise.

816. — As regards the constitution of the arbitral tribunal, the scope of the rule contained in Article IV, paragraph 1 is evident: all aspects of the process of appointing the arbitrators, including their number, their qualifications and the possibility of challenging and replacing them, are governed exclusively by the rules of the chosen institution, and the parties need not provide for them in their arbitration agreement.[126] In most cases, the rules leave the parties with a predominant role, but they also empower the institution to supervise or assist the parties to a greater or lesser extent.[127] The European Convention thus confirms the validity of the methods of appointing the arbitrators adopted by arbitral institutions.

817. — The Convention ensures that institutional arbitration is favored even in borderline situations. Article IV, paragraph 5 provides that:

> Where the parties have agreed to submit their disputes to a permanent arbitral institution without determining the institution in question and cannot agree thereon, the claimant may request the determination of such institution in conformity with the procedure referred to in paragraph 3 above.

Using a rather complicated procedure,[128] an external non-judicial authority will give effect to a somewhat uncertain common intention whereby the parties, although in favor of an institutional arbitration, have not agreed on the institution to which their dispute is to be submitted. This issue came before the German Federal Court in a case where a German and an Italian party disagreed as to the identity of the arbitral institution they had chosen in

---

[125] *See infra* paras. 822 *et seq.*

[126] *See* Spanish *Tribunal Supremo*, Apr. 26, 1984, Mondial Grain Distributors Co. Inc. v. Atlántica Canarias SA, XVI Y.B. COM. ARB. 599 (1991).

[127] On the different institutional systems for appointing arbitrators, see *infra* paras. 974 *et seq.*

[128] *See infra* paras. 924 *et seq.*

Hamburg.[129] The Federal Court upheld the decision of the lower court to set aside the award on the grounds that the arbitral tribunal appointed by the institution chosen by the plaintiff had no jurisdiction, thus disregarding Article IV, paragraph 5 of the European Convention. Admittedly, it is difficult for a Supreme Court to perfect the parties' consent at such a late stage. However, if used at the appropriate juncture, this mechanism could salvage at least some pathological arbitration agreements.

c) The 1965 Washington Convention

818. — The 1965 Washington Convention makes a more concrete contribution to institutional arbitration by establishing a permanent arbitral institution operating in a particular context: the International Centre for Settlement of Investment Disputes (ICSID). Its headquarters are located at the World Bank in Washington, D.C., and the World Bank was the driving force behind the institution's creation. ICSID arbitration procedure is determined either by the Convention, or by its rules of arbitration.[130]

2° Recent Arbitration Statutes

819. — The trend of international conventions recognizing the legitimacy of institutional arbitration has had a direct influence on national legal systems. Although in the past certain courts were wary of institutionalizing a private form of justice,[131] the ratification of the New York Convention led to acceptance of institutional arbitration in national law. As a matter of principle, the courts nowadays will, during the arbitral proceedings, refuse to review the exercise by arbitral institutions of their powers regarding the constitution of the arbitral tribunal.[132] Recent statutes have also recognized the distinction between *ad hoc* and institutional arbitration. For example, Article 2 of the UNCITRAL Model Law states that:

---

[129] *See* P. Schlosser, note following German *Bundesgerichtshof*, Dec. 2, 1982, Firma Wunsche Handelsgesellschaft v. Firma Coop. "S. Maria" s.a.r.l., 1983 REV. ARB. 353.

[130] On this Convention, see *supra* para. 301; among an extensive bibliography, see Aron Broches, *The Convention on the Settlement of Investment Disputes Between States and Nationals of Other States*, in COLLECTED COURSES OF THE HAGUE ACADEMY OF INTERNATIONAL LAW, Vol. 136, Year 1972, Part II, at 331; Georges R. Delaume, *Le Centre International pour le Règlement des Différends Relatifs aux Investissements (C.I.R.D.I.)*, 109 J.D.I. 775 (1982); Christoph Schreuer, *Commentary on the ICSID Convention*, 11 ICSID REV. – FOREIGN INV. L.J. 318 (1996); 12 ICSID REV. – FOREIGN INV. L.J. 59 and 365 (1997); 13 ICSID REV. – FOREIGN INV. L.J. 150 (1998); Emmanuel Gaillard, *Centre International pour le Règlement des Différends Relatifs aux Investissements (C.I.R.D.I.) – Chronique des sentences arbitrales*, published yearly in the JOURNAL DU DROIT INTERNATIONAL since 1986; ARON BROCHES, SELECTED ESSAYS – WORLD BANK, ICSID, AND OTHER SUBJECTS OF PUBLIC AND PRIVATE INTERNATIONAL LAW (1995).

[131] For example in Switzerland; *see supra* para. 811.

[132] For example, the Belgian courts held that they had no jurisdiction to order an arbitral institution to constitute a three-member arbitral tribunal where the institution, applying its rules, had appointed a sole arbitrator (Brussels Trib. of First Inst., réf., Dec. 24, 1993, *Koninklijke Sphinx*, *supra* note 57).

for the purposes of this Law:

(*a*) 'arbitration' means any arbitration whether or not administered by a permanent arbitral institution.

3° French Law

820. — We have seen that in French domestic arbitration law[133] a juridical person may organize an arbitration, but that there are some restrictions on its power to appoint arbitrators.

821. — In international arbitration, however, arbitral institutions did not need express recognition by statute. Nevertheless, by imposing no specific restrictions, Article 1493, paragraph 1 of the New Code of Civil Procedure, together with Article 1495, endorses the prominent role played by arbitral institutions in the appointment of arbitral tribunals.

Further, in giving priority to the arbitration agreement, Article 1493 specifies that that agreement may appoint the tribunal either "directly" or "by reference to arbitration rules," thus recognizing the importance of such rules in practice. Of course, there are a number of *ad hoc* arbitration rules, such as the UNCITRAL Rules,[134] but Article 1493 principally refers to rules drawn up by arbitral institutions.

822. — The French courts have consistently confirmed that a reference in an arbitration agreement to an arbitral institution entails the application of that institution's rules.[135] For example, the *Cour de cassation* ruled in one case that:

---

[133] *See* Arts. 1451 and 1455 of the New Code of Civil Procedure.

[134] On these rules, see *supra* paras. 200 and *infra* paras. 963 *et seq.*

[135] Cass. civ., Feb. 26, 1941, Compagnie continentale d'importation du Sud-Ouest v. Passerieux, Sirey, Pt. I, at 53 (1941); FOUCHARD, *supra* note 15, ¶ 472, and the references cited n. 3; CA Paris, Feb. 21, 1980, General National Maritime Transport Co. v. Götaverken Arendal A.B., 107 J.D.I. 660 (1980), and P. Fouchard's note; 1980 REV. ARB. 524, and F.C. Jeantet's note; Dalloz, Jur. 568 (1980), and J. Robert's note; 1980 REV. CRIT. DIP 763, and E. Mezger's note; JCP, Ed. G., Pt. II, No. 19,512 (1981), and P. Level's note; for an English translation, see VI Y.B. COM. ARB. 221 (1981); 20 I.L.M. 883 (1981), with an introductory note by F.C. Jeantet; CA Paris, Dec. 9, 1980, Aksa v. Norsolor, 1981 REV. ARB. 306, and F.C. Jeantet's note; 1981 REV. CRIT. DIP 545, and E. Mezger's note; for an English translation, see 20 I.L.M. 887 (1981); CA Paris, Jan. 22, 1982, Appareils Dragon v. Construimport, 1982 REV. ARB. 91, 2d decision, and E. Mezger's note; *see also* Cass. 2e civ., June 8, 1983, Appareils Dragon v. Empresa central de abastecimientas y vantas de equipos, and CA Paris, May 17, 1983, Techni Import Professionnel (T.I.P.) v. Electro Scientific Industries (E.S.I.), 1987 REV. ARB. 309; CA Paris, Nov. 18, 1983, Intercontinental Hotels NV v. Istanbul Turizm Ve Otelcilik, 1987 REV. ARB. 77, and observations by T. Bernard; CA Paris, Jan. 15, 1985, Opinter France v. Dacomex, 1986 REV. ARB. 87, and E. Mezger's note; CA Paris, Apr. 26, 1985, Abess Bros. and Sons Ltd. v. Société des Grands Moulins de Pantin, 1986 REV. ARB. 98, and observations by T. Bernard; CA Paris, Nov. 29, 1985, Société commerciale de produits agricoles (S.C.P.A.) v. Société coopérative de la Roche Clermault, 1987 REV. ARB. 335.

the 'Synacomex clause,' whereby the parties were to submit their disputes to the Paris Arbitration Chamber, necessarily implied that the parties would adopt the rules of that institution.[136]

Likewise, the Paris Court of Appeals held in a different matter that:

> In the present case, [the parties] agreed to resort to arbitration by the ICC Court of Arbitration and thereby subjected themselves, in the absence of any contrary provision, to the rules of that Court.[137]

823. — The rule was also applied, in connection with the appointment of arbitrators, in the *République de Guinée* case.[138] The Paris Tribunal of First Instance held, for example, that:

> the Republic of Guinea and the defendant companies, by appointing the Paris Arbitration Chamber to organize their arbitration, accepted that its rules would govern their proceedings, thus empowering that permanent institution to organize the arbitral proceedings in accordance with its statutes and rules.[139]

824. — The issue also arose in the *Raffineries de pétrole d'Homs et de Banias* case, where the ICC Court of Arbitration dismissed an arbitrator[140] on the basis of the ICC Rules. The Paris Tribunal of First Instance held that:

> the common intentions of the parties . . . may validly provide for a third party to organize and supervise the arbitral proceedings . . . . Thus, the mutual and unequivocal intention of the parties was to grant that role to a single third party (the ICC Court of Arbitration) and to resolve all problems concerning the nomination and the confirmation of the arbitrators by reference to one rule only (Article 13 of the Internal Rules).[141]

The Paris Court of Appeals subsequently confirmed the jurisdiction of the ICC and the exclusive application of its rules in clearer terms still:

---

[136] Cass. com., May 19, 1987, Caille v. Peter Cremer France, 1987 Bull. Civ. IV, No. 117; 1988 REV. ARB. 142, and P. Ancel's note.

[137] CA Paris, July 7, 1987, Pia Investments Ltd. v. Cassia, 1988 REV. ARB. 649, and E. Mezger's note.

[138] CA Paris, Nov. 18, 1987 and May 4, 1988, *Chambre arbitrale de Paris*, *supra* note 56.

[139] TGI Paris, réf., June 23, 1988, République de Guinée v. MM. R... et O..., 1988 REV. ARB. 657, 3d decision, and P. Fouchard's note.

[140] On challenges of arbitrators, see *infra* paras. 871 *et seq.*

[141] TGI Paris, réf., Mar. 28, 1984, *supra* note 50.

It has been established that the arbitration in question . . . is an international arbitration governed by the intentions of the parties. In this case, the rules of domestic law have a purely subsidiary role and apply only in the absence of a specific agreement by the parties . . . . Since the seat of arbitration is outside France, and no reference has been made to French procedural law, the rules of the Court of Arbitration, which constitute the law of the parties, must be applied to the exclusion of all other laws.[142]

825. — Similarly, in the *Philipp Brothers* case, the Paris Tribunal of First Instance held that:

in this instance, by agreeing to the arbitration clause in the disputed contracts designating the Chambre arbitrale de l'Association Française pour le Commerce des Cacaos as the organization administering the arbitration, Philipp Brothers agreed with full knowledge and without any reservation to the application of the rules of that chamber.[143]

And, in the same case, the Paris Court of Appeals refused to hold the composition of the arbitral tribunals to be irregular, on the grounds that:

the method of appointing the arbitrators is determined by the Rules of the Chambre arbitrale de l'Association Française pour le Commerce des Cacaos. The parties, having referred to those rules in their arbitration agreement, accepted them as constituting their procedural law.[144]

826. — The role of arbitral institutions is therefore fully recognized because their rules have been held to be binding where the parties have incorporated them in their arbitration agreements.[145] More specifically, by giving full effect to Article 1493 of the New Code of Civil Procedure, the French courts refuse to interfere with the mechanisms for appointing the arbitral tribunal or to review the exercise of the powers conferred by institutional rules on the institutions themselves. This was the case in the various decisions discussed above (including *Raffineries d'Homs et de Banias*, *République de Guinée*, *Philipp Brothers* and *Dutco*), where the applicable institutional rules could only be contested by way of an action to enforce or set aside any award rendered under the auspices of the institution chosen by

---

[142] CA Paris, May 15, 1985, Raffineries de pétrole d'Homs et de Banias v. Chambre de Commerce Internationale, 1985 REV. ARB. 141, 2d decision; JCP, Ed. G., Pt. II, No. 20,755 (1987), and P. Level's note.

[143] TGI Paris, réf., Oct. 28, 1988, *Drexel Burnham Lambert*, and June 29, 1989, *Philipp Brothers*, *supra* note 32.

[144] CA Paris, Apr. 6, 1990, *Philipp Brothers*, *supra* note 33.

[145] The French *Cour de cassation* has underlined that, when the parties refer to institutional rules, those rules "serve as the procedural law" (Cass. 1e civ., June 17, 1997, Thomson CSF v. Groupement Sanitec Megco (Beyrouth),1998 REV. ARB. 414, and L. Kiffer's note).

the parties.[146] In particular, the courts will not consider the rules to give rise to an action in tort, nor will they interfere in the setting up of the arbitral tribunal by the arbitral institution.[147]

827. — Arbitral institutions are at liberty to provide in their rules that the institution will only intervene on a subsidiary basis to resolve difficulties with the appointment of the arbitrators. Equally, they may provide that the institution will play a more active role, either by compiling lists of arbitrators from which the parties are free to choose, or by reserving a right to confirm (or reject) the arbitrators proposed by the parties or the party-appointed arbitrators, or even by itself directly appointing some or all of the arbitrators (usually the sole arbitrator or the third arbitrator).[148]

§2. – Difficulties in the Constitution of the Arbitral Tribunal

828. — The Achilles' heel of arbitration is the situation where the parties disagree as to the appointment of the arbitral tribunal, especially once the dispute has arisen. For an arbitration to be efficient, the parties need the assistance of an appointing authority empowered to prevent paralysis in the process of constituting the arbitral tribunal, to appoint the arbitrator or arbitrators in the event that the parties (or the arbitrators already appointed) refuse to do so or disagree, and to resolve problems concerning the challenge and replacement of the members of the tribunal.

829. — In institutional arbitration, the predetermined third party acting as an appointing authority will be the institution itself. In *ad hoc* arbitration, that third party may be identified in the arbitration clause or in the rules to which the clause refers, and its powers will therefore be those conferred, directly or indirectly, by the parties. Not surprisingly, international arbitral practice on this question is very varied and merits a separate discussion.[149]

830. — National laws give the parties absolute freedom in this area. The primacy of the parties' agreement, as we have already seen with regard to the appointment of the tribunal, necessarily applies to difficulties encountered in its constitution.

831. — Recent arbitration statutes go further still. Seeking to give full effect to the arbitration agreement, and following the example set by French law (A), they now provide for the intervention of the courts to assist with the constitution or reconstitution of the

---

[146] *See* Philippe Fouchard, *Les institutions permanentes d'arbitrage devant le juge étatique (A propos d'une jurisprudence récente)*, 1987 REV. ARB. 225.

[147] *See infra* para. 849.

[148] On the mechanisms used in practice and in arbitration rules to appoint arbitrators, see *infra* paras. 974 *et seq.*

[149] *See infra* paras. 951 *et seq.*

arbitral tribunal (B). In contrast, the 1961 European Convention and the 1965 Washington Convention do not provide for recourse to the courts in such circumstances (C).

A. – FRENCH LAW

832. — Article 1493, paragraph 2 of the French New Code of Civil Procedure provides that:

> If a difficulty arises in the constitution of the arbitral tribunal in an arbitration which takes place in France or which the parties have agreed shall be governed by French procedural law, the most diligent party may, in the absence of a clause to the contrary, apply to the President of the *Tribunal de Grande Instance* of Paris in accordance with the procedures of Article 1457.

This provision thus allows a French judge to intervene in international arbitrations to resolve difficulties concerning the constitution of the arbitral tribunal. There was no equivalent rule in the old Code of Civil Procedure, but the new text has adopted and expanded upon the position taken in earlier case law. That case law reflected the fundamental principle that since the arbitration clause is fully effective in its own right, it is the duty of the courts, if requested, to ensure that the clause be enforced. Effective enforcement of an arbitration agreement can only mean requiring it to be performed. This leads the court to intervene in the initial phase of organizing the arbitration, which may involve appointing the arbitrators themselves.

833. — The French decree of 1980 had already attributed a similar role to the same judge in domestic arbitration, under the provision which later became Article 1444 of the New Code of Civil Procedure.[150]

French domestic arbitration law also singles out certain other situations in which the courts may assist with the constitution of the arbitral tribunal. For example, Article 1454 authorizes the courts to appoint an arbitrator to an arbitral tribunal initially constituted with an even number of arbitrators. That provision is of course irrelevant in international arbitration as an arbitral tribunal need not comprise an uneven number of arbitrators.[151] However, there are doubts as to whether Article 1463, which stipulates that difficulties concerning a party's challenge of an arbitrator shall be referred to the courts, applies to international arbitration.[152] On the other hand, Article 1457, which concerns the procedure for seeking court intervention, clearly does apply to international arbitration, as Article 1493, paragraph 2 expressly refers to it.

---

[150] *See infra* paras. 851 *et seq.*

[151] *See supra* para. 770.

[152] *See infra* para. 872.

834. — The involvement of the courts in the constitution of the arbitral tribunal is nevertheless a fairly recent phenomenon. Far from constituting unacceptable interference with the functioning of private justice, the courts' involvement is in fact a form of assistance sought and granted when necessary for the arbitration agreement to be fully effective.[153]

The relatively broad scope of Article 1493, paragraph 2 has facilitated the development of the courts' role, especially in an international context, without reducing the autonomy of arbitration from national laws. Anticipating the success of the system of court intervention, one commentator queried as early as 1981 whether Article 1493, paragraph 2 might not give the President of the Paris Tribunal of First Instance "the opportunity . . . to become a sort of permanent arbitral institution."[154]

835. — However, when parties apply to the courts at the beginning of arbitral proceedings, they are not always seeking help in constituting the arbitral tribunal on the grounds that their agreement does not work in practice and that some difficulty has therefore arisen. The parties sometimes attempt to rely on Article 1493, paragraph 2 in order to avoid the consequences of the strict application of the arbitration agreement or the relevant arbitration rules, in the hope that the judge might stay the proceedings or organize them differently. In such a case, the role of the judge will no longer be one of assistance but one of control, which is one of the difficulties with the application and interpretation of Article 1493, paragraph 2.

We shall now examine in turn the conditions governing the intervention of the courts (1), the purpose of such intervention (2) and the procedure involved (3).

1° Conditions Governing Judicial Intervention

836. — Certain of the conditions governing the intervention of the courts under Article 1493, paragraph 2 of the New Code of Civil Procedure are clearly set out in the code itself. These include, in particular, provisions concerning the international jurisdiction of the French courts (a) and its subsidiary nature (b). Article 1493, paragraph 2 does not, however, address the validity and content of the arbitration clause (c).

a) The International Jurisdiction of the French Courts

837. — The President of the Paris Tribunal of First Instance will only have jurisdiction to assist with difficulties concerning the constitution of the arbitral tribunal if there is a connection between the arbitration in question and France. In short, either the arbitration

---

[153] For an analysis of the situation in 1985, see Fouchard, *supra* note 55.

[154] Jean-Louis Delvolvé, observations made during the colloquium organized by the Comité français de l'arbitrage on September 23, 1981 concerning the French reform of its international arbitration law in 1981, 1981 REV. ARB. 486.

must take place in France, or the parties must have agreed that it is to be governed by French procedural law.[155]

838. — This requirement of a link between the arbitration and France has been unanimously approved by commentators of the 1981 reform of French international arbitration law.[156] It is, after all, perfectly reasonable to confine the international jurisdiction of the French courts to arbitrations that concern either the French legal system or French economic interests. The role of the French courts is not intended to be that of the good Samaritan in arbitrations taking place throughout the world. Such interventionism would not be tolerated outside France, and there would be a substantial risk that the validity of the constitution of an arbitral tribunal with which a French court had assisted would be challenged on the basis that the court had exceeded its jurisdiction.

839. — This limitation of the French courts' jurisdiction[157] was established by the President of the Paris Tribunal of First Instance in a case prior to the 1981 reform of French international arbitration law. When requested by the plaintiff to appoint an arbitrator for the defendant (the multinational corporation Air Afrique), the judge found that the contract containing the arbitration clause had no element that connected it with French law. In particular, the contract had been signed in Gabon and was subject to Gabonese law. The judge therefore ruled that:

> [the parties] appear to have made no reference, even implicitly, to French procedural law, either in determining the seat of the arbitral tribunal, or in choosing the law applicable to both the arbitration agreement and the powers of the arbitrators, it being noted that the arbitrators were instructed to 'make their award on the basis of equity and the fundamental principles governing French and Gabonese law.'

---

[155] On this issue in other legal systems, *see infra* para. 916.

[156] Goldman, *supra* note 85, at 473; Pierre Bellet and Ernst Mezger, *L'arbitrage international dans le nouveau code de procédure civile*, 1981 REV. CRIT. DIP 611, 623; Patrice Level, *La réforme de l'arbitrage international (D. n° 81-500, 12 mai 1981, Nouveau Code de procédure civile, art. 1492 à 1507)*, JCP, Ed. E., No. 9899 (1981); Philippe Fouchard, *L'arbitrage international en France après le décret du 12 mai 1981*, 109 J.D.I. 374, 387 (1982); Yves Derains and Rozabel E. Goodman-Everard, *France, in* ICCA INTERNATIONAL HANDBOOK ON COMMERCIAL ARBITRATION (1998).

[157] *See* TGI Paris, réf., June 3, 1985, Europe Etudes Gecti v. E.T.P.O., 1987 REV. ARB. 179, 1st decision, and P. Fouchard's note; TGI Paris, réf., Jan. 10, 1996, National Iranian Oil Co. v. Israel, 1996 BULL. ASA 319, and the commentary by Homayoon Arfazadeh, *Juge d'appui et for de nécessité – A propos d'une récente décision du Président du Tribunal de grande instance de Paris dans l'affaire NIOC c. Etat d'Israël, id.* at 325; for an English translation, see 11 INT'L ARB. REP. B1 (Feb. 1996). In this case, the French judge considered that his international jurisdiction could only result from the fact the parties "entrusted the President of the ICC, a non-governmental international organization with its headquarters in Paris, with a mission limited to the appointment, where necessary, of a third arbitrator."

The judge thus took the international nature of the arbitration clause into consideration and refused to apply French domestic law.[158] He instructed the plaintiff to "seek redress under the law of contract with respect to the other party's refusal to perform its agreement and to appoint its arbitrator."[159]

The President of the Tribunal of First Instance thus considered that the contractual provision whereby the general principles of French law governed the substance of the dispute on a non-exclusive basis, and the French nationality of the plaintiff, were not sufficient for him to have jurisdiction.

840. — In the same case, the judge implicitly refused to apply Article 14 of the French Civil Code, which gives the French courts jurisdiction on the basis of the plaintiff's nationality. The judge's decision is somewhat controversial, and for a time some authors preferred the opposite view,[160] considering that Article 14 (and indeed Article 15 of the same Code, which justifies the jurisdiction of the French courts on the basis of the defendant's nationality) were of general application.

A number of arguments have been put forward in defense of the judge's position. Some are irrelevant, such as those contending that the ordinary effect of an arbitration clause is to exclude the jurisdiction of national courts,[161] or that the arbitration clause itself constitutes a waiver of Articles 14 and 15.[162] Although French case law is consistently in favor of that interpretation,[163] the exclusion of the jurisdiction of national courts and the waiver of Articles 14 and 15 only concern the jurisdiction of the courts over the merits of the dispute. They do not concern the assistance provided by the courts in order to give effect to an arbitration clause. It would certainly be unfortunate if the extension of the international jurisdiction of the French courts over the constitution of the arbitral tribunal were to weaken any subsequent award in other countries, and that would be the consequence of applying Article 14 of the Civil Code.

There is a simpler and better reason for excluding the application of Article 14, as is set out very clearly in a 1987 decision rendered after the New Code of Civil Procedure had come into effect. It confirms the solution reached in the 1981 decision in the following terms:

---

[158] At the time of the judge's ruling, Article 1493 of the New Code of Civil Procedure had yet to be adopted: the applicable provision was Article 4 of the 1980 Decree, which later became Article 1444 of the New Code of Civil Procedure.

[159] TGI Paris, réf., Apr. 2, 1981, Stern v. Air Afrique, 1983 REV. ARB. 191, and P. Fouchard's note.

[160] JEAN ROBERT, L'ARBITRAGE – DROIT INTERNE – DROIT INTERNATIONAL PRIVÉ ¶ 299 (5th ed. 1983). In the 6th edition the author did not maintain this position (¶ 291).

[161] See supra paras. 661 et seq.

[162] See DE BOISSÉSON, supra note 30, ¶ 641 at 562.

[163] See, e.g., CA Paris, Nov. 30, 1988, Korsnas Marma v. Durand-Auzias, 1989 REV. ARB. 691, 1st decision, and P.-Y. Tschanz' note; André Huet, Compétence "privilégiée" des tribunaux français ou compétence fondée sur la nationalité française de l'une des parties, J.-CL. DR. INT., Fasc. 581-32, ¶¶ 29–32 (1995).

In international arbitration—a dispute resolution method where the parties agree to exclude the jurisdiction of national courts over the merits of the dispute, in favor of a jurisdiction and procedural rules of their choice— Article 1493 of the New Code of Civil Procedure derogates from Articles 14 and 15 of the French Civil Code, which entitle French parties to submit their disputes to the French courts and which confer full jurisdiction on those courts to hear disputes where the other party is of foreign nationality.[164]

This decision thus confirms that Article 1493, paragraph 2 must be viewed as excluding the effects of Articles 14 and 15 in its specific field. It is an accepted principle of interpretation that where two provisions apparently contradict each other, the more recent shall prevail and, more importantly, that the more specific provision shall prevail over the more general. The spirit and the letter of Article 1493, paragraph 2 both support that solution: by clearly determining the conditions under which a particular French court has international jurisdiction to perform a specific function, the text excludes the application of other provisions which do not specifically contemplate those circumstances.

841. — The first of the two situations where the court will have international jurisdiction under Article 1493, paragraph 2—where the arbitration "takes place in France"—occurs more frequently than the second. Its application is not confined to arbitrations actually in progress in France, as most of the difficulties that prompt a request for assistance from the French courts arise prior to or at the very beginning of the proceedings. In such cases, it must simply be established that the arbitration agreement provides that the proceedings are to take place in France. This form of international jurisdiction based on territoriality is perfectly legitimate as, although having the seat of the arbitration in France does not in itself mean that the arbitration is subject to French law, the parties' agreement to conduct the arbitration in France provides sufficient grounds for the French court to intervene in the constitution of the arbitral tribunal.

The second situation where the French judge will have international jurisdiction is where the parties have chosen to apply French procedural law to their arbitration. At first sight this second ground may seem surprising, as French international arbitration law—and especially the New Code of Civil Procedure—does not generally require the selection and application of a particular national law. Nevertheless, this ground is also legitimate because the parties sometimes do specifically choose the law governing the arbitral procedure, and particularly French law because of its liberal attitude towards international arbitration. To allow the French courts to intervene in those circumstances is to give effect to the intentions of the parties to have their arbitral procedure governed by French law, as required by Article 1494

---

[164] TGI Paris, réf., May 11, 1987, Les Silos du Sud-Ouest S.A. v. Société des Engrais du Bénin (S.E.B.), 1988 REV. ARB. 699, 1st decision, and P. Fouchard's note.

of the New Code of Civil Procedure.[165] It also rightly assumes that the constitution of the arbitral tribunal is a matter of arbitral procedure.[166]

842. — In the *Les Silos du Sud-Ouest* case, the President of the Paris Tribunal of First Instance was called upon to interpret Article 1493, paragraph 2. He held that the international arbitration with which he was asked to assist did not correspond to either of the scenarios envisaged in that article. The case concerned a turnkey contract between a French and a Beninese firm. On the basis of the arbitration clause in the contract, the French company asked the French court to appoint the second arbitrator in place of the defendant. The judge declined jurisdiction on the following grounds:

> In the present case, the arbitration clause states that the arbitral tribunal must have its seat in a neutral country, thus excluding France and the Republic of Benin. The parties have not explicitly referred to French law as the law governing procedure. Finally, the fact that the defendant has abstained from presenting its arguments at the present interim hearing does not mean that it has accepted, even implicitly, that French procedural law should apply.[167]

It is important to note that the judge suggested that where a foreign defendant does participate in French judicial assistance proceedings without challenging the international jurisdiction of French courts, it can be inferred that it tacitly accepts the application of French law regarding the constitution of the arbitral tribunal as requested by the French plaintiff. That would be a broad interpretation of the justification of the jurisdiction of French courts based on the fact that the parties have chosen French law to govern the arbitral procedure. However, that kind of broad interpretation is not unreasonable in the circumstances. In practice, the arbitration clause seldom refers explicitly to the law governing the arbitral procedure, and French law does not encourage the parties to do so. A lack of formalism is therefore justified on this point. Further, where both parties actually participate in proceedings regarding the constitution of the arbitral tribunal without challenging the jurisdiction of the French courts, it is clear that they tacitly but unequivocally agree not only that French procedural law applies, but also that the French courts are entitled to intervene.

843. — Thus, in addition to the two cases set forth in Article 1493, paragraph 2, the French courts (through the President of the Paris Tribunal of First Instance) may also intervene where a party requests their assistance in connection with a difficulty concerning the constitution of the arbitral tribunal and the other party does not challenge their jurisdiction. For instance, this will be the case where the other party confines its arguments to questions such as the identity of the arbitrator or arbitrators or the other statutory conditions governing the judge's involvement. The parties will be considered to have tacitly

---

[165] *See infra* para. 1200.

[166] *See supra* paras. 742 and 745.

[167] TGI Paris, réf., May 11, 1987, *supra* note 164.

accepted the judge's intervention as an appointing authority, just as they could have agreed on any other predetermined third party.

844. — In the absence of a tacit agreement between the parties, the French courts may even derive their jurisdiction from the conduct of the arbitrators who, under Article 1494, paragraph 2 of the New Code of Civil Procedure, have the power to determine the procedural law where the parties fail to do so in their arbitration agreement. In a 1985 case, the President of the Paris Tribunal of First Instance retained jurisdiction when challenged by the defendant, ruling that as the arbitrators had appeared at the hearing without disputing his jurisdiction or his power to extend deadlines "[the arbitrators themselves] must be deemed to have decided to apply French procedural law, which allows the courts to intervene in order to ensure the smooth operation of the arbitral proceedings."[168] The judge's position was rather controversial, given that Article 1493, paragraph 2 seems to require that the choice of French law be directly made by the parties themselves. However, the judge did also take into account—and this was probably sufficient to justify his jurisdiction—the fact that the arbitrators had chosen to locate the seat of the arbitration in France.

845. — It is also possible for the French courts to extend their jurisdiction where the treatment of the plaintiff by the foreign courts that would otherwise have jurisdiction amounts to a denial of justice.

That at least is what seems to be implied by the decision of the President of the Paris Tribunal of First Instance rendered in the *Les Silos du Sud-Ouest* matter. The French company involved in that case raised a subsidiary argument that because of the defendant's deliberate stalling tactics the arbitration clause had become impossible to perform and the arbitral tribunal could not be constituted. The judge, however, instructed the plaintiff to apply first to the Beninese courts to have this refusal sanctioned under Beninese law. The French judge declared that he had no jurisdiction "as things stood," and that he would only be able to intervene if the plaintiff were to prove that the Beninese courts had neither awarded damages nor enforced the arbitration agreement by appointing the second arbitrator. Only in those circumstances would there be a denial of justice.

The same approach was taken in a more recent case involving a dispute between the Iranian oil company NIOC and the Government of Israel. The mere fact that two non-French parties had agreed that in the event of any difficulty they would invite the President of the ICC to appoint the third arbitrator did not mean that they had chosen France as the seat of arbitration. The President of the Paris Tribunal of First Instance declined jurisdiction and instructed the plaintiff to apply to the courts of the defendant's home country, adding that "with respect to the conditions governing jurisdiction, a French judge, like any other judge" should ensure that the arbitration agreement is performed and that the parties receive equal

---

[168] TGI Paris, réf., Apr. 3, 1985, Application des gaz v. Wonder Corp. of America, 1985 REV. ARB. 170.

treatment as regards the appointment of the arbitrators, but only if a denial of justice by the courts of the defendant's home country is proved.[169]

846. — The President of the Paris Tribunal of First Instance also has jurisdiction to resolve problems concerning the constitution of the arbitral tribunal where the parties have so designated him or her in their agreement. In such a case, however, the President's jurisdiction (and the jurisdiction of any court designated by the parties) is not based on Article 1493, paragraph 2. It is nevertheless entirely legitimate, as with any voluntary extension of jurisdiction in international commercial matters. Article 1493 authorizes this indirectly by specifying that the jurisdiction of the President of the Paris Tribunal of First Instance is not mandatory.

b) Non-Mandatory Character of French Courts' Jurisdiction

847. — Under Article 1493, paragraph 2 of the French New Code of Civil Procedure the jurisdiction of the President of the Paris Tribunal of First Instance is conditional upon the parties not having agreed otherwise. The parties are thus free to choose their own method of resolving difficulties concerning the constitution of the arbitral tribunal, in the same way that they are free to determine the method of appointing the arbitrators and the authority responsible for appointing them where the parties disagree. The parties may choose to submit such issues to any other individual or organization: a different court, whether in France or elsewhere, a predetermined third party or, of course, an arbitral institution. This solution is consistent with the primacy of the parties' agreement,[170] and we will examine the other consequences of that principle at a later stage.[171]

848. — Although it is seldom mentioned by the courts, the language "in the absence of a clause to the contrary" plays a major part in the case law concerning Article 1493, paragraph 2. It clearly denotes that the courts will only have jurisdiction if the parties have not chosen another mechanism for resolving difficulties relating to the constitution of the arbitral tribunal. It is thus a plain indication of the fact that the jurisdiction of the President of the Paris Tribunal of First Instance is not mandatory. For instance, the President must refuse to intervene if an arbitral institution has been designated by the parties and its rules specify that it has the power to resolve difficulties arising from the constitution of the tribunal. However, the President's jurisdiction is also subsidiary in the sense that he or she

---

[169] TGI Paris, réf., Jan. 10, 1996, *National Iranian Oil Co.*, *supra* note 157. In this case, although the Israeli state opposed the constitution of the arbitral tribunal on the grounds that the claims concerned an "act of state" and that it was protected by its immunity from jurisdiction (on these points, see *infra* para. 855), the court found there to be no denial of justice, as there could be no presumption that the Israeli courts which would have international jurisdiction to assist in the constitution of the arbitral tribunal would, if hearing the question, necessarily adopt the same position as the Israeli government.

[170] *See supra* paras. 752 *et seq.*

[171] *See infra* paras. 951 *et seq.*

will only lend assistance if the system initially adopted by the parties to resolve such difficulties proves, in practice, to be inadequate or impracticable.[172]

849. — The courts have frequently had occasion to apply this rule. In the *Raffineries de pétrole d'Homs et de Banias* case, a difficulty arose with the constitution of the tribunal in an ICC arbitration. The Paris Court of Appeals specifically denied the possibility of recourse to the courts, thus reversing the decision of the President of the Paris Tribunal of First Instance.[173] Similarly, in the various *Philipp Brothers* decisions,[174] the President of the Paris Tribunal of First Instance accepted jurisdiction over the challenges made against the arbitrators because at that time the rules of the chosen institution—the AFCC—did not provide for a mechanism enabling it to resolve that type of problem.

Likewise, by an order dated October 29, 1996 in the *General Establishments for Chemical Industries (GECI) v. Industrialexport* case, the President of the Paris Tribunal of First Instance retained jurisdiction to hear the challenge of an arbitrator, despite the fact that the arbitration clause referred to the ICC Rules, although only for the initial constitution of the arbitral tribunal. The judge considered that the clause did not express an unequivocal mutual intention to have the full ICC Rules govern the arbitral proceedings and any incidents arising.[175] The ICC itself, and later the Paris Court of Appeals, had considered the arbitration to be an *ad hoc* proceeding.[176] As the same judge stated in another case:

> [the judge] is not entitled . . . to substitute himself for the pre-appointed arbitral institution, unless there is an acknowledged or proven default by that institution, for the purposes of organizing and implementing the arbitral proceedings in accordance with its rules which the parties have agreed to adopt.[177]

In arguably the most significant case on this issue, a party to an *ad hoc* international arbitration taking place in France requested the President of the Paris Tribunal of First Instance to confirm the default, and proceed with the replacement, of the arbitrator appointed by its adversary. However, the arbitration was subject to the UNCITRAL Arbitration Rules,

---

[172] *See* TGI Paris, réf., June 4, 1998, Euton v. Ural Hudson Ltd., No. 56510/98, unpublished; TGI Paris, réf., Nov. 26, 1998, République de Tanzanie v. DTT, 1999 REV. ARB. 131, and observations by A. Hory.

[173] CA Paris, May 15, 1985, *supra* note 142; *comp. with* TGI Paris, Mar. 28, 1984, *Raffineries de pétrole d'Homs et de Banias, supra* note 50.

[174] TGI Paris, réf., Oct. 28, 1988, *Drexel Burnham Lambert*, June 14, 1989, June 29, 1989, and July 15, 1989, *Philipp Brothers, supra* note 32, 1990 REV. ARB. 497.

[175] Unpublished decision, No. 60194/96. Recourse taken against this decision was ruled inadmissible by the Paris Court of Appeals (*see* CA Paris, 1e Ch., Sec. C., Sept. 30, 1997, General Establishments for Chemical Industries (GECI) v. Industrialexport, Case No. 96/88637 and 97/455, unpublished).

[176] CA Paris, July 9, 1992, Industrialexport-Import v. GECI, 1993 REV. ARB. 303, and C. Jarrosson's note; see also, in the same case, TGI Paris, réf., Feb. 15, 1995, Industrialexport v. K., 1996 REV. ARB. 503, 2d decision, and P. Fouchard's note.

[177] TGI Paris, réf., Jan. 18, 1991, Société chérifienne des pétroles v. Mannesmann Industria Iberica, 1996 REV. ARB. 503, 1st decision, and P. Fouchard's note.

which provide a mechanism for the replacement of arbitrators. That mechanism is admittedly fairly complex, in that it requires the Secretary General of the Permanent Court of Arbitration in The Hague to nominate the authority which is to resolve the difficulty, unless the parties agree otherwise.[178] It is therefore understandable that the plaintiff preferred to apply directly to the French courts. The reaction of the President of the Paris Tribunal of First Instance to the challenge of his jurisdiction was that the UNCITRAL Rules on the procedure for replacing defaulting arbitrators did not prohibit him from intervening to "confirm that the proceedings had come to a stand-still and to assist in re-establishing the necessary co-operation between the parties." He therefore instructed the parties, the arbitrator alleged to be in default and the chairman of the arbitral tribunal to supply him with more detailed information on the situation. Having considered that information, he concluded at a later hearing that the arbitral tribunal had in fact recently convened and that the purported default had not been proved. Without violating the replacement procedure agreed by the parties—and thereby fully respecting Article 1493, paragraph 2—the President of the Tribunal of First Instance nevertheless took the position that he held a general power of assistance, which in this case undoubtedly helped to set the proceedings back on course.[179]

850. — The non-mandatory character of the jurisdiction of the President of the Paris Tribunal of First Instance also accounts for the relatively restrictive interpretation by the courts of the concept of "a difficulty . . . in the constitution of the arbitral tribunal" which the President is empowered to resolve under Article 1493, paragraph 2.[180]

On the other hand, if the arbitration clause provides for the intervention of a third party only for the purposes of appointing a third arbitrator, and the defendant refuses to appoint the second arbitrator, the President will consider that the requirement of good faith entitles him or her to appoint the second arbitrator in the defendant's place.[181]

c) Validity and Content of the Arbitration Clause

851. — Unlike Article 1444—which applies to French domestic arbitration—Article 1493, paragraph 2 of the New Code of Civil Procedure does not expressly state that:

> if the arbitration clause is either manifestly void or inadequate for the purpose of constituting the arbitral tribunal, the President shall so state and declare that no appointment need be made.

---

[178] On these rules, see *infra* para. 963.

[179] TGI Paris, réf., Feb. 24 and Apr. 15, 1992, *Icori Estero*, *supra* note 54.

[180] *See infra* paras. 856 *et seq.*

[181] TGI Paris, réf., Oct. 20, 1997, *Boulois v. UNESCO*, 1997 REV. ARB. 575, and C. Jarrosson's note, *aff'd*, CA Paris, 14e Ch., Sec. B, June 19, 1998, *UNESCO v. Boulois*, No. 97/26549, unpublished.

How should one construe the absence of this wording in the provision applicable in international arbitration? Several differing interpretations have been put forward, but the courts have not yet clearly taken sides.

852. — The simplest and most radical interpretation is that since the wording[182] is not included in Article 1493, paragraph 2, it does not apply to international arbitration.[183] In favor of that view is the argument that the draftsmen, with the domestic law provision in front of them, must have departed from it deliberately in an attempt to facilitate the constitution of the arbitral tribunal in international arbitration, and to limit any debate on the issue before the judge whose assistance is sought. Furthermore, Article 1495 specifically permits the application of the more liberal rule found in Article 1493 even if the parties agree that French law governs the arbitral proceedings.[184]

853. — The opposing view is that the two conditions that apply in domestic law must be extended to international arbitration. This is based on the belief that the reference in Article 1493, paragraph 2 to Article 1457 is insufficient to address the issue because Article 1457 only concerns the procedure for judicial intervention.[185] As a result, it is argued that the substantive conditions of Article 1444, paragraphs 1 and 3, should be extended to international arbitration.[186]

854. — Midway between those two views, a third interpretation is that in international arbitration the court should only verify that the clause is not patently void,[187] as it would be unreasonable to require it to appoint an arbitrator where there is no indication that an arbitration clause exists. The court should not be seen to automatically appoint arbitrators in cases where the arbitration clearly has no contractual basis and the award has no chance of being recognized in any jurisdiction. In international arbitration, however, the court's involvement should not be subject to the condition that the arbitration clause must be "adequate for the purpose of constituting the arbitral tribunal" within the meaning of Article 1444 of the New Code of Civil Procedure. That would amount to extending to international arbitration the domestic prohibition affecting "blank clauses,"[188] which the very liberal wording of Article 1493, paragraph 1 clearly rejects.[189]

---

[182] On the application of this wording in domestic arbitration, see Rubellin-Devichi and Loquin, *supra* note 47, ¶¶ 38 *et seq.*

[183] *See* TGI Paris, réf., June 3, 1985, *Europe Etudes Gecti*, *supra* note 157.

[184] *See* Cohen, *supra* note 86, at 201.

[185] *See infra* paras. 885 *et seq.*

[186] *See* TGI Paris, réf., Feb. 21, 1983, A. v. W., 1983 REV. ARB. 479, lst decision, and B. Moreau's note; CA Paris, July 9, 1986, Alexandre Giuliani v. Colas, 1987 REV. ARB. 179, 5th decision, and P. Fouchard's note.

[187] Fouchard, *supra* note 156, and note at 1987 REV. ARB. 195. For a decision that is implicitly in favor, see TGI Paris, réf., Jan. 10, 1996, *National Iranian Oil Co.*, *supra* note 157.

[188] *See* Article 1443, paragraph 2 of the French New Code of Civil Procedure.

[189] *See supra* para. 486.

855. — It has also been suggested that a distinction can be drawn according to the basis of the court's jurisdiction.[190] If it were to have jurisdiction because the arbitration was subject to French procedural law, Article 1444 would apply,[191] although other more favorable substantive rules stemming either from French case law on international arbitration, or from a foreign law governing the arbitration clause, could prevail. If, on the other hand, the court were to have jurisdiction because the arbitration was to be held in France, Article 1444 would not apply, and establishing that "the arbitration clause is either manifestly void or inadequate" would not be a matter for the court, but for the arbitrators, subject to any subsequent action to set the award aside.[192]

The principle generally guiding the court in situations where its involvement is contested is thus that it is not its role to prejudge the jurisdiction and powers of the arbitrator to be appointed. This applies particularly to questions of arbitrability,[193] the limits of the arbitrator's mission,[194] and the possibility of a stay of the arbitral proceedings.[195] The court will also firmly reject any objections based on the immunity from jurisdiction of a state or international organization.[196]

2° The Purpose of Judicial Intervention

856. — According to Article 1493, paragraph 2 of the New Code of Civil Procedure, the President of the Paris Tribunal of First Instance may be seized if "a difficulty arises in the constitution of the arbitral tribunal." The judge's role in international arbitration thus seems clearly defined: it is to resolve difficulties concerning the constitution of the arbitral tribunal. The word "difficulty" is broad enough to cover a number of incidents. In contrast, the

---

[190] Fouchard, *supra* note 55, at 31 *et seq.*, and note at 1987 REV. ARB. 195; DE BOISSÉSON, *supra* note 30, ¶ 643; Emmanuel Gaillard, *Les manœuvres dilatoires des parties et des arbitres dans l'arbitrage international*, 1990 REV. ARB. 759, 779.

[191] *See* TGI Paris, réf., Sept. 8, 1983, M. v. C., 1983 REV. ARB. 479, 4th decision, and B. Moreau's note; 1984 RTD CIV. 546, and observations by J. Normand.

[192] *See* TGI Paris, réf., Apr. 10, 1990, European Country Hotels Ltd. v. Consorts Legrand, 1994 REV. ARB. 545, 1st decision, and observations by P. Fouchard.

[193] *See* TGI Paris, réf., Jan. 10, 1996, *National Iranian Oil Co.*, *supra* note 157.

[194] TGI Paris, réf., Apr. 23, 1997, G.M.F. Assistance Internationale v. Alba Compania General de Seguros, No. 66532/96, unpublished, which left the task of coordinating the arbitration and foreign proceedings concerning a related contract, if the need were to arise, to the arbitral tribunal to be appointed.

[195] Despite the French law rule whereby civil proceedings must be stayed pending the outcome of related criminal proceedings, the President of the Paris Tribunal of First Instance nevertheless went forward with the constitution of the arbitral tribunal, holding that only the arbitral tribunal could determine whether or not to stay the arbitration (TGI Paris, réf., Feb. 12, 1996, Augier v. Hawker, 1996 REV. ARB. 135, 2d decision, and observations by J. Pellerin). On the issue, see also *infra* para. 1660.

[196] In its order of January 10, 1996 (*see supra* note 157), the President of the Paris Tribunal of First Instance held that "in agreeing to an arbitration clause, a state waives its immunity from jurisdiction, not only with respect to the arbitrators, but also with respect to the competent state courts, when they intervene to assist with the implementation of the arbitral procedure." Similarly, in a case where UNESCO's claims regarding immunity from jurisdiction were rejected, see TGI Paris, réf., Oct. 20, 1997, *Boulois, aff'd*, CA Paris, June 19, 1998, *UNESCO*, *supra* note 181.

"constitution" of the arbitral tribunal appears to concern only a particular stage of the arbitral proceedings—the initial phase of setting up the arbitral tribunal (a). However, the courts have held, rightly in our opinion, that the judge will have jurisdiction to resolve difficulties occurring at a later stage, provided that they are related to the constitution (or re-constitution) of the arbitral tribunal (b). However, this interpretation of the law has not been extended so far as to "create real interference by the courts in the normal course of arbitral proceedings," which would be both undesirable and inconsistent with the judge's role of "help and assistance."[197]

a) Resolving Initial Difficulties Concerning the Constitution of the Arbitral Tribunal

857. — When arbitral proceedings begin, both plaintiffs and defendants often bring a variety of actual or imagined problems before the President of the Paris Tribunal of First Instance. In keeping with the spirit of the New Code of Civil Procedure, the President will only agree to intervene in cases where the problem genuinely concerns the constitution of the arbitral tribunal.

1) Difficulties Warranting Judicial Intervention

858. — Article 1493, paragraph 2 of the New Code of Civil Procedure unquestionably applies to the appointment of the arbitrators at the outset of the arbitral proceedings. Difficulties arise, particularly in *ad hoc* arbitrations, where the arbitration clause fails to designate a third party to resolve any difficulties regarding the appointment process, and merely states that the parties shall agree to appoint the arbitrator or arbitrators. The most common obstacles are a defendant who refuses to appoint the second arbitrator, and disagreement between the parties or the first two arbitrators as to the identity of the sole arbitrator or the third arbitrator. In such cases, the President of the Tribunal of First Instance will either appoint the required arbitrator or arbitrators, or take the necessary measures to ensure that the arbitrators are appointed.[198] Generally, the judge will order the defaulting party to appoint the missing arbitrator, or order the two arbitrators to appoint a third one.[199] If this is unsuccessful, the President will then appoint the missing arbitrator.

859. — A problem may arise at an even earlier stage, if the arbitration clause does not specify either the method for appointing the arbitrators or the number of arbitrators comprising the tribunal. A "blank clause" of that kind might state, for example, that all

---

[197] Gérard Pluyette, *Le point de vue du juge*, 1990 REV. ARB. 355.

[198] On the appointment of a second arbitrator, see TGI Paris, réf., Feb. 21, 1983, *supra* note 186; TGI Paris, réf., Apr. 23, 1997, *G.M.F. Assistance Internationale*, *supra* note 194; TGI Paris, réf., Oct. 20, 1997, *Boulois*, *aff'd*, CA Paris, June 19, 1998, *UNESCO*, *supra* note 181; on the appointment of a third arbitrator, see TGI Paris, réf., May 22, 1987 and June 23, 1987, *Transportacion Maritima Mexicana*, *supra* note 25.

[199] *See* TGI Paris, Aug. 11, Sept. 20, and Dec. 30, 1983, Cofitra v. Cattin Machines, 1985 REV. ARB. 81, 2d decision.

disputes arising from the contract must be resolved "by arbitration in Paris." Blank clauses are permitted under French international arbitration law.[200] In such cases the court may, after hearing the parties, decide on the number of arbitrators and the method of their appointment. It can also directly appoint the required arbitrator or arbitrators.[201] However, as yet, no such cases appear to have come before the President of the Paris Tribunal of First Instance.

860. — Another type of difficulty occurs where the arbitration agreement does not precisely identify the third party responsible for designating the arbitrators or the institution chosen to administer the arbitration. This was the original ground for court intervention in the *République de Guinée* case. The three contracts in question (for the construction of 3,000 homes) each contained an arbitration clause. The first referred to "the International Chamber of Commerce," the second to "the arbitral Chamber . . . in Paris" and the third to "the Paris Arbitration Chamber." The plaintiffs had all submitted their disputes to the latter institution, whereas the Republic of Guinea argued that in view of the nature of the disputes, the parties could only have intended to submit them to the ICC, which has its headquarters in Paris. The President of the Tribunal of First Instance considered that this problem was a difficulty concerning the constitution of the arbitral tribunal, and he held that the ICC had been appointed to organize the arbitration arising from the first contract alone, and that the Paris Arbitration Chamber was the institution chosen to resolve disputes arising from the other two contracts.[202]

Similarly, in a 1988 decision, the President of the Tribunal of First Instance was required to rule on an arbitration clause in a contract between a company incorporated in the United States and a company incorporated in Spain. The parties had agreed that the law of Arkansas would govern the contract and that they would refer their disputes to "the official Chamber of Commerce in Paris, France." The judge held that:

> although there is no 'official Chamber of Commerce' in Paris, the ICC—a private institution—clearly is the arbitration center in Paris that is recognized in international practice, in France and abroad, for organizing dispute resolution by arbitration, regardless of the nature of the dispute, the parties' nationality or the applicable law.[203]

2) Difficulties Not Warranting Judicial Intervention

861. — The President of the Paris Tribunal of First Instance will refuse to rule on the jurisdiction of the arbitral tribunal and, more generally, to interfere with the organization and functioning of an arbitration, if the arbitral tribunal is considered to be already constituted. This can be seen from a number of decisions.

---

[200] *See supra* paras. 486 and 854.

[201] On the procedure for this judicial assistance, *see infra* para. 901.

[202] TGI Paris, réf., May 30, 1986, *République de Guinée, supra* note 68.

[203] TGI Paris, réf., Dec. 13, 1988, Asland v. European Energy Corp., 1990 REV. ARB. 521.

862. — A party to a contract containing an ordinary ICC arbitration clause claimed before the President of the Paris Tribunal of First Instance that it had tried in vain to commence arbitral proceedings. The judge was asked either to declare that the arbitration clause was "manifestly void" and that the arbitral tribunal could therefore not be constituted or, alternatively, to declare that the agreement was inapplicable and to "refer the case to the court with jurisdiction to hear the merits of the dispute, namely the Paris Commercial Court." The judge refused, on the grounds that "the claim is not based on a difficulty concerning the constitution of the arbitral tribunal but on the fact that the arbitration agreement is patently void," and he declined jurisdiction.[204]

863. — Another example concerned the jurisdiction of an arbitral tribunal constituted under the Rules of the Paris Arbitration Chamber which was challenged by the defendant on the grounds that the arbitration clause only referred to "arbitration in Paris." The arbitral tribunal fixed a deadline before which the most diligent party was to:

> apply to the President of the Paris Tribunal of First Instance for a provisional ruling as to which Parisian arbitration institution has jurisdiction to organize the arbitral proceedings.

On the basis of Article 1493, paragraph 2 one of the parties then asked the judge to "confirm the validity of the nomination of the arbitrators." The judge declared that there were "no grounds for a provisional ruling," on the basis that "although [the judge] can hear actions regarding difficulties concerning the constitution of the arbitral tribunal, his role does not involve determining the jurisdiction of that tribunal." He considered that the parties had voluntarily participated in the constitution of the arbitral tribunal, and that the tribunal, thus vested with judicial powers, was now responsible for determining the applicable procedural rules.[205]

864. — Similarly, a defendant in an ICC arbitration unsuccessfully applied to the ICC International Court of Arbitration seeking to be discharged from the proceedings on the grounds that it had entered into no arbitration agreement with the plaintiff. It then seized the President of the Paris Tribunal of First Instance on the basis of both Article 809 of the New Code of Civil Procedure, which entitles the judge to prevent imminent damage or to stop plainly illegal acts of interference, and Article 1493, paragraph 2 of the same Code. Again, the judge held that there were no grounds for a provisional ruling. A decision by the ICC International Court of Arbitration did not cause illegal interference, provided that the decision was within the powers of that institution. Neither did it cause imminent damage, as the arbitral tribunal was able to rule on its own jurisdiction if need be, and the defendant could bring an action to set the award aside. The judge added that:

---

[204] TGI Paris, réf., June 3, 1985, *Europe Etudes Gecti, supra* note 157.

[205] TGI Paris, réf., Oct. 14, 1985, Chayaporn Rice Ltd. v. Ipitrade International, 1987 REV. ARB. 179, 2d decision, and P. Fouchard's note.

in this case, the fact that the [defendant] was summonsed to appear in the arbitral proceedings is not, *prima facie*, a difficulty concerning the constitution of the arbitral tribunal, such as might justify judicial intervention on the basis of Article 1493 of the New Code of Civil Procedure.[206]

It is true that in seeking its discharge from the arbitral proceedings, the defendant did not, strictly speaking, raise a difficulty concerning the constitution of the arbitral tribunal. However, it did also claim that the ICC International Court of Arbitration had ordered it and the other defendants to appoint an arbitrator jointly, which it alleged was a "violation of the principle of equal treatment of the parties." The judge did not address that objection, despite the fact that it concerns the constitution of the arbitral tribunal and raises a genuine difficulty, namely the right of each party with a distinct interest in the dispute to participate on an equal basis in the appointment of the arbitral tribunal. This issue, which often arises in multiparty arbitration, was later addressed by the *Cour de cassation* in the *Dutco* case.[207]

In the same way, the President of the Paris Tribunal of First Instance refused to intervene where a party defending an ICC arbitration alleged that the claimant company could not invoke the arbitration clause, because it was contained in a contract to which the claimant was neither party nor assignee. The judge ruled that this "challenge of the existence of an arbitration agreement . . . is to be examined by the arbitrators themselves, who are to decide on the validity and limits of their powers."[208]

b) Resolving Subsequent Difficulties Affecting the Constitution of the Arbitral Tribunal

865. — In its first decision in the *République de Guinée* case, the Paris Tribunal of First Instance stated that it had jurisdiction to hear claims founded on Article 1493, paragraph 2 of the New Code of Civil Procedure, provided that the arbitral tribunal "is not yet constituted, that is to say, when the arbitrators have not yet accepted their brief expressly and unequivocally."[209] The Court thus clearly sought to give a narrow interpretation of its powers. However, French case law as a whole tends to take a less restrictive position.

866. — First, and although this issue concerns not so much the constitution of the arbitral tribunal as the duration of its functions, the President of the Tribunal of First Instance will agree to extend the deadline before which the arbitral tribunal must make its award. This is despite the fact that while the court has such a power in French domestic arbitration pursuant to Article 1456, paragraph 2 of the New Code of Civil Procedure, there is no equivalent provision expressly granting the court such powers in international arbitration. There are a number of cases confirming that the court may exercise this prerogative provided that the

---

[206] TGI Paris, réf., July 13, 1988, R.E.D.E.C. v. Uzinexport Import, 1989 REV. ARB. 97, and P. Bellet's note.

[207] *See* CA Paris, May 5, 1989, and Cass. 1e civ., Jan. 7, 1992, *Dutco, supra* notes 74 and 75.

[208] TGI Paris, réf., Nov. 26, 1998, *République de Tanzanie, supra* note 172.

[209] TGI Paris, réf., May 30, 1986, *République de Guinée, supra* note 68.

extension is applied for in due time.[210] Certain of these expressly refer to Article 1456 of the New Code of Civil Procedure, thus confirming its application to international arbitration. This seems legitimate, even in situations where the parties have not expressly specified that the arbitration is governed by French procedural law.

867. — However, the limits of the court's "role of assistance to the arbitration" were clearly set forth in a decision of the Paris Tribunal of First Instance of October 30, 1990. It was held that, although the court may rule on an application for an extension, its role is not to give the arbitrators a form of "legal opinion" advising them whether the arbitral tribunal is entitled to continue with its brief and make an award on the merits of the case.[211] In this case, the arbitrators asked if the fact that a preliminary award was the object of an action to set aside should lead them to stay the proceedings.[212]

868. — The duration of the jurisdiction of the President of the Paris Tribunal of First Instance was defined in general terms in a decision of that Tribunal dated July 12, 1989:

> Article 1493, paragraph 2 of the New Code of Civil Procedure . . . does not confine the intervention of the judge, in exercising his role of 'technical assistance' and 'judicial co-operation' in favor of the arbitration, to the initial aspects of the constitution of the arbitration tribunal. It also empowers him or her to resolve, in accordance with the common intention of the parties, difficulties concerning subsequent events affecting the constitution of the arbitral tribunal and preventing it from continuing to exercise its decision-making powers.[213]

The same position has been taken in numerous subsequent decisions.[214]

869. — The court will thus agree to intervene after the arbitral tribunal has started to carry out its brief, provided that it is only asked to enable the tribunal to pursue its functions and, more precisely, to remain validly "constituted." The Paris Court of Appeal, rejecting an

---

[210] *See* TGI Paris, réf., May 9, and June 19, 1984, Font Laugière Chimie (Manufactures Jacques Dugniolles) v. Moaco, 1985 REV. ARB. 161; TGI Paris, réf., Apr. 3, 1985, *Application des gaz, supra* note 168; Fouchard, *supra* note 55, at 45 *et seq.*; TGI Paris, réf., Jan. 12, 1988, Omnium de Travaux v. République de Guinée, June 3, 1988, Tribunal arbitral v. Bachmann, May 10, and Oct. 30, 1990, European Country Hotels Ltd. v. Consorts Legrand, July 6, 1990, Irridelco International Corp. v. Ets. Marcel Sebin, 1994 REV. ARB. 538, and observations by P. Fouchard. On the issue, see *infra* para. 1387.

[211] TGI Paris, réf., Oct. 30, 1990, *European Country Hotels, supra* note 210.

[212] On the answer, which is in the negative, see *infra para* 1659.

[213] TGI Paris, réf., July 12, 1989, La Belle Créole S.A. v. The Gemtel Partnership, 1990 REV. ARB. 176, 1st decision, and P. Kahn's note.

[214] TGI Paris, réf., Apr. 10, 1990, *European Country Hotels, supra* note 192; TGI Paris, réf., Jan. 18, 1991, *Société chérifienne des pétroles, supra* note 177; TGI Paris, réf., Feb. 24, 1992, *Icori Estero, supra* note 54; TGI Paris, réf., Feb. 15, 1995, *Industrialexport, supra* note 176.

appeal in the *La Belle Créole* case, confirmed and reinforced that liberal interpretation of the scope of judicial intervention under Article 1493, paragraph 2:

> the President of the [Paris] Tribunal [of First Instance], who referred expressly to the provisions of Article 1493, paragraph 2 of the New Code of Civil Procedure when justifying his decisions, intervened in the exercise of the powers conferred on him by that text. Those powers entitle him to assist in furthering the progress of an international arbitration where the constitution of the arbitral tribunal raises a difficulty, that is to say, where the necessary co-operation between the parties is lacking and the arbitration has come to a standstill.[215]

870. — Where the tribunal has already been constituted, two kinds of difficulties may arise: one or more of the arbitrators may be challenged, or the arbitral tribunal may need a new arbitrator. The challenge (1) and replacement (2) of an arbitrator are therefore the two further areas where the President of the Paris Tribunal of First Instance will agree to intervene, within the limits described above.

1) The Challenge of an Arbitrator

871. — A party may challenge an arbitrator if it considers that arbitrator to lack the independence and impartiality which it is entitled to expect of a judge.[216]

872. — In international arbitration there is no express provision that such difficulties are to be resolved by the courts. In contrast, Article 1463, paragraph 2 of the New Code of Civil Procedure stipulates that in domestic arbitration "difficulties relating [to the challenge or default] of an arbitrator shall be brought before the President of the competent court." That text has, however, been extended to international arbitration although, as in domestic law, it is only of subsidiary application. In other words, the President of the Paris Tribunal of First Instance will accept jurisdiction over a challenge which the arbitrator in question has chosen to reject, but only on condition that the arbitration agreement does not provide for any other body or individual to resolve the problem.[217]

The judge will thus refuse to hear a challenge of an arbitrator if that challenge has already been, or could have been, properly submitted to the institution chosen by the parties or, in *ad hoc* arbitration, to the third party appointed for that purpose.

---

[215] CA Paris, Nov. 24, 1989, The Gemtel Partnership v. La Belle Créole S.A., 1990 REV. ARB. 176, 3d decision, and P. Kahn's note.

[216] On these concepts, the grounds for challenging arbitrators and the attributes required of arbitrators, see *infra* paras. 1021 *et seq.*

[217] TGI Paris, réf., Oct. 29, 1996, *General Establishments for Chemical Industries*, *supra* note 175: "It is undisputed that the President of the Tribunal of First Instance only has jurisdiction over a challenge of an arbitrator where the arbitration agreement does not specify that any other authority shall resolve such an incident."

873. — That was the position taken by the court in the *République de Guinée* case. Following a number of difficulties arising between the Republic and the institution organizing the arbitration, the Republic challenged two arbitrators before the court. It argued that the decision to remove an arbitrator was a judicial matter subject to the exclusive jurisdiction of the courts, whereas the President of the arbitral institution was only empowered to organize the arbitration. The Republic also argued that in this instance one of the challenged arbitrators was in fact the President of the arbitral institution, and that he could not be both judge and party. All of these arguments were rejected.

The Paris Tribunal of First Instance observed first of all that:

> by choosing the Paris Arbitration Chamber as the institution responsible for organizing their arbitration, [the parties] agreed to adhere to its procedural rules and thereby empowered that institution to organize the arbitral proceedings in accordance with its statutes and rules, and to resolve any difficulties which might arise.

The court then stated that although the decision to remove an arbitrator is a judicial matter, in that it involves ruling on a challenge against the arbitrator in person, all that is required is that the institution chosen by the parties to organize the arbitration should comply with the essential principles of due process. It continued that "the courts have not been granted exclusive jurisdiction, overriding the parties' intentions, to hear all challenges of arbitrators." With regard to the specific jurisdiction of the President of the Paris Arbitration Chamber, the court noted that in accordance with the rules of the Chamber, he would be replaced by a vice-president appointed for the purpose of ruling on the challenges in question. The court therefore instructed the Republic to submit its challenges to that vice-president.[218]

874. — The President of the Paris Tribunal of First Instance also declined jurisdiction when asked to order the ICC to appoint an arbitrator of non-EC nationality instead of the third arbitrator, a Greek national, whom the ICC had already appointed.[219] The judge declined jurisdiction, not because the problem had arisen after the tribunal had been constituted[220] and concerned one of the arbitrators, but simply because by accepting jurisdiction he would in effect have substituted himself for the arbitral institution chosen by the parties, which had acted in accordance with its rules.

875. — In contrast, where the chosen arbitration institution has no internal mechanism to deal with challenges of arbitrators, the President of the Tribunal of First Instance will retain jurisdiction over any action concerning the independence or impartiality of an arbitrator.

---

[218] TGI Paris, réf., June 23, 1988, *République de Guinée*, *supra* note 139.

[219] TGI Paris, réf., Jan. 18, 1991, *Société chérifienne des pétroles*, *supra* note 177.

[220] *See supra* paras. 865 *et seq.*

876. — That position can be seen in the various decisions made in the *Philipp Brothers* case. We described earlier[221] how Philipp Brothers, a British trading company defending a number of arbitrations organized by and held before the Chambre arbitrale de l'Association Française pour le Commerce des Cacaos (AFCC), had refused to select its arbitrators from the list drawn up by the AFCC in accordance with its rules. The arbitrators were ultimately appointed by the AFCC, but Philipp Brothers claimed that the appointees all had close business links with its opponents. Philipp Brothers therefore challenged the arbitrators, both as a tribunal and individually. Since the rules of the AFCC contained no mechanism for examining and deciding upon such challenges, the claims were submitted to the President of the Paris Tribunal of First Instance.

The challenge of the arbitral tribunal as a whole was rejected for two reasons. First, it was held to be contrary to the arbitration rules which all parties had agreed to adopt with full knowledge of their content. Second, it was

> based on a general criticism of the conditions governing appointments, which is not a problem of constitution of the arbitral tribunal within the meaning of Article 1493, paragraph 2 of the New Code of Civil Procedure. It is therefore solely a matter of assessing the validity of the constitution of the arbitral tribunal.[222]

The judge thus refused to examine the legality of the constitution of the arbitral tribunal, as the Court of Appeals had exclusive jurisdiction to do so when reviewing any subsequent award.[223] The Court of Appeals can set aside an award, or refuse to enforce it in France, on the grounds that the arbitral tribunal is "irregularly constituted,"[224] whereas "difficulties . . . in the constitution of the arbitral tribunal" are within the jurisdiction of the President of the Paris Tribunal of First Instance under Article 1493, paragraph 2 of the same Code.

Nevertheless, neither the defendants, nor the AFCC, nor the court queried the latter's jurisdiction to hear the individual challenges, some of which were ultimately held to be well-founded.[225]

877. — The intervention of the court is particularly useful in *ad hoc* arbitration because, unless the arbitration agreement refers to existing arbitration rules, it will rarely provide a specific mechanism for challenging the arbitrators. In such cases, the Paris Tribunal of First Instance will accept jurisdiction over any such challenge.[226]

---

[221] *See supra* para. 768.

[222] TGI Paris, réf., June 29, 1989, *Philipp Brothers, supra* note 32.

[223] *See infra* para. 1620.

[224] Article 1502, paragraph 2 and Article 1504 of the New Code of Civil Procedure.

[225] TGI Paris, réf., Oct. 28, 1988, *Drexel Burnham Lambert*, June 14, June 29, and July 15, 1989, *Philipp Brothers, supra* note 174.

[226] *See* TGI Paris, réf., Sept. 21, 1989, La Belle Créole S.A. v. The Gemtel Partnership, 1990 REV. ARB. 176, 2d decision, and P. Kahn's note.

878. — The jurisdiction of the President of the Paris Tribunal of First Instance is of course limited in time: it expires when the arbitral proceedings come to an end. This was confirmed in a 1990 decision where the sole arbitrator in an international arbitration delivered his award on the day that one of the parties sought to challenge him. The court held that it no longer had jurisdiction over the matter

> as the arbitrator has discharged his duties, there can no longer be any difficulty regarding the constitution of the arbitral tribunal such as might warrant the intervention of the President of the Paris Tribunal of First Instance. The plaintiff should therefore resort to the recourse available against the arbitral award if it considers that there are grounds on which to set aside the award.[227]

2) The Replacement of an Arbitrator

879. — It may be necessary to replace an arbitrator in a number of circumstances. These include a successful challenge, an arbitrator's default or resignation (whether as a result of a genuine impediment or a deliberate intention to obstruct),[228] removal of an arbitrator by mutual agreement of the parties, and finally an arbitrator's death. These are events occurring after the initial constitution of the arbitral tribunal which affect its existence or the validity of its composition. In each of these cases, the tribunal must be "reconstituted." However, such reconstitution presents a number of difficulties which are resolved more or less successfully in French domestic arbitration law, but are totally ignored in French international arbitration law.

880. — As we have seen,[229] the President of the Paris Tribunal of First Instance will agree to help resolve difficulties with the reconstitution of the arbitral tribunal, rightly avoiding an overly literal construction of Article 1493, paragraph 2 of the New Code of Civil Procedure in favor of a more practical interpretation. The President's involvement is subject to one condition: the agreement between the parties (and particularly any institutional arbitration rules they have chosen) must not contain provisions already allowing for the replacement of an arbitrator.

881. — The few occasions on which such applications have been heard by the President of the Paris Tribunal of First Instance show that difficulties arising during the arbitration and affecting the composition of the arbitral tribunal are not always easy to resolve.

882. — For instance, French domestic arbitration law provides that arbitrators must pursue their functions until they are completed (Art. 1462) and that they can only refrain from doing so if a ground for challenge arises after they have been appointed (Art. 1463).

---

[227] TGI Paris, réf., July 2, 1990, Annahold BV v. L'Oréal, 1996 REV. ARB. 483, 1st decision.

[228] See Gaillard, supra note 190, at 781 et seq.

[229] See supra para. 868.

However, is a French judge, in the absence of a stipulation to the contrary in the parties' agreement or in the rules to which they refer, empowered to extend those provisions to international arbitration so as to prevent an arbitrator from refusing to act?

The answer appears to be in the negative.[230] In a 1995 case, the President of the Paris Tribunal of First Instance expressly refused to rule on a claim that an arbitrator had resigned unlawfully, holding that "[the judge] cannot attempt, by issuing an injunction against the defaulting arbitrator, to compel the latter to resume and pursue a task as personal as that of judging." The judge did agree, however, to ensure the arbitrator in question was replaced.[231]

Another decision demonstrates the caution exercised by the court when asked to replace an arbitrator allegedly in default. The arbitration in question was governed by the UNCITRAL Rules, which provide that the Secretary General of the Permanent Court of Arbitration in the Hague is to designate the authority who is to intervene in the event that an arbitrator defaults. As the jurisdiction of the judge is subject to any mechanism chosen by the parties, he was unable to replace the arbitrator as requested. However, without declining jurisdiction, he observed that Article 1493 empowered him

> to assist in furthering an international arbitration and, without interfering with the actual procedure for replacement, . . . to declare that the arbitration has come to a standstill and to help in re-establishing the necessary co-operation between the parties.[232]

However, since there was a disagreement as to whether the arbitrator was actually in default, the judge issued various requests for information. By the time the arbitrator in question appeared before the judge to explain his position, the complete arbitral tribunal had in fact convened. As a result, the judge held that the arbitrator's alleged default had not been established and that there were no grounds for judicial intervention.[233]

883. — Article 1464 of the New Code of Civil Procedure, which provides, in the context of French domestic arbitration, that the arbitral proceedings shall come to an end in the event of the dismissal, death, impediment, default or successful challenge of an arbitrator, is somewhat unfortunate. It tends to encourage stalling tactics, or at least to extend the proceedings considerably, as it obliges the parties to return to their arbitration agreement and start again from scratch.

Admittedly, Article 1464 does allow the parties to agree to derogate from its provisions. In institutional arbitration this generally involves resuming the arbitral proceedings with a replacement arbitrator from the position reached prior to the departure of the previous arbitrator. However, would it be possible for the parties to agree, or for the applicable arbitration rules to stipulate, that an arbitrator resigning in bad faith should not be replaced

---

[230] Gaillard, *supra* note 190, at 785.

[231] TGI Paris, réf., Feb. 15, 1995, *Industrialexport, supra* note 176. *See also* TGI Paris, réf., Apr. 10, 1990, *European Country Hotels, supra* note 192.

[232] TGI Paris, réf., Feb. 24, 1992, *Icori Estero, supra* note 54.

[233] TGI Paris, réf., Apr. 15, 1992, *Icori Estero, supra* note 54.

if the truncated arbitral tribunal so decided? Some might argue that such a solution[234]—which in practice is highly effective in discouraging the use of such tactics by biased arbitrators—is too brutal and should, at the very least, be reviewed by the courts.

In any event, in the absence of an agreement to that effect, the French courts do not seem prepared to allow the validity of a truncated tribunal, even where an arbitrator resigns in bad faith.[235]

However, the President of the Paris Tribunal of First Instance was flexible in his interpretation of institutional arbitration rules which did not expressly provide for the replacement of an arbitrator in the event of his or her death. He held that the death of an arbitrator could be treated as an impediment,[236] which was covered by the rules in question. Of course, such an indirect means of dealing with the problem is not available in *ad hoc* arbitration.

884. — In international arbitration, the case law is not entirely settled. The question arose in the *La Belle Créole* case where, of the three arbitrators forming the arbitral tribunal, the arbitrator appointed by La Belle Créole died in the course of the arbitral proceedings. La Belle Créole replaced him, but this move was challenged by its opponent who claimed, on the basis of Article 1464, that the arbitral proceedings had come to an end. La Belle Créole applied to the President of the Paris Tribunal of First Instance for a declaration that it was entitled to appoint a new arbitrator and that the replacement took effect on the date on which the previous arbitrator had died, in accordance with the principles of the proper administration of justice and with the usages of international arbitration.

In his decision of July 12, 1989, the judge held that the death of an arbitrator in the course of the arbitral proceedings is an event which affects the constitution of the arbitral tribunal, regardless of the time it occurs.[237] He considered that the provisions of Articles 1442 to 1480 of the New Code of Civil Procedure, and particularly Article 1464, did not apply to an international arbitration taking place in France where the parties had not chosen to apply French procedural law. Relying solely on the common intention of the parties, he then observed that the replacement of the deceased arbitrator and the continuation of the arbitral proceedings had not been accepted by one of the parties. From this he concluded that the arbitral proceedings had indeed come to an end on the date of the arbitrator's death. However, he did rule that the parties remained bound by their arbitration agreements and ordered them to constitute a new arbitral tribunal, instructing each of them to appoint an

---

[234] This solution has been adopted in the rules of a number of arbitral institutions; *see infra* paras. 1006 and 1136. On the issue, see Stephen M. Schwebel, *The Authority of a Truncated Tribunal*, in ICCA CONGRESS SERIES NO. 9, IMPROVING THE EFFICIENCY OF ARBITRATION AGREEMENTS AND AWARDS: 40 YEARS OF APPLICATION OF THE NEW YORK CONVENTION 314 (A.J. van den Berg ed., 1999); Emmanuel Gaillard, *When an Arbitrator Withdraws*, N.Y.L.J., June 4, 1998, at 3.

[235] TGI, Paris, réf., Feb. 15, 1995, *Industrialexport, supra* note 176; CA Paris, July 1, 1997, Agence Transcongolaise des Communications-Chemins de fer Congo Océan (ATC-CFCO) v. Compagnie minière de l'Ogooué (Comilog), 1998 REV. ARB. 131, and D. Hascher's note. On these decisions, see *infra* para. 1136.

[236] TGI Paris, Jan. 12, 1988, *Omnium de Travaux, supra* note 210.

[237] On this point, see *supra* para. 868.

arbitrator as soon as possible and arranging for a further hearing in the event that any difficulty should arise in re-constituting the tribunal.[238]

As it happened, that approach proved to be effective,[239] but it does not resolve all the problems that currently result from the shortcomings of French law on the point. When it is necessary to replace an arbitrator, the courts should have the power to decide whether the arbitral proceedings have merely been suspended and to determine exactly how they will be resumed with the new arbitrator.

3° The Procedure for Judicial Intervention

885. — Article 1493, paragraph 2 of the New Code of Civil Procedure governs the procedural aspects of judicial intervention. It states that:

> the most diligent party may, in the absence of a clause to the contrary, apply to the President of the *Tribunal de Grande Instance* of Paris in accordance with the procedures of Article 1457.[240]

The rules contained in Article 1457 are relatively succinct, dealing in turn with the determination of the relevant jurisdiction (a), the organization of the hearing (b), and the finality of the resulting decision (c).

a) Relevant Jurisdiction

886. — As discussed earlier, under French international arbitration law, jurisdiction to hear all difficulties regarding the constitution of the arbitral tribunal is conferred on one judge: the President of the Paris Tribunal of First Instance. This centralization of all disputes arising out of the constitution of an arbitral tribunal having its situs in France is an important feature of French international arbitration law.

887. — The President of the Paris Tribunal of First Instance is not obliged to rule in person. In accordance with the practice of the court, the task maybe delegated by the President to another judge, often a vice-president or senior judge of the same court.

In addition, if a case is particularly important or sensitive, the President (or the judge to whom the case has been delegated) will sometimes hear it together with other judges. In such

---

[238] TGI Paris, réf., July 12, 1989, *supra* note 213.

[239] On the subsequent constitution of the new tribunal and the resolution of the challenge raised at that hearing, see TGI Paris, réf., Sept. 21, 1989, *La Belle Créole, supra* note 226.

[240] Article 1457 contains a number of procedural rules applicable to judicial intervention in domestic arbitration in matters regarding the application of Articles 1444, 1454, 1456 and 1463 of the same Code. It is Article 1493, paragraph 2 which enables these procedural rules to be extended to international arbitration by the reference it makes to Article 1457.

cases, the court itself delivers the judgment, as in the *République de Guinée* case, for example.

888. — The reason why all such litigation is heard by a single court in France, irrespective of where the arbitration is held, is simple. The vast majority of international arbitrations with their seat in France take place in Paris, where many of the law firms involved in arbitration are located. As a result, a number of judges from the Paris Tribunal of First Instance have acquired broad experience of both the law and practice of a relatively specialized field. It allows them to perform their delicate role of co-operation most capably. In other words, judicial specialization was essential, and it is clear from the quality of decisions made on the basis of Article 1493, paragraph 2 that it has been successfully achieved.[241]

889. — In international arbitration[242] the parties are free to choose a different judge, or indeed any other predetermined third party, to help them constitute the arbitral tribunal.[243] The jurisdiction of the President of the Paris Tribunal of First Instance is thus neither mandatory nor exclusive—the parties can choose any other authority instead.

However, if the chosen authority is a French court or a judge (the President of a Commercial Court, for example, or the President of a Tribunal of First Instance outside Paris), the intervention of that judge appears to be governed not by Article 1457 of the New Code of Civil Procedure, but by ordinary French procedural rules.[244]

---

[241] Having these cases heard by only one court has also proved to be beneficial in eliminating domestic conflicts of jurisdiction *ratione materiae* and *ratione loci*. In French domestic arbitration, Article 1457, paragraph 3 of the New Code of Civil Procedure sets out precise rules governing territorial jurisdiction which do not apply in international arbitration. However, that article does cover cases where the defendant in the court proceedings is not resident in France (in which case, if the seat of arbitration is undetermined, the president of the court where the defendant is resident will have jurisdiction). That text, which was drafted in 1980, no longer applies to international arbitration, because specific rules covering international arbitration were added to the Code in 1981. It remains of relevance only in exceptional cases where, despite the fact that one of the parties to the arbitration (the defendant) is resident abroad, the dispute does not involve the interests of international trade (on this concept, see *supra* paras. 107 *et seq.*). As far as jurisdiction *ratione materiae* is concerned, it should be noted that the President of the Commercial Court is no longer involved. This is perhaps unfortunate as that court plays an important role in the French business world. The desire to simplify matters prevailed and the President of the Commercial Court will only have jurisdiction if the parties have expressly provided so in their agreement (Art. 1444, para. 2, and Art. 1456).

[242] In French domestic arbitration, the *Cour de cassation* overturned a decision of a Court of Appeals which failed to comply with the choice of assisting jurisdiction set out in the arbitration clause. *See* Cass. 2e civ., Mar. 29, 1995, Bouyssou v. Gaillard, 1995 Bull. Civ. II, No. 110; 1995 REV. ARB. 605, 1st decision, and A. Hory's note.

[243] This is the significance of the words "in the absence of a clause to the contrary" found in Article 1493, paragraph 2.

[244] This view appears to be implicit in a 1995 decision of the *Cour de cassation*, overruling a July 7, 1992 decision of the Paris Court of Appeals (Laiguède v. Ahsen Inc., 1994 REV. ARB. 728, and observations by T. Bernard). In that case, which arose out of an international arbitration, the arbitration clause stipulated that all disputes were to be resolved by an arbitrator appointed by the President of the Paris Commercial Court acting as a sole judge in expedited proceedings ("*référé*"). However, the arbitrator appointed by that judge declined jurisdiction, whereupon the judge authorized the claimant to argue the issue before the full Paris Commercial Court. On the

(continued...)

b) Organization of the Proceedings

890. — The rules of procedure contained in the New Code of Civil Procedure regarding the organization of the proceedings are somewhat brief (1), which has led the President of the Paris Tribunal of First Instance to develop an important body of case law (2).

1) Rules of Procedure

891. — Article 1457 of the New Code of Civil Procedure provides that "the President of the *Tribunal*, seized as in expedited proceedings (*référé*) by a party or by the arbitral tribunal, shall rule by way of an order."

892. — By stating that the President is to be seized in the same way as for expedited proceedings, the text merely provides an analogy as far as the commencement of the action is concerned. It is not intended to suggest a full assimilation with expedited proceedings, as we shall see when we discuss the finality of the decisions eventually made.[245] In particular, the President's jurisdiction is not conditional upon the question needing urgent resolution or the absence of serious opposition to the measure.[246]

893. — In principle, the judge is seized by means of a summons (*assignation*), as that is the normal way of initiating expedited proceedings. However, the parties may also file a joint application (*requête conjointe*) with the clerk of the tribunal.[247]

As with a summons, a joint application enables both parties to appear before the judge and thus allows both sides a full hearing. That is an essential requirement of the procedure for resolving difficulties regarding the constitution of the arbitral tribunal. It would be

---

[244](...continued)
basis of Article 1457, paragraph 1 of the New Code of Civil Procedure, the Court of Appeals held inadmissible an appeal of the decision of the Paris Commercial Court, which had eventually nominated an arbitrator. However, the *Cour de cassation*, referring to that Article but also to Articles 1493, 1504 and 1502, paragraph 2 of the same Code, ruled that: "the arbitrator was appointed without regard to the parties' intentions or to the aforementioned texts, and was therefore appointed unlawfully, and the appeal against the decision of the judge who made that appointment without having the power to do so is therefore admissible" (Cass. 1e civ., May 10, 1995, Laiguède v. Ahsen Inox, 1995 Bull. Civ. I, No. 191; 1995 REV. ARB. 605, 2d decision, and A. Hory's note). The *Cour de cassation* thus did not apply the rule in Article 1457, paragraph 1 whereby a court decision appointing an arbitrator is not capable of appeal, first because the parties had chosen a judge other than the President of the Paris Tribunal of First Instance, but perhaps also because the Commercial Court had exceeded its powers by substituting itself for its President, who was of course the judge chosen by the parties to appoint the arbitrator (on the admissibility of an appeal on the grounds that the President of the Paris *Tribunal de grande instance* ruled *ultra vires*, see *infra* paras. 905 *et seq.*).

[245] *See infra* paras. 902 *et seq.*

[246] *See* Philippe Bertin, *L'intervention des juridictions au cours de la procédure arbitrale*, 1982 REV. ARB. 331, 335.

[247] *See* Articles 54 and 57 of the New Code of Civil Procedure. For an example of a motion filed jointly, in French domestic arbitration, see TGI Paris, Feb. 22, 1984, Cordier v. Ruzé, 1985 REV. ARB. 91.

inconceivable for the courts to interfere in an international arbitration unless all parties had been heard or at least summonsed.

894. — Article 1457 enables the arbitral tribunal itself to seize the judge, and arbitrators have used it on several occasions. At times, as we have seen, they have even requested that the judge go beyond his powers in this area, by asking for a ruling on their own jurisdiction[248] or even for a form of legal opinion.[249]

Provided that the arbitrators do observe the limits of the judge's powers, it is appropriate for them to apply to the judge if both parties fail to take the necessary action. It is in the arbitrators' personal interest that their tribunal be lawfully and rapidly constituted and that any problems which might arise in that process, including the challenge of an arbitrator, be resolved by the proper authority. If need be, they may also apply to the judge to obtain an extension of the deadline for completion of the arbitral proceedings, assuming they fail to obtain the parties' agreement on the matter in due time.[250] By accepting their brief, the arbitrators become contractually bound to the parties,[251] and if they fail to act with due diligence in carrying out that brief, they could ultimately be liable to the parties.[252]

895. — Although Article 1457 expressly confers the right to apply to the judge on the arbitral tribunal alone, that right has been extended to each of the arbitrators individually. In the *République de Guinée* case, one of the Republic's opponents, together with each of the arbitrators forming the arbitral tribunal, applied to the judge for an extension of the deadline for completion of the arbitral proceedings. The action on the part of the arbitrators was contested, but the court allowed it in the following terms:

> each of the arbitrators has *locus standi* to apply for the extension, provided that the judge, as far as possible, seeks the opinion of the other arbitrators. The arbitral tribunal is not an autonomous legal entity distinct from each of the arbitrators. Although the arbitrators may act together to ensure that the arbitration progresses smoothly, each of them can be personally liable in the exercise of their functions. The expiration of an arbitration deadline is an event which could potentially give rise to such liability.[253]

The court could hardly have been clearer: it is the individuals within the arbitral tribunal who perform the arbitrators' brief and who have an interest in doing so. It is more than likely that they will not all share the same views regarding the difficulty with the constitution of the tribunal which has arisen, either because they simply do not have the same opinions as to what their role and duties entail, or because of their respective positions within the arbitral

---

[248] TGI Paris, réf., Oct. 14, 1985, *Chayaporn Rice*, *supra* note 205.

[249] TGI Paris, réf., Oct. 30, 1990, *European Country Hotels*, *supra* note 210.

[250] On this issue, see *supra* para. 866.

[251] On this acceptance, see *infra* paras. 941 *et seq.*

[252] On arbitrators' liability, see *infra* paras. 1142 *et seq.*

[253] TGI Paris, réf., Nov. 29, 1989, Omnium de Travaux v. République de Guinée, 1990 REV. ARB. 525.

tribunal—a party-appointed arbitrator will not necessarily behave in the same way as the tribunal's chairman.

In addition, if the arbitral tribunal is either not yet or no longer complete, the initiative of applying to the judge will necessarily be taken by one or two arbitrators, acting individually.

896. — On these questions the courts display considerable flexibility. For instance, the President of the Paris Tribunal of First Instance had no hesitations in hearing an application filed solely in the name of the arbitral tribunal followed by the name and address of its attorney. He allowed the tribunal's claim against both parties, neither of which appeared, for an extension of the proceedings.[254]

897. — The same flexibility is evident with regard to the participation of arbitrators in cases where they are not themselves claimants. It is not uncommon for them to be involved, collectively or individually, in proceedings before the judge. Whether or not they participate often depends on whether they are personally implicated in the difficulty with the constitution of the arbitral tribunal.

898. — Even where they are not personally implicated, they may be summonsed by the claimant, if only to ensure that the resulting decision will be enforceable against them. Depending on the circumstances, they may[255] or may not be represented by an attorney.[256] Irrespective of whether they are represented or not, the judge will hear them if they wish to express their point of view on the problem to be resolved, or if the judge wishes to hear it. The judge may want to establish, for example, if and when the arbitrator accepted his or her brief, so that with full knowledge of those facts a decision can then be made whether or not to extend the arbitral proceedings.[257] A less formal alternative is for the judge to simply take into account a memorandum[258] or letter[259] in which the arbitrator informs the court of the status of the arbitral proceedings and comments on the measures, such as an extension, sought by one of the parties. The judge even noted in one case that the arbitrators had appeared voluntarily, without challenging his jurisdiction or disputing his power to grant an extension. He therefore concluded that the arbitrators were deemed to have subjected the arbitration to French procedural law, and on that basis he confirmed his international jurisdiction to grant the extension.[260]

899. — Where the arbitrators are personally involved, the claimant will sometimes summons them personally, and the judge will be keen to hear them. This will be the case,

---

[254] TGI Paris, réf., June 3, 1988, *Bachmann, supra* note 210.

[255] TGI Paris, réf., Jan. 12, 1988, *Omnium de Travaux, supra* note 210.

[256] TGI Paris, réf., May 10, and Oct. 30, 1990, *European Country Hotels, supra* note 210.

[257] TGI Paris, réf., May 9, and June 19, 1984, *Font Laugière Chimie, supra* note 210.

[258] TGI Paris, réf., Apr. 3, 1985, *Application des gaz, supra* note 168.

[259] TGI Paris, réf., July 6, 1990, *Irridelco International, supra* note 210.

[260] TGI Paris, réf., Apr. 3, 1985, *Application des gaz, supra* note 168.

for instance, where a party seeks to have an arbitrator replaced for refusing to act.[261] In such a case, it will be useful for the judge to hear the arbitrator in person.[262] That situation can obviously create considerable tension between the arbitrator and a party, but fortunately it rarely happens in practice. Generally, the arbitrator does not attend the proceedings, which simply involve the parties to the arbitration, but the judge will be informed by one of the parties of the position taken by the arbitrator with regard to the challenge.[263]

900. — In the *Philipp Brothers* case, the President of the Paris Tribunal of First Instance sought to go beyond previous practice and establish precise rules governing the question. Addressing Philipp Brothers' challenge of nine arbitrators, he held that:

> the judge must, in all cases, ensure that all parties have a fair hearing and the opportunity to present their case. He cannot reach a decision on a challenge based on an arbitrator's personal qualities without having informed that arbitrator of the existence and basis of the proceedings and, in particular, without having allowed the arbitrator to make any observations he considers appropriate.[264]

It is not necessary for a party challenging an arbitrator to join that arbitrator in the proceedings, as such proceedings can properly take place between the two parties alone. The judge must, however, ensure that the arbitrator is informed of the existence of the proceedings and give the arbitrator the opportunity to comment on the challenge.

2) Practice of the Court

901. — The handful of statutory rules governing the proceedings are complemented by the practice of the courts, as can be seen from the numerous interventions by the President of the Paris Tribunal of First Instance since 1981. The various decisions discussed above undoubtedly reveal a degree of empiricism, which is inevitable given the diversity of the cases brought before the judge. The Tribunal's two major objectives are nonetheless clearly discernible.

The first of those objectives is to involve the parties directly in the choice of replacement arbitrators. Thus, after rejecting any objections raised by the defendant to the appointment of an arbitrator, the Tribunal will allow the defendant, or the two parties jointly, enough time either to nominate the arbitrators, or to provide a list of names, or to express their opinion

---

[261] TGI Paris, réf., Apr. 10, 1990, *European Country Hotels, supra* note 192.

[262] TGI Paris, réf., June 23, 1988, *République de Guinée, supra* note 139; TGI Paris, réf., July 2, 1990, *Annahold, supra* note 227.

[263] TGI Paris, réf., Jan. 13, 1986, S.A. Setec Bâtiment v. Société Industrielle et Commerciale des Charbonnages, 1987 REV. ARB. 63, and P. Bellet's note; TGI Paris, réf., Sept. 21, 1989, *La Belle Créole, supra* note 226.

[264] TGI Paris, réf., June 14, 1989, *Philipp Brothers, supra* note 174.

on the arbitrator or arbitrators whom they wish to appoint. In each case the court will have regard to the common intention of the parties.

The Tribunal's second objective is to ensure that the proceedings are not unduly delayed by new objections or sustained disagreements. Thus, although it will grant the parties time to make their decision regarding the replacement arbitrator or arbitrators, it will invariably impose a short deadline for doing so (a few weeks at the most). In addition, it will instruct the parties (and the arbitrators, if appropriate) to attend a further hearing in the course of which it will verify that the necessary appointments have been made, and will rule on any unresolved difficulty.[265]

This line of practice is an original blend of liberalism and interventionism, which is all the more effective for the fact that the Tribunal's decisions can only rarely be appealed.

c) Finality of the Court's Decisions

902. — Under Article 1457 of the New Code of Civil Procedure

> the President of the *Tribunal* . . . shall rule by way of an order against which no recourse is available.
>
> However, such order may be appealed when the President holds that no appointment shall be made for one of the reasons set forth in Article 1444 (paragraph 3). The appeal shall be brought, heard and decided as for recourse against jurisdictional decisions (*contredit de compétence*).

In a clear attempt to restrict appeals and any other litigation subsequent to the judge's decision, recent case law has drawn the following consequences from Article 1457, some of which are not self-evident.

1) An Ordinary Appeal Is Inadmissible

903. — In this respect, the text is clear. Apart from cases where the court refuses to appoint an arbitrator on the grounds that the arbitration agreement is manifestly void or inadequate (under Article 1444, paragraph 3, which is not directly applicable to international arbitration),[266] its decision is not capable of appeal.

Nevertheless, several appeals have been filed against decisions where the appellant claimed that the rule set out in Article 1457 did not apply to international arbitration. The appellants argued that the reference to Article 1457 in Article 1493, paragraph 2 only concerns the procedure for petitioning the court, and not the possibility of appealing against

---

[265] See, for decisions prior to 1986, Fouchard, *supra* note 55, at 37 *et seq.*, and the references cited therein; more recent decisions of importance include *Philipp Brothers* (*supra* note 32), *La Belle Créole* (*supra* notes 213 and 226) and *European Country Hotels* (*supra* notes 192 and 210); *see also* TGI Paris, réf., Apr. 23, 1997, *G.M.F. Assistance Internationale, supra* note 194.

[266] *See supra* paras. 832 *et seq.* and 851.

its decision. In support of that restrictive interpretation it was also noted that, in listing the situations in which a decision is not capable of appeal, Article 1457 does not refer expressly to the situation described in Article 1493, paragraph 2. That very literal interpretation of the two texts is in total contradiction with the spirit of the 1981 reform of French international arbitration law. There is no reason to broaden the scope for appeals against the court decisions in international arbitration as compared to court decisions in domestic arbitration. Consequently, the appeals were all held to be inadmissible.[267] The most recent of these decisions clearly explains the court's reasoning:

> That reference [in Article 1493, paragraph 2], which is not confined to provisions concerning domestic arbitration, means that the procedure provided for in Article 1457 is applicable to international arbitration, and it should not be interpreted as referring solely to the manner in which the judge is to be petitioned. The judge's decisions are not therefore capable of appeal. The reasons for excluding a second tier of jurisdiction in domestic arbitration, which stem from the need to prevent the use of an appeal as a stalling tactic, remain entirely valid in international arbitration.[268]

The *Cour de cassation* likewise appears to have rejected the idea of a special system of recourse against decisions concerning the appointment of arbitrators in international arbitration.[269]

2) No Recourse to the *Cour de cassation*

904. — Although there can be no ordinary appeal against the decision of the President of the Paris Tribunal of First Instance, is it possible to appeal to the French Supreme Court, the *Cour de cassation*? Some commentators considered that to be the case, arguing that Article 1457 refers only to ordinary appeals, and that recourse to the *Cour de cassation*, which is an extraordinary form of recourse, is always available in respect of decisions which cannot be appealed. That would enable the Supreme Court not only to exercise "disciplinary" control over the decisions of the lower court, but also to maintain a uniform interpretation of the law. Without an express provision to that effect, these commentators were of the view that such an action could not be excluded. However, the *Cour de cassation* took a different view, holding the action filed by Philipp Brothers against the decision of the President of the Paris Tribunal of First Instance discussed above to be inadmissible:

---

[267] CA Paris, Nov. 9, 1983, Wasteels v. Ampafrance, 1985 REV. ARB. 81, 11th decision; CA Paris, July 9, 1986, *Alexandre Giuliani*, *supra* note 186; CA Paris, June 19, 1998, *UNESCO*, *supra* note 181.

[268] CA Paris, Nov. 24, 1989, *The Gemtel Partnership*, *supra* note 215.

[269] Cass. 1e civ., May 10, 1995, *Laiguède*, *supra* note 244.

The court has considered Articles 1444, 1457 and 1493 of the New Code of Civil Procedure. In the field of international arbitration, the President of the Paris Tribunal of First Instance, seized as in summary proceedings, rules on problems concerning the constitution of the arbitral tribunal by making a decision from which no appeal lies. The [present] action has been filed against a decision delivered by the President of a Tribunal of First Instance who rejected the challenges brought by Philipp Brothers against the arbitrators and held that the tribunals responsible for deciding the disputes between Philipp Brothers and various other companies were constituted. Recourse of that kind is not admissible.[270]

In support of that decision, it was pointed out that the *Cour de cassation* had always interpreted such provisions in that way, so that where statute stipulates that a court rules "without recourse," or that "no recourse" lies from a court decision, recourse to the *Cour de cassation* is also excluded.[271]

3) An Appeal on the Grounds that a Judge Has Ruled *Ultra Vires* Is Admissible in Exceptional Circumstances

905. — As the exclusion of all forms of appeal against a judicial decision may be considered somewhat disconcerting,[272] some authors have suggested that an appeal against a decision made *ultra vires* should be admissible, as is generally the case with regard to any decision described in statute as being incapable of appeal.[273]

906. — The French courts now tend to allow this form of appeal against decisions of the assisting judge.

Initially, an appeal was held to be inadmissible on the basis of either the existence of an action to set the award aside,[274] or an examination of the facts of each case, which showed

---

[270] Cass. 2e civ., Nov. 22, 1989, Philipp Brothers v. Drexel Burnham Lambert, 1989 Bull. Civ. II, No. 209; 1990 REV. ARB. 142, and S. Guinchard's note.

[271] S. Guinchard, note following Cass. 2e civ., Nov. 22, 1989, *Philipp Brothers*, *supra* note 270, and the references cited therein.

[272] See the observations made by Gérard Pluyette at the January 27, 1992 colloquium organized by the Comité français de l'arbitrage on *Les perspectives d'évolution du droit français de l'arbitrage*, 1992 REV. ARB. 312, 318.

[273] S. Guinchard, note following Cass. 2e civ., Nov. 22, 1989, *Philipp Brothers*, *supra* note 270; A. Hory, note following Cass. 2e civ., Mar. 10, 1993, Laiguède v. Ahsen Inox, CA Paris, Apr. 16, 1992, Perma v. S.a.r.l. Maxime, and CA Paris, May 26, 1992, Guyapêche v. Export AB Frantz Witte, 1993 REV. ARB. 431.

[274] CA Paris, Nov. 14, 1991, Consorts Legrand v. European Country Hotels Ltd., 1994 REV. ARB. 545, 2d decision, and observations by P. Fouchard.

that the President of the Paris Tribunal of First Instance had exercised his powers in accordance with the provisions of the New Code of Civil Procedure.[275]

Subsequently, however, the *Cour de cassation* held that a decision in which a judge appoints an arbitrator "without being empowered to do so" can be appealed. That decision would have provided clear confirmation of the admissibility of appeals against *ultra vires* decisions, had the judge's absence of jurisdiction resulted from a violation of the law and not from a breach of the arbitration agreement alone.[276]

More recently, the Paris Court of Appeals clearly authorized this form of appeal, where the decision of the President of the lower court is "seriously defective as a result of the violation of a fundamental principle or of public policy,"[277] if it is *ultra vires*, or if it "contravenes the parties' fundamental rights."[278] The *Cour de cassation*, in cases concerning French domestic arbitration, has endorsed the availability of an appeal where the lower courts exceed their powers,[279] and has fixed the time period within which such an appeal must be brought.[280]

4) Finality of the Decision when the Award Is Subsequently Reviewed by the Courts

907. — One last question concerning the finality of a decision made under Articles 1493, paragraph 2 and 1457 of the New Code of Civil Procedure arose in the *Philipp Brothers* case.

Was the decision *res judicata*, given that the judge was seized "as in expedited proceedings" and that, in principle, a decision in expedited proceedings is not *res judicata*?[281] The simple answer is that the assimilation with expedited proceedings only goes to the manner in which the President of the Tribunal of First Instance is seized. The President's decision is not provisional, unlike the provisional rulings described in Article 484 of the New Code of Civil Procedure. It is a final decision on the merits of the question.[282]

908. — However, we also need to consider whether the Court of Appeals, when hearing an action to set aside an award or reverse an enforcement order, can overrule the decision of the President of the Tribunal of First Instance. For example, is the Court of Appeals

---

[275] CA Paris, Apr. 16, 1992, *Perma, supra* note 273; Cass. 2e civ., May 16, 1994, Perma v. Entreprise Maxime, 1994 REV. ARB. 715, 2d decision, and A. Hory's note; Dalloz, Jur. 423 (1994), and Y. Chartier's note.

[276] Cass. 1e civ., May 10, 1995, *Laiguède, supra* note 244.

[277] CA Paris, Dec. 19, 1995, GECI v. Industrialexport, 1996 REV. ARB. 110, and A. Hory's note; 1996 RTD COM. 454, and observations by J.-C. Dubarry and E. Loquin.

[278] CA Paris, Sept. 30, 1997, *GECI, supra* note 175.

[279] Cass. 2e civ., Dec. 18, 1996, Spedidam v. Adami, 1997 REV. ARB. 361, 1st decision, and A. Hory's note; Cass. 2e civ., Apr. 8, 1998, Doux v. Fidimesc, 1998 REV. ARB. 373, and A. Hory's note.

[280] Cass. 2e civ., Jan. 21, 1998, Consorts Bailly v. Ets. H. Binetruy, 1998 REV. ARB. 113, and A. Hory's note.

[281] *See* Art. 488 of the New Code of Civil Procedure.

[282] *See* S. Guinchard, note following Cass. 2e civ., Nov. 22, 1989, *Philipp Brothers, supra* note 270; DE BOISSÉSON, *supra* note 30, ¶ 648 at 572.

bound by the judge's findings as to the identity of the arbitral institution or appointing authority, or the interpretation of the provisions of the arbitration agreement concerning the method of appointing the arbitrators or, most importantly, by the judge's decision on a challenge of an arbitrator? All of these questions can be raised before the Court of Appeals on the basis of Articles 1502 and 1504 of the New Code of Civil Procedure, by way of a claim that the arbitration agreement is void (Art. 1502 1°), that the constitution of the arbitral tribunal is irregular (Art. 1502 2°), or that there has been a violation of international public policy (1502 5°).

909. — In the *Philipp Brothers* case[283] it was argued that the Court of Appeals had complete freedom to review the lower court's decision, because one of the three conditions governing the *res judicata* effect of decisions laid down by Article 1351 of the Civil Code was not satisfied: even if the action before the Court of Appeals was based on the same grounds and involved the same parties, the object of the two proceedings was different. Before the President of the Tribunal of First Instance, the object of the action was to replace an arbitrator; before the Court of Appeals, it was to have the award set aside.

910. — The apparent strength of this argument[284] failed to convince the Paris Court of Appeals in the action to set aside the awards made following the various decisions of the President of the Paris Tribunal of First Instance. The action to set aside was based, in particular, on a claim that the arbitral tribunals were unlawfully constituted. In a carefully reasoned judgment, the Court of Appeals held that:

> the decisions rejecting the challenges against all of the arbitrators who were subsequently required to make an award, which are not open to appeal, constituted irrevocable decisions as to the independence of the challenged arbitrators, and that issue cannot be reviewed in an action to set aside the award. This is because, first, the object of the claim (a qualitative assessment of the arbitrators) is identical in both the challenge and the action to set aside, each of which is based on a lack of independence on the part of the arbitrators illustrated by the same facts; and, second, by deciding the challenges concerning the arbitrators themselves, without the possibility of an appeal, the intervention of the judge in the constitution of the arbitral tribunal established and guaranteed the lawfulness of the constitution of the tribunal in that respect.

That being the case, the Court of Appeals considered that "a further challenge concerning the lawfulness of the constitution of the tribunal could only be based on the subsequent discovery of a defect affecting its constitution."[285]

The Court of Appeals rejected all of the new complaints leveled at the arbitrators and dismissed the action to set aside the award. Its decision, which did not subsequently go

---

[283] TGI Paris, réf., June 29, 1989, *Philipp Brothers*, *supra* note 32.

[284] *See* DE BOISSÉSON, *supra* note 30, ¶ 648 at 572.

[285] CA Paris, Apr. 6, 1990, *Philipp Brothers*, *supra* note 33.

before the *Cour de cassation*, was not universally well-received.[286] However, apart from the specific case of the refusal to replace an arbitrator, decisions made by the President of the Tribunal of First Instance will not usually restrict the Court of Appeals' powers in an action to set aside an award based on a ground directly concerning the award. Thus, the fact that the President of the Tribunal of First Instance may have extended the deadline for the completion of the arbitral proceedings will not prevent the Court of Appeals from making its own decision as to whether the arbitration agreement had already expired when the first instance judge intervened.[287] There is always a need for review by the courts of the essential aspects of the legality of an arbitral award, but one tier of control suffices. French law is consistent in its desire to avoid multiplying the means of recourse to the courts in international arbitration.

B. – OTHER LEGAL SYSTEMS

911. — The French approach to court assistance with the constitution of the arbitral tribunal very much reflects the change in attitude of law-makers worldwide towards arbitration, and particularly towards international arbitration. Legislators now want the courts to provide support for arbitration, if necessary, both at the beginning and during the course of proceedings, so as to ensure that the parties' intentions are fully complied with. The role of the courts is thus no longer confined to reviewing and enforcing arbitral awards. It also involves ensuring that the arbitration agreement is fully effective and, in particular, helping to set up the arbitral tribunal.[288]

912. — The same trends appear in recent arbitration legislation promulgated around the world.

913. — First—and although this is not really a novelty—the parties are free to determine how difficulties concerning the constitution (or reconstitution) of the arbitral tribunal are to be resolved. To take only one example, the UNCITRAL Model Law, and all legislation adopting it,[289] provides that the parties are free to agree on a procedure for challenging an arbitrator (Art. 13(1)). They also allow the parties to agree to terminate the arbitrator's mandate in the event of default (Art. 14), and stipulate that whenever an arbitrator is to be replaced, the replacement arbitrator is to be nominated under the rules that governed the appointment of the arbitrator being replaced (Art. 15).

---

[286] See the criticisms made by DE BOISSÉSON, *supra* note 30, ¶ 648 at 572–73 and, in favor, S. Guinchard, note following Cass. 2e civ., Nov. 22, 1989, *Philipp Brothers, supra* note 270.

[287] CA Paris, Nov. 14, 1991, *Consorts Legrand, supra* note 274.

[288] *See* Berthold Goldman, *The Complementary Roles of Judges and Arbitrators in Ensuring that International Commercial Arbitration is Effective, in* INTERNATIONAL ARBITRATION – 60 YEARS OF ICC ARBITRATION – A LOOK AT THE FUTURE 257 (ICC Publication No. 412, 1984).

[289] On the worldwide influence of the Model Law, see *supra* para. 205.

914. — Second, and more importantly, comparative law shows that the trend in favor of judicial assistance is universal.[290] It can be seen, for example, in arbitration provisions incorporated in the Belgian Judicial Code in 1972 (Arts. 1684 to 1687), in the Netherlands Code of Civil Procedure in 1986 (Arts. 1026 to 1035), in the Swiss Private International Law Statute in 1987 (Arts. 179, 180 and 185), in the Italian Code of Civil Procedure in 1994 (Art. 810), in the English Arbitration Act in 1996 (Sec. 18), and in the German ZPO in 1997 (Arts. 1034, 1035, 1037, 1038, and 1062).

915. — Difficulties concerning the constitution of the arbitral tribunal and the exact role of the "assisting judge" (*juge d'appui*), to use the Swiss terminology,[291] raise the same issues in other jurisdictions as they do in France.

In Switzerland, for instance, Article 179, paragraph 2 of the Private International Law Statute provides that in the absence of an agreement between the parties, the court of the district where the arbitral tribunal has its seat can hear claims regarding the appointment, removal and replacement of arbitrators. Under paragraph 3 of the same article

> [w]here a court is called upon to appoint an arbitrator, it shall make the appointment, unless a summary examination shows that no arbitration agreement exists between the parties.

Although the Statute is silent on the point, the Swiss Federal Tribunal held in one decision that appeals against a cantonal judge's decision to appoint an arbitrator were inadmissible, and that such an approach was "entirely in keeping with the intentions of the legislator and the aim of the Private International Law Statute, which is, in particular, to limit appeals and the grounds on which they can be brought."[292] However, in a later decision, the Federal Tribunal held that the cantonal judge had not made an arbitrary ruling by deciding that the dispute for which he was asked to appoint an arbitrator was not covered by the arbitration agreement.[293] This solution was criticized by Swiss authors for having gone beyond the summary examination of the arbitration agreement to which the assisting judge should be confined, and for having infringed on the jurisdiction of the arbitral tribunal to determine its own jurisdiction under Article 186, paragraph 1 of the Swiss Private International Law Statute.[294] Our view is that, although judicial assistance in constituting the arbitral tribunal should not be granted automatically, the discretion of the court at such an early stage of the arbitral proceedings must be as limited as possible.

---

[290] See, for example, the legislation and case law listed by country in "Judicial appointment and removal of arbitrators," in PARKER SCHOOL OF FOREIGN AND COMPARATIVE LAW, COLUMBIA UNIVERSITY, INTERNATIONAL COMMERCIAL ARBITRATION AND THE COURTS 135–43 (1990).

[291] LALIVE, POUDRET, REYMOND, *supra* note 35, at 327 *et seq.*

[292] Swiss Fed. Trib., Sept. 11, 1989, 1989 BULL. ASA 371, and J.-F. Poudret's note; 1991 REV. SUISSE DR. INT. ET DR. EUR. 332, and F. Knoepfler's note.

[293] Swiss Fed. Trib. Feb. 27, 1992, F. Anstalt v. T. Company Ltd., 1992 BULL. ASA 347; 1993 REV. SUISSE DR. INT. ET DR. EUR. 203, and P. Schweizer's note.

[294] Paul Volken, *A propos de la nomination d'arbitres par le juge étatique*, 1993 BULL. ASA 3.

On the other hand, if the assisting judge rules on the challenge of an arbitrator, the Swiss Private International Law Statute (Art. 180, para. 3) expressly provides that the judge's decision will be final. This has been interpreted by the Swiss Federal Tribunal as excluding recourse under administrative law.[295] However, and in contrast with the position of the French courts,[296] the Swiss Federal Tribunal has held admissible recourse against an award made by an arbitral tribunal the members of which have not previously been challenged before the assisting judge.[297]

916. — The most recent non-French legislation also shares the French desire to limit the international jurisdiction of a court hearing a claim concerning a difficulty with the constitution of the arbitral tribunal. This can be seen in Austria, Switzerland, the Netherlands and Germany, for example.[298] The first two of those countries confine their courts' jurisdiction to cases where the seat of the arbitration is on their territory,[299] as does the UNCITRAL Model Law. Dutch and German law, on the other hand, allow the court to appoint the arbitrators even where the parties have not agreed on the seat of the arbitration, on the condition that at least one of the parties has its domicile or *de facto* residence in the Netherlands or in Germany, respectively.[300] This does not create a true jurisdictional privilege, because the jurisdiction of the Dutch or German courts is not based on the nationality of one of the parties. It may, however, cause problems if, before the courts of another country, the party with no connection with the Netherlands or Germany contests the jurisdiction of the Dutch or German court on the grounds that such jurisdiction is based solely on the fact that its opponent is *de facto* resident or domiciled in the Netherlands or in Germany. The 1994 Italian law on arbitration likewise extends the jurisdiction of the courts: they are able to intervene not only if the seat of the arbitration is in Italy, but also

> If the parties have not yet determined the seat of arbitration, the petition is presented to the President of the Court (*tribunale*) in the place where the submission to arbitration or the contract to which the arbitration clause refers has been executed or, if such place is abroad, to the President of the Court (*tribunale*) of Rome.[301]

---

[295] Feb. 9, 1998, I. SA v. V. (Hong Kong), 1998 BULL. ASA 634.

[296] *See supra* para. 910.

[297] Fed. Trib., Feb. 9, 1998, *supra* note 295. The recourse held admissible in this case (but rejected on the merits) was also an administrative law action, based on the violation of citizens' constitutional rights.

[298] *See also* P. Fouchard, notes following TGI Paris, réf., May 11, 1987, *Les Silos du Sud-Ouest*, *supra* note 164 and TGI Paris, réf., May 22 and June 23, 1987, *Transportacion Maritima Mexicana*, *supra* note 25, at 708.

[299] A tacit localization may suffice, however, according to the Geneva Court of Justice, Feb. 7, 1991, X v. Y and Z, 1991 BULL. ASA 155.

[300] Art. 1073, para. 2 of the Netherlands Code of Civil Procedure; Art. 1025(3) of the German ZPO (in force as of January 1, 1998).

[301] Art. 810, para. 2 of the Code of Civil Procedure. *See Italy* (Annex I), *in* ICCA INTERNATIONAL HANDBOOK ON COMMERCIAL ARBITRATION (1994).

The same preoccupation with directing all difficulties concerning the constitution of international arbitral tribunals to a single court for an entire country (such as Paris in France and Rome in Italy) can be seen outside Europe. Examples include Tunisia[302] and Egypt. Drawing inspiration from the UNCITRAL Model Law, in 1994 the Egyptian legislature decided that the Cairo Court of Appeals would have exclusive jurisdiction to exercise subsidiary powers over the constitution of the arbitral tribunal for all arbitrations taking place in Egypt, as well as those which, by agreement between the parties, are governed by Egyptian law.[303]

917. — The provisions of the UNCITRAL Model Law (Arts. 11, 13 and 14) are of particular importance because of their influence on worldwide legislation. The Model Law also addresses the concern that an arbitration could be delayed by disagreements as to the appointment of the arbitrator or arbitrators.

918. — First, it enables the parties to request "a third party, including an institution" to perform functions (which are not further defined) under a procedure for appointing arbitrators (Art. 11(4)(c)). It thereby recognizes the autonomy of institutional arbitration and of the arbitral institutions' power to intervene in the appointment of the arbitrators.

919. — Second, if the appointment of the arbitrator cannot be effected by the third party or institution chosen by the parties, a request can be submitted to the court or authority on which that role of assistance was conferred by the legislature when it introduced the Model Law into its legal system (Art. 11(3), and Art. 6). The provisions covering this form of judicial assistance (Art. 11(4) and (5)) are mandatory (Art. 11(2)), which is perfectly legitimate provided that such assistance remains subsidiary. As a result of these provisions, a disagreement between the parties or the negligence of an arbitral institution cannot prevent the constitution of the arbitral tribunal if at least one of the parties is relying on the arbitration agreement. Following the example of other modern laws, the Model Law adds that a decision by the appropriate court or authority to appoint an arbitrator is not open to appeal (Art. 11(5)). It also contains guidelines for selecting the arbitrator, concerning qualifications (which should be consistent with the intentions of the parties), nationality (which in some cases should differ from the nationalities of the parties), independence and impartiality.

920. — Other mandatory rules suggested by the Model Law are intended not only to organize judicial assistance, but also to restrict the autonomy of the parties and arbitral institutions.

---

[302] The Tunisian Code of Arbitration entrusts this mission to the First President of the Tunis Court of Appeals (Art. 56).

[303] Arts. 1, 9, 17, 19 and 20 of Law No. 27 for 1994 Promulgating the Law Concerning Arbitration in Civil and Commercial Matters; see also the commentary by Bernard Fillion-Dufouleur and Philippe Leboulanger, *Le nouveau droit égyptien de l'arbitrage*, 1994 REV. ARB. 665, 674 *et seq.*

921. — The first such rule, which governs the procedure for challenging arbitrators, is somewhat unsatisfactory. Having stated the principle that the parties are free to agree upon their own procedure for challenging arbitrators, the Model Law provides that failing such agreement the challenge is to be submitted to the arbitral tribunal itself (Art. 13(2)). This is unsatisfactory in that it may be difficult, in the event of a disagreement, for two arbitrators to dismiss the third. For that reason, Article 13, paragraph 3 provides that "[i]f a challenge under any procedure agreed upon by the parties or under the procedure of paragraph (2) of this article is unsuccessful" the challenge can then be submitted to a court or other chosen authority. The Model Law thus imposes an appeal to the courts (or other authority defined in Article 6) against any decision refusing to remove an arbitrator, irrespective of whether that decision was made by the arbitral institution, by a pre-appointed third party, or by the arbitral tribunal. This demonstrates a worrying lack of confidence in any form of privately-organized arbitration, and it also clearly incites parties to engage in delaying tactics. Furthermore, these disadvantages are hardly mitigated by the fact that an appeal to the courts or other authority would not entail staying the proceedings, as one can scarcely imagine that "while such a request is pending, the arbitral tribunal, including the challenged arbitrator, [would] continue the arbitral proceedings and make an award" (Art. 13(3)). Even if the tribunal were to consider that to be the appropriate course of action, would it have the necessary moral authority to do so? It would of course be preferable to allow the arbitral institution to rule without the possibility of an appeal, subject, possibly, to subsequent review of the award by the courts, which would enable them to address allegations regarding an arbitrator's independence and impartiality as potential violations of public policy (Arts. 34 and 36).

922. — The second restriction imposed by the Model Law concerns the conduct of the arbitral proceedings and must also apply to the constitution of the arbitral tribunal. Article 18 provides that "[t]he parties shall be treated with equality." That principle, which is now enshrined in a number of arbitration laws, is of course entirely laudable. It protects the parties from any negligence or bias on the part of the appointing authorities or arbitral institutions which the parties may have chosen.

C. – INTERNATIONAL CONVENTIONS

923. — Unlike the national laws examined above, two international conventions have preferred to resort to a non-judicial authority to resolve difficulties concerning the constitution of the arbitral tribunal. That is not so surprising in the case of the 1965 Washington Convention, as it created an institutional form of arbitration, the International Centre for Settlement of Investment Disputes (ICSID) (2°). The 1961 European Convention, however, also departs from the model found in national law (1°).

1° The 1961 European Convention

924. — Long before the adoption of modern arbitration laws providing for the intervention of the courts to resolve difficulties with the constitution of the arbitral tribunal, the 1961 European Convention set up an innovative mechanism aimed at facilitating the appointment of arbitrators in *ad hoc* arbitrations.[304]

925. — Paragraphs 2 to 7 of Article IV of the Convention establish a fairly complex system intended to operate where an arbitration agreement is inadequate or where there is disagreement among the parties, particularly as to the constitution of the arbitral tribunal. Its complexity stems primarily from the diversity of measures which may be required to constitute (or reconstitute) the arbitral tribunal if there are defects in the arbitration agreement or disagreements between the parties after the dispute has arisen. However, that complexity also has a more "political" origin: the predominant concern of the negotiators of the Convention was to enhance the efficiency of East-West international arbitration, and the economic and political divide which then separated the East and the West prevented them from seeking such measures from a national court. The authority or pre-appointed third party to which the parties could apply would therefore have to be a national or international economic organization. It was only after considerable effort that it was agreed that the role would be assumed by the Presidents of Chambers of Commerce, organizations which at least had the merit of existing in both the East and the West (although they were hardly similar institutions), and by an East-West organization with equal representation of both sides (the Special Committee), the composition of which was defined in the Annex to the Convention.

926. — The first and most elementary difficulty with the constitution of the arbitral tribunal arises where one of the parties refuses to appoint an arbitrator (or replace the arbitrator it appointed). In that case, in the absence of an agreement to the contrary, the other party (generally the plaintiff in the arbitration) may, within thirty days, request the President of the Chamber of Commerce where its opponent has its residence to appoint an arbitrator (Art. IV(2)).

In a 1991 decision, the Lyon Court of Appeals applied that provision to an arbitration agreement providing for an *ad hoc* arbitration where each party was to appoint an arbitrator. When the French defendant refused to do so, the Italian plaintiff applied to the President of the Milan Commercial Court, asking him to appoint the second arbitrator. Overruling an order enforcing the award made thereafter, the Lyon Court of Appeals held that, as the European Convention was applicable in that case, the Italian plaintiff ought to have applied not to the Italian courts but to the President of the Chamber of Commerce where the French defendant had its headquarters.[305] However, the application of Article IV, paragraph 2 in that

---

[304] For institutional arbitration, the Geneva Convention simply refers back to the rules of the institution chosen by the parties. *See supra* para. 814.

[305] CA Lyon, July 4, 1991, France-Embryon v. Argonauta, 118 J.D.I. 1000 (1991), and P. Kahn's note; for an English translation, see XIX Y.B. COM. ARB. 859 (1994).

case was questionable, given that it had been replaced, as between France and Italy, by the 1962 Paris Agreement Relating to Application of the European Convention.[306]

927. — Further difficulties with the constitution of the arbitral tribunal result from defective arbitration agreements. For example, the agreement may not set forth a method for appointing a sole arbitrator or the third arbitrator, or for replacing an arbitrator, and it may not indicate the seat of the arbitration (Art. IV(3)). In some cases, the parties may only have agreed upon a "blank" arbitration clause, simply stating that any disputes are to be resolved by arbitration, without specifying whether the arbitration is to be institutional or *ad hoc* (Art. IV(6)).[307] Where no subsequent agreement is reached by the parties, the measures to be taken will be determined as follows: if the parties have agreed on the seat of arbitration, the plaintiff may choose to apply either to the President of the Chamber of Commerce of the host country, or to the President of the Chamber of Commerce where the defendant has its residence; if there is no agreement as to the seat, the plaintiff may apply either to the President of the Chamber of Commerce where the defendant has its residence or, if it prefers, to the Special Committee.

928. — The Special Committee is a body in which East and West are equally represented. In theory, its seat is located in Geneva, and its composition initially raised considerable difficulties. Equal representation is only achieved by alternation, since the Special Committee always comprises three members, the first two being elected by the Chambers of Commerce of the East and the West, respectively, while the third—the President—is appointed on an alternating basis by the East or by the West. This system of rotation every two years ensures that the Committee remains impartial.[308]

929. — The Special Committee has been set up and renewed as planned, and the member states have designated the authorities that constitute "the Chambers of Commerce or other institutions" in their respective countries.[309]

930. — In practice, the system created by Article IV of the Convention has rarely been used. The Economic Commission for Europe, which was empowered to receive requests regarding the organization of arbitrations, dealt with less than ten cases, according to available information.[310]

931. — The entire mechanism contained in Article IV is particularly unwieldy. It reflects the political and legal hurdles which the Convention's negotiators had to overcome in order

---

[306] *See infra* para. 934.

[307] On this issue, see *supra* para. 486.

[308] For more details, see FOUCHARD, *supra* note 15, ¶¶ 426 *et seq*.

[309] This List, which is regularly updated, can be consulted on the T.M.C. Asser Instituut Website <http://www.asser.nl/ica/eur-c.htm>.

[310] *See* Dominique T. Hascher, *European Convention on International Commercial Arbitration of 1961 – Commentary*, XVII Y.B. COM. ARB. 711, ¶ 35 at 726 (1992); XX Y.B. COM. ARB. 1006, ¶ 35 at 1021 (1995).

to create a balanced system in which an external non-judicial authority could intervene to assist in the constitution of the arbitral tribunal.

As far as the institutions chosen in 1961 are concerned, the system has aged badly, particularly over the last few years. Following the demise of the CMEA and the privatization of the economies of Central and East European countries, there is no longer anything unique about the difficulties arising in East-West relations concerning the constitution of the arbitral tribunal. In addition, the changes which have affected the former chambers of foreign commerce in the East, and the likely creation in those countries of national committees of the International Chamber of Commerce, will soon deprive the Special Committee of any utility.

Nevertheless, at the time it was adopted, Article IV had the merit of overcoming the divisions and barriers that accompanied the partition of Europe. It enabled parties which had failed to agree on the choice of their arbitrators to resort to a mutually-acceptable "escape route." In that respect, the main advantage of Article IV was preventative.[311]

For the future, the system should be simplified. Applying to the Presidents of the national chambers of commerce has become unworkable in countries which have turned away from a centrally-planned economy. The East-West distinction based on the existence of an ICC national committee is now obsolete, and there is no longer any justification for equal representation in the Special Committee. A solution would be to repeal paragraphs 2 to 7 of Article IV, together with the Annex concerning the Special Committee, and to give subsidiary jurisdiction to a national court.[312]

932. — In any case, the original system did not apply to arbitrations that did not concern East-West relations. Within the CMEA, a number of socialist countries signed the Moscow Convention of May 26, 1972 on the Settlement by Arbitration of Civil Law Disputes Arising out of Economic, Scientific and Technical Co-operation Relationships, which gave jurisdiction over difficulties with the constitution of the arbitral tribunal to the arbitration commission for foreign trade of the defendant's country.[313] Similarly, several Western countries departed from the Article IV system in their mutual relations by signing the 1962 Paris Agreement.

933. — Although resorting to the Presidents of Chambers of Commerce or to the Special Committee seemed the best solution available in relations between East and West, in Western Europe a number of countries felt that those bodies were not the most appropriate institutions for the appointment of arbitrators in purely Western European disputes. Western European Chambers of Commerce are not national bodies, and it was considered debatable, at the very least, whether the Special Committee had jurisdiction to organize arbitrations

---

[311] Ottoarndt Glossner, *The Institutional Appointment of Arbitrators: The Special Committee of the European Convention on Commercial Arbitration of Geneva, 21 April 1961*, 12 ARB. INT'L 95 (1996).

[312] On preparatory work aimed at revising the Convention commenced by the Economic Commission for Europe and the UNCITRAL, see *supra* para. 284.

[313] Entered into force on Aug. 17, 1973. For an English translation, see 13 I.L.M. 5 (1974). On this Convention, see *supra* paras. 292 *et seq.*

between private corporations from the West, given that its members included representatives of socialist countries, who would sometimes be in the majority.

934. — These reservations led to the Paris Agreement, which was signed on December 17, 1962 under the auspices of the Council of Europe, and which now binds eight European states.[314] Having stated, in diplomatic terms, that the system created by the European Convention was not always suited to arbitrations between Western parties, and that by virtue of Article X, paragraph 7 of the Convention they were free to conclude other international instruments on arbitration, the signatories agreed (Art. 1) that for relations between parties established on their territory, paragraphs 2 to 7 of Article IV of the European Convention would be replaced by the following provision:

> If the arbitral Agreement contains no indication regarding the measures referred to in paragraph 1 of Article IV of the European Convention on International Commercial Arbitration as a whole, or some of these measures, any difficulties arising with regard to the constitution or functioning of the arbitral tribunal shall be submitted to the decision of the competent authority at the request of the party instituting proceedings.

935. — At the time, some commentators deplored the fact that this text allowed a national court to constitute an international arbitral tribunal and, worse, did not even specify exactly what was meant by the "competent authority."[315] This provision thus gave rise to possible conflicts between different jurisdictions which was precisely what the European Convention sought to avoid.

That criticism is less pertinent nowadays, as judicial assistance in arbitration exists in all Western European countries. Resorting to a national court has become a normal way of resolving difficulties with the constitution of the arbitral tribunal, and as a result the 1962 Paris Agreement has lost almost all its significance.[316] Nevertheless, the purely negative effect of the Agreement (the exclusion of the Convention's pre-designated third parties) should have been matched by something more positive. The drafters of the Agreement should have determined which court would have international jurisdiction, thus resolving the conflict between jurisdictions. In that respect, they could usefully have stipulated that the courts of the seat of the arbitration would have exclusive jurisdiction or, failing that, the courts of the defendant's domicile or residence. The 1991 case decided by the Lyon Court of Appeals[317] clearly shows that even if the 1962 Paris Agreement had been applied, it would not have provided the Court with directions as to international jurisdiction, and the Court

---

[314] On the Paris Agreement, see *supra* paras. 288 *et seq.*

[315] FOUCHARD, *supra* note 15, ¶ 454.

[316] This was successfully argued before the President of the District Court of Luxembourg on June 7, 1993, (XX Y.B. COM. ARB. 1067 (1995)) but was rejected by the Kortrijk Commercial Court in Belgium on October 1, 1993 (Société Lorraine de Matériel Radio-électrique (SLORA) v. NV Barco Electronic (XX Y.B. COM. ARB. 1057 (1995)).

[317] *See* CA Lyon, July 4, 1991, *France-Embryon*, *supra* note 305.

could not have ruled against the Italian plaintiff on the basis of that text for having asked the Italian courts, rather than the French courts, to appoint an arbitrator where the French defendant had refused to do so. Given that the 1968 Brussels Convention on Jurisdiction and Enforcement of Judgments in Civil and Commercial Matters has rightly been held to be inapplicable to any "litigation pending before a national court concerning the appointment of an arbitrator,"[318] the conflict between jurisdictions remains.

2° The 1965 Washington Convention

936. — No such problems arise under the Washington Convention of March 18, 1965, because it established a permanent arbitral institution, the International Centre for Settlement of Investment Disputes (ICSID), to resolve disputes relating to international investments.[319] Where the parties disagree over the appointment of the arbitrators, the institution will intervene.

937. — In the case of such a disagreement, if the arbitral tribunal has not been constituted within a period of 90 days, the Chairman of the Administrative Council of ICSID shall "at the request of either party and after consulting both parties as far as possible, appoint the arbitrator or arbitrators not yet appointed" (Art. 38 of the Convention). In principle, the arbitrators are drawn from a list and should be of a nationality other than that of the parties to the dispute, but this rule is less strict for arbitrators nominated by the parties (Arts. 39 and 40).

938. — The same rules apply to the replacement of an arbitrator. However, to prevent delaying tactics, the Convention stipulates that if a party-nominated arbitrator resigns without the approval of the arbitral tribunal as a whole, a replacement will be chosen by the Chairman of the Administrative Council (Art. 56).

Where a party challenges an arbitrator, the challenge is resolved by the other members of the arbitral tribunal, except where those members disagree or where there is only one arbitrator. In those cases, the decision is taken by the Chairman of the Administrative Council (Arts. 57 and 58).

---

[318] *See* Court of Justice of the European Communities, July 25, 1991, Case C–190/89, Marc Rich and Co. AG v. Società Italiana Impianti PA, 1991 E.C.R. I–3894, with the opinion of the adovcate general, Mr. Darmon; 1991 REV. ARB. 677, and D. Hascher's note; 119 J.D.I. 488 (1992), and observations by A. Huet; 1993 REV. CRIT. DIP 310, and P. Mayer's note; Riccardo Monaco, *Compétence arbitrale et compétence selon la Convention communautaire de 1968, in* ETUDES DE DROIT INTERNATIONAL EN L'HONNEUR DE PIERRE LALIVE 587 (1993); Bernard Audit, *L'arbitre, le juge et la Convention de Bruxelles, in* L'INTERNATIONALISATION DU DROIT – MÉLANGES EN L'HONNEUR DE YVON LOUSSOUARN 15 (1994); Dominique T. Hascher, *Recognition and Enforcement of Arbitration Awards and the Brussels Convention*, 12 ARB. INT'L 233 (1996); Hans van Houtte, *May Court Judgments that Disregard Arbitration Clauses and Awards be Enforced under the Brussels and Lugano Conventions?*, 13 ARB. INT'L 85 (1997).

[319] On this Convention, see *supra* para. 301.

939. — The precise conditions for appointing arbitrators and for resolving subsequent difficulties with the composition of the arbitral tribunal are set out in detail in the arbitration rules.[320]

940. — In practice, the application of those rules seems to have raised few problems. In particular, the intervention of the Chairman of the Administrative Council, who is careful to consult the parties before appointing an arbitrator, has generally proved effective.[321] Only one case (*Holiday Inns v. Morocco*) has given rise to a difficulty of note, when it became necessary to replace a party-appointed arbitrator who had become a non-executive director of the party that appointed him. As the two other arbitrators did not agree on his resignation, he was replaced, not by the party which had appointed him, but by a decision of the Chairman of the Administrative Council.[322]

§ 3. – Acceptance by the Arbitral Tribunal of Its Brief

941. — This is the last stage in the constitution of the arbitral tribunal. Although there are no requirements of form (B), it is necessary for the tribunal to accept its brief (A) and important consequences result from that acceptance (C).

A. – NECESSITY FOR ACCEPTANCE BY THE TRIBUNAL OF ITS BRIEF

942. — The French New Code of Civil Procedure contains no express provision covering the acceptance of an international arbitrator's brief. However, that omission is not surprising, as the 1981 Decree reforming French international arbitration law deliberately set out to avoid creating a procedural regime governing international arbitration. The situation is different in French domestic arbitration, where Article 1452 of the New Code of Civil Procedure provides that "[t]he constitution of the arbitral tribunal is complete only if the arbitrator or arbitrators accept the mission entrusted to them." Under Articles 1494 and 1495 of the New Code of Civil Procedure,[323] Article 1452 will apply where French procedural law has been chosen, by the parties or by the arbitrators, to govern the arbitration. In the absence

---

[320] Rules of Procedure for Arbitration Proceedings (Arbitration), Chapter I – Establishment of the Tribunal, Arts. 1–12; *see also* Pierre Lalive, *Aspects procéduraux de l'arbitrage entre un Etat et un investisseur étranger dans la Convention du 18 mars 1965 pour le règlement des différends relatifs aux investissements entre Etats et ressortissants d'autres Etats, in* CENTRE DE RECHERCHE SUR LE DROIT DES MARCHÉS ET DES INVESTISSEMENTS INTERNATIONAUX DE LA FACULTÉ DE DROIT ET DES SCIENCES ÉCONOMIQUES DE DIJON, INVESTISSEMENTS ÉTRANGERS ET ARBITRAGE ENTRE ÉTATS ET PERSONNES PRIVÉES – LA CONVENTION B.I.R.D. DU 18 MARS 1965, at 111 (1969).

[321] Georges R. Delaume, *ICSID Arbitration Proceedings: Practical aspects*, 5 PACE L. REV. 563 (1985).

[322] Holiday Inns S.A. v. Government of Morocco, ICC Case No. ARB/72/1. On this case, see Frédéric Eisemann, *La double sanction prévue par la Convention de la B.I.R.D. en cas de collusion ou d'ententes similaires entre un arbitre et la partie qui l'a désigné*, 1977 AFDI 436.

[323] Cohen, *supra* note 86.

of such a choice, and assuming that the arbitration in question is not subject to a national law or to institutional rules containing a similar provision, a French court would certainly hold that the requirement set out in Article 1452 can and must be extended to that arbitration.

943. — The requirement that the arbitrators appointed should accept their brief stems from the fundamental principle that arbitrators are private judges, appointed on a case-by-case basis that demands the consent of the parties and the arbitrators. The arbitrators' consent is no less important than that of the parties, because the role which they assume is not a mandatory, public adjudicating role, and no obligation of that kind can be imposed on an ordinary citizen by other private parties.[324] Such an obligation can only really result from a contract binding the arbitrators to the parties (and to any institution organizing the arbitration).[325]

944. — The requirement for acceptance by the arbitrators of their brief is thus a substantive rule applicable to all arbitrations, whether domestic or international.[326]

The acceptance requirement is so self-evident that the courts have rarely had occasion to reaffirm it. Nevertheless, the President of the Paris Tribunal of First Instance did so in a 1990 decision,[327] and he even pointed out that although the third arbitrator, when approached by the other two in connection with his appointment, had agreed in principle to accept it, that agreement in principle did not constitute a "personal and irrevocable acceptance" of his brief.

In other legal systems, the acceptance by the arbitrators of their brief is seldom the subject of a specific legislative provision, as the need for such acceptance is evident. However, explicit reference is made to such acceptance in the Belgian Judicial Code, which states in its Article 1689 that "[t]he arbitrator who has accepted his office may not resign, unless so authorized by the Court of First Instance at his request," and the Netherlands Code of Civil Procedure, Article 1029, paragraph 1 of which provides that "[a]n arbitrator shall accept his mandate in writing."

B. – FORM OF ACCEPTANCE

945. — Although the intention of arbitrators to accept their brief must be unequivocal, there is no requirement in French law that such acceptance be expressed in a particular form, or even that it be expressed at all. Acceptance may be tacit, and it can be inferred, for example, from an arbitrator's conduct. If the arbitrators call a meeting and hear the parties,

---

[324] DE BOISSÉSON, *supra* note 30, ¶¶ 202 and 634.

[325] On this contractual aspect of the arbitrator's status, see *infra* paras. 1101 *et seq.*

[326] Compare, in favor of the application of Article 1458 of the New Code of Civil Procedure to international arbitration, Cass. 1e civ., June 28, 1989, Eurodif v. République Islamique d'Iran, 1989 Bull. Civ. I, No. 255; 1989 REV. ARB. 653, 2d decision, and P. Fouchard's note; 117 J.D.I. 1004 (1990), 2d decision, and P. Ouakrat's note.

[327] TGI Paris, réf., May 10, 1990, *European Country Hotels*, *supra* note 210.

they are deemed to have accepted their brief. In any case, as confirmed by the President of the Paris Tribunal of First Instance in relation to a French domestic arbitration, such acceptance must be "a fact of which all parties are duly made aware during the arbitral proceedings and which is entirely unequivocal and unambiguous."[328]

Similarly, although this time in a case concerning an international arbitration, the same judge required

> proof of the exact date on which the third arbitrator accepted his functions, personally and unequivocally, and notified the parties of his acceptance.[329]

On appeal, the Paris Court of Appeals confirmed that the third arbitrator's acceptance

> in the absence of a specific agreement expressing it, must stem from a personal and irrevocable manifestation of his intention.[330]

946. — In most cases, however, the arbitrator's consent is given in writing. Examples include an exchange of letters, minutes recording the opening of the arbitral proceedings, the drafting of the terms of reference by the arbitrators, or a submission agreement signed by them. In each of those cases it must of course be established that all the arbitrators have personally accepted their own brief, without which the arbitral tribunal would not be legally constituted.

The Netherlands Code of Civil Procedure is the only recent statute which provides that "[a]n arbitrator shall accept his mandate in writing" (Art. 1029(1)).

C. – CONSEQUENCES OF ACCEPTANCE

947. — The first consequence of the arbitrators' acceptance of their brief is the completion of the constitution of the arbitral tribunal. However, although it may be presented as being the final stage of the constitution of the arbitral tribunal, that acceptance will not in fact suffice to render the tribunal definitively constituted. As we have seen, various difficulties may subsequently arise, prompting changes to the initial composition of the tribunal: resignations, default, deaths and, most frequently, challenges of arbitrators.

948. — The second consequence of the arbitrators' acceptance is more significant. Their acceptance marks the start of their functions. They are obliged thereafter to carry out their duties as private judges, conducting the arbitral proceedings diligently and impartially.[331]

---

[328] Réf., Oct. 28, 1983, Tréfilunion v. Bauchet Lemaire et Cie., 1985 REV. ARB. 151.

[329] TGI Paris, réf., May 10, 1990, *European Country Hotels*, *supra* note 210.

[330] CA Paris, Nov. 14, 1991, *Consorts Legrand*, *supra* note 274.

[331] On arbitrators' contractual obligations, see *infra* paras. 1101 *et seq.*

949. — More importantly still, the date of their acceptance also marks the start of the period within which they are required to make their award. While French international arbitration law, unlike domestic law,[332] does not fix the duration of the proceedings or specify the means of extending it,[333] the French courts have confirmed—although there was little doubt on this point—that the deadline for making the award (fixed by the arbitration agreement or by the arbitration rules, for example) begins to run as soon as the arbitrators have accepted their brief.[334] It was held that if arbitrators appointed by the ICC have not accepted their functions, then the various time periods set forth in the arbitration agreement and in the ICC Rules will not have started to elapse, and as a result there will be no grounds for extending them. Similarly, where an *ad hoc* arbitration agreement gave the arbitrators six months to make their award and an extension was requested, the court held that:

> since the defendants have failed to supply sufficient proof to establish that the third arbitrator gave his personal and definitive acceptance before November 10, 1989, the deadline for delivery of the award has not expired.[335]

The request for an extension was therefore granted.

950. — It has also been held that the arbitrators' acceptance of their brief has a further consequence as regards the extent of the courts' jurisdiction in the presence of an arbitration agreement. Some provisions governing the jurisdiction of the courts to decide certain types of provisional measures require that the arbitral tribunal be not yet constituted and therefore unable to hear the dispute.[336] Those measures are thus no longer available once all the arbitrators have accepted their brief.[337]

SECTION II
INTERNATIONAL PRACTICE

951. — Even if a number of awards made under the ICC Rules have addressed the issue of the constitution of the arbitral tribunal,[338] international practice on this question does not result primarily from arbitral awards because, in theory, by the time an award is made, difficulties concerning the constitution of the arbitral tribunal will already have been

---

[332] Philippe Grandjean, *La durée de la mission des arbitres*, 1995 REV. ARB. 39, and the decisions cited therein.

[333] *See infra* paras. 1246 *et seq.* and 1379 *et seq.*

[334] TGI Paris, réf., May 9, 1984, *Font Laugière Chimie, supra* note 210.

[335] TGI Paris, réf., May 10, 1990, *European Country Hotels, supra* note 210.

[336] See, for example, in France, Cass. 1e civ., Mar. 6, 1990, Horeva v. Sitas, 1990 Bull. Civ. I, No. 64; 1990 REV. ARB. 633, 2d decision, and H. Gaudemet-Tallon's note.

[337] On this issue, generally, see *infra* paras. 1302 *et seq.*

[338] *See infra* paras. 976 *et seq.* See also the application and interpretation of the ICC Rules on the appointment, challenge and replacement of arbitrators in ICC Awards No. 6209 (1990) and 6476 (1994), ICC BULLETIN, Vol. 8, No. 1, at 57 and 59 respectively (1997); No. 7001 (1994), ICC BULLETIN, Vol. 8, No. 2, at 60 (1997).

resolved. Instead, the decisions of the various arbitral institutions as to the appointment, challenge and replacement of arbitrators are of greater importance. Although such decisions are generally only administrative in character, they have considerable practical significance. However, arbitral institutions rarely publish or otherwise disclose these decisions.[339]

International arbitral practice is also reflected in the private instruments providing for and organizing the constitution of the arbitral tribunal: arbitration agreements, institutional or *ad hoc* arbitration rules, inter-institutional agreements[340] and other texts or codes produced by professional bodies concerning arbitration practice. These private sources[341] are too numerous, too diverse and, on the constitution of the arbitral tribunal, too lengthy to warrant an exhaustive study here.

952. — However, certain arbitration rules provide a fairly faithful representation of current trends, because of their considerable and ongoing influence on arbitral practice.[342] This is the case of both the UNCITRAL Arbitration Rules, which are chiefly used in *ad hoc* proceedings, and the ICC Rules of Arbitration, which play a major role in international institutional arbitration. In addition, the arbitration commissions for foreign trade found in formerly socialist countries in Europe and Asia are "internationalizing" themselves, thus adding to the convergence of institutional arbitral practice.

953. — Despite being intended for *ad hoc* arbitration, the UNCITRAL Rules are of much more general application. They have provided a model, whether in full[343] or in part,[344] for several arbitral institutions, certain of which have adopted the Rules as they stand, but have provided that different rules appearing in their own governing legislation and arbitration rules may prevail in some cases.[345]

---

[339] But see, in ICC arbitration, Dominique Hascher, *ICC Practice in Relation to the Appointment, Confirmation, Challenge and Replacement of Arbitrators*, ICC BULLETIN, Vol. 6, No. 2, at 4 (1995); Renzo Morera, *The Appointment of Arbitrators by the Court (in accordance with Article 2(6) of the Arbitration Rules)*, ICC BULLETIN, Vol. 7, No. 2, at 32 (1996); YVES DERAINS AND ERIC A. SCHWARTZ, A GUIDE TO THE NEW ICC RULES OF ARBITRATION 173 *et seq.* (1998).

[340] On these agreements, see *supra* paras. 317 *et seq.*; on the diversity of the systems for choosing institutional or *ad hoc* arbitration in the model clauses in the Inter-Association arbitration agreements concluded between the American Arbitration Association and other arbitral institutions, see AMERICAN ARBITRATION ASSOCIATION, THE INTERNATIONAL ARBITRATION KIT 301 (4th ed. 1993).

[341] See *supra* paras. 303 *et seq.*

[342] See Marc Blessing, *The Major Western and Soviet Arbitration Rules – A comparison of the Rules of UNCITRAL, UNCITRAL Model Law, LCIA, ICC, AAA and the Rules of the USSR Chamber of Commerce and Industry*, 6 J. INT'L ARB. 7 (Sept. 1989).

[343] An example of an institution adopting the UNCITRAL Rules in full is the Inter-American Commercial Arbitration Commission (IACAC).

[344] An example of an institution adopting the UNCITRAL Rules in part is the International Energy Agency Dispute Settlement Centre.

[345] Two examples are the arbitration centers set up under the auspices of the Asian-African Legal Consultative Committee: the Kuala Lumpur Regional Centre for Arbitration, created in 1978 (*see* Homayoon Arfazadeh, *New Perspectives in South East Asia and Delocalised Arbitration in Kuala Lumpur*, 8 J. INT'L ARB. 103 (Dec. 1991)), and the Cairo Regional Centre for International Commercial Arbitration, created in 1980 (*see* ABDUL
(continued...)

954. — The International Chamber of Commerce, with seventy-six years of experience of international commercial arbitration, is perhaps the most widely-imitated model in institutional arbitration. Its success in practice has grown with the expansion of its geopolitical base.[346] The System of Conciliation, Arbitration and Expertise developed by the Euro-Arab Chambers of Commerce was strongly influenced by the ICC.[347] Many other nationally-based arbitral institutions, such as the London Court of International Arbitration or the AAA, based themselves on the ICC model, particularly with regard to the appointment and removal of arbitrators. In 1985 the LCIA changed its name from the London Court of Arbitration, and adopted new rules.[348] The AAA also has a distinct set of rules for international arbitration.[349]

955. — However, the success (or at least the greater public awareness) of institutional arbitration should not be allowed to distort the picture. Although by definition it is more discreet, or even totally confidential, *ad hoc* arbitration plays and will always play a significant role, even in international disputes.

We shall therefore now provide an overview, discussing in turn the constitution of the arbitral tribunal in *ad hoc* arbitration (§ 1) and in institutional arbitration (§ 2).

As both forms of arbitration are based on the discretion of the parties and arbitral institutions, the mechanisms devised for constituting the arbitral tribunal are quite varied in nature. Nevertheless, they have features in common, as can be seen from the applicable arbitration rules.

§ 1. – *Ad hoc* Arbitration

956. — The main characteristics of *ad hoc* arbitration can be seen particularly clearly in the process of constituting the arbitral tribunal (A). Those characteristics are at the same time the strengths and weaknesses of *ad hoc* arbitration as compared to institutional arbitration.[350] Because of their popularity internationally, the UNCITRAL Rules (B) provide an important illustration of the attempts to reconcile flexibility and efficiency in the constitution of an *ad hoc* arbitral tribunal.

---

[345](...continued)
    HAMID EL-AHDAB, ARBITRATION WITH THE ARAB COUNTRIES 245 *et seq.* (1990); this no longer appears in the second edition).

[346] On ICC arbitration in general, see *supra* paras. 349 *et seq.*

[347] These Rules became effective on January 10, 1983.

[348] The 1985 Rules were subsequently replaced by a new set of Rules effective as of January 1, 1998.

[349] Since 1982, the AAA Supplementary Procedures for International Commercial Arbitration, amended on February 1, 1986 and, since 1991, the AAA International Arbitration Rules, last amended in 1997; *see supra* para. 344.

[350] Gerald Aksen, *Ad hoc Versus Institutional Arbitration*, ICC BULLETIN, Vol. 2, No. 1, at 8 (1991); Pierre Lalive, *Avantages et inconvénients de l'arbitrage "ad hoc"*, in ETUDES OFFERTES À PIERRE BELLET 301 (1991).

A. – COMMON METHODS OF APPOINTING *AD HOC* ARBITRATORS

957. — In *ad hoc* arbitration, the constitution of the arbitral tribunal is the exclusive domain of the parties. They are entirely free to determine its composition and to decide on the number of arbitrators, the qualifications required of them and the method for appointing them. That freedom, which is widely recognized in national legal systems,[351] promotes flexibility by enabling the parties to adapt the constitution of the arbitral tribunal to suit the particular nature of each dispute. Furthermore, because the arbitrators are usually appointed directly by the parties, the constitution process is, in theory at least, faster and less costly than in institutional arbitration. Finally and most importantly, the direct choice of the arbitrators by the parties is undoubtedly the method of appointment most in keeping with the spirit of arbitration: it implies a personal relationship of trust between each of the parties and the private judge it appoints, and that trust provides the best guarantee that the proceedings will run smoothly and the award will be enforced voluntarily.

958. — On the other hand, there is a risk that, precisely when it is being set up, an *ad hoc* arbitration may prove to be more vulnerable to various obstacles than an arbitration which has the benefit of an intermediary in the shape of an arbitral institution. In that respect, the efficiency of the arbitration depends heavily on the drafting of the arbitration agreement. A "blank" arbitration clause, which merely provides for disputes to be resolved by arbitration, will require the intervention of the courts to be effective, unless the parties agree upon the choice of arbitrators. The courts will also be asked to intervene if the arbitration clause contains various criteria for appointing the arbitrators, but does not specify how to deal with obstacles resulting from disagreements or default. Although many legal systems now allow the courts, at the request of a party, to resolve difficulties with the constitution of the arbitral tribunal,[352] the efficiency of international arbitration should not be dependent on court intervention.

959. — Practitioners have gradually become familiar with the main difficulties which can arise when constituting an *ad hoc* arbitral tribunal. As a result, although arbitration agreements are obviously not all drafted identically, there are a number of constants or dominant trends. These are also found in the numerous drafting guidelines produced by arbitration experts.[353]

---

[351] *See supra* paras. 752 *et seq.*

[352] *See supra* paras. 828 *et seq.*

[353] See, for example, Lazare Kopelmanas, *La rédaction des clauses d'arbitrage et le choix des arbitres, in* HOMMAGE À FRÉDÉRIC EISEMANN 23 (ICC Publication No. 321, 1978); Charley del Marmol, *Rédaction d'une clause d'arbitrage et choix d'arbitres compétents*, 1977 DPCI 277; Xavier Tandeau de Marsac, *Comment se négocie l'insertion d'une clause d'arbitrage dans un contrat international?*, Gaz. Pal., Doct. 268 (1980); Michel Dubisson, *La négociation d'une clause de règlement des litiges*, 1981 DPCI 77; Philippe Fouchard, *La rédaction des conventions d'arbitrage, in* LES ENTREPRISES TUNISIENNES ET L'ARBITRAGE COMMERCIAL INTERNATIONAL – COLLOQUE 2, 3 ET 4 NOVEMBRE 1981 CERP 97 (1983); Piero Bernardini, *The Arbitration Clause of an International Contract*, 9 J. INT'L ARB. 45 (June 1992); Markham Ball, *Just Do It – Drafting the*
(continued...)

960. — It is exceptional for the arbitrators to be appointed in the arbitration agreement. At that stage it is not known whether a dispute will ever arise during the performance of the contract and, if it does, when it will arise and what it will concern. The appointment of an arbitrator at that stage is therefore likely to be premature, and could prove to be very awkward if a dispute does occur. For example, the arbitrators appointed in the agreement might be totally unsuited to the nature of the dispute, or might die before the dispute arises.

961. — The most common form of arbitration agreement will stipulate that any dispute which may arise in the course of the contract shall be resolved by a three-member arbitral tribunal, with each party appointing one arbitrator and the third appointed by mutual agreement between the first two arbitrators. This system owes its success to the fact that parties value their freedom to appoint one of the arbitrators. Admittedly, the status of party-appointed arbitrators raises delicate issues concerning their independence and their relations with the party appointing them, and neither international arbitral practice nor national legal systems are unanimous as to how those issues are best resolved.[354] Nonetheless, practitioners remain undaunted by such difficulties. They generally attach considerable importance to the personal relationship of trust between each party and the arbitrator it appoints. The role of the third arbitrator—whose contribution in such circumstances will often be decisive—will, in practice, be made easier by the relationship of trust on which his or her appointment by the other two arbitrators was based. In addition, it is easier for two arbitrators, rather than the parties themselves, to agree upon the identity of the third arbitrator. As a result, the choice of a sole arbitrator, although less costly, is usually only optional. At any rate, the continental tradition is that the parties generally retain their right to opt for a tribunal of three arbitrators.

962. — There are no other major areas of convergence on this subject in the drafting of arbitration agreements. In particular, arbitration agreements do not systematically identify the third party responsible for appointing the necessary arbitrator or arbitrators in the event of disagreement between the parties. That omission is unfortunate, as it compromises the efficiency of *ad hoc* arbitration. However, in such cases, most legal systems allow the tribunal to be constituted with the help of the courts, as we have seen.

---

[353](...continued)
  Arbitration Clause in an International Agreement, 10 J. INT'L ARB. 29 (Dec. 1993); Maurice Cozian and François Ruhlmann, *Réflexions sur la négociation et la mise en forme d'une clause d'arbitrage en droit commercial international*, Gaz. Pal., Doct. 1002 (1993); ROGER P. BUDIN, LES CLAUSES ARBITRALES INTERNATIONALES BIPARTITES, MULTIPARTITES ET SPÉCIALES DE L'ARBITRAGE *AD HOC* ET INSTITUTIONNEL – CLAUSES MODÈLES (1993); MARTIN HUNTER, JAN PAULSSON, NIGEL RAWDING & ALAN REDFERN, THE FRESHFIELDS GUIDE TO ARBITRATION AND ADR: CLAUSES IN INTERNATIONAL CONTRACTS (1993); Marc Blessing, *Drafting an Arbitration Clause*, *in* ASA SPECIAL SERIES NO. 8, THE ARBITRATION AGREEMENT – ITS MULTIFOLD CRITICAL ASPECTS 32 (1994); Richard Kreindler, *Practical Issues in Drafting International Arbitration Clauses*, 63 ARBITRATION 47 (1997); Dana H. Freyer, *Practical Considerations in Drafting Dispute Resolution Provisions in International Commercial Contracts – A US Perspective*, 15 J. INT'L ARB. 7 (Dec. 1998).

[354] On this question, and on the notion of the "non neutral" arbitrator, see *infra* paras. 1041 *et seq.*

Similarly, there is no dominant trend in international arbitral practice as to the choice of third party responsible for appointing the third arbitrator. Alternatives include presidents of chambers of commerce or of arbitral institutions, individuals representing the legal profession (the president of a bar or the dean of a university law faculty) or the sector in question, politicians, diplomats, representatives of the international community and presidents of national courts. The spectrum is thus very broad. This can lead to difficulties if the third party has no experience in the exercise of such functions or of international commercial arbitration in general, or if the third party refuses to act when requested to do so.

B. – THE CONSTITUTION OF THE ARBITRAL TRIBUNAL UNDER THE UNCITRAL ARBITRATION RULES

963. — The UNCITRAL Arbitration Rules were published in 1976[355] and were intended for use in international commerce by parties who found it difficult to agree upon a choice of arbitral institution. By offering a universally acceptable *ad hoc* arbitration system, formulated by a wide range of experts with different backgrounds, UNCITRAL met a significant need. Its Arbitration Rules have been well-received by practitioners. A number of arbitral institutions have even adopted them, referred to them in their own rules, or at least drawn inspiration from them.

964. — As with any *ad hoc* arbitration, the constitution of the arbitral tribunal under the UNCITRAL Rules is above all a matter for the parties. However, the resulting flexibility carries with it a risk of inefficiency which is liable to materialize if the parties disagree, once the dispute has arisen, as to the appointment of the arbitrators. For that reason, the Rules provide for the intervention of a pre-designated third party, thus creating a "semi-organized" arbitration.[356]

965. — All of the provisions of the Rules are optional, in that when adopting them the parties are free to depart from them by written agreement. In addition, in the event of a conflict between a provision of the Rules and a mandatory rule of law applicable to the arbitration, the Rules specify that the latter shall prevail (Arts. 1(1) and 1(2)).

966. — The seat of the arbitration is determined by the parties or, failing that, by the arbitrators (Art. 16). The number of arbitrators is also determined by the parties, but their choice is restricted to either one or three. If they fail to make such a choice, three arbitrators will be appointed (Art. 5).

---

[355] On these rules, see *supra* paras. 200 *et seq.*, and Annex X, especially Section II: Composition of the arbitral tribunal, Arts. 5–14.

[356] Philippe Fouchard, *Les travaux de la C.N.U.D.C.I. – Le règlement d'arbitrage*, 106 J.D.I. 816 (1979).

1° The Appointment of the Arbitrators

967. — In principle, the parties are responsible for appointing the arbitrators. A sole arbitrator is appointed by mutual agreement between the parties. If three arbitrators are to be appointed, each party appoints one arbitrator, with the third appointed by mutual agreement between the first two. The main concern of the Rules is, however, to address the situation where the parties cannot agree on the appointment of an arbitrator, or where a party refuses to make such an appointment.[357]

968. — The parties are therefore invited to choose an "appointing authority" responsible for appointing the missing arbitrator or arbitrators. Where a party (usually the defendant) fails to appoint an arbitrator, the appointing authority will make that appointment directly. In contrast, for the appointment of a sole arbitrator or a third arbitrator the appointing authority resorts to a fairly complex list procedure. It supplies the parties with a list of at least three candidates. Each party must strike out the candidates to which it objects, and must number the remaining candidates in order of preference. The appointing authority will then appoint the sole or third arbitrator according to the parties' preferences.

The same list system is used by the AAA and by the Netherlands Arbitration Institute, and the American and Dutch practitioners involved in drafting the UNCITRAL Rules pushed for the adoption of that system. Its advantage lies in the fact that the parties are involved in choosing the arbitrator, without there being any risk of obstructing the system. In that respect, the system reconciles efficiency with the need to maintain a relationship of trust between the arbitrator and the parties. However, because it is fairly complex, the list procedure is of subsidiary application. The parties can agree to exclude it, and it can also be excluded by the appointing authority, if it considers that the system "is not appropriate for the case."

969. — Finally, a difficulty can arise in any *ad hoc* arbitration where the parties fail to agree on the choice of an appointing authority. In that case, the UNCITRAL Rules provide for the appointing authority to be designated by the Secretary-General of the Permanent Court of Arbitration at The Hague. Although that venerable institution has been semi-dormant for several decades and might therefore seem an odd choice, it does at least have the merit of having received the approval of representatives of a great number of countries in the negotiations of the UNCITRAL Rules. The role of the Secretary-General is modest, but sufficient to overcome delaying tactics (and hence to deter the parties from engaging in them). The Secretary-General is not of course the "appointing authority," and does not actually appoint the arbitrators, but instead designates the appointing authority, which then goes on to compile the list of arbitrators from which the parties are to choose.[358]

970. — The system is rather cumbersome, because it involves a number of different stages (there were twelve in one particularly complex case). Although the deadline imposed

---

[357] *See* Arts. 6 and 7 of the Rules.

[358] *See* PERMANENT COURT OF ARBITRATION, 97TH ANNUAL REPORT 12–15, ¶¶ 35–49 (1997).

for each stage is fairly short, each one allows an uncooperative party a further opportunity to delay the constitution of the arbitral tribunal.

971. — Nevertheless, the system has worked fairly well so far. On the rare occasions when the matter does reach the Secretary-General of the Permanent Court of Arbitration, the Secretary-General consults specialists in the field and, taking into account the nature of the dispute and the parties involved, designates the most appropriate appointing authority.

To avoid this rather onerous procedure, it is in the parties' interest to select an appointing authority when drafting their arbitration clause. The arbitration rules of the European Development Fund, which are closely based on the UNCITRAL Rules, strongly encourage the parties to do so and provide that if no such choice is made

> either party may request the most senior in rank from amongst the judges of the International Court of Justice at the Hague who are nationals of the ACP States and the Member States to exercise the powers of the Appointing Authority.[359]

Another illustration of the success of the UNCITRAL Rules is that several prominent arbitral institutions now offer to act as appointing authority. That is the case, in particular, with the AAA,[360] the LCIA,[361] the Arbitration Institute of the Stockholm Chamber of Commerce, the Japan Commercial Arbitration Association[362] and the ICC International Court of Arbitration.[363] This development, and the total or partial adoption of the UNCITRAL Rules by a number of arbitral institutions, led UNCITRAL to publish "Recommendations to assist arbitral institutions and other interested bodies with regard to arbitration under the UNCITRAL Arbitration Rules (1982),"[364] to avoid confusion and contradiction between different sets of rules.

---

[359] *See* Arts. 8 and 9 of the Procedural Rules on Conciliation and Arbitration of Contracts Financed by the European Development Fund (EDF), in force since June 1, 1991 (Annex V to the Decision No. 3/90 of the ACP-EEC Council of Ministers of 29 March 1990 adopting the general regulation, general conditions, and procedural rules on conciliation and arbitration for works, supply and service contracts financed by the European Development Fund (EDF) and concerning their application), 1990 O.J. (L 382) 95; XVII Y.B. COM. ARB. 323 (1992).

[360] AAA, Procedures for Cases under the UNCITRAL Arbitration Rules.

[361] LCIA, Services for Arbitrations under the UNCITRAL Arbitration Rules.

[362] *See* the Administrative and Procedural Rules for Arbitration under the UNCITRAL Arbitration Rules, effective June 1, 1991, XVII Y.B. COM. ARB. 352 (1992).

[363] *See* ICC AS APPOINTING AUTHORITY UNDER THE UNCITRAL ARBITRATION RULES (ICC Publication No. 409, 1983); *see also* INTERNATIONAL COURT OF ARBITRATION 18 (ICC Publication No. 800, 1998).

[364] *See Report of the United Nations Commission on International Trade Law on the work of its fifteenth session (New York, 26 July–6 August 1982)*, Official Records of the General Assembly, Thirty-seventh session, Supplement No. 17 (A/37/17) (19 August 1982), *reprinted in* UNCITRAL YEARBOOK – Vol. XIII: 1982, Part Three, II, at 420.

2° The Challenge and Replacement of an Arbitrator

972. — The primary aim of the UNCITRAL Rules with respect to the challenge and replacement of arbitrators is to provide a degree of transparency: under Article 9, an arbitrator approached in connection with a possible appointment must disclose "any circumstances likely to give rise to justifiable doubts as to his impartiality or independence." It is circumstances of this kind that can lead to an arbitrator being challenged (Art. 10). A party making a challenge must give written notice of the challenge to the challenged arbitrator, the other members of the arbitral tribunal and the other party, informing them of the reasons for the challenge (Art. 11). If the other party does not agree to the challenge and the challenged arbitrator does not withdraw from office, the decision will be taken by the appointing authority, irrespective of whether it originally appointed the arbitrator in question, and regardless of whether the appointing authority has already been designated (Art. 12).

973. — An arbitrator can be replaced in the event of a successful challenge, death or resignation, as well as "in the event that [he] fails to act or in the event of the *de jure* or *de facto* impossibility of his performing his functions" (Art. 13(2)). Such a failure or impossibility is established using a procedure similar to that used for challenges. Whatever the cause of the replacement, the substitute arbitrator is appointed or chosen pursuant to the procedure which governed the appointment or choice of the arbitrator being replaced (Arts. 12(2) and 13).[365]

Finally, the Rules specify that if a sole or presiding arbitrator is replaced, any hearings held previously must be repeated, whereas if any other arbitrator is replaced, the arbitral tribunal decides whether or not to repeat them (Art. 14). That provision is very useful in practice, since it allows the tribunal to minimize the delay caused by the untimely resignation of an arbitrator.

§ 2. – Institutional Arbitration

974. — The characteristic features of institutional arbitration, and hence its advantages and disadvantages, are in direct contrast to those of *ad hoc* arbitration. The involvement of an institution and the application of its rules undoubtedly help in constituting the arbitral tribunal, because although the parties retain a role in that process everything is geared to ensure that they cannot obstruct it. However, the greater efficiency of this form of arbitration is gained at the expense of a certain weakening of the relationship of trust which the parties and the arbitrators are supposed to share. It may also entail a more laborious process for setting up the arbitral tribunal, and yet it does not always provide the parties with the

---

[365] On the compatibility of the jurisdiction of the Secretary General of the Permanent Court of Arbitration and the involvement of the President of the Paris *Tribunal de grande instance*, limited to helping "reestablish the necessary cooperation between the parties," see TGI Paris, réf., Feb. 24, 1992 and Apr. 15, 1992, *Icori Estero*, *supra* note 54.

procedural guarantees that they expect from the courts. That may be the case, in particular, with some of the newer organizations, the founders of which do not necessarily have extensive experience of international business and arbitration.[366]

975. — The proliferation of international arbitral institutions[367] makes it impossible to give an exhaustive account of the procedures for constituting an arbitral tribunal adopted in the rules of each of them.

The diversity of institutional rules has increased with the publication, over the past ten years or so, of fast-track arbitration rules.[368] We will therefore examine first the ICC Rules (A), which are typical of the institutional approach to constituting the arbitral tribunal and have inspired many other institutional rules.

We will then discuss the procedures adopted in a small number of other major arbitral institutions (B). As a result of the influence of the ICC and the generality of the needs and constraints of international institutional arbitration, the rules of these various institutions are sufficiently similar to provide a true reflection of international practice in the constitution of the arbitral tribunal.

A. – THE RULES OF ARBITRATION OF THE INTERNATIONAL COURT OF ARBITRATION OF THE ICC

976. — In the latest version of the ICC Rules,[369] which entered into force on January 1, 1998, the arbitral tribunal is the subject of Articles 7 to 12 (replacing Article 2 of the previous Rules, which contained 13 paragraphs). Its essential provisions concern the appointment (2°), the challenge and the replacement (3°) of the arbitrators, while Article 14 deals with the seat of the arbitration (4°). First, however, Article 1 states that the

---

[366] See for example, in France, the report of the January 19, 1990 symposium of the Comité français de l'arbitrage on arbitral institutions, 1990 REV. ARB. 227.

[367] For a general description, see *supra* paras. 323 *et seq.*

[368] See, for example, the fast-track arbitration rules adopted by the AAA (Arts. 53–57 of the 1991 Commercial Arbitration Rules), the Geneva Chamber of Commerce and Industry (1992), the China International Economic Arbitration Commission (CIETAC) and the China Maritime Arbitration Commission (1994), the World Intellectual Property Organization (1994), the Arbitration Institute of the Stockholm Chamber of Commerce (1995), the CEPANI in Brussels (1997 Rules, Section V on "Arbitration of Limited Financial Importance") and the Japan Commercial Arbitration Association (1997). On international fast-track arbitration, see Eva Müller, *Fast-Track Arbitration – Meeting the Demands of the Next Millennium*, 15 J. INT'L ARB. 5 (Sept. 1998). *See also infra* para. 1248.

[369] For a general description of the ICC, see *supra* paras. 349 *et seq.*, and the references cited therein; as the applicable provisions have not been substantially modified, commentary on the previous Rules remains pertinent; see especially Alain Prujiner, *La gestion des arbitrages commerciaux internationaux: l'exemple de la Cour d'arbitrage de la CCI*, 115 J.D.I. 663 (1988); W. LAURENCE CRAIG, WILLIAM W. PARK, JAN PAULSSON, INTERNATIONAL CHAMBER OF COMMERCE ARBITRATION 203 *et seq.* (1990); Christophe Imhoos, *The ICC Arbitral Process – Part I: Constituting the Arbitral Tribunal*, ICC BULLETIN, Vol. 2, No. 2, at 3 (1991). For commentary on the new Rules, see the references at para. 350 above, note 579.

International Court of Arbitration is the permanent organ of the ICC which is to provide for the settlement by arbitration of disputes submitted to it (1°).

1° Nature and Purpose of the International Court of Arbitration

977. — The ICC International Court of Arbitration is a body which, in principle, meets once a month. It comprises a Chairman (who is empowered to take urgent decisions on behalf of the Court), 8 vice-chairmen and 56 members representing a total of 56 different nationalities.[370] The Court is backed up by a substantial Secretariat, which forms the real working machinery of the institution. Finally, as the ICC is an international organization comprising a large number of National Committees, the Court often seeks the views of those Committees when appointing an arbitrator.

978. — Article 1(2) of the ICC Rules states that the Court "does not itself settle disputes." This provision, contained in Article 2(1) of the previous Rules, has two important consequences.

979. — First, because the Court is not the arbitral tribunal, when it decides that an arbitration is to take place and rules on the composition of the arbitral tribunal, its decision is "administrative in nature."[371] As this is therefore not a judicial decision, it is not capable of appeal, and the Court need not state the grounds on which it is based (Art. 7(4), replacing Art. 2(13) of the previous Rules). Second, when the Court decides to accept a request for arbitration, determines which parties are involved and declares that the arbitration shall take place, it takes organizational steps which do not bind the arbitrators. In particular, where the Court considers that "it is *prima facie* satisfied that an arbitration agreement under the Rules may exist," despite the default of the defendant or the challenge by one party of the existence, validity or scope of the arbitration agreement (Art. 6(2)), it requires the arbitrators to rule on their own jurisdiction. In so doing, the Court takes a further administrative decision.[372]

---

[370] For the composition of the Court from April 8, 1997 to December 31, 1999, see ICC BULLETIN, Vol. 8, No. 1, at 13 (1997).

[371] Y. Derains, observations following ICC Award No. 6519 (1991), French shareholder v. English company, 118 J.D.I. 1065, 1071 (1991), and observations by Y. Derains.

[372] The previous Rules (Arts. 7 and 8(3), and Art. 12 of the Internal Rules) stated that the Court's decisions were of an administrative nature. The authors of the revised 1998 Rules rightly believed that it was not for the ICC to characterize its own decisions. However, commentators consider, correctly in our view, that the ICC's 1988 characterization remains accurate: see Herman Verbist and Christophe Imhoos, *The New 1998 ICC Rules of Arbitration/Le nouveau Règlement d'arbitrage de la Chambre de Commerce Internationale de 1998*, 1997 INT'L BUS. L.J. 989, 1004; Andreas Reiner, *Le règlement d'arbitrage de la CCI, version 1998*, 1998 REV. ARB. 25, 32.

The French courts, like their Swiss counterparts, have endorsed that characterization,[373] and it has been confirmed in numerous ICC awards. For instance, in a 1979 award the arbitrator referred to Article 8, paragraph 3 and held that:

> the fact that the Court accepted the present arbitration does not imply, by any means, a decision on its admissibility; this matter is submitted expressly to the judgment of the appointed arbitrator.[374]

Likewise, the arbitrators are solely responsible for ruling on the interpretation of an ambiguous or pathological arbitration agreement,[375] and for determining which parties are actually bound by the arbitration.[376]

980. — However, in matters regarding the appointment of the arbitrators, the Court exercises a jurisdiction of its own. Thus, one arbitrator rightly observed that:

---

[373] *See* Fouchard, *supra* note 146, at 231 *et seq.*, and the references cited therein; *see also* TGI Paris, réf., July 13, 1988, *R.E.D.E.C.*, *supra* note 206; more generally, for the acts of management of the arbitral proceeding, see TGI Paris, May 21, 1997, Cubic Defense Systems Inc. v. Chambre de commerce internationale, 1997 REV. ARB. 417, *aff'd*, CA Paris, Sept. 15, 1998, 1999 REV. ARB. 103, and P. Lalive's note; 126 J.D.I. 162 (1999), and E. Loquin's note. This decision holds—correctly in our view—that "the [International Court of Arbitration of the ICC] does not perform a judicial role, the measures it takes only being part of the administration of the arbitral procedure." *But see* CA Paris, 11e Ch., Sec. B, Oct. 2, 1997, X v. Y, No. 452496, unpublished. According to this decision, "the judicial character of the institution applies not only to the arbitral tribunal, which is only an emanation of the Court of Arbitration, but also to the Court itself." This incorrect characterization was made by a criminal court in a very specific context: it allowed a lawyer being sued for defamatory remarks allegedly made in challenging an arbitrator before the Court of Arbitration to benefit from immunity from prosecution.

[374] Award No. 3383 (1979), Belgian party v. Iranian party, 107 J.D.I. 978 (1980), and observations by Y. Derains; for an English translation, see VII Y.B. COM. ARB. 119 (1982); *see also* S. Jarvin, observations following award No. 3790 (1983), French contractor v. Libyan owner, 110 J.D.I. 910 (1983).

[375] Examples include a clause referring to the Zurich International Chamber of Commerce (ICC Award No. 4472 (1984), German party v. German party, 111 J.D.I. 946 (1984), and observations by S. Jarvin), or to the ICC "sitting in Geneva" (ICC Award No. 4023 (1984), French company v. Ministry of an Arab country, 111 J.D.I. 950 (1984), and observations by S. Jarvin). On this issue, generally, see *supra* para. 485.

[376] ICC Award 4504 (1985 and 1986) states that the Court's decision [that the arbitration will take place] "only serves as an instruction to the Tribunal to examine the question" (Petroleum producer v. Two companies, 113 J.D.I. 1118 (1986), and observations by S. Jarvin); *see also* ICC Awards No. 5065 (1986), Lebanese party v. Two Pakistani companies, 114 J.D.I. 1039 (1987), and observations by Y. Derains; No. 5423 (1987), Datel-productions v. King productions SARL, 114 J.D.I. 1048 (1987), and observations by S. Jarvin; 1988 Partial Award in ICC Case No. 5730, Société de lubrifiants Elf Aquitaine v. A.R. Orri, 117 J.D.I. 1029 (1990), and observations by Y. Derains; 1992 REV. ARB. 125. On arbitrators' powers to determine their own jurisdiction, see *supra* paras. 650 *et seq.*

[a]lthough the parties . . . [had] agreed upon a method of appointing the sole arbitrator, . . . when this method later proved to be ineffective because of the refusal of the [authority empowered] to appoint an arbitrator . . . then the arbitrator shall be appointed by the Court.[377]

Similarly, another arbitrator stated that "[t]he Court of Arbitration has exclusive jurisdiction to decide whether one or three arbitrators are to sit and this decision is in itself not to be challenged before the arbitrator or before the Geneva courts."[378]

The French courts also consider that they should not "substitute [themselves] for the pre-designated arbitral institution in organizing and implementing the arbitral proceedings in accordance with its rules, unless that institution is proved to have failed to do so," and that "decisions of the Court [of Arbitration] concerning the appointment of the arbitrators are not open to appeal."[379]

981. — Article 9, paragraph 1 of the ICC Rules (Art. 2(1) of the previous Rules) stipulates that in appointing or confirming the appointment of arbitrators, the Court shall "consider the prospective arbitrator's nationality, residence and other relationships with the countries of which the parties or the other arbitrators are nationals." This allows the Court to ensure the respect of the general principle that every arbitrator must be and remain independent of the parties (Art. 7(1)). Subject to this restriction, the parties are entitled to depart from the provisions governing the constitution of the arbitral tribunal (Art. 7(6), replacing Art. 2(1) of the previous Rules). The French *Cour de cassation* therefore upheld a decision to set aside an award on the grounds that the arbitral tribunal was unlawfully constituted because the ICC Court of Arbitration had set up the arbitral tribunal without taking into account various derogations from its Rules provided for in the arbitration agreement.[380]

2° The Appointment of the Arbitrators

982. — The arbitral tribunal comprises one or three arbitrators (Art. 8(1), replacing Art. 2(2) of the previous Rules). The number of arbitrators is determined by the parties,

---

[377] ICC Award No. 2321 (1974), Two Israeli companies v. Government of an African state, I Y.B. COM. ARB. 133 (1976); for a French translation, see 102 J.D.I. 938 (1975), and observations by Y. Derains.

[378] ICC Award No. 2114 (1972), Meiki Co. Ltd. v. Bucher-Guyer S.A., V Y.B. COM. ARB. 186 (1980).

[379] TGI Paris, réf., Jan. 18, 1991, *Société chérifienne des pétroles, supra* note 177, where a party challenged the appointment of the chairman of the arbitral tribunal by the ICC Court. On the recognition of the powers of arbitral institutions in this area, see *supra* paras. 808 *et seq.*

[380] Cass. 1e civ., Dec. 4, 1990, *E.T.P.M.*, rejecting an appeal against CA Paris, Feb. 11, 1988, *Gas del Estado, supra* note 60.

either in their arbitration agreement[381] or by means of a later agreement.[382] Failing that, the number is decided by the Court.[383] The Court will, in principle, opt for a sole arbitrator[384] unless it considers that the scale or nature of the dispute warrants a tribunal of three arbitrators (Art. 8(2), replacing Art. 2(5) of the previous Rules). The practice of the Court is public and has been the subject of a number of studies.[385] In 1998, 47.4% of cases submitted to the ICC were heard by three arbitrators.[386] In most cases, the parties made that choice,[387] indicating that they still favor having three arbitrators and thereby enabling each party to nominate one of the arbitrators.

983. — Sole arbitrators are nominated by mutual agreement between the parties, which is then confirmed by the Court. In the absence of an agreement between the parties, the Court appoints the arbitrator directly (Art. 8(3), replacing Art. 2(3) of the previous Rules). Where three arbitrators are to be appointed, each party nominates an independent arbitrator, and the appointment is confirmed by the Court. Where a party fails to make its appointment, the Court makes the appointment directly, in place of the party in default. The third arbitrator, the Chairman of the arbitral tribunal,[388] is nominated by agreement between the two party-appointed arbitrators, and that nomination is confirmed by the Court. If the party-appointed arbitrators fail to make an appointment in due time, the Court will appoint the third arbitrator (Art. 8(4), replacing Art. 2(4) of the previous Rules).

In order to accelerate the constitution of the arbitral tribunal, the 1998 Rules now allow the Secretary-General of the Court alone to confirm the appointment of arbitrators where the declaration of independence is not qualified or, if it is qualified, does not give rise to objections. In such a case, the confirmation is reported to the Court at its next session (Art. 9(2)).[389]

---

[381] The number of arbitrators was determined in the arbitration agreement in 41 % of the cases submitted to the Court in 1998; *see 1998 Statistical Report*, ICC BULLETIN, Vol. 10, No. 1 (1999).

[382] The number of arbitrators was determined in a later agreement in 32 % of the cases submitted to the Court in 1998, *id.*

[383] The Court determined the number of arbitrators in 27 % of the cases submitted to the Court in 1998, *id.*

[384] A sole arbitrator was appointed in 23.1% of the cases (76 cases) and three arbitrators were appointed in 3.9 % of the cases (13 cases), *id.*

[385] Other than the references given above, note 320, see Hascher, *supra* note 339.

[386] This figure is gradually decreasing over the years; see the statistics in the JOURNAL DU DROIT INTERNATIONAL annual review or in the ICC BULLETIN.

[387] In 1998, the parties chose three arbitrators in 143 cases, and a sole arbitrator in 97 cases (*see 1998 Statistical Report, supra* note 381).

[388] The ICC Rules give the Chairman an important prerogative: the ability to reach a decision alone if there is no majority decision (Art. 25, replacing Art. 19 of the previous Rules); in practice, the Chairman directs the conduct of the proceedings and this is reflected in fees that are slightly higher than those of the co-arbitrators.

[389] *See* Yves Derains, *The main objectives of the revision, in* ICC BULLETIN, SPECIAL SUPPLEMENT, THE NEW 1998 ICC RULES OF ARBITRATION 10 (ICC Publication No. 586, 1997); Reiner, *supra* note 372, at 32.

984. — Where the Court is required to make an appointment, such appointment will be "upon a proposal from a National Committee" of the ICC.[390] The relevant National Committee will be that of the country where the party which failed to make the appointment is based, if such a Committee exists. For sole or third arbitrators, the relevant Committee will be that of a third country which the Court considers to be appropriate. The latter rule is not absolute: under certain conditions the Court itself can choose the sole or third arbitrator from a country having no National Committee. Further, unless a party objects, the sole or third arbitrator can be chosen from a country of which one of the parties is a national (Art. 9(3) to (6), replacing Art. 2(6) of the previous Rules).[391]

985. — Although it is relatively flexible, this system sometimes gives rise to difficulties, particularly where the dispute involves more than two parties with different interests at stake. If the parties have stipulated that the dispute is to be decided by three arbitrators, two or more co-defendants may refuse—and in practice the Secretariat of the Court invites them to do so—to make a joint appointment of one arbitrator (the second arbitrator). Such a refusal has been held to be legitimate by the French *Cour de cassation* in the *Dutco* case,[392] on the basis of the "principle of equality between the parties in the appointment of the arbitrators."

The *Dutco* decision gave rise to some concern among practitioners.[393] They had been trying for many years, particularly within the ICC, to put forward a model clause and special rules for multiparty arbitration, but had met with little success because of the diversity of the situations described using the adjective "multiparty."[394] Nevertheless the main difficulty stems from the privity of the arbitration agreement which means, in principle, that third parties to the contract containing the arbitration agreement cannot be required (or allowed) to participate in arbitral proceedings based on such agreement.[395]

986. — The most usual scenario—and that encountered in the *Dutco* case—is less complicated. It concerns only one contract involving more than two parties, one arbitration agreement, and one dispute arising out of the contract. The principle of equality between the

---

[390] This wording used in the 1998 Rules allows the Secretariat of the Court to itself ask for a proposal from a National Committee, and thus to appoint that arbitrator in place of the Court. On the benefits and dangers of this development, see Reiner, *supra* note 372, at 33.

[391] These provisions were applied in ICC Award No. 7001 (1994), ICC BULLETIN, Vol. 8, No. 2, at 62 (1997).

[392] Cass. le civ., Jan. 7, 1992, *Dutco*, *supra* note 75, where the dispute was between three members of a consortium.

[393] *See supra* para. 792.

[394] MULTI-PARTY ARBITRATION – VIEWS FROM INTERNATIONAL ARBITRATION SPECIALISTS (ICC Publication No. 480/1, 1991); see, previously, MULTI-PARTY ARBITRATION (ICC Publication No. 404, 1982); Delvolvé, *supra* note 76. In 1994, the Working Party on multi-party arbitration established by the ICC Commission on International Arbitration, chaired by Jean-Louis Delvolvé, issued a Final Report on Multi-party Arbitration which is very detailed on the various aspects of this question and the available solutions (*see* ICC BULLETIN, Vol. 6, No. 1, at 26 (1995)).

[395] On these problems of multiparty arbitration, see *supra* paras. 518 *et seq.*

parties seldom led to unsurmountable difficulties in such a situation, even under the 1988 Rules. Problems were only likely to arise where the following circumstances co-existed:
— the parties had not adopted the standard ICC arbitration clause (which provides for "one or more arbitrators"), but had expressly stipulated that there were to be three arbitrators;
— in its request for arbitration the claimant sued more than one defendant;
— the co-defendants did not belong to one same group and had different interests at stake;
— the co-defendants refused, on grounds of equality, to appoint an arbitrator jointly.

Even in such a case, which was in practice fairly rare, the Court was not entirely powerless. In order to uphold the principle of equality, it could still order the claimant either to split its action and bring claims against each defendant separately, or to waive its right to appoint an arbitrator so that the Court alone appointed either one or three arbitrators. To justify either of those measures, the Court needed only refer to Article 26 of the Rules (Art. 35 of the 1998 Rules), which required it to make every effort "to make sure that the award is enforceable at law."

987. — That was certainly the spirit of a 1993 memorandum from the Secretariat of the Court,[396] which read as follows:

> The judgment of the *Cour de Cassation* leaves parties wishing to institute proceedings against multiple defendants with a number of different options in order to avoid violating the principle of equality upon which the *Dutco* decision is founded. One would be to seek to reach an agreement with the defendants concerning the constitution of the tribunal. This would not offend the principles upon which the *Cour de Cassation*'s judgment is based, provided, however, that the dispute has arisen. In the event that agreement with the defendants were no longer possible, or that the defendants cannot agree on the joint nomination of a co-arbitrator or do not accept that an appointment be made on their behalf by the ICC Court, the claimant might then consider requesting the ICC to appoint an arbitrator on its behalf. In such case, the defendants could not claim to be disadvantaged if a joint appointment were made by or for them. Nor would any such argument be available to them if a sole arbitrator were appointed by the ICC in accordance with Article 2, paragraph 5 of its Rules. Of course, it may also be possible for the claimant to introduce separate arbitration proceedings against the different defendant parties concerned.

988. — The 1998 ICC Rules seek to resolve the problem more directly, by introducing at Article 10 a special provision for arbitration where there is more than one claimant or defendant. Article 10 thus reflects the common intention of parties who agree to have their disputes settled by ICC arbitration.

The principle remains that if the arbitration clause provides for three arbitrators, the multiple claimants jointly, and/or the multiple defendants jointly, nominate one arbitrator.

---

[396] *Note from the Secretariat of the ICC International Court of Arbitration on the Constitution of Arbitral Tribunals in Multi-Party Cases*, ICC BULLETIN, Vol. 4, No. 2, at 6 (1993).

If the parties fail to make a joint nomination and all parties are unable to agree on a method for the constitution of the arbitral tribunal, the Court may appoint every member of the tribunal and shall designate one of them to act as chairman. The Court has full discretion to appoint any person it regards as suitable to act as arbitrator.

The new system is legally watertight and is welcome in practice.[397] Contrary to the opinion of certain commentators, the *Dutco* decision did not state that the principle of the equality of the parties gave each party the right to appoint "its" arbitrator. Each party will receive equal treatment where all the arbitrators are appointed by third parties. In fact, it is probable that the Court will seldom need to appoint all three arbitrators, as the mere fact that it may do so will either encourage the parties to agree on the method of appointment, or will discourage a claimant from initiating a single arbitration proceeding against multiple defendants or from requesting arbitration together with other claimants. Furthermore, the appointment of all the arbitrators by the Court is only an option: the Court could consider that, because all multiple claimants or multiple defendants have the same interests (as in the case of a parent company and its subsidiary), those parties are required to make a joint nomination of one arbitrator.

989. — By confirming the appointment of an arbitrator, and *a fortiori* by appointing one directly, the Court is able to verify that the requirement of independence is satisfied, particularly by means of the "statement of independence" which all prospective arbitrators must submit, whether their appointment is proposed by a party, by the other two arbitrators, by a National Committee or by the Court (Art. 7(2), replacing Art. 2(7) of the previous Rules).[398]

3° The Challenge and Replacement of an Arbitrator

990. — The requirement of independence on the part of the arbitrators brings with it the requirement that each party should have the right, exercisable within a limited time frame,[399] to challenge an arbitrator "for an alleged lack of independence or otherwise" (Art. 11(1), replacing Art. 2(8) of the previous Rules). A party making a challenge must submit a written statement "specifying the facts and circumstances on which the challenge is based." The Court decides on the admissibility and, if need be, on the merits of the challenge, having first provided "an opportunity for the arbitrator concerned, the other party or parties and any

---

[397] Commentators appear unanimous in their approval of this new system: see in particular Stephen Bond, *The Constitution of the Arbitral Tribunal, in* ICC BULLETIN, SPECIAL SUPPLEMENT, THE NEW 1998 ICC RULES OF ARBITRATION 22 (ICC Publication No. 586, 1997); DERAINS AND SCHWARTZ, *supra* note 339, at 165 *et seq.*

[398] On the requirement that arbitrators be independent, which is one aspect of their status, see *infra* paras. 1021 *et seq.* On the ICC's practice of requiring arbitrators to sign a statement of independence, see Hascher, *supra* note 339.

[399] The expiration of this deadline obviously does not affect the admissibility of an action to set aside based on an arbitrator's lack of independence; *see* CA Paris, June 1, 1995, Paris Hotel Associates Ltd. v. Hotel Gray d'Albion Cannes S.A., 1996 REV. ARB. 528; *see also* Philippe Fouchard, *Le statut de l'arbitre dans la jurisprudence française, id.* at 325, especially ¶ 43 at 346–47.

other members of the Arbitral Tribunal to comment in writing within a suitable period of time" (Art. 11(3), replacing Art. 2(9) of the previous Rules).[400]

The 1998 Rules add that such comments are to be communicated to the parties and to the arbitrators (Art. 11(3)).

991. — As with the appointment, confirmation or replacement of an arbitrator, the Court's decision on a challenge is "final" (Art. 7(4), replacing Art. 2(13) of the previous Rules). This provision must not be misunderstood. First, there is no doubt that it prohibits any form of appeal within the ICC arbitration system. Second, because the ICC Rules are merely contractual, the fact that the Court's decision is "final" simply means that by agreeing to submit disputes to arbitration under the ICC Rules the parties waive their right to bring any available appeal, to the extent that such a waiver is valid.

Prior to the entry into force of the Swiss Private International Law Statute, the Swiss courts did not consider this waiver to be valid. Relying on the mandatory nature of Article 21 of the Intercantonal *Concordat* on arbitration, they held that when a decision of the Court of Arbitration was contested, the Swiss courts had exclusive jurisdiction to rule on the challenge. Nowadays, however, Article 7(4) applies, because Article 180, paragraph 3 of the Swiss Private International Law Statute provides that the Swiss courts shall only intervene "to the extent to which the parties have not determined the procedure for the challenge."[401]

In French law, as we have seen,[402] the courts will only be involved in the challenge of an arbitrator if the parties have not agreed on an alternative procedure. The President of the Paris Tribunal of First Instance will thus refuse to intervene if the dispute has already been, or could have been, submitted to the relevant arbitral institution. Similarly, the Paris Court of Appeals rejected both an appeal against a decision of the International Court of Arbitration upholding a challenge and a secondary action which the same party brought against the International Court of Arbitration. The grounds given by the Court of Appeals were that there was no allegation that the International Court of Arbitration had breached the ICC Rules.[403] In that case, the Paris Tribunal of First Instance had carefully discussed the legal nature of the decision of the International Court of Arbitration on the challenge, considering it to be no more than "a measure of an administrative nature, . . . a decision . . . remaining outside the exercise of the power to judge and decide a dispute." The Tribunal nevertheless noted that the arbitrator had been removed after a discussion on the matter and that the absence of grounds for the decision was justified by the common intention of the parties.[404]

---

[400] On the procedure and grounds for challenges before the ICC International Court of Arbitration, see Hascher, *supra* note 339, at 11 *et seq.*; DERAINS AND SCHWARTZ, *supra* note 339, at 173 *et seq.*

[401] *See* LALIVE, POUDRET, REYMOND, *supra* note 35, at 119 and 343, and the references cited therein.

[402] *See supra* paras. 871 *et seq.*

[403] CA Paris, May 15, 1985, *Raffineries de pétrole d'Homs et de Banias, supra* note 142, and the commentary by Fouchard, *supra* note 55, at 21 *et seq.*

[404] TGI Paris, Mar. 28, 1984, *Raffineries de pétrole d'Homs et de Banias, supra* note 50.

In a different case, the *Cour de cassation* in turn made a clear statement as to the status of the International Court of Arbitration's decision on a challenge. It held that the Court of Appeals

> rightly observed that the decision, concerning a challenge, taken . . . by the ICC Court of Arbitration, which was only responsible for organizing the arbitration and which was not exercising a judicial function, cannot be considered to be an arbitral award.[405]

The *Cour de cassation* also held it to be perfectly legitimate for the Court not to give grounds for its decision, given that "the Rules upon which the parties had agreed provide . . . that the grounds of the decision shall not be communicated."[406]

992. — A decision of the International Court of Arbitration on the replacement of an arbitrator is also final (Art. 7(4), replacing Art. 2(13) of the previous Rules). An arbitrator will be replaced upon death, upon acceptance by the Court of a challenge, or upon acceptance by the Court of the arbitrator's resignation (Art. 12(1), replacing Art. 2(10) of the previous Rules). The new Rules add a fourth case: an arbitrator will be replaced at the request of all the parties. This dismissal by mutual agreement is likely to be very rare, occurring only where all the parties have lost all confidence in the arbitrator.[407] On the other hand, an arbitrator cannot simply resign as he chooses: to avoid an untimely or deliberately obstructive resignation by an arbitrator who is overly sensitive to the interests of the appointing party,[408] the Court will examine the grounds of such resignation.[409]

The Court can also replace an arbitrator who is "prevented *de jure* or *de facto* from fulfilling his functions," or who is "not fulfilling his functions in accordance with the or within the prescribed time-limits" (Art. 12(2), replacing Art. 2(11) of the previous Rules). The Court thus has the power to remove negligent arbitrators. However, the Rules do contain procedural safeguards: the arbitrator in question, the remainder of the tribunal and the parties are to be informed, and they are all invited to submit written comments to the Secretariat of the Court. The 1998 Rules specify that these comments are to be communicated to the parties and to the arbitrators (Art. 12(3)).

---

[405] Cass. 2e civ., Oct. 7, 1987, Opinter France v. S.a.r.l. Dacomex, 1987 REV. ARB. 479, and E. Mezger's note; 1987 Bull. Civ. II, No. 184. The Paris Court of Appeals thus ignored this leading decision of the *Cour de cassation* when, in order to reject a complaint of defamation brought by one lawyer against another, it held that the International Court of Arbitration was a body of a judicial nature when deciding on the challenge of an arbitrator. *See supra* para. 979.

[406] Cass. 2e civ., Oct. 7, 1987, *supra* note 405.

[407] *See infra* paras. 1138 *et seq.*

[408] *See* Gaillard, *supra* note 190, at 784 *et seq.*

[409] *See* Jean-Jacques Arnaldez and Ebun Jakande, *Les amendements apportés au Règlement d'arbitrage de la Chambre de Commerce Internationale (CCI) (en vigueur depuis le 1er janvier 1988)*, 1988 REV. ARB. 67, 81; for statistics on resignations accepted by the ICC, see Hascher, *supra* note 339; DERAINS AND SCHWARTZ, *supra* note 339, at 181 *et seq.*

Although it is rarely applied,[410] this provision is a powerful deterrent, and is perfectly justified. Although in their capacity as private judges arbitrators may enjoy a form of immunity vis-à-vis the parties,[411] they remain contractually liable for the proper performance of their functions to the institution which appointed them or confirmed their appointment. That institution could incur liability towards the parties if it were established that it had been at fault or negligent in organizing and supervising the arbitration.

In order to discourage a party or an arbitrator from seeking to delay proceedings by requiring an arbitrator to be replaced, the 1998 Rules contain two important new provisions:
- first, the Court need not follow the procedure set forth for the arbitrator's initial appointment (Art. 12(4)). The Court can thus itself directly appoint an arbitrator to replace an arbitrator initially appointed by a party;
- second, the Court is not obliged to replace an arbitrator who has died or been removed by the Court pursuant to Articles 12(1) and 12(2) subsequent to the closing of the proceedings (Art. 12(5)). In other terms, at that stage the Court can authorize a "truncated" arbitral tribunal to decide the case.[412]

4° The Seat of the Arbitration

993. — The seat of the International Court of Arbitration in Paris is of course not to be confused with the seat of the arbitration, which the parties are free to determine. The seat of arbitration is chosen by the parties in the great majority of cases.[413] In the absence of a choice by the parties, the Court will choose the seat (Art. 14(1), replacing Art. 12 of the previous Rules), having regard to the wishes of the parties, the localization of the dispute and the local law on international arbitration.

The Court will also take into account any factor from which an implied choice by the parties can be inferred.[414] Thus, where the arbitration agreement refers to arbitration under the auspices of the ICC "in Paris" or "of Paris," the Court considers that the parties have indirectly chosen Paris as the seat of their arbitration. The Court's view is that there is only one International Chamber of Commerce, and as the words "in Paris" or "of Paris" are therefore unnecessary for the purpose of identifying the arbitral institution, they can be interpreted as providing an indication of the location of the seat of the arbitration. In any event, France remains the country which is most often chosen as the seat of ICC arbitrations,

---

[410] It has been applied in less than one per cent of cases, according to CRAIG, PARK, PAULSSON, *supra* note 369, at 236; DERAINS AND SCHWARTZ, *supra* note 339, at 184 *et seq.*

[411] On this point, see *infra* paras. 1074 *et seq.*

[412] On truncated tribunals, see *infra* para. 1136. On these issues, see, in particular, DERAINS AND SCHWARTZ, *supra* note 339, at 188 *et seq.*

[413] In 1998, this occurred in 81% of the cases; *see 1998 Statistical Report*, ICC BULLETIN, Vol. 10, No. 1 (1999).

[414] *See* CRAIG, PARK AND PAULSSON, *supra* note 369, at 204; Herman Verbist, *The Practice of the ICC International Court of Arbitration With Regard to the Fixing of the Place of Arbitration*, 12 ARB. INT'L 347 (1996), and for the French version, 1995 INT'L BUS. L.J. 1000; DERAINS AND SCHWARTZ, *supra* note 339, at 201 *et seq.*

ahead of Switzerland.[415] Nevertheless, ICC arbitrators sit in a very wide variety of jurisdictions: ICC arbitrations took place in 25 different countries in 1992, and in 35 different countries in 1997. The majority of those cases were in Europe, but a significant percentage also took place in the four other continents,[416] underlining the universal reach of ICC arbitration.

B. – RULES OF OTHER ARBITRAL INSTITUTIONS

994. — Despite their diversity,[417] arbitral institutions often play very similar roles, not only during the initial stage of constituting the arbitral tribunal (1°), but also in resolving subsequent difficulties affecting the composition of the tribunal arising during the course of proceedings (2°).

1° The Initial Constitution of the Arbitral Tribunal

995. — All arbitral institutions will of course provide a mechanism in their rules for appointing the arbitrators, and they all retain a role in the appointment process. However, the various sets of rules do diverge over the respective roles of the parties and the institutions in determining not only who is to choose the arbitrators, but also which arbitrators can be chosen.

996. — In most cases, the institutions allow the parties to determine the number of arbitrators, but their choice is restricted to one or three. Some rules give the parties the final say, but express a preference for a sole arbitrator,[418] or for three arbitrators.[419] Other rules determine the number of arbitrators according to the size of the dispute.[420]

997. — The method of appointment is generally as follows:
— a sole arbitrator is appointed by mutual agreement;

---

[415] In 1998, France was chosen in 77 out of 328 cases (with the choice made by the parties in 51 of those cases). Switzerland was second (66 cases, with the choice made by the parties in 58 of these cases), and England third (50 cases, with the choice made by the parties in 46 of these cases). *See 1998 Statistical Report, supra* note 413.

[416] See the list *id.*

[417] For a typology of international arbitration centers, see *supra* paras. 323 *et seq.*

[418] *See* Art. 5 of the AAA International Arbitration Rules; Art. 5.4 of the LCIA Arbitration Rules; Art. 18(3) of the 1997 Rules of the Belgian Centre for Arbitration and Mediation (CEPANI).

[419] *See* Arts. 21-1 and 21-2 of the Rules of Conciliation, Arbitration and Expertise of the Euro-Arab Chambers of Commerce; Art. 16(1) of the 1999 Arbitration Rules of the Arbitration Institute of the Stockholm Chamber of Commerce.

[420] *See* Art. 20 of the 1988 Rules of the Quebec National and International Commercial Arbitration Centre (CACNIQ); Rule 21 of the 1998 Indian Council of Arbitration Rules.

— where three arbitrators are to be appointed, each party appoints one arbitrator, and the third is appointed by mutual agreement between the first two arbitrators;

— the institution only intervenes where a party has failed to make an appointment, or to appoint the sole or third arbitrator in the event of a disagreement between the parties or the other arbitrators, as the case may be.

That is the minimum role retained by most institutions, and it is one which shows most respect for the parties' freedom to choose the arbitrators. If that were the extent of the institutions' involvement, they would act exactly like any pre-designated appointing authority in an *ad hoc* arbitration.

998. — It is much rarer for the institution to retain exclusive power to appoint the sole arbitrator, the third arbitrator or even the whole arbitral tribunal directly.[421] However, institutions do so in rules organizing fast-track arbitration.[422]

999. — On the other hand, many institutions do retain the power to refuse the appointment of arbitrators[423] or, rather, to confirm their appointment (or decline to do so).[424] That enables the institution to verify the qualifications and independence of all the arbitrators, and to avoid subsequent difficulties caused by a poorly conducted arbitration or by challenges.[425]

1000–1001. — Finally, many institutional rules follow the example of the ICC in requiring prospective arbitrators to disclose any circumstances which would be liable to cast doubt on their impartiality or independence.[426] The institution will thereby be in a position to monitor the choices made by the parties and to confirm the appointment of the arbitrators in each particular case.

1002–1005. — As to the determination, in general terms, of which arbitrators can be appointed, the different rules have varying standards. They often contain no restrictions, requiring no particular qualifications. That is the approach favored by arbitral institutions which organize a broad range of arbitrations.

Conversely, other rules provide that only individuals named on a list drawn up in advance by the institution can be appointed as arbitrators. This system, which is far more restrictive,

---

[421] This is the case with the LCIA, which, by way of an exception, allows the parties to appoint the first two arbitrators (although never the third arbitrator) if provided for in the arbitration agreement (Arts. 5.5, 5.6 and 7).

[422] *See* Sec. E-5 of the AAA Commercial Arbitration Rules (which provides for a list of five arbitrators, from which two names may be struck; Art. 65 of the 1998 CIETAC Rules; Art. 1 of the 1995 Rules for Expedited Arbitrations of the Arbitration Institute of the Stockholm Chamber of Commerce, XXII Y.B. COM. ARB. 439 (1997); Art. 40 of the 1997 CEPANI Rules.

[423] This is also the case with the LCIA, if the arbitrators are not considered "suitable or independent or impartial" (Art. 7.1).

[424] As provided by the ICC Rules; see *supra* para. 983.

[425] *See also* Arts. 22 and 24 of the CACNIQ Rules; Art. 18(2) of the of the 1997 CEPANI Rules.

[426] *See infra* paras. 1055 *et seq.* and 1058.

is rarely found in non-specialized institutions.[427] It is instead often used in trade institutions, because of the highly technical nature of most of the disputes submitted to them. In such cases, it is considered preferable for the arbitrators to be professionals drawn from the relevant business sector.[428] On the other hand, there is a risk that the institution might be overly selective in compiling its lists, as a result of which one of the parties might consider that its choice is unduly limited, or that, not belonging to the organization, it has not been treated on an equal footing.

There are also intermediate systems, where the lists exist but remain optional, with the parties retaining the right to appoint arbitrators not appearing on the list.[429]

2° Resolving Subsequent Difficulties

1006. — One of the advantages of institutional arbitration as compared to *ad hoc* proceedings is that it invariably provides for the resolution of problems that are liable to affect an arbitral tribunal which is already constituted or is on the verge of being constituted.

The death or incapacity of an arbitrator will obviously lead to a process of replacement. The same applies in the case of an arbitrator's resignation, although that can create problems if it is untimely, or where its effect or aim is to stall the proceedings (hence the option, which is still rarely found in institutional rules, of allowing the arbitral tribunal to pursue its functions with only two arbitrators).[430] Conversely, institutional rules often allow the institution to remove a negligent or unsuitable arbitrator.[431] Incidents of this kind often raise delicate questions as to the status of arbitrators and the nature of their relationship with the institution organizing the arbitration.[432]

1007. — The arbitral institution may also have to resolve challenges by the parties of the arbitrators appointed. If the challenged arbitrator does not resign, the matter is submitted to the institution, which rules on the merits of the challenge. That is one of the important functions of arbitral institutions, because the increasing intensity of the arbitral process and the excesses resulting from the unilateral appointment of an arbitrator by each party have led to an escalation in the number of challenges. Some rules stipulate that the institution will not

---

[427] It is the case of the Indian Council of Arbitration (Rules 9 *et seq.* and 22).

[428] *See* Art. 8 of the Rules of the Chambre arbitrale de l'Association Française pour le Commerce des Cacaos; Art. 3.4 of the Grain and Feed Trade Association (GAFTA) Rules; Art. 1 of the Federation of Oils, Seeds and Fats Associations Ltd. (FOSFA) Rules.

[429] *See* Art. 5 of the 1991 Rules of the Austrian Federal Economic Chamber (the Vienna Rules); Art. VI of the Paris Maritime Arbitration Chamber Rules.

[430] *See infra* para. 1136.

[431] *See* Art. 10 of the LCIA Arbitration Rules; Rule 26(a) of the Indian Council of Arbitration; Art. 19 of the 1999 Arbitration Rules of the Arbitration Institute of the Stockholm Chamber of Commerce; Art. 31 of the CACNIQ Rules; Art. 18(4) of the 1997 CEPANI Rules; Art. 12(2).of the Rules of the Italian Arbitration Association (AIA).

[432] *See infra* paras. 1128 *et seq.*

give reasons for its decisions[433] and that its decisions are final.[434] National laws generally consider such provisions to be legitimate, although they do allow for subsequent review of the award by the courts where a challenge is alleged to have been wrongly rejected.

1008. — Lastly, in almost all cases where arbitrators stop performing their functions, they must be replaced.[435] In principle, institutional rules provide for such replacement to occur under the same conditions as those that governed the initial appointment of the arbitrator being replaced. However, in some cases, to save time (or to prevent delay), the institution may retain the power to replace the arbitrator directly, and its rules may provide that the proceedings will not necessarily be repeated.[436]

---

[433] *See* Art. 29.1 of the LCIA Arbitration Rules; Art. 12(1) of the Rules of the Italian Arbitration Association (AIA).

[434] *See* Art. 29.1 of the LCIA Arbitration Rules.

[435] The exception to this rule is if the rules allow the proceedings to continue before a tribunal that is incomplete; see *infra* para. 1136.

[436] *See* Art. 11(2) of the AAA International Arbitration Rules; Art. 33 of the CACNIQ Rules.

CHAPTER II
THE STATUS OF THE ARBITRATORS

1009. — In both international and domestic arbitration, difficulties with the arbitral tribunal generally arise during its constitution. These difficulties, whether resulting from a defective arbitration agreement or the attitude of the parties, are resolved by the relevant arbitral institution or by the courts. They often relate to the arbitrators themselves, or to the qualities and conduct expected of them.[1]

However, determining the status of the arbitrators is a task which goes far beyond the resolution of difficulties with the constitution of the arbitral tribunal. In its broadest sense, the status of the arbitrators covers all their rights and duties throughout the arbitral proceedings. This extends to the arbitral hearings themselves, the determination of the law governing the substance of the dispute, and the making of the award—all matters where arbitrators enjoy considerable powers.

The purpose of the present chapter is more limited. We shall focus not so much on the arbitral tribunal but rather on the individual arbitrators, the nature of their functions, their relations with the parties that appointed them and with any arbitral institution organizing or supervising the arbitration.

1010. — The status of the arbitrators in this more limited sense is not covered in any depth by the traditional sources of international arbitration law such as national legislation, arbitral case law and international conventions. Those sources are more concerned with the arbitral proceedings than with the individuals who conduct them. Even today, the status of the arbitrators is largely a matter for private rules and ethical codes. However, the development of arbitration has been accompanied by a perceived deterioration of its moral standards. The rights and obligations of arbitrators are called into question increasingly often, and while national law often remains highly elliptical on these issues,[2] they have become a matter of some concern to the courts and practitioners.[3] It is therefore important

---

[1] *See supra* paras. 870 *et seq.*

[2] However, court decisions concerning arbitrators' rights and obligations are becoming increasingly frequent; *see* Philippe Fouchard, *Le statut de l'arbitre dans la jurisprudence française*, 1996 REV. ARB. 325, and the decisions cited and reproduced therein.

[3] For example, the ICC Commission on International Arbitration created a working group to examine the "status of the arbitrator." The final report published by the group in 1995 set forth certain fundamental principles. *See Final Report on the Status of the Arbitrator*, ICC BULLETIN, Vol. 7, No. 1, at 27 (1996). See also the reports of the joint symposium organized by the ICC, the AAA and the ICSID, held in Paris on November 17, 1995 (ICC BULLETIN, SPECIAL SUPPLEMENT, THE STATUS OF THE ARBITRATOR (ICC Publication No. 564, 1995)).

to examine the questions that arise and outline how they are addressed in comparative law and international arbitral practice.

1011. — Given the paucity of strictly national sources, and because there is a general consensus among the few national sources that do exist as to the major principles applicable to the issues raised, the status of international arbitrators is almost never considered in choice of law terms. However, in so far as it might be necessary to determine the law applicable to that status, various connecting factors are theoretically possible.

In principle, the law governing the substance of the dispute and hence, in practice, the law governing the disputed contract, should be disregarded in favor of the law governing the arbitral procedure, because the arbitrator's brief is linked by its nature to the arbitral proceedings. However, because of its autonomy, international arbitration is often detached from all national procedural laws.[4] If that is the case, the law of the seat of the arbitration will be the most appropriate connection for three reasons: first, in comparative private international law the law of the seat will often govern the arbitral procedure, usually on a subsidiary basis; second, the law of the seat has the advantage of being easy to identify in most cases; finally, the status of the arbitrators is in part modeled on that of the judge, and it therefore follows that it should be determined by reference to the law of the place where the arbitrators perform their duties.

However, this principle should be qualified. In institutional arbitration, it may be preferable to apply the law of the seat of the arbitral institution, because the duties and prerogatives of the arbitrators will be shaped by the institution's rules, practices and legal environment. The institution will also participate in the appointment of the arbitrators and exercise a degree of control over the performance by the arbitrators of their functions. Further, although the arbitrator's brief is of a judicial nature, its origins are contractual. It is based on two successive agreements: the arbitration agreement between the parties and, as we shall see,[5] the contract binding the parties (and the arbitral institution, if one is involved) to the arbitrators. That second, *sui generis* contract is rarely in the form of a distinct document, and it is exceptional for it to contain an express choice of law provision. The most natural connection would therefore be to the procedural law chosen to govern the arbitration and, only in the absence of such a law, the law of the seat of the arbitration.

Under the Rome Convention of June 19, 1980 on the Law Applicable to Contractual Obligations, the law governing a contract will be that of the country to which the contract is "most closely connected" (Art. 4(1)). However, as the Rome Convention does not apply to arbitration agreements (Art. 1(2)(d)), neither should it apply to the contractual relations between the arbitrator, on the one hand, and the parties and the arbitral institution on the other. If one were nevertheless to refer to the Convention for guidance, the presumption in its Article 4, paragraph 2 would operate so that the contract would be deemed to be most closely connected to the country "where the party who is to effect the performance characteristic of the contract has . . . his habitual residence." In the contractual relationship between the arbitrator and the parties (and any arbitral institution), the party which is to

---

[4]   *See infra* paras. 1171 *et seq.*

[5]   *See infra* paras. 1102 *et seq.*

effect the performance characteristic of the contract is undoubtedly the arbitrator. The law of the arbitrator's place of residence would therefore govern his or her status. However, if the arbitral tribunal were to comprise several arbitrators residing in different countries, the use of that connection would be fraught with difficulties. For example, the liability of each arbitrator would be determined in the light of different laws. One would then have to resort to the "escape clause" contained in Article 4, paragraph 5 of the Rome Convention, so that, in that case at least, the law of the seat of the arbitration or the law of the seat of any arbitral institution would prevail.

In any event, the arbitrator's national law should not be taken into account, not only because of the legal uncertainty to which it leads where the tribunal comprises several arbitrators of differing nationalities, but also because, strictly speaking, the status of the arbitrators has nothing to do with their personal status. It concerns not their civil standing or capacity, but their role as private judges.

1012. — There is another preliminary question which is perhaps of greater importance in practice: which court will have jurisdiction to hear a dispute between a party (or an arbitral institution) and an arbitrator, or an action brought by arbitrators to obtain payment of their fees?

Neither the Brussels Convention nor the Lugano Convention on Jurisdiction and Enforcement in Civil and Commercial Matters appear to apply to such disputes. Article 1, paragraph 4 of each excludes arbitration from its scope. Furthermore, in the *Marc Rich* decision, the European Court of Justice gave full effect to that exclusion, holding that it

> extends to litigation pending before a national court concerning the appointment of an arbitrator, even if the existence or validity of an arbitration agreement is a 'preliminary issue in that litigation.'[6]

It would be logical for that exclusion to cover disputes concerning relations between the arbitrators and the parties or arbitral institutions.

One should therefore apply either other treaties on international jurisdiction that do cover arbitration, or the rules adopted on this issue in the country where the action is heard. For example, under French rules of conflicts of jurisdiction,[7] the special rules contained in Articles 14 and 15 of the Civil Code confer special jurisdiction on the French courts in favor of a French plaintiff or defendant, while ordinary rules[8] confer jurisdiction on the court of the place where the defendant has its residence, or the place where "the service is performed" (which in our context will be the country of the seat of the arbitration).

---

[6] Court of Justice of the European Communities, July 25, 1991, Case C–190/89, Marc Rich and Co. AG v. Società Italiana Impianti PA, 1991 E.C.R. I–3894, with the opinion of the advocate general, Mr. Darmon; 1991 REV. ARB. 677, and D. Hascher's note; 119 J.D.I. 488 (1992), and observations by A. Huet; 1993 REV. CRIT. DIP 310, and P. Mayer's note.

[7] *See* André Huet, *Compétence "privilégiée" des tribunaux français ou compétence fondée sur la nationalité française de l'une des parties*, J.-CL. DR. INT., Fascs. 581-30, 581-31 and 581-32 (1995).

[8] Arts. 42 and 46 of the New Code of Civil Procedure.

1013. — For the reasons explained above, we shall confine ourselves hereafter to a discussion of the substantive rules determining the status of the arbitrator. We shall begin by briefly re-examining the rules considered above with respect to the constitution of the arbitral tribunal, which concern the conditions the arbitrator, as an individual, must satisfy.

1014. — First, arbitrators are natural persons. It is very rare for national laws to allow arbitral institutions to act as arbitrators.[9]

1015. — Second, most legal systems contain no requirement as to arbitrators' nationality. The same is true of the 1961 European Convention. However, in order to ensure that the arbitrators possess the necessary independence and impartiality, in some cases it may be legitimate to specify that they must not be of the same nationality as the parties.[10] The absence of a nationality requirement is now clearly expressed in the UNCITRAL Model Law, which provides, in its Article 11, paragraph 1, that "no person shall be precluded by reason of his nationality from acting as an arbitrator, unless otherwise agreed by the parties."

1016. — Finally, in order to be appointed as an arbitrator, ordinary legal capacity is required in principle.[11]

1017. — More important are the rules directly relating to the arbitrators' functions. They act as judges, but as private judges. They assume a judicial function, but are generally paid, under contract, to perform that function. As a result, they provide services to the parties and to the arbitral institution, if one is involved. We shall now examine these two facets of an arbitrator's status: arbitrators as judges (Section I) and arbitrators as providers of services (Section II).

SECTION I
ARBITRATORS AS JUDGES

1018. — Arbitrators are empowered by the parties to decide the parties' dispute. That judicial power is the principal characteristic of their role and enables arbitration to be distinguished from superficially similar concepts such as expert proceedings, conciliation and mediation.[12] This appears clearly in a recent decision of the European Court of Justice, which held that "the services of an arbitrator are principally and habitually those of settling a dispute between two or more parties" and could not therefore be assimilated to the

---

[9]   On this issue, see *supra* para 797.

[10]   *See infra* para. 1037.

[11]   On these points, see *supra* paras. 762 *et seq.*

[12]   *See* CHARLES JARROSSON, LA NOTION D'ARBITRAGE 111 *et seq.* (1987). *See supra* paras. 12 *et seq.*

representation of a party and the defense of its interests, services performed by lawyers.[13] The fact that arbitrators are judges imposes on them a number of requirements (§ 1), but also offers them a certain degree of protection (§ 2).

§ 1. – Requirements Imposed on Arbitrators

1019. — Arbitrators must satisfy various conditions in order to perform the functions of a judge. We shall consider in turn the nature of these conditions (A) and their implementation (B).

A. – NATURE OF THE REQUIREMENTS

1020. — The most important requirements imposed on arbitrators are of a general nature: an arbitrator must be independent and impartial vis-à-vis the parties. Other more specific conditions are only imposed on arbitrators in certain cases.

1° Independence and Impartiality

1021. — The principle that arbitrators must be independent and impartial is now universally accepted in international arbitration (a). We shall define the meaning of independence and impartiality (b) before examining the scope of the principle (c).

a) Universal Acceptance of the Principle

1022. — Most national laws, international conventions and arbitration rules provide that arbitrators must be independent and impartial.[14]

---

[13] *See* Court of Justice of the European Communities, Sept. 16, 1997, Case C–145/96, von Hoffmann v. Finanzamt Trier, 1997 E.C.R. I–4857, and the opinion of the advocate general N. Finelli; 1998 REV. ARB. 166; 125 J.D.I. 562 (1998), and observations by M. Aurillac. On the impact of this characterization on the tax treatment of arbitrators' fees, see Jean-Pierre Le Gall, *Les honoraires d'arbitrage au regard du droit fiscal communautaire (à propos de l'arrêt von Hoffmann de la CJCE)*, 1998 REV. ARB. 83; Christian Amand, *TVA communautaire et arbitrage*, 1999 BULL. ASA 13; Pierre A. Karrer, Christian Roos, Michael Nordin, *Do Arbitrators and Lawyers Do Completely Different Things? The European Court Of Justice Subjects Arbitrators To Value Added Tax In The von Hoffmann Case*, 13 INT'L ARB. REP. 26 (Dec. 1998); *see also infra* para. 1158.

[14] For a collection of articles on this issue, see THE ARBITRAL PROCESS AND THE INDEPENDENCE OF ARBITRATORS (ICC Publication No. 472, 1991). *See also* Aldo Berlinguer, *Impartiality and Independence of Arbitrators in International Practice*, 6 AM. REV. INT'L ARB. 339 (1995); Doak Bishop and Lucy Reed, *Practical Guidelines for Interviewing, Selecting and Challenging Party-Appointed Arbitrators in International Commercial Arbitration*, 14 ARB. INT'L 395 (1998).

1023. — In national legislation, the requirement of independence and impartiality does not necessarily apply specifically to international arbitration. It is generally a rule found in domestic law, which is extended to international arbitration.

1024. — That is the case in French law. The New Code of Civil Procedure barely addresses the personal qualities of arbitrators, merely alluding, in two places,[15] to "grounds for challenge," which are not further defined. The *Cour de cassation* recently held that a prospective arbitrator's duty to disclose such grounds for challenge could only relate to matters provided for by statute. The statutory provision in question could only be Article 341 of the same Code, which lists the admissible grounds for challenging a judge.[16]

On the other hand, when they are invited to decide disputes regarding which facts and circumstances an arbitrator is obliged to disclose, the French courts will more readily refer to the general requirement of independence. In its *Ury v. Galeries Lafayette* decision, which concerned a domestic arbitration, the *Cour de cassation* held that:

> an independent mind is indispensable in the exercise of judicial power, whatever the source of that power may be, [and it is] one of the essential qualities of an arbitrator.[17]

The Paris Court of Appeals reiterated the same statement in several decisions concerning international arbitration,[18] and the requirement of an independent mind is also found in several more recent French decisions.[19] Other decisions simply refer to the arbitrator's independence as being "the essence of his judicial role"[20] or "an absolute requirement of all arbitral proceedings."[21]

---

[15] Arts. 1452, para. 2, and 1463, para. 1.

[16] Cass. 2e civ., Nov. 14, 1990, Graine d'élite Clause v. Gérin, 1990 Bull. Civ. II, No. 230; 1991 REV. ARB. 75, and C. Jarrosson's note; 1992 RTD COM. 167, and observations by J.-C. Dubarry and E. Loquin; Cass. com., Oct. 29, 1991, Reliure Sill v. Papeteries de l'Aa, 1991 Bull. Civ. IV, No. 313; 1996 REV. ARB. 398, and the commentary by Fouchard, *supra* note 2.

[17] Cass. 2e civ., Apr. 13, 1972, Consorts Ury v. S.A. des Galeries Lafayette, JCP, Ed. G., Pt. II, No. 17,189 (1972), and P. Level's note; Dalloz, Jur. 2 (1973), and J. Robert's note; 1975 REV. ARB. 235, and E. Loquin's note.

[18] CA Paris, June 8, 1972, Woltz v. S.O.D.I.P.A.R., 1973 REV. ARB. 38, and J. Rubellin-Devichi's note; CA Paris, Dec. 12, 1996, Commercial Agraria Hermanos Lucena v. Transgrain France, 1998 REV. ARB. 699, and observations by D. Bureau.

[19] TGI Paris, réf., Mar. 22, 1983, V. and L. v. C., 1983 REV. ARB. 479, 2d decision, and B. Moreau's note; JCP, Ed. G., Pt. II, No. 20,004 (1983), and O. d'Antin and M. Lacorne's note; TGI Paris, réf., Sept. 21, 1989, La Belle Créole S.A. v. The Gemtel Partnership, 1990 REV. ARB. 176, 2d decision, and P. Kahn's note; Cass. 2e civ., Nov. 8, 1989, Editions Médicafrique v. Le Concours médical, No. 88-18.035, unpublished.

[20] CA Paris, June 2, 1989, T.A.I. v. S.I.A.P.E., and Gemanco v. S.A.E.P.A., 2 decisions, 1991 REV. ARB. 87; CA Paris, June 28, 1991, KFTCIC v. Icori Estero, 1992 REV. ARB. 568, and P. Bellet's note; for an English translation, see 6 INT'L ARB. REP. E1 (Aug. 1991); CA Paris, June 13, 1996, KFTCIC v. Icori Estero, 1997 REV. ARB. 251, and E. Gaillard's note; 124 J.D.I. 151 (1997), and E. Loquin's note; for an English translation, see 11 INT'L ARB. REP. D1 (July 1996).

[21] CA Paris, Apr. 6, 1990, Philipp Brothers v. Icco, 1990 REV. ARB. 880, and M. de Boisséson's note.

In other cases, particularly concerning international arbitration, the courts have expressly added the condition of impartiality to that of independence.[22] On occasions the courts have also required neutrality[23] or objectivity[24] on the part of the arbitrators.

1025. — In other jurisdictions, arbitration legislation is fairly similar. Some laws simply require independence on the part of arbitrators.[25] However, the UNCITRAL Model Law adds the condition of impartiality (Art. 12(2)) and was followed in that respect by the Netherlands Code of Civil Procedure (Art. 1033(1)), the Tunisian Arbitration Code (Art. 57), the German Arbitration Statute of December 22, 1997 (Art. 1036 of the ZPO), and the Belgian Judicial Code (Art. 1690, para. 1 (Law of May 19, 1998)). The 1996 English Arbitration Act only contains the requirement of impartiality (Sec. 24(1)(a)) as does the 1999 Swedish Arbitration Act (Sec. 8).

1026. — The same trends emerge in institutional arbitration rules.[26] Some, such as the ICC Rules (Art. 7(1), replacing Art. 2(7) of the previous Rules), only require arbitrators to be independent from the parties involved,[27] but most require both impartiality and independence, as is the case of the UNCITRAL Rules (Art. 9).

1027. — Of the international conventions on arbitration, only the 1965 Washington Convention, which operates a list system for its arbitration center (ICSID), addresses the qualities required of an arbitrator. It specifies that "[p]ersons designated to serve on the Panels shall be persons . . . who may be relied upon to exercise independent judgment" (Art. 14(1)).

---

[22] Cass. 2e civ., Feb. 20, 1974, Forges et Ateliers de Commentry Oissel v. Hydrocarbon Engineering, 1975 REV. ARB. 238; TGI Paris, réf., Oct. 28, 1988, Drexel Burnham Lambert Ltd. v. Philipp Brothers, and June 29, 1989, Philipp Brothers v. Drexel, 1990 REV. ARB. 497, 1st and 3d decisions.

[23] TGI Paris, réf., Jan. 15, 1988, Société des Equipements Industriels Stolz S.A. v. Ets. Letierce, 1988 REV. ARB. 316, and J. Robert's note; CA Paris, May 4, 1988, Chambre arbitrale de Paris v. République de Guinée, 1988 REV. ARB. 657, 2d decision, and P. Fouchard's note.

[24] CA Paris, May 4, 1988, *Chambre arbitrale de Paris, supra* note 23.

[25] This is the case of Article 180, paragraph 1 of the Swiss Private International Law Statute which, according to some Swiss authors, is a more realistic approach. *See* PIERRE LALIVE, JEAN-FRANÇOIS POUDRET, CLAUDE REYMOND, LE DROIT DE L'ARBITRAGE INTERNE AND INTERNATIONAL EN SUISSE 340 (1989). On the difficulty of distinguishing between the two concepts of independence and impartiality, see Swiss Fed. Trib., June 30, 1994, Hitachi Ltd. V. SMS Schloemann Siemag AG, 1997 BULL. ASA 99; 1997 REV. SUISSE DR. INT. ET DR. EUR. 587, and observations by F. Knoepfler.

[26] See, for example, the rules of the Quebec National and International Commercial Arbitration Centre (CACNIQ) (Art. 24); the LCIA (Art. 10.3); the China International Economic and Trade Arbitration Commission (CIETAC) (Art. 29 of the 1998 Rules); the Indian Council of Arbitration (Rule 25); the Arbitration Institute of the Stockholm Chamber of Commerce (Art. 17 of the 1999 Rules); the AAA which, in its 1997 International Arbitration Rules (Art. 7), states that arbitrators "shall be impartial and independent" and no longer authorizes the parties to agree to depart from this rule (in contrast with the 1993 Rules). On this amendment, see *infra* paras. 1043 *et seq.*

[27] *See* Michel A. Calvo, *The Challenge of the ICC Arbitrators – Theory and Practice*, 15 J. INT'L ARB. 63 (Dec. 1998).

Finally, Article 6 of the European Convention for Protection of Human Rights and Fundamental Freedoms provides that "everyone is entitled to a fair and public hearing . . . by an independent and impartial tribunal established by law." It is true that there are doubts as to whether the Convention is directly applicable to arbitrators, because an arbitral tribunal is not "established by law" and the obligations contained in the Convention are directed at governments and government entities. However, the fundamental principle contained in Article 6 must inspire both private and public justice, and courts in jurisdictions bound by the Convention would in any case be obliged to enforce the principle in any review of an arbitral award.[28]

b) Definition of Independence and Impartiality

1028. — It is not easy to provide a comprehensive definition of the qualities of independence and impartiality required of arbitrators. Independence is a situation of fact or law, capable of objective verification. Impartiality, on the other hand, is more a mental state, which will necessarily be subjective.[29] Impartiality is of course the essential quality required of a judge. However, as it is rarely possible to provide direct proof of impartiality, the arbitrators should at least be required to be independent, which is easier to prove and which, in principle, guarantees the arbitrators' freedom of judgment. Whereas the bias of arbitrators will very rarely be revealed by their conduct, links of dependence with one of the parties—even though they will not necessarily lead the arbitrator to be biased—will provide a sufficient basis on which to consider that they do not satisfy the conditions required of a judge. The 1999 Swedish Arbitration Act lists the different situations in which a party might suspect the impartiality of an arbitrator and mount a challenge.[30] The concept of an independent mind, which often appears in French case law,[31] shows the extent to which the two concepts of independence and impartiality are intertwined.

1029. — The French courts have adopted the following definition of the independence required of arbitrators:

---

[28] See Charles Jarrosson, L'arbitrage et la Convention européenne des droit de l'homme, 1989 REV. ARB. 573.

[29] See Emmanuel Gaillard, Les manoeuvres dilatoires des parties et des arbitres dans l'arbitrage commercial international, 1990 REV. ARB. 759, 761; JEAN ROBERT, L'ARBITRAGE – DROIT INTERNE – DROIT INTERNATIONAL PRIVÉ ¶ 135 (6th ed. 1993); see also Pierre Lalive, Conclusions, in THE ARBITRAL PROCESS AND THE INDEPENDENCE OF ARBITRATORS 119 (ICC Publication No. 472, 1991).

[30] The three main situations are, according to Section 8 of this Act. "1. where the arbitrator or a person closely associated to him is a party, or otherwise may expect significant benefit or detriment, as a result of the outcome of the dispute; 2. where the arbitrator or person closely associated to him is the director of a company or any other association which is a party, or otherwise represents a party or any other person who may expect significant benefit or detriment as a result of the outcome of the dispute; 3. where the arbitrator has taken a position in the dispute, as an expert or otherwise, or has assisted a party in the preparation or conduct of his case in the dispute."

[31] See the decisions cited supra para. 1024.

the independence of the arbitrator is essential to his judicial role, in that from the time of his appointment he assumes the status of a judge, which excludes any relation of dependence, particularly with the parties. Further, the circumstances relied on to challenge that independence must constitute, through the existence of material or intellectual links, a situation which is liable to affect the judgment of the arbitrator by creating a definite risk of bias in favor of a party to the arbitration.[32]

The various factors which may deprive the arbitrators of their independence are generally, although not exclusively, their links with the parties.

1030. — For example, arbitrators have been found to be insufficiently independent in the following cases:
— where, at the same time as the arbitral proceedings, an arbitrator was personally paid to provide advice and technical assistance to one of the parties to the arbitration;[33]
— where, at the time of signature of a submission agreement in which he was appointed as a replacement arbitrator, an arbitrator was acting as a paid consultant to a company of the same group as that of one of the parties to the arbitration;[34]
— where the arbitrator was employed by a party on the day after he had made his award.[35]
In all of those cases, the interests shared by the arbitrator and one of the parties (generally the party that appointed him) sufficed to call his independence into question.

The situation is different in trade arbitrations where, by definition, the parties and the arbitrators are all professionals in the same field. It was held in the *Philipp Brothers* case that the parties and the arbitrators

> will necessarily be in business relationships with or adverse to the others but, in principle, the existence of such business relationships need not bring into doubt, or even into question, their independence from the party which appointed them, or indeed their impartiality to decide the dispute as an arbitrator, and consequently as a 'judge.'[36]

---

[32] CA Paris, June 2, 1989, *T.A.I.* and *Gemanco*, *supra* note 20; CA Paris, June 28, 1991, *KFTCIC*, *supra* note 20; CA Paris, Apr. 9, 1992, Annahold BV v. L'Oréal, 1996 REV. ARB. 483, 2d decision, and the commentary by Fouchard, *supra* note 2; 1993 REV. CRIT. DIP, Som. 760; for an English translation, see 7 INT'L ARB. REP. A1 (July 1992); CA Paris, Jan. 12, 1996, Gouvernement de l'Etat du Qatar v. Creighton Ltd., 1996 REV. ARB. 428, 2d decision, and P. Fouchard's note, *aff'd*, Cass. le civ., Mar. 16, 1999, Etat du Qatar v. Creighton Ltd., No. Q 96-12.748, unpublished.

[33] TGI Paris, réf., Jan. 15, 1988, *Société des Equipements Industriels Stolz*, *supra* note 23.

[34] CA Paris, Apr. 9, 1992, *Annahold*, *supra* note 32.

[35] CA Paris, July 2, 1992, Raoul Duval v. Merkuria Sucden, 1996 REV. ARB. 411, 1st decision; compare with CA Reims, July 23, 1981, which is less restrictive, allowing an arbitrator who acted as such at first instance to represent one of the parties in an appeal before a second arbitral body, as that practice is admitted in English law, which the parties had agreed would govern their arbitral procedure (Denis Coakley v. Reverdy, 1982 REV. ARB. 303, and P. Gastambide's note; for an English translation, see IX Y.B. COM. ARB. 400 (1984)).

[36] TGI Paris, réf., Oct. 28, 1988, *Drexel Burnham Lambert*, and June 29, 1989, *Philipp Brothers*, *supra* note 22.

However, that statement is less controversial than it may seem, because in that case the judge simply held that a "professional" party could not bring a global challenge against all of the arbitrators, who were professionals in the same field and named on the list drawn up by the arbitral institution. The Court went on to examine each of these "business relationships" individually, and where Philipp Brothers failed to provide "proof of a relationship of dependence upon, a friendship with or enmity towards one of the parties," it rejected the challenge. On the other hand, the professional subordination of one arbitrator to another or the involvement of the same arbitrator in similar disputes in a first tier of arbitral jurisdiction led the same court to accept the challenges against two arbitrators "who cannot have sufficient independence of mind, or indeed the necessary impartiality, to carry out their role as a judge."

1031. — In some cases, the reason for the challenge will be the arbitrator's links not with one of the parties, but with a party's counsel. This will rarely be accepted as the basis for removing an arbitrator, because the international arbitration community is a small world, where it is not uncommon for the arbitrators, often lawyers themselves, to know and meet the parties' counsel, or for them to be appointed with the agreement or even the support of the latter.[37]

The issue came before the French courts in a case involving two English barristers belonging to the same chambers. One of the barristers was acting as counsel for one party to the arbitration, while the other was the chairman of the arbitral tribunal, which the other party considered as affecting the chairman's independence. The Paris Court of Appeals rejected this contention and observed that belonging to the same chamber of barristers

> is essentially a matter of sharing premises and staff, without creating professional ties—as in a French law *association*—involving shared interests or any form of economic or intellectual dependency between the members of chambers. Members of the same chambers, because of the specialization of the chambers, often argue cases against one another, or participate in arbitral tribunals before which other members of the same chambers are acting as counsel.[38]

---

[37] On this point and its impact on the independence of the arbitrators, and the content of the statement of independence required of arbitrators nominated by the ICC, see the debate between Alain Hirsch, *Les arbitres peuvent-ils connaître les avocats des parties?* (1990 BULL. ASA 7), Stephen R. Bond, *The ICC Arbitrator's Statement of Independence: A Response to Prof. Alain Hirsch* (1990 BULL. ASA 226) and Andreas F. Lowenfeld, *An Arbitrator's Declaration of Independence* (1991 BULL. ASA 85); *see also* Dominique Hascher, *ICC Practice in Relation to the Appointment, Confirmation, Challenge and Replacement of Arbitrators*, ICC BULLETIN, Vol. 6, No. 2, at 4 (1995).

[38] CA Paris, June 28, 1991, *KFTCIC, supra* note 20.

This liberal approach, which is shared by the Swiss Federal Tribunal,[39] is commendable, although the "transparency" of such situations must be maintained from the outset.[40]

1032. — Arbitrators' links with the arbitral institution under the auspices of which they operate have sometimes formed the basis for a challenge. This means that the arbitral institution itself is in conflict with one of the parties, which is occasionally the case in particularly intense trade arbitrations. In the only matter where a French court examined the issue, the arbitrators appointed by the institution were its president and vice-president, and the court referred the challenge against them to the institution itself.[41]

1033. — The impartiality of an arbitrator is even more difficult to define. It amounts to the absence of risk of bias on the part of the arbitrator towards one of the parties. The courts approach the issue with great caution. As the Swiss Federal Tribunal rightly observed, accusations will be rejected if based solely on "a subjective feeling of one of the parties, [rather than] solid facts objectively and reasonably justifying [mistrust] in a person reacting normally."[42]

In practice, parties generally base their accusations of bias on two grounds.

1034. — First, the impartiality of an arbitrator is often disputed on the grounds that he or she is already familiar with the dispute, or a connected dispute, from a previous arbitration.[43] Aside from the allegations of breach of due process which frequently arise in such cases, it is often claimed that as the arbitrator will have reached a decision in the first arbitration he or she will no longer have the objectivity required of a judge taking on a new case. Such a claim was held to be founded by the court in the *Philipp Brothers* case.[44] The same was true in a construction dispute where the arbitrator appointed by the owner in the main dispute against the contractor was again appointed by the owner in a dispute under the warranties given by the engineer. The judge began by stating that, in principle,

---

[39] Fed. Trib., Feb. 9, 1998, I. SA v. V. (Hong Kong), 1998 BULL. ASA 634, which held that the fact that two attorneys, one being an arbitrator and the other acting as counsel, together own a law firm and therefore have a common business does not suffice to justify a challenge.

[40] *See* John Kendall, *Barristers, Independence and Disclosure*, 8 ARB. INT'L 287 (1992); *see infra* para. 1055.

[41] TGI Paris, réf., June 23, 1988, République de Guinée v. MM. R... et O..., 1988 REV. ARB. 657, 3d decision, and P. Fouchard's note.

[42] May 11, 1992, D. v. A., 1992 BULL. ASA 381, 392; 1994 REV. SUISSE DR. INT. ET EUR. 117, and the commentary by P. Schweizer. The American courts are equally cautious: *see* York Hannover Holding A.G. v. American Arbitration Ass'n, No. 92 Civ. 1643, 1993 WL 159961 (S.D.N.Y. May 11, 1993); XX Y.B. COM. ARB. 856 (1995); Spector v. Torenberg, 852 F. Supp. 201 (S.D.N.Y. 1994); XX Y.B. COM. ARB. 962 (1995).

[43] *See* Claude Reymond, *Des connaissances personnelles de l'arbitre à son information privilégiée – Réflexions sur quelques arrêts récents*, 1991 REV. ARB. 3; Mohammed Bedjaoui, *Des fortes vérités de Cassandre aux modestes correctifs de Némésis (Ou le souci communément partagé de voir la liberté fondamentale de choisir un arbitre n'être ni un danger ni en danger)*, *in* ETUDES DE DROIT INTERNATIONAL EN L'HONNEUR DE PIERRE LALIVE 385 (1993).

[44] TGI Paris, June 29, 1989, *Philipp Brothers*, *supra* note 22.

that arbitrator's knowledge of the previous proceedings is not such as to cast doubt on his impartiality, his objectivity, or his ability to reach a fair decision regarding the new dispute, as there are no serious personal allegations against him.

However, the judge then observed that the first award had addressed the liability of the engineer, despite the fact that it was not a party to that main arbitration, and therefore decided to exclude the arbitrator from the second proceeding.[45]

Similarly, if an arbitrator serving in two related arbitrations has communicated false information to the second arbitral tribunal which may influence that tribunal's decision, the resulting imbalance between the parties will constitute a breach of due process.[46]

Nonetheless, in the absence of any prior decision by the arbitrator which may be characterized as prejudice with respect to the subsequent case, the courts have held that there is no reason to prevent that arbitrator from participating in connected proceedings.[47]

The same approach was adopted where, following an initial award made against a principal debtor, the same chairman was appointed in proceedings initiated by the creditors against the guarantors. The Paris Court of Appeals ruled that, in principle, the same arbitrator could serve in parallel proceedings, except

> where a decision has been made in the other proceedings by that arbitrator which can be seen as prejudice, particularly if, in the first proceeding, the arbitrator has participated in an award which will logically have certain repercussions on the issues to be decided in the second proceeding. However, the earlier decision must have a bearing on indivisible set of factual and legal circumstances which characterizes the second dispute submitted to the arbitrator. There is neither prejudice nor bias where the arbitrator is required to rule on a factual situation similar to that examined earlier in connection with different parties, and even less so where he is to decide a question of law on which he has already ruled.[48]

The court's liberal interpretation was particularly justified, in that case, by the fact that by seeking to appoint their own arbitrator, the guarantors had made it necessary to have two

---

[45] TGI Paris, réf., Jan. 13, 1986, S.A. Setec Bâtiment v. Société Industrielle et Commerciale des Charbonnages, 1987 REV. ARB. 63, and P. Bellet's note.

[46] Cass. 1e civ., Mar. 24, 1998, Excelsior Film TV v. UGC-PH, Dalloz, IR 105 (1998); JCP, Ed. G., Pt. IV, No. 2128 (1998); 126 J.D.I. 155 (1999), and A.-E. Kahn's note.

[47] CA Paris, June 2, 1989, *Gemanco, supra* note 20; CA Paris, Jan. 12, 1996, *Gouvernement de l'Etat du Qatar, aff'd*, Cass. 1e civ., Mar. 16, 1999, *supra* note 32; Reymond, *supra* note 43, at 7 *et seq.*; CA Paris, 1e Ch., Sec. C, Apr. 2, 1998, Compagnie Française d'Etudes et de Construction TECHNIP v. Entreprise Nationale des Engrais et des Produits Phytosanitaires dite ASMIDAL (Algérie), No. 97/6929, unpublished.

[48] CA Paris, Oct. 14, 1993, Ben Nasser v. BNP, 121 J.D.I. 446 (1994), and E. Loquin's note; 1994 REV. ARB. 380, and P. Bellet's note; in Australia, on April 15, 1996, the Court of Appeal of the Supreme Court of Victoria refused to disqualify an arbitrator who had already participated in similar disputes (*see* Gascor v. Ellicott, 11 INT'L ARB. REP. A1 (June 1996)).

separate sets of proceedings and had also expressly agreed that the ICC International Court of Arbitration could appoint the same chairman for both arbitral tribunals. In addition, the chairman had drawn their attention to the situation in his statement of independence.

Similarly, it was held in another case that a replacement arbitrator

> by studying the file given to him by the secretariat of the deceased arbitrator, and by declaring . . . that he considered himself to be 'in agreement with' the decisions which had been made, . . . cannot be criticized for having had knowledge of the dispute, or even for having expressed an opinion which was liable to cast doubt on his independence of mind and freedom of judgment.[49]

1035. — A second situation where accusations of bias arise results from an arbitrator's prior conduct. Such prior conduct may be the position taken by an arbitrator in a general discussion on a legal or professional matter, which a party claims is contrary to its interests. A claim of this kind will generally be rejected. The Paris Court of Appeals held so in a dispute between franchisers and franchisees,

> where the submitted documents do not raise doubt as to the impartiality of the arbitrator, and the statements which he has made do not reveal excessive vehemence or systematic hostility such as might raise a presumption that the arbitrator is biased towards one of the parties.[50]

A party may also seek to challenge an arbitrator on the basis of that arbitrator's attitude earlier in the proceedings, provided that it clearly reveals that he or she is biased in favor of one of the parties. That "definite risk of bias" was not considered to exist where, in a preliminary award on the law applicable to a state contract, the legal system of the state in question (Dubai) had been described as being "somewhat autocratic." As the Paris Tribunal of First Instance observed,

> that statement does not demonstrate any form of hostility on the part of the arbitrator towards one of the parties, or indeed reveal a prejudice against the arguments defended by them.[51]

Likewise, the Swiss Federal Tribunal rightly noted that:

> procedural mistakes or a decision containing errors as to its substance are not sufficient to constitute bias on the part of an arbitrator, except in the case of

---

[49]   TGI Paris, réf., Sept. 21, 1989, *La Belle Créole, supra* note 19.

[50]   CA Paris, July 5, 1990, Uni-Inter v. Maillard, 1991 REV. ARB. 359, and observations by B. Moreau.

[51]   Apr. 1, 1993, Etat de Dubai v. Halcrow, 1993 REV. ARB. 455, and P. Bellet's note. See also TGI Paris, Oct. 29, 1996, General Establishments for Chemical Industries (GECI) v. Industrialexport, No. 60194/96, unpublished, which held that criticism by the chairman of an arbitral tribunal of the attitude of co-arbitrators successively appointed by a party did not reveal either prejudice against or animosity towards that party.

particularly serious or recurring errors, which would constitute a blatant breach of his obligations.[52]

1036. — In international arbitration, the twin qualities of independence and impartiality take on a slightly different emphasis with the addition of a requirement of neutrality. References to this requirement are sometimes found in court decisions.[53]

It has been suggested that the concept of neutrality involves "the arbitrator taking a certain distance in relation to his legal, political and religious culture,"[54] not confining himself or herself to his or her own traditions, or an intellectual openness to other ways of thinking.[55] It is a state of mind (and is therefore subjective), which is sometimes easier to assess by using concrete terms, such as the reference to the "residence and other relationships with the countries of which the parties or the other arbitrators are nationals" (Art. 9(1) of the ICC Rules).

1037. — The independence of arbitrators, and likewise their neutrality, can be enhanced by their nationality: if their nationality is different from that of the parties, it can be assumed that they will have greater freedom of judgment. This explains the requirement found in some arbitration rules that a third or sole arbitrator must not share the nationality of any of the parties.[56] However, although that condition is legitimate and often observed in practice, several institutional arbitration rules containing it also allow the institution to disregard it in certain circumstances.[57] Furthermore, the Paris Tribunal of First Instance held in one case that:

> although the practice is adopted in a number of arbitration rules, it does not necessarily oblige the President of the Tribunal of First Instance to reject the choice of an arbitrator who is of the same nationality as one of the parties . . . . The arbitrator, who is a judge and not a party's representative, cannot be suspected of bias solely on the basis of his nationality, and the requirement of impartiality which determines the choice of the individual . . . is sufficient to guarantee that the hearings will be conducted fairly.

The court therefore considered itself justified in appointing a French chairman where one of the parties was French, although its opponent, a Mexican corporation, had asked for the

---

[52] Swiss Fed. Trib., May 11, 1992, *supra* note 42.

[53] TGI Paris, réf., Jan. 15, 1988, *Société des Equipements Industriels Stolz, supra* note 23; CA Paris, May 4, 1988, *Chambre arbitrale de Paris, supra* note 23.

[54] MATTHIEU DE BOISSÉSON, LE DROIT FRANÇAIS DE L'ARBITRAGE INTERNE ET INTERNATIONAL ¶ 770 at 782 (2d ed. 1990).

[55] *See* Lalive, *supra* note 29.

[56] *See, e.g.,* Art. 9(6) of the ICC Rules (Art. 2(6), para. 3 of the previous Rules); Art. 6.1 of the LCIA Rules; Rule 22 of the Indian Council of Arbitration Rules; Art. 5.2 of the arbitration rules annexed to the exchange of letters between France and Algeria dated March 27, 1983, 111 J.D.I. 989 (1984); 1986 REV. ARB. 311.

[57] See the articles of the ICC Rules and of the Indian Council of Arbitration Rules cited *supra* note 56.

appointment of a "neutral" individual.[58] The court cannot be reproached in law for considering that an arbitrator's nationality cannot constitute an element of partiality in itself. However, it should have taken such nationality into account as a factual matter, the appearance of neutrality being as important in international arbitration as neutrality itself.

By contrast, the court did not have to address the claims raised by a Moroccan plaintiff in a case where the ICC International Court of Arbitration had appointed a Greek chairman in a dispute where the two defendants were Spanish and German. The Moroccan party claimed that the Greek arbitrator belonged to the same political, legal and economic world as its opponents, and it suggested that European Community "citizenship" could be assimilated with nationality. The court, however, considered that it could not substitute itself for the arbitrators (who alone were entitled to determine their jurisdiction), or indeed for the arbitral institution which had acted in accordance with its rules.[59] Although the plaintiff was undoubtedly wrong in assimilating EC membership with nationality within the meaning of the ICC Rules, its argument at least had the merit of raising the question of the exact meaning of the neutrality of international arbitrators in terms of their nationality.

The LCIA now specifically addresses this argument, at Article 6.3 of its 1998 Rules, which provides that "citizens of the European Union shall not be treated as having the same nationality."

1038. — One final point should be noted regarding the meaning of independence and impartiality. As it is clear that those qualities cannot be assessed objectively, the French courts have sensibly decided that the relevant test is that of a party's "reasonable doubt" as to the arbitrator's independence or impartiality.[60] The UNCITRAL Model Law shows the same caution, referring merely to "justifiable doubts" (Art. 12(1)), as do the new arbitration laws of Germany and Belgium (Art. 1036 of the ZPO and Art. 1690, para. 1 of the Judicial Code respectively). One should therefore consider the point of view of a "reasonable man" in the different circumstances encountered in each case. Given this uncertainty, the duty of prospective arbitrators to disclose facts that may affect their independence becomes essential.[61]

c) Scope of the Requirement that Arbitrators Be Independent and Impartial

1039. — It is not enough to simply state that arbitrators must be independent and impartial, and to define what those characteristics mean. The scope of the requirement of independence and impartiality must also be determined.

---

[58] TGI Paris, réf., May 22 and June 23, 1987, Transportacion Maritima Mexicana S.A. v. Alsthom, 1988 REV. ARB. 699, 2d and 3d decisions, and P. Fouchard's note.

[59] TGI Paris, réf., Jan. 18, 1991, Société chérifienne des pétroles v. Mannesmann Industria Iberica, 1996 REV. ARB. 503, 1st decision, and P. Fouchard's note.

[60] *See* CA Paris, Apr. 9, 1992, *Annahold, supra* note 32.

[61] *See infra* para. 1055.

1040. — First, there is the question of the duration of the arbitrators' independence and impartiality. The answer is simple: the arbitrators must be independent and impartial from the time they assume their functions until an award on the last item in dispute is made.[62] That requirement is clearly expressed in the ICC Rules, which state that "[e]very arbitrator must be and remain independent of the parties involved in the arbitration" (Art. 7(1) of the 1998 Rules, replacing Art. 2(7) of the previous Rules). That position is shared by the French courts, which considered in one case that an employment contract signed by an arbitrator after making his award implied that he had prior—and undisclosed—relations with the party which subsequently became his employer.[63] Conversely, the courts allowed an arbitrator who had participated in a first instance award to represent a party before the arbitral appellate court, because that practice was permitted under English arbitral procedure, which the parties had agreed to follow.[64]

1041. — Second, are all arbitrators affected by the requirement of independence and impartiality? This deceptively simple question is in fact the subject of considerable controversy, at least in international practice. Are all arbitrators subject to exactly the same requirements of independence and impartiality, or should a distinction be drawn between party-appointed arbitrators, on the one hand, and the third, presiding arbitrator or sole arbitrator, on the other? One might perhaps expect party-appointed arbitrators not to be entirely neutral, and to pay particular attention to the interests of the parties that appointed them.

1042. — As we have seen,[65] international practice remains very much in favor of the system that enables each party to appoint "its own" arbitrator. Any attempt to resist that preference would be as futile as to hope that, in unilaterally choosing a member of the arbitral tribunal, a party will not seek to appoint an arbitrator who is at least favorably disposed towards it.

Under those circumstances, there are two possible approaches to the question, both of which find support.

1043. — The first approach, which has been followed in U.S. domestic arbitration, is to acknowledge what is perceived as the reality of the situation. There is an officially recognized distinction between party-appointed arbitrators, described as being "non-neutral," and other arbitrators. Only the latter are subject to all the requirements of independence and impartiality.

This distinction is found in the AAA Commercial Arbitration Rules. Party-appointed arbitrators are not required to be neutral, and they are therefore neither obliged to disclose

---

[62] *See* Swiss Fed. Trib., May 11, 1992, *supra* note 42, which considers the situation and the conduct of arbitrators after a draft award has been established but not signed.

[63] CA Paris, Apr. 9, 1992, *Annahold, supra* note 32.

[64] CA Reims, July 23, 1981, *Denis Coakley, supra* note 35.

[65] *See supra* paras. 961, 983, and 997.

circumstances likely to affect their impartiality, nor subject to any challenge procedure. That regime only applies to the "neutral arbitrator," unless the parties agree otherwise.[66]

The distinction between neutral and non-neutral arbitrators has been approved by the United States courts[67] and was confirmed and clarified in the "Code of Ethics for Arbitrators in Commercial Disputes" jointly adopted in 1977 by the AAA and the American Bar Association.[68] Arbitrators' obligations of independence and impartiality were set forth in six canons, with a seventh canon covering "ethical considerations relating to arbitrators appointed by one party." According to the Code, a party-appointed arbitrator is not expected to be neutral and, unless the parties or the rules applicable to the arbitration provide otherwise, is not obliged to comply with the same standards as the third arbitrator. In particular, the party-appointed arbitrator is entitled to be predisposed towards the party which appointed him or her, and to communicate with that party about the case, provided that the other arbitrators and the parties are warned that the arbitrator intends to do so.

1044. — The second approach is more common, especially in international arbitration.

Perhaps as a response to the position in U.S. domestic arbitration,[69] in 1987 the International Bar Association adopted "Rules of Ethics for International Arbitrators."[70] These Rules state from the outset that "international arbitrators should be impartial, independent" (Introductory Note), and that they "shall be and shall remain free from bias" (Article 1: Fundamental Rule). The essential point is that the Rules are aimed at all arbitrators, irrespective of how they are appointed.

The Paris Bar adopted the same approach in 1983. In its resolution concerning the ethics of lawyers appointed as arbitrators, it concluded that "the arbitrator cannot consider himself to be the advocate, let alone the representative, of the party that appointed him," and that an arbitrator's duties included "independence and impartiality . . . in relation to all parties to the arbitration."[71] Other ethical rules, such as those of the ICC,[72] the CEPANI[73] and the Chamber

---

[66] *See* Secs. R-12 and R-19 of the 1999 Commercial Arbitration Rules of the American Arbitration Association.

[67] *See* Pierre Bellet, *Des arbitres neutres et non neutres, in* ETUDES DE DROIT INTERNATIONAL EN L'HONNEUR DE PIERRE LALIVE 399 (1993), and the references cited therein.

[68] *See* X Y.B. COM. ARB. 132 (1985), with an introductory note by Howard M. Holtzmann at 131.

[69] *See* Martin Hunter, *Ethics of the International Arbitrator*, 1986 BULL. ASA 173, and Pierre Lalive, *Message du Président – Faut-il codifier la déontologie arbitrale?*, 1986 BULL. ASA 113.

[70] *See* XII Y.B. COM. ARB. 199 (1987); for a French translation, see 1988 REV. ARB. 333, and the commentary by Xavier de Mello, *Réflexions sur les règles déontologiques élaborées par l'International Bar Association pour les arbitres internationaux, id.* at 339; David J. Branson, *Ethics for International Arbitrators*, 3 ARB. INT'L 72 (1987).

[71] *See* the December 20, 1983 *Délibération du Conseil de l'Ordre des Avocats au Barreau de Paris*, 1984 REV. ARB. 438, with an introductory note by Jean-Louis Delvolvé, *Devoirs et responsabilités de l'avocat exerçant la fonction d'arbitre, id.* at 435.

[72] *See Final Report on the Status of the Arbitrator, supra* note 3, especially Part I, "Defining a status for international arbitrators: elementary principles", at 29.

[73] Arts. 3 to 6 of the *Règles de bonne conduite pour les arbitrages CEPANI.*

of National and International Arbitration of Milan[74] take the same position, requiring all arbitrators to be both independent and impartial. The position taken in international practice led the AAA, in its International Arbitration Rules, to substantially modify its position. Those Rules initially provided that unless the parties agreed otherwise, arbitrators were to be impartial and independent.[75] Then, in its 1997 Rules, the AAA removed the option allowing the parties to agree to appoint non-neutral arbitrators.[76] This edition of the Rules also prohibits any communication between the arbitrators and the parties concerning the dispute, except to inform a prospective arbitrator of the "general nature of the controversy," "to discuss the candidate's qualifications, availability or independence . . . , or to discuss the suitability of candidates for selection as third arbitrator."[77] In so doing, the AAA brought its international rules into line with the practice most commonly accepted throughout the world.[78]

1045. — The status of party-appointed arbitrators remains a subject of controversy.[79] Following the lead of certain American practitioners,[80] there is now some support in Europe for denouncing the supposed hypocrisy behind the requirement that party-appointed arbitrators are and must be independent.[81] Other commentators point to the pressure placed on party-appointed arbitrators nominated by governments, and advocate removing the requirement of independence and impartiality so that the parties should be free to appoint partisan arbitrators if they wish. These commentators consider that only a minimum level of good faith on the part of arbitrators will suffice.[82]

However, in international arbitration, most practitioners still favor unmitigated independence on the part of all arbitrators.[83] They consider any intermediate solution to be dangerous, and that there should be no compromise over the arbitrator's judicial role. The

---

[74] Ethics for Arbitrators, Arts. 3 and 4.

[75] Art. 7 of the International Arbitration Rules, as amended and effective on November 1, 1993.

[76] Art. 7(1) of the International Arbitration Rules, as amended and effective on April 1, 1997.

[77] *Id.*, at Art. 7(2).

[78] Compare the position taken by the Geneva group of the Swiss Arbitration Association (ASA), 1997 BULL. ASA 188.

[79] THE ARBITRAL PROCESS AND THE INDEPENDENCE OF ARBITRATORS, *supra* note 14; Andreas F. Lowenfeld, *The Party-Appointed Arbitrator in International Controversies: Some Reflections*, 30 TEXAS INT'L L.J. 59 (Winter 1995); Jacques Werner, *The Independence of Arbitrators in Totalitarian States – Tackling the Tough Issues*, 14 J. INT'L ARB. 141 (Mar. 1997); Michele Taruffo, *Note sull'imparzialità dell'arbitrato di parte*, 1997 RIV. DELL'ARB. 481; Alan Scott Rau, *On Integrity in Private Judging*, 1998 ARB. INT'L 115; Jean-Flavien Lalive, *Some Practical Suggestions on International Arbitration, in* DROIT ET JUSTICE – MÉLANGES EN L'HONNEUR DE NICOLAS VALTICOS 287 (1999).

[80] Robert Coulson, *An American Critique of the IBA's Ethics for International Arbitrators*, 4 J. INT'L ARB. 103 (June 1987).

[81] *See* Lalive, *supra* note 29, at 130; Martin Hunter, *in* THE ARBITRAL PROCESS AND THE INDEPENDENCE OF ARBITRATORS 25 (ICC Publication No. 472, 1991).

[82] Bellet, *supra* note 67, at 406 *et seq.*

[83] *See* Charles Jarrosson, Report on the 6th ICC – ICSID – AAA joint symposium on "The arbitral process and the independence of arbitrators" held in Paris on October 27, 1988, 1988 REV. ARB. 748; *see also* THE ARBITRAL PROCESS AND THE INDEPENDENCE OF ARBITRATORS (ICC Publication No. 472, 1991).

same approach has been adopted in comparative law and international conventions, as well as in the rules and practice of international arbitral institutions.

1046. — Arbitral practice remains broadly in favor of having each party appoint an arbitrator in whom it has a particular relationship of trust. Does that necessarily entail encouraging that arbitrator to abandon his or her duty of impartiality and to take the side of the appointing party, thus transforming the arbitrator into little more than the advocate of the appointing party. Given the delaying tactics sometimes adopted by party-appointed arbitrators,[84] it is not enough to require arbitrators to act in good faith. The better solution is to adhere to the requirements of independence and impartiality, in the hope that in practice they will discourage arbitrators from being systematically one-sided.

1047. — That at least is the position currently adopted in most legal systems. With the exception of U.S. law, which recognizes the concept of the non-neutral arbitrator,[85] no international convention or modern arbitration statute has undermined the requirement that party-appointed arbitrators be independent and impartial. However, the Swiss Federal Tribunal has held that the independence and impartiality of party-appointed arbitrators need not be examined as strictly as those of arbitrators nominated by a third party or by the courts.[86]

In contrast, the French courts are particularly firm on this matter. Beginning with the *Ury v. Galeries Lafayette* decision, they have required the same independence and impartiality of all arbitrators. In that case, the *Cour de cassation* held that:

> the appointment of each arbitrator is not a unilateral act, even when initiated by one party alone. [It] results from the common intention of the parties, who take into account the qualities of the person whom they call upon to judge their dispute.[87]

Similarly, before going on to uphold the removal of a party-appointed arbitrator by the ICC Court of Arbitration, the Paris Tribunal of First Instance found that:

> an arbitrator—who is a judge, not a representative of the party that appointed him—must derive his judicial powers from a single, common manifestation of the intentions of the parties to the proceedings, even though his appointment may have been initiated by one party alone.[88]

---

[84] *See* Gaillard, *supra* note 29.

[85] *See supra* para. 1043.

[86] Aug. 18, 1992, K v. X, ATF 118 II 359; 1994 REV. SUISSE DR. INT. ET DR. EUR. 127, and P. Schweizer's note.

[87] Cass. 2e civ., Apr. 13, 1972, *Ury*, *supra* note 17.

[88] TGI Paris, Mar. 28, 1984, Raffineries de pétrole d'Homs et de Banias v. Chambre de Commerce Internationale, 1985 REV. ARB. 141, 1st decision.

It is therefore almost invariably the party-appointed arbitrators who are reminded by the courts of their obligations of independence and impartiality.

2° Special Conditions Imposed on Arbitrators

1048. — Arbitrators are private judges, and as such they may be chosen because of certain qualities they possess, or for their experience in a particular field. The parties are free to determine these special conditions by mutual agreement.

1049. — The arbitrators may also be required to have special skills. The 1965 Washington Convention provides an example with respect to the drawing up of lists of arbitrators by contracting states. Under Article 14, individuals selected to appear on such lists "shall be persons of high moral character and recognized competence in the field of law, commerce, industry or finance."

The same Article adds that "competence in the field of law," is particularly important, and that in making his appointments, the Chairman of the Center's Administrative Council

> shall in addition pay due regard to the importance of assuring representation on the Panels of the principal legal systems of the world and of the main forms of economic activity.

These provisions are of unequal value: "high moral character," and "competence in the field of law" are qualities which one can expect of any judge. However, skills in particular fields are mentioned only on an alternative basis, in order to enhance the representativeness of the institution's list of arbitrators.

1050. — In trade arbitrations, the rules of the association organizing the proceeding often stipulate that the arbitrators must be professionals of the trade. In such cases, the list of arbitrators drawn up by the association will only include practitioners who have, for example, experience of cocoa trading and processing,[89] or of any other trade in which the professional body is specialized.

1051. — Generally speaking, the parties are free to define any particular qualities which the arbitrators must have, such as professional experience in a particular financial or technical field, knowledge of a specific legal system and/or branch of the law, and language skills. These are the various "qualifications" of the arbitrator referred to, *inter alia*, in Quebec's CACNIQ Arbitration Rules (Arts. 24 and 27), and at Article 180 of the Swiss Private International Law Statute. The Rules of the International Arbitral Centre of the

---

[89]   This is the case of the Association Française pour le Commerce des Cacaos; *see* CA Paris, Apr. 6, 1990, *Philipp Brothers*, *supra* note 21.

Austrian Federal Economic Chamber also specify that "[a]rbitrators should have specific knowledge and experience in legal, commercial, or other pertinent matters" (Art. 5.1).

An example of an arbitration clause containing numerous conditions as to the qualifications of the arbitrators was contained in the general conditions of an international construction contract which came before the Paris Tribunal of First Instance.[90] The clause stipulated that:

> all of the arbitrators shall have a perfect knowledge of the English language and substantial experience of international construction disputes. The president of the Arbitral Tribunal shall be a lawyer.

1052. — Such requirements are both lawful and legitimate: lawful, because the parties have specifically provided for them or, in trade arbitrations, are familiar with them and accept them by adopting an arbitration clause referring to a specialized institutional arbitration;[91] legitimate, because the intentions of the parties are, by means of arbitration, to obtain private justice adapted to their needs.

We must now consider how the requirements of independence and impartiality are actually implemented in practice.

B. – IMPLEMENTATION OF THE REQUIREMENTS

1053. — There are a number of ways in which the parties, arbitral institutions and the courts can ensure that arbitrators are and remain independent and impartial.

Some measures are preventative (1°), others are punitive (2°).

1° Preventative Measures

1054. — The first preventative measure is the arbitrators' duty of disclosure (a), while the second consists of the powers of the appointing authority to verify that prospective arbitrators do in fact satisfy the applicable conditions (b).

a) Duty of Disclosure

1055. — Any person asked to assume the functions of an arbitrator must inform the parties and, as the case may be, the appointing authority or arbitral institution, of all circumstances which, from the parties' point of view, might be liable to affect his or her

---

[90] Réf., Dec. 12 and 20, 1991, Campenon Bernard v. Eurodisneyland SCA, 1996 REV. ARB. 516, and P. Fouchard's note; *see also infra* para. 1065.

[91] *See supra* paras. 808 *et seq.*

independence or impartiality. As such, the duty of disclosure is almost universally recognized.

1056. — In French domestic arbitration law, under Article 1452, paragraph 2 of the New Code of Civil Procedure,

> [a]n arbitrator who is aware of a ground for challenge regarding his or her person shall so inform the parties. In such a case, he or she may accept his or her mission only with the agreement of the parties.

This same issue arises in international arbitration. A number of decisions seemed to consider, implicitly at least, that the rule found in domestic arbitration should be extended to international cases.[92] However, in its more recent decisions, the Paris Court of Appeals uses the same phrase but no longer tracks the language of the domestic law provision.[93] The French courts thus now seem to consider that an arbitrator's duty of disclosure is not founded upon the extension of the domestic law rule found in the New Code of Civil Procedure to international arbitration. Instead, they rightly impose that duty on all arbitrators, thereby creating a substantive rule directly applicable in international arbitration.

1057. — In other legal systems, the same rule is becoming more widespread, as a result of the influence of the UNCITRAL Model Law, which provides in its Article 12, paragraph 1 that:

> When a person is approached in connection with his possible appointment as an arbitrator, he shall disclose any circumstances likely to give rise to justifiable doubts as to his impartiality or independence. An arbitrator, from the time of his appointment and throughout the arbitral proceedings, shall without delay disclose any such circumstances to the parties unless they have already been informed of them by him.

The same wording is also found, in particular, in Canada's federal and provincial arbitration laws,[94] the Tunisian Arbitration Code of 1993 (Art. 57) and the 1997 German Arbitration Law (Art. 1036(1) of the ZPO). In the United States, the international

---

[92] This can be seen from references to "the arbitrator's statutory duty of disclosure, which enables the parties to exercise their right to challenge." (CA Paris, June 2, 1989, *T.A.I.* and *Gemanco*, *supra* note 20). In French law, the only "statutory" source of such a duty is Article 1452, paragraph 2.

[93] CA Paris, June 28, 1991, *KFTCIC*, *supra* note 20; CA Paris, Apr. 9, 1992, *Annahold*, *supra* note 22; CA Paris, Jan. 12, 1996, *Gouvernement de l'Etat du Qatar*, *aff'd*, Cass. 1e civ., Mar. 16, 1999, *supra* note 32. On the question generally, see Fouchard, *supra* note 2, at 347 *et seq.*

[94] For Quebec, see Art. 942.1 of the Code of Civil Procedure, as amended on November 11, 1986.

commercial arbitration laws of California[95] and Texas[96] go beyond a general formulation of the duty of disclosure and include a long but non-exhaustive list of all circumstances which a prospective arbitrator is obliged to reveal.

Article 1034 of the Netherlands Code of Civil Procedure imposes a "duty of disclosure," which is defined as follows:

> (1) A prospective arbitrator . . . who presumes that he could be challenged shall disclose in writing to the person who has approached him the existence of such grounds.
> (2) A person who has been appointed as arbitrator . . . shall, if the parties have not previously been notified, immediately notify the parties as prescribed in the preceding paragraph.

1058. — International arbitration rules consistently impose a duty of disclosure. Examples include the UNCITRAL Rules (Art. 9), the ICC Rules (Art. 7(2) of the 1998 Rules, replacing Art. 2(7) of the previous Rules), the ICSID Rules (Art. 6), the AAA International Arbitration Rules (Art. 7), the LCIA Rules (Art. 5.3 of the 1998 Rules), the Italian Arbitration Association Rules (Art. 14(1)), the CACNIQ Rules (Art. 27), the Rules of the Arbitration Institute of the Stockholm Chamber of Commerce (Art. 17 of the 1999 Rules), the China International Economic and Trade Arbitration Commission (Art. 28) and the Indian Council of Arbitration (Rule 24) .

In the words of one commentator,[97] the international arbitrator's duty to disclose is entirely undisputed. Irrespective of the applicable procedural rules, it is an obligation which constitutes a general principle of international arbitration.

1059. — Some laws[98] and arbitration rules are careful to specify that the duty of disclosure is permanent. Arbitrators must disclose any new circumstance which, in the minds of the parties, will be liable to affect their independence. Even in the absence of an express provision to that effect, the arbitrators' duty of disclosure must continue until they make their award, because they are required to remain independent until they have fulfilled their role as judges.[99] Thus, even where an arbitrator was employed by one of the parties on the day after the award was made, the Paris Court of Appeals nevertheless set the award aside

---

[95] CAL. CIV. PROC. CODE § 1297.121; on the development of Californian law on domestic arbitration and views from a comparative law standpoint, see J. Lani Bader, *Arbitrator Disclosure – Probing the Issues*, 12 J. INT'L ARB. 39 (Sept. 1995).

[96] TEX. REV. CIV. STAT. ANN. Art. 249-12, § 1, redesignated as TEX. CIV. PROC. & REM. CODE ANN. §§ 172.101 to 172.106 (West 1999).

[97] Lalive, *supra* note 29, at 134.

[98] Such as the UNCITRAL Model Law (Art. 12(1)) and the Netherlands Code of Civil Procedure (Art. 1034).

[99] *See supra* para. 1040.

on the grounds that the other party was not informed of the situation, which must have involved prior negotiations, before the award had been made.[100]

The purpose of the arbitrator's duty of disclosure is to ensure that the parties are able to challenge that arbitrator if, in their view, the arbitrator does not meet (or no longer meets) the applicable conditions of independence and impartiality. The challenge procedure, whether before an arbitral institution, appointing authority or court, requires the challenging party to prove the facts on which the challenge is based. That party cannot therefore take any action until it is aware of such facts.[101]

1060. — The real problem is not the existence of a duty of disclosure but determining which facts prospective arbitrators should disclose. Clearly, the principle is that they should disclose all circumstances affecting their independence or impartiality. However, the courts already find that principle difficult enough to implement,[102] so can it provide adequate guidance for prospective arbitrators?

A recent debate concerning ICC practice[103] highlighted the fact that subjectivity is inevitable in this area, in two respects. In the "statement of independence" that prospective arbitrators are required to submit to the International Court of Arbitration prior to receiving confirmation of their appointment, the arbitrators must first declare that they are and intend to remain independent of each of the parties. They are then faced with a choice between either declaring that no fact or circumstance need be disclosed, or stating that

> however . . . I wish to call your attention to the following facts or circumstances which I hereafter disclose because I consider that they might be of such a nature as to call into question my independence in the eyes of any of the parties.

The prospective arbitrators are thus expected to decide what they should disclose by putting themselves in the position of the parties. One can well imagine the dilemma faced by arbitrators in deciding whether to disclose an inconsequential circumstance: if they reveal it, their appointment may not be confirmed by the International Court of Arbitration, but if they do not reveal it, it may later resurface and create a potentially serious incident. Of course, one possible solution consists in disclosing all such circumstances and specifying that, in the arbitrator's opinion, they do not raise doubts as to his or her independence. This is also an option open to the arbitrator in the "statement of independence" form.

1061. — The courts themselves have to take account of the element of subjectivity inherent in the diversity of the situations that arise in this area. They do sometimes try to

---

[100] July 2, 1992, *Raoul Duval, supra* note 35. *See also* CA Paris, Jan. 12, 1996, *Gouvernement de l'Etat du Qatar, aff'd*, Cass. 1e civ., Mar. 16, 1999, *supra* note 32.

[101] On the options available once a party is aware of the facts, see *infra* paras. 1067 *et seq.*

[102] *See supra* paras. 1028 *et seq.*

[103] *See supra* para. 1031.

clarify the scope of the duty of disclosure. For example, in a 1992 decision in which it reiterated a formula used consistently over ten years,[104] the Paris Court of Appeals held that:

> the arbitrator's duty of disclosure, which enables the parties to exercise their right to challenge, should be examined not only in the light of the extent to which the situation at issue is common knowledge, but also in the light of the impact that it may reasonably be expected to have on the arbitrator's judgment.

The Court of Appeals went on to observe that the functions exercised by an arbitrator as a consultant to the chairman of a company within the group to which one of the parties belonged, for which he was paid significant sums of money,

> were not, by their very nature, of a sufficiently public nature to release [M.M.] from his duty to inform, or to exonerate him from the duty of transparency which is inherent in the role of an arbitrator . . . . At the time when the submission agreement in which [M.M.] was appointed as a substitute arbitrator was signed, he and a company of the group to which one of the parties to the arbitration belonged had shared interests. This situation would have raised reasonable doubts as to the independence of the arbitrator and would, at the very least, have justified a challenge against him.[105]

Facts which need not be disclosed should thus satisfy either of the following two conditions: they should either be publicly known, rendering any further disclosure pointless,[106] or they should raise no "reasonable doubt" as to the arbitrator's independence. This double test was used again in a more recent decision of the same Court of Appeals,[107] and arbitrators should apply these two alternative conditions when determining what should be disclosed. It is also the test used by the French courts when considering the personal liability of arbitrators who choose to remain silent and pursue their functions despite the existence of a circumstance or the occurrence of an event which, according to a party, should have been disclosed.[108]

---

[104] CA Paris, June 2, 1989, *T.A.I.* and *Gemanco*, June 28, 1991, *KFTCIC*, *supra* note 20; CA Paris, July 8, 1994, Siab v. Valmont, 1996 REV. ARB. 428, 1st decision, and P. Fouchard's note.

[105] CA Paris, Apr. 9, 1992, *Annahold*, *supra* note 32.

[106] *See* CA Paris, June 2, 1989, *T.A.I.* and *Gemanco*, *supra* note 20, where an arbitrator's position as a state employee was "obvious and well-known."

[107] CA Paris, July 2, 1992, *Raoul Duval*, *supra* note 35.

[108] *See infra* paras. 1091 *et seq.*, in the *Annahold* and *Raoul Duval* cases.

b) Powers of the Authority Appointing the Arbitrators

1062. — Where arbitrators are appointed by a pre-designated third party, or by the courts, or where their appointment is confirmed by an arbitral institution,[109] the appointing authority or the institution will be entitled to refuse to make or confirm the appointment if it considers that the prospective arbitrators do not satisfy the conditions of independence and impartiality.

1063. — In institutional arbitration, the institution's rules generally grant the appointing authority that power. For example, Article 7, paragraph 2 of the ICC Rules (replacing Art. 2(7) of the previous Rules) makes it clear that the International Court of Arbitration, duly informed by means of the prospective arbitrators' statement of independence and any comments made by the parties regarding the nominees, will only appoint or confirm arbitrators if it is satisfied, in the light of that information, that they are independent of all parties involved in the arbitration.[110] The same is true of the LCIA,[111] and, generally speaking, all arbitral institutions which have the power to make the final appointment of prospective arbitrators on the basis of both the information received from the candidates and the comments made by the parties.

1064. — In *ad hoc* arbitration, it is less certain that the appointing authority will always have the power or even sufficient information to exercise a *prima facie* review of the judicial qualities of prospective arbitrators. In most cases, neither the arbitration agreement nor any applicable arbitration rules (the UNCITRAL Rules, for instance) contain any indication as to the third party's powers in this respect. However, the appointing authority, chosen and trusted by the parties, should verify the independence and impartiality of arbitrators that it intends to appoint, as the duty of disclosure is a general principle applicable in any international arbitration.

1065. — Where, as a result of the intentions of the parties or the law governing the arbitration, a court is responsible for appointing an arbitrator, it will undoubtedly have the authority to verify that arbitrator's independence and impartiality. The practice of the French courts suggests that they carefully ensure that they appoint only independent and impartial arbitrators, although this will not be reflected in the very brief court order making such appointments.[112]

However, two rulings of the Paris Tribunal of First Instance in the *Eurodisney* case are significant in this respect. An arbitration agreement in a construction contract stipulated that

---

[109] On these scenarios, and on the constitution of the arbitral tribunal with the support of these various appointing authorities, see *supra* para. 952.

[110] For ICC practice, see Hascher, *supra* note 27.

[111] Art. 5.3 and 7.1 of the 1998 Rules (Art. 3.1 *et seq.* of the previous Rules).

[112] *See* Philippe Fouchard, *La coopération du président du Tribunal de grande instance à l'arbitrage*, 1985 REV. ARB. 5.

the arbitrators were required to have various linguistic, technical and legal skills.[113] The owner argued that the list of arbitrators which the ICC compiled did not allow those criteria to be satisfied, and therefore petitioned the judge to order the ICC to extend its list as well as the "information attached to it, so as to enable an informed choice to be made." In both decisions, the court replied that:

> in order to exercise the functions of assistance and cooperation in constituting the arbitral tribunal, conferred on him in the event of a difficulty not only through the intentions of the parties, but also by Articles 1444 or 1493 of the New Code of Civil Procedure, to which the arbitration agreement expressly refers, the President of the Paris Tribunal of First Instance must be fully informed as to the personal qualities of the arbitrators liable to be appointed.

Having heard the parties and examined the documents produced by the parties, the Paris Tribunal then invited the Chairman and the Secretary General of the ICC International Court of Arbitration to provide it with

> further details, purely by way of information, regarding the personal qualities and experience of the prospective arbitrators named on the list.[114]

It was only when the Paris Tribunal had considered the views of the representatives of the International Court of Arbitration concerning the personal qualities and experience of the arbitrators, and had interpreted the arbitration agreement, that it ruled that it had an adequate list and proceeded to appoint the arbitrators.

Had the independence or impartiality of a prospective arbitrator been at issue, the Paris Tribunal would certainly have examined those requirements and, if necessary, refused to appoint any arbitrator not clearly in possession of those qualities.

2° Punitive Measures

1066. — Certain steps can be taken after arbitrators have been appointed where a party contests their independence or impartiality, or argues that they do not possess the particular qualities required to enable them to fulfil their functions.

The party making such a claim has two possible courses of action: it can challenge the arbitrator (b) or seek to have the award set aside (c). Before briefly discussing these procedures, we shall set out a few principles common to each of them and show how the two interrelate (a).

---

[113] TGI Paris, réf., Dec. 12 and 20, 1991, *Campenon Bernard, supra* note 90.

[114] TGI Paris, réf., Dec. 12, 1991, *Campenon Bernard, supra* note 90.

a) Interrelation of the Two Procedures

1067. — In the case of both a challenge and an action to set aside, the admissibility of the claim is generally subject to compliance with a common rule: the party bringing the claim must demonstrate that the facts and circumstances on which it relies were not known to it prior to the appointment of the arbitrator. If the party was aware of such facts and circumstances at that time, it will be presumed to have waived its right to rely on them. To be more precise, it would be deemed to have considered that those facts and circumstances did not affect the qualities which it expected of an arbitrator. This is the key benefit of the arbitrator's duty of disclosure: if it has been scrupulously observed, it allows both the prospective arbitrator to assume his or her judicial role uncontested, and the arbitration to proceed without the risk of subsequent—and no doubt disruptive—challenges.

This rule reflects a principle widely accepted in international arbitration, and is described by UNCITRAL as a waiver of a party's "right to object."[115] Good faith prevents a party who remains silent prior to the appointment of the arbitrator from using facts of which it was aware at that time to challenge, at a later stage, the independence of an arbitrator or the validity of an award.

The rule is found in most contemporary arbitration statutes,[116] and is accepted by the French[117] and Swiss[118] courts in the absence of such a statute. The UNCITRAL Model Law, together with all laws based upon it, clearly sets forth the rule in its Article 12, paragraph 2:

> [a] party may challenge an arbitrator appointed by him, or in whose appointment he has participated, only for reasons of which he becomes aware after the appointment has been made.

1068. — A challenge and an action to set aside cannot be combined, at least in principle. If the award has already been made when a party becomes aware of the circumstances affecting the arbitrators' independence and impartiality, the arbitrators can no longer be challenged, and only an action to set the award aside (or to prevent its enforcement) will be admissible.[119] If, on the other hand, the award has yet to be made when it is discovered that the arbitrators do not meet the requirements of independence and impartiality, they can be

---

[115] Art. 4 of the Model Law.

[116] *See, e.g.*, Art. 1033(2) of the Netherlands Code of Civil Procedure; Art. 180, para. 2 of the Swiss Private International Law Statute.

[117] *See, e.g.*, CA Paris, June 2, 1989, *T.A.I.*, *supra* note 20; CA Paris, May 10, 1994, Sheik Mahfouz Salem Bin Mahfouz v. Al Tayar, 1996 REV. ARB. 66, and the commentary by Loïc Cadiet, *La renonciation à se prévaloir des irrégularités de la procédure arbitrale*, *id.* at 3; CA Paris, Dec. 12, 1996, *Commercial Agraria Hermanos Lucena*, *supra* note 18; Cass. 1e civ., Mar. 24, 1998, *Excelsior Film TV*, *supra* note 46.

[118] See, for example, Fed. Trib., Feb. 9, 1998, *supra* note 39, which held that "a party that fails to react immediately loses its rights to invoke its grounds for challenge at a later stage."

[119] TGI Paris, July 2, 1990, Annahold BV v. L'Oréal, 1996 REV. ARB. 483, 1st decision, and CA Paris, Apr. 9, 1992, *Annahold*, *supra* note 32.

challenged. If no challenge is made, or if the challenge is unsuccessful, an action against the award or against the enforcement of the award will no longer be admissible.[120]

1069. — However, the courts draw a distinction according to whether the challenge has been rejected by a third party, such as an arbitral institution, or by a court.[121] In the former case, as the decision is merely an administrative measure within the arbitral proceedings, it is not *res judicata*[122] and will not prevent the courts from determining, after the award has been made, whether the challenge raised against the arbitrator and rejected by the arbitral institution constitutes a ground on which to refuse the action to enforce, or set aside the award.[123] If, however, the challenge has been rejected by a court, the issue of the arbitrators' independence is deemed to be finally decided and can no longer be re-examined by the courts when hearing an action to set the award aside, unless a defect affecting the constitution of the arbitral tribunal has since come to light.[124]

The case law of the Swiss Federal Tribunal illustrates this distinction. In one decision, the rejection by the ICC of the challenge of an arbitrator was held not to prevent the challenging party from bringing an action to set aside under Article 190 of the Swiss Private International Law Statute on grounds of the alleged absence of independence.[125] In another case, where the cantonal court had jurisdiction over the challenge of an arbitrator pursuant to Article 180 of the Private International Law Statute (because the parties had not agreed on an alternative procedure), the court's decision was held to be final and no action to set aside was available against the award.[126] However, recourse against the award may be available based on the administrative law theory of the violation of a citizen's constitutional rights.[127]

---

[120] CA Paris, June 2, 1989, *T.A.I.* and *Gemanco, supra* note 20; CA Paris, May 10, 1994, *Sheikh Mahfouz Salem, supra* note 117.

[121] On the subsidiary nature of court intervention, see *supra* paras. 847 *et seq.*, particularly para. 875 as regards the challenge of arbitrators.

[122] Cass. 2e civ., Oct. 7, 1987, Opinter France v. S.A.R.L. Dacomex, 1987 REV. ARB. 479, and E. Mezger's note; *see also supra* para. 991.

[123] CA Paris, May 15, 1985, Raffineries de pétrole d'Homs et de Banias v. Chambre de Commerce Internationale, 1985 REV. ARB. 141, 2d decision; CA Paris, May 4, 1988, *Chambre arbitrale de Paris, supra* note 23; CA Paris, Jan. 12, 1996, *Gouvernement de l'Etat du Qatar, aff'd*, Cass. 1e civ., Mar. 16, 1999, *supra* note 32; CA Paris, June 13, 1996, *KFTCIC, supra* note 20.

[124] CA Paris, Apr. 6, 1990, *Philipp Brothers, supra* note 21.

[125] Fed. Trib., June 30, 1994, *Hitachi Ltd., supra* note 25.

[126] Fed. Trib., Aug. 13, 1996, T v. G, 1997 BULL. ASA 108; 1997 REV. SUISSE DR. INT. ET DR. EUR 609, and observations by P. Schweizer.

[127] Fed. Trib., Feb. 9, 1998, *supra* note 39.

b) Challenging Arbitrators

1070. — A party can challenge an arbitrator on discovering, after that arbitrator's appointment, that he or she does not possess the qualities required of a private judge, namely independence and impartiality,[128] and any special qualifications imposed by the arbitration agreement.[129] However, the attitude of the courts will differ according to the nature of the grounds for the challenge. If the arbitrators' independence or impartiality are at issue, the court will carefully examine the circumstances giving rise to the challenge. If, on the other hand, the challenge is based on the alleged absence of the special technical, linguistic or legal skills required of an arbitrator in a particular dispute, the court will generally be more reluctant to assess whether or not the arbitrator reaches the appropriate standard.[130]

1071. — We have seen that the principles governing the challenge procedure are now well established.[131] The challenge must be initiated by the party disputing an arbitrator's independence or impartiality as soon as that party becomes aware of circumstances which raise doubts as to the arbitrator's possession of those qualities. The challenge is submitted to the arbitral institution or appointing authority duly empowered, under the arbitration agreement or the applicable arbitration rules, to decide the matter. In French law, only where no such authority has been chosen by the parties will the challenge be submitted to the Paris Tribunal of First Instance.[132] The UNCITRAL Model Law (Art. 13), the Swiss Private International Law Statute (Art. 180, para. 3), and the 1994 Italian Arbitration Statute,[133] in particular, also provide for judicial intervention only on a subsidiary basis. Parties rarely resort to the courts, in practice, as nearly all current arbitration rules organize a challenge procedure (before the appointing authority[134] in *ad hoc* arbitration, or before the institution[135] in institutional arbitration). When the parties go before the courts, the aim is usually to contest the decision of the arbitral institution. However, at this early stage of the proceedings, the courts will not hear such an application, which will only be reviewed in the context of an action to set aside (or to resist enforcement of) the award.

---

[128] On these concepts, see *supra* paras. 1020 *et seq.*

[129] See *supra* paras. 1048 *et seq.*

[130] See TGI Paris, Sept. 21, 1989, *La Belle Créole*, *supra* note 19; TGI Paris, Apr. 1, 1993, *Etat de Dubai*, *supra* note 51.

[131] See *supra* paras. 871 *et seq.*

[132] See TGI Paris, Apr. 1, 1993, *Etat de Dubai*, *supra* note 51.

[133] Art. 836 of the Code of Civil Procedure; *see* Guiseppe Tarzia, *Assistenza e non interferenza guidiziaria nell'arbitrato internazionale*, 1996 RIV. DELL'ARB. 473.

[134] Art. 12 of the UNCITRAL Rules.

[135] See *supra* para. 1006.

c) Actions to Set Aside or Prevent Enforcement of the Award

1072. — If the grounds for a challenge do not emerge until after the award is made,[136] or where the challenge is rejected by the arbitral institution or appointing authority,[137] a party can seek redress for the arbitrators' failure to satisfy the conditions imposed by contesting the award.

1073. — Several of the grounds admissible in an action to set aside may be relied on in those circumstances.[138] In some cases, the claimant has based its action on all admissible grounds.[139]

Thus, a party unaware of links existing between the arbitrator and its opponent may argue that the arbitration agreement is void for mistake as to the substantive qualities of the arbitrator and that, as a result, the award is also void for want of a valid arbitration agreement. This approach was endorsed by the French *Cour de cassation* for the first time in its *Ury v. Galeries Lafayette* decision, which concerned a domestic arbitration.[140] If the claimant can show proof of the mistaken consent, this is undoubtedly the best ground on which to contest the award.

The challenging party may also rely on specific grounds regarding the constitution of the arbitral tribunal. For example, the Paris Court of Appeals held in one case that an arbitral tribunal was

> unlawfully constituted, within the meaning of Article 1502, paragraph 2 of the New Code of Civil Procedure, as a result of the appointment of an arbitrator who did not provide the guarantees of independence, vis-à-vis each of the parties, which any litigant is entitled to expect of him.[141]

This second, more specific ground will be preferred particularly where—as in this case —the disputed links between an arbitrator and one of the parties did not exist at the time the arbitrator was appointed.

Finally, and although strictly speaking the principle of due process is not at issue, the making of an award by an arbitrator who is proved to have been biased towards, or

---

[136] *See supra* para. 1068.

[137] *See supra* para. 1069.

[138] In French law, see Article 1502 of the New Code of Civil Procedure. On the grounds for setting aside an award, see *infra* paras. 1601 *et seq.*

[139] *See, e.g.,* CA Paris, Apr. 9, 1992, *Annahold, supra* note 32.

[140] Cass. 2e civ., Apr.13, 1972, *Ury, supra* note 17; *see also* Cass. 2e civ., Feb. 20, 1974, *Forges et Ateliers de Commentry Oissel, supra* note 22; for international arbitration, see CA Paris, Apr. 9, 1992, *Annahold, supra* note 32, which applied Article 1502 1° of the French New Code of Civil Procedure.

[141] CA Paris, July 2, 1992, *Raoul Duval, supra* note 35.

dependent upon, one of the parties may constitute a breach of international public policy.[142] This would obviously be a matter of procedural public policy, as a party's right to a fair hearing would be adversely affected by the relationship between the arbitrator and the other party.[143] Likewise, the principle of equal treatment of the parties, which in the context of the appointment of arbitrators has been held to be a matter of public policy,[144] means that each arbitrator should be equally independent of all of the parties.[145]

§ 2. – Protection of the Arbitrators

1074. — As arbitrators carry out a judicial function, they should benefit from protection similar to that enjoyed by judges, both during and after the proceedings.

1075. — The stringent conditions governing challenges of arbitrators already provide a relatively effective form of protection. Provided that the arbitrators carefully observe their duty of disclosure, the parties will not, in the course of the arbitration, be able to unilaterally challenge either the arbitrators in person or the performance of their functions.

The fact that arbitrators exercise a judicial role also accounts for the fact that they cannot easily be removed, either by the parties or by the arbitral institution which appointed them or confirmed their appointment. The removal of arbitrators, which might seem the normal remedy for a breach of contract, will only be possible under exceptional circumstances due to the specificity of the arbitrators' task.[146]

1076. — It is essentially after the award has been made that the arbitrators become vulnerable to the feelings of a party dissatisfied with their decision. Accordingly, to allow them peace of mind in the exercise of their functions, the arbitrators are protected against the risk of legal action subsequent to the award.

The principle of the immunity of arbitrators is widely recognized (A). However, that immunity is subject to various limits and exceptions, the extent of which has increased in recent years (B).

---

[142] See, for example, in France, Article 1502 5° of the New Code of Civil Procedure.

[143] See, in French domestic arbitration, CA Paris, Mar. 13, 1981, Ets. Cornet et Fils v. Union Nationale des Coopératives Agricoles (U.N.C.A.C.), 1983 REV. ARB. 83, and B. Moreau's note.

[144] See, in France, Cass. 1e civ., Jan. 7, 1992, B.K.M.I. v. Dutco, 1992 Bull. Civ. I, No. 2; 1992 REV. ARB. 470, and P. Bellet's note; 119 J.D.I. 707 (1992), 2d decision, and C. Jarrosson's note; 1992 RTD COM. 796, and observations by J.-C. Dubarry and E. Loquin; for an English translation, see XVIII Y.B. COM. ARB. 140 (1993); 7 INT'L ARB. REP. B1 (Feb. 1992).

[145] However, in upholding the principle of "impartiality in judicial decision-making," the Paris Court of Appeals preferred to base its findings on the specific rules of Article 1502. See CA Paris, Dec. 20, 1984, G.P.L.A. v. The Canal Harbour Worms Co., 1987 REV. ARB. 49, and E. Mezger's note.

[146] See infra paras. 1138 et seq.

A. – THE PRINCIPLE OF IMMUNITY

1077. — The word "immunity" in this context is used primarily by the courts and authors in common law countries to refer to the principle that arbitrators cannot be held liable for the manner in which they perform their judicial functions. It can also be used in a civil law context where the immunity from prosecution traditionally enjoyed by judges may or may not be extended to arbitrators. The word immunity also underlines that only public authorities (the legislature or the courts) are liable to grant it and that it is intended to serve the public interest by guaranteeing that arbitral justice can function properly. It is therefore not to be confused with contractual provisions aimed at avoiding or restricting liability, which only concern the strictly contractual aspects of the arbitrator's functions. In other words, in the absence of an international convention on this issue, an arbitrator's immunity can only be conferred by national law. Thus, with one exception (the CACNIQ),[147] arbitral institutions which seek to exclude or restrict the contractual liability of their arbitrators do not use the word "immunity." We shall consider provisions excluding or restricting liability when we come to examine the contractual status of the arbitrator as a provider of services.[148]

1° French Law

1078. — In a case before the Paris Court of Appeals, a party contesting an arbitral award requested the Court to order the arbitrators to appear in person before the Court. That request was rejected on the following grounds:

> The arbitrator . . . is not a third party in relation to the dispute which he has decided . . . . On accepting his functions, he assumes the status of a judge, as a result of the contract appointing him. He therefore enjoys the same rights and is subject to the same duties as a judge, and it is not legally possible for a judge to be heard in person in proceedings to which he is not a party.[149]

Although the issue raised was somewhat peripheral and the case concerned a domestic arbitration, the position of the Court was expressed in general, carefully measured terms, and should be extended to international arbitration. That position was based on the similarity between the respective roles of judge and arbitrator, and models the protection of the arbitrator on that of the judge. However, that approach must be clarified and qualified as far as an arbitrator's liability is concerned.

---

[147] Art. 25 of the Arbitration Rules.

[148] *See infra* paras. 1151 *et seq.*

[149] CA Paris, May 29, 1992, Consorts Rouny v. S.A. Holding, 1992 RTD COM. 588, and observations by J.-C. Dubarry and E. Loquin; 1996 REV. ARB. 408, and Fouchard, *supra* note 2, ¶ 16.

1079. — Under French law, the state must compensate parties for loss caused by the defective operation of the courts, and such liability can only be incurred in cases of gross negligence or denial of justice.[150] Only professional judges who are personally at fault enjoy immunity from jurisdiction, other than where sued by the state itself[151] to recover its liability vis-à-vis a third party.[152]

1080. — These rules do not apply to arbitrators. As arbitration is a private form of justice, "the arbitrator does not become a judge, even for a short time, but remains an ordinary citizen," as a result of which "an arbitrator can incur liability under a regime more straightforward than that applicable to a judge."[153]

The *Cour de cassation* has held that:

> as arbitrators assume no public office and can therefore not cause the state to incur liability under Article 505 of the Code of Civil Procedure . . . , an action for damages in respect of the performance of their functions can only be brought under ordinary tort or contract law.[154]

1081. — That position also needs to be qualified, and a number of more recent decisions, albeit concerning domestic arbitrations, have done so.

1082. — First, in a case before the Reims Tribunal of First Instance, a party brought an action against the arbitrators seeking to recover the loss suffered as a result of their award. The court held that:

> all of the claimant's arguments essentially amount to the general criticism that the arbitrators reached the wrong decision. In this context, the arbitrators could only incur liability in the event of gross fault, fraud, or connivance with one of the parties. Otherwise the protection, independence and authority of the arbitrators would be restricted to an extent that would be incompatible with the task of judging which is conferred on them.

---

[150] Art. L. 781-1 of the Code of Judicial Organization.

[151] *See* Art. 11-1 of the Ordinance No. 58-1270 of Dec. 22, 1958, as amended on Jan. 18, 1979 and Art. 505 *et seq.* of the old Code of Civil Procedure.

[152] On this issue generally, see Guy Pluyette and Pascal Chauvin, *Responsabilité du service de la justice et des magistrats*, J.-CL. PROC. CIV., Fasc. 74 (1993).

[153] HENRI MOTULSKY, ECRITS – VOL. 2 – ETUDES ET NOTES SUR L'ARBITRAGE 5, 15 (1974).

[154] Cass. 2e civ., Jan. 29, 1960, Veuve J. Houdet et Fils v. Chambre arbitrale de l'union syndicale de grains et farines de Bordeaux, Dalloz, Jur. 262 (1960); 1960 REV. ARB. 121; 1960 RTD CIV. 348, and observations by P. Hébraud; see also, more recently, CA Paris, Oct. 12, 1995, 1e Ch., Sec. C, Van Luijk v. Raoul Duval, No. 93.16203, unpublished.

As none of these grounds of liability was either justified or even alleged, the court dismissed the claim. Furthermore, because it considered the action to be abusive and offensive, the court upheld the arbitrators' counterclaims and awarded the token damages sought by each of them.[155]

1083. — In another case, where the arbitrators were being sued by a party on the grounds of an alleged breach of the applicable procedural rules, and themselves filed a counterclaim, the Paris Tribunal of First Instance took the same position, emphasizing the need to protect the arbitrators' authority and dignity:

> Apart from an action to set aside an arbitral award, a party cannot claim to have a right to be indemnified by arbitrators whom it alleges are at fault . . . . By suing the arbitrators and impugning their personal conduct . . . the plaintiffs have acted irresponsibly and imprudently, and are at fault within the meaning of Article 1382 of the Civil Code, as they have undermined the honor of the arbitrators and disregarded the consideration which is due to any arbitrator performing the functions entrusted to him in accordance with the rules and requirements of an objective procedural technique.[156]

In a more recent case, a party considered that in their award the arbitrators had made a clerical error in calculating the amounts due. That party began by asking the arbitrators to amend the award. The arbitrators refused to do so, believing that the party was really asking them to change their reasoning. The arbitrators were then summonsed before the courts, on the grounds that they were contractually liable under Articles 1142 and 1147 of the Civil Code. Without actually excluding the possibility of such liability,[157] the Paris Tribunal of First Instance held that, because of the judicial functions assumed by the arbitrators,

> such an action cannot be substituted for the actions available against the award, and neither can it indirectly empower the court to review the arbitral award . . . . Thus, as a matter of principle, it is not the role of a Tribunal of First Instance, seized of an ordinary contractual dispute, to review the arbitrators' decision.[158]

On appeal, the Paris Court of Appeals took an even firmer stance. Again, the possibility that an arbitrator might incur contractual liability for his or her own fault was not excluded,[159] but the Court held that:

---

[155] TGI Reims, Sept. 27, 1978, Florange v. Brissart et Corgié, No. 482/77, unpublished.

[156] Oct. 2, 1985, Castin v. Gomez, 1987 REV. ARB. 84, and observations by B. M.

[157] On this issue, see *infra* para. 1148.

[158] June 13, 1990, Bompard v. Consorts C., 1996 REV. ARB. 476, 1st decision, and the commentary by Fouchard, *supra* note 2; for an English translation, see 6 INT'L ARB. REP. F10 (Aug. 1991).

[159] *See infra* para. 1148.

in this case, the allegation leveled at the arbitrators was effectively that they had made a gross miscalculation . . . and relates to the substance of the award. As such, it could only have formed the basis of an action to set aside the award under Article 1484 of the New Code of Civil Procedure . . . . The alleged fault is therefore directly connected to the substance of the judicial act . . . . Consequently, the claimant has no *locus standi* and the action must be declared inadmissible.[160]

1084. — There is no reason why these domestic law principles should not apply in international arbitration. The same justification applies in both cases: it is to protect the arbitrators in the exercise of their judicial role by preventing the parties from bringing an action against them in person, over and above an action to set the award aside, which would clearly have a destabilizing effect, not only in each particular case, but also for arbitration in general. Although the decisions described above do not refer expressly to the concept of immunity, the protection which they afford arbitrators is very similar.

2° Other Legal Systems

1085. — National legal systems appear to differ in their conception of the immunity of arbitrators. When UNCITRAL was preparing the Model Law, the issue was deemed too controversial for a satisfactory uniform solution to be attainable.[161] A survey covering thirteen countries,[162] and the summary prepared by its editor,[163] suggest that the United States is the only country in favor of full immunity. Of the other countries, some granted limited immunity (Austria, England, Germany and Norway), others did not preclude liability (France, Spain and Sweden), while the remainder had yet to express a clear position.

1086. — The principle of the immunity of arbitrators is primarily found in common law countries.[164] In the United States, several statutes as well as case law dating back to 1884 exclude all civil liability for arbitrators in respect of acts committed in that capacity.[165] This immunity is intended to protect the function (in other words, the integrity and independence

---

[160] May 22, 1991, Bompard v. Consorts C., 1996 REV. ARB. 476, 2d decision, and the commentary by Fouchard, *supra* note 2; for an English translation, see 6 INT'L ARB. REP. F8 (Aug. 1991).

[161] *See United Nations Commission on International Trade Law, Fourteenth Session, Vienna, 19–26 June 1981, International Commercial Arbitration – Possible features of a model law on international commercial arbitration – Report of the Secretary General*, UN Doc. A/CN.9/207, ¶ 70.

[162] THE IMMUNITY OF ARBITRATORS (Julian D. M. Lew ed., 1990).

[163] *Id.*, at 4.

[164] *See Final Report on the Status of the Arbitrator – Appendix II – Comparative Synthesis of Current Substantive Law in Various Countries*, ICC BULLETIN, Vol. 7, No. 1, at 27, 37 (1996).

[165] *See* Christian Hausmaninger, *Civil Liability of Arbitrators—Comparative Analysis and Proposals for Reform*, 7 J. INT'L ARB. 7 (Dec. 1990); Michael Hoellering, *Arbitral Immunity Under American Law, in* AAA GENERAL COUNSEL'S ANNUAL REPORT 1990-91, at 162.

of the judicial process) rather than the individual.[166] In New Zealand, the 1996 Arbitration Act provides that "an arbitrator is not liable for negligence in respect of anything done or omitted to be done in the capacity of arbitrator" (Art. 13). The English courts also granted arbitrators immunity, although this was not the case for experts (such as architects, accountants and valuers) as they do not perform a judicial function.[167] The 1996 Arbitration Act confirms this case law, although it does allow certain exceptions with respect to arbitrators' immunity.[168]

The Canadian courts take the same position. In one case, the Quebec Court of Appeal treated accountants alleged to have failed to make the accurate stock evaluation required of them as arbitrators, and held them to be protected by their immunity in the same way as judges.[169] However, the Canadian Supreme Court considered that the brief of an expert accountant did not involve resolving a dispute and that the issue of their immunity therefore did not arise.[170]

1087. — Legal systems which clearly afford arbitrators no immunity include that of Spain, where the Arbitration Statute of December 5, 1988 provides that arbitrators can be sued for loss caused by misrepresentation or fault on their part (Art. 16(1)). The Austrian Code of Civil Procedure also admits such liability in the event of an unjustified default or delay (Art. 584(2)).

1088. — Because many countries have no relevant laws or precedents, it is in fact a fairly hazardous task to attempt to classify the various positions taken in different jurisdictions. In any event, the distinctions between the different positions are perhaps less marked than suggested by the classifications described above. No legal system allows arbitrators to be fully liable for any error of judgment they commit, in order to avoid judicial harassment of arbitrators by losing parties. Conversely, even in the United States, where immunity is often depicted as being absolute, it is hard to imagine arbitrators being able to avoid liability for acts which clearly constitute a breach of their fundamental duties as judges.

---

[166] *See, e.g.,* Corey v. New York Stock Exchange, 691 F.2d 1205 (6th Cir. 1982); Austern v. Chicago Bd. Options Exchange, Inc., 898 F.2d 882 (2d Cir. 1990); Feichtinger v. Conant, 893 P.2d 1266 (Alaska 1995); for an analysis of recent U.S. case law by Carl F. Salans, see *Arbitrator Immunity in the United States,* ICC BULLETIN, Vol. 7, No. 1, at 48 (1996).

[167] Sutcliffe v. Thackrah, [1974] A.C. 727; [1974] 1 All E.R. 859; [1974] 1 Lloyd's Rep. 319 (H.L. 1974); Arenson v. Arenson, [1977] A.C. 405 (H.L. 1974); Alan Redfern, *The Immunity of Arbitrators, in* ICC BULLETIN, SPECIAL SUPPLEMENT, THE STATUS OF THE ARBITRATOR 121 (ICC Publication No. 564, 1995); Alan Redfern, *Status of Arbitrators under English law,* ICC BULLETIN, Vol. 7, No. 1, at 43 (1996).

[168] Sec. 29; *see infra* para. 1097.

[169] Zittrer v. Sport Maska Inc., 1985 C.A. 386.

[170] Sport Maska Inc. v. Zittrer, [1988] 1 S.C.R. 564.

1088-1.— Some legal systems extend immunity to arbitral institutions. This is the case in U.S. case law[171] and in the 1996 English Arbitration Act (Sec. 74). It is certainly appropriate to protect institutions against legal actions brought by dissatisfied parties unable to pursue the arbitrators. However, in our view, the institutions receive sufficient protection from the recognition of their power to exercise their discretion in administering the arbitration and from the requirement that proof of gross fault be adduced against them. It is therefore unnecessary to treat them as judicial bodies, which of course they are not. This position has been taken by the French courts in cases brought against the ICC. Nevertheless, those courts have yet to find that an institution committed an act or omission triggering its liability, given the powers granted to the institution by the parties when agreeing to its arbitration rules.[172]

B. – The Limits of Arbitrator Immunity

1089. — Each legal system takes broadly the same approach when it comes to defining the cases where arbitrators cannot rely on their immunity and are therefore personally liable. These cases are where the arbitrators have failed to comply with their duty of disclosure (1°), and where they have knowingly violated their duties as judges (2°).

1° Liability for Failure to Comply with Duty of Disclosure

1090. — Apart from any other measures of redress in respect of the non-disclosure of facts and circumstances raising doubts as to their independence and impartiality,[173] it is reasonable to have the arbitrators bear any losses caused through their fault. In particular, by challenging the arbitrator or bringing an action to set aside the award, the parties will incur costs and other losses, and will spend considerable time in the process.

The French courts so decided in two cases concerning international arbitration.

1091. — In the *Annahold* case, that company discovered, on June 25, 1990, that the sole arbitrator appointed by the parties on December 22, 1989 was a financial consultant to the chairman of the other party. An investigation revealed that in his capacity as a consultant the arbitrator had been paid net quarterly fees of 125,000 French francs until the end of 1989. On the very next day—June 26, 1990—Annahold asked the arbitrator to resign from his functions and applied to the courts for an interim ruling on its challenge against the arbitrator. However, on June 27 the arbitrator made his award. The Paris Tribunal of First

---

[171] *See Corey* and *Austern*, *supra* note 166; see also the other decisions analyzed by Salans, *supra* note 166.

[172] *See* TGI Paris, May 21, 1997, Cubic Defense Systems Inc. v. Chambre de commerce internationale, 1997 Rev. Arb. 417, *aff'd*, CA Paris, Sept. 15, 1998, 1999 Rev. Arb. 103, and P. Lalive's note; 126 J.D.I. 162 (1999), and E. Loquin's note; *see also infra* paras. 1142 and 1153.

[173] *See supra* paras. 1066 *et seq.*

Instance therefore decided that there were no grounds for an interim ruling on the challenge, and it instructed the plaintiff to "exercise the only available actions against the award, if it considers that there are grounds on which to set it aside."[174] The Paris Court of Appeals subsequently set the award aside on the grounds of invalid consent to the arbitration agreement.[175] On the basis of the decision of the Court of Appeals, the Paris Tribunal of First Instance then heard various claims brought by the same company against its opponent and the arbitrator. It criticized the arbitrator for having responded to the request that he resign in view of his connections with one of the parties, by stating, on June 26, 1990, that he was unaware of any such connections. The court also considered that the newspaper articles on which he relied in seeking to demonstrate that his position as a financial consultant were public knowledge did not establish that his involvement with the opponent company was sufficiently well-publicized to exempt him from his duty to disclose such involvement to the other party. Consequently,

> on the basis of Article 1382 of the Civil Code, the victim of such fraudulent maneuvers can sue the person who committed them, so as to obtain reparation in respect of the loss it has suffered . . . . [The victim] is entitled to obtain from [the arbitrator], by way of compensation, restitution of the sum of 600,000 French francs, which it paid to him in fees, together with interest at the legal rate calculated from the date of the payment.[176]

1092. — In the *Raoul Duval* case, that company claimed against the arbitrator appointed by the arbitral institution as chairman of the first instance arbitral tribunal on the grounds that he was employed by its opponent on the day after making his award. The Paris Court of Appeals considered that he was not independent and set aside the award on the grounds of the unlawful constitution of the arbitral tribunal.[177] Raoul Duval then sued the arbitrator to obtain compensation for the loss caused by his conduct. Relying on the findings of the Court of Appeals in the action to set aside, the Paris Tribunal of First Instance held that the arbitrator should have informed the parties of his connections with one of them, and that in accordance with Article 1452 of the New Code of Civil Procedure he should only have pursued his functions if the parties had agreed that he should do so. The Tribunal considered that he had "undoubtedly incurred liability by committing the fault of not disclosing the situation to Raoul Duval," and it refused to apply the provisions of Article 505 of the Code of Civil Procedure,[178] on which the arbitrator sought to rely, holding that an arbitrator does not assume a public function and is not assimilated with the non-professional judiciary governed by that provision. The Court concluded that:

---

[174] July 2, 1990, *supra* note 119.

[175] Apr. 9, 1992, *supra* note 32.

[176] TGI Paris, Dec. 9, 1992, Annahold BV v. L'Oréal, 1996 REV. ARB. 438, 3d decision.

[177] CA Paris, July 2, 1992, *supra* note 35.

[178] On the liability of non-professional judges, see *supra* para. 1079.

The relationship between the arbitrator and the parties, which is contractual in nature, justifies his liability being assessed in the light of the ordinary legal conditions set out in Article 1142 of the Civil Code . . . . [The arbitrator] is therefore ordered to pay Raoul Duval the sum of 22,500 French francs by way of damages in respect of the arbitration fees paid to the AFCC by the plaintiff. With regard to the remaining claims, while [the plaintiff company] has failed to establish that it genuinely lost its chances of success in the proceedings, or indeed the result of those proceedings, the Court nevertheless considers that it has sufficient grounds to award 25,000 French francs in damages in respect of the additional loss caused by [the arbitrator's] misconduct.[179]

1093. — A comparison of those two decisions raises certain questions regarding arbitrators' personal liability.

1094. — First, although the French courts will hold arbitrators liable where they fail to meet their disclosure obligations, the basis of their liability varies. In the first decision considered above, the arbitrator was held liable in tort whereas, in the second, the arbitrator was found liable in contract. That situation is not necessarily contradictory because, in the first case, the submission agreement (which included the contract between the arbitrator and the parties) had been avoided for misrepresentation, and contractual liability was therefore excluded. In the second case, the award had been set aside because the arbitral tribunal was unlawfully constituted. As a result, the contract between the parties and the arbitrator subsisted and the court was able to find the arbitrator liable for a subsequent breach of his contractual duty of disclosure. There is no doubt that a contract exists between the arbitrator and the parties and, although the services provided under it are highly specific, there is no reason why redress for a breach of the arbitrator's obligations should not be founded in contract.[180]

1095. — The second difficulty encountered by a court that finds arbitrators liable concerns the determination of the loss resulting from their misconduct.

There is no doubt that where an award is set aside because of the arbitrators' fault, the parties' expenses and costs incurred in the course of the arbitral proceedings are wasted, and that loss is recoverable. The two decisions discussed above allowed compensation for both the administrative costs paid to the arbitral institution and the arbitrators' fees. In addition to an award of costs against the arbitrator in the court proceedings, the courts can also order the arbitrator to indemnify the parties for all or part of the costs incurred in their defense in

---

[179] TGI Paris, May 12, 1993, Raoul Duval v. V., 1996 REV. ARB. 411, 2d decision. This decision was confirmed in equally severe terms by the Paris Court of Appeals, which held that "the arbitrator had the positive obligation to inform the parties of this situation . . . , violated due process and committed a personal fault triggering his liability." (CA Paris, Oct. 12, 1995, *Van Luijk, supra* note 154). The *Cour de cassation* subsequently held that it was bound by the determination of the lower court and rejected the action brought by the arbitrator (Cass. 1e civ., Dec. 16, 1997, Van Luijk v. Raoul Duval, No. 1988D, unpublished).

[180] On this contract, see *infra* paras. 1103 *et seq.*

the arbitral proceedings (such as lawyers' fees and travel expenses) because, as a result of the arbitrator's conduct, those proceedings were unable to culminate in a valid award. The court can also award damages for the costs of the new arbitral proceedings required after the setting aside of the award as a result of the arbitrator's conduct.[181] Those losses are direct and certain, as is the loss incurred through the delay in obtaining justice, but evaluating them is more delicate. On the other hand, it seems that the plaintiff cannot obtain compensation in respect of the loss of its opportunity to win the arbitral proceedings. Once the award has been set aside, the plaintiff should start a new arbitration on the basis of the arbitration agreement. The risks involved in so doing are, in principle, not increased by the failure of the first proceedings, or by the resulting delays and changes in the "arbitral personnel."

2° Liability of Arbitrators for the Wilful Violation of Their Obligations

1096. — Leaving aside any liability which arbitrators may incur for having failed to disclose circumstances calling into question their independence and impartiality, they still cannot enjoy absolute immunity. As suggested earlier,[182] comparative law in this area reveals certain similarities between different legal systems.

1097. — Even the United States courts, often portrayed as favoring absolute immunity for arbitrators, make exceptions for wilful misconduct.[183] That is also the statutory position adopted in the state of Maryland, for example.[184]

Similarly, in England, because of doubts expressed in the legal community regarding absolute immunity,[185] the 1996 Arbitration Act removes arbitrators' immunity when it is established that they acted in bad faith,[186] and allows them to be held liable for losses resulting from their resignation.

The Australian international arbitration statute is comparable, but more specific. It sets forth the principle that arbitrators are not liable for their own negligence, but adds that they can be liable for fraud in acts and omissions committed in their capacity as arbitrators.[187] The same terms were adopted in the laws of several Australian states, while in Bermuda, the

---

[181] *See* CA Paris, Oct. 12, 1995, *Van Luijk, supra* note 154.

[182] *See supra* para. 1085.

[183] Lundgren v. Freeman, 307 F.2d 104 (9th Cir. 1962).

[184] Health Care Malpractice Claims, MD. CODE ANN., CTS. & JUD. PROC. § 3-2A-04 (g) (1998), cited by Hausmaninger, *supra* note 165, at 33.

[185] *See* Julian D. M. Lew, *Immunity of arbitrators under English law, in* THE IMMUNITY OF ARBITRATORS 21 (1990).

[186] Secs. 29(1) and (3) and 25.

[187] Sec. 28 of the International Arbitration Act 1974, Part III of which ("International Commercial Arbitration") is based on the UNCITRAL Model Law; *see* Clyde Croft, *Australia Adopts the UNCITRAL Model Law*, 5 ARB. INT'L 189, 198 (1989); Michael C. Pryles, *Australia, in* ICCA INTERNATIONAL HANDBOOK ON COMMERCIAL ARBITRATION (1992).

1993 International Conciliation and Arbitration Act likewise grants arbitrators immunity, except in respect of the "consequences of conscious and deliberate wrongdoings" (Art. 34).

Greek legislation is ambiguous: under Article 881 (formerly Art. 942) of the 1968 Code of Civil Procedure, which is still in force, "the arbitrators . . . shall be liable solely for fraud or gross negligence." However, under the law introducing the Code (in 1971), proceedings against arbitrators (who in this case are treated as non-judicial legal auxiliaries) will only be admissible if based on misrepresentation, gross negligence, or a denial of justice (Art. 73, para. 4).[188] Although misrepresentation is an exception found in the examples described earlier, the grounds of denial of justice and especially gross negligence give the courts wider discretion to assess the arbitrators' conduct.

1098. — The French courts have been more restrictive. In the *Bompard* case, the Paris Tribunal of First Instance held that "civil liability can only be incurred [by the arbitrators] . . . where it is established that they have committed fraud, misrepresentation, or gross fault."[189]

The Court of Appeals was less specific, only requiring there to be a "personal fault" on the part of the arbitrator. The words "personal fault" should be strictly construed, consistent with the definition given by the Court:

> the duties of a judge . . . can give rise to civil liability in the event of a personal fault, that is to say, a fault which is incompatible with his judicial functions.[190]

1099. — Authors and practitioners seeking to determine when arbitrators will not enjoy immunity are broadly in agreement: any intentional fault, and any misrepresentative or fraudulent conduct will render them liable.[191] In such cases, the arbitrators violate their judicial obligations to act fairly and treat the parties equally, and they therefore no longer deserve to be protected in the same way as a judge. Personal faults of that kind are "separable" from the arbitrators' professional role, and do not even require proof of a contractual basis in order for the arbitrators to be liable.

A more delicate question arises as to whether gross fault or gross negligence will also cause the arbitrators' immunity to be lifted. That proposition finds support in some jurisdictions because of their traditional assimilation of gross fault and wilful misconduct.[192]

---

[188] *See* ANGHELOS C. FOUSTOUCOS, L'ARBITRAGE INTERNE ET INTERNATIONAL EN DROIT PRIVÉ HELLÉNIQUE 114 (1976).

[189] TGI Paris, June 13, 1990, *supra* note 158.

[190] CA Paris, May 22, 1991, *supra* note 160.

[191] *See* Hausmaninger, *supra* note 165, at 33; *see also* Philippe Fouchard, *Final report on the Status of the Arbitrator – A Report of the ICC's Commission on International Arbitration*, ICC BULLETIN, Vol. 7, No. 1, at 27 (1996).

[192] In French law, see the cases cited by GENEVIÈVE VINEY, LES OBLIGATIONS: LA RESPONSABILITÉ: EFFETS ¶ 226 at 311 (1988).

However, although the assimilation of the two is legitimate for the purposes of defeating clauses excluding or limiting contractual liability,[193] the same is not necessarily true where the goal is to restrict the arbitrators' immunity in their capacity as judges. In that context, the normal remedy for default by arbitrators is, in principle, the setting aside of, or refusal to enforce, the award. A serious error of fact or law committed by arbitrators in deciding the dispute, or even a serious error in conducting the proceedings, will not lead them to incur personal liability.[194] Given that they act as judges, the arbitrators should be protected by their immunity to ensure that they do not become the target of actions based on allegations of serious errors of judgment. In France, that was the view taken in the *Bompard* case, while in the English case of *Sutcliffe v. Thackrah*, Lord Reid strongly suggested this to be the proper approach on public policy grounds.[195]

1100. — However, the arbitrators are not just judges. Their functions were conferred on them by the parties, and they have contractually undertaken to perform them. We must therefore consider whether, in their capacity as service providers, their liability can be incurred, excluded or limited—in contract alone.

SECTION II
ARBITRATORS AS SERVICE PROVIDERS

1101. — Although they are judges, arbitrators assume that role as a result of a contract under which they have agreed with the parties (and the arbitral institution, if one is involved) to perform a brief which is well-defined and usually remunerated. Their status is therefore contractual (§ 1), as a result of which it carries with it a number of rights and obligations (§ 2).

§ 1. – The Contractual Nature of the Arbitrators' Status

1102. — Despite the judicial role of the arbitrators and their resulting assimilation with judges, the source of their status remains contractual. There is no longer any serious dispute as to the existence of a contract between the arbitrators and the parties (A), but there remains some disagreement as to its exact nature (B).

---

[193] *See infra* paras. 1151 *et seq.*

[194] *See supra* paras. 1077 *et seq.*

[195] *See supra* note 167.

A. – THE EXISTENCE OF A CONTRACT BETWEEN THE ARBITRATORS AND THE PARTIES

1103. — Certain authors consider that the rights and obligations of arbitrators should be treated, if not as a quasi-contract, then at least as a "status" resulting directly from law and comprising rights and obligations assumed by the arbitrators in the public interest.[196] However, the reluctance of those authors to recognize the existence of a contract stems primarily from the "ingenuity" required to identify it and the unusual nature of the relationship between the parties and the arbitrators.[197]

Most authors in fact support the contractual approach.[198] However, the contract in question has rarely been the subject of a detailed examination,[199] and is therefore worth considering more thoroughly.

1104. — The idea that arbitrators have a "status" is obviously not incorrect. Their role as private judges is too particular to result solely from the intentions of private parties. In order for them to assume the judicial power which national laws and the courts recognize them as possessing, the arbitrators (and with them the entire arbitration) move within a legal and procedural framework which goes beyond the parties and their judges chosen on a case-by-case basis. That is not to say that their judicial role is necessarily governed by a particular national law, as the development of international arbitration is marked by the decline of the choice of law method in favor of substantive transnational rules which are sufficiently robust and cohesive to constitute a self-standing legal framework well adapted to this private form of justice.[200] In other words, the fact that international arbitrators have a "status" simply

---

[196] MICHAEL J. MUSTILL, STEWART C. BOYD, COMMERCIAL ARBITRATION 220 *et seq.* (2d ed. 1989).

[197] *Id.* at 222 *et seq.*

[198] See, in England, ALAN REDFERN AND MARTIN HUNTER, LAW AND PRACTICE OF INTERNATIONAL COMMERCIAL ARBITRATION (2d ed. 1991); Murray L. Smith, *Contractual Obligations Owed by and to Arbitrators: Model Terms of Appointment*, 8 ARB. INT'L 17 (1992); in Germany, Bernd von Hoffmann, *Die internationale Schiedsrichtervertrag – eine kollisionsrechtliche Skizze*, in FESTSCHRIFT FÜR OTTOARNDT GLOSSNER ZUM 70 GEBURTSTAG 143 (1993); in Italy, Giuseppe Mirabelli, *Contratti nell'arbitrato (con l'arbitrato; con l'istituzione arbitrale)*, 30 RASS. DELL'ARB. 3 (1990), and the references cited therein; in Belgium: MARCEL HUYS, GUY KEUTGEN, L'ARBITRAGE EN DROIT BELGE ET INTERNATIONAL ¶ 174 (1981); in France, DE BOISSÉSON, *supra* note 54, at 174 *et seq.* and 575 *et seq.*; in comparative law, RENÉ DAVID, ARBITRATION IN INTERNATIONAL TRADE ¶¶ 292 *et seq.* (1985); Gaillard, *supra* note 29, at 792.

[199] *See* FRANZ HOFFET, RECHTLICHE BEZIEHUNGEN ZWISCHEN SCHIEDSRICHTER UND PARTEIEN (1991); Alexandre Ditchev, *Le "contrat d'arbitrage" – Essai sur le contrat ayant pour objet la mission d'arbitrer*, 1981 REV. ARB. 395; Mirabelli, *supra* note 198.

[200] See, for the French concept that international arbitration is not necessarily governed by national law, *supra* paras. 139 *et seq.* and, on the idea that an international arbitral award does not form part of the legal order of the jurisdiction where it was made, Cass. 1e civ., Mar. 23, 1994, Hilmarton v. OTV, 1994 Bull. Civ. I, No. 104; 1994 REV. ARB. 327, and C. Jarrosson's note; 121 J.D.I. 701 (1994), and E. Gaillard's note; 1994 RTD COM. 702, and observations by J.-C. Dubarry and E. Loquin; 1995 REV. CRIT. DIP 356, and B. Oppetit's note; for an English translation, see 9 INT'L ARB. REP. 6 (May 1994); XX Y.B. COM. ARB. 663 (1995).

means that the contract from which their powers are derived cannot exclude the application of the fundamental principles which govern the resolution of disputes before any forum.

1105. — Nevertheless, in recent years, the courts of various jurisdictions have expressly recognized the existence of a contract between the arbitrators and the parties to the arbitration, and the consequences that result from that relationship. In England, for example, the courts have confirmed that by accepting their appointment, arbitrators contractually undertake to fulfil their brief diligently, in return for remuneration,[201] and that by accepting their functions, they become a party to an arbitration contract.[202] The French courts have developed similar jurisprudence.[203]

National arbitration statutes, on the other hand, are more circumspect. They do not formally recognize that alongside the arbitration agreement (which is concluded solely between the parties to the arbitration), there is another contract between the parties and the arbitrators. This is probably because the legislators would have to put the contract into a particular legal category, and define its exact conditions and effects, thus adding another stage and further complications to the implementation of any arbitration. In both law and practice, in all legal systems and under all arbitration rules, the formation, performance and expiration of the contract between the parties and the arbitrators occur gradually and informally.

1106. — Nonetheless, a contract does necessarily exist between the parties and the arbitrators. The contractual relationship is straightforward. First, the parties appoint the arbitrators: whatever method is used to appoint them, there is no doubt as to the parties' intention to empower particular individuals to resolve their dispute. It is irrelevant that in some cases a predetermined third party or institution may ultimately be responsible for appointing the arbitrators or confirming that appointment. They do so on behalf of the parties, who will have agreed beforehand that the arbitrators may be chosen indirectly. Second, as nobody is ever under an obligation to assume the role of arbitrator in a given dispute, the arbitrators' consent to act in that capacity is a prerequisite. They give that consent by accepting their functions, thereby completing the constitution of the arbitral tribunal.[204] The arbitrators' consent may be given by signing the submission agreement, by

---

[201] K/S Norjarl A/S v. Hyundai Heavy Industries Co. Ltd, [1992] 1 Q.B. 863; [1991] 3 All E.R. 211; [1991] 3 W.L.R. 1025; [1991] 1 Lloyd's Rep. 524 (C.A. 1990).

[202] Compagnie Europeene de Cereals SA v. Tradax Export S.A., [1986] 2 Lloyd's Rep. 301 (High Ct., Q.B. (Com. Ct.) 1986).

[203] TGI Paris, June 13, 1990 and CA Paris, May 22, 1991, *Bompard*, *supra* notes 158 and 160, which holds that arbitrators can be contractually liable; CA Paris, May 4, 1988, *Chambre arbitrale de Paris*, *supra* note 23, which prevents the courts from breaking the "contractual links" between validly appointed arbitrators and the parties to the dispute. *See also* CA Paris, Dec. 19, 1996, Qualiconsult v. Groupe Lincoln, 1988 REV. ARB. 121, and C. Jarrosson's note: this decision refers specifically to the "arbitration contract" between the parties and the arbitrators, and defines their reciprocal obligations.

[204] *See*, *e.g.*, Art. 1452 of the French New Code of Civil Procedure.

drawing up terms of reference, or by any manifestation of an intention to perform the functions conferred on them by the parties.[205]

1107. — The contract between the arbitrators and the parties is bilateral: as we shall see, it creates rights and obligations for both the arbitrators and the parties.[206] Its performance takes place throughout the arbitral proceedings. It normally comes to an end when an arbitral award has been made, which releases the arbitrators from their functions.[207] In exceptional cases, the duration of the contract may be extended where the arbitrators are empowered to interpret or correct clerical errors in their award.[208] It may also be curtailed, either because the parties decide not to pursue the arbitral proceedings (by reaching a settlement, for example), or for a reason pertaining to the arbitrators themselves (such as death, incapacity, resignation, challenge or removal).

1108. — With a few minor variations arising from procedural peculiarities imposed by law or stipulated by the parties, the existence of such a contract is universally recognized, in both *ad hoc* and institutional arbitration.

1109. — However, where an arbitral institution is chosen to organize the proceedings, the contractual relationship becomes triangular.[209]

1110. — An initial contract is concluded between the parties and the arbitral institution.[210] By drafting and publishing its arbitration rules, the arbitral institution effectively puts out a permanent offer to contract, aimed at an indeterminate group of persons (those potential litigants operating in the field or fields covered by the institution), but made under fixed conditions. By concluding their arbitration agreement, the parties accept that offer and agree to empower their chosen institution to organize and oversee the arbitration in the event that a dispute arises between them.[211] This is a contract of adhesion, even though the parties have some scope to add to or depart from the rules laid down by the institution. When the request for arbitration is submitted to the institution and it begins to organize the proceedings, the contract is perfected. Generally it will not be perfected before that point, because the institution will not know whether its offer has been accepted.

---

[205] *See supra* paras. 942 *et seq.*

[206] *See infra* paras. 1126 *et seq.*

[207] Art. 1475 of the French New Code of Civil Procedure.

[208] *See infra* paras. 1414 *et seq.* and 1628.

[209] On the exact content of these three contracts, see Mirabelli, *supra* note 198; *see also* Ditchev, *supra* note 199.

[210] On this contract, see Philippe Fouchard, *Les institutions permanentes d'arbitrage devant le juge étatique (A propos d'une jurisprudence récente)*, 1987 REV. ARB. 225, 248 *et seq.*, and note following CA Paris, May 4, 1988, *Chambre arbitrale de Paris*, 1988 REV. ARB. 674; Charles Jarrosson, *Le rôle respectif de l'institution, de l'arbitre et des parties dans l'instance arbitrale*, 1990 REV. ARB. 381.

[211] On the formation and content of this contract, see TGI Paris, May 21, 1997, *Cubic Defense Systems*, and particularly the confirmation on appeal by the Paris Court of Appeals on September 15, 1998, *supra* note 172.

With a few exceptions, arbitral institutions do not act as arbitrators. The French courts consider that they simply "police the arbitral proceedings," and the Swiss courts have held that "they administer the proceedings."[212] Under French law, the relationship between the parties and the institution is similar to a contract of agency, in so far as the institution is responsible for performing various acts on behalf of the parties. However, it is also comparable to a contract for the provision of services, in that the institution also undertakes to perform various tasks listed in its rules and accepted by the parties, implicitly at least, when they choose that institution in their arbitration agreement. This can be seen very clearly in the *République de Guinée* case, where the Paris Tribunal of First Instance held that:

> by choosing the Paris Arbitral Chamber as the institution responsible for organizing their arbitration, [the parties] agreed to adhere to its procedural rules and thereby empowered that institution to organize the arbitral proceedings in accordance with those rules, and to resolve any difficulties which might arise, without entitling it to interfere in the judicial function conferred solely on the arbitrators.[213]

In an action against that decision, the Paris Court of Appeals declined to interfere and refused to terminate this contract, which it characterized as a contract of agency in the parties' mutual interest (*mandat d'intérêt commun*).[214]

Arbitral institutions may be liable for their failure to perform their contractual obligations. Certain legal systems grant them quasi-judicial immunity, while others recognize their broad discretion in the administration of arbitration proceedings and are therefore reluctant to allow claims brought by dissatisfied parties.[215]

Some institutions protect themselves further by including in their rules a clause excluding their liability. This is the case of the ICC, which introduced the following provision at Article 34 of its 1998 Rules:

> Neither the arbitrators, nor the Court and its members, nor the ICC and its employees, nor the ICC National Committees shall be liable to any person for any act or omission in connection with the arbitration.[216]

It is not certain that these provisions enhance the institution's appeal to its users. Further, it may well be that the courts hold such clauses to be ineffective in the case of gross fault by the institution or, in certain cases, abusive or unconscionable conduct, given, in particular,

---

[212] Regarding France, see *supra* para. 824. On Switzerland, see Fouchard, *supra* note 210, ¶ 46 at 262.

[213] Réf., June 23, 1988, *République de Guinée*, *supra* note 41.

[214] May 4, 1988, *Chambre arbitrale de Paris*, *supra* note 23.

[215] *See supra* para. 1088-1.

[216] *See also* Art. 35 of the 1997 AAA International Arbitration Rules; Art. 31 of the 1998 LCIA Arbitration Rules.

that such clauses are contained in a contract of adhesion.[217] The real question is whether the institution, which is a service provider and not a judicial body, can benefit from the same regime as arbitrators in this respect.[218]

1111. — There is also a contract between the arbitral institution and each of the arbitrators. The institution appoints or confirms the appointment of the arbitrators after verifying their suitability; it agrees to treat them as arbitrators in the exercise of its own organizational, administrative and supervisory role; it undertakes to reimburse their expenses and to pay their fees (which it receives from the parties). As for the arbitrators, by accepting their brief they agree to perform it under the auspices and in accordance with the rules of the institution. They agree that the institution shall exercise its functions under those rules, such as its powers to challenge or remove an arbitrator, to grant extensions of time, to monitor the proceedings, to examine a draft version of the award before it is rendered, and to determine the arbitrators' fees. This is a contract where each party independently promises and performs services for the benefit of the other, and particularly for the benefit of third parties (the parties to the arbitration).

1112. — Finally, the involvement of an arbitral institution does not cause the contractual relationship between the parties and the arbitrators to disappear. The parties may sometimes have less freedom in their choice of arbitrator, and the institution may intervene or interfere in the relations between them, but on the whole the contractual relationship between the arbitrator and the parties remains the same. They agree that the arbitrators should carry out a judicial role, and their rights and obligations[219] are not fundamentally different, although the way in which those rights and obligations are exercised is affected by the presence and the rules of the institution.

B. – THE CHARACTERIZATION OF THE CONTRACT BETWEEN THE ARBITRATORS AND THE PARTIES

1113. — There are two reasons why it is helpful to characterize the contract between the arbitrators and the parties. First, from a theoretical point of view, it clarifies the arbitrators' status. But there is a second, more practical reason: as the contract is concluded progressively,[220] with no single legal document setting forth the rights and obligations of the

---

[217] Thus the Paris Court of Appeals, in its *Cubic* decision (*supra* note 172) cast doubt, in an *obiter dictum*, on the validity of the ICC exemption clause. It stated that "as [the exemption clause] appears in the new Rules, which were adopted after the date of the contract in dispute, and even supposing that it is effective, it has no application in the present case."

[218] On the question of the validity of clauses excluding arbitrators' liability, see *infra* paras. 1151 *et seq.*

[219] *See infra* paras. 1126 *et seq.*

[220] *See supra* paras. 1105 *et seq.*

parties, it is helpful to liken it to an existing category of contracts, so that if need be it can be subjected to the legal regime governing such contracts.

1114. — The contract between the arbitrators and the parties is similar in some respects to an agency agreement (1°) and in others to an agreement for the provision of services (2°). Nevertheless, it must ultimately be recognized as being a *sui generis* contract on which is difficult to pin a name, despite the fact that its content is quite clear (3°).

1° Agency

1115. — According to Swiss authors, the contract between the arbitrators and the parties is one of agency, or a form of agency, jointly conferred on the arbitrator by both parties.[221] Article 14 of the Swiss *Concordat* refers to the arbitrators' acceptance of their "mandate" (although the German version of the same text uses the word "*Amt*," which is closer to the idea of an office or function). Admittedly, Article 394 of the Swiss Code of Obligations takes a broad view of the relationship of agency, in that the agent undertakes "to carry out the tasks entrusted to him or render the services which he has promised to provide." More generally, some of the rules governing the creation and expiration of a relationship of agency are broadly compatible with those governing the arbitrator's functions. Agency is granted *intuitu personae*; it can only be revoked by both parties acting jointly and, under the French case law on agency in the mutual interest of the parties, that revocation must be justified by a fault on the part of the agent, failing which the latter is entitled to receive damages. The agent cannot resign from his or her functions without indemnifying the principal in respect of any loss which such resignation might cause.

1116. — However, characterizing the contract between arbitrators and parties as one of agency would be unacceptable in French law, because the specific object of a contract of agency is to confer a power of representation on the agent (Art. 1984 of the Civil Code). The arbitrator does not "represent" the parties, and certainly not the party which appointed him or her.[222] Rather, the arbitrators assume a judicial power of their own. That power should be carefully distinguished from that of the parties to add to or modify the contract, for example, which when conferred on a third party can indeed give rise to a relationship of agency.[223]

1117. — There are other reasons why the contract between the arbitrators and the parties should not be assimilated with an agency agreement. In particular, without being in a

---

[221] PIERRE JOLIDON, COMMENTAIRE DU CONCORDAT SUISSE SUR L'ARBITRAGE 231 (1984); PIERRE LALIVE, JEAN-FRANÇOIS POUDRET, CLAUDE REYMOND, LE DROIT DE L'ARBITRAGE INTERNE ET INTERNATIONAL EN SUISSE 332 (1989).

[222] *See supra* paras. 1041 *et seq.*

[223] On these institutions similar to, but still distinct from, arbitration, see CHARLES JARROSSON, LA NOTION D'ARBITRAGE ¶¶ 209 *et seq.*, 302 *et seq.*, and 685 *et seq.* (1987). *See also supra* paras. 33 *et seq.*

position of subordination, the agent is obliged to follow the principal's instructions[224] and to account to the principal for the performance of its functions.[225]

1118. — As a result, the French courts have consistently refused to treat arbitrators (whether acting in domestic or international cases) as agents of the parties.[226] The grounds given are that the arbitrators' judicial role excludes any form of dependence on or representation of the parties, individually or collectively. In a 1992 decision, the Paris Court of Appeals even set aside an arbitral award made on the basis of a clause whereby any disputes were to be submitted to "representatives," considering the clause to be an invalid arbitration agreement:

> A stipulation of that kind is incompatible with the actual concept of arbitration, since the arbitrators, though appointed by the parties, can under no circumstances become their representatives. That would imply, in particular, that they represent the parties and account for their functions. Such a role, and the obligation it entails, are alien to the functions of an arbitrator, which are judicial in nature.[227]

2° A Contract for the Provision of Services

1119. — The contract between the arbitrators and the parties undoubtedly comes closer to a contract for the provision of services, because its object is wider in scope than that of an agency agreement. The arbitrators' brief can be seen as a set of intellectual services, which the arbitrators provide for the benefit of the parties, in return for remuneration.[228] The arbitrators, in common with other professionals, undertake to give the parties the benefit of their experience and knowledge, and to accomplish tasks such as investigating the case and hearing the parties within a certain period of time. The arbitrators thus agree to provide services which constitute either best efforts undertakings or undertakings to achieve a particular result.[229]

From a macro-economic point of view, the same picture emerges. The international arbitration "market" brings together clients (corporations) and professionals who compete with one another to offer their highly specialized services.

---

[224] Art. 397 of the Swiss Code of Obligations.

[225] Art. 1993 of the French Civil Code; Art. 400 of the Swiss Code of Obligations.

[226] TGI Reims, Sept. 27, 1978, *Florange, supra* note 155; TGI Paris, réf., Mar. 22, 1983, *V. and L., supra* note 19; TGI Paris, Mar. 28, 1984, *Raffineries de pétrole d'Homs et de Banias, supra* note 88; TGI Paris, June 13, 1990 and CA Paris, May 22, 1991, *Bompard, supra* notes 158 and 160; CA Paris, Mar. 24, 1992, Pelfanian v. Nurit, 1993 REV. ARB. 277, 2d decision; Cass. 2e civ., July 3, 1996, SOMES v. de Saint Rapt, 1996 REV. ARB. 405.

[227] CA Paris, Mar. 24, 1992, *Pelfanian, supra* note 226.

[228] *See* PHILIPPE MALAURIE AND LAURENT AYNÈS, LES CONTRATS SPÉCIAUX ¶ 1211 (7th ed. 1993/1994).

[229] *See infra* para. 1149.

1120. — From a legal standpoint, that analysis is insufficient. It does not account for the specific function of the arbitrators, which is judicial. Dispute resolution is not, strictly speaking, a "service." The arbitrators are certainly obliged to comply with the arbitration agreement and arbitration rules adopted by the parties, but the parties cannot go so far as to give "instructions" to the arbitrators as to the way in which the proceedings are to be conducted, let alone the content of their award.

1121. — In fact, although in some respects the arbitrators are clearly in the contractual position of service providers, that characterization is of little assistance in determining their contractual status. A contract for the provision of services is the "jack-of-all-trades" among specific contracts,[230] and is not always governed by a set of modern, precise rules, although some civil law systems, such as those of Germany, Switzerland and Italy, have gradually developed an appropriate regime.[231] However, because of the diversity of the "services" such a contract might encompass, that regime still does not provide the contract between parties and arbitrators with a satisfactory legal framework. A further consequence of such classification is that it would then become useful, if not essential, to connect the contract to a particular national law. That, as we have seen, is another complicating factor,[232] as this is an area where it is infinitely preferable to apply substantive rules of international arbitration. Those rules become easier to determine if we recognize the specific nature of the contract between the arbitrators and the parties.

3° A *Sui Generis* Contract

1122. — The contractual relationship between the arbitrators and the parties cannot be reduced to a familiar category found in civil law systems. It shares the hybrid nature of arbitration itself: its source is contractual, but its object is judicial, and authors worldwide are now virtually unanimous on that point.[233] Its judicial object must not be confused with the purely contractual consequences to which it gives rise.[234]

1123. — To describe this contract as being *sui generis*, as most authors now do, is not to say that its legal regime cannot be determined, or that it varies from one case to the next. The principal features of the contract are nowadays broadly accepted in practice, and the rules applied to it by national legal systems are essentially similar.[235]

---

[230] *See* MALAURIE AND AYNÈS, *supra* note 228, ¶ 700.

[231] For example, the contract for services (*Werkvertrag*) of Article 611 of the German BGB.

[232] *See supra* para. 1011.

[233] *See* Philippe Fouchard, *Arbitrage commercial international – Notion*, J.-CL. DR. INT., Fasc. 585-1 or J.-CL. PROC. CIV., Fasc. 1050 (1989).

[234] *See* HOFFET, *supra* note 199.

[235] *See infra* paras. 1126 *et seq.*

1124. — Authors are almost unanimous in considering that the contract has a specific nature and invariably produces the same effects. They differ only as to the terminology to be used to distinguish the contract from other agreements, particularly the arbitration agreement (which only binds the parties to the dispute) and the agreements between any arbitral institution and the parties or the arbitrators.[236]

To establish those distinctions, and in the absence of more appropriate terminology, some authors refer to the contract between the parties and arbitrators as the "arbitration contract."[237] An alternative is the German expression "*schiedsrichtlicher Vertrag*," meaning "arbitrator's contract" (as distinct from the arbitration agreement, which is referred to as the "*Schiedsvertrag*"). An equivalent expression, "*contratto di arbitrato*," is used in Italy.[238] That terminology has the merit of showing that the arbitrators themselves are at the heart of the contract, but it fails to give a clear indication as to who the parties are. Another suggested name for the contract between the arbitrators and the parties, which is supported by several French court decisions, is the "contract of empowerment"[239] (*contrat d'investiture*). This reveals the precise object of the contract: the parties empower one or more arbitrators to resolve their dispute, and those arbitrators undertake to exercise that power and to perform that task. As the Paris Court of Appeals rightly observed,

> as soon as he accepts his brief, the arbitrator undertakes, by virtue of the contract of empowerment, the source of which lies in the parties' intentions, to accomplish his arbitral functions in full, in his capacity as a Judge . . . . Correlatively, the parties undertake to accept the arbitrators' decision.[240]

Finally, perhaps the majority view is in favor of returning to or maintaining Roman law terminology. In Roman law the contract was referred to as the *receptum arbitrii*,[241] because it was the contract whereby the arbitrators "received" the arbitration or, in other words, accepted their functions.

1125. — Of course, the terminology used is not the most important aspect of the contract between the parties and the arbitrators. The specificity of that contract, and the importance of the contractual element of the arbitrators' status, can only be seen from an analysis of the rights and obligations it contains.

---

[236] *See supra* paras. 1109 *et seq.*

[237] *See* Ditchev, *supra* note 199, at 397.

[238] Mirabelli, *supra* note 198.

[239] DE BOISSÉSON *supra* note 54, at 175 *et seq.* and 575 *et seq.*; *see also* TGI Paris, June 13, 1990 and CA Paris, May 22, 1991, *Bompard, supra* notes 158 and 160.

[240] CA Paris, May 22, 1991, *Bompard, supra* note 160.

[241] DAVID, *supra* note 198, ¶¶ 267 and 292; FOUSTOUCOS, *supra* note 188, ¶ 149; JOLIDON, *supra* note 221, at 232 *et seq.*; LALIVE, POUDRET, REYMOND, *supra* note 221, at 92 *et seq.* and 332 *et seq.*

§ 2. – The Arbitrators' Contractual Rights and Obligations

1126. — Without returning to the requirements imposed on and protection afforded to the arbitrators in their capacity as judges,[242] we shall consider the purely contractual aspects of their status, namely, their obligations (A) and rights (B) as service providers.

This subject has long remained unsettled, although nowadays arbitral practice and recent rules of private origin provide a relatively satisfactory framework for the contractual relationship between the arbitrators and the parties.[243] Sources which contribute to the definition of the rights and obligations of arbitrators include guidelines for arbitrators, the practice of arbitral institutions, certain provisions of institutional rules, as well as the codes of ethics adopted by such institutions[244] and, before them, by Bars and Bar Associations.[245]

A. – THE ARBITRATORS' OBLIGATIONS

1127. — National legislation, arbitration rules and codes of ethics show strong similarities in determining not only the arbitrators' obligations (1°), but also the means used to obtain compliance with them or to remedy their breach (2°).

1° Determining the Arbitrators' Obligations

1128. — Broadly speaking, the obligations of arbitrators fall into four categories.

1129. — Although essential, the first set of obligations requires only a brief mention. All arbitrators are obliged to act equitably and impartially, and to treat the parties equally throughout the proceedings. They must also give the parties a proper opportunity to argue their case. These requirements are already imposed on the arbitrators as a result of their status as private judges,[246] but they also constitute specific contractual obligations as a direct consequence of the arbitrators' acceptance of their appointment.

---

[242] *See supra* paras. 1018 *et seq.*

[243] *See* ICC Commission on International Arbitration, *Defining a Status for International Arbitrators: Elementary Principles*, ICC BULLETIN, Vol. 7, No. 1, at 29 (1996); Philippe Fouchard, *The Status of the Arbitrator as Defined by Codified Practice*, *id.* at 55.

[244] See, for example, the *Norme di comportamento dell'arbitrato* adopted by the Chamber of National and International Arbitration of Milan, 1997 RIV. DELL'ARB. 463; the *Règles de bonne conduite pour les arbitrages CEPANI*, published by the Belgian Centre for Arbitration and Mediation.

[245] For example, the Rules of Ethics for International Arbitrators of the International Bar Association, *supra* note 70; the December 20, 1983 *Délibération* of the Paris Bar and the commentary by Delvolvé, *supra* note 71.

[246] *See supra* paras. 1018 *et seq.*

A sign of the times is that, undoubtedly influenced by the UNCITRAL Rules,[247] arbitration rules increasingly remind arbitrators of these obligations,[248] as do codes of ethics.[249] This is unnecessary in our view, because arbitrators are already bound to comply with those obligations pursuant to international conventions, national laws and court decisions. Such obligations are directly applicable to the arbitral proceedings and should be treated as such, although from the point of view of the arbitrators' status they can also be considered as an integral part of their contractual duties.

1130. — The second set of obligations of the arbitrators also concerns the way in which the proceedings are to be conducted, but is more directly related to the arbitrators' contractual position.

The arbitrators must complete their functions within the legal or contractual deadlines that they have been given. This rule is universally accepted, but is now rarely expressed in the form of an explicit obligation imposed upon the arbitrators. One exception is the Italian Code of Civil Procedure, which provides in its Article 813 that "the arbitrators must make their award within the deadline fixed by the parties or by law."[250]

As a result, where the arbitral tribunal comprises more than one arbitrator, each of them is responsible for applying to the competent court to obtain any extension of the deadline for completion of the proceedings that may be required, especially if none of the parties has done so. If an arbitrator fails to apply to the courts in this way, he or she may be personally liable.[251]

In any case, by accepting their functions the arbitrators also undertake to perform them diligently. Again, this rule is universally recognized, although it is seldom expressed as such. It mirrors the "reasonable time" requirement found in international conventions and declarations concerning the protection of human rights in court proceedings.[252]

Where an arbitral tribunal comprises more than one arbitrator, arbitrators who fail to participate in the hearings or deliberation will likewise breach their duty to act diligently. If by doing so they are attempting to obstruct the proceedings, particularly in the interests of the party that appointed them, they will be liable for wilful misconduct.

---

[247] Art. 15 of the UNCITRAL Rules.

[248] Art. 26 of the Rules of the Italian Arbitration Association; Art. 17 of the 1999 Rules of the Arbitration Institute of the Stockholm Chamber of Commerce; Art. 16 of the 1997 AAA International Arbitration Rules; Art. 15(2) of the 1998 ICC Rules; Art. 14 of the 1998 LCIA Rules.

[249] See Art. 1 of the Rules of Ethics for International Arbitrators of the International Bar Association, *supra* note 70; Art. 3.25.3 of the *Règlement intérieur* of the Paris Bar.

[250] On the consequences of failing to do so, see *infra* para. 1146.

[251] See TGI Paris, réf., Nov. 29, 1989, Omnium de Travaux v. République de Guinée, 1990 REV. ARB. 525.

[252] See the IBA Rules of Ethics for International Arbitrators, *supra* note 70, whose Article 1, entitled "Fundamental Rule," provides that "[a]rbitrators shall proceed diligently and efficiently." *See also* Art. 6-1 of the European Convention for Protection of Human Rights and Fundamental Freedoms.

1131. — The third set of arbitrators' duties ties in with the second set, but is more often covered by statutory provisions or arbitration rules. The arbitrators are required to pursue their functions until their conclusion or, in other words, until the final award is made.[253] Therefore, once they have accepted their functions, in principle they cannot resign without proper grounds.

Although it is rare for arbitration rules to contain an express provision to that effect,[254] such a rule is common to many arbitration statutes, and is found, *inter alia*, in French law (Art. 1462 of the New Code of Civil Procedure), Italian law (Art. 813 of the Code of Civil Procedure), Belgian law (Art. 1689 of the Judicial Code) and Dutch law (Art. 1029(2) of the Code of Civil Procedure). It penalizes irresponsible conduct by arbitrators who may be tiring of their arduous duties. However, its aim is above all to prevent delay: it is not unknown for arbitrators, sensing that they are in the minority within the arbitral tribunal, to resign in an attempt to prevent the tribunal from making an award against the party which appointed them. For that reason, the Netherlands Code of Civil Procedure and the UNCITRAL Model Law (Art. 14) provide that an arbitrator's resignation must be accepted, either by both parties, or by the pre-designated third party, or by the "assisting judge."[255]

In Switzerland, the Private International Law Statute remains silent on this issue, but authors consider that, in accordance with the "ordinary law of arbitration" found in the French and Belgian texts referred to above, "an arbitrator who has accepted his functions must, in principle, pursue them to their conclusion," and that "he may only resign on proper grounds."[256] However, another Swiss author has described that view as wishful thinking.[257] In any event, the Swiss Federal Tribunal considered in one decision that where the ICC had rejected an arbitrator's resignation, an award made by the two remaining arbitrators alone was invalid.[258]

Although there are means of reducing the impact of an arbitrator's dilatory conduct,[259] it is understandable that several institutions' arbitration rules likewise prohibit untimely resignations by the arbitrators.[260] The most severe are undoubtedly those of the Iran-United

---

[253] *See* DE BOISSÉSON, *supra* note 54, ¶ 213.

[254] Article 7(5) of the 1998 ICC Rules provides that "[b]y accepting to serve, every arbitrator undertakes to carry out his responsibilities in accordance with these Rules."

[255] *See* Gaillard, *supra* note 29.

[256] LALIVE, POUDRET, REYMOND, *supra* note 221, at 333.

[257] F. Knoepfler, observations following Swiss Fed. Trib., Apr. 30, 1991, X v. Y A.G., 1993 REV. SUISSE DR. INT. ET DR. EUR. 187, 192.

[258] Apr. 30, 1991, *supra* note 257. The case was also published in ATF 117 Ia 166; JT 1992 I 313; 1992 BULL. ASA 259; 1993 REV. SUISSE DR. INT. ET DR. EUR. 187, with observations by F. Knoepfler; *see also* Stephen M. Schwebel, *The Validity of an Arbitral Award Rendered by a Truncated Tribunal*, ICC BULLETIN, Vol. 6, No. 2, at 19, especially at 21 *et seq.* (1995).

[259] *See infra* para. 1136.

[260] See Article 8 of the ICSID Rules, which allows the arbitral tribunal to accept or reject the resignation of a party-appointed arbitrator; Article 12(1) of the 1998 ICC Rules, replacing Article 2(10) of the previous Rules, which provides that an arbitrator's resignation must be accepted by the International Court of Arbitration; Article

(continued...)

States Claims Tribunal which, at Article 13, paragraph 5, provide that arbitrators must continue to serve in all cases where they have already participated in a hearing on the substance of the dispute.

Arbitrators can of course resign, with or without the approval of the arbitral institution or their colleagues, if there are proper grounds to justify their resignation. For example, it may become impossible for them to pursue their functions, or a circumstance may arise, through no fault of their own, which affects their independence vis-à-vis the parties.

1132. — The fourth contractual obligation assumed by the arbitrators is a duty of confidentiality. It is increasingly common for this obligation to be specifically set forth in arbitration rules and codes of ethics.[261] Thus, Article 34 of the AAA International Arbitration Rules provides that:

> Confidential information disclosed during the proceedings by the parties or by witnesses shall not be divulged by an arbitrator or by the administrator. Unless otherwise agreed by the parties, or required by applicable law, the members of the tribunal and the administrator shall keep confidential all matters relating to the arbitration or the award.

The ICC also refers to the confidential nature of arbitration, although this only concerns the work of the International Court of Arbitration, the ICC's permanent administrative body.[262]

It matters little that these provisions are phrased in relatively cautious terms. One of the fundamental principles—and one of the major advantages—of international arbitration is that it is confidential. The Paris Court of Appeals even went so far as to criticize a party for having brought an action to set aside an award before a court which clearly lacked jurisdiction and which had led to the public examination of facts which ought to have remained confidential.[263] Uncertainties remain regarding the extent and the justification of the confidentiality of arbitration, as well as the determination of who is bound by it.[264]

---

[260](...continued)
18(4) of the 1997 Belgian CEPANI Rules.

[261] Art. 5.5 of the Rules of Arbitration and Conciliation of the Austrian Federal Economic Chamber; Art. 51 of the Rule of the Zurich Chamber of Commerce; Art. 27 of the International Arbitration Rules of the Chamber of National and International Arbitration of Milan; Art. 30.2 of the 1998 LCIA Rules.

[262] Art. 6 of the Statutes of the International Court of Arbitration of the ICC and Art. 1 of its Internal Rules (Appendices I and II to the 1998 Rules); Art. 2 of the previous Internal Rules of the Court.

[263] CA Paris, Feb. 18, 1986, Aïta v. Ojjeh, 1986 REV. ARB. 583, and G. Flécheux's note; Dalloz, Jur. 339 (1987); *see* Emmanuel Gaillard, *Le principe de confidentialité de l'arbitrage commercial international*, Dalloz, Chron. 153 (1987).

[264] *See, e.g.*, High Court of Australia, Apr. 7, 1995, Esso Australia Resources Ltd. v. Plowman, 10 INT'L ARB. REP. A1 (May 1995); 11 ARB. INT'L 235 (1995), and the Expert Reports filed in that case, *id.* at 265; 6 WORLD ARB. & MED. REP. 133 (1995); XXI Y.B. COM. ARB. 137 (1996); for a French translation, see 1996 REV. ARB. 539, and D. Kapelink-Klinger's note; *see also* Jan Paulsson and Nigel Rawding, *The Trouble with Confidentiality*,
(continued...)

Nevertheless, it is clear that the rule applies to arbitrators, who are service providers with no personal interest in the case, and who must ensure that the dispute remains confidential, as the parties clearly intended.

However, ensuring compliance with this obligation is an altogether more difficult matter.

2° Remedies for Non-Compliance with the Arbitrators' Obligations

1133. — The means of ensuring that arbitrators comply with their duties are themselves fairly diverse.[265]

1134. — Strictly speaking, certain of these measures are not taken against the defaulting arbitrators personally. They concern arbitration law in general, rather than the status of the arbitrator, and we shall therefore consider them only briefly.

1135. — First, the normal consequence of default by an arbitrator will generally arise after the award is made, when a party relies on that default to contest the validity or enforceability of the award. One of the guarantees enjoyed by arbitrators as private judges lies in the fact that they are protected from the possibility of actions against them personally based on alleged errors of judgment.[266] In principle, it is the award, and not the arbitrator, that will be under attack.[267] This will be the case where the arbitrators have failed to observe the principles of equality or due process, or if they have made their award after the applicable deadline has expired.

That is not to say that in such cases the arbitrators cannot be personally liable.[268] However, as the French *Cour de cassation* has held: "one cannot be both judge and party."[269]

---

[264] (...continued)
ICC BULLETIN, Vol. 5, No. 1, at 48 (1994); Edouard Bertrand, *Confidentialité de l'arbitrage: évolution ou mutation après l'affaire Esso/BHP v Plowman/The Confidentiality of Arbitration: Evolution or Mutation Following Esso/BHP vs. Plowman*, 1996 INT'L BUS. L.J. 169; Patrick Neill, *Confidentiality in Arbitration*, 12 ARB. INT'L 287 (1996); Jean-Louis Delvolvé, *Vraies et fausses confidences, ou les petits et grands secrets de l'arbitrage*, 1996 REV. ARB. 373; François Dessemontet, *Arbitration and Confidentiality*, 7 AM. REV. INT'L ARB. 229 (1996), and, for a French version, *in* LE DROIT EN ACTION 61 (papers published by the Law Faculty of the Lausanne University, J.-M. Rapp and M. Jaccard eds., 1996). *See also infra* para. 1412.

[265] *See* Andrew I. Okekeifere, *The Parties' Rights Against a Dilatory or Unskilled Arbitrator – Possible New Approaches*, 15 J. INT'L ARB. 129 (June 1998).

[266] *See supra* paras. 1074 *et seq.*

[267] This principle was confirmed by the Paris Court of Appeals in the *L'Oréal* case, which held that "according to the rules of public policy to which an action to set aside an arbitral award is subject, the proceedings can only deal with the award, and not the arbitrator, who is not a party to this controversy . . ." (CA Paris, Apr. 9, 1992, *supra* note 32).

[268] *See infra* paras. 1142 *et seq.*

[269] Cass. 1e civ., Dec. 16, 1997, *Van Luijk, supra* note 179, rejecting an arbitrator's action against the decision of the Paris Court of Appeals dated December 6, 1994, V. v. Raoul Duval, 1996 REV. ARB. 411, 3d decision, and
(continued...)

The Swiss Federal Tribunal has held that arbitrators are not entitled to recover expenses incurred when invited by a court to make observations during an action to set aside their award.[270] Also, arbitrators are not entitled to appeal against a decision setting aside their award on the grounds that they are the authors of that judicial act.[271]

1136. — A number of mechanisms have been set up, in both national arbitration statutes and arbitration rules, to defeat disruptive steps sometimes taken by arbitrators for the benefit of the party which appointed them. These measures do not, however, involve actually penalizing the arbitrators themselves.

This is the case of untimely resignations, for example. Where such resignations are not directly or indirectly prohibited,[272] the replacement of the resigning arbitrator is essentially a stopgap measure, entailing additional delay and expenditure. In order to limit such delay and expenditure, it is increasingly frequent for the applicable law or arbitration rules to allow the arbitral tribunal not to repeat earlier procedural steps.[273] A further—and very effective—dissuasive rule is for the replacement arbitrator to be appointed directly by the appointing authority or the competent court.[274] This solution has now been adopted in the arbitration rules of a number of institutions,[275] and certain arbitration statutes expressly provide for it.[276]

However, the most effective way of dealing with the delaying tactics of arbitrators resigning in the interests of the party that appointed them is to allow the proceedings to continue with a "truncated" tribunal, without replacing the resigning arbitrators. This remedy, which some commentators consider too radical, is gaining considerable support.

---

[269](...continued)
Fouchard, *supra* note 2, ¶ 19, which prohibited the arbitrator from seeking a declaration that he was not bound by a decision setting aside his award.

[270] Fed. Trib., Dec. 7, 1994, X v. Y, 1995 BULL. ASA 233; 1996 REV. SUISSE DR. INT. ET DR. EUR. 542, and observations by P. Schweizer.

[271] Cass. 1e civ., Dec. 16, 1997, *Van Luijk*, *supra* note 179, *affirming* CA Paris, Dec. 6, 1994, *V.*, *supra* note 269.

[272] *See supra* para. 1131.

[273] *See*, *e.g.*, the Netherlands Code of Civil Procedure (Art. 1030(3)); the 1996 English Arbitration Act (Sec. 27(4)); the UNCITRAL Rules (Art. 14); the ICC Rules (Art. 12(4) of the 1998 Rules, replacing Art. 2(12) of the previous Rules); the 1997 AAA International Arbitration Rules (Art. 11(2)); the International Arbitration Rules of the Chamber of National and International Arbitration of Milan (Art. 7(6)); see ICC Award No. 6476 (1994), ICC BULLETIN, Vol. 8, No. 1, at 59 (1997), for a careful application of this principle in an extremely conflictual arbitration.

[274] *See* Gaillard, *supra* note 29.

[275] Art. 12.4 of the 1998 ICC Rules provides that "[w]hen an arbitrator is to be replaced, the Court has discretion to decide whether or not to follow the original nominating process." A similar provision can be found at Article 11 of the 1998 LCIA Rules. *See also* Art. 7(5) of the International Arbitration Rules of the Chamber of National and International Arbitration of Milan.

[276] *See* Sec. 16 of the 1999 Swedish Arbitration Act (replacing Sec. 10, para. 3 of the 1929 Act); see also Section 17 of the 1999 Act, according to which "[w]here an arbitrator has delayed the proceedings, the District Court shall, upon request by a party, remove the arbitrator from his post and appoint another arbitrator;" Art. 813, para. 3 of the Italian Code of Civil Procedure.

This has emerged primarily from the practice of public international law arbitration,[277] and from arbitrations held before the Iran-United States Claims Tribunal. Several English and American authors are clearly in favor and consider that their respective legal systems allow truncated tribunals.[278] By contrast, it seems that the Swiss Federal Tribunal will not allow proceedings to continue with a truncated arbitral tribunal, unless the parties themselves have expressly provided for such an eventuality.[279]

The French courts have shown similar reluctance. The President of the Paris Tribunal of First Instance has held that "no statutory provision permits the courts to allow the arbitral tribunal to continue with the proceedings once an arbitrator has resigned without replacing him."[280] Likewise, the Paris Court of Appeals held that, despite "the possible dilatory and abusive character" of the resignation of an arbitrator during deliberations, the decision made by the arbitral tribunal deprived of one of its members and thus no longer in compliance with the parties' agreement had to be set aside.[281]

These Swiss and French decisions do not affect agreements and arbitration rules that allow proceedings to continue with a truncated arbitral tribunal. Provisions to that effect have recently been included in a number of arbitration rules.

The AAA was the first to do so in 1991, with the International Arbitration Rules stipulating in their Article 11, paragraph 1 that:

> if an arbitrator on a three-person tribunal fails to participate in the arbitration, the two other arbitrators shall have the power in their sole discretion to continue the arbitration and to make any decision, ruling or award, notwithstanding the failure of the third arbitrator to participate.[282]

The AAA Rules add that in determining whether to continue the arbitration or to make any decision, the two arbitrators shall take into account the stage reached in the arbitration and any reason expressed by the resigning arbitrator for his or her failure to participate. More recently, two other arbitral institutions have adopted exactly the same text as

---

[277] *See* STEPHEN M. SCHWEBEL, INTERNATIONAL ARBITRATION: THREE SALIENT PROBLEMS 144 *et seq.* (1987).

[278] See, prior to the 1996 English Arbitration Act, REDFERN AND HUNTER, *supra* note 198, at 190 *et seq.* and the references cited and, subsequently, Section 27(1)(a) of the 1996 Act which allows the parties to decide "whether . . . the vacancy is to be filled" where an arbitrator ceases to hold office; in the United States, see Schwebel, *supra* note 258.

[279] Swiss Fed. Trib., Apr. 30, 1991, *supra* note 257; see also the commentary by Schwebel, *supra* note 258.

[280] TGI Paris, réf., Feb. 15, 1995, Industrialexport v. K, 1996 REV. ARB. 503, 2d decision, and P. Fouchard's note. *See* Emmanuel Gaillard, *When an Arbitrator Withdraws*, N.Y.L.J., June 4, 1998, at 3.

[281] CA Paris, July 1, 1997, Agence Transcongolaise des Communications-Chemins de fer Congo Océan (ATC–CFCO) v. Compagnie minière de l'Ogooué (Comilog), 1998 REV. ARB. 131, and D. Hascher's note.

[282] This rule has not been affected by the revision of the rules in 1997, which simply reserved the case of withdrawal, challenge or death of the arbitrator pursuant to Article 10.

Article 11, paragraph 1 of the AAA Rules,[283] which also heavily influenced Article 12 of the 1998 LCIA Rules.

The ICC's 1998 Rules, after heated debate at the drafting stage, also introduce the possibility of having an incomplete arbitral tribunal, but only after the proceedings have closed and an arbitrator dies or is removed by the International Court of Arbitration. In such a case, the International Court of Arbitration may decide not to replace the arbitrator and "[i]n making such determination, the Court shall take into account the views of the remaining arbitrators and of the parties and such other matters that it considers appropriate in the circumstances."[284] Is this requirement of any utility in practice? As a tribunal can only be truncated after the closing of the proceedings, would it not be sufficient for the Court to exercise its entitlement[285] to refuse to accept the resignation of arbitrators in bad faith, rather than to remove them? In fact, the two remaining arbitrators can circumvent the passivity or obstruction of the first arbitrator and deliberate validly by putting questions to the first arbitrator in writing and by forwarding him or her a draft of the award.[286] By considering the first arbitrator's silence to constitute a negative response or disagreement, the award can be made by a majority decision of the two remaining arbitrators, without infringing the requirement for collegial deliberation.[287]

There are, as a result, legitimate doubts as to the usefulness of provisions allowing for truncated arbitral tribunals. Nonetheless, such provisions should be considered valid, on the basis of the common intention of the parties in adopting arbitration rules containing them.

One question that does arise is whether such provisions infringe on a party's rights to a fair hearing and to equal treatment and, if that is the case, whether a party is entitled to waive those rights.[288] The response to this concern[289] is that if a party is deprived of the participation in the deliberations of the arbitrator it appointed, that will be exclusively the result of that arbitrator's conduct. To avoid any doubt on this point, the remaining arbitrators or the arbitral institution should not accept a truncated tribunal until they have determined that it is the result of the patently dilatory behavior of the minority arbitrator, which is not unconnected to the position of the party that appointed him or her.

---

[283] Art. 13(3) of the Hague Permanent Court of Arbitration Optional Rules for Arbitration Between International Organizations and Private Parties, effective July 1, 1996, *reprinted in* PERMANENT COURT OF ARBITRATION, BASIC DOCUMENTS – CONVENTIONS, RULES, MODEL CLAUSES AND GUIDELINES 125, 138 (1998); Art. 35 of the 1994 WIPO Arbitration Rules.

[284] *See* Marc Blessing, *Keynotes on Arbitral Decision-Making, in* ICC BULLETIN, SPECIAL SUPPLEMENT, THE NEW 1998 ICC RULES OF ARBITRATION 44 (ICC Publication No. 586, 1997); YVES DERAINS AND ERIC A. SCHWARTZ, A GUIDE TO THE NEW ICC RULES OF ARBITRATION 193 *et seq* (1998).

[285] The Rules provide that the arbitrator shall only be replaced "upon the acceptance by the court of the arbitrator's resignation" (Art. 12(1) of the 1998 Rules, replacing Art. 2(10) of the previous Rules) .

[286] *See* LALIVE, POUDRET, REYMOND, *supra* note 25, at 411 *et seq.*

[287] *See* D. Hascher, note following CA Paris, July 1, 1997, *Agence Transcongolaise*, *supra* note 281, at 137.

[288] In France, the question must be assessed in the light of the *Dutco* decision (Cass. 1e civ., Jan. 7, 1992, *supra* note 144).

[289] As expressed, for instance, by certain ICC National Committees during the drafting of the 1998 Rules; *see* Andreas Reiner, *Le règlement d'arbitrage de la CCI, version 1998*, 1998 REV. ARB. 25, especially at 62 *et seq.*

As emphasized by those promoting this approach, its utility would thus be chiefly as a deterrent.

1137. — However effective these various remedies may be, some of the forms of conduct by arbitrators described above will constitute serious contractual breaches which may result in the termination of the arbitrators' contract (a) or in their personal liability (b) or both.

a) Termination of the Arbitrators' Contract

1138. — In the event of negligence or misconduct on the part of arbitrators, it is universally recognized that the contract between them and the parties, as well as the contract between them and any arbitral institution, can be terminated. It is interesting that the term most commonly found in national laws and arbitration rules is "dismissal" (*révocation*), which discreetly suggests an analogy with agency agreements.[290]

This termination of the arbitrators' functions should of course be distinguished from the dismissal of an arbitrator following a challenge. An arbitrator will be dismissed where he or she does not satisfy the qualities required of persons acting in a judicial capacity. Dismissal is generally sought by one party only and, in the event that the challenge is contested, the matter is decided by the arbitral institution, the appointing authority or the courts.[291] In contrast, the termination of the arbitrators' functions generally results from a joint decision by all parties, failing which the matter will be decided by the arbitral institution or by the competent court.

1139. — The grounds for termination are generally expressed in similar terms in national arbitration statutes[292] and arbitration rules.[293] Arbitrators can be removed if they become unable or refuse to pursue their functions, and especially where it is established that they

---

[290] *See supra* paras. 1115 *et seq.*

[291] *See supra* paras. 1070 *et seq.*

[292] Secs. 23 and 24 of the 1996 English Arbitration Act; Art. 14(1) of the UNCITRAL Model Law; Art. 1687, para. 1 of the Belgian Judicial Code; Art. 1031 of the Netherlands Code of Civil Procedure; CAL. CIV. PROC. CODE § 1297.141; TEX. REV. CIV. STAT. ANN. Arts. 249-14 and 249-15, redesignated as TEX. CIV. PROC. & REM. CODE ANN. §§ 172.101 to 172.106 (West 1999); Art. 813(3) of the Italian Code of Civil Procedure, which was introduced by the January 5, 1994 statute; *see also* the commentary by Piero Bernardini, *L'arbitrage en Italie après la récente réforme*, 1994 REV. ARB. 479; Sec. 17 of the 1999 Swedish Arbitration Act which applies "[w]here an arbitrator has delayed the proceedings."

[293] Art. 13(2) of the UNCITRAL Rules; Art. 12(2) of the ICC Rules (Art. 2(11) of the previous Rules); Art. 8(1) of the ICSID Rules; Art. 10.2 of the 1998 LCIA Rules; Art. 18(4) of the 1997 Belgian CEPANI Rules; Art. 15(2) of the Rules of the Italian Arbitration Association; Art. 31 of the CACNIQ Rules; Art. 19 of the 1999 Rules of the Arbitration Institute of the Stockholm Chamber of Commerce; Art. 17 of the Rules of the Zurich Chamber of Commerce; Art. 12 of the Rules of Arbitration and Conciliation of the Austrian Federal Economic Chamber; Rule 26(a) of the 1998 Arbitration Rules of the Indian Council of Arbitration.

have acted negligently or are guilty of misconduct.[294] No reasons need to be given for arbitrators to be removed in this way. The agreement of the parties suffices.

1140. — In France, the provisions of the New Code of Civil Procedure with regard to the removal of arbitrators are particularly brief. Not only is there no pertinent provision specific to international arbitration, but the only relevant domestic law provision is Article 1462, paragraph 2, which simply states that an arbitrator can only be removed with the unanimous consent of the parties.

However, the President of the Paris Tribunal of First Instance has jurisdiction, under Article 1493, paragraph 2 of the New Code of Civil Procedure, to resolve difficulties concerning the constitution of the arbitral tribunal in international arbitration. We have seen that, on the basis of that provision, the judge can resolve questions concerning challenges of arbitrators,[295] and also seems willing to rely on it to decide an application by one party for the replacement of an arbitrator. In an international arbitration taking place in France, the judge was requested to replace an arbitrator whom one party considered to be in default. Although the arbitration rules governing the proceedings (the UNCITRAL Rules) provided a replacement procedure for such cases, the President of the Tribunal of First Instance nevertheless held that he had jurisdiction, "without interfering in the actual replacement procedure," to "establish that the arbitration had come to a standstill" as a result of the alleged default.[296] The judge could do no more than that, as an appointing authority had been contractually chosen to implement the requested measures. In fact, he did not have the opportunity to take any further action as he concluded in a subsequent decision that since the entire arbitral tribunal had recently convened, the alleged default on the part of one of the arbitrators was not established.[297]

1141. — As we noted in connection with an arbitrator's resignation, the removal of an arbitrator is not always an appropriate remedy. Where the arbitrator's negligence is deliberate, the replacement of that arbitrator by a substitute appointed by the parties will not prevent the replacement from continuing to disrupt proceedings. It is therefore preferable to have the appointing authority or competent court appoint the replacement.[298] Of course, a more radical solution, enabling considerable savings of cost and time, would be not to replace the defaulting arbitrator at all.[299]

---

[294] *See* J. Kodwo Bentil, *Arbitration in Construction or Building Works Disputes and the Removal of an Arbitrator for Misconduct under Anglo-Australian Laws*, 10 INT'L CONSTR. L. REV. 88 (1993).

[295] *See supra* para. 871.

[296] Réf., Feb. 24, 1992, Icori Estero S.p.A. v. Kuwait Foreign Trading Contracting & Investment Co. (KFTCIC), 1994 REV. ARB. 557, 1st decision, and observations by P. Fouchard.

[297] TGI Paris, réf., Apr. 15, 1992, Icori Estero S.p.A. v. Kuwait Foreign Trading Contracting & Investment Co. (KFTCIC), 1994 REV. ARB. 557, 2d decision, and observations by P. Fouchard.

[298] *See supra* para. 1136.

[299] *Id.*

The removal of defaulting arbitrators may also be accompanied by an action against them for damages.

b) Arbitrators' Personal Liability

1142. — We only propose to address hereafter the personal civil liability of arbitrators and to leave aside the question of criminal liability (which might arise, for example, where arbitrators fail to satisfy their duties as independent and impartial judges). Certain legal systems do however impose certain special forms of criminal liability on arbitrators, particularly in the case of "passive" corruption.[300] The only other possible liability to consider is that of any arbitral institution involved. Such liability might be incurred for acts of arbitrators where the institution is itself at fault for choosing them or for negligently exercising its powers to supervise the arbitral proceedings.[301] Institutions are rarely found liable on these grounds,[302] although that has not prevented certain of them from including in their Rules a clause purporting to exclude their liability.[303]

1143. — There is no longer any disagreement among commentators as to the principle that arbitrators can incur civil liability, although the principle is seldom expressed in statute and has rarely been applied in practice.

1144. — Of course, in their judicial capacity arbitrators will enjoy a degree of immunity which, for example, prevents them from being sued in respect of errors—even those of a serious nature—made in reaching their award. However, a fault committed in conducting the arbitral proceedings constitutes a breach of contract, and as remunerated providers of services the arbitrators are accountable for such breaches under the ordinary law of contract.

1145. — Civil law systems have sometimes expressed this principle of liability in very general terms. For instance, the Austrian Code of Civil Procedure provides in its Article 584, paragraph 2 that arbitrators who have failed to perform, or failed to perform in due time, the obligations they assumed on accepting their functions, are liable to the parties for any loss caused by their default or delay, without prejudice to the parties' right to request that the arbitral proceedings be terminated.[304]

---

[300] See Final Report on the Status of the Arbitrator – Appendix II – Comparative Synthesis of Current Substantive Law in Various Countries, ICC BULLETIN, Vol. 7, No. 1, at 37, 39 (1996).

[301] See Philippe Fouchard, La responsabilité des institutions permanentes d'arbitrage (Presentation made at the Journées Jean Robert, at the CACNIQ, Montreal, on October 7, 1988).

[302] See supra para. 1088-1.

[303] See infra para. 1153.

[304] See Hausmaninger, supra note 165.

1146. — Without actually setting forth a general principle as to arbitrators' liability, other more recent statutes emphasize that if a particular failing on the part of the arbitrators is established, they may be liable to repair the damage caused through their fault. This applies to untimely resignations and to deliberate default under the Lebanese New Code of Civil Procedure of 1983,

> Once he has accepted his functions, the arbitrator cannot resign without serious grounds for doing so, in the absence of which he will be liable to pay damages to the party which has suffered a loss.[305]

Similarly, the 1986 Portuguese Law on Voluntary Arbitration provides, in Article 9.3, that:

> An arbitrator who, having accepted his or her functions, refuses, without justification, to exercise them, shall be liable for any damage which he or she may cause.[306]

The Italian Code of Civil Procedure goes further, holding arbitrators liable to pay damages, not only if they resign without justification, but also where the award is set aside on the grounds that it has not been made within the legal or contractual deadline (Art. 813(2)).

1147. — In the absence of statutory provisions, the French courts also hold arbitrators to be liable for their default. However, although the *Cour de cassation* clearly stated in 1960 that this could only be ordinary civil liability,[307] more recent first instance decisions are not always consistent in their determination of what conduct gives rise to liability. These decisions have held such conduct to include "fault in the exercise of [the arbitrator's] judicial role,"[308] "fault in the implementation or conduct of the arbitral proceedings,"[309] "a personal fault,"[310] failure to comply with the applicable deadlines,[311] and unjustified resignation.[312]

---

[305] Art. 769, para. 3; *see* Marie Sfeir-Slim, *Le nouveau droit libanais de l'arbitrage a dix ans*, 1993 REV. ARB. 543, 560; Abdul Hamid El-Ahdab, *The Lebanese Arbitration Act*, 13 J. INT'L ARB. 39, 64 (Sept. 1996).

[306] Law No. 31/86 of August 29, 1986; *see* Dário Moura Vicente, *L'évolution récente du droit de l'arbitrage au Portugal*, 1991 REV. ARB. 419, 425.

[307] Cass. 2e civ., Jan. 29, 1960, *Veuve J. Houdet et Fils*, *supra* note 154.

[308] CA Paris, Mar. 24, 1977, Gouault v. Gouault, 1978 REV. ARB. 31.

[309] TGI Paris, June 13, 1990, *Bompard*, *supra* note 158.

[310] CA Paris, May 22, 1991, *Bompard*, *supra* note 160.

[311] TGI Paris, réf., Nov. 29, 1989, *Omnium de Travaux*, *supra* note 251.

[312] TGI Paris, réf., Feb. 15, 1995, *Industrialexport*, *supra* note 280; CA Paris, July 1, 1997, *Agence Transcongolaise*, *supra* note 281.

1148. — On this issue, the position has changed in common law systems, which were initially in favor of the principle of arbitrator immunity. A number of more recent decisions, notably in England, have held that the situation of the arbitrators is governed by contract, and that by accepting their appointment and remuneration, the arbitrators undertake to perform their obligations diligently.[313] However, the 1996 English Arbitration Act grants arbitrators immunity except where an arbitrator resigns or there is evidence of bad faith: "the parties are free to agree with an arbitrator as to the consequences of his resignation as regards . . . any liability thereby incurred by him."[314] In the absence of such agreement, however, the resigning arbitrator may ask the courts "to grant him relief from any liability thereby incurred by him" (Sec. 25).

1149. — In order to determine more clearly the cases in which arbitrators may incur liability, it is helpful to distinguish between best efforts obligations and obligations to achieve a given result.[315] Arbitrators who resign without good reason, or who fail to comply with the applicable deadlines, or fail to extend those deadlines in due time, breach an obligation to achieve a given result. That breach in itself renders them liable for any resulting loss. As regards their other duties, however, provided that they do not act in a manner which is clearly contrary to the general obligations which they assumed, they are only required to exercise the diligence and care that can be expected of experienced professionals, and do not undertake to achieve a particular result. They cannot do so in any event, as the outcome of the dispute is inherently uncertain.

1150. — In the light of these developments, arbitrators have become increasingly concerned that they might be the targets of legal action by parties dissatisfied with the services they provided. This concern is also prompted by the fact that court actions against the award are subject to increasingly stringent formal and substantive requirements: some arbitrators consider that, with no hope of obtaining satisfactory recourse against the award, or having already failed to obtain it, a party dissatisfied with the award might turn against the arbitrators responsible for making it.

1151. — These concerns have led to provisions being proposed which exclude or restrict the arbitrators' liability. Such provisions are somewhat controversial in practice.

1152. — It is in fact difficult for arbitrators, in their relations with the parties, to require a clause limiting or excluding their liability. As we have seen, the acceptance of their functions is rarely embodied in a formal contract, and it is hard to imagine how prospective arbitrators could make that acceptance conditional on the inclusion of a clause restricting or excluding liability. One author has suggested a rather unusual model of "Terms of Appointment": the first clause stipulates that the arbitrators agree to be free on dates which

---

[313] Sec. 29; *see supra* para. 1097.

[314] See the English cases cited *supra* para. 1105; *see also* REDFERN AND HUNTER, *supra* note 198, at 217.

[315] *See* JACQUELINE LINSMEAU, L'ARBITRAGE VOLONTAIRE EN DROIT PRIVÉ BELGE 118 *et seq.* (1991).

are reasonable having regard to the nature of the dispute and to their own personal and professional availability; the next sixteen clauses simply determine their expenses, fees and methods of payment; the eighteenth clause states that the contract is to be governed by English law and disputes resolved by the English courts, and the final clause provides that:

> (19) The arbitrator is exempt from liability for breach of any legal duty or for any act or omission in connection with or related to the conduct of the arbitration whether or not such act or omission is within jurisdiction.[316]

This clause purports to grant total immunity to the arbitrators by mutual agreement between the arbitrators and the parties. It would be unwise for parties to arbitration to accept this kind of blanket waiver.

1153. — In practice, clauses restricting arbitrators' liability are more frequently found in arbitration clauses prepared in advance for institutional or *ad hoc* arbitrations.

A number of institutions have followed this approach.[317] Their primary and sometimes exclusive[318] concern is to exclude their own liability. Certain arbitration rules do also exclude the liability of arbitrators in principle, but make an exception for serious misconduct. For example, the 1998 LCIA Rules state that arbitrators are not liable for "any act or omission" in connection with any arbitration conducted in accordance with those rules, but that they can be liable for the consequences of "conscious and deliberate wrongdoing" (Art. 31.1). Similarly, the rules of the German Institution of Arbitration exonerate the arbitrators from liability "in connection with arbitral proceedings . . . provided such acts do not constitute an intentional or grossly negligent breach of duty" (Sec. 44.2). The Rules of the CACNIQ simply state that "arbitrators enjoy the same immunity as do judges."[319] The AAA, having changed its rules several times on this point, now stipulates that, by way of an exception, arbitrators "may be liable for the consequences of conscious and deliberate wrongdoing."[320]

The ICC introduced a clause excluding liability in its 1998 Rules, but made no exception for gross or intentional fault. This turnaround is rather surprising as it goes against the recommendation of the internal working group, and was considered by several national committees as being unlikely to enhance the ICC's appeal.[321]

---

[316] Smith, *supra* note 198.

[317] Art. 31.1 of the 1998 LCIA Rules; Art. 35 of the 1997 AAA International Arbitration Rules; Art. 34 of the 1998 ICC Rules; Arts. 9 and 25 of the CACNIQ Rules; Art. 77 of the WIPO Arbitration Rules.

[318] This is the case of the Italian Arbitration Association.

[319] Art. 25; on these Rules, see the commentary by Joëlle Thibault, *Le Centre d'arbitrage commercial national et international du Québec et son règlement général d'arbitrage commercial*, 1994 REV. ARB. 69, 87.

[320] Art. 35 of the 1997 International Arbitration Rules.

[321] *See Final Report on the Status of the Arbitrators – Appendix IV – The Status of the Arbitrator As Defined by Codified Practice*, ICC BULLETIN, Vol. 7, No. 1, at 27, 55 (1996).

1154. — Are these clauses valid? It seems unlikely that private arbitration rules have the power to confer judicial immunity on the arbitrators. A judge's immunity results from a status which is not really contractual. Further, no legal system allows unrestricted exclusion clauses. Civil law countries generally prevent the exclusion of liability for gross or intentional fault. Common law countries limit the effectiveness of exclusion clauses where they are held to be unconscionable (in the United States)[322] or, as in the 1996 English Arbitration Act, where an arbitrator is in bad faith.[323] In most jurisdictions, the courts will be particularly unwilling to enforce an exclusion clause, such as those contained in arbitration rules, that has been imposed upon, rather than negotiated by the parties to the arbitration.[324]

1155. — There is a last form of pecuniary liability which may be incurred by arbitrators, although this is less problematic. This is the reduction, or a claim for restitution, of the arbitrators' fees. This is a matter of ordinary contract law,[325] and it is therefore not surprising that, in France for instance, there is no statutory provision relating specifically to arbitration and referring directly to this form of redress.

If the arbitrators fail to honor their contractual obligations, the bilateral nature of the arbitration contract enables the parties (or any institution, acting in the name of the parties) either to rely on the *exceptio non adimpleti contractus* so as to suspend payment of the arbitrators' fees, or to invoke incomplete performance or claim for the loss suffered, so as to obtain at least a partial restitution of the sums paid as the parties' side of the bargain.

In a number of French cases,[326] arbitrators who failed to reveal links between themselves and one of the parties were ordered to reimburse the fees paid to them. The courts could make a similar order with respect to other breaches of the arbitrators' duties.

Few arbitration rules provide for this form of redress, despite the fact that it would be straightforward for an arbitral institution, which will have collected advance payments from the parties intended to cover the arbitrators' expenses and fees, to refrain from transferring those sums to a defaulting arbitrator. Only two sets of arbitration rules, both Italian, contain such a provision. For example, Article 15, paragraph 3 of the International Arbitration Rules of the Italian Arbitration Association states that "[t]he Court may decide not to pay the fees of an arbitrator who has resigned without good cause or who has not properly performed his functions."[327]

---

[322] *See* § 2–719(3) of the Uniform Commercial Code (1952).

[323] *See* MARGARET RUTHERFORD, JOHN SIMS, ARBITRATION ACT 1996: A PRACTICAL GUIDE 98 *et seq.* (1996). On this provision, see *supra* para. 1097.

[324] *See* EID ABOU RAWACH, RECHERCHES SUR LES CLAUSES EXONÉRATOIRES DE RESPONSABILITÉ DANS LES CONTRATS DU COMMERCE INTERNATIONAL (Thesis, University of Paris I (France), 1998).

[325] *See* Gaillard, *supra* note 29, at 794.

[326] *See supra* paras. 1091 *et seq.*

[327] *See also* Art. 7(5) of the Rules of the Chamber of National and International Arbitration of Milan.

1156. — Of course, the arbitrators' entitlement to be remunerated constitutes one of their most important rights.

B. – RIGHTS OF THE ARBITRATORS

1157. — The arbitrators' rights fall into two categories: pecuniary rights and moral rights.

1° Arbitrators' Pecuniary Rights

1158. — In providing the services which they have undertaken to perform, the arbitrators incur a variety of expenses for which they can invariably seek reimbursement.

Furthermore, as it is rare for arbitrators to serve on an unpaid basis, they are also entitled to remuneration from the parties who appointed them to decide their dispute. That remuneration is made by way of the payment of fees.

These monetary rights themselves give rise to fiscal obligations for the arbitrators, which lead to certain difficulties in international cases. The principle is that each country's tax authorities has full discretion to decide which taxes (on income or on turnover) and which territorial rule (that of the arbitrators' residence or, particularly as regards value added tax, that of the jurisdiction of the debtor) will apply to arbitrators' fees.

In the determination of an arbitrator's tax status, national law generally considers that arbitrator to be a service provider.[328] However, in 1997 the European Court of Justice held that arbitrators should not be assimilated to "consultants . . . lawyers " and that the special territorial regime found in the Directive 77/388/EEC (Art. 9 (2)(e)) did not apply.[329] The precise meaning and consequences of this decision seem to have perplexed specialists in the field,[330] and are the subject of ongoing discussions between national tax authorities and the European Commission.

1159. — The conditions governing the reimbursement of expenses, advances on fees, and the amount of those fees are determined primarily by practice.

The Italian Code of Civil Procedure is one of the few statutes dealing with these issues. It begins by stating that arbitrators are entitled to be reimbursed in respect of their expenses, and to receive fees for work which they have carried out, unless they have waived such rights. It then stipulates that the parties are jointly liable to pay those fees, without prejudice to their right to recover such payments from one another. Lastly, Article 814 of the Code

---

[328] *See* Jean-Pierre Le Gall, *Le statut fiscal de l'arbitre international en Europe*, *in* L'INTERNATIONALISATION DANS LES INSTITUTIONS ET LE DROIT: CONVERGENCES ET DÉFIS – ETUDES OFFERTES À ALAIN PLANTEY 331 (1995); Jean-Pierre Le Gall, *Fiscalité et arbitrage*, 1994 REV. ARB. 3, especially at 6 *et seq.*

[329] *See* Court of Justice of the European Communities, Sept. 16, 1997, *von Hoffman, supra* note 13.

[330] *See* Le Gall, *supra* note 13; Karrer, Roos, Nordin, *supra* note 13; Aurillac, observations following Court of Justice of the European Communities, Sept. 16, 1997, *von Hoffmann, supra* note 13.

provides that if the parties do not accept the assessment of fees and expenses carried out by the arbitrators, they will be determined by a court.

These principles are also found in some other legal systems,[331] and are often set forth in arbitration rules.

a) Determining the Amount of Arbitrators' Fees

1160. — In *ad hoc* arbitration, arbitrators' fees are determined by the arbitrators themselves.[332] In institutional arbitration, they are determined either by the arbitrators, or by the institution,[333] depending on the applicable arbitration rules.[334] The fee scales contained in arbitration rules, and likewise the decisions taken by the administrative bodies within the arbitral institutions responsible for applying those scales, are contractually binding. Institutional arbitration is sometimes criticized for being expensive, as administrative costs are added to the arbitrators' fees.[335] In fact, where arbitration rules provide scales for arbitrators' fees and administrative costs, as in the case of ICC arbitration, the parties can be sure that they will not face excessive fee claims from the arbitrators.[336]

These rules lay down an implicit but fundamental principle: they prohibit any unilateral financial arrangement between an arbitrator and the appointing party. The IBA Rules of Ethics[337] also adopt that principle, which constitutes a vital safeguard for the independence of all arbitrators.

The question arises as to whether a court, at the request of the parties, can review the level of the arbitrators' fees, and reduce them if it considers them to be excessive. It could certainly do so in legal systems which, as in France, allow the courts to reduce excessive levels of remuneration fixed unilaterally by agents or contractors. However, if the fees have been calculated on the basis of a scale appearing in arbitration rules, it is less likely that a court will be entitled to adjust them, because the parties will be deemed to have been aware

---

[331] See, for example, in Belgian law, HUYS AND KEUTGEN *supra* note 198, ¶ 333 *et seq.*

[332] See, for example, Articles 38 and 39 of the UNCITRAL Rules, which describe the category of arbitration "costs" as including arbitrators' fees, and provide that the appointing authority's views as to fees should be taken into account although that authority cannot actually fix the amount of such fees.

[333] Fees of arbitrators acting in cases under the auspices of the LCIA (*see* Schedule of costs), of the AAA (Art. 32 of the 1997 International Arbitration Rules) and of ICSID (Art. 14 of the Administrative and Financial Regulations) are fixed as a function of an hourly or daily rate, and not, as in ICC arbitration, as a function of the amount in dispute.

[334] On this issue, generally, see J. Gillis Wetter and Charl Priem, *Costs and Their Allocation in International Commercial Arbitrations*, 2 AM. REV. INT'L ARB. 249 (1991).

[335] See, for example, for a critical assessment of the ICC system, Robert H. Smit, *An Inside View of the ICC Court*, 10 ARB. INT'L 53, especially at 73 *et seq.* (1994).

[336] On the question of fees and expenses in ICC arbitration, see Eric A. Schwartz, *The ICC Arbitral Process – Part IV: The Costs of ICC Arbitration*, ICC BULLETIN, Vol. 4, No.1, at 8 (1993), and the excerpts of awards, *id.* at 31; DERAINS AND SCHWARTZ, *supra* note 284, at 303 *et seq.*

[337] IBA Rules of Ethics for International Arbitrators, *supra* note 70.

of the fee scale and to have accepted it. A party would have to argue that the terms in question were those of a contract of adhesion, imposed by another party abusing its stronger bargaining position. However, in a case involving sophisticated parties with experience of arbitration, it is unlikely that such a claim would succeed.

On the other hand, if arbitrators fail to exercise their functions in a proper manner, their fees may be reduced or restituted, in whole or in part.[338] This is the principal reason why it is inappropriate for arbitrators to fix the amount of their fees in their award and, worse still, to order the parties, in the award, to pay those fees.[339]

b) Methods of Payment

1161. — The conditions governing advances and the payment of fees are clearly defined in institutional rules, and they cannot be disputed by the parties (who agree to comply with them in their arbitration agreement), or indeed by the arbitrators (who accept them when accepting the functions conferred on them by the institution).[340] However, the parties are sometimes reluctant to pay the specified advance in equal shares, as is generally required. It is also not unheard of for arbitrators to complain that arbitral institutions are too slow in paying over the arbitrators' fees.

c) Who Ultimately Bears the Costs of an Arbitration?

1162. — A number of practical difficulties may arise in determining who ultimately bears the costs of the arbitration.

It is well established—and perfectly legitimate—that the arbitrators, in their award, should determine who should ultimately pay the costs. Most arbitration rules so provide,[341] and an order to pay all or part of the costs of the arbitration is commonly found in the award, based on the success and conduct of each party in the arbitration.

However, in some cases, the arbitrators do not confine themselves to allocating the burden of the costs. They may also fix the amount of the costs in their award. Do they thus provide themselves with a basis on which to recover remuneration which they may not yet have received, or to prevent any subsequent challenge by a party as to the amount of the costs under the principle that their award is binding? Such a position would not be accepted by the courts. An arbitrator cannot be both judge and party, and the level of fees fixed in an

---

[338] *See supra* para. 1155.

[339] *See infra* para. 1162.

[340] On this issue, see *infra* paras. 1253 *et seq.*

[341] *See* Art. 40 of the UNCITRAL Rules; Art. 31(3) of the 1998 ICC Rules (Art. 20(1) of the previous Rules). See, generally, *infra* para. 1255.

award will therefore not be definitive. A party contesting the level of such fees would have to do so by a separate court action, and not by seeking to have the award set aside.[342]

2° Arbitrators' Moral Rights

1163. — The moral rights enjoyed by arbitrators have already been considered[343] and do not require an extensive commentary here.

1164. — As they are required to dispense justice, the arbitrators are service providers of a particular kind. Although they must comply with the arbitration agreement and the applicable procedural rules, they are not subordinated to the parties in the conduct of the arbitral proceedings.[344] Because their functions are judicial in nature, they enjoy a number of prerogatives in conducting the proceedings. Those judicial prerogatives are examined elsewhere.[345]

1165. — It is also widely recognized that the arbitrators can legitimately expect the parties to cooperate throughout the arbitral proceedings. That principle is self-evident although, regrettably, it does not appear in most rules of arbitral procedure.

1166. — In addition, the arbitrators have the right to pursue their brief until its conclusion. They can only be dismissed with the consent of all parties.[346] Clearly, if the parties agree to end the arbitration, the arbitrators cannot prevent them from doing so. However, the arbitrators cannot be subject to the whims of one of the parties and, in particular, their mandate cannot be unilaterally revoked by the party that appointed them. This rule is essential to ensure that the arbitrators retain their authority and independence vis-à-vis that party. Unfortunately, this rule is not always followed, especially where the arbitrators have been appointed by their own state or by an entity owned by that state.

1167. — The confidentiality of the arbitral process is both an obligation imposed upon the arbitrators[347] and a right they can exercise vis-à-vis the parties, any arbitral institution

---

[342] Cass. 2e civ., Oct. 28, 1987, S.A.R.L. Bureau Qualitas v. Viet, 1988 REV. ARB. 149, and C. Jarrosson's note; Cass. 2e civ., Oct. 10, 1990, S.A.R.L. Bureau Qualitas v. Viet, 1990 Bull. Civ. II, No. 187, at 95; 1991 JOURN. NOT. AV. 729, and P. Laroche de Roussane's note; 1996 REV.ARB. 393, 1st decision, and the commentary by Fouchard, *supra* note 2; *see also* CA Paris, Sept. 23, 1994, Société Hôtelière de Montagne v. Epoux d'Amade, 1996 REV. ARB. 393, 2d decision; CA Paris, Dec. 19, 1996, *Qualiconsult, supra* note 203; CA Paris, Nov. 25, 1997, VRV v. Pharmachim, 1998 REV. ARB. 684, and G. Bolard's note.

[343] *See supra* paras. 1074 *et seq.*

[344] *See supra* para. 1118.

[345] *See infra* paras. 1197 *et seq.* and 1226.

[346] *See, e.g.,* Art. 1462 of the French New Code of Civil Procedure.

[347] *See supra* para. 1132.

that is involved, and even, subject to review by the courts, third parties.[348] It is also a prerogative inherent in their judicial function,[349] as is the case with the rule that all deliberations between the arbitrators must remain confidential.[350]

1168. — It is, however, increasingly common for journals to publish arbitral awards and administrative decisions concerning arbitral proceedings.[351] This raises a question as to whether arbitrators enjoy any rights with respect to the publication of their award or procedural decisions. It is accepted that the anonymity of the parties is and should be maintained. However, one columnist of a Swiss arbitration review[352] considers that, for reasons of copyright, arbitrators deserve to have their identity disclosed.

In our view, arbitrators have no valid claim to intellectual property rights over their awards. An award is not a protected intellectual work. It is intended for the parties, who pay the arbitrators for the task of preparing the award and who become the owners of the award once it is made.

---

[348] *See* Art. 30.1 of the 1998 LCIA Rules.

[349] *See supra* para. 1078.

[350] *See infra* para. 1374.

[351] *See* DOMINIQUE HASCHER, COLLECTION OF PROCEDURAL DECISIONS IN ICC ARBITRATION – RECUEIL DES DÉCISIONS DE PROCÉDURE DANS L'ARBITRAGE CCI 1993-1996 (1997), and the latest published decisions in 124 J.D.I. 1058 (1998); see also the BULLETIN ASA, which, since the second issue in 1993, gives the names of the arbitrators involved.

[352] 1993 BULL. ASA 296.

PART FOUR

THE ARBITRAL PROCEDURE

1169. — Although the courts will sometimes assist in setting up the arbitral tribunal[1] and may subsequently hear actions to set aside or enforce the award,[2] once the arbitral tribunal is constituted they are generally required to refrain from interfering in the arbitral proceedings.

The principle that arbitral proceedings should remain free of court interference until the award is made was clearly stated by the Paris Court of Appeals in a 1987 decision in a case between the Republic of Guinea and a number of French companies. In a provisional ruling, the President of the Paris Tribunal of First Instance had considered that he was entitled to suspend the arbitral proceedings on the grounds that there was

> a serious risk that each of the parties might not enjoy the essential guarantees intended to provide an equitable hearing, within the meaning of French domestic law and of the international commitments assumed by France.[3]

Despite the serious nature of the judge's concerns, the Paris Court of Appeals rightly overruled his decision on the grounds that:

> the exercise of the prerogatives attached to [the arbitrators' judicial power], which is legitimate and autonomous in its own right, must be guaranteed in a totally independent manner, as befits any judge, without any interference with the organization which set up the arbitral tribunal and thus exhausted its powers, and without any intervention by the courts.[4]

Only when the award is reviewed can the courts verify that the arbitration was held in circumstances providing all the necessary procedural guarantees.[5]

---

[1] *See infra* paras. 742 *et seq.*

[2] *See infra* paras. 1559 *et seq.*

[3] TGI Paris, réf., Oct. 30, 1986, République de Guinée v. Chambre arbitrale de Paris, 1987 REV. ARB. 371, 379, and the commentary by Philippe Fouchard, *Les institutions permanentes d'arbitrage devant le juge étatique (A propos d'une jurisprudence récente)*, *id.* at 225. *See also supra* paras. 780 and 790.

[4] CA Paris, Nov. 18, 1987, Chambre arbitrale de Paris v. République de Guinée, 1988 REV. ARB. 657, 1st decision, and P. Fouchard's note. *See also* TGI Paris, réf., Feb. 15, 1995, Industrialexport v. K., 1996 REV. ARB. 503, 2d decision, and P. Fouchard's note; Emmanuel Gaillard, *Les manoeuvres dilatoires des parties et des arbitres dans l'arbitrage commercial international*, 1990 REV. ARB. 759, especially at 761 *et seq.*

[5] *See infra* para. 1203.

The principle of the autonomy of the arbitral procedure has long been recognized in French law, and it is tending to become the rule in other jurisdictions as well.[6] The UNCITRAL Model Law puts it differently, clearly confining the intervention of the courts to "certain functions of arbitration assistance and supervision" (Arts. 5 and 6). Even English law, which traditionally promoted resolution by the courts of any kind of difficulty arising during the arbitration, has substantially limited the cases where the courts can intervene during the course of arbitral proceedings.[7]

The autonomy of the arbitral procedure also prohibits states from using their legislative powers to obstruct the normal course of arbitration proceedings. In the 1994 *Stran Greek Refineries* case, the European Court of Human Rights held invalid the purported rescission by the Greek legislator of a contract for the construction of a refinery, together with its arbitration clause, despite the fact that an arbitral award had already been made in proceedings brought by the Greek State itself. The Court held that:

> [t]he principle of the rule of law and the notion of fair trial enshrined in Article 6 [of the European Convention on Human Rights] preclude any interference by the legislature with the administration of justice designed to influence the judicial determination of the dispute.[8]

1170. — The involvement of the courts is only justified where urgent provisional or protective measures are required (Chapter III). That exception aside, it is up to the parties and the arbitral tribunal to determine, if need be, the law applicable to the arbitral procedure (Chapter I), and to decide how the arbitration is to be conducted (Chapter II), a process which culminates in the making of the award (Chapter IV).

---

[6] *See, e.g.,* Christine Lécuyer-Thieffry and Patrick Thieffry, *L'évolution du cadre législatif de l'arbitrage international dans les années 1980*, 118 J.D.I. 947, 954 (1991); Sigvard Jarvin, *To What Extent Are Procedural Decisions of Arbitrators Subject to Court Review?*, *in* ICCA CONGRESS SERIES No. 9, IMPROVING THE EFFICIENCY OF ARBITRATION AGREEMENTS AND AWARDS: 40 YEARS OF APPLICATION OF THE NEW YORK CONVENTION 366 (A.J. van den Berg ed., 1999), and for a French version, 1998 REV. ARB. 611.

[7] *See* Secs. 1(c), 24, 42 *et seq.* and 66 *et seq.* of the 1996 Arbitration Act.

[8] European Court of Human Rights, Stran Greek Refineries and Stratis Andreadis v. Greece, Dec. 9, 1994, Series A, No. 301-B; for the French version, see 1996 REV. ARB. 283, and the commentary by Ali Bencheneb, *La contrariété à la Convention européenne des droits de l'homme d'une loi anéantissant une sentence arbitrale, id.* at 181; 122 J.D.I. 796 (1995), and observations by P. Tavernier.

CHAPTER I
THE LAW GOVERNING THE PROCEDURE

1171. — One often sees references to the "law governing the arbitral procedure," or to "procedural law," as opposed to the "law governing the substance" or "the merits" of a dispute. It is important, however, to remember that in most modern legal systems the parties and the arbitrators are by no means obliged to have a particular national law govern any procedural issues which may arise in the course of the arbitration. As is often the case in practice, they may simply refer to private rules of arbitral procedure, prepared by an arbitral institution or used in *ad hoc* arbitration.[1] They may also apply transnational rules derived from an analysis of comparative law or arbitral case law.[2] If they wish, they can combine provisions of a number of different laws, or even refrain from choosing any procedural rules or law at all, leaving the arbitrators to resolve any procedural difficulties as and when they arise.[3] The parties and, in the absence of agreement between them, the arbitrators thus have a great deal of freedom in this respect. Their freedom is explained by the fact that rules governing arbitral procedure, the determination of which is examined in Section II, have gradually become autonomous of those governing other aspects of the dispute, as we shall now see in Section I.

SECTION I
AUTONOMY OF THE LAW GOVERNING THE ARBITRAL PROCEDURE

1172. — It is nowadays generally accepted that the law governing the arbitral procedure will not necessarily be the same as that governing the merits of the dispute (§ 1), or indeed that of the seat of the arbitration (§ 2). The only rules that will prevail over those of the law which otherwise governs the procedure will be the mandatory procedural rules of the law of the jurisdiction where any action to set aside or enforce the award is heard (§ 3).

---

[1]   On these rules, see *supra* paras. 321 *et seq.*

[2]   *See infra* para. 1203.

[3]   *See infra* para. 1203.

§ 1. – The Law Governing the Procedure and the Law Governing the Merits

1173. — "The law governing the arbitral procedure will not necessarily be that governing the merits of the dispute." That principle was clearly stated by the Paris Court of Appeals in 1974 in the *Diefenbacher* case[4] and, in France, it has not been contested since.[5] As a result, the parties can choose to submit their main contract and the arbitral procedure to two different laws. Further, where the parties have not chosen a procedural law, the arbitrators are not obliged to apply the law which the parties, or the arbitrators themselves, have chosen to govern the main contract. The same principle is found in other modern arbitration laws.[6]

Arbitral case law also recognizes that there is not necessarily a link between the law governing the merits and the law governing the procedure.[7]

1174. — Several reasons have been put forward to justify this principle.

1175. — First, it has been argued that the principle is a consequence of the autonomy of the arbitration agreement, as the arbitral procedure is an extension of that agreement.[8] This argument is unconvincing, because the grounds on which the principle of the autonomy of the arbitration agreement[9] is based are entirely different to those which dictate the choice of a procedural law. In addition, this theory presupposes that the law governing the arbitral

---

[4]   CA Paris, June 18, 1974, O.C.P.C. v. Wilhelm Diefenbacher K.G., and O.C.P.C. v. Diefenbacher, 1975 REV. ARB. 179, and J. Robert's note.

[5]   *See, e.g.*, Cass. 1e civ., Mar. 18, 1980, Compagnie d'Armement Maritime (CAM) v. Compagnie Tunisienne de Navigation (COTUNAV), 1980 Bull. Civ. I, No. 87; 1980 REV. ARB. 476, and E. Mezger's note; 107 J.D.I. 874 (1980), and E. Loquin's note; Cass. 1e civ., May 10, 1988, Wasteels v. Ampafrance, 1989 REV. ARB. 51, and J.-L. Goutal's note.

[6]   See, for example, on Swiss law, PIERRE LALIVE, JEAN-FRANÇOIS POUDRET, CLAUDE REYMOND, LE DROIT DE L'ARBITRAGE INTERNE ET INTERNATIONAL EN SUISSE 351 (1989). On the issue, see also YVES DERAINS AND ERIC A. SCHWARTZ, A GUIDE TO THE NEW ICC RULES OF ARBITRATION 208 *et seq.* (1998).

[7]   See, for example, the August 23, 1958 award by Messrs. Sauser-Hall, referee, Hassan and Habachy, arbitrators, in Saudi Arabia v. Arabian American Oil Co. (ARAMCO), 27 INT'L L. REP. 117 (1963); for a French translation, see 1963 REV. CRIT. DIP 272. *See also* Henri Batiffol, *La sentence Aramco et le droit international privé*, 1964 REV. CRIT. DIP 647; the May 26, 1965 Ruling of the Bulgarian Chamber of Commerce and Industry in Case No. 52/65, I Y.B. COM. ARB. 123 (1976); ICC Award No. 5029 (1986), by Mr. Malmberg, French contractor v. Egyptian employer, XII Y.B. COM. ARB. 113 (1987).

[8]   *See, e.g.*, Frédéric-Edouard Klein, *Du caractère autonome de la clause compromissoire, notamment en matière d'arbitrage international (Dissociation de la nullité de cette clause de celle du contrat principal)*, 1961 REV. CRIT. DIP 499, 500; AHMED BUZGHAIA, LE PRINCIPE DE L'AUTONOMIE DE LA CLAUSE D'ARBITRAGE – ESSAI D'INTERPRÉTATION DE LA JURISPRUDENCE FRANÇAISE (Thesis, University of Nice (France), 1980); *see also* CA Paris, Feb. 21, 1980, General National Maritime Transport Co. v. Götaverken Arendal A.B., 107 J.D.I. 660 (1980), and P. Fouchard's note, especially at 671; 1980 REV. ARB. 524, and F.C. Jeantet's note; Dalloz, Jur. 568 (1980), and J. Robert's note; 1980 REV. CRIT. DIP 763, and E. Mezger's note; JCP, Ed. G., Pt. II, No. 19,512 (1981), and P. Level's note; for an English translation, see VI Y.B. COM. ARB. 221 (1981); 20 I.L.M. 883 (1981), with an introductory note by F.C. Jeantet.

[9]   *See supra* paras. 388 *et seq.*

procedure will be the same as that governing the arbitration agreement, which is not necessarily the case.[10]

1176. — It has also been pointed out that to assimilate the law governing the arbitral procedure with that governing the merits would be to unduly favor the contractual element of arbitration over its judicial element. As arbitrators administer justice, it is appropriate to determine the rules governing the arbitral procedure using specific connecting factors.[11]

1177. — Another more pragmatic view is that the considerations likely to guide the parties or the arbitrators in choosing the applicable law are not necessarily the same in the case of the substance of the contract and the arbitral procedure.[12] This is the more persuasive argument. To take just one example, the parties may wish to adopt Anglo-American style procedure, with discovery and examination of witnesses, while having the merits of any dispute governed by a law which they consider to be more suitable in view of the nature of the contract or the circumstances of the case. Arbitrators may share the same concerns, and are therefore in no way required to reason in the same way when determining the law governing the arbitral procedure and that governing the merits.

§ 2. – The Procedural Law and the Law of the Seat

1178. — In the past, whenever the parties had indicated no choice of procedural law, it was not uncommon for the arbitral procedure to be governed by the law of the seat of the arbitration. It is widely accepted today that the seat of the arbitration, often chosen for reasons of convenience or because of the neutrality of the country in question,[13] does not necessarily cause the procedure to be governed by the law of that jurisdiction. As the choice of a seat by the parties, the arbitral institution or the arbitrators themselves is often made on grounds entirely unrelated to the arbitral procedure, that choice will not automatically have an impact upon the conduct of the arbitral proceedings. This approach is endorsed by a

---

[10] For a discussion of this argument, see P. Fouchard, note following CA Paris, Feb. 21, 1980, *Götaverken*, *supra* note 8, at 671.

[11] On this argument, see especially E. Loquin, note following Cass. 1e civ., Mar. 18, 1980, *Compagnie d'Armement Maritime*, *supra* note 5, at 880.

[12] *See* J. Robert, note following CA Paris, June 18, 1974, *O.C.P.C.*, *supra* note 4, at 189; Loquin, *supra* note 11, at 880.

[13] On this issue, see especially Yves Derains, *Le choix du lieu de l'arbitrage/The Choice of the Place of Arbitration*, 1986 INT'L BUS. L.J. 109. *See also* THE PLACE OF ARBITRATION (M. Storme and F. de Ly eds., 1992).

majority of authors,[14] and is also evident in the development of national legislation (A), international conventions (B), arbitration rules (C) and arbitral case law (D).

A.– NATIONAL LEGISLATION

1179. — In French law, the rule whereby arbitral procedure was governed by the law of the seat was based not so much on the mechanical application of a subsidiary choice of law rule where the seat was the exclusive connecting factor, as on the identification of elements indicating the parties' implied intention as to the procedural law. The choice by the parties of the seat of arbitration supposedly revealed that implied intention.[15]

The same position was also widely followed in other legal systems, including the 1929 Swedish Arbitration Act,[16] and the 1969 Swiss *Concordat*, which contains numerous mandatory provisions applying to all arbitrations held in Switzerland.[17] The same thinking inspired the resolution adopted in Siena in 1952 by the Institute of International Law.[18] In resolving procedural issues, the arbitrator was, by analogy with the courts, to apply the law of the "arbitral forum."

1180. — Recent legislation has departed from this traditional rule. The French reform of 1981 makes no reference to the law of the seat in its provisions concerning the determination of the law governing the procedure.[19] The Netherlands[20] and Portuguese[21] arbitration statutes

---

[14] *See, e.g.,* Philippe Fouchard, *L'arbitrage international en France après le décret du 12 mai 1981*, 109 J.D.I. 374, ¶ 25 at 388 (1982); Bernardette Demeulenaere, *The place of arbitration and the applicable procedural law: The case of Belgium, in* THE PLACE OF ARBITRATION 67 (M. Storme and F. de Ly eds., 1992); Gabrielle Kaufmann-Kohler, *Identifying and Applying the Law Governing the Arbitration Procedure – The Role of the Law of the Place of Arbitration, in* ICCA CONGRESS SERIES NO. 9, IMPROVING THE EFFICIENCY OF ARBITRATION AGREEMENTS AND AWARDS: 40 YEARS OF APPLICATION OF THE NEW YORK CONVENTION 336 (A.J. van den Berg ed., 1999).

[15] *See, e.g.,* Cass. req., Dec. 8, 1914, Salles v. Hale, D.P., Pt. I, at 194 (1916); 1914 REV. DR. INT. PR. ET DR. PÉN. INT. 433. For an analysis of this case law, see PHILIPPE FOUCHARD, L'ARBITRAGE COMMERCIAL INTERNATIONAL ¶¶ 504 *et seq.* (1965).

[16] For a commentary, see THE STOCKHOLM CHAMBER OF COMMERCE, ARBITRATION IN SWEDEN 45 (2d. ed. 1984). No similar provision is found in the 1999 Swedish Arbitration Act which replaced the 1929 Act as of April 1, 1999 although, on the law applicable to the arbitration agreement, see Section 48 of the Act.

[17] This text no longer applies to international arbitrations taking place in Switzerland unless the parties have specifically so provided. *See supra* para. 162.

[18] ANN. INST. DR. INT., Year 1952, Pt. I, at 469, 535.

[19] Art. 1494 of the New Code of Civil Procedure; for a commentary, see *infra* paras. 1203 *et seq.*

[20] Art. 1036 of the Code of Civil Procedure.

[21] Art. 15 of Law No. 31/86 of August 29, 1986 on Voluntary Arbitration; *see* Dário Moura Vicente, *L'évolution récente du droit de l'arbitrage au Portugal*, 1991 REV. ARB. 419, 434, who emphasizes that local procedural rules must be respected, although that is not imposed by the law.

of 1986, the Swiss Private International Law Statute of 1987,[22] the Algerian legislative decree of 1993[23] and the Egyptian[24] and Italian[25] arbitration statutes of 1994 have taken a similar approach. English law long attached important consequences to the choice of the seat, which even prevailed over an apparently clear choice of procedural law by the parties.[26] The 1996 Arbitration Act, however, now recognizes the freedom of the parties (and the arbitrators, in the absence of a choice by the parties) to choose the law applicable to the arbitral procedure, subject to a limited number of mandatory provisions (Sec. 4). The UNCITRAL Model Law of 1985 likewise opted for a considerably reduced role of the seat in determining the law applicable to procedure. Under the heading "Determination of rules of procedure," it provides in Article 19, paragraph 1 that "[s]ubject to the provisions of this Law," which in fact means subject to those provisions of the Model Law considered to be mandatory, "the parties are free to agree on the procedure to be followed by the arbitral tribunal." The article then specifies that "[f]ailing such agreement, the arbitral tribunal may, subject to the provisions of this Law, conduct the arbitration in such manner as it considers appropriate."[27]

1181. — The changing position in national legislation is often summarized as being that, unlike a national court, the arbitrator "has no forum."[28] It would be, however, equally true

---

[22] Art. 182, para. 2; for a commentary, see LALIVE, POUDRET, REYMOND, *supra* note 6, at 351; ANDREAS BUCHER AND PIERRE-YVES TSCHANZ, INTERNATIONAL ARBITRATION IN SWITZERLAND (1989). On the discussion in the Swiss parliament arising from the abandonment of the mandatory application of certain provisions of the law of the seat, see Marc Blessing, *The New International Arbitration Law in Switzerland – A Significant Step Towards Liberalism*, 5 J. INT'L ARB. 9, 47 (June 1988).

[23] Art. 458 bis 6 of the Algerian Code of Civil Procedure (Legislative Decree No. 93-09 of April 25, 1993); *see* Mohand Issad, *Le décret législatif algérien du 25 avril 1993 relatif à l'arbitrage international*, 1993 REV. ARB. 377; Mohammed Bedjaoui and Ali Mebroukine, *Le nouveau droit de l'arbitrage international en Algérie*, 120 J.D.I. 873 (1993).

[24] Art. 25 of Law No. 27 for 1994 Promulgating the Law Concerning Arbitration in Civil and Commercial Matters; *see* Bernard Fillion-Dufouleur and Philippe Leboulanger, *Le nouveau droit égyptien de l'arbitrage*, 1994 REV. ARB. 665, 676.

[25] Art. 816 of the Code of Civil Procedure; *see* Piero Bernardini, *L'arbitrage en Italie après la récente réforme*, 1994 REV. ARB. 479, 490.

[26] Union of India v. McDonnell Douglas Corp., [1993] 2 Lloyd's Rep. 48; XIX Y.B. COM. ARB. 235 (1994) (High Ct., Q.B. (Com. Ct.) 1992).

[27] Art. 19, para. 2. For a commentary, see Klaus Lionnet, *Should the Procedural Law Applicable to International Arbitration be Denationalised or Unified? The Answer of the Uncitral Model Law*, 8 J. INT'L ARB. 5 (Sept. 1991); *comp. with* Philippe Fouchard, *La Loi-type de la C.N.U.D.C.I. sur l'arbitrage commercial international*, 114 J.D.I. 861 (1987), especially at 875 *et seq*. For the incorporation of this provision into German law since January 1, 1998, see Article 1042 of the ZPO. On the 1999 Swedish Arbitration Act, see *supra* note 16.

[28] *See, e.g.*, Berthold Goldman, *La volonté des parties et le rôle de l'arbitre dans l'arbitrage international*, 1981 REV. ARB. 469, 471; Eric Loquin, *Les pouvoirs des arbitres internationaux à la lumière de l'évolution récente du droit de l'arbitrage international*, 110 J.D.I. 293 (1983), especially at 298 *et seq*.

to state that the forum of an international arbitrator consists of all legal systems willing, under certain conditions, to recognize an award made by that arbitrator.[29]

B.– INTERNATIONAL CONVENTIONS

1182. — The earliest international conventions clearly favored the application of the law of the seat to questions of procedure. The Protocol on Arbitration Clauses in Commercial Matters, signed in Geneva on September 24, 1923,[30] provides in its Article 2 that:

> [t]he arbitral procedure, including the constitution of the arbitral tribunal, shall be governed by the will of the parties and by the law of the country in whose territory the arbitration takes place.

Here, compliance with the provisions of the procedural law of the seat of the arbitration is a condition for the mutual recognition of awards.

The Convention on the Execution of Foreign Arbitral Awards signed in Geneva on September 26, 1927,[31] provides that the recognition or enforcement of an award may be refused or suspended

> [i]f the party against whom the award was made proves that, under the law governing the arbitration procedure, there is a ground . . . entitling him to contest the validity of the award in a court of law (Art. 3).

Although it does not impose compliance with the law of the seat, the Convention does thus require the parties to respect the mandatory provisions of a law chosen by applying a traditional choice of law rule which the Convention does not itself determine. However, the Convention does admit that laws other than that of the forum of an action to set aside or enforce an award can govern the arbitral procedure on a mandatory basis. This was the first sign of progress.

1183. — The 1958 New York Convention still attributes an important but subsidiary role to the law of the seat of the arbitration.[32] Article V, paragraph 1(d) enables contracting states to refuse recognition or enforcement of an award where

---

[29] On this issue, see Emmanuel Gaillard, *Thirty Years of Lex Mercatoria: Towards the Selective Application of Transnational Rules*, 10 ICSID REV. – FOREIGN INV. L.J. 208 (1995), and, for a French version, *Trente ans de Lex Mercatoria – Pour une application sélective de la méthode des principes généraux du droit*, 122 J.D.I. 5 (1995).

[30] This Convention no longer applies to relationships between states that are party to the 1958 New York Convention. *See supra* para. 241.

[31] This Convention, like the 1923 Protocol, is no longer in force between states that are party to the 1958 New York Convention. *See supra* para. 244.

[32] *See* ALBERT JAN VAN DEN BERG, THE NEW YORK ARBITRATION CONVENTION OF 1958, at 325–30 (1981).

the arbitral procedure was not in accordance with the agreement of the parties, or, failing such agreement, was not in accordance with the law of the country where the arbitration took place.

This approach is unsatisfactory. Article V, paragraph 1(e) of the Convention already allows a court to refuse enforcement of an award set aside in the country of the seat and, under Article VI, a court can stay enforcement proceedings if an action to set aside is pending in the country of the seat. Where the breach of the procedural rules of the seat is sufficiently serious, it is likely to give rise to an action to set aside before the courts of that jurisdiction, which may defeat the enforcement procedure by virtue of Articles V, paragraph 1(e), and VI. Conversely, if the breach of a procedural rule of the "arbitral forum" did not open up the possibility of an action before the courts of that "forum" to set aside the award, it would be inappropriate for such a breach to constitute a ground on which to refuse enforcement elsewhere.

For a party seeking to prevent enforcement of the award, Article V, paragraph 1(d), does have the advantage of dispensing with the need to bring an action before the courts of the seat for the breach of the procedural rules of the seat to produce effects in other legal systems. However, that is precisely what is wrong with the approach adopted in the Convention. If the breach of a procedural rule of the "arbitral forum" can form the basis of an action before the local courts, and if such an action has not been commenced, it is going too far to allow other legal systems to examine that breach without requiring the party relying on it to bring an action before the courts of the country whose procedural rules have been violated. Those courts are, after all, best positioned to hear such an action. If, on the other hand, the laws of the jurisdiction where recognition or enforcement is sought do contain the same requirement, the award could be rejected simply by application of Article V, paragraph 2, on the basis of a breach of local public policy, and the issue of compliance with the rules of the state where the seat is located would not arise.

In modern arbitration law, the existence of legislation which allows parties to exclude any action to set aside the award at the place of the seat[33] highlights the paradox in the concern of the authors of the New York Convention that compliance with the procedural rules of the seat of the arbitration be policed by the courts of other jurisdictions where enforcement is sought. For example, where an award is made in Belgium, Sweden or Switzerland, the parties are entitled to exclude all actions to set aside the award before the local courts, unless at least one of the parties to the dispute has Belgian, Swedish or Swiss nationality or residence. If the parties have not determined the law governing the arbitral procedure, either directly or by reference to arbitration rules, the New York Convention allows the court hearing a request for enforcement of the award to refuse such enforcement on the grounds of a breach of the procedural law of the situs. The paradox is evident in that the legal system of the forum has specifically declared that it is not willing to impose its rules on the conduct of the arbitration.

Under such circumstances, a court hearing the enforcement proceedings should exercise its discretion under Article V of the New York Convention so as to avoid refusing to give

---

[33] *See infra* para. 1594.

effect to an award solely on the grounds of a breach of the procedural law of the seat. A court hearing a request for enforcement is by no means obliged to refuse enforcement on such grounds, and it can therefore ignore a breach of the procedural rules of the law of the seat. At the very least, the court should construe the waiver of the action to set aside as an implicit decision not to have the law of the forum govern the procedure, pursuant to the option granted to the parties by Article V, paragraph 1(d) of the New York Convention.

1184. — The 1961 European Convention on International Commercial Arbitration contains the first modern expression of the currently accepted principles used to determine the law applicable to arbitral procedure. It provides, in Article IV, paragraph 1 (b)(iii), that the parties to an arbitration agreement shall be free "to lay down the procedure to be followed by the arbitrators." Where the parties have refrained from doing so, the Convention provides in Article IV, paragraph 4(d) that the arbitrators themselves can determine the procedural rules to be followed. Failing that, the Convention provides a fall-back whereby the authority responsible under the Convention for organizing the arbitration can "establish directly or by reference to the rules and statutes of a permanent arbitral institution the rules of procedure to be followed by the arbitrator(s)."[34]

The Convention thus provides that the parties and, absent agreement between the parties, the arbitrators are free to determine how the arbitral proceedings are to be conducted, without any reference to the law of the seat of the arbitration.

1185. — The 1965 Washington Convention, establishing ICSID, likewise took a modern approach to the conduct of the arbitral proceedings. It confined itself to affirming the autonomy of the parties to determine the rules governing the arbitral procedure, and helpfully specifies that the parties' autonomy enables them to exclude various provisions of the ICSID Arbitration Rules, thus underlining the optional character of those rules.[35] In the absence of any choice by the parties, the arbitrators are fully empowered to resolve procedural difficulties as they see fit. To do so they may choose whether or not to apply any particular law. However, a reference to the law of the seat would be meaningless in this context, given the genuinely delocalized nature of ICSID arbitration which, unlike other forms of arbitration, is based solely on an international treaty.[36]

---

[34] For a commentary, see Lazare Kopelmanas, *La place de la Convention européenne sur l'arbitrage commercial international du 21 avril 1961 dans l'évolution du droit international de l'arbitrage*, 1961 AFDI 331; FOUCHARD, *supra* note 15, ¶¶ 513 *et seq.*; Dominique T. Hascher, *European Convention on International Commercial Arbitration of 1961 — Commentary*, XX Y.B. COM. ARB. 1003, ¶ 29 at 1019 (1995), and the cases cited therein.

[35] Art. 44. On this issue, see E. Gaillard, note following Cass. 1e civ., Nov. 18, 1986, Atlantic Triton v. République populaire révolutionnaire de Guinée, 114 J.D.I. 125, 129 (1987).

[36] *See* Aron Broches, *The Convention on the Settlement of Investment Disputes Between States and Nationals of Other States*, *in* COLLECTED COURSES OF THE HAGUE ACADEMY OF INTERNATIONAL LAW, Vol. 136, Year 1972, Part II, at 331; Emmanuel Gaillard, *Centre International pour le Règlement des Différends Relatifs aux Investissements (C.I.R.D.I) – Chronique des sentences arbitrales*, 113 J.D.I. 197, 198 (1986).

C.- ARBITRATION RULES

1186. — Arbitration rules have developed along similar lines.

1187. — The best illustration of this is to be found in the amendments to the ICC Rules of Arbitration concerning the law applicable to the arbitral procedure.

The Rules which entered into force on June 1, 1955 stipulated that, for matters not covered by the Rules and in the absence of an indication to the contrary by the parties, the rules "of the law of the country in which the arbitrator holds the proceedings" would apply (Art. 16). In the version which entered into force on June 1, 1975, Article 11 of the Rules, which remained unchanged following the amendments of January 1, 1988, stated that:

> [t]he rules governing the proceedings before the arbitrator shall be those resulting from these Rules and, where these Rules are silent, any rules which the parties (or, failing them, the arbitrator) may settle, and whether or not reference is thereby made to a municipal procedural law to be applied to the arbitration.

One author observed that:

> there has thus been a move away from the subsidiary and mandatory application of the law of the 'forum,' in favor of a combination of the powers of the parties and those of the arbitrator, without the need to refer to any national law whatsoever, and that combination is adopted and confirmed by Article 1494 of the French New Code of Civil Procedure.[37]

The 1998 Rules slightly modified the formulation of the principle, with Article 15(1) reading as follows:

> [t]he proceedings before the Arbitral Tribunal shall be governed by these Rules, and, where these Rules are silent, by any rules which the parties or, failing them, the Arbitral Tribunal may settle on, whether or not a reference is thereby made to the rules of procedure of a national law to be applied to the arbitration.

The 1998 Rules simply add that certain fundamental tenets of procedural justice must be respected by the arbitrators in every case, following the example of the UNCITRAL

---

[37] Goldman, *supra* note 28, at 476. On this issue, see also Karl-Heinz Böckstiegel, *The Legal Rules Applicable in International Commercial Arbitration Involving States or State-controlled Enterprises, in* INTERNATIONAL ARBITRATION – 60 YEARS OF ICC ARBITRATION – A LOOK AT THE FUTURE 117 (ICC Publication No. 412, 1984). For a critical view of this evolution, see Lionnet, *supra* note 27.

Arbitration Rules[38] and the Swiss Private International Law Statute.[39] Thus, Article 15(2) provides that "[i]n all cases, the Arbitral Tribunal shall act fairly and impartially and ensure that each party has a reasonable opportunity to present its case."[40]

1188. — The 1976 UNCITRAL Arbitration Rules provide in Article 15, paragraph 1 that:

> [s]ubject to these Rules, the arbitral tribunal may conduct the arbitration in such manner as it considers appropriate, provided that the parties are treated with equality and that at any stage of the proceedings each party is given a full opportunity of presenting his case.

This is in keeping with the modern conception of the law of international arbitral procedure,[41] and it influenced the authors of the 1985 UNCITRAL Model Law.[42] The principles contained in the UNCITRAL Rules have thus had a much greater impact than other rules because, unlike recognition by statute, the recognition of party autonomy in arbitration rules which the parties themselves choose to apply is of limited relevance.

1189. — Article 16 of the 1997 AAA International Arbitration Rules also confers broad discretion on the arbitrators as to the conduct of the arbitral procedure without making any reference to the law of the place of arbitration. Similarly, the 1998 LCIA Rules give the parties and the arbitrators substantial freedom (Arts. 14.1 and 14.2) but, in a change from the 1985 Rules, specify that the law of the seat of the arbitration governs the procedure unless the parties agree otherwise (Art. 16.3). This new provision reflects an unfortunate resurgence of the traditional view[43] that the seat of the arbitration is the equivalent of a court's forum, and that the law of the seat therefore has a role to play as the *lex fori*, albeit only in the absence of an agreement between the parties.

D.– ARBITRAL CASE LAW

1190. — International arbitral practice has also moved away from applying the law of the seat of the arbitration in the absence of a contrary intention of the parties. Instead it now allows the arbitrators complete freedom in choosing the applicable procedure, or in simply resolving procedural issues as and when they arise.

---

[38]   *See infra* para. 1188.

[39]   Art. 182, para. 3. *See infra* para. 1194.

[40]   On this issue, see DERAINS AND SCHWARTZ, *supra* note 6, at 208 *et seq.*

[41]   On this issue, see Karl-Heinz Böckstiegel, *Die UNCITRAL-Verfahrensordnung für Wirtschafts- schiedsgerichtsbarkeit und das anwendbare nationale Recht*, 28 RIW 706 (1982).

[42]   *See supra* para. 1180.

[43]   *See* F.A. Mann, *Lex Facit Arbitrum, in* INTERNATIONAL ARBITRATION – LIBER AMICORUM FOR MARTIN DOMKE 157 (P. Sanders ed., 1967), *reprinted in* 2 ARB. INT'L 241 (1986). *See also supra* para. 1180.

1191. — For many years, where the parties had not determined the arbitral procedure, arbitrators would generally apply the law of the seat of the arbitration. This was quite natural in ICC arbitration, as it was the position taken in the ICC Rules.[44] However, it was of more significance in *ad hoc* cases. It was widely accepted that "in default of agreement by the parties, the arbitration is submitted to the judicial sovereignty of the seat of the arbitration at the place where the case is heard," as observed in the 1963 award in the *Sapphire v. NIOC* case.[45]

1192. — Another trend has emerged, however, which rejects the idea of having the law of the seat necessarily govern the arbitral procedure. This could be clearly seen in ICC arbitration even prior to the amendment of the ICC Rules in 1975.[46] For example, in a 1971 award made in an arbitration in Geneva involving an Indian party and a Pakistani party, it was held that "by virtue of the ICC Rules . . . , the arbitrator has a broad discretion in procedural matters." The tribunal added that limits to that discretion exist because "the arbitrator cannot avoid his duty to comply with the fundamental general principles of procedure," and not because of the requirements of a particular national law.[47] The same tendency to go beyond applying a particular national law, be it the law of the seat or any other, can be seen in *ad hoc* arbitration. The 1958 award in the *Saudi Arabia v. ARAMCO* arbitration is a good illustration. The case concerned a state contract, and it was held that the procedure should be governed solely by the provisions of public international law, and not by those of the Canton of Geneva, where the arbitration took place. The grounds given were that an arbitration involving a sovereign state could not be governed by the law of another country.[48] Similarly, at a preliminary meeting held on June 9, 1975 in the *LIAMCO v. Libya* case, the arbitrator decided that:

---

[44]   *See, e.g.*, ICC Award No. 2272 (1975), Italian claimant A. v. Belgian respondent B., II Y.B. COM. ARB. 151 (1977).

[45]   Sapphire International Petroleums Ltd. v. National Iranian Oil Co., 35 INT'L L. REP. 136, 169 (1967); *see also* December 22, 1954 Award by L. Python, The Alsing Trading Co., Ltd. v. Etat Hellénique, 23 INT'L L. REP. 633 (1956) and, for a commentary, Stephen M. Schwebel, *The Alsing Case*, 8 INT'L & COMP. L.Q. 320 (1959); for excerpts of the French original, see 1955 REV. ARB. No. 2, at 27; the October 10, 1973 Award by G. Lagergren in BP Exploration Co. (Libya) Ltd. v. Government of the Libyan Arab Republic, which held that Danish law would govern the procedure in a case with no link with Denmark other than the location of the seat (53 INT'L L. REP. 297 (1979); V Y.B. COM. ARB. 143, 147 (1980); see excerpts in French reproduced in 1980 REV. ARB. 117; for a commentary, see Brigitte Stern, *Trois arbitrages, un même problème, trois solutions – Les nationalisations pétrolières libyennes devant l'arbitrage international, id.* at 3, especially at 8 *et seq.*); Robert B. von Mehren and P. Nicholas Kourides, *International Arbitrations Between States and Foreign Private Parties: The Libyan Nationalization Cases*, 75 AM. J. INT'L L. 476 (1981).

[46]   *See supra* para. 1187.

[47]   ICC Award No. 1512 (1971), Indian cement company v. Pakistani bank, I Y.B. COM. ARB. 128 (1976); for a French translation, see 101 J.D.I. 905 (1974), and observations by Y. Derains.

[48]   Aug. 23, 1958 award, *supra* note 7.

in his procedure [the arbitrator] shall be guided as much as possible by the general principles contained in the Draft Convention on Arbitral Procedure elaborated by the International Law Commission of the United Nations in 1958.[49]

Likewise, in its 1977 award, the arbitral tribunal in the *Texaco v. Libya* case applied rules of international law and not the law of the seat.[50]

These awards reflect the dominant trend now found in international arbitral case law.[51]

§ 3. – Procedural Law and the Law of the Country Where the Award Is Subject to Court Review

1193. — Irrespective of the law or the rules of law which govern the procedure, the mandatory provisions of laws of jurisdictions where the award is liable to be reviewed by

---

[49] *See* April 12, 1977 award in Libyan American Oil Co. (LIAMCO) v. Government of the Libyan Arab Republic, 20 I.L.M. 1 (1981), VI Y.B. COM. ARB. 89, 91 (1981); for a French translation, see 1980 REV. ARB. 132, especially at 147 *et seq.*, and the commentary by Stern, *supra* note 45.

[50] Texaco Overseas Petroleum Co./California Asiatic Oil Co. v. Government of the Libyan Arab Republic, 17 I.L.M. 1, ¶ 16 at 9 (1978); 53 INT'L L. REP. 389 (1979); IV Y.B. COM. ARB. 177 (1980); for extracts of the French original text, see 104 J.D.I. 350 (1977), with a commentary by Jean-Flavien Lalive, *Un grand arbitrage pétrolier entre un Gouvernement et deux sociétés privées étrangères (Arbitrage Texaco/Calasiatic c/ Gouvernement Libyen), id.* at 319. *See also* Gérard Cohen Jonathan, *L'arbitrage Texaco-Calasiatic contre Gouvernement Libyen (Sentence au fond du 19 janvier 1977),* 1977 AFDI 452; François Rigaux, *Des dieux et des héros – Réflexions sur une sentence arbitrale,* 1978 REV. CRIT. DIP 435; Joe Verhoeven, *Droit international des contrats et droit des gens (A propos de la sentence rendue le 19 janvier 1977 en l'affaire California Asiatic Oil Company et Texaco Overseas Oil Company c. Etat libyen),* REV. BELGE DR. INT. 1978–1979, at 209; Stern *supra* note 45.

[51] *See, e.g.,* ICC Award No. 2879 (1978): "where the arbitration rules are silent the arbitral tribunal will apply the rules it deems appropriate" (French buyer v. Yugoslavian seller, 106 J.D.I. 989 (1979), and observations by Y. Derains); ICC Award No. 5103 (1988): "[a]s regards the law applicable to the arbitral procedure, this was subject, as set forth in the terms of reference, to the Rules of the ICC Court of Arbitration and to the provisions of the terms of reference. Where an issue was not covered by such rules and provisions, according to Article 11 of the Rules and Article 1494, paragraph 2 of the French New Code of Civil Procedure, to which the parties expressly referred in the terms of reference, the arbitral tribunal itself determined the rules to be followed and took the measures necessary for the conduct of the case and the assessment of the evidence" (Three European companies v. Four Tunisian companies, 115 J.D.I. 1206 (1988), and observations by G. Aguilar Alvarez); ICC Award No. 7489 (1993), ICC BULLETIN, Vol. 8, No. 2, at 68 (1997). However, references to the law of the place of the arbitration have not altogether disappeared in certain awards. *See, e.g.,* ICC Award No. 5029 (1986), *supra* note 7; the November 3, 1977 *ad hoc* Award, Mr. Gastambide presiding, Mechema Ltd. v. S.A. Mines, Minerais et Métaux, 1980 REV. ARB. 560, and J. Schapira's note; for an English translation, see VII Y.B. COM. ARB. 77 (1982), which provided that "it is generally accepted that, failing an agreement of the parties, the arbitral procedure is governed by the law of the country in which the arbitration takes place;" ICC Award No. 7184 (Paris, 1994), ICC BULLETIN, Vol. 8, No. 2, at 63 (1997). Compare with the February 5 and May 31, 1988 *ad hoc* Awards by J. Stevenson, president, I. Brownlie and B. Cremades, arbitrators, in Wintershall A.G. v. Government of Qatar, which applied the mandatory provisions of Dutch law (the Netherlands being the seat of the arbitration) as required by that law (28 I.L.M. 795, 801 (1989); XV Y.B. COM. ARB. 30 (1990); *see infra* para. 1194).

the courts cannot be entirely ignored by the arbitrators. Those are, in fact, the only laws which limit the autonomy of the parties and the arbitral tribunal in the conduct of the arbitral proceedings.

1194. — The first constraint results from the public policy provisions of the country where an action may be brought to set the award aside. It is for this reason that the arbitrators must take into account the requirements of the law of the seat of the arbitration, and not because that law should necessarily govern the arbitral procedure as the *lex fori*. In most legal systems, an action to set aside will be brought before the courts of the country of the seat of the arbitration, and it is there that a breach of certain procedural rules may provide the basis for such an action. This can be seen in a number of national arbitration laws. For example, under Article 1693 of the Belgian Judicial Code, the parties are entitled to determine the rules of arbitral procedure, but only subject to the provisions of Article 1694, which is intended to guarantee the parties' rights to a fair hearing and equal treatment throughout the arbitral proceedings.[52] Similarly, Article 182, paragraph 3 of the Swiss Private International Law Statute specifies that "whatever procedure is chosen, the arbitral tribunal shall ensure equal treatment of the parties and the right of the parties to be heard in an adversarial procedure." Likewise, under Article 1036 of the Netherlands Code of Civil Procedure, the principle of freedom of choice in determining the rules of procedure applies "[s]ubject to the provisions of this Title," which concerns "arbitration in the Netherlands." Some of those provisions, such as compliance with the requirements of due process and equal treatment of the parties, are mandatory (Art. 1039(1) and (2)). However, most of them, such as the right to present witnesses and experts, the submission of evidence, and the rules governing default by a party, apply only where the parties do not specify otherwise. Similarly, the 1996 English Arbitration Act uses general terms in Section 33, paragraph 1 regarding the arbitrators' duties in the conduct of the procedure:

> The tribunal shall—
> (a) act fairly and impartially as between the parties, giving each party a reasonable opportunity of putting his case and dealing with that of his opponent, and
> (b) adopt procedures suitable to the circumstances of the particular case, avoiding unnecessary delay or expense, so as to provide a fair means for the resolution of the matters falling to be determined.

The fact that the French legislature considered it unnecessary to stipulate expressly that the principles of due process and equal treatment of the parties apply to all international arbitrations held in France should not be interpreted as meaning that those principles do not apply in every case, as a breach of those principles constitutes a ground for setting the award aside. Article 1502 4° of the French New Code of Civil Procedure includes a breach of the

---

[52] *See* MARCEL HUYS, GUY KEUTGEN, L'ARBITRAGE EN DROIT BELGE ET INTERNATIONAL ¶¶ 137 *et seq.* (1981); Marcel Huys, *Belgium, in* INTERNATIONAL CHAMBER OF COMMERCE, ARBITRATION LAW IN EUROPE 31 (ICC Publication No. 353, 1981).

principle of due process among the grounds for setting an award aside or refusing its enforcement, while Article 1502 5° of the same code lists among such grounds the violation of international public policy, which certainly includes the principle of equal treatment of the parties.[53]

1195. — Although they are under no obligation to do so, arbitrators wishing to ensure the international effectiveness of their award should comply with the principles which, if breached, would justify the refusal of enforcement in the main jurisdictions where, given the circumstances of the case, attempts may be made to enforce their award.[54] In practice, those rules will often coincide with the rules of the country where an action may be brought to set the award aside, although that will not always be the case. Also, the law of the seat of the arbitration may allow the parties to exclude actions to set aside the award in certain circumstances, as in Belgium, Sweden and Switzerland.[55] In such cases, the procedural public policy of the jurisdictions where enforcement is sought will be the only point of reference for arbitrators who wish to ensure that their award is internationally enforceable.[56]

However, in the rare case of a conflict between the public policy rules of the seat of the arbitration, or those of the place where the award is liable to be enforced, and the arbitrators' own conception of the requirements of genuinely international public policy, our view is that the arbitrators should allow the latter to prevail.[57]

SECTION II
DETERMINING THE LAW GOVERNING THE ARBITRAL PROCEDURE

1196. — Before examining the criteria for determining the law governing the arbitral procedure (§ 2) and the consequences of the determination of that law (§ 3), we shall consider whether it is necessary or appropriate to determine that law in advance (§ 1).

---

[53] *See infra* para. 1654.

[54] In favor of the consideration by the arbitrators of the procedural principles of public policy the breach of which could justify the refusal of enforcement (to the extent that it is possible to identify the jurisdictions in which the award could be enforced), see also Derains, observations following ICC Award No. 2879 (1978), *supra* note 51.

[55] *See infra* para. 1594.

[56] *See infra* paras. 1652 *et seq.*

[57] See the November 1984 Interim Award in ICC Case No. 4695, Parties from Brazil, Panama and U.S.A. v. Party from Brazil, XI Y.B. COM. ARB. 149 (1986). On awards recognized in one jurisdiction but set aside in another, see *infra* para. 1595.

§ 1.– Is It Necessary or Appropriate to Determine the Procedural Law in Advance?

1197. — In their arbitration agreement, or once the dispute has arisen, the parties are free to choose or refrain from choosing the law governing the arbitral procedure. More significantly, in the absence of a choice by the parties, the arbitrators enjoy the same freedom. In France, the arbitrators' freedom to determine the procedure "to the extent that is necessary" is enshrined in Article 1494, paragraph 2 of the New Code of Civil Procedure. French arbitration law, in keeping with its liberal tradition, thus does not oblige the arbitrators to determine the law governing the arbitral procedure at the outset of the proceedings, although the option of doing so does remain open to them. The arbitrators will only be obliged to determine the procedural law in advance where the parties have expressly required them to do so.[58] If the parties have given no such instructions, the arbitrators must simply decide whether it is an appropriate course of action.[59] The Swiss courts have taken the same approach.[60]

1198. — There is still a considerable divergence of opinion as to whether it is appropriate for arbitrators to determine in advance the law applicable to all procedural issues which may arise during the arbitration. As the parties usually do not specify a procedural law in their arbitration agreement, it is generally up to the arbitrators to determine the rules governing the procedure, or to obtain an agreement between the parties on the matter once the dispute has arisen. However, the arbitrators themselves may disagree as to how the proceedings should be conducted. Some arbitrators prefer to choose the procedural law—or rules of law—at the outset of the arbitration, when the parties will be unaware of the particular difficulties which may arise and therefore more likely to reach an agreement as they are not in dispute on any specific issue. This approach is considered to enhance the predictability of the arbitration.

Other arbitrators deem it wiser not to resolve questions of procedure until they know exactly what is at stake, and are reluctant to bind themselves in advance by choosing a given law which may prove ill-suited to resolve subsequent specific difficulties. For example, the suitability of hearing witnesses (based on Anglo-American methods of direct and cross-examination), or the parties themselves (as traditionally occurs in Switzerland), can best be judged after the arbitrators have heard the parties' respective arguments and have acquainted themselves with the evidence already submitted. The fact that the arbitrators are not obliged

---

[58] *See* Goldman, *supra* note 28, at 475.

[59] On the freedom of the arbitrators and its limits in this area, see Pierre Mayer, *Comparative Analysis of Power of Arbitrators to Determine Procedures in Civil and Common Law Systems*, in ICCA CONGRESS SERIES NO. 7, PLANNING EFFICIENT ARBITRATION PROCEEDINGS/THE LAW APPLICABLE IN INTERNATIONAL ARBITRATION 24 (A.J. van den Berg ed., 1996) and, for a French version, *Le pouvoir des arbitres de régler la procédure – Une analyse comparative des systèmes de civil law et de common law*, 1995 REV. ARB. 163; Patrice Level, *Brèves réflexions sur l'office de l'arbitre*, in NOUVEAUX JUGES, NOUVEAUX POUVOIRS – MÉLANGES EN L'HONNEUR DE ROGER PERROT 259 (1996).

[60] *See* Swiss Fed. Trib., Aug. 17, 1994, Türkiye Elektrik Kurumu v. Osuuskunta METEX Andelslag, 1995 BULL. ASA 198, and F.R. Ehrat's note; 1996 REV. SUISSE DR. INT. ET DR. EUR. 539, and observations by F. Knoepfler.

to resolve each difficulty by reference to the same procedural law[61] makes it all the more appropriate for them to avoid limiting their options by making an early decision covering all incidents that may arise, and instead to pick and choose the means of resolving each incident as it happens.

The divergence of views on this issue is gradually losing its significance. This is because national legislation in this area is converging and is less often of mandatory application, at least in international arbitration. As a result, most national laws now only require compliance with a few fundamental principles.

§ 2. – Criteria for Determining the Law Applicable to the Arbitral Procedure

1199. — To the extent that they consider it appropriate, the parties (A) and, in the absence of a choice by the parties, the arbitrators (B) are free to determine the rules of law governing the arbitral procedure.

A. – CHOICE MADE BY THE PARTIES

1200. — Subject only to the mandatory provisions of laws liable to conflict with the procedural law when an award is reviewed by the courts,[62] all modern arbitration legislation endorses the principle that the parties are free to choose the law or rules of law governing the arbitral procedure. That principle has long been recognized by the French courts,[63] and it is now found in Article 1494, paragraph 1 of the French New Code of Civil Procedure, which provides that:

> [t]he arbitration agreement may, directly or by reference to arbitration rules, determine the procedure to be followed in the arbitral proceedings; it may also submit the proceedings to a specified procedural law.

1201. — This provision is often considered a substantive rule of French international arbitration law which applies to all international arbitrations taking place in France.[64]

---

[61] *See infra* para. 1202.

[62] *See supra* paras. 1193 *et seq.*

[63] *See, e.g.*, Cass. req., July 17, 1899, Ospina v. Ribon, Sirey, Pt. I, at 393 (1900); D.P., Pt. I, at 225 (1904), and P. Pic's note; 26 J.D.I. 1024 (1899). For a more recent illustration, see, for example, CA Paris, Jan. 17, 1992, Guangzhou Ocean Shipping Co. v. Société Générale des Farines, 1992 REV. ARB. 656, and observations by D. Bureau; CA Paris, June 17, 1997, Eiffage v. Butec, which specifies that, in such a case, the non-compliance by the arbitrators with the provisions of the procedural law thus chosen does not constitute a ground for setting aside or refusing to enforce the award (1997 REV. ARB. 583, and observations by D. Bureau).

[64] *See, e.g.*, Fouchard, *supra* note 14, ¶ 25; Pierre Bellet and Ernst Mezger, *L'arbitrage international dans le nouveau code de procédure civile*, 1981 REV. CRIT. DIP 611.

1202. — Article 1494, paragraph 1 is particularly important for the wide-ranging freedom it confers on the parties. It treats the idea of submitting the procedure to a particular law as simply one of a number of options. The parties can also choose to marry principles drawn from several national laws, selecting and combining them however they see fit. They may also submit procedural issues to rules of law other than those of a particular legal system, such as procedural principles shared by several legal systems, general procedural principles common to most legal systems, or *lex mercatoria*.[65] The parties are also entitled to resolve all procedural issues themselves, in their arbitration agreement. French international arbitration law thus gives them total freedom to "invent their procedure."[66] In practice, the parties usually confine themselves to referring to the provisions of a set of arbitration rules,[67] as suggested by Article 1494 of the New Code of Civil Procedure. That reference is sometimes implicit: for example, it is generally implicit in institutional arbitration that the rules of a chosen institution will govern the arbitration.[68] The reference to arbitration rules will need to be explicit where the parties want to apply *ad hoc* arbitration rules such as the UNCITRAL Rules. Armed with the freedom conferred on them by French law, the parties can even allow the arbitrators simply to seek guidance from a particular law or set of rules, without having to apply its provisions to the letter. This approach is also found in Swiss law, and the expressions "rules of reference" or "law of reference" are used in such circumstances.[69]

B. – CHOICE MADE BY THE ARBITRATORS

1203. — French law is equally liberal in the absence of a choice of procedural law made by the parties. Article 1494, paragraph 2 of the French New Code of Civil Procedure provides only that, in the absence of any indication as to the parties' intentions, "the arbitrator shall determine the procedure, if need be, either directly or by reference to a law or to arbitration rules." The arbitrators are thus given the same freedom of choice as the parties. Like the parties, they may choose a particular national law, combine several national laws, refer to supra-national principles or to a set of arbitration rules, or simply select "rules

---

[65] Among those principles, it was held, for example, that the parties "are obliged to co-operate in the production of evidence, particularly in arbitration" (ICC Award No. 1434 (1975), Multinational group A v. State B, 103 J.D.I. 978 (1976), and observations by Y. Derains); ICC Award No. 3410, unpublished, cited by Sigvard Jarvin, *The sources and limits of the arbitrator's powers*, 2 ARB. INT'L 140, 151 (1986). On an agreement regarding the duty not to aggravate existing disputes, see the December 21, 1994 Procedural Order in ICC Case No. 8238, 123 J.D.I. 1063 (1996), and observations by D. Hascher. Similarly, the requirement that a party have standing has been presented as a general procedural principle (*see* ICC Award No. 7155 (1993), Norwegian company v. Three French companies, 123 J.D.I. 1037 (1996), and observations by J.-J. Arnaldez). For a general presentation of these principles, see MATTHIEU DE BOISSÉSON, LE DROIT FRANÇAIS DE L'ARBITRAGE INTERNE ET INTERNATIONAL ¶¶ 714 *et seq.* (2d ed. 1990).

[66] Goldman, *supra* note 28, at 474.

[67] See the observations by G. Muller, sole arbitrator, in ICC Award No. 5505 (1987), Buyer from Mozambique v. Seller from the Netherlands, XIII Y.B. COM. ARB. 110, 115 (1988).

[68] *See supra* paras. 321 *et seq.*

[69] *See, e.g.*, LALIVE, POUDRET, REYMOND, *supra* note 6, at 352.

of reference" or a "law of reference."[70] They are also entitled to make no choice until such time as a particular procedural difficulty needs to be resolved. Alternatively, they can confine themselves to stating that they will determine, to the extent necessary, the rules governing the arbitral procedure. In this context, French international arbitration law clearly endorses the theory of a contract with no governing law ("*contrat sans loi*"), and allows the arbitrators to take "decisions" on a case-by-case basis, rather than lay down "rules" of general application.[71]

1204. — The extremely liberal position of French law with regard to the discretion available to both the parties and the arbitrators has been the subject of some criticism. Certain commentators have described it as "cosmopolitan liberalism" likely to increase "legal uncertainty in international commerce."[72] We believe that such concerns are unjustified. The absolute freedom conferred on the parties and the arbitrators in determining—or even creating—the arbitral procedure has to be judged in the light of the constraints resulting from the regime covering actions to set aside or resist enforcement of the award.[73] The rule which grants the parties and the arbitrators full autonomy can therefore be considered a substantive rule allowing absolute discretion.[74] However, full court control returns in the form of the application of procedural public policy in jurisdictions where actions lie to set aside or resist enforcement of the award. The liberal approach adopted in French law is accordingly less radical than it may seem. Only the method has changed. In French and other modern laws, as well as in the more recent international conventions, this new-found liberalism is invariably allied to the requirement of compliance with principles essential to the proper administration of justice, including the principles of equal treatment of the parties, due process and, more generally, international procedural public policy.

Courts with jurisdiction over actions to set aside or resist enforcement of an award generally confine themselves to ensuring that there is compliance with such principles and with their understanding of international procedural public policy.[75] International arbitrators, who by definition are independent of any legal system, will take those principles into account as part of their own conception of truly international public policy, and practical considerations based on the efficacy of the award ought not, in our opinion, prevail over the arbitrators' own sense of the fundamental requirements of procedural justice.[76]

---

[70] *See supra* para. 1202.

[71] On these notions, see especially PIERRE MAYER, LA DISTINCTION ENTRE RÈGLES ET DÉCISIONS ET LE DROIT INTERNATIONAL PRIVÉ (1973).

[72] *See* Bellet and Mezger, *supra* note 64, at 621.

[73] *See supra* paras. 1193 *et seq.*

[74] *See* JEAN-MICHEL JACQUET, PRINCIPE D'AUTONOMIE ET CONTRATS INTERNATIONAUX (1983).

[75] *See infra* para. 1638.

[76] On the potential conflict between the concern that the award be effective and the arbitrators' conception of truly international public policy, see *supra* para. 1195 and the references cited therein.

§ 3. – The Consequences of the Determination of the Law Governing the Arbitral Procedure

1205. — The consequences of the determination of the law governing the arbitral procedure go beyond simply providing the parties and the arbitrators with a body of rules enabling all procedural issues arising in the course of the arbitration to be resolved.

In some cases, the choice of a procedural law also has an impact on the jurisdiction of the courts which may be involved in constituting the arbitral tribunal and, in some legal systems, reviewing the award. However, these indirect consequences have diminished, without disappearing altogether, in modern arbitration legislation. This is a welcome development, as the law governing the arbitral procedure, where there is one,[77] is a highly artificial means of connecting an arbitration to a legal system.

1206. — In some jurisdictions, access to the courts to obtain assistance in constituting the arbitral tribunal still depends on the choice of procedural law. In most legal systems, that assistance depends solely on the location of the seat of the arbitration.[78] French law gives wider access to its courts, by providing that they will have jurisdiction to resolve difficulties concerning the constitution of the arbitral tribunal not only if the seat is in France, but also, irrespective of the location of the seat, if French law has been chosen to govern the arbitral procedure.[79] It is therefore only where the arbitration agreement has no connection with French law, in that it neither locates the seat in France nor provides that French law will govern the procedure, that the French courts will refuse to assist in the constitution of the arbitral tribunal.[80] Other recent statutes, such as the 1996 English Arbitration Act (Section 2(4)) and the German Arbitration Statute of December 22, 1997 (Art. 1025 ZPO) either require, using general terms, some form of connection with the jurisdiction (as in England), or base the jurisdiction of the courts on the place of business or habitual residence of the parties. Neither statute refers to the law chosen to govern the arbitral procedure.

1207. — An increasingly small number of legal systems connect the procedural law, as well as the seat of the arbitration, to the "nationality of the award," which in turn triggers jurisdiction over actions to set the award aside.

This was the case, as regards actions against awards, in French law prior to the 1981 reform. An award made in an arbitration governed by French law could thus be considered a "French" award, and as such it would be governed by the rules applicable to actions to set aside or resist enforcement of awards made in France.[81] Conversely, the connection between the choice of a procedural law and the "nationality" of the award led the French courts to

---

[77] On the freedom of the parties and the arbitrators to refrain from determining a procedural law, see *supra* para. 1197.

[78] *See, e.g.*, Art. 11(3) of the UNCITRAL Model Law and Art. 176, para. 1 of the Swiss Private International Law Statute.

[79] Art. 1493, para. 2 of the New Code of Civil Procedure. *See supra* paras. 832 *et seq.*

[80] On this issue, see *supra* para. 839 and, on the situation in other legal systems, see *supra* para. 916.

[81] *See* E. Loquin, note following Cass. 1e civ., Mar. 18, 1980, *Compagnie d'Armement Maritime*, *supra* note 5.

refuse to hear actions against awards made in France in an international arbitration for which no procedural law had been chosen.[82] Happily, the 1981 reform of French international arbitration law now dissociates these issues and ensures that the choice of a procedural law will have no impact on actions to set aside or enforce the award, which now depend exclusively on the location of the seat of the arbitration.[83] Similarly, the reform of English arbitration law in 1996 reversed the previous case law of the House of Lords which had held the jurisdiction of the English courts to hear an action to set aside to be dependent upon the choice of English law as that governing the arbitral procedure.[84] German law has evolved in a similar fashion. Prior to the December 1997 reform, the nationality of the award and, as a result, jurisdiction over actions to set aside were dependent on the law governing the arbitral procedure.[85] This has also been changed by Article 1025, paragraph 1 of the ZPO, which provides that the new statute shall apply where the seat of the arbitration is in Germany.[86]

1208. — The New York Convention, which governs the recognition and enforcement of "foreign awards," also frames the issue in terms of the "nationality of the award," raising a question as to whether that nationality depends solely on the seat of the arbitration, or whether it can also result from the choice of a procedural law. By stating that it applies not only to awards made in the territory of countries other than that where recognition and enforcement are sought, but also to "arbitral awards not considered as domestic awards in the State where their recognition and enforcement are sought" (Art. I(1), *in fine*), the Convention provides no uniform answer to this question. Legal systems where, for the purpose of determining the jurisdiction of the courts to hear actions to set aside, the "nationality of the award" depends on the choice of a procedural law should logically adopt

---

[82] *See* CA Paris, Feb. 21, 1980, *Götaverken, supra* note 8; CA Paris, Dec. 9, 1980, Aksa v. Norsolor, 1981 REV. ARB. 306, and F.C. Jeantet's note; 1981 REV. CRIT. DIP 545, and E. Mezger's note; for an English translation, see 20 I.L.M. 887 (1981).

[83] *See infra* para. 1593.

[84] *See* Hiscox v. Outhwaite, (No. 1) [1992] 1 A.C. 562; [1991] 3 All E.R. 641; [1991] 3 W.L.R. 297; [1991] 2 Lloyd's Rep. 435; XVII Y.B. COM. ARB. 599 (1992) (H.L. 1991); see also the disapproving commentary by Claude Reymond, *Where is an arbitral award made?*, 108 L.Q. REV. 1 (1992); the disapproving observations by Albert Jan van den Berg, *New York Convention of 1958 – Consolidated Commentary – Cases Reported in Volumes XVII (1992) – XIX (1994)*, XIX Y.B. COM. ARB. 475, 483 (1994); Albert Jan van den Berg, *New York Arbitration Convention 1958: Where is an arbitral award "made"? Case comment House of Lords, 24 July 1991, Hiscox v. Outhwaite, in* THE PLACE OF ARBITRATION 113 (M. Storme and F. de Ly eds., 1992); Michael E. Schneider, *L'arrêt de la Chambre des Lords dans l'affaire Hiscox v. Outhwaite*, 1991 BULL. ASA 279. *See also infra* para. 1593.

[85] *See* Article 2 of the Law Concerning the Convention of June 10, 1958 on the Recognition and Enforcement of Foreign Arbitral Awards v. March 15, 1961 (BGBl.II S. 121). *See also* J. Van Compernolle, *L'arbitrage dans les relations commerciales internationales: questions de procédure*, 1989 REV. DR. INT. DR. COMP. 101.

[86] *See* Peter Schlosser, *La nouvelle législation allemande sur l'arbitrage*, 1998 REV. ARB. 291; Klaus Peter Berger, *Germany Adopts the UNCITRAL Model Law*, 1 INT'L ARB. L. REV. 121 (1998); Karl-Heinz Böckstiegel, *An Introduction to the New German Arbitration Act Based on the UNCITRAL Model Law*, 14 ARB. INT'L 19, 23 (1998).

the same approach in applying the New York Convention.[87] Prior to the 1981 reform, the French courts took that view,[88] which was rightly criticized.[89] By opting for the criterion of the seat of the arbitration, the 1981 reform definitively resolved the question. Similarly, prior to the December 1997 reform, German law based the nationality of the award for the purposes of the application of the New York Convention on the choice of procedural law, but that approach was reversed by the new arbitration statute.

---

[87] See the references cited *supra* para. 1207.

[88] *See* CA Paris, Feb. 21, 1980, *Götaverken*, *supra* note 8.

[89] *See* P. Fouchard, note following CA Paris, Feb. 21, 1980, *Götaverken*, *supra* note 8, at 672 *et seq.*; VAN DEN BERG, *supra* note 32, at 20 *et seq*

CHAPTER II
THE ARBITRAL PROCEEDINGS

1209. — Following the chronological sequence of a typical international arbitration,[1] we shall examine the commencement (Section I) and the organization (Section II) of the arbitral proceedings before considering the parties' pleadings and evidence (Section III).

SECTION I
COMMENCEMENT OF THE ARBITRAL PROCEEDINGS

1210. — Although default by one of the parties generally does not give rise to the application of a specific procedure governed by its own set of rules, it does constitute a sufficiently serious incident to warrant being considered separately from adversarial proceedings with all parties present. We shall therefore examine adversarial proceedings and default proceedings in turn.

---

[1] On the proceedings in ICC arbitration, see Marc Blessing, *The ICC Arbitral Procedure Under the 1998 ICC Rules – What Has Changed?*, ICC BULLETIN, Vol. 8, No. 2, at 16 (1997); Horacio A. Grigera Naon, *The Appendixes to the 1998 ICC Arbitration Rules*, ICC BULLETIN, Vol. 8, No. 2, at 37 (1997); Andreas Reiner, *Le règlement d'arbitrage de la CCI, version 1998*, 1998 REV. ARB. 25; Herman Verbist and Christophe Imhoos, *The New 1998 ICC Rules of Arbitration/Le nouveau Règlement d'arbitrage de la Chambre de Commerce Internationale de 1998*, 1997 INT'L BUS. L.J. 989; YVES DERAINS AND ERIC A. SCHWARTZ, A GUIDE TO THE NEW ICC RULES OF ARBITRATION 197 *et seq.* (1998).

§ 1. – Adversarial Proceedings

1211. — An arbitration will generally be commenced[2] by a request for arbitration, followed by an answer, enabling each of the parties to present its initial claims.

A. – THE REQUEST FOR ARBITRATION

1212. — As noted in one French decision,

> the purpose of a request for arbitration, which is delivered by one party to the other, is to inform the latter that its co-contractor intends to resort to arbitration, and to give notice to the other party to appoint its arbitrator and to set out its position in the proceedings.[3]

1° Form and Content of the Request

1213. — French international arbitration law contains no mandatory requirements as to the form of the request for arbitration. For there to be such a request, a party must simply give an unequivocal indication of its intention to initiate legal proceedings. However, that indication must be sufficiently explicit, as the Paris Court of Appeals held in a 1986 decision stating that the mere mention of an intention to make a claim "to be evaluated subsequently . . . conveys a sense of contingency excluding any actual manifestation of an intention to initiate legal proceedings."[4]

---

[2] On the argument put forward in some cases that an attempt at conciliation must be made before arbitration can begin, see, for example, the October 27, 1989 *ad hoc* Award by S. Schwebel, chairman, D. Wallace and M. Leigh, arbitrators, Biloune v. Ghana Investment Centre, which held such a condition to be satisfied (XIX Y.B. COM. ARB. 11 (1994), especially ¶ 2 at 14); the Interim Award of July 17, 1992 and the Final Award of July 13, 1993 made under the auspices of the Stockholm Chamber of Commerce, Licensor and buyer v. Manufacturer, XXII Y.B. COM. ARB. 197 (1997); the *ad hoc* Award rendered in Geneva on October 13, 1997, by Messrs. Faurès, chairman, Hirsch and Veeder, arbitrators, Cayman Islands company v. African state, unpublished. On the consequences of non-compliance, in French domestic law, see Cass. com., Nov. 28, 1995, Peyrin v. Polyclinique des Fleurs, 1996 REV. ARB. 613, and C. Jarrosson's note. For an example of the requirement for preliminary conciliation through prayer, see Performance Unlimited, Inc. v. Questar Publishers, Inc., 52 F.3d 1373 (6th Cir. 1995); 6 WORLD ARB. & MED. REP. 130 (1995).

[3] CA Paris, Feb. 5, 1980, Intertradex v. L.B.S., 1980 REV. ARB. 519, 521.

[4] CA Paris, 1e Ch., Sec. Supp., Jan. 16, 1986, Europmarkets v. Argolicos Gulf Shipping Co., No. L 12357; unpublished, cited by MATTHIEU DE BOISSÉSON, LE DROIT FRANÇAIS DE L'ARBITRAGE INTERNE ET INTERNATIONAL ¶ 727 at 702 (2d. ed. 1990). The fact that the claim here was a counterclaim does not affect the principle. See also, in Swedish law, the requirement that the request for arbitration include "an express and unconditional regard for arbitration" (Sec. 19, para. 2 of the 1999 Arbitration Act).

However, any conditions of form agreed by the parties, directly or by reference to institutional arbitration rules, must be enforced by the arbitrators.[5] The same is true of any statements or documents to be submitted with the request. For example, the ICC Rules of Arbitration require the parties to submit, together with their request for arbitration, a statement of claim and evidential documents establishing, in particular, the existence of the arbitration agreement.[6] Other institutional rules allow the parties to confine themselves, initially at least, to a statement of claim alone.[7]

2° Time Limits

1214. — The request for arbitration must be sent to the other party or parties directly by the claimant or, if its rules so provide, by the arbitral institution. The time limits for submitting a claim, and likewise the applicable conditions of form, are determined by the arbitration agreement and by any rules which the parties may have incorporated in it by reference. The ICC Rules provide no time limit for the submission of claims, as is confirmed in arbitral case law.[8]

1215. — The French courts have sometimes been very flexible in interpreting the time limits set forth in institutional rules. This is illustrated in a decision of the Paris Court of Appeals in a case concerning the Rules of the Paris Arbitration Chamber, which stipulated that any claim not received by the Secretariat of the Chamber within a certain period would be void. In this case, the arbitrators disregarded a failure to meet that deadline, on the grounds that "the delay did not deprive the defendant company of the opportunity to present its claims and to be accurately informed of the claimant's case against it." The Court of Appeals declined to set the award aside.[9]

---

[5] For an example of the application of rules requiring notification by registered mail, see CA Paris, Jan. 17, 1992, Guangzhou Ocean Shipping Co. v. Société Générale des Farines, 1992 REV. ARB. 656, and observations by D. Bureau.

[6] *See* Art. 4(3) of the Rules, replacing Art. 3(2) of the previous Rules. On the content of the Request in ICC Arbitration, see DERAINS AND SCHWARTZ, *supra* note 1, at 51 *et seq.* (1998); Blessing, *supra* note 1, at 16 *et seq.*; Reiner, *supra* note 1, at 28 *et seq.* On the absence of formalism in ICC arbitration and the fact, in particular, that the request for arbitration need not be signed, see ICC Award No. 6228 (1990), ICC BULLETIN, Vol. 8, No. 1, at 54 (1997); ICC Award No. 6784 (1990), *id.*

[7] Art. 1.1(c) of the 1998 LCIA Rules; Art. 2(3) of the 1997 AAA International Arbitration Rules. On the changes resulting from the revision of the ICC Rules in 1998, see Reiner, *supra* note 1, especially at 28 *et seq.*; on the diversity of national practices, not all of which require the parties to set out all their legal and factual arguments in their first submission, see PIERRE LALIVE, JEAN-FRANÇOIS POUDRET, CLAUDE REYMOND, LE DROIT DE L'ARBITRAGE INTERNE ET INTERNATIONAL EN SUISSE 356–57 (1989). The ICC Rules do not go so far: although they give certain deadlines for new claims, they do not prevent the parties from raising new factual or legal arguments during the arbitral proceedings. *See infra* para. 1233.

[8] *See, e.g.*, ICC Award No. 2626 (1977), German company v. Italian company, 105 J.D.I. 980 (1978), and observations by Y. Derains. The same solution would be reached under the 1998 Rules.

[9] CA Paris, Nov. 15, 1979, Saronis Shipping Co. v. Soules, 1980 REV. ARB. 513, and J. Viatte's note.

Nevertheless, as a general rule, arbitrators will ensure that deadlines stipulated by the parties are complied with, and the courts will not set aside or refuse to enforce the arbitrators' award for having done so.[10]

1216. — Compliance with time limits fixed by the parties, directly or by reference to institutional rules, for the submission of a request for arbitration will not affect the fact that the request may be declared inadmissible for non-compliance with the requirements of the law governing the substance of the contract.[11] A typical example will be where the law governing a contract for the sale of goods provides that actions in respect of latent defects must be brought within a certain time limit. Apart from complying with the relevant procedural rules, arbitrators hearing a dispute arising from such a contract must, when ruling on the merits of the dispute, act on a failure to meet those deadlines by applying the consequences of that failure as prescribed by the law governing the contract.[12]

3° Receipt

1217. — Receipt of the request by the other party or parties generally marks the start of the period of time within which an answer must be filed. The duration of that period is fixed either by the parties' agreement, or by any relevant arbitration rules, or by the law governing the procedure. Receipt of the request sometimes marks the formal commencement of the arbitral proceedings.[13] In some legal systems, if an application is made to the courts in connection with the same issues, the courts will only decline jurisdiction if the request for

---

[10] See, for example, CA Paris, Jan. 16, 1986, *Europmarkets, supra* note 4, in a case where a counterclaim was "declared out of time because it was made after the expiration of the contractual deadline." See also, in French domestic arbitration, CA Paris, Jan. 24, 1992, Ferruzzi v. Ucacel, 1992 REV. ARB. 640, and observations by J. Pellerin, *aff'd*, Cass. 2e civ., Jan. 26, 1994, 1994 Bull. Civ. II, No. 38, at 21; 1995 REV. ARB. 443.

[11] *See also* Y. Derains, observations following ICC Award No. 2626 (1977), *supra* note 8, at 984.

[12] For an illustration of this rule, see the May 27, 1980 Award of the Arbitration Court of the Chamber of Commerce and Industry of Czechoslovakia, Austrian buyer v. Czechoslovak foreign trade company, XI Y.B. COM. ARB. 114 (1986); the June 20, 1980 Award by the Netherlands Oils, Fats and Oilseeds Trade Association, Argentinian seller v. German buyer, VI Y.B. COM. ARB. 144 (1981); on the question of time limits laid down by the procedural law, see the October 25, 1972 Award of the Court of Arbitration at the Bulgarian Chamber of Commerce and Industry in Case No. 40/1972, Bulgarian State enterprise v. Lebanese enterprise, IV Y.B. COM. ARB. 190 (1979); on the admissibility of a request for arbitration that did not comply with certain requirements of the FIDIC Conditions, see ICC Awards No. 3790 (1983), French contractor v. Libyan owner, 110 J.D.I. 910 (1983), and observations by S. Jarvin, for an English translation, see XI Y.B. COM. ARB. 119 (1986); No. 5600 (1987), ICC BULLETIN, Vol. 2, No. 1, at 16 (1991); No. 5634 (1987), ICC BULLETIN, Vol. 2, No. 1, at 19 (1991); No. 6216 (1989), ICC BULLETIN, Vol. 2, No. 1, at 25 (1991).

[13] See, for example, Article 21 of the UNCITRAL Model Law which provides that "[u]nless otherwise agreed by the parties, the arbitral proceedings . . . commence on the date on which a request . . . is received by the respondent." This provision is transposed into German law at Article 1044 of the ZPO (Law of Dec. 22, 1997). In ICC arbitration, it is on the date of receipt of the request by the ICC Secretariat that the arbitration begins (Art. 4(2) of the 1998 Rules). On this issue, see DERAINS AND SCHWARTZ, *supra* note 1, at 50 *et seq.*

arbitration has been received.[14] The date of receipt can also affect the merits of the dispute. For example, it is not uncommon for arbitrators to decide that interest will accrue on sums awarded to a party with effect from the date on which the request for arbitration was received, thus ensuring that the burden of the duration of the arbitration will not be borne by that party.

4° Amending the Request

1218. — Whether the claimant will be entitled to modify its initial claim during the course of the proceedings depends on the agreement between the parties or the applicable arbitration rules.[15]

The ICC Rules seek to limit the introduction of new claims after the terms of reference have been drawn up.[16] However, a request for ICC Arbitration may be amended at any time prior to the terms of reference, unless a new party is introduced by that amendment. If a new party is introduced by that amendment, due process requires that the amended request be considered an entirely new request, causing the original deadlines for the filing of the answer to run again.[17] In the absence of the kind of provision found in ICC arbitration, the parties can modify their claims throughout the arbitral proceedings, although the arbitral tribunal may set a deadline beyond which no new claims will be admissible. Such an approach is preferable to that found in Article 23, paragraph 2 of the UNCITRAL Model Law, whereby both the claimant and the defendant can modify or add to their claims throughout the arbitral proceedings, although the arbitral tribunal will be entitled to reject a new or modified claim "having regard to the delay in making it."[18] This assessment, after the fact, of the reasons why a party failed to present all of its claims at the outset is liable to give rise to serious unpredictability. The parties' reasons may vary considerably, from poor organization to the desire to avoid aggravating the dispute in the hope of reaching a settlement, and they will always be difficult to evaluate. It is therefore preferable for the arbitrators themselves to determine in advance a date beyond which claims may no longer be amended unless there are serious grounds for disregarding that deadline.

5° Who is the Claimant?

1219. — In some cases, both parties hope to gain the psychological advantage—real or imagined—of being the claimant in the dispute, and thus to benefit from the procedural

---

[14] On Iraqi law, see Hans van Houtte, *Conduct of the Arbitral Proceedings, in* ESSAYS ON INTERNATIONAL COMMERCIAL ARBITRATION 113, 120 (P. Sarcevic ed., 1989).

[15] On this issue, generally, see François Perret, *Les conclusions et les chefs de demande dans l'arbitrage international*, 1996 BULL. ASA 7.

[16] *See* Art. 19 of the 1998 Rules (replacing Art. 16 of the previous Rules). *See also infra* para. 1233.

[17] *See* DERAINS AND SCHWARTZ, *supra* note 1, at 57–58.

[18] *See also* Art. 4 of the 1997 AAA International Arbitration Rules.

consequences of that status (such as the right to file pleadings before the defendant). This has sometimes led to arbitrations where there is neither a claimant nor a defendant, with all parties simultaneously submitting their claims and then simultaneously responding to the claims made against them. This happened in the *Government of Kuwait v. Aminoil* case.[19] Despite what has sometimes been suggested,[20] a simultaneous exchange of memorials is in no way contrary to the principle of due process, provided that the parties remain entitled to reply.[21] However, this method does run the risk of making the parties' written submissions more difficult to confront, and it should only be adopted under particular circumstances or where the parties so agree. Furthermore, a successive exchange should not be interpreted as suggesting that a counterclaim is, by definition, less credible than a principal claim.

1220. — Another problem may arise where an award made in an initial arbitral proceeding has been set aside and the defendant in the initial proceeding starts a second round of proceedings, purporting to be the claimant. In such circumstances, however, as the setting aside of the award does not affect the existence of the initial request for arbitration, the respective positions of the parties should remain unchanged.

B. – THE ANSWER TO THE REQUEST FOR ARBITRATION

1221. — In its answer, the defendant will be able to counter the claimant's request with arguments of all kinds (including absence of jurisdiction, inadmissibility and defenses on the merits).

1222. — The defendant will also be able to enter a counterclaim, within the conditions and time limits stipulated in the parties' agreement or in any applicable rules. Generally, there is no requirement that there be a connection between the principal claim and the counterclaim, provided that the latter is based on the same arbitration agreement as the former.

The 1965 Washington Convention, establishing ICSID, is now virtually alone in stipulating that incidental and additional claims, as well as counterclaims, must arise "directly out of the subject-matter of the dispute" (Art. 46) in order for the arbitral tribunal

---

[19] *See* the March 24, 1982 *ad hoc* Award by P. Reuter, chairman, H. Sultan and G. Fitzmaurice, arbitrators, The Government of the State of Kuwait v. The American Independent Oil Co. (AMINOIL), 21 I.L.M. 976 (1982); IX Y.B. COM. ARB. 71 (1984); for a French translation, see 109 J.D.I. 869 (1982), and the commentary by Philippe Kahn, *Contrats d'Etat et nationalisation, id.* at 844. *See also* Pierre-Yves Tschanz, *The Contributions of the Aminoil Award to the Law of State Contracts,* 18 INT'L LAW. 245 (1984).

[20] *See, e.g.,* Eugen Bucher, *Die Schweiz als traditioneller Sitzort internationaler Schiedsgerichte, in* DIE INTERNATIONALE SCHIEDSGERICHTSBARKEIT IN DER SCHWEIZ, Vol. 2, at 119, 129 (K.-H. Böckstiegel ed., 1989).

[21] *See* LALIVE, POUDRET, REYMOND, *supra* note 7, at 358; in French law, see CA Paris, June 21, 1990, Compagnie Honeywell Bull S.A. v. Computacion Bull de Venezuela C.A., 1991 REV. ARB. 96, and J.-L. Delvolvé's note. It does not violate due process to allow memorials to be filed otherwise than at the same time, enabling one party to have the last word. As held by the Paris Court of Appeals in its decision of June 21, 1990, "one of the parties [must] bring the procedure to an end, as in any litigation" (*id.* at 99).

to be required to hear them. This approach is somewhat unsatisfactory, because in theory it may oblige a party with a claim who receives a request for arbitration based on a particular arbitration agreement to submit another request for arbitration, which is likely to come before different arbitrators, despite the fact that it is based on the same arbitration agreement. In practice, it is to be hoped that arbitrators—who decide their own jurisdiction and the admissibility of claims submitted to them—will interpret this requirement with sufficient flexibility to avoid such results. Indeed, it is fair to assume that any claim based on a contract which has already given rise to a claim by another party will, by definition, be held to be directly related to the earlier claim.

The time limit within which a counterclaim must be filed will not necessarily coincide with the deadline fixed by the parties or by the institutional rules for principal claims. A party may choose not to bring a principal claim, but if its opponent enters a claim against it, the first party will still be able to present its case in the form of a counterclaim.[22] However, in ICC arbitration, there are limits as to when a counterclaim can be submitted: under Article 5(5) of the ICC Rules, it must be filed at the same time as the answer to the request for arbitration. This rule may seem harsh, but it is designed to speed up the proceedings. Also it is standard ICC practice to qualify the rule by admitting additional claims or counterclaims at any time until the signature of the terms of reference. This rule was developed on the basis of Article 13, paragraph 1 of the previous Rules, which provided that the terms of reference were to be defined "in the light of [the parties'] most recent submissions."[23] The same rule applies under the 1998 Rules, as the language of Article 13, paragraph 1 has been incorporated in the new Article 18, paragraph 1, with the same meaning.[24] By contrast, the LCIA Rules allow a party to wait until it submits its statement of defense to file any counterclaim (Art. 15.3).

1223. — There is great controversy as to whether the defendant can join a party other than that which submitted the request for arbitration. For example, the contract containing the arbitration agreement may have been signed by more than two parties, without determining how a multi-party arbitration would be organized.[25] The party which is put in the position of defendant by the initial claimant may have an interest in suing another party to the arbitration agreement. It may, for example, wish to seek redress from that third party for its failure to perform, call a guarantee provided by it, or simply raise new claims against it. Under those circumstances, is the defendant entitled to submit a claim in the same arbitral proceedings, or is it required to commence separate proceedings? If separate proceedings are needed, there will be a risk that a different arbitral tribunal will be constituted and that contradictory awards may result. The injustice of such an outcome is all the more severe for

---

[22] *See* ALAN REDFERN AND MARTIN HUNTER, LAW AND PRACTICE OF INTERNATIONAL COMMERCIAL ARBITRATION 319 *et seq.* (2d ed. 1991).

[23] *See infra* para. 1233.

[24] *See* DERAINS AND SCHWARTZ, *supra* note 1, at 72–73.

[25] On the different issue of the extension of the effects of the arbitration agreement to non-signatories of that agreement, see *supra* paras. 498 *et seq.* On the other aspects of multiparty arbitration, and for a bibliography, see *supra* paras. 385 and 521.

the fact that the parties will all have signed the same arbitration agreement. This suggests that all of the issues should be decided by the same arbitral tribunal, whenever it is not incompatible with the requirement of equality between the parties in the constitution of the arbitral tribunal. That requirement would not be met were the third party obliged to accept the choice of arbitrators made by the first two parties.[26] Under French law, that problem can be resolved at the time the arbitral tribunal is constituted, as any party is entitled to apply to the President of the Paris Tribunal of First Instance in connection with difficulties concerning the constitution of the arbitral tribunal, under Article 1493 of the New Code of Civil Procedure. The judge would then have to reconcile the principle of equality between the parties with the fact that they have all signed the same arbitration agreement, even if that entails appointing a sole arbitrator or all three arbitrators. On the other hand, contrary to what has sometimes been suggested, this problem clearly cannot be resolved by simply allowing a "counterclaim" to be filed by the defendant against the third party.[27] Nothing in the 1998 ICC Rules will change this situation, as Article 4(6) only allows consolidation of arbitrations between the same parties, subject to certain conditions.[28]

§ 2. – Default Proceedings

1224. — Certain legal systems, such as that of France, contain no provisions specifically governing default proceedings. Nevertheless, two general principles necessarily apply.[29]

First, default does not constitute an admission of liability and does not automatically validate the arguments of the claimant. Without going so far as acting as advocate for the defaulting party, the arbitral tribunal must examine the merits of the claimant's legal and factual arguments.[30] This rule is clearly stated in the 1965 Washington Convention, establishing ICSID. Article 45, paragraph 1 of the Convention provides that "failure of a party to appear or to present his case shall not be deemed an admission of the other party's assertions." The UNCITRAL Model Law,[31] following the UNCITRAL Rules of Arbitration,

---

[26] For a similar scenario where two co-defendants were obliged to appoint one arbitrator together, see Cass. 1e civ., Jan. 7, 1992, B.K.M.I v. Dutco, 1992 Bull. Civ. I, No. 2; 1992 REV. ARB. 470, and P. Bellet's note; 119 J.D.I. 707 (1992), 2d decision, and C. Jarrosson's note; 1992 RTD COM. 796, and observations by J.-C. Dubarry and E. Loquin; for an English translation, see XVIII Y.B. COM. ARB. 140 (1993); 7 INT'L ARB. REP. B1 (Feb. 1992).

[27] On this issue, generally, compare with DE BOISSÉSON *supra* note 4, ¶ 610 and the discussion held under the auspices of the International Law Association in Helsinki, 1996 REV. ARB. 563, and observations by E. Gaillard; Patrice Level, *Joinder of Proceedings, Intervention of Third Parties, and Additional Claims and Counterclaims*, ICC BULLETIN, Vol. 7, No. 2, at 36 (1996); on set-off issues, see Klaus Peter Berger, *Set-Off in International Economic Arbitration*, 15 ARB. INT'L 53 (1999).

[28] *See supra* para. 521.

[29] On this issue, generally, see Daniel E. Tunik, *Default Proceedings in International Commercial Arbitration*, 1 INT'L ARB. L. REV. 86 (1998).

[30] *See* REDFERN AND HUNTER, *supra* note 22, at 268 *et seq.*; DE BOISSÉSON, *supra* note 4, ¶ 789 at 796.

[31] Art. 25: "Unless otherwise agreed by the parties, if, without sufficient cause, . . . (b) the respondent fails to communicate his statement of defense [within the applicable deadlines], the arbitral tribunal shall continue the

(continued...)

takes the same position, as does arbitral case law.[32] The 1996 English Arbitration Act invites the arbitrators in the case of default by one party to "make an award on the basis of the evidence before [them]" (Sec. 41(4)). It also allows the arbitral tribunal to take a rather radical step where the plaintiff is found to be prosecuting its claim with "inordinate and inexcusable delay": it may "mak[e] an award dismissing the claim" (Sec. 41(3)).

The second governing principle is that default by a party must not paralyze or even slow the progress of the arbitral proceedings. The arbitrators must go forward despite the absence of the defaulting party. In order to satisfy the requirements of due process, all that is necessary is that the defaulting party be notified of the commencement of the arbitral proceedings and of the progress thereof, and be given an opportunity to present its case at each stage of the proceedings.[33] If the defendant then fails to appear at any stage of the proceedings or, indeed, at all,[34] a default award can be made against it.[35] As noted earlier, a default award has more serious consequences than a default judgment made by a court, because it is generally not open to appeal or other recourse and, once they have made their award, the arbitrators no longer have jurisdiction over the dispute.[36] Nevertheless, a party cannot simply refuse to participate in proceedings so as to obstruct the arbitration. Again, the Washington Convention articulates this widely-accepted rule as follows: "if a party fails to appear or to present his case at any stage of the proceedings the other party may request the Tribunal to deal with the questions submitted to it and to render an award."[37] Similarly, Article 25 of the UNCITRAL Model Law, followed in this respect by the 1996 English Arbitration Act (Sec. 41(4)), also provides that if a party fails to appear without showing sufficient cause, "the arbitral tribunal may continue the proceedings and make the award on

---

[31]   (...continued)
   proceedings without treating such failure in itself as an admission of the claimant's allegations." In German Law, see Article 1048(2) of the ZPO, in force as of January 1, 1998.

[32]   *See, e.g.*, ICC Award No. 6670 (1992), Financial institution based in France v. Two companies, 119 J.D.I. 1010 (1992), and observations by J.-J. Arnaldez; ICC Award No. 7153 (1992), Austrian party v. Yugoslavian party, 119 J.D.I. 1005 (1992), and observations by D. Hascher; ICC Award No. 7701 (1994), ICC BULLETIN, Vol. 8, No. 2, at 66 (1997).

[33]   On these issues, see Emmanuel Gaillard, *Law and Court Decisions in Civil Law Countries, in* ICCA CONGRESS SERIES NO. 5, PREVENTING DELAY AND DISRUPTION OF ARBITRATION/EFFECTIVE PROCEEDINGS IN CONSTRUCTION CASES 106 (A.J. van den Berg ed., 1991).

[34]   The ICC Rules were modified in 1998 to reflect the fact that a party can default throughout the whole proceedings or at "any stage thereof." *See* DERAINS AND SCHWARTZ, *supra* note 1, at 102.

[35]   *See, e.g.*, CA Paris, Feb. 7, 1991, Dovert et Tabourdeau v. Confex, 1992 REV. ARB. 634, and observations by J. Pellerin; CA Paris, Mar. 24, 1995, Bin Saud Bin Abdel Aziz v. Crédit Industriel et Commercial de Paris, 1996 REV. ARB. 259, and J.-M. Talau's note.

[36]   *See* Stephen M. Schwebel and Susan G. Lahne, *Public Policy and Arbitral Procedure, in* ICCA CONGRESS SERIES No. 3, COMPARATIVE ARBITRATION PRACTICE AND PUBLIC POLICY IN ARBITRATION 205 (P. Sanders ed., 1987); Bernard Hanotiau, *Le défaut d'une partie dans la procédure d'arbitrage international, in* MÉLANGES OFFERTS À RAYMOND VANDER ELST, Vol. I, at 375 (1986).

[37]   Art. 45(2). On the application of these rules by ICSID arbitral tribunals, see, for example, the March 31, 1986 Award by B. Cremades, president, J. Goncalves Pereira and A. Redfern, arbitrators, in ICSID Case No. ARB/83/2 Liberian Eastern Timber Corp. v. The Government of the Republic of Liberia, 26 I.L.M. 647 (1987); XIII Y.B. COM. ARB. 35 (1988); 2 ICSID REP. 346 (1994); for a French translation, see 115 J.D.I. 166 (1988), and observations by E. Gaillard.

the evidence before it."[38] Most arbitration rules contain a similar provision.[39] Further, a party which initially defaulted may appear during the course of the proceedings, even without justifying its failure to appear at an earlier stage. However, due process does not require that the proceedings begin afresh. Provided that the defaulting party has been given the opportunity to participate in each of the previous stages of the arbitration, the requirements of due process and equal treatment of the parties will have been satisfied.[40]

SECTION II
ORGANIZATION OF THE ARBITRAL PROCEEDINGS

1225. — The commencement of the arbitral proceedings brings the claims of each party to the attention of the others. It also puts the constitution of the arbitral tribunal in motion and reveals any difficulties which may arise in the appointment of the arbitrators.[41] A number of procedural issues will also arise. Some are fundamental, such as the choice of the seat of the arbitration or the rules governing the hearing of witnesses. Others are of lesser importance, such as the place where the hearings are to be held or where the evidence of witnesses is to be taken. All these issues must be determined by agreement between the parties or, failing such agreement, by the arbitral tribunal.

1226. — Along with many other legal systems, French law allows the arbitral tribunal to resolve such issues as and when they arise, unless the parties agree otherwise.[42] The tribunal will do so by taking administrative measures often referred to as procedural orders. Provided that they do not decide any substantive aspect of the dispute, these decisions or orders do not constitute arbitral awards and therefore cannot be the subject of an action to set aside.[43] It is common practice to ask the parties for their views on these matters as soon as the

---

[38] Art. 25(c). *See also* Art. 28 of the UNCITRAL Rules.

[39] See Article 6(3) of the 1998 ICC Rules: "[i]f any of the parties refuses or fails to take part in the arbitration or any stage thereof, the arbitration shall proceed notwithstanding such refusal or failure," and Article 21(2) (replacing Arts. 8(2) and 15(2) of the previous Rules); Art. 15.8 of the 1998 LCIA Rules: "[i]f the respondent fails to submit a Statement of Defence or the Claimant a Statement of Defence to Counterclaim, or if at any point any party fails to avail itself of the opportunity to present its case . . . , the Arbitral Tribunal may nevertheless proceed with the arbitration and make an award;" Art. 23 of the 1997 AAA International Arbitration Rules.

[40] *See, e.g.,* CA Paris, Feb. 7, 1991, *Dovert et Tabourdeau, supra* note 35; CA Paris, Mar. 11, 1993, Al-Kawthar Investment Co. Ltd. v. BNP, 1994 REV. ARB. 735, and observations by D. Cohen; for an English translation, see 8 INT'L ARB. REP. F1 (Apr. 1993).

[41] *See supra* paras. 750 *et seq.*

[42] *See supra* paras. 1197 *et seq.*

[43] CA Paris, July 7, 1987, Pia Investments Ltd. v. Cassia, 1988 REV. ARB. 649, and E. Mezger's note; CA Paris, Mar. 25, 1994, Sardisud v. Technip, 1994 REV. ARB. 391, and C. Jarrosson's note. On the concept of the arbitral award, see *infra* paras. 1349 *et seq.,* especially para. 1355.

arbitral tribunal is constituted.[44] This will sometimes involve a hearing, sometimes referred to as a "pre-trial conference" or "pre-hearing conference."[45] It may also consist of an exchange of letters between the tribunal and the parties, which must of course respect the principles of due process. The pre-trial conference, and a list of questions generally discussed on that occasion, were the subject of an UNCITRAL project to produce "Guidelines for Preparatory Conferences in Arbitral Proceedings," intended to help parties unfamiliar with arbitration in the conduct of the arbitral proceedings. That initiative met with a mixed response.[46] UNCITRAL subsequently amended the project, taking into account the risk of systematically burdening arbitral proceedings by recommending one or more preliminary conferences, and it published only "Notes on Organizing Arbitral Proceedings."[47]

1227. — The exchange of views by the parties may or may not lead to the preparation of "terms of reference."

Although they are an essential element of ICC arbitration,[48] terms of reference are also found in proceedings not held under the auspices of the ICC. In view of both the importance of terms of reference in the continental tradition and the controversy that surrounds them, we shall begin by examining their utility and nature (§ 1), before going on to consider the procedural issues generally encountered by the arbitral tribunal, whether or not terms of reference are used (§ 2).

§ 1. – Terms of Reference

1228. — Terms of reference consist of a document signed by the parties and the arbitrators or, if the parties do not agree to sign, by the arbitrators alone or by the arbitral

---

[44] On the "provisional advance" that, in ICC arbitration, the claimant is invited to pay at the start of the arbitration "to cover the costs of arbitration until the Terms of Reference have been drawn up," see Article 30(1) of the 1998 Rules. The new ICC Rules do not expressly subordinate the transmittal of the file to the arbitrators to the payment of such "provisional advance" but such a practice is expected to be followed. On this issue, see DERAINS AND SCHWARTZ, *supra* note 1, at 306 *et seq.* and *infra* para. 1253.

[45] *See* Michael F. Hoellering, *The Pre-arbitration Conference: Can the Big Case Be Expedited?*, N.Y.L.J., Aug. 12, 1972, at 3.

[46] U.N. Doc. A/CN.9/396/Add. 1. On this issue, see Philippe Fouchard, *Une initiative contestable de la CNUDCI – A propos du projet de "Directives pour les conférences préparatoires dans le cadre des procédures arbitrales"*, 1994 REV. ARB. 461 and 1994 BULL. ASA 369; Pierre Lalive, *De la fureur réglementaire*, 1994 BULL. ASA 213; *see also* Jernej Sekolec, *UNCITRAL Project for Improving Methods of Planning Arbitral Proceedings*, *in* ICCA CONGRESS SERIES No. 7, PLANNING EFFICIENT ARBITRATION PROCEEDINGS/THE LAW APPLICABLE IN INTERNATIONAL ARBITRATION 100 (A.J. van den Berg ed., 1996); Howard M. Holtzmann, *Questions Concerning the Desirability and Text of the UNCITRAL Project to Improve Planning of Arbitral Proceedings, id.* at 173.

[47] U.N. Doc. V. 96–84935, U.N. Sales No. E.97.V.II (1996). *See* XXII Y.B. COM. ARB. 448 (1997), with background remarks by J. Sekolec; 1998 REV. ARB. 273, and observations by P. Fouchard; Roberto Ceccon, *UNCITRAL Notes on Organizing Arbitral Proceedings and the Conduct of Evidence – A New Approach to International Arbitration*, 14 J. INT'L ARB. 67 (June 1997).

[48] *See infra* para. 1229.

institution.[49] The purpose of the terms of reference is to set out the parties' claims, to identify the issues which the arbitral tribunal must resolve and to determine the main procedural rules governing the arbitral proceedings.[50]

The terms of reference originate from a rule, which once applied in French law and applied until recently in certain legal systems of the continental tradition, whereby an arbitration agreement can only bind the parties if their consent to arbitration is renewed, by means of a submission agreement, once the dispute has arisen.[51] Where the terms of reference record the parties' agreement, they can indeed serve that purpose. With the disappearance of the requirement for a submission agreement from most arbitration laws, certain authors, particularly those of the common law tradition, consider that terms of reference retain no more than an historic interest. The institution of the terms of reference is therefore controversial as regards both its utility (A) and its nature (B).

A. – UTILITY OF TERMS OF REFERENCE

1229. — The requirement that terms of reference be drawn up is a characteristic feature of ICC arbitration.[52] They are also found in the Belgian CEPANI Arbitration Rules (Art. 17), and are not uncommon in continental-style *ad hoc* arbitrations. By contrast, they are generally not found in legal systems belonging to the common law tradition, and are not required under either the AAA Rules or the LCIA Rules. Neither the Arbitration Rules of the Geneva Chamber of Commerce and Industry,[53] nor those of the Arbitration Institute of the Stockholm Chamber of Commerce require terms of reference, whereas the Rules of Arbitration of the Euro-Arab Chambers of Commerce allow the arbitrators to draw up terms of reference if they see fit (Art. 23-7).[54]

---

[49] On the mechanism in ICC arbitration for the approval by the International Court of Arbitration of Terms of Reference which one party refuses to sign, see Article 18(3) of the 1998 Rules, replacing Article 13(2) of the previous Rules.

[50] On this issue, generally, see Jean-Jacques Arnaldez, *L'acte déterminant la mission de l'arbitre*, in ETUDES OFFERTES À PIERRE BELLET 1 (1991); DERAINS AND SCHWARTZ, *supra* note 1, at 228 *et seq.*

[51] On the requirements of French domestic arbitration law in this respect, which were repealed by a 1925 statute, see *supra* para. 386 and, on the laws of Latin American countries which have only recently dispensed with such requirements, see *supra* para. 632.

[52] *See* Art. 18 of the 1998 Rules (replacing Art. 13 of the previous Rules). For a commentary, see Michael E. Schneider, *The Terms of Reference*, in ICC BULLETIN, SPECIAL SUPPLEMENT, THE NEW 1998 ICC RULES OF ARBITRATION 26 (ICC Publication No. 586, 1997); Blessing, *supra* note 1, at 26 *et seq.*; Reiner, *supra* note 1, at 41 *et seq.*

[53] On these Rules, in force as of January 1, 1992, see P.-Y. Tschanz, *Le règlement d'arbitrage de la Chambre de commerce et d'industrie de Genève (éd. 1992)*, 1992 REV. ARB. 690; Gabrielle Kaufmann, *The Geneva Chamber of Commerce and Industry Adopts Revised Arbitration Rules*, 9 J. INT'L ARB. 71 (June 1992).

[54] On the refusal to set aside an award made under these Rules without terms of reference, where it was claimed that the subject-matter of the arbitrator's brief was inadequately defined, see CA Paris, May 10, 1994, Sheikh Mahfouz Salem Bin Mahfouz v. Al Tayar, 1996 REV. ARB. 66, and C. Jarrosson's note.

1230. — The requirement of terms of reference is the subject of some criticism, which initially came from common lawyers, who considered that the parties' claims could only be accurately determined by means of an exchange of the documents held by each party and the examination of witnesses. They were therefore opposed to the idea of prematurely fixing the terms of the debate by listing, in advance, the points to be decided by the arbitral tribunal. For such authors, terms of reference complicate the proceedings without providing any real benefit.[55] The same view has been echoed by some civil lawyers,[56] and there is no doubt that, under the previous ICC Rules, the preliminary terms of reference stage often neutralized several months of the arbitral proceedings during which the examination of the merits of the case could not progress. The measures provided for in the 1998 ICC Rules to accelerate the adoption of terms of reference, in particular by removing the requirement that a list of issues be included where the tribunal "considers it inappropriate," should provide a satisfactory response to the objection.[57]

1231. — The benefits of drawing up terms of reference are three-fold and explain why many practitioners, from both civil and common law traditions,[58] nevertheless favor their use.

1232. — The first advantage of terms of reference is that the parties' initial written statements are not always as clear as one might expect, and in drawing up terms of reference they are obliged to present their claims concisely but completely. In practice, the parties are generally invited to comment on their position as set forth in a draft of the terms of reference produced by the tribunal (or by the chairman of the tribunal, who is usually responsible for preparing the text). This provides the parties with an opportunity to clarify any of their allegations that may require further explanation, as well as to specify which issues remain disputed and those upon which they agree.

As the arbitrators are required to comply with the brief conferred upon them,[59] it is important to involve the parties, from the outset of the proceedings, in the process of defining that brief and in determining exactly which issues are to be resolved by the tribunal. Some authors even claim that the terms of reference thus enable a number of grounds for setting the award aside to be eliminated. They suggest that terms of reference which are clearly drafted by the tribunal and the parties together help the arbitrators to understand the

---

[55] *See, e.g.*, Hans Smit, *The Future Of International Commercial Arbitration: A Single Transnational Institution?*, 25 COLUM. J. TRANSNAT'L L. 9, 21 (1986).

[56] For a radical critique of the institution, see especially ANTOINE KASSIS, RÉFLEXIONS SUR LE RÈGLEMENT D'ARBITRAGE DE LA CHAMBRE DE COMMERCE INTERNATIONALE – LES DÉVIATIONS DE L'ARBITRAGE INSTITUTIONNEL 226–269 (1988).

[57] *See* Art. 18 of the 1998 ICC Rules; DERAINS AND SCHWARTZ, *supra* note 1, at 233 *et seq.* See also, on the fact that the 1998 Rules no longer make the effectiveness of the terms of reference conditional upon payment of the advance on costs, *infra* para. 1254, note 140.

[58] *See, e.g.*, W. LAURENCE CRAIG, WILLIAM W. PARK, JAN PAULSSON, INTERNATIONAL CHAMBER OF COMMERCE ARBITRATION 251–68 (2d ed. 1990); Stephen R. Bond, *ICC Terms of Reference Rule Saves Time and Money While Promoting Common Understanding*, 6 INT'L ARB. REP. 33 (Aug. 1991).

[59] *See, e.g.*, Art. 1502 3° of the French New Code of Civil Procedure; *infra* paras. 1626 *et seq.*

issues submitted to them and thus contribute to the validity of the award.[60] However, the reverse may also be true: in some cases, the terms of reference create difficulties for the arbitrators in defining their brief which would not have arisen had they confined themselves to ruling on the claims stated in the parties' written pleadings.[61] In fact, badly-drafted terms of reference can clearly prejudice the parties' positions,[62] and where terms of reference are required, they should be prepared with great care.[63] On the other hand, provided that they are carefully drafted, they can simplify the work of the arbitral tribunal and contribute to the smooth running of the proceedings. They can also eliminate certain grounds for setting the award aside, where they state, as is sometimes the case, that the parties have no objection to the constitution of the arbitral tribunal.[64]

The French courts have substantially reduced the risk of awards being set aside by holding that the arbitrators' brief is confined within the limits of the dispute, as defined by the parties' claims and not by the list of issues to be resolved drawn up by the parties and included in the terms of reference.[65] Thus, when hearing an action to set aside or resisting enforcement of an award on the grounds of Articles 1502 3° or 1504 (non compliance with the arbitrators' brief), the French courts need not verify the consistency of the award with the list of issues to be resolved contained in the terms of reference. This is a sensible approach, as the parties' claims evolve as their memorials are exchanged and the arbitration progresses.

1233. — The second advantage of terms of reference is that they create a proper framework for the proceedings, by enabling the parties and the arbitrators to put forward their views from the outset on a number of issues which are essential to the functioning of the arbitration,[66] and by limiting the parties' right to submit new claims to the tribunal at a later stage. It is of course possible to insert language in the terms of reference giving the arbitral tribunal considerable freedom in its conduct of the proceedings, but it may also be useful to determine a number of procedural rules in advance.

In ICC arbitration, one of the most important consequences of the terms of reference—whether or not the parties actually sign them—is to limit the submission of new claims by the parties. Prior to 1998, this resulted from Article 16, which provided that:

> [t]he parties may make new claims or counter-claims before the arbitrator on condition that these remain within the limits fixed by the Terms of Reference

---

[60] CRAIG, PARK, PAULSSON, *supra* note 58, at 252.

[61] KASSIS, *supra* note 56, ¶ 314.

[62] *See infra* para. 1236.

[63] On this issue, see Jean-Claude Goldsmith, *How to draft Terms of Reference*, 3 ARB. INT'L 298 (1987).

[64] On the impact of these provisions on actions to set aside, see *infra* para. 1606.

[65] Cass. 1e civ., Mar. 6, 1996, Farhat Trading Co. v. Daewoo, 1997 REV. ARB. 69, and J.-J. Arnaldez' note; 1997 REV. CRIT. DIP 313, and D. Cohen's note.

[66] *See infra* paras. 1238 *et seq.*

provided for in Article 13 or that they are specified in a rider to that document, signed by the parties and communicated to the Court.

The 1998 Rules are more flexible. Article 19 allows the arbitral tribunal, if it sees fit, to authorize the parties to submit new claims:

> After the Terms of Reference have been signed or approved by the Court, no party shall make new claims or counterclaims which fall outside the limits of the Terms of Reference unless it has been authorized to do so by the Arbitral Tribunal, which shall consider the nature of such new claims or counterclaims, the stage of the arbitration and other relevant circumstances.

These provisions are intended to prevent the parties from continually altering their claims in the course of the proceedings. To allow that would unduly prolong the arbitration by requiring the other party to respond to the new claims, unless that party were to waive its right to do so, a right it enjoys by virtue of the principle of due process.

The limits for submitting new claims or counterclaims are those fixed in the terms of reference. Under the previous Rules, they bound both the arbitrators and the parties, who could only depart from them by mutual agreement. However, the 1998 Rules give the arbitrators broad discretion to hear new claims, particularly as the factors which Article 19 requires the arbitrators to take into account are not, in our view, subject to subsequent review by the courts.

However, the precise meaning and scope of Article 16 of the previous ICC Rules gave rise to a number of difficulties in practice.[67] Certain of these difficulties will also arise under Article 19 of the 1998 Rules.

Interpreted *a contrario*, these provisions mean, first, that until the terms of reference have been adopted by the parties or by the Court, the parties are free to submit any claims or counterclaims as they see fit, provided of course that they fall within the scope of the arbitration agreement.[68]

---

[67] On this issue, see especially Perret, *supra* note 15.

[68] The principle, which also results from the language of Article 18(1) of the 1998 Rules (Art. 13(1) of the previous Rules), which provides that the terms of reference are drawn up "in light of [the parties'] most recent submissions," see *supra* para. 1222, was recognized in Award No. 3987 (1983), Austrian company v. Greek company, 111 J.D.I. 943 (1984), and observations by Y. Derains; *see also* ICC Award No. 3281 (1981), French licensor v. Spanish licensee, 109 J.D.I. 990 (1982), and observations by Y. Derains; ICC Award No. 2626 (1977), *supra* note 8; ICC Award No. 4367 (Nov. 16, 1984), U.S. supplier v. Indian buyer, XI Y.B. COM. ARB. 134 (1986); ICC Award No. 6039 (1992), ICC BULLETIN, Vol. 8, No. 1, at 54 (1997); No. 6437 (1990), *id.* at 63; No. 8083 (1994), *id.* at 64; No. 7237 (1993), *id.* at 65; No. 6000 (1988), French textile company v. U.S. distributor, *id.* at 67; the December 19, 1996 Award in ICC Case No. 8197, by Messrs. Lazareff, chairman, Rubino-Sammartano and Crivellaro, arbitrators, *affirmed by* CA Paris, May 19, 1998, Torno SpA v. Kumagai Gumi Co. Ltd., 13 INT'L ARB. REP. E1 (July 1998); Arnaldez, *supra* note 50, at 26–27; Erik Schäfer, *The ICC Arbitral Process – Part II: Terms of Reference*, ICC BULLETIN, Vol. 3, No. 1, at 8, 12 (1992); GUIDE TO ICC ARBITRATION 40 (ICC Publication No. 448, 1994); DERAINS AND SCHWARTZ, *supra* note 1, at 57–58. It has been suggested that arbitrators could nonetheless hold inadmissable new claims made before this date where a party makes a series of new claims one by one in order to delay proceedings (Y. Derains, observations

(continued...)

Second, these provisions mean that the final deadline for submitting new claims does not necessarily coincide with the adoption of the terms of reference. The only requirement is that new claims should be within the limits of the terms of reference. It would therefore be quite possible for parties seeking greater freedom to file new claims to stipulate in the terms of reference that such claims will be admissible if submitted before a certain date (the deadline fixed for filing a memorial, for example), or even at any time in the proceedings. However, if the terms of reference do not mention the possibility of altering claims or submitting counterclaims, the dispute will be confined to the claims set forth in the terms of reference, unless of course, under the 1998 Rules, the arbitrators otherwise allow in their discretion.

Third, these provisions mean that claims submitted outside the deadlines fixed by the terms of reference should be declared inadmissible by the arbitral tribunal unless, again, it sees fit to allow them.[69] By contrast, any new argument or plea submitted in support of an existing claim will be admissible, provided of course it complies with the requirements of due process. Thus, for instance, any new theory in support of a claim for damages not exceeding the sum initially claimed would certainly be admissible outside the limits fixed for new claims by the terms of reference.[70] That may not be the case, however, where damages subsequently claimed are greater than those which were initially sought, unless the terms of reference expressly[71] or implicitly[72] allow the parties to update their claims. The suggestion that a request for a different amount of damages does not constitute a new claim

---

[68] (...continued)
following ICC Award No. 3987 (1983), *supra* at 946). This seems questionable. Given Article 19 (replacing Article 16 of the previous Rules), an arbitral tribunal declaring inadmissible a claim made before the deadline fixed in the terms of reference or before the adoption of the terms of reference themselves would run the risk of ruling *infra petita* and having its award set aside as a result (*see infra* para. 1628). However, nothing would prevent the tribunal from drawing the appropriate conclusions regarding the merits of such a party's case in such circumstances.

[69] See, for example, ICC Award No. 3267 (Mar. 28, 1984), which rightly notes that the fact that arbitrators are able to rule in equity has no impact on the application of Article 16 (today Art. 19) (Mexican construction company v. Belgian company (member of a consortium), XII Y.B. COM. ARB. 87, 91 (1987)). *See also* ICC Award No. 6503 (1990), French company v. Spanish company , 122 J.D.I. 1022 (1995), and observations by Y. Derains.

[70] For an illustration, see ICC Award No. 4462 (Feb. 23, 1987), National Oil Corp. v. Libyan Sun Oil Co., by R. Schmelck, chairman, H. Koetz and E. Muskie, arbitrators. The arbitral tribunal rightly found that arguments based on the co-contractor's breach of contract did not constitute a new claim under Article 16 of the 1975 ICC Rules, where the original arguments were based on a party's right to withdraw from the petroleum exploration project at issue, given that both sets of arguments were based on the same facts and had the same purpose (29 I.L.M. 601 (1990); XVI Y.B. COM. ARB. 54, 71 (1991)); *see also* ICC Award No. 6223 (1991), ICC BULLETIN, Vol. 8, No. 2, at 69 (1997); ICC Award No. 6618 (1991), *id.* at 70; No. 6657 (1993), *id.* at 72.

[71] See, for example, CA Paris, June 30, 1988, which rejected an argument based on an arbitral tribunal allegedly exceeding its brief where a claim for damages in the terms of reference was for a sum "not less than" a certain amount (Industrie Pama v. Schultz Steel, 1991 REV. ARB. 351, and observations by J.-H. Moitry and C. Vergne). On the inadmissibility of a counterclaim failing to satisfy the conditions set forth in the terms of reference, see ICC Award No. 7314 (1995), ICC BULLETIN, Vol. 8, No. 2, at 72 (1997).

[72] See, for example, ICC Award No. 5514 (1990), where the terms of reference did not specify the amount of damages claimed (French company v. Government committed to the provision of financing, 119 J.D.I. 1022 (1992), and observations by Y. Derains).

is questionable.[73] The same is true where the nature of the right in respect of which redress is sought is different,[74] or of course where the claim is directed at different parties.[75]

Several arbitral awards have endorsed the principle that although new claims cannot be made, new legal pleas ("*moyens*") are admissible after the terms of reference.[76] This, admittedly, is hardly explicit in the English language version of the ICC Rules, which uses the ambiguous term "claim" for both the claim, strictly speaking (Art. 19), and its justification (Art. 18(1)(c)), whereas the French language version uses different terms, respectively *demandes* and *prétentions des parties*. The French language version is thus arguably clearer.[77]

In order to forestall such difficulties, ICC arbitral practice under the 1975 and 1988 Rules favored the adoption of clauses simply defining the dispute and the arbitrators' brief by reference to the parties' subsequent written submissions. The greater flexibility of the 1998 Rules makes such a precaution less necessary.

1234. — The third advantage of terms of reference lies in the fact that they bring the parties together at the outset of the proceedings. A meeting of the parties to agree on how the proceedings are to be conducted and to clarify their respective cases may provide an opportunity to open a dialogue leading to the amicable settlement of the dispute. In practice, it is not unusual for a settlement to be reached at the terms of reference stage.[78] On the other hand, if a party refuses to participate in the preparation of the terms of reference, that will not affect the validity of the subsequent award.[79]

---

[73] *But see* CRAIG, PARK, PAULSSON, *supra* note 58, at 255; DERAINS AND SCHWARTZ, *supra* note 1, at 250; ICC Award No. 7076 (1993), ICC BULLETIN, Vol. 8, No. 1, at 66 (1997). One of the cases these authors cite (Carte Blanche (Singapore) PTE, Ltd. v. Carte Blanche Int'l, Ltd., 683 F. Supp. 945 (S.D.N.Y. 1988); 3 INT'L ARB. REP. 3 (Apr. 1988)) is based, however, on the ambiguities in the terms of reference adopted. For a case declaring a new counterclaim to be inadmissible, see ICC Award No. 6647 (1991), ICC BULLETIN, Vol. 8, No. 2, at 71 (1997).

[74] See, for example, for the application of Article 16 of the 1975 Rules to a claim for damages based on a violation of a commercial property right when the terms of reference only mentioned a claim for payment of the balance of an invoice, ICC Award No. 6309 (1991), German company v. Dutch company, 118 J.D.I. 1046 (1991), and observations by J.-J. Arnaldez.

[75] Compare with ICC Award No. 3742 (1983), which refused the extension, after the signature of the terms of reference, of the proceedings to two entities which succeeded to a party (European contractor v. Three Middle Eastern state-owned entities, 111 J.D.I. 910 (1984), and observations by Y. Derains).

[76] *See, e.g.*, ICC Award No. 4504 (1985 and 1986), Petroleum producer v. Two companies, 113 J.D.I. 1118 (1986), and observations by S. Jarvin; ICC Award No. 5302, American party v. American party, cited by Jarvin, *id.* at 1128. A diminution of the initial claim would also be admissible (*see* ICC Award No. 3281 (1981), *supra* note 68).

[77] On this issue, see Perret, *supra* note 15.

[78] "Over the last five years, one arbitration request out of three has made its way through the process up to the rendering of an arbitration award." One quarter of the withdrawals takes place during the drafting of the terms of reference (*see 1996 Statistical Report, A Historical Breakthrough*, ICC BULLETIN, Vol. 8, No. 1, at 6, 8 (1997)).

[79] CA Paris, June 28, 1991, KFTCIC v. Icori Estero, 1992 REV. ARB. 568, and P. Bellet's note, especially at 572; for an English translation, see 6 INT'L ARB. REP. El (Aug. 1991); CA Paris, Mar. 11, 1993, *Al-Kawthar Investment*, *supra* note 40, at F8.

B. – NATURE OF THE TERMS OF REFERENCE

1235. — The legal nature of terms of reference, and in particular their relation to the arbitration agreement,[80] are also a subject of some contention. However, a distinction should be drawn between two situations.

1236. — The first situation is where the terms of reference have been signed by the parties. In that case, they constitute an agreement which, in itself, amounts to consent by the parties to refer their disputes to arbitration. On that basis, the Paris Court of Appeals held in one case that:

> in the absence of any arbitration agreement, the fact that the parties submitted their disputes to arbitration, as evidenced in particular by their signing of terms of reference . . . can amount to a submission agreement.[81]

Likewise, terms of reference accepted without reservation by the parties can modify the scope of the initial arbitration agreement, either restricting or widening it. The parties must therefore carefully ensure that by signing the terms of reference they do not inadvertently limit or extend the jurisdiction of the arbitral tribunal.

In general, any agreement between the parties evidenced by the terms of reference is binding not only on the parties, but also on the arbitrators, who must comply with the parties' intentions. The Paris Court of Appeals applied this principle when, having held that the terms of reference signed by the parties required the arbitrators to rule on their own jurisdiction in a separate award, set aside the award in which the issue of jurisdiction had been addressed together with the merits of the dispute.[82] However, the *Cour de cassation* overruled that decision on the grounds that:

> by reaching such a decision, where the terms of reference contained no express, precise clause requiring the arbitrators to rule by means of two separate, successive awards on their jurisdiction and on the merits of the dispute,

---

[80] *See supra* paras. 385 *et seq.*

[81] CA Paris, Mar. 19, 1987, Kis France v. A.B.S., 1987 REV. ARB. 498, and L. Zollinger's note; *see also* CA Paris, Jan. 12, 1988, S.A. Replor v. S.A.R.L. Ploemeloise de financement, de participation, d'investissement, 1988 REV. ARB. 691, and L. Zollinger's note; CA Paris, 1e Ch., Sec. C, Jan. 19, 1999, CIC International Ltd. v. Ministre de la Défense de la République Fédérale d'Allemagne, No. 1998/03375, unpublished. Compare, for a critique of the assimilation of the terms of reference and the submission agreement, B. Goldman, note following CA Paris, July 12, 1984, République Arabe d'Egypte v. Southern Pacific Properties Ltd., 112 J.D.I. 129, 152 (1985); for an English translation, see 23 I.L.M. 1048 (1984); X Y.B. COM. ARB. 113 (1985).

[82] CA Paris, Dec. 19, 1986, O.I.A.E.T.I. v. SOFIDIF, 1987 REV. ARB. 359, and the commentary by Emmanuel Gaillard, *L'affaire SOFIDIF ou les difficultés de l'arbitrage multipartite (à propos de l'arrêt rendu par la Cour d'appel de Paris le 19 décembre 1986)*, *id.* at 275.

the Court of Appeals had misinterpreted the provisions of French law concerning the setting aside of an award where the arbitrators exceed the terms of their brief. Nevertheless, the *Cour de cassation* observed that:

> in international arbitration, the task conferred on the arbitrators may include special obligations as to the procedure to be followed and may, in particular, require them to make separate awards concerning jurisdiction, admissibility and the substance of the dispute, . . . provided that those obligations arise from explicit and precise clauses in the terms of reference.[83]

Likewise, if the parties agree in the terms of reference to change the location of the seat of the arbitration, that agreement will produce all the legal consequences attached to the determination of the seat.[84]

Of course, the position will be different where a party challenges the jurisdiction of the arbitral tribunal and appears before the arbitrators, who have jurisdiction to rule on their own jurisdiction, and signs terms of reference which mention the challenge. Such conduct cannot be construed as a waiver of that party's right to argue, in a subsequent court action, that the arbitral tribunal lacked jurisdiction, even if the same party submitted its arguments on the merits of the dispute to the arbitral tribunal as a precautionary measure.[85] Similarly, whenever the terms of reference, or the submission agreement signed on the basis of the initial arbitration agreement, clearly refer to that initial agreement and to its limitations, the parties remain entitled to rely on those limitations in later submissions.[86]

1237. — The second situation to be distinguished is that where at least one of the parties has refused to sign the terms of reference or to subscribe unreservedly to all of the provisions they contain. In that case, the entire document, or the provisions recording a difference of opinion between the parties, will have no value other than that which is

---

[83]   Cass. 1e civ., Mar. 8, 1988, Sofidif v. O.I.A.E.T.I., 1988 Bull. Civ. I, No. 64, at 42; 1989 REV. ARB. 481, and C. Jarrosson's note.

[84]   *See infra* para. 1239.

[85]   *See* CA Paris, July 12, 1984, *République Arabe d'Egypte, supra* note 81, *aff'd,* Cass. 1e civ., Jan. 6, 1987, Southern Pacific Properties Ltd. v. République Arabe d'Egypte, 114 J.D.I. 638 (1987), and B. Goldman's note; 1987 REV. ARB. 469, and P. Leboulanger's note; 1988 RTD CIV. 126, and J. Mestre's note; for an English translation, see 26 I.L.M. 1004 (1987); XIII Y.B. COM. ARB. 152 (1988); 2 INT'L ARB. REP. 17 (Jan. 1987).

[86]   See, for example, CA Paris, Oct. 27, 1994, which held that a submission agreement, signed in application of an international arbitration clause that was void because it provided for an appeal (*see infra* para. 1597), was also void because it too referred to the possibility of appeal provided for in the arbitration clause (de Diseno v. Mendes, 1995 REV. ARB. 263, 2d decision, and P. Level's note).

conferred on them by the arbitration rules adopted by the parties.[87] In any event, the terms of reference can never be treated as an award and cannot be reviewed accordingly by the courts.[88]

§ 2. – Issues Relating to the Organization of the Proceedings

1238. — When drawing up the terms of reference, the arbitrators will often mention the instrument by which the parties conferred jurisdiction on them,[89] or the difficulties yet to be resolved on that issue. They may also refer to the parties' agreement as to the law governing the merits of the dispute, or the fact that the arbitral tribunal is to decide that issue.[90] If they have been empowered to act as *amiable compositeurs*,[91] they will say so. However, the organization of the proceedings raises other questions, which depend primarily on the intentions of the parties, expressed directly or by reference to any arbitration rules they may have chosen. If nothing has been agreed by the parties, they are matters for the arbitral tribunal to decide. Some of these questions will be resolved in the terms of reference, if terms of reference are used. Others will be resolved by way of separate procedural orders, issued by the arbitral tribunal or by its chairman alone immediately after the signature of terms of reference or at a later stage.

A. – SEAT OF THE ARBITRATION

1239. — Although its role is tending to diminish,[92] the location of the place of arbitration,[93] also known as the seat of the arbitration,[94] still carries important legal consequences. In particular, it gives access to the courts if that is required during the process

---

[87] On the ICC system, see *supra* para. 1233; on this issue generally, see Gaillard, *supra* note 82, at 288 *et seq.*; KASSIS, *supra* note 56, ¶¶ 309 *et seq.*; CRAIG, PARK, PAULSSON, *supra* note 58, ¶ 15-05 at 261 *et seq.*

[88] *But see* Supreme Court of Argentina, Oct. 24, 1995, Compañia Naviera Pérez Companc S.A.C.F.I.M.F.A. v. Ecofisa S.A., 11 INT'L ARB. REP. 9 (Feb. 1996).

[89] On the possibility of modifying the limits of such jurisdiction, see *supra* para. 1236.

[90] On the determination of the law applicable to the merits, see *infra* paras. 1420 *et seq.*

[91] On *amiable composition*, see *infra* paras. 1500 *et seq.*

[92] See, for example, with respect to the determination of the law applicable to the procedure, *supra* paras. 1199 *et seq.*, with respect to the law applicable to the merits, *infra* paras. 1541 *et seq.*, and on the possibility of an award set aside in one jurisdiction being recognized in another, *infra* para. 1595.

[93] On this issue, generally, see THE PLACE OF ARBITRATION (M. Storme and F. De Ly eds., 1992).

[94] The trend in recent years has been to substitute the words "place of the arbitration" for "seat of the arbitration." Following the 1985 UNCITRAL Model Law (Art. 20), the 1998 ICC Rules retained the expression "place of *the* arbitration" (in French "*lieu de l'arbitrage*," instead of "*siège de l'arbitrage*" used in the former Rules), the article "the" being thought to connote, in the English version, the existence of a legal link between a country and the arbitration. *See* DERAINS AND SCHWARTZ, *supra* note 1, at 201 *et seq.* The 1997 AAA International Rules followed the same approach (Art. 13). See, however, the use of the word "seat" in the 1996 English Arbitration Act (Sec. 3) and in the LCIA Rules (Art. 16).

of constituting the arbitral tribunal,[95] and it sometimes leads to the application of mandatory procedural rules of the country where the seat is located.[96] It also has an impact on the jurisdiction of the courts to hear actions to set an award aside,[97] and on compliance with any reciprocity condition that sometimes affects the application of conventions concerning the recognition and enforcement of awards.[98]

1240. — As a result, it is increasingly common for the parties themselves to determine the seat of the arbitration in their arbitration agreement or at the beginning of the arbitral proceedings.[99] According to ICC statistics, this is true of over 80% of ICC arbitrations.[100] In some cases, the arbitration agreement fixes the seat of arbitration in the country of the defendant's domicile. The seat thus varies according to which party begins the proceedings. These clauses, which are often found in contracts involving Japanese parties, mirror the principle of giving jurisdiction to the courts of the defendant's domicile. A similar mechanism is to allow the defendant to choose between two possible seats, which leads to the same result. The courts generally consider such clauses to be valid.[101]

Where the parties have made no such choice, the seat is determined in accordance with the mechanisms provided for by the parties to that end, directly or, more often, by reference to arbitration rules. In ICC arbitration, for example, the seat is determined by the International Court of Arbitration when the parties themselves have not selected it.[102] The LCIA Rules take a more directive approach: in the absence of a choice by the parties, it is presumed that the seat of the arbitration will be located in London, unless the arbitral

---

[95] *See supra* paras. 837 *et seq.*

[96] French law does not accept this mandatory intervention of the law of the seat, but its liberal approach is not shared by all legal systems and caution is therefore advisable. On the movement towards the detachment of arbitral procedure from the seat of the arbitration, see *supra* paras. 1199 *et seq.*

[97] *See infra* paras. 1589 and 1593.

[98] *See* CA Paris, July 12, 1984, *République Arabe d'Egypte*, *supra* note 81, *aff'd*, Cass. 1e civ., Jan. 6, 1987, *Southern Pacific Properties*, *supra* note 85.

[99] For a discussion of the factors that the parties should take into consideration when choosing the seat of the arbitration, see, for example, Piero Bernardini, *The Arbitration Clause of an International Contract*, 9 J. INT'L ARB. 45, 51 (June 1992); Sigvard Jarvin, *The ICC Arbitral Process – Part V: The Place of Arbitration*, ICC BULLETIN, Vol. 4, No. 2, at 7 (1993); William W. Park, *Illusion and Reality in International Forum Selection*, 30 TEXAS INT'L L.J. 135 (1995), especially at 180 *et seq.* On the validity of a provision allowing a party to select the place of arbitration, see CA Versailles, Dec. 14, 1995, SA MSC v. GAN Aticam, 1996 DALLOZ AFF. 296; 1996 RTD COM. 250, and observations by J.-C. Dubarry and E. Loquin.

[100] The ICC Annual Reports show that this number was between 80 per cent (in 1988 and 1993, for example) and 87.8 per cent (in 1996). It was 86 per cent in 1989 and 1990, and 87.3 per cent in 1994. For the latest statistics, see ICC BULLETIN, Vol. 10, No. 1 (1999).

[101] In English law, see Star Shipping AS. v. China National Foreign Trade Transportation Corp. (The "STAR TEXAS"), [1993] 2 Lloyd's Rep. 445; XXII Y.B. COM. ARB. 815 (1997) (C.A. 1993). *See also* CA Versailles, Dec. 14, 1995, *SA MSC*, *supra* note 99.

[102] Art. 14(1) of the 1998 Rules (replacing Art. 12 of the previous Rules). On the criteria applied by the Court in making its decision, see CRAIG, PARK, PAULSSON, *supra* note 58, at 204; DERAINS AND SCHWARTZ, *supra* note 1, at 201 *et seq.*; Herman Verbist, *The Practice of the ICC International Court of Arbitration With Regard to the Fixing of the Place of Arbitration*, 12 ARB. INT'L 347 (1996), and for a French version, 1995 INT'L BUS. L.J. 1000.

tribunal infers from all the circumstances of the case that another location would be more appropriate.[103] In that respect, the LCIA differs from the ICC: the latter has always emphasized its truly international nature and does not favor any particular location in determining the seat of the arbitration.[104] In the absence of any direct or indirect indication by the parties, including through the choice of arbitration rules, the seat is determined by the arbitral tribunal.[105]

It is common practice—now enshrined in Article 16 of the UNCITRAL Rules, Article 14, paragraph 2 of the 1998 ICC Rules, Article 16.2 of the 1998 LCIA Rules, Article 13(2) of the 1997 AAA International Arbitration Rules, and Article 20 of the 1999 Rules of the Arbitration Institute of the Stockholm Chamber of Commerce—to specify that the arbitral tribunal may, for reasons of convenience, hold hearings at locations other than the place of arbitration without causing the seat itself to change. As the legal consequences attached to the determination of the seat depend on the choice made by the parties, the arbitral institution or the arbitrators, rather than on the place where the arbitration actually takes place, such clauses are unquestionably valid. Such validity was recognized by the UNCITRAL Model Law in its Article 20, paragraph 2, by the Belgian Judicial Code in its Article 1693, paragraph 2 (Law of May 19, 1998) and by the 1999 Swedish Arbitration Act in its Section 22. Even without such a clause, the French courts acknowledge that it is perfectly legitimate for some procedural steps to be performed in a place other than the seat chosen by the parties, as "no legal provision [obliges arbitral tribunals] to perform all tasks

---

[103] Art.16. Compare with Article 13 of the 1997 AAA International Arbitration Rules, which provides that, if the parties are silent, the arbitrators may, within 60 days, change the place of arbitration initially chosen by the institution. The Rules provide, however, that the award must be made at that place (Art. 27(3)). The LCIA, which previously required the award to be made at the seat, relaxed this condition in its 1998 Rules: an award made elsewhere than at the seat is now deemed made at the seat (Art. 16.2). The extremely formalistic requirement that an award be made at the seat may lead to problems in some jurisdictions, even those which do not confuse the seat and the actual place where the award is signed. On this confusion found in English law prior to the 1996 Arbitration Act, see Hiscox v. Outhwaite, (No. 1) [1992] 1 A.C. 562; [1991] 3 All E.R. 641; [1991] 3 W.L.R. 297; [1991] 2 Lloyd's Rep. 435; XVII Y.B. COM. ARB. 599 (1992) (H.L. 1991); *see also* Claude Reymond, *Where is an Arbitral Award Made?*, 108 L.Q. REV. 1 (1992); the disapproving observations by Albert Jan van den Berg, *New York Convention of 1958 – Consolidated Commentary – Cases Reported in Volumes XVII (1992) – XIX (1994)*, XIX Y.B. COM. ARB. 475, 483 (1994); Albert Jan van den Berg, *New York Arbitration Convention 1958: Where is an arbitral award "made"?* Case comment House of Lords, 24 July 1991, Hiscox v. Outhwaite, in THE PLACE OF ARBITRATION 113 (M. Storme and F. De Ly eds., 1992); Michael E. Schneider, *L'arrêt de la Chambre des Lords dans l'affaire Hiscox v. Outhwaite*, 1991 BULL. ASA 279. Happily, neither the UNCITRAL Model Law (Art. 20) nor the 1996 English Arbitration Act (Sec. 3) contains any such restrictions.

[104] Every year, the ICC International Court of Arbitration fixes or confirms the seat of arbitration in over thirty different countries (*see* ICC BULLETIN, Vol. 10, No. 1 (1999)). It should be noted, however, that if an arbitration agreement refers to arbitration at the ICC "in Paris" or "of Paris," the Court will consider that to be an indirect choice of Paris as seat of the arbitration (*see* CRAIG, PARK, PAULSSON, *supra* note 58, at 204). In 1995, this was the case in 23 matters (*see* 1995 Statistical Report, ICC BULLETIN, Vol. 7, No. 1, at 7 (1996)).

[105] See, for example, Section 3 of the 1996 English Arbitration Act, which states that the seat of the arbitration results from the will of the parties, expressed either directly or indirectly by delegation to the arbitral tribunal or other authority, or "in the absence of any such designation, having regard to the parties' agreement and all the relevant circumstances." *See also* Art. 20(1) of the UNCITRAL Model Law, or Art. 1693(1) of the Belgian Judicial Code (Law of May 19, 1998).

required for the performance of each aspect of their brief in the same place, including the hearings and the delivery of the award."[106]

B. – REPRESENTATION OF THE PARTIES

1241. — Most arbitration laws place no restrictions on the possibility for each of the parties to be assisted or represented by the person of its choice.[107] Some countries, however, still restrict the rights of foreign lawyers, or lawyers domiciled abroad, to represent parties before arbitral tribunals sitting in their territory, even in international disputes.[108]

1242. — The issue of the entitlement of counsel or other persons to represent a party to an international arbitration should not be confused with the differences that may result from the various ways in which parties' representatives are required to establish that they are duly empowered to represent their clients, depending on the professional organization to which they belong. It is acceptable that arbitrators dealing with lawyers belonging to organized bars with codes of ethics strict enough to warrant such exemptions refrain from requiring such lawyers to establish the existence of their powers of attorney, in the same way as if they were appearing before courts of their own country. The Netherlands Arbitration Act of 1986 has been interpreted in that way, providing expressly that "the parties may . . . be represented by a practicing lawyer, or . . . by any other person expressly authorized in writing for this purpose" (Art. 1038 of the Code of Civil Procedure). Commentators generally agree that the exemption whereby Dutch lawyers are not required to prove their powers applies equally to

---

[106] See, in French domestic arbitration, Cass. 2e civ., Feb. 9, 1994, Gautier v. Astra plastique, 1995 REV. ARB. 127, and observations by P. Véron; 1994 RTD COM. 477, and observations by J.-C. Dubarry and E. Loquin. On the question of whether the award must be made at the seat of arbitration, see *infra* para. 1410 and, on the determination of the seat as a jurisdictional criterion establishing which court shall hear actions to set an award aside, see *infra* para. 1590.

[107] See, for example, Section 36 of the English Arbitration Act, which provides that "[u]nless otherwise agreed by the parties, a party to arbitral proceedings may be represented in the proceedings by a lawyer or other person chosen by him." Most arbitration rules take a similar position. *See, e.g.,* Art. 4 of the UNCITRAL Rules: "The Parties may be represented or assisted by persons of their choice;" Art. 21(4) of the 1998 ICC Rules (replacing Art. 15(5) of the previous Rules). In French case law, see Cass. 1e civ., June 19, 1979, S.A.R.L. Primor v. Société d'exploitation industrielle de Bétaigne, 1979 REV. ARB. 487, and G. Bolard's note; Gaz. Pal., Jur. 492 (1979), and J. Viatte's note.

[108] For a comparative law analysis, see David W. Rivkin, *Keeping Lawyers Out of International Arbitrations*, 9 INT'L FIN. L. REV. 11 (Feb. 1990) and *Restrictions on Foreign Counsel in International Arbitrations*, XVI Y.B. COM. ARB. 402 (1991). On the liberal interpretation of Malaysian law, see Supreme Court of Malaysia, Jan. 2, 1990, Government of Malaysia v. Zublin–Muhibbah Joint Venture, XVI Y.B. COM. ARB. 166 (1991). In Japan, see Charles R. Stevens, *Japan Commercial Arbitration Rules Revisited*, 9 ARB. INT'L 317 (1993). On the lifting of this restriction by China, see 1995 BULL. ASA 50. As regards Portugal, see Dário Moura Vicente, *L'évolution récente du droit de l'arbitrage au Portugal*, 1991 REV. ARB. 419, especially at 426 *et seq.*

foreign lawyers whose laws contain a similar exemption.[109] Other legal systems require the parties' representatives to establish the existence of their powers in every case.[110]

The safest practice is undoubtedly for the arbitrators or the arbitration institution to systematically require the parties to establish the existence of such powers. Article 21, paragraph 4 of the 1998 ICC Rules (replacing Article 15(5) of the previous Rules) specifies that the parties may appear in person or "through duly authorized representatives," which suggests that the latter must prove the existence of their powers. Similarly, the LCIA Rules expressly reserve the right for the arbitral tribunal to require the parties' representatives to submit proof of their authority (Art. 18.2).

C. – COMMUNICATIONS

1243. — The parties or, if the parties fail to agree, the arbitral tribunal must determine the rules governing communications during the course of the proceedings between the parties, the arbitral tribunal and, where appropriate, the arbitral institution.

This entails specifying the addresses of the parties and their representatives, as well as those of the arbitrators, to whom documents can validly be sent. The permitted methods of communication (ordinary mail, courier delivery, telex or facsimile, for example) should also be specified, as should items such as when time limits for exchanges of evidence or memorials will be considered to have been met (on dispatch or receipt of the documents in question), the starting point for deadlines for the recipient's response and any extension of deadlines falling on public holidays or weekends.

D. – LANGUAGE OF THE ARBITRATION

1244. — The arbitration will take place in the language or languages chosen by the parties or, if the parties fail to make such a choice, by the arbitral tribunal.

Where there is no indication to the contrary, the language chosen by the arbitrators will usually be that of the contract containing the arbitration agreement. In ICC arbitration, Article 16 of the 1998 ICC Rules (replacing Article 15(3) of the previous Rules) states that the language or languages of the arbitration shall be determined by the arbitral tribunal, "due regard being given to all relevant circumstances, including the language of the contract." The 1997 AAA International Arbitration Rules state that the language of the arbitration will be that of the contract containing the arbitration agreement, unless the parties provide otherwise (Art. 14). The LCIA, which took the same position in its 1985 Rules, now provides that, unless the parties agree otherwise, the language of the arbitration agreement will be the "initial language" of the arbitration, but that the arbitral tribunal shall, on its formation, decide upon the language of the arbitration, taking into account the comments of the parties,

---

[109] PIETER SANDERS AND ALBERT JAN VAN DEN BERG, THE NETHERLANDS ARBITRATION ACT 1986, at 74 (1987).
[110] *See* Rivkin, *supra* note 108; DE BOISSÉSON, *supra* note 4, ¶ 736.

the initial language of the arbitration and any other relevant matters (Art. 17). The UNCITRAL Arbitration Rules are more neutral in this respect and simply state that the language of the arbitration is to be determined by the parties or, if they fail to do so, by the arbitral tribunal (Art. 17). The fact that in international commerce the language of the contract will often be English may have contributed to the position taken by the AAA and, previously, the LCIA.[111]

Admittedly, the other solutions put forward are not satisfactory. Apart from the difficulties which it creates where the applicable law has not been chosen by the parties, the idea that it would be preferable to have the language of the arbitration coincide with that of the country whose laws govern the substance of the dispute[112] is certainly much less consistent with the parties' expectations than the rule which gives greater weight to the language of the contract. It has also sometimes been argued, in connection with Swedish law, that a general principle exists whereby, in the absence of an agreement to the contrary, the parties are entitled to express themselves in their own language.[113] However, there is no basis for the existence of such a right. Quite the reverse, in fact: most legal systems, including that of Sweden, give full discretion to the arbitrators, in the absence of an agreement between the parties, to determine the language of the proceedings.[114]

In some cases, arbitrations are held in several languages simultaneously. Given the considerable expense involved—an expense which is often underestimated by the parties—caution should be exercised before choosing that option. Furthermore, the choice of a language for the arbitration proceedings does not necessarily imply that all documents submitted to the arbitrators must be translated into that language. Although, unless the parties agree otherwise, it is common practice for the parties' written submissions and pleadings to be in the language chosen, the arbitrators will often agree that documentary evidence which can be understood in its original language by all parties and by the arbitral tribunal need not be translated. Likewise, where a translation is required, the arbitrators may decide that it need not be officially certified unless it is disputed by the other party.

1245. — Where there is a failure to comply with the provisions as to the language of proceedings agreed by the parties, or determined by the arbitrators failing agreement of the parties, an action to set aside or refuse enforcement of the award may be entertained but will generally prevail only where the principles of due process and equal treatment of the parties are considered to have been violated. Thus, in a case where the agreed language for the

---

[111] On this issue, see Serge Lazareff, *The Language of Institutional Arbitration*, ICC BULLETIN, Vol. 8, No. 1, at 18 (1997).

[112] *See* Detlev von Breitenstein, *La langue de l'arbitrage – Une langue arbitraire?*, 1995 BULL. ASA 18.

[113] *See* THE STOCKHOLM CHAMBER OF COMMERCE, ARBITRATION IN SWEDEN 109 (2d ed. 1984).

[114] See, in the absence of specific requirements in the 1999 Swedish Arbitration Act, Article 23 of the 1999 Rules of the Arbitration Institute of the Stockholm Chamber of Commerce. See also Article 22 of the UNCITRAL Model Law and, for its implementation in German law, Article 1045 of the ZPO, in force as of January 1, 1998; Art. 835 of the Italian Code of Civil Procedure (Law of Jan. 5, 1994); Sec. 34(2)(b) of the 1996 English Arbitration Act. Compare with Article 29 of Egyptian Law No. 27 for 1994 Promulgating the Law Concerning Arbitration in Civil and Commercial Matters, which sets forth a presumption in favor of the Arabic language, but allows the parties or, failing their agreement, the arbitrators to disregard it.

proceedings was English and one of the parties had sent memorials in Spanish to the two Spanish-speaking members of the arbitral tribunal, the Paris Court of Appeals held that as the content of the memorials was identical and as the arbitrators had struck evidence in Spanish from the record, strict equality between the parties had been maintained, and that, as a result, the award was valid.[115]

E. – DEADLINES

1246. — French international arbitration law does not restrict arbitral proceedings to any mandatory time-frame, other than that which may have been laid down by the parties themselves. That principle was reaffirmed by the *Cour de cassation* in its 1994 decisions in the *Sonidep* and *Degrémont* cases.[116]

The logic of that position is that it is for the arbitral tribunal, by agreement with the parties or acting under its own authority, to fix a timetable for the arbitral proceedings. In a typical continental arbitration, the tribunal will set deadlines within which the parties must submit their memorials, produce their documentary evidence (the deadline for which is often the same as that for the memorials), indicate the names of witnesses they wish to call and the subject-matter of their testimony, and file their witness statements.[117] In proceedings that follow the common law tradition, the arbitral tribunal will often allow some discovery of documents and the deposition of witnesses before giving the parties an opportunity to present their claims in detailed memorials, for which the tribunal is sometimes reluctant to fix deadlines in advance. In many continental jurisdictions, however, the parties, or the arbitrators absent agreement between the parties, are entirely free to determine the nature and the pace of proceedings, employing every possible combination of the continental and common law traditions as they see fit.

1247. — In order to retain maximum flexibility with regard to deadlines, arbitrators nowadays generally prefer to specify the timetable in a procedural order, which will be distinct from the terms of reference and less cumbersome to amend, unless the terms of reference themselves contain provisions allowing the arbitrators to alter deadlines.[118] The UNCITRAL Arbitration Rules take a similarly cautious approach. They provide, in

---

[115] CA Paris, June 21, 1990, *Compagnie Honeywell Bull, supra* note 21.

[116] Cass. 1e civ., June 15, 1994, Sonidep v. Sigmoil, 1995 REV. ARB. 88, 1st decision, and E. Gaillard's note; Cass. 1e civ., June 15, 1994, Communauté urbaine de Casablanca v. Degrémont, 1995 REV. ARB. 88, 2d decision, and E. Gaillard's note; 1994 REV. CRIT. DIP 681, and D. Cohen's note. On the question of the duration of the arbitrators' brief in general, see *infra* paras. 1379 *et seq.* and the references cited therein. In Swiss law, see Fed. Trib., Mar. 24, 1997, T AG v. H Company, 1997 BULL. ASA 316, and the commentary by Richard H. Kreindler and Timothy J. Kautz, *Agreed Deadlines and the Setting Aside of Arbitral Awards*, 1997 BULL. ASA 576; for an English translation, see 12 INT'L ARB. REP. H1 (Sept. 1997).

[117] On the arbitrators' discretion where a party fails to comply with the deadlines laid down, see, for a liberal approach, ICC Award No. 6192 (1992), ICC BULLETIN, Vol. 8, No. 2, at 64 (1997).

[118] Compare, on the English practice of "orders for directions," CRAIG, PARK, PAULSSON, *supra* note 58, ¶ 15-02 at 258.

principle, for a period of forty-five days within which each party must communicate its written pleadings, but "the arbitral tribunal may extend the time-limits if it concludes that an extension is justified" (Art. 23). The AAA International Arbitration Rules take a comparable position (Art. 17(2)). Other rules merely seek to confine the submission of new claims or counterclaims within certain limits, so as to ensure that the parties do not belatedly raise claims in a deliberate attempt to obstruct the proceedings.[119]

1248. — It is increasingly common, however, for the parties to set strict contractual time-limits for the arbitrators to complete their brief, if not for each stage of the proceedings. This will necessarily have an impact on the determination of the timetable for the proceedings and, when the deadlines are very stringent, is referred to as "fast-track" arbitration. Thus, for example, in an ICC arbitration which was widely publicized (with the consent of the arbitrators, the parties and their counsel) the parties had stipulated that in the event of a dispute, certain issues were to be resolved by the arbitrators within two months of the request for arbitration. These issues concerned the determination of the price in a long-term gas supply contract between Canada and the United States. The ICC organized the arbitration with remarkable speed and the award was made nine weeks after the request for arbitration was submitted, the parties having agreed to extend the time-limit by one week. During that period, the arbitral tribunal dealt with the challenge of an arbitrator, the drawing up of terms of reference, questions as to the extent of its jurisdiction and the merits of the dispute, memorials were exchanged, the witnesses and parties were heard, and the award was approved by the ICC.[120]

The development of such procedures is welcome because they depart from the traditional image of arbitration as a process which is often less rapid than one might wish for. They reflect the tendency to accelerate resolution of business disputes and the need for increased

---

[119] On the conditions set forth in the ICC Rules, see *supra* para. 1233.

[120] For a description of what is known as the *Panhandle* case, see Arthur W. Rovine, *International Fast-Track Arbitration – Part I: An Overview*, 5 WORLD ARB. & MED. REP. 165 (1994) and the 1992 Awards in ICC Cases No. 7385, Ultimate buyer v. Intermediary buyer/seller, and No. 7402, Intermediary buyer/seller v. Primary seller, XVIII Y.B. COM. ARB. 68 (1993); ICC BULLETIN, Vol. 8, No. 1, at 56 (1997). *See also Fast-Track Arbitration: Different Perspectives*, ICC BULLETIN, Vol. 3, No. 2, at 4 (1992), with the contributions of Benjamin Davis (*The case viewed by a counsel at the ICC Court's Secretariat*), Peter J. Nickles, Moses Silverman and David K. Watkiss (*Three perspectives from the parties' counsels*), and Hans Smit (*A chairman's perspective*) and the contributions of the same authors in 2 AM. REV. INT'L ARB. 138 *et seq.* (1991); Benjamin Davis, *Fast-Track Arbitration and Fast-Tracking Your Arbitration*, 9 J. INT'L ARB. 43 (Dec. 1992); Arthur W. Rovine, *Fast-Track Arbitration – An ICC Breakthrough*, 7 INT'L ARB. REP. 14 (Apr. 1992); David C. Downie, Jr., *"Fast-Track" International Commercial Arbitration: Proposed Institutional Rules*, 2 AM. REV. INT'L ARB. 473 (1991). See also the contributions made during the 1993 Geneva Global Arbitration Forum on the theme of "The drive towards speedier arbitral justice" by Pierre-Yves Tschanz (*The Chamber of Commerce and Industry of Geneva's Arbitration Rules and their Expedited Procedure*, 10 J. INT'L ARB. 51 (Dec. 1993)), Stephen Smid (*The Expedited Procedure in Maritime and Commodity Arbitrations, id.* at 59), and Benjamin Davis, Odette Lagacé Glain and Michael Volkovitsch (*When Doctrines Meet – Fast-Track Arbitration and the ICC Experience, id.* at 69). On other means of accelerating the arbitral proceedings, see, for example, Howard M. Holtzmann, *Streamlining Arbitral Proceedings: Some Techniques of the Iran-United States Claims Tribunal*, 11 ARB. INT'L 39 (1995).

certainty.[121] It is therefore not surprising that studies have recently been conducted to assess the feasibility of fast-track arbitration under various legal systems.[122] Nevertheless, parties would be well advised to use these accelerated procedures only for issues where they are truly warranted, and which are capable of being resolved on a fast-track basis. A dispute relating to price determination is a good example of an issue which both warrants and is capable of fast-track arbitration. In contrast, the whole array of disputes liable to arise out of the delivery of a complex industrial plant would obviously be unsuited to a fast-track procedure. In particular, equality between the parties and compliance with due process would be almost impossible, as the claimant would have ample time to prepare its case in depth before initiating the proceedings, whereas the defendant would be unable to do so. That consideration also highlights the importance of locating the seat of a fast-track arbitration in a country such as France or England, where the courts can hear applications to extend the time-limit within which the arbitrators are to make their award when due process so requires.[123]

F. – POWERS OF THE CHAIRMAN OF THE ARBITRAL TRIBUNAL

1249. — The parties may confer certain powers on the chairman of the arbitral tribunal which the chairman is entitled to exercise either alone or after informally consulting his or her co-arbitrators. These powers may include the option of extending deadlines for one of the parties where its delay is justifiable, fixing the dates of hearings and, more generally, the power to rule on any procedural difficulty.[124] However, unless the parties have agreed otherwise, the proceedings must, for the most part, be conducted by the arbitral tribunal itself. In particular, evidence must be submitted to the entire tribunal, and not to one arbitrator to whom the examination of such evidence is delegated. Article 1461, paragraph 1 of the French New Code of Civil Procedure, which applies on a subsidiary basis where the parties have stipulated that the proceedings are to be governed by French procedural law,[125] expressly provides that "[p]rocedural orders and minutes shall be made by all the arbitrators unless the arbitration agreement authorizes them to delegate this task to one of them."

---

[121] On the issue generally, see IMPROVING INTERNATIONAL ARBITRATION – THE NEED FOR SPEED AND TRUST – LIBER AMICORUM MICHEL GAUDET (B. Davis ed., 1998). See also the optional expedited procedure made available to the parties at Article 31 of the Arbitration Rules of the 1992 Geneva Chamber of Commerce and Industry. For a commentary, see Tschanz and Kaufmann, *supra* note 53.

[122] *See International Fast-Track Commercial Arbitration, in* COMP. L.Y.B. OF INT'L BUS., SPECIAL ISSUE, DISPUTE RESOLUTION METHODS 357–455 (1994).

[123] On these issues, see *infra* para. 1387.

[124] On these powers, generally, see Claude Reymond, *The President of the Arbitral Tribunal,* 9 ICSID REV. – FOREIGN INV. L.J. 1 (1994) and for a French version, *in* ETUDES OFFERTES À PIERRE BELLET 467 (1991).

[125] *See infra* para. 1257.

The same rule applies in Swiss law: Article 184, paragraph 1 of the Private International Law Act specifies that "[t]he arbitral tribunal shall itself take the evidence."[126]

The chairman of the arbitral tribunal, acting alone, may thus only take a number of purely administrative measures.[127] It is also widely accepted that he or she is responsible for keeping order at the hearings, as well as for chairing them.[128]

The LCIA Rules confer special powers on the chairman of the tribunal, even in the absence of a specific agreement between the parties to that effect. They provide, in Article 14, paragraph 3, that if the arbitral tribunal comprises three members, the chairman may, after consulting his co-arbitrators, make procedural decisions alone. This is an indication of the persistent English preference in favor of sole arbitrators.

G. – SECRETARY OF THE ARBITRAL TRIBUNAL

1250. — In large international arbitrations, the arbitrators' workload will be considerable. The amount of evidence submitted, the size of the memorials exchanged and the number and length of witness hearings are often extremely significant. In addition, the facilities available to the parties' representatives in managing such extensive documentation are often disproportionate to those available to the arbitral tribunal. As a result, it is now common in large international disputes to follow the Swiss practice[129] of allowing the arbitral tribunal to appoint a secretary. The secretary will essentially provide administrative assistance, and obviously cannot replace the arbitral tribunal in the decision-making process.[130] In 1988, the ICC International Court of Arbitration recognized the arbitral tribunal's entitlement to a secretary by means of an amendment to the explanatory note which is sent to the parties and to the arbitrators at the beginning of the proceedings.[131] The French courts clearly endorsed this practice in an action to set aside an award based on an alleged breach of due process and of equality between the parties, purportedly caused by the presence of the secretary of the arbitral tribunal at some of the hearings and his alleged interference in the proceedings. The

---

[126] On this issue, generally, see J. Van Compernolle, *L'arbitrage dans les relations commerciales internationales: questions de procédure*, 66 REV. DR. INT. DR. COMP. 101, 115–16 (1989).

[127] CA Paris, April 26, 1985, Aranella v. Italo-Ecuadoriana, 1985 REV. ARB. 311, and E. Mezger's note; 113 J.D.I. 175 (1986), and J.-M. Jacquet's note.

[128] See, for example, Article 1693, paragraph 3 of the Belgian Judicial Code; Art. 14 of the ICSID Rules.

[129] *See* Arts. 7 and 15 of the 1969 *Concordat*.

[130] Compare the English notion of registrar, REDFERN AND HUNTER, *supra* note 22, at 246 *et seq.*

[131] See the December 29, 1988 letter from the Secretary General, 1989 BULL. ASA 82, and the observations by Pierre Lalive, *Secrétaire des tribunaux arbitraux: le bon sens l'emporte, id.* at 1; the ICC Secretariat subsequently specified in an October 1, 1995 note that the remuneration of an administrative secretary should normally be covered by the arbitrators' fees, and not reimbursed separately as an expense. *See Note from the Secretariat of the ICC Court Concerning the Appointment of Administrative Secretaries by Arbitral Tribunals,* ICC BULLETIN, Vol. 6, No. 2, at 77 (1995). On the resulting controversy, see Pierre Lalive, *Un post-scriptum et quelques citations,* 1996 BULL. ASA 35; Eric Schwartz, *On the Subject of "Administrative Secretaries",* 1996 BULL. ASA 32. On the issue, see also DERAINS AND SCHWARTZ, *supra* note 1, at 334 *et seq.* In ICSID arbitration, each tribunal has a secretary appointed by the ICSID Secretary-General, who is generally drawn from the Secretariat of the Centre (ICSID Administrative and Financial Regulation 25).

court dismissed the action and held that the tribunal "was entitled to appoint a secretary" and that it had not been established "how he had interfered in the proceedings."[132]

H. – TAKING OF EVIDENCE

1251. — One of the most important procedural issues to be resolved by the arbitrators concerns the taking of evidence, both written and oral. The decision to allow a common law-style discovery procedure, or to call and have the parties examine numerous witnesses, will have a substantial impact on the conduct of the arbitration. Similarly, the appointment of an independent expert, or the decision to allow the parties to submit the findings of their own experts, may be very significant. As noted earlier,[133] these issues can be determined either at the beginning of the proceedings or as and when they arise.[134]

I. – PARTIAL AWARDS

1252. — From the outset of the proceedings, the parties can stipulate that the arbitrators shall make separate awards on different aspects of the dispute. The parties may, for example, ask the arbitrators to rule successively on jurisdiction and the merits, or successively on the principle of liability and the quantum of damage, if need be. Where it is expressed with sufficient clarity, the intention of the parties that these issues be dealt with in separate awards will bind the arbitrators.[135] In the absence of any agreement between the parties on the matter, the arbitrators may themselves choose to decide the various issues before them by way of partial awards, or to dispose of all the issues in a single award.[136]

J. – COSTS OF THE ARBITRATION

1253. — The costs of the arbitration include the arbitrators' fees,[137] all expenses connected with the hearings (such as hiring premises and stenotypists' fees), fees and expenses of any experts engaged by the tribunal and the administrative expenses of the arbitral institution, if one is involved.

---

[132] CA Paris, June 21, 1990, *Compagnie Honeywell Bull*, *supra* note 21, at 100.

[133] *See supra* para. 1197.

[134] These issues are examined in more detail *infra* paras. 1257 *et seq.*

[135] *See* Cass. 1e civ., Mar. 8, 1988, *Sofidif*, *supra* note 83.

[136] On this issue, generally, see *infra* para. 1360.

[137] *See supra* paras. 1158 *et seq.*

In institutional arbitration, the arbitral institution is responsible for obtaining an advance from the parties in respect of these fees and expenses.[138] In *ad hoc* arbitration, the tribunal should consider asking the parties to provide an advance on the costs of the arbitration at the beginning of the proceedings.[139]

1254. — The costs of the arbitration are generally advanced by the parties in equal shares. However, the party in whose interest it is to resort to arbitration may have to pay the entire advance where the other party fails to put forward its share.[140] In that case, the party advancing the costs will ask the arbitral tribunal to order the defaulting party, in the final award or even in a partial award confined to that issue, to pay its share because, by agreeing to refer disputes to arbitration, the defaulting party had undertaken to do so.[141] A French lower court even went so far as to uphold its jurisdiction to order a party to pay damages where, having filed a request for arbitration, it then refused to pay the advance required to enable the arbitration to go ahead.[142] Other courts have intervened to order the defaulting party to pay its share of the arbitration costs.[143]

1255. — Even where the parties initially agree to advance the costs of the arbitration in equal shares, the arbitrators are generally required to rule on the ultimate allocation of the arbitration costs, including the fees and expenses incurred by the parties in preparing their case.[144] In the absence of an agreement between the parties,[145] the arbitral tribunal is free to

---

[138] On the advantages of a fee scale applied by certain arbitral institutions, see *supra* para. 1160.

[139] *See, e.g.*, Art. 41 of the UNCITRAL Arbitration Rules.

[140] In order to accelerate proceedings, the 1998 ICC Rules no longer make the effectiveness of the terms of reference conditional upon payment by the parties of the advance on costs. Instead, after consultation with the arbitral tribunal and the expiration of a final deadline fixed by the ICC, any claims put forward by the non-paying party are deemed to have been withdrawn (Art. 30(4)). On the costs mechanisms in ICC arbitration, see Grigera Naon, *supra* note 1, at 44 *et seq.*; DERAINS AND SCHWARTZ, *supra* note 1, at 303 *et seq*. On the finding that a failure by a claimant to pay an advance on fees constitutes a withdrawal of its claim, see also, in French domestic arbitration law, Cass. 2e civ., Jan. 26, 1994, *Ferruzzi, supra* note 10.

[141] On this issue, generally, see ICCA CONGRESS SERIES NO. 5, PREVENTING DELAY AND DISRUPTION OF ARBITRATION/EFFECTIVE PROCEEDINGS IN CONSTRUCTION CASES (A.J. van den Berg, ed., 1991).

[142] Trib. com. Beaune, July 8, 1994, Wenko Wenselaar v. S.A. GB Industries, 1995 REV. ARB. 132, and observations by P. Véron.

[143] *See* TGI Beauvais, réf., Apr. 9, 1998, Fertalge Euromade Alger v. Kaltenbach Thuring SA, No. 5087/98, unpublished. *Comp. with* Trib. com. Paris, réf., Dec. 18, 1998, SARL Sifamos v. Grammer AG, No. 98 099216 - n° 25, unpublished.

[144] *Comp.* Art. 31(3) of the 1998 ICC Rules (replacing Art. 20(1) of the previous Rules); Art. 40 of the UNCITRAL Arbitration Rules; Art. 28 of the 1998 LCIA Rules and Art. 31 of the 1997 AAA International Arbitration Rules. On the questionable practice of the arbitrators incorporating an order to pay their fees in the award itself, see *supra* para. 1162.

[145] Two types of agreement are often seen: those which have each party bear their own costs, and those which have the losing party bear all the costs. The latter requires interpretation only where the losing party is only partially unsuccessful. A proportional split would appear to be consistent with the intentions of the parties in that case. On the setting aside of an award which did not follow such provisions on the grounds that the arbitrators exceeded their brief, see, in French domestic arbitration, CA Paris, Mar. 20, 1986, Mondeil v. de Ligaut, 1987

(continued...)

apportion these costs as it sees fit.[146] It is increasingly common for the arbitral tribunal to order the party which is defeated on the merits of a dispute to pay all or a substantial part of the costs of the arbitration. That is traditionally the practice in some common law countries[147] and now frequently occurs when the arbitral tribunal has its seat in continental jurisdictions such as France[148] or Switzerland.[149] In reaching their decision on the allocation of costs between the parties, arbitrators may take into account the attitude of the parties during the arbitral proceedings.[150] This issue is of considerable importance, because arbitration proceedings—particularly where the dispute is complex and large amounts are at stake—can be extremely costly.[151]

1256. — When confronted with the prospect of incurring such expenses, one of the parties, usually the defendant, may ask that its opponent be ordered to provide a guarantee to cover the costs incurred in the course of the arbitration, including lawyers' fees. This application will often be made before the proceedings have even begun. That request for

---

[145] (...continued)
REV. ARB. 82, and observations by B. Moreau.

[146] *See, e.g.*, Vaud Cantonal Trib., Feb. 16, 1993, Brega v. Techint, 1995 BULL. ASA 57, 62, and observations by J.-F. Poudret. On the finding that arbitrators do not violate due process by ruling on the costs of the arbitration, when so requested by one party and having questioned each party on the amount of costs incurred, see, in the United States, Compagnie des Bauxites de Guinée v. Hammermills, Inc., Civ. A. No. 90-0169 (JGP), 1992 WL 122712 (D.D.C. May 29, 1992); XVIII Y.B. COM. ARB. 566 (1993).

[147] On the practice in England, see, for example, Channel Island Ferries Ltd. v. Cenargo Navigation Ltd. ("The Rozel"), [1994] 2 Lloyd's Rep. 161; 1994 BULL. ASA 439 (High Ct., Q.B. (Com. Ct.) 1994). The principle is now found in Section 61 of the 1996 Arbitration Act.

[148] For examples of ICC arbitral tribunals sitting in Paris requiring the losing party to bear the prevailing party's costs, see ICC Award No. 6962 (1992), Seller v. Buyer, XIX Y.B. COM. ARB. 184 (1994); ICC Award No. 6917 (1993), unpublished.

[149] In Switzerland, see, for example, the Award by T. Giovannini in ICC Case No. 7419 (1995), European company B. S.p.A. v. North African company S. S.A., 1995 BULL. ASA 535, and the award cited *infra* note 149.

[150] *See* ICC Award No. 8486 (1996), Dutch party v. Turkish party, 125 J.D.I. 1047 (1998), and observations by Y. Derains.

[151] In the *Westland* case, which lasted thirteen years, the final award made in Switzerland on June 28, 1993 awarded costs of 18 million pounds sterling against the losing party on this basis (ICC Award No. 3879 (June 28, 1993), Westland Helicopters Ltd. v. Arab Organization for Industrialization, unpublished, cited in 1994 BULL. ASA 404); the award was upheld by the Swiss Fed. Trib., Apr. 19, 1994, Les Emirats Arabes Unis v. Westland Helicopters Ltd., 1994 BULL. ASA 404, 426; 1995 BULL. ASA 186, and P. Schweizer's note; 1995 REV. SUISSE DR. INT. ET DR. EUR. 564, and P. Schweizer's note. In *Southern Pacific Properties*, which lasted fourteen years and in which an ICSID proceeding followed an ICC arbitration, the arbitral tribunal awarded SPP over 5 million U.S. dollars in compensation for expert and legal fees on top of damages for loss suffered as a result of expropriation (*see* May 20, 1992 Award by E. Jimenez de Arechaga, president, R. Pietrowski, Jr. and M.A. El Mahdi, arbitrators (M.A. El Mahdi dissenting), in ICSID Case No. ARB/84/3, Southern Pacific Properties (Middle East) Ltd. v. Arab Republic of Egypt, 32 I.L.M. 933 (1993), with correction at 32 I.L.M. 1470 (1993); 8 ICSID REV. – FOREIGN INV. L.J. 328 (1993), XIX Y.B. COM. ARB. 51 (1994); 8 INT'L ARB. REP. A1 (Aug. 1993); 3 ICSID REP. 189 (1995); for a French translation, see 121 J.D.I. 229, 237–38 (1994), and observations by E. Gaillard). On ways of controlling costs, see Michael E. Schneider, *Lean Arbitration: Cost Control and Efficiency Through Progressive Identification of Issues and Separate Pricing of Arbitration Services*, 10 ARB. INT'L 119 (1994).

security for costs, or a *cautio judicatum solvi*, raises two questions which should be carefully distinguished.

The first concerns the arbitrators' jurisdiction to order such measures. It has been held on occasions that arbitrators hearing the merits of a dispute do not have jurisdiction to hear applications for security for costs, which is the exclusive preserve of the courts. That was the position in English law prior to the 1996 reform.[152] That approach is clearly unsatisfactory[153] as the arbitrators have jurisdiction to take any protective measure justified by the circumstances.[154] The arbitration agreement is usually drafted in sufficiently broad terms for the arbitrators' jurisdiction to include granting protective measures to ensure that it will be possible to compel a party to pay the costs in the event that they are awarded against it. Thus, it was to the general satisfaction that the 1996 English Arbitration Act reversed prior case law by specifically providing that "[t]he tribunal may order a claimant [or a counterclaimant but not a mere defendant] to provide security for the costs of the arbitration."[155] The same position is implicitly accepted in most legal systems.

The second question raised by requests for security for costs is whether such a measure should be granted in international arbitration. It would be particularly unfortunate if the granting of security for costs were to become the norm, as is the case before the courts of a number of countries when the plaintiff is foreign. Access to arbitral justice would be systematically obstructed, which would be odd at a time when arbitration has become the normal means of resolving disputes in international commerce.[156]

In particular, it would be unacceptable—and probably contrary to international public policy in many countries—for security for costs to be ordered on the grounds of the

---

[152] On English law prior to the 1996 Arbitration Act, see the May 5, 1994 decision of the House of Lords, Coppée-Lavalin SA/NV v. Ken-Ren Chemicals and Fertilizers Ltd., [1994] 2 W.L.R. 631; [1994] 2 All E.R. 449; XX Y.B. COM. ARB. 223 (1995); 9 INT'L ARB. REP. 3 (May 1994); for a French translation, see 1995 REV. ARB. 513, and D. Kapelink-Klinger's note. See also the November 12, 1991 Order of an arbitral tribunal constituted under the aegis of the Zurich Chamber of Commerce, 1995 BULL. ASA 84, 90. For a decision against requiring security for costs in arbitration, see the December 9, 1994 *ad hoc* Award made in Geneva by P.A. Recordon, Panamanian party v. Party domiciled in Geneva, 1995 BULL. ASA 529.

[153] For criticism of the English law approach prior to the 1996 Arbitration Act, see Claude Reymond, *Security for Costs in International Arbitration*, 110 L.Q. REV. 501 (1994); John Beechey, *International Arbitrations and the Award of Security for Costs in England*, 1994 BULL. ASA 179; Jan A.S. Paulsson, *The Unwelcome Atavism of Ken-Ren: the House of Lords Shows its Meddle*, 1994 BULL. ASA 439; Brian Davenport, *The Ken-Ren Case: Much Ado About Nothing Very Much*, 10 ARB. INT'L 303 (1994); David J. Branson, *The Ken-Ren Case: It is an Ado Where More Aid is Less Help*, 10 ARB. INT'L 313 (1994); Sophie Nappert, *The Ken-Ren Appeals: the House of Lords on Security for Costs and ICC Arbitration*, 1994 INT'L BUS.L.J. 643.

[154] *See infra* paras. 1314 *et seq.*

[155] Sec. 38(3). For a commentary, see V.V. Veeder, *England* (at 43), *in* ICCA INTERNATIONAL HANDBOOK ON COMMERCIAL ARBITRATION (1997); Claude Reymond, *L'Arbitration Act, 1996 – Convergence et originalité*, 1997 REV. ARB. 45, 61; Peter Fitzpatrick, *Security for Costs under the Arbitration Act 1996*, 1 INT'L ARB. L. REV. 139 (1998); Otto Sandrock, *The Cautio Judicatum Solvi in Arbitration Proceedings or The Duty of an Alien Claimant to Provide Security for the Costs of the Defendant*, 14 J. INT'L ARB. 17 (June 1997). On the issue, see also Andreas Reiner, *Les mesures provisoires et conservatoires et l'Arbitrage international, notamment l'Arbitrage CCI*, 125 J.D.I. 853, 890 (1998). On the conditions under which such security will be granted, see *infra* note 158.

[156] *See supra* para. 1.

nationality or domicile of one of the parties.[157] That is why the 1996 English Arbitration Act specifically states that the fact that a party has its habitual residence outside the United Kingdom, or is a foreign company or one "whose central management and control is exercised outside the United Kingdom" is not a valid ground for security for costs to be ordered (Sec. 38(3)(a) and (b)). On the other hand, the arbitral tribunal may consider such measures to be justified in some specific situations. The fact that a party is suffering financial difficulties or is the subject of bankruptcy proceedings is certainly not sufficient, in itself, to form the basis of a request for security. However, that may not be the case where a party appears to have deliberately organized its insolvency while commencing what may prove to be lengthy and expensive arbitral proceedings against its co-contractor. In that situation, the arbitrators may consider it necessary, as a protective measure, to order the insolvent party—or both parties—to deposit the sums required to cover the reimbursement of the other party's arbitration costs, in the event that at the end of the proceedings an award of costs is made.[158]

SECTION III
PLEADINGS AND EVIDENCE

1257. — Most recent arbitration statutes also give the parties and, on a subsidiary basis, the arbitral tribunal broad powers to resolve any procedural questions that may arise.[159] In international arbitrations held in France, for instance, the parties and, absent agreement of the parties, the arbitrators are free to submit the arbitral proceedings to any law, rule of law or body of rules they consider appropriate. For the arbitrators, that freedom goes as far as

---

[157] See for example the exclusion of security for costs on the basis of nationality, domicile or residence under the Hague Convention of March 1, 1954 on Civil Procedure (Art. 17, para. 1).

[158] ICC Award No. 6632 (Brussels, Jan. 27, 1993), unpublished, bases its decision to order both parties to provide security for costs (including legal fees) on similar grounds and also on the parties' obligation to refrain from "any act liable to have an adverse effect on the enforcement of the forthcoming award," using the expression coined in the December 23, 1982 Partial Award in ICC Case No. 3896 (Framatome S.A. v. Atomic Energy Organization of Iran (AEOI), 110 J.D.I. 914 (1983), and observations by S. Jarvin; for an English translation, see X Y.B. COM. ARB. 47 (1985)). See also the posting of security for costs ordered by the December 26, 1990 award by Messrs. Robine, chairman, Decker and Mayrand, arbitrators, in ICC Case No. 6697 (Casa v. Cambior, 1992 REV. ARB. 135, 145, and P. Ancel's note); and the December 21, 1998, Procedural Order in *ad hoc* arbitration, X v. Y, 1999 BULL. ASA 59, in a case where the plaintiff was involved in bankruptcy proceedings. Compare, on the refusal to grant such a measure in a case where one party had contracted from the outset with a company with very limited financial resources, ICC Award No. 7047 (Feb. 28, 1994) Corporation W. v. State agency F., 1995 BULL. ASA 301, 306; for an English translation, see XIX Y.B. COM. ARB. 79 (1994); ICC BULLETIN, Vol. 8, No. 1, at 61 (1997); Dec. 11, 1995 Procedural Order in ICC Case No. 8479, 1997 BULL. ASA 363; Oct. 15, 1992 Procedural Order incorporated in ICC Award No. 7489 (1993), ICC BULLETIN, Vol. 8, No. 2, at 68 (1997).

[159] *See, e.g.*, Art. 19 of the UNCITRAL Model Law; Art. 1042 of the German ZPO (Law of Dec. 22, 1997); Art. 1693 of the Belgian Judicial Code; Art. 816 of the Italian Code of Civil Procedure; Art. 182 of the Swiss Private International Law Statute; Art. 1036 of the Netherlands Code of Civil Procedure; Sec. 34 of the 1996 English Arbitration Act; Sec. 21 of the 1999 Swedish Arbitration Act.

allowing them to refrain from determining the applicable rules in advance, so as to retain the possibility of resolving each procedural difficulty as and when it arises.[160]

Where the parties or the arbitrators have chosen French law to govern the arbitral procedure, that law only applies in the absence of an agreement between the parties determining the procedure. Article 1495 of the New Code of Civil Procedure provides that:

> [w]here the international arbitration is governed by French law, the provisions of Titles I [arbitration agreements], II [the arbitral proceedings] and III [arbitral awards] of the present Book shall only apply in the absence of a specific agreement, and subject to Articles 1493 [the constitution of the arbitral tribunal] and 1494 [the freedom of the parties or, subsidiarily, the arbitrators to determine the procedure].[161]

For the arbitrators, the only limits, other than those resulting from the intentions of the parties, derive from the requirements of international procedural public policy. These include, in particular, equality between the parties and compliance with the requirements of due process, a breach of which would allow the award to be set aside.[162]

1258. — Arbitrations organized in countries which have adopted such a liberal regime can therefore draw on a variety of different legal systems for rules governing pleadings and evidence.

In particular, advantage can be taken of the differences between common law and civil law systems as to the conduct of the proceedings and the taking of evidence, and parties or arbitrators can pick and choose the rules which are best suited to a particular case.[163]

Before the courts those differences remain marked. For example, the pre-trial discovery procedure used in England and the United States is undoubtedly one of the features of common law proceedings that continental lawyers find most difficult to accept. It enables a party to obtain from its opponent the disclosure of all the documents in its possession that are relevant to the dispute and not covered by privilege. The extent of discovery obligations varies from one legal system to the next: for example, more discovery is generally available

---

[160] *See supra* para. 1197.

[161] For an in-depth commentary of this provision, see Daniel Cohen, *La soumission de l'arbitrage international à la loi française (Commentaire de l'article 1495 NCPC)*, 1991 REV. ARB. 155; Eric Loquin, *Arbitrage – Instance arbitrale – Procédure devant les arbitres*, J.-CL. PROC. CIV., Fasc. 1036, ¶¶ 7 *et seq.* (1994).

[162] See, for example, in France, Articles 1502 and 1504 of the New Code of Civil Procedure; *see infra* para. 1638.

[163] *See, e.g.*, Georges Rouhette, *L'administration de la preuve au cours des arbitrages commerciaux se déroulant selon les systèmes de droit français et de common law*, 1974 REV. ARB. 237; J. Gillis Wetter, *The Conduct of the Arbitration*, 2 J. INT'L ARB. 7 (June 1985); Arthur L. Marriott, *Evidence in International Arbitration*, 5 ARB. INT'L 280 (1989); Mauro Rubino-Sammartano, *Rules of Evidence in International Arbitration – A Need for Discipline and Harmonization*, 3 J. INT'L ARB. 87 (June 1986); Christian Dieryck, *Procédure et moyens de preuve dans l'arbitrage commercial international*, 1988 REV. ARB. 267; Enrico Righetti, *L'istruzione probatoria nell'arbitrato istituzionale commerciale e marittimo*, 1993 RIV. DELL'ARB. 315; Justin Thorens, *L'arbitre international au point de rencontre des traditions du droit civil et de la common law – Deux problèmes liés, l'un à la communication des pièces et l'autre à l'audition des témoins*, in ETUDES DE DROIT INTERNATIONAL EN L'HONNEUR DE PIERRE LALIVE 693 (1993).

in the United States than in England.[164] Continental systems are familiar with the principle of compulsory disclosure of documents, but they implement it in a far more limited way.[165]

The examination of witnesses by the lawyers of each party is also a feature of common law systems.[166] This contrasts with the methods used in continental systems, where witness evidence is given less weight, witness statements are generally in writing and the court is responsible for the oral examination of witnesses, with the parties only suggesting questions.

1259. — Various explanations for these differences have been put forward. Traditionally, continental proceedings are perceived as being more inquisitorial, whereas common law proceedings are seen as more adversarial.[167] The importance of the oral stage of proceedings in common law countries has also been explained by the presence of a jury in some civil trials.[168] In addition, the common law systems attach considerable importance to strict equality between the parties.[169] This requirement prevails over other concerns, such as business secrecy, and will only be fully satisfied where each of the parties has had access to all the documents of the case and an opportunity to examine all witnesses directly.[170]

Despite the harmonization of national arbitration statutes, which all give wide discretion to the arbitrators, the factors described above account for the differences between an arbitration held in England or the United States and a continental arbitration, as the lawyers and arbitrators involved will naturally tend to transpose the approach they would follow before their own courts.

1260. — In practice, however, international commercial arbitrations now tend to follow an increasingly uniform pattern. The written stage is essentially based on continental procedure, whereas the oral stage has been influenced to a greater extent by Anglo-American techniques. As regards the written submission of a party's case, common lawyers themselves recognize the predominance of the "European model," whereby a party's arguments are

---

[164] On U.S. discovery, see Federal Rules of Civil Procedure, Rules 26–37; for a comparison of English and American laws on this issue, see Charles N. Brower, *Discovery and Production of Evidence in the United States: theory and practice, in* TAKING OF EVIDENCE IN INTERNATIONAL ARBITRAL PROCEEDINGS 7 (ICC Publication No. 440/8, 1990); David St. J. Sutton, *Discovery and Production of Evidence in Arbitral Proceedings – the U.S. and England distinguished, id.* at 57.

[165] On blocking statutes designed to prevent extraterritorial discovery, see especially CAHIERS DU CEDIN, L'APPLICATION EXTRA-TERRITORIALE DU DROIT ÉCONOMIQUE (1987).

[166] *See* John P. Madden, *How to present witness evidence in an arbitration – American style*, 1993 BULL. ASA 438.

[167] *But see* Lord Justice Staughton, *Common Law and Civil Law Procedures. Which Is the More Inquisitorial? A Common Lawyer's Response*, 5 ARB. INT'L 351 (1989); Claude Reymond, *Civil Law and Common Law Procedures: Which Is the More Inquisitorial? A Civil Lawyer's Response*, 5 ARB. INT'L 357 (1989).

[168] *See, e.g.*, Reymond, *supra* note 167, at 359.

[169] See also the comparative law analysis of DE BOISSÉSON, *supra* note 4, at 729.

[170] *See* Emmanuel Gaillard, *La réaction américaine aux lois de blocage, in* CAHIERS DU CEDIN, L'APPLICATION EXTRA-TERRITORIALE DU DROIT ÉCONOMIQUE 115, 118 (1987).

presented together with the supporting written evidence.[171] Initially at least, each party must choose from among the documents in its possession those which actually support its claims, whereas the common law approach is for each party to be given an opportunity to consult all the documents of the case before deciding on its arguments. On the other hand, during the oral stage—even where the arbitration is held in a civil law country—it is not unusual for the parties to be able to examine the witnesses using common law methods.[172]

Given this procedural convergence, it is possible to describe the conduct of an international arbitration in general terms, by considering in turn the submission of memorials and evidence (§ 1), the examination of witnesses (§ 2), the use of experts (§ 3) and the hearings (§ 4).

§ 1. – The Submission of Memorials and Evidence

1261. — The submission of memorials and evidence is essentially governed by agreement between the parties, whether or not that agreement is embodied in terms of reference, and by the provisions of any applicable arbitration rules, subject to the procedural public policy requirements of due process and equal treatment of the parties.

In anything but the smallest arbitrations, the parties will usually exchange two sets of written submissions (referred to, for example, as memorial, counter-memorial, reply and rejoinder). In most cases, that exchange will be successive, rather than simultaneous.[173] The parties are sometimes able to submit further observations after the examination of witnesses or even after the final hearing, in what is often referred to as a post-hearing brief. The arbitral tribunal may at any time request the parties to provide a written explanation of any issue on which it considers that further information is required.[174]

The presentation of evidence to the tribunal and to the other party or parties often raises more difficult issues.

A. – EVIDENCE TO BE SUBMITTED

1262. — When evidence is presented to the arbitral tribunal, it must also be communicated to the other party. The communication to the other party must cover all elements of fact and law submitted to the tribunal. The tribunal must ensure that this

---

[171] Andreas Lowenfeld, *The Two-Way Mirror: International Arbitration as Comparative Procedure*, 10 MICH. Y.B. INT'L STUD. 163 (1985). For an example of a court decision refusing to set aside an award for not having ordered extensive discovery, see CA Paris, Jan. 19, 1999, *CIC International*, *supra* note 81.

[172] For an attempt to strike a compromise between continental and common law procedures regarding evidence, see the IBA Rules on the Taking of Evidence in International Commercial Arbitration, to be adopted by the IBA Concil at its Boston meeting on June 1, 1999. These Rules will replace the 1983 IBA Rules of Evidence (1 ARB. INT'L 125 (1985), and the commentary by D.W. Shenton, *An Introduction to the IBA Rules of Evidence*, *id.* at 118; for a French translation, see 1986 REV. ARB. 655, with a commentary by Xavier de Mello at 660).

[173] *See supra* para. 1219.

[174] On the deadlines for producing these documents, see *supra* paras. 1246 *et seq.*

fundamental requirement is complied with, as its breach could cause the award to be set aside[175] or its enforcement denied.[176]

1263. — In litigation before the courts of certain jurisdictions, documents aimed at establishing the content of the applicable law (such as legislative texts and case law) need not be produced because they are considered matters of law and are therefore supposedly public knowledge. This practice—which is unsatisfactory even in court proceedings—should be rejected in international arbitration. For example, it would be unacceptable if, when submitting its pleading notes to the tribunal at a hearing, a party were to include case law without simultaneously communicating them to the other party and, when appropriate, without the tribunal allowing the other party the opportunity to respond. As an arbitral tribunal has no forum, it should consider all laws to be foreign laws, the content of which should be established as though it were an element of fact. The idea that foreign laws should be treated as issues of fact is well established in both common law[177] and civil law[178] systems and should apply in international arbitral practice.[179]

1264. — Pleading notes[180] themselves can only be submitted to the arbitral tribunal if a copy is communicated to the other party at the same time.[181]

1265. — Parties sometimes invoke confidentiality concerns in seeking to limit their obligation to disclose to their opponent all documents which they submit to the arbitral tribunal. This is liable to create considerable difficulties. A party may legitimately wish to

---

[175] See, for example, on the setting aside of an award that referred to an opinion which was not communicated to one of the parties, CA Paris, Jan. 18, 1983, Sporprom Service B.V. v. Polyfrance Immo, 1984 REV. ARB. 87, and P. Mayer's note.

[176] See CA Paris, Feb. 12, 1993, Unichips Finanziaria v. Gesnouin, 1993 REV. ARB. 255, 3d decision, and D. Hascher's note; 1993 RTD COM. 646, and observations by J.-C. Dubarry and E. Loquin; 1993 BULL. ASA 564; for an English translation, see XIX Y.B. COM. ARB. 658 (1994). On this issue, generally, see *infra* para. 1638.

[177] For England, see Wetter, *supra* note 163, at 25. The 1996 English Arbitration Act simply states that the arbitral tribunal should, unless the parties agree otherwise, determine "whether and to what extent the tribunal should itself take the initiative in ascertaining the facts and the law" (Sec. 34(2)(g)).

[178] See, e.g., HENRI BATIFFOL AND PAUL LAGARDE, DROIT INTERNATIONAL PRIVÉ, Vol. 1, ¶ 328 (8th ed. 1993); PIERRE MAYER, DROIT INTERNATIONAL PRIVÉ ¶ 193 (6th ed. 1998).

[179] But see Wetter, *supra* note 163, at 25. On the extent of the review by the French courts of these issues, see *infra* para. 1639.

[180] Parties submit pleading notes to the court during or immediately after hearings in a number of continental jurisdictions, including France and Switzerland. The same procedure is often adopted in international arbitration, particularly when conducted in the continental tradition. Pleading notes usually consist of a compilation or summary of a party's earlier written pleadings, in the form of notes on each of the issues raised. In the French tradition, evidence and legal materials pertinent to each issue will be inserted after the note on that issue for the court's convenience. No new evidence or legal materials should be produced, and no new arguments raised. However, if it transpires that a party has failed to comply with that rule, due process will only be respected if its opponent is given sufficient opportunity to respond to the new evidence, legal materials or arguments, or if they are struck from the record. See also *infra* para. 1301.

[181] Comp. Dieryck, *supra* note 163, at 271.

avoid revealing certain documents to its opponent. Know-how or pricing information, for example, might provide an opponent who is also a competitor with an undeserved advantage. The 1998 ICC Rules recognize this concern, providing at Article 20, paragraph 7 that "[t]he Arbitral Tribunal may take measures for protecting trade secrets and confidential information." A party may in fact ask for documents to be submitted only to the arbitral tribunal, or only to its chairman, without communicating them to the other party. However, this might be construed as a breach of due process and, thus, as a ground for setting aside the award. The party intending to rely on such a document might therefore have to choose between producing it or protecting its confidentiality. Only if all parties agree that their rights will not be unduly affected would it be acceptable for documents to be submitted to the tribunal and not to the other side. However, a question remains as to whether the arbitrators could allow that to happen, even with the parties' consent, as due process is a matter of public policy.[182] If the parties do consent in full knowledge of the facts—that is, once the problem has arisen—it would appear that they can validly agree that certain documents may be submitted to the tribunal alone and can therefore waive their right to contest the award on those grounds. The question will also arise where a party simply makes no objection when a breach of due process is committed, which raises the issue as to whether by remaining silent that party forfeits its right to challenge the award at a later stage. The answer will generally be in the affirmative.[183] On the other hand, we believe it to be doubtful whether an agreement given in advance to the mechanism found in Article 20, paragraph 2 of the 1998 ICC Rules, through the reference to those Rules in one's arbitration agreement, is sufficient to allow the arbitrators to see documents provided by one party which are not shown to the other party.[184]

Where a party seeks to rely on the confidentiality of certain documents so as to defeat the other party's request for compulsory disclosure, it is up to the arbitral tribunal to decide whether there are valid grounds for not disclosing the documents in question.

One solution may be for a party disclosing confidential documents to do so on condition that the opposing party or parties, the arbitral tribunal and any arbitral institution that receives copies of the documents sign a confidentiality agreement. The aim of such an agreement is to oblige each signatory to limit the use of the disclosed documents to purposes strictly related to the arbitration, if need be to limit the number of individuals who will have access to the documents, and to return all original documents and copies after the arbitration. However, the difficulty with confidentiality agreements becomes apparent if a document does become public knowledge. It will never be easy to establish which party is responsible for the document's release, and it may be difficult for the disclosing party to prove that it suffered loss as a result of any breach by its adversary.[185]

---

[182] See, e.g., CA Paris, June 14, 1985, S.A.R.L. Anciens Ets. Harognan Comptoir Euro-Turc v. Turkish Airlines "Turk Hava Yollari A.O.", 1987 REV. ARB. 395, and observations by J. Pellerin.

[183] For an answer in the affirmative, see CA Paris, June 14, 1985, *Harognan*, *supra* note 182, and on this issue generally, *infra* para. 1606.

[184] See Reiner, *supra* note 1, at 58; DERAINS AND SCHWARTZ, *supra* note 1, at 263 *et seq.*

[185] For an example of a confidentiality order adopted by consent, see the July 12, 1994 Order in ICC Case No. 7893, 125 J.D.I. 1069 (1998), and observations by D. Hascher.

1266. — Where an argument as to the confidentiality of a party's documents is based on a law or regulation prohibiting the disclosure of certain documents (on the grounds of national security, for example), on what basis can that law can be taken into consideration? Will it be procedural, substantive, or a mandatory rule? As this is a matter of evidence, over which arbitrators have unfettered discretion, arbitrators sitting in a country other than that which issued the regulation in question are generally under no obligation to give effect to it. At the very most, they may take such regulations into consideration as an element of fact which might constitute a legitimate reason for non-disclosure. Arbitrators sitting in the country which enacted the regulation might have a more difficult task, as their award will be generally subject to an action to set aside in that country and the rule in question may be held to be a requirement of public policy.

B. – METHOD OF PRESENTING EVIDENCE

1267. — Due process requires that written submissions and evidence be communicated simultaneously and in an identical form to each member of the arbitral tribunal and to the other party. The communication of memorials and evidence may be performed directly or, under some arbitration rules, via the arbitral institution. Of course, using the latter option does not constitute a breach of due process.[186]

1268. — No particular system for identifying evidence—such as the French "*bordereau de communication de pièces*"[187] or the English "agreed bundle of documents"[188]—is required. What matters is that the arbitrators and the parties receive exactly the same documents. The French courts have sometimes held there to be a presumption that items of evidence referred to or discussed in the award were properly given to the other side by the party that produced them.[189] That is in fact nothing more than a clumsy reference to the more general rule that the burden of proof is on the party seeking to rely on a ground for setting aside an award, such as a breach of due process.[190] Nonetheless, it is in the parties' interest to keep written evidence of all communications of documents. It is common practice for the party receiving a document, or its representative, to be asked to sign a copy of the letter accompanying and describing the document in question by way of an acknowledgment of receipt.

1269. — The time-limits for filing memorials and evidence are determined by agreement between the parties or, if no such agreement is reached, by the arbitral tribunal. This raises

---

[186] CA Paris, Apr. 24, 1980, Progilor v. Intergras, 1981 REV. ARB. 176.

[187] On document production in France, see DE BOISSÉSON, *supra* note 4, at 738 *et seq.*

[188] *See* MICHAEL J. MUSTILL, STEWART C. BOYD, COMMERCIAL ARBITRATION 326 (2d ed. 1989).

[189] Cass. 2e civ., Jan. 28, 1970, Union Economique et Financière (U.N.E.F.) v. SCARCOC, 1973 REV. ARB. 66, and P. Fouchard's note.

[190] *See, e.g.*, CA Paris, Jan. 13, 1984, Centre d'information pour groupements d'achats (C.I.G.A.) v. La Margeride, 1984 REV. ARB. 530, and observations by T. Bernard.

the important issue of the position the arbitrators should take if a party fails to comply with the specified deadlines.

In international commercial arbitration, there is a tendency to avoid taking severe measures to penalize a party who submits evidence and other documents out of time.[191] In the absence of a specific agreement between the parties concerning compliance with deadlines, an award cannot generally be set aside or refused enforcement by the courts for having allowed the late submission of documents.[192] On the other hand, if the arbitrators do allow such non-compliance, they must ensure the observance of the principles of due process and equality of the parties.[193] Thus, where a party submits a document after an agreed deadline, the arbitrators will have to extend the other party's deadlines and ensure that the latter will then have sufficient time to prepare for the next stage of the arbitration, which will often be the hearings. Equal treatment of the parties does not necessarily mean that each party must have exactly the same number of days to produce its written submissions and evidence. They must simply have been able to present their arguments of fact and law under broadly similar conditions.

1270. — However, it is important to note that the arbitrators are under no obligation to depart from the deadlines initially agreed, provided that those deadlines were adequate in the first place. The arbitral tribunal will only be obliged to accept the belated submission of documents or evidence where the party submitting them has a valid excuse for its delay. In the absence of a legitimate reason, the tribunal can take a firm position and simply reject the memorials or evidence submitted late. Admittedly, the legitimacy of the reasons for the delay may be re-examined later by the courts responsible for reviewing the compliance of the award with the rules of due process, although that should not encourage arbitrators to continually extend the applicable deadlines. The concern felt by some arbitrators that their awards might be set aside if they refuse requests for such extensions is often founded on an erroneous conception of the principle of due process. The requirements of due process are

---

[191] *See* DE BOISSÉSON, *supra* note 4, at 740: "in practice, given the flexibility required in arbitration, evidence produced late will be admissible (but not after a closing order, unless the arbitrator considers it possible to re-open the proceedings);" see ICC Award No. 3327 (1981), which relies—wrongly as it only concerns the merits—on the fact that the arbitrators were required to rule as *amiables compositeurs*, in refusing to reject memorials submitted late by one party (French company v. African state, 109 J.D.I. 971 (1982), and observations by Y. Derains). On the broad discretion of arbitrators on this question, see the very liberal decision in ICC Award No. 6192 (1992), ICC BULLETIN, Vol. 8, No. 2, at 64 (1997). The 1996 English Arbitration Act specifies that "[t]he tribunal may fix the time within which any directions given by it are to be complied with, and may if it thinks fit extend the time so fixed (whether or not it has expired)" (Sec. 34(3)).

[192] See, for example, in France, Cass. 2e civ., Oct. 15, 1980, Société des établissements Soulès et Cie. v. Saronis Shipping Co., 1982 REV. ARB. 40, and P. Courteault's note. Although dating from before the 1981 reform, this decision is still good law.

[193] On the requirements of due process where documents are submitted late, see, for example, CA Paris, Dec. 20, 1977, GEOSTOCK v. Entreprise de Travaux Publics A. Borie, 1978 REV. ARB. 501, and P. Roland-Lévy's note; CA Paris, Nov. 13, 1980, Société industrielle et commerciale des charbonnages v. Les Chantiers Modernes, 1984 REV. ARB. 129, and observations by T. Bernard; Cass. 1e civ., Jan. 7, 1992, Pakistan Atomic Energy Commission v. Société générale pour les techniques nouvelles, 1992 REV. ARB. 659, and observations by D. Bureau; CA Paris, July 7, 1994, Uzinexportimport Romanian Co. v. Attock Cement Co., 1995 REV. ARB. 107, and S. Jarvin's note; for an English translation, see 10 INT'L ARB. REP. D1 (Feb. 1995).

in fact satisfied if the initial deadline was sufficient to enable the party in question to present its arguments and evidence.[194] Thus, as one chairman of an ICC arbitral tribunal rightly observed:

> The arbitrators have a duty to take into account the fundamental right of each party to present its case properly, but they also have a duty to ensure that the arbitration progresses at a reasonable pace and to avoid unwarranted or deliberate delays. If a party which has had ample opportunity to prepare its case or to submit requests to the arbitral tribunal at an earlier stage of the proceedings, applies to the tribunal, belatedly and without giving legitimate reasons for its tardiness, with requests which are liable to cause substantial delays, it may well be the duty of the arbitrators to continue the arbitration without accepting the request of the tardy party.[195]

1271. — Arbitrators sometimes implement the French practice of issuing a closing order (*"ordonnance de clôture"*), setting a date beyond which no new document or evidence can be submitted. This practice, which has been introduced by the ICC at Article 22 of its 1998 Rules,[196] does not substantially affect the consequences of belatedly filing written submissions and evidence, as the closing order can always be put back. A closing order will, however, lend a degree of solemnity to the deadline it fixes. That said, it would be wrong to assume that the deadline contained in the closing order is the only truly binding deadline, and that the other aspects of the timetable fixed by the arbitrators can be disregarded without serious consequences. Interpreted in that way, having a closing order would do more harm than good.[197]

C. – POWERS OF THE ARBITRATORS

1272. — Under both French international and domestic arbitration law, "[i]f a party is in possession of an item of evidence, the arbitrator may . . . order that party to produce it."[198] This provision could provide the basis for requests for the disclosure of documents modeled on common law discovery procedures. Article 20, paragraph 5 of the ICC Rules gives arbitral tribunals similar powers: "[a]t any time during the proceedings, the Arbitral Tribunal may summon any party to provide additional evidence." However, despite the trend towards

---

[194] On this issue, generally, see Gaillard, *supra* note 33, at 108. *See also* CA Paris, May 19, 1998, *Torno, supra* note 68.

[195] Letter of the Chairman of the arbitral tribunal in Case No. 6465, 121 J.D.I. 1088, 1090 (1994), and observations by D. Hascher.

[196] *See also* Art. 29 of the UNCITRAL Rules; Art. 24 of the 1997 AAA International Arbitration Rules; Art. 57 of the WIPO Arbitration Rules.

[197] *See also* DERAINS AND SCHWARTZ, *supra* note 1, at 270–71.

[198] See Article 1460, paragraph 3 of the French New Code of Civil Procedure, which is applicable, unless the parties agree otherwise, to international arbitration governed by French procedural law, under Article 1495 of the same Code.

harmonization that can be seen in international arbitral practice,[199] arbitral tribunals sitting on the continent generally take a relatively conservative approach to requests for compulsory disclosure.[200]

1273. — Since arbitrators lack *imperium*, their procedural injunctions are less effective than those of the courts.[201] As a result it is sometimes necessary to apply to the courts to seek enforcement of an arbitral tribunal's order.[202]

1274. — There is controversy as to whether arbitrators can attach penalties to their procedural orders. It has been argued that their lack of *imperium* and the absence of statutory basis prevents them from doing so.[203] However, we consider that where the arbitration agreement is drafted in terms sufficiently broad so as not to exclude that option (such as "all disputes arising out of the present contract"), there is no reason why international commercial arbitrators should not attach penalties to their injunctions, provided that the measures are incorporated, in the interests of enforcement, in an interim award.[204] The French courts have held this approach to be valid.[205] Both the Dutch[206] and Belgian[207] legislatures have enacted provisions specifically allowing arbitrators to impose penalties in these circumstances. However, the 1999 Swedish Arbitration Act expressly prohibits the imposition of penalties in this context (Sec. 25, para. 3).

---

[199] *See supra* para. 1260.

[200] Compare, for the practice of arbitrators sitting in London, MUSTILL AND BOYD, *supra* note 188, at 324 *et seq.*; REDFERN AND HUNTER, *supra* note 22, at 330 *et seq.* For an example of a decision regarding a request for document production, see the January 7, 1991 Order made in ICC Case No. 6401, 123 J.D.I. 1055 (1996), and observations by D. Hascher.

[201] But see, on the powers of injunction confered on arbitrators in the United States, Wetter, *supra* note 163, at 20; Brower, *supra* note 164, at 29; on English law, see Sutton, *supra* note 164, at 72; on French law, see Charles Jarrosson, *Réflexions sur l'imperium*, in ETUDES OFFERTES À PIERRE BELLET 245, 269 *et seq.* (1991).

[202] *See infra* paras. 1302 *et seq.*

[203] *See* Berthold Goldman, *The Complementary Roles of Judges and Arbitrators in Ensuring that International Commercial Arbitration Is Effective*, in INTERNATIONAL ARBITRATION – 60 YEARS OF ICC ARBITRATION – A LOOK AT THE FUTURE 257, 278 (ICC Publication No. 412, 1984); Eric Loquin, *Les pouvoirs des arbitres internationaux à la lumière de l'évolution récente du droit de l'arbitrage international*, 110 J.D.I. 293, 307–08 (1983); in French domestic arbitration, see Roger Perrot, *L'application à l'arbitrage des règles du nouveau Code de procédure civile*, 1980 REV. ARB. 642, 645; Gérard Cornu, *Le décret du 14 mai 1980 relatif à l'arbitrage – Présentation de la réforme*, 1980 REV. ARB. 583, 587.

[204] *See* DE BOISSÉSON, *supra* note 4, at 743; Jarrosson, *supra* note 201, at 273.

[205] See, in French domestic arbitration, CA Paris, June 8, 1990, Hoche Friedland v. Le Grand Livre du mois, 1990 REV. ARB. 917, and observations by J.-H. Moitry and C. Vergne; CA Paris, Mar. 10, 1995, Tardivel v. Cejibe, 1996 REV. ARB. 143, and observations by Y. Derains.

[206] Art. 1056 of the Code of Civil Procedure (Law of July 2, 1986).

[207] New Art. 1709 bis of the Judicial Code (Law of May 19, 1998).

1275. — Arbitrators faced with a party refusing, for no valid reason, to comply with their order to disclose certain documents can also "draw all necessary inferences" from that refusal and thus effectively penalize that party in their award on the merits.[208]

1276. — The arbitrators will assess the weight of the evidence submitted to them by the parties, which may entail resolving challenges as to the authenticity of documents.[209]

§ 2. – Witness Testimony

A. – THE DECISION TO ALLOW WITNESS TESTIMONY

1277. — The decision to allow witness testimony is taken by the arbitral tribunal, which may refuse to hear witnesses introduced by one of the parties if it considers itself to be sufficiently well-informed through other evidence. Its award is unlikely to be set aside on the basis of such a refusal.[210] This is true even in jurisdictions, such as England, which are traditionally far more open to the admission of witness testimony.[211] Conversely, the arbitral tribunal can instruct a party to produce a witness if it considers it to be essential to its understanding of the case. The arbitral tribunal will only be deprived of that option where the parties restrict the use of witness testimony in their arbitration agreement or in a subsequent agreement.

1278. — Comparative law reveals a divergence of opinions as to whether it is appropriate to hear witnesses. In common law systems, witness testimony is considered an essential element of proof without which the tribunal cannot really judge the truth of the parties'

---

[208] *See, e.g.,* ICC Award No. 8694 (1996), American company v. Belgian company, 124 J.D.I. 1056 (1997), and observations by Y. Derains.

[209] See, for example, Article 1467 of the French New Code of Civil Procedure, declared applicable to international arbitration by Article 1495; Art. 1696, para. 2 of the Belgian Judicial Code, as amended by the Law of May 19, 1998; Art. 184 of the Swiss Private International Law Statute. On this issue, see Roger Perrot, *L'administration de la preuve en matière d'arbitrage (Le droit continental de la preuve)*, 1974 REV. ARB. 159, 163 *et seq.*; *The Standards and Burden of Proof in International Arbitration*, 10 INT'L ARB. 317 (1994) (contributions from Alan Redfern, Claude Reymond, Andreas Reiner, Bernard Hanotiau, Sir Edward Everleigh, Ian W. Menzies and Allan Philip in a colloquium held in London in 1992).

[210] See, for example, in France, CA Paris, Mar. 15, 1984, Soubaigne v. Limmareds Skogar, 1985 REV. ARB. 285, and the commentary by Eric Loquin, *Pouvoirs et devoirs de l'amiable compositeur. A propos de trois arrêts de la Cour d'appel de Paris, id.* at 199; CA Paris, 1e Ch., Sec. Supp., July 13, 1987, P.A.E.C. v. S.G.N., No. 85.17852, unpublished, cited by DE BOISSÉSON, *supra* note 4, at 745–46. On the discretionary powers of the arbitrators in ICC arbitration in this respect, see CA Paris, Sept. 9, 1997, Heilmann v. Graziano Transmissioni, 1998 REV. ARB. 712, and observations by Y. Derains. *See also* RENÉ DAVID, ARBITRATION IN INTERNATIONAL TRADE ¶ 323 (1985).

[211] See the Court of Appeal's decision in Dalmia Dairy Industries Ltd. v. National Bank of Pakistan, [1978] 2 Lloyd's Rep. 223, 270, following the refusal by Professor Lalive, sitting as sole arbitrator in London, to hear certain witnesses, and particularly the reasons given by Lord Justice Kerr in support of this decision. Compare, in the U.S., *In re* Arbitration between Iron Ore Co. of Canada v. Argonaut Shipping, Inc., No. 85 Civ. 3460 (GLG), 1985 U.S. Dist. LEXIS 15572 (S.D.N.Y. Sept. 26, 1985); XII Y.B. COM. ARB. 173 (1987).

allegations. That view is based on the idea that the judge—or the jury—will uncover the truth by hearing the witnesses in person, especially where the latter are subjected to "vigorous" cross-examination.[212] Continental lawyers are generally more skeptical as to the sincerity of witness testimony and the benefit of calling for it in every case. They believe that the best form of proof is written evidence, although a number of differences exist between the various continental systems.

In international commercial arbitration, continental opposition to witness testimony is on the decline. Many continental arbitrators now recognize that hearing witnesses is often useful. Conversely, among English and American arbitrators there is a growing tendency to limit the number of witnesses and to restrict the time for witness examination.[213] Thus, there was no misconduct when a tribunal sitting in an international arbitration in New York refused to hear witnesses introduced by one of the parties.[214] Further proof of the harmonization of arbitral practice can be found in the fact that the ICC introduced, at Article 20, paragraph 3 of its 1998 Rules, the possibility for the arbitral tribunal to hear witnesses.[215]

1279. — The arbitral tribunal is free to organize the hearing of witnesses as it sees fit.[216] It is also free to assess the weight of the evidence provided by the testimony of witnesses that it has agreed to hear.[217]

B. – WHO CAN BE A WITNESS?

1280. — Some legal systems fully accept that the parties themselves can appear as witnesses. This is the case in common law jurisdictions.[218] Others, such as Germany, prohibit appearances by the parties altogether, whereas in French law the parties may appear as witnesses subject to special rules governing their testimony. In an international arbitration,

---

[212] *See* Rouhette, *supra* note 163, at 254 *et seq.*

[213] *See* Marriott, *supra* note 163, at 284. See also, confirming that the different traditions are moving closer, REDFERN AND HUNTER, *supra* note 22, at 335 and, for an analysis of arbitral practice, together with various procedural measures in arbitration concerning witnesses, Michael E. Schneider, *Witnesses in International Arbitration/Les témoins dans la procédure arbitrale*, 1993 BULL. ASA 302 and 568.

[214] *In re* Arbitration Between Intercarbon Bermuda, Ltd. v. Caltex Trading and Transport Corp., 146 F.R.D. 64 (S.D.N.Y. 1993); XIX Y.B. COM. ARB. 802 (1994).

[215] On this issue, see DERAINS AND SCHWARTZ, *supra* note 1, at 255 *et seq.* On the powers of arbitrators, recognized by certain legal systems, to compel, by way of a subpoena, third parties to appear before them as witnesses, and on the merits of such a step, see the April 13, 1993 letter by the sole arbitrator in ICC Case No. 7453 (1993), 124 J.D.I. 1082 (1997), and observations by D. Hascher. On the assistance of courts in this respect, see *infra* paras. 1336 *et seq.*

[216] For an example of a procedural order organizing the hearing of witnesses, see the September 4, 1990 Order in ICC Case No. 6401, 125 J.D.I. 1058 (1998).

[217] On the consequences of false testimony, see Marianne Roth, *False Testimony at International Arbitration Hearings Conducted in England and Switzerland – A Comparative View*, 11 J. INT'L ARB. 5 (Mar. 1994).

[218] *See, e.g.*, Rouhette, *supra* note 163, at 254.

in the absence of an agreement between the parties to the contrary, the arbitral tribunal can allow the parties to appear as witnesses. It is up to the arbitral tribunal to decide whether it is appropriate to hear them in the circumstances, and to assess the evidentiary weight of their testimony. Some arbitral tribunals prefer to use a different term (such as "*sachant*") to refer to officers or employees of a party whose testimony they wish to hear.[219] Others draw a distinction between the parties' officers, who can only be heard as parties, and their employees, who can be heard as witnesses.[220] In fact, these distinctions are of little significance, as the witnesses themselves generally do not testify under oath[221] and the arbitrators always have the power to assess the weight to be given to their testimony. A similar approach was followed by the Iran-United States Claims Tribunal, which allowed the parties' representatives to be heard by the tribunal and examined by the parties, without describing them as witnesses.[222] Where representatives of the parties are authorized to appear as witnesses, they are often not allowed to attend hearings other than those at which they are to give evidence. The reverse would only be acceptable if all witnesses were likewise allowed to attend all of the hearings, which is not usually the case.[223] It is therefore a wise precaution for a party intending to produce its representatives as witnesses to ensure—in the absence of an agreement between the parties—that those representatives do not participate in the previous hearings, so as to avoid a challenge as to the admissibility of their testimony.[224]

1281. — A similar difference between common and civil law traditions exists in relation to experts called to provide an opinion on technical issues. Common lawyers generally prefer to ask the arbitral tribunal to hear technical explanations from the experts engaged by each party whereas, in the continental tradition, the parties often ask the arbitral tribunal to appoint an independent expert.[225] In spite of these differences, international arbitrators are free to choose between the two systems, both of which are used in practice. Likewise, the ICC Rules, as revised in 1998, give arbitrators the possibility of hearing "experts appointed by the parties" (Art. 20(3)) or of "appoint[ing] one or more experts, defin[ing] their terms

---

[219] See, for example, the Procedural Order in ICC Case No. 6657, cited by D. Hascher in 121 J.D.I. 1106 (1994). On the discretion of ICC arbitrators to hear a party's technical consultant, see CA Paris, Apr. 13, 1995, Thomson v. Groupement Sanitec Megco, 1996 REV. ARB. 536, and observations by L. Kiffer.

[220] See, for example, the October 30, 1992 decision of a German arbitrator sitting in Paris in ICC Case No. 7319, 121 J.D.I. 1102 (1994), and observations by D. Hascher.

[221] *See infra* para. 1286.

[222] *See* Howard M. Holtzmann, *Chapter 16 – Some Lessons of the Iran-United States Claims Tribunal, in* THE SOUTHWESTERN LEGAL FOUNDATION, PRIVATE INVESTORS ABROAD – PROBLEMS AND SOLUTIONS IN INTERNATIONAL BUSINESS IN 1987, ¶¶ 16.04 (J.R. Moss ed., 1987).

[223] *See infra* para. 1287.

[224] Compare, for a more liberal view, CRAIG, PARK, PAULSSON, *supra* note 58, at 402.

[225] On the characteristics of the two systems and their use in international arbitration, see ARBITRAGE ET EXPERTISE, colloque Paris, Nov. 23-24, 1993, ICC Publication No. 480/7 (1994). For illustrations, see the decisions rendered in ICC Case No. 5926 (Sept. 26, 1988) and the procedural calendar in ICC Case No. 5082, 122 J.D.I. 1037 and 1041 (1995), and observations by D. Hascher. On the distinction between witnesses and experts, see the June 9, 1987 Order made in ICC Case No. 4815, 123 J.D.I. 1042 (1996), and observations by D. Hascher.

of reference and receiv[ing] their reports" (Art. 20(4)). In some cases, the arbitral tribunal will draw from both systems, hearing the views of the experts engaged by the parties but then deciding that it needs to appoint an independent expert on some issues. Of course, the tribunal is under no obligation to endorse the findings of either the parties' experts or the expert that it appoints.[226]

1282. — Legal opinions are the subject of similar differences between the common and civil law traditions. In the continental tradition written opinions are preferred. The common law tradition favors an oral presentation by the opining lawyer, which provides the other party with an opportunity to test the strength of the other side's legal arguments by questioning. In international arbitration, both methods are used, sometimes in the same proceedings.

C. – THE PROCEDURE FOR HEARING WITNESS EVIDENCE

1283. — In most cases, at the beginning of the proceedings, the arbitral tribunal will provide the parties with a deadline before which they must submit the names of any witnesses they wish to produce and the subject-matter of their testimony. In addition, the arbitral tribunal itself may call witnesses.[227]

1284. — The parties are often invited to submit witness evidence in writing,[228] with the resulting document referred to as a witness statement or affidavit. This does not necessarily exclude the possibility of hearing witnesses orally at a later stage, but it may help the arbitral tribunal to assess the utility of doing so and enable it to shorten the duration of the witness hearings.[229] In addition, following the common law tradition, it may be agreed that the affidavits of witnesses who refuse to appear may be struck from the record.[230]

1285. — Difficulties often arise as to whether the parties are entitled to communicate with the witnesses they wish to produce before their testimony is presented. In common law systems, it is perfectly legitimate for a party to "prepare" witnesses.[231] Other systems prohibit

---

[226] *See also* Loquin, *supra* note 203, ¶ 67.

[227] *See* Goldman, *supra* note 203, at 278.

[228] For an example of the organization of the procedure of hearing witnesses, see the February 17, 1994 Order made in ICC Case No. 7314, 123 J.D.I. 1045 (1996), and observations by D. Hascher.

[229] *See supra* para. 1278.

[230] This solution is specifically provided for at Article 20.4 of the 1998 LCIA Rules.

[231] Article 20.6 of the 1998 LCIA Rules expressly provides that: "[s]ubject to the mandatory provisions of any applicable law, it shall not be improper for any party or its legal representatives to interview any witness or potential witness for the purpose of presenting his testimony in written form or producing him as an oral witness." The reference to the mandatory rules of the applicable law is not accompanied by any indication of which choice of law rules are to be used to determine such applicable law. In any event, it is certainly arguable that prohibitions on contact with witnesses found in certain legal systems apply only in court proceedings, and

(continued...)

such a practice, particularly where it is contrary to lawyers' ethical rules.[232] In international arbitration, either approach is permissible, the only condition being that the same rules should apply to all the parties and their counsel and their representatives. This must be verified by the arbitral tribunal, especially where the parties and their counsel belong to different legal traditions.[233]

1286. — In French law, it is generally accepted that as the arbitrators are private individuals, they are not empowered to take oaths from witnesses.[234] Other legal systems take the reverse position.[235] A practice which is accepted everywhere and is used in international arbitration is to have the witnesses state that they will be truthful and that they are aware that false declarations may lead to criminal penalties.

1287. — How witnesses are examined is also left to the discretion of the arbitral tribunal, unless the parties have decided that issue themselves by mutual agreement. The witness examination can be performed by the arbitral tribunal, as would happen in a continental court, or by the parties' representatives, as in the common law tradition. The latter approach is now frequently adopted in continental arbitrations, but to varying degrees. In the pure common law tradition, witnesses produced by a party may be examined first by that party (direct examination), then by the other party (cross-examination) and then again by each of the parties (re-direct and re-cross). However, unless the parties have made an express stipulation to that effect, the arbitral tribunal will not be obliged to enforce all the rules which, in England or the United States, dictate how that questioning is to be carried out.[236]

---

[231] (...continued)
not in international arbitration, especially where the arbitration is subject to rules allowing such contacts.

[232] In Belgium, see Dieryck, *supra* note 163, at 270; Lambert Matray, *Quelques problèmes de l'arbitrage commercial international (doctrine et jurisprudence)*, in L'ARBITRAGE – TRAVAUX OFFERTS AU PROFESSEUR ALBERT FETTWEIS 289 (1989).

[233] *See also* Van Compernolle, *supra* note 126, at 111–12; François Dessemontet, *Les Usages du Barreau et l'arbitrage international*, in L'AVOCAT MODERNE – REGARDS SUR UNE PROFESSION QUI CHANGE – MÉLANGES PUBLIÉS PAR L'ORDRE DES AVOCATS VAUDOIS À L'OCCASION DE SON CENTENAIRE 177 (F. Chaudet and O. Rodondi eds., 1998).

[234] Goldman, *supra* note 203, at 278; Loquin, *supra* note 203, at 308; Perrot, *supra* note 209, at 172; in French domestic arbitration, see Article 1461, paragraph 2 of the New Civil Code of Procedure. *See also* Sec. 25, para. 3 of the 1999 Swedish Arbitration Act.

[235] *See, e.g.*, Art. 1041(1) of the Netherlands Code of Civil Procedure; Art. 211 of the Law of March 8, 1992 on Civil Procedure in the United Arab Emirates, 1993 REV. ARB. 343, and the commentary by Abdul Hamid El-Ahdab, *La nouvelle loi sur l'arbitrage de l'Etat des Emirats Arabes Unis, id.* at 229; Abdul Hamid El-Ahdab, *The New Arbitration Act of the State of The United Arab Emirates*, 11 INT'L ARB. REP. 32 (Aug. 1996); Sec. 38(5) of the 1996 English Arbitration Act. Compare, for United States arbitral practice, Howard Holtzmann and Robert Coulson, *L'administration de la preuve dans les arbitrages commerciaux américains – 2e partie: La pratique procédurale*, 1974 REV. ARB. 128, 140.

[236] On the prohibition, in common law countries, of "leading questions in direct examination" and the prohibition on questioning witnesses as to their "opinions," see Rouhette, *supra* note 163, at 254 *et seq.* On the fact that, even in the United States, the absence of cross-examination is not a breach of due process, see *In re* Arbitration between Generica Ltd. v. Pharmaceutical Basics, Inc., No. 95 C 5935, 1996 U.S. Dist. LEXIS 13716 (N.D. Ill. Sept. 16, 1996), *aff'd*, Generica Ltd. v. Pharmaceutical Basics, Inc., 125 F.3d 1123 (7th Cir. 1997); XXII Y.B.
(continued...)

The witnesses may also be examined solely by the party not presenting their testimony, if it is considered that their written affidavits are the equivalent of direct examination. They may also be examined by the parties and the arbitrators using less formal methods. In all cases, the arbitral tribunal must ensure that the hearings run smoothly, asking any question which it considers to be necessary and curtailing discussions which appear to be irrelevant. The arbitral tribunal will not usually allow witnesses to attend hearings other than those at which they are to be examined, so that they will neither be influenced by nor gain an advantage from a first-hand knowledge of previous testimony.

1288. — Witness statements are sometimes transcribed in full by stenotype or audio recording. The latter is more difficult for the parties to use, but may prove useful if the content of the testimony is contested. In some cases, witness testimony is simply summarized in minutes drawn up by the arbitral tribunal. The arbitral tribunal will often send these minutes to the parties to obtain their comments or objections, and in the absence of any response from the parties within a certain period of time, the minutes will be declared to be the definitive record.

1289. — The arbitral tribunal must at all times enforce and comply with due process. In particular, it cannot hear a witness unless all parties are present (except, of course, where a party is in default).[237]

§ 3. – Expert Evidence and Site Inspections

1290. — Unlike a number of legal systems, such as that of the Netherlands (Art. 1042 of the Code of Civil Procedure), England (Sec. 37(1) of the 1996 Arbitration Act) and countries which have adopted the UNCITRAL Model Law,[238] French international arbitration law contains no specific provisions concerning expert evidence.

Nevertheless, it is well established that under French law,[239] as in the different legal systems where this possibility is expressly provided for, the tribunal may, at the request of a party or on its own initiative, appoint its own expert to give evidence.[240] That principle is

---

[236] (...continued)
COM. ARB. 1029, 1036 (1997).

[237] *Comp. with* DAVID, *supra* note 210, ¶ 324.

[238] *See, e.g.*, Art. 1049 of the German ZPO, in force as of January 1, 1998.

[239] See Article 10 of the New Code of Civil Procedure to which Article 1460, paragraph 2 of the same Code refers. Article 1460, paragraph 2 is applicable in international arbitration governed by French procedural law, unless the parties agree otherwise.

[240] On the importance of technical experts in international arbitration, see for example, Lazare Kopelmanas, *Le rôle de l'expertise dans l'arbitrage commercial international*, 1979 REV. ARB. 205; Charles Jarrosson, *Chambre de Commerce Internationale: arbitrage et expertise*, 1991 REV. ARB. 501; Pierre-Yves Günter, *Arbitrage et expertise*, 1993 BULL. ASA 538; *see also* ARBITRAGE ET EXPERTISE, *supra* note 225.

found in most institutional arbitration rules.[241] However, the arbitral tribunal is never required to grant a party's request for the appointment of an expert. In its 1980 decision in the *Air Intergulf v. S.E.C.A.* case, the Paris Court of Appeals held that where the tribunal considers that it has sufficient information to make its decision, "its refusal to order . . . the expert investigation requested by a party does not contravene the rights of the defense."[242]

Swiss law is less straightforward on this point, as it considers the involvement of an expert to be linked to a party's right to a fair hearing, and does not exclude the possibility of the refusal to appoint an expert constituting grounds for an action to set aside. However, the Swiss Federal Tribunal held in 1996 that an award can only be set aside where the arbitrators fail to appoint an expert in very limited circumstances. The appointment must have been requested, the requesting party must have offered to bear the cost and the expert's mission would have had to have concerned relevant issues of which the arbitrators did not have special knowledge. Further, the review of the exercise of the arbitrators' discretion performed by the Federal Tribunal can only be carried out on public policy grounds.[243] Thus, in practice, the arbitrators' discretion remains very broad.

1291. — The chosen expert must be independent of the parties, failing which a challenge can be brought. Also, to ensure that no doubt can arise as to the expert's neutrality, he or she should not be chosen from among the competitors of either party which, in some fields, limits the choice considerably.

1292. — The arbitral tribunal is responsible for determining the expert's brief. It will be in the interest of the tribunal to define that brief precisely, but the tribunal should also avoid using terms that prevent the expert from addressing certain questions, the importance of which might well only emerge once a greater familiarity of the relevant technical issues is acquired. Both questions of fact, especially of a technical nature, and legal issues can give rise to the appointment of an expert.[244]

---

[241] *See, e.g.,* Art. 20(4) of the 1998 ICC Rules, replacing Art. 14(2) of the previous Rules; Art. 27 of the UNCITRAL Arbitration Rules; Art. 21 of the 1998 LCIA Rules; Art. 22 of the 1997 AAA International Arbitration Rules; Art. 27(1) of the 1999 Rules of the Arbitration Institute of the Stockholm Chamber of Commerce.

[242] CA Paris, 1e Ch., Sec. Supp., May 13, 1980, Air Intergulf, Ltd. v. Société d'exploitation et de construction aéronautique (S.E.C.A.), No. G 9097, unpublished, cited by DE BOISSÉSON, *supra* note 4, at 748; CA Paris, 1e Ch., Sec. C, Dec. 3, 1998, Interpipe v. Hunting Oilfield Services, No. 1997/14112, unpublished. *Comp. with* Van Compernolle, *supra* note 126, at 114. See also Article 26 of the UNCITRAL Model Law and, in arbitral practice, the letter of the Chairman of the arbitral tribunal in ICC Case No. 6465, giving the reasons for refusing to order expert proceedings (121 J.D.I. 1088 (1994), and observations by D. Hascher, especially at 1093 *et seq.*).

[243] Fed. Trib., Sept. 6, 1996, X. v. Y., 1997 BULL. ASA 291.

[244] For an example of the appointment of an expert on a question of law, see the Order made on June 25, 1992 in ICC Case No. 6848, 122 J.D.I. 1047 (1995), and observations by D. Hascher.

1293. — Like the arbitrators, the expert must observe the principles of due process and equal treatment of the parties.[245] Any correspondence from the expert must be sent simultaneously to all parties, and any meeting convened must be held with the representatives of all parties afforded a possibility to attend, in the absence of an agreement to the contrary. Likewise, any communication between the arbitral tribunal and the expert must be brought to the attention of the parties. The expert must also invite all parties to participate in the expert's factual inquiry sessions, and each must have an equal opportunity to put their case. It is true that in a 1997 decision the Paris Court of Appeals did refuse to set aside an award where the arbitral tribunal refused to take account of the fact that an expert had taken some steps in the absence of one of the parties, because the arbitrators considered that the party subsequently had sufficient opportunity to challenge the expert's findings.[246] As suggested by one commentator,[247] that solution seems too permissive. Indeed, the possibility for the absent party to challenge the expert's findings after the fact does not allow it to convey its arguments as convincingly as its opponent.[248]

1294. — In general, the expert's investigation will culminate in the submission of a written report. The parties must be given the opportunity to comment upon the content of the report before the tribunal.[249] The tribunal may also choose to hear the expert's findings orally.[250] All meetings for that purpose must be held in the presence of the parties or their representatives, who will usually be authorized by the arbitral tribunal to question the expert directly.[251]

1295. — The arbitral tribunal is also entitled, where it considers such measures to be necessary, to order a site inspection. This, like the expert's investigation, must comply with

---

[245] *See* CA Paris, Feb. 12, 1993, *Unichips Finanziaria, supra* note 176. In arbitral case law, see, for example, the Order made on February 28, 1989 in ICC Case No. 5715, 123 J.D.I. 1049 (1996), and observations by D. Hascher. On this issue, generally, see Jean-François Poudret, *Expertise et droit d'être entendu dans l'arbitrage international, in* ETUDES DE DROIT INTERNATIONAL EN L'HONNEUR DE PIERRE LALIVE 607 (1993).

[246] CA Paris, Feb. 6, 1997, Carter v. Alsthom, 1997 REV. ARB. 556, and P. Mayer's note.

[247] *See* P. Mayer, note following CA Paris, Feb. 6, 1997, *Carter, supra* note 246.

[248] On the requirements of due process, see *infra* paras. 1638 *et seq.*

[249] *See* CA Paris, Mar. 13, 1973, Baumajs v. S.C.I. Martin Nadaud Cimarna, 1973 REV. ARB. 176; CA Paris, Feb. 12, 1993, *Unichips Finanziaria, supra* note 176; CA Paris, June 25, 1993, Schönenberger Systemtechnik GmbH v. S.A. Vens, 1993 REV. ARB. 685, and observations by D. Bureau. Section 37(1) of the 1996 English Arbitration Act allows the arbitral tribunal to authorize the experts to attend the proceedings. For an example of a decision regarding expert proceedings, see the Order made on November 21, 1989 in ICC Case No. 5082, 122 J.D.I. 1043 (1995) and observations by D. Hascher.

[250] Article 20(4) of the 1998 ICC Rules obliges the arbitral tribunal to hear the expert and to allow the parties to put questions to him or her.

[251] For an expert's point of view on these issues, see François Vermeille, *Le choix de l'expert et le déroulement de l'expertise*, 1994 BULL. ASA 192.

the requirements of due process and equality of the parties.[252] The arbitrators have sole discretion to decide whether a site inspection is appropriate.[253]

§ 4. – Hearings

1296. — Unless the parties agree otherwise, the arbitrators are free to organize the hearings as they see fit, subject only to compliance with the principles of due process and equal treatment of the parties. In France[254] and in Switzerland[255] they can even decide to dispense with hearings and reach their decision on the basis of the parties' written submissions without violating due process, although that rarely occurs in practice. By contrast, certain arbitration statutes[256] and most arbitration rules[257] do require the arbitrators to hear the parties unless the parties have specifically waived that right. As a result, in the vast majority of cases, the parties are entitled to present their arguments in a hearing, if one of them so requests.

1297. — Lawyers with a common law background often wish to have an opportunity to present their case orally immediately prior to the hearing of witnesses. These short preliminary pleadings are known as opening statements.[258] Although opening statements are sometimes permitted, international arbitral practice generally follows the continental tradition, in which the oral pleadings are the final stage of the proceedings. The purpose of the oral pleadings is to enable the parties to recapitulate and present in an organized fashion most of the factual and legal points on which the parties disagree. That presupposes that the parties will be given sufficient time, particularly after the final witness hearings, to prepare their pleadings accordingly.

1298. — In large cases, it is not uncommon for the pleadings to last several days or even, in arbitrations held in the common law tradition, several weeks. In order to be able to organize the hearings, the arbitral tribunal expects each party to inform it of the time it needs to present its case. Although in the English and American traditions the plaintiff has the last

---

[252] For an example of such measures being delegated to the chairman of the arbitral tribunal alone, see CA Paris, April 26, 1985, *Aranella, supra* note 127, 1985 REV. ARB. 316 *et seq.*

[253] See, for example, in French domestic arbitration law, CA Paris, July 8, 1982, Caliqua v. Cifal, 1983 REV. ARB. 345, and observations by T. Bernard.

[254] *See* CA Paris, June 21, 1990, *Compagnie Honeywell Bull, supra* note 21, especially at 100.

[255] *See* LALIVE, POUDRET, REYMOND, *supra* note 7, at 357–58.

[256] *See, e.g.*, Art. 24 of the UNCITRAL Model Law; Art. 1047 of the German ZPO (Law of Dec. 22, 1997); Art. 1694, para. 3 of the Belgian Judicial Code; Art. 1039(2) of the Netherlands Code of Civil Procedure; Sec. 24, para. 1 of the 1999 Swedish Arbitration Act.

[257] *See, e.g.*, Art. 15(2) of the UNCITRAL Arbitration Rules; Art. 20(6) of the 1998 ICC Rules (Art. 14(3) of the previous Rules); Art. 19.1 of the 1998 LCIA Rules; Art. 25(1) of the 1999 Rules of the Arbitration Institute of the Stockholm Chamber of Commerce.

[258] *See, e.g.*, REDFERN AND HUNTER, *supra* note 22, at 349. For an example, see the September 4, 1990 Order in ICC Case No. 6401, *supra* note 216.

word, in international arbitration this is another area where the continental tradition generally prevails. The oral pleadings usually follow the order in which the memorials were submitted. The plaintiff speaks first. The defendant then presents its response and any counterclaims. The parties will often be able to present a relatively brief rebuttal and rejoinder.

1299. — The principle of equal treatment of the parties requires that both must have the opportunity to present their case orally, but not, as some parties claim, that they should have exactly the same amount of time to do so.

The content of their oral pleadings is a matter for the parties or their representatives to decide, although the arbitral tribunal may curtail discussion of aspects it considers irrelevant. An argument presented in the course of the pleadings but not contained in a party's written submissions will generally be admissible, provided the principle of due process is observed[259] and subject to any restrictions imposed by applicable arbitration rules on the submission of new claims.[260]

1300. — The attitude of the arbitral tribunal during the pleadings varies from one legal tradition to another, but continental lawyers generally prefer not to be interrupted when presenting their case.[261]

1301. — If they so agree or the arbitral tribunal so requires, the parties may submit their pleading notes ("*dossier de plaidoirie*") to the tribunal, either immediately before or immediately after the hearing. The submission of pleading notes is subject of course to an identical copy being given to the other party. This French practice, which tends to come as a surprise to lawyers from other legal systems, is sometimes found in international arbitration. It is therefore advisable to discuss this issue in advance of the hearing in order to reach agreement between the parties or obtain a decision of the arbitral tribunal on the question. A party's pleading notes may respond to the opponent's arguments, but can contain neither new claims nor evidence which has not been produced earlier in the proceedings.[262]

---

[259] See, for example, in the context of an ICC arbitration, Award No. 5346 (1988), Egyptian company X v. French company Y, 118 J.D.I. 1059 (1991), and observations by Y. Derains.

[260] *See supra* para. 1233.

[261] *See, e.g.*, DE BOISSÉSON, *supra* note 4, at 795.

[262] *See supra* para. 1264. On the arbitrators' entitlement to refuse the filing of pleading notes, even in French domestic arbitration, see CA Paris, Mar. 12, 1998, Doux v. FTT, 1999 REV. ARB. 95, and G. Flécheux's note.

CHAPTER III
PROVISIONAL AND CONSERVATORY MEASURES IN THE COURSE OF THE ARBITRATION PROCEEDINGS

1302. — Despite the principle of the autonomy of the arbitral proceedings,[1] it is sometimes necessary for a court to intervene, not only in the constitution of the arbitral tribunal,[2] but also during the course of the proceedings in order to grant provisional or conservatory measures.[3]

1303. — The terminology generally used in this context is not always helpful. First, the expressions "interim" or "provisional measures" and "protective" or "conservatory measures" are often used interchangeably. However, the former expressions refer to the nature of the decision made (an interim or provisional order does not bind the court or arbitrator hearing the merits of the dispute), whereas the latter refer to the purpose of the decision (a protective or conservatory ruling preserves a party's rights, the status quo or evidence).[4] Admittedly, a protective or conservatory order will generally be provisional in nature, but that is not necessarily the case. A protective measure may have fulfilled its purpose by the time the decision on the merits of the dispute is made, and for that reason it

---

[1] *See supra* para. 1169.

[2] *See supra* paras. 750 *et seq.*

[3] On this issue, generally, see SÉBASTIEN BESSON, ARBITRAGE INTERNATIONAL ET MESURES PROVISOIRES – ETUDE DE DROIT COMPARÉ (1998); CONSERVATORY AND PROVISIONAL MEASURES IN INTERNATIONAL ARBITRATION (ICC Publication No. 519, 1993); François Knoepfler, *Les mesures provisoires et l'arbitrage international, in* SCHIEDSGERICHTSBARKEIT 307 (1997); L. Collins, *Provisional and Protective Measures in International Litigation, in* COLLECTED COURSES OF THE HAGUE ACADEMY OF INTERNATIONAL LAW, Vol. 234, Year 1992, Part III, especially Chapter V; Alexandre Hory, *Mesures d'instruction in futurum et arbitrage*, 1996 REV. ARB. 191; B. Moreau, *L'intervention du tribunal au cours de la procédure arbitrale en droit français et droit comparé*, 1978 REV. ARB. 323; Francisco Ramos Mendez, *Arbitrage international et mesures conservatoires*, 1985 REV. ARB. 51; Philippe Ouakrat, *L'arbitrage commercial international et les mesures provisoires: étude générale*, 1988 DPCI 239; Claude Goldman, *Mesures provisoires et arbitrage international/Provisional Measures in International Arbitration*, 1993 INT'L BUS. L.J. 3; Andreas Reiner, *Les mesures provisoires et conservatoires et L'Arbitrage international, notamment l'Arbitrage CCI*, 125 J.D.I. 853 (1998). In French domestic arbitration, see Eric Loquin, *Arbitrage – Compétence arbitrale – Conflits entre la compétence arbitrale et la compétence judiciaire*, J.-CL. PROC. CIV., Fasc. 1034, ¶¶ 9 *et seq.* (1994).

[4] On this issue, see Stephen R. Bond, *The Nature of Conservatory and Provisional Measures, in* CONSERVATORY AND PROVISIONAL MEASURES IN INTERNATIONAL ARBITRATION, *supra* note 3, at 8; BESSON, *supra* note 3, ¶¶ 38 *et seq.* at 39.

may have been intended from the outset to stand alone. An example in the construction context is a decision to place a works site under the surveillance of a security firm. Conversely, a provisional order will not necessarily be protective. This is the case of the French *référé-provision*, the purpose of which is to enforce without delay a creditor's rights, provided its claim cannot seriously be contested, by means of a summary order issued without prejudice to the subsequent decision on the merits.[5] In addition, the general nature of the expressions "provisional measures" and "protective measures" tends to cloud often essential distinctions between certain of the measures granted. In particular, these terms fail to convey the genuine specificity of measures designed to facilitate the enforcement of the subsequent award.[6]

1304. — We shall therefore examine the different categories of measures which may be granted by the courts in actions connected with the arbitral proceedings (Section II). First, however, we shall consider the principles governing the allocation of jurisdiction between arbitral tribunals and the courts over provisional and protective measures ordered despite the existence of an arbitration agreement or pending arbitral proceedings (Section I).

SECTION I
JURISDICTION OF THE ARBITRAL TRIBUNAL AND THE COURTS

1305. — The principle that the courts and arbitrators have concurrent jurisdiction to take provisional or protective measures[7] is increasingly recognized in modern arbitration law (§ 1). However, the principle operates subject to certain limits (§ 2).

---

[5] *See infra* para. 1339.

[6] *See infra* para. 1334.

[7] On the applicability of the Brussels and Lugano Conventions on Jurisdiction and Enforcement in Civil and Commercial Matters to provisional measures—as opposed, in most circumstances, to provisional orders to pay a sum of money, see the November 17, 1998 decision of the Court of Justice of the European Communities in Case C–391/95, Van Uden Maritime BV, trading as Van Uden Africa Line v. Kommanditgesellschaft in Firma Deco-Line e.a., 1998 E.C.R. I–7122; 14 INT'L ARB. REP. CI (Jan. 1999); 1998 ECJ CELEX LEXIS 3138; 1999 REV. ARB. 143, and H. Gaudemet-Tallon's note; 1999 BULL. ASA 68, and the commentary by M. Scherer at 83; see also the opinion of the advocate general, Mr. Léger, presented on June 10, 1997, 1998 BULL. ASA 166.

§ 1. – The Principle of Concurrent Jurisdiction

1306. — The various sources of arbitration law—statute, institutional rules, international conventions and arbitral awards—reveal a growing acceptance of the principle that courts and arbitral tribunals have concurrent powers to order provisional or protective measures.[8] This principle has three consequences, each of which will be discussed in turn.

A. – JURISDICTION OF THE COURTS

1307. — The first consequence of the principle of concurrent jurisdiction is that the parties are entitled to apply to the courts, despite the existence of an arbitration agreement, to obtain provisional or protective measures.

The thinking is that parties to an arbitration agreement should not be deprived of the benefit of emergency measures available from the courts. It is considered more effective to apply to the courts where emergency measures are needed both because the courts will hear an application as a matter of urgency, and because their decisions will be readily enforceable.[9]

It has sometimes been argued that the principle whereby the courts lack jurisdiction to hear disputes covered by an arbitration agreement[10] prevents the courts from ordering provisional or conservatory measures. This argument has been raised particularly in connection with the 1958 New York Convention. Although the Convention contains no specific provisions on this issue, it has sometimes been held that by ordering a protective

---

[8] *See* Gérard Couchez, *Référé et arbitrage (Essai de bilan... provisoire)*, 1986 REV. ARB. 155; B. Audit, note following Cass. 1e civ., Nov. 18, 1986, Atlantic Triton v. République populaire révolutionnaire de Guinée, 1987 REV. CRIT. DIP 760, 764; Ouakrat, *supra* note 3, at 263 *et seq.*

[9] On the positions taken in different legal systems, see *The role of the courts and problems related to the execution of conservatory and provisional measures*, *in* CONSERVATORY AND PROVISIONAL MEASURES IN INTERNATIONAL ARBITRATION, *supra* note 3, with the contributions by Gérard Pluyette (*The French Perspective*, at 72), Richard W. Hulbert, (*The American Law Perspective*, at 92) and Samir El-Sharkawi (*The Arab Perspective*, at 104). In Italy, Article 818 of the Code of Civil Procedure, which was not modified by the law of January 5, 1994, is more radical and provides that "the arbitrators cannot authorize attachments or other interim measures;" *see* Piero Bernardini, *Italy*, *in* ICCA INTERNATIONAL HANDBOOK OF COMMERCIAL ARBITRATION (forthcoming in 1999). On the unusual position taken in English law prior to the 1996 Arbitration Act in this respect, see Channel Tunnel Group Ltd. v. Balfour Beatty Construction Ltd., [1993] A.C. 334; [1993] 2 W.L.R. 262; [1993] 1 All E.R. 664; [1993] 1 Lloyd's Rep. 116; XIX Y.B. COM. ARB. 736 (1994), in which the House of Lords, upholding the 1992 decision of the Court of Appeal, [1992] 1 Q.B. 656; [1992] 2 All E.R. 609; [1992] 2 W.L.R. 741; [1992] 2 Lloyd's Rep. 291; XVIII Y.B. COM. ARB. 446 (1993), refused to order emergency measures because the arbitration was held in Belgium and English law was not applicable to the merits. For a summary in French, see V.V. Veeder, *L'arrêt Channel Tunnel de la Chambre des Lords (1993) A.C. 335 – L'affaire du tunnel sous la Manche et les mesures conservatoires*, 1993 REV. ARB. 705). It is to be hoped that this case law will not survive the enactment of Section 38 of the 1996 Act which suggests no such distinctions.

[10] *See supra* paras. 661 *et seq.*

measure designed to facilitate the enforcement of a subsequent award,[11] the court contravenes Article II, paragraph 3 of the Convention, which provides that the courts must decline jurisdiction where there is an arbitration agreement between the parties. That was the view taken in 1974 by the US Federal Court of Appeals (3d Circuit) in the *McCreary & Tire & Rubber Co. v. CEAT S.p.A.* case.[12] That decision divided the subsequent case law to the extent that even now the question of whether an attachment order can be obtained in the United States before the award has been made remains uncertain and depends, in practice, on the place where the measure is sought.[13] The position taken in *McCreary* ostensibly upholds the arbitrators' jurisdiction, but in fact it may render the subsequent award ineffective and is plainly wrong. Protective measures aimed at ensuring that the subsequent award will be enforceable fall within the exclusive jurisdiction of the courts, as do measures of enforcement themselves.[14] The New York Convention does not contradict that principle, and its authors never intended to prevent the courts from ordering protective measures.[15] Although the *McCreary* controversy focused on attachment procedures, the same observation applies to the various other protective measures which may be sought in an emergency, despite the existence of an arbitration agreement or pending arbitral proceedings.[16] In the absence of uniform provisions on this issue in the New York

---

[11] *See infra* para. 1334.

[12] 501 F.2d 1032 (3d Cir. 1974).

[13] On United States case law, see ALBERT JAN VAN DEN BERG, THE NEW YORK ARBITRATION CONVENTION OF 1958, at 139 *et seq.* (1981); Lawrence F. Ebb, *Flight of Assets from the Jurisdiction "In the Twinkling of a Telex": Pre- and Post-Award Conservatory Relief in International Commercial Arbitrations,* 7 J. INT'L ARB. 9 (Mar. 1990). *Comp. with* Performance Unlimited, Inc. v. Questar Publishers, Inc., 52 F.3d 1373 (6th Cir. 1995); 6 WORLD ARB. & MED. REP. 130 (1995); see also Section 8 of the Federal Arbitration Act (9 U.S.C.A. § 8 (West 1999)), which expressly gives jurisdiction to the federal courts to authorize seizures in shipping disputes submitted to arbitration, and resulting case law (for example Unitramp, Ltd. v. Mediterranean Brokerage & Agents, S.A.S., Civ. Action No. 93-2831 Section "I", 1993 U.S. Dist. LEXIS 13304 (E.D. La. Sept. 13, 1993); 8 INT'L ARB. REP. 6 (Oct. 1993)). *See also* Lawrence W. Newman and Robert Davidson, *Provisional Remedies in International Arbitration – Part I: U.S. Courts,* 6 WORLD ARB. & MED. REP. 32 (1995); GARY B. BORN, INTERNATIONAL COMMERCIAL ARBITRATION IN THE UNITED STATES – COMMENTARY & MATERIALS 735 *et seq.* (1994). For a comparative law analysis, see MAURO RUBINO-SAMMARTANO, INTERNATIONAL ARBITRATION LAW 355 *et seq.* (1990).

[14] *See infra* paras. 1323 *et seq.*

[15] *See* VAN DEN BERG, *supra* note 13, at 144; Ouakrat, *supra* note 3, ¶ 64 at 258; for a criticism of the 3d Circuit court in the *McCreary* case, see Joseph D. Becker, *Attachments in aid of international arbitration – the American position,* 1 ARB. INT'L 40 (1985); Pierre-Yves Tschanz, *International Arbitration in the United States: the Need for a New Act,* 3 ARB. INT'L 309 (1987); Ebb, *supra* note 13; Collins, *supra* note 3, at 79; YVES DERAINS AND ERIC A. SCHWARTZ, A GUIDE TO THE NEW ICC RULES OF ARBITRATION 272 (1998); BESSON, *supra* note 3, ¶¶ 261 *et seq.* at 166 *et seq.*

[16] The possibility for parties to obtain pre-trial discovery from United States courts for the purposes of an arbitration taking place outside the United States, which would mean that the arbitral tribunal would be considered as a "foreign or international tribunal" within the meaning of 28 U.S.C. §1782, has been addressed in a number of decisions. After some decisions in the affirmative (*see, e.g., In re* Application of Euromepa S.A. v. Esmerian, Inc., 51 F.3d 1095 (2d Cir. 1995); 1996 BULL. ASA 199), the trend is now to refuse such an assimilation: *see In re* Application of Medway Power Ltd., 985 F. Supp. 402 (S.D.N.Y. 1997); *In re* National Broadcasting Co., No. M–77 (RWS), 1998 WL 19994 (S.D.N.Y. Jan. 16, 1998), *aff'd,* National Broadcasting Co. v. Bear Stearns & Co., 165 F.3d 184 (2d Cir. 1999); Application of the Republic of Kazakhstan v.

(continued...)

Convention, each country must determine whether, and under what conditions, such measures can be taken by its own courts.[17]

1308. — The 1961 European Convention clearly favors having the parties apply to the courts for provisional measures. It states, in Article VI, paragraph 4, that:

> [a] request for interim measures or measures of conservation addressed to a judicial authority shall not be deemed incompatible with the arbitration agreement . . .

This provision has been applied in practice by arbitrators[18] and the courts. For example, in one case a Spanish judge rightly held that it should prevail over his own law.[19]

1309. — The issue of whether the parties can apply to the courts for protective measures where there is an arbitration agreement or where arbitral proceedings are pending has proved more controversial in ICSID arbitration. The 1965 Washington Convention states in general terms that ICSID arbitration is exclusive (Art. 26) and empowers the arbitrators to recommend any protective measures aimed at safeguarding the rights of the parties (Art. 47). Thus the question arose as to whether this latter provision was intended to create an exclusive right for the arbitrators to decide on provisional measures, including the attachment of assets which, in practice, cannot be effectively decided by an arbitral tribunal.

The Centre has consistently expressed the opinion that the autonomy of ICSID arbitration prevents the ordering of protective measures by the courts, including those aimed at ensuring the enforceability of the subsequent award (such as attachments), until an award has been made on the merits of the dispute.[20] The Rennes Court of Appeals took that view in its 1984 decision in the *République de Guinée v. Atlantic Triton* case.[21] However, the history of the

---

[16] (...continued)
Biedermann Int'l, 168 F.3d 880 (5th Cir. 1999), reversing a December 3, 1998 decision of the U.S. District Court for the Southern District of Texas (35 F. Supp. 2d 567). *See also* David W. Rivkin and Barton Legum, *Attempts to Use Section 1782 to Obtain US Discovery in Aid of Foreign Arbitrations*, 14 ARB. INT'L 213 (1998); Eric A. Schwartz and Rolf B. Johnson, *Court-Assisted Discovery in Aid of International Commercial Arbitrations – Two Recent US Cases Regarding the Applicability of 28 U.S.C. § 1782*, 15 J. INT'L ARB. 53 (Sept. 1998); Emmanuel Gaillard, *Court-Ordered Production of Evidence*, N.Y.L.J., Apr. 1, 1999, at 3; Hans Smit, *American Judicial Assistance to International Arbitral Tribunals*, 8 AM. REV. INT'L ARB. 153 (1997).

[17] On the question of a reform of the New York Convention on this point, see Bernardo M. Cremades, *Is Exclusion of Concurrent Courts' Jurisdiction over Conservatory Measures to be Introduced through a Revision of the Convention?*, 6 J. INT'L ARB. 105 (Sept. 1989).

[18] ICC Award No. 4415 (1984), French company v. Two Italian companies, 111 J.D.I. 952 (1984), and observations by S. Jarvin.

[19] *Audiencia provincial* of Cadiz, June 12, 1991, Bahia Industrial, S.A. v. Eintacar-Eimar, S.A., XVIII Y.B. COM. ARB. 616 (1993).

[20] *See, e.g.,* ICSID: INTERNATIONAL CENTRE FOR SETTLEMENT OF INVESTMENT DISPUTES (Doc. ICSID 12 (1980)).

[21] CA Rennes, Oct. 26, 1984, République populaire révolutionnaire de Guinée v. Atlantic Triton, 112 J.D.I. 925 (1985), and E. Gaillard's note; 1985 REV. ARB. 439, and G. Flécheux's note; for an English translation, see 24 I.L.M. 340 (1985); XI Y.B. COM. ARB. 215 (1986).

Convention suggests that this approach is no more consistent with the intentions of the authors of the Washington Convention[22] than it is with the needs of arbitral practice.[23] The French *Cour de cassation* thus vacated the decision of the Rennes Court of Appeals on the grounds that Article 26 of the Washington Convention "was not intended to prohibit applications to the courts for protective measures aimed at ensuring the enforcement of the forthcoming award."[24] In Belgium, the lower court of Antwerp took the reverse position and followed the approach advocated by the ICSID guide.[25] In Switzerland, the issue was raised in the *Mine v. Guinea* case but was never properly addressed by the courts due to other preliminary procedural difficulties.[26] As a result, the question of the exact scope of Article 26 of the Washington Convention has remained a matter of controversy.[27] However, the issue was rendered moot, for all practical purposes, by the revision of the ICSID Rules which took place in 1984. The Rules now exclude the possibility of resorting to the courts for such provisional measures unless the parties have otherwise provided.[28] Since it is not disputed that, where applicable, the principle recognizing the jurisdiction of the courts to order provisional measures is not of a mandatory nature,[29] the issue of the exact meaning of Article 26 of the Washington Convention will no longer arise in the same terms. When the parties adopt the Rules without specifying their intent to reserve the possibility to resort to the courts for provisional measures, this will be construed by some authors as the parties' waiver of their rights, and by others simply as confirmation of the absence of such rights. The result, however, will be identical. When the parties have expressly provided for such a possibility, their agreement is likely to be held valid, as Article 26 of the Washington

---

[22]   *See* E. Gaillard, note following CA Rennes, Oct. 26, 1984, *République de Guinée, supra* note 21, at 941. *But see* Collins, *supra* note 3, at 104.

[23]   *See* G. Flécheux, note following CA Rennes, Oct. 26, 1984, *République de Guinée, supra* note 21, at 453; *but see* Paul D. Friedland, *Provisional Measures and ICSID Arbitration*, 2 ARB. INT'L 335 (1986).

[24]   Cass. 1e civ., Nov. 18, 1986, Atlantic Triton v. République populaire révolutionnaire de Guinée, 114 J.D.I. 125 (1987), and E. Gaillard's note; 1987 REV. CRIT. DIP 760, and B. Audit's note; 1987 REV. ARB. 315, and G. Flécheux's note; for an English translation, see 2 INT'L ARB. REP. 306 (May1987); XII Y.B. COM. ARB. 183 (1987). *See also* Bertrand P. Marchais, *Mesures provisoires et autonomie du système d'arbitrage C.I.R.D.I. – Réflexions sur l'arrêt de la Cour de cassation du 18 novembre 1986 (Société Atlantic Triton c. République populaire révolutionnaire de Guinée)*, 1988 DPCI 275; Philippe Ouakrat, *La pratique du CIRDI*, 1987 DPCI 273, 298 *et seq.*; Paul D. Friedland, *ICSID and Court-Ordered Provisional Remedies: An Update*, 4 ARB. INT'L 161 (1988).

[25]   See Court of First Instance of Antwerp (Belgium), Sept. 27, 1985, Guinea v. Maritime International Nominees Establishment, 24 I.L.M. 1639 (1985); 1 ICSID REV. – FOREIGN INV. L.J. 372 (1986); XII Y.B. COM. ARB. 181 (1987).

[26]   On the *MINE v. Guinea* case, in which one party also obtained an AAA award by default in the same matter, which explains why the admissibility of escrow procedures where there is an ICSID arbitration clause has never been addressed in Switzerland in a normal context, see E. Gaillard, note following Cass. 1e civ., Nov. 18, 1986, *Atlantic Triton, supra* note 24, at 131–33; BESSON, *supra* note 3, ¶¶ 276 *et seq.*

[27]   On this issue generally, see Gaillard, note following Cass. 1e civ., Nov. 18, 1986, *Atlantic Triton, supra* note 24; Collins, *supra* note 3, at Chap. VII; Antonio R. Parra, *The Practices and Experience of the ICSID, in* CONSERVATORY AND PROVISIONAL MEASURES IN INTERNATIONAL ARBITRATION, *supra* note 3, at 39.

[28]   *See infra* para. 1320; *comp. with* Collins *supra* note 3, at 105.

[29]   *See infra* para. 1319.

Convention has not so far been construed as an implicit but mandatory exclusion of the jurisdiction of the courts.

B. – No WAIVER OF THE ARBITRATION AGREEMENT

1310. — The second consequence of the principle of concurrent jurisdiction is that by applying to the courts for provisional or protective relief, a party does not waive the application of the arbitration agreement to the merits of the dispute.

1311. — The fact that provisional or protective measures are compatible with the arbitration agreement is set forth in the ICC Rules of Arbitration (Art. 23(2) of the 1998 Rules; Art. 8(5) of the previous Rules),[30] the UNCITRAL Arbitration Rules (Art. 26(3)), the AAA International Arbitration Rules (Art. 21(3) of the 1997 Rules) and the Rules of the Arbitration Institute of the Stockholm Chamber of Commerce (Art. 31(2) of the 1999 Rules). The same would be true in most legal systems even in the absence of an agreement between the parties to that effect.[31] The UNCITRAL Model Law expressly provides so in its Article 9.[32] Arbitral case law likewise recognizes that by applying for such measures before a court, a party has not necessarily waived its rights under the arbitration agreement.[33]

1312. — The 1961 European Convention also endorses the principle, stating in Article VI, paragraph 4 that "[a] request for interim measures or measures of conservation addressed to a judicial authority shall not be . . . regarded as a submission of the substance of the case to the court."

---

[30] On ICC practice prior to the 1998 Rules, see Eric A. Schwartz, *The Practices and Experience of the ICC Court*, in CONSERVATORY AND PROVISIONAL MEASURES IN INTERNATIONAL ARBITRATION, *supra* note 3, at 45, and on the 1998 Rules, Andreas Reiner, *Le Règlement d'arbitrage de la CCI, version 1998*, 1998 REV. ARB. 3, 16 (1998); DERAINS AND SCHWARTZ, *supra* note 15, at 272 *et seq. Comp. with* Art. 25.3 of the 1998 LCIA Rules.

[31] See, for example, in the United States, for a case where a request for pre-trial discovery was held to be compatible with a subsequent request for arbitration, Envirex v. Schussler, 832 F. Supp. 1293 (E.D. Wis. 1993); 5 WORLD ARB. & MED. REP. 62 (1994).

[32] *See also* Art. 1022(2) of the Netherlands Code of Civil Procedure; Act. 1033 of the German ZPO (Law of Dec. 22, 1997). *Comp. with* Sec. 4, para. 3 of the 1999 Swedish Arbitration Act.

[33] See, as regards requests for expert proceedings, ICC Award No. 4156 (1983), French company v. French company, 111 J.D.I. 937 (1984), and observations by S. Jarvin; ICC Award No. 2444 (1976), Italian company v. Yugoslavian company, 104 J.D.I. 932 (1977), and observations by Y. Derains. Compare with ICC Award No. 5650 (1989), U.S. contractor v. African State employer, XVI Y.B. COM. ARB. 85 (1991). See also, in a case where the court had been requested to appoint an expert, to enjoin a party to cease an allegedly illegal activity and to pay an advance to the plaintiff, the 1991 partial award in ICC Case No. 6709, which rightly held the arbitral tribunal to have jurisdiction (German licensor v. French licensee, 119 J.D.I. 998 (1992), and observations by D. Hascher). For a decision that a seizure carried out as retaliation against a party commencing arbitration proceedings can be considered to be a breach of the arbitration agreement, see ICC Award No. 5835 (1988), ICC BULLETIN, Vol. 8, No. 1, at 67 (1997).

1313. — In this context, a decision of the French *Cour de cassation* in 1990 was particularly unwelcome. In that case,[34] an ICC arbitration was pending and the arbitral tribunal had appointed experts. These experts submitted their report to the tribunal, but the claimant in the arbitration then applied to the courts for the appointment of another expert. The Paris Court of Appeals considered that the claimant had thereby waived its rights to continue the arbitration, and its decision was upheld by the *Cour de cassation*. It is arguable that the circumstances of the case, and particularly the fact that an expert's report had already been issued in the arbitration, significantly influenced both courts in reaching their decisions. Nevertheless, the principle should remain that a request for provisional measures does not imply a waiver of the arbitration agreement.[35]

C. – JURISDICTION OF THE ARBITRATORS

1314. — The third consequence of the principle of concurrent jurisdiction is that the arbitrators themselves have jurisdiction to order provisional or protective measures.[36]

1315. — Some early arbitration laws gave the courts exclusive jurisdiction to order provisional measures.[37] However, modern legislation has taken a different position. Most laws now recognize that the courts and the arbitrators have concurrent powers to take certain

---

[34] Cass. 1e civ., Oct. 9, 1990, Bin Seoud Bin Abdul Aziz v. Banque Rivaud, 1991 REV. ARB. 305, and M.-L. Niboyet-Hoegy's note.

[35] *See also* M.-L. Niboyet-Hoegy, note following Cass. 1e civ., Oct. 9, 1990, *Bin Seoud Bin Abdul Aziz, supra* note 34.

[36] On this issue, generally, see Piero Bernardini, *The Powers of the Arbitrator, in* CONSERVATORY AND PROVISIONAL MEASURES IN INTERNATIONAL ARBITRATION, *supra* note 3, at 21.

[37] See, for example, Article 26 of the Swiss *Concordat* and, for an illustration, ICC Award No. 4998 (1985), French company v. Moroccan company, 113 J.D.I. 1139 (1986), and observations by S. Jarvin; Art. 685 of the Greek Code of Civil Procedure and the commentary in ANGHELOS C. FOUSTOUCOS, L'ARBITRAGE INTERNE ET INTERNATIONAL EN DROIT PRIVÉ HELLÉNIQUE ¶¶ 112 *et seq.* (1976); Art. 1036 of the German ZPO, which applied prior to the entry into force on January 1, 1998 of the new German arbitration statute (new Art. 1041 ZPO); Art. 818 of the Italian Code of Civil Procedure, left untouched by the 1994 reform, according to which "[t]he arbitrators may not grant attachment or other interim measures of protection." On this issue, generally, see RUBINO-SAMMARTANO, *supra* note 13, ¶ 17.1.2; Piero Bernardini, *Italy, in* ICCA INTERNATIONAL HANDBOOK ON COMMERCIAL ARBITRATION (forthcoming in 1999).

conservatory measures.[38] Some even allow the arbitrators themselves to apply to the courts to ensure that their decision will be enforceable.[39]

1316. — Arbitral case law also recognizes that arbitrators can take conservatory measures. Many examples of this can be seen in a variety of arbitration systems.[40] The ICC specifically provides for this possibility at Article 23(1) of its Rules.[41] These measures can be incorporated by the arbitrators in a provisional award.[42] Other arbitral institutions have followed this approach.[43]

1317. — The principle of concurrent jurisdiction is thus well established. It is however confined within certain limits.

---

[38] *See, e.g.*, Art. 183 of the Swiss Private International Law Statute; Art. 1696, para. 1, of the Belgian Judicial Code (Law of May 19, 1998); Art. 17 of the UNCITRAL Model Law; compare with Article 1051 of the Netherlands Code of Civil Procedure (Law of July 2, 1986), which only states that "[a]n arbitration agreement shall not preclude a party from requesting a court to grant interim measures of protection, or from applying . . . for a decision in summary proceedings." For a comparative law analysis, see Ouakrat, *supra* note 3; Ramos Mendez, *supra* note 3; Neil E. McDonell, *The Availability of Provisional Relief in International Commercial Arbitration*, 22 COLUM. J. TRANSNAT'L L. 273 (1984); BESSON, *supra* note 3, ¶¶ 441 *et seq.* at 263 *et seq.* Arbitration rules generally confirm the jurisdiction of the arbitrators to grant provisional relief (see the references cited *supra* para. 1311), but as their authority is no greater than the intentions of the parties, one should really refer to national law to determine whether such jurisdiction is conferred upon the arbitrators.

[39] *See* Art. 183(2) of the Swiss Private International Law Statute. On the provisions of the UNCITRAL Model Law and Swiss Law authorizing the arbitrators to apply to the courts regarding the production of evidence, see *infra* para. 1337. *Comp. with* Sec. 26 of the 1999 Swedish Arbitration Act.

[40] *See* ICC Award No. 4126 (1984), European contractor v. African State owner, 111 J.D.I. 934 (1984), and observations by S. Jarvin; "Interim Ruling Award" No. 2015 of August 24, 1985 by a tribunal constituted under the aegis of the Society of Maritime Arbitrators, Southern Seas Navigation Ltd. v. Petroleos Mexicanos, XI Y.B. COM. ARB. 209 (1986); the December 9, 1983 Decision Regarding Provisional Measures by B. Goldman, president, I. Foighel and E.W. Rubin, arbitrators, in ICSID Case No. ARB/81/1, Amco Asia Corp. v. Republic of Indonesia, to put an end to the breach of the confidentiality of the arbitral process (24 I.L.M. 365 (1985); XI Y.B. COM. ARB. 159 (1986); 1 ICSID REP. 410 (1993)); see also the commentary by Emmanuel Gaillard, *Le principe de confidentialité de l'arbitrage commercial international*, Dalloz, Chron. 153 (1987). See, in addition, the decisions of ICC arbitral tribunals sitting in Geneva, in 1989 regarding the absence of proof of irreparable loss, in 1993 regarding the restriction on the communication of confidential information, and the 1989 decision of an *ad hoc* arbitral tribunal regarding the payment of an advance prior to an expert's ruling on price review (1994 BULL. ASA 142 *et seq.*).

[41] For a commentary, see Marc Blessing, *The ICC Arbitral Procedure Under the 1998 Rules – What Has Changed?*, ICC BULLETIN, Vol. 8, No. 2, at 16, especially at 31 *et seq.* (1997); DERAINS AND SCHWARTZ, *supra* note 15, at 272 *et seq.*

[42] *See, e.g.*, ICC Award No. 3540 (1980), French contractor v. Yugoslavian sub-contractor, 108 J.D.I. 914 (1981), and observations by Y. Derains; for an English translation, see VII Y.B. COM. ARB. 124 (1982).

[43] *See* Art. 26 of the UNCITRAL Rules; Art. 25 of the 1998 LCIA Rules; Art. 21 of the 1997 AAA International Rules; Art. 31(1) of the 1999 Rules of the Arbitration Institute of the Stockholm Chamber of Commerce.

§ 2. – Limits to Concurrent Jurisdiction

1318. — The concurrent jurisdiction of the courts and the arbitrators to grant provisional or protective measures is limited in two respects. First, the parties may agree to depart from the principle of concurrent jurisdiction (A). Second, there are areas where the courts have exclusive jurisdiction (B).

A. – AGREEMENT BETWEEN THE PARTIES

1319. — The principle of concurrent jurisdiction is not a matter of public policy. The parties are therefore perfectly entitled to agree to remove certain measures from the jurisdiction of the arbitrators. That is simply an application of the more general principle that the parties are free to define the scope of their arbitration agreement as they see fit. Any selective exclusion of that kind must be drafted with great care, so as to avoid ambiguous borderline cases, but there is no doubt as to the legality of such agreements. In practice, the parties often stipulate that their arbitration agreement does not prevent them from applying to the courts for provisional or protective measures, or even that the courts will have exclusive jurisdiction to take such measures.

Conversely, it is generally accepted that the parties can agree not to apply to the courts for provisional or protective measures during the course of the arbitration.[44]

1320. — That, in effect, is what the parties do when they sign an ICSID arbitration agreement, unless they specifically agree otherwise. Indeed, at a time when the issue of the exact meaning of Article 26 of the Washington Convention was in dispute in a case pending before the French courts,[45] the Centre added a fifth paragraph to Article 39 of its Rules, specifying that:

> [n]othing in this Rule shall prevent the parties, provided that they have so stipulated in the agreement recording their consent, from requesting any judicial or other authority to order provisional measures, prior to the institution of the proceeding, or during the proceeding, for the preservation of their respective rights and interests.[46]

---

[44] See, in France, Cass. 1e civ., Nov. 18, 1986, *Atlantic Triton*: "The power of the courts to order provisional measures . . . can only [be excluded] by an explicit agreement between the parties or by an implicit agreement resulting from the adoption of arbitration rules which contain such an exclusion" (*supra* note 24). Compare, as regards "*référé-provision*," Cass. 2e civ., Mar. 20, 1989, L.F.P. Danel v. Sotiaf Informatique, 1989 REV. ARB. 494, and G. Couchez' note. See also Article 17 of the UNCITRAL Model Law, which confirms the parties' freedom of choice. However, see the reservations discussed at paragraph 1334 below regarding measures intended to facilitate enforcement of an award.

[45] *See supra* para. 1309.

[46] ICSID BASIC DOCUMENTS 80 (1985); for the French version, see 113 J.D.I. 253 (1986).

This provision clearly excludes the possibility of applying to the courts unless that option has been expressly provided for by the parties. The statement that the parties can nevertheless so agree is of course superfluous, as the Rules themselves are only binding to the extent agreed by the parties. Thus, the only value of the added clause is to reverse the presumption accepted in other forms of arbitration according to which, unless otherwise specified, the courts still retain a power to order provisional measures. Accordingly, unless the parties have provided otherwise, in ICSID arbitration the courts can grant no measures to protect evidence,[47] or to prevent irreparable harm (for instance by ordering the continuation of works or the discontinuation of an illegal activity),[48] irrespective of whether or not the arbitral tribunal has been constituted.[49]

1321. — A similar exclusion of the jurisdiction of the courts results implicitly where the parties use the ICC pre-arbitral referee procedure, which entered into force on January 1, 1990.[50] These Rules, which were modeled on the French *référé* procedures, enable a third party, nominated by agreement between the parties or by the Chairman of the ICC International Court of Arbitration, to take any measures required as a matter of urgency.[51] The decision of the referee is provisional (Art. 6.3), and the referee cannot later act as an arbitrator to decide the merits of the dispute, unless the parties provide otherwise in writing (Art. 2.3).[52] The referee's decision binds neither the arbitral tribunal nor the court responsible for deciding the merits of the dispute where there is no arbitration clause. The decision must be made within thirty days of the date of submission of the file to the third party. The competent jurisdiction "may determine whether any party who refuses or fails to carry out an order of the Referee is liable to any other party for loss or damage caused by such refusal or failure" (Art. 6.8.1), and may rule on any liability resulting from the carrying out of an order requested in unjustified circumstances (Art. 6.8.2). In our opinion, where a pre-arbitral referee clause is provided for, the parties waive their rights to apply to the courts for all measures within the referee's jurisdiction. Such a waiver is perfectly legitimate and can be inferred from the intention to resort to a referee for the provisional measures covered by the Rules.[53] Determining the true intentions of the parties is a more delicate task where

---

[47] *See infra* paras. 1331 *et seq.*

[48] *See infra* paras. 1327 *et seq.*

[49] On this issue, see G. Flécheux, note following Cass. 1e civ., Nov. 18, 1986, *Atlantic Triton, supra* note 24.

[50] ICC PRE-ARBITRAL REFEREE PROCEDURE (ICC Publication No. 482, 1990); 1990 REV. ARB. 937; ICC BULLETIN, Vol. 1, No. 1, at 19 (1990). For a commentary, see Jean-Jacques Arnaldez and Erik Schafer, *Le Règlement de référé pré-arbitral de la Chambre de commerce internationale (en vigueur depuis le 1er janvier 1990)*, 1990 REV. ARB. 835; Jan A.S. Paulsson, *An Introduction to the 1990 ICC Rules for a Pre-Arbitral Referee Procedure*, 5 INT'L ARB. REP. 18 (Mar. 1990); on a preliminary draft, see Yves Derains, *Expertise technique et référé arbitral*, 1982 REV. ARB. 239. On the express recognition by national law of the possibility of empowering the arbitral tribunal or its chairman to render an award in summary proceedings (*référé arbitral*), see Article 1051 of the Netherlands Code of Civil Procedure (Law of July 2, 1986).

[51] On the measures liable to be taken, see Article 2.1 of the Rules.

[52] On the terminology, see *supra* para. 1303.

[53] See, on this issue, CA Paris, 14e Ch., Sec. B, July 3, 1992, Euro Disney v. Impresa Pizzarotti, No. 92/11058, unpublished, which, in the context of an ICC arbitration, justified the jurisdiction of the courts to order

(continued...)

they have opted for accelerated procedures which are liable to culminate in an actual arbitral award.[54] In such cases, courts hearing requests for protective measures must determine whether, by resorting to an accelerated arbitral procedure, the parties intended to waive their right to apply to the courts for urgent measures, and whether the imminence of an award is such that the urgency allegedly justifying the application to the court is unfounded. If in doubt, as with any waiver, it should not be presumed that the parties waived their right to apply to the courts.

1322. — There is, however, a limit to the influence of the parties' intentions on the allocation of jurisdiction between the courts and the arbitrators. Measures aimed at facilitating the enforcement of a forthcoming award fall within the exclusive jurisdiction of the courts, even where they are taken on a protective basis. Although the parties can agree to refrain from applying to the courts for such measures until the outcome of the dispute is known, they cannot empower the arbitrators to make attachment or other orders connected with the enforcement of the decision, because the courts have a monopoly over such measures.

This rule also constitutes the second exception to the principle of concurrent jurisdiction.

B. – THE COURTS HAVE EXCLUSIVE JURISDICTION IN MATTERS OF ENFORCEMENT

1323. — The courts' exclusive jurisdiction over the enforcement of judicial decisions, whether court judgments or arbitral awards, prevents arbitrators from hearing such issues. This rule is found in most arbitration laws and also applies in ICSID arbitration. Article 54, paragraph 3 of the Washington Convention states that "[e]xecution of the award shall be governed by the laws concerning the execution of judgments in force in the state in whose territories such execution is sought." The parties therefore cannot depart from applicable arbitration rules in order to empower the arbitrators to take measures designed to facilitate the enforcement of the award.

1324. — In the light of these principles, we shall examine in greater detail the various provisional or protective measures which are liable to be requested by the parties.

---

[53] (...continued)
provisional or protective measures on the grounds that "the [ICC] Rules do not provide for the possibility of an arbitral tribunal ordering such measures before the constitution of the arbitral tribunal" (*aff'd*, Cass. 2e civ., Oct. 11, 1995, 1996 REV. ARB. 228, 1st decision, and the commentary by Hory, *supra* note 3; 1996 RTD COM. 664, and observations by J.-C. Dubarry and E. Loquin). See also, in French domestic arbitration, in favor of such a waiver, and thus the absence of jurisdiction of the courts on the basis of the adoption by the parties of the emergency procedures provided for by the Rules of the Paris Arbitration Chamber, see TGI Bressuire, réf., Feb. 6, 1994, S.A. Cargill Division Soja France v. S.A.R.L. Cipa, 1995 REV. ARB. 32, 2d decision, and observations by P. Véron. See, however, the more reserved position of Hory, *supra* note 3, at 201.

[54] *See supra* para. 1248.

SECTION II
DIFFERENT TYPES OF PROVISIONAL OR CONSERVATORY MEASURES

1325. — Courts and arbitral tribunals can generally hear applications for a variety of conservatory measures (§ 1) and for measures concerning the production of evidence (§ 2). In France, the parties can also seek a *référé-provision* (§ 3).

§ 1. – Conservatory Measures

1326. — Although they are generally discussed as a single topic, conservatory measures include some very diverse concepts. A clear distinction should be drawn between conservatory measures intended to prevent irreparable harm, those designed to preserve evidence and those that facilitate the enforcement of an award.[55]

A. – CONSERVATORY MEASURES INTENDED TO PREVENT IRREPARABLE HARM

1327. — Even where an arbitration agreement exists, or where arbitral proceedings are pending, it may sometimes be necessary to take urgent measures to maintain the status quo or to prevent irreparable harm. A party may, for example, wish to obtain an immediate ban on illegal competition, or an authorization to sell perishable goods without delay.[56] Where an arbitration agreement exists, or where arbitral proceedings are in progress, there is a question as to whether the party seeking urgent measures should address its request to the courts or to the arbitrators. Where the arbitral tribunal has yet to be constituted, a party might be denied justice in an emergency if it were obliged to seek relief from the arbitrators. Even where the arbitral tribunal is constituted, it may be more effective to apply to a court, whose decision will be provisionally enforceable, rather than to the arbitrators, whose award is subject to enforcement proceedings before the courts.

---

[55] For a typology of "provisional or protective measures," compare François Knoepfler and Philippe Schweizer, *Les mesures provisoires et l'arbitrage, in* RECUEIL DE TRAVAUX SUISSES SUR L'ARBITRAGE INTERNATIONAL 221 (1984); Ouakrat, *supra* note 3, ¶¶ 10 *et seq.*; in French domestic law, see Jean-Régis Mirbeau-Gauvin, *Réflexions sur les mesures conservatoires*, Dalloz, Chron. 39 (1989); Hans van Houtte, *Provisional Measures in Arbitration, in* T.M.C. ASSER INSTITUUT, HAGUE-ZAGREB-GHENT ESSAYS 8 – ON THE LAW OF INTERNATIONAL TRADE 133 (C.C.A. Voskuil and J.A. Wade eds., 1991).

[56] This situation is specifically intended to be covered by Article 26(1) of the UNCITRAL Arbitration Rules, which allows the arbitrators to take all provisional measures that they consider necessary.

1328. — Unless the parties themselves have determined how jurisdiction is to be allocated between the arbitrators and the courts,[57] the French courts consider that their jurisdiction will be justified if the situation is urgent.[58] In domestic arbitration, the French courts consistently hold that "where a state of urgency has been duly established, the existence of an arbitration agreement cannot prevent the exercise of the powers of the courts to grant interim relief."[59] That approach is equally applicable to international arbitration, as the courts are the only authorities capable of taking urgent measures which are immediately enforceable, regardless of whether or not the arbitral tribunal is constituted.[60] Thus, the Paris Court of Appeals held in one case that it was able, given the urgency, to order the escrow of disputed shares pending a decision by the arbitrators on the substance of the dispute and to prohibit a company from issuing new shares intended for the directors in breach of a shareholders' agreement.[61] In the same way, the Rouen Court of Appeals retained jurisdiction to take protective measures if necessary, "regardless of whether or not the arbitral tribunal is constituted," although it considered in that case that neither the alleged urgency or "patently illegal breach" had been proved.[62]

1329. — This approach is entirely consistent with the regime for protective measures organized in ICC arbitration. Article 23, paragraph 2 of the ICC Rules provides that:

> [b]efore the file is transmitted to the Arbitral Tribunal, and in appropriate circumstances even thereafter, the parties may apply to any competent judicial authority for interim or conservatory measures. The application of a party to a judicial authority for such measures or for the implementation of any such measures ordered by an Arbitral Tribunal shall not be deemed to be an infringement or a waiver of the arbitration agreement and shall not affect the relevant powers reserved to the Arbitral Tribunal.

This provision thus broadens the possibilities for the parties to apply to the courts for provisional measures after the transmission of the file to the arbitral tribunal, as that is permitted in "appropriate circumstances." In contrast, such an application was only possible,

---

[57] *See supra* para. 1319.

[58] On urgency as a basis for jurisdiction, see PHILIPPE JESTAZ, L'URGENCE ET LES PRINCIPES CLASSIQUES DU DROIT CIVIL (1968).

[59] *See, e.g.*, Cass. 3e civ., June 7, 1979, Société d'exploitation du cinéma REX v. Rex, 1979 Bull. Civ. III, No. 122; 1980 REV. ARB. 78, and P. Courteault's note; Cass. 2e civ., July 17, 1957, Ufremine v. Société nouvelle de Saint-Elie A Dieu Vat, 1957 Bull. Civ. II, No. 546, at 354; compare with Cass. 2e civ., Feb. 1, 1989, S.C.A.C. v. Brajeux, the precedential value of which is questionable given the facts of the case (1989 REV. ARB. 494, and G. Couchez' note). On this issue, generally, see Loquin, *supra* note 3, ¶¶ 10 *et seq.*

[60] *See* Couchez, *supra* note 8, at 161.

[61] CA Paris, Dec. 12, 1990, Terex v. Banexi, 1991 BULL. JOLY 595.

[62] CA Rouen, Sept. 7, 1995, Rotem Amfert Negev v. Grande Paroisse, 1996 REV. ARB. 275, and the commentary by Hory, *supra* note 3.

prior to January 1, 1998, "before the file is transmitted to the arbitrator, and in exceptional circumstances even thereafter" (Art. 8(5) of the previous Rules).[63]

1330. — The jurisdiction of the courts does not deprive the arbitrators of the possibility of ruling in the last resort. The provisional nature of interim orders enables the arbitrators to review measures taken by the courts. Thus, for example, where a court orders the continuation of works, but the arbitral tribunal considers that to be unwarranted, there is nothing to prevent the tribunal from subsequently ordering the works to cease. Where there is a conflict between provisional decisions of this kind, the decision of the arbitral tribunal, which has jurisdiction to rule on the merits of the dispute, should prevail. This is because the only justification for applying to the courts lies in the presumption that they are equipped to take the protective measure required in the circumstances more rapidly.[64] That principle was correctly stated in the 1984 ICSID award made in the *Amco Asia v. Indonesia* case. As the arbitrators observed,

> an international Tribunal is not bound to follow the result of a national court. One of the reasons for instituting an international arbitration procedure is precisely that parties—rightly or wrongly—feel often more confident with a legal institution which is not entirely related to one of the parties. If a national judgement was binding on an international Tribunal such a procedure could be rendered meaningless.
>
> Accordingly, no matter how the legal position of a party is described in a national judgement, an International Arbitral Tribunal enjoys the right to evaluate and examine this position without accepting any *res judicata* effect of a national Court. In its evaluation, therefore, the judgements of a national court can be accepted as one of the many factors which have to be considered by the arbitral tribunal.[65]

Arbitrators are therefore in a position to order the parties to abandon the implementation of a protective measure previously obtained from a court.[66]

---

[63] On this evolution, see DERAINS AND SCHWARTZ, *supra* note 15, at 276 *et seq.*; W. LAURENCE CRAIG, WILLIAM W. PARK, JAN PAULSSON, ANNOTATED GUIDE TO THE 1998 ICC ARBITRATION RULES 137 *et seq.* (1998).

[64] *See supra* para. 1307.

[65] Nov. 20, 1984 Award by B. Goldman, president, I. Foighel and E.W. Rubin, arbitrators, in ICSID Case No. ARB/81/1, Amco Asia Corp. v. Republic of Indonesia, 24 I.L.M. 1022, 1026–27 (1985); 1 INT'L ARB. REP. 601 (1986); 1 ICSID REP. 413 (1993); for a French translation, see 114 J.D.I. 145, 149 (1987), and observations by E. Gaillard.

[66] See, for example, the January 6, 1988 Award by D. Zubrod, president, J. Berg and D. Sharpe, arbitrators, in ICSID Case No. ARB/84/4, Maritime International Nominees Establishment v. Government of the Republic of Guinea, 3 INT'L ARB. REP. A1 (Jan. 1988); XIV Y.B. COM. ARB. 82, 85 (1989). *Comp. with* ICC Award No. 5835 (1988), *supra* note 33. But see the December 20, 1983 Award in Case No. 1923 by a tribunal constituted under the aegis of the Society of Maritime Arbitrators, Sea Dragon, Inc. v. Uni-Ocean Singapore Pte, Ltd., X Y.B. COM. ARB. 95 (1985).

B. – CONSERVATORY MEASURES TO PRESERVE EVIDENCE

1331. — The preservation of evidence sometimes requires urgent action, which means that the courts must have jurisdiction over such questions. In French law, for example, applications before the courts can be made on the basis of two different provisions, each of which is subject to its own conditions.[67]

1332. — The first provision is found in Article 145 of the New Code of Civil Procedure, which reads:

> if there are legitimate grounds for preserving or establishing, prior to any legal proceedings, proof of facts which may determine the outcome of a dispute, statutory investigative measures may be ordered at the request of any interested person, in *ex parte* or emergency proceedings.

To rely on Article 145, it is not necessary to establish the urgency of the situation.[68] However, that provision will no longer be applicable once the case has been submitted to the tribunal with jurisdiction over the merits of the case.[69]

It has long been established in French case law that the existence of an arbitration agreement does not prevent the application of Article 145. The *Cour de cassation* observed in one decision that:

> the existence of an arbitration agreement does not affect the power conferred on the courts by Article 145 of the New Code of Civil Procedure to order statutory investigative measures before the case goes before the authority competent to hear the merits, where there are legitimate grounds for preserving

---

[67] On the practicalities of the appointment of an expert and expert proceedings in French law, see Jean de Hauteclocque, *French Judicial Expertise Procedure and International Arbitration*, 4 J. INT'L ARB. 77 (June 1987).

[68] Cass. ch. mixte, May 7, 1982, B.N.P. v. S.A.R.L. Fransucre, Dalloz, Jur. 541 (1982), and the opinion of the advocate general Mr. Cabannes; 1982 RTD CIV. 786, and observations by R. Perrot; 1983 RTD CIV. 185, and observations by J. Normand; 1982 RTD COM. 543, and observations by A. Benabent and J.-C. Dubarry. However, measures under Article 145 can only be ordered *ex parte* if the circumstances so require (*see* Cass. 2e civ., May 13, 1987, Comité d'entreprise de la société anonyme "Les Porcelaines de Limoges Castel" v. S.A. Les Porcelaines de Limoges Castel, 1987 Bull. Civ. II, No. 112, at 65; 1988 RTD CIV. 181, and observations by R. Perrot).

[69] *See, e.g.*, Cass. com., Nov. 15, 1983, La société à responsabilité limitée Fonssagrives–Tiel v. Sdow, 1983 Bull. Civ. IV, No. 307; 1984 RTD CIV. 561, and observations by R. Perrot; JCP, Ed. G., Pt. IV, at 29 (1984); Cass. 3e civ., Dec. 9, 1986, Société de Caution Mutuelle des Professions Immobilières et Foncières "SO.CA.F." v. Syndicat des copropriétaires, JCP, Ed. G., Pt. IV, No. 62 (1987). On the question, generally, of the application of Article 145 to arbitration, see Hory, *supra* note 3.

or establishing proof of facts which may determine the outcome of the dispute.[70]

The fact that arbitrators have jurisdiction over the merits of a dispute does not alter the conditions governing the application of Article 145. Urgency is not required,[71] but no request can be based on Article 145 once the arbitral tribunal has been constituted.

As Article 145 is not considered to be a matter of public policy, the parties can choose to exclude it, either directly or by reference to arbitration rules which, for example, confine the jurisdiction of the courts to situations where a state of urgency exists.[72]

This was the case of the 1955 ICC Rules, which provided in Article 13, paragraph 5 that the parties could only apply to the courts for protective or provisional measures in cases of urgency.[73] That requirement was eliminated when the Rules were amended in 1975. Article 8, paragraph 5 of the amended Rules simply referred to obtaining interim or conservatory measures,[74] which undoubtedly included the measures covered by Article 145. In this respect, neither the 1988 nor 1998 revisions of the Rules changed the substance of the corresponding provision, which is now found at Article 23(2).[75]

1333. — The second possible basis for the jurisdiction of the courts lies in the ordinary provisions of French law regarding urgent measures. Where urgency is established, the courts can take measures to preserve evidence even if the merits of the dispute are before the arbitral tribunal. As discussed earlier, the existence of an arbitration agreement does not

---

[70] Cass. 3e civ., Dec. 20, 1982, S.C.I. Le Panorama v. Société immobilière et mobilière du Tertre (S.I.M.T.), 1986 REV. ARB. 233, and the commentary by Couchez, *supra* note 8 (regarding an expert proceeding as to the constructibility of land). *See also* Cass. com., Mar. 24, 1954, Dreyfus et Cie. v. Muller, 1955 REV. ARB. 95 (regarding an expert proceeding as to the nature and quality of goods); TGI Seine, Dec. 20, 1962, Barrière v. Kreutler, Dalloz, Jur. 108 (1963) (regarding an expert proceeding as to the description of the works carried out). For other examples of the application of Article 145 of the New Code of Civil Procedure and the confirmation of the principle, see CA Paris, July 30, 1986, Burmeister v. Alsthom Atlantique, 1989 REV. ARB. 113, and observations by J. Pellerin and CA Paris, July 3, 1992, *Euro Disney, aff'd*, Cass. 2e civ., Oct. 11, 1995, *supra* note 53; two other decisions made the same day concerning Euro Disney and regarding an expert proceeding which included the task of "describing the works completed at the date the contract was terminated, assessing the extent of such works in the light of the contractual provisions, indicating whether such works are consistent with the initial specifications and, if not, indicating how and to what extent they are not" (Cass. 2e civ., Oct. 11, 1995, Euro Disney v. Torno, 1996 REV. ARB. 228, 2d and 3d decisions, and the commentary by Hory, *supra* note 3). See also the approval by A. Hory of this case law, *supra* note 3.

[71] Cass. ch. mixte, May 7, 1982, *B.N.P.*, *supra* note 68.

[72] See, for example, regarding a clause imposing an expert proceeding, TGI Paris, réf., Feb. 10, 1983, Syndicat des copropriétaires du 206, boulevard Jean-Jaurès v. La Sovim compagnie d'assurance I.A.R.D. Groupe Drouot, Gaz. Pal., Jur. 573 (1983).

[73] According to the 1955 text: "[t]he parties may, in case of urgency, whether prior to or during the proceedings before the arbitrator, apply to any competent judicial authority for interim measures of protection . . . ."

[74] ICC Publication No. 291.

[75] *See supra* para. 1329.

affect the emergency jurisdiction of the courts in these circumstances.[76] However, the urgency of the situation will be assessed in the light of whether the arbitrators themselves could reach an effective decision on the requested measures.

C. – CONSERVATORY MEASURES DESIGNED TO FACILITATE THE ENFORCEMENT OF THE AWARD

1334. — Some conservatory measures are intended to facilitate the enforcement of the subsequent arbitral award by freezing assets against which the award is likely to be enforced. This is the case with attachment orders, for example. The courts have exclusive jurisdiction to grant coercive measures of that kind, and their jurisdiction is not affected by the existence of an arbitration agreement or by the fact that arbitral proceedings are pending.[77]

Again taking attachment orders as an example, French law provides that the applicant must establish a claim which appears to be "well founded in principle."[78] The courts' decision as to whether that condition is satisfied does not infringe upon the arbitrators' jurisdiction over the merits of the dispute. The mere fact that the arbitrators cannot order an enforcement measure provides the justification for the courts' jurisdiction, irrespective of the conditions governing the application of such measures. Here, there is no risk of conflicting jurisdiction, whether or not the arbitral tribunal is constituted.

The French courts clearly endorse this approach, which they justify on the grounds that an attachment "does not imply examining the merits of the dispute, which is a matter for the arbitrators."[79] The same approach is often followed in other jurisdictions.[80]

1335. — Contrary to the much-criticized position taken by the Swiss courts with regard to assets belonging to governments,[81] to make an attachment order the French courts require no connection with French territory other than the presence of attachable assets in France.

---

[76] *See supra* para. 1307. For an example, see CA Versailles, Oct. 8, 1998, Akzo Nobel v. Elf Atochem, 1999 REV. ARB. 57, and A. Hory's note.

[77] See, however, on the particularity of ICSID arbitration in this respect, *supra* paras. 1309 and 1320.

[78] Article 67 of Law No. 91-650 of July 9, 1991, J.O., July 9, 1991, p. 9228. For a commentary of the impact on French arbitration law of the law of July 9, 1991, see Philippe Théry, *Quelques observations à propos de la loi du 9 juillet 1991 portant réforme des procédures civiles d'exécution*, 1991 REV. ARB. 727, and *Les procédures civiles d'exécution et le droit de l'arbitrage*, 1993 REV. ARB. 159.

[79] Cass. 1e civ., Mar. 20, 1989, République islamique d'Iran v. Framatome, 1989 REV. ARB. 653, and P. Fouchard's note; 117 J.D.I. 1004 (1990), and P. Ouakrat's note; Cass. 2e civ., June 8, 1995, SNTM Hyproc v. SNACH, 1996 REV. ARB. 125, and observations by J. Pellerin.

[80] See, for example, in English law,The Rena K, [1979] Q.B. 377; [1979] 1 All E.R. 397; [1978] W.L.R. 431; [1978] 1 Lloyd's Rep. 545; IV Y.B. COM. ARB. 323 (1979) (High Ct., Q.B., Admiralty Div. 1978); in Italian law, the May 12, 1977 decision of the *Corte di Cassazione*, Scherk Enter. Aktiengesellschaft v. Société des Grandes Marques, IV Y.B. COM. ARB. 286 (1979); on the hesitations in the United States, see McDonell, *supra* note 38.

[81] *See, e.g.*, Fed. Trib., June 19, 1980, Libya v. Libyan American Oil Co. (LIAMCO), ATF 106 Ia 142; J.T. 1982 II 66; for an English translation, see 20 I.L.M. 151 (1981). See also the criticism of this case in 1983 BULL. ASA 11 and by P. Lalive and A. Bucher in 1981 ANNUAIRE SUISSE DE DROIT INTERNATIONAL 463 *et seq.*

§ 2. – Measures Designed to Facilitate the Production of Evidence

1336. — Arbitrators have no *imperium*, even vis-à-vis the parties. Further, the privity of the arbitration agreement prevents them from issuing injunctions to third parties.[82] It is therefore sometimes necessary to apply to the courts for an order to produce evidence. Only a court can effectively compel a party to the proceedings or a third party to produce evidence which is considered to be essential in gaining an understanding of the case, or to provide witness testimony. Some laws therefore allow the parties—and in certain cases the arbitrators—to apply to the courts for assistance in obtaining such evidence.

1337. — This position is well established in the English[83] and American[84] legal systems, both of which have always had a strong tradition of judicial intervention. It can also be seen in several continental systems. For example, Swedish law has long allowed a party, where the arbitral tribunal considers such action to be necessary, to apply to the courts to obtain compulsory disclosure of documents in the possession of a party or third party, if need be with daily penalties in case of refusal, or to obtain the sworn testimony of a party, or the testimony of a third party.[85] More recently, similar provisions were adopted in the 1985 UNCITRAL Model Law (Art. 27)[86] and the 1987 Swiss Private International Law Statute (Art. 184(2)). Both expressly authorize the arbitrators themselves to apply, if need be, for court assistance in obtaining the production of evidence. Thus, at the request of an ICC arbitral tribunal sitting in Geneva, the Geneva Tribunal of First Instance ordered the

---

[82] In French domestic arbitration, this restriction on the powers of the arbitral tribunal is confirmed by Article 1460, paragraph 1 of the New Code of Civil Procedure, which does not list Article 11, paragraph 2 of the same Code (according to which a court can order "the production of any documents held by third parties, where there are no legitimate grounds to prevent disclosure") among the other provisions of the Code applicable to arbitration. On this issue, see Roger Perrot, *L'application à l'arbitrage des règles du nouveau Code de procédure civile*, 1980 REV. ARB. 642, 645; Gérard Cornu, *Le décret du 14 mai 1980 relatif à l'arbitrage – Présentation de la réforme*, 1980 REV. ARB. 583, 587. In international arbitration, in the absence of a specific provision, it is generally considered that the same solution should apply, based on the nature of arbitration which is to bind only the parties that consent to it. *See* Eric Loquin, *Les pouvoirs des arbitres internationaux à la lumière de l'évolution récente du droit de l'arbitrage international*, 110 J.D.I. 293, especially ¶ 28 (1983).

[83] *See* Sec. 44 of the 1996 Arbitration Act.

[84] *See* Sec. 7 of the U.S. 1925 Federal Arbitration Act (9 U.S.C.A. § 7). But see, on the fact that 28 U.S.C. § 1782 is not applicable in arbitrations having their seat outside the United States, *supra* note 16.

[85] *See* Section 26 of the 1999 Swedish Arbitration Act, which replaces Section 15 of the 1929 Act; for a commentary of the latter, see THE STOCKHOLM CHAMBER OF COMMERCE, ARBITRATION IN SWEDEN 188 *et seq.* (2d ed. 1984).

[86] For its transposition in Germany, see Article 1050 of the ZPO, in force as of January 1, 1998, which broadens the scope of the rule to any measure the arbitral tribunal is not empowered to take.

appearance of witnesses resident in Switzerland[87] and, by means of rogatory letters, of witnesses resident abroad.[88]

1338. — In French law the situation is not as clear. The New Code of Civil Procedure is silent as to the role of the courts in the production of evidence, and there appears to be no case law on the point. Most authors consider that, under ordinary legal principles, the courts can order a third party to produce documents.[89] As regards documents held by the parties, or the testimony of a party, the risk of infringement of the arbitrators' jurisdiction is greater. Some authors consider that the arbitrators themselves can apply to the courts to obtain the compulsory disclosure of evidence or sworn testimony.[90] However, in the absence of a statutory provision to that effect, it is debatable whether the arbitrators have the necessary standing to apply to a court in such circumstances.[91] Where the request is made by a party, the obstacle is likely to be the concern of the courts not to infringe the arbitrators' jurisdiction to take evidence. In order to avoid such an infringement, it is considered necessary to obtain the arbitrators' consent beforehand. Nevertheless, if this is the case, it might be simpler for the arbitrators to issue an interim award ordering the measure in question subject to its enforcement by the courts.[92]

§ 3. – The *Référé-Provision* Procedure

1339. — The *référé-provision* is a peculiarity of French and Dutch law. It enables a creditor to benefit from emergency procedures, not so as to obtain measures required as a matter of urgency, but to rapidly have its rights enforced, fully or in part,[93] where those

---

[87] Order dated Oct. 15, 1990, 1994 BULL. ASA 307.

[88] Order dated Jan. 31, 1991, 1994 BULL. ASA 310; Order dated Feb. 16, 1993, 1994 BULL. ASA 314; Order dated Jan. 5, 1993, 1994 BULL. ASA 316. See also the October 1, 1990 Order of the Arbitral Tribunal in ICC Case No. 6401, 125 J.D.I. 1065 (1998), and observations by D. Hascher.

[89] *See* Moreau, *supra* note 3, at 333; Loquin, *supra* note 82, ¶¶ 28 and 37; *comp. with* Roger Perrot, *L'administration de la preuve en matière d'arbitrage (Le droit continental de la preuve)*, 1974 REV. ARB. 159, 168.

[90] Loquin, *supra* note 82, ¶ 37.

[91] See, however, on the recognition by the courts, in similar circumstances, of the possibility for the arbitrators to apply to the courts for an extension of time for the making of their award, *infra* para. 1387, note 119.

[92] *See supra* para. 1274.

[93] On the possibility of obtaining the full payment of a debt in an emergency hearing in France, see Cass. com., Jan. 20, 1981, Société anonyme d'économie mixte du tunnel de Sainte-Marie-aux-Mines v. SETEC TP, 1981 Bull. Civ. IV, No. 40, at 30; 1981 RTD CIV. 679, and observations by J. Normand; CA Paris, Jan. 20, 1988, V.S.K. Electronics v. Sainrapt et Brice International S.B.I., 1990 REV. ARB. 651, and the commentary by Bruno Oppetit, *La clause arbitrale par référence, id.* at 551; 116 J.D.I. 1032 (1989), and E. Loquin's note.

rights are "not seriously disputable."[94] Before the courts, no condition of urgency is attached to a *référé-provision*. It is based essentially on

> the wish to provide immediate protection for the creditor, and thus to . . . defeat the tactics of those who, despite the absence of doubt surrounding the existence of their debt, rely on their opponent's reluctance to initiate legal proceedings and on the delays inherent in any such proceedings to postpone a payment which they must know to be inevitable.[95]

We shall consider in turn the principle of the *référé-provision* (A) and the conditions for its implementation (B) where an arbitration agreement exists.

A. – THE PRINCIPLE

1340. — The issue of whether a party which has agreed to be bound by an arbitration agreement can nevertheless seek a *référé-provision* is a delicate matter, because of the hybrid nature of that measure.

In order to decide whether to grant a *référé-provision*, the court hearing the request must examine the substantive claims of the party alleging that it is the creditor. Of course, the question of whether the creditor's claim is "seriously disputable" is a substantive issue. In ruling on the *référé-provision*, a court is therefore liable to infringe the arbitrators' jurisdiction over the merits.

On the other hand, the decision taken by the court is by nature provisional and in no way binds the arbitral or judicial authority with jurisdiction over the merits. The risk of infringing the arbitrators' jurisdiction is therefore temporary. However, the decision taken by the courts is liable to reverse the parties' roles in the arbitration, as the party whose claim has been satisfied, albeit temporarily, no longer has the burden of maintaining the pace of the arbitral proceedings, and is no longer exposed to the risk of its contractual partner becoming insolvent.[96]

---

[94] *See* Arts. 809, para. 2 and 873, para. 2 of the French New Code of Civil Procedure and Arts. 289 *et seq.* of the Netherlands Code of Civil Procedure. Compare with Section 39 of the 1996 English Arbitration Act which recognizes the freedom of the parties to empower the arbitrators themselves to make such provisional decisions. For an example of such a decision, see the award rendered on December 12, 1996 by C.J.H. Brunner, chairman, H. Beckhuis and A.J. van den Berg, arbitrators, under the aegis of the Netherlands Arbitration Institute, Producer v. Construction company, XXIII Y.B. COM. ARB. 97 (1998). See also Section 4, paragraph 2 of the 1999 Swedish Arbitration Act regarding the compatibility of expedited collection procedures before the Debt Enforcement Authority with the existence of an arbitration agreement.

[95] Jacques Normand, *Observations: Arbitrage et référé provision*, 1985 RTD CIV. 208, 210. For a comprehensive analysis of the *référé-provision* mechanism, see Wallace R. Baker, Patrick de Fontbressin, *The French Référé Procedure – A Legal Miracle?*, II U. MIAMI Y.B. INT'L L. 1 (1992-1993).

[96] See also the discussion of the nature of such measures in the November 17, 1998 decision of the Court of Justice of the European Communities, *Van Uden, supra* note 7.

1341. — The French courts accept that the option of applying to court for a *référé-provision* remains open, under certain conditions, where the claim on which the application is founded is a substantive issue covered by the jurisdiction of an arbitral tribunal. In a case concerning a domestic arbitration, the *Cour de cassation* held that:

> since the existence of an arbitration agreement does not exclude the jurisdiction of the court, who had in fact established the urgency of the situation, to order a provisional payment in favor of a creditor whose claim was not seriously disputable, the Court of Appeals rightly rejected the argument that the court lacked jurisdiction to do so.[97]

In spite of the criticism this decision attracted,[98] it has been widely followed in subsequent case law.[99] The only area of doubt has been the conditions governing the admissibility of a *référé-provision* where the arbitrators have jurisdiction to rule on the merits of the dispute.[100]

1342. — Of course, as with other provisional measures, the courts' jurisdiction to order a *référé-provision* can be expressly excluded by the parties, either directly or by reference to arbitration rules containing such an exclusion.[101] However, the ICC Rules of Arbitration contain no such exclusion. There was some doubt on this point because the *Cour de cassation* held in 1984 that a *référé-provision* was not included in the "interim or conservatory measures" referred to in Article 8, paragraph 5 (now Article 23, paragraph 2) of the ICC Rules of Arbitration.[102] That finding is incorrect.[103] Article 8, paragraph 5 of the previous Rules and Article 23, paragraph 2 of the 1998 Rules refer to measures which are characterized by their provisional nature, and there can be no doubt that a *référé-provision* shares that characteristic. Furthermore, as the ICC Rules have abandoned the requirement of urgency for interim or conservatory measures ordered by the courts under these

---

[97] Cass. 3e civ., July 9, 1979, S.C.I. La Lagune v. S.A.R.L. SERCIF, JCP, Ed. G., Pt. II, No. 19,389 (1980), and observations by G. Couchez; 1980 REV. ARB. 78, and P. Courteault's note.

[98] See especially, in favor of excluding the possibility of *référé-provision* where there is an arbitration agreement, H. Gaudemet-Tallon, note following Cass. 1e civ., Mar. 6, 1990, Horeva v. Sitas, 1990 Bull. Civ. I, No. 64; 1990 REV. ARB. 633, 2d decision, and H.Gaudemet-Tallon's note, especially at 645 *et seq.*

[99] See the decisions cited *infra* para. 1345. But see the more restrictive decision of CA Paris, 14e Ch., Sec. C, Oct. 29, 1993, Ets. Metallurgiques Brun Frères v. S.A. Stanko France, No. 93/16786, unpublished, which overturned an order which granted a *référé-provision* on the grounds that the matter was not yet before the arbitral tribunal.

[100] *See infra* para. 1343.

[101] *See supra* para. 1319.

[102] Cass. 1e civ., Mar. 14, 1984, République islamique d'Iran v. Commissariat à l'Energie Atomique, Dalloz, Jur. 629 (1984), and J. Robert's note; 1985 REV. ARB. 69, and G. Couchez' note; JCP, Ed. G., Pt. II, No. 20,205 (1984), and H. Synvet's note; 1985 RTD CIV. 208, and observations by J. Normand.

[103] See also, for a criticism of the decision of the *Cour de cassation*, Couchez, note following Cass. 1e civ., Mar. 14, 1984, *République islamique d'Iran, supra* note 102, at 75. In that case, the solution reached could have been justified by the additional requirement of urgency which courts have added to the normal conditions of the *référé-provision* (*see infra* paras. 1343 *et seq.*), without any reference to the—non existent—specificity of ICC arbitration in this respect.

provisions, a *référé-provision* cannot be considered as being excluded from the urgency exception to the arbitrators' jurisdiction on the basis of the parties' intentions in incorporating the ICC Rules in their arbitration agreement.[104]

B. – CONDITIONS FOR THE IMPLEMENTATION OF THE *RÉFÉRÉ-PROVISION*

1343. — Although they have accepted the principle that a *référé-provision* can be granted despite the existence of an arbitration agreement, the French courts have been sensitive to the fact that it involves the examination of the substantive issues which fall within the arbitrators' jurisdiction. The jurisdiction of the courts is therefore subject to two conditions which are specific to the context of arbitration: the arbitral tribunal must not be constituted and there must be urgency.

1° The Arbitral Tribunal Must Not Be Constituted

1344. — In a 1984 decision, the *Cour de cassation* rejected an application for a *référé-provision* where an ICC arbitration was "in progress," on the grounds that the requested measure was not an interim or conservatory measure over which the ICC Rules recognize the jurisdiction of the courts.[105] As we have seen, there is little weight in the argument that Article 23, paragraph 2 of the current ICC Rules (Art. 8(5) of the previous Rules) does not include the *référé-provision* among the provisional measures which the courts can take despite the existence of an ICC arbitration agreement.[106] However, the court's decision could be interpreted as restricting the option of requesting a *référé-provision* to cases where the arbitral tribunal is not yet constituted. In a 1986 decision concerning a domestic arbitration, the *Cour de cassation* held—this time without referring to the purported specificity of ICC arbitration—that "where a dispute submitted to an arbitral tribunal under an arbitration agreement is also put before a national court, the latter must decline jurisdiction." It thus overruled a decision of a Court of Appeals in which a *référé-provision* had been granted on the grounds that the claim could not seriously be contested and that the situation was urgent.[107] The condition that the arbitral tribunal not be constituted is perfectly understandable. Where the tribunal is constituted, it is possible to request that it award, within a short time frame, a provisional payment representing all or part of a claim which

---

[104] On the removal in 1975 of the reference to urgency found at Article 13(5) of the 1955 Rules, see *supra* para. 1332.

[105] Cass. 1e civ., Mar. 14, 1984, *République islamique d'Iran*, *supra* note 102.

[106] *See supra* para. 1342.

[107] Cass. 2e civ., June 18, 1986, Buzzichelli v. S.a.r.l. S.E.R.M.I., 1986 REV. ARB. 565, 1st decision, and G. Couchez' note.

appears to be beyond serious dispute.[108] However, this condition that the tribunal not be constituted was still not properly formulated. A dispute may be brought before an arbitral tribunal as a result of a request for arbitration,[109] but several weeks or even months may elapse before the arbitral tribunal is actually constituted and hence able to make a rapid decision on the matter. Although the 1986 decision described above referred to cases where the dispute is before the arbitral tribunal, it is generally interpreted as meaning that the courts no longer have jurisdiction to rule on a *référé-provision* once the arbitral tribunal is constituted.[110] Nevertheless, the ambiguity remained in a 1989 decision of the *Cour de cassation*, concerning an international arbitration.[111] However, in a later decision the same court adopted a more realistic approach by deciding that the courts had jurisdiction provided that the arbitral tribunal was "not yet constituted and hence incapable of actually hearing the question."[112] The case law of the Paris Tribunal of First Instance is consistent with this approach.[113] As this requires the tribunal to be fully constituted, it allays the concerns prompted by the earlier decisions. In ICC arbitration, the cut-off date should be that of the transmission of the file to the arbitral tribunal, pursuant to Article 13 of the 1998 Rules (Art. 10 of the previous Rules).

2° Urgency

1345. — The first decisions confirming that a *référé-provision* could be requested from the courts despite the existence of an arbitration agreement referred to the urgency of the measure.[114] Where the authority which would normally have jurisdiction over the merits of the dispute is a court,[115] no condition of urgency applies, but where that authority is an arbitral tribunal, the condition of urgency limits the infringement by the courts of the arbitral tribunal's jurisdiction over the merits of the dispute. In the absence of urgency, the claimant

---

[108] But see Normand, *supra* note 95, who considers that the provisional nature of *référé-provision* should suffice to justify the jurisdiction of the courts.

[109] *See supra* para. 1210.

[110] *See, e.g.,* E. Loquin, observations following CA Paris, Jan. 20, 1988, *V.S.K. Electronics, supra* note 93, at 1041; MATTHIEU DE BOISSÉSON, LE DROIT FRANÇAIS DE L'ARBITRAGE INTERNE ET INTERNATIONAL ¶ 759 at 760 (2d ed. 1990).

[111] Cass. 1e civ., Mar. 20, 1989, The Authority for Supply Commodities Cairo Estram v. Ipitrade International, 1989 REV. ARB. 494, 3d decision, and G. Couchez' note; 116 J.D.I. 1045 (1989), and B. Oppetit's note.

[112] Cass. 1e civ., Mar. 6, 1990, *Horeva, supra* note 98.

[113] *See, e.g.,* TGI Paris, réf., June 17, 1998, Commisimpex v. République du Congo, Case No. 55138/98, unpublished.

[114] *See, e.g.,* Cass. 3e civ., July 9, 1979, *S.C.I. La Lagune, supra* note 97. Compare with CA Rouen, Sept. 26, 1985, Société des Engrais de Saint-Wandrille v. Les Engrais de Gabès, which states simply that the condition of urgency is relevant (1986 REV. ARB. 233).

[115] *See, e.g.,* Cass. 1e civ., Nov. 4, 1976, La Cordialité Baloise v. Ben Khelifa, Gaz. Pal., Jur. 352, (1977); 1977 RTD CIV. 361, and observations by J. Normand.

could simply prompt the constitution of the arbitral tribunal and ask the arbitrators to rule on its request.[116]

In a 1989 decision concerning an international arbitration, the *Cour de cassation* held, without referring to the condition of urgency, that:

> provided that the dispute is not yet before the arbitral tribunal, and in the absence of an express stipulation, the existence of an arbitration agreement applying without further indications to all disputes cannot exclude the jurisdiction of the courts to order a provisional payment to a creditor whose claim cannot seriously be contested.[117]

The *Cour de cassation* later returned to a more restrictive approach. In a 1990 decision, it held that:

> in the absence of a contrary intention of the parties to international arbitration, and provided that the *ad hoc* arbitral tribunal is not yet constituted and hence incapable of actually hearing the dispute, the existence of an arbitration agreement does not, in an urgent situation such as that established in the present case, exclude the exceptional jurisdiction of the courts to order a provisional payment where the claim cannot seriously be contested.[118]

---

[116] *See* Loquin, note following CA Paris, Jan. 20, 1988, *V.S.K. Electronics*, *supra* note 93, at 1041; *comp. with* Couchez, *supra* note 8.

[117] Cass. 1e civ., Mar. 20, 1989, *Cairo Estram*, *supra* note 111; *see also* CA Paris, Jan. 20, 1988, *V.S.K. Electronics*, *supra* note 93; *but see* CA Paris, Feb. 13, 1990, Sunkyong Ltd. v. Interagra Ipitrade International: "[i]n international arbitration, the existence of an arbitration clause does not, in principle, prevent the courts from having jurisdiction, as their decisions are provisional and will not prejudice the final decision, and as they have the power to grant a *référé-provision* when the existence of the obligation cannot seriously be contested; however, this international jurisdiction of the French courts, justified by urgency, is excluded where the matter is properly before the arbitral tribunal, and can in any event be excluded by agreement of the parties" (Dalloz, Jur. 593 (1990), and G. Peyrard's note).

[118] Cass. 1e civ., Mar. 6, 1990, *Horeva*, *supra* note 98.

In its 1997 *Rantec* decision,[119] the *Cour de cassation* put an end to the hesitations of the lower courts,[120] and confirmed that the requirement of urgency, widely supported by commentators,[121] continues to apply.

---

[119] Cass. 1e civ., Oct. 21, 1997, Rantec v. SIDT Europe, 1998 REV. ARB. 673, 2d decision, and L. Degos' note. See also, in domestic arbitration, Cass. 2e civ., Apr. 2, 1997, Société Fiduciaire Européenne v. Jerusalmi, 1998 REV. ARB. 673, 1st decision, and L. Degos' note.

[120] On the requirement of urgency, see, for example, CA Paris, Jan. 30, 1992, Air Charter v. Euralair, 1992 REV. ARB. 666, and observations by J.-H. Moitry; CA Versailles, May 22, 1992, Dumez International v. Laurent Bouillet Entreprise, which confirms both the condition of urgency and that whereby the matter must not already be before the arbitral tribunal (1992 REV. ARB. 666, and observations by J.-H. Moitry). *But see* CA Paris, Oct. 27, 1995, Forouzan v. Valhôtel, 1996 REV. ARB. 275, and the commentary by Hory, *supra* note 3; 1996 RTD COM. 663 and observations by J.-C. Dubarry and E. Loquin; CA Nancy, May 23, 1995, Tamrock v. Mogliarini, 1996 REV. ARB. 660, and observations by A. Hory.

[121] *See* Oppetit, note following Cass. 1e civ., Mar. 20, 1989, *Cairo Estram, supra* note 111, at 1048–49; Couchez, note following Cass. 2e civ., Mar. 20, 1988, *L.F.P. Danel, supra* note 44, at 500; Loquin, note following CA Paris, Jan. 20, 1988, *V.S.K. Electronics, supra* note 93, at 1042; DE BOISSÉSON, *supra* note 110, ¶ 760 at 762; Philippe Fouchard, *La coopération du Président du Tribunal de grande instance à l'arbitrage*, 1985 REV. ARB. 5, especially at 7–8; Ouakrat, *supra* note 3.

CHAPTER IV
THE ARBITRAL AWARD

1346–1347. — We shall consider in turn the concept and the classification of arbitral awards (Section I), the process of making an award (Section II), the form of the award (Section III) and its effects (Section IV).

SECTION I
CONCEPT AND CLASSIFICATION OF ARBITRAL AWARDS

1348. — The concept of the arbitral award has been the subject of considerable debate. The same is true of attempts to define the various types of award that exist. Awards are described as being final, preliminary, interim, interlocutory, or partial, but these terms are often used without sufficient precision. For example, the UNCITRAL Arbitration Rules state that "[i]n addition to making a final award, the arbitral tribunal shall be entitled to make interim, interlocutory, or partial awards," without actually defining those terms (Art. 32(1)). Similarly, Article 2(iii) of the 1998 ICC Rules states that in those Rules "Award" includes *inter alia* "an interim, partial or final Award," again without elaborating on the distinction.[1]

It is therefore not only the concept of the arbitral award which requires clarification (§ 1), but also the definition of the various categories of award (§ 2).

§ 1. – The Concept of Arbitral Award

1349. — It is not always easy to identify an arbitral award. In some cases, the arbitrators themselves do not describe their decision as such. One arbitral tribunal will give its decision the title "Findings of the Amiable Compositeur,"[2] while another will describe a purely administrative measure as an award.[3]

---

[1] *See* YVES DERAINS AND ERIC A. SCHWARTZ, A GUIDE TO THE NEW ICC RULES OF ARBITRATION 36 *et seq.* (1998).

[2] *See* CA Paris, 1e Ch., Sec. Supp., Jan. 13, 1987, T.F.E. v. L'Haridon, No. 86.4496, unpublished.

[3] *See, e.g.,* December 23, 1982 Partial Award in ICC Case No. 3896, Framatome S.A. v. Atomic Energy Organization of Iran (AEOI), 110 J.D.I. 914 (1983), and observations by S. Jarvin; for an English translation,

(continued...)

1350. — Defining an arbitral award is made more difficult by the fact that most instruments governing international arbitration themselves contain no such definition.

This is the case with many international arbitration laws, including French law.[4] The UNCITRAL Model Law does not give a definition of an arbitral award either, despite such a definition being considered during the drafting stages. The following definition was suggested:

> 'award' means a final award which disposes of all issues submitted to the arbitral tribunal and any other decision of the arbitral tribunal which finally determine[s] any question of substance or the question of its competence or any other question of procedure but, in the latter case, only if the arbitral tribunal terms its decision an award.[5]

This text, however, was the subject of so much disagreement, particularly with regard to whether decisions by the arbitrators concerning the jurisdiction of the arbitral tribunal and procedural issues should be considered to be awards,[6] that it was eventually abandoned. The authors of the Model Law instead decided not to give a definition at all.[7] The ICC working group on interim and partial awards likewise found it impossible to reach a consensus on the issue.[8]

Even international conventions on the recognition and enforcement of arbitral awards fail to define the concept of an award. The 1958 New York Convention merely states that:

> [t]he term 'arbitral awards' shall include not only awards made by arbitrators appointed for each case but also those made by permanent arbitral bodies to which the parties have submitted (Art. I(2)).

---

[3]   (...continued)
see X Y.B. COM. ARB. 47 (1985).

[4]   On this issue, generally, see IBRAHIM NAGUIB SAAD, LA SENTENCE ARBITRALE (ESSAI D'UNE DÉFINITION EN DROIT FRANÇAIS ET EN DROIT ÉGYPTIEN) (Thesis, University of Paris (France), 1969); Yves Derains, *La sentence arbitrale, in* FONDATION POUR L'ETUDE DU DROIT ET DES USAGES DU COMMERCE INTERNATIONAL, DROIT ET PRATIQUE DE L'ARBITRAGE INTERNATIONAL EN FRANCE 69 (Y. Derains ed., 1984).

[5]   *See United Nations Commission on International Trade Law, Seventeenth Session, New York, 25 June – 13 July 1984, Report of the Working Group on International Contract Practices on the Work of its Seventh Session (New York, 6–17 February 1984),* UN Doc. A/CN.9/246, Mar. 6, 1984, ¶ 192.

[6]   On this issue, see *infra* para. 1357.

[7]   On this issue, see François Knoepfler and Philippe Schweizer, *Making of Awards and Termination of Proceedings, in* ESSAYS ON INTERNATIONAL COMMERCIAL ARBITRATION 160 (1989); HOWARD M. HOLTZMANN AND JOSEPH E. NEUHAUS, A GUIDE TO THE UNCITRAL MODEL LAW ON INTERNATIONAL COMMERCIAL ARBITRATION – LEGISLATIVE HISTORY AND COMMENTARY 154 (1989).

[8]   *See* Martin Hunter, *Final Report on Interim and Partial Awards,* ICC BULLETIN, Vol. 1, No. 2, at 26, 27 (1990).

Similarly, the main institutional rules do not define what is meant by an award. At best, they simply describe the conditions governing the making of an award[9] and its form.[10]

1351. — Nevertheless, it is essential to identify precisely which of an arbitrator's decisions can be classified as awards and, in particular, to distinguish awards from procedural orders, from orders for provisional measures, and even from agreements between the parties. These distinctions have significant legal consequences, the main one being that only a genuine award can be the subject of an action to set it aside or to enforce it.[11] As a result, the deadlines laid down in such proceedings will only begin to elapse when a genuine award is made. Similarly, only genuine awards are covered by international conventions on the recognition and enforcement of arbitral awards.[12] The characterization of a decision as an award may also have an impact on the application of certain provisions of arbitration rules. For example, Article 27 of the ICC Rules states that an "award" must be submitted in draft form to the International Court of Arbitration for approval prior to being signed.

1352. — However, as with contracts, the characterization of a decision as an award does not depend on the terminology employed by the arbitrators. It is determined solely by the nature of the decision itself. The inclusion or omission of items such as the names of the arbitrators, the date and the arbitrators' signatures should be irrelevant in the characterization of an award.[13] Those formal aspects may, however, affect the validity of a document which, on the basis of its subject-matter, can be characterized as an award.[14]

1353. — An arbitral award can be defined[15] as a final decision by the arbitrators on all or part of the dispute submitted to them, whether it concerns the merits of the dispute, jurisdiction, or a procedural issue leading them to end the proceedings.[16]
Several aspects of this definition require further examination.

---

[9] *See infra* paras. 1367 *et seq.*

[10] *See infra* paras. 1389 *et seq.*

[11] *See, e.g.,* CA Paris, Feb. 18, 1986, Péchiney v. Marlio, 1990 REV. ARB. 727, and observations by C. Jarrosson.

[12] *See, e.g.,* CA Paris, Nov. 21, 1991, Foroughi v. Eshragh, 1992 REV. ARB. 494, and M.-C. Rondeau-Rivier's note; Supreme Court of Queensland, Oct. 29, 1993, Resort Condominiums Int'l Inc. v. Bolwell, in which the court refused to treat as an award covered by the New York Convention an order to adopt a certain form of conduct during the arbitral proceedings (9 INT'L ARB. REP. A1 (Apr. 1994); see also the commentary by Michael Pryles, *Interlocutory Orders and Convention Awards: the Case of Resort Condominiums v. Bolwell*, 10 ARB. INT'L 385 (1994)).

[13] But see the unsatisfactory decisions on this point of the Paris Court of Appeals which has refused to characterize as awards documents which do not comply with certain requirements of form, when that should only lead the court to set such awards aside (CA Paris, Feb. 18, 1986, *Péchiney, supra* note 11; CA Paris, Nov. 21, 1991, *Foroughi, supra* note 12).

[14] *See infra* para. 1406.

[15] This definition is taken almost verbatim from the reasoning given in CA Paris, Mar. 25, 1994, Sardisud v. Technip, 1994 REV. ARB. 391, and C. Jarrosson's note.

[16] On this last point see, in the context of the discussion of the 1987 Swiss Private International Law Statute, PIERRE LALIVE, JEAN-FRANÇOIS POUDRET, CLAUDE REYMOND, LE NOUVEAU DROIT DE L'ARBITRAGE INTERNE ET INTERNATIONAL EN SUISSE 405–06 (1989).

1354. — First, an award is made by the arbitrators. Decisions taken by an arbitral institution, rather than by arbitrators acting in proceedings that the institution administers, are not arbitral awards. Thus, for example, a decision by the ICC International Court of Arbitration rejecting a challenge against an arbitrator does not constitute an award against which an action to set aside can be brought.[17]

1355. — Second, an award resolves a dispute. Measures taken by arbitrators which do not decide the dispute either wholly or in part are not awards. This is true of orders for the hearing of witnesses and document production, for example, which are only procedural steps and as such are incapable of being the subject of an action to set aside. While acknowledging that principle, the Paris Court of Appeals has nevertheless adopted a broad understanding of what constitutes a dispute, holding that:

> the reasoned decision by the arbitrator . . . whereby, having examined the parties' conflicting arguments, he refused to stay the proceeding, is judicial in nature and constitutes an arbitral award against which an action to set aside can be brought.[18]

1356. — Third, an award is a binding decision. Decisions which only bind the parties on condition that they expressly accept them are not awards. Thus, the decision of an "arbitral tribunal of first instance" which "makes a draft award which is only to become an award if the parties accept it, failing which the dispute is to be submitted to a tribunal of second instance for a definitive award," could not be the subject of an immediate action to set it aside.[19] On that basis, the Paris Court of Appeals held in a 1995 case that "a principle exists whereby, in an arbitration involving two tiers of jurisdiction, an action to set aside can only be brought against the award made at second instance."[20] The same applies to recommendations made by the "neutral" in the various forms of Alternative Dispute Resolution in which the parties have stipulated that such recommendations will not be binding unless expressly accepted by them, directly or through a more sophisticated system of exchanging settlement offers.

---

[17] CA Paris, Jan. 15, 1985, Opinter France v. Dacomex, 1986 REV. ARB. 87, and E. Mezger's note, *aff'd*, Cass. 2e civ., Oct. 7, 1987, 1987 REV. ARB. 479, and E. Mezger's note.

[18] CA Paris, July 7, 1987, Pia Investments Ltd. v. Cassia, 1988 REV. ARB. 649, and E. Mezger's note. See also the case law cited *supra* para. 1226, note 43.

[19] *See* Cass. 1e civ., June 1, 1987, Société Commerciale de Produits Agricoles v. Société Coopérative de la Roche Clermault, No. 86-11.457, unpublished, in a case where the appealing party unsuccessfully argued only that there had been a breach of due process in the commencement of the second-tier arbitral proceedings. *See also* CA Paris, Oct. 24, 1991, Sicopag v. Ets. Louis Laprade, 1992 REV. ARB. 494, and M.-C. Rondeau-Rivier's note.

[20] CA Paris, July 7, 1995, Corelf v. Worldwide, 1996 REV. ARB. 270, and E. Loquin's note, which concerns the Rules of the Paris Maritime Arbitration Chamber, which provide for two arbitral instances where the amount in dispute exceeds a certain level, and specify that "where the dispute is heard by the higher instance, the award made by that instance will be considered the only award made in the proceeding."

1357. — Fourth, an award may be partial.[21] Decisions by the arbitrators on issues such as jurisdiction, the applicable law, the validity of a contract or the principle of liability are in our opinion genuine arbitral awards, despite the fact that they do not decide the entire dispute and may not lead to an immediate award of damages or other redress. However, the opposite view has found support in Switzerland. Certain leading Swiss authors consider that "decisions, and even substantive decisions, which do not rule on a claim, only constitute partial awards if they put an end to all or part of the arbitral proceedings." According to those authors, all decisions which "decide substantive issues, such as the validity of the main contract, the principle of liability as opposed to the level of damages, etc." do not constitute arbitral awards; they are simply "preparatory or interlocutory decisions" which cannot be the subject of an action to set aside independent of the subsequent award on the parties' claims on the merits.[22] That analysis is based on a narrow understanding of the concept of a claim which, according to these authors, covers a request for an award of damages or other redress but not for an initial finding as to liability. Along with other Swiss authors,[23] we disagree with this view. A decision on jurisdiction, the applicable law or the principle of liability, for example, is a final decision on one aspect of the dispute. It should therefore be considered as an award, against which an immediate action to set aside can be brought. We are not convinced, from a theoretical standpoint, that there is a compelling justification for deferring the possibility for the parties to bring an action to set aside once the arbitrators have made a decision which they present as being final, as far as that aspect of the dispute is concerned, and binding on the parties. From a practical standpoint, such deferral would also lead to unnecessary delay and expense. If, for instance, the award on the principle of liability is to be set aside, the parties have a clear interest in knowing the outcome as soon as possible, as that may save them all or part of the cost of an expert proceeding or lengthy hearings on the quantum of damages. This is the position taken by the French courts.[24] In Switzerland, the Federal Tribunal has held that, under the 1987 Private International Law Statute, an action to set aside can only be brought against awards regarding the constitution of the arbitral tribunal and its jurisdiction—even where the tribunal finds in favor of its jurisdiction—where it would cause irreparable harm not to accept the immediate action to set aside or where the award puts an end to the entire dispute.[25]

A peculiarity of ICSID arbitration should be noted in this respect. Contrary to the position generally adopted in other types of arbitrations, a decision by the arbitrators on jurisdiction is not considered by the Centre as being an award, and it cannot be the subject of an immediate action in annulment before an *ad hoc* committee unless it puts an end to the

---

[21] On the concept of partial awards, see *infra* paras. 1360 *et seq.*

[22] LALIVE, POUDRET, REYMOND, *supra* note 16, at 406–07.

[23] *See, e.g.*, ANDREAS BUCHER, PIERRE-YVES TSCHANZ, INTERNATIONAL ARBITRATION IN SWITZERLAND 129 (1988); Marc Blessing, *The New International Arbitration Law in Switzerland – A Significant Step Towards Liberalism*, 5 J. INT'L ARB. 9, 65 (June 1988).

[24] CA Paris, Mar. 25, 1994, *Sardisud*, *supra* note 15.

[25] Fed. Trib., Oct. 3, 1989, M.G. v. P.G., 1990 BULL. ASA 44; Fed. Trib., Feb. 6, 1990, Deutsche Babcock AG v. House of Trade and Contracting Co., 1990 BULL. ASA 163, and the critical commentary by Jean-François Poudret, *La recevabilité du recours au tribunal fédéral contre la sentence partielle de l'art. 188 LDIP*, 1990 [SW.] JOURN. TRIB. 354.

dispute. This explains why the 1984 decision on jurisdiction made in the *SOABI v. Senegal*[26] case, for example, was carefully entitled "decision" rather than "award,"[27] although ICSID arbitrators have not always been as cautious.[28]

§ 2. – Different Categories of Award

1358. — The concepts of final award (A), partial award (B), award by default (C) and award by consent (D) each require explanation.

A. – FINAL AWARDS AND INTERIM AWARDS

1359. — The expression "final award" ("*sentence definitive*") is used to mean very different things.

It sometimes refers to an award which includes a decision on the last aspect of a dispute and which, as a result, terminates the arbitrators' jurisdiction over that dispute as a whole. In that sense, "final" awards are distinguished from "interim," "interlocutory," or "partial" awards, none of which puts an end to the arbitrators' brief. That was the definition used by the working group preparing the UNCITRAL Model Law, although it is important to note that it was precisely the controversy over this terminology which led UNCITRAL to abandon its attempts to define the concept of an award.[29] Traces of the working group's definition can be found in the Model Law, which states in Article 32, paragraph 1 that a final award terminates the arbitral proceedings. Prior to 1998, Article 21 of the ICC Rules of Arbitration drew a distinction between "partial" and "definitive" awards. The 1998 rules simply refer to interim, partial and final awards, without defining those terms (Art 2(iii)).[30] Many English-speaking commentators also use the term "final" to describe an award deciding the last aspects of a dispute.[31]

---

[26] Decision of Aug. 1, 1984, by A. Broches, president, K. M'Baye and H. van Houtte, arbitrators, in ICSID Case No. ARB/82/1, Société Ouest Africaine des Bétons Industriels v. State of Senegal, 113 J.D.I. 221 (1986), and observations by E. Gaillard; *see also* 117 J.D.I. 211 (1990); 6 ICSID REV. – FOREIGN INV. L.J. 217 (1991).

[27] On this issue, generally, see E. Gaillard, observations following the May 16, 1986 decision of the *Ad hoc* Committee in ICSID Case No. ARB/81/1, Amco Asia Corp. v. Republic of Indonesia, 114 J.D.I. 174, 185–86 (1987).

[28] See, for example, the September 25, 1983 "Award" on Jurisdiction in Case No. ARB/81/1, Amco Asia Corp. v. Republic of Indonesia, 23 I.L.M. 351 (1984); X Y.B. COM. ARB. 61 (1985); 1 ICSID REP. 389 (1993); for a French translation, see 1985 REV ARB. 259; 113 J.D.I. 201 (1986), and observations by E. Gaillard.

[29] *See supra* para. 1350 and HOLTZMANN AND NEUHAUS, *supra* note 7, at 867.

[30] *See* DERAINS AND SCHWARTZ, *supra* note 1, at 36.

[31] *See, e.g.*, MICHAEL J. MUSTILL, STEWART C. BOYD, COMMERCIAL ARBITRATION 24 (2d ed. 1989); ALAN REDFERN AND MARTIN HUNTER, LAW AND PRACTICE OF INTERNATIONAL COMMERCIAL ARBITRATION 356–57 (2d ed. 1991); W. LAURENCE CRAIG, WILLIAM W. PARK, JAN PAULSSON, INTERNATIONAL CHAMBER OF COMMERCE ARBITRATION 321 (2d ed. 1990); RUSSELL ON ARBITRATION ¶ 6.003 (D. Sutton, J. Kendall, J. Gill
(continued...)

The expression "final award" is also sometimes used to describe an award which puts an end to at least one aspect of the dispute. In that sense, a final award is distinguished from an interim award (or from a procedural order) which do not terminate any aspect of the dispute, nor the last stage of that dispute. Thus interpreted, a final award does not necessarily cover the entire dispute, nor the last stage of that dispute. An award on liability, for example, is a final award, despite the fact that it may also order expert proceedings to provide the arbitrators with an evaluation of the damage or loss, following which further hearings will take place. That approach can be seen in the Dutch Code of Civil Procedure, Article 1049 of which provides that "the arbitral tribunal may render a final award, a partial final award, or an interim award."[32] The Belgian legislature followed suit, at first implicitly, then explicitly in its statute of May 19, 1998. Article 1699 of the Belgian Judicial Code now reads "[t]he arbitral tribunal takes a final decision or renders interlocutory decisions, through one or more awards." A number of Swiss commentators appear to take the same position.[33] We believe this approach to be consistent with contractual practice, as it reflects what is meant by the words "final and binding," which are often used in arbitration agreements to describe any award or awards to be rendered by the arbitral tribunal. Interestingly, this is also how the 1996 English Arbitration Act uses the same words.[34]

We consider the latter interpretation to be the better one: as discussed above, an award is a decision putting an end to all or part of the dispute;[35] it is therefore final with regard to the aspect or aspects of the dispute that it resolves.[36]

B. – PARTIAL AWARDS AND GLOBAL AWARDS

1360. — The parties may decide that the arbitrators shall rule on a particular aspect of a dispute (such as jurisdiction, the governing law or liability) by making a separate award, referred to as a partial award. To avoid confusion, we suggest that partial awards should be contrasted with global awards, rather than with final awards. As discussed above, the term "final" refers to the impact of the award, whether partial or not, on the portion of the dispute resolved by the arbitrators.[37]

---

[31] (...continued)
eds., 21st ed. 1997).

[32] *See also* the commentary on this provision in PIETER SANDERS, ALBERT JAN VAN DEN BERG, THE NETHERLANDS ARBITRATION ACT 1986, at 28 (1987).

[33] *See* LALIVE, POUDRET, REYMOND, *supra* note 16, at 412. *But see* Fed. Trib., Oct. 3, 1989, *supra* note 25, at 48.

[34] *See* Sec. 58(1) of the 1996 English Arbitration Act; RUSSELL ON ARBITRATION, *supra* note 31, ¶ 6.006.

[35] *See supra* paras. 1355 and 1357.

[36] On the distinction between the definitive nature of an award and the fact that it is made "in the last resort," which must be specified in French domestic arbitration in order to avoid an appeal before the courts, see *infra* para. 1597.

[37] *See supra* para. 1359. See the "Partial Final Arbitral Award" made under the auspices of the Geneva Chamber of Commerce and Industry on March 7, 1996, L. Ltd. v. The Foreign Trade Association of the Republic of U., 1997 BULL. ASA 494.

In the absence of an agreement between the parties on this matter, the arbitrators are responsible for deciding whether it is appropriate to decide by way of partial awards.

Some laws expressly give the arbitrators freedom to do so. In particular, Article 188 of the Swiss Private International Law Statute provides that "[u]nless the parties have agreed otherwise, the arbitral tribunal may make partial awards."[38] The arbitrators are given the same option by Article 1049 of the Dutch Code of Civil Procedure, Article 1699 of the Belgian Judicial Code and Section 29 of the 1999 Swedish Arbitration Act. Similarly, English law provides that unless the parties agree otherwise the arbitration agreement is deemed to empower the arbitrators to make partial awards at their discretion.[39] Although the French New Code of Civil Procedure does not mention it explicitly, the same rule applies in French law.

Some arbitration rules also expressly refer to the arbitrators' power to render partial awards.[40]

1361. — The arbitrators' freedom to determine whether it is appropriate to make partial awards can only be exercised within the limits set forth by the parties themselves. For instance, in the *SOFIDIF* case, the Paris Court of Appeals interpreted the terms of reference as stipulating that the arbitrators were to rule by separate awards on jurisdiction and on the merits of the dispute. The Court concluded that the award, which had disregarded that provision, should be set aside under Article 1502 3° of the New Code of Civil Procedure on the grounds that the arbitrators had exceeded the limits of their brief.[41] The *Cour de cassation* overruled that decision on the grounds that the Court of Appeals could only reach that conclusion if the obligation to make separate awards resulted from an "express, precise clause of the terms of reference."[42] Thus, under French international arbitration law, directions by the parties on this point, provided that they are sufficiently clear and precise, may lead an award to be set aside if they are disregarded by the arbitrators.[43]

---

[38]   The Swiss *Concordat* already contained this rule at Article 32.

[39]   Sec. 47 of the 1996 English Arbitration Act ("Awards on different issues"). For a comparative law analysis, see MAURO RUBINO-SAMMARTANO, INTERNATIONAL ARBITRATION LAW 405 *et seq.* (1990).

[40]   *See, e.g.*, Art. 2(iii) of the 1998 ICC Arbitration Rules (Art. 21 of the previous Rules); Art. 26.7 of the 1998 LCIA Rules; Art. 32(1) of the UNCITRAL Arbitration Rules; Art. 27(7) of the 1997 AAA International Arbitration Rules; Art. 34 of the 1999 Rules of the Arbitration Institute of the Stockholm Chamber of Commerce.

[41]   CA Paris, Dec. 19, 1986, O.I.A.E.T.I. v. SOFIDIF, 1987 REV. ARB. 359, and the commentary by Emmanuel Gaillard, *L'affaire SOFIDIF ou les difficultés de l'arbitrage mulitpartite (à propos de l'arrêt rendu par la Cour d'appel de Paris le 19 décembre 1986)*, id. at 275.

[42]   Cass. 1e civ., Mar. 8, 1988, Sofidif v. O.I.A.E.T.I., 1988 Bull. Civ. I, No. 64; 1989 REV. ARB. 481, and C. Jarrosson's note; for an English translation, see 3 INT'L ARB. REP. B1 (Mar. 1988).

[43]   *See supra* para. 1236.

1362. — In the absence of any stipulation by the parties, the arbitrators' decision as to whether it is appropriate to make partial awards will depend on the circumstances of the case.[44]

The usefulness of partial awards on jurisdiction will mainly depend on whether the issues of jurisdiction will be determined by the same facts as those determining the merits. If that is the case, it will be preferable to make a single award covering both jurisdiction and, assuming the arbitrators' jurisdiction is confirmed, the merits. If, on the other hand, jurisdiction appears to be a separate issue and the substantive issues to be resolved by the tribunal if it retains jurisdiction are complex, it will generally be appropriate to decide by way of a separate award. By stating that "[i]n general, the arbitral tribunal should rule on a plea concerning its jurisdiction as a preliminary question. However, the arbitral tribunal may proceed with the arbitration and rule on such a plea in their final award," the UNCITRAL Rules appear to encourage the use of partial awards on jurisdiction (Art. 21(4)), as does the Swiss Private International Law Statute, which provides in Article 186, paragraph 3, that "[t]he arbitral tribunal shall, in general, decide on its jurisdiction by a preliminary decision."[45] The more cautious approach found in the Arbitration Rules of the Arbitration Institute of the Stockholm Chamber of Commerce, which previously required the arbitrators to invoke "special reasons" in order to render a partial award in the absence of an agreement of the parties to that effect (Art. 27 of the 1988 Rules), is no longer found in the 1999 Rules (Art. 34).

The question of whether it is appropriate to make a separate award on the applicable law also depends on the circumstances of the dispute. If the governing law is determined in a separate award, the parties will not need to present their arguments on the merits in the light of each different law which might otherwise apply to the dispute, including general principles of law.[46] However, to do so may delay the outcome of the dispute and oblige the arbitrators to choose a governing law without being fully aware of the impact this decision may have on the merits.[47]

---

[44] On this issue, see ICC Awards No. 3790 (1983), French contractor v. Libyan employer, 110 J.D.I. 910 (1983), and observations by S. Jarvin; for an English translation, see XI Y.B. COM. ARB. 119 (1986); No. 5639 (1987), Bank v. African owner, 114 J.D.I. 1054 (1987), and observations by S. Jarvin; No. 5073 (1986), U.S. exporter v. Argentine distributor, XIII Y.B. COM. ARB. 53 (1988); the February 5, 1988 Partial Award on Liability by J. Stevenson, president, I. Brownlie and B. Cremades, arbitrators, Wintershall A.G. v. Government of Qatar, 28 I.L.M. 795 (1989); XV Y.B. COM. ARB. 30 (1990).

[45] However, once a partial award on jurisdiction is made, the party which wants to contest it in an action to set aside must bring this action without delay; see Swiss Fed. Trib., Apr. 19, 1994, Les Emirats Arabes Unis v. Westland Helicopters Ltd., 1994 BULL. ASA 404, 406 and the references cited therein. *See also supra* para. 1357. In Austria, see, in favor of a partial award on certain substantive issues being subject to an immediate action to set aside, Austrian *Oberster Gerichtshof*, June 25, 1992, S Establishment for Commerce v. H Corporation, XXII Y.B. COM. ARB. 619 (1997).

[46] *See infra* paras. 1594 *et seq.*

[47] For an example of a partial award on the applicable law, see ICC Award No. 3267 (1979), Mexican construction company v. Belgian company (member of a consortium), VII Y.B. COM. ARB. 96 (1982); for a French translation, see 107 J.D.I. 961 (1980), and observations by Y. Derains; for an example of a refusal to rule on the applicable law in a partial award, see the letter of the chairman of the arbitral tribunal in ICC Case No. 6465, 121 J.D.I. 1088 (1994), and observations by D. Hascher, especially at 1092–93.

It is impossible to assess in the abstract when separate awards on liability and quantum of damages are appropriate. A partial award on liability may encourage a settlement and enable the arbitrators to determine more accurately the brief of any expert appointed to assist in the evaluation of damages. On the other hand, it may delay the outcome of the proceedings and bind the arbitrators before they are fully aware of all the facts of the case. In short, the decision depends entirely on the circumstances of each case.

C. – DEFAULT AWARDS

1363. — As discussed earlier, default by one of the parties does not bring the arbitral proceedings to an end. In order to satisfy the requirements of due process and equal treatment of the parties, it is sufficient for each party to be given an equal opportunity to present its case.[48] Default by a party does not therefore prevent the making of a valid award. There is no obligation on the arbitrators to simply accept the arguments of the party which is present or represented, nor indeed to increase the burden of proof on that party so as to compensate for the other's failure to participate, provided the defaulting party has been properly invited to attend. In other words, an award made following default proceedings is no different from one made following proceedings where all parties participate. In both cases, the rules of due process are satisfied. Thus, having established that the various documents submitted to the arbitral tribunal had invariably been sent to the defaulting party by means of two different couriers, a court was founded to reject an action to set aside brought against a default award, on the grounds that "the provisions of the [ICC] Rules adopted by the parties had been observed and no specific formal requirements were required to ensure that the proceedings complied with the rules of due process."[49]

D. – CONSENT AWARDS

1364. — In some cases, the parties succeed in reaching a settlement in the course of the proceedings. If they do so, they may simply formalize their agreement in a contract and terminate the arbitral proceedings. Alternatively, they may want their decision to be recorded by the arbitral tribunal in the form of an award. This is referred to as a consent award. In obtaining a consent award, the parties expect their settlement to benefit from the authority and effects attached to an award. Admittedly, in certain legal systems,[50] a settlement is *res judicata* in any event, so in that respect it gains nothing from being embodied in an award. However, the parties may seek a consent award in order to enjoy the recognition and

---

[48]   On this issue, generally, see *supra* para. 1224.

[49]   CA Paris, Mar. 24, 1995, Bin Saud Bin Abdel Aziz v. Crédit Industriel et Commercial de Paris, 1996 REV. ARB. 259, and J.-M. Talau's note.

[50]   See, for example, in France, Article 2052, paragraph 1 of the Civil Code.

enforcement procedures provided for in widely-ratified international conventions on arbitration.[51]

1365. — The first question that arises here is whether the arbitrators are obliged to make a consent award where the parties so request. Most modern arbitration laws, which promote the principle of party autonomy, will require them to do so. This is clearly the case in French law. A number of arbitration rules also expressly invite the arbitrators to record the agreement reached by the parties in a consent award. The 1998 ICC Rules provide, in Article 26 (Art. 17 of the previous Rules), that:

> [i]f the parties reach a settlement after the file has been transmitted to the Arbitral Tribunal . . . , the settlement shall be recorded in the form of an Award made by consent of the parties if so requested by the parties and if the Arbitral Tribunal agrees to do so.

Similar provisions appear in the 1998 LCIA Rules (Art. 26.8), the 1999 Stockholm Chamber of Commerce Rules (Art. 32(5)) and the Euro-Arab Chambers of Commerce Rules (Art. 24-1). In ICSID arbitration, the parties' settlement may give rise to an order recording the discontinuance of the proceedings. If the parties so request, the arbitral tribunal can incorporate the settlement in an award under Article 43 of the ICSID Rules.

1366. — The second question arising in connection with consent awards is whether, like ordinary awards, they benefit from the recognition and enforcement mechanisms provided for in international conventions and national legislation. Neither the 1958 New York Convention nor the 1961 European Convention expressly refers to consent awards. Nevertheless, in determining whether those conventions apply, one should, in our opinion, interpret those instruments in order to determine their scope rather than consider the position in the jurisdiction where the disputed award is made.[52]

The lack of case law on this issue[53] makes it difficult to take a firm view.[54] If an award is defined as being restricted to a decision whereby the arbitrators resolve all or part of a

---

[51] On these conventions, see *infra* paras. 1663 *et seq.*

[52] But see ALBERT JAN VAN DEN BERG, THE NEW YORK ARBITRATION CONVENTION OF 1958, at 50 (1981), for the view that a consent award may be covered by the New York Convention if considered to be an award in the country in which it was made.

[53] Consent awards themselves are rarely published. But see the interesting case of a partial award recording the agreement of the parties on the law governing the merits of a dispute, ICC Award No. 4761 (1984), Italian consortium v. Libyan company, 113 J.D.I. 1137 (1986), and observations by S. Jarvin. Given its subject-matter, the contractual nature of this consent award is particularly clear. In fact, the award is simply a formal means of documenting the choice of law agreed by the parties.

[54] On this issue, see MATTHIEU DE BOISSÉSON, LE DROIT FRANÇAIS DE L'ARBITRAGE INTERNE ET INTERNATIONAL 808–09 (2d ed. 1990); RUBINO-SAMMARTANO, *supra* note 39, at 438; Richard H. Kreindler, *Settlement Agreements and Arbitration in the Context of the ICC Rules*, ICC BULLETIN, Vol. 9, No. 2, at 22 (1998) and, in the context of Article 34 of the Swiss *Concordat*, which explicitly allows an arbitral tribunal to record, in an award, the agreement bringing a dispute to an end, see PIERRE JOLIDON, COMMENTAIRE DU CONCORDAT SUISSE SUR L'ARBITRAGE 485–87 (1984) and LALIVE, POUDRET, REYMOND, *supra* note 16, at 192–93.

dispute, it seems doubtful that a decision which simply endorses the agreement of the parties could be considered to be an award.[55] However, the UNCITRAL Model Law provides a strong argument in favor of applying the ordinary regime for awards by stating in Article 30, paragraph 2 that a consent award "has the same status and effect as any other award on the merits of the case." Thus, in countries which have adopted the Model Law, the issue will be resolved by simply applying the ordinary legal rules governing the recognition and enforcement of awards. It could be that the position of the Model Law will have a wider impact, as the adoption of the rule set out in Article 30, paragraph 2 reveals the existence of a consensus which is liable to support a similar interpretation of other international instruments.

SECTION II
THE MAKING OF THE AWARD

1367. — An arbitral award[56] is made by the arbitrators (§ 1) subject, in some cases, to approval by an arbitral institution (§ 2). The award must be made within any time-limit fixed by the parties or by law (§ 3).

§ 1. – Role of the Arbitrators

1368. — The role of the arbitrators is to resolve all of the disputed issues by one or more decisions,[57] and to express those decisions in a document which is subject to certain formal requirements, and which is known as the arbitral award. The process which enables the arbitrators to reach such a decision is referred to as the deliberations. Although one cannot go as far as to say that there can be no deliberations where the dispute is heard by a sole arbitrator, the regime governing the deliberations is of practical importance only where there is an arbitral tribunal comprising more than one member.

1369. — The requirement for deliberations is not always expressly set out in international arbitration statutes. For instance, no such requirement exists in French international arbitration law, and none of the grounds for setting aside an award listed in Article 1502 of the New Code of Civil Procedure refers directly to deliberations. Nevertheless, they do constitute a fundamental condition under French law, which will apply even where neither the parties nor their chosen arbitration rules make reference to them. It might be argued that the absence of proper deliberations constitutes a violation of due process justifying the

---

[55] On this definition, see *supra* paras. 1353 *et seq.*

[56] On awards in ICC arbitration, see Marcel Fontaine, *The ICC Arbitral Process – Part IV: The Award – Drafting the Award – A Perspective from a Civil Law Jurist*, ICC BULLETIN, Vol. 5, No. 1, at 30 (1994); Humphrey Lloyd, *Writing Awards – A Common Lawyer's Perspective*, *id.* at 38.

[57] For an example of an invitation made by the arbitrators to the parties to negotiate, see the June 7, 1988 Order in ICC Case No. 5282, 121 J.D.I. 1086 (1994), and observations by D. Hascher.

setting aside of an award. However, this would run contrary to the principle of the arbitrators' independence, as it is only where the arbitrators are not independent of the parties that any unequal treatment of the party-appointed arbitrators in the conduct of the deliberations would amount to a breach of due process or equality of the parties.[58] It is therefore generally considered that the existence of proper deliberations is in itself a requirement of international procedural public policy, a breach of which will also constitute a ground for the setting aside of the award.[59]

1370. — Similarly, international arbitration statutes generally give no further indication as to how deliberations are to be conducted. They must, however, satisfy certain conditions, which we shall now examine.

A. – THE DECISION-MAKING PROCESS

1371. — Where the arbitral tribunal comprises more than one arbitrator, it is necessary to determine how its decisions are to be made in the event that the arbitrators are not unanimous.

Some arbitration rules simply state that in such circumstances the decision is to be taken by a majority of the arbitrators. That is the position taken in the UNCITRAL Arbitration Rules (Art. 31(1)), the AAA International Arbitration Rules (Art. 26) and the ICSID Rules (Art. 16(1)). The case law generated under the UNCITRAL Rules by the Iran-United States Claims Tribunal illustrates one of the difficulties which may arise when a majority is required. Where one arbitrator does not participate in the deliberations or takes a position which the other arbitrators consider to be unreasonable, in order to avoid delaying the award indefinitely, another arbitrator—generally a co-arbitrator—must accept the views of the third arbitrator—generally the chairman—which may lead the first arbitrator to endorse an award with which he is not in agreement. Some arbitrators have gone as far as stating in a separate opinion that they consider the result to be unsatisfactory but endorse it only in order to create a majority which complies with the requirements of the rules.[60]

Other rules have chosen to specify that where a majority cannot be obtained, the chairman of the arbitral tribunal can decide alone. That system was introduced by the ICC Rules of

---

[58] On the relationships between these two principles, see *infra* para. 1638.

[59] *See* DE BOISSÉSON, *supra* note 54, at 800; P. Fouchard, note following Cass. 2e civ., Jan. 28, 1981, Industrija Motora Rakovica v. Lynx Machinery Ltd., 1982 REV. ARB. 425. Compare, in French domestic arbitration, with CA Paris, Apr. 5, 1973, Le Parisien Libéré v. Ancelot, 1974 REV. ARB. 17, and G. Flécheux's note.

[60] *See, e.g.,* H. Holtzmann's opinion in the June 14, 1983 Award of the Iran-U.S. Claims Tribunal in Economy Forms Corp. v. Iran, Award No. 55-165-1, 3 Iran-U.S. Cl. Trib. Rep. 42, 55, and the observations by D. Hascher, 121 J.D.I. 1084 (1994). On this issue, generally, see Stephen M. Schwebel, *The Majority Vote of an International Arbitral Tribunal, in* ETUDES DE DROIT INTERNATIONAL EN L'HONNEUR DE PIERRE LALIVE 671 (1993); Karl-Heinz Böckstiegel, *Experiences as an Arbitrator Using the UNCITRAL Arbitration Rules, id.* at 423, 428.

Arbitration in 1955, and is found today in Article 25, paragraph 1 of the 1998 Rules.[61] It has since been followed by the Euro-Arab Chambers of Commerce,[62] the LCIA Arbitration Rules (Art. 26.3) and the 1999 Rules of the Arbitration Institute of the Stockholm Chamber of Commerce (Art. 30) among others. Article 46 of the International Arbitration Rules of the Zurich Chamber of Commerce adopts a similar approach, but restricts the chairman's discretion by stipulating that an award in favor of the winning party can be neither less than the lowest proposal made by the co-arbitrators, nor greater than their highest proposal.

These two different approaches are also found in arbitration legislation. The UNCITRAL Model Law (Art. 29), the Netherlands Code of Civil Procedure (Art. 1057), the 1996 English Arbitration Act (Sec. 22(1))[63] and the new German law on arbitration (Art. 1052 ZPO) have followed the traditional position found in the UNCITRAL Arbitration Rules. In contrast, the 1987 Swiss Private International Law Statute (Art. 189, para. 2), the 1988 Spanish Arbitration Statute (Art. 34) and the 1999 Swedish Arbitration Act (Sec. 30, para. 2) have followed the ICC Rules in this respect and provide that if no majority is possible, the award can be made by the chairman alone.

Provisions enabling the chairman to reach a decision alone are intended to ensure that where the arbitrators have strongly differing views, the chairman need not side with one or other of the co-arbitrators so as to obtain a majority. Although the chairman is entitled to decide alone, he or she may prefer to opt for a compromise solution. In practice, there have been very few cases where the decision-making process might have failed but for a clause of this kind. In 1995, of the 203 awards submitted to the Court of Arbitration, none was made by the chairman alone under Article 19 of the ICC Rules (now Art. 25(1)).[64] In 1996, of the 217 awards submitted to the Court, only one was made by the chairman alone and in 1997, of the 227 awards submitted, just two were made by the chairman.[65] In 1998, of the 242 awards submitted, again only one was made by the chairman alone. Nevertheless, the very existence of the possibility for the chairman to decide alone will probably persuade the co-arbitrators to take a more reasonable attitude in certain cases.

As French law is silent on this issue, it is not inconceivable that where the parties do not agree otherwise the French courts would accept such a practice, even where it is not

---

[61] On Article 25(1) of the 1998 Rules, see DERAINS AND SCHWARTZ, *supra* note 1, at 284 *et seq.*

[62] *See, e.g.,* Art. 24-2 of the Rules of Conciliation, Arbitration and Expertise of the Euro-Arab Chambers of Commerce.

[63] *See also* Section 16 of the 1929 Swedish Arbitration Act, in force until April 1, 1999.

[64] On the mechanism contained in Article 19 of the previous ICC Rules, see CRAIG, PARK, PAULSSON, *supra* note 31, at 329. For an example of an award made following such a procedure, see ICC Award No. 1703 (1973), by G. Lagergren, chairman, with the dissenting opinions by S. Efron and A. El Shalakany, arbitrators, Société Générale de l'Industrie du Papier "RAKTA" v. Parsons and Whittemore Overseas Co., Inc., *reprinted in* J. GILLIS WETTER, THE INTERNATIONAL ARBITRAL PROCESS: PUBLIC AND PRIVATE, Vol. V, at 361 (1979); ICC Award No. 3881 (1984), Swiss and German (FRG) companies v. Syrian state-owned company, 113 J.D.I. 1096 (1996), and observations by S. Jarvin. *See also* DERAINS AND SCHWARTZ, *supra* note 1, at 284 *et seq.*

[65] *See* Dominique Hascher, *Scrutiny of Draft Awards by the Court – 1995 Overview*, ICC BULLETIN, Vol. 7, No. 1, at 14 (1996); Dominique Hascher, *Scrutiny of Draft Awards by the Court – 1996 Overview*, ICC BULLETIN, Vol. 8, No. 1, at 17 (1997); Dominique Hascher, *The Application of the Rules by the Court – 1997 Overview*, ICC BULLETIN, Vol. 9, No. 1, at 12, 13 (1998); Fabien Gélinas, *The Application of the Rules by the Court – 1998 Overview*, ICC BULLETIN, Vol. 10, No. 1 (1999).

expressly provided for in the applicable arbitration rules. This seems preferable to compelling the chairman of the arbitral tribunal to side with one of the co-arbitrators or to declare that, in the absence of a majority, no award can be made. Nonetheless, all of the arbitrators must have been given the opportunity to participate in the deliberations.[66]

B. – METHODS OF COMMUNICATION BETWEEN THE ARBITRATORS

1372. — Most modern laws contain no requirements as to the form of the deliberations. As stated by the French *Cour de cassation* in a decision of January 28, 1981, which remains valid following the reform of May 12, 1981, "no particular form is required for the deliberations of the arbitrators."[67] By majority voting or by virtue of the powers of the chairman under the rules governing decision-making,[68] the arbitral tribunal is free to determine the conduct of the deliberations.[69] The arbitrators can thus meet to deliberate, or exchange questionnaires,[70] notes or draft awards, or communicate by telephone, fax or video-conference.[71] In this respect, the Swiss Federal Court has rightly ruled that an award made by circulating a draft among the arbitrators satisfied the requirement for deliberations.[72]

C. – REFUSAL OF AN ARBITRATOR TO PARTICIPATE IN THE DELIBERATIONS

1373. — An arbitrator cannot obstruct the making of an award by simply refusing to participate in the deliberations. Just as compliance with the rules of due process only entails providing the parties with an opportunity to present their case even though they may choose not to do so,[73] the requirement for deliberations will be satisfied if each of the arbitrators is given an equal opportunity to take part, in a satisfactory manner, in the discussions among the arbitrators and in the drafting of the award. The French *Cour de cassation* has

---

[66] *See supra* para. 1369.

[67] Cass. 2e civ., Jan. 28, 1981, *Industrija Motora Rakovica*, *supra* note 59, *upholding* CA Paris, Dec. 22, 1978, 1979 REV. ARB. 266, and J. Viatte's note.

[68] *See supra* para. 1371.

[69] *See* Claude Reymond, *The President of the Arbitral Tribunal*, 9 ICSID REV. – FOREIGN INV. L.J. 1, 12 *et seq.* (1994), and for a French version, *in* ETUDES OFFERTES À PIERRE BELLET 467, especially at 477 *et seq.* (1991); D. Hascher, observations following the questionnaire to co-arbitrators issued by the chairman of the arbitral tribunal in ICC Case No. 5082, 121 J.D.I. 1081, 1083 (1994).

[70] For an example of a questionnaire drawn up by the chairman of an ICC arbitral tribunal, see 121 J.D.I. 1081 (1994), and observations by D. Hascher.

[71] Compare with Article 837 of the Italian Code of Civil Procedure (Law No. 25 of Jan. 5, 1994) which provides that "[t]he award shall be made by a majority of the votes of the arbitrators *meeting in person or in video conference*, unless the parties have provided otherwise, and shall be subsequently set forth in writing" (emphasis added).

[72] Oct. 23, 1985, SEFRI S.A. v. Komgrap, ATF 111 Ia 336; 1986 BULL. ASA 77.

[73] *See supra* para. 1224.

recognized that a party's right to a fair hearing, which was claimed to have been breached where no deliberations took place, was satisfied where the missing arbitrator was "given the opportunity to make comments on the proposed amendments to the initial draft of the award."[74] The same solution is also embodied in certain modern arbitration statutes, such as the 1999 Swedish Arbitration Act (Sec. 30, para. 1). Article 26.2 of the LCIA Rules thus expresses a widely accepted rule in providing that where an arbitrator refuses to participate in the making of the award "having been given a reasonable opportunity to do so, the remaining arbitrators may proceed in his absence and state in their award the circumstances of the other arbitrator's failure to participate in the making of the award."[75] The 1998 revision of the ICC Rules introduced, as a means of accelerating the procedure, Article 12, paragraph 5, pursuant to which:

> [s]ubsequent to the closing of the proceedings, instead of replacing an arbitrator who has died or been removed by the Court . . . , the Court may decide, when it considers it appropriate, that the remaining arbitrators shall continue the arbitration.

The application of this provision, which raises certain difficulties concerning the principle of the equality of the parties,[76] should, in our view, remain the exception in practice. Nevertheless, Article 12, paragraph 5 is likely to dissuade arbitrators from resigning for the sole purpose of delaying the outcome of the arbitration.[77]

D. – SECRECY OF DELIBERATIONS

1374. — Although, again, most laws do not explicitly require deliberations in international arbitration to be secret,[78] such secrecy is generally considered to be the rule.[79] This means that views exchanged during the deliberations cannot be communicated to the parties. However, this does not prevent the arbitrators from indicating in their award that their decision was reached by a majority or unanimously.[80] Non-compliance with the

---

[74]   Cass. 2e civ., Jan. 28, 1981, *Industrija Motora Rakovica*, *supra* note 59.

[75]   On this issue, generally, see Emmanuel Gaillard, *Les manoeuvres dilatoires des parties et des arbitres dans l'arbitrage commercial international*, 1990 REV. ARB. 759.

[76]   On the issue, see Emmanuel Gaillard, *When an Arbitrator Withdraws*, N.Y.L.J., June 4, 1998, at 3, and *supra* para. 1136.

[77]   *See* Andreas Reiner, *Le Règlement d'arbitrage de la CCI, version 1998*, 1998 REV. ARB. 25, 62 *et seq.*; DERAINS AND SCHWARTZ, *supra* note 1, at 193 *et seq.*

[78]   Compare, in French domestic arbitration, with Article 1469 of the New Code of Civil Procedure.

[79]   *See* DE BOISSÉSON, *supra* note 54, at 802; *comp. with* JEAN ROBERT, L'ARBITRAGE – DROIT INTERNE – DROIT INTERNATIONAL PRIVÉ 310 (5th ed. 1983), whose remarks in this respect were not included in the 6th edition published in 1993.

[80]   *See* LALIVE, POUDRET, REYMOND, *supra* note 16, at 414. On dissenting opinions, see *infra* paras. 1396 *et seq.* and on the confidentiality of the award, see *infra* para. 1412. See also, on the limits to the confidentiality of the
(continued...)

requirement of secrecy could render the arbitrator in breach personally liable,[81] but would not invalidate the award.[82]

§ 2. – Role of the Arbitral Institution

1375. — In *ad hoc* arbitration, the award is the work of the arbitrators alone. However, where the parties have chosen to submit their dispute to institutional arbitration, the institution is sometimes responsible for reviewing a draft of the arbitrators' award. The purpose of that review is usually to enable the institution to maximize the chances of awards made under its supervision being enforced.

1376. — Most international arbitration laws are silent on this issue, and arbitral institutions are therefore free to determine how they review awards and, by adopting their arbitration rules, the parties confer contractual status on the involvement of the institution.

Under the heading "Scrutiny of the Award by the Court," the ICC Rules provide, in Article 27 (Art. 21 of the previous Rules), that:

> [b]efore signing any Award, the Arbitral Tribunal shall submit it in draft form to the Court. The Court may lay down modifications as to the form of the Award and, without affecting the Arbitral Tribunal's liberty of decision, may also draw its attention to points of substance. No Award shall be rendered by the Arbitral Tribunal until it has been approved by the Court as to its form.[83]

The ICC International Court of Arbitration thus has the power to review the form of the award, and to draw the attention of the arbitrators to substantive issues which it considers to be problematic. This distinction between form and substance is sometimes delicate. Contrary to the view put forward by some authors,[84] the scrutiny by the International Court of Arbitration of the form of the award does not extend to ensuring compliance with the entire arbitral procedure. For example, it does not entail checking whether proper adversarial

---

[80] (...continued)
deliberations that may result from the review of arbitral awards by the courts, Mary T. Reilly, *The Court's Power to Invade the Arbitrators' Deliberation Chamber*, 9 J. INT'L. ARB. 27 (Sept. 1992) and on this issue, generally, Jean-Denis Bredin, *Le secret du délibéré arbitral*, in ETUDES OFFERTES À PIERRE BELLET 71 (1991).

[81] On arbitrators' liability, see *supra* paras. 1074 *et seq.*

[82] On the grounds for challenging the award, see *infra* para. 1603.

[83] On the exercise of this scrutiny in practice, see especially Alain Prujiner, *La gestion des arbitrages commerciaux internationaux: l'exemple de la Cour d'arbitrage de la CCI*, 115 J.D.I. 663, 708 (1988); CRAIG, PARK, PAULSSON, *supra* note 31, at 341 *et seq.*; David T. McGovern, *The ICC Arbitral Process – Part VI: Scrutiny of the Award by the ICC Court*, ICC BULLETIN, Vol. 5, No. 1, at 46 (1994); DERAINS AND SCHWARTZ, *supra* note 1, at 289 *et seq.*

[84] *See* CRAIG, PARK, PAULSSON, *supra* note 31, at 343; ANTOINE KASSIS, RÉFLEXIONS SUR LE RÈGLEMENT D'ARBITRAGE DE LA CHAMBRE DE COMMERCE INTERNATIONALE – LES DÉVIATIONS DE L'ARBITRAGE INSTITUTIONNEL 69 (1988).

hearings took place on each disputed issue, unless the existence of a procedural flaw in that area is evident from simply reading the award.[85] In 1998, of the 242 draft awards submitted to the Court for scrutiny, 18 were returned to the arbitrators, 5 for reasons of form, 3 for reasons of substance, and 3 on both grounds; 62 awards were approved subject to modifications as to their form, after which the Court, through a smaller committee, reviewed compliance with the Court's decision.[86]

Some arbitration rules, such as those of the Euro-Arab Chambers of Commerce (Art. 24-4) or those of the Chambre franco-allemande de commerce et d'industrie (COFACI) (Art. 23), contain provisions similar to those of the ICC Rules. Others, such as the LCIA Rules or the AAA Rules, have no such system and leave the arbitrators solely responsible for both the form and the substance of the award.

1377. — The ICC being headquartered in Paris, the French courts have had the occasion to specify that as the review exercised by arbitral institutions is merely "administrative," the institution need not state the reasons for any amendments it may require.[87] In the context of ICC arbitration, the French courts have also held that as the ICC International Court of Arbitration is not an "arbitrator of second instance," it is not obliged to examine all the documents submitted to the arbitrators by the parties.[88]

1378. — Some authors have questioned both the benefit of submitting draft awards to an arbitral institution for approval and even the validity of awards made under such conditions.[89]

The difficulty is whether the draft award submitted by the arbitrators for review by the institution is in fact a true award which terminates the arbitrators' jurisdiction over the case and is *res judicata*. If that were the case, any subsequent intervention by the arbitral institution would infringe upon the independence of the arbitral tribunal and, because the award effectively terminates the arbitrators' mandate,[90] the institution would be powerless to alter it. However, because arbitration is based essentially on the principle of party autonomy, the award is not properly made until it is delivered in accordance with the conditions which the parties themselves have fixed by adopting the institution's arbitration rules.[91] Courts which have had to review the scrutiny of awards exercised by arbitral institutions—in practice, the ICC—have generally rejected the arguments of parties

---

[85]   *See also* Eric Loquin, *L'examen du projet de sentence par l'institution et la sentence au deuxième degré – Réflexions sur la nature et la validité de l'intervention de l'institution arbitrale sur la sentence*, 1990 REV. ARB. 427.

[86]   Gélinas, *supra* note 65.

[87]   CA Paris, Jan. 22, 1982, Appareils Dragon v. Construimport, 1982 REV. ARB. 91, 2d decision, and E. Mezger's note.

[88]   CA Paris, Apr. 20, 1972, Schutte Lanz v. Gallais, 1973 REV. ARB. 84, and E. Loquin's note; Cass. 2e civ., Jan. 23, 1974, Schutte Lanz v. Gallais, 1974 REV. ARB. 296, and E. Loquin's note.

[89]   *See* KASSIS, *supra* note 84, ¶¶ 76 *et seq.*; PETER SCHLOSSER, DAS RECHT DER INTERNATIONALEN PRIVATEN SCHIEDSGERICHTSBARKEIT, Vol. I, 480–83 (1975).

[90]   *See infra* para. 1414.

[91]   *See* Loquin, *supra* note 85, at 443.

challenging the validity of an award solely on the grounds that it was rendered after scrutiny by an arbitral institution.[92] Likewise, an arbitral institution reviewing an award in accordance with the conditions contained in its arbitration rules cannot be accused of infringing upon the arbitrators' independence, which concerns the relationships between the arbitrators and the parties, or of failing to keep the deliberations secret, provided that the institution itself observes that secrecy.[93]

§ 3. – Time-Limits for Making the Award

1379. — The question of when the arbitral tribunal must make its award, which raises the issue of the duration of the arbitrators' functions,[94] depends on whether or not the parties have specified a time-limit for that purpose.

A. – WHERE THE PARTIES HAVE SPECIFIED NO TIME-LIMIT

1380. — Where the parties have not set a deadline before which the arbitrators are to make their award, the next question is whether they have nevertheless chosen a mechanism for doing so.

1° Where the Parties Have Chosen a Mechanism for Fixing a Deadline

1381. — Where the parties have not set a time-limit within which the arbitrators are to make their award, a mechanism for fixing that time-limit may be found in rules incorporated by reference in their arbitration agreement.

1382. — They may have adopted a procedural law specifying a deadline or designating the authority responsible for setting that deadline. For example, if French law is chosen to govern the proceedings, the six month period provided for in Article 1456, paragraph 1 of

---

[92] *See* Superior Court of the Zurich Canton, June 29, 1979, Banque Yougoslave de l'Agriculture v. Robin International Inc., unpublished, cited by CRAIG, PARK, PAULSSON, *supra* note 31, at 348. Compare with Bank Mellat v. GAA Development and Construction Co., [1988] 2 Lloyd's Rep. 44 (Q.B. (Com. Ct.) 1988), which rejected a challenge based on alleged "misconduct" in that the arbitrators failed to meet to discuss the comments of the arbitral institution. But see, for a case where the award was set aside, the March 10, 1976 decision of the Supreme Court of Turkey discussed in KASSIS, *supra* note 84, at 121.

[93] For a rebuttal of this argument which is sometimes raised with respect to the institutional review of awards, see also Loquin, *supra* note 85, at 455 *et seq.*; P. Fouchard, 1990 REV. ARB. 527 (reviewing ANTOINE KASSIS, RÉFLEXIONS SUR LE RÈGLEMENT D'ARBITRAGE DE LA CHAMBRE DE COMMERCE INTERNATIONALE – LES DÉVIATIONS DE L'ARBITRAGE INSTITUTIONNEL (1988)).

[94] On this issue, generally, in French domestic arbitration law, see Philippe Grandjean, *La durée de la mission des arbitres*, 1995 REV. ARB. 39; Eric Loquin, *Arbitrage – Compétence arbitrale – Etendue*, J.-CL. PROC. CIV., Fasc. 1032, ¶¶ 48 *et seq.* (1994).

the New Code of Civil Procedure will apply,[95] and can be extended, under paragraph 2 of the same Article, by the parties or by the courts.[96]

1383. — The parties may also have incorporated in their agreement arbitration rules containing provisions as to the deadline for making the award.

The French courts have firmly established the principle that time-limits and extensions fixed by a pre-designated third party—in practice, an arbitral institution—are binding on the parties just as if they had been established by the parties themselves.[97]

Arbitration rules vary considerably on this issue. For example, the ICC Rules of Arbitration fix a time-limit for rendering the award of six months from the signature or approval by the International Court of Arbitration of the terms of reference.[98] However, the International Court of Arbitration may "pursuant to a reasoned request from the arbitrator or if need be on its own initiative, extend this time-limit if it decides it is necessary to do so."[99] The previous ICC Rules made the effectiveness of the terms of reference, and thus the point of departure of the six months time period, subject to payment of the advance on costs. This condition has been removed in the 1998 Rules and is replaced by the striking out of any claims made by the non-paying party. This allows the six-month period to run from the date of the last signature of the terms of reference or from that of the notification by the secretariat to the arbitral tribunal of the Court's approval of the terms of reference (Art. 24(1)). The decision to extend a deadline is made by the International Court of Arbitration.[100] The Court need not inform the parties of its intention to extend the deadline,

---

[95] On the date on which this period commences, which requires the arbitrators' brief to have been defined, see CA Paris, July 4, 1991, Etude Rochechouart Immobilier v. Banque Vernes, 1992 REV. ARB. 626, and observations by J. Pellerin.

[96] For a discussion of the effectiveness of this provision, despite the ambiguities in certain aspects of the decision of Cass. 1e civ., June 15, 1994, Communauté urbaine de Casablanca v. Degrémont, 1995 REV. ARB. 88, 2d decision, see E. Gaillard's note following that decision, especially at 97.

[97] See, on the fixing of deadlines by the ICC International Court of Arbitration, CA Paris, Jan. 22, 1982, *Appareils Dragon, supra* note 87; on the extension of a contractual deadline granted by the ICC International Court of Arbitration, Cass. 1e civ., June 16, 1976, Krebs v. Milton Stern, 104 J.D.I. 671 (1977), and P. Fouchard's note; 1977 REV. ARB. 269, and E. Mezger's note; 1978 REV. CRIT. DIP 767; Dalloz, Jur. 310 (1978), and J. Robert's note. *See also* CA Paris, Feb. 28, 1980, Financière MOCUPIA v. INVEKO France, 1980 REV. ARB. 538, and E. Loquin's note. On the fact that, in institutional arbitration, the provisions of the institution's rules regarding the deadline for making the award prevail over those of Article 1456 of the French New Code of Civil Procedure, see ICC Award No. 2730 (1982), Two Yugoslavian companies v. Dutch and Swiss group companies, 111 J.D.I. 914 (1984), and observations by Y. Derains. On the other hand, if the institution's rules give the institution, rather than the arbitrators, the power to extend deadlines, the arbitrators would be exceeding their powers were they themselves to rule on that question (*see* CA Versailles, Jan. 24, 1992, Degrémont v. Communauté urbaine de Casablanca, 1992 REV. ARB. 626, and observations by J. Pellerin).

[98] Art. 24(1) of the 1998 Rules, replacing Art. 18(1) of the previous Rules. On the terms of reference, see *supra* paras. 1228 *et seq.*

[99] Art. 24(2) of the 1998 Rules, replacing Art. 18(2) of the previous Rules.

[100] CA Paris, Dec. 3, 1981, Comptoirs Industriels Réunis Blachère et Cie. v. Société de Développement Viticole (SODEVI), 1982 REV. ARB. 91, and E. Mezger's note; CA Paris, Mar. 24, 1995, *Bin Saud Bin Abdel Aziz, supra* note 49.

or even advise them of the date on which such extension may be decided.[101] Its decision is of an administrative nature, and no grounds need be given.[102] Where an excessive delay is attributable to the arbitrators, the International Court of Arbitration may resort to the provisions of the Rules concerning the replacement of arbitrators, which apply where the arbitrators fail to perform their duties within the stipulated time-limits.[103]

Conversely, the LCIA Rules, which are silent on this issue, and the AAA International Rules (Art. 24) leave the arbitrators and the arbitral institution in full control of the deadlines before which the award must be made, unless the parties have provided otherwise. In the case of *ad hoc* arbitration, the UNCITRAL Rules of course take a similar approach.

2° Where the Parties Have Not Chosen a Mechanism for Fixing a Deadline

1384. — Where the parties have determined neither the deadline within which the arbitral tribunal must make its award, nor any mechanism for fixing that deadline, French international arbitration law imposes no limit on the period within which the arbitrators are to make their award. Even prior to the 1981 reform, it had been held that the old Article 1007 of the Code of Civil Procedure, which required the award to be rendered within the deadline fixed by the submission agreement or, in the absence of such a deadline, within three months, applied only to arbitrations governed by French procedural law and was not a requirement of international public policy.[104] That position was reinforced by the fact that the 1981 Decree remained silent on this point.[105] Thus, Article 1456, paragraph 1 of the New Code of Civil Procedure, which provides that "[i]f the arbitration agreement does not specify a time-limit, the arbitrators' mission shall last only six months from the day when the last arbitrator accepted his or her mission," does not apply to international arbitration unless the parties have chosen French law to govern the procedure.[106] In the 1994 *Sonidep* case, the *Cour de cassation* confirmed that "in international arbitration, French law . . . does not

---

[101] Cass. 2e civ., June 8, 1983, Appareils Dragon v. Empresa central de abastecimientas y vantas de equipos, 1987 REV. ARB. 309, and the commentary by Philippe Fouchard, *Les institutions permanentes d'arbitrage devant le juge étatique (A propos d'une jurisprudence récente), id.* at 225; CA Paris, May 19, 1998, Torno SpA v. Kumagai Gumi Co. Ltd., 13 INT'L ARB. REP. E1 (July 1998).

[102] CA Paris, Jan. 22, 1982, *Appareils Dragon, supra* note 87. On the rules governing administrative decisions made by arbitral institutions, see *supra* para. 32; CA Paris, May 17, 1983, Techni Import Professionnel (T.I.P.) v. Electro Scientific Industries (E.S.I.), 1987 REV. ARB. 309, and the commentary by Fouchard, *supra* note 101.

[103] *See* Art. 12(2) of the 1998 Rules, replacing Art. 2(11) of the previous Rules.

[104] Cass. 1e civ., June 30, 1976, Bruynzeel Deurenfabrik N.V. v. Ministre d'Etat aux Affaires Etrangères de la République Malgache, 104 J.D.I. 114 (1977), and B. Oppetit's note; 1977 REV. ARB. 317, and J. Rubellin-Devichi's note; Gaz. Pal., Jur. 70 (1977), and J. Viatte's note.

[105] *See, e.g.,* Philippe Fouchard, *La coopération du Président du Tribunal de grande instance à l'arbitrage,* 1985 REV. ARB. 5, 45.

[106] On this issue, see *supra* para. 1346.

require the arbitrators' powers to be confined, in the absence of a contractual deadline, within a statutory deadline."[107]

This liberal approach has been followed in Dutch law, which underlines the arbitral tribunal's discretion on this issue (Art. 1048 of the Code of Civil Procedure), and by Swiss or Swedish law which, like French law, remain silent on the question. Other legal systems, such as those of Sweden prior to the 1999 Arbitration Act[108] and Belgium,[109] provide that even in international cases the arbitrators must make their award within six months, although they differ as to the starting-point for that time-limit. The UNCITRAL Model Law offers a more flexible approach, providing that where an arbitrator fails to complete his or her functions within a reasonable period of time and does not resign, and the parties do not agree to terminate his or her mandate, either party can ask the court responsible for the constitution of the arbitral tribunal to decide on the termination of that mandate (Art. 14). No recourse is available against such a decision.

B. – WHERE THE PARTIES HAVE SPECIFIED A TIME-LIMIT

1385. — In both institutional and *ad hoc* arbitration, the parties are free to fix a precise deadline within which the arbitrators must make their award. Arbitration agreements sometimes contain express provisions to that effect. The benefit of such clauses depends on the circumstances, because the parties will often have difficulty in making a realistic assessment of the time required to resolve disputes which may arise between them.[110] The use of such clauses is justified where they are confined to particular issues capable of being quickly resolved by the arbitrators.[111] However, they are liable to become pathological where the chosen arbitral institution is unable to enforce them or, in the case of an *ad hoc* arbitration, where the seat of the arbitration prevents rapid, easy access to the courts for the purpose of constituting the arbitral tribunal. The main danger of such clauses stems from the time required to constitute the arbitral tribunal. Certain clauses stipulate that the period of time within which the award is to be made will begin to elapse at a date prior to the constitution of the arbitral tribunal. In that case, any party keen to obstruct the arbitration need only delay its appointment of an arbitrator in order to jeopardize the entire proceedings.[112] The only means of ensuring that such tactics do not prevent the arbitration

---

[107] Cass. 1e civ., June 15, 1994, Sonidep v. Sigmoil, 1995 REV. ARB. 88, 1st decision, and E. Gaillard's note.

[108] Sec. 18, para. 2, of the 1929 Arbitration Act, which applied until April 1, 1999.

[109] Article 1698, paragraph 2, of the Judicial Code, which provides for a flexible approach to the application of the deadline, subject to review by the courts.

[110] On this issue, see also P. Fouchard, note following CA Paris, Jan. 17, 1984, Bloc'h et Fils v. Delatrae Mockfjaerd, 1984 REV. ARB. 498, where the parties had agreed a period of ten days from the appointment of the arbitrators for the making of the award.

[111] On fast-track arbitration, see *supra* para. 1248 and the references cited therein.

[112] A pathological clause occasionally found in practice provides for the period of time for the rendering of the award to run from the date of the arbitration clause.

from taking place is to obtain rapid support from the court responsible for assisting with the constitution of the arbitral tribunal.

1386. — Clauses in which the parties limit the duration of the arbitrators' mission raise two questions: the first concerns the possibility of extending the deadline, and the second concerns the arbitrators' failure to comply with it.

1° Extending the Deadline Fixed by the Parties

1387. — The deadline set by the parties for the delivery of the award can of course be extended by their mutual agreement, which may be express or implied.[113]

In the absence of such an agreement, can the deadline initially fixed by the parties nevertheless be extended? Of course, as they are bound by the parties' agreement, the arbitrators would create grounds on which their award could be set aside if they were to disregard a deadline fixed by the parties. This was established by the French *Cour de cassation* in its 1994 decision in the *Degrémont* case:

> the principle that the time-limit fixed by the parties, either directly or by reference to arbitration rules, cannot be extended by the arbitrators themselves is a requirement of both domestic and international public policy, in that it is inherent in the contractual nature of arbitration.[114]

Where French law has been chosen to govern the procedure, the problem is resolved by Article 1456, paragraph 2 of the New Code of Civil Procedure,[115] which provides that:

---

[113] For an example of the courts finding an implicit agreement between the parties to extend such a deadline, see TGI Paris, réf., May 21, 1984, Vivent v. Reflets de Paris, 1985 REV. ARB. 165, and the commentary by Fouchard, *supra* note 105, at 5; CA Paris, June 26, 1987, Entreprise Guy Broussail v. Marbrerie du Bel Air, 1990 REV. ARB. 905, and observations by B. Moreau; CA Paris, June 8, 1990, Lucas v. Perez Arroyo, 1992 REV. ARB. 625, 2d decision, and observations by J. Pellerin; CA Paris, Jan. 17, 1992, Armand Colin v. Diffusion du Livre scolaire Dilco, 1992 REV. ARB. 625, and observations by J. Pellerin; CA Paris, Feb. 9, 1995, Marchand v. Sogea Atlantique, which requires that a tacit extension result from "positive" and unequivocal acts (1996 REV. ARB. 137, and observations by J. Pellerin); CA Paris, May 19, 1998, *Torno*, *supra* note 101, which, more satisfactorily, holds that participation without reservation in the arbitration after the expiration of the deadline is sufficient.

[114] Cass. 1e civ., June 15, 1994, Communauté urbaine de Casablanca v. Degrémont, 1995 REV. ARB. 88, 2d decision, and E. Gaillard's note; 1994 REV. CRIT. DIP 681, and D. Cohen's note. *See also* CA Paris, Sept. 22, 1995, Dubois et Vanderwalle v. Boots Frites BV, where the same grounds were used to justify the refusal to enforce an award made outside France after the expiry of the three month deadline contained in the arbitration clause (1996 REV. ARB. 100, and E. Gaillard's note).

[115] On the extension provided for in this Article and its application by the courts, see Grandjean, *supra* note 94. On the application of Article 1456, paragraph 2, to an international arbitration governed by French procedural law, see TGI Paris, réf., June 3, 1988, Tribunal arbitral v. Bachmann, 1994 REV. ARB. 538, 2d decision, and observations by P. Fouchard; *see also supra* para. 877.

> [t]he contractual time-limit may be extended either by agreement of the parties
> or, at the request of either of them or of the arbitral tribunal, by the President
> of the *Tribunal de Grande Instance* or, [if the arbitration agreement has
> expressly referred to him as nominating authority,] by the President of the
> *Tribunal de Commerce.*

In the event that the law governing the procedure does not contain a similar provision, it is necessary to determine whether the courts can intervene. In France, it has been suggested that their jurisdiction should be based on Article 1493, paragraph 2, which confers jurisdiction on the President of the Paris Tribunal of First Instance to resolve difficulties with the constitution of the arbitral tribunal in international arbitrations held in France.[116] The intervention of the courts to extend unrealistic time-limits is appropriate, at least where the seat of the arbitration is located in France. However, strictly speaking, this is not a difficulty which concerns the constitution of the arbitral tribunal. In the absence of any statutory provision expressly allowing for such intervention, the courts have had to create such a rule themselves. They have done so by interpreting the intentions of the parties. In a case where neither the parties nor the arbitrators had chosen French law to govern the proceedings, the President of the Paris Tribunal of First Instance retained jurisdiction over a request for an extension of a time-limit on the grounds that the arbitrators had implicitly chosen French law to govern the procedure, which enabled him to base his decision on Article 1456 of the New Code of Civil Procedure.[117] The validity of that approach has been confirmed by several decisions concerning international arbitrations held in France but not expressly governed by French law: in each case,[118] the President of the Paris Tribunal of First Instance applied Article 1456, paragraph 2. That extensive application of Article 1456, paragraph 2 is both legitimate, as the arbitration has a connection with France, and appropriate, because the only consequence of such court intervention is to maintain the effectiveness of an arbitration agreement which has not provided a mechanism for extending the deadline for making the award. It has also been held that each of the arbitrators, acting alone, is entitled to apply for an extension, as they could incur personal liability by allowing the time-limit to expire.[119] This safety net for the parties under French law can prove to be invaluable. However, for it to be successful, the request for an extension must be made prior

---

[116] *See* DE BOISSÉSON, *supra* note 54, at 776.

[117] TGI Paris, réf., Apr. 3, 1985, Application des gaz v. Wonder Corp. of America, 1985 REV. ARB. 170, and the commentary by Fouchard, *supra* note 105. *See also* TGI Paris, réf., May 9, and June 19, 1984, Font Laugière Chimie (Manufactures Jacques Dugniolles) v. Moaco, 1985 REV. ARB. 161, and the commentary by Fouchard, *supra* note 105, at 45 *et seq.*

[118] TGI Paris, réf., Jan. 12, 1988, Omnium de Travaux v. République de Guinée, May 10, 1990 and Oct. 30, 1990, European Country Hotels Ltd. v. Consorts Legrand, July 6, 1990, Irridelco International Corp. v. Ets. Marcel Sebin, 1994 REV. ARB. 538, and observations by P. Fouchard; *see also supra* para. 866.

[119] TGI Paris, réf., Nov. 29, 1989, Omnium de Travaux v. République de Guinée, 1990 REV. ARB. 525, and the commentary by Charles Jarrosson, *Le rôle respectif de l'institution, de l'arbitre et des parties dans l'instance arbitrale, id.* at 381.

to the expiration of the deadline fixed by the parties, as the courts cannot resurrect proceedings once the deadline has passed.[120]

Since the 1996 reform, English law has shared the concerns found in French law, and allows the courts to intervene, where necessary, to extend the deadlines fixed by the parties. Under Section 50 of the 1996 Arbitration Act, the court may, if requested by a party or the arbitral tribunal, and after remedies available in the arbitration have been exhausted, extend the deadline for making an award "if satisfied that a substantial injustice would otherwise be done." This is different from French law[121] in that the court may extend a deadline that has expired (Sec. 50(4)). Similar provisions apply to extensions of deadlines fixed by the parties for the beginning of arbitral proceedings or of other dispute resolution procedures which must be exhausted before arbitral proceedings can begin (Sec. 12). These decisions can only be appealed with leave from the court (Secs. 12(6) and 50(5)).

2° Breach of the Time-Limit Fixed by the Parties

1388. — Under French law, an award made after the expiration of the deadline fixed by the parties for the making of the award may be set aside on the grounds that it was made on the basis of an expired agreement, under Article 1502 1° of the New Code of Civil Procedure. An award made abroad under the same circumstances could be refused enforcement in France on the same grounds.[122] Further, the making of an interim or partial award[123] does not cause the deadline for making subsequent awards to be suspended even where an action is pending to set aside the interim or partial award.[124]

In ICC arbitration, it is important to remember that the award is made not when the draft award is submitted by the arbitrators to the International Court of Arbitration,[125] but after the Court has approved the draft. The award must therefore be approved within the agreed time-limit.[126] However, this did not prevent the ICC, in a case which provides a perfect illustration

---

[120] TGI Paris, réf., Apr. 3, 1985, *Application des gaz, supra* note 117.

[121] *See supra* note 120.

[122] *See* CA Paris, Jan. 17, 1984, *Bloc'h et Fils, supra* note 110; CA Paris, Sept. 22, 1995, *Dubois et Vanderwalle, supra* note 114. See also, in French domestic arbitration, Cass. 2e civ., May 14, 1997, Sofiger v. Touchais, 1998 REV. ARB. 703, and observations by Y. Derains. On the consequences on that part of the proceedings held prior to the expiration of the specified time period, see, in French domestic arbitration, Cass. 2e civ., May 18, 1989, S.a.r.l. Hostin Armes Blanches v. Prieur Sports, 1990 REV. ARB. 903, and observations by B. Moreau.

[123] On these concepts, see *supra* paras. 1359 and 1360.

[124] See, in French domestic arbitration law, Cass. 2e civ., Apr. 5, 1994, S.a.r.l. Hostin Armes Blanches v. Prieur Sports, 1995 REV. ARB. 85, and C. Jarrosson's note; Dalloz, Jur. 363 (1994), and Y. Chartier's note; 1994 RTD COM. 477, and observations by J.-C. Dubarry and E. Loquin; CA Paris, Nov. 10, 1995, Verbiese v. SEE, 1997 REV. ARB. 596, and observations by J. Pellerin.

[125] *See supra* para. 1376.

[126] *See* Cass. 2e civ., Apr. 27, 1981, Ripolin Georget Freitag v. Henry Clark & Sons, 1983 REV. ARB. 105, and observations by T. Bernard. *Comp. with* TGI Paris, May 6, 1976, Clark & Sons Ltd. v. Ripolin Georget, 1977 REV. ARB. 292, and P. Level's note.

of fast-track arbitration, from ensuring that an award was made within nine weeks of the request for arbitration, as required by the parties.[127]

SECTION III
FORM OF THE AWARD

1389. — As a general rule, an arbitral award will be in writing.

Some legal systems expressly require an award to be in writing.[128] This rule exists in French domestic arbitration law,[129] but it has been considered unnecessary to specifically require an award in writing in international arbitration.[130] Oral awards are thus not precluded, but they remain extremely rare, which is fortunate given the evidential difficulties which they are liable to create at the enforcement stage.[131]

Most institutional arbitration rules provide that the award must be made in writing.[132]

1390. — Most arbitration laws and rules also contain provisions concerning the language of the award (§ 1), the reasons for the award (§ 2), dissenting opinions (§ 3), and information which must appear in any award (§ 4). In some legal systems, there are certain formal requirements concerning the filing of the award (§ 5).

§ 1. – Language of the Award

1391. — In principle, the award is made in the language of the arbitral proceedings.[133] The parties could of course agree otherwise and ask for the award to be made in a different language. If and when enforcement is sought, the award may have to be translated into the

---

[127] *See supra* para. 1248.

[128] *See, e.g.,* Art. 1057(2) of the Netherlands Code of Civil Procedure; Art. 1701(4) of the Belgian Judicial Code; Art. 1054(1) of the German ZPO; Art. 31(1) of the UNCITRAL Model Law; Sec. 31 of the 1999 Swedish Arbitration Act. *See also* Art. 48(2) of the 1965 Washington Convention. On the requirement for notarization under Spanish law before the 1988 reform, see Spanish *Tribunal Supremo*, Mar. 28, 1994, ABC v. C. Española, SA, 1994 REV. ARB. 749, and F. Mantilla-Serrano's note.

[129] Art. 1471 of the New Code of Civil Procedure.

[130] *Comp. with* Art. 189, para. 2 of the Swiss Private International Law Statute; Section 52 of the 1996 English Arbitration Act, which requires the award to be in writing unless the parties agree otherwise.

[131] See, for example, in France, Article 1498 of the New Code of Civil Procedure, which requires that the existence of the award be established by the party invoking it.

[132] *See, e.g.,* Art. 32(2) of the UNCITRAL Arbitration Rules; Art. 26.1 of the 1998 LCIA Arbitration Rules; Art. 27(1) of the 1997 AAA International Arbitration Rules. Compare with Articles 24 *et seq.* of the 1998 ICC Arbitration Rules (Arts. 21 *et seq.* of the previous Rules) where the same principle is implicit. *See* DERAINS AND SCHWARTZ, *supra* note 1, at 281 *et seq. See also* Article 32 of the 1999 Rules of the Arbitration Institute of the Stockholm Chamber of Commerce.

[133] On this issue, see *supra* para. 1244.

language of the country where it is to be enforced, under Article IV, paragraph 2 of the 1958 New York Convention.

§ 2. – Reasons for the Award

1392. — Most recent statutes on international arbitration do require the arbitrators to state the reasons for their decision in their award. Such a requirement is found, for example, in the Belgian Judicial Code (Art. 1701(6)), in the Netherlands Code of Civil Procedure, except for awards by consent and awards in quality arbitrations (Art. 1057 (4)(e)), and in the German ZPO (new Article 1054(2) in force as of January 1, 1998). Even in the English tradition, which has long been in favor of not giving grounds for awards, the advantages of stating reasons are gaining recognition in international arbitration.[134] Both English case law[135] and the 1996 Arbitration Act[136] now reflect this trend. Thus, the position most often taken is that adopted in Article VIII of the 1961 European Convention:

> [t]he parties shall be presumed to have agreed that reasons shall be given for the award unless they
> (*a*) either expressly agree that reasons shall not be given; or
> (*b*) have assented to an arbitral procedure under which it is not customary to give reasons for awards, provided that in this case neither party requests before the end of the hearing, or if there has not been a hearing then before the making of the award, that reasons be given.

The approach of the UNCITRAL Model Law is similar, allowing the parties to choose that no reasons be given, but presumes that, in the absence of any indication to the contrary, their intention was that the arbitrators should state the grounds for their award (Art. 31(2)).

Where the choice is left to the parties, their preference may be indicated in the arbitration agreement, or it may result from their choice of a procedural law[137] or of arbitration rules which require reasons to be given.[138] The additional provision in some rules that the grounds for the award need only be given where the parties do not provide otherwise is self-evident. Arbitration rules, by definition, are only binding because the parties have chosen to adopt them, and the parties can agree to depart from them as they see fit.

---

[134] *See, e.g.*, Lord Justice Bingham, *Reasons and Reasons for Reasons: Differences Between a Court Judgment and an Arbitration Award*, 4 ARB. INT'L 141 (1988).

[135] *See* Johan Steyn, *England*, VIII Y.B. COM. ARB. 3, 23 (1983).

[136] *See* Sec. 52(4).

[137] See, for example, in a case where the parties chose French law to govern the proceedings, CA Paris, May 15, 1997, Sermi et Hennion v. Ortec, 1998 REV. ARB. 558, and P. Fouchard's note.

[138] *See, e.g.*, Art. 32(3) of the UNCITRAL Arbitration Rules; Art. 32(1) of the 1999 Rules of the Arbitration Institute of the Stockholm Chamber of Commerce; Art. 26.1 of the 1998 LCIA Arbitration Rules; Art. 27(2) of the 1997 AAA International Arbitration Rules; Art. 25(2) of the 1998 ICC Rules. In ICSID arbitration, the Washington Convention specifies itself that reasons must be given (Art. 48(3)); *see also* Art. 47 of the ICSID Rules.

1393. — Where the procedural law or arbitration rules which the parties may have chosen are silent as to whether reasons are to be given, as was the case with the ICC Rules in force prior to January 1, 1998, will there be a presumption in favor of or against requiring grounds to be stated?[139] The French courts consider that unless the parties agree otherwise, grounds for the award should be given. Thus, in a case concerning an ICC arbitration held in France under the 1975 ICC Rules, the Paris Court of Appeals reviewed whether reasons for the award had been given because:

> since it was not established that, in the absence of any indication in the ICC Rules, the parties or the arbitrators had intended to submit the dispute to a procedural law which does not oblige the arbitrators to state the grounds for the award, that obligation applied.[140]

This solution reflects the parties' expectations, particularly in ICC arbitration, where the scrutiny of the International Court of Arbitration over the draft award submitted by the arbitrators[141] has always implied that the reasons for their decision will be given. This is now explicitly stated in the 1998 Rules, Article 25(2) of which provides that "[t]he Award shall state the reasons upon which it is based."

As a result, virtually all international arbitral awards give reasons, with the exception of certain quality arbitrations.[142]

1394. — In French domestic arbitration, the grounds for the award must be stated.[143] No such requirement exists in French international arbitration law, and the parties therefore have the option of requiring the arbitrators to give reasons. The mere fact that an award contains no reasons does not cause it to violate the French notion of international public policy and make it incapable of being recognized or enforced in France.[144]

---

[139] For a commentary in favor of the adoption of a legislative provision on this question, see Eric Loquin, *Perspectives pour une réforme des voies de recours*, 1992 REV. ARB. 321, 340.

[140] CA Paris, June 16, 1988, Swiss Oil v. Petrogab, 1989 REV. ARB. 309, and C. Jarrosson's approving note; for an English translation, see XVI Y.B. COM. ARB. 133 (1991); CA Paris, Mar. 30, 1995, Fabre v. Espitalier, 1996 REV. ARB. 131, and observations by J. Pellerin; CA Paris, June 20, 1996, PARIS v. Razel, 1996 REV. ARB. 657, and observations by D. Bureau.

[141] *See supra* para. 1376.

[142] *See supra* para. 1392.

[143] Art. 1471 of the New Code of Civil Procedure.

[144] Cass. 1e civ., Nov. 22, 1966, Gerstlé v. Merry Hull, JCP, Ed. G., Pt. II, No. 15,318 (1968), and observations by H. Motulsky; 94 J.D.I. 631 (1967), and B. Goldman's note; 1967 REV. CRIT. DIP 372, and P. Francescakis' note; CA Paris, Mar. 25, 1983, Sorvia v. Weinstein International Disc Corp., 1984 REV. ARB. 363, and J. Robert's note; CA Paris, Jan. 22, 1988, C.F.I.D. v. Ets. A. Arnaud, 1989 REV. ARB. 251, and Y. Derains' note; CA Paris, Nov. 29, 1990, Payart v. Morgan Crucible Co., 1991 REV. ARB. 659, 1st decision, and observations by J. Pellerin; 118 J.D.I. 414 (1991), and P. Kahn's note; CA Paris, June 28, 1991, KFTCIC v. Icori Estero, 1992 REV. ARB. 568, and P. Bellet's note, especially at 571; for an English translation, see 6 INT'L ARB. REP. El (Aug. 1991); CA Paris, Mar. 26, 1992, Société nigérienne des produits pétroliers (SONIDEP) v. Sigmoil Resources N.V., Dalloz, IR 161 and 169 (1992); CA Paris, May 10, 1994, Sheikh Mahfouz Salem Bin Mahfouz v. Al Tayar, 1996 REV. ARB. 66, and C. Jarrosson's note.

The French courts would only censure the failure to give reasons if the law governing the proceedings required reasons to be given,[145] or if the failure to give reasons concealed a violation of due process.[146] In both such cases the award would be set aside or refused enforcement.[147]

1395. — Where the grounds for the award must be stated, that does not mean that they must be well-founded in fact or law. A court reviewing the award to ensure that reasons have been given will not of course review the substantive findings of the award. Thus, even grounds that are clearly wrong will satisfy the requirement that the arbitrators state the reasons for their award.[148] However, the French *Cour de cassation* has held that giving contradictory reasons could be considered as amounting to giving no reasons at all.[149] Nevertheless, a contradiction in the grounds for an award will only be contrary to international public policy if it is "established that the . . . arbitral proceedings were governed by a law requiring that grounds be stated."[150]

The Belgian Courts, on the other hand, have ruled that the potential contradiction between two reasons in the award could not be reviewed by the courts, as it pertained to the merits

---

[145] Cass. 1e civ., Nov. 22, 1966, *Gerstlé, supra* note 144; CA Paris, June 28, 1988, Total Chine v. E.M.H., which sets aside an award for the failure to give reasons where the parties had chosen French law to govern the procedure and where the Court made the somewhat superfluous finding that the parties had specified in their arbitration clause that reasons were to be given in the award (1989 REV. ARB. 328, and J. Pellerin's note).

[146] CA Paris, Apr. 28, 1976, Compagnie d'Armement Maritime (CAM) v. Compagnie Tunisienne de Navigation (COTUNAV), 1977 REV. ARB. 151, and M. Boitard's note; CA Paris, July 11, 1978, Compagnie d'Armement Maritime (CAM) v. Compagnie Tunisienne de Navigation (COTUNAV), 1979 REV. ARB. 258, and M. Boitard's note; Cass. 1e civ., Mar. 18, 1980, Compagnie d'Armement Maritime (CAM) v. Compagnie Tunisienne de Navigation (COTUNAV), 1980 Bull. Civ. I, No. 87; 1980 REV. ARB. 496, and E. Mezger's note; 107 J.D.I. 874 (1980), and E. Loquin's note .

[147] See, even before the 1987 Swiss Private International Law Statute, Fed. Trib., Dec. 12, 1975, Provenda S.A. v. Alimenta S.A., 1977 REV. ARB. 195.

[148] Cass. 1e civ., Jan. 22, 1975, Krebs v. Milton Stern, 1975 REV. ARB. 309, and E. Mezger's note; CA Paris, Feb. 28, 1992, Freyssinet International v. Renardet, 1992 REV. ARB. 649, and observations by D. Cohen.

[149] *See, e.g.,* Cass. 1e civ., Dec. 11, 1979, Elettronica v. Thomson-C.S.F., 1982 REV. ARB. 419, and the commentary by Jean Robert, *La dénaturation par l'arbitre – Réalités et perspectives, id.* at 405. *But see* Cass. 1e civ., Feb. 28, 1995, Société Générale pour l'Industrie v. Ewbank, 1995 REV. ARB. 597, and D. Bureau's note; 1996 RTD COM. 446, and observations by J.-C. Dubarry and E. Loquin; Cass. 2e civ., Oct. 25, 1995, GIE commerçants réunis indépendants v. Multimob, 1996 REV. ARB. 127, and observations by J. Pellerin; CA Paris, June 20, 1996, *Paris, supra* note 140; CA Paris, Dec. 11, 1997, Cubana v. Consavio International Ltd., 1999 REV. ARB. 124, and observations by D. Bureau; CA Paris, Mar. 5, 1998, Forasol v. CISTM, 1999 REV. ARB. 86, and E. Gaillard's note; CA Paris, 1e Ch., Sec. C, Apr. 2, 1998, Compagnie Française d'Etudes et de Construction TECHNIP v. Entreprise Nationale des Engrais et des Produits Phytosanitaires dite ASMIDAL (Algérie), No. 97/6929, unpublished; CA Paris, 1e Ch., Sec. C, Jan. 19, 1999, CIC International Ltd. v. Ministre de la Défense de la République Fédérale d'Allemagne, No. 1998/03375, unpublished.

[150] CA Paris, May 6, 1988, Unijet S.A. v. S.A.R.L. International Business Relations Ltd. (I.B.R.), 1989 REV. ARB. 83, and E. Loquin's note. On this issue, generally, see Jean-Louis Delvolvé, *Essai sur la motivation des sentences arbitrales,* 1989 REV. ARB. 149.

of the dispute.[151] This solution is, in our view, preferable to that accepted in French law, although it would still be extremely rare for the French courts to set aside an award on the basis of the existence of contradictory reasons in the award.[152]

§ 3. – Dissenting Opinions

1396. — Where an award is made by a majority of the arbitrators, an arbitrator in the minority may want to express his or her views as to what the outcome of the dispute should have been, in a document intended for the parties and generally referred to as a dissenting or minority opinion.[153]

In international arbitration, several issues surrounding dissenting opinions need to be distinguished: their admissibility (A), their usefulness (B) and the applicable legal regime (C).

A. – ADMISSIBILITY OF DISSENTING OPINIONS

1397. — Influenced by the practice followed by their courts, lawyers trained in common law systems generally consider the issuance of dissenting opinions to be normal practice.[154] Authors of the civil law tradition, on the other hand, tend to consider dissenting opinions to be inappropriate, if not unlawful.[155]

---

[151] CA Brussels, Jan. 24, 1997, Compagnie Inter-Arabe de Garantie des Investissements (CIAGI) v. Banque Arabe et Internationale d'Investissement (BAII), 1998 REV. ARB. 181, and J. Linsmeau's note, especially at 198; 1997 BULL. ASA 334; XXII Y.B. COM. ARB. 643 (1997) (*upholding* Brussels Tribunal of First Instance, Jan. 25, 1996, 1997 [BELG.] JOURN. TRIB. 6, and G. Block's note), *aff'd*, Belgian *Cour de cassation*, June 5, 1998, CIAGI v. BAII, 1998 BULL. ASA 719, with an introductory note by G. Block at 715; 1998 REV. ARB. 715, and J. Linsmeau's note.

[152] E. Gaillard, note following CA Paris, Mar. 5, 1998, *Forasol, supra* note 149.

[153] A dissenting opinion should be distinguished from a separate or distinct opinion, by which an arbitrator expresses agreement with the decision of the majority, but gives different reasons. Such an opinion is less frequently encountered in arbitration than in certain national courts.

[154] But see REDFERN AND HUNTER, *supra* note 31, at 398, who appear to attach substantial importance to the difficulties to which they believe dissenting opinions may give rise in continental legal systems. *See also infra* paras. 1403 *et seq.*

[155] See, for example, for a disapproving analysis of dissenting opinions in French international arbitration, ROBERT, *supra* note 79, at 310; these remarks were not included in the 6th edition of 1993; Bredin, *supra* note 80, at 79. See also the reservations expressed by DE BOISSÉSON, *supra* note 54, at 802.

1398. — Some civil law commentators[156] have argued that dissenting opinions are prohibited in so far as they constitute a breach of the secrecy of the deliberations provided for in certain domestic arbitration statutes.[157] This argument is unconvincing. First, such domestic arbitration provisions apply only where the parties have expressly chosen them to govern the procedure. Even in that case, a breach of the secrecy of the deliberations may not be considered a ground on which the award can be set aside. For instance, it is the case neither in French domestic law[158] nor, pursuant to Articles 1502 and 1504 of the New Code of Civil Procedure, in French international arbitration law. Second, and more importantly, expressing a dissenting opinion does not necessarily entail breaching the secrecy of the deliberations, provided that the dissenting arbitrator does not reveal the views expressed individually by the other arbitrators.[159]

This latter view represents the dominant trend in civil law jurisdictions which, without actually encouraging dissenting opinions, generally do not consider them to be unlawful.[160] A number of civil law commentators share that view.[161] However, given the controversy which arose during the drafting stage, the authors of the UNCITRAL Model Law preferred to avoid expressly taking sides on this issue.[162]

---

[156] ROBERT, *supra* note 79, at 310. See also, in French domestic arbitration law, C. Jarrosson, note following CA Paris, Oct. 15, 1991, Affichage Giraudy v. Consorts Judlin, 1991 REV. ARB. 643, 648. This argument was raised before the Paris Court of Appeals, although for procedural reasons the court was not required to decide the issue (*see* CA Paris, July 7, 1994, Uzinexportimport Romanian Co. v. Attock Cement Co., 1995 REV. ARB. 107, and S. Jarvin's note; for an English translation, see 10 INT'L ARB. REP. D1 (Feb. 1995)).

[157] *See, e.g.*, Art. 1469 of the French New Code of Civil Procedure.

[158] CA Paris, Mar. 19, 1981, Barre v. Les Solidaires, 1982 REV. ARB. 84, and J. Viatte's note.

[159] See the views of Claude Reymond, in LALIVE, POUDRET, REYMOND, *supra* note 16, at 416–17. As the opinions of the authors of that publication diverge on this question, the views at 416–17 can be attributed to Claude Reymond alone. Article 945 of Quebec's Code of Civil Procedure specifies that the confidentiality of the deliberations does not exclude dissenting or separate opinions. On the freedom for the arbitrators to express minority opinions unless the parties agree otherwise, see Derains, *supra* note 4, at 73 *et seq.*

[160] See, for example, Article 33, paragraph 1 of Spanish Law 36/1988 on Arbitration of December 5, 1988, which states that arbitrators may give dissenting opinions.

[161] See, in Swiss law, Reymond, *supra* note 159; BUCHER AND TSCHANZ, *supra* note 23, ¶ 262; Laurent Levy, *Dissenting Opinions in International Arbitration in Switzerland*, 5 ARB. INT'L 35 (1989); Jacques Werner, *Dissenting Opinions – Beyond Fears*, 9 J. INT'L ARB. 23 (Dec. 1992); P. Schweizer, note following Swiss Fed. Trib., May 11, 1992, D. v. A., 1994 REV. SUISSE DR. INT. ET DR. EUR. 117, 126; in Italian law, RUBINO-SAMMARTANO, *supra* note 39, at 429; in Dutch law, SANDERS AND VAN DEN BERG, *supra* note 32, at 86. For an example of a separate opinion in an *ad hoc* arbitration with its seat in The Hague, see the February 5, 1988 Partial Award on Liability, *Wintershall*, *supra* note 44; for a dissenting opinion in an *ad hoc* arbitration with its seat in Paris, see the December 29, 1993 Award by D.G. Wright, president, P. Mayer and C. Molineaux, arbitrators (C. Molineaux dissenting), Icori Estero S.p.A. v. Kuwait Foreign Trading Contracting & Investment Co., 9 INT'L ARB. REP. A1 (Dec. 1994); for a dissenting opinion of the chairman of an arbitral tribunal in an award made in Switzerland, see the Interim Award in ICC Case No. 3879 (Mar. 5, 1984), by E. Bucher, chairman, P. Bellet and N. Mangård, arbitrators, Westland Helicopters Ltd. v. Arab Organization for Industrialization, 112 J.D.I. 232 (1985); 1989 REV. ARB. 547; for an English translation, see 23 I.L.M. 1071 (1984); XI Y.B. COM. ARB. 127 (1986).

[162] *See* HOLTZMANN AND NEUHAUS, *supra* note 7, at 837. Article 1054 of the ZPO, which entered into force on January 1, 1998, is also silent on the point. On the fact that dissenting opinions are uncommon in Germany, see OTTOARNDT GLOSSNER, COMMERCIAL ARBITRATION IN THE FEDERAL REPUBLIC OF GERMANY 18 (1984).

B. – USEFULNESS OF DISSENTING OPINIONS

1399. — It is sometimes argued, in support of dissenting opinions, that the open criticism of flaws allegedly affecting the arbitral proceedings, or the public expression of differing views on a particular issue, tends to strengthen the legitimacy of the arbitral proceedings and to lead to more thorough reasoning on the part of the majority.[163] It is also suggested that dissenting opinions give some arbitrators or parties cosmetic satisfaction. Rightly or wrongly, dissenting opinions are often felt to be particularly useful in arbitrations where one or more of the parties is a government.[164] For example, the 1965 ICSID Convention specifically allows for dissenting opinions (Art. 48(4)).

1400. — Against dissenting opinions it has been argued that they provide an arbitrator with an easy alternative: instead of pursuing the deliberations so as to reach a unanimous award, arbitrators may prefer not to do so if, by means of a dissenting opinion, they can demonstrate to the party that appointed them that they "defended its interests." Also, dissenting opinions are sometimes thought to encourage bias, as they reveal the views of party-appointed arbitrators. Above all, they are felt to weaken the authority of the award.[165] In many cases, a dissenting opinion is intended by its author as a critique of the majority decision, setting the scene for an action to set the award aside. For example, the dissenting opinion issued by the minority arbitrator in the *Klöckner* case[166] was the basis of the subsequent setting aside of the award by an *ad hoc* committee.[167] However, the practice of issuing dissenting opinions is successfully implemented in the vast majority of cases, and should not be prohibited solely because it is liable to be abused. Besides, such a prohibition would be futile in that the only remedy would be the personal liability of the dissenting arbitrator, as opposed to any effect on the award itself. Indeed, it would be paradoxical, to say the least, if the attitude of the arbitrator representing the minority view were to affect the validity of the award to which he or she is opposed.

1401. — Although it would be unfortunate for dissenting opinions to become common practice, one should not, on the other hand, overestimate their importance. In particular, it

---

[163] See, for example, the book review by Laurent Lévy and William W. Park, *The French Law of Arbitration by Jean Robert and Thomas E. Carbonneau*, 2 ARB. INT'L 266 (1986); Levy, *supra* note 161, at 39.

[164] *See, e.g.,* Levy, *supra* note 161, at 38.

[165] *See, e.g.,* DE BOISSÉSON, *supra* note 54, at 802.

[166] Award of October 21, 1983 by E. Jimenez de Arechaga, president, W.D. Rogers and D. Schmidt, arbitrators (D. Schmidt dissenting), in ICSID Case No. ARB/81/2, Klöckner Industrie-Anlagen GmbH v. United Republic of Cameroon, 111 J.D.I. 409 (1984), and observations by E. Gaillard; the dissenting opinion by M.-D. Schmidt appears at 441; for an English translation, see 1 J. INT'L ARB. 145 and 332 (1984); X Y.B. COM. ARB. 71 (1985); 2 ICSID REP. 9 and 77 (1994).

[167] See the *Ad hoc* Committee Decision of May 3, 1985, by P. Lalive, president, A.-L. Cocheri and I. Seidl-Hohenveldern, arbitrators, 114 J.D.I. 163 (1987), and observations by E. Gaillard at 184; for an English translation, see 1 ICSID REV. – FOREIGN INV. L.J. 89 (1986); XI Y.B. COM. ARB. 162 (1986); 2 ICSID REP. 95 (1994).

would not be appropriate to give too much consideration to the dissenting arbitrator's views on the merits of the dispute in an action to set aside the award rendered by the majority.

Those who believe in the effectiveness of professional codes of ethics suggest that the practice of giving dissenting opinions should be regulated only by ethical rules of conduct drawn up for use by arbitrators.[168]

1402. — The various institutional arbitration rules deal with dissenting opinions in different ways.

The UNCITRAL Model Law does not take sides on the issue. Neither do the Rules of the LCIA (Art. 26), the AAA (Art. 27 of the International Arbitration Rules) or the Euro-Arab Chambers of Commerce. This does not amount to a rejection of the practice of issuing dissenting opinions. It simply leaves the issue to be resolved either by the law governing the arbitral proceedings, by custom, or by the arbitration agreement.

Article 47, paragraph 3 of the ICSID Rules, which reproduces Article 48, paragraph 4 of the Washington Convention, provides that "[a]ny member of the Tribunal may attach his individual opinion to the award, whether he dissents from the majority or not, or a statement of his dissent."[169] The Rules of the Arbitration Institute of the Stockholm Chamber of Commerce likewise allow for dissenting opinions (Art. 32(4) of the 1999 Rules). By contrast, the arbitration rules of the Franco-German Chamber of Commerce and Industry (COFACI) expressly prohibit arbitrators from giving dissenting opinions (Art. 21.4).

The ICC Rules of Arbitration have evolved on this point. In the version in force prior to January 1, 1998, the Internal Rules of the International Court of Arbitration, which formed an annex to the ICC Rules, provided in Article 17 that the Court "pays particular attention to the respect of . . . the mandatory rules of the place of arbitration, notably with regard to . . . the admissibility of dissenting opinions." Since January 1, 1998, Article 6 of the Internal Rules has replaced the previous Article 17, and maintains the earlier rule, but without referring to the particular case of dissenting opinions. This reflects the fact that the ICC Rules are not hostile to the principle of dissenting opinions, and no longer even underline the fact that, in certain legal systems, such opinions can jeopardize the validity of the award. In principle, if a dissenting opinion has been prepared, it is submitted to the Court in draft form together with the draft award made by the majority, and the Court will then decide, on the basis of the requirements of the applicable law, whether to send the dissenting

---

[168] See, for example, Levy, *supra* note 161, at 42, and the draft of the International Bar Association's Code of Ethics for International Arbitrators, which provides that the dissenting arbitrator "should not breach the confidentiality of the deliberations" of the tribunal but that he or she "retains the right . . . to draw the attention of the parties to any fundamental procedural irregularity" (cited by Levy, *id.*). *See also* Canon VI of the Code of Ethics for Arbitrators in Commercial Disputes, jointly adopted by the AAA and the American Bar Association in 1977 (X Y.B. COM. ARB. 132 (1985), with an introductory note by Howard M. Holtzmann at 131).

[169] For an example of an award stated to have been made "unanimously," but which was accompanied by two individual opinions, see the Award dated February 21, 1997 in ICSID Case No. ARB/93/1, American Manufacturing & Trading, Inc. v. Republic of Zaire, 125 J.D.I. 243 (1998), and observations by E. Gaillard; for an English translation, see XXII Y.B. COM. ARB. 60 (1997); 36 I.L.M. 1531 (1997); 12 INT'L ARB. REP. A1 (Apr. 1997).

opinion to the parties.[170] In practice, the Court cannot prevent an arbitrator from sending a dissenting opinion directly to the parties, although any court reviewing the award would not then consider the dissenting opinion as forming part of the award.[171] In 1998, of the 242 awards submitted to the International Court of Arbitration, 15 were accompanied by a dissenting opinion.[172]

C. – THE LEGAL REGIME GOVERNING DISSENTING OPINIONS

1403. — A dissenting opinion can only be issued when the majority has already made the decision which constitutes the award. Until then, any document issued by the minority arbitrator can only be treated as part of the deliberations. However, once the majority decision has been reached, it is preferable for the author of the dissenting opinion to communicate a draft to the other arbitrators so as to enable them to discuss the arguments put forward in it. The award made by the majority could then be issued after the dissenting opinion, or at least, after the draft dissenting opinion.[173] Admittedly, unlike a judge issuing a separate opinion within a permanent court such as the International Court of Justice, the dissenting arbitrator will generally be less inclined to follow such a procedure.[174]

1404. — As regards the legal nature of a dissenting opinion, authors generally conclude from the fact that the award is rendered by a majority that the dissenting opinion is not part of the award.[175] That analysis is correct, except where the arbitration rules chosen by the parties or the law applicable to the procedure provide otherwise. In ICC arbitration, the dissenting opinion is not examined by the International Court of Arbitration under Article 27 of the Rules (Art. 21 of the previous Rules), as the Court takes the dissenting opinion into account for purposes of information only.[176] In other words, the dissenting opinion does not

---

[170] On the procedure followed by the ICC, see CRAIG, PARK, PAULSSON, *supra* note 31, at 332 *et seq.*; D. Hascher, observations following the questionnaire in ICC Case No. 5082, *supra* note 69, at 1085; Martin Hunter, *Final Report on Dissenting and Separate Opinions*, ICC BULLETIN, Vol. 2, No. 1, at 32 (1991); DERAINS AND SCHWARTZ, *supra* note 1, at 285–86.

[171] *See infra* para. 1404.

[172] *See* Gélinas, *supra* note 65. The number of dissenting opinions in previous years was 20 in 1994 (of 182 awards) (*see* Dominique Hascher, *Scrutiny of Draft Awards by the Court: 1994 Overview*, ICC BULLETIN, Vol. 6, No. 1, at 51 (1995)); 12 in 1995 (of 203 awards) (*see* Dominique Hascher, *Scrutiny of Draft Awards by the Court – 1995 Overview*, ICC BULLETIN, Vol, 7, No. 1, at 14 (1996)); 19 in 1996 (of 217 awards) (*see* Dominique Hascher, *Scrutiny of Draft Awards by the Court – 1996 Overview*, ICC BULLETIN, Vol. 8, No. 1, at 17 (1997)); 3 in 1997 (of the 227 awards) (*see* Dominique Hascher, *The Application of the Rules by the Court – 1997 Overview*, ICC BULLETIN, Vol. 9, No. 1, at 12 (1998)).

[173] *See* Reymond, *supra* note 161, at 417.

[174] For an example, see the response by the president of the arbitral tribunal to a dissenting opinion in ICSID Case No. ARB/82/1, Société Ouest Africaine des Bétons Industriels v. State of Senegal, 117 J.D.I. 209 (1990); 6 ICSID REV. – FOREIGN INV. L.J. 289 (1991).

[175] *See, e.g.,* ROBERT, *supra* note 79; DE BOISSÉSON, *supra* note 54, at 801; Reymond, *supra* note 161, at 417.

[176] Hascher, *supra* note 65.

form part of the award.[177] In any event, the issue is of little consequence in practice, as the dissenting opinion will, in proceedings reviewing the award, have no effect on the award's validity or enforceability.[178] On the other hand, it is preferable for the dissenting opinion to accompany the award when the latter is communicated to the parties, or if it is filed with a court or even published.[179] However, it will not be considered unlawful to disregard the dissenting opinion. As the Swiss Federal Tribunal rightly observed,

> the dissenting opinion is not part of the award. Unless the arbitration agreement so provides or the majority agrees otherwise, the minority arbitrator cannot require it to be attached to the award or communicated to the parties together with the award . . . . The dissenting opinion is separate from the award; it affects neither the reasons nor the result. Consequently, any procedural flaws with regard to its drafting or communication will have no effect on the award.[180]

1405. — In an action to set aside or resist enforcement of the award, a dissenting opinion, regardless of whether or not it was permitted by the arbitration rules or by the law of the seat, has no authority except as an element of fact. Thus, if the dissenting arbitrator states that a procedural breach was committed—for example, that a document was sent by one party to the arbitral tribunal but was not communicated to the other party—that is simply a fact which a court may take into consideration as evidence, but to which it is not obliged to attribute special importance. Both the dissenting arbitrator's assessment of the facts of the case and the legal reasoning used have no particular authority. In this respect, the minority opinion will not affect the outcome of an action against the award made by the majority, especially where, as is usually the case, no review of the merits can take place in the context of that action.

§ 4. – Information Which Must Appear in the Award

1406. — Failing agreement between the parties, some legal systems leave it to the arbitrators or, in practice, to the applicable arbitration rules to decide what information must be included in the award. This is the case in French law on international arbitration. In French domestic arbitration,

---

[177] See the October 17, 1980 decision of the Geneva Court of Justice, unpublished, cited by Levy, *supra* note 161, at 40.

[178] *See* Levy, *supra* note 161, at 40.

[179] On the confidentiality of awards, see *infra* para. 1412.

[180] Fed. Trib., May 11, 1992, D. v. A., 1992 BULL. ASA 381, 386; 1994 REV. SUISSE DR. INT. ET DR. EUR. 117, and the commentary by P. Schweizer.

[t]he arbitral award shall indicate:
- the names of the arbitrators who made it;
- its date;
- the place where it was made;
- the last names, first names or denomination of the parties, as well as their domicile or corporate headquarters;
- if applicable, the names of the counsel or other persons who represented or assisted the parties.[181]

The award must be signed by all the arbitrators or, "if a minority among them refuses to sign it, the others shall mention the fact."[182] Although French international arbitration law makes no reference to those provisions, the parties may nevertheless choose to apply them by having French law govern the procedure. In any case, the requirements contained in those provisions are generally observed in international arbitration practice. Some of them, such as the identification of the parties and the arbitrators, as well as the signature of the award by a majority of the latter, are matters of common sense. To disregard them could create difficulties in enforcing the award, if only on a practical level.[183] However, it is important to note that if one or other of those items were omitted, that alone would not invalidate an award made in France in an international arbitration.[184] In a domestic arbitration, an action against the award based on the claim that the name of one of the parties was incomplete and hence incorrect was held to be inadmissible, as such a case was not provided for by Article 1484 of the New Code of Civil Procedure.[185] The same would necessarily apply in French international arbitration law.

Some legal systems do explicitly require that similar details be included in international arbitral awards, although they do not provide that the failure to do so will constitute a ground on which the award can be set aside.[186]

---

[181] Art. 1472 of the French New Code of Civil Procedure. On the refusal, in French domestic arbitration law, to set aside an award that did not specify a party's forename, see CA Paris, June 28, 1991, Boumeddane v. Jardin, 1992 REV. ARB. 633, and observations by J. Pellerin.

[182] Art. 1473 of the French New Code of Civil Procedure. On the setting aside, in French domestic arbitration law, of an award which did not include an arbitrator's signature and did not refer to his refusal to sign, see CA Paris, Oct. 27, 1988, Proux v. Guerton, 1990 REV. ARB. 908, and observations by B. Moreau. Compare with CA Paris, July 5, 1990, Uni-Inter v. Maillard, which held a statement that the arbitrators were deciding by majority vote to be sufficient (1991 REV. ARB. 359, and observations by B. Moreau) and CA Paris, October 15, 1991, *Affichage Giraudy, supra* note 156, which held that it was not necessary to give the reasons for an arbitrator's refusal to sign an award for the requirements of Article 1473 to be satisfied.

[183] On the case law which wrongly refuses to characterize as awards documents where certain formal requirements are not complied with, see *supra* para. 1352.

[184] See Articles 1502 and 1504 of the French New Code of Civil Procedure, which differ on this point from the French domestic law provisions at Article 1484 5°.

[185] CA Paris, Mar. 22, 1985, Ets. Crucke v. Frahuil, 1987 REV. ARB. 78, and observations by B. Moreau.

[186] *See* Arts. 1057 and 1065 of the Netherlands Code of Civil Procedure; Sec. 52 of the 1996 English Arbitration Act.

1407. — Where the procedural law is silent on this question, arbitral institutions will have a free rein. The rules of most institutions contain provisions concerning the date and the signature of the award, and the place where it was made.[187]

A. – DATE OF THE AWARD

1408. — Arbitration rules and legislation do not always contain an explicit requirement that the date of the award be specified.[188] However, the date is particularly important because "[o]nce it is made, the arbitral award is *res judicata* in relation to the dispute it resolves."[189]

B. – SIGNATURE OF THE ARBITRATORS

1409. — Where the decision is not unanimous, one or more of the arbitrators may refuse to sign the award. As they could hardly allow such a refusal to obstruct the arbitration, all institutional arbitration rules enable the majority to overcome that difficulty, subject to certain conditions. The UNCITRAL Rules (Art. 32(4)), the LCIA Rules (Art. 26.4 of the 1998 Rules), and the AAA International Rules (Art. 26(1) of the 1997 Rules) provide that in such cases the reason for the arbitrator's failure to sign should be stated in the award. Under the Rules of the Arbitration Institute of the Stockholm Chamber of Commerce, the award must contain the confirmation by the remaining arbitrators that the arbitrator whose signature is missing took part in the deliberations.[190] In French international arbitration law, the signatures of a majority of the arbitrators is sufficient, although the requirements discussed above reflect good practice and should be systematically followed. Some legal systems have taken a less formal approach: Swiss law, for example, provides that "[t]he signature of the presiding arbitrator shall suffice."[191] Such a position would only be acceptable in French law if agreed by the parties, directly or by reference to arbitration rules.

---

[187] *See, e.g.*, Art. 32 of the UNCITRAL Arbitration Rules; Art. 25(3) of the 1998 ICC Arbitration Rules (Art. 22 of the previous Rules); Art. 32(1) of the 1999 Rules of the Arbitration Institute of the Stockholm Chamber of Commerce; Art. 27 of the 1997 AAA International Arbitration Rules; Art. 26 of the 1998 LCIA Arbitration Rules.

[188] For such a requirement, see, for example, Section 52(5) of the 1996 English Arbitration Act.

[189] See the reference in Article 1500 of the New Code of Civil Procedure to Article 1476 of the same Code. On this issue, generally, see *infra* para. 1419.

[190] Art. 32(1) of the 1999 Rules. The International Arbitration Rules of the AAA, as revised in 1997, remove the requirement that arbitrators attach a declaration to their award stating that a colleague who did not sign was given the opportunity to do so (Art. 28(3) of the 1993 Rules).

[191] Art. 189, para. 2, *in fine* of the Swiss Private International Law Statute. This is also possible under the 1999 Swedish Arbitration Act if the parties have so agreed (Sec. 32, para. 1).

As held by the Paris Court of Appeals in a 1997 decision regarding an award made under the ICC Rules, the fact that the arbitrators did not sign the award on the same day is not a ground for setting aside the award or refusing to enforce it.[192]

C. – PLACE WHERE THE AWARD IS MADE

1410. — In international arbitration, the place where the award is made must be mentioned in the award only if the parties have specified, either directly or by reference to arbitration rules, that it should be included. This raises a question as to whether the award should necessarily be made at the place of the seat of the arbitration. Some commentators consider that it should, suggesting that if the award were to be made elsewhere, the seat of the arbitration might move as a result. This would have a number of consequences, particularly with regard to the law applicable to the proceedings, access to the courts for an action to set aside, and the applicability of the 1958 New York Convention.[193] In fact, however, the seat of the arbitration depends on the choice made by the parties or, in the absence of such a choice, by the arbitral institution or the arbitrators. It cannot depend on the place where, perhaps for reasons of convenience, the award is made.[194] The real issue is whether the arbitrators are required, given that a particular place has been fixed as the seat of the arbitration, to make the award in that place, and if so, what would be the consequences of their making the award elsewhere. In legal systems which do not specifically address this point, such as French law, the most liberal approach should be adopted. The arbitrators will only be obliged to make the award in a specific place if that is the intention of the parties. That will be the case in particular where the arbitration rules chosen by the parties provide for the award to be made in a certain place. For example, Article 16, paragraph 4 of the UNCITRAL Arbitration Rules, adopted in 1976, provides that the award must be made at the place of the seat of the arbitration. By contrast, the ICC Rules of Arbitration state that "the arbitral award shall be deemed to be made at the place of the arbitration proceedings" as fixed by the parties or by the Court (Art. 25(3), replacing Art. 22 of the previous Rules), it being specified that the arbitral tribunal "may deliberate at any location it considers appropriate" (Art. 14(3)). The trend in recent arbitration rules is to follow this approach. For example, the 1999 version of the Arbitration Rules of the

---

[192] CA Paris, June 17, 1997, Eiffage v. Butec, 1997 REV. ARB. 583, and observations by D. Bureau.

[193] *See, e.g.,* REDFERN AND HUNTER, *supra* note 31, at 304.

[194] *See* CA Versailles, 1e Ch., 1e Sec., Jan. 14, 1987, Chimimportexport v. Tournant Thierry, No. 7298/85, unpublished. In this case, the award contained the words "done in Brussels," although the parties had agreed on a seat in Paris. The award was treated as having been made in France for the purposes of actions to set aside. See also CA Paris, Sept. 22, 1995, *Dubois et Vanderwalle, supra* note 114, which held the fact that the award was signed by an arbitrator in France to be of no consequence, and determined the seat of the arbitration on the basis, in particular, of the organization responsible for appointing the arbitrators; CA Paris, Oct. 28, 1997, Procédés de préfabrication pour le béton v. Libye, 1998 REV. ARB. 399, and B. Leurent's note; in French domestic arbitration, see CA Paris, Jan. 11, 1996, Algotherm v. DEP, 1996 REV. ARB. 100, and E. Gaillard's note. On this issue, generally, see *infra* para. 1590, and on the uncertainties of English law on this point prior to the 1996 reform, see *infra* para. 1593.

Arbitration Institute of the Stockholm Chamber of Commerce has been modified to that effect (Art. 32(1), replacing Art. 28(1) of the 1988 Rules). The UNCITRAL Model Law contains a similar provision.[195]

§ 5. – Recipients of the Award

1411. — The award is communicated to the parties directly by the arbitrators or, if the arbitration rules so provide, via the arbitral institution.[196]

In France, there is no requirement that the award be filed with any judicial authority, unlike in Switzerland, for example, in the case of arbitrations governed by the 1969 *Concordat*,[197] in Belgium (Art. 1702, para. 2 of the Judicial Code), and in the Netherlands (Art. 1058 of the Code of Civil Procedure[198]). It is only when the recognition or enforcement of an award is sought in France that it becomes necessary to establish the existence of the award by producing the original award or a certified copy (Art. 1499 of the New Code of Civil Procedure). However, in practice, it is not unusual for a copy of the award to be filed with the clerk of the Tribunal of First Instance.[199]

1412. — It is generally considered that the arbitral award, like the existence of the arbitral proceedings, is confidential. The confidentiality of both the proceedings and the award is of course one of the attractions of arbitration in the eyes of arbitration users. It is expressly endorsed by the UNCITRAL Arbitration Rules, which provide that "[t]he award may be made public only with the consent of both parties."[200] The 1965 ICSID Convention and the ICSID Arbitration Rules likewise prohibit the Centre from publishing the award without the consent of the parties.[201] Some arbitral awards refer to the principle of confidentiality, occasionally adding qualifications.[202] The principle is not threatened by the fact that anonymous extracts from awards may be published, as is the case in the *Yearbook*

---

[195] *See* Art. 31(3), *in fine*. *See also* Art. 1693, paragraph 1, *in fine* of the Belgian Judicial Code (Law of May 19, 1998).

[196] *See, e.g.*, Art. 28(1) of the 1998 ICC Arbitration Rules (Art. 23(1) of the previous Rules); Art. 26.5 of the 1998 LCIA Arbitration Rules; Art. 27(5) of the 1997 AAA International Arbitration Rules; Art. 48 of the ICSID Arbitration Rules.

[197] Art. 35, paras. 1 and 5; under the Swiss Private International Law Statute, filing the award with the court is optional (Art. 193, para. 1).

[198] On the fact that, in the Netherlands, the deposit of an award is not a condition precedent to a request for enforcement or an application to set aside, see SANDERS AND VAN DEN BERG, *supra* note 32.

[199] On the reasons for the filing of these awards in the absence of an application for enforcement, see SOPHIE CRÉPIN, LES SENTENCES ARBITRALES DEVANT LE JUGE FRANÇAIS ¶¶ 138 *et seq.* (1995).

[200] Art. 32(5). *Comp. with* Art. 27(4) of the 1997 AAA International Arbitration Rules.

[201] *See* Art. 48(5) of the Convention and Art. 48(4) of the Arbitration Rules.

[202] *See, e.g.*, ICC Award No. 6931 (Geneva, 1992), which, while refusing to grant the party's request in the case being heard, did not rule out the possibility of publishing the award by way of compensation for defamation or passing-off (Austrian party v. French party, 121 J.D.I. 1064 (1994), and observations by Y. Derains).

Commercial Arbitration and the *Journal du Droit International*, particularly for ICC and ICSID awards.[203]

On the other hand, the award will become public if court proceedings are initiated concerning its validity or enforcement. In addition, the only remedy available where a party breaches confidentiality will be damages. That involves establishing not only the source and unlawful nature of the disclosure, but also the existence of resulting loss, which will never be easy.[204] Nevertheless, the principle remains intact. It was reiterated in a 1986 decision by the Paris Court of Appeals in a case where an action to set aside an award made in England was brought before the French courts, which clearly had no jurisdiction, so as to allow "a public debate on facts which should have remained confidential" to take place. That breach of confidentiality led to a substantial award of damages against the party at fault, and the Court observed that "it is inherent in the nature of arbitral proceedings that the utmost confidentiality should be maintained in resolving private disputes as both parties had agreed."[205] The principle of confidentiality was enforced in even harsher terms on September 10, 1998 by the Stockholm City Court in the *Bulbank* matter. In this case, the attorneys of the party which obtained a favorable award on jurisdiction from an arbitral tribunal sitting in Stockholm published the award without the consent of the other side. The other party demanded that the arbitration proceedings be discontinued because of that publication. The arbitral tribunal rejected the argument and went on to make an award on the merits. This award was held invalid by the Stockholm City Court on the grounds of the breach of confidentiality which occurred in the proceedings. This decision was unquestionably too severe and has been rightly reversed by the Svea Court of Appeals on

---

[203] On the gradual establishment of arbitral case law, see *supra* paras. 371 *et seq.*

[204] See the December 9, 1983 Decision Regarding Provisional Measures in ICSID Case No. ARB/81/1, Amco Asia Corp. v. Republic of Indonesia, where the confidentiality issue was decided by an ICSID arbitral tribunal composed of B. Goldman, president, E. Rubin and I. Foighel, arbitrators (24 I.L.M. 365 (1985); XI Y.B. COM. ARB. 159 (1986); 1 ICSID REP. 410 (1993)).

[205] CA Paris, Feb. 18, 1986, Aïta v. Ojjeh, 1986 REV. ARB. 583, and G. Flécheux's note; Dalloz, Jur. 339 (1987). On this issue, generally, see Emmanuel Gaillard, *Le principe de confidentialité de l'arbitrage commercial international*, Dalloz, Chron. 153 (1987); Jean-Louis Delvolvé, *Vraies et fausses confidences ou les petits et les grands secrets de l'arbitrage*, 1996 REV. ARB. 373. *See also* Jan A.S. Paulsson and Nigel Rawding, *The Trouble with Confidentiality*, ICC BULLETIN, Vol. 5, No. 1, at 48 (1994). On the limits of confidentiality, see in Australian law, High Court of Australia, Apr. 7, 1995, Esso Australia Resources Ltd. v. Plowman, 10 INT'L ARB. REP. A1 (May 1995), and the commentary by Marcus S. Jacobs, *Arbitration Confidentiality in Australia*, 10 INT'L ARB. REP. 21 (July 1995); 11 ARB. INT'L 235 (1995); 6 WORLD ARB. & MED. REP. 133 (1995); XXI Y.B. COM. ARB. 137 (1996); for a French translation, see 1996 REV. ARB. 539, and D. Kapelink-Klinger's note; *see also* Edouard Bertrand, *Confidentialité de l'arbitrage: évolution ou mutation après l'affaire Esso/BHP v Plowman/The Confidentiality of Arbitration: Evolution or Mutation Following Esso/BHP vs. Plowman*, 1996 INT'L BUS. L.J.169. But see, in England, Ali Shipping Corp. v. Shipyard Trogir, [1998] 2 All E.R. 136; [1999] 1 W.L.R. 314; [1998] 1 Lloyd's Rep. 711 (C.A. 1997); for a French translation, see 1998 REV. ARB. 579, and L. Burger's note; *see also* Peter Sheridan, *Privacy and Confidentiality – Recent Developments: The Divergence Between English and Australian Law Confirmed*, 1 INT'L ARB. L. REV. 171 (1998). On the question of whether documents obtained in an arbitration proceeding, or the award itself, can be used in a related court proceeding, see, in English law, Hassneh Insurance Co. of Israel v. Stuart J. Mew, [1993] 2 Lloyd's Rep. 243; XIX Y.B. COM. ARB. 223 (1994) (High Ct., Q.B. (Com. Ct.) 1992); on this issue, generally, see 11 ARB. INT'L 231 (1995) (Special issue on the Confidentiality of International Commercial Arbitration).

March 30, 1999.[206] The incident nevertheless shows that the confidentiality of the arbitral process is not to be taken lightly.

SECTION IV
IMMEDIATE EFFECTS OF THE AWARD

1413. — The making of the arbitral award has a number of immediate effects. It terminates the arbitrators' jurisdiction over the dispute which they have resolved (§ 1) and marks the point in time from which the award is *res judicata* with regard to that dispute (§ 2). From that time onwards, the award can be voluntarily performed by the parties. However, to obtain recognition or enforcement of the award, a number of formalities must be satisfied. These will be addressed as part of our examination of actions to enforce and set aside arbitral awards.[207]

§ 1. – Termination of the Arbitrators' Jurisdiction

1414. — Certain recent statutes on international arbitration contain provisions empowering the arbitrators to interpret the award, correct clerical errors, issue an additional award on claims which may have been omitted, and sometimes modify or cancel an award obtained by fraud. Provisions on some or all of these issues are found in the UNCITRAL Model Law (Art. 33), the 1986 Netherlands Arbitration Act (Arts. 1060 and 1061 of the Code of Civil Procedure), the 1996 English Arbitration Act (Sec. 57), the 1997 German arbitration statute (Art. 1058 of the ZPO), the 1998 Belgian arbitration statute (new Art. 1702 bis of the Judicial Code) and the 1999 Swedish Arbitration Act (Sec. 32). Other legal systems, including French international arbitration law,[208] are silent, leaving these questions to the parties who are free to select an appropriate procedural law or arbitration rules.[209]

Even where not provided for in the applicable procedural law, an arbitral award should certainly be considered as ending the arbitrators' jurisdiction over the dispute it resolves.

---

[206] Svea Ct. of App., Mar. 30, 1999, A.I. Trade Finance Inc. v. Bulgarian Foreign Trade Bank Ltd., 14 INT'L ARB. REP. A1 (Apr. 1999). On the City Court decision, see Constantine Partasides, *Bad News from Stockholm: Bulbank and Confidentiality Ad Absurdum*, 13 INT'L ARB. REP. 20 (Dec. 1998).

[207] On this issue, see *infra* paras. 1560 *et seq.*

[208] Article 1475 of the New Code of Civil Procedure provides that in French domestic arbitration "the award brings an end to the arbitrator's jurisdiction over the dispute it resolves" but that "the arbitrator has the power to interpret the award, to rectify clerical errors and omissions affecting it and to complete it, where he or she has failed to rule on a claim". For an illustration, see CA Paris, Apr. 18, 1991, Letierce v. Stolz, 1992 REV. ARB. 631, and observations by J. Pellerin. In international arbitration, Article 1500 of the New Code of Civil Procedure makes no reference to Article 1475.

[209] On this issue, generally, see Nathalie Garnier, *Interpréter, rectifier et compléter les sentences arbitrales internationales*, 1995 REV. ARB. 565; David D. Caron and Lucy F. Reed, *Post Award Proceedings Under the UNCITRAL Arbitration Rules*, 11 ARB. INT'L 429 (1995); Andrew N. Vollmer and Angela J. Bedford, *Post-Award Arbitral Proceedings*, 15 J. INT'L ARB. 37 (Mar. 1998).

That results from the nature of the agreement between the parties and the arbitral tribunal to resolve the dispute.[210] On the other hand, the absence of provisions of French law applicable to international arbitration is particularly unfortunate when a question arises as to the exceptions that can be made to the principle that the award terminates the arbitrators' jurisdiction. There is an equally great need in international arbitration to provide the parties with a mechanism enabling them to obtain the interpretation of the award (A), to correct clerical errors (B), or even to have the award extended to cover issues which the arbitrators have failed to address (C). The same is true of the possibility of requesting that the arbitrators withdraw an award obtained by fraud (D).

A. – INTERPRETATION OF THE AWARD

1415. — The interpretation of an arbitral award is only really helpful where the ruling, which is generally presented in the form of an order, is so ambiguous that the parties could legitimately disagree as to its meaning. By contrast, any obscurity or ambiguity in the grounds for the decision does not warrant a request for interpretation of the award. It is probably for that reason that institutional arbitration rules have traditionally considered it unnecessary to provide for the possibility of asking the arbitral tribunal to interpret their award. However, in 1976, the UNCITRAL Rules so provided at Article 35. This provision sets out the relevant time-limits (thirty days from receipt of the award within which to submit the request, and forty-five days from receipt of the request to reply) and indicates that the party submitting the request must notify the other party. Once the interpretation has been given, it forms part of the award.[211] The same system is now also provided for at Article 30 of the AAA International Arbitration Rules, although the deadline for the arbitrators' reply is reduced to thirty days. A similar mechanism exists in ICSID arbitration,[212] but the request is not subject to a deadline, and if the request cannot be submitted to the initial arbitral tribunal, it is even possible to constitute a new tribunal for that purpose.[213] Similarly, and in contrast to the previous Rules, the revised ICC Rules which entered into force on January 1, 1998 allow the parties to seek the interpretation of an award within 30 days of it being made

---

[210] In Swiss law, see Fed. Trib., Nov. 1, 1996, P.v. A., 1997 BULL. ASA 116.

[211] For an example of the application of this principle, see the May 31, 1988 *ad hoc* Award, Wintershall A.G. v. Government of Qatar, 28 I.L.M. 795 (1989); XV Y.B. COM. ARB. 30 (1990), especially ¶ 89 at 57.

[212] *See* Art. 50 of the Washington Convention; Arts. 50 and 51 of the ICSID Arbitration Rules.

[213] Art. 50(2) of the Washington Convention. On the issue of the interpretation of awards, generally, see Jean-François Poudret, *L'interprétation des sentences arbitrales (étude de droit suisse et de droit comparé), in* RECUEIL DE TRAVAUX SUISSES SUR L'ARBITRAGE INTERNATIONAL 269 (1984); Roger Perrot, *L'interprétation des sentences arbitrales*, 1969 REV. ARB. 7; Robert D.A. Knutson, *The Interpretation of Arbitral Awards – When is a Final Award not Final?*, 11 J. INT'L ARB. 99 (June 1994); Pierre-Yves Gunter, *L'interprétation de la Sentence: examen de quelques questions à la lumière d'un cas réel*, 1996 BULL. ASA 574. For an example of interpretation performed by a second arbitral tribunal, see ICC Award No. 6233 (1992), Owner of company registered in Lebanon v. African state, XX Y.B. COM. ARB. 58 (1995).

(Art. 29).[214] In contrast, the LCIA rules allow corrections of the award, but not its interpretation.[215]

Arbitration statutes now provide for the possibility of having the award interpreted by the arbitral tribunal. The UNCITRAL Model Law was the first to do so (Art. 33),[216] followed by the Belgian and the Swedish legislatures in 1998 and 1999 respectively.[217] The 1996 English Arbitration Act, like the LCIA Rules, only provides for the correction and not for the interpretation of the awards.[218]

B. – CORRECTING CLERICAL ERRORS

1416. — In the absence of any corrective mechanism, the presence of a clerical error in the arbitrators' ruling can create serious problems. One need only consider the example of an error in calculating the total award of damages to appreciate the absurdity of the situation where a party is definitively ordered by the award to pay a sum higher or lower than that intended by the arbitral tribunal.[219]

As a result, arbitration rules generally contain provisions enabling the arbitral tribunal itself, subject to certain time-limits and to compliance with the requirements of due process, to correct any clerical errors which arise.[220] One of the weaknesses of the ICC Rules of Arbitration prior to their 1998 revision lay in their failure to provide for such a mechanism, as the scrutiny of awards by the International Court of Arbitration does not always prevent clerical errors from appearing in the final award. Admittedly, the courts were sometimes able to correct an error during proceedings to set aside or enforce an award,[221] but these were only indirect remedies. Happily, the 1998 ICC Rules do now provide, at Article 29, for the correction of the award, which can be requested by a party or be carried out by the arbitral tribunal on its own initiative. In the latter case, the correction must be submitted for approval

---

[214] DERAINS AND SCHWARTZ, *supra* note 1, at 298 *et seq.*

[215] *See infra* para. 1416.

[216] For its implementation in German law, see Article 1058 of the ZPO.

[217] New Article 1702 bis, paragraph 1(b) of the Belgian Judicial Code (Law of May 19, 1998); Sec. 32 of the 1999 Swedish Arbitration Act.

[218] *See infra* para. 1416.

[219] For an example of a clerical error, which was easily corrected in a system that so permitted, see the October 17, 1990 Decision on Supplemental Decisions and Rectification in ICSID Case No. ARB/81/1, Amco Asia Corp. v. Republic of Indonesia (5 INT'L ARB. REP. D1 (Nov. 1990); XVII Y.B. COM. ARB. 73 (1992); 1 ICSID REP. 569 (1993)), which constituted a rectification of the June 5, 1990 ICSID Award on the merits (5 INT'L ARB. REP. D4 (Nov. 1990); XVII Y.B. COM. ARB. 73 (1992); 1 ICSID REP. 569 (1993); for a French translation, see 118 J.D.I. 172, 181 (1991), and observations by E. Gaillard).

[220] *See, e.g.,* Art. 36 of the UNCITRAL Arbitration Rules; Art. 30 of the 1997 AAA International Arbitration Rules; Art. 27 of the 1998 LCIA Arbitration Rules; Art. 37 of the 1999 Rules of the Arbitration Institute of the Stockholm Chamber of Commerce. *See also* Art. 49(2) of the Washington Convention and Art. 49 of the ICSID Arbitration Rules.

[221] *See, e.g.,* CA Paris, Feb. 2, 1978, Elettronica v. Thomson-C.S.F., 1978 REV. ARB. 501, and P. Roland-Lévy's note, *aff'd*, Cass. 1e civ., Dec. 11, 1979, *supra* note 149.

to the ICC International Court of Arbitration within thirty days of the award. In the former case, the party's request must be made within thirty days of the award, with the tribunal reaching a decision after rapidly obtaining comments from the other party. Correction is only possible with respect to a "clerical, computational or typographical error or any errors of similar nature contained in an Award" (Art. 29(1)). This means that where the arbitration rules or the procedural law allow the arbitrators to correct clerical errors,[222] that remedy cannot be used to alter the meaning of the decision.[223]

In the absence of any similar statutory provision, the courts in certain jurisdictions have held that arbitrators are entitled to rectify their award where there is a clerical error.[224] However, more recent arbitration statutes often explicitly allow for the correction of errors where the parties have not so agreed. This is the case of the UNCITRAL Model Law,[225] the 1994 Italian arbitration statute,[226] the 1996 English Arbitration Act,[227] the 1998 Belgian arbitration statute and the 1999 Swedish Arbitration Act,[228] as well as French law on domestic arbitration.[229]

C. – ADDITIONAL AWARDS

1417. — In some cases, the arbitral tribunal fails to decide one of the heads of claim. This situation is not to be confused with that where the tribunal does not respond to all the allegations, or even all the arguments put forward by the parties. A failure to decide on certain heads of claim is sometimes easy to remedy, where the procedural law[230] or the arbitration rules allow a party to seek an additional award from the arbitral tribunal in such circumstances. Such a mechanism is found in Belgian law (Art. 1708 of the Judicial Code), the UNCITRAL Model Law (Art. 33(3)), the 1986 Netherlands Arbitration Act (Art. 1061 of the Code of Civil Procedure), the 1994 Italian arbitration statute (Art. 826 of the Code of Civil Procedure), the 1996 English Arbitration Act (Sec. 57(3)(b)), the 1997 German Act (Art. 1058(1)(3) of the ZPO) and the 1999 Swedish Arbitration Act (Sec. 32).

---

[222] *See* Cass. 1e civ., June 16, 1976, *Krebs, supra* note 97.

[223] On Article 29 of the ICC Rules, see DERAINS AND SCHWARTZ, *supra* note 1, at 298 *et seq.*

[224] See, for example, in the United States, Danella Constr. Corp. v. MCI Telecommunications Corp., 993 F.2d 876 (3d Cir. 1993); 8 INT'L ARB. REP. D1 (Oct. 1993).

[225] Article 33 and, in German law, Article 1058 of the ZPO.

[226] Art. 826 of the Code of Civil Procedure (Law of Jan. 5, 1994).

[227] Sec. 57 of the English Arbitration Act 1996.

[228] See Article 1702 bis, paragraph 1(a) of the Belgian Judicial Code (Law of May 19, 1998), which also allows the parties to apply to the enforcement court to have the award rectified where the arbitral tribunal cannot be reconstituted (Art. 1702 bis, paragraph 5) and Section 32 of the 1999 Swedish Arbitration Act.

[229] Art. 1475, paragraph 2 of the New Code of Civil Procedure, referring to Article 461 of the same Code, which deals with the correction of clerical mistakes in court decisions. *See* JEAN ROBERT, L'ARBITRAGE – DROIT INTERNE – DROIT INTERNATIONAL PRIVÉ ¶ 211 (6th ed. 1993).

[230] *See supra* para. 1414.

In addition, the UNCITRAL Arbitration Rules (Art. 37), the AAA International Arbitration Rules (Art. 30(1)), the LCIA Rules (Art. 27.3) and the ICSID Rules[231] all contain provisions to that effect. This is not the case of the 1998 ICC Rules, where the issue was discussed at the drafting stage and the proposal was ultimately rejected.[232]

Where there is no mechanism enabling the arbitrators to make an additional award, their failure to decide one of the heads of claim will be a ground on which the award may be set aside.[233]

D. – WITHDRAWAL OF AN AWARD OBTAINED BY FRAUD

1418. — Until 1981, the French courts were able to correct an award made in France and obtained by fraud. There has been considerable discussion as to whether such an action is still available in the absence of a specific statutory provision to that effect. The possibility of fraud, through the submission of false documents or otherwise, seemed so serious that many commentators were of the view that such an action should remain available.[234]

Doubtless wishing to avoid directly conflicting with the objectives of the French legislation enacted in 1981, the French courts will allow a defrauded party to seek redress from the arbitral tribunal itself, provided that the latter is still constituted or "can be reconvened."[235] This cumbersome solution, which entails reconvening the arbitral tribunal within an undetermined period following the making of the award, has rightly been the subject of some criticism.[236] We shall consider the issue in more detail when examining the actions which lie against arbitral awards.[237]

§ 2. – *Res Judicata*

1419. — Certain legal systems specify that, once rendered, an arbitral award is *res judicata*. This is the case for instance in Belgium (Art. 1703 of the Judicial Code) or in the Netherlands (Art. 1059 of the Code of Civil Procedure). Similarly, the German Statute of December 22, 1997, unlike the UNCITRAL Model Law on which it is largely based,

---

[231] Article 49, which implements Article 49, paragraph 2 of the Washington Convention.

[232] On the modifications made concerning the interpretation of the award and rectification of clerical errors, *see supra* paras. 1415 and 1416.

[233] In French law, this would be the case under Articles 1502 3° and 1504 of the New Code of Civil Procedure. On this issue, see *infra* para. 1628.

[234] See the authors cited *infra* para. 1599.

[235] Cass. 1e civ., May 25, 1992, Fougerolle v. Procofrance, 119 J.D.I. 974 (1992), and E. Loquin's note; 1992 REV. CRIT. DIP 699, and B. Oppetit's note; 1993 REV. ARB. 91, and the commentary by Matthieu de Boisséson, *L'arbitrage et la fraude (à propos de l'arrêt Fougerolle, rendu par la Cour de cassation le 25 mai 1992)*, *id.* at 3; for an English translation, see XIX Y.B. COM. ARB. 205 (1994).

[236] *See* E. Loquin, note following Cass. 1e civ., May 25, 1992, *Fougerolle*, 119 J.D.I. 974, 978 (1992).

[237] *See infra* para. 1599.

provides, in Article 1055 of the ZPO, that "[t]he arbitral award has the same effect between the parties as a final and binding court judgment."

In France, Article 1476 of the New Code of Civil Procedure stipulates that "[o]nce it is made, the arbitral award is *res judicata* in relation to the dispute it resolves." This provision applies to "awards made abroad or made in international arbitration" as a result of the cross-reference in Article 1500 of the same Code.

This means that once an award has been made, the same dispute between the same parties cannot be submitted to the courts. Before the award is made, the courts are obliged to decline jurisdiction where they find that an arbitration agreement exists.[238] Only if the resulting award were to be set aside or refused recognition or enforcement on the grounds that the arbitrator had ruled "in the absence of an arbitration agreement or on the basis of an agreement that was void or had expired" (Art. 1502 1° of the New Code of Civil Procedure) would it be possible to submit the same dispute to the French courts, provided of course that they have international jurisdiction to hear the case.[239]

Although in 1981 the French legislature may have sought to attribute a leading role in international arbitration to party autonomy, it could not have overlooked the need to establish a rule confirming the *res judicata* effect of arbitral awards. This rule is primarily directed at the French courts, which must hold inadmissible any action seeking resolution of a dispute which has already been decided by arbitration. Neither the intentions of the parties nor arbitration rules can provide otherwise, as the issue concerns the functioning of the French judicial system.

As a corollary of the fact that an arbitral award is *res judicata*, the French courts consider that, as soon as it is made, it

> constitutes a title in respect of which protective measures can be sought, the only effect of the suspensive nature of an action to set it aside[240] being to prevent its enforcement—subject to the possibility of requesting provisional enforcement from the court hearing the action to set the award aside.[241]

---

[238] *See supra* paras. 661 *et seq.*

[239] Compare, on the conditions governing the *res judicata* effect of foreign awards, the distinctions discussed by ROBERT, *supra* note 79, at 355. These observations are not included in the 6th edition of 1993.

[240] *See infra* para. 1591.

[241] CA Paris, July 9, 1992, Norbert Beyrard France v. République de Côte d'Ivoire, 1994 REV. ARB. 133, and P. Théry's note.

PART FIVE

THE LAW APPLICABLE TO THE MERITS OF THE DISPUTE

1420. — The law applicable to the merits of the dispute is chosen by the parties or, in the absence of any agreement between the parties, by the arbitrators. It is important to clearly distinguish these two situations, particularly because issues which appear to arise in similar terms in both, such as the role of trade usages or the impact of international mandatory rules, have in reality very different implications depending on whether they are matters affecting a choice made by the parties[1] or simply aspects of a decision reached by the arbitrators.[2] We shall examine first the situation where the parties have chosen the applicable law (Chapter I), and then that where it is chosen by the arbitrators (Chapter II).

---

[1] *See infra* para. 1515.
[2] *See infra* para. 1557.

CHAPTER I
APPLICABLE LAW CHOSEN BY THE PARTIES

1421. — Virtually all modern arbitration laws recognize that, in international situations, the parties are free to determine the law applicable to the merits of the dispute which the arbitrators are to resolve. This principle, traditionally referred to as the principle of party autonomy, is binding on the arbitrators. In French international arbitration law, the rule is set forth in Article 1496 of the New Code of Civil Procedure, which states that "[t]he arbitrator shall resolve the dispute in accordance with the rules of law chosen by the parties." This provision is generally considered to be a substantive rule of international arbitration.[1] As a result, under French law arbitrators confronted with a choice of law made by the parties need not consider the validity of such a choice under the law which they consider governs the choice of law agreement. By providing, in a rule applicable to all international arbitrations, that party autonomy governs, French law avoids that additional step. By contrast, when discussing Article 187 of the Private International Law Statute, which is the corresponding provision in Swiss law, some authors have felt it necessary to allude to, if not to fully examine, the law applicable to the choice of law agreement, while recognizing at the same time the theoretical nature of doing so as the principle of party autonomy is widely accepted in comparative law.[2] We believe this detour to be unnecessary. In fact, when the party autonomy principle is framed in sufficiently broad terms, as is the case in France and Switzerland for example, the law chosen by the parties will govern all substantive aspects of the dispute, and not just the issues covered by the *lex contractus*: the principle of party autonomy has an even greater scope in the context of arbitration than it does before national courts, and thus cannot be based exclusively on the recognition of the parties' freedom to select the law applicable to contracts in traditional choice of law rules applicable before the courts.

1422. — Most modern arbitration laws recognize the principle of party autonomy in similar terms.[3]

---

[1] On the nature of the party autonomy principle, see *supra* para. 1201 and the references cited.

[2] *See, e.g.*, PIERRE LALIVE, JEAN-FRANÇOIS POUDRET, CLAUDE REYMOND, LE DROIT DE L'ARBITRAGE INTERNE ET INTERNATIONAL EN SUISSE 392 (1989).

[3] *See, e.g.*, Art. 1054 of the Netherlands Code of Civil Procedure (Law of July 2, 1986); Art. 187 of the Swiss Private International Law Statute; Art. 28 of the UNCITRAL Model Law; Sec. 46 of the 1996 English Arbitration Act; Art. 1051(1) of the German ZPO (Law of Dec. 22, 1997); MARCEL HUYS, GUY KEUTGEN,

(continued...)

1423. — The resolution adopted by the International Law Institute on September 12, 1989 at Santiago de Compostela also endorses the principle, by providing in Article 6 that "[t]he parties have full autonomy to determine the procedural and substantive rules and principles that are to apply in the arbitration."[4]

1424. — Most of the international conventions which address the issue of the governing law in international commercial arbitration contain similar provisions.[5]

1425. — The principle of autonomy also appears in many institutional arbitration rules.[6] However, as those rules are only binding by virtue of the intentions of the parties, their restatement of the principle of autonomy amounts to no more than an affirmation by the parties themselves of their own autonomy. Strictly speaking, only national law can provide the basis for party autonomy and determine the conditions and limits within which it can be exercised. That law will be either that of the place of the arbitration, which will generally govern actions to set the award aside, or the laws of all the jurisdictions willing to recognize an award which has given effect to the parties' choice of applicable law.[7] Nevertheless, the fact that the main international conventions on the recognition of arbitral awards prevent the courts from reviewing the merits of disputes has furthered the development of private

---

[3]   (...continued)
L'ARBITRAGE EN DROIT BELGE ET INTERNATIONAL ¶¶ 796 *et seq.* (1981); ALAN REDFERN AND MARTIN HUNTER, INTERNATIONAL COMMERCIAL ARBITRATION 97 *et seq.* (2d ed. 1991); MAURO RUBINO-SAMMARTANO, INTERNATIONAL ARBITRATION LAW (1990); ARBITRATION IN SPAIN 122 *et seq.* (B. Cremades ed., 1991); J. STEWART MCCLENDON AND ROSABEL E. EVERARD GOODMAN, INTERNATIONAL COMMERCIAL ARBITRATION IN NEW YORK 114 *et seq.* (1986); Delia Revoredo de Mur, *Law Applicable to International Contracts in Latin America,* in ICCA CONGRESS SERIES NO. 7, PLANNING EFFICIENT ARBITRATION PROCEEDINGS/THE LAW APPLICABLE IN INTERNATIONAL ARBITRATION 501 (A.J. van den Berg ed., 1996). But see, on the mandatory application to arbitration proceedings taking place in certain Arab countries of the law of the place of performance of the contract or of the place of arbitration, ABDUL HAMID EL-AHDAB, ARBITRATION WITH THE ARAB COUNTRIES (2d ed. 1999); RUBINO-SAMMARTANO, *supra* at 263. On the question of the applicable law in international commercial arbitration in general, see JULIAN D.M. LEW, APPLICABLE LAW IN INTERNATIONAL COMMERCIAL ARBITRATION – A STUDY IN COMMERCIAL ARBITRATION AWARDS (1978); Marc Blessing, *Choice of Substantive Law in International Arbitration,* 14 J. INT'L ARB. 39 (June 1997).

[4]   Resolution on Arbitration Between States, State Enterprises or State Entities, and Foreign Enterprises, XVI Y.B. COM. ARB. 236, 238 (1991), and observations by A.T. von Mehren at 233; for the French version, see 1990 REV. ARB. 933. See also the references cited *infra* para. 1446.

[5]   See Art. VII of the 1961 European Convention and the commentary by Frédéric-Edouard Klein, *La Convention européenne sur l'arbitrage commercial international,* 1962 REV. CRIT. DIP 621; P.I. Benjamin, *The European Convention on International Commercial Arbitration,* 37 BRIT. Y.B. INT'L L. 478 (1961); Art. 42 of the 1965 ICSID Convention.

[6]   See Art. 17(1) of the 1998 ICC Arbitration Rules (Art. 13(3) of the previous Rules); Art. 33(1) of the UNCITRAL Arbitration Rules; Art. 28 of the 1997 AAA International Arbitration Rules; Art. 22.3 of the 1998 LCIA Rules; Art. 24(1) of the 1999 Rules of the Arbitration Institute of the Stockholm Chamber of Commerce.

[7]   See Arthur Taylor von Mehren, *To what Extent Is International Commercial Arbitration Autonomous?,* in LE DROIT DES RELATIONS ÉCONOMIQUES INTERNATIONALES – ETUDES OFFERTES À BERTHOLD GOLDMAN 217 (1982).

sources of international arbitration law (such as arbitration rules and arbitral case law), which have tended to strengthen the principle of autonomy.[8]

1426. — Thus, all these sources must be considered when examining how and when the parties select the applicable law (Section I), the subject matter of their choice (Section II) and the limits on the effectiveness of that choice (Section III).

SECTION I
FORMULATION AND TIMING OF THE PARTIES' CHOICE OF LAW

We shall now discuss how the parties' choice of law must be formulated in order to be effective (§ 1) and when that choice can be made (§ 2).

§ 1. – Formulation of the Parties' Choice of Law

1427. — The parties' choice of applicable law may be express or tacit. Under French law (Art. 1496 of the New Code of Civil Procedure), Swiss law (Art. 187, para. 1 of the Private International Law Statute) and the UNCITRAL Model Law (Art. 28(1)), for example, there are no particular requirements of form and, provided the parties have made a clear choice, it will be binding on the arbitrators.

However, these rules have generated a certain amount of controversy. Unlike a number of international conventions on the law applicable to contracts, modern arbitration statutes do not specify that the parties' choice must "unambiguously result from the provisions of the contract"[9] or "be demonstrated with reasonable certainty by the terms of the contract or the circumstances of the case."[10] Does this mean that the choice of the law to be applied by the arbitrators must be express,[11] or that it can simply be tacit and not result clearly from the terms of the contract or from the circumstances of the case?[12] Or does it mean that one should follow a middle path, where evidence as to the intentions of the parties should be

---

[8]   On private sources of arbitration law, see *supra* paras. 364 *et seq.*

[9]   *See* Art. 2(2) of the Hague Convention of June 15, 1955 on the Law Applicable to International Sales of Goods.

[10] *See* Art. 3(1) of the Rome Convention of June 19, 1980 on the Law Applicable to Contractual Obligations.

[11] *See* Philippe Fouchard, *L'arbitrage international en France après le décret du 12 mai 1981*, 109 J.D.I. 374, ¶ 40 at 396–97 (1982).

[12] In favor of the latter approach, in the context of Article 187, paragraph 1 of the Swiss Private International Law Statute, which is similar to Article 1496 of the French New Code of Civil Procedure, see LALIVE, POUDRET, REYMOND, *supra* note 2, at 389–90.

drawn solely from the provisions of the contract?[13] In our view, none of these three solutions is satisfactory. There is a clear distinction between the existence of the parties' consent as to the applicable law and the form such consent takes. Virtually no modern arbitration statute contains requirements as to the form of the parties' consent. Consequently, there is nothing to prevent the arbitrators from inferring from the conduct of the parties that there is an implied agreement as to the applicable law where, for example, the parties argue their case on the basis of the same law, even though they have not expressly agreed to apply it.[14] However, the parties' intentions must be certain.[15] That is a substantive requirement that the arbitrators cannot disregard.

1428. — It is important to note that, in the continental legal tradition, the choice of a place of arbitration cannot, in itself, be considered a choice of applicable law. In contrast, English law has long held the decision to resort to arbitration in England to be, at the very least, a strong indication that English law has been chosen as the applicable law by the parties.[16] For example, in a 1968 decision in the *Tzortzis and Another v. Monark Line A/B* case,[17] the English Court of Appeal held that although the transaction in question had closer links with Sweden, the parties had implicitly chosen English law to govern the contract by agreeing on London as the seat of the arbitration. This position is considered by commentators to remain valid under the 1996 Arbitration Act, which contains no specific provision in this respect.[18] In practice, this means that—contrary to what happens with respect to Paris or Geneva, for example—where London is chosen as the seat of an arbitration and no further indication is given as to the applicable law, that may be interpreted as an implicit election of English law. Where the ties between jurisdiction and the applicable law lead to the application of a law

---

[13]   *See* Berthold Goldman, *La nouvelle réglementation française de l'arbitrage international, in* THE ART OF ARBITRATION – ESSAYS ON INTERNATIONAL ARBITRATION – LIBER AMICORUM PIETER SANDERS 153, 163 (J. Schultz and A.J. van den Berg eds., 1982).

[14]   Compare ICC Award No. 1434 (1975), in which, in a similar situation, the arbitral tribunal discussed the applicable law at length before deciding that there was an implicit agreement between the parties to apply the law referred to in their pleadings (Multinational group A v. State B, 103 J.D.I. 978 (1976), and observations by Y. Derains), and ICC Award No. 2438 (1975), in which a similar conclusion was reached, wrongly, where there was an express agreement between the parties (Spanish company v. French company, 103 J.D.I. 969 (1976), and observations by Y. Derains). See also the June 27, 1990 Award by A.S. El-Kosheri, president, S.K.B. Asante and B. Goldman, arbitrators (S.K.B. Asante dissenting), in ICSID Case No. ARB/87/3, Asian Agricultural Products Ltd. (AAPL) v. Democratic Socialist Republic of Sri Lanka, which inferred from the positions of the parties during the proceedings an agreement that an investment contract was the principal source of law applicable in the matter (30 I.L.M. 577 (1991); 6 ICSID REV. – FOREIGN INV. L.J. 526 (1991); 6 INT'L ARB. REP. A1 (May 1991); XVII Y.B. COM. ARB. 106 (1992); for a French translation, see 119 J.D.I. 216 (1992), and observations by E. Gaillard).

[15]   For an example of a choice of law resulting from a reference to general conditions of sale containing a choice of law provision, see ICC Award No. 5865 (1989), Panamanian company v. Finnish company, 125 J.D.I. 1008 (1998), and observations by D. Hascher.

[16]   *See* MICHAEL J. MUSTILL, STEWART C. BOYD, COMMERCIAL ARBITRATION 71 (2d ed. 1989).

[17]   [1968 1 All E.R. 949; [1968] 1 W.L.R. 406; [1968] 1 Lloyd's Rep. 337 (C.A. 1968). See the remarks of Lord Denning, [1968] 1 All E.R. 949.

[18]   *See, e.g.,* RUSSELL ON ARBITRATION 69 *et seq.* (D. Sutton, J. Kendall, J. Gill eds., 21st ed. 1997).

other than English law, the English courts sometimes feel the need to justify the application of that law on the basis of other considerations, such as the neutrality desired by the parties.[19] The Singapore High Court took the same approach in a decision dated September 29, 1995, which made reference to English law.[20] Similar ties between jurisdiction and the applicable law are found in some arbitration rules. For example, by submitting to the Hamburg Friendly Arbitration Rules, and in the absence of an indication to the contrary as to the governing law, the parties will be deemed to have chosen German law.[21] This is an example of a choice of law made by reference, which is generally held to be valid.[22]

Contemporary international arbitration practice tends to give less importance to the choice of the seat of arbitration. In an award made in Paris in 1976 in ICC Case No. 2735, it was considered that the choice of applicable law could be inferred from the determination of the seat of the arbitration.[23] By contrast, a 1988 award made in London in ICC Case No. 5717 rightly stated, with regard to the law applicable to the merits of the case and despite an awkward reference to the "agreement to arbitrate," that:

> [t]he choice of London as the place of arbitration and English as the language of the contract does not, in itself, indicate an intention of the parties that English law should govern the validity of the agreement to arbitrate.[24]

In practice, it is always in the parties' interest to specify the applicable law as clearly as possible in their arbitration agreement, so as to avoid difficulties of the kind discussed above.

---

[19] See, for example, the reasoning of the Court of Appeal in an oil and gas case between a German company on the one hand and a United Arab Emirates company and an English company on the other hand, concerning an arbitration taking place in Switzerland. The Court considered that the choice by the parties of a neutral forum implied that they also intended that a neutral law (held to be Swiss law) would apply (Deutsche Schachtbau-und Tiefbohrgesellschaft mbH v. Ras Al Khaimah National Oil Co., [1990] A.C. 295; [1987] 2 All E.R. 769; [1987] 3 W.L.R. 1023; [1987] 2 Lloyd's Rep. 246; XIII Y.B COM. ARB. 522 (1988)). On the limits to this reasoning where the seat is chosen by the defendant exercising its option to that effect, see Star Shipping AS. v. China National Foreign Trade Transportation Corp. (The "Star Texas"), [1993] 2 Lloyd's Rep. 445; XXII Y.B. COM. ARB. 815 (1997) (C.A. 1993). On this issue, see Ole Lando, *The Law Applicable to the Merits of the Dispute, in* ESSAYS ON INTERNATIONAL COMMERCIAL ARBITRATION 129, 135 *et seq.* (P. Šarčević ed., 1989).

[20] Hainam Machinery Import and Export Corp. v. Donald & McArthy Pte Ltd., XXII Y.B. COM. ARB. 771, 778 (1997).

[21] See OTTOARNDT GLOSSNER, COMMERCIAL ARBITRATION IN THE FEDERAL REPUBLIC OF GERMANY 27 and 63 (1984). Similarly, the standard European Contract for Coffee contains a provision under which the choice of the place of arbitration also constitutes a choice of the law of the seat as that governing the merits of the dispute (see the March 19, 1987 Award under the aegis of the Arbitration Court of the German Coffee Association, U.S. buyer v. U.K. seller, XIX Y.B. COM. ARB. 44 (1994)).

[22] For an example of the validation of a choice of law carried out by reference to a standard form contract, see ICC Award No. 5865 (1989), *supra* note 15.

[23] ICC Award No. 2735 (1976), Yugoslavian seller v. U.S. purchaser, 104 J.D.I. 947 (1977), and observations by Y. Derains.

[24] ICC BULLETIN, Vol. 1, No. 2, at 22 (1990).

1429. — The choice of applicable law made by the parties is generally taken to mean the designation of the internal provisions of that law, to the exclusion of its choice of law rules. In continental legal systems at least, that exclusion has long been recognized in contract law.[25] This position has prevailed in international arbitration law, as demonstrated by Article 28, paragraph 1 of the UNCITRAL Model Law:

> Any designation of the law or legal system of a given State shall be construed, unless otherwise expressed, as directly referring to the substantive law of that State and not to its conflict of laws rules.

The same rule is found in Section 46(2) of the 1996 English Arbitration Act.[26]

Of course, the arbitrators are not prevented from considering whether the parties' choice of applicable law covers all of the disputed subject-matter or merely the main contract from which the dispute has arisen. In the latter case, the arbitrators will be free to determine, whether by using choice of law rules or not, the law applicable to other aspects of the dispute (such as agency or tortious liability).[27]

§ 2. – The Timing of the Parties' Choice of Law

1430. — It is settled law that the parties can choose the applicable law not only at the time of signing the arbitration agreement but also at any other time before or after the dispute has arisen. The drafting of a submission agreement or terms of reference may provide an opportunity for the parties to reach an agreement on this issue. In addition, concurring written submissions by the parties concerning the applicable law would be equally binding on the arbitrators.[28] This view is widely accepted in comparative law.[29]

---

[25]   *See, e.g.*, HENRI BATIFFOL AND PAUL LAGARDE, DROIT INTERNATIONAL PRIVÉ, Vol. 1, ¶ 311 at 509 (8th ed. 1993); PIERRE MAYER, DROIT INTERNATIONAL PRIVÉ ¶ 706 (6th ed. 1998); Art. 15 of the June 19, 1980 Rome Convention on the Law Applicable to Contractual Obligations. But see, in the United States, RESTATEMENT (SECOND) OF CONFLICTS OF LAWS § 8(2)–(3) (1971).

[26]   *See also* ICC Award No. 5505 (1987), Buyer from Mozambique v. Seller from the Netherlands, XIII Y.B. COM. ARB. 110, 117 (1988). *But see* ICC Award No. 1704 (1977), French bank v. Indian company, 105 J.D.I. 977 (1978), and observations by Y. Derains.

[27]   *See infra* paras. 1537 *et seq.*

[28]   In favor of the validity of a choice after the dispute has arisen, see, for example, Yves Derains, *L'ordre public et le droit applicable au fond du litige dans l'arbitrage international*, 1986 REV. ARB. 375, 392. See also the references cited *supra* para. 1427.

[29]   *See, e.g.*, HUYS AND KEUTGEN, *supra* note 3, at 579 and ICC Awards No. 1026 (1962) and 1525 (1969), unpublished, cited by these authors. *See also* the December 17, 1975 Award by the Court of Arbitration of the Bulgarian Chamber of Commerce and Industry, Bulgarian State enterprise v. State enterprise from the German Democratic Republic, IV Y.B. COM. ARB. 192 (1979); ANDREAS BUCHER, PIERRE-YVES TSCHANZ, INTERNATIONAL ARBITRATION IN SWITZERLAND ¶ 200 (1988). But see, on the questionable conclusion that a choice of law made during the arbitral proceedings is "less mandatory" than an earlier choice of law, the reasons of the first instance court cited in the decision of the German *Bundesgerichtshof* of September 26, 1985, 1986
(continued...)

SECTION II
THE SUBJECT MATTER OF THE PARTIES' CHOICE

1431. — In 1981, the French legislature deliberately chose to refer to "rules of law" rather than to "law" in describing the subject-matter of the parties' choice with respect to the merits of the dispute.[30] It was followed in this respect by several modern arbitration statutes[31] and by the major institutional arbitration rules.[32] The expression "rules of law" is intended to signal that the parties may choose not only a national law, with the different nuances that might entail (§ 1), but also, if they see fit, transnational rules, often referred to as *lex mercatoria* (§ 2). The parties can also empower the arbitrators to act as *amiables compositeurs*[33] (§ 3).

§ 1. – National Laws

1432. — In international arbitration, as in private international law, the word "law" encompasses all rules belonging to the legal system in question, with each source (including statute, case law and custom) having the authority attributed to it by that legal system. Thus, for example, by referring to "Venezuelan law," the parties include all of the sources recognized by the Venezuelan legal system, following the hierarchy established therein.

1433. — Some choice of law clauses are more difficult to construe. Sometimes, for example, the parties refer without further indication to the law of a federal state. If contract law in that country is governed by federal law, as is the case in Switzerland, the absence of any further indication in the clause is of no consequence. Indeed, it is preferable to submit a contract to "Swiss law" rather than to the law of a particular canton.[34] However, if contract law in the chosen legal system is a matter of state law rather than federal law, the clause

---

[29] (...continued)
BULL. ASA 153, 154.

[30] Art. 1496 of the New Code of Civil Procedure.

[31] *See, e.g.*, Art. 28 of the UNCITRAL Model Law; Art. 1054 of the Netherlands Code of Civil Procedure; Art. 187 of the Swiss Private International Law Statute; Art. 1051 of the German ZPO (in force as of January 1, 1998) and the discussion *infra* para. 1444.

[32] *See* Art. 17 of the 1998 ICC Arbitration Rules. For a commentary, see YVES DERAINS AND ERIC A. SCHWARTZ, A GUIDE TO THE NEW ICC RULES OF ARBITRATION 217 *et seq.* (1998). See also Article 28(1) of the 1997 AAA International Arbitration Rules, which requires the tribunal to "apply the substantive law(s) or rules of law designated by the parties as applicable to the dispute," and Article 22.3 of the 1998 LCIA Rules according to which "the arbitral tribunal shall decide the parties' dispute in accordance with the law(s) or rules of law chosen by the parties as applicable to the merits of their dispute;" Art. 24(1) of the 1999 Rules of the Stockholm Chamber of Commerce.

[33] *See, e.g.*, Art. 1497 of the French New Code of Civil Procedure.

[34] On the effect of such a provision, particularly with respect to public law, see Blaise Knapp, *Le droit suisse est applicable au présent contrat, in* ETUDES DE DROIT INTERNATIONAL EN L'HONNEUR DE PIERRE LALIVE 81 (1993).

becomes difficult to interpret. This is the case, for example, with clauses submitting a contract to "U.S. law." In such a situation, the arbitrators must determine which of the various state laws will govern the contract, first by interpreting the intentions of the parties, as an intention has been expressed, and only then by resorting to the methods which they would have used to determine the applicable law in the absence of any choice whatsoever, which often means leaving the matter entirely to the discretion of the arbitrators.[35] The same difficulties are encountered with clauses referring to "British law," which might mean English or Scots law, or to "the law of the member states of the European Community."[36]

Other contracts contain contradictory governing law clauses. In ICC Case No. 5864, the arbitral tribunal had to reconcile a clause that referred to Libyan law and custom with a second that referred to the law with the closest connection to the case and custom. The tribunal found that in both clauses the parties intended Libyan law to apply, supplemented by custom where no provision of Libyan law was applicable.[37]

1434. — Leaving aside these issues of interpretation, the parties' freedom in choosing a national law is virtually unfettered. International arbitration law, as expressed in international conventions, comparative law and arbitral practice, reinforces the parties' autonomy, which was already widely recognized in the private international law of contract.[38] The parties may choose a "neutral" law, with no connection with the dispute (A), or they may choose several national laws, using the technique of *dépeçage* (B). They may decide to stabilize their chosen law at a particular point in time (C) or they may even choose a law which partly or entirely renders the contract in question void (D). However, in our opinion, the parties cannot choose to have their contract governed by no rules of law at all (E).

A. – CHOICE OF A NEUTRAL LAW

1435. — Historically, in order for the parties' choice of law to be valid under the private international law of contract, the chosen law had to have an objective connection with the

---

[35] *See infra* paras. 1537 *et seq.*

[36] See, for example, ICC Award No. 7319 (1992), which held such a choice to be valid, provided that it was supplemented by the law of a member state, determined according to the ordinary choice of law method (cited in ICC BULLETIN, SPECIAL SUPPLEMENT, INTERNATIONAL COMMERCIAL ARBITRATION IN EUROPE 41 (1994)). The application of principles common to the members of the European Community might have been more in keeping with the intentions of the parties; *see infra* para. 1447.

[37] ICC Award No. 5864 (1989), U.S. company v. Libyan company, 124 J.D.I. 1073 (1997), and observations by Y. Derains.

[38] *See, e.g.*, Art. 3 of the June 19, 1980 Rome Convention on the Law Applicable to Contractual Obligations.

substance of the contract. In other words, the parties could not choose a law having no connection with the dispute.[39]

In contemporary international arbitration law, that approach has generally been abandoned.[40] The emphasis today is on the need to allow the parties to choose a neutral law or, in other words, a law which has no connection with either the parties or the subject-matter of the contract.[41]

Thus, for example, Swedish law was often chosen, because of Sweden's neutrality, to govern contracts between Western corporations and state-owned entities in the USSR or communist China. Swiss law is sometimes chosen for similar reasons. In fact, parties have a variety of different reasons for choosing neutral laws, although that choice is frequently based on considerations which are more political than legal. Nevertheless, prior to reaching their agreement, the parties will sometimes conduct a comparative law analysis.[42] Another approach, which is more intuitive but probably more appropriate than a choice based solely on political considerations, is for each party to attempt to impose an applicable law drawn from a legal system similar to that party's own.[43]

Whatever the parties' reasons may be, a choice of a law which is objectively unconnected with the contract is undoubtedly valid in most legal systems. This is certainly the case under Article 1496 of the French New Code of Civil Procedure. It has also consistently been recognized in arbitral case law.[44]

---

[39] See, in the United States, RESTATEMENT (SECOND) OF CONFLICTS OF LAWS § 187 (1971) which still requires a substantial relationship between the transaction or the parties and the law chosen, unless there is another reasonable basis for the parties' choice.

[40] Compare with the approach of the June 19, 1980 Rome Convention on the Law Applicable to Contractual Obligations, which also requires no connection with the dispute (Art. 3) (see also Giuliano and Lagarde Report, 1973 RIV. DIR. INT. E PROC. 217).

[41] See, e.g., RENÉ DAVID, ARBITRATION IN INTERNATIONAL TRADE ¶ 388 (1985); MATTHIEU DE BOISSÉSON, LE DROIT FRANÇAIS DE L'ARBITRAGE INTERNE ET INTERNATIONAL 597 (2d ed. 1990); RUBINO-SAMMARTANO, supra note 3, at 253; LALIVE, POUDRET, REYMOND, supra note 2, at 393; Lando, supra note 19, at 134; compare the more reserved position of HUYS AND KEUTGEN, supra note 3, at 597 and of Article 62 of the Spanish Law 36/1988 on Arbitration of December 5, 1988, according to which "the arbitrators shall decide according to the law expressly chosen by the parties, provided that it has some connection with the main legal transaction or with the dispute." See also the commentary in ARBITRATION IN SPAIN, supra note 3, at 122.

[42] See Emmanuel Gaillard, The Use of Comparative Law in International Commercial Arbitration, in ICCA CONGRESS SERIES NO. 4, ARBITRATION IN SETTLEMENT OF INTERNATIONAL COMMERCIAL DISPUTES INVOLVING THE FAR EAST AND ARBITRATION IN COMBINED TRANSPORTATION 283 (P. Sanders ed., 1989).

[43] On the parties' reasons for their decisions as to the choice of applicable law, see also Yves Derains, The ICC Arbitral Process – Part VIII: Choice of the Law Applicable to the Contract and International Arbitration, ICC BULLETIN, Vol. 6, No. 1, at 10 (1995).

[44] On the possibility for arbitrators to apply a law with no connection to the dispute (in this case Swiss law), see, for example, ICC Award No. 1598 (1971), Danish party v. Bulgarian and Ethiopian parties, III Y.B. COM. ARB. 216 (1978); see also, on the validity of the choice of Swiss law in a contract with no connection to Switzerland, ICC Award No. 4629 (Paris, 1989), Contractors v. Owner, XVIII Y.B. COM. ARB. 11 (1993), especially ¶ 7 at 16.

B. – CHOICE OF SEVERAL LAWS (*DÉPEÇAGE*)

1436. — The parties may also wish to choose different laws to govern different aspects of disputes which may arise between them. This situation, which is known as "*dépeçage,*" should not be confused with the situation where the parties declare that principles common to several laws apply.[45]

Applying different laws to different aspects of a dispute is becoming increasingly accepted, even before the courts. In the European Union, Article 3, paragraph 1 of the 1980 Rome Convention on the Law Applicable to Contractual Obligations enables the parties to opt for several laws to be applied selectively to different "parts" of an international contract. There is no doubt that such a choice by the parties would be validated by international arbitrators. By allowing the parties to choose the applicable "rules of law," modern statutes on arbitration[46] clearly validate such a choice, and it is not even necessary to justify that choice by establishing that certain "parts" of the contract can be distinguished. Thus, for example, the *Aramco* award allowed *dépeçage* on the basis that:

> [s]ince the Parties themselves declared that the Concession was not to be governed by a single law, the Tribunal can justifiably split the contract into parts, to be governed by several laws.[47]

The International Law Institute has also endorsed this approach. In its resolution adopted in Athens in September 1979, it suggested, specifically in connection with state contracts but in terms which are of general application, that "[t]he parties may choose as the proper law of the contract . . . one or several domestic legal systems . . . ."[48] The Institute subsequently expressed the rule in general terms in Article 6 of its resolution adopted in Santiago de Compostela on September 12, 1989: "[t]he parties have full autonomy to determine the procedural and substantive rules and principles that are to apply in the

---

[45] *See infra* para. 1457.

[46] *See supra* para. 1431.

[47] Aug. 23, 1958 *ad hoc* Award by G. Sauser-Hall, referee, M. Hassan and S. Habachy, arbitrators, Saudi Arabia v. Arabian American Oil Co. (ARAMCO), 27 INT'L L. REP. 117, 166 (1963); for a French translation, see 1963 REV. CRIT. DIP 272, 313. See also the references cited *supra* para. 1173.

[48] Article 2 of the Resolution on The Proper Law of the Contract in Agreements between a State and a Foreign Private Person, *in* INSTITUT DE DROIT INTERNATIONAL, TABLEAU DES RÉSOLUTIONS ADOPTÉES (1957–1991), at 332, 333 (1992); 1980 REV. CRIT. DIP 427.

arbitration."[49] Several arbitration rules have expressly recognized that parties may agree to *dépeçage* by requiring the arbitrators to apply "the law(s)" chosen by the parties.[50]

However, the fact that *dépeçage* is valid does not mean that it is necessarily appropriate. A multiplicity of applicable laws is liable to create unnecessary disputes over the scope of each, and may generate inconsistencies or imbalances as a result of their juxtaposition.

C. – CHOICE OF A STABILIZED LAW

1437. — Stabilization clauses—which in effect freeze the content of the applicable law at a particular point in time—have given rise to a wealth of commentary in the context of state contracts.[51]

When negotiating with a state, the private party will often feel the need to protect itself from the legislative power of its contractual partner. As the state usually insists on submitting the contract to its own law, the parties frequently adopt a compromise position whereby the contract is submitted to the law of that state as it stands at a particular point in time, which is generally the date the contract is signed. It is true that, in any event, if a state were to use its sovereign powers to enact new legislation in order to improve its contractual

---

[49] *Supra* note 4 and the references cited *infra* para. 1446. On the question of *dépeçage*, see also Jean-Flavien Lalive, *Contrats entre Etats ou entreprises étatiques et personnes privées – Développements récents*, in COLLECTED COURSES OF THE HAGUE ACADEMY OF INTERNATIONAL LAW, Vol. 181, Year 1983, Part III, at 49; Craig M. Gertz, *The Selection Of Choice Of Law Provisions In International Commercial Arbitration: A Case For Contractual Depeçage*, 12 NW. J. INT'L L. & BUS. 163 (1991).

[50] *See* Art. 28(1) of the 1997 AAA International Arbitration Rules, Art. 22.3 of the 1998 LCIA Rules or Art. 24(1) of the 1999 Rules of the Stockholm Chamber of Commerce. Although they do not use this language, the 1998 ICC Rules also endorse this approach by enabling the parties to choose the "rules of law" to be applied by the arbitral tribunal (Art. 17(1)). *See supra* para. 1431.

[51] *See* Bernard Audit, *Transnational Arbitration and State Contracts: Findings and Prospects*, in THE HAGUE ACADEMY OF INTERNATIONAL LAW, CENTRE FOR STUDIES AND RESEARCH IN INTERNATIONAL LAW AND INTERNATIONAL RELATIONS, TRANSNATIONAL ARBITRATION AND STATE CONTRACTS (in the French version at 23 and in an English translation at 77 (1988)); Nicolas David, *Les clauses de stabilité dans les contrats pétroliers. Questions d'un praticien*, 113 J.D.I. 79 (1986); JEAN-MICHEL JACQUET, PRINCIPE D'AUTONOMIE ET CONTRATS INTERNATIONAUX ¶¶ 176 *et seq.* (1983); Philippe Kahn, *Contrats d'Etat et nationalisation – Les apports de la sentence arbitrale du 24 mars 1982*, 109 J.D.I. 844 (1982); Jean-Flavien Lalive, *Un grand arbitrage pétrolier entre un Gouvernement et deux sociétés privées étrangères (Arbitrage Texaco/Caliastic c/ Gouvernement Libyen)*, 104 J.D.I. 319 (1977); PHILIPPE LEBOULANGER, LES CONTRATS ENTRE ETATS ET ENTREPRISES ÉTRANGÈRES (1985); Pierre Mayer, *La neutralisation du pouvoir normatif de l'Etat en matière de contrats d'Etat*, 113 J.D.I. 5 (1986); Brigitte Stern, *Trois arbitrages, un même problème, trois solutions – Les nationalisations pétrolières libyennes devant l'arbitrage international*, 1980 REV. ARB. 3; Prosper Weil, *Les clauses de stabilisation ou d'intangibilité insérées dans les accords de développement économique*, in MÉLANGES OFFERTS À CHARLES ROUSSEAU – LA COMMUNAUTÉ INTERNATIONALE 301 (1974); Nigel Rawding, *Protecting Investments Under State Contracts: Some Legal and Ethical Issues*, 11 ARB. INT'L 341, 346 *et seq.* (1995); Wolfgang Peter, *Stabilization Clauses in State Contracts/Les clauses de stabilisation dans les contrats d'Etat*, 1998 INT'L BUS. L.J. 875; Charles Leben, *Retour sur la notion de contrat d'Etat et sur le droit applicable à celui-ci*, in MÉLANGES OFFERTS À HUBERT THIERRY – L'ÉVOLUTION DU DROIT INTERNATIONAL 247 (1998). See also the clauses cited by Georges R. Delaume, *L'affaire du Plateau des Pyramides et le CIRDI. Considérations sur le droit applicable*, 1994 REV. ARB. 39, 42; Georges R. Delaume, *The Proper Law of State Contracts Revisited*, 12 ICSID REV. – FOREIGN INV. L.J. 1 (1997).

position, that may be characterized as an abuse of its powers and contested as such.[52] However, incorporating a clause freezing the applicable law remains the best guarantee for the private party that its rights under the contract cannot be unilaterally altered by the state.

It has sometimes been considered necessary to distinguish between stabilization clauses, which are intended to freeze the applicable legislation, and "intangibility" clauses.[53] However, the distinction appears to make no significant difference to the regime governing the contract.

The validity of stabilization clauses has traditionally been examined primarily from a public international law standpoint. In particular, is the abdication of legislative power which they entail compatible with the principles governing state sovereignty?[54] The answer is generally in the affirmative, on the basis that such clauses do not prevent the state from legislating, but merely enable a particular contract to avoid the effects of that legislation. It has also been suggested, somewhat tautologically, that a state's sovereignty provides sufficient justification for the irrevocable waiver of some its powers.[55]

Arbitral case law generally validates stabilization clauses.[56] The International Law Institute has also affirmed, in Article 3 of its 1979 resolution, that "[t]he parties may agree that domestic law provisions referred to in the contract shall be considered as being those in force at the time of conclusion of the contract."[57]

---

[52] On this issue, see especially E. Gaillard, observations following the November 20, 1984 Award in ICSID Case No. ARB/81/1, Amco Asia Corp. v. Republic of Indonesia, 114 J.D.I. 145, 161 (1987), and observations following the June 5, 1990 ICSID award in *Amco*, 118 J.D.I. 186 (1991).

[53] *See, e.g.*, Weil, *supra* note 51.

[54] *See* François Rigaux, *Des dieux et des héros – Réflexions sur une sentence arbitrale*, 1978 REV. CRIT. DIP 435; Wilhelm Wengler, *Les principes généraux du droit en tant que loi du contrat*, 1982 REV. CRIT. DIP 467, especially at 490 *et seq.*; Eduardo Jimenez de Arechaga, *International Law in the Past Third of a Century*, in COLLECTED COURSES OF THE HAGUE ACADEMY OF INTERNATIONAL LAW, Vol. 159, Year 1978, Part I, at 9.

[55] For an approach that places significant emphasis on the will of the state, see, for example, MAMOUDOU DEME, QUALITÉ DES PARTIES ET CONTRAT D'ETAT (Thesis, University of Rouen (France), 1993).

[56] See, for example, the January 19, 1977 Award by R.-J. Dupuy, sole arbitrator, Texaco Overseas Petroleum Co./ California Asiatic Oil Co. v. Government of the Libyan Arab Republic, 104 J.D.I. 350 (1977), ¶¶ 69 *et seq.*, and the commentary by Lalive, *supra* note 51; for an English translation, see 17 I.L.M. 1 (1978); 53 INT'L L. REP. 389 (1979); IV Y.B. COM. ARB. 177 (1980); the March 24, 1982 *ad hoc* Award by P. Reuter, president, H. Sultan and G. Fitzmaurice, arbitrators, The Government of the State of Kuwait v. The American Independent Oil Co. (AMINOIL), 21 I.L.M. 976 (1982); IX Y.B. COM. ARB. 71 (1984); for a French translation, see 109 J.D.I. 869 (1982), ¶¶ 83 *et seq.*, and the commentary by Kahn, *supra* note 51; the November 30, 1979 Award by J. Trolle, president, R.-J. Dupuy and F. Rouhani, arbitrators, in ICSID Case No. ARB/77/1, AGIP S.p.A. v. Government of the People's Republic of the Congo, 1982 REV. CRIT. DIP 92, and H. Batiffol's note; for an English translation, see 21 I.L.M. 726 (1982); VIII Y.B. COM. ARB. 133 (1983); 1 ICSID REP. 306 (1993); the March 31, 1986 Award by B. Cremades, president, J. Goncalves Pereira and A. Redfern, arbitrators, in ICSID Case No. ARB/83/2, Liberian Eastern Timber Corp. v. Government of the Republic of Liberia, 26 I.L.M. 647 (1987); XIII Y.B. COM. ARB. 35 (1988); 2 ICSID REP. 346 (1994); for a French translation, see 115 J.D.I. 166 (1988), and observations by E. Gaillard; the January 14, 1982 *ad hoc* Preliminary Award by B. Gomard, sole arbitrator, Elf Aquitaine Iran v. National Iranian Oil Co. (NIOC), XI Y.B. COM. ARB. 97 (1986); for a French translation, see 1984 REV. ARB. 401, and the observations by Philippe Fouchard, *L'arbitrage Elf Aquitaine Iran c/ National Iranian Oil Company – Une nouvelle contribution au droit international de l'arbitrage*, *id.* at 333.

[57] *Supra* note 48, at 334.

1438. — Clauses stabilizing the applicable law can also be found in contracts that do not involve states, where they provide the parties with the certainty that, at the time they sign the contract, they know—or can ascertain—the content of the law governing that contract.

In traditional private international law thinking, doubts remain as to the validity of clauses freezing the applicable law.[58] Admittedly, the courts have had little opportunity to address the issue, as stabilization clauses are usually found in contracts containing an arbitration clause, as a result of which most of the relevant litigation is heard by arbitral tribunals.

When the issue arises in arbitration, the general trend is, as indicated above,[59] to admit the validity of such clauses, whether or not they appear in a state contract. Even in the absence of a stabilization clause, one arbitral tribunal considered, admittedly applying transitional provisions of the law chosen by the parties, that it should apply the law as it stood at the time the contract was signed.[60] This would be all the more appropriate where there is a stabilization clause.[61] As the law governing the merits of the dispute is not a matter that can be reviewed by the courts,[62] there is nothing in modern arbitration legislation enabling a court confronted with the issue—in the context of an action to set aside the award, for example—to question the validity of an award giving effect to a stabilization clause.

D. – CHOICE OF A LAW WHICH RENDERS THE CONTRACT VOID

1439. — It has sometimes been argued that the parties cannot, without contradicting themselves, choose a law the application of which leads all or part of their contract to be void. As the parties cannot have intended to conclude an invalid contract, the argument goes, they cannot have chosen a law which causes it to be void, even in part. That reasoning, which is sometimes made before the courts,[63] may seem more convincing before an arbitral tribunal, as arbitrators themselves derive their power from a contract between the parties.[64] However, the argument should, in our view, be rejected. It is based on a mistaken conception of the intention of the parties when choosing the applicable law. When entering into a contract, the parties seek to place themselves under the general protection of a legal system

---

[58] *See* MAYER, *supra* note 25, ¶ 708.

[59] *See supra* note 56.

[60] *See, e.g.,* ICC Award No. 3093 (1979), Primary Coal v. Compania Valenciana, 107 J.D.I. 951 (1980), and observations by Y. Derains.

[61] In favor of the validity of clauses stabilizing the applicable law, see, for example, Derains, *supra* note 28, at 390; but see, for a criticism of such clauses based on their "unrealistic" character, REDFERN AND HUNTER, *supra* note 3, at 105 and 121.

[62] *See infra* para. 1603.

[63] See, in the United States, RESTATEMENT (SECOND) OF CONFLICT OF LAWS § 187, Comment b (1971).

[64] *See* Y. Derains, observations following ICC Award No. 5953 (1989), U.S. company v. Spanish company, 117 J.D.I. 1056, 1062 (1990). Compare, in the case of a pathological clause where the parties chose two laws, one of which caused the agreement to be void, ICC Award No. 4145 (1984), Establishment of Middle East country v. South Asian construction company, XII Y.B. COM. ARB. 97 (1987); for a French translation, see 112 J.D.I. 985 (1985), and observations by Y. Derains.

which they trust, admittedly without always being familiar with its content, to resolve all difficulties which are liable to arise in connection with their contract. If resolving those difficulties entails having a provision of the contract declared void (an overly-restrictive non-competition clause, for example), or even the entire contract (as in the case where the price is considered to be abusive under applicable regulations), the intentions of the parties are respected by holding the relevant clause or contract to be void.[65] Arbitral case law therefore generally considers, and rightly so, that the mandatory provisions of the law chosen by the parties should prevail over the terms of the contract.[66]

While approving of that approach, some authors have suggested that the situation is different where the contract itself provides that in the event of a conflict between the applicable law and the terms of the contract, the latter shall prevail.[67] Such clauses are now sometimes included in international contracts.[68] In such a case, the parties intend that the provisions of their contract should not be invalidated by the law that they choose to govern the contract. However, the parties' intention that certain contractual clauses should evade the application of provisions of the governing law will not necessarily be effective. As a result of the intention of the parties, clauses conflicting with the chosen law will no longer be governed by any law. Thus, if one were to give full effect to the parties' intentions, part of the contract would have no governing law. As we shall see, this option is not available to the parties.[69] The arbitrators will therefore have to determine, by reference to the rules which they would apply in the absence of any choice of law, the rules of law governing

---

[65] On this issue, see Emmanuel Gaillard, *La distinction des principes généraux du droit et des usages du commerce international, in* ETUDES OFFERTES À PIERRE BELLET 203, 213 (1991).

[66] *See, e.g.,* ICC Award No. 2119 (1978), Dutch company v. French shipyard, 106 J.D.I. 997 (1979), and observations by Y. Derains. But see, for a case where, despite the choice by the parties of French law to govern their dispute, arbitrators did not apply Article 14 of the French law of December 31, 1975 on subcontracts, which holds subcontracts void if certain conditions are not met, ICC Award No. 7528 (1994), Sub-contractor v. Contractor, XXII Y.B. COM. ARB. 125 (1997), and comments by Ibrahim Fadlallah, *L'ordre public dans les sentences arbitrales, in* COLLECTED COURSES OF THE HAGUE ACADEMY OF INTERNATIONAL LAW, Vol. 249, Year 1994, Part V, ¶ 75. The arbitral tribunal based its decision on the will of the parties, as they were held to have elected to apply French contract law other than this particular statute. *See also infra* para. 1527.

[67] *See* Derains, *supra* note 28, at 390 *et seq.;* DE BOISSÉSON, *supra* note 41, at 600.

[68] See, for example, the clause that gave rise to ICC Case No. 6257, which stated that the applicable law was "French law, subject to the explicit exceptions contained in this contract" (unpublished), or the clause that gave rise to ICC Case No. 6136, which provided that "to the extent that they are not contrary to the provisions of this contract . . . and the present transaction, the following shall apply in this order [general principles of law and the law of the state in which the contract was to be performed]" (unpublished). See also the clause pursuant to which the arbitrators could not apply sources of law other than the contract unless such contract was ambiguous, cited by Delaume, *L'affaire du Plateau des Pyramides et le CIRDI, supra* note 51, at 43; and the clause found in Banque Arabe et Internationale d'Investissement (BAII) v. The Inter-Arab Investment Guarantee Corp., *ad hoc* Award of November 17, 1994, 11 INT'L ARB. REP. A1, ¶ 11 at A14 (Apr. 1996); for a French translation, see 1998 REV. ARB. 211, and F. Horchani's note.

[69] *See infra* para. 1440.

those provisions.[70] It is only where such rules of law lead the contractual clauses at issue to be valid that the arbitrators will be able to salvage them.[71]

E. – CONTRACTS WITH NO GOVERNING LAW

1440. — The considerable freedom enjoyed by the parties and, in the absence of any choice by the parties, by the arbitrators in determining the rules of law governing the merits of a dispute raises a question as to whether the parties can go so far as to stipulate that their contract is self-sufficient and is not governed by any rules of law.

In current practice, such clauses are very rarely encountered, which tends to indicate that the parties themselves have doubts as to their effectiveness. However, some clauses do attempt, by more or less contrived means, to achieve the same result. In particular, the parties may seek to give the governing law a purely subsidiary role, by specifying that in the event of a conflict between the provisions of that law and those of the contract, the latter are to prevail.[72] In such a case, the parties are clearly trying to ensure that the examination of the validity and scope of the contract will be performed, either entirely or in part, without any reference to rules that would otherwise prevail over the contract.

This situation is not to be confused with contracts where the parties have opted for the application of general principles of law, or transnational rules of one form or another.[73] In such a case, provided that they do not take an excessively restrictive view of the general principles chosen by the parties,[74] arbitrators can indeed examine the validity of the contract, interpret it, or even refuse to give effect to provisions which they consider to be excessive (such as penalty clauses), by applying those principles.[75] Although it is governed by no national law, the contract will then have a governing law in the sense that it does not seek to avoid compliance with rules that are hierarchically superior to its own terms.

Likewise, a contract with no governing law should not be confused with *amiable composition*, where the arbitrators can apply their own conception of equity to the parties' contract. Even in the case of *amiable composition*, the parties' contract will not be self-sufficient.[76]

---

[70] *See infra* para. 1538.

[71] For reasoning in favor of recognizing the autonomy or separability of the choice of law clause in the same way that the arbitration clause is recognized as being autonomous, see ICC Award No. 6476 (1994), ICC BULLETIN, Vol. 7, No. 1, at 86 (1996).

[72] See the examples cited *supra* note 68.

[73] On the different types of transnational rules, see *infra* para. 1457.

[74] On the use of transnational rules as a substitute for a contract with no governing law, see *infra* paras. 1451 *et seq.*

[75] On the content of these principles, see *infra* paras. 1459 *et seq.*

[76] On the powers of arbitrators acting as *amiables compositeurs* with respect to the provisions of the contract, see *infra* para. 1507.

1441. — What attitude should arbitrators take when confronted not with a clause providing for the application of transnational rules or empowering the arbitrators to act as *amiable compositeurs*, but with a clause purporting to remove the contract from any governing law or rules of law?

Two arguments have been put forward in support of the validity of such clauses.

The first is based on the idea that the contract itself is a set of rules, and that it therefore qualifies as a "rule of law"[77] which the parties can choose to govern their contract.[78] That argument is unconvincing in so far as the contract itself only becomes a "rule of law" where a superior rule grants it that legal status. It seems doubtful that by referring to the "rules of law" which the parties can instruct the arbitrators to apply to the merits of the dispute, the various legal systems which validate such a choice intend to confer a status of rule of law on provisions which would not otherwise enjoy such standing.[79]

The second argument used in international arbitration in favor of contracts with no governing law is based on the nature of international arbitration. The idea is that as the arbitrators derive their powers from the intentions of the parties, they do not need a *lex fori* on which to base the binding nature of a contract. Proponents of this theory argue that the intentions of the parties bind the arbitrators and they must uphold them "without seeking to justify that obligation;" they consider that the fact that, in most legal systems, there is no review by the courts of the law applied by the arbitrators provides sufficient justification for the arbitrators to comply with the parties' intention to exclude a governing law.[80] However, to pursue that line of reasoning would amount to giving absolute freedom to the arbitrators,[81] and would entitle them just as much to ignore the parties' intention to free their contract from all rules of law as to give effect to it. Besides, however liberal a law may be in the field of international arbitration, there will be more to it than those provisions the breach of which gives rise to an action to set aside or resist enforcement of the award. In most modern arbitration statutes, although it does not appear among the grounds for refusing to enforce or for setting aside an award, there is a specific provision requiring the parties' contract to be governed by "rules of law."[82] That requirement is binding on arbitrators even if not expressly constituting grounds on which to set aside or refuse enforcement of an award.

---

[77] These terms are used, for example, in Article 1496 of the French New Code of Civil Procedure, Article 28 of the UNCITRAL Model Law and similar provisions in other modern arbitration statutes. *See supra* para. 1431.

[78] *See* JEAN ROBERT, L'ARBITRAGE – DROIT INTERNE – DROIT INTERNATIONAL PRIVÉ ¶ 330 at 288 (5th ed. 1983): "the choice may be . . . that of contractual rules to the exclusion of a law." This view no longer appears in the 6th edition published in 1993 (¶ 300 at 226).

[79] On the case law which acknowledges the legal character of *lex mercatoria* in terms which accept that such legal character is required for the parties to be able to validly choose *lex mercatoria* as the governing law under Article 1496 of the French New Code of Civil Procedure, see *infra* para. 1636.

[80] MAYER, *supra* note 25, ¶ 702 at 458.

[81] On the limits to the freedom of the parties and, in consequence, of the arbitrators, and particularly that resulting from international public policy, see *infra* paras. 1533 *et seq.*

[82] See, for example, in France, Article 1496 of the New Code of Civil Procedure and the corresponding provisions in other modern arbitration statutes cited *supra* para. 1431.

Thus, in our opinion, the parties' freedom to choose the applicable rules of law does not extend to allowing them to reject the need for the contract to be governed by some rules.[83] If faced with a contractual provision inviting them to apply no rule of law to all or part of the dispute which they are to resolve, the arbitrators will nevertheless be at liberty to apply the rules of law they consider to be appropriate, just as if the parties had simply expressed no choice at all.[84] In such cases, one way of giving effect to the parties' intentions, without going so far as to allow contracts with no governing law, would be to apply general principles of law rather than the rules of a particular national law. A careful analysis of awards which state that they accept the theory of contracts with no governing law[85] shows that they in fact consider it necessary to apply general principles of law.[86] This does not amount to accepting that the contract is self-sufficient and hence free from the effects of any rule of law.

1442. — However, parties may validly agree to exercise a "partial negative choice" according to which the arbitrators are required not to apply certain laws identified in the parties' contract. Such provisions are generally intended to ensure the neutrality of the choice of law vis-à-vis the parties in situations where the parties themselves cannot agree on a particular applicable law. As such, they do not actually prevent the contract from being governed by rules of law. Provided that the clause does not prevent the arbitrators from having the dispute governed by rules of law which they are free to choose from the options remaining open to them, the requirement that the contract be governed by some "rules of law" as opposed to being considered self-sufficient will be satisfied. The same is true where the parties choose to have the dispute governed by rules which do not belong to any particular legal system.

§ 2. – Transnational Rules

1443. — Although the validity of choosing transnational rules to govern an international contract is now widely accepted in international arbitration (A), those rules, often referred to under the heading *lex mercatoria*,[87] continue to be a highly controversial subject (B). However, by examining the method and content of transnational rules we may be able to help dispel some of that controversy (C).

---

[83] *See, e.g.*, Lalive, *supra* note 49, at 45 *et seq.*

[84] *See infra* paras. 1538 *et seq.*

[85] *See, e.g.*, ICC Award No. 2152 (1972), cited by Y. Derains, observations following ICC Award No. 1641 (1969), 101 J.D.I. 888, 889 (1974).

[86] On this issue, see *infra* para. 1443.

[87] On the terminology, see *infra* para. 1447.

A. – VALIDITY OF THE CHOICE OF TRANSNATIONAL RULES AS GOVERNING LAW

1444. — Parties sometimes prefer not to have their contract governed by a particular national law, but instead elect to have it governed by transnational rules, which are often referred to collectively, together with trade usages, as *lex mercatoria*.[88] The freedom enjoyed by the parties to apply such rules is signaled, in contemporary international arbitration, by the use of the words "rules of law" as opposed to "the law" or "laws" when describing the rules which the parties are free to select pursuant to the principle of party autonomy.

This terminology was first used by the 1981 French decree on international arbitration, which provided in Article 1496 of the New Code of Civil Procedure that the parties (and, in the absence of a choice by them, the arbitrators)[89] were free to select the "rules of law" applicable to their dispute. Commentators were unanimous in recognizing the implicit reference to transnational rules in the text[90] and the courts have never questioned that interpretation.[91] Several other legal systems have used the same expression with the same meaning. When Article 1054 of the Netherlands Code of Civil Procedure was presented to the legislature in 1986, the Dutch government emphasized in an explanatory memorandum that the expression "rules of law" encompassed not only national rules of law but also *lex mercatoria*.[92] Likewise, Article 187 of the 1987 Swiss Private International Law Statute provides that "[t]he arbitral tribunal shall decide the case according to the rules of law

---

[88] See, generally, Berthold Goldman, *Frontières du droit et "lex mercatoria"*, in ARCHIVES DE PHILOSOPHIE DU DROIT, VOL. IX, LE DROIT SUBJECTIF EN QUESTION 177 (1964); Berthold Goldman, *La lex mercatoria dans les contrats et l'arbitrage internationaux: réalité et perspectives*, 106 J.D.I. 475 (1979); Berthold Goldman, *Nouvelles réflexions sur la Lex Mercatoria*, in ETUDES DE DROIT INTERNATIONAL EN L'HONNEUR DE PIERRE LALIVE 241 (1993); Emmanuel Gaillard, *Thirty Years of Lex Mercatoria: Towards the Selective Application of Transnational Rules*, 10 ICSID REV. – FOREIGN INV. L.J. 208 (1995) and, for the French version, *Trente ans de lex mercatoria – Pour une application sélective de la méthode des principes généraux du droit*, 122 J.D.I. 5 (1995); TRANSNATIONAL RULES IN INTERNATIONAL COMMERCIAL ARBITRATION (E. Gaillard ed., ICC Publication No. 480/4, 1993); FELIX DASSER, INTERNATIONALE SCHIEDSGERICHTE UND LEX MERCATORIA – RECHTSVERGLEICHENDER BEITRAG ZUR DISKUSSION ÜBER EIN NICHTSTAATLICHES HANDELSRECHT (1989); Jan A.S. Paulsson, *La Lex Mercatoria dans l'arbitrage C.C.I.*, 1990 REV. ARB. 55; FILALI OSMAN, LES PRINCIPES GÉNÉRAUX DE LA *LEX MERCATORIA* – CONTRIBUTION À L'ÉTUDE D'UN ORDRE JURIDIQUE ANATIONAL (1992); FILIP J.M. DE LY, INTERNATIONAL BUSINESS LAW AND LEX MERCATORIA (1992); DOMINIQUE BUREAU, LES SOURCES INFORMELLES DU DROIT DANS LES RELATIONS PRIVÉES INTERNATIONALES (Thesis, University of Paris II (France), 1992); Ning Jin, *The Status of Lex Mercatoria in International Commercial Arbitration*, 7 AM. REV. INT'L ARB. 163 (1996); LEX MERCATORIA AND ARBITRATION (T.E. Carbonneau ed., rev. ed., 1998); KLAUS PETER BERGER, THE CREEPING CODIFICATION OF THE LEX MERCATORIA (1999).

[89] On this issue, see *infra* paras. 1554 *et seq.*

[90] See Fouchard, *supra* note 11, ¶ 39, Goldman, *supra* note 13, at 164; DE BOISSÉSON, *supra* note 41, ¶ 661 at 591; ROBERT, *supra* note 78, ¶ 1440 (who goes as far as suggesting that the parties may be able to choose to have no law govern their contract). On this issue, see the discussion *supra* para. 1441.

[91] See, e.g., CA Paris, June 25, 1993, Schönenberger Systemtechnik GmbH v. S.A. Vens, 1993 REV. ARB. 685, and observations by D. Bureau.

[92] See A.V.M. Struycken, *La lex mercatoria dans le droit des contrats internationaux*, in L'ÉVOLUTION CONTEMPORAINE DU DROIT DES CONTRATS – JOURNÉES RENÉE SAVATIER, POITIERS, 24-25 OCTOBRE 1985, at 207, 227 (1986).

chosen by the parties," thus giving the parties the option of applying *lex mercatoria*, in one form or another.[93] A large number of laws, including those of Italy,[94] Egypt,[95] Mexico[96] and Germany[97] followed suit.[98] This is largely due to the fact that, in 1985, the UNCITRAL Model Law embraced the trend by providing in its Article 28 that "the arbitral tribunal shall decide the dispute in accordance with such rules of law as are chosen by the parties[99] as applicable to the substance of the dispute." Some authors have argued, rather curiously, that the expression "rules of law" found in the UNCITRAL Model Law covers certain transnational rules, such as international conventions, but that it is not intended to enable the parties to submit their dispute to general principles of law or to *lex mercatoria*.[100] However, neither the terminology employed, nor the Model Law's *travaux préparatoires* justify such a restrictive interpretation.[101]

---

[93] See LALIVE, POUDRET, REYMOND, *supra* note 2, at 393; BUCHER AND TSCHANZ, *supra* note 29, ¶¶ 211 *et seq.*; Marc Blessing, *The New International Arbitration Law in Switzerland – A Significant Step Towards Liberalism*, 5 J. INT'L ARB. 9, 60 (June 1988); Pierre Lalive and Emmanuel Gaillard, *Le nouveau droit de l'arbitrage international en Suisse*, 116 J.D.I. 905, 945 (1989).

[94] See Art. 834 of the Italian Code of Civil Procedure, as amended by Law No. 25 of January 5, 1994, and the commentary by Piero Bernardini, *L'arbitrage en Italie après la récente réforme*, 1994 REV. ARB. 479, 492. *See also* Piero Bernardini, *Italy*, in ICCA INTERNATIONAL HANDBOOK ON COMMERCIAL ARBITRATION (forthcoming in 1999).

[95] See Art. 39 of Egyptian Law No. 27 of 1994 Promulgating the Law Concerning Arbitration in Civil and Commercial Matters, and the commentary by Bernard Fillion-Dufouleur and Philippe Leboulanger, *Le nouveau droit égyptien de l'arbitrage*, 1994 REV. ARB. 665, 678.

[96] See Art. 1445(2) of the Mexican Law on Arbitration of July 22, 1993.

[97] See Art. 1051 of the ZPO, in force as of January 1, 1998.

[98] See also Art. 813 of the 1983 Lebanese New Code of Civil Procedure, and the commentary by Marie Sfeir-Slim, *Le nouveau droit libanais de l'arbitrage a dix ans*, 1993 REV. ARB. 543, 589; Abdul Hamid El-Ahdab, *The Lebanese Arbitration Act*, 13 J. INT'L ARB. 39, 93 (Sept. 1996); Art. 458 bis 14 of the Algerian Code of Civil Procedure (Legislative Decree No. 93-09 of 1993), and the commentary by Mohand Issad, *Le décret législatif algérien du 25 avril 1993 relatif à l'arbitrage international*, 1993 REV. ARB. 377, 386; Art. 2 of the Brazilian law on Arbitration dated September 23, 1996, which refers to "rules of law" and "general principles of law, usage and customs and the rules of international commerce;" *see* João Bosco Lee, *Le nouveau régime de l'arbitrage au Brésil*, 1997 REV. ARB. 199. On the meaning of Article 73 of the Tunisian Arbitration Code (Law No. 93-42 of April 26, 1993), and the divergence between the Arab language version and the translation into French, see Kalthoum Meziou and Ali Mezghani, *Le Code tunisien de l'arbitrage*, 1993 REV. ARB. 521, 533. On the situation in China, see Hong-Lin Yu, *Some Thoughts on the Legal Status of A-national Principles in China*, 1 INT'L ARB. L. REV. 185 (1998).

[99] On the more conservative position adopted when the arbitrators are to select the applicable law, see *infra* para. 1556.

[100] See HOWARD HOLTZMANN AND JOSEPH E. NEUHAUS, A GUIDE TO THE UNCITRAL MODEL LAW ON INTERNATIONAL COMMERCIAL ARBITRATION – LEGISLATIVE HISTORY AND COMMENTARY 768 (1989); RUDOLF MEYER, BONA FIDES UND LEX MERCATORIA IN DER EUROPAISCHEN RECHTSTRADITION (1994), and the review by Ignaz Seidl-Hohenveldern, 121 J.D.I. 1114 (1994), although the author is generally in favor of the existence of a law common to the community of merchants.

[101] On the issue, see, in particular, the observations made by A. Broches during the August 21, 1990 working session of the International Law Association's Committee on International Commercial Arbitration, on the Committee's Report on "The Applicability of Transnational Rules in International Commercial Arbitration," INTERNATIONAL LAW ASSOCIATION, REPORT OF THE SIXTY-FOURTH CONFERENCE – BROADBEACH,

(continued...)

Even in legal systems which, like that of England, have traditionally been extremely skeptical with respect to the application of transnational rules, it has been recognized, first by the courts[102] and then in the 1996 Arbitration Act,[103] that the parties can validly choose transnational rules as their applicable law.[104]

1445. — The acceptance of the validity of general principles of law as the law governing the contract is in keeping with international arbitral practice. The resolution adopted in 1979 in Athens by the Institute of International Law endorsed that approach in relation to state contracts, by providing that:

> [t]he parties may in particular choose as the proper law of the contract either one or several domestic legal systems or the principles common to such systems, or the general principles of law, or the principles applied in international economic relations, or international law, or a combination of these sources of law.[105]

The resolution adopted by the Institute in 1989 in Santiago de Compostela, again in connection with state contracts, was more general in scope, and provided that:

> these rules and principles [chosen by the parties] may be derived from different national legal systems as well as from non-national sources such as principles of international law, general principles of law and the usages of international commerce.

---

[101] (...continued)
QUEENSLAND, AUSTRALIA 126, 147 (1991); Lando, *supra* note 19, at 154; Philippe Fouchard, *La Loi-type de la C.N.U.D.C.I. sur l'arbitrage commercial international*, 114 J.D.I. 861, 878 (1987). For a discussion of the position of the principal international conventions in this respect, see Horacio A. Grigera Naon, *Enforceability of Awards Based on Transnational Rules Under the New York, Panama, Geneva and Washington Conventions*, *in* TRANSNATIONAL RULES IN INTERNATIONAL COMMERCIAL ARBITRATION, *supra* note 88, at 89.

[102] See, in particular, *Deutsche Schachtbau*, *supra* note 19; Pierre Lalive, *Arbitrage en Suisse et "Lex mercatoria" (Note sur un important arrêt anglais)*, 1987 BULL. ASA 165; David W. Rivkin, *Enforceability of Arbitral Awards Based on Lex Mercatoria*, 9 ARB. INT'L 67, especially at 72 *et seq.* (1993).

[103] After having established, in its Section 46(1)(a), the principle that the arbitrators shall decide the dispute "in accordance with the law chosen by the parties," the 1996 Arbitration Act states in its Section 46(1)(b) that "if the parties so agree," the arbitral tribunal shall decide the dispute "in accordance with such other considerations as are agreed by them or determined by the tribunal." This euphemism obviously covers any form of *lex mercatoria*. On the issue, see Stewart R. Shackleton, *The Applicable Law in International Arbitration Under the New English Arbitration Act 1996*, 13 ARB. INT'L 375 (1997); Claude Reymond, *L'Arbitration Act 1996 – Convergence et Originalité*, 1997 REV. ARB. 45, 63.

[104] For an early example of an award rendered in London on the basis of general principles of law, see the September 2, 1930 *ad hoc* Award, Lena Goldfields Ltd. v. USSR, discussed in V.V. Veeder, *The Lena Goldfields Arbitration: the Historical Roots of Three Ideas*, 47 INT'L & COMP. L.Q. 747 (1998).

[105] Art. 2, *supra* note 48.

In even clearer terms, the International Law Association adopted a resolution following its conference held in Cairo in April 1992, which reads as follows:

> [t]he fact that an international arbitrator has based an award on transnational rules (general principles of law, principles common to several jurisdictions, international law, usages of trade, etc.) rather than on the law of a particular State should not in itself affect the validity or enforceability of the award;
>
> (1) where the parties have agreed that the arbitrator may apply transnational rules.[106]

1446. — Nevertheless, the terminology used remains vague in both contractual practice and academic commentary.

Parties resort to a variety of expressions to convey their intention that the contract be governed by transnational rules, such as "general principles of international commercial law," "generally-recognized legal principles" and "principles common to several legal systems."[107] In state contracts, governing law clauses are complicated by references borrowed from public international law such as "international custom," "international law" and "general principles of law within the meaning of Article 38 of the Statute of the International Court of Justice."[108]

Authors have endeavored to be more systematic by giving a precise definition to each of the expressions used, but the terminology still varies considerably from one author to the next.[109] One has suggested that general principles in the public international law sense should be distinguished from general principles of international commercial law and that "general principles" should in any event be distinguished from "usages" and from "principles common to the parties' national laws."[110] For a generic description of rules other than those of a particular national law, some authors use the expression "a-national law"[111]

---

[106] Report of the Sixty-Fifth Conference, Cairo 1992 and the commentary in TRANSNATIONAL RULES IN INTERNATIONAL COMMERCIAL ARBITRATION, *supra* note 88, at 36 and 65. On the case where the parties are silent, see *infra* para. 1556.

[107] See, for example, the clauses cited by Rivkin, *supra* note 102.

[108] See, for example, the numerous clauses cited by Prosper Weil, *Principes généraux du droit et contrats d'Etat, in* LE DROIT DES RELATIONS ÉCONOMIQUES INTERNATIONALES – ETUDES OFFERTES À BERTHOLD GOLDMAN 387, especially at 389 *et seq.* (1982). For an example of the use of the words "international law" in a private law contract, see ICC Award No. 8365 (1996), Spanish bank v. German bank, 124 J.D.I. 1078 (1997), and observations by J.-J. Arnaldez.

[109] *See, e.g.*, Michel Virally, *Un tiers droit? Réflexions théoriques, in* LE DROIT DES RELATIONS ÉCONOMIQUES INTERNATIONALES – ETUDES OFFERTES À BERTHOLD GOLDMAN 373 (1982); Weil, *supra* note 109, at 405 *et seq.*; CLIVE SCHMITTHOFF, INTERNATIONAL TRADE USAGES (ICC Publication No. 440/4, 1987); for a discussion of the distinctions put forward, see Bruno Oppetit, *Arbitrage et contrats d'Etat – L'arbitrage Framatome et autres c/ Atomic Energy Organization of Iran*, 111 J.D.I. 37 (1984).

[110] Oppetit, *supra* note 110, at 45–46.

[111] PHILIPPE FOUCHARD, L'ARBITRAGE COMMERCIAL INTERNATIONAL ¶¶ 576 *et seq.* (1965).

or "a-national rules,"[112] while others refer to "international trade usages,"[113] or to transnational rules.[114] However, the term most frequently used in a generic sense, whether to promote the concept or to criticize it, is *lex mercatoria*.[115]

1447. — At the risk of adding to the confusion, and with little hope of being able to impose definitive meanings for each expression, we shall simply give the meaning attributed to each of those expressions as used hereafter. Indeed, the terminological debate is only important in so far as it facilitates discussion, on a substantive level, of the way in which the various concepts fit together.

To denote rules other than those of a given jurisdiction, we shall use the generic expression *lex mercatoria*. The expression appears essentially in academic writing, and it covers not only transnational rules (which can only be described negatively as all rules which do not originate exclusively from a particular national legal system), but also international trade usages (meaning the practices usually followed in a particular trade).

In general, we prefer the term "transnational rules" to "a-national rules," because such rules derive from the convergence of the main legal systems from which they are drawn. It is therefore counterintuitive to suggest that they have no link with national legal orders. Transnational rules in turn embrace two separate concepts: first, rules which are common to several legal systems, determined on the basis of the "*tronc commun*" method;[116] and,

---

[112] Eric Loquin, *L'application de règles anationales dans l'arbitrage commercial international*, *in* L'APPORT DE LA JURISPRUDENCE ARBITRALE 67 (ICC Publication No. 440/1, 1986); DE BOISSÉSON, *supra* note 41, at 611.

[113] E. Loquin, *La réalité des usages du commerce international*, 1989 RID ÉCO. 163.

[114] Lalive, *supra* note 49, at 31; the preliminary reports by Horacio A. Grigera Naon ("Civil Law Countries") and Paul Bowden ("Common Law Countries"), *The Applicability of Transnational Rules in International Commercial Arbitration*, *in* INTERNATIONAL LAW ASSOCIATION, REPORT OF THE SIXTY-FOURTH CONFERENCE, *supra* note 101, at 127 and 136.

[115] See, for example, in addition to the authors cited *supra* note 88, Michael J. Mustill, *The New Lex Mercatoria: The First Twenty-five Years*, *reprinted in* LIBER AMICORUM FOR THE RT. HON. LORD WILBERFORCE 149 (M. Bos and I. Brownlie eds., 1987), *reprinted in* 4 ARB. INT'L 86 (1988); Paulsson, *supra* note 88; Andreas F. Lowenfeld, *Lex Mercatoria: An Arbitrator's View*, 6 ARB. INT'L 133 (1990); Christoph W.O. Stoecker, *The Lex Mercatoria: To What Extent Does It Exist?*, 7 J. INT'L ARB. 101 (Mar. 1990); Ole Lando, *The Lex Mercatoria in International Commercial Arbitration*, 34 INT'L & COMP. L.Q. 747 (1985); Keith Highet, *The Enigma of the Lex Mercatoria*, 63 TUL. L. REV. 613 (1989); Georges R. Delaume, *The Proper Law of State Contracts and the Lex Mercatoria: A Reappraisal*, 3 ICSID REV. – FOREIGN INV. L.J. 79 (1988); Georges R. Delaume, *Comparative Analysis as a Basis of Law in State Contracts: the Myth of the Lex Mercatoria*, 63 TUL. L. REV. 575 (1989); Philippe Kahn, *Droit international économique, droit du développement, lex mercatoria: concept unique ou pluralisme des ordres juridiques?*, *in* LE DROIT DES RELATIONS ÉCONOMIQUES INTERNATIONALES – ETUDES OFFERTES À BERTHOLD GOLDMAN 97 (1982); Vanessa L.D. Wilkinson, *The New Lex Mercatoria – Reality or Academic Fantasy?*, 12 J. INT'L ARB. 103 (June 1995); JACK J. COE, JR., INTERNATIONAL COMMERCIAL ARBITRATION: AMERICAN PRINCIPLES AND PRACTICE IN A GLOBAL CONTEXT 80 *et seq.* (1997).

[116] On this method, see especially RUBINO-SAMMARTANO, *supra* note 3, at 274 *et seq.*, who distinguishes it from that of "*lex mercatoria*;" *see also* Mauro Rubino-Sammartano, *Le "tronc commun" des lois nationales en présence (Réflexions sur le droit applicable par l'arbitre international)*, 1987 REV. ARB. 133; Mauro Rubino-Sammartano, *The Channel Tunnel and the Tronc Commun Doctrine*, 10 J. INT'L ARB. 59 (Sept. 1993). *Comp. with* Bertrand Ancel, *The Tronc Commun Doctrine: Logics and Experience in International Arbitration*,

(continued...)

second, general principles of international trade law, drawn from all the main legal systems and from international sources such as international arbitral case law and international conventions, which demonstrate widespread acceptance of the rule in question by the international legal community. The adoption of the UNIDROIT "Principles of International Commercial Contracts" shows that attempts at unification can actually bear fruit. The authors of the UNIDROIT principles recognize that their principles can be chosen by parties to govern contracts and that they can be applied when the parties have agreed that their contract is governed by "general principles of law," "*lex mercatoria*" or similar concepts.[117] It is also important to focus on the relationship between general principles of international commercial law and principles of public international law. In any situation, principles of public international law, themselves often drawn from comparative law, can provide a source of inspiration for principles of international commercial law because, like international conventions, they demonstrate the general acceptance of a set of rules. In the specific context of state contracts, the application of principles of public international law, modified where appropriate by the requirements of international commercial law, may well be more directly justifiable than in a purely private law context, particularly in defining the obligations of the state towards the private party.

It is also essential, for reasons which we shall consider in detail later, not to confuse transnational rules with international trade usages. The latter are practices generally followed in a specific industry, as opposed to genuine rules of law.[118]

1448. — The parties' freedom to have their dispute governed by "rules of law" allows them to resort to any of the components of *lex mercatoria* described above. The arbitrators must therefore establish exactly what the parties had in mind when they used a particular expression to describe the rules of law applicable to the dispute. In so doing, they must take into account the continuing linguistic fluctuations and search for the true intention of the parties by going beyond the terms actually used. Thus, although we consider that the expression "trade usages" has a specific meaning and should not be confused with general principles of international trade law,[119] that does not necessarily mean that parties do not actually intend to apply general principles when referring to "usages." As the arbitrators are required to give effect to the intentions of the parties, it would be perfectly legitimate for them to apply general principles in such cases.[120]

---

[116] (...continued)
7 J. INT'L ARB. 65 (Sept. 1990).

[117] UNIDROIT, PRINCIPLES OF INTERNATIONAL COMMERCIAL CONTRACTS (1994). See especially the preamble and the comment at 3–4. See also the references cited *infra* para. 1458, note 174.

[118] *See infra* para. 1513.

[119] The expression "trade usages" is used in Article 17(2) (formerly 13(5)) of the ICC Rules) and in certain arbitration statutes. *See infra* para. 1514.

[120] On this issue, see Gaillard, *supra* note 65, at 212 and n. 33.

B. – CRITICAL ANALYSIS OF TRANSNATIONAL RULES

1449. — Ever since it appeared in the 1960s,[121] the concept of *lex mercatoria* has been heavily criticized. In fact, if—as we believe they should—trade usages are defined restrictively as meaning only practices which are usually followed in a specific sector of business activity,[122] the criticism concerns primarily transnational rules and, in particular, general principles of international commercial law drawn from international sources and from the analysis of comparative law.

The criticism leveled at transnational rules is broadly of three kinds.

1° Conceptual Criticism

1450. — The first kind of criticism is conceptual. It involves the rejection of the idea that *lex mercatoria* can constitute a genuine legal order in the same way as national laws or public international law. In this respect, the strongest criticism[123] is essentially based on the argument that the diverse rules grouped together under the heading *lex mercatoria*[124] are not sufficiently organized to satisfy the criteria which traditionally define the existence of a legal order.[125]

Two arguments can be put forward against that view.

First, general principles of law, which are the most significant constituent of *lex mercatoria*, are becoming increasingly specialized in arbitral practice. With specialization, they tend to form a coherent set of rules which, though incomplete, presents one of the characteristic features of a legal order: it contains general rules which lead to the creation of specific ones.[126]

---

[121] On the analysis of early applications of *lex mercatoria*, see, for example, DE LY, *supra* note 88, ¶¶ 8 *et seq.*

[122] *See infra* para. 1514.

[123] Paul Lagarde, *Approche critique de la lex mercatoria*, in LE DROIT DES RELATIONS ÉCONOMIQUES INTERNATIONALES – ETUDES OFFERTES À BERTHOLD GOLDMAN 125 (1982); *see also* ANTOINE KASSIS, THÉORIE GÉNÉRALE DES USAGES DU COMMERCE ¶¶ 584 *et seq.* (1984).

[124] *See infra* paras. 1454 *et seq.*

[125] On these criteria, see SANTI ROMANO, L'ORDRE JURIDIQUE (1975).

[126] See on the example of estoppel, which, in this context, is derived from the more general principle of good faith, Emmanuel Gaillard, *L'interdiction de se contredire au détriment d'autrui comme principe général du droit du commerce international (le principe de l'estoppel dans quelques sentences arbitrales récentes)*, 1985 REV. ARB. 241; *comp. with* Philippe Pinsolle, *Distinction entre le principe de l'estoppel et le principe de bonne foi dans le droit du commerce international*, 125 J.D.I. 905 (1998); more generally, on the numerous rules derived from the principle of good faith in the performance of contracts, see E. Gaillard, observations on the October 21, 1983 Award in ICSID Case No. ARB/81/2, Klöckner Industrie-Anlagen GmbH v. United Republic of Cameroon, 114 J.D.I. 137, 141 (1987); on the various rules derived from the obligation of the parties to cooperate in good faith, see Loquin, *supra* note 114, at 190. Significantly, there is now an increasing number of references to specialized branches of *lex mercatoria*. *See, e.g.*, Charles Molineaux, *Moving Toward a Construction Lex Mercatoria – A Lex Constructionis*, 14 J. INT'L ARB. 55 (Mar. 1997); Aboubacar Fall, *Defence and Illustration of Lex Mercatoria in Maritime Arbitration – The Case Study of "Extra–Contractual*

(continued...)

Second, and more importantly, it is by no means evident that to be the object of a valid choice of governing law the rules chosen must necessarily be organized in a distinct legal order. Although the insistence by some advocates of *lex mercatoria* that it fulfils the criteria that traditionally define a legal order[127] may have fueled the controversy on this point, it is the idea that the parties' choice of applicable law is necessarily restricted to a complete legal order which is questionable.[128] The justification based on that idea, whatever the order may be, is inoperative here. As long as the arbitrator can use a set of rules, whether complete or not, to avoid blindly giving effect to the terms of the contract,[129] this criticism is misconceived. Furthermore, the control exercised by the courts in international commercial arbitration is largely based on the concept of international public policy, as applied when actions are brought to set aside or resist enforcement of an award. While we do not believe that arbitrators should automatically apply the provisions of a contract irrespective of its content,[130] the fact remains that the subsequent review of the arbitrators' award by the courts to ensure its consistency with international public policy should dispel any fears arising from provisions which leave the arbitrators free to apply general principles of law rather than a national law.

In any event, it is quite clear that by allowing the parties to refer to "rules of law" rather than to a "law," all of the statutes which have chosen to follow Article 1496 of the French New Code of Civil Procedure in this respect contradict the theory that, in order to be capable of being a valid choice of governing law, *lex mercatoria* must constitute a complete legal order.

2° Ideological Criticism

1451. — The second form of criticism leveled at *lex mercatoria* is ideological. *Lex mercatoria* is sometimes presented as only being to the benefit of the stronger parties to a contractual relationship and, in particular, to parties from developed nations in relations between developed and developing countries.[131] One commentator has observed, without actually endorsing such criticism, that:

---

[126] (...continued)

Detention" in Voyage Charter-party Disputes, 15 J. INT'L ARB. 83 (Mar. 1998); R. Doak Bishop, *International Arbitration of Petroleum Disputes: the Development of Lex Petrolea*, XXIII Y.B. COM. ARB. 1131 (1998).

[127] Criteria defined by ROMANO, *supra* note 126. For such an approach, see, for example, Loquin, *supra* note 113, especially Part II, "*L'existence d'un ordre juridique a-national.*"

[128] *See* BUCHER AND TSCHANZ, *supra* note 29, ¶ 226.

[129] *See infra* paras. 1454 *et seq.*

[130] *See supra* para. 1440.

[131] See, for example, Wengler, *supra* note 54, at 501; AMOR ZAHI, L'ETAT ET L'ARBITRAGE 225 *et seq.* (1985).

how often parties involved in international commerce and their counsels have . . . called to be released from the 'shackles' of national laws, so as to submit themselves to more suitable rules, which they would impose on themselves 'spontaneously,' and how often, in return, their attempt has met with the suspicion that it conceals a 'law of the strong' imposed by powerful corporations on weaker ones, or even a take-over of the transnational legal 'space' by private economic powers.[132]

In other words, it has been suggested that "[e]ssentially, the *lex mercatoria* is a doctrine of *laissez-faire*."[133]

This criticism is connected in two respects to that of the idea that *lex mercatoria* is a legal order.[134] First, *lex mercatoria* being an incomplete set of rules, any contract selecting it as the applicable law will only partially be governed by rules of law. According to this view, *lex mercatoria* thus leads to the recognition of a contract which has, to some extent, no governing law ("*contrat sans loi*"). Second, the content of *lex mercatoria* prompts some authors to conclude that it is merely another way of affirming the primacy of the contract over the law. If one considers the principle *pacta sunt servanda* to be the most fundamental—if not the only—principle of *lex mercatoria*, having the contract governed by *lex mercatoria* could result in the terms of the contract prevailing over any other rule. That, once again, would lead to a contract with no governing law.

1452. — Such criticism is not altogether unfounded. It is true that some awards give the impression that the only achievement, if not the only aim, of the substantial efforts that some authors devote to the subject of *lex mercatoria* has been the justification of the principle of the binding character of contracts. The principle of good faith in the performance of contracts[135] is often included, as is the principle of the protection of vested rights.[136] However, those additions scarcely add anything to the principle *pacta sunt servanda* if "bad faith" is simply defined, as is the case in some arbitral awards, as the failure to comply with the contract, and "vested rights" as those rights which result from a straightforward application of the contract.[137]

1453. — However, although this misguided application of the *lex mercatoria* doctrine is sometimes found, it does not necessarily follow from the general principles of law method. Nothing in the elaboration of transnational rules restricts the method to the principle of the binding authority of contracts. It is equally evident, from comparing national laws and

---

[132] Lagarde, *supra* note 124, at 125–26.

[133] Mustill, *supra* note 116, at 181.

[134] *See supra* para. 1450.

[135] See the awards cited *infra* para. 1460.

[136] See the awards cited *infra* para. 1461.

[137] On this issue, see *infra* para. 1461.

international sources, that only validly concluded contracts are binding on the parties and that there are a number of exceptions to the principle of the binding character of contracts.[138] This allows a perfectly clear distinction to be drawn between the doctrine of transnational rules and that of contracts with no governing law.

In addition, it is by no means clear that a strict application of the *pacta sunt servanda* principle is necessarily unfavorable to the weaker party, and in particular to developing countries and their nationals, who are nowadays more often claimants in arbitral proceedings than they were in the past. Neither is it clear that arbitral awards based on general principles are systematically unfavorable to the weaker party. For example, in the *Klöckner* case, the 1983 ICSID award found in favor of the Republic of Cameroon on the basis of the principle of "the duty of full disclosure to a partner."[139] In 1985, amidst much criticism, an *ad hoc* Committee annulled that award on the grounds that in that case it was not legitimate to apply exclusively general principles of law.[140] Principles such as the sovereignty of states over their natural resources, the protection of humanity's cultural heritage[141] and the interpretation of a contract against the party that drafted it,[142] all of which tend to protect the State or the weaker party, equally form part of the general principles of international commercial law. Transnational rules therefore cannot be suspected of being inherently unfavorable to developing countries.[143]

3° Practical Criticism

1454. — The third kind of criticism raised against the use of transnational rules and, more specifically, general principles of law concerns the difficulty of determining their exact content. This criticism is particularly prevalent in common law countries. There has been much cynicism as to the vague nature of general principles, described in ironic terms as being so difficult to define that they appear to boil down to what the arbitrators decide in each particular case. That has prompted some commentators to ask whether *lex mercatoria* offers "a set of rules which is sufficiently accessible and certain to permit the efficient conduct of . . . transactions."[144] Compared to a given national law, *lex mercatoria* is

---

[138] *See infra* paras. 1464 *et seq.*

[139] October 21, 1983 Award by E. Jimenez de Arechaga, president, W.D. Rogers and D. Schmidt, arbitrators (D. Schmidt dissenting), in ICSID Case No. ARB/81/2, Klöckner Industrie-Anlagen GmbH v. United Republic of Cameroon, 111 J.D.I. 409, 426 (1984), and observations by E. Gaillard, 114 J.D.I. 137 (1987); for an English translation, see 1 J. INT'L ARB. 145 (1984); X Y.B. COM. ARB. 71 (1985); 2 ICSID REP. 9 (1994).

[140] Decision of May 3, 1985, by P. Lalive, president, A. El-Kosheri and I. Seidl-Hohenveldern, arbitrators, 114 J.D.I. 163 (1987), and observations by E. Gaillard at 185; for an English translation, see 1 ICSID REV. – FOREIGN INV. L.J. 89 (1986); XI Y.B. COM. ARB. 162 (1986); 2 ICSID REP. 95 (1994).

[141] *See infra* para. 1468.

[142] *See infra* para. 1475.

[143] *See* Philippe Leboulanger, *L'arbitrage international Nord-Sud, in* ETUDES OFFERTES À PIERRE BELLET 323, especially at 338 *et seq.* (1991).

[144] Mustill, *supra* note 116, at 180.

described as being vague and incomplete. Contradictions sometimes arise from the grey areas surrounding certain rules, and critics point out, for example, that the principle *pacta sunt servanda* and the doctrine of change in circumstances ("*imprévision*")—which is presented for the purposes of their reasoning as the negation of the principle *pacta sunt servanda*—are both included among the rules of *lex mercatoria*.[145] It has also been suggested that in quantitative terms the results of twenty-five years of applying *lex mercatoria* are somewhat disappointing.[146]

We consider that although these observations do contain an element of truth, this owes more to the nature of arbitration than to the use of general principles. As arbitral tribunals are neither permanent nor organized in a hierarchy aimed at providing a uniform interpretation of the law by a supreme court, the case law they generate cannot aspire to the same degree of consistency as that of the courts of a particular jurisdiction. If, from the point of view of the predictability of the applicable rules, the ideal is national law as applied by the relevant supreme court, there is no doubt that arbitral tribunals offer a lesser degree of predictability. However, in the context of international commerce, the real question is whether arbitrators ruling on the basis of general principles of international commercial law are significantly less predictable than arbitrators ruling on the basis of a national law, or even than a national court applying a law other than its own national law. Given the nature of international arbitration, the striking feature of arbitral case law is in fact the remarkable consistency of the decisions reached in spite of the diversity of the reasoning employed.[147] Further, and although its importance should not be exaggerated, the flexibility gained by the arbitrators in being able to apply general principles of law is perfectly legitimate, provided that the parties clearly intended that they should do so.[148]

The argument that some of the principles of *lex mercatoria* are contradictory also fails to take into account the way the rules of *lex mercatoria* tend to be organized. Assuming that the doctrine of *imprévision* is a transnational rule, which is sometimes recognized in arbitral case law,[149] there is no incompatibility with the principle *pacta sunt servanda*. It is simply an exception to that principle, and an exception which only comes into play where a number of conditions are satisfied. In legal systems where the doctrine applies, there is no contradiction between the provisions implementing the doctrine of *imprévision* and those implementing the principle *pacta sunt servanda*. On the contrary, those provisions are

---

[145] *See, e.g.,* KASSIS, *supra* note 124, at 349 *et seq.* But see, on the reality of arbitral case law, *infra* para. 1458 and on this issue, generally, *supra* paras. 371 *et seq.*

[146] Mustill, *supra* note 116, at 180; *comp. with* Georges R. Delaume, *The Proper Law of State Contracts and the Lex Mercatoria: A Reappraisal,* 3 ICSID REV. – FOREIGN INV. L.J. 79 (1988); Stoecker, *supra* note 116, at 125; Emmanuel Gaillard, *Centre International pour le Règlement des Différends Relatifs aux Investissements (C.I.R.D.I.) – Chronique des sentences arbitrales,* 113 J.D.I. 197, 199 (1986).

[147] *See infra* paras. 1459 *et seq.* On the relative predictability of transnational rules, see Emmanuel Gaillard, *Use of General Principles of International Law in International Long-Term Contracts,* 27 INT'L BUS. LAW. 214 (1999).

[148] For the situation where the parties are silent as to the applicable law, see *infra* paras. 1554 *et seq.*

[149] *See infra* para. 1482.

linked, often in a single article, by the logic of principle and exception.[150] *Lex mercatoria*, which is becoming increasingly structured,[151] is perfectly capable of resolving such supposed contradictions although, in the absence of a supranational court responsible for maintaining uniformity in arbitral case law, differences of interpretation may continue to arise.

Finally, we need to address the argument based on what is perceived as inadequacy of *lex mercatoria* in quantitative terms. It will only be impossible to find within *lex mercatoria* "a set of rules which is sufficiently accessible and certain to permit the efficient conduct of ... transactions"[152] if one's objective is to draw up a *list* of general principles which already appear in arbitral case law. However, to seek to draw up such a list is to misunderstand the aims of the *lex mercatoria* doctrine: the application of general principles is essentially a *method*—as opposed to a list—enabling almost any number of principles to be identified and applied to each disputed situation. We shall now examine that method, and the results it produces.

C. – METHOD AND CONTENT OF TRANSNATIONAL RULES

1455. — When faced with a clause which, in one form or another,[153] provides that a dispute is to be governed by transnational rules, the arbitrators, the parties and their counsels will have to determine, once the dispute has arisen, the actual content of the rules applicable to the dispute. This is the true test of the effectiveness of *lex mercatoria* as an instrument for resolving disputes in international trade. Again, it cannot be too strongly emphasized that applying transnational rules involves understanding and implementing a method, rather than drawing up a list of the general principles of international commercial law.[154]

Therefore, after first discussing the transnational rules method, we shall examine a few examples of rules generally considered as being general principles of international commercial law.

1° Method

1456. — Two issues should be borne in mind with respect to the method to be used when identifying and applying general principles.

---

[150] A good illustration of this structure can be seen in the 1994 UNIDROIT Principles of International Commercial Contracts, *supra* note 118, Arts. 6.2.1 *et seq.*, at 145 *et seq.*

[151] *See supra* para. 1450.

[152] *See* Mustill, *supra* note 116, at 180.

[153] *See supra* para. 1446.

[154] On this issue, generally, see TRANSNATIONAL RULES IN INTERNATIONAL COMMERCIAL ARBITRATION, *supra* note 88; Gaillard, *supra* note 88, 10 ICSID REV. – FOREIGN INV. L. J. 224–28 (1995); 122 J.D.I 22–26 (1995); *but see* BERGER, *supra* note 88, at 218 *et seq.*

1457. — The first is that the starting point for any analysis of the method for determining applicable rules of law must be the choice of law clause itself. In using the generic term *lex mercatoria* to cover all of the different situations where the parties do not simply choose a particular national law, it is important not to lose sight of the diversity of the concepts liable to be included under that heading.[155] Amid the controversy over the legal nature of *lex mercatoria* and the various criticisms it has attracted,[156] it is equally important to take full account of the diversity of the contractual provisions submitting certain disputes to rules other than those of a particular legal system. The task of the arbitrators—and hence that of the parties when presenting their case—is invariably to give effect to the choice initially made by the parties. The parties and the arbitrators should therefore begin by examining the choice of law clause for guidance as to the method to be used to determine the relevant rules for resolving the dispute.

Some clauses provide that principles common to several specified legal systems are to apply. In such a case, the arbitrators must use the *"tronc common"* method[157] and conduct a comparative analysis limited to that of the listed legal systems, unless the clause itself allows other rules to be used on a subsidiary basis.

Thus, for example, the construction contract for the Channel Tunnel stated that it was governed by

> common principles of English and French law, and in the absence of such common principles by such principles of international trade law as have been applied by national and international tribunals.[158]

On several occasions, the panel of experts appointed under Article 67 of that same contract was required to draw up such common or general principles, and succeeded in doing so.[159]

It is fairly frequent for the application of a national law to be combined with that of principles of international origin. Thus, for example, an Iranian petroleum agreement signed in 1954 was governed by

---

[155] *See supra* para. 1447.

[156] *See supra* paras. 1450 *et seq.*

[157] See, for example, ICC Case No. 5163 where the arbitrators had to apply "the principles common to the laws of the Arab Republic of Egypt and the United States of America" (unpublished clause cited in Gaillard, *supra* note 88, 10 ICSID REV. – FOREIGN INV. L.J. 225 (1995); 122 J.D.I. 23 (1995)). On the terminology, see *supra* para. 1447.

[158] Clause 68 of the contractual conditions attached to the construction contract signed on August 13, 1986 by Eurotunnel and Transmanche Link (ed. of Jan. 27, 1987).

[159] On this panel, see *supra* para. 28.

principles of law common to Iran and to the various countries to which the other parties belong and, failing that, by principles of law generally recognized by civilized nations, including such principles applied by international tribunals.[160]

Similarly, the Libyan nationalization arbitrations were governed by

principles of law of Libya common to the principles of international law and, in the absence of such common principles . . . then by and in accordance with the general principles of law as may have been applied by international tribunals.[161]

More recently, the arbitrators who made the *ad hoc* award in the *Banque Arabe et Internationale d'Investissements* case on November 17, 1994 in Amman were required to apply to a contract, in the absence of provisions to the contrary, "common legal principles prevailing in the member countries of the Corporation, and the recognized principles of International Law."[162]

Other clauses refer exclusively to rules of international origin, with or without indicating how those rules should be determined. Such clauses are less common than combinations of rules from different legal systems, and they tend to be formulated in a variety of ways.[163]

In all cases, any indications given by parties as to the method of determining the applicable rules must take precedence. Such indications would include a specified hierarchy between the various given sources or instructions to apply only principles common to certain regions of the world.[164]

---

[160] Article 46 of the Tehran petroleum agreements of October 1954, 1956 REV. ARB. 63, 69. See also the unpublished arbitration clause in ICC Case No. 5331, cited in Gaillard, *supra* note 88, 10 ICSID REV. – FOREIGN INV. L.J. 225, n. 71; 122 J.D.I. 23, n. 71 (1995).

[161] *See* Apr. 12, 1977 *ad hoc* Award by S. Mahmassani, Libyan American Oil Co. (LIAMCO) v. Government of the Libyan Arab Republic, 20 I.L.M. 1, 33 (1981); VI Y.B. COM. ARB. 89 (1981); for a French translation, see 1980 REV. ARB. 132. *See also* Robert B. von Mehren and P. Nicholas Kourides, *International Arbitrations Between States and Foreign Private Parties: The Libyan Nationalization Cases*, 75 AM. J. INT'L L. 476 (1981). On the validity of these provisions, see, for example, Derains, *supra* note 28, at 390.

[162] Award by O. Nabulsi, chairman, Z. Hashem and A. El Kosheri, arbitrators, *supra* note 68.

[163] For example, "generally recognized principles of international commercial law," ICC Case No. 5333, unpublished. See also Article 3.4 of the Multilateral Investment Guarantee Agency General Conditions of Guarantee for Equity Investments, dated January 25, 1989, 4 ICSID REV. – FOREIGN INV. L.J. 112, 114, which refers to the contract, the convention establishing MIGA, and general principles of law. On this issue, see Jean Touscoz, *Le règlement des différends dans la Convention instituant l'Agence Multilatérale de Garantie des Investissements (A.M.G.I.): un développement de l'arbitrage international et du droit des investissements internationaux*, 1988 REV. ARB. 629, 636; Ibrahim F.I. Shihata, *Towards a Greater Depoliticization of Investment Disputes: The Roles of ICSID and MIGA*, 1 ICSID REV. – FOREIGN INV. L.J. 1 (1986).

[164] For example, "principles of law applicable in Western Europe," ICC Case No. 6378 (1991), 120 J.D.I. 1018 (1993), and observations by D. Hascher; principles of law applicable "in Northern Europe," unpublished clause. On regional transnational rules, see Gaillard, *supra* note 88, 10 ICSID REV. – FOREIGN INV. L.J. 230–31 (1995); 122 J.D.I. 28–30 (1995).

1458. — The second point to bear in mind is that where the parties submit their disputes to general principles of international commercial law, or behave in a manner which can reasonably be interpreted as conveying the same intention,[165] the arbitrators should determine the applicable rules by examining comparative law, international instruments and international case law.[166]

Comparative law is a fundamental source of transnational rules. Arbitrators often identify general principles by drawing them from various legal systems in which they are recognized, sometimes in different forms.[167] However, in order to be considered as a general principle, a rule need not be found in every legal system. That would amount to giving a veto to systems which take an isolated position, whereas the goal is precisely to find a generally accepted tendency rather than to select, often somewhat randomly, a particular legal system to govern disputes.[168]

International instruments and, in particular, international conventions are also a common source of inspiration for arbitrators seeking to determine the rules of *lex mercatoria*. This is entirely justified, in so far as these texts reflect the agreement of a number of countries on a particular issue. Thus, for example, arbitrators deciding a dispute concerning international sales of goods on the basis of general principles are likely to refer to the Vienna Convention of April 11, 1980, on Contracts for the International Sale of Goods.[169] Likewise, the

---

[165] *See supra* para. 1448.

[166] On the sources of *lex mercatoria*, see especially Lando, *supra* note 19, at 144 *et seq.*

[167] See, for example, on estoppel by representation, known in German and Swiss law as the principle of *non concedit venire contra factum proprium*, *infra* para 1462.

[168] See, with regard to the arbitration agreement, the example of the principle of separability set forth *supra* para. 405, note 43. On this issue, generally, see Gaillard, *supra* note 88, 10 ICSID REV. – FOREIGN INV. L.J. 228–30 (1995); 122 J.D.I. 26–28 (1995).

[169] On the application by arbitrators of the 1964 Hague Convention on the International Sale of Goods, which was the predecessor of the 1980 Vienna Convention, see ICC Award No. 2879 (1978), French buyer v. Yugoslavian seller, 106 J.D.I. 989 (1979), and observations by Y. Derains. But see, on the refusal to apply the 1980 Vienna Convention on the grounds that the Convention was not in force on the date the contract was signed, ICC Award No. 6281 (1989), Egyptian buyer v. Yugoslavian seller, 116 J.D.I. 1114 (1989), and observations by G. Aguilar Alvarez; 118 J.D.I. 1054 (1991), and D. Hascher's note; for an English translation, see XV Y.B. COM. ARB. 96 (1990). On the use of the Vienna Convention as a means of determining international trade usages, see ICC Award No. 5713 (Paris, 1989), Seller v. Buyer, XV Y.B. COM. ARB. 70 (1990); ICC Award No. 7331 (1994), Yugoslavian seller v. Italian buyer, 122 J.D.I. 1001 (1995), and observations by D. Hascher; ICC BULLETIN, Vol. 6, No. 2, at 73 (1995). On the use of the Vienna Convention to support the position of a national law, see ICC Award No. 6281 (1989), *supra*, 118 J.D.I. 1056 (1991); on the finding that the 1964 Convention had been incorporated into German law, see ICC Award No. 6309 (1991), German company v. Dutch company, 118 J.D.I. 1046 (1991), and observations by J.-J. Arnaldez; and, on the application of the Vienna Convention as the applicable law, ICC Award No. 7153 (1992), Austrian party v. Yugoslavian party, 119 J.D.I. 1006 (1992), and D. Hascher's note; ICC Award No. 8324 (1995), Seller v. Buyer, 123 J.D.I. 1019 (1996), and D. Hascher's note; ICC Award No. 8128 (1995), Buyer v. Seller, 123 J.D.I. 1024 (1996), and D. Hascher's note. On this issue, generally, see Jean-Paul Béraudo, *The United Nations Convention on Contracts for the International Sale of Goods and Arbitration*, ICC BULLETIN, Vol. 5, No. 1, at 60 (1994); Andrea Giardina, *International Conventions on Conflict of Laws and Substantive Law*, in ICCA CONGRESS SERIES NO. 7, PLANNING EFFICIENT ARBITRATION PROCEEDINGS/THE LAW APPLICABLE IN INTERNATIONAL ARBITRATION 459 (A.J. van den Berg ed., 1996). On the use of international treaties to establish transnational

(continued...)

resolutions of sufficiently representative international organizations can certainly lead to the creation of new general principles. For example, it is not surprising that, on the basis of the measures taken by the United Nations and the European Communities during the Gulf crisis, an arbitral tribunal identified and applied principles which effectively justify the non-performance of certain contracts signed with Iraqi parties.[170] In the same way, the work of an organization such as UNIDROIT is particulary influential in determining general principles of law.[171] In May 1994, UNIDROIT published a set of Principles of International Commercial Contracts. These principles are intended to apply particularly "where the parties have agreed that their contract be governed by 'general principles of law,' the '*lex mercatoria*' or the like."[172] The Principles consist of 108 rules presented in the form of a restatement and accompanied by a commentary. It is a remarkable work of comparative law, which has undoubtedly made a vital contribution to the development of transnational rules.[173]

Arbitrators also often refer to international case law in determining the content of transnational rules. This is naturally true of arbitral awards, which are now accessible as a result of their publication in various periodicals. It is in the area of general principles of law that it is most clear that the previously contentious issue of whether "arbitral case law" actually exists has been overtaken by arbitral practice. In arbitral practice, of course, arbitrators very often use precedents established by other arbitral awards rendered in similar

---

[169] (...continued)
choice of law rules, see *infra* para. 1549.

[170] *See* the July 20, 1992 Award rendered under the auspices of the Chamber of National and International Arbitration of Milan, Subcontractor v. Contractor, 1993 INT'L CONSTR. L. REV. 201; XVIII Y.B. COM. ARB. 80 (1993). For a compilation of the legislation passed following the Gulf conflict, see, for example, THE IMPACT OF THE FREEZE OF KUWAITI AND IRAQI ASSETS ON FINANCIAL INSTITUTIONS AND FINANCIAL TRANSACTIONS (B.R. Campbell & D. Newcomb eds., 1990); THE KUWAIT CRISIS: SANCTIONS AND THEIR ECONOMIC CONSEQUENCES (D.L. Bethlehem ed., 1991) (2 vols.); more generally, see Yves Derains, *L'impact des crises politiques internationales sur les contrats internationaux et l'arbitrage commercial international/The Impact of International Political Crises on International Contracts and International Commercial Arbitration*, 1992 INT'L BUS. L.J. 151; Lambert Matray, *Embargo and Prohibition of Performance*, *in* ACTS OF STATE AND ARBITRATION 69 (K.-H. Böckstiegel ed., 1997).

[171] *See, e.g.*, Michael Joachim Bonell, *The UNIDROIT Initiative for the Progressive Codification of International Trade Law*, 27 INT'L & COMP. L.Q. 413 (1978).

[172] *Supra* note 118, at 1. For an example of an award solely based on UNIDROIT Principles pursuant to the intention of the parties, see ICC Award No. 8331 (1996), Vehicle supplier v. Purchaser, 125 J.D.I. 1041 (1998), and observations by Y. Derains.

[173] On this issue, generally, see UNIDROIT PRINCIPLES FOR INTERNATIONAL COMMERCIAL CONTRACTS: A NEW LEX MERCATORIA? (ICC Publication No. 490/1, 1995); Klaus Peter Berger, *The Lex Mercatoria Doctrine and the UNIDROIT Principles of International Commercial Contracts*, 28 LAW & POL'Y INT'L BUS. 943 (1997); BERGER, *supra* note 88; Andrea Giardina, *Les Principes UNIDROIT sur les contrats internationaux*, 122 J.D.I. 547 (1995); Jean-Paul Béraudo, *Les principes d'Unidroit relatifs au droit du commerce international*, JCP, Ed. G, Pt. I, No. 3842 (1995); MICHAEL J. BONELL, AN INTERNATIONAL RESTATEMENT OF CONTRACT LAW – THE UNIDROIT PRINCIPLES OF INTERNATIONAL COMMERCIAL CONTRACTS (1994); Michael Joachim Bonell, *The UNIDROIT Principles of International Commercial Contracts: Towards a New Lex Mercatoria?/Les principes UNIDROIT relatifs aux contrats du commerce international: vers une nouvelle Lex Mercatoria?*, 1997 INT'L BUS. L.J. 145; Michael Joachim Bonell, *The UNIDROIT Principles in Practice: The Experience of the First Two Years*, 1997 UNIFORM L. REV. 34; Hans van Houtte, *The UNIDROIT Principles of International Commercial Contracts*, 11 ARB. INT'L 373 (1995).

circumstances.[174] The case law generated by permanent international courts, such as the International Court of Justice, will also be relevant, both when the parties expressly provide that it should apply[175] and when, more generally, it reflects widely accepted rules of law.[176]

2° Content

1459. — As the theory of general principles of international commercial law essentially resides in a method of determining such principles,[177] to present them in the form of a list will inevitably be too simplistic an approach.

As a result, the debate among certain authors as to whether a list of some twenty principles is long or short is irrelevant. A list of principles often quoted by commentators discussing *lex mercatoria* is that compiled in an article that seeks to demonstrate the inadequacy of the method.[178] The author of that article listed twenty principles of varying importance which had been considered in arbitral awards as constituting general principles. His goal was to illustrate the dearth of such principles. Ironically, his list has subsequently been used to support *lex mercatoria*.[179]

Another author presented and discussed a number of principles more convincingly in an article on "the reality of international trade usages." He lists the principles under the following headings: (1) the predictability of transactions (including the "presumption of competence of parties in international trade," "the effectiveness of the arbitration agreement," "the principle of non-reliance on the lack of power of a contractual negotiator" and "the prohibition on contradicting oneself to the detriment of another;" (2) the adaptability of contracts (including "the presumption of acquiescence in an act of performance other than that which was defined in the contract" and "the obligation to re-negotiate"); (3) the cooperation of the parties (including "the obligation to mitigate damages," "equal distribution of the burden of risks" and "the obligation to be candid");

---

[174] On this issue, generally, and on the affirmative response to the question of whether arbitral case law actually exists, see *supra* paras. 371 *et seq.*

[175] See the examples cited *supra* para. 1446.

[176] On the use of the case law of the International Court of Justice as a basis for the principle of estoppel by representation in international trade law, see, for example, the September 25, 1983 Jurisdictional Decision by B. Goldman, president, I. Foighel and E.W. Rubin, arbitrators, in ICSID Case No. ARB/81/1, Amco Asia Corp. v. Republic of Indonesia, 23 I.L.M. 351, 381 (1984); X Y.B. COM. ARB. 61 (1985); 1 ICSID REP. 389 (1993); for a French translation, see 1985 REV. ARB. 259; 113 J.D.I. 200, 220 (1986), and observations by E. Gaillard.

[177] See *supra* paras. 1455 *et seq.*

[178] See Mustill, *supra* note 116.

[179] See, *e.g.*, Philippe Kahn, *Les principes généraux du droit devant les arbitres du commerce international*, 116 J.D.I. 305, 325 (1989); Andreas F. Lowenfeld, *Lex Mercatoria: An Arbitrator's View*, *in* LEX MERCATORIA AND ARBITRATION 71 (T.E. Carbonneau ed., rev. ed. 1998), who responds to Mustill's criticism that the Ten Commandments or the U.S. Bill of Rights might also be considered "modest," at 89. See also Goldman, *Nouvelles réflexions sur la Lex Mercatoria*, *supra* note 88.

(4) ethical business practices (which essentially means "the unenforceability of contracts involving corruption").[180]

However valuable they may be, these lists are by no means exhaustive. The same is true of the list of principles drawn up by UNIDROIT[181] and the examples discussed below.

1460. — Illustrations of general principles of international commercial law found in arbitral case law naturally include rules with an extremely broad scope. This is the case of both the principle of the binding force of contracts, often expressed in arbitral awards as *pacta sunt servanda*, and the principle of good faith.

There are now countless arbitral awards recognizing that both rules[182] are general principles of international commercial law. In most cases, arbitrators simultaneously characterize the two rules as general principles.[183]

1461. — In fact, some awards treat the principle of good faith as simply another expression of the principle *pacta sunt servanda*. That will be the case if bad faith is defined as the failure to honor one's contractual commitments. That is a position that contributes little to the development of *lex mercatoria*.[184] Likewise, a general principle that contracts are binding is hardly revolutionary given that the same principle appears in all legal systems. Besides, awards which restrict themselves to applying that principle are most exposed to the criticism that *lex mercatoria* is merely a device enabling the hierarchy of norms to be altered

---

[180] *See* Loquin, *supra* note 114, at 168 *et seq.*

[181] *See supra* para. 1458.

[182] For awards which recognize the rule *pacta sunt servanda* as a general principle, see, for example, ICC Award No. 3540 (1980), French contractor v. Yugoslavian sub-contractor, 108 J.D.I. 914, 917 (1981), and observations by Y. Derains; for an English translation, see VII Y.B. COM. ARB. 124 (1982); ICC Award No. 2321 (1974), Two Israeli companies v. Government of an African state, I Y.B. COM. ARB. 133 (1976); for a French translation, see 102 J.D.I. 938 (1975), and observations by Yves Derains; the November 20, 1984 Award in ICSID Case No. ARB/81/1, Amco Asia Corp. v. Republic of Indonesia, which was later annulled on different grounds, 24 I.L.M. 1022, 1034–35 (1985); 1 INT'L ARB. REP. 601 (1986); 1 ICSID REP. 413 (1993); for a French translation, see 114 J.D.I. 145, 154 (1987), and observations by E. Gaillard. For awards recognizing the principle of good faith to be a general principle, see, for example, the October 26, 1979 Award by Messrs. Cremades, chairman, Ghestin and Steiner, arbitrators, in ICC Case No. 3131, Pabalk Ticaret Limited Sirketi v. Norsolor, 1983 REV. ARB. 525, 531. On this issue, generally, see Pierre Mayer, *Le principe de bonne foi devant les arbitres du commerce international, in* ETUDES DE DROIT INTERNATIONAL EN L'HONNEUR DE PIERRE LALIVE 543 (1993).

[183] See, for example, the April 12, 1977 *LIAMCO* Award, *supra* note 162, 20 I.L.M. 54–58; 1980 REV. ARB. 158–162; VI Y.B. COM. ARB. 89 (1981); for a French translation, see 1980 REV. ARB. 132, especially at 158–62; see also the commentaries by Patrick Rambaud, *Un arbitrage pétrolier: la sentence LIAMCO*, 26 AFDI 274 (1980), and by Brigitte Stern, *Trois arbitrages, un même problème, trois solutions – Les nationalisations pétrolières libyennes devant l'arbitrage international*, 1980 REV. ARB. 3; the January 19, 1977 Award by R.-J. Dupuy in *Texaco, supra* note 56; ICC Award No. 5953 (1989), *supra* note 64.

[184] But see, on the potential implications of the notion of good faith, GÉRARD CORNU, REGARDS SUR LE TITRE III DU LIVRE III DU CODE CIVIL. DES CONTRATS ET DES OBLIGATIONS CONVENTIONNELLES EN GÉNÉRAL, LES COURS DE DROIT, 1976–77, at 200.

by putting the contract before the law.[185] The same applies to the principle of the protection of vested rights, found in certain arbitral awards.[186]

1462. — However, the principle of good faith is particularly useful when understood as providing the basis for more specific rules, which may in turn become general principles. This is the case, for example, of the principle that a party cannot contradict itself to the detriment of another. This principle is known in German and Swiss law by the maxim *non concedit venire contra factum proprium* and, in common law countries, as estoppel by representation. It is found in French law in the form of a principle of consistency[187] and has also been recognized in arbitral case law.[188] It enables arbitrators to take concrete measures where the conditions for the application of the principle are satisfied, which occurs far less frequently than parties suggest.[189] Even the most reticent observers of a phenomenon which they perceive as a means allowing arbitrators to create new rules of law recognize that the principle of good faith potentially constitutes one of the richest sources of *lex mercatoria*.[190]

1463. — In any case, the principle *pacta sunt servanda* is subject to certain limits in all legal systems. It only applies if the contract is validly entered into, and exceptions to the

---

[185] *See supra* paras. 1451 *et seq.*

[186] *See, e.g.,* the August 23, 1958 Award in the *ARAMCO* case, *supra* note 47; the 1984 Award of the Iran-U.S. Claims Tribunal in Starrett Hous. Corp. v. Iran (Case No. 24), Interlocutory Award No. ITL 32-24-1, 4 Iran-U.S. Cl. Trib. Rep. 122; the November 20, 1984 Award in *Amco*, *supra* note 183, 24 I.L.M. 1035 (1985); 114 J.D.I. 154 (1987).

[187] *See, e.g.,* CA Paris, Feb. 13, 1990, Sunkyong Ltd. v. Interagra Ipitrade International, Dalloz, Jur. 593 (1990), and G. Peyrard's note. *See also* Philippe Blondel, *Les "principes généraux" dans la jurisprudence de cassation – Rapport de synthèse*, JCP, Ed. E., Suppl. 5-1989, at 16 (1989), especially at 20; Horatia Muir Watt, *Pour l'accueil de l'estoppel en droit privé français*, *in* L'INTERNATIONALISATION DU DROIT – MÉLANGES EN L'HONNEUR DE YVON LOUSSOUARN 303 (1994).

[188] See, for example, the September 25, 1983 Jurisdictional Decision in *Amco*, *supra* note 177, 23 I.L.M. 377–82 (1984); 113 J.D.I. 218–21 (1986), and observations by E. Gaillard at 250–52; the September 2, 1983 Award of the Iran-U.S. Claims Tribunal in Woodward-Clyde Consultants v. Iran, Award No. 73-67-3, 3 Iran-U.S. Cl. Trib. Rep. 239 (1983); for a French translation, see 1985 REV. ARB. 272; the June 5, 1990 Award in ICSID Case No. ARB/81/1, Amco Asia Corp. v. Republic of Indonesia, 5 INT'L ARB. REP. D4, D37 (Nov. 1990); XVII Y.B. COM. ARB. 73 (1992); 1 ICSID REP. 569 (1993); for a French translation, see 118 J.D.I. 172, 177 (1991), and observations by E. Gaillard, at 183–84; see also the preliminary award in ICC Case No. 1512 (Jan. 14, 1970), Indian cement company v. Pakistani bank, 1992 BULL. ASA 505; V Y.B. COM. ARB. 174 (1980); ICC Award No. 5926 (1989), unpublished, in which the parties, from Latin America and North America respectively, both recognized the existence of the principle but each sought to invoke it to support its case. See, for the same situation, ICC Award No. 6363 (1991), Licensor v. Licensee, XVII Y.B. COM. ARB. 186 (1992), especially ¶ 44 at 201. See also the April 8, 1999 *ad hoc* Award made in Paris, Construction companies v. Middle East State, unpublished, which decides that a party which has assigned a contract without the prior consent of its co-contractor cannot rely on this circumstance in the context of the determination of the parties to the arbitration agreement (at 75).

[189] On this issue, generally, see Gaillard, *supra* note 127; Loquin, *supra* note 114, at 173; SCHMITTHOFF, *supra* note 110, ¶ 70; Kahn, *supra* note 180, at 323; Pinsolle, *supra* note 127; Paul Bowden, *L'interdiction de se contredire au détriment d'autrui (estoppel) as a Substantive Transnational Rule in International Commercial Arbitration*, *in* TRANSNATIONAL RULES IN INTERNATIONAL COMMERCIAL ARBITRATION, *supra* note 88, at 125.

[190] Mayer, *supra* note 183.

principle may be justified by the need to protect the weaker party or the general interest. The solemn formulation of principles such as *pacta sunt servanda* and the principle of good faith does not mean that similar prerequisites and exceptions do not exist when the transnational rules method applies.[191] Arbitral case law shows that general principles are not confined to a few rules so broad in scope that they add nothing to the provisions of the contract, but that, on the contrary, they cover in some detail most of the major issues of international contract law.

This can be seen with respect to the validity of contracts, as well as to their interpretation and performance.

a) Principles Relating to the Validity of Contracts

1464. — The issues of a contracting party's capacity and power have given rise to a number of general principles. It has been suggested that there is a principle according to which "a party cannot rely on the absence of power of the person negotiating a contract." This would prevent "one of the parties to a contract from relying on the fact that its own representative did not have the requisite powers, provided that the other party was unaware of that fact."[192] Expressed in this way, this principle goes too far, as the fact that the other party is required to be reasonably diligent should also be taken into account.[193] As one author has observed, there is "a tendency among arbitrators in international commerce to consider . . . that the law should only protect parties to the extent that are not under a duty to protect themselves."[194] The real principle in this context is therefore that a reasonably diligent party can rely on its legitimate ignorance of the fact that the person who signed the contract was not empowered to do so.[195]

1465. — Arbitral case law has also given rise to principles concerning invalid consent given by parties to a contract. In particular, it has established a principle that "in international trade parties are presumed to be competent." This principle makes it more difficult for a professional party to seek to have a contract declared void on the basis of its

---

[191] *Comp. with* Virally, *supra* note 110, at 381.

[192] Loquin, *supra* note 114, at 173. *See also* Pierre Lalive, *Transnational (or Truly International) Public Policy and International Arbitration*, *in* ICCA CONGRESS SERIES NO. 3, COMPARATIVE ARBITRATION PRACTICE AND PUBLIC POLICY IN ARBITRATION 257 (P. Sanders ed., 1987), and, for a French version, 1986 REV. ARB. 329, 345.

[193] See, for example, in French law, Patrice Jourdain, *Le devoir de "se" renseigner (Contribution à l'étude de l'obligation de renseignement)*, Dalloz, Chron. 139 (1983). On this issue, see also XAVIER BOUCOBZA, L'ACQUISITION INTERNATIONALE DE SOCIÉTÉ ¶¶ 673 *et seq.* (1998).

[194] GEORGES RIPERT, LA RÈGLE MORALE ¶ 43, cited by Y. Derains, observations following ICC Award No. 1990 (1972), Italian company v. Spanish company, 101 J.D.I. 897 (1974).

[195] On the widely accepted idea that the doctrine of apparent authority serves to correct the absence of necessary powers, see Article 11 of the June 19, 1980 Rome Convention on the Law Applicable to Contractual Obligations. See also on this issue, with regard to state contracts, Audit, *supra* note 51, at 38 *et seq.* Compare, with regard to the arbitration clause, *supra* para. 470.

own mistake.[196] In some cases, that principle has been extended to mean that "an error of fact or law cannot be recognized in international commercial relations, as it is incompatible with the presumption of competence established through usage."[197] Once again, it would no doubt be sufficient—at least with regard to errors of fact—for the effect of this presumption of competence to be to increase the burden of proof on the party seeking to rely on its own error. It certainly cannot be excluded that in some circumstances an error of fact, even one committed by a professional, might lead to a contract being held void.

1466. — The principles of apparent authority and the presumption of competence tend to favor the validity of contracts. However, this is not to say that there is a general principle of *favor validitatis*.[198] The validity of a contract, in itself, is not something deserving protection. Instead, that validity is conditioned on the compliance with the applicable rules of law, be they those of a national law or general principles.[199] In fact, a number of general principles tend to clarify the conditions under which a contract can be held void.

1467. — As in national laws, the aim of some general principles is to protect only one of the parties. Thus, for example, arbitrators would have no difficulty in finding rules in comparative law as to vitiated consent which are accepted on a sufficiently wide scale to be considered as forming general principles of international commercial law.[200] In the same vein, it has sometimes been argued that the unlawfulness of the abuse of a dominant economic position is also a general principle.[201]

1468. — By contrast, some principles are based on the protection of the general interest. In particular, arbitral case law has established a principle that contracts obtained by corruption are void. Early awards referred to the existence of

---

[196] *See* ICC Award No. 1990 (1972), Italian company v. Spanish company, 101 J.D.I. 897 (1974), and observations by Y. Derains; ICC Award No. 3776 (1982), cited by Guy Horsmans, *L'interprétation des contrats internationaux*, *in* L'APPORT DE LA JURISPRUDENCE ARBITRALE, *supra* note 113, at 123, 146; the October 27, 1975 Award by the Czechoslovak Chamber of Commerce, *id.* at 146.

[197] Loquin, *supra* note 114, at 169.

[198] *But see* ICC Award No. 4145 (1984), *supra* note 64.

[199] On the different question of the principle of interpretation whereby sense should be given to the provisions agreed by the parties, see *infra* para. 1471.

[200] On the affirmation that "contractual principles such as the invalidity of contracts where the parties' consent is defective are general principles of law which are applicable here," see ICC Award No. 3327 (1981), French company v. African state, 109 J.D.I. 971 (1982), and observations by Y. Derains. On the affirmation of the general principle that misrepresentation constitutes a cause of nullity of contracts, see the award cited by FOUCHARD, *supra* note 112, at 433. Compare the more conservative position taken by Paulsson, *supra* note 88, at 96, which, in our view, overestimates the differences in national laws on these issues although, admittedly, the terminology used differs significantly from one jurisdiction to the next.

[201] Kahn, *supra* note 180, at 317. But see the reservations expressed by DE BOISSÉSON, *supra* note 41, at 636. Compare, for the idea that the lifting of the corporate veil can be based on *lex mercatoria*, with ICC Award No. 8385 (1995), U.S. company v. Belgian company, 124 J.D.I. 1061 (1997), and observations by Y. Derains.

a general principle of law recognized by civilized nations that contracts which seriously violate *bonos mores* or international public policy are invalid or at least unenforceable and that they cannot be sanctioned by courts or arbitrators.[202]

In later cases, the arbitrators did not find such disputes to be non-arbitrable or that the *nemo auditur* principle applied, but instead held the contract in question to be void.[203] Thus, for example, where a fictitious contract was designed to provide a party with credit to which it was not entitled, a 1982 ICC award made in Case No. 2730 found the transaction in question to be contrary

not only to Yugoslavian legislation [which was held to be applicable to the contract] but also to morals and *bonos mores*. In general, any contract the object of which is contrary to mandatory laws, rules of public policy, morals and *bonos mores* will be void . . . . This principle is accepted in all countries and by all legal systems. It constitutes an international rule, an element of the ordinary law of contract in international transactions.[204]

---

[202] ICC Award No. 1110 (1963) by Mr. G. Lagergren, Mr. X, Buenos Aires v. Company A, 10 ARB. INT'L 282, ¶ 16 at 293 (1994).

[203] *See, e.g.*, ICC Award No. 3916 (1982), Iranian party v. Greek party, 111 J.D.I. 930 (1984), and observations by S. Jarvin; ICC Award No. 3913 (1981), cited by Y. Derains, observations following ICC Award No. 2730 (1982), Two Yugoslavian companies v. Dutch and Swiss group companies, 111 J.D.I. 914, 920 (1984); ICC Award No. 5943 (1990), 123 J.D.I. 1014 (1996), and observations by D. Hascher.

[204] *Supra* note 204, at 917–18. On the issue of the nullity of contracts for corruption, see EXTORTION AND BRIBERY IN BUSINESS TRANSACTIONS (ICC Publication No. 315, 1977); Ahmed S. El Kosheri and Philippe Leboulanger, *L'arbitrage face à la corruption et aux trafics d'influence*, 1984 REV. ARB. 3; François Knoepfler, *Corruption et arbitrage international*, *in* LES CONTRATS DE DISTRIBUTION – CONTRIBUTIONS OFFERTES AU PROFESSEUR FRANÇOIS DESSEMONTET À L'OCCASION DE SES 50 ANS 357 (1998); Loquin, *supra* note 114, at 180; Lalive, *supra* note 193, at 345; Kahn, *supra* note 180, at 314. For a more reserved position on the ground that the nullity of contracts for corruption is less frequently pronounced than is sometimes alleged to be the case, see Bruno Oppetit, *Le paradoxe de la corruption à l'épreuve du droit du commerce international*, 114 J.D.I. 5 (1987). The broad ratification of the OECD Convention on Combating Bribery of Foreign Public Officials in International Business Transactions, signed in Paris on December 17, 1997, should put an end to this minority view. *See also* ICC Award No. 5622 (Geneva, Aug. 19, 1988), Hilmarton v. OTV (1993 REV. ARB. 327, and the commentary by Vincent Heuzé, *La morale, l'arbitre et le juge*, *id.* at 179; 1992 RIV. DELL'ARB. 773, and A. Giardina's note; for an English translation, see XIX Y.B. COM. ARB. 105 (1994)) and, on the subsequent proceedings to which this award gave rise, *infra* para 1595; for a case where the arbitrators considered that corruption could lead to the nullity of the contract but where there was insufficient evidence of such corruption, see the March 21, 1992 ICC Award upheld by CA Paris, Sept. 30, 1993, European Gas Turbines v. Westman International Ltd., 1994 REV. ARB. 359, and D. Bureau's note; 1994 REV. CRIT. DIP 349, and V. Heuzé's note; 1994 RTD COM. 703, and observations by J.-C. Dubarry and E. Loquin; 1994 BULL. ASA 105, and the commentary by Adel Nassar, *Ordre public international et arbitrage? Y a-t-il eu une évolution?*, *id.* at 110; XX Y.B. COM. ARB. 198 (1995); ICC Award No. 7047 (Feb. 28, 1994), by H. Raeschke-Kessler, chairman, J. Patry and D. Mitrovic, arbitrators, Corporation W. v. State Agency F., 1995 BULL. ASA 301, *upheld by* Swiss Fed. Trib., Dec. 30, 1994, 1995 BULL. ASA 217; 1996 REV. SUISSE DR. INT. ET DR. EUR. 545, and observations by P. Schweizer. See also the awards cited *supra* para. 586.

Authors generally favor the approach whereby an arbitrator dealing with an illegal contract should not decline jurisdiction, but should instead declare the contract to be void.[205] The only situation in which it is unclear if this is still true is that where neither party requests the arbitral tribunal to rule on the issue of nullity. This would leave the arbitrators with no other choice than to ignore the issue of nullity or to resign if they believe that they should not become involved in a breach of international public policy.[206]

Similarly, the general principle that contracts contravening "public morality" are void might affect contracts such as those which facilitate drug trafficking, terrorism, agreements intended to incite subversion (the hiring of mercenaries, for example) and human rights violations.[207]

The protection of humanity's cultural heritage, as illustrated in particular by the work of UNESCO, can also provide a basis for the creation of general principles. This was discussed at length in the *Pyramids* case.[208]

Likewise, antitrust law has also given rise to an analysis in terms of general principles.[209]

b) Principles Relating to the Interpretation of Contracts

1469. — Arbitral case law recognizes the existence of a number of principles concerning the interpretation of contracts.[210] These principles are fairly similar to Articles 1156 *et seq.* of the French Civil Code,[211] and comparable provisions in other legal systems, and even more so to the UNIDROIT Principles of International Commercial Contracts.[212]

---

[205] *See* Berthold Goldman, *The Complementary Roles of Judges and Arbitrators in Ensuring that International Commercial Arbitration is Effective, in* INTERNATIONAL ARBITRATION – 60 YEARS OF ICC ARBITRATION – A LOOK AT THE FUTURE 257, 272 (ICC Publication No. 412, 1984); El Kosheri and Leboulanger, *supra* note 205, at 14; Lalive, *supra* note 193, at 337. More generally, on the arbitrability of issues of corruption, see *supra* para. 586.

[206] *See* Pierre Mayer, *La règle morale dans l'arbitrage international, in* ETUDES OFFERTES À PIERRE BELLET 379, ¶ 34 (1991). On the fact that these principles are part of international public policy, see *infra* para. 1535.

[207] *See* Lalive, *supra* note 193, at 341.

[208] *See supra* para. 508 and especially Kahn, *supra* note 180, at 317–18; DE BOISSÉSON, *supra* note 41, at 639.

[209] *See* Jean-Hubert Moitry, *Arbitrage international et droit de la concurrence: vers un ordre public de la lex mercatoria?,* 1989 REV. ARB. 3. *But see* Laurence Idot, *Les conflits de lois en droit de la concurrence,* 122 J.D.I. 321, 328 (1995).

[210] On this issue, generally, see Philippe Kahn, *L'interprétation des contrats internationaux,* 108 J.D.I. 5 (1981); Horsmans, *supra* note 197; FOUCHARD, *supra* note 112, at 434 *et seq.* On the principles of construction of arbitration agreements, see *supra* paras. 476 *et seq.*

[211] *See, e.g.,* ICC Award No. 1434 (1975), *supra* note 14. On these rules, see especially Jacques Dupichot, *Pour un retour aux textes: défense et illustration du "petit guide-âne" des articles 1156 à 1164 du Code civil, in* ETUDES OFFERTES À JACQUES FLOUR 179 (1979); CORNU, *supra* note 185, ¶¶ 44 *et seq. See also* J. LOPEZ SANTA MARIA, LES SYSTÈMES D'INTERPRÉTATION DES CONTRATS (Thesis, University of Paris (France), 1968), with a foreword by J. Flour.

[212] *Supra* note 118, especially Arts. 4.1 to 4.8, at 90–100.

1470. — The most general principle of contractual interpretation is that contracts should be interpreted in good faith.[213] Despite the tendency for many parties to see bad faith in any interpretation whereby one of the parties seeks to limit its undertakings, bad faith cannot be defined by reference to the restrictive or extensive nature of the interpretation proposed. A party only interprets a contract in bad faith where the interpretation it puts forward at the time of the dispute does not coincide with what the parties genuinely intended when they signed the contract. The requirement that contracts be interpreted in good faith is merely another way of saying that a literal interpretation should not prevail over an interpretation reflecting the parties' true intentions. As observed in an early award, "the fundamental principle of good faith . . . entails searching for the common intention of . . . the parties."[214] Similarly, in the *Aramco* award of August 23, 1958, it was held that "the interpreter must . . . remember that the Parties intended by their agreements to establish a reasonable contractual situation, in conformity with the common aim they had in view."[215] Likewise, the award made in 1975 in ICC Case No. 1434 stated that:

> the disputed limitation of liability clause should be interpreted in the light of general principles of the interpretation of contracts, and particularly those which appear in Articles 1156 *et seq.* of the [French] Civil Code, beginning with a literal and grammatical interpretation of the words used, without failing to place them in their context and to consider the contract as a whole, so as to discover the genuine common intention of the parties, referring in particular, if the terms are ambiguous, to the principle of good faith (cf. Article 1134 Civil Code) and resorting, if need be, to extrinsic interpretational indicators, which may be found, for example, in the historic context and in the relations between the parties.[216]

1471. — The principle of effectiveness, whereby "it should be assumed that the authors of a clause intended it to have a real significance and impact,"[217] is also applied in arbitral practice. As set forth in the 1975 award in ICC Case No. 1434,

---

[213] *See, e.g.,* ICC Award No. 2291 (1975), French transporter v. English company, 103 J.D.I. 989 (1976), and observations by Y. Derains; the September 25, 1983 Jurisdictional Decision in *Amco, supra* note 177.

[214] Award of June 10, 1955 by President Cassin, Gouvernement Royal Hellénique v. Gouvernement de sa Majesté Britannique, 1956 REV. CRIT. DIP 279, and H. Batiffol's note; 1956 REV. ARB. 15.

[215] *Supra* note 47, 27 INT'L L. REP. 173 (1963); for a French translation, see 1963 REV. CRIT. DIP 272, 319. See also the reasons given for an award made by a Dutch arbitrator on December 23, 1932, according to which the examination of the contract "cannot be limited to its literal terms as contracts must be performed in good faith" (European company v. European company cited by FOUCHARD, *supra* note 112, ¶ 619 at 439).

[216] *Supra* note 14. With respect to the arbitration agreement, see *supra* para. 477.

[217] *See* the June 10, 1955 Award by President Cassin, *supra* note 215.

there is a universally-recognized rule of interpretation whereby, if the terms of a contract are capable of two contrary interpretations or can convey two different meanings, one should favor the interpretation which gives a certain effect to the words, rather than the interpretation which renders them redundant or even absurd. This 'principle of useful effect,' which is also known as 'the effectiveness principle' (*ut res magis valeat quam pereat*) is endorsed, in particular, by Article 1157 of the [French] Civil Code.[218]

1472. — The arbitrators will also take into account the conduct of the parties subsequent to their entry into the contract and until the dispute arises, as that conduct will reflect the parties' own interpretation of the disputed contract on entering into it. This rule of interpretation is sometimes described as "practical and quasi-authentic interpretation," "contemporary practical interpretation" or "proof by the subsequent conduct of the parties."[219] It can be applied in situations such as that where a party has performed the contract, without reserving its rights, under conditions different to those initially provided for.[220]

1473. — It has sometimes been suggested that there is a principle whereby silence should be interpreted as acquiescence.[221] One author rightly criticized that proposition, noting that no such principle was accepted in English law.[222] In fact, there is no such rule in continental legal systems either,[223] and it cannot therefore be considered as constituting a general principle.[224]

---

[218] ICC Award No. 1434 (1975), *supra* note 14. *See also* ICC Award No. 3380 (1980), Italian entreprise v. Syrian enterprise, 108 J.D.I. 927 (1981), and observations by Y. Derains; for an English translation, see VII Y.B. COM. ARB. 116 (1982); ICC Award No. 3460 (1980), French company v. Ministry of an Arab country, 108 J.D.I. 939 (1981), and observations by Y. Derains; the March 24, 1982 *ad hoc* Award in *AMINOIL, supra* note 56, ¶ 89; the September 25, 1983 Jurisdictional Decision in *Amco, supra* note 177; ICC Award No. 8365 (1996), *supra* note 109; ICC Award No. 8331 (1996), *supra* note 173. *See also* Paulsson, *supra* note 88, at 92; SCHMITTHOFF, *supra* note 110, ¶ 70; with respect to the arbitration agreement, see *supra* para. 478.

[219] *See, e.g.,* the August 23, 1958 Award in *ARAMCO, supra* note 47, 27 INT'L L. REP. 197–98 (1963); 1963 REV. CRIT. DIP 338; ICC Award No. 7792 (1994), 122 J.D.I. 993 (1995), and observations by D. Hascher.

[220] Compare, on the "presumption of acquiescence to an act of performance different from that defined by the contract," Loquin, *supra* note 114, at 175. With respect to the arbitration agreement, see *supra* para. 477.

[221] *See* ICC Award No. 543 (1934), French company v. Belgian company, cited by FOUCHARD, *supra* note 112, ¶ 615 at 432; ICC Award No. 3344 (1981), Arab State Enterprise v. Arab State Enterprise, 109 J.D.I. 978 (1982), and observations by Y. Derains; ICC Award No. 8365 (1996), *supra* note 109.

[222] Mustill, *supra* note 116, at 177, n. 106. *Comp. with* Loquin, *supra* para. 1459 and note 114.

[223] See, for example, in French law, JACQUES GHESTIN, TRAITÉ DES CONTRATS – LA VENTE ¶ 120 (1990); HENRI AND LÉON MAZEAUD, JEAN MAZEAUD, FRANÇOIS CHABAS, LEÇONS DE DROIT CIVIL – TOME II / PREMIER VOLUME – OBLIGATIONS ¶ 137 (F. Chabas ed., 9th ed. 1998).

[224] *But see* Paulsson, *supra* note 88, at 89.

1474. — There is, however, a principle of consistency whereby within a particular document a recurring word is deemed to have the same meaning throughout.[225] This rule is set forth in more general terms in Article 1161 of the French Civil Code, which states that "all clauses of a contract are interpreted one by reference to another, the meaning of each clause being determined in the light of the entire document." The need for an interpretation of the contract or of its various constituent parts as a whole has also been recognized in arbitral case law.[226]

1475. — Although there have been fewer opportunities to apply it in arbitral case law, there is also a general principle whereby, if in doubt, a clause should be interpreted *contra proferentem*, or against the party that drafted it. This rule is usually, although not exclusively, applied when construing contracts of adhesion. It prevents the party that drafted the disputed provision from relying on any ambiguity in that provision in support of a position which is favorable to that party but which was not made clear when the provision was drafted. In other words, the rule requires the party drafting the provision in question to enlighten the other party as to what might be the least favorable interpretation from the other party's point of view. As a result there should be no temptation for the party drafting the terms of the contract to leave deliberate ambiguities in the hope of exploiting them at a later stage.[227]

1476. — Contractual interpretation is not based exclusively on intrinsic factors. It has been held that the parties' intentions should be examined in context and, in particular, in the light of current usages in the relevant business sector. In the absence of any indication to the contrary, the parties will be deemed to have agreed that such usages should apply.[228]

1477. — Lastly, it is a generally recognized principle that arbitrators are not bound by the characterization given by the parties to their contract. In the same way as the courts, arbitrators are entitled to recharacterize the parties' agreements as they see fit.[229] Given the convergence of different legal systems on this issue, the existence of such a principle is not in doubt. However, the arbitral awards usually cited in support of its existence are irrelevant,

---

[225] *See, e.g.,* ICC Award No. 1434 (1975), *supra* note 14, and Kahn, *supra* note 211, at 18.

[226] *See, e.g.,* ICC Award No. 1434 (1975), *supra* note 14, and the September 25, 1983 Jurisdictional Decision in *Amco, supra* note 177, 23 I.L.M. 377 *et seq.* (1984); 113 J.D.I. 218 *et seq.* (1986), and the observations by E. Gaillard at 231. With respect to the arbitration agreement, see *supra* para. 477.

[227] *See, e.g.,* ICC Award No. 2795 (1977), Swiss buyer v. Enterprise of socialist country, seller, IV Y.B. COM. ARB. 210 (1979). *Comp. with* ICC Award No. 3460 (1980), *supra* note 219; the April 26, 1993 Award under the aegis of the Society of Maritime Arbitrators, Inc., New York, in Case No. 2972, Nordic American Shipping A/S v. Bayoil (USA) Inc., XX Y.B. COM. ARB. 126, 131 (1995). *See also* Art. 4.6 of the UNIDROIT Principles, *supra* note 118. With respect to the arbitration agreement, see *supra* para. 479.

[228] *See, e.g.,* ICC Award No. 2583 (1976), Spanish contractor v. Libyan owner, 104 J.D.I. 950 (1977), and observations by Y. Derains.

[229] Goldman, *La lex mercatoria dans les contrats et l'arbitrage internationaux: réalité et perspectives, supra* note 88, at 489; Paulsson, *supra* note 88, at 92.

as one involved recharacterizing the parties' claims[230] and in the other Moroccan law applied.[231]

c) Principles Relating to the Performance of Contracts

1478. — Some principles help to clarify the parties' obligations in the performance of their contracts.

1479. — Arbitrators often apply the principle found in Article 1134, paragraph 3 of the French Civil Code, as well as in many subsequent codifications in civil law systems,[232] according to which "contracts must be performed in good faith."[233] Again,[234] the principle of good faith is often simply another way of formulating the principle that the failure to perform contractual obligations renders the defaulting party liable.[235]

1480. — The question of whether the parties' obligations should be assessed differently in economic development contracts is too controversial to generate general principles of law.[236] On the other hand, there appears to be no doubt that contracts which require long-term cooperation between the parties can give rise to specific principles.[237]

1481. — It is in the context of these long-term contracts that the obligation to keep one's co-contractor fully informed, which was expressed in the *Klöckner* award as "the duty of full disclosure," is at its strongest.[238] However, the requirement that each party inform its co-

---

[230] ICC Award No. 3540 (1980), *supra* note 183.

[231] ICC Award No. 3243 (1981), U.S. company v. Moroccan company, 109 J.D.I. 968 (1982), and observations by Y. Derains. See also, on the basis of Portuguese law, ICC Award No. 7518 (1994), Italian party v. Portuguese party, 125 J.D.I. 1034 (1998), and observations by Y. Derains.

[232] See, for example, Article 148 of the Egyptian Civil Code, which was used as a model in many other Arab countries.

[233] *See, e.g.*, ICC Award No. 3131 (Oct. 26, 1979), *Norsolor*, *supra* note 183, and the commentary by Berthold Goldman, *Une bataille judiciaire autour de la lex mercatoria – L'affaire Norsolor*, 1983 REV. ARB. 379. On this issue in the context of state contracts, see Pierre Lalive, *Sur la bonne foi dans l'exécution des contrats d'Etat, in* MÉLANGES OFFERTS À RAYMOND VANDER ELST 425 (1986).

[234] *See supra* para. 1461.

[235] See, for example, the *Norsolor* award, *supra* note 183.

[236] In favor of a specific assessment of such contracts, see, for example, Patrick Rambaud, *L'annulation des sentences Klöckner et Amco*, 32 AFDI 259 (1986); the January 19, 1977 *Texaco* Award by R.-J. Dupuy, *supra* note 56; but see the October 21, 1983 Award in *Klöckner*, subsequently annulled on different grounds, *supra* note 140, 111 J.D.I. 426 (1984), and observations by E. Gaillard, 114 J.D.I. 141 (1987). *See also* Prosper Weil, *Droit international et contrats d'Etat, in* MÉLANGES OFFERTS À PAUL REUTER – LE DROIT INTERNATIONAL: UNITÉ ET DIVERSITÉ 549 (1981); Kahn, *supra* note 51.

[237] Gérard Morin, *Le devoir de coopération dans les contrats internationaux – Droit et pratique*, 1980 DPCI 9, 13.

[238] *Supra* note 140. See also Loquin, *supra* note 114, at 179 *et seq.*, according to which it is a general principle of law, and Audit, *supra* note 51, at 111.

contractor of circumstances liable to jeopardize the performance of the contract has sometimes been presented as a rule with a more general scope. Thus, as observed in an ICC award made in 1985, "the parties' obligation to collaborate with a view to ensuring that the contract is properly performed imposes . . . on each party a duty to inform, in particular."[239]

1482. — It is also in relation to long-term contracts that the question arises as to whether the doctrine of change in circumstances (*"imprévision"*) is a general principle.[240] Awards sometimes state in general terms that the parties' reciprocal obligations should be properly balanced as a matter of principle. For example, in the 1975 award in ICC Case No. 2291, the arbitral tribunal observed that:

> any commercial transaction is based on a balance between the reciprocal obligations and . . . to deny that principle would amount to deprive commercial contracts of all certainty, and to have them based on speculation or chance. *Lex mercatoria* contains a rule whereby the obligations should remain balanced from a financial point of view.[241]

Similarly, it was held in another award that:

> in an international contract concluded without any speculative intention, the parties can be considered, in the absence of an express agreement, to have wanted a guarantee against devaluation; furthermore, it would be contrary to good faith if the government of a State, having ordered and received services, were to refuse to pay for them at their true value, thereby intending to benefit from a substantial devaluation of the payment currency.[242]

---

[239] Award cited by Sigvard Jarvin, *L'obligation de coopérer de bonne foi; Exemples d'application au plan de l'arbitrage international*, *in* L'APPORT DE LA JURISPRUDENCE ARBITRALE, *supra* note 113, at 157, 167–68. *See also* ICC Award No. 3093 (1979), *supra* note 60. On this issue, see also Piero Bernardini, *Is the Duty to Cooperate in Long-Term Contracts a Substantive Transnational Rule in International Commercial Arbitration?*, *in* TRANSNATIONAL RULES IN INTERNATIONAL COMMERCIAL ARBITRATION, *supra* note 88, at 137. On the corresponding obligation of reasonable diligence in seeking out information, see *supra* para. 1464.

[240] On this issue, see especially Denis Philippe, *"Pacta sunt servanda" et "Rebus sic stantibus"*, *in* L'APPORT DE LA JURISPRUDENCE ARBITRALE, *supra* note 113 at 181; ANTOINE KASSIS, THÉORIE GÉNÉRALE DES USAGES DU COMMERCE ¶¶ 548 *et seq.* (1984); Paulsson, *supra* note 88, at 95.

[241] *Supra* note 214. *See also* SCHMITTHOFF, *supra* note 110, ¶ 70.

[242] *Ad hoc* Award of July 2, 1956 by Messrs. Ripert and Panchaud, Société Européenne d'Etudes et d'Entreprises v. République fédérale de Yougoslavie, 86 J.D.I. 1074 (1959), and the statement of the Yugoslav Government in connection with the arbitral award, 87 J.D.I. 760 (1960). *See also* Guy Horsmans and Michel Verwilghen, *Stabilité et évolution du contrat économique international*, *in* LE CONTRAT ÉCONOMIQUE INTERNATIONAL – STABILITÉ ET ÉVOLUTION 451 (Report of the *VIIe Journées d'études juridiques Jean Dabin*, held at Louvain-la-Neuve (Belgium) on November 22–23, 1973 (1975)).

However, arbitrators will not generally go so far as to conclude that, on the basis of general principles, they can adapt a contract to meet a change in economic circumstances,[243] unless of course the parties have so provided by means of a hardship clause.[244] This is an appropriate solution, given the significant divergence of views among different legal systems as to the admissibility of the change in circumstances doctrine in private law.[245]

1483. — However, arbitral case law tends to recognize that in long-term contracts the parties have a duty to re-negotiate in good faith. Arbitral case law also tends to reject, in this context, the English doctrine according to which an "agreement to agree" has no binding effect.[246]

1484. — Other principles serve to determine the consequences of the failure by a party to perform its contractual obligations.

1485. — Arbitral case law has established a general principle that the failure to perform a contract renders the defaulting party liable.[247]

1486. — The fact that the co-contractor of a defaulting party can rely on that party's failure to perform to withhold performance itself has also been held to be a transnational rule.[248] The award rendered in 1980 in ICC Case No. 3540 states that "the *non adimpleti*

---

[243] See, for example, the reservations expressed in ICC Award No. 1512 (1971), Indian cement company v. Pakistani bank, I Y.B. COM. ARB. 128 (1976); for a French translation, see 101 J.D.I. 904 (1974), and observations by Y. Derains; ICC Award No. 2404 (1975), Belgian seller v. Romanian purchaser, 103 J.D.I. 995 (1976), and observations by Y. Derains. *See also* Goldman, *La lex mercatoria dans les contrats et l'arbitrage internationaux: réalité et perspectives, supra* note 88, at 495. On this issue, generally, see Hans van Houtte, *Changed Circumstances and Pacta Sunt Servanda, in* TRANSNATIONAL RULES IN INTERNATIONAL COMMERCIAL ARBITRATION, *supra* note 88, at 105.

[244] On this issue, see *supra* paras. 35 *et seq.*

[245] For a comparative law analysis, see René David, *L'imprévision dans les droits européens, in* ETUDES OFFERTES À ALFRED JAUFFRET 211 (1974). For the position of the UNIDROIT principles with respect to hardship, see Articles 6.1.2 to 6.2.3; *see also* P. Kahn, review of the Principles in 121 J.D.I. 1115 (1994). For an application of the doctrine of change in circumstances under Algerian law, which expressly accepts the rule, see, for example, the *ad hoc* Award rendered in Paris on December 29, 1993 by D.G. Wright, chairman, P. Mayer and C. Molineaux, arbitrators (C. Molineaux dissenting), Icori Estero S.p.A. v. Kuwait Foreign Trading Contracting & Investment Co., 9 INT'L ARB. REP. A1 (Dec. 1994). For an example of the refusal to apply the doctrine of change in circumstances recognized, within certain limits, by Dutch law, see ICC Award No. 8486 (1996), Dutch party v. Turkish party, 125 J.D.I. 1047 (1998), and observations by Y. Derains.

[246] On the duty to renegotiate in good faith, see, for example, ICC Award No. 2291 (1975): "reasonable re-negotiation [is] customary in international contracts" (*supra* note 214); ICC Award No. 8365 (1996), *supra* note 109. See also Loquin, *supra* note 114, at 175 and, on the similar concept of the "equal sharing of the burden of risks," at 178; Goldman, *La lex mercatoria dans les contrats et l'arbitrage internationaux: réalité et perspectives, supra* note 88, at 492. On the fact that the invalidity of an "agreement to agree" is not a transnational rule, see ICC Award No. 8540 (Sept. 4, 1996), unpublished.

[247] *See, e.g.,* ICC Award No. 3131 (Oct. 26, 1979), *Norsolor, supra* note 183, and Kahn, *supra* note 180, at 321.

[248] *See, e.g.,* ICC Award No. 2583 (1976), *supra* note 229.

contractus rule . . . should be considered as belonging to the general principles of law forming the *lex mercatoria*."[249]

Awards generally provide that this principle is not effective where the failure to perform relied on by the co-contractor is of far less significance than its own non-performed obligations. In other words, a party can only properly withhold performance if it complies with the principle of proportionality.[250] As one author has observed, "it would be contrary to good faith to rely on . . . the non-performance of a relatively minor obligation . . . in an attempt to avoid performance of an essential obligation of one's own."[251]

1487. — Termination of the contract for failure to perform or lack of proper performance, which is closely related to the withholding of performance, is also considered by some arbitrators to be a general principle of law.[252]

1488. — The release of a party from its obligations by an event satisfying the conditions of *force majeure*,[253] and the fact that *force majeure* has a purely suspensive effect,[254] provided that it is not long-lasting,[255] are also recognized as general principles.[256]

---

[249] *Supra* note 183. *See also* ICC Award No. 7539 (1995), French company v. Greek company, 123 J.D.I. 1030 (1996), and observations by Y. Derains; the October 21, 1983 Award in *Klöckner, supra* note 140, and observations by E. Gaillard, 114 J.D.I. 142 (1987); ICC Award No. 8365 (1996), *supra* note 109; Paulsson, *supra* note 88, at 93. On this issue, see Philip D. O'Neill, Jr. and Nawaf Salam, *Is the Exceptio Non Adimpleti Contractus Part of the New Lex Mercatoria?*, in TRANSNATIONAL RULES IN INTERNATIONAL COMMERCIAL ARBITRATION, *supra* note 88, at 147.

[250] For another application of this principle, see *infra* para. 1496.

[251] JEAN CARBONNIER, DROIT CIVIL – Vol. 4 – LES OBLIGATIONS ¶ 84, considered to reflect a rule of *lex mercatoria* by Y. Derains, observations following ICC Award No. 2583 (1976), Spanish contractor v. Libyan owner, 104 J.D.I. 950, 951 (1977). *See also* the October 21, 1983 *Klöckner* Award, *supra* note 140, and the observations by E. Gaillard, 114 J.D.I. 143 (1987). On whether there is a general principle under which the right to withhold performance is subject to the prior formal notification by the party invoking it to its co-contractor, see Gaillard, *id.* at 143–44 (1987).

[252] Compare, on the effect of express termination clauses, ICC Award No. 2520 (1975), Two Czechoslovak companies v. Italian company, 103 J.D.I. 992 (1976), and observations by Y. Derains.

[253] Compare, on the definition of *force majeure*, ICC Award No. 2478 (1974), which was subject to Swiss law, but was expressed in general terms (French company v. Romanian company, 102 J.D.I. 925 (1975), and observations by Y. Derains); ICC Award No. 2142 (1974), 101 J.D.I. 892 (1974), and observations by R.T.

[254] See, for example, the November 25, 1971 Preliminary Award in ICC Award No. 1703, Société Générale de l'Industrie du Papier "RAKTA" v. Parsons and Whittmore Overseas Co., Inc., *reprinted in* J. GILLIS WETTER, THE INTERNATIONAL ARBITRAL PROCESS: PUBLIC AND PRIVATE, Vol. V, at 361, 369 (1979); for a French translation, see 101 J.D.I. 894 (1974), and observations by R. Thompson. *Comp. with* ICC Award No. 7539 (1995), *supra* note 250.

[255] On the consequences of the long-lasting embargo against Iraq, held to be a cause of termination of a construction contract, see ICC Award No. 8095 (Sept. 25, 1997), unpublished.

[256] On this issue, see David W. Rivkin, *Lex Mercatoria and Force Majeure*, in TRANSNATIONAL RULES IN INTERNATIONAL COMMERCIAL ARBITRATION, *supra* note 88, at 161; Henry Lesguillons, *Pratique arbitrale concernant la "force majeure" et la "frustration"*, in INADEMPIMENTO, ADATTAMENTO, ARBITRATO – PATOLOGIE DEI CONTRATTI E RIMEDI 457 (1992).

1489. — Another general principle will be that the party to which a non-performed obligation is owed cannot rely on the non-performance if it has not objected to that non-performance within a reasonable period of time.[257]

1490. — Another set of general principles governs the evaluation of damages resulting from a total or partial failure to perform the contract.[258]

1491. — One of the most well-established general principles in arbitral case law is the duty of the party to which the non-performed obligation is owed to mitigate its losses.[259]

1492. — Arbitral case law also accepts the principle of full compensation for the loss sustained, with damages covering both the loss actually suffered and loss of profit.[260] Certain distinctions are made in some cases regarding state contracts, depending on whether the

---

[257] See, for example, ICC Award No. 2520 (1975), in which the arbitrators took into account, in their assessment of damages, the absence of any adverse reaction by one party to the failure by the other party to perform its obligations (*supra* note 253); ICC Award No. 8365 (1996), *supra* note 109. Compare, in a case governed by Moroccan law, ICC Award No. 3243 (1981), *supra* note 232.

[258] On this issue, see Marcel Fontaine, *Il danno risarcibile nella giurisprudenza arbitrale della Camera di Commercio Internazionale, in* INADEMPIMENTO, ADATTAMENTO, ARBITRATO – PATOLOGIE DEI CONTRATTI E RIMEDI 541 (1992); JÉRÔME ORTSCHEIDT, LA RÉPARATION DU DOMMAGE DANS L'ARBITRAGE COMMERCIAL INTERNATIONAL (Thesis, University of Paris XII (France), 1999).

[259] *See, e.g.,* ICC Award No. 2478 (1974), *supra* note 254; ICC Award No. 3344 (1981), *supra* note 222; ICC Award No. 4761 (1987), Italian consortium v. Libyan company, 114 J.D.I. 1012 (1987), and observations by S. Jarvin; ICC Award No. 5910 (1988), Belgian purchaser v. Belgian seller, 115 J.D.I. 1216 (1988), and observations by Y. Derains; ICC Award No. 5514 (1990), French company v. Government committed to the provision of financing, 119 J.D.I. 1022, 1024–25 (1992), and observations by Y. Derains; ICC Award No. 6840 (1991), Egyptian seller v. Senegalese buyer, 119 J.D.I. 1030, 1034 (1992), and observations by Y. Derains; the June 5, 1990 Award by R. Higgins, president, M. Lalonde and P. Magid, arbitrators, in *Amco , supra* note 189, 5 INT'L ARB. REP. D41 *et seq.* (Nov. 1990); 118 J.D.I. 178 (1991), and observations by E. Gaillard, especially at 187; on this issue, generally, see Yves Derains, *L'obligation de minimiser le dommage dans la jurisprudence arbitrale,* 1987 INT'L BUS. L.J. 375; Kahn, *supra* note 180, at 321–22; Loquin, *supra* note 114, at 177–78; Goldman, *La lex mercatoria dans les contrats et l'arbitrage internationaux: réalité et perspectives, supra* note 88, at 495. On the application of this rule in awards where different national laws apply, see the references cited by Y. Derains, observations following ICC Award No. 5910 (1988), *supra,* at 1222; in French law, see ICC Award No. 2404 (1975), *supra* note 244; *see also* CA Paris, 1e Ch., Sec. C, Dec. 8, 1998, Peter Van Vugt Agrow Products B.V. v. Hydro Agri France Nouvelle Denomination Hydro Azote, No. 1997/04763, unpublished; in English law, see ICC Award No. 5885 (1989), Seller v. Buyer, XVI Y.B. COM. ARB. 91 (1991); in Algerian law, see ICC Award No. 5865 (1989), *supra* note 15. For a convincing demonstration that, in spite of the fact that it is not formulated in the same way, this principle is recognized under French law, see ORTSCHEIDT, *supra* note 259, ¶¶ 200 *et seq.*

[260] *See, e.g.,* ICC Award No. 1526 (1968), Belgian parties v. African state, 101 J.D.I. 915 (1974), and observations by Y. Derains; the November 20, 1984 Award, set aside on other grounds, in *Amco, supra* note 183, 24 I.L.M. 1036 (1985); 114 J.D.I. 155 (1987).

dispute concerns a lawful[261] or an unlawful[262] expropriation. These distinctions remain, however, controversial.

1493. — In contrast, the rule whereby punitive damages can be awarded against the defaulting party in some circumstances is not sufficiently established in comparative law to be considered a general principle.[263]

1494. — However, in cases where the contract does stipulate that the arbitrators may make an award of damages exceeding the value of the actual loss, it is possible for them to apply a principle, based on comparative law, whereby the effects of excessive penalty clauses should be tempered. The precise remedy varies in different legal systems, but reducing the effects of penalty clauses (rather than holding such clauses void altogether) would be more in keeping with the spirit of international commercial law, particularly in cases where the parties have submitted their disputes to general principles of law or remained silent as to the applicable law.[264]

1495. — Some awards have held, by way of a general principle, that only direct and foreseeable losses are capable of giving rise to compensation.[265]

1496. — In the case of partial non-performance, damages are to be assessed on the basis of what proportion of the entire set of obligations provided for in the contract has been performed.[266] That, again, is an application of the principle of proportionality.[267]

---

[261] On the recovery of compensation in cases of lawful expropriation, see the discussion in the June 5, 1990 Award in *Amco, supra* note 189, 5 INT'L ARB. REP. D41 *et seq.* (Nov. 1990); 118 J.D.I. 179 (1991), and observations by E. Gaillard, especially at 187. *See also* the May 20, 1992 Award by E. Jimenez de Arechaga, president, R. Pietrowski, Jr. and M. El Mahdi, arbitrators (M. El Mahdi dissenting), in ICSID Case No. ARB/84/3, Southern Pacific Properties (Middle East) Ltd. v. Arab Republic of Egypt, 8 ICSID REV. – FOREIGN INV. L.J. 328 (1993); 32 I.L.M. 933 (1993), with correction at 32 I.L.M. 1470 (1993); XIX Y.B. COM. ARB. 51 (1994); 8 INT'L ARB. REP. A1 (Aug. 1993); 3 ICSID REP. 189 (1995); for a French translation, see 121 J.D.I. 229 (1994), and observations by E. Gaillard. On the issue, see ORTSCHEIDT, *supra* note 259, ¶¶ 426 *et seq.*

[262] On the recovery of compensation in cases of unlawful expropriation, see, for example, the June 5, 1990 Award in *Amco, supra* note 189, 5 INT'L ARB. REP. D41 *et seq.* (Nov. 1990); 118 J.D.I. 187 (1991).

[263] On this issue, see E. Allan Farnsworth, *Punitive Damages in Arbitration*, 7 ARB. INT'L 3 (1991); ORTSCHEIDT, *supra* note 259, ¶¶ 604 *et seq.* But see, on the arbitrability of the question, *supra* para. 579.

[264] *See* UNIDROIT Principles, *supra* note 118, Art. 7.4.13, para. 2; see *infra* para. 1556.

[265] ICC Award No. 1526 (1968), in which the arbitral tribunal reasoned in terms of general principles although it had declared a specific law to be applicable (*supra* note 261); ICC Award No. 2404 (1975), *supra* note 244; the November 20, 1984 Award in *Amco*, set aside on other grounds, *supra* note 183, 24 I.L.M. 1037 (1985); 114 J.D.I. 155 (1987); the June 5, 1990 Award in *Amco, supra* note 189, 5 INT'L ARB. REP. D41 *et seq.* (Nov. 1990); 118 J.D.I. 179 (1991), and observations by E. Gaillard, especially at 187.

[266] See, for example, the November 1, 1978 ICC Award in Banque du Proche-Orient v. Fougerolle, *upheld by* CA Paris, June 12, 1980, 1981 REV. ARB. 292, and G. Couchez' note; 109 J.D.I. 931 (1982), 2d decision, and B. Oppetit's note.

[267] *See supra* para. 1486.

1497. — It is even possible that an issue as technical as the method of calculating reparable loss could give rise to general principles.[268]

1498. — Likewise, the conditions governing the set-off of the respective sums which parties to a contract may owe one another have been treated as general principles in some awards.[269] We may also witness the development of transnational rules governing interest.[270]

1499. — To summarize, it is essential to recognize that the system of general principles cannot be reduced to the application of a list of rules which have already been formally codified, but that it consists instead of a method enabling the underlying principles of comparative law to be uncovered, if required.[271] It is hard to deny that such a method is an appropriate tool for resolving all disputes liable to arise out of contracts which the parties intended to be governed by transnational rules or to which arbitrators choose to apply transnational rules where the parties fail to elect a governing law.[272]

---

[268] On this issue, particularly in the context of state contracts, see Ignaz Seidl-Hohenveldern, *L'évaluation des dommages dans les arbitrages transnationaux*, 33 AFDI 7 (1987); William C. Lieblich, *Determinations by International Tribunals of the Economic Value of Expropriated Enterprises*, 7 J. INT'L ARB. 37 (Mar. 1990). On this issue, generally, see Bernard Hanotiau, *La détermination et l'évaluation du dommage réparable: principes généraux et principes en émergence*, in TRANSNATIONAL RULES IN INTERNATIONAL COMMERCIAL ARBITRATION, *supra* note 88, at 209; Yves Derains, *Intérêts moratoires, dommages-intérêts compensatoires et dommages punitifs devant l'arbitre international*, in ETUDES OFFERTES À PIERRE BELLET 100, especially at 114 *et seq.* (1991); ORTSCHEIDT, *supra* note 259, ¶¶ 21 *et seq.*

[269] *See* ICC Award No. 3540 (1980), *supra* note 183, and the observations by Kahn, *supra* note 180, at 323. *See also* Paulsson, *supra* note 88, at 93. *See also* Klaus Peter Berger, *Set-Off in International Economic Arbitration*, 15 ARB. INT'L 53 (1999).

[270] Pierre A. Karrer, *Transnational Law of Interest in International Arbitration*, in TRANSNATIONAL RULES IN INTERNATIONAL COMMERCIAL ARBITRATION, *supra* note 88, at 223; Derains, *supra* note 269, at 102 *et seq.*; Yves Derains, *La jurisprudence arbitrale de la Chambre de commerce internationale en matière de monnaie de compte et de monnaie de paiement*, in INADEMPIMENTO, ADATTAMENTO, ARBITRATO – PATOLOGIE DEI CONTRATTI E RIMEDI 477 (1992); ORTSCHEIDT, *supra* note 259, ¶¶ 482 *et seq.*; Herbert Schönle, *Intérêts moratoires, intérêts compensatoires et dommages-intérêts de retard en arbitrage international*, in ETUDES DE DROIT INTERNATIONAL EN L'HONNEUR DE PIERRE LALIVE 649 (1993); Martin Hunter and Volker Triebel, *Awarding Interest in International Arbitration – Some Observations Based on a Comparative Study of the Laws of England and Germany*, 6 J. INT'L ARB. 7 (Mar. 1989); David J. Branson and Richard E. Wallace, Jr., *Awarding Interest in International Commercial Arbitration: Establishing a Uniform Approach*, 28 VIRG. J. INT'L L. 919 (1988). On the starting point for interest, see the May 20, 1992 Award in *Southern Pacific Properties, supra* note 262. On the question of interest, see excerpts of ICC Awards No. 4629 (1989), No. 5428 (1988), No. 5440 (1991), No. 5597 (1990), No. 5694 (1989), No. 5721 (1990), No. 5731 (1989), No. 5789 (1988), No. 5864 (1989), No. 6162 (1990), and No. 6219 (1990), ICC BULLETIN, Vol. 3, No. 1, at 15 *et seq.* (1992); No. 5029 (1991), No. 5285 (1992), No. 5289 (1986), No. 5324 (1989), No. 5834 (1989), No. 5881 (1989), No. 5900 (1989), No. 5904 (1989), No. 6058 (1990), No. 6075 (1990), No. 6256 (1990), No. 6281 (1989), No. 6360 (1990), and No. 6573 (1991), ICC BULLETIN, Vol. 3, No. 2, at 46 *et seq.* (1992); No. 8128 (1995), *supra* note 170.

[271] *See supra* paras. 1458 and 1459.

[272] *See infra* para. 1556.

§ 3. – *Amiable Composition*

1500. — Just as the parties can choose to have the resolution of their disputes governed by a national law or by transnational rules, they can also instruct the arbitrators to act as *amiables compositeurs*.[273] In France, Article 1497 of the New Code of Civil Procedure provides that "[t]he arbitrator shall rule as *amiable compositeur* if the agreement of the parties conferred this mission upon him or her." This provision was inspired by Article VII, paragraph 2 of the 1961 European Convention, which states that "[t]he arbitrators shall act as *amiables compositeurs* if the parties so decide and if they may do so under the law applicable to the arbitration." Article 1497 does not add the condition that the applicable law should allow *amiable composition*, as French law does so. This is hardly surprising, given that the concept of *amiable composition* is often considered as being a product of French law[274] although, despite hesitations in common law countries, it is now recognized in most legal systems.

1501. — As with choice of law clauses,[275] French law contains no requirements as to the form of clauses providing for *amiable composition*. The only restriction is the requirement for a definite intention of the parties to resort to that particular method of dispute resolution. In the absence of a common intention of the parties to that effect, arbitrators would "fail to comply with the terms of their brief"[276] if they were to decide to act as *amiables compositeurs*, even if the parties had given no indication as to the law governing the dispute. To allow *amiable composition* only where the parties have expressly provided so is an approach widely accepted in comparative law.[277] The 1965 Washington Convention takes the same position,[278] as do most institutional arbitration rules.[279]

---

[273] On this issue, generally, see ERIC LOQUIN, L'AMIABLE COMPOSITION EN DROIT COMPARÉ ET INTERNATIONAL – CONTRIBUTION À L'ÉTUDE DU NON-DROIT DANS L'ARBITRAGE INTERNATIONAL (1980); Eric Loquin, *Arbitrage – Instance arbitrale – Arbitrage de droit et amiable composition*, J.-CL. PROC. CIV., Fasc. 1038 (1994); Ion I. Nestor, *L'amiable compositeur et l'arbitrage selon les règles du droit, in* COMMERCIAL ARBITRATION – ESSAYS IN MEMORIAM EUGENIO MINOLI 341 (1974); PETER RIEDBERG, DER AMIABLE COMPOSITEUR IN INTERNATIONALEN PRIVATEN SCHIEDSGERICHTSVERFAHREN (1962). In ICSID arbitration, see Christoph Schreuer, *Decisions Ex Aequo et Bono Under the ICSID Convention*, 11 ICSID REV. – FOREIGN INV. L.J. 37 (1996).

[274] *See, e.g.*, REDFERN AND HUNTER, *supra* note 3, at 36 *et seq.*

[275] *See supra* para. 1427.

[276] This is a ground for setting aside the award under Article 1502 3° of the French New Code of Civil Procedure; *see infra* paras. 1626 *et seq.*, especially para. 1635.

[277] *See, e.g.*, Art. 1054(3) of the Netherlands Code of Civil Procedure; Art. 187, para. 2 of the Swiss Private International Law Statute; Art. 1700(1) of the Belgian Judicial Code (Law of May 19, 1998), which specifically excludes the possibility of public law entities resorting to *amiable composition*; Art. 28(3) of the UNCITRAL Model Law; Art. 1051(3) of the German ZPO (Law of Dec. 22, 1997).

[278] Art. 42(3). See also the November 30, 1979 Award in *AGIP*, by J. Trolle, president, and R.-J. Dupuy and F. Rouhani, arbitrators, which refused to accept the suggestion of the state party to the dispute that the tribunal should rule in equity despite the fact that the contract provided that Congolese law would apply, supplemented, if necessary, by principles of international law (*supra* note 56); compare with the August 8, 1980 Award by

(continued...)

1502. — Nevertheless, considerable controversy remains as to the exact meaning of *amiable composition* and, in particular, as to the need to distinguish it from the concept of equity and from the arbitrators' power to rule *ex aequo et bono*. A distinction has sometimes been drawn between arbitration "in equity" as found in Switzerland, for example,[280] and *amiable composition* under French law. It has been suggested that the former is "detached from legal rules, even if they are mandatory," while the latter merely allows the arbitrator, "ruling in law, to moderate the effects of the application of that [law]."[281] The authors of the UNCITRAL Model Law preferred not to take sides in that debate, or indeed to restrict the parties' freedom by adopting a dogmatic approach. It therefore provides, at Article 28, paragraph 3, that "[t]he arbitral tribunal shall decide *ex aequo et bono* or as *amiable compositeur* only if the parties have expressly authorized it to do so." The same position prevails in the ICC Rules in force since January 1, 1998, whereby "[t]he Arbitral Tribunal shall assume the powers of an *amiable compositeur* or decide *ex aequo et bono* only if the parties have agreed to give it such powers" (Art. 17(3)).[282] However, the distinction between *amiable composition* and equity seems artificial given that, in either case, the arbitrators could choose to have their sense of what justice requires prevail over any other consideration. The French courts appear to use the expressions "*amiable composition*" and "judgment in equity" interchangeably, often holding that arbitrators deciding as *amiables compositeurs* must "seek the fairest solution."[283] However, unless otherwise specified by the

---

[278] (...continued)
J. Trolle, president, R. Bystricky and E. Razafindralambo, arbitrators, in Case No. ARB/77/2, S.A.R.L. Benvenuti & Bonfant v. Government of the People's Republic of the Congo, which records the agreement between the parties during the proceedings to confer powers of *amiables compositeurs* on the arbitrators (for an English translation, see 21 I.L.M. 740 (1982), with corrections at 21 I.L.M. 1478 (1982); VIII Y.B. COM. ARB. 144 (1983); 1 ICSID REP. 330 (1993)).

[279] *See, e.g.*, Art. 17(3) of the 1998 ICC Arbitration Rules (Art. 13(4) of the previous Rules); Art. 33(2) of the UNCITRAL Arbitration Rules; Art. 28(3) of the 1997 AAA International Arbitration Rules; Art. 22.4 of the 1998 LCIA Rules; Art. 24(3) of the 1999 Rules of the Stockholm Chamber of Commerce.

[280] Art. 31, para. 3 of the Swiss 1969 *Concordat* and Art. 187, para. 2 of the Swiss Private International Law Statute; Pierre Jolidon, *La sentence en équité dans le Concordat suisse sur l'arbitrage*, in ASSOCIATION SUISSE DE L'ARBITRAGE, RECUEIL DE TRAVAUX SUISSES SUR L'ARBITRAGE INTERNATIONAL 259 (C. Reymond and E. Bucher eds., 1984); ICC Award No. 6503 (1990), French company v. Spanish company, 122 J.D.I. 1022 (1995), and observations by Y. Derains.

[281] LALIVE, POUDRET, REYMOND, *supra* note 2, at 401 and the references cited therein. Compare, in French law, the idea that equity is only one of the elements of *amiable composition*, LOQUIN, *supra* note 274, ¶¶ 587 *et seq.* and in Italian law, RUBINO-SAMMARTANO, *supra* note 3, at 273. *See also* Mauro Rubino-Sammartano, *Amiable Compositeur (Joint Mandate to Settle) and Ex Bono et Aequo (Discretionary Authority to Mitigate Strict Law) – Apparent Synonyms Revisited*, 9 J. INT'L ARB. 5 (Mar. 1992); Otto Sandrock, *"Ex aequo et bono"- und "Amiable composition"- Vereinbarungen: ihre Qualifikation, Anknüpfung und Wirkungen*, in JAHRBUCH FÜR DIE PRAXIS DER SCHIEDSGERICHTSBARKEIT II, at 120 (1988); Gerardo Broggini, *Réflexions sur l'Equité dans l'arbitrage international*, 1991 BULL. ASA 95.

[282] DERAINS AND SCHWARTZ, *supra* note 32, at 226 *et seq.*

[283] CA Paris, Mar. 15, 1984, Soubaigne v. Limmareds Skogar, 1985 REV. ARB. 285, and the commentary by Eric Loquin, *Pouvoirs et devoirs de l'amiable compositeur. A propos de trois arrêts de la Cour d'appel de Paris*, *id.* at 199; CA Paris, May 6, 1988, Unijet S.A. v. S.A.R.L. International Business Relations Ltd. (I.B.R.), 1989 REV. ARB. 83, and E. Loquin's note.

parties, arbitrators acting as *amiables compositeurs* are in fact free to either apply a national law as a starting point, and then exclude its effects if need be,[284] or to look directly for the solution which they consider to be most equitable.[285]

Amiable composition can thus be defined in an essentially negative fashion as the arbitrators' power not to restrict themselves to applying rules of law, thereby allowing them not only to ignore rules of law altogether, but also to depart from them to the extent that their conception of equity requires.

1503. — A 1981 award in ICC Case No. 3327, inspired by the views taken by one French commentator,[286] described the philosophy of *amiable composition* as follows:

> Arbitration, in this perspective, addresses aims different from those of conventional court proceedings. It is characterized by less emphasis on the legal nature of the dispute and more on its technical, psychological and commercial aspects. An *amiable composition* clause provides the arbitrator with a means to limit the bearing of law on the dispute and to give precedence to other factors, and it enables factual situations, which under a healthy commercial policy warrant different treatment, to be removed from the application of rigid rules.[287]

1504. — The parties themselves sometimes provide indications as to the approach they expect the arbitrators to adopt. It is not unusual for them to combine an *amiable composition* clause with a clause selecting a governing law.[288] In such cases, the arbitrators will begin by applying the chosen law and will depart from it where they consider that it would lead to an inequitable result.

1505. — Where the parties have simply included an *amiable composition* clause without giving any further detail, the arbitrators are by no means obliged to apply a national law or transnational rules. It has sometimes been argued that in such cases the arbitrators ought to take into account general principles of law

---

[284] *See, e.g.*, ICC Award No. 5118 (1986), Italian party v. Two Tunisian parties, 114 J.D.I. 1027 (1987), and observations by S. Jarvin; ICC Award No. 3755 (1988), ICC BULLETIN, Vol. 1, No. 2, at 25 (1990).

[285] *See, e.g.*, ICC Award No. 5103 (1988), Three European companies v. Four Tunisian companies, 115 J.D.I. 1206 (1988), and observations by G. Aguilar Alvarez.

[286] LOQUIN, *supra* note 274, ¶ 583.

[287] *Supra* note 201.

[288] *See, e.g.*, ICC Award No. 2139 (1974), 102 J.D.I. 929 (1975), and observations by Y. Derains, at 920; ICC Award No. 2216 (1974), State-owned company, seller v. Norwegian purchaser, 102 J.D.I. 917 (1975), and observations by Y. Derains.

a reference to equity or, in a different form, the instruction given to him or her to rule *ex aequo et bono*, should lead the arbitrator acting as *amiable compositeur* to take into account general principles of law and international trade practices. Interpreted in this way, an *amiable composition* clause can be considered as referring implicitly to *lex mercatoria*.[289]

It is true that arbitral tribunals resolving a dispute on the basis of equity tend to seek guidance from general principles rather than from a particular national law, even though they may ultimately depart from those principles if their direct application conflicts with the arbitrators' sense of what is equitable.[290] However, the temptation to assimilate *amiable composition* with the application of general principles of law should be avoided. Arbitrators deciding as *amiables compositeurs* are not in any way required to apply transnational rules.[291] Conversely, the application of transnational rules by arbitrators does not necessarily require that the arbitrators be empowered to rule in equity, or indeed—and this is an essential difference between the regime of *lex mercatoria* and that of *amiable composition*—that the parties expressly empower the arbitrators to apply transnational rules, as those rules may be chosen by the arbitrators in the absence of any choice by the parties.[292]

There is in fact an historic explanation for this confusion. During the 1950s and 1960s, the aim of *amiable composition* was not simply to avoid the strict application of a national law. Commentators also considered it to be a means for the arbitrator to apply and, above all, to gradually develop the rules of *lex mercatoria*.[293] As *lex mercatoria* now has more substance, its applicability no longer depends on the existence of an *amiable composition*

---

[289] Goldman, *La lex mercatoria dans les contrats et l'arbitrage internationaux: réalité et perspectives, supra* 88, at 480–81.

[290] *See, e.g.,* ICC Award No. 3327 (1981), *supra* note 201; ICC Award No. 3267 (1979), Mexican construction company v. Belgian company (member of a consortium), VII Y.B. COM. ARB. 96 (1982); for a French translation, see 107 J.D.I. 961 (1980), and observations by Y. Derains; the November 3, 1977 *ad hoc* Award in Mechema Ltd. v. S.A. Mines, Minerais et Métaux, 1980 REV. ARB. 560, and J. Schapira's note; for an English translation, see VII Y.B. COM. ARB. 77 (1982).

[291] *See, e.g.,* ICC Award No. 3267 (1979), *supra* note 291; ICC Award No. 3742 (1983), European contractor v. Three Middle-Eastern state-owned entities, 111 J.D.I. 910 (1984), and observations by Y. Derains. *See also* LALIVE, POUDRET, REYMOND, *supra* note 2, at 402.

[292] *See infra* para. 1556; compare, on the distinction between the two situations, Y. Derains, observations following ICC Award No. 3267 (1979), *supra* note 291, 107 J.D.I. 967 (1980); and, on the fact that a clause declaring the general principles of law and justice to be applicable does not give the arbitrators the powers of *amiables compositeurs*, see ICC Award No. 3380 (1980), *supra* note 219. *See also* Jean-Denis Bredin, *A la recherche de l'Aequitas Mercatoria, in* L'INTERNATIONALISATION DU DROIT – MÉLANGES EN L'HONNEUR DE YVON LOUSSOUARN 109 (1994).

[293] *See, e.g.,* PHILIPPE KAHN, LA VENTE COMMERCIALE INTERNATIONALE 38 (1961); FOUCHARD, *supra* note 112, ¶ 582.

clause.[294] In fact, an *amiable composition* clause will enable arbitrators to decide not to apply a general principle which they consider to be inequitable in the circumstances.[295]

1506. — On the other hand, arbitrators ruling in equity cannot be criticized for applying general principles of law, or even a particular national law if they consider that to be appropriate. Thus, in a case in which arbitrators empowered to act as *amiables compositeurs* reached their decision without making reference to equity, the Paris Court of Appeals refused to set aside the award for non-compliance by the arbitrators with the terms of their brief, on the grounds that the arbitrators had "necessarily been guided equally by rules of law and by their sense of equity."[296]

1507. — A more delicate issue—and one which is more indicative of the differences between certain legal systems—is whether arbitrators empowered to act as *amiables compositeurs*, or to rule in equity, can depart from the provisions of the contract where they consider that to apply them directly would lead to an unfair result.

It has sometimes been argued that an arbitrator acting as *amiable compositeur* must observe the provisions of the disputed contract. In a 1982 award made in ICC Case No. 3938, it was held that:

> the view most widely accepted by authors and international arbitral practice is that an arbitrator acting as *amiable compositeur* remains bound by the contract . . . ; the considerations which may lead the arbitrator to correct distortions which may result from a strict application of the provisions of the law to the particular circumstances of the case are not valid with regard to the contract, which is a special set of rules resulting from the parties' own intentions.[297]

Certain authors share that view and consider that an *amiable compositeur* cannot "directly transgress contractual provisions."[298] The UNCITRAL Model Law provides some support for that position. Although in certain legal systems, including French law, *amiable composition* is the subject of a distinct statutory provision, the Model Law includes *amiable composition* in the article concerning the "Rules Applicable to Substance of Dispute" (Art. 28). *Amiable composition* is therefore also subject to paragraph 4 of the same Article,

---

[294] On the decline of this "function as a substitute for the applicable law," see LOQUIN, *supra* note 274, ¶¶ 562 *et seq.* and 570 *et seq.*

[295] The content of paragraphs 1 and 2 of Article VII of the 1961 European Convention, Articles 1496 and 1497 of the French New Code of Civil Procedure, and corresponding provisions in other modern arbitration statutes (*see supra* para. 1502), as well as the order in which those provisions appear, give clear support for this interpretation. *See also* Fouchard, *supra* note 11, at 399 *et seq.*

[296] CA Paris, Mar. 15, 1984, *Soubaigne, supra* note 284. On this issue, generally, see *infra* para. 1635.

[297] French purchaser v. Dutch seller, 111 J.D.I. 926 (1984), and observations by S. Jarvin.

[298] *See* JEAN ROBERT, L'ARBITRAGE – DROIT INTERNE – DROIT INTERNATIONAL PRIVÉ 186 (6th ed. 1993). *Comp. with* Jean-Denis Bredin, *L'amiable composition et le contrat*, 1984 REV. ARB. 259.

which provides that "[i]n all cases, the arbitral tribunal shall decide in accordance with the terms of the contract and shall take into account the usages of the trade applicable to the transaction." This would seem to imply that in legal systems which have adopted the Model Law, the powers of arbitrators ruling in equity are limited in that they must comply with the provisions of the contract, even if the arbitrators consider that to apply them would lead to an inequitable result.

However, a majority of authors accept that, without going so far as to modify the contract, arbitrators ruling as *amiables compositeurs* can "refuse to apply rights created by the contract, or make them less severe, or even extend their effects."[299]

Having shown signs of leaning towards the first approach,[300] the French courts now consider that arbitrators acting as *amiables compositeurs* can depart from the contract. As stated by the Paris Court of Appeals in a 1988 decision in the *Société Unijet* case, arbitrators ruling as *amiables compositeurs* "have the power to mitigate rights created by the contract, to exclude the consequences of the strict application of the terms of the contract."[301] However, the courts have also held that arbitrators acting as *amiables compositeurs* are not at liberty to "alter the structure of the agreement"[302] "by replacing the contractual obligations with new obligations which do not reflect the parties' common intention."[303]

Arbitral practice also tends to recognize that arbitrators acting as *amiables compositeurs* can choose to depart from the contract.[304]

We consider this latter approach to be the right one. Unlike the parties' agreement as to the choice of governing law, which is binding on the parties pursuant to the provisions of the relevant international arbitration statutes, the binding nature of the contract derives exclusively from the applicable substantive rules. As arbitrators empowered to rule in equity are entitled not to apply such rules where they consider that those rules would lead to an inequitable result, they could of course decide, on the same basis, not to apply the rule that contracts are binding. However, it has been argued that the limitation of the powers of an *amiable compositeur* with respect to the contract owes less to the nature of *amiable composition* than it does to the nature of arbitration in general: the role of the arbitrators is not to act as agents for both parties, but to resolve a dispute, and for that reason they cannot rewrite the contract. This is an attractive argument, but it too has its limits. If a rule of law

---

[299] Loquin, *supra* note 284, at 208; *see also* LOQUIN, *supra* note 274, ¶¶ 462 *et seq.*; DE BOISSÉSON, *supra* note 41, ¶ 663; Mayer, *supra* note 207, ¶ 3.

[300] *See* Cass. 1e civ., June 16, 1976, Krebs v. Milton Stern, 104 J.D.I. 671 (1977), and P. Fouchard's note; 1977 REV. ARB. 269, and E. Mezger's note; 1978 REV. CRIT. DIP 767; Dalloz, Jur. 310 (1978), and J. Robert's note.

[301] CA Paris, May 6, 1988, *Unijet*, *supra* note 284. *See also* CA Paris, Mar. 12, 1985, Intrafor Cofor v. Gagnant, 1985 REV. ARB. 299, and the commentary by Loquin, *supra* note 284; Dalloz, IR 467 (1985), and observations by P. Julien; Cass. 1e civ., Apr. 28, 1987, Krebs v. Milton Stern, 1987 Bull. Civ. I, No. 128; 1991 REV. ARB. 345, and observations by J.-H. Moitry and C. Vergne; CA Paris, Apr. 19, 1991, Parfums Stern France v. CFFD, 1991 REV. ARB. 673, and observations by E. Loquin; CA Paris, Nov. 4, 1997, Taurus Films v. SARL Les Films du Jeudi, 1998 REV. ARB. 704, and observations by Y. Derains.

[302] See the decisions cited *supra* note 302.

[303] CA Paris, Apr. 19, 1991, *Parfums Stern France*, *supra* note 302.

[304] *See, e.g.,* ICC Award No. 3327 (1981), *supra* note 201; ICC Award No. 3344 (1981), *supra* note 222; ICC Award No. 4972 (1989), X & Y v. Z & Mr. W, 116 J.D.I. 1100 (1989), and observations by G. Aguilar Alvarez.

recognizing the doctrine of change in circumstances were to be applied on the basis that it satisfied the requirements of equity, the opposite result could be obtained: under that doctrine, the arbitrators could alter the structure of rights and obligations set forth in the contract.[305]

1508. — Like any other arbitrators, arbitrators acting as *amiables compositeurs* cannot disregard rules of international public policy, a breach of which would provide grounds for setting aside or refusing to enforce the award.[306]

Likewise, arbitrators ruling in equity are still obliged to comply with and ensure that the parties comply with the fundamental requirements of procedural fairness. Unless the parties agree otherwise, *amiable composition* concerns the substance of the dispute and not the procedure, and the *amiable compositeur* will remain a judge, bound to observe the fundamental principles that are required for the proper administration of justice.[307]

SECTION III
LIMITS ON THE EFFECTIVENESS OF THE PARTIES' CHOICE OF LAW

1509. — In the vast majority of cases, the arbitrators comply with the choice expressed by the parties as to the law governing the merits of the dispute, and simply apply that law. In a 1971 award made in ICC Case No. 1512, the arbitral tribunal held that:

> the arbitrator has no power to substitute his own choice to that of the parties, as soon as there exists an expressed, clear and unambiguous choice, and no sufficient reason has been put forward to refuse effects to such a choice.[308]

---

[305] On this point, see, in the context of French domestic arbitration, Patrice Level, *L'amiable composition dans le décret du 14 mai 1980 relatif à l'arbitrage*, 1980 REV. ARB. 651, especially at 656 *et seq.*

[306] On the requirement that arbitrators comply with international public policy even when acting as *amiables compositeurs*, see, for example, ICC Award No. 4265 (1984), Egyptian company v. Dutch company, 111 J.D.I. 922 (1984), and observations by Y. Derains; ICC Award No. 6503 (1990), *supra* note 281, at 1024; CA Paris, Mar. 12, 1985, *Intrafor Cofor*, *supra* note 302; Loquin, *supra* note 284, at 225 *et seq.*

[307] On compliance with due process, see *infra* para. 1638. But see, for an example of an award which founded the refusal to reject memorials submitted out of time on the arbitrators' status as *amiables compositeurs*, ICC Award No. 3327 (1981), *supra* note 201. On the obligation for arbitrators acting as *amiables compositeurs* to comply with due process, see *infra* para. 1638. See also, on their duty, in French domestic law, to comply with mandatory rules, CA Paris, Mar. 16, 1995, SARL Enodis v. SNC Prodim, 1996 REV. ARB. 146, and observations by Y. Derains.

[308] Award No. 1512 (1971), *supra* note 244, I Y.B. COM. ARB. 130 (1976).

Even where the choice made by the parties is considered by the arbitrators to be "surprising," the arbitrators will not contest it.[309]

1510. — However, several theories have been put forward to allow the arbitrators to apply rules of law other than those chosen by the parties to govern the contract.[310] Certain of those theories as to the limits of the effectiveness of the parties' choice are, in our opinion, unsatisfactory (§ 1). Others, however, do clearly restrict the effectiveness of the parties' choice (§ 2).

§ 1. – Unsatisfactory Restrictions of the Effectiveness of the Parties' Choice of Governing Law

1511. — Authors have developed several theories, based on a number of different considerations, intended to allow arbitrators, in certain circumstances, to disregard the choice of governing law made by the parties. These include the theory of the incompleteness of the chosen law (A), the extensive understanding of international trade usages (B) and the theory of international mandatory rules (*lois de police*) (C).

A. – THE THEORY OF THE INCOMPLETENESS OF THE LAW CHOSEN BY THE PARTIES

1512. — One of the earliest theories on the basis of which arbitrators considered themselves entitled to disregard the law chosen by the parties is that of the incomplete character of that law. This involves the arbitrators establishing that the law chosen by the parties does not provide an answer to the issues in dispute, and using that finding to justify resolving those issues by reference to another law or to general principles of law. The most extreme example of this approach, and one which did much to discredit arbitration in certain parts of the world, remains the 1951 award made by Lord Asquith in the *Petroleum Development Ltd. v. The Sheikh of Abu Dhabi* case. Although the contract referred to the law of Abu Dhabi, admittedly in ambiguous terms, the distinguished arbitrator considered that the law of Abu Dhabi, which had yet to be codified, was not sufficiently sophisticated to provide a solution to the dispute. He therefore decided that he should apply not English law as such, but English law in so far as it reflected universal legal principles:

---

[309] *See, e.g.,* ICC Award No. 1581 (1971), quoted by Y. Derains, observations following ICC Award No. 1422 (1966), 101 J.D.I. 887 (1974).

[310] On this issue, see Jean-Christophe Pommier, *La résolution du conflit de lois en matière contractuelle en présence d'une élection de droit: le rôle de l'arbitre*, 119 J.D.I. 5 (1992).

Albeit English municipal law is inapplicable as such, some of its rules are, in my view, so firmly grounded in reason, as to form part of this broad body of jurisprudence—this modern law of nature.[311]

The 1958 award made in the *Aramco* case also relied on the argument that the applicable law was inadequate in order to apply transnational rules. The arbitral tribunal considered that it need not apply Saudi Arabian law, which the contract specified would govern "matters within the jurisdiction of Saudi Arabia," on the grounds that:

> [b]ecause of this fundamental similarity [between Saudi Arabian law and the laws of Western countries on oil concession], the Tribunal will be led, in the case of gaps in the law of Saudi Arabia, of which the Concession Agreement is a part, to ascertain the applicable principles by resorting to the world-wide custom and practice in the oil business and industry; failing such custom and practice, the Tribunal will be influenced by the solutions recognized by world case-law and doctrine and by pure jurisprudence.[312]

This approach has not entirely disappeared from contemporary arbitration law. For example, authors with considerable experience of international arbitral practice only criticize the *Petroleum Development* and *Aramco* awards because, in their view, the respective laws of Abu Dhabi and Saudi Arabia are now sufficiently developed to provide answers to the issues which were in dispute. At no stage do those authors question the validity of the approach whereby the actual or perceived inadequacy of the law chosen by the parties is invoked to justify the application of other rules of law in resolving the dispute.[313] Similarly, in a 1984 award in ICC Case No. 4145, the arbitrators interpreted a clause which referred to both the law of an Arab country and Swiss law by observing that "Swiss law constitutes a highly sophisticated system of law, which answers all the questions that may arise from the interpretation or fulfilment of an agreement of the kind of the one entered into."[314]

An even clearer illustration of this trend is provided by the 1992 ICSID award made in the *SPP* case. The arbitral tribunal considered that even if the parties had chosen Egyptian law to govern the substance of the dispute—which was not clearly established—the arbitrators would nevertheless have been entitled to fill any gaps in that law by applying supranational rules. The tribunal applied that principle to issues as specific as the starting-point for the accrual of interest, and decided, on the basis that Egyptian law was allegedly insufficiently developed to adequately address that subject, to apply rules of public

---

[311] In the Matter of an Arbitration Between Petroleum Dev. (Trucial Coast) Ltd. and the Sheikh of Abu Dhabi, 1 INT'L & COMP. L.Q. 154 and 247 (1952).

[312] Aug. 23, 1958 Award by G. Sauser-Hall, referee, and M. Hassan and S. Habachy, arbitrators, *supra* note 47, 27 INT'L L. REP 171 (1963); for a French translation, see 1963 REV. CRIT. DIP 317. See also the references cited *supra* para. 1173.

[313] REDFERN AND HUNTER, *supra* note 3, at 103.

[314] *Supra* note 64, XII Y.B. COM. ARB. 101 (1987).

international law.[315] This approach is wholly unsatisfactory in that it presupposes that some legal systems are not sufficiently sophisticated to provide answers to all of the issues liable to arise in international commerce. Taking the *SPP* case as an example, it is self-evident that when the Egyptian courts award interest, they resolve the issue of the starting-point for interest by applying their own law. It is therefore hardly credible to suggest that Egyptian law provides no answer to that issue.[316]

It is in fact the proposition that a legal system can be incomplete and therefore can require arbitrators to apply rules from another source that is unsatisfactory. It disregards the structure according to which legal systems are organized, with rules of varying levels of generality. To express the same criticism in purely procedural terms, if the courts of the country whose law has been chosen by the parties were to have jurisdiction to hear the dispute, there is every reason to believe that they would find a solution to each case, even if that entailed reasoning by analogy or resorting to the general principles of their own legal system. Those are therefore the principles that the arbitrators should apply in resolving the dispute in order to respect the choice made by the parties, as opposed to general principles drawn from a variety of other legal systems.[317]

B. – THE EXTENSIVE INTERPRETATION OF INTERNATIONAL TRADE USAGES

1513. — A certain understanding of international trade usages suggests that, in a number of situations, arbitrators are entitled to add to or even modify the provisions of the law chosen by the parties.

Under this conception, "trade usages" include not only the practices usually followed in a particular business sector—an interpretation which is unanimously accepted—but also rules of law derived from comparative law or other international sources. Trade usages are

---

[315] Award by E. Jimenez de Arechaga, president, R. Pietrowski, Jr. and M. El Mahdi, arbitrators (M. El Mahdi dissenting), *supra* note 262, 32 I.L.M. 933, ¶ 234 at 981 (1993); XIX Y.B. COM. ARB. 51, ¶ 234 at 87 (1994); Patrick Rambaud, *L'affaire "des pyramides": suite et fin*, 39 AFDI 567 (1993); Georges R. Delaume, *The Pyramids Stand—The Pharaohs Can Rest in Peace*, 8 ICSID REV. – FOREIGN INV. L.J. 231 (1993); Ibrahim F.I. Shihata and Antonio R. Parra, *Applicable Substantive Law in Disputes Between States and Private Foreign Parties: The Case of Arbitration under the ICSID Convention*, 9 ICSID REV. – FOREIGN INV. L.J. 183 (1994).

[316] For a criticism of the award, see all authors cited *supra* note 316, with the exception of Rambaud.

[317] On the issue of whether national laws contain gaps, see PIERRE MAYER, LA DISTINCTION ENTRE RÈGLES ET DÉCISIONS ET LE DROIT INTERNATIONAL PRIVÉ ¶¶ 102 *et seq.* (1973); E. Gaillard, observations following the June 5, 1990 Award in *Amco*, 118 J.D.I. 173, 183 (1991); Gaillard, *supra* note 88, 10 ICSID REV. – FOREIGN INV. L.J. 215–16 (1995); 122 J.D.I. 12–14 (1995). See also the report of the ILA Committee on International Arbitration's Working Session *in* TRANSNATIONAL RULES IN INTERNATIONAL COMMERCIAL ARBITRATION, *supra* note 88, at 25, especially at 30 *et seq.* See also, in the context of ICSID arbitration, against the idea that arbitrators can apply international law in cases where the parties have made an express choice of a given law, Okezie Chukwumerije, *International Law and Article 42 of the ICSID Convention*, 14 J. INT'L ARB. 79, 85 *et seq.* (Sept. 1997); Nagla Nassar, *Internationalization of State Contracts – ICSID, the Last Citadel*, 14 J. INT'L ARB. 185 (Sept. 1997).

thus assimilated with general principles of international commercial law.[318] This conception is implicit in the work of several proponents of *lex mercatoria*.[319]

The determination of the exact meaning of "trade usages" is important because in numerous instances arbitrators are required to apply them irrespective of the law chosen by the parties. For example, Article 1496 of the French New Code of Civil Procedure instructs arbitrators to take into account international trade usages "in all cases," that is, even where the parties have expressly chosen the law governing the dispute. The same is true of the 1961 European Convention, the Codes of Civil Procedure of the Netherlands and Germany and, more generally, all statutes inspired by the UNCITRAL Model Law.[320] The ICC Rules and the UNCITRAL Rules also contain similar wording.[321] Some commentators consider that the inclusion of the word "usages" in those rules and statutes tacitly authorizes the application of non-national rules of law.[322]

If one were to accept this extensive view of trade usages, arbitrators would be able, on the basis that trade usages are taken to include general principles of law, to extend or modify provisions of the law expressly chosen by the parties.

A small number of arbitral awards appear to have followed this approach. However, although the arbitrators state in those awards that they have not confined themselves to applying the law chosen by the parties, the conclusions that they reach are no different from those that would have resulted from a straightforward application of the chosen law. An example can be found in the 1982 award in ICC Case No. 3896, between Framatome and other plaintiffs and the Atomic Energy Organization of Iran. Although the applicable law chosen by the parties was Iranian law, the tribunal referred on several occasions to general principles of law "found enshrined in particular in international trade usages and international law." In that case, those principles were in fact also found in Iranian law, but the arbitrators nevertheless underlined that they did not consider themselves to be strictly limited to applying the law chosen by the parties.[323]

---

[318] On this latter concept, see *supra* para. 1447.

[319] *See, e.g.*, Goldman, *La lex mercatoria dans les contrats et l'arbitrage internationaux: réalité et perspectives, supra* note 88, at 478; Y. Derains, observations following ICC Award No. 3380 (1980), *supra* note 219, at 930; Loquin, *supra* notes 114 and 113.

[320] *See* Art. VII of the 1961 European Convention; Art. 1054(4) of the Netherlands Code of Civil Procedure; Art. 1051(4) of the German ZPO, in force as of January 1, 1998; Art. 28(4) of the UNCITRAL Model Law.

[321] Art. 17(2) of the 1998 ICC Rules (Art. 13(5) of the previous Rules); Art. 33(3) of the UNCITRAL Rules.

[322] *See, e.g.*, BUCHER AND TSCHANZ, *supra* note 29, ¶ 237.

[323] Apr. 30, 1982 Award on Jurisdiction by P. Lalive, chairman, and B. Goldman and J. Robert, arbitrators, Framatome S.A. v. Atomic Energy Organization of Iran (AEOI), 111 J.D.I. 58 (1984), and the commentary by Oppetit, *supra* note 110. See also the February 16, 1983 ICC Award in Case No. 3493 (set aside by the French courts on different grounds), S.P.P. (Middle East) Ltd. v. Arab Republic of Egypt, 22 I.L.M. 752 (1983); IX Y.B. COM. ARB. 111 (1984); for a French translation, see 1986 REV. ARB. 105, 115, and the commentary by Philippe Leboulanger, *Etat, politique et arbitrage – L'affaire du Plateau des Pyramides, id.* at 3. See also the confusion between trade usages and *lex mercatoria* found in ICC Award No. 5314 (1988), U.S. manufacturer v. Italian licensor, XX Y.B. COM. ARB. 35 (1995).

1514. — The problem is avoided if one favors the strict conception of trade usages as practices usually followed in a particular business sector. The fact that such practices must be taken into account in all cases should never enable arbitrators to ignore the applicable law. At the very most, it will enable them to interpret the intentions of the parties who, in the absence of an express agreement to the contrary, may be considered to have agreed to comply with trade usages.[324]

This strict view is, in our opinion, the right one. It reflects the importance of the role of the principle of party autonomy in contemporary arbitration law.[325] The wording found in Article 1496 of the French New Code of Civil Procedure, Article 1054 of the Netherlands Code of Civil Procedure and other similar provisions of modern arbitration statutes is in fact directly inspired by that of Article VII, paragraph 1 of the 1961 European Convention. Given the date of that Convention, it can hardly have been intended to endorse an extensive view of trade usages which had yet to be developed.[326] In our view, arbitrators are therefore not entitled, under French law, Dutch law, the ICC Rules and the UNCITRAL Rules, to exclude or amend provisions of the law chosen by the parties on the pretext that they are applying trade usages.[327]

In our opinion, the same conclusion can be extended to state contracts. Where the parties have chosen the law of a state to govern their contract, whether or not that state is party to the contract, arbitrators must comply with that choice.[328] If the state uses its sovereign prerogatives for the sole purpose of improving its contractual position, there are other means of censuring its conduct—such as the theory of the abuse of power[329] or other rules contained in the governing law chosen by the parties—and there is no justification for departing from the parties' agreement. That is the position taken in the 1965 Washington Convention, which does not allow the arbitrators to examine whether the law chosen by the parties complies with international law (Art. 42). The only exception to this approach is that the law chosen by the parties must comply with international public policy, but that of course is an entirely different matter.

---

[324] In favor of this conception of the term "usages," see, for example, Kahn, *supra* note 180, at 319; Oppetit, *supra* note 110, at 41. *See also* CA Paris, Mar. 5, 1998, Forasol v. CISTM, which defines trade usages within the meaning of Article 1496 of the New Code of Civil Procedure as "the practices usually followed in international commerce" (1999 REV. ARB. 86, and E. Gaillard's note). For an example of an award refusing to apply the UNIDROIT Principles on hardship in a case where the parties referred exclusively to Spanish law, see ICC Award No. 8873 (1997), Contractor v. Algerian owner, 125 J.D.I. 1017 (1998), and observations by D. Hascher.

[325] *See supra* paras. 1421 *et seq.*

[326] On this argument, see especially Pierre Mayer, *L'autonomie de l'arbitre international dans l'appréciation de sa propre compétence, in* COLLECTED COURSES OF THE HAGUE ACADEMY OF INTERNATIONAL LAW, Vol. 217, Year 1989, Part V, at 45.

[327] On this issue, generally, see Gaillard, *supra* note 65. *Comp. with* Gerald Aksen, *The Law Applicable in International Arbitration – Relevance of Reference to Trade Usages, in* ICCA CONGRESS SERIES NO. 7, PLANNING EFFICIENT ARBITRATION PROCEEDINGS/THE LAW APPLICABLE IN INTERNATIONAL ARBITRATION 471 (A.J. van den Berg ed., 1996).

[328] *But see* Oppetit, *supra* note 110, at 46 and n. 26.

[329] *See supra* para. 1437.

C. – THE THEORY OF INTERNATIONAL MANDATORY RULES (*LOIS DE POLICE*)

1515. — The theory of international mandatory rules (*lois de police*) has also been presented as allowing the arbitrators to take into account rules belonging to a legal system other than that chosen by the parties to govern their dispute.[330]

As with the theory of the incompleteness of the applicable law[331] and that of the extensive interpretation of trade usages,[332] the theory of international mandatory rules enables arbitrators to avoid a strict application of the law chosen by the parties. However, this theory is entirely different in spirit. International mandatory rules reflect a strong degree of interventionism, with the failure to apply the contract being justified on the basis of certain national policies. In contrast, the aim of both the incompleteness theory and the extensive interpretation of trade usages is to allow provisions of the law governing the contract to be disregarded in favor of a direct application of the terms of the contract.[333]

1516. — Nowadays, mandatory rules are generally defined from a purely functional point of view as rules that would not meet their objectives if not applied to a number of situations which they define themselves.[334]

---

[330] On this issue, generally, see especially Yves Derains, *Les normes d'application immédiate dans la jurisprudence arbitrale internationale*, *in* LE DROIT DES RELATIONS ÉCONOMIQUES INTERNATIONALES – ETUDES OFFERTES À BERTHOLD GOLDMAN 29 (1982); Derains, *supra* note 28, at 394 *et seq.*; Yves Derains, *Les tendances de la jurisprudence arbitrale internationale*, 120 J.D.I. 829 (1993), especially at 845 *et seq.*; Pierre Mayer, *L'interférence des lois de police*, *in* L'APPORT DE LA JURISPRUDENCE ARBITRALE, *supra* note 113, at 31; Pierre Mayer, *Les lois de police*, *in* TRAVAUX DU COMITÉ FRANÇAIS DE DROIT INTERNATIONAL PRIVÉ, JOURNÉE COMMÉMORATIVE DU CINQUANTENAIRE, PARIS, 23 NOVEMBRE 1985, at 105 *et seq.* (1988); Pierre Mayer, *Mandatory rules of law in international arbitration*, 2 ARB. INT'L 274 (1986); Mayer, *supra* note 207, ¶¶ 14 *et seq.*; Pierre Mayer, *La sentence contraire à l'ordre public au fond*, 1994 REV. ARB. 615, especially at 640 *et seq.*; François Knoepfler, *L'article 19 LDIP est-il adapté à l'arbitrage international?*, *in* ETUDES DE DROIT INTERNATIONAL EN L'HONNEUR DE PIERRE LALIVE 531 (1993); Daniel Hochstrasser, *Choice of Law and "Foreign" Mandatory Rules in International Arbitration*, 11 J. INT'L ARB. 57 (Mar. 1994); Serge Lazareff, *Mandatory Extraterritorial Application of National Law Rules*, *in* ICCA CONGRESS SERIES NO. 7, PLANNING EFFICIENT ARBITRATION PROCEEDINGS/THE LAW APPLICABLE IN INTERNATIONAL ARBITRATION 538 (A.J. van den Berg ed., 1996); 11 ARB. INT'L 137 (1995); Bernd von Hoffmann, *Internationally Mandatory Rules of Law Before Arbitral Tribunals*, *in* ACTS OF STATE AND ARBITRATION 3 (K.-H. Böckstiegel ed., 1997); COE, *supra* note 116, at 79-80; Marc Blessing, *Mandatory Rules of Law versus Party Autonomy in International Arbitration*, 14 J. INT'L ARB. 23 (Dec. 1997); Marc Blessing, *Impact of Mandatory Rules on International Contracts*, Paper submitted to the Second IBA International Arbitration Day, Düsseldorf, November 12-13, 1998; Nathalie Voser, *Mandatory Rules of Law as a Limitation on the Law Applicable in International Commercial Arbitration*, 7 AM. REV. INT'L ARB. 319 (1996).

[331] *See supra* para. 1511.

[332] *See supra* para. 1513.

[333] *See* the examples cited *supra* paras. 1511 and 1513.

[334] On this issue, generally, see especially Pierre Mayer, *Les lois de police étrangères*, 108 J.D.I. 277 (1981); for a substantive definition of mandatory rules, see P. Francescakis, *Quelques précisions sur les "lois d'application immédiate" et leurs rapports avec les règles de conflits de lois*, 1966 REV. CRIT. DIP 1.

In European choice of law thinking, it is widely accepted that the courts must always apply the mandatory rules of the forum, that they must apply the mandatory rules of the governing law chosen by the parties, provided that those rules are not contrary to international public policy and, although this point is still somewhat controversial, that they may take into account the mandatory rules of a law other than the governing law chosen by the parties, provided that those mandatory rules are closely connected with the dispute.[335] That is the position taken in Article 7, paragraph 1 of the 1980 Rome Convention, which has been in force since April 1, 1991.[336] Three states however—Germany, Luxembourg and the United Kingdom—have made the reservation pursuant to which their courts cannot take foreign mandatory rules into account.

1517. — The issue arises in similar terms before arbitrators, the only difference being that, as arbitrators have no forum, for them all mandatory rules are necessarily "foreign" mandatory rules. There is no doubt that arbitrators must apply the mandatory rules of the governing law chosen by the parties, subject only to compliance with genuinely international public policy requirements.[337] Thus, for example, arbitrators might be entitled not to apply mandatory rules relating to the boycott of one country found in the laws of the other countries—even if the parties had elected that such a law should govern their contract—if they hold those rules to be contrary to international public policy requirements as to religious or racial discrimination.[338] The impact of international public policy considerations will be the same regardless of whether or not the provisions they purport to exclude are mandatory rules. The only truly difficult issue is whether the arbitrators must—or may—take into account international mandatory rules of a legal system other than that which the parties have chosen to govern their contract when there is a close connection between that other legal system and the subject-matter of the dispute.

---

[335] On this issue, see BATIFFOL AND LAGARDE, *supra* note 25, ¶ 254; MAYER, *supra* note 25, ¶¶ 121 *et seq.*; BERNARD AUDIT, DROIT INTERNATIONAL PRIVÉ 97 *et seq.* (2d ed. 1997); DICEY & MORRIS, THE CONFLICT OF LAWS, Vol. 2, at 1239 *et seq.* (12th ed. 1993 and 4th cumulative supp. 1997).

[336] 1980 O.J. (L266); 19 I.L.M. 1492 (1980).

[337] *See infra* para. 1533.

[338] In favor of the possibility of excluding a mandatory rule of the law chosen by the parties that violates international public policy, see Yves Derains, *Les normes d'application immédiate dans la jurisprudence arbitrale internationale, supra* note 331, at 37. Compare, for an example of a case where, on the basis of the legitimate expectations of the parties, the arbitrator did not apply the RICO Act, although the parties had chosen "New York law" to govern their contract, with ICC Award No. 8385 (1995), *supra* note 202, and, for the refusal to apply mandatory dispositions of the French law of December 31, 1975 on subcontracts, despite the choice by the parties of French law to govern their contract, see ICC Award No. 7528 (1993), *supra* note 66.

This question has provoked serious differences of academic opinion.[339] The controversy can, however, be scaled down by drawing a distinction between the aspects of the question that are not in dispute and those that lie at the heart of the debate.

1518. — The first point that is clear is that the arbitrators can take into account, as elements of fact, mandatory rules liable to have an impact on the performance of the contract. They can therefore draw from those factual elements the various conclusions provided for in the governing law chosen by the parties.

Thus, for example, a law other than that governing the contract which prohibits the export of goods under the conditions set forth in the contract could be considered, under the law governing the contract, to be a *force majeure* event.[340]

Similarly, arbitrators may have to decide whether a breach of a law other than that chosen by the parties to govern their contract could have the effect of rendering the purpose of the contract immoral, thus providing grounds on which to hold it void. The best-known example was the subject of a 1967 award in ICC Case No. 1399. The case concerned a contract between a French party and a Mexican party which was submitted to French law and was intended to circumvent Mexican customs laws. The arbitrators refused to avoid the contract for illegality, observing that "French law is not concerned with foreign customs laws."[341] Some authors approve of that approach, arguing that there is nothing "immoral or illegal in breaking a law which is not applicable."[342] The situation is not, however, that clear-cut. Of course, the law chosen by the parties should be the one determining whether a contract the purpose of which is to contravene a foreign law can be considered as being, if not fundamentally illegal, then at least immoral. As a result, there can be no general solution to the question. For instance, the position under French law is that the illegality of conduct in another country can render a contract immoral under French law.[343] The French courts consider that their examination of the morality of a situation is not confined to events occurring on French territory, particularly if the same facts would have been illegal had they

---

[339] In favor of the application of international mandatory rules by arbitrators, see especially, Derains, articles cited *supra* note 331; Mayer, articles cited *supra* note 331; Knoepfler, *supra* note 331; HORACIO A. GRIGERA NAON, CHOICE OF LAW PROBLEMS IN INTERNATIONAL COMMERCIAL ARBITRATION 238 (Thesis, Harvard Law School (U.S.A.), 1985); Lando, *supra* note 19, at 158; Philippe Fouchard, remarks made at the *Journée du cinquantenaire* of the Comité français de droit international privé, *supra* note 331, at 115; regarding antitrust law, see Idot, *supra* note 210, at 328; Hochstrasser, *supra* note 331; A.F.M. Maniruzzaman, *International Arbitrator and Mandatory Public Law Rules in the Context of State Contracts: An Overview*, 7 J. INT'L ARB. 53 (Sept. 1990). For the reverse position, see, for example, Berthold Goldman, remarks made at the *Journée du cinquantenaire* of the Comité français de droit international privé, *supra* note 331, at 116; ROBERT, *supra* note 299, ¶ 356; Arthur T. von Mehren, Limitations on Party Choice of the Governing Law: Do they Exist for International Commercial Arbitration? 13 (paper published by The Mortimer and Raymond Sackler Institute of Advanced Studies, Tel Aviv, 1986); LALIVE, POUDRET, REYMOND, *supra* note 2, at 187.

[340] For further examples, see Derains, *Les normes d'application immédiate dans la jurisprudence internationale*, *supra* note 331, at 38.

[341] Mexican licensee v. French licensor; see the excerpts cited by LEW, *supra* note 3, ¶ 422 at 550–52.

[342] Mayer, *L'interférence des lois de police*, *supra* note 331, ¶ 44.

[343] *But see* Trib. civ. Seine, Jan. 4, 1956, Spitzer v. Amunategui, 1956 REV. CRIT. DIP 679, and H. Batiffol's note.

taken place in France.[344] In a 1961 decision, the French *Cour de cassation* rightly rejected the argument that French public policy only outlaws bribery of the French authorities, and not foreign officials. The Court therefore held void for illegality a contract where the payment of a commission concealed the remuneration of improper steps taken to secure approval of a transaction taking place outside France.[345]

1519. — The second uncontested point is that arbitrators sitting in any Member State of the European Union are under no obligation to apply principles governing court decisions—including, in particular, Article 7, paragraph 1 of the 1980 Rome Convention—which allow courts to take into account foreign mandatory rules. It has been suggested, in connection with Swiss law on international arbitration, that arbitrators sitting in Switzerland are required to apply Article 19 of the Swiss Private International Law Statute, which also allows the courts to apply foreign mandatory rules. Among the commentators taking such a position, some have criticized the resulting uncertainties,[346] while others consider it to be appropriate for arbitrators to apply foreign mandatory rules.[347] However, in our opinion, this reasoning is founded on an unsatisfactory premise, as there is no basis for the assimilation of arbitrators with the courts of the seat of the arbitration. It is now accepted that arbitrators are under no obligation to apply the private international law of the seat of the arbitration,[348] particularly where there are other specific rules governing international arbitration, as is the case in France, Switzerland, and now England.[349]

1520. — The third point which is beyond dispute is that mandatory rules must be applied by arbitrators where to refrain from doing so would lead to a result contrary to genuinely international public policy. In such cases, however, the grounds for the application of such rules do not lie in the mandatory rules doctrine but in that of international public policy.[350]

The controversy surrounding the application of mandatory rules by arbitrators therefore only takes on significance in practice when arbitrators encounter mandatory rules which

---

[344] *See also* ICC Case No. 1399 (1967), *supra* note 342.

[345] Cass. com., Mar. 7, 1961, Laburthe v. Sauveroche, 1961 Bull. Civ. III, No. 125. In English law, compare with Soleimany v. Soleimany, [1998] 3 W.L.R. 811; 13 INT'L ARB. REP. A1 (Mar. 1998) (C.A. 1998) and the discussion *infra* para. 1528. On the reaction of the *lex mercatoria* to corruption, see *supra* para. 1468 and on international public policy, *infra* para. 1533.

[346] Francis A. Mann, *New Dangers of Arbitration in Switzerland*, FIN. TIMES, Nov. 24, 1988, at 43.

[347] Knoepfler, *supra* note 331.

[348] On the approach which consists in following as a model Article 7, paragraph 1 of the Rome Convention, see the Dutch award cited by Mayer, *supra* note 207, ¶ 14; ICC Award No. 6500 (1992), Lebanese Traders Distributors & Consultants v. Reynolds Tobacco International, 119 J.D.I. 1015 (1992); see also the draft recommendations on the law applicable by arbitrators to international contracts proposed by Ole Lando, *Conflict-of-Law Rules for Arbitrators*, in FESTSCHRIFT FÜR KONRAD ZWEIGERT ZUM 70. GERBURTSTAG 157, 173 (1981).

[349] *See* Sec. 46(3) of the 1996 Arbitration Act. But see, with respect to mandatory rules other than that of the *lex contractus*, the case law cited *infra* para. 1528.

[350] *See infra* para. 1533.

neither belong to the governing law chosen by the parties nor reflect the requirements of truly international public policy.

1521. — Most authors express the concern that arbitrators should be allowed, when reaching their decisions, to take proper account of the overriding requirements of justice. To achieve that goal, some favor the application of international mandatory rules, while others rely solely on the more conventional concept of international public policy which, in international arbitration, must mean genuinely international public policy.[351]

It is therefore not surprising to find that the same examples (such as corruption, customs offences, breaches of embargoes, and antitrust violations) are used as illustrations of the application of both mandatory rules and the requirements of international public policy. Proponents of the mandatory rules method tend to adopt a very restrictive view of international public policy, thus leaving sufficient space for other imperative rules. For example, as corruption is not unanimously outlawed, it is sometimes considered to be contrary

> neither to an international trade usage (it is in fact a widely-used instrument), nor to a general principle of law, as it is encouraged by some States when their exporters resort to it on foreign territory.[352]

Another question is whether the condemnation of drug trafficking is a rule of *lex mercatoria* or of international public policy, given that some countries do not actively prohibit it.[353] However, as previously noted, in order to be considered as a general principle, a rule need not be recognized in all legal systems.[354] The same is true of genuinely international public policy which, in our opinion, international arbitrators must apply.[355] They are perfectly entitled to take into account the necessity to fight against corruption or drug trafficking, and indeed they must do so to ensure that their award will not be set aside or refused enforcement.[356]

1522. — Nevertheless, the divergence of views between the proponents of international mandatory rules and those who prefer to rely exclusively on the concept of international public policy is more than a matter of terminology. The crux of the problem is the determination of the reasoning arbitrators should adopt when faced with an allegation that a contract is illegal in the light of rules other than those of the law governing the contract.

---

[351] *See infra* para. 1648.

[352] Mayer, *supra* note 207, ¶ 26.

[353] *Id.,* ¶ 27.

[354] See, regarding the principle of the autonomy of the arbitration clause, *supra* para. 405, note 43 and on this issue, generally, *supra* para. 1458.

[355] *See infra* paras. 1533 *et seq.*, especially para. 1535.

[356] *See infra* para. 1662.

The mandatory rules method involves identifying rules which, in their own legal system, reflect essential policy, and then evaluating, given the closeness of the connections between the case and that legal system and the "consequences of their application or non-application," if it is appropriate to apply those rules in the case at hand.[357] Where the courts apply foreign mandatory rules, and where arbitrators are invited to apply mandatory rules other than those of the *lex contractus*, the underlying philosophy is essentially the spirit of international cooperation in defending vital national policies.

The emphasis is thus not so much on the moral value of the rule as on the strength of the legislator's intention and the closeness of the objective connections between the rule and the situation in dispute. As one author rightly observed,

> it is impossible to base the application of mandatory rules solely on a value judgment; the essence of the method is to base it on the existence of a close connection between the rule and the legal situation. However, the rule which should thus be applied may be no more compatible with good morals than the *lex contractus*, and it may even lead to an even more inequitable result.[358]

For an example of this, we need only consider the numerous occasions where a court or an arbitral tribunal is confronted not with a mandatory rule which might prevail over the *lex contractus*, but with a conflict of mandatory rules. A good illustration can be seen in the measures taken by Iraq in response to the freezing by most countries of assets belonging to Iraqi nationals.[359] As with the laws to which they respond, these measures are mandatory rules in the legal system in which they originate. If the issue of their applicability were to arise in the context of contracts to be performed in Iraq, the requirement of a close connection between the mandatory rule and the situation in dispute would be satisfied.[360] It would then be necessary to assess "the consequences of the application or non-application of such rules" which, for the court or arbitral tribunal deciding whether or not to apply them, is a directive which often leads to confusion. In its modern form, the mandatory rules theory provides no guidance other than functional criteria on which courts or arbitrators can decide whether or not to apply such rules in a particular case. It is therefore hardly surprising that the theory inevitably reintroduces moral considerations in deciding between the various mandatory rules at issue, or simply in determining whether a particular mandatory rule connected with the situation should in fact be taken into account. Neither is it surprising that the result of the mandatory rules approach is to leave a great deal of room for subjective appreciation by the arbitrators. This has led to the view that, as the arbitrators are, by

---

[357] This is the criterion of Article 7, paragraph 1 of the Rome Convention, which supporters of the method suggest should be applied in arbitration, directly or as a source of inspiration.

[358] Mayer, *supra* note 207, ¶ 16.

[359] Iraqi Law No. 57 of September 16, 1990 on Protection of Iraqi properties, interests and rights inside and outside Iraq, 5 INT'L ARB. REP. C1 (Dec. 1990).

[360] Compare with the 1957 decision of the House of Lords in Regazzoni v. K.C. Sethia (1944), Ltd., [1958] A.C. 301; [1957] 3 All E.R. 286; [1957] 3 W.L.R. 752; [1957] Lloyd's Rep. 289, where the mandatory rules of the place of performance were taken into account (for a French translation, see 88 J.D.I. 1140 (1961)).

definition, the sole judges of the contract, without restricting themselves to the governing law chosen by the parties they can "contrive to uphold the general interest and to protect the interests of the weaker party by applying the mandatory rules of the country in question whenever such interests are threatened," and that "as the principle alien to the law chosen by the parties is not intrinsically superior . . . , the exclusion of that law is founded on the will of the arbitrator, who seeks to uphold good morals."[361] Interpreted to the letter, this is not particularly reassuring for parties involved in international commerce, for whom predictability is an important consideration.

The transnational public policy method is based on a different philosophy. Where arbitrators have to address the argument that a contract is illegal, despite the fact that it complies with the *lex contractus*, under the transnational public policy theory they should decide on the basis of values very widely accepted by the international community, and not according to their own discretion as to whether it would be appropriate to give effect to a particular national policy. For example, the fact that apartheid, drug trafficking and corruption are condemned on almost all sides of the international community should provide sufficient justification for the exclusion, through the application of international public policy, of any contrary provisions of the *lex contractus*, or of the contract where the *lex contractus* takes no position. The same should be true of the resolutions taken by the United Nations and by many countries following the Iraqi invasion of Kuwait, even though that invasion was not universally condemned. The reasoning is based on the fact that the rules in question are widely accepted by the international community. The advantage of this approach is that it avoids both the subjectivism of leaving the arbitrators free to apply only the requirements of their own sense of justice, and the permissiveness of having no public policy reaction at all.

In any event, it is important to note that the international mandatory rules method is itself sometimes tempered by more global considerations. For example, Article 9 of the 1991 Resolution of the Institute of International Law, concerning "the autonomy of the parties in international contracts between private persons or entities," provides that:

> If regard is to be had to mandatory provisions . . . of a law other than that of the forum or that chosen by the parties, then such provisions can only prevent the chosen law from being applied if there is a close link between the contract and the country of that law *and if they further such aims as are generally accepted by the international community*.[362](emphasis added)

Interpreted in this way, the theory of "foreign" mandatory rules has much more in common with the doctrine of genuinely international public policy.

---

[361] Mayer, *supra* note 207, ¶ 22.

[362] Resolution adopted during the Basel Session, August 26–September 3, 1991, *reprinted in* INSTITUT DE DROIT INTERNATIONAL, TABLEAU DES RÉSOLUTIONS ADOPTÉES (1957–1991), at 408, 413 (1992); for the original French version, see 1992 REV. CRIT. DIP 198.

We consider that, for arbitrators even more so than for national courts (before which the concern of inter-state cooperation may also play an important role), the need to sustain universal values should constitute the first guideline in ascertaining international legality.

1523. — Although the results obtained by arbitrators applying one or other of these methods often coincide, this will not always be the case.

A perfect example can be seen in the 1988 award in ICC Case No. 5622. The French corporation OTV had engaged Hilmarton, an English company, to provide legal and tax advice, and "to coordinate administrative matters" with a view to obtaining and performing a public works contract concerning the sewage processing system in Algiers. The contract was governed by Swiss law. A dispute arose concerning payment of the agreed commissions and the sole arbitrator sitting in Geneva considered that, as "[the] claimant essentially gathered confidential information, surveyed and observed and also used its influence on the Algerian authorities," the claimant's "mission" was contrary to Algerian law, which prohibits the use of intermediaries. He declared the contract void on the grounds that it contravened an Algerian mandatory rule and hence *bonos mores* within the meaning of Article 20, paragraph 1 of the Swiss Code of Obligations.[363] This was thus a clear application of the mandatory rules approach, under which the arbitrator felt entitled to give effect to the mandatory rules of a law other than that governing the contract. The award was set aside by the Court of Justice of the canton of Geneva, on the grounds that it was "arbitrary." The Court held that, unlike corruption, the use of intermediaries did not offend Swiss law, which was applicable to the merits of the case.[364]

There is little doubt that the decision reached by the arbitrator was based on the feeling that "coordination in administrative matters" was in fact a euphemism for acts of corruption which would be universally condemned. However, from a technical standpoint, the grounds for the award were the rules of a national law that prohibit intermediaries. Although those rules are intended to prevent corruption, they do not in themselves reflect a universally accepted moral standard. In the absence of such universality, it was possible to construe the rules as being incapable of overriding the law which would normally apply. For that reason, we believe that the arbitrator ought to have pursued his line of reasoning to its logical conclusion by examining whether the services in dispute in fact constituted acts of corruption. In that case, the arbitrator could have reached the same result by basing his decision on considerations of transnational public policy.[365] That would have been much less

---

[363] ICC Award No. 5622 (1988), *supra* note 205, 1993 REV. ARB. 332; XIX Y.B. COM. ARB. 112 (1994).

[364] Nov. 17, 1989, Hilmarton v. OTV, 1993 REV. ARB. 315, 320–21; for an English translation, see XIX Y.B. COM. ARB. 214 (1994). The decision was upheld by the Swiss Federal Tribunal on April 17, 1990 (OTV v. Hilmarton, 1993 REV. ARB. 315, and the commentary by Heuzé, *supra* note 205; for an English translation, see XIX Y.B. COM. ARB. 214 (1994)).

[365] *See infra* para. 1525.

controversial and would not have required him to apply a specific rule of Algerian law over the *lex contractus*.[366]

1524. — Admittedly, the *Hilmarton* case also demonstrates that it is easier for an arbitrator to simply apply mandatory rules of a jurisdiction which is closely connected with the dispute, as opposed to going to the trouble of determining the content of genuinely international public policy. Given that it is always difficult to prove corruption, the arbitrator, guided by his intimate convictions on the question, confined himself to applying the Algerian law prohibiting intermediaries as a mandatory rule. The burden of proof on the party contesting the legality of the contract was thus considerably reduced as compared to the burden of proving the existence of universally condemned conduct. The same is true with respect to the task of the arbitrators in giving reasons for their award. For some authors, this simplification justifies the application by arbitrators of both genuinely international public policy and mandatory rules of a jurisdiction other than that of the *lex contractus* when assessing the legality of a party's behavior.

Antitrust law provides another example in support of the international mandatory rules theory. Despite the efforts made to bring about a convergence of laws in this field,[367] this highly technical subject is more easily analyzed in terms of mandatory rules, rather than in terms of universal moral standards.[368]

1525. — However pertinent the foregoing considerations may be, it would seem that basing a decision on transnational public policy is nevertheless more consistent with the transnational source of the arbitrators' decision-making powers than the application of mandatory rules other than those of the law chosen by the parties. Having no forum, arbitrators draw the legitimacy of their decisions from the broad recognition of the rules they apply. That is undoubtedly true of the principle that in international transactions the parties are free to choose the law governing their agreement. It is also true of the principle that the arbitrators' powers are limited by international public policy considerations. However, resorting to mandatory rules other than those of the *lex contractus* or, in the case of courts, other than those of the *lex fori*, remains highly controversial. This can be seen in the reservations made, even within the European Union, with regard to Article 7, paragraph 1 of the Rome Convention.[369]

---

[366] *See* E. Gaillard, observations following Cass. 1e civ., Mar. 23, 1994, Hilmarton v. OTV, 121 J.D.I. 701, 706 (1994). On this case, see also Heuzé, *supra* note 205; Ali Mebroukine, *Le choix de la Suisse comme siège de l'arbitrage dans les clauses d'arbitrage conclues entre entreprises algériennes et entreprises étrangères*, 1994 BULL. ASA 4; Andrea Giardina, *Norme imperative contro le intermediazioni nei contratti e arbitrato internazionale*, 1992 RIV. DELL'ARB. 784. On the procedure before the French courts, see *infra* para. 1595.

[367] *See* Moitry, *supra* note 210.

[368] *See* Idot, *supra* note 210, at 328.

[369] *See supra* para. 1516.

Where the goal is to defeat conduct widely viewed as unacceptable (such as apartheid, drug trafficking, corruption or even antitrust violations),[370] the best approach seems to be to avoid the concept of mandatory rules altogether and to hold that to apply the provisions of the contract or the provisions of laws which allow such practices would be contrary to genuinely international public policy.

If, on the other hand, the goal is to give effect to national policies which do not reflect widely-shared moral values, the use of the mandatory rule concept is inappropriate.

By clearly setting out the fact that the goal of the application of mandatory rules is the furtherance of generally accepted moral standards, arbitrators can avoid giving a moralizing role to those rules which is alien to their primary purpose, namely inter-state co-operation. Above all, it helps prevent the all too frequent criticism that international arbitration is arbitrary.

1526. — Arbitral case law appears to be divided on this issue, with some awards recognizing that the arbitrators have the power to apply rules of law other than those of the *lex contractus*, and others refusing to do so. However, on closer examination it in fact appears that arbitrators have so far remained particularly reluctant to apply mandatory rules other than those of the *lex contractus*.

Examples of cases where the arbitrators have held themselves entitled to apply mandatory rules not belonging to the governing law chosen by the parties include a 1973 award in ICC Case No. 1859, which found that "the importer . . . was obliged to comply with the mandatory rules of the importing countries," and that the co-contractor "could not claim that those laws are not enforceable against it."[371] Likewise, a 1991 award in ICC Case No. 6294 considered the applicability of German rules prohibiting employee transfers to a contract governed by Swiss law and entered into by a Hungarian party and a German party. The arbitral tribunal rejected the application of German law, but only on the grounds that the interest of a party in releasing itself from obligations which it had failed to honor vis-à-vis the other party did not deserve protection, and was certainly not an overriding interest.[372] It is not uncommon to find arbitrators taking such a position.[373] However, we know of virtually no cases where the arbitrators have relied on the application of a mandatory rule to justify

---

[370] *See* Berthold Goldman, *L'arbitrage international et le droit de la concurrence*, 1989 BULL. ASA 260; Xavier de Mello, *Arbitrage et droit communautaire*, 1982 REV. ARB. 349, 362; Georges Van Hecke, *Arbitrage et règles de concurrence*, 1978 REV. ARB. 191. On this issue, generally, see the references cited *supra* para. 575. *See also* the awards cited *infra* para. 1533.

[371] Cited by Derains, *Les normes d'application immédiate dans la jurisprudence arbitrale internationale*, *supra* note 331, at 40.

[372] Hungarian sub-contractor v. German contractor, 118 J.D.I. 1050 (1991), and observations by J.-J. Arnaldez.

[373] *See, e.g.*, ICC Award No. 6320 (1992), which accepts the principle of the extra-territorial application of a United States mandatory rule against corruption where the contract was governed by Brazilian law, on the condition (which was not met in the case) that the rule reflected "an important and legitimate interest of that state" and that there was a sufficient connection (Owner v. U.S. contractor, ICC BULLETIN, Vol. 6, No. 1, at 59 (1995); 122 J.D.I. 986, 989 (1995), and observations by D. Hascher; for an English translation, see XX Y.B. COM. ARB. 62 (1995)); ICC Award No. 6773 (1992), which did not apply United States antitrust laws to a contract governed by French law "although the arbitral tribunal can take such laws into consideration" (Belgian and U.S. companies v. Luxembourg and Italian companies, ICC BULLETIN, Vol. 6, No. 1, at 66 (1995)).

a decision other than that would have resulted from the application of the law chosen by the parties.[374] This cautious attitude has led some authors to describe arbitral awards which state that the arbitrators are at liberty to apply mandatory rules other than those of *lex contractus* as complying with "the parties' legitimate expectations."[375] However, that view is completely at odds with the philosophy underlying the mandatory rules theory, the purpose of which is to enable a national policy to prevail over the parties' intentions. The fact that arbitral case law can be understood in terms of the parties' "legitimate expectations" only reinforces the proposition that arbitrators are in fact unwilling to take into account mandatory rules, except as elements of fact or where the parties have tacitly chosen to have them apply as rules which by their nature should prevail over the provisions of the law chosen by the parties to govern their relationship.

1527. — Other awards, in both the terms used and the decisions reached, are more clearly hostile towards the application of mandatory rules other than those of the *lex contractus*. For example, in an ICC award made in 1992 in the *Reynolds* case, the arbitrators refused to take into account Lebanese customs regulations when evaluating the loss suffered by an exclusive distributor following the termination of a distribution contract.[376] Likewise, in a 1987 award made under the aegis of the Court of Arbitration of the German Coffee Association, the arbitrators would not allow customs regulations of the place of origin of a consignment of coffee to prevail over German law, which the parties had implicitly chosen to govern the substance of the dispute.[377] Similarly, in a 1990 award made in Cologne in ICC Case No. 6379, the arbitrators would not allow Italian law, which had been chosen by the parties to govern their contract, to be disregarded in favor of the mandatory rules contained in paragraph 4 of the Belgian statute of July 27, 1961, as amended on April 13, 1971, which provides that Belgian law applies to the termination of exclusive sales agreements "producing [their] effects in all or in part of Belgium."[378]

Another example is provided by the 1994 award made in ICC Case No. 7047. The parties had entered into a contract governed by Swiss law for sales assistance in support of various

---

[374] *See also* von Mehren, *supra* note 340, at 14; the analysis of arbitral case law in LEW, *supra* note 3, ¶¶ 415 *et seq.* and, more recently, the conclusions reached by Derains, *supra* note 28, ¶¶ 46–51. Also, in the April 27, 1992 ICC Award cited *infra* para. 1527, the arbitrators took an openly restrictive position. Compare with the August 19, 1988 Award in ICC Case No. 5622, *Hilmarton*, subsequently set aside, *supra* note 205.

[375] *See* Derains, *Les normes d'application immédiate dans la jurisprudence arbitrale internationale*, *supra* note 331, at 45; Yves Derains, *Attente légitime des parties et droit applicable au fond en matière d'arbitrage commercial international*, *in* TRAVAUX DU COMITÉ FRANÇAIS DE DROIT INTERNATIONAL PRIVÉ 1984–1985, at 81 (1987).

[376] Apr. 27, 1992 Award by K.H. Böckstiegel, chairman, B. Goldman and M., arbitrators, *upheld by* CA Paris, Oct. 27, 1994, Lebanese Traders Distributors & Consultants LTDC v. Reynolds, 1994 REV. ARB. 709, and the commentary by Mayer, *La sentence contraire à l'ordre public au fond*, *id.* at 615, 649; for an English translation, see 10 INT'L ARB. REP. E1 (Feb. 1995).

[377] *See supra* para. 1428 and note 21.

[378] Italian principal v. Belgian distributor, XVII Y.B. COM. ARB. 212 (1992); 1993 REV. DR. COM. BELGE 1146, and B. Hanotiau's note; ICC BULLETIN, Vol. 7, No. 1, at 83 (1996); *see also* Bernard Hanotiau, *L'arbitrabilité et la favor arbitrandum: un réexamen*, 121 J.D.I. 899 (1994), especially ¶¶ 67 *et seq.* On this last issue, see *supra* paras. 580 *et seq.*

products. In an attempt to avoid performance of its obligations, the defendant relied on the regulations of the country where the main contract was to be performed, which prohibited the use of intermediaries in the field of activity in question. The arbitral tribunal rejected the defendant's argument, on the grounds that:

> the parties are entitled to submit their legal relations to whatever law they choose, and to exclude national laws which would apply in the absence of a choice. Consequently, the provisions of the law thus excluded can only prevail over the chosen law in so far as they are matters of public policy.[379]

1528. — Courts reviewing an award in an action to set aside or at the enforcement stage are also reluctant to apply mandatory rules other than those of the *lex contractus*.[380] This is certainly the case in France. One author who favors arbitrators applying mandatory rules other than those of the law chosen by the parties has remarked that, when reviewing arbitral awards, the French courts "are not inclined to take into account foreign mandatory rules."[381]

It may even be that, by applying mandatory rules other than that of the *lex contractus* without justifying their application on the basis of international public policy,[382] arbitrators run the risk of exceeding the terms of their brief, thus leaving their award vulnerable to an action to set aside in certain jurisdictions.[383] Swiss case law provides some examples of this risk materializing.[384]

Using slightly different terminology, English law is more receptive to the reasoning underlying the mandatory rules theory. Following long-established case law,[385] the Court of Appeal recently refused to enforce an award made in London under Jewish law in a dispute between two Iranian refugees on the ground that the award gave effect to a contract which violated Iranian customs regulations.[386] This solution is particularly paradoxical because the

---

[379] February 28, 1994, Corporation W. v. State agency F., Award by H. Raeschke-Kessler, chairman, J. Patry and D. Mitrovic, arbitrators, 1995 BULL. ASA 301, 330–32, *upheld by* Swiss Fed. Trib., Dec. 30, 1994, *supra* note 205. See also, for an example of hostility towards the French mandatory rules contained in Article 14 of the Law of December 31, 1975 on subcontracts, even where French law is chosen by the parties, ICC Award No. 7528 (1994), *supra* note 66, and, for a holding that mandatory rules are only mandatory in their jurisdiction of origin, ICC Award No. 6379 (1990), *supra* note 379.

[380] See, for example, in French law, CA Paris, Oct. 27, 1994, *Reynolds*, *supra* note 377; in Swiss law, see Court of Justice of the Geneva Canton, Nov. 17, 1989, *Hilmarton*, *supra* note 365. But see Swiss Fed. Trib., Dec. 30, 1994, *supra* note 205, which held that it was not necessary to address the question as the arbitrators had stated that the mandatory nature of the rule at issue had not been established and that such a finding was not a violation of international public policy (1995 BULL. ASA 223).

[381] Pierre Mayer, *La sentence contraire à l'ordre public au fond*, *supra* note 331, at 649. On the extent of the review of awards by the courts, generally, see *infra* paras. 1645 *et seq.*

[382] *See infra* para. 1533.

[383] This may be the case, for example, in French law, pursuant to Articles 1502 3° and 1504 of the New Code of Civil Procedure. For similar situations, see *infra* paras. 1635 *et seq.*

[384] See, in the *Hilmarton* matter, the decisions cited *supra* note 365.

[385] *See Regazzoni*, *supra* note 361.

[386] *Soleimany*, *supra* note 346.

English courts are required, in principle, to reject arguments based on mandatory rules other than those of the applicable law and the forum. This results from the fact that the United Kingdom has made the reservation excluding the application of Article 7, paragraph 1 of the 1980 Rome Convention.[387]

§ 2. – Legitimate Restrictions of the Effectiveness of the Parties' Choice of Governing Law

1529. — The effectiveness of the parties' choice of governing law may be limited in at least two ways. First, certain issues may not be covered by the law chosen by the parties (A). Second, the arbitrators can exclude the law that would normally apply on the basis of international public policy (B), albeit in a very limited number of situations.

A. – SCOPE OF THE LAW CHOSEN BY THE PARTIES

1530. — A number of recent statutes on international arbitration allow the parties to choose the law applicable to the "dispute," rather than simply to the contract to which their arbitration agreement relates.[388] It is legitimate to infer from such provisions that other non-contractual issues which may arise between the parties (such as tortious liability, questions of title to property and abuse of rights issues) will be governed by the law they have chosen, despite the fact that, according to traditional private international law thinking, the principle of party autonomy does not apply in such matters. Commentators have not universally approved this position.[389]

The answer to the question of whether the law chosen by the parties covers all aspects of the dispute depends on several considerations.

1531. — First, the scope of the law chosen by the parties can clearly be no greater than that intended by the parties entering into the contract. Thus, where the parties have referred to the law applicable "to the present contract," or have used an equivalent phrase, the arbitrators remain free to determine the law applicable to issues which cannot be

---

[387] *See supra* para. 1516. It is interesting to consider the observations of F.A. Mann in this connection (*supra* note 347). He was critical, in 1988, of the "new dangers" of arbitration in Switzerland. The particular "danger" he feared—the application of mandatory rules other than those of the governing law—was unfounded as far as Switzerland was concerned, because Article 19 of the Swiss Private International Law Statute does not apply to arbitration (*see supra* para. 1319). However, through one of those twists of fate, that "danger" is now found in English law.

[388] *See, e.g.*, Art. 1496 of the French New Code of Civil Procedure; Art. 28(1) of the UNCITRAL Model Law; Sec. 46(1) of the 1996 English Arbitration Act.

[389] Compare the views of Pierre Bellet and Ernst Mezger, *L'arbitrage international dans le nouveau code de procédure civile*, 1981 REV. CRIT. DIP 611, 631; Fouchard, *supra* note 11, at 394; DE BOISSÉSON, *supra* note 41, ¶ 660.

characterized as contractual issues, assuming of course that the arbitration agreement is drafted in sufficiently broad terms to give the arbitrators jurisdiction over such issues.[390] In reaching their decision on this question, the arbitrators will follow the method that they would have used had the parties failed to make any choice of governing law at all.

1532. — Second, it has been argued that the principle of autonomy does not apply to the determination of the law governing issues such as a party's capacity to enter into a contract. According to one author, "the capacity of each party should be assessed in the light of its own law, except where the other party could reasonably have been unaware of its content."[391] The same analysis could be made with respect to one party's power to enter into a contract on behalf of another party. The justification for this approach lies in the fact that both a party's capacity and its power to contract are questions that logically arise before that of the choice of the law governing the contract. It is therefore understandable that those issues should be governed by a law determined objectively. The choice of the applicable law will thus generally be made using the method that would apply to determine the law governing the contract in the absence of a choice by the parties.[392] If the arbitrators follow the civil law tradition, capacity will be governed by the national law of the party in question. If they follow the common law tradition, the law of the party's domicile will generally be preferred. In both cases, powers will usually be governed by the law of their source. Thus, for example, the powers of corporate representatives will be governed by the law under which the corporation represented is organized. An exception should, however, be made for the doctrine of apparent authority as set out, for example, in Article 11 of the 1980 Rome Convention. This reflects a very widely accepted rule, namely that only where a party is legitimately unaware of the other party's lack of capacity or power will such lack of capacity or power constitute a ground for avoiding the contract.[393]

B. – INTERNATIONAL PUBLIC POLICY

1533. — There is no doubt that arbitrators are entitled to disregard the provisions of the governing law chosen by the parties where they consider those provisions to be contrary to

---

[390] On this issue, generally, see Claude Reymond, *Conflits de lois en matière de responsabilité délictuelle devant l'arbitre international*, in TRAVAUX DU COMITÉ FRANÇAIS DE DROIT INTERNATIONAL PRIVÉ 1988–1989, at 97 (1991); Wolfgang Kühn, *Express and Implied Choice of the Substantive Law in the Practice of International Arbitration*, in ICCA CONGRESS SERIES NO. 7, PLANNING EFFICIENT ARBITRATION PROCEEDINGS/THE LAW APPLICABLE IN INTERNATIONAL ARBITRATION 380 (A.J. van den Berg ed., 1996).

[391] Fouchard, *supra* note 11, at 395.

[392] *See infra* paras. 1537 *et seq.* On the application of the national law of the defendant, as opposed to the law governing the contract, to the issue (characterized as preliminary by the award) of whether the defendant was an autonomous legal entity, see the September 9, 1983 *ad hoc* Award, F.R. German engineering company v. Polish buyer, XII Y.B. COM. ARB. 63 (1987).

[393] On the law applicable to powers of attorney in French law, see EMMANUEL GAILLARD, LE POUVOIR EN DROIT PRIVÉ ¶¶ 338 *et seq.* (1985). On the application of the doctrine of apparent authority to the arbitration agreement, see *supra* para. 470.

international public policy.[394] Even if the arbitrators are extremely reluctant in practice to disregard the provisions of the governing law on such a ground,[395] such a possibility is generally acknowledged even by those commentators who attach the most weight to the principle of party autonomy.[396]

In virtually every country, an award can be set aside or denied recognition if it is contrary to international public policy. This is acknowledged by arbitration statutes,[397] as well as by international treaties. Most significantly, in all countries which have ratified the 1958 New York Convention, an award contravening the requirements of international public policy can be refused recognition and enforcement (Art. V(2)(b)). This must mean that arbitrators themselves have the power to disregard the provisions of a law chosen by the parties which would lead to the violation of a principle which is part of international public policy. It would hardly be consistent to criticize arbitrators for rendering an award contravening international public policy without having given them the opportunity to exclude the provisions of the law chosen by the parties which were contrary to international public policy in the first place. Support for this view can be found in Article 2 of the Resolution adopted by the Institute of International Law at Santiago de Compostela on September 12, 1989, which states that "[i]n no case shall an arbitrator violate principles of international public policy as to which a broad consensus has emerged in the international community."[398]

Accordingly, arbitrators have the right—and even the obligation—to themselves raise the issue of whether disputed contracts or legal provisions put before them satisfy the requirements of international public policy.[399]

As a result of this consensus, the controversy in this area has focused not so much on the principle that international public policy can prevail over the law chosen by the parties, as on the determination of the content of international public policy.

1534. — The first question that arises in determining the content of international public policy is whether arbitrators should look to one or several identified legal systems, or whether they should take a more global approach. The answer differs according to whether one places emphasis on the arbitrators' decision satisfying the fundamental requirements of justice, in the same way as a court decision, or on their making an award which will not be set aside by the courts at the seat of the arbitration and which will be capable of recognition

---

[394] On this issue, generally, see JEAN-BAPTISTE RACINE, L'ARBITRAGE COMMERCIAL INTERNATIONAL ET L'ORDRE PUBLIC (1999) and, on "transnational public policy" in particular, ¶¶ 628 et seq.

[395] See, e.g., Fadlallah, supra note 66, at 369 and infra para. 1536.

[396] See, e.g., von Mehren, supra note 340, at 14.

[397] See, e.g., Art. 1502 5° and 1504 of the French Code of Civil Procedure; Art. 190 of the Swiss Private International Law Statute. Compare with Article 34 of the UNCITRAL Model Law or Section 68(2)(g) of the 1996 English Arbitration Act, which refer to "public policy."

[398] Supra note 4, and the references cited supra para. 1446.

[399] See, for example, regarding European Community antitrust law, ICC Awards No. 7315 (Madrid, 1992) and No. 7181 (Paris, 1992), Parties to a joint venture agreement for the development of software packages, cited in ICC BULLETIN, SPECIAL SUPPLEMENT, INTERNATIONAL COMMERCIAL ARBITRATION IN EUROPE 42 and 44 (1994) and in ICC BULLETIN, Vol. 6, No. 1, at 55 (1995).

and enforcement in jurisdictions where attachable assets are located. The former approach does not require the arbitrators to draw on a particular legal system in order to determine the content of international public policy. The latter approach, however, does oblige them to consider the conception of international public policy which prevails at the seat, as well as that of the jurisdictions connected with the dispute, which entails proceeding in a manner very similar to that used to determine the law applicable to the dispute when no choice has been made by the parties.[400]

Were they to have regard only for the effectiveness of the award, the arbitrators would take into account international public policy as understood in countries where the award is likely to be enforced. However, in our opinion the arbitrators' approach should not be restricted in such a way. As their brief is to decide a dispute, arbitrators cannot disregard the fundamental requirements of justice. Further, as the basis of their power to decide a dispute is derived not from the law of a single country, but from those of all jurisdictions willing to recognize an award under certain conditions, arbitrators hearing an international dispute cannot confine themselves to applying one particular conception of international public policy. Concerns as to the enforceability of the award should therefore not prevail over the universal requirements of justice. Thus, to take an extreme example, an international arbitral tribunal sitting in a country where racial or religious discrimination forms part of the national conception of public policy should not depart from a global view of the requirements of international public policy exclusively on the basis that its award might be set aside for failing to reflect the public policy of the country of the seat, regardless of whether or not the case is connected with that country.[401]

There is no contradiction between this position and the idea that the application of international public policy by arbitrators is justified by the fact that most laws on arbitration and most international conventions on the recognition and enforcement of awards provide for the award to be reviewed in the light of international public policy.[402] Of course, the conception of public policy of the jurisdiction where that review takes place will be that of the countries where an action is brought to set aside or resist enforcement of the award.[403]

---

[400] For an example of the consideration, admittedly in an *obiter dictum*, of the public policy of the seat of the arbitration and of each of the states concerned by the transaction, see ICC Award No. 4338 (1984), U.S. party v. Syrian minister, 112 J.D.I. 981 (1985), and observations by Y. Derains. For an example of the consideration of the public policy of the place of enforcement of the award, see ICC Award No. 3281 (1981), French licensor v. Spanish licensee, 109 J.D.I. 990 (1982), and observations by Y. Derains. Compare the draft recommendations on the law applicable by arbitrators to international contracts made by Ole Lando, which combine the requirements of truly international public policy and the public policy of the place of enforcement (*supra* note 349).

[401] For an award that is indifferent towards the public policy of the place of enforcement of the award, compare, regarding the jurisdiction of the arbitral tribunal, ICC Award No. 2476 (1976), Swiss company v. Italian company, 104 J.D.I. 936 (1977), and observations by Y. Derains, and the November 1984 Interim Award in ICC Case No. 4695, Parties from Brazil, Panama and U.S.A. v. Party from Brazil, XI Y.B. COM. ARB. 149 (1986).

[402] *See supra* para. 1533.

[403] See Article V(2)(b) of the 1958 New York Convention, which lists among the grounds for refusal to recognize and enforce an award non-compliance with the public policy of the country of recognition or enforcement. On
(continued...)

That is not to say, however, that the award derives its validity from one of those legal systems. The validity of the award instead results from the laws of all jurisdictions liable to recognize and enforce the award, regardless of whether the losing party has assets located there.[404]

1535. — If one rejects the narrow view which requires arbitrators to adopt the conception of public policy of one or more identified jurisdictions, a question remains as to whether the arbitrators are free to determine the content of international public policy according to their own conscience, or whether they should base their judgment on values widely recognized in the international community.

The latter view is more generally accepted.[405] However, it has been criticized on the grounds that the unanimity which it requires does not in fact exist, as countries cannot all reach agreement even on fundamental values.[406] That criticism has led to suggestions that international conventions, the resolutions of international organizations and the almost total convergence of national laws "merely serve as justification and do not constitute the source of legal rules which the arbitrator would simply apply."[407] On the other hand, the same criticism has led a moralizing role to be attributed to mandatory rules connected with the dispute—a role which international public policy is purportedly ill-equipped to play.[408]

We have already discussed why it is going too far to insist that a rule must be adopted in all jurisdictions worldwide for it to be considered as reflecting the requirements of a genuinely international public policy. The condemnation of racial discrimination, corruption, or drug trafficking need not be absolutely unanimous for it to reflect a universal moral standard. To require total unanimity would be to deprive the application of public policy of all meaning in international arbitration as, by definition, for public policy to come into play, at least one law—the law which would otherwise apply—must be contrary to the fundamental conception of justice which is reflected by public policy.[409]

---

[403] (...continued)
this issue, see *infra* para. 1648.

[404] On this conception of arbitration and its consequences, see Emmanuel Gaillard, *Enforcement of Awards Set Aside in the Country of Origin: The French Experience*, in ICCA CONGRESS SERIES No. 9, IMPROVING THE EFFICIENCY OF ARBITRATION AGREEMENTS AND AWARDS: 40 YEARS OF APPLICATION OF THE NEW YORK CONVENTION 505 (A.J. van den Berg ed., 1999) and, for a French version, 125 J.D.I. 645 (1998).

[405] *See, e.g.*, Berthold Goldman, *Les conflits de lois dans l'arbitrage international de droit privé*, in COLLECTED COURSES OF THE HAGUE ACADEMY OF INTERNATIONAL LAW, Vol. 109, Year 1963, Part II, at 347; Goldman, *supra* note 206, at 274; Lambert Matray, *Arbitrage et ordre public transnational*, in THE ART OF ARBITRATION – ESSAYS ON INTERNATIONAL ARBITRATION – LIBER AMICORUM PIETER SANDERS 241 (J. Schultz and A.J. van den Berg eds., 1982); Lalive, *supra* note 193; BUCHER AND TSCHANZ, *supra* note 29, ¶ 239; Moitry, *supra* note 210. *See also* the September 12, 1989 Resolution of the Institute of International Law, *supra* note 4.

[406] Mayer, *supra* note 207, ¶¶ 26–27.

[407] *Id.*, ¶¶ 25–26.

[408] On this issue, see *supra* para. 1522.

[409] On these issues, see *supra* para. 1521.

Furthermore, it seems neither correct nor appropriate to suggest that to apply these fundamental principles of justice (which only partially overlap with general principles of law)[410] would amount to

> implicitly denying that the country whose law departs from the majority view is a 'civilized nation,' which [would] ultimately [be] more unacceptable than having an arbitrator tip the balance in favor of his own moral judgment.[411]

When considering examples such as racial discrimination, drug trafficking or corruption, such a disinterested attitude is out of place. On the other hand, to base the whole approach on the complete subjectivity of the arbitrators is equally inappropriate.

Although it may not be part of the substantive law of every sovereign state, genuinely international public policy is nevertheless a reality, and it is perfectly able to operate so as to override the law which would otherwise apply, just as the local conception of international public policy would operate in a national court.

1536. — Nonetheless, the fact remains that in practice it is extremely rare for arbitrators to decide not to apply the rules of the governing law chosen by the parties.[412]

---

[410] *See supra* para. 1468.

[411] Mayer, *supra* note 207, ¶ 26.

[412] *See* Fadlallah, *supra* note 66, at 369; von Mehren, *supra* note 340, at 14. See, for example, the refusal, in two awards made in Switzerland in 1990 and 1993 (ICC Cases No. 6503 and 7097), to allow European antitrust law to prevail over Swiss law and the *amiable composition* agreed by the parties (ICC BULLETIN, SPECIAL SUPPLEMENT, INTERNATIONAL COMMERCIAL ARBITRATION IN EUROPE 39 and 38 (1994); 122 J.D.I. 1022 (1995), and observations by Y. Derains).

CHAPTER II
APPLICABLE LAW CHOSEN BY THE ARBITRATORS

1537. — Where the parties have not determined the law governing the dispute, the arbitrators are responsible for doing so.

In performing this task, the arbitrators now generally enjoy broad discretion, which applies not only to the method they use (Section I), but also to the subject matter of their choice (Section II). The extent of their discretion is such that, whereas the effectiveness of the choice of governing law made by the parties is liable to be restricted in some respects,[1] that of the choice of law made by the arbitrators is virtually unlimited[2] (Section III).

SECTION I
THE METHOD USED BY ARBITRATORS IN SELECTING THE APPLICABLE LAW

1538. — In some cases, without actually determining the law applicable to the dispute, the parties give an indication as to the method to be followed by the arbitrators in making their choice. The parties may agree on the method during the proceedings: this may be the case when the memorials are exchanged, for example.[3] Alternatively, guidance may be found in the provisions of the arbitration rules chosen by the parties. With the entry into force of the new AAA, ICC and LCIA Rules in 1997 and 1998 and the Rules of the Stockholm Chamber of Commerce in 1999, the UNCITRAL Rules, which were adopted in 1976, are the only major set of rules which still state that in the absence of an indication by the parties as to the applicable law, the arbitrators shall apply the law designated by the rule of conflict which they consider appropriate.[4] The new AAA, ICC, LCIA and Stockholm Chamber of Commerce Rules all depart from this approach, rejecting the requirement that arbitrators use

---

[1]   *See supra* paras. 1509 *et seq.*

[2]   *See* Arthur T. von Mehren, Limitations on Party Choice of the Governing Law: Do They Exist for International Commercial Arbitration? 14 (paper published by The Mortimer and Raymond Sackler Institute of Advanced Studies, Tel Aviv, 1986).

[3]   *See, e.g.*, ICC Award No. 1250 (1964), Lebanese distributor v. Western European car manufacturer, V Y.B. COM. ARB. 168 (1980); ICC Award No. 2680 (1977), cited by Y. Derains, 105 J.D.I. 997 (1978), in which the parties agreed to request the arbitrators to apply the choice of law rules of a given country.

[4]   Art. 33(1) of the UNCITRAL Arbitration Rules.

a choice of law rule to select the law or rules of law applicable to the dispute.[5] The AAA International Arbitration Rules which came into force on April 1, 1997 provide that "failing . . . a designation by the parties, the tribunal shall apply such law or laws as it determines to be appropriate" (Art. 28(1)); the 1998 LCIA Rules also state that when the parties have made no choice of law "the Arbitral Tribunal shall apply the law(s) or rules of law which it considers appropriate" (Art. 22.3); the 1998 ICC Rules provide that in the absence of agreement by parties upon the applicable rules of law, "the Arbitral Tribunal shall apply the rules of law which it determines to be appropriate" (Art. 17(1)). The 1999 Rules of the Stockholm Chamber of Commerce also state that "[i]n the absence of an agreement [by the parties] the arbitral tribunal shall apply the law or rules of law which it considers to be the most appropriate" (Sec. 24(1)). In each case, the arbitrators are granted the widest possible discretion, which extends to allowing them to use the direct choice method.[6] This will be so regardless of the method retained by the international arbitration law of the seat of the arbitration in the absence of a choice of governing law by the parties, provided that such law recognizes, as is almost invariably the case, the principle of party autonomy in the choice of the law governing the substance of the dispute.[7] Thus, by selecting arbitration rules which in turn give broad discretion to the arbitrators, the parties simply benefit, albeit indirectly, from the principle of party autonomy. This means, for example, that in an LCIA or ICC arbitration held in London, in the absence of any further indication by the parties, the arbitrators will not apply Section 46(3) of the 1996 Arbitration Act, which still requires them to resort to a choice of law rule. They will instead apply the rules selected by the parties, which free them from the statutory requirement and thus bring such a proceeding in line with the methodology followed in arbitrations taking place in jurisdictions such as France or the Netherlands even where no arbitration rules have been chosen by the parties.[8]

1539. — In the absence of any indication by the parties as to how the arbitrators should determine the applicable law, the relevant arbitration statutes do not always impose a specific method on the arbitrators (§ 1). Like the AAA, ICC or LCIA Rules, they instead often allow the arbitrators to choose from a number of different methods used to select the rules of law applicable to the dispute (§ 2).

---

[5] For a description of the evolution of the practice followed by the arbitrators in the past forty years, even under the early ICC Rules, which, in their Art. 13(3), used terms similar to those of the UNCITRAL Rules, see YVES DERAINS AND ERIC A. SCHWARTZ, A GUIDE TO THE NEW ICC RULES OF ARBITRATION 221 et seq. (1998).

[6] See infra para. 1552.

[7] See Berthold Goldman, Les conflits de lois dans l'arbitrage international de droit privé, in COLLECTED COURSES OF THE HAGUE ACADEMY OF INTERNATIONAL LAW, Vol. 109, Year 1963, Part II, at 347; in the case of the previous ICC Arbitration Rules, ICC Award No. 4237 (Feb. 17, 1984), Syrian State trading organization v. Ghanaian State enterprise, X Y.B. COM. ARB. 52 (1985); Partial Award in ICC Case No. 6719 (1994), where arbitrators sitting in Geneva held, under Article 13(3) of the previous ICC Rules, that they were entitled to apply a choice of law rule as they saw fit, including a rule other than Article 187 of the Swiss Private International Law Statute, which they nevertheless decided to apply (Syrian party v. Two Italian companies, 121 J.D.I. 1071, 1077 (1994), and observations by J.-J. Arnaldez).

[8] See infra para. 1540.

§ 1. – Is a Method Imposed on the Arbitrators?

1540. — Since the 1981 reform, French international arbitration law has adopted a position which could hardly be more liberal with respect to the determination by the arbitrators of the law applicable to the merits of the dispute. Article 1496, paragraph 1 of the New Code of Civil Procedure simply indicates that, in the absence of a choice by the parties, the arbitrators shall decide the dispute in accordance with the rules of law they "consider appropriate." Paragraph 2, which applies whether or not the parties have made a choice as to the governing law, further provides that the arbitrators must "[i]n all cases . . . take trade usages into account." Paragraph 2 thus barely limits the arbitrators' discretion, as they are invited to determine themselves the content of any trade usages that are liable to be taken into account in any given case. These provisions have been adopted verbatim by the 1986 Netherlands Arbitration Act (Art. 1054(2) of the Code of Civil Procedure) and in a number of other countries such as Algeria, Tunisia and Lebanon.[9] When these provisions are applicable, the arbitrators do not have to determine the governing law by resorting to the choice of law rules applied by the courts in the country where the arbitration takes place, an approach which is now considered outdated in most legal systems (A).

In France, unlike certain other countries such as Switzerland, arbitrators are not even required to apply choice of law rules specifically designed to meet the needs of international arbitration (B).

A. – ORDINARY CHOICE OF LAW RULES OF THE SEAT OF THE ARBITRATION

1541. — Under one outdated theory, which placed excessive emphasis on the judicial nature of arbitration in that it effectively assimilated arbitrators and judges of the seat of the arbitration,"the rules of choice of law in force in the state of the seat of the arbitral tribunal must be followed to settle the law applicable to the substance of the difference." That was the formulation adopted by the Institute of International Law in its 1957 Amsterdam Resolution following the Sauser-Hall report.[10]

---

[9]   *See* Art. 458 bis 14 of the Algerian Code of Civil Procedure (Legislative Decree No. 93-08 of April 25, 1993); Art. 73 of the Tunisian Arbitration Code of April 26, 1993; Art. 813 of the Lebanese New Code of Civil Procedure of September 16, 1983.

[10] Art. 11 of the Institute of International Law's Resolution on Arbitration in Private International Law, adopted during the Amsterdam session held on September 18–27, 1957, *reprinted in* INSTITUT DE DROIT INTERNATIONAL, TABLEAU DES RÉSOLUTIONS ADOPTÉES (1957–1991), at 236, 243 (1992). In favor of this position, see also F.A. Mann, *Lex Facit Arbitrum, in* INTERNATIONAL ARBITRATION – LIBER AMICORUM FOR MARTIN DOMKE 157 (P. Sanders ed., 1967), *reprinted in* 2 ARB. INT'L 241 (1986). For a discussion of this issue, see JEAN-MICHEL JACQUET, PRINCIPE D'AUTONOMIE ET CONTRATS INTERNATIONAUX ¶¶ 192 *et seq.* (1983); Steven J. Stein, *The Drafting of Effective Choice-of-Law Clauses,* 8 J. INT'L ARB. 69 (Sept. 1991); Filip J.M. de Ly, *The Place of Arbitration in the Conflict of Laws of International Commercial Arbitration: an Exercise in Arbitration Planning,* 12 NW. J. INT'L L. & BUS. 48 (1991); Julian D.M. Lew, *The place of arbitration and the applicable procedural law in the English common law, in* THE PLACE OF ARBITRATION 77 (M. Storme and F. de Ly eds., 1992); Otto Sandrock, *The place of arbitration and the law applicable to the*

(continued...)

This theory has been heavily criticized[11] for disregarding both the transnational nature of the sources of an international commercial arbitrator's powers[12] and the reasons why the parties, the arbitral institution, or the arbitrators themselves choose a place of arbitration (which generally will have nothing to do with the law governing the merits or the private international law of the seat of the arbitration).[13] The approach taken in the 1957 resolution is now obsolete, as is the related notion of the arbitral forum, with most modern arbitration laws having now abandoned all reference to the private international law "of the forum."[14] Laws which grant, as is the case in France, the arbitrators total freedom to select the applicable law when the parties have not done so do not prevent arbitrators from drawing inspiration from the choice of law rules of the place of arbitration. However, arbitrators sitting in France, for example, would be wrong to consider that such rules should take priority over other rules, or indeed that they should be taken into account at all.[15] In a Resolution on encouraging recourse to arbitration to settle legal disputes, the European Parliament underlined "the special nature of arbitration inasmuch as an arbitration tribunal has a greater degree of freedom to choose the body of law to be applied to a dispute without being bound by *lex fori* . . . as normal courts are."[16]

---

[10](...continued)
   merits of the dispute, id. at 89; Charles Jarrosson, *De quelques aspects spécifiques tenant au lieu de l'arbitrage pour certaines matières ou dans certains pays, id.* at 123.

[11]   *See* PHILIPPE FOUCHARD, L'ARBITRAGE COMMERCIAL INTERNATIONAL ¶¶ 546 *et seq.* (1965); MATTHIEU DE BOISSÉSON, LE DROIT FRANÇAIS DE L'ARBITRAGE INTERNE ET INTERNATIONAL ¶ 652 (2d. ed. 1990); Pierre Lalive, *Le droit applicable au fond par l'arbitre international, in* DROIT INTERNATIONAL ET DROIT COMMUNAUTAIRE 33, 41 (1991); Gabrielle J. Kaufmann-Kohler, *Aspects de la mise en œuvre du droit en arbitrage*, 1988 REV. DR. SUISSE 403, 414.

[12]   *See supra* paras. 1525 and 1534, note 405.

[13]   *See supra* para. 1178.

[14]   *See, e.g.,* Art. 1054 of the Netherlands Code of Civil Procedure; Art. 187, para. 1 of the Swiss Private International Law Statute; Art. 834 of the Italian Code of Civil Procedure (Law of Jan. 5, 1994); Art. 28(2) of the UNCITRAL Model Law, which follows the UNCITRAL Arbitration Rules. *See also* W. LAURENCE CRAIG, WILLIAM W. PARK, JAN PAULSSON, INTERNATIONAL CHAMBER OF COMMERCE ARBITRATION 285 (2d ed. 1990). For a systematic analysis of the evolution, in arbitration statutes, arbitration rules and international conventions, from the "classical approach" which treated the seat of arbitration as the forum of a court, to the "modern approach," which does not, see Marc Blessing, *Regulations in Arbitration Rules on Choice of Law, in* ICCA CONGRESS SERIES NO. 7, PLANNING EFFICIENT ARBITRATION PROCEEDINGS/THE LAW APPLICABLE IN INTERNATIONAL ARBITRATION 391 (A.J. van den Berg ed., 1996).

[15]   On the fact that the choice of law rules of the seat are irrelevant, see, for example, ICC Award No. 1512 (1971), Indian cement company v. Pakistani Bank, I Y.B. COM. ARB. 128 (1976); for a French translation, see 101 J.D.I. 904, 907 (1974), and observations by Y. Derains; ICC Award No. 2730 (1982), Two Yugoslavian companies v. Dutch and Swiss group companies, 111 J.D.I. 914 (1984), and observations by Y. Derains; ICC Award No. 6527 (1991), Buyer v. Seller, ICC BULLETIN, Vol. 7, No. 1, at 88 (1996); XVIII Y.B. COM. ARB. 44 (1993); ICC Award No. 8385 (1995), U.S. company v. Belgian company, 124 J.D.I. 1061 (1997), and observations by Y. Derains. *But see, e.g.,* ICC Award No. 5551 (1988), French buyer v. Spanish seller, ICC BULLETIN, Vol. 7, No. 1, at 82 (1996).

[16]   1994 O.J. (C 205) 519; 1995 BULL. ASA 42. See also on the gradual abandonment of this latter approach in international practice, A.F.M. Maniruzzaman, *Conflict of Laws Issues in International Arbitration: Practice and Trends*, 9 ARB. INT'L 371 (1993). On the fact that arbitrators have no forum, see *supra* para. 1181.

1542. — Institutional arbitration rules can, however, require the application of the choice of law rules of the seat of the arbitration. This is the case, for example, of the International Arbitration Rules of the Zurich Chamber of Commerce, which provide, in their Article 4, that the choice of law rules found in the Swiss Private International Law Statute apply unless the choice of law rules of the domicile or habitual residence of each party coincide. In such cases, those choice of law rules must be applied in order to comply with the intentions of the parties, in the same way as a direct choice of law made by the parties should be followed.

1543. — The same considerations necessarily come into play with respect to the application by the arbitrators of the domestic law of the seat of the arbitration to the merits of the dispute.[17]

B. – CHOICE OF LAW RULES OF THE SEAT OF THE ARBITRATION SPECIFICALLY DESIGNED FOR INTERNATIONAL ARBITRATION

1544. — The issue of whether arbitrators are required to apply a choice of law rule of the seat of the arbitration specifically designed for international arbitration is not resolved in the same way by different legal systems.

While recognizing that there is no justification for applying the ordinary choice of law rules of the seat of the arbitration, a number of recent arbitration statutes do contain choice of law rules specifically intended to be applied by arbitrators. For example, Article 187 of the 1987 Swiss Private International Law Statute provides that in the absence of a choice of governing law by the parties, "[t]he arbitral tribunal shall decide the dispute according to the rules of law . . . with which the case has the closest connection." This choice of law rule, which is specific to international arbitration, is intended to guide arbitrators sitting in Switzerland in their determination of the applicable law, and therefore denies the arbitrators the option of applying other choice of law rules or of exercising greater discretion in their choice of the governing law. The position taken by the Swiss legislature has been followed in several recent arbitration statutes, including those of Italy,[18] Mexico[19] and Germany,[20] all of which departed from the UNCITRAL Model Law[21] in this respect. As far as the method is concerned, the Swiss approach is thus, in theory, less liberal than that adopted in French

---

[17] On laws which regard the selection of the seat, at least when made by the parties, as an indication of an implicit choice of the law governing the merits of the dispute, see *supra* para. 1428.

[18] *See* Art. 834 of the Code of Civil Procedure (Law of Jan. 5, 1994).

[19] *See* Art. 1445 of the Mexican Commercial Code (Law of July 22, 1993).

[20] *See* Art. 1051(2) of the ZPO, in force as of January 1, 1998.

[21] *See also* Art. 39(2) of the Egyptian Law No. 27 for 1994 Promulgating the Law Concerning Arbitration in Civil and Commercial Matters. See also, in Swedish law, before the 1999 Arbitration Act, which remained silent in this respect, Kaj I. Hobér, *In Search for the Center of Gravity – Applicable Law in International Arbitration in Sweden, in* SWEDISH AND INTERNATIONAL ARBITRATION 1994, at 7.

and Dutch arbitration law,[22] which grant complete freedom to the arbitrators, or even in the UNCITRAL Model Law, which grants the arbitrators the freedom to select the choice of law rules it considers appropriate.[23] However, it has been argued that the choice of law rule contained in Article 187 of the Swiss law is so flexible that in practice it barely restricts the arbitrators' freedom to apply the law they favor.[24] The first examples of the application of the rule in arbitral case law support that view. In a 1993 award made in Geneva in ICC Case No. 7154, it was held that the contract in dispute had closer connections with "the law which preserves its existence than with the law which denies it."[25] Ensuring that a law validating a contract prevails over a law leading to its avoidance[26] has, of course, little in common with the approach based on a close connection test, which enables a court or an arbitrator to measure, on a case-by-case basis, the strength of the links between the various laws and the case being heard. Understood in such a broad manner, the Swiss choice of law rule barely differs from the absolute discretion enjoyed by arbitrators under French or Dutch law.[27]

Other awards comply more strictly with the spirit of Article 187 of the Swiss Private International Law Statute, and evaluate the strength of the connections between each of the laws that might apply and the situation in dispute. In an award made in 1994 in ICC Case No. 6719, the arbitrators attached most weight to the place where the contractual goods were manufactured, having noted that it was also the place where the contract was signed,[28] and to the fact that the manufacture of such goods was closely supervised by the authorities of that State.[29] In practice, such reasoning is not dissimilar to the approach endorsed by legal systems which have adopted the direct choice method.[30]

Unlike Swiss law and the laws it has inspired, French arbitration law and the laws it has influenced[31] have chosen not to compel the arbitrator to use a particular choice of law rule. Although the arbitrators are simply required to apply the law or the rules of law which they consider to be "appropriate," they are perfectly entitled to apply a choice of law rule or to use any other method of selecting the applicable law as they see fit.

---

[22] *See supra* para. 1540.

[23] *See infra* para. 1546.

[24] On this issue, see especially PIERRE LALIVE, JEAN-FRANÇOIS POUDRET, CLAUDE REYMOND, LE DROIT DE L'ARBITRAGE INTERNE ET INTERNATIONAL EN SUISSE 396 *et seq.* (1989); ANDREAS BUCHER AND PIERRE-YVES TSCHANZ, INTERNATIONAL ARBITRATION IN SWITZERLAND ¶¶ 197 *et seq.* (1988); Blessing, *supra* note 14, at 430–31; *comp. with* Emmanuel Gaillard, *Le point de vue d'un utilisateur étranger/The Point of View of a Foreign User*, 1989 INT'L BUS. L.J. 793, 798.

[25] Algerian shipowner v. French shipyard, 121 J.D.I. 1059 (1994), and observations by Y. Derains.

[26] For criticism of the systematic preference for the law favoring arbitration in the context of the arbitration agreement, which also applies to the choice of the law governing the merits of the dispute, see *supra* para. 481.

[27] *See supra* para. 1540. For another illustration of the application of Article 187 of the Swiss Private International Law Statute, see *supra* note 7.

[28] On the weakness as a connecting factor of the place of signature of the contract, see *infra* para. 1549.

[29] *Supra* note 7, at 1077.

[30] *See infra* para. 1552.

[31] *See supra* para. 1540.

§ 2. – The Different Methods Used by Arbitrators to Choose the Applicable Law

1545. — In exercising the freedom to determine the governing law that they are granted by a number of arbitration statutes, openly as in France or the Netherlands, or under the cover of a very flexible choice of law rule, as in Switzerland, Italy, Mexico and Germany,[32] arbitrators may (A) or may not (B) decide to resort to specific choice of law rules.

A. – APPLICATION OF A CHOICE OF LAW RULE

1546. — The 1961 European Convention provides in its Article VII, paragraph 1 that "[f]ailing any indication by the parties as to the applicable law, the arbitrators shall apply the proper law under the rule of conflict that the arbitrators deem applicable." The same rule was adopted in 1985 in the UNCITRAL Model Law, which states in Article 28, paragraph 2 that "[f]ailing any designation [of the applicable rules of law] by the parties, the arbitral tribunal shall apply the law determined by the conflict of laws rules which it considers applicable." The 1996 English Arbitration Act takes a similar approach (Sec. 46(3)). Comparable provisions appeared in the ICC Rules applicable prior to January 1, 1998 and in the 1976 UNCITRAL Rules, although the 1998 ICC Rules has now adopted the direct choice method, as have the AAA International Rules and the LCIA Rules.[33] The fact that French and Dutch arbitration laws are less restrictive and do not require the arbitrators to apply a choice of law rule does not prevent them from doing so. The arbitral case law generated by awards made where such a requirement is found can serve as a model for arbitrators who may wish to follow the choice of law approach even where they are not bound to do so.

Where the arbitrators do apply choice of law rules, the two most common methods in arbitral case law are the "cumulative" method and the method of general principles of private international law.[34] However, the arbitrators sometimes have the option of selecting, at their entire discretion, what they consider to be the most appropriate choice of law rule.

---

[32] *See supra* para. 1544.

[33] *See supra* para. 1538; compare the hybrid method found in the Spanish Arbitration Law of December 5, 1988 which provides in its Article 62 that where the parties have not chosen the applicable law, the arbitrators shall apply the law governing the relationship from which the dispute arises or, if there is none, the law they consider to be the most appropriate in the circumstances. For a commentary, see ARBITRATION IN SPAIN 123 *et seq.* (B. Cremades ed., 1991).

[34] *See* Pierre Lalive, *Les règles de conflit de lois appliquées au fond du litige par l'arbitre international siégeant en Suisse*, 1976 REV. ARB. 155. On the different methods, see also Yves Derains, *Attente légitime des parties et droit applicable au fond en matière d'arbitrage commercial international, in* TRAVAUX DU COMITÉ FRANÇAIS DE DROIT INTERNATIONAL PRIVÉ 1984–1985, at 81, especially at 83 *et seq.* (1987); Y. Derains, observations following ICC Award No. 4132 (1983), Italian company v. Korean company, 110 J.D.I. 891 (1983), and observations by Y. Derains and S. Jarvin; for an English translation, see X Y.B. COM. ARB. 44 (1985); Beda Wortmann, *Choice of Law by Arbitrators: The Applicable Conflict of Laws System*, 14 ARB. INT'L 97 (1998).

1° The Cumulative Method

1547. — The cumulative method involves simultaneously applying choice of law rules of all the legal systems connected with the dispute. The fact that the rules differ is of little consequence, provided that in the case at hand they lead to the same result.[35]

This method has the merit of providing the most predictable outcome. If the choice of law rules of all legal systems connected with the situation in dispute (such as those of the parties and the place where the contract was performed) point to the same law, the parties cannot complain that their expectations have not been met by the application of that law. Under this approach, among the various choice of law rules which they apply cumulatively, the arbitrators do not necessarily have to include the choice of law rules of the seat of the arbitration. Indeed, this approach is based on the idea of not defeating the parties' expectations, assuming that they exist. It implies that the arbitrators should only consider the choice of law rules of legal systems which had a connection with the case at a time when the parties were required to act in a certain way, under the contract or otherwise. At such time, the parties would only have been in a position to know the choice of law rules of those legal systems, should they have wanted to foresee the applicable law. Private international law specialists will note that in that respect the underlying philosophy of the cumulative method is similar to that of the "conflicts of systems" (*conflits de systèmes*) theory.[36]

However, the inherent limits of the cumulative method are evident where the various choice of law rules of the legal systems connected with the dispute lead to different results.

---

[35] On this method, see especially Yves Derains, *L'application cumulative par l'arbitre des systèmes de conflit de lois intéressés au litige (A la lumière de l'expérience de la Cour d'Arbitrage de la Chambre de Commerce Internationale)*, 1972 REV. ARB. 99; Lalive, *supra* note 34, at 180. For illustrations of the method, see, in addition to the numerous examples cited by Derains and Lalive, ICC Award No. 4996 (1985), French agent of an Italian company v. Italian company, 113 J.D.I. 1131 (1986), and observations by Y. Derains; ICC Award No. 3043 (1978), South African company v. German company, 106 J.D.I. 1000 (1979), and observations by Y. Derains; ICC Award No. 5717 (1988), ICC BULLETIN, Vol. 1, No. 2, at 22 (1990) (which applies, because it is common, the criterion of the closest connection); ICC Award No. 6281 (1989), Egyptian buyer v. Yugoslavian seller, 116 J.D.I. 1114 (1989), and observations by G. Aguilar Alvarez; 118 J.D.I. 1054 (1991), and observations by D. Hascher; for an English translation, see XV Y.B. COM. ARB. 96 (1990); ICC Award No. 6283 (1990), Agent (Belgium) v. Principal (U.S.A.), XVII Y.B. COM. ARB. 178 (1992); ICC Award No. 6149 (1990), Seller (Korea) v. Buyer (Jordan), XX Y.B. COM. ARB. 41 (1995); ICC Award No. 7250 (1992), American distributor v. Dutch producer, ICC BULLETIN, Vol. 7, No. 1, at 92 (1996).

[36] On this theory, see, for example, HENRI BATIFFOL, PAUL LAGARDE, DROIT INTERNATIONAL PRIVÉ, Vol. 1, ¶ 322 (8th ed. 1993); PIERRE MAYER, DROIT INTERNATIONAL PRIVÉ ¶¶ 232 *et seq.* (6th ed. 1998). See also the observations by Dominique Holleaux, *in* TRAVAUX DU COMITÉ FRANÇAIS DE DROIT INTERNATIONAL PRIVÉ 1984–1985, at 99 (1987).

2° General Principles of Private International Law

1548. — General principles of private international law are the choice of law equivalent of general principles of substantive law.[37] Using them involves finding common or widely-accepted principles in the main systems of private international law.[38]

1549. — It is true that significant differences subsist between the various systems of private international law of contracts with regard to situations where the choice of governing law has not been made by the parties. For example, for some time it was unclear whether the law of the place of characteristic performance[39] should be preferred to the law of the place of habitual residence of the party which effected that performance. The latter criterion prevailed in the 1980 Rome Convention on the Law Applicable to Contractual Obligations.[40] In addition, the awards which proclaimed the existence of a "common or universal private international law" in the context of the selection of "the law governing the contract where the parties have made an express choice"[41] are of limited relevance. Most recent arbitration statutes expressly recognize the parties' freedom to select the applicable law and little can be drawn from these general statements in cases where no choice has been made by the parties themselves. Other awards which claim to apply general principles are so undermined by the reality of comparative private international law that they tend to illustrate the limits rather than the benefits of the method. This is true of the award made in 1967 in ICC Case No. 1404, in which the arbitrators, on the basis of "constant theory and case law concerning the conflict of laws in private international law" held that "preference has to be given to the law of the place where the contract has been made and, subsidiarily, to that of the place

---

[37] *See supra* paras. 1443 *et seq.*

[38] On this issue, see Berthold Goldman, *La lex mercatoria dans les contrats et l'arbitrage internationaux: réalité et perspectives*, 106 J.D.I. 475, 492 (1979); Lalive, *supra* note 34, at 181; Emmanuel Gaillard, *Thirty Years of Lex Mercatoria: Towards the Selective Application of Transnational Rules*, 10 ICSID REV. – FOREIGN INV. L.J. 208, 216 (1995), and for the French version, *Trente ans de Lex Mercatoria – Pour une application sélective de la méthode des principes généraux du droit*, 122 J.D.I. 5, 14 (1995); JULIAN D.M. LEW, APPLICABLE LAW IN INTERNATIONAL COMMERCIAL ARBITRATION – A STUDY IN COMMERCIAL ARBITRATION AWARDS 436 *et seq.* (1978); Maniruzzaman, *supra* note 16; Wortmann, *supra* note 34.

[39] For an example of the application of the law of the place of performance of a turnkey project, see ICC Award No. 3755 (1988), ICC BULLETIN, Vol. 1, No. 2, at 25 (1990). In favor of the law of the place of performance of the contractual obligations, see ICC Award No. 6560 (1990), which also held that the place of signature and the language of the contract are not important localization factors (Seller (Netherlands Antilles) v. Buyer (France), XVII Y.B. COM. ARB. 226 (1992)); the February 5, 1988 Partial Award on Liability rendered in The Hague by J. Stevenson, chairman, I. Brownlie and B. Cremades, arbitrators, Wintershall A.G. v. Government of Qatar, which applied, on the basis of the criterion of the closest connection, the law of the country in which the contract for petroleum exploration was to be performed (28 I.L.M. 795, 802 (1989); XV Y.B. COM. ARB. 30, 34 (1990)).

[40] For a discussion on this issue, see, for example, HENRI BATIFFOL, PAUL LAGARDE, DROIT INTERNATIONAL PRIVÉ, Vol. 2, at 292 (7th ed. 1983); more generally, for an illustration of the diversity of private international law systems, see the comparative law analysis of Ole Lando, *Chapter 24 – Contracts*, in INTERNATIONAL ENCYCLOPEDIA OF COMPARATIVE LAW – VOLUME III – PRIVATE INTERNATIONAL LAW (1976).

[41] *See, e.g.*, ICC Award No. 1512 (1971), *supra* note 15.

where it has to be performed."[42] More convincingly, a 1989 award in ICC Case No. 5713 stated that "the general tendency in choice of law thinking is to apply the domestic law of the current residence of the party which is to perform the characteristic performance."[43]

However, the existence of these outdated decisions is not sufficient to discredit the general principles method as a whole. In recent years, it has gained vital support from the convergence of international conventions on the law applicable to contracts. When arbitrators use the method of general principles of private international law, they often look for those principles in both arbitral case law[44] and international conventions on the subject, whether or not in force.[45] By definition, those instruments reflect a certain consensus, which is reinforced if the convention in question has been widely ratified.[46] Thus, the 1980 Rome Convention on the Law Applicable to Contractual Obligations,[47] the 1955 Hague Convention on the Law Applicable to International Sales of Goods[48] and the Convention revised in 1986 under the joint auspices of the Hague Conference and UNCITRAL on the Law Applicable

---

[42]   French company v. Five companies from the same group, cited by LEW, *supra* note 38, at 332–33.

[43]   Seller v. Buyer, XV Y.B. COM. ARB. 70 (1990). For an example of an award applying the law of the place of performance of the seller's principal obligation, in the absence of a single place of signature of the contract, see ICC Award No. 5865 (1989), Panamanian company v. Finnish company, 125 J.D.I. 1008 (1998), and observations by D. Hascher; ICC BULLETIN, Vol. 1, No. 2, at 23 (1990). On the law applicable to interest, see ICC Award No. 7585 (1994), Italian company v. Finnish company, 122 J.D.I. 1015 (1995), and observations by Y. Derains.

[44]   On the concept, see *supra* paras. 371 *et seq.*

[45]   On the use as a model of an international convention which was not in force in any of the countries concerned by a dispute, see, for example, ICC Award No. 1717 (1972), 101 J.D.I. 890 (1974), and observations by Y. Derains; on the use of an international convention which was in force in only one of the countries concerned by a dispute, see ICC Award No. 5713 (1989), Seller v. Buyer, XV Y.B. COM. ARB. 70 (1990); ICC BULLETIN, Vol. 1, No. 2, at 24 (1990).

[46]   On the use of international conventions by arbitrators, see Andrea Giardina, *International Conventions on Conflict of Laws and Substantive Law*, *in* ICCA CONGRESS SERIES NO. 7, PLANNING EFFICIENT ARBITRATION PROCEEDINGS/THE LAW APPLICABLE IN INTERNATIONAL ARBITRATION 459 (A.J. van den Berg ed., 1996).

[47]   *See, e.g.*, ICC Award No. 4996 (1985), *supra* note 35; ICC Award No. 6360 (The Hague, 1990), where the Rome Convention, which reflected the choice of law rule of the seat of the arbitration, was presented as an example of "a generally accepted rule of private international law" (ICC BULLETIN, Vol. 1, No. 2, at 24 (1990)); ICC Award No. 7205 (1993), French company v. Owner of Saudi company, 122 J.D.I. 1031 (1995), and observations by J.-J. Arnaldez; ICC Award No. 7319 (1992), French supplier v. Irish distributor, ICC BULLETIN, Vol. 5, No. 2, at 56 (1994); ICC Award No. 7177 (1993), Greek agent of an Antiguan corporation v. Greek company, ICC BULLETIN, Vol. 7, No. 1, at 89 (1996). For a view hostile to the application of the 1980 Rome Convention in international arbitration, see ANTOINE KASSIS, LE NOUVEAU DROIT EUROPÉEN DES CONTRATS INTERNATIONAUX ¶¶ 474 *et seq.* (1993). For a reference to Article 7 of the Rome Convention, see ICC Award No. 6500 (1992), Lebanese Traders Distributors & Consultants v. Reynolds Tobacco International, 119 J.D.I. 1015 (1992), and J.-J. Arnaldez' note; ICC Award No. 7407 (1994), Italian bank v. Company of the Netherlands Antilles, ICC BULLETIN, Vol. 7, No. 1, at 93 (1996). On the question of international mandatory rules, see *supra* paras. 1515 *et seq.*, especially para. 1519.

[48]   *See, e.g.*, ICC Award No. 1717 (1972), *supra* note 45; ICC Award No. 5885 (1989), Seller v. Buyer, XVI Y.B. COM. ARB. 91, 92 (1991); ICC BULLETIN, Vol. 7, No. 1, at 83 (1996); ICC Award No. 5713 (1989), *supra* note 45. Also, for references to the 1955 Hague Convention in an *obiter dictum*, ICC Award No. 6281 (1989), *supra* note 35.

to Contracts for the International Sale of Goods[49] are often cited by arbitrators as sources of transnational choice of law rules. The same is true of the Hague Convention of March 14, 1978, on the Law Applicable to Intermediary Agreements and Agency.[50]

If they are unable to determine' general principles of private international law, the arbitrators will either have to decide what they consider to be the most appropriate choice of law rule, or they will be obliged to abandon choice of law rules altogether.

3° The Free Selection of a Choice of Law Rule

1550. — The method which involves the free selection—or even creation—of what appears to be the most suitable choice of law rule is not uncommon in arbitral practice.[51] Where there are serious differences between the various possible choice of law rules, the arbitrators have little option but to adopt a normative approach. The idea will no longer be to look for the convergence of various choice of law systems—whether or not connected with the case—but to determine what appears to be the best or the "most appropriate" choice of law rule. Of course, it is hard to see how a choice of law rule, which is abstract by nature, could be "appropriate" for a particular case.[52] Nonetheless, in certain legal systems or under certain Rules,[53] the arbitrators are free to select the choice of law rule which, in their opinion, best satisfies the various imperatives of private international law (such as predictability, realism, and consistency with other choice of law rules). Moreover, they are not obliged to choose from existing choice of law rules. They are perfectly entitled to invent new ones.

1551. — However, in order to avoid burdening arbitrators with the delicate task of creating a new choice of law rule or with simply determining the "appropriate" choice of law rule, certain statutes and arbitration rules have abandoned the reference to choice of law rules and adopted what is generally referred to as the "*voie directe*" or direct choice method.

---

[49]   *See, e.g.*, ICC Award No. 6527 (Rome, 1991), Buyer v. Seller, ICC BULLETIN, Vol. 7, No. 1, at 88 (1996); XVIII Y.B. COM. ARB. 44 (1993), especially ¶¶ 1 *et seq.* at 45.

[50]   *See, e.g.*, ICC Award No. 4996 (1985), *supra* note 35; ICC Award No. 6523 (1991), Austrian company v. Turkish company, ICC BULLETIN, Vol. 7, No. 1, at 88 (1996); ICC Award No. 7329 (1994), French agent v. Italian manufacturer, ICC BULLETIN, Vol. 7, No. 1, at 93 (1996).

[51]   On this issue, see especially FOUCHARD, *supra* note 11, ¶¶ 556 *et seq.*

[52]   Philippe Fouchard, *L'arbitrage international en France après le décret du 12 mai 1981*, 109 J.D.I. 374, 397 (1982).

[53]   *See supra* para. 1546.

B. – DIRECT CHOICE METHOD

1552. — The direct choice method (*voie directe*) involves the arbitrators choosing the applicable law without referring to any choice of law rule, not even a rule they create themselves.[54] The freedom to select the applicable law or rules of law in this way was first granted by the 1981 French decree on international arbitration (Art. 1496 of the New Code of Civil Procedure) followed by the 1986 Netherlands Arbitration Statute (Art. 1054(2) of the Code of Civil Procedure). By contrast, the UNCITRAL Model Law (Art. 28(2)) and the 1996 English Arbitration Act (Sec. 46(3)) preferred to retain the reference to a choice of law rule unless, of course, the parties have decided otherwise (which they do when they choose to apply the AAA, ICC or LCIA Rules, which have all endorsed the direct choice method,[55] unlike the UNCITRAL Rules).[56]

The determination made by arbitrators applying the direct choice method may be based on the connections between the case and the chosen law, as in the choice of law method, but it may also be guided by the content of the chosen law. The arbitrators might decide that a particular law, being more modern, is better suited to governing the dispute,[57] or that a law belonging to the continental tradition—or, conversely, to the common law tradition—is more suited to the disputed contract given, for example, how the contract is drafted, or the concepts to which it refers. Likewise,[58] the arbitrators may, where the parties have not chosen the applicable law, decide not to apply a law which would lead the contract to be held void.[59] Here, the word "appropriate," applied to the law governing the merits of the dispute rather than to the choice of law rule,[60] has real meaning.[61]

---

[54] See Lalive, *supra* note 34, at 181; Derains, *supra* note 34, ¶ 10; DE BOISSÉSON, *supra* note 11, ¶ 655.

[55] See Art. 28(1) of the 1997 AAA International Arbitration Rules; Art. 17(1) of the 1998 ICC Rules; Art. 22.3 of the 1998 LCIA Rules. For a commentary, see DERAINS AND SCHWARTZ, *supra* note 5, at 221 *et seq.*

[56] See *supra* para. 1538.

[57] On the dangers of this kind of reasoning, which is inappropriate when the parties have chosen the applicable law, but which becomes available, given the flexibility of the direct choice method, where the parties fail to choose the applicable law, see *supra* para. 1511 and, for an example under Article 187 of the Swiss Private International Law Statute, see ICC Award No. 7154 (1993), *supra* note 25.

[58] The fact that the law chosen by the parties leads the contract to be void does not allow the arbitrators to refuse to apply it; *see supra* para. 1439.

[59] See, *e.g.*, ICC Award No. 4145 (1984), Establishment of Middle East country v. South Asian construction company, XII Y.B. COM. ARB. 97 (1987); for a French translation, see 112 J.D.I. 985 (1985), and observations by Y. Derains; ICC Award No. 4996 (1985), where, in a case between a French party and an Italian party, it was held that French law applied, on the grounds, in particular, that the nullification of the contract under Italian law constituted "a further and important reason for applying French law in this case" (*supra* note 35); ICC Award No. 8540 (Sept. 4, 1996), where the application of English law would have led a contract to be void, as an "agreement to agree:" "In view of the parties' intention . . . , we are of the opinion that this tribunal cannot designate as the proper law a system of law under which the [agreement] would be found a legal nullity or under which the [agreement's] key obligation would be found to be unenforceable" (unpublished).

[60] See *supra* para. 1550.

[61] On the concept of the law appropriate to a contract, see Henri Batiffol, *La loi appropriée au contrat, in* LE DROIT DES RELATIONS ÉCONOMIQUES INTERNATIONALES – ETUDES OFFERTES À BERTHOLD GOLDMAN 1 (1982).

1553. — It has rightly been observed, however, that the direct choice method often conceals the implicit consideration of a choice of law rule.[62] Awards which are described as illustrating the direct choice method often reveal the existence of connecting factors relied upon by the arbitrators. In such cases, the arbitrators' approach is very similar to the conventional choice of law method. For example, the award made in 1983 in ICC Case No. 4132—often considered an illustration of the direct choice method—held that Korean law should apply, because "the Agreement is for an important part to be performed within the territory of the Republic of Korea."[63] Similarly, a 1977 award in ICC Case No. 2694 applied the *lex societatis* to the authority of a company's directors,[64] and the 1983 award in ICC Case No. 3880 found that it was not "necessary to establish which private international law would be applicable in designating the law applicable to the sale contract in the absence of a choice by the parties," although the arbitrators in fact cumulatively applied the criteria of "the headquarters of the seller, the place where the contract was performed and the place where the contract was signed."[65] In these awards, the direct choice method simply amounts to dispensing with the need to give reasons for the selection of the choice of law rule or connecting factor used by the arbitrators in determining the applicable law. The same can be said of the choice of law rule pursuant to which the arbitrators apply the law with the closest connection to the case.[66] The recurrence of certain situations creates precedents in arbitral case law as to the value of particular connecting factors, which in turn leads to the development of more specific choice of law rules, providing guidance for arbitrators[67] where they are not bound either by the intentions of the parties[68] or by a choice of law rule of the seat of the arbitration.[69]

---

[62] Lalive, *supra* note 34, at 181–82; BUCHER AND TSCHANZ, *supra* note 24, ¶ 204.

[63] *See supra* note 34.

[64] French company v. Swiss, French and Luxembourg companies, 105 J.D.I. 985 (1978), and observations by Y. Derains.

[65] Belgian purchaser v. Belgian company, seller, 110 J.D.I. 897 (1983), and observations by Y. Derains and S. Jarvin; for an English translation, see X Y.B. COM. ARB. 44 (1985). *See also* ICC Award No. 6840 (1991), which is presented as being an illustration of the direct choice method, but which is, in reality, an example of the application of the law which has the closest connections with the dispute (Egyptian seller v. Senegalese buyer, 119 J.D.I. 1030 (1992), and observations by Y. Derains).

[66] On the legal systems that apply this criterion, such as that of Switzerland (Art. 187 of the Swiss Private International Law Statute), see *supra* para. 1544.

[67] *See, e.g.,* ICC Award No. 6719 (1994), *supra* note 7.

[68] *See supra* para. 1538.

[69] *See supra* para. 1541.

SECTION II
THE SUBJECT MATTER OF THE ARBITRATORS' CHOICE

1554. — Just as it does in defining the scope of the parties' choice of applicable law,[70] Article 1496 of the French New Code of Civil Procedure uses the expression "rules of law" rather than the word "law" with respect to the subject matter of the arbitrators' choice. Thus, in the absence of an express choice by the parties, the arbitrators are given the same freedom as the parties to consider a wide variety of sources when determining the applicable law. By using the same words to define the subject-matter of the arbitrators' choice, a number of arbitration statutes have similarly chosen to allow the arbitrators to apply rules other than those of a particular national law where the parties have remained silent on the question.[71]

Other arbitration statutes are more conservative[72] and follow in this respect the example of the UNCITRAL Model Law, which allows the parties to choose the applicable "rules of law" but which instructs the arbitrators, in the absence of such a choice, to apply the law[73] designated by the application of a choice of law rule.[74] However, most such statutes do not allow the courts reviewing an award to re-examine the choice of governing law made by the arbitrators.[75]

Nevertheless, here again, when the parties have elected, in the absence of a specific choice of law, to have their arbitration governed by rules which give the arbitrators the freedom to choose the "rules of law"—and not necessarily "the law"—applicable to the merits, their election will be complied with. This is the case, in particular, when the parties

---

[70] *See supra* para. 1431.

[71] Art. 187, para. 1 of the Swiss Private International Law Statute; Art. 1054(2) of the Netherlands Code of Civil Procedure; Art. 813 of the 1983 Lebanese New Code of Civil Procedure; Art. 458 bis 14 of the Algerian Code of Civil Procedure (Legislative Decree No. 93-08 of April 25, 1993), and the commentary by Mohand Issad, *Le décret législatif algérien du 25 avril 1993 relatif à l'arbitrage international*, 1993 REV. ARB. 377, 391.

[72] *See, e.g.*, Art. 1445 of the Mexican Commercial Code (Law of July 22, 1993); Art. 834 of the Italian Code of Civil Procedure (Law No. 25 of Jan. 5, 1994), and the commentary by Piero Bernardini, *L'arbitrage en Italie après la récente réfome*, 1994 REV. ARB. 479, 492, where the author is clearly against applying a-national rules in these circumstances; Art. 39 of Egyptian Law No. 27 for 1994 Promulgating the Law Concerning Arbitration in Civil and Commercial Matters, and the commentary by Bernard Fillion-Dufouleur and Philippe Leboulanger, *Le nouveau droit égyptien de l'arbitrage*, 1994 REV. ARB. 664, 679, where the authors do not completely exclude recourse to transnational rules despite the language of the statute. On the meaning of Article 73 of the Tunisian Arbitration Code, see Kalthoum Meziou and Ali Mezghani, *Le Code tunisien de l'arbitrage*, 1993 REV. ARB. 521, 534; Sec. 46(3) of the 1996 English Arbitration Act; Art. 1051(2) of the German ZPO (Law of Dec. 22, 1997).

[73] Art. 28. On the legislative history, see especially HOWARD M. HOLTZMANN AND JOSEPH E. NEUHAUS, A GUIDE TO THE UNICITRAL MODEL LAW ON INTERNATIONAL COMMERCIAL ARBITRATION – LEGISLATIVE HISTORY AND COMMENTARY 769–70 (1989); ARON BROCHES, SELECTED ESSAYS – WORLD BANK, ICSID, AND OTHER SUBJECTS OF PUBLIC AND PRIVATE INTERNATIONAL LAW (1995) ("The 1985 UNCITRAL Model Law on International Commercial Arbitration: An Exercise in International Legislation," at 375, 401).

[74] On how to determine this choice of law rule, see *supra* paras. 1546 *et seq.*

[75] *See, e.g.*, Art. 34 of the UNCITRAL Model Law.

have adopted the 1997 AAA International Arbitration Rules, the 1998 ICC Rules, or the 1998 LCIA Rules.[76]

1555. — When given the freedom to select the applicable "rules of law," the arbitrators, like the parties themselves, may simply apply a given national law which has objective connections with the case. Alternatively, they may choose a "neutral" law,[77] or apply several laws to different aspects of the dispute using the "*dépeçage*" method.[78] They may also stabilize the applicable law at a particular point in time, which will generally be when the contract was signed.

1556. — In the same circumstances, the arbitrators will be able to apply rules other than those of a particular national law,[79] such as general principles of law[80] or principles common to the legal systems connected to the case.[81]

On several occasions, the French courts have held valid awards where, in the absence of a choice of law by the parties, the arbitrators decided to apply transnational rules (or *lex mercatoria*) rather than a particular national law.[82] In a 1989 decision in the *Valenciana*

---

[76] *See supra* para. 1538.

[77] On the example of the law of the seat of the arbitration, see *supra* paras. 1428 and 1543.

[78] *See* Fouchard, *supra* note 52, at 398. For an example of a case where the arbitrators found the *dépeçage* method to be inappropriate, see the May 31, 1996 Award made under the aegis of the Zurich Chamber of Commerce, by P.A. Karrer, chairman, and C. Kälin-Nauer and B.F. Meyer-Hauser, arbitrators, in Case No. 273/95, Raw material processor v. Processing group, XXIII Y.B. COM. ARB. 128, 139 (1998).

[79] On the idea that the application of transnational rules is particularly suitable where the connecting factors are dispersed, see ICC Award No. 6500 (1992), *supra* note 47; ICC Award No. 8385 (1995), *supra* note 15; the March 8, 1996 Award under the auspices of the Paris Arbitration Chamber, Agent (Austria) v. Principal (Egypt), XXII Y.B. COM. ARB. 28 (1997).

[80] See, for example, the *Norsolor* (ICC Case No. 3131) and *Valenciana* (ICC Case No. 5953) Awards which gave rise to the litigation described *infra* notes 82 *et seq. See also* ICC Award No. 7331 (1994), Yugoslavian seller v. Italian buyer, 122 J.D.I. 1001 (1995), and observations by D. Hascher; ICC Award No. 7375 (June 5, 1996), Ministry of Defence and Support for Armed Forces of the Islamic Republic of Iran v. Westinghouse Electric Corp., by M. Blessing, chairman, P. Bernardini and A. Movahed, arbitrators (A. Movahed dissenting), 11 INT'L ARB. REP. A1 (Dec. 1996), especially ¶¶ 217 *et seq.*

[81] *See, e.g.,* ICC Award No. 5103 (1988), which, after finding that the legal systems in question where fairly closely related, decided to apply, whenever possible, "rules common to French and Tunisian law of contracts" (Three European companies v. Four Tunisian companies, 115 J.D.I. 1206 (1988), and observations by G. Aguilar Alvarez; ICC BULLETIN, Vol. 1, No. 2, at 25 (1990)).

[82] *See* Cass. 2e civ., Dec. 9, 1981, Fougerolle v. Banque du Proche-Orient, 1982 REV. ARB. 183, and G. Couchez' note; 109 J.D.I. 931 (1982), 3d decision, and observations by B. Oppetit, *upholding* CA Paris, June 12, 1980, 109 J.D.I. 931 (1982), 2d decision, and B. Oppetit's note; 1981 REV. ARB. 292, and G. Couchez' note; CA Paris, Nov. 19, 1982, Norsolor v. Pabalk Ticaret Sirketi, 1983 REV. ARB. 465, 3d decision, and the commentary by Berthold Goldman, *Une bataille judiciaire autour de la lex mercatoria: l'affaire Norsolor, id.* at 379; for an English translation, see XI Y.B. COM. ARB. 484 (1986); *aff'd,* Cass. 1e civ., Oct. 9, 1984, Pabalk Ticaret Sirketi v. Norsolor, 1985 REV. CRIT. DIP 551, 2d decision, and B. Dutoit's note; 1985 REV. ARB. 431, and B. Goldman's note; Dalloz, Jur. 101 (1985), and J. Robert's note; 112 J.D.I. 679 (1985), and P. Kahn's note; for an English translation, see 2 J. INT'L ARB. 67 (June 1985), with comments by D. Thompson; XI Y.B. COM. ARB. 484 (1986); 24 I.L.M. 360 (1985), with an introductory note by E. Gaillard; *see also* Philippe Fouchard, *Les usages, l'arbitre et le juge – A propos de quelques récents arrêts français, in* LE DROIT DES

(continued...)

case, the Paris Court of Appeals held that an arbitrator who had decided to apply *lex mercatoria*, in the absence of any indication by the parties as to the governing law, had not exceeded the terms of his brief. The Court described the rules of *lex mercatoria* as "rules which are international in nature and which, in the absence of a predetermined governing law, can be applied to resolve a dispute of that kind."[83] An action to overturn that decision was rejected by the *Cour de cassation* on the grounds that by applying the rules of international commerce established through practice and endorsed by national courts, the arbitrator had founded his decision in law and had not disregarded his brief.[84] In 1982, the Austrian Supreme Court similarly held in the *Norsolor* matter that an award could not be set aside for having applied, in the absence of any indication by the parties as to the governing law, general principles of law also referred to as *lex mercatoria*.[85]

A number of other legal systems have similarly accepted that where the parties have not chosen the governing law, the arbitrators are entitled to apply *lex mercatoria*.[86] Article 6 of the resolution adopted by the International Law Institute at its Santiago de Compostela session in 1989 endorses that approach, in the context of state contracts, by providing that "[t]o the extent that the parties have left such issues open, the tribunal shall supply the necessary rules and principles drawing on the sources indicated in Article 4." Those sources are "general principles of public or private international law, general principles of international arbitration" and national law.[87] Likewise, the resolution adopted in Cairo in 1992 by the International Law Association recognizes that the application of transnational rules by international commercial arbitrators should not affect the validity or enforceability of the award "where the parties have remained silent concerning the applicable law."[88] The only situation where arbitrators exceed the terms of their brief by applying *lex mercatoria*

---

[82](...continued)
RELATIONS ÉCONOMIQUES INTERNATIONALES – ETUDES OFFERTES À BERTHOLD GOLDMAN 67 (1982).

[83] CA Paris, July 13, 1989, Compania Valenciana de Cementos Portland v. Primary Coal, 1990 REV. ARB. 663, and P. Lagarde's note; 117 J.D.I. 430 (1990), and B. Goldman's note; 1990 REV. CRIT. DIP 305, and B. Oppetit's note; for an English translation, see XVI Y.B. COM. ARB. 142 (1991); 4 INT'L ARB. REP. B1 (Dec. 1989).

[84] Cass 1e civ., Oct. 22, 1991, Compania Valenciana de Cementos Portland v. Primary Coal Inc., 1991 Bull. Civ. I, No. 275; 1992 REV. ARB. 457, and P. Lagarde's note; 1992 REV. CRIT. DIP 113, and B. Oppetit's note; 119 J.D.I. 177 (1992), and B. Goldman's note; 1992 RTD COM. 171, and observations by J.-C. Dubarry and E. Loquin; for an English translation, see 6 INT'L ARB. REP. B1 (Dec. 1991).

[85] *Oberster Gerichtshof*, Nov. 18, 1982, Norsolor v. Pabalk, 1983 REV. ARB. 519 (1983), *reversing* CA Vienna, Jan. 29, 1982, 1983 REV. ARB. 516 (1983), *setting aside* ICC Award No. 3131 (1979), Pabalk Ticaret Limited Sirketi v. Norsolor, 1983 REV. ARB. 525 (1983). For a commentary, see Goldman, *supra* note 82.

[86] On this issue, see Ole Lando, *The Law Applicable to the Merits of the Dispute*, *in* ESSAYS ON INTERNATIONAL COMMERCIAL ARBITRATION 129, 150 *et seq.* (P. Sarcevic ed., 1989); FILIP J.M. DE LY, INTERNATIONAL BUSINESS LAW AND LEX MERCATORIA ¶¶ 316 *et seq.* (1992); KLAUS PETER BERGER, THE CREEPING CODIFICATION OF LEX MERCATORIA (1999).

[87] XVI Y.B. COM. ARB. 233 (1991), and observations by A.T. von Mehren; for the French text, see 1990 REV. ARB. 931, and observations by P. Fouchard. See also the commentaries cited *supra* para. 1445.

[88] Report of the Sixty Fifth Conference, Cairo 1992, and the commentary in TRANSNATIONAL RULES IN INTERNATIONAL COMMERCIAL ARBITRATION 65 (E. Gaillard ed., ICC Publication No. 480/4, 1993). Compare, for the case where the parties expressly choose the applicable law, *supra* paras. 1443 *et seq.*

is that where the parties do not agree on the applicable law, but do require the arbitrators to select a national law to govern the dispute.[89]

Legal systems which, like French law, allow arbitrators to apply transnational rules when the parties are silent as to the governing law, consider that all species of transnational rules are acceptable: principles common to legal systems connected with the dispute, determined by the "*tronc commun*" method;[90] general principles of international commercial law,[91] whether used as such or in conjunction with a national law;[92] general principles of public international law, where a state is involved;[93] or even trade usages which, according to some laws or arbitration rules,[94] should be taken into account "in all cases."[95] The controversy surrounding the meaning of trade usages[96] is largely irrelevant in this context, given the extent of the powers conferred on arbitrators in the absence of a choice of law by the parties.

SECTION III
LIMITS ON THE EFFECTIVENESS OF THE ARBITRATORS' CHOICE

1557. — When the arbitrators (rather than the parties) determine the governing law, there is no place for the various theories put forward to allow the arbitrators to decline to apply the law chosen by the parties. Where the parties are silent as to the governing law, a number

---

[89] *See* Lando, *supra* note 86, at 154–55.

[90] On this method, see especially MAURO RUBINO-SAMMARTANO, INTERNATIONAL ARBITRATION LAW 274 *et seq.* (1990), who contrasts the method with that of "*lex mercatoria;*" *see also* Mauro Rubino-Sammartano, *Le "tronc commun" des lois nationales en présence (Réflexions sur le droit applicable par l'arbitre international)*, 1987 REV. ARB. 133; Mauro Rubino-Sammartano, *The Channel Tunnel and the Tronc Commun Doctrine*, 10 J. INT'L ARB. 59 (Sept. 1993). *Comp. with* Bertrand Ancel, *The Tronc Commun Doctrine: Logics and Experience in International Arbitration*, 7 J. INT'L ARB. 65 (Sept. 1990); Fouchard, *supra* note 52, at 398; DE BOISSÉSON, *supra* note 11, ¶ 672; for an illustration of the method, see, for example, ICC Award No. 2886 (1977), 105 J.D.I. 996 (1978), and observations by Y. Derains and, for a critical analysis of the method, ICC Award No. 4145 (1984), *supra* note 59.

[91] *See, e.g.*, ICC Award No. 5065 (1986), Lebanese party v. Two Pakistani companies, 114 J.D.I. 1039 (1987), and observations by Y. Derains; ICC Award No. 4338 (1984), U.S. party v. Syrian minister, 112 J.D.I. 981 (1985), and observations by Y. Derains; ICC Award No. 2291 (1975), French transporter v. English company, 103 J.D.I. 989 (1976), and observations by Y. Derains. On the content of these principles, see *supra* paras. 1459 *et seq.*

[92] *See, e.g.*, ICC Award No. 8540 (Sept. 4, 1996), unpublished, which refers to the UNIDROIT Principles for this purpose.

[93] On the differences to which this gives rise in relations between a state and a private party, see *supra* para. 1447.

[94] *See, e.g.*, Art. 1496 of the French New Code of Civil Procedure and *supra* para. 1513.

[95] *See, e.g.*, ICC Award No. 1641 (1969), French parties v. Swedish party, 101 J.D.I. 888 (1974), and observations by Y. Derains.

[96] *See supra* para. 1513.

of legal systems and the major arbitration rules[97] give the arbitrators total freedom when determining the applicable rules of law. In exercising that freedom, they are entitled to apply—or to refuse to apply—a particular rule because it constitutes a mandatory rule;[98] they may seek to overcome the perceived inadequacy of a particular law; they are free to adopt a broad or narrow conception of trade usages; they have the discretion to apply different choice of law rules to the contract and to other aspects of the dispute (such as title to property and tortious liability) pursuant to a "*dépeçage*" approach, or to apply a single law to the entire dispute; they may even declare that their decision is based on what they perceive as being the requirements of genuinely international public policy. All of these possibilities are simply manifestations of the unlimited freedom enjoyed by arbitrators in choosing the applicable rules of law.

Where an action lies at the seat of the arbitration to set aside the award on the basis of a breach of international public policy, as is the case in most legal systems,[99] arbitrators who want to ensure that their award will be effective internationally will be mindful of the conception of international public policy of the seat of the arbitration. However, as the basis of their powers is genuinely transnational, they could, if the conception of international public policy of the seat differs from their notion of truly international public policy, restrict themselves to satisfying the requirements of the latter.[100] The same reasoning leads to the conclusion that arbitrators should not be required, solely on the basis that they want their award to be internationally enforceable, to comply with the conceptions of international public policy of all the jurisdictions where the award is liable to be enforced. To return to an example discussed earlier,[101] the fact that the award is to be enforced in a jurisdiction where religious or racial discrimination is a requirement of public policy should not lead international arbitrators to abandon their own conception of the requirements of genuinely international public policy or, for those who choose to put the test in more subjective terms, their own conception of the requirements of justice.[102]

---

[97] *See supra* para. 1554.

[98] For an affirmation that the mandatory rules of the country of the place of performance of an agency contract should be taken into account where the parties have not chosen the applicable law, see ICC Award No. 6500 (1992), *supra* note 47.

[99] *See infra* paras. 1645 *et seq.*

[100] On this issue, see *supra* para. 1534.

[101] *See supra* para. 1534.

[102] *See* Pierre Mayer, *La règle morale dans l'arbitrage international, in* ETUDES OFFERTES À PIERRE BELLET 379, ¶¶ 26–27 (1991), and the discussion *supra* para. 1535.

PART SIX

COURT REVIEW OF ARBITRAL AWARDS

1558. — Being made by private judges, arbitral awards have no authority in national laws other than that which those laws choose to confer upon them. Most legal systems now view international arbitration favorably and recognize awards as being similar in authority to court judgments. In fact, given the widespread ratification of international conventions on the recognition and enforcement of arbitral awards,[1] an arbitral award will generally be easier to enforce than a foreign court judgment. However, the international enforceability conferred on arbitral awards by national legal systems would be inconceivable without some form of review of the content of the award and of the conditions in which it was made.

The natural time for that review to occur is after the making of the award, when the question arises as to how to incorporate it into national legal orders and thus make it enforceable. The existence of judicial control is the corollary of the policy found in legal systems favorable to arbitration whereby the courts are prevented from interfering during the arbitral process.[2] Thus, for instance, the "competence-competence" rule, whereby the courts cannot rule on the arbitrators' jurisdiction until the arbitrators themselves have had the opportunity to do so, can only exist because the courts are able to review the arbitrators' jurisdiction once the award has been made.[3]

1559. — The review of awards occurs both at the seat of the arbitration (where, as a general rule,[4] actions to set aside will take place) and in all countries where enforcement of the award is sought (as the enforcement of the award in those jurisdictions will invariably be subject to the examination of a number of issues of both a procedural and a substantive nature).[5]

Any discussion of the review of arbitral awards necessarily centers on the procedures of each jurisdiction's national courts, none of which will be identical. Rather than examine the relevant procedure in a number of different jurisdictions, we will focus primarily on French

---

[1] *See supra* paras. 248, 275, and 295.

[2] *See supra* para. 1169. But see, on court assistance with the setting up of the arbitral tribunal, *supra* paras. 750 *et seq.*

[3] *See supra* para. 650.

[4] See the exceptions discussed *infra* para. 1593.

[5] Adam Samuel, *The effect of the place of arbitration on the enforcement of the agreement to arbitrate*, in THE PLACE OF ARBITRATION (M. Storme and F. de Ly eds., 1992). On the advantages of negotiating a model law on the question, see Jan Paulsson, *Towards Minimum Standards of Enforcement: Feasibility of a Model Law*, in ICCA CONGRESS SERIES NO. 9, IMPROVING THE EFFICIENCY OF ARBITRATION AGREEMENTS AND AWARDS: 40 YEARS OF APPLICATION OF THE NEW YORK CONVENTION 574 (A.J. van den Berg ed., 1999).

law, which in this area as in many others takes a liberal approach (Chapter I). We will then consider the most relevant international conventions (Chapter II).[6]

CHAPTER I
FRENCH LAW

1560. — In France, the rules governing recourse against international arbitral awards are found in the May 12, 1981 Decree which applies to "arbitral awards made abroad or in international arbitration."[1] As a result, only awards made in France in arbitrations which do not involve the interests of international commerce within the meaning of Article 1492 of the New Code of Civil Procedure[2] are outside the scope of Articles 1498 *et seq.* of that Code.[3] The fact that awards made outside France in cases which may be purely domestic are governed by the same rules as awards made in international cases has the merit of simplicity. The fact that an award was made outside France, which is usually easy to establish, will suffice to trigger the application of the 1981 Decree.[4] The distinction between domestic arbitration and international arbitration is therefore only relevant to awards made in France.

1561. — The only possible drawback of this simplification lies in the fact that awards made abroad in disputes involving exclusively local interests are treated by French law as international awards and are therefore not subject to any special treatment. This has sometimes been criticized.[5] However, the mere fact that the issue of the enforceability of such awards can arise in France, as opposed to the country in which the award was made, is a sufficiently foreign element to justify the application of the 1981 Decree on international awards, which is more liberal than the regime governing French domestic awards.

1562. — Awards made outside France in cases involving only French parties and affecting exclusively French interests have also given rise to some concern. Certain

---

[1] This language is found in Title VI of Book IV of the New Code of Civil Procedure. It appears in the headings of both chapters in that Title, which deal respectively with the recognition and enforcement of awards (Arts. 1498 to 1500) and actions against the award (Arts. 1501 to 1507).

[2] *See supra* paras. 78 *et seq.*

[3] Because they are based on an international treaty, ICSID awards are subject to a specific regime, which is independent of national legal orders; *see* Cass. 1e civ., June 11, 1991, Société ouest-africaine de bétons industriels (SOABI) v. Sénégal, 118 J.D.I. 1005 (1991), and E. Gaillard's note; 1991 REV. ARB. 637, and A. Broches' note; 1992 REV. CRIT. DIP 331, and P.L.'s note; for an English translation, see 30 I.L.M. 1167 (1991), with an introductory note by G. Delaume; XVII Y.B. COM. ARB. 754 (1992).

[4] On the determination of the place where the award was made, see *infra* para. 1590.

[5] *See* Pierre Bellet and Ernst Mezger, *L'arbitrage international dans le nouveau code de procédure civile*, 1981 REV. CRIT. DIP 611, 647, with respect to the review of compliance with public policy; Pierre Mayer, *L'insertion de la sentence dans l'ordre juridique français*, in FONDATION POUR L'ETUDE DU DROIT ET DES USAGES DU COMMERCE INTERNATIONAL, DROIT ET PRATIQUE DE L'ARBITRAGE INTERNATIONAL EN FRANCE 81, 101–03 (Y. Derains ed., 1984).

commentators have argued that such awards should be characterized as French domestic awards, thus bringing them under the stricter regime of the May 14, 1980 Decree. In particular, those commentators find it unacceptable that, merely because an arbitration has been held abroad, the review of compliance with public policy be performed in the light of the requirements of international public policy (Art. 1502 5° of the New Code of Civil Procedure), and not those of French domestic public policy (Art. 1484 6° of the same Code).[6] However, early commentators of the 1981 Decree objected that such awards were exceptional and did not deserve special treatment.[7] Arbitration practice has since confirmed that view, as it appears that the issue of how to treat an award made abroad in a purely French dispute has not arisen since 1981. Besides, there is little doubt that where it is clear that the seat of the arbitration in a purely domestic French case was located abroad in a fraudulent attempt to avoid the application of French law, the courts would be in a position to use the flexibility of the concept of international public policy to uphold the provisions of French law. A French court might even be tempted to apply the rules of international public policy differently according to the closeness of the connections between the case and the French legal system, as the courts do on other issues.[8] Alternatively, it might take a less controversial stance and consider that the fraudulent avoidance of French law is contrary to the French notion of international public policy and that as such it should be rejected on the basis of Article 1502 5° of the New Code of Civil Procedure.[9]

1563. — Having determined the scope of the rules concerning the recognition and enforcement of foreign awards under the system established by the 1981 Decree, we shall now consider in turn the procedure applicable to the review by the French courts of international awards (Section I) and the extent of that review (Section II).

SECTION I
PROCEDURE FOR THE REVIEW BY THE COURTS

1564. — Arbitral awards are reviewed by the courts when a party applies for their recognition and enforcement, or when actions are brought to set them aside. With a few minor distinctions,[10] the rules governing the recognition and enforcement of awards apply both to international awards made in France and to awards made outside France. In contrast,

---

[6] Bellet and Mezger, *supra* note 5, at 647; Mayer, *supra* note 5, at 103–04.

[7] Philippe Fouchard, *L'arbitrage international en France après le décret du 12 mai 1981*, 109 J.D.I. 374, 403 (1982).

[8] See, for example, in family law, Cass. 1e civ., Apr. 22, 1986, Riahi v. Aboultabi, 1987 REV. CRIT. DIP 374, and P. Courbe's note; 114 J.D.I. 629 (1987), and P. Kahn's note; Cass. 1e civ., May 17, 1993, E.M. v. A., 1993 REV. CRIT. DIP 684, and P. Courbe's note; Cass. 1e civ., Feb. 10, 1993, L. v. B., 1993 REV. CRIT. DIP 620, and J. Foyer's note.

[9] *See* Fouchard, *supra* note 7, at 405. For an example of similar reasoning, see CA Paris, June 18, 1964, Gunzburg v. Schrey, 91 J.D.I. 810 (1964), and J.-D. Bredin's note.

[10] See, for example, on recourse available against an enforcement order, *infra* paras. 1580 *et seq.*

the rules governing actions to set awards aside apply only to awards made in France. It is widely accepted that the courts of the seat of the arbitration have exclusive jurisdiction to hear any action to set an award aside, within the conditions and limits determined by the law of that country.[11]

1565. — We shall now examine both forms of review by the French courts, beginning with applications for recognition and enforcement (§ 1), before moving on to actions to set aside (§ 2). We will conclude by discussing the exclusive character of these forms of recourse (§ 3).

§ 1. – Recognition and Enforcement

1566. — In France, the New Code of Civil Procedure devotes several provisions, either directly or by reference to the regime governing domestic arbitration, to the recognition (A) and enforcement (B) of arbitral awards (Arts. 1498 to 1500). It also sets forth the recourse available against an order granting or refusing recognition or enforcement (Arts. 1501 to 1507) (C).

A. – RECOGNITION OF ARBITRAL AWARDS

1567. — Following the 1958 New York Convention[12] and modern treaties on the enforcement of foreign court judgments,[13] French arbitration law goes further than merely providing a regime for the enforcement of arbitral awards. It also establishes a system governing the "recognition" of awards. However, the concept of recognition is difficult to situate between the rule whereby an award is *res judicata* as soon as it is made[14] and a rules governing enforcement.[15]

To justify the existence of a concept of recognition distinct from the concept of enforcement, authors point to two different situations. First, it may be in the interest of a party in some cases to introduce an award into the French legal order without actually having

---

[11] On the position in French law, see *infra* para. 1589, and on that of the relevant international conventions, see *infra* paras. 1676 *et seq.*

[12] *See infra* para. 1667.

[13] See, for example, the September 27, 1968 Brussels Convention on Jurisdiction and Enforcement of Judgments in Civil and Commercial Matters (Consolidated and updated version at 29 I.L.M. 1413 (1990)) or the September 16, 1988 Lugano Convention which, in essence, extended the rules of the Brussels Convention to the Member States of the European Free Trade Association (28 I.L.M. 620 (1989)).

[14] Article 1476 of the New Code of Civil Procedure, which applies in international arbitration by way of the reference contained in Article 1500 of the same Code.

[15] *See infra* para. 1568.

it enforced, as in the case of an award which simply rejects all claims made by a plaintiff.[16] However, it is arguable that in such a situation the need to distinguish between recognition and enforcement is merely a result of the confusion created by the 1981 Decree between the concepts of "*exequatur*" and "enforcement" ("*exécution forcée*")."[17] Having elected to refer to enforcement rather than to *exequatur* when defining the principal method of incorporating an award into the French legal order, the Decree needed to resort to the further concept of recognition to cover situations where a party seeks to have the award incorporated into the French legal order without having it enforced. However, the uncertainty as to the nature of the action is of little practical importance, as the 1981 Decree makes recognition and "enforcement" subject to the same substantive conditions: the existence of the award must be established and the award must not be patently contrary to international public policy.[18] In addition, although this is not stated in the Decree, it is accepted that the court which has jurisdiction to hear a claim for recognition will be the same as that with jurisdiction to hear an application to make the award enforceable.[19] The terminological uncertainty and the overlap in the use of the concepts of recognition and enforceability therefore create no difficulties in practice.

The second situation where the concept of recognition of an arbitral award is of significance is where it is raised as an incidental claim before a French court. Under Article 1498 of the New Code of Civil Procedure, the court hearing the incidental claim may give effect to the award without declining jurisdiction in favor of the court competent to hear an application for enforcement. However, that rule is not easy to reconcile with the rule whereby an award is automatically *res judicata*. Interpreted to the letter, the rule that an award is automatically *res judicata* as soon as it is made (Arts. 1476 and 1500) would lead the court hearing the incidental claim to take the award into account without reviewing it at all. Yet, under Article 1498, the recognition of an award is subject to verification of the award's existence and of its *prima facie* compliance with international public policy. Most authors agree that in such cases the award's *res judicata* effect means only that, if the award is challenged, the court hearing the incidental claim should ensure that such award complies, *prima facie*, with the two conditions laid down by French law for the introduction of an award into the French legal order. This is the only way to reconcile the two apparently contradictory rules of Articles 1476 and 1498.[20] The fact remains that on this issue the 1981 Decree is hardly a model of clarity.

It has also been argued that an incidental claim for recognition before a French court involves a review extending to the five grounds for refusing enforcement—or for setting aside the award—listed in Article 1502 of the New Code of Civil Procedure. Although

---

[16] Fouchard, *supra* note 7, at 405; Jean Robert, *L'arbitrage en matière internationale – Commentaire du décret n° 81-500 du 12 mai 1981 (art. 1492 à 1507 nouv. c. pr. civ.)*, Dalloz, Chron. 209, 213 (1981).

[17] *See infra* para. 1568.

[18] *See infra* paras. 1575 *et seq.*

[19] *See* Mayer, *supra* note 5, at 86.

[20] *See* Robert, *supra* note 16, at 213. But see, in favor of having no review of the *res judicata* effect of the award, Bellet and Mezger, *supra* note 5, at 650.

Article 1498 of the Code only refers to verifying the existence of the award and its *prima facie* compliance with international public policy, some authors have suggested that:

> in the case of an incidental claim for recognition in the course of adversarial proceedings, the court is entitled to rule on any plea submitted by the party objecting to such recognition which is admissible under Article 1502.[21]

That view is plainly contrary not only to the provisions of Article 1498 of the New Code, but also to the spirit of the 1981 Decree, one of the principal aims of which was to have all disputes which might arise on review of arbitral awards heard by the Court of Appeals. The Court of Appeals may hear actions either on appeal from an enforcement order, or directly by means of an action to set the award aside, although the latter will only lie in respect of awards made in France.[22] The fact that an award's automatic *res judicata* effect may be conditional, in the event that the award is contested, on a review of the award under Article 1498 of the New Code of Civil Procedure does not in any way imply that such a review will extend, contrary to the intention clearly expressed by the legislature, to the grounds on which actions lie under Articles 1502 and 1504 of that Code.[23]

B. – ENFORCEMENT OF ARBITRAL AWARDS

1568. — Unlike the 1980 Decree on French domestic arbitration, the 1981 Decree on international arbitration does not use the term *"exequatur,"* except indirectly by reference to certain provisions of domestic arbitration law (Art. 1500). Instead it refers to "enforcement (*exécution forcée*) of awards."[24] It also refers on several occasions to the order granting or refusing "enforcement" of the award (Arts. 1501, 1502 and 1504, para. 2 of the New Code of Civil Procedure).

This is unfortunate in that there is no distinction between the declaration that an award can be enforced in the same way as a local judgement (*exequatur*) and the actual enforcement of the award against identified assets. However, the courts do distinguish between the two situations in cases concerning a state's immunity from enforcement,[25] which prevents the actual enforcement of the award against assets but not necessarily the award being declared enforceable (through being granted *exequatur*) in France.

The procedure for enforcement of foreign awards and awards made in France in international arbitration is governed in part by the reference in Article 1500 of the New Code

---

[21] Bellet and Mezger, *supra* note 5, at 638; Fernand Charles Jeantet, *L'accueil des sentences étrangères ou internationales dans l'ordre juridique français*, 1981 REV. ARB. 503, 510–11; Mayer, *supra* note 5, at 86–87. On the grounds listed in Article 1502, see *infra* paras. 1601 *et seq.*

[22] See *infra* para. 1589.

[23] On the fact that the review of the existence of the award does not include a review of the validity and scope of the arbitration agreement, see *infra* para. 1576.

[24] See the headings of Chapters I and II of Title VI of Book IV.

[25] *See* Cass. 1e civ., June 11, 1991, *SOABI, supra* note 3.

of Civil Procedure to Articles 1476 to 1479 of the same Code, which concern domestic arbitration. We shall examine in turn the rules regarding the courts' jurisdiction (1°), the rules governing the procedure to be followed before the courts (2°) and the extent of the review exercised by the courts (3°).

1° Jurisdiction

1569. — The 1981 Decree addressed the issue of subject-matter jurisdiction (a), but did not expressly consider territorial jurisdiction (b).

a) Subject-Matter Jurisdiction

1570. — Applications for enforcement of an award are submitted to the Tribunal of First Instance ("*Tribunal de grande instance*"), and the ruling is made by a single judge.[26] Thus, the enforcement order is not made by the "enforcement judge" initially referred to in Article 1477 of the New Code of Civil Procedure.[27] The *Cour de cassation* has confirmed that:

> the enforcement judge referred to in Article 1498 of the New Code of Civil Procedure, for the purpose of declaring that arbitral awards made abroad are enforceable in France, is the Tribunal of First Instance, ruling through a single judge.

It went on to hold that in ordering enforcement of an award, a judge hearing an interlocutory application had exceeded his powers by substituting himself for the enforcement judge designated by Article 1498 of the New Code of Civil Procedure and by Article L. 311-11 of the Code of Judicial Organization.[28]

---

[26] *See* Article L. 311-11 of the Code of Judicial Organization, resulting from Law No. 91-650 of July 9, 1991. *See* Philippe Théry, *Quelques observations à propos de la loi du 9 juillet 1991 portant réforme des procédures civiles d'exécution*, 1991 REV. ARB. 727.

[27] *See* Article 305 of Decree No. 92-755 of July 31, 1992, which repeals the second sentence of the first paragraph of Article 1477 of the New Code of Civil Procedure; *see also* Philippe Théry, *Les procédures civiles d'exécution et le droit de l'arbitrage*, 1993 REV. ARB. 159.

[28] Cass. 1e civ., June 29, 1994, Caisse régionale d'assurances mutuelles agricoles de La Réunion v. Mediterranean Shipping Co., 1994 Bull. Civ. I, No. 224; 1996 REV. ARB. 400, and A. Hory's note. See also, for case law prior to the 1991 and 1992 reforms on enforcement procedures, which holds a request for enforcement to be inadmissible if brought before the Tribunal of First Instance and not its President alone, TGI Paris, Nov. 22, 1989, Acteurs Auteurs Associés (A.A.A.) v. Hemdale Film Corp., 1990 REV. ARB. 693, and B. Moreau's note; 1991 REV. CRIT. DIP 107, and M.-N. Jobard-Bachellier's note.

b) Territorial Jurisdiction

1571. — Article 1477 specifies that the court with territorial jurisdiction will be the court "of the place where the award was made." That criterion can only apply to awards made in France. For awards made outside France, the 1981 Decree provides no alternative criterion. This omission creates a difficulty similar to that which arises in determining which French court has jurisdiction where, under Articles 14 and 15 of the Civil Code, the French courts generally speaking have jurisdiction on the sole basis of the existence of a French litigant. Several solutions have been put forward.

Some authors suggest that the Paris Tribunal of First Instance should be the only court with jurisdiction. This approach is based on an analogy with the system for resolving difficulties concerning the constitution of the arbitral tribunal under Article 1493, paragraph 2 of the New Code of Civil Procedure. It has the merit of directing all such applications towards a court which has sufficient experience in the field.[29] However, it is difficult to justify in the absence of a statutory provision to that effect. In practice, other courts have in fact heard applications for enforcement of awards made outside France.[30]

Other authors propose that the approach adopted in previous case law should still apply.[31] That was to attribute jurisdiction to the courts of the domicile of the defendant in enforcement proceedings or, more generally, to the courts of the place where the plaintiff intended enforcement to take place.[32]

A further group of authors is in favor of applying the criteria used to determine the special jurisdiction which arises where an application is made before the French courts on the basis of Articles 14 and 15 of the Civil Code.[33] This approach has the advantage of flexibility. The courts have held that in such cases

> the plaintiff can validly apply to a French court, which may be chosen because of the grounds connecting the case to France or, failing that, according to the requirements of the proper administration of justice.[34]

---

[29] See Patrice Level, *La réforme de l'arbitrage international (D. n° 81-500, 12 mai 1981, Nouveau Code de procédure civile, art. 1492 à 1507)*, JCP, Ed. C.I., Pt. I, No. 9899, ¶ 25 (1981).

[30] See, e.g., TGI Lyon, réf., Feb. 12, 1987, Ferrara v. Markling Micoud, 1988 RTD CIV. 173, and observations by J. Normand and, on appeal, CA Lyon, Jan. 7, 1988, 1988 REV. ARB. 685, and M.-C. Rondeau-Rivier's note; 1988 RTD CIV. 570, and observations by J. Normand.

[31] See, e.g., Cass. req., July 27, 1937, Roses v. Moller et Cie., D.P., Pt. I, at 25 (1938), and the report by Judge Castets; JCP, Ed. G., Pt. II, No. 449 (1937); Sirey, Pt. I, at 25 (1938); 65 J.D.I. 86 (1938).

[32] See Fouchard, *supra* note 7, ¶ 63; André Huet, *Les procédures de reconnaissance et d'exécution des jugements étrangers et des sentences arbitrales en droit international privé français*, 115 J.D.I. 5, 21 n.47 (1988). Compare, in favor of the jurisdiction of the courts of the place of actual enforcement, Jeantet, *supra* note 21, at 508; Robert, *supra* note 16, at 214; Mayer, *supra* note 5, at 87.

[33] See Bellet and Mezger, *supra* note 5, at 642.

[34] Cass. 1e civ., June 13, 1978, Mora v. La Fédérale, 1978 REV. CRIT. DIP 722, and B. Audit's note; 106 J.D.I. 414 (1979), and observations by P. Kahn.

This justifies the jurisdiction of the courts of the defendant's domicile or of the place where attachable property is located, as well as that of the Paris courts, "on account of their geographically central situation,"[35] and that of the courts of the plaintiff's domicile, provided that the plaintiff is not acting with the intention to disadvantage the defendant. We favor this approach, which simply adds flexibility to the previous solutions in the absence of precise statutory criteria. It was endorsed by the Paris Court of Appeals in a 1992 decision in the *GL Outillage v. Stankoimport* case, where an award made in Stockholm was submitted for enforcement to the President of the Tribunal of First Instance in Paris, although the French defendant company in the enforcement proceedings was headquartered in the French provincial town of Troyes.[36]

2° Procedure

1572. — The court hearing the enforcement action is seized by way of an *ex parte* application.

Enforcement is therefore granted (or refused) without any adversarial proceedings between the parties at this stage. However, the practice of the Paris courts allows the enforcement court the right (which it rarely exercises) to summon the other party if the court considers it necessary to obtain information, particularly in cases where there is an issue of manifest violation of international public policy in the award.[37]

The fact that enforcement can be obtained by means of an *ex parte* order rather than by issuing an ordinary writ has sometimes been disputed on the grounds that under Article 812 of the New Code of Civil Procedure a court can only hear *ex parte* applications in cases provided for by statute.[38] Most authors reject that view, rightly arguing that the 1980 Decree on domestic arbitration, and hence the 1981 Decree which refers to it, were not intended to depart from prior practice.[39] Having an *ex parte* procedure ensures the avoidance of any discussion before the enforcement court of the potential grounds on which enforcement might be refused. It therefore reflects the legislature's intention to direct such claims towards the Court of Appeals, thus leaving the first instance court to perform no more than a *prima facie* review.[40] The practice of the Paris Tribunal of First Instance shows a consistent

---

[35] Cass. 1e civ., June 13, 1978, *Mora, supra* note 34.

[36] CA Paris, July 10, 1992, GL Outillage v. Stankoimport, 1994 REV. ARB. 142, and P. Level's note; for an English translation, see 7 INT'L ARB. REP. B1 (Sept. 1992). This decision also held that the claim that the enforcement judge has no territorial jurisdiction is not admissible under Article 1502 of the New Code of Civil Procedure. On this issue, see *infra* para. 1584.

[37] On the scope of the review performed by the enforcement judge, see *infra* paras. 1575 *et seq.*

[38] *See* CA Lyon, Jan. 7, 1988, *Ferrara, supra* note 30.

[39] See especially the note by M.-C. Rondeau-Rivier and the observations by J. Normand following CA Lyon, Jan. 7, 1988, *Ferrara, supra* note 30.

[40] *See infra* para. 1575.

preference for *ex parte* proceedings, and it would appear that the same practice has also been adopted by the Lyon Tribunal of First Instance.[41]

1573. — The party applying for enforcement must submit not only the original or a certified copy of the arbitral award, but also an original or a certified copy of the arbitration agreement. These requirements are set out in Article 1499, paragraph 1 of the New Code of Civil Procedure. If those documents are not in French, the applicant must also provide a "translation certified by a translator registered on the list of experts" (Art. 1499, para. 2).

Article 1499 partly duplicates Article 1477, paragraph 2, which applies as a result of the reference to it in Article 1500. Article 1477, paragraph 2 provides that:

> the original of the award, together with a copy of the arbitration agreement, shall be filed by one of the arbitrators or by the most diligent party with the secretariat of the court [which has jurisdiction to hear the enforcement application].

The only difference between these two statutory provisions concerns the filing of the award by one of the arbitrators. It is not inconceivable, as a result of the reference in Article 1500 to Article 1477, paragraph 2, that one of the arbitrators might file the award with the clerk of the relevant court. However, that rarely occurs in international cases, where it is almost invariably the party applying for enforcement which files the award in support of its application. In any event, under French international arbitration law, there is no need for the award to be filed except in an application for enforcement.[42] The purpose of the rule is simply to enable the enforcement court to perform the *prima facie* review required of it.[43]

1574. — The court making an order granting enforcement need not give its reasons. It will simply affix the enforcement order on the text of the arbitral award.[44] In practice, this consists of an official stamp at the bottom of the award, accompanied by the date and the judge's signature.[45] Reasons need only be stated in decisions refusing enforcement.[46] However, an award of which enforcement has been granted cannot be enforced in the month following the notification of the enforcement decision to the other party. This gives the other party an opportunity to bring the case before the Court of Appeals in adversarial proceedings.[47]

---

[41] *See* J. Normand, observations following CA Lyon, Jan. 7, 1988, *Ferrara, supra* note 30, at 571.

[42] *See supra* para. 1411.

[43] *See infra* para. 1575.

[44] See Article 1478 of the New Code of Civil Procedure, which applies as a result of the reference contained in Article 1500 of the same Code.

[45] On recourse available against a decision granting enforcement, see *infra* para. 1583.

[46] See Article 1478, paragraph 2, which applies as a result of the reference contained in Article 1500. On recourse available against a decision refusing enforcement, see *infra* para. 1581.

[47] *See infra* para. 1584.

3° Extent of the Review by the Court

1575. — The enforcement court is seized by way of an *ex parte* application[48] and performs only a *prima facie* review of the award. In the words of Article 1498 of the New Code of Civil Procedure, the court will verify only that the existence of the award has been "proven by the party relying on the award" and that recognition is not "manifestly contrary to international public policy." Under no circumstances can the court alter the award by adding to the decision reached by the arbitrators.[49] However, the enforcement court can specifically censure frivolous recourse against the award.[50]

1576. — Doubts have been raised as to the exact extent of the review of the existence of the award by the enforcement court. Under Article 1499, paragraph 1 of the New Code of Civil Procedure, the existence of the award is established by producing an original or certified copy of the award and the arbitration agreement.[51]

This requirement has been criticized on the grounds that it places an unwarranted restriction, in the case of international arbitration, on the acceptance by the French legal order of awards based on oral arbitration agreements.[52] Yet, in international practice, the number of arbitration agreements for which no written evidence exists is insignificant. The requirement that an original of the arbitration agreement be submitted is not therefore too restrictive. However, it is quite conceivable that a court hearing an application for enforcement of an award made on the basis of an oral arbitration agreement could disregard the procedural requirement for an original or certified copy of the award and make do with other forms of evidence appropriate to the situation. This would bring procedural requirements into line with the substantive rule that the essential issue is the certainty of the parties' consent to go to arbitration, regardless of how that consent is evidenced.[53]

The requirement that the arbitration agreement be produced also raises a question as to the extent of the control by the enforcement court implied by this condition. Requiring the arbitration agreement to be filed has been interpreted as indicating that verifying the existence of the award entails verifying the existence and extent of the arbitrators' jurisdiction. It has therefore been suggested that the enforcement court should ensure that, *prima facie*, the award "decides a dispute falling within the terms of arbitration

---

[48] *See supra* para. 1572.

[49] Cass. 1e civ., Dec. 14, 1983, Epoux Convert v. Droga, 1984 REV. ARB. 483, and M.-C. Rondeau-Rivier's note; JCP, Ed. G., Pt. IV, at 60 (1984). Nor can it join a counterclaim; see, similarly, in the United States, Kwong Kam Tat Trading Co. v. Comsup Commodities, Inc., No. 92-3299 (JCL) (D.N.J. 1992); XIX Y.B. COM. ARB. 797 (1994); 8 INT'L ARB. REP. E1 (Jan. 1993).

[50] Cass. 1e civ., Dec. 14, 1983, *Epoux Convert, supra* note 49.

[51] *See supra* para. 1573.

[52] Bellet and Mezger, *supra* note 5, at 639. On the form of the arbitration agreement, see *supra* paras. 590 *et seq.*, especially para. 610.

[53] *See* Mayer, *supra* note 5, at 87. Compare, in favor of the sufficiency of a text produced by one party only and accepted by the other, E. Mezger, *Dix questions relatives au Titre VI du Livre IV NCPC*, 1981 REV. ARB. 543, 544.

agreement."[54] However, the statutory provision governing the substantive aspects of the review performed by the enforcement court—namely, Article 1498 of the New Code of Civil Procedure—makes no reference whatsoever to the arbitrators' jurisdiction. This is quite logical given that their jurisdiction is an issue entirely distinct from that of the existence of the award. As questions of jurisdiction are rarely straightforward, and the intention of the French legislature was to allocate the substantive review of arbitral awards to the Court of Appeals alone, the enforcement court should refrain from addressing issues relating to the existence, validity or extent of the arbitration agreement.[55] Those issues are thoroughly reviewed by the Court of Appeals pursuant to Articles 1502 1°, and 1504 of the New Code of Civil Procedure.[56]

1577. — The review covering manifest violations of international public policy raises fewer difficulties of interpretation. The principle of an initial review of this kind is perfectly justified. The French legislature could not allow an award plainly contravening fundamental principles to be received into the French legal order, even subject to subsequent recourse based on a claim that recognition or enforcement of the award would be contrary to international public policy.[57] However, in terms not repeated in Article 1502 with respect to the substantive review of the award by the Court of Appeals, Article 1498 provides that only awards in respect of which recognition or enforcement would be "manifestly" contrary to international public policy will be refused enforcement. The review of compliance with international public policy exercised by the enforcement court in *ex parte* proceedings is thus clearly no more than a *prima facie* control.

The public policy review by the court is performed solely in the light of the requirements of "international public policy," rather than the "public policy" considerations which apply in domestic arbitration. As the awards in question are either international or have been made abroad—and even though they may concern only one legal order—there is no justification for applying the rules of French domestic public policy.[58]

1578. — The enforcement judge can either grant or refuse enforcement, but is never entitled to modify the decision reached by the arbitrators. The *Cour de cassation* thus overruled a decision of the Lyon Court of Appeals, which had added an award of damages in respect of additional loss resulting from a late payment, "in view of the low interest rate granted in the award."[59] The only situation in which a court would be justified in intervening substantively would be to censure a frivolous action against the award.[60]

Given that the powers of the enforcement court are thus confined to either granting or refusing enforcement, it cannot add to an award by ordering provisional enforcement. For

---

[54] Fouchard, *supra* note 7, ¶ 64.

[55] Compare, in favor of having no review of the validity of the arbitration agreement, Huet, *supra* note 32, at 22.

[56] *See infra* paras. 1608 *et seq.*

[57] *See* Arts. 1502 5° and 1504 of the New Code of Civil Procedure; *see also infra* paras. 1645 *et seq.*

[58] For a more detailed critical analysis of the reverse position, see *supra* paras. 1561 and 1562.

[59] Cass. 1e civ., Dec. 14, 1983, *Epoux Convert, supra* note 49.

[60] Cass. 1e civ., Dec. 14, 1983, *Epoux Convert, supra* note 49. For another example, see *infra* para. 1590.

the same reason, if the arbitrators have ordered provisional enforcement, the court cannot alter their decision, except by refusing enforcement if the arbitrators' decision is found to be patently contrary to international public policy.[61] This rule is easy to apply to awards made in France in international cases. However, for awards made outside France, the effect of the rule has sometimes been disregarded on the grounds that the benefit of provisional enforcement granted outside France "loses its effects by crossing national boundaries."[62] It has been argued that in such cases, as a result of Articles 524 and 525 of the New Code of Civil Procedure (which apply through a chain of cross-references triggered by Articles 1479 and 1500 of the same Code), only the Court of Appeals can grant provisional enforcement.[63] That analysis is unsatisfactory. Although provisional enforcement ordered by a court, in common with all enforcement measures ordered by the courts, has strict territorial limits, there is no reason why an award of provisional enforcement by arbitrators should only be effective in the territory where the arbitral tribunal has its seat. In fact, each legal system liable to be involved in the enforcement of the award should determine the effects of arbitrators' decisions regarding provisional enforcement, as that is a matter which, by definition, falls within the jurisdiction of the national courts.

However, a partial refusal of enforcement is perfectly conceivable as, for example, in the case of an award where one aspect which plainly contravenes international public policy is separable from the other parts of the award.[64]

1579. — Once issued, a decision granting enforcement cannot be reversed in summary proceedings.[65] The only available recourse against such a decision is that provided for in the New Code of Civil Procedure before the Court of Appeals.[66]

---

[61] On this issue, generally, see P. Bellet, note following CA Paris, Nov. 27, 1984, Lalanne v. Deutsche Gesellschaft für Wirtschaftliche Zusammenarbeit, 1985 REV. ARB. 289, and P. Bellet's note.

[62] Mezger, *supra* note 53, at 548; P. Bellet, note following CA Paris, Nov. 27, 1984, *Lalanne, supra* note 61, at 297; B. Moreau, observations following CA Paris, May 20, 1988, T.A.I. v. Siape, 1990 REV. ARB. 907.

[63] On the powers of the court hearing an appeal from a decision refusing enforcement, see *infra* para. 1581.

[64] *See* Philippe Bertin, *Le rôle du juge dans l'exécution de la sentence arbitrale*, 1983 REV. ARB. 281; M.-C. Rondeau-Rivier, note following Cass. 1e civ., Dec. 14, 1983, *Epoux Convert, supra* note 49, at 490. Compare, on the possibility of setting aside part of the award suggested by Article 1490 of the New Code of Civil Procedure, to which Article 1507 of the same Code refers, *infra* para. 1591. Similarly, see, for example, Supreme Court of Hong Kong, High Court, Aug. 12, 1992, J.J. Agro Industries (P) Ltd. v. Texuna International Ltd., XVIII Y.B. COM. ARB. 396 (1993).

[65] *See* CA Paris, réf., Mar. 10, 1986, Ets. Croullet Céréales v. Ets. Michel Blanc & Fils, 1988 REV. ARB. 325; TGI Paris, réf., Sept. 13, 1984, Les Huileries de l'Arceau v. Frahuil, 1985 REV. ARB. 327, and T. Bernard's note.

[66] See, in French domestic arbitration, TGI Paris, réf., Jan. 22, 1997, France Quick v. Carlest, 1997 REV. ARB. 569, and M.-C. Rivier's note.

C. – RECOURSE AGAINST AN ORDER REFUSING OR GRANTING RECOGNITION OR ENFORCEMENT

1580. — The recourse available against a decision concerning the recognition or enforcement of an arbitral award differs according to whether recognition or enforcement is refused (1°) or granted (2°).

1° Appeal Against a Decision Refusing Recognition or Enforcement

1581. — Under Article 1501 of the New Code of Civil Procedure, "a decision which refuses recognition or enforcement[67] of an award may be appealed." Such an appeal must be brought "before the Court of Appeals having jurisdiction over the judge who made the decision" (Art. 1503). It must be filed within one month of notification of the decision to the other party or parties (Art. 1503, *in fine*). It has rightly been noted that as a decision refusing recognition or enforcement will necessarily have been made in *ex parte* proceedings, only the applicant will be aware of it, and is clearly not going to notify the other party or parties. In practice, the result in such cases will be that there is no deadline for bringing an appeal.[68] The fact that an appeal suspends enforcement, under Article 1506, is irrelevant in this context, as the award has been refused recognition or enforcement.

The only difficult question is whether the Court of Appeals, when hearing an appeal against a decision refusing recognition or enforcement, must confine its review to the two aspects of the award considered by the enforcement judge and on the basis of which enforcement was refused.[69] Alternatively, is the Court entitled to perform a full review of the award in adversarial proceedings? In that case it could only reverse the decision to refuse enforcement by establishing that none of the five grounds for refusing enforcement under Article 1502 has been satisfied.

Some authors have suggested that the Court of Appeals must confine itself to performing the same review as the enforcement judge.[70] This view is based on the differences in the wording of Articles 1501 and 1502, and on the fact that in international arbitration there is no text equivalent to Article 1489, which provides that an appeal against a decision refusing enforcement of a domestic award allows the Court of Appeals to consider all the grounds under which the award can be challenged.

Other authors point to the legislature's intention to centralize all actions against the award before a single court—the Court of Appeals—and argue that even where it is hearing an appeal from a decision refusing enforcement, the Court of Appeals must, in adversarial

---

[67] On this terminology, see *supra* para. 1568.

[68] *See* Bellet and Mezger, *supra* note 5, at 650–51.

[69] These are the non-existence of the award and its manifest non-compliance with international public policy; see *supra* para. 1575.

[70] Jean Robert, *La réforme de l'arbitrage international en France – Décret du 12 mai 1981– Synthèse*, 1981 REV. ARB. 530, 537–38.

proceedings, decide on all the grounds that can be raised in connection with the award.[71] The reverse approach would prejudice the party opposing recognition or enforcement, by obliging it to bring two successive actions before the same Court of Appeals, the first on the limited grounds on which the enforcement judge is able to decide, and the second on the five grounds on which the Court of Appeals can review the award. The absurdity of that scenario confirms that, although the drafting of the law is undoubtedly clumsy, the legislature cannot have intended to require two successive actions.[72] The view that the Court of Appeals can decide on the five grounds found in Article 1502 is also supported by Article 1507 of the New Code of Civil Procedure. That article itself refers to Article 1487, paragraph 1 of the same Code, which states that "[a]ppeals and actions to set aside shall be brought, heard and decided in accordance with the rules relating to procedure in litigation before the Court of Appeals." Relying on the general scope of that text, it has been argued that an appeal against an order refusing recognition or enforcement is itself litigation before the Court of Appeals, unlike enforcement proceedings, and that as a result all grounds liable to be raised in an action under Article 1502 can be heard by the Court.[73] Although the text-based argument alone is not particularly compelling,[74] the general structure of the system of recourse established by the legislature in 1981 implies that the Court of Appeals must be able to hear argument on all grounds found in Article 1502, irrespective of the way in which the Court was seized.

1582. — The court responsible for hearing the appeal from an order refusing enforcement may be required to rule on the provisional enforcement of the award. Article 1479 of the New Code of Civil Procedure, which applies to international arbitration by virtue of the reference to it in Article 1500 of the same Code, provides that:

> [t]he rules on provisional enforcement of judgments are applicable to arbitral awards.
> In the case of an appeal or an action to set aside, the First President or magistrate conducting the procedure, once the matter is referred to him or her, may . . . order provisional enforcement pursuant to the procedure provided for in Articles 525 and 526.

Articles 525 and 526 provide that provisional enforcement "can only be ordered in the decision which is intended to be made enforceable," except where there is an appeal to the First President or the judge in charge of the proceedings, who may grant provisional enforcement if it has not already been ordered in the decision enforceability of which is sought. In the context of arbitration this means, in practice, that for international awards made in France or to be enforced in France, to be provisionally enforceable, a declaration

---

[71] Fouchard, *supra* note 7, at 412–13; Bellet and Mezger, *supra* note 5, at 650; Mayer, *supra* note 5, at 88; MATTHIEU DE BOISSÉSON, LE DROIT FRANÇAIS DE L'ARBITRAGE INTERNE ET INTERNATIONAL 819 (2d ed. 1990).

[72] *See* Bellet and Mezger, *supra* note 5, at 650.

[73] *See* Fouchard, *supra* note 7, at 413.

[74] For a critical analysis of this argument, see Mayer, *supra* note 5, at 88.

to that effect should appear in the award itself. If provisional enforcement has been ordered in the award, the First President may, on appeal, terminate it "if it is prohibited by law" (Art. 524, para. 1) or "if it is liable to have patently excessive consequences" (Art. 524, para. 2).[75]

2° Appeal Against a Decision Granting Recognition or Enforcement

1583. — The appeals which lie against a decision granting recognition or enforcement depend on whether or not the award in question was made in France.

1584. — Where the award was made outside France (whether or not in an international arbitration), the order granting recognition or enforcement can be appealed. Article 1502 of the New Code of Civil Procedure states, without any restriction similar to that contained in Article 1504 relating to awards made in France,[76] that "an appeal against a decision which grants recognition or enforcement"[77] is available in the five cases listed in that same text.[78] Any other ground for appeal, such as the lack of territorial jurisdiction of the court hearing the application, is inadmissible.[79]

From a purely procedural standpoint, it suffices for present purposes to note that the appeal must be brought before the Court of Appeals which has jurisdiction over the judge who granted recognition or enforcement, and that it must be brought within one month of the notification of that order (Art. 1503). Here, the starting-point for the one month deadline is extremely important,[80] as it will obviously be in the interest of the party which has obtained recognition or enforcement to notify its opponent of the order, so as to be able to begin enforcement of the award. Enforcement is suspended during the one month period which begins on notification, and continues to be so once an appeal is filed within that deadline. Thus, unless otherwise specified in the award or by the Court of Appeals, the party seeking to enforce the award cannot do so until the Court of Appeals has ruled on the issues listed in Article 1502.[81] The appeal is filed, heard and decided in accordance with the procedural rules governing ordinary litigation before the Court of Appeals.[82] The rejection of the appeal will automatically render the arbitral award enforceable.[83]

---

[75] On the difficulties resulting from the transposition of these principles of domestic law to international arbitration, see P. Bellet, note following CA Paris, Nov. 27, 1984, *Lalanne, supra* note 61, at 295 *et seq.*

[76] See *infra* para. 1585.

[77] On this terminology, see *supra* para. 1568.

[78] See *infra* paras. 1601 *et seq.*

[79] CA Paris, July 10, 1992, *GL Outillage, supra* note 36.

[80] *Comp. supra* para. 1581.

[81] Art. 1506. On provisional enforcement, see *infra* para. 1591.

[82] Article 1487, paragraph 1, which applies as a result of the reference contained in Article 1507.

[83] Article 1490, which applies as a result of the reference contained in Article 1507.

1585. — In the case of an international award made in France,

> [n]o form of recourse is available against an order granting enforcement[84] of such an award. However, an action to set aside[85] shall, within the limits of the court's jurisdiction, be deemed to constitute recourse against the decision of the judge who granted enforcement or to bring an end to that judge's jurisdiction. (Art. 1504, para. 2).

The aim of this rule is to simplify the appeals system. The review performed by the Court of Appeals of international awards made in France is identical in scope to the review of awards made abroad[86] in an appeal against recognition or enforcement of such awards. Enforcement of the award is suspended during both the period for filing the appeal and the appeal itself (Art. 1506), and the procedural regime for both forms of review exercised by the Court of Appeals over arbitral awards is thus perfectly consistent.

§ 2. – Actions to Set Aside

1586. — French arbitration law is of course more concerned with actions heard by the French courts to set awards aside (A) than with the effect in France of the setting aside of awards outside France or of the commencement of proceedings outside France, particularly at the seat of the arbitration, to set awards aside (B).

A. – ACTIONS BEFORE THE FRENCH COURTS TO SET AWARDS ASIDE

1587. — We shall consider in turn which awards can be the subject of an action to set aside in France (1°) and the conditions governing the setting aside procedure before the Court of Appeals (2°).

1° Awards Which Can Be the Subject of an Action to Set Aside in France

1588. — The determination of which awards can be the subject of actions to set aside before the French courts has been made in the clearest possible terms by the 1981 Decree. Article 1504 of the New Code of Civil Procedure provides, in paragraph 1, that "[a]n arbitral award made in France in an international arbitration may be the subject of an action to set

---

[84] On this terminology, see *supra* para. 1568.

[85] *See infra* para. 1587.

[86] *See* the reference to Article 1502 contained in Article 1504 of the New Code of Civil Procedure.

aside in the cases set forth in Article 1502."[87] That wording has two consequences, one positive, the other negative.

1589. — The positive consequence of paragraph 1 of Article 1504 is that the 1981 Decree departs from the previous case law of the Paris Court of Appeals, which considered that actions to set aside "non-French" awards were inadmissible. Non-French awards were defined as awards made under a procedural law other than French law and having "no connection whatsoever with the French legal system," despite the fact that the arbitration was held in France. The Paris Court of Appeals had applied these criteria to an award made in an ICC arbitration that took place in France between a Libyan company and a Swedish company concerning a dispute arising from the performance of a contract for the construction and delivery in Sweden of a number of ships.[88] Following the 1981 Decree, the fact that an award is made in France will suffice to give the French courts jurisdiction over an action to set it aside. This will be the case even where the award is made in an international arbitration which has no connection with the French legal system other than the fact that the seat of the arbitration is located in France.

We consider the position taken in the 1981 Decree to be the better approach. It is based on what is now a widely-accepted view[89] of the distribution of jurisdiction among the various countries concerned by the arbitral award, a view which has also influenced the main international conventions on the recognition and enforcement of arbitral awards:[90] the country in which the seat of the arbitration is located has exclusive jurisdiction[91] to hear actions to set an arbitral award aside, whereas countries in which enforcement of the award is sought can only agree or refuse to give effect to it in their territory.

This jurisdictional rule therefore cannot give rise to "floating" awards, which may contain serious flaws but which no national courts are able to set aside. In addition, it avoids the drawback inherent in the application of the law governing the arbitral procedure to determine which court has international jurisdiction to set an award aside, namely the fact that in many cases no choice of procedural law is ever made.[92]

Of course, the trend in favor of allowing awards set aside in the country of origin to be enforced elsewhere[93] will diminish the international impact of the proceedings organized at the seat. However, an award set aside in one jurisdiction will clearly have to be scrutinized very closely prior to its enforcement in other jurisdictions, and the place where the

---

[87] On the binding nature of an award, as opposed to decisions of the first instance arbitral tribunal in cases where there are two tiers of arbitral jurisdiction, see *supra* para. 1356.

[88] CA Paris, Feb. 21, 1980, General National Maritime Transport Co. v. Götaverken Arendal A.B., 107 J.D.I. 660 (1980), and P. Fouchard's note; 1980 REV. ARB. 524, and F.C. Jeantet's note; Dalloz, Jur. 568 (1980), and J. Robert's note; 1980 REV. CRIT. DIP 763, and E. Mezger's note; JCP, Ed. G., Pt. II, No. 19,512 (1981), and P. Level's note; for an English translation, see VI Y.B. COM. ARB. 221 (1981); 20 I.L.M. 883 (1981), with an introductory note by F.C. Jeantet.

[89] See *infra* para. 1593.

[90] See *infra* paras. 1685 *et seq.*

[91] See *infra* para. 1590.

[92] On this issue, see *supra* para. 1197.

[93] See *infra* para. 1595.

arbitration is held remains the most appropriate criterion—as opposed to the law governing the proceedings—to be used in the determination of where actions to set aside an award will be available.

1590. — The negative consequence of the wording of Article 1504 is that the French courts only have jurisdiction to hear actions to set aside awards made in France. In particular, this means that where the parties or the arbitrators have chosen French law to govern the arbitral proceedings, that in itself does not bring the award under French jurisdiction with respect to actions to set aside. This approach differs from that followed in defining the international jurisdiction of the French courts for the purposes of resolving difficulties concerning the constitution of the arbitral tribunal, where the President of the Paris Tribunal of First Instance may intervene in both arbitrations held in France and arbitrations governed by French procedural law.[94] Article 1504 also departs from the case law of the Paris Court of Appeals prior to the 1981 reform. In a manner similar to that of the case law giving precedence to the governing law over the seat in refusing to hear actions to set aside "non-French" awards made in France,[95] the Paris Court of Appeals had suggested that it would uphold the jurisdiction of the French courts to examine the validity of awards rendered abroad under French procedural law. It was only because the award in question had been "made under a procedure other than that of French law" that the Paris Court of Appeals held inadmissible an action to set aside an award made in Vienna, in a case between a French and a Turkish corporation.[96] The 1981 Decree reversed that line of case law, in the same way as it reversed the decisions which held that actions to set aside certain awards made in France were inadmissible. The position taken in the Decree is perfectly justifiable. To use the procedural law criterion would undoubtedly lead to serious conflicts of jurisdiction, given that the seat of the arbitration is the criterion generally favored in comparative law[97] and in major international conventions on the recognition and enforcement of awards.[98] For example, were they to retain jurisdiction on the basis of the procedural law, the French courts might set aside awards held valid by the courts of the seat of the arbitration. Accepting a more universally-recognized criterion for determining jurisdiction, such as that of the seat of the arbitration, avoids those difficulties. Nevertheless, the choice of the seat as the basis for jurisdiction to hear actions to set aside does not pre-judge the issue of whether an award set aside by the courts of the foreign seat of the arbitration can nevertheless be recognized in France.[99]

The rule that the French courts have no jurisdiction to hear actions to set aside awards made outside France is now so clear that a party disregarding it may be ordered to pay damages for frivolous suit. The Paris Court of Appeals so held in a case in which an action

---

[94] Art. 1493, para. 2. *See supra* paras. 837 *et seq.*

[95] *See supra* para. 1589.

[96] CA Paris, Dec. 9, 1980, Aksa v. Norsolor, 1981 REV. ARB. 306, and F.C. Jeantet's note; 1981 REV. CRIT. DIP 545, and E. Mezger's note; for an English translation, see 20 I.L.M. 887 (1981).

[97] See *infra* para. 1593 which considers, in particular, the recent conversion of English law to this criterion.

[98] *See infra* para. 1687.

[99] On this issue, generally, see *infra* para. 1595.

was brought in France to set aside an award made in London. Having referred to the principle that actions to set aside an award are confined "by Article 1504 of the New Code of Civil Procedure to awards made in France in matters of international arbitration," the Court held that the plaintiff, "acting in bad faith, [had] submitted its challenge of the arbitral award to a court which patently lacked jurisdiction, thereby allowing the public examination of facts which were intended to remain confidential."[100]

In light of Article 1504 of the New Code of Civil Procedure, it is important to be able to determine where an award has been made. This is not always easy. In particular, where the parties, an arbitral institution or the arbitrators have fixed the seat of the arbitration at a given place, it may be that, for reasons of convenience, part of the arbitral proceedings will take place at another location.[101] If, for similar reasons, the arbitral award is signed and dated at a place other than that chosen as the seat of the arbitration by the parties, the arbitral institution, or the arbitrators, it may prove difficult to establish where the award was made within the meaning of Article 1504. If, for example, the award was signed in France, whereas the seat of the arbitration was located in another country, a party might be tempted to argue that the award was "made" in France and that, as a result, the French courts have jurisdiction to hear an action to set the award aside.[102] That risk of dissociating the legal seat of the arbitration from the place where the award was actually made is substantially reduced in ICC arbitration, as Article 25(3) of the ICC Rules (Art. 22 of the former Rules) provides that the award is deemed to have been made at the seat of the arbitration. One might nevertheless argue in such cases that the terms of the parties' agreement or of the applicable arbitration rules (which have no more weight than the intentions of the parties) cannot alter the public policy rules governing actions against awards.[103] In fact, the answer to these difficulties lies in the interpretation of the concept of the making of an award. It is legitimate to suggest that by making the distinction between arbitral awards made in France in international cases and those made outside France of paramount importance for procedural purposes, the French legislature chose not to rely on a criterion which is purely accidental or which depends on the decision as to where to sign the award made by the arbitrators for reasons of convenience. Rather, the legislature's position is based more fundamentally on the recognition of the parties' freedom to choose—directly or indirectly—the place where the arbitral proceedings are to take place and hence the legal environment surrounding the arbitration. That legal environment may of course differ considerably from one jurisdiction to the next, especially as regards actions against the award.[104] From the point of view of the French legislature, the jurisdiction of the French courts to hear all actions to set aside international awards made in France is undoubtedly based on the idea of providing those involved in international commerce with an arbitral forum which takes a particular view of the control which the courts should exercise over awards. It would not be in keeping with

---

[100] CA Paris, Feb. 18, 1986, Aïta v. Ojjeh, 1986 REV. ARB. 583, and G. Flécheux's note; Dalloz, Jur. 339 (1987).

[101] *See supra* para. 1240.

[102] For another example where it might be legitimate to have doubts as to the place where the award was made, see Bellet and Mezger, *supra* note 5, at 637.

[103] *See infra* para. 1596.

[104] *See infra* para. 1594.

that policy if the jurisdiction of the French courts over actions to set aside were to depend on the random factor of where the arbitrators signed the award, particularly where the parties had chosen another place as the seat of the arbitration. Thus, for the purposes of Article 1504, the award should be deemed to have been made at the seat of the arbitration. The French courts have clearly adopted that approach. For example, a Court of Appeals held that an award stating that it was "done in Brussels," although the parties had chosen Paris as the seat of the arbitration, was to be considered as having been made in France for the purposes of the action to set the award aside.[105] Conversely, the French courts declined jurisdiction over an action to set aside an award made after proceedings held for the most part in Paris, although the arbitration agreement and the terms of reference designated Geneva as the seat of the arbitration. The Paris Court of Appeals rightly held that "the seat of the arbitration is a purely legal concept which has important consequences, notably the jurisdiction of state courts in actions to set aside, and which is dependent on the intentions of the parties. It is not a factual concept dependent on the place of the hearing or the signature of the award, which are liable to vary according to the whims or the carelessness of the arbitrators."[106] After much hesitation, the same approach is now found in England and India, which have fallen in line with the general trend.[107]

2° Procedure Before the Court of Appeals

1591. — Under Article 1504 of the New Code of Civil Procedure, the grounds on which an action to set aside can be brought against an international award made in France are the same as those which can be raised against the recognition or enforcement in France of an award made outside France. We shall examine those grounds in detail at a later stage.[108]

As far as procedure is concerned, the action to set an award aside must be brought before the Court of Appeals of the place where the award was made (Art. 1505). It can be brought as soon as the award has been made, but no later than one month following notification of the enforcement order (Art. 1505). Notification of the award sent by registered post to the parties' counsels by the arbitrators or by the arbitral institution does not amount to notification for the purposes of Article 1505.[109] Such notification must be made by process

---

[105] CA Versailles, 1e Ch., 1e Sec., Jan. 14, 1987, Chimimportexport v. Tournant Thierry, No. 7298/85, unpublished.

[106] CA Paris, Oct. 28, 1997, Procédés de préfabrication pour le béton v. Libye, 1998 REV. ARB. 399, and B. Leurent's note; *see also* CA Paris, 1e Ch., Sec. C, Dec. 3, 1998, Interpipe v. Hunting Oilfield Services, No. 1997/14112, unpublished.

[107] *See infra* para. 1593.

[108] *See infra* paras. 1601 *et seq.*

[109] CA Paris, Mar. 14, 1989, Murgue Seigle v. Coflexip, 1991 REV. ARB. 355, and observations by J.-H. Moitry and C. Vergne; 1991 RTD COM. 575, and observations by J.-C. Dubarry and E. Loquin; CA Paris, Feb. 22, 1996, Karl Schlueten GmbH et Co. Kg. v. Société Industrielle et Minière (SNIM), and CA Paris, Mar. 22, 1996, N.V. Lernout v. Compumedia SI, 1997 REV. ARB. 83, and observations by Y. Derains. On the requirement that there be an enforcement order prior to notification, compare, in French domestic arbitration, Cass. 2e civ., Feb. 15, 1995, Sorco v. Rail applique, 1996 REV. ARB. 223, and B. Moreau's note.

server under ordinary French rules of procedure. The one month period following notification, like the proceedings to set aside themselves, has a suspensive effect, so that in principle the award cannot be enforced until the deadline for bringing an action to set it aside has expired, or before the Court of Appeals has reached a decision in such an action. However, because of the reference in Article 1500 to Article 1479 of the New Code of Civil Procedure, which in turn refers to Articles 525 and 526 of the same Code, the Court of Appeals can order provisional enforcement of an award submitted to it for review.[110]

The action to set aside is heard under the ordinary rules of procedure applicable to litigation before the Court of Appeals.[111]

If the action to set the award aside is rejected by the Court of Appeals, the award, or any part of the award which has not been held void, becomes immediately enforceable.[112] Only part of an award may be set aside. This can happen where various aspects of the award are separable and the grounds for setting aside do not affect all of them. Where the action is clearly ill-founded, the Court of Appeals can include an award of damages in its decision, on the basis of the frivolous nature of the suit brought by the plaintiff.[113] On the other hand, it cannot add to the award.[114] If the Court of Appeals sets the award aside, its decision entirely or partially annuls the award, but unlike the situation in domestic arbitration (Art. 1485), the Court of Appeals cannot itself review the merits of the dispute. Where the award is set aside by the Court, the arbitration agreement on which the award was based remains effective and the dispute can be re-submitted to an arbitral tribunal.[115]

The decision of the Court of Appeals can itself be brought before the *Cour de cassation*, in accordance with the ordinary rules of French law. If the Court of Appeals rejected the action to set aside, the award must be enforced before a party can seek to have that decision overturned before the *Cour de cassation*, under Article 1009-1 of the New Code of Civil Procedure.[116]

---

[110] On this issue, generally, see especially P. Bellet, note following CA Paris, Nov. 27, 1984, *Lalanne*, *supra* note 61.

[111] Article 1487, paragraph 1, which applies by way of the reference found in Article 1507.

[112] Article 1490, which applies by way of the reference found in Article 1507.

[113] *See, e.g.*, CA Paris, Feb. 18, 1986, *Aïta*, *supra* note 100.

[114] CA Paris, Sept. 11, 1997, Alfalfas v. Comexol, 1998 REV. ARB. 564, and the commentary by Xavier Boucobza, *La clause compromissoire par référence en matière d'arbitrage commercial international*, *id.* at 495.

[115] For a justification of this solution in international arbitration, see for example, Fouchard, *supra* note 7, ¶ 75 at 412. On the more delicate issue of whether the setting aside of an award leaves the first arbitral tribunal intact or whether a new arbitral tribunal should be constituted, see especially Bertrand Moreau, *Les effets de la nullité de la sentence arbitrale*, *in* ETUDES OFFERTES À PIERRE BELLET 403 (1991).

[116] On this issue, see Marc Lévis, *L'effectivité du pourvoi en cassation et l'arbitrage (à propos de l'article 1009-1 NCPC)*, 1997 REV. ARB. 169.

B. – THE EFFECT OF PROCEEDINGS PENDING OUTSIDE FRANCE TO SET ASIDE AN AWARD OR OF A DECISION SETTING IT ASIDE

1592. — Most jurisdictions with modern arbitration legislation have a procedure for bringing actions against international awards made on their territory. The extent of the review performed by the courts still varies considerably from one country to the next, but with very few exceptions the principle of such review is accepted in comparative law.[117]

1° Jurisdiction of Courts Outside France to Set Aside Awards

1593. — The criterion relied on by courts to uphold their jurisdiction to set aside an arbitral award is usually the fact that the award was made on their territory.[118] This simple geographical criterion has been adopted by the UNCITRAL Model Law, which provides in its Article 34 that an award can be set aside, in a limited number of cases derived from the New York Convention, by the courts specified by each country in Article 6 as having jurisdiction to hear the main issues arising in connection with the arbitral proceedings. Article 1, paragraph 2 further provides that those courts have jurisdiction "only if the place of arbitration is in the territory" of the country in question.[119] Most modern arbitration laws also use the seat of the arbitration as the factor determining which awards can be the subject of an action to set aside before the local courts.[120]

Until recently, English law and Indian law took a different approach on this issue.[121] However, the position of English law has considerably evolved. The difficulty resulted, before the reform of English arbitration law in 1996, from a House of Lords decision of July 24, 1991 which, admittedly, was made in very unusual circumstances. An arbitrator deciding a dispute where the parties had chosen London as the seat of arbitration had nevertheless dated and signed his award in Paris. The House of Lords refused to infer from the fact that the seat of arbitration was in London that the English courts had jurisdiction to hear an

---

[117] For a comparative law analysis, see, for example, William Laurence Craig, *Uses and Abuses of Appeal from Awards*, 4 ARB. INT'L 174 (1988).

[118] Compare, in French law, *supra* para. 1589.

[119] *See also* HOWARD M. HOLTZMANN AND JOSEPH E. NEUHAUS, A GUIDE TO THE UNCITRAL MODEL LAW ON INTERNATIONAL COMMERCIAL ARBITRATION – LEGISLATIVE HISTORY AND COMMENTARY 241 (1989).

[120] *See, e.g.*, Arts. 1037 and 1064(2) of the Netherlands Code of Civil Procedure (Law of July 2, 1986); Art. 1717, para. 2 of the Belgian Judicial Code; Art. 46 of the Spanish Law 36/1988 on Arbitration of December 5, 1988; Arts. 176, para. 1 of the 1987 Swiss Private International Law Statute; Sec. 46 of the 1999 Swedish Arbitration Act; in Hong Kong, see Supreme Court, High Court, Mar. 2, 1991, Shenzhen Nan Da Industrial and Trade United Co. Ltd. v. FM International Ltd., XVIII Y.B. COM. ARB. 377, ¶ 19 at 382 (1993).

[121] Compare, in the United States, International Standard Electric Corp. v. Bridas Sociedad Anonima Petrolera, which, following tortuous reasoning, declined jurisdiction over an action to set aside an ICC award made in Mexico, on the grounds, wrongly based on the New York Convention (see *infra* para. 1666), that only the courts of the seat of the arbitration or of the country whose law governed the arbitral procedure had jurisdiction (745 F. Supp. 172 (S.D.N.Y. 1990); XVII Y.B. COM. ARB. 639 (1992); for a French translation, see 1994 REV. ARB. 739, and Y. Derains' note).

action to set aside the award, and decided that, being "made" in Paris,[122] the award was in fact a foreign award within the meaning of the 1958 New York Convention. The House of Lords concluded that an action to set aside the award could nevertheless be brought before the English courts, because the arbitration was governed by English procedural law.[123] The decision thus applied the criterion used in the French *Götaverken* and *Aksa* cases, which was abandoned in French law under the 1981 Decree.[124] The reasoning used in order to obtain an equitable result was therefore unfortunate. It was liable to create serious conflicts of jurisdiction, because if the approach adopted by the House of Lords were also adopted by the courts of the place where the award was actually signed, the award could be the subject of a concurrent action to set it aside, and it is by no means certain that the outcome of a concurrent action would be the same as that of the action before the English courts. It would certainly have been preferable, and more in keeping with the jurisdictional criteria becoming established in comparative law, to have avoided giving an overly literal interpretation of the place where the award was actually "made" for the purposes of applying provisions concerning the jurisdiction of the English courts, and instead to have linked the availability of actions against the award to the seat of arbitration intended by the parties. This was accomplished by Section 53 of the 1996 Arbitration Act, which provides that "where the seat of the arbitration is in England and Wales or Northern Ireland, any award in the proceedings shall be treated as made there, regardless of where it was signed, despatched, or delivered to any of the parties." This provision, which applies unless the parties agree otherwise, resolves the problem in English law.

Indian law has followed the same path. On May 7, 1992, the Supreme Court upheld the jurisdiction of the Indian courts to set aside an award made in London in an ICC case between an Indian party and a non-Indian party on the grounds that the law applicable to the arbitration agreement was Indian law, the choice of that law having been determined on the basis of a presumption that it coincided with the law governing the merits of the dispute, particularly as the latter had been chosen by the parties.[125] That approach disregarded the intentions of the parties which, by providing that the arbitrators were to be free to determine the seat of the arbitration, intended to entrust the arbitrators with the task of determining the

---

[122] On the position in French law, see *supra* para. 1590.

[123] Hiscox v. Outhwaite, (No. 1) [1992] 1 A.C. 562; [1991] 3 All E.R. 641; [1991] 3 W.L.R. 297; [1991] 2 Lloyd's Rep. 435; XVII Y.B. COM. ARB. 599 (1992) (H.L. 1991); see also the disapproving commentary by Claude Reymond, *Where is an arbitral award made?*, 108 L.Q. REV. 1 (1992); the disapproving observations by Albert Jan van den Berg, *New York Convention of 1958 – Consolidated Commentary – Cases Reported in Volumes XVII (1992) – XIX (1994)*, XIX Y.B. COM. ARB. 475, 483 (1994); Albert Jan van den Berg, *New York Arbitration Convention 1958: Where is an arbitral award "made"? Case Comment House of Lords, 24 July 1991, Hiscox v. Outhwaite*, *in* THE PLACE OF ARBITRATION 113 (M. Storme and F. de Ly eds., 1992); Michael E. Schneider, *L'arrêt de la Chambre des Lords dans l'affaire Hiscox v. Outhwaite*, 1991 BULL. ASA 279.

[124] CA Paris, Feb. 21, 1980, *Götaverken*, *supra* note 88; CA Paris, Dec. 9, 1980, *Aksa*, *supra* note 96; *see supra* para. 1590.

[125] National Thermal Power Corp. v. The Singer Corp., [1992] 2 S.C.J. 431; 7 INT'L ARB. REP. C1 (June 1992); XVIII Y.B. COM. ARB. 403 (1993).

legal environment in which the award would be made.[126] It also ignored the principle of separability of the arbitration agreement.[127] The adoption, on January 16, 1996, of an Arbitration and Conciliation Ordinance in India based on the UNCITRAL Model Law should make this case law obsolete.

2° Grounds on Which an Award May Be Set Aside Outside France

1594. — The grounds on which an award may be set aside under recent international arbitration legislation are generally based on the same philosophy underlying the grounds for refusing recognition or enforcement found in the relevant international conventions,[128] and they differ only in certain limited respects from the grounds found in French law.[129]

The grounds on which an award can be set aside in England are traditionally somewhat broader than those found in other legal systems. The ground of "misconduct" previously found in English law[130] was replaced, in the 1996 Arbitration Act, by that of "serious irregularity,"[131] which is still considered to be excessively vague by continental standards.[132] In this respect, it is unfortunate that the drafters of the UNCITRAL Model Law confined themselves to reproducing at Article 36, as grounds for setting aside an award, the grounds for refusing enforcement listed in Article V of the New York Convention. Those grounds

---

[126] See also the analysis by Albert J. van den Berg, *New York Convention of 1958 – Consolidated Commentary – Cases Reported in Volumes XVII (1992) – XIX (1994)*, *supra* note 123, at 489; Jan A.S. Paulsson, *The New York Convention's Misadventures in India*, 7 INT'L ARB. REP. 18 (June 1992). *Comp. with* V.S. Deshpande, *"Foreign Award" in the 1958 New York Convention*, 9 J. INT'L ARB. 51 (Dec. 1992).

[127] *See supra* para. 412.

[128] *See infra* paras. 1694 *et seq.*

[129] *See infra* paras. 1601 *et seq.*

[130] On this concept, see, for example, MICHAEL J. MUSTILL, STEWART C. BOYD, COMMERCIAL ARBITRATION 550 *et seq.* (2d ed. 1989).

[131] On the concept of "serious irregularity" see, for example, RUSSELL ON ARBITRATION 415 *et seq.* (D. Sutton, J. Kendall, J. Gill eds., 21st ed. 1997)

[132] *See, e.g.*, Claude Reymond, *L'Arbitration Act, 1996 – Convergence et originalité*, 1997 REV. ARB. 45, 64; Matthieu de Boisséson, *The Arbitration Act 1996 and the New ICC Arbitration Rules 1998: A Comparative Approach*, 1 INT'L ARB. L. REV. 68, 72 (1998); on the question of the appropriate extent of court control of arbitral awards, see, for example, I.N. Duncan Wallace, *Control by the Courts: A Plea for More, Not Less*, 6 ARB. INT'L 253 (1990), and the response of Pierre Mayer, *Seeking the Middle Ground of Court Control: A Reply to I.N. Duncan Wallace*, 7 ARB. INT'L 311 (1991). On the situation in the United States, see, for example, Jan Paulsson, *Means of Recourse Against Arbitral Awards Under U.S. Law*, 6 J. INT'L ARB. 101 (June 1989); GARY B. BORN, INTERNATIONAL COMMERCIAL ARBITRATION IN THE UNITED STATES 459 *et seq.* (1994). Barry H. Garfinkel and Rona G. Shamoon, *A Dangerous Expansion of "Manifest Disregard"*, ADR CURRENTS, Vol. 3, No. 4, Dec. 1998. For a comparative law analysis, see, for example, F. De Ly, *Judicial Review of the Substance of Arbitral Awards*, *in* COMPARABILITY AND EVALUATION – ESSAYS ON COMPARATIVE LAW, PRIVATE INTERNATIONAL LAW AND INTERNATIONAL COMMERCIAL ARBITRATION 341 *et seq.* (1994).

are somewhat outdated and a new model law on this fundamental issue would be welcome.[133]

At the other end of the spectrum, certain arbitration laws have now completely eliminated, in certain circumstances, any action to set aside at the seat of the arbitration. In Belgium, a law dated March 27, 1985 introduced a new Article 1717, paragraph 4 into the Judicial Code, providing that:

> the Belgian courts can only hear an action to set an award aside if at least one of the parties to the dispute decided by the arbitral award is either an individual having Belgian nationality or residence, or a legal entity constituted in Belgium or having a subsidiary or other establishment in Belgium.

This innovative provision, which was intended to promote arbitration in Belgium, had some success.[134] In particular, it may well be the case that this provision influenced the choice of Brussels as the seat of arbitration made in the Channel Tunnel contract between ten Anglo-French construction contractors and a pool of banks.[135]

The total suppression in Belgium of all recourse may also have discouraged arbitration users looking for a limited but effective review of arbitral awards. Thus, two years later, the Swiss legislature took the same approach, but made it optional. Article 192 of the 1987 Swiss Private International Law Statute introduced a provision stating that:

> [w]here none of the parties has its domicile, its habitual residence, or a business establishment in Switzerland, they may, by an express statement in the arbitration agreement or by a subsequent agreement in writing, exclude all setting aside proceedings, or they may also limit such proceedings to one or several of the grounds [on which an award can be set aside] listed in Article 190, paragraph 2.

Unlike the Belgian system introduced in 1985, Swiss law thus gave the parties the option to exclude recourse against an award. If they intend to do so, they must expressly provide for such an exclusion. The Swiss courts have rightly been strict when examining the parties' intentions to make such an exclusion. For example, they held that Article 24 of the previous ICC Rules (Art. 28(6) of the 1998 Rules), which provides that the parties are deemed to have "waived their right to any form of recourse insofar as such waiver can validly be made," does not in itself constitute an exclusion of actions to set aside the award under Article 192

---

[133] *See* Jan Paulsson, *Towards Minimum Standards of Enforcement: Feasibility of a Model law, in* ICCA CONGRESS SERIES NO. 9, IMPROVING THE EFFICIENCY OF ARBITRATION AGREEMENTS AND AWARDS: 40 YEARS OF APPLICATION OF THE NEW YORK CONVENTION 574 (A.J. van den Berg ed., 1999) and, for a French version, *L'exécution des sentences arbitrales dans le monde de demain*, 1998 REV. ARB. 637.

[134] *See* H. van Houtte, *La loi belge du 27 mars 1985 sur l'arbitrage international*, 1986 REV. ARB. 29; Jan Paulsson, *Arbitration unbound in Belgium*, 2 ARB. INT'L 68 (1986).

[135] *See supra* para. 1457.

of the Swiss Statute.[136] The same was held to be true with respect to the provision whereby an award is to be "final."[137]

The principle adopted in Switzerland was followed in the 1993 Tunisian Arbitration Code (Art. 78(6)). Then in 1998, the Belgian legislature decided to abandon its rather radical approach, and adopted instead the Swiss model. The Belgian law of May 19, 1998, thus replaced Article 1717, paragraph 4 of the Judicial Code with a provision whereby

> [t]he parties may, by an explicit declaration in the arbitration agreement or by a later agreement, exclude any application for the setting aside of an arbitral award, in case none of them is a physical person of Belgian nationality or a physical person having his normal residence in Belgium or a legal person having its main seat or a branch office in Belgium.[138]

In 1999, the same rule was adopted in Sweden. Section 51 of the new Swedish Arbitration Act, in force as of April 1, 1999, reads:

> [w]here none of the parties is domiciled or has its place of business in Sweden, such parties may in a commercial relationship through an express written agreement exclude or limit the application of the grounds for setting aside an award . . . .
> An award which is subject to such an agreement shall be recognized and enforced in Sweden in accordance with the rules applicable to a foreign award.

The adoption of this rule, which had long been contemplated,[139] is not surprising in light of the previous case law of the Swedish Supreme Court which refused to hear actions to set aside awards made in Sweden in cases which had no connection with Sweden other than the seat of the arbitration.[140]

Even if the approach found in Switzerland, Tunisia, Belgium and Sweden is somewhat isolated in comparative law, it is of considerable importance to the conception of the review of arbitral awards by the courts of the seat. The fact that parties can now choose to exclude all control at the seat of the arbitration substantially affects the philosophy underlying that control. Even where such control is exercised, because it has not been waived, it does not

---

[136] *See, e.g.,* Fed. Trib., Apr. 9, 1991, Clear Star Ltd. v. Centrala Morska Importowo-Eksportova "Centromor", 1991 REV. ARB. 709, and P.-Y. Tschanz' note; Fed. Trib., Dec. 19, 1990, Sonatrach v. K.C.A. Drilling Ltd., 6 INT'L ARB. REP. B9 (Apr. 1991). *See also* PIERRE LALIVE, JEAN-FRANÇOIS POUDRET, CLAUDE REYMOND, LE DROIT DE L'ARBITRAGE INTERNE ET INTERNATIONAL EN SUISSE 449 (1989).

[137] Fed. Trib., July 2, 1997, L. Ltd. v. The Foreign Trade Association of the Republic of U., 1997 BULL. ASA 494, 496.

[138] *See* Bernard Hanotiau and Guy Block, *La loi du 19 mai 1998 modifiant la legislation belge relative à l'arbitrage*, 1998 BULL. ASA 528.

[139] *See also* Sec. 52 of the 1994 draft and, for a commentary, THE DRAFT NEW SWEDISH ARBITRATION ACT – A PRESENTATION (1994).

[140] Supreme Court of Sweden, Apr. 18, 1989, *Solel Boneh, supra* note 120, and the commentary by Paulsson, *supra* note 120.

have the same significance. It is no longer the manifestation of a state's sovereign will to ensure that activities taking place on its territory comply with certain rules considered fundamental by that state. Those rules are no longer considered fundamental by Switzerland, Tunisia, Belgium and Sweden where the award is not liable to be enforced in those countries, as shown by the fact that the parties can agree to exclude review by the courts. When there is court review today, it sometimes exists only because the parties are presumed to have wanted some form of control over their award by the courts of the jurisdiction in which the arbitration took place. Rather than being imposed, review of awards by the courts in Switzerland, Tunisia, Belgium and Sweden has become a means of assisting the parties, in the same way as the courts assist the parties in constituting the arbitral tribunal. This philosophy is not in fact limited to Swiss, Tunisian, Belgian or Swedish law. It was also found in French case law prior to the 1981 reform: the courts refused to hear actions to set aside awards made in France but governed by a foreign procedural law.[141] This solution has been repealed by the 1981 reform, as a result of which actions to set awards aside cannot be excluded, even if the awards are not liable to be enforced in France. The rationale behind this approach is not so much, in our view, to give international effect to the views of the seat of the arbitration—after all, decisions made outside France setting aside awards are not recognized as such in France[142]—than to provide a limited review reflecting what is assumed to be the expectations of the parties. Thus, the philosophy of court review being intended to assist the parties is not limited to optional court review. However, optional court review is of course the most tangible manifestation of that philosophy. Against this background, it would not be surprising to see more arbitration statutes following the Swiss, Tunisian, Belgian and Swedish examples.

3° Consequences in France of a Foreign Judgment Setting Aside an Arbitral Award

1595. — Where an arbitral award has been set aside outside France, can it nevertheless be recognized and enforced in France, or should the French courts give effect to the judgment of the foreign court setting the award aside? This question gives rise to a conflict between the arbitral award and the foreign ruling setting it aside. In fact, the conflict is only really troublesome if the award has been set aside at the seat of the arbitration, as the courts of no other country will be recognized as having jurisdiction to set the award aside.[143] On this ground alone, the French courts would refuse to take into account a decision by a non-French court setting the award aside in a country other than that of the seat of the arbitration. On the other hand, there is no doubt that an award set aside by the courts at the seat of the arbitration no longer enjoys the benefit of the provisions of the 1958 New York

---

[141] CA Paris, Feb. 21, 1980, *Götaverken, supra* note 88; on this issue, see *supra* para. 141.

[142] *See infra* para. 1595.

[143] *See supra* para. 1589.

Convention.[144] Similarly, it is clear that, under the provisions of that Convention, an award in respect of which an action to set aside is pending at the seat of arbitration may be refused recognition and enforcement until a final decision has been made at the seat.[145] However, in the *Pabalk v. Norsolor* matter, the French courts held that the provisions of the New York Convention merely represent the minimum recognition of awards that the contracting States undertake to provide, and that they do not prevent the recognition and enforcement in France, under the ordinary rules of French arbitration law, of an award which has been set aside at the seat of the arbitration.[146] This approach is perfectly in keeping with Article VII of the New York Convention. However, the circumstances of the case did not provide the *Cour de cassation* with an opportunity to discuss the conditions of French law governing the recognition and enforcement of awards set aside at the seat. As the Austrian Supreme Court had reversed the decision setting aside the award at issue,[147] the French courts were not required to address the question. Nevertheless, some authors understood the decisions rendered in the *Norsolor* matter as allowing awards set aside at the seat to be recognized in France.[148] The *Cour de cassation* took an even clearer position in its 1993 *Polish Ocean Line* decision, where it held that a ruling by the courts of the seat of the arbitration suspending the enforceability of an award could not prevent enforcement of the award in France under the ordinary rules of French arbitration law.[149] This approach was then unequivocally confirmed by the *Cour de cassation* in its 1994 *Hilmarton* decision. It was held that the award, which had been set aside in Switzerland,

---

[144] *See* Art. V(1)(e) of the Convention.

[145] Art. VI of the Convention. On this issue, see *supra* paras. 267 *et seq.*

[146] Cass. 1e civ., Oct. 9, 1984, Pabalk Ticaret Sirketi v. Norsolor, 1985 REV. ARB. 431, and B. Goldman's note; 112 J.D.I. 679 (1985), and P. Kahn's note; 1985 REV. CRIT. DIP 551, 2d decision, and B. Dutoit's note; Dalloz, Jur. 101 (1985), and J. Robert's note; for an English translation, see 24 I.L.M. 360 (1985), with an introductory note by E. Gaillard; 2 J. INT'L ARB. 67 (June 1985), with comments by D. Thompson; XI Y.B. COM. ARB. 484 (1986); *see also* Jean Robert, *Retour sur l'arrêt Pabalk –Norsolor (Civ. 1re, 9 oct. 1984, D. 1985.101)*, Dalloz, Chron. 83 (1985).

[147] Supreme Court of Austria (*Oberster Gerichtshof*), Nov. 18, 1982, Norsolor v. Pabalk, 1983 REV. ARB. 519.

[148] *See* Berthold Goldman, *Une bataille judiciaire autour de la lex mercatoria – L'affaire Norsolor*, 1983 REV. ARB. 379, 385; Fouchard, *supra* note 7, ¶ 58 at 404.

[149] Cass. 1e civ., Mar. 10, 1993, Polish Ocean Line v. Jolasry, 1993 REV. ARB. 255, 2d decision, and D. Hascher's note; 120 J.D.I. 360 (1993), 1st decision, and P. Kahn's note; for an English translation, see XIX Y.B. COM. ARB. 662 (1994).

[was] an international award which [was] not integrated in the legal system of that State, so that it remains in existence even if set aside and its recognition in France [was] not contrary to international public policy.[150]

The recognition in the French legal order of an award set aside outside France obviously prevents the recognition or enforcement in France of a second award made after the setting aside of the first award at the seat of arbitration. The French *Cour de cassation* clarified this point in its June 10, 1997 decision in the *Hilmarton* matter.[151]

The only question left open by the *Hilmarton* decision is that of the scope of the principle that it establishes. Which awards are to be considered not incorporated into the legal order of the jurisdiction of the seat and are thus capable of being recognized under French law regardless of the fact that they have been set aside by the courts of the seat? The reference to the absence of incorporation of the award in any legal system appears to have borrowed from a French commentator, who justified the approach taken in the *Norsolor* case on the basis that the decision setting aside the award at the seat would not bind the courts of all other jurisdictions if it concerned "an international award, since such an award would not be incorporated in the legal order of the place it was made."[152] One can therefore conclude that only domestic awards set aside in their country of origin cannot be recognized in France on the basis of the *Hilmarton* decision. The Paris Court of Appeals followed this reasoning in its 1997 *Chromalloy* decision. It held an award made in Egypt to be an international award

---

[150] Cass. 1e civ., Mar. 23, 1994, Hilmarton v. OTV, 1994 Bull. Civ. I, No. 104; 1994 REV. ARB. 327, and C. Jarrosson's note; 121 J.D.I. 701 (1994), and E. Gaillard's note; 1994 RTD COM. 702, and observations by J.-C. Dubarry and E. Loquin; 1995 REV. CRIT. DIP 356, and B. Oppetit's note; for an English translation, see XX Y.B. COM. ARB. 663, ¶ 5 at 665 (1995); 9 INT'L ARB. REP. E1 (May 1994), *upholding* CA Paris, Dec. 19, 1991, 1993 REV. ARB. 300. *Comp.* CA Versailles, June 29, 1995 (2 decisions), OTV v. Hilmarton, 123 J.D.I. 120 (1996), and E. Gaillard's note; 1995 REV. ARB. 639, and C. Jarrosson's note; for an English translation, see XXI Y.B. COM. ARB. 524 (1996). On the award dated August 19, 1988 (ICC Case No. 5622) and the Swiss case law to which it gave rise, see *supra* para. 1523.

[151] Cass. 1e civ., June 10, 1997, OTV v. Hilmarton, 1997 REV. ARB. 376, and P. Fouchard's note; 124 J.D.I. 1033 (1997), and E. Gaillard's note; for an English translation, see XXII Y.B. COM. ARB. 696 (1997); 12 INT'L ARB. REP. I1 (July 1997), *overturning* CA Versailles, June 29, 1995, *supra* note 150. On this issue, generally, see Philippe Fouchard, *La portée internationale de l'annulation de la sentence arbitrale dans son pays d'origine*, 1997 REV. ARB. 329; Emmanuel Gaillard, *Enforcement of Awards Nullified in the Country of Origin: The French Experience, in* ICCA CONGRESS SERIES No. 9, IMPROVING THE EFFICIENCY OF ARBITRATION AGREEMENTS AND AWARDS: 40 YEARS OF APPLICATION OF THE NEW YORK CONVENTION 105 (A.J. van den Berg ed., 1999), and, for the French version, *L'exécution des sentences annulées dans leur pays d'origine*, 125 J.D.I. 645 (1998); Jan Paulsson, *Enforcing Arbitral Awards Notwithstanding a Local Standard Annulment (LSA)*, ICC BULLETIN, Vol. 9, No. 1, at 14 (1998). For a critical view, see Jean-François Poudret, *Quelle solution pour en finir avec l'affaire Hilmarton*, 1998 REV. ARB. 7; Sébastien Besson and Luc Pittet, *La reconnaissance à l'étranger d'une sentence annulée dans son Etat d'origine – Réflexions à la suite de l'affaire Hilmarton*, 1998 BULL. ASA 498; Dana H. Freyer and Hamid G. Gharavi, *Finality and Enforceability of Foreign Arbitral Awards: From "Double Exequatur" to the Enforcement of Annulled Awards: A Suggested Path to Uniformity Amidst Diversity*, 13 ICSID REV. – FOREIGN INV. L.J. 101 (1998); Richard W. Hulbert, *Further Observations on Chromalloy: A Contract Misconstrued, a Law Misapplied, and an Opportunity Foregone*, 13 ICSID REV. – FOREIGN INV. L.J. 124 (1998); Albert Jan van den Berg, *Enforcement of Annulled Awards?*, ICC BULLETIN, Vol. 9, No. 2, at 15 (1998).

[152] Goldman, *supra* note 148, at 391.

which, by definition, is not integrated in the legal order of that State so that its existence remains established despite its being annulled and its recognition in France is not in violation of international public policy.[153]

Conversely, the fact that the courts of the place of the seat of the arbitration have refused to set aside an award, the enforcement of which is sought in France, does not affect the extent of the review performed by the French courts for the purposes of recognition and enforcement of the award.[154]

The solution adopted by the French courts is reflected in United States jurisprudence. In a decision dated July 31, 1996, again in the *Chromalloy* matter, the District Court of the District of Columbia granted the enforcement of an award against the Arab Republic of Egypt which had been set aside at the seat of the arbitration by the Egyptian courts.[155]

§ 3. – Exclusivity of Recourse Against Arbitral Awards

1596. — In its attempt to simplify proceedings arising in connection with awards made outside France and in international awards made in France, in 1981 the French legislature sought to exclude all recourse except that relating to recognition and enforcement,[156] and

---

[153] CA Paris, Jan. 14, 1997, République arabe d'Egypte v. Chromalloy Aero Services, 1997 REV. ARB. 395, and P. Fouchard's note; 125 J.D.I. 750 (1998), and E. Gaillard's note; for an English translation, see XXII Y.B. COM. ARB. 691, 693 (1997). For the Egyptian decision to set aside, see CA Cairo, Dec. 5, 1995, 1998 REV. ARB. 723, and P. Leboulanger's note.

[154] CA Paris, Feb. 12, 1993, Unichips Finanziara v. Gesnouin, 1993 REV. ARB. 255, 3d decision, and D. Hascher's note; 1993 RTD. COM. 646, and observations by J.-C. Dubarry and E. Loquin; 1993 BULL. ASA 564; for an English translation, see XIX Y.B. COM. ARB. 658 (1994); *see also* Bruno Leurent, *Reflections on the International Effectiveness of Arbitration Awards*, 12 ARB. INT'L 269 (1996), and, for a French version, *Réflexions sur l'efficacité internationale des sentences arbitrales*, *in* TRAVAUX DU COMITÉ FRANÇAIS DE DROIT INTERNATIONAL PRIVÉ 1993–1995, at 181 (1996); Bruno Leurent and Nathalie Meyer Fabre, *La reconnaissance en France des sentences rendues à l'étranger, l'exemple franco-suisse*, 1995 BULL. ASA 118. But see, in the United States, Seetransport Wiking Trader Schiffahrtsgesellschaft MBH & Co. v. Navimpex Centrala Navala, which accepted the decision of the Paris Court of Appeals to uphold an arbitral award (29 F.3d 79 (2d Cir. 1994); 9 INT'L ARB. REP. 10 (July 1994)).

[155] *In re* Arbitration of Certain Controversies between Chromalloy Aeroservices v. the Arab Republic of Egypt, 939 F. Supp. 907 (D.D.C. 1996); 11 INT'L ARB. REP. C64 (Aug. 1996); XXII Y.B. COM. ARB. 1001 (1997); 35 I.L.M. 1359 (1996); for a French translation, see 1997 REV. ARB. 439, and the commentary by Fouchard, *supra* note 151. *See also* David W. Rivkin, *The Enforcement of Awards Nullified in the Country of Origin: The American Experience*, *in* ICCA CONGRESS SERIES No. 9, IMPROVING THE EFFICIENCY OF ARBITRATION AGREEMENTS AND AWARDS: 40 YEARS OF APPLICATION OF THE NEW YORK CONVENTION 528 (A.J. van den Berg ed., 1999), and the references cited therein. See, for the recognition in Austria, on the basis of Article IX of the 1961 European Convention, of an award set aside in Slovenia, Supreme Court of Austria (*Oberster Gerichtshof*), Oct. 20, 1993, Radenska v. Kajo; for an English translation, XX Y.B. COM. ARB. 1051 (1995); for a French translation, see 1998 REV. ARB. 419, and P. Lastenouse and P. Senkovic's note; 125 J.D.I. 1003 (1998).

[156] *See supra* paras. 1581 *et seq.*

actions to set aside the award.[157] Thus, none of an appeal, *stricto sensu*, against an award (A), a third party action (B), an action to revise the award in cases of fraud (C), or an action to declare the award non-binding on a specific party (D) will be admissible.[158]

The parties cannot agree on other arrangements in their contracts, as the organization of recourse available under French law is traditionally considered to be a matter of public policy.[159]

A. – NO APPEAL

1597. — The inadmissibility of appeals against arbitral awards—which would allow the Court of Appeals to re-examine the merits of the dispute—is easy to justify in international arbitration, even in cases where the parties have not expressly provided for it.[160] It would be meaningless to recognize the effectiveness of arbitration agreements if, in the absence of an agreement to the contrary, the final outcome of the dispute were necessarily to be determined by the courts. The requirement, in French domestic arbitration[161] (Art. 1482 of the New Code of Civil Procedure), for an express waiver by the parties to ensure that the courts cannot review the merits is unfortunate. It would have been totally archaic in international arbitration. Importantly, the exclusion of all forms of appeal in international arbitration applies even where the parties have chosen French law to govern the arbitral procedure.[162]

On the question of whether parties can agree that an award will be appealable before the courts, it has been held that as the organization of recourse is of a mandatory nature, such provisions are void.[163] This solution raises a further issue: what will be the effect on the arbitration agreement itself? The Paris Court of Appeals has taken a radical position in

---

[157] *See supra* paras. 1586 *et seq.*

[158] See also, on the inadmissibility of an application to annul the contract containing the arbitration agreement, TGI Paris, Nov. 20, 1996, République du Congo v. Qwinzy, No. 21 749/95, unpublished.

[159] Cass. 1e civ., Apr. 6, 1994, Buzzichelli Holding v. Hennion, 1995 REV. ARB. 263, and P. Level's note; CA Paris, Dec. 12, 1989, Binaate Maghreb v. Sereg Routes, 1990 REV. ARB. 863, and P. Level's note; CA Paris, Oct. 27, 1994, de Diseno v. Mendes, 1995 REV. ARB. 263, 2d decision, and P. Level's note. But see, in the United States, Lapine Tech. Corp. v. Kyocera Corp., 130 F.3d 884 (9th Cir. 1997), *reversing* 909 F. Supp. 697 (N.D. Cal. 1995); Eric Schwartz, *Choosing Between Broad Clauses and Detailed Blueprints, in* ICCA CONGRESS SERIES No. 9, IMPROVING THE EFFICIENCY OF ARBITRATION AGREEMENTS AND AWARDS: 40 YEARS OF APPLICATION OF THE NEW YORK CONVENTION 105 (A.J. van den Berg ed., 1999); Abby Cohen Smutny, *Judicial Review of Arbitral Awards: Comment on the Ninth Circuit Decision in Lapine Technology Corp. v. Kyocera Corp.*, 13 INT'L ARB. REP. 18 (Feb. 1998); James B. Hamlin, *Defining the Scope of Judicial Review by Agreement of the Parties, id.* at 25; Nancy B. Turck, *Lapine Technology Corporation v. Kyocera Corporation*, 1 INT'L ARB. L. REV. 127 (1998); Hans Smit, *Contractual Modification of the Scope of Judicial Review of Arbitral Awards*, 8 AM. REV. INT'L ARB. 147 (1997).

[160] *See* CA Paris, 1e Ch., Sec. C, Dec. 1, 1995, Orkem v. ABS Holding Ltd., No. 95.17178, unpublished; CA Paris, Dec. 3, 1998, *Interpipe, supra* note 106.

[161] For an unsatisfactory interpretation of this provision, according to which the word "final" does not mean "without any recourse," see Cass. 2e civ., July 1, 1992, Perma v. Entreprise Maxime, 1995 REV. ARB. 63, and C. Jarrosson's disapproving note.

[162] *See* Jeantet, *supra* note 21, at 514.

[163] *See supra* para. 1596.

certain decisions, considering that the nullity of clauses providing for rights of appeal invalidates the entire arbitration agreement on the grounds that the possibility of an appeal was a decisive factor in the parties' decision to submit their disputes to arbitration.[164] However, in other decisions the same court salvaged the arbitration agreement through interpretation.[165] For example, it held in one case that a clause stipulating that "the forthcoming award shall be capable of recourse before the Paris Court of Appeals" did not express a clear intention on the part of the parties to have the award reviewed on the merits, and that such clause therefore did not constitute a factor which determined the parties' consent to enter into the arbitration agreement.[166] The clause was validated in that case because of the ambiguity as to the nature of the appeal: it was unclear whether the parties intended there to be a review of the merits of the award, or simply included a superfluous reminder of the possibility of an action to set any award aside. However, the formulation used by the parties in the *Diseno* case ("nevertheless, the parties reserve the right to appeal the award before the Court of Appeals") did not leave any scope for such clemency from the Court.[167]

The contrary position has been taken in other legal systems. For example, Article 1703 of the Belgian Judicial Code, introduced by the law of May 19, 1998, now provides that there can be no appeal against an award unless the parties have so agreed. In the United States, the courts adopted a similar approach in the *Lapine Technology* case.[168]

B. – No Third Party Action

1598. — Third party actions against international arbitral awards are also inadmissible. This form of recourse would lead the courts, upon request by third parties, to review the merits of the dispute. That would be directly contrary both to the intention of the parties to have their disputes resolved by arbitration and to the recognition of the legitimacy of choosing arbitration as a private dispute resolution method, particularly in international cases. In any event, the privity of the arbitration agreement and of the *res judicata* effect of the arbitrators' decision suffices to protect third parties from any negative impact which they consider the award might have on them.[169]

---

[164] CA Paris, Dec. 12, 1989, *Binaate Maghreb, supra* note 159; CA Paris, Oct. 27, 1994, *de Diseno, supra* note 159.

[165] On the interpretation of pathological arbitration agreements, see *supra* paras. 484 *et seq.*

[166] CA Paris, May 23, 1991, Thomson CSF v. Baudin Chateauneuf, 1991 REV. ARB. 661, and observations by J. Pellerin.

[167] CA Paris, Oct. 27, 1994, *de Diseno, supra* note 159.

[168] *See supra* note 159.

[169] *See* Bellet and Mezger, *supra* note 5, at 654.

C. – No Action to Revise the Award for Fraud

1599. — The inadmissibility of an action in revision for fraud—a form of recourse which was available against awards made in France prior to the 1981 reform[170]— has proved to be more controversial. Actions in revision were allowed before the reform in the event that, after the award had been made, fraud, falsification of documents or the concealment of decisive evidence came to light. Some commentators considered that such cases were very rare and that even then the parties had other means of obtaining redress, "if only on the basis of due process or public policy."[171] The majority view, however, was one of regret that the possibility of bringing an action in revision for fraud was removed by the 1981 Decree. Such actions were considered to be particularly useful where the deadline for bringing an action to set aside the award had expired prior to the discovery of the fraud or falsification.[172]

In its decision in the *Fougerolle v. Procofrance* case, the *Cour de cassation* relaxed the rule prohibiting actions in revision. Although it rejected the claim in that case, it held that:

> [a]s a consequence of the general principles of law relating to fraud—notwithstanding the revision of review by Article 1507 of the New Code of Civil Procedure—the revision of an award made in France concerning international arbitration is, by way of exception, to be admitted in the case of fraud, as long as the arbitral tribunal remains constituted after the making of the award (or can be reconstituted).[173]

In other words, the *Cour de cassation* did not introduce a new form of action against the award before the courts, but enabled the arbitrators themselves—at least where the arbitral tribunal could be reconvened—to take into account circumstances of which they were unaware as a result of fraud.[174] A question remains as to how redress can be obtained in respect of fraud where the arbitral tribunal can no longer be reconvened. Certain commentators have called for the introduction of recourse to the courts in that case.[175]

Without allowing any new forms of recourse, the courts have also relied on the concept of public policy within the meaning of Article 1502 5° of the New Code of Civil Procedure. They consider that the existence of tactics aimed at deceiving the arbitrators will, if they

---

[170] *See, e.g.,* JACQUELINE RUBELLIN-DEVICHI, L'ARBITRAGE – NATURE JURIDIQUE – DROIT INTERNE ET DROIT INTERNATIONAL PRIVÉ ¶ 421 (1965); Fouchard, *supra* note 7, ¶ 78 at 413.

[171] Fouchard, *supra* note 7, ¶ 77 at 413.

[172] *See* Bellet and Mezger, *supra* note 5, at 654; Mayer, *supra* note 5, at 89; Camille Bernard, observations made at the January 27, 1992 Colloquium organized by the Comité français de l'arbitrage on *Perspectives d'évolution du droit français de l'arbitrage,* 1992 REV. ARB. 351; Eric Loquin, *Perspectives pour une réforme des voies de recours,* 1992 REV. ARB. 321, 332–33.

[173] Cass. 1e civ., May 25, 1992, Fougerolle v. Procofrance, 119 J.D.I. 974 (1992), and E. Loquin's note; 1992 REV. CRIT. DIP 699, and B. Oppetit's note; 1993 REV. ARB. 91, and the commentary by Matthieu de Boisséson, *L'arbitrage et la fraude (à propos de l'arrêt Fougerolle, rendu par la Cour de cassation le 25 mai 1992), id.* at 3; for an English translation, see XIX Y.B. COM. ARB. 205, 206 (1994).

[174] *See supra* para. 418.

[175] See especially Loquin, note following Cass. 1e civ., May 25, 1992, *Fougerolle, supra* note 174.

prove to be effective, lead the enforcement of an award delivered under those circumstances to be contrary to international public policy. That was the position taken by the Paris Court of Appeals in a 1993 decision in the *European Gas Turbines* case, where documents produced after the award revealed that the detailed statement of expenses submitted to the arbitrators, on the basis of which the award had been made, was entirely fictitious.[176] This was also the position taken by the same court in 1998 in the *Thomson C.S.F.* matter.[177]

A similar debate has arisen in other countries. A number of recent statutes allow an action in revision in international arbitration,[178] while other laws exclude it. The UNCITRAL Model Law, for example, does not treat fraud, corruption or falsification as separate grounds on which an award can be set aside, the idea being that the possibility of setting the award aside for a breach of international public policy is sufficient to cover the majority of such cases.[179] The same approach is adopted in the 1987 Swiss Private International Law Statute and in Italian law following the 1994 reform.[180] However, a number of commentators considered the omission in Swiss law to be involuntary and take the view that the courts can address the situation in the absence of a statutory provision.[181] The Swiss Federal Tribunal did so in a 1992 decision, taking a position similar to that of the French *Cour de cassation*, although the Federal Tribunal held that it had jurisdiction to hear an action in revision which, if successful, would lead the Federal Tribunal to remit the case to the arbitrators for a decision on the merits.[182]

---

[176] CA Paris, Sept. 30, 1993, European Gas Turbines SA v. Westman International Ltd., 1994 REV. ARB. 359, and D. Bureau's note; 1994 REV. CRIT. DIP 349, and V. Heuzé's note; 1994 RTD COM. 703, and observations by J.-C. Dubarry and E. Loquin; 1994 BULL. ASA 105, and the commentary by Adel Nassar, *Ordre public international et arbitrage? Y a-t-il eu une évolution?*, *id.* at 110; for an English translation, see XX Y.B. COM. ARB. 198 (1995); 8 INT'L ARB. REP. B1 (Nov. 1995), *upheld by* Cass. 1e civ., Dec. 19, 1995, 1996 REV. ARB. 49, and D. Bureau's note; 1996 RTD COM. 667, and observations by J.-C. Dubarry and E. Loquin. *See also* CA Paris, Jan. 21, 1997, Nu Swift PLC v. White Knight, 1997 REV. ARB. 429, and observations by Y. Derains; CA Paris, June 17, 1997, Eiffage v. Butec, 1997 REV. ARB. 583, and observations by D. Bureau; CA Paris, 1e Ch., Sec. C, Feb. 27, 1997, Banque Franco-Tunisienne v. Arab Business Consortium Finance and Investment Company (ABCI), No. 94/14769, unpublished, where the court reviewed the allegation of fraud under Article 1502 5° before finding the allegation to be unsubstantiated.

[177] CA Paris, 1e Ch., Sec. C, Sept. 10, 1998, Thomson C.S.F. v. Brunner, No. 96/88554, unpublished.

[178] *See, e.g.*, Art. 1068 of the Netherlands Code of Civil Procedure. See also, in ICSID arbitration, Art. 51(1) of the Washington Convention.

[179] *See* HOLTZMANN AND NEUHAUS, *supra* note 119, at 912; ARON BROCHES, COMMENTARY ON THE UNCITRAL MODEL LAW ON INTERNATIONAL COMMERCIAL ARBITRATION 191 *et seq.* (1990).

[180] Article 838 of the Code of Civil Procedure excludes the application of Article 831 regarding actions in revision and third-party opposition, unless the parties agree otherwise. *See* Piero Bernardini, *L'arbitrage en Italie après la récente réforme*, 1994 REV. ARB. 479; Piero Bernardini, *Italy*, *in* ICCA INTERNATIONAL HANDBOOK ON COMMERCIAL ARBITRATION (forthcoming in 1999).

[181] *See, e.g.*, LALIVE, POUDRET, REYMOND, *supra* note 136, at 443–44; ANDREAS BUCHER, PIERRE-YVES TSCHANZ, INTERNATIONAL ARBITRATION IN SWITZERLAND ¶ 324 (1988).

[182] Fed. Trib., Mar. 11, 1992, P. v. S. Ltd., 1993 REV. ARB. 115, and P.-Y. Tschanz' note; Fed. Trib., July 2, 1997, L Ltd., *supra* note 137; Fed. Trib., July 9, 1997, N. Aluminium Plant v. E. and S., 1997 BULL. ASA 506.

D. – NO ACTION TO HAVE THE AWARD DECLARED NON-BINDING

1600. — The New Code of Civil Procedure also rules out the possibility of bringing an action before the French courts to have an award made outside France declared non-binding ("*inopposable*"). In the case of an award made in France, if the losing party considers that the award is invalid on one of the five grounds listed in Article 1502,[183] it can immediately bring an action before the French courts to set the award aside.[184] However, if the award is made outside France, the losing party can only bring an action in France against a decision of the French courts granting recognition or enforcement.[185] Thus, if the party defeated in the arbitration owns attachable assets in France, it will be in the uncomfortable position of having to wait until the successful party attempts to enforce the award before bringing its claims against the award to court. For that reason, certain commentators consider that it would be appropriate to allow an action to declare the award non-binding,[186] just as the French courts have done for foreign court judgments.[187] Other commentators are more conservative on this point,[188] and the courts tend to be opposed to the idea.[189] One of the major disadvantages of the introduction by the courts of an action to declare awards non-binding is that it would be liable to interfere with the statutory organization of recourse. In the absence of a statutory provision, the courts could not empower the first instance courts to perform only a summary review and limit any appeal against a decision declaring the award to be binding or not to the five grounds of review of non-French awards listed in Article 1502 of the New Code of Civil Procedure.[190] It has been suggested that the losing party could circumvent the problem by itself applying for enforcement of the award, in order to be able to bring an immediate appeal against the enforcement order before the Court of Appeals.[191] However, the difficulty with that approach is that the party requesting enforcement would have no standing to appeal against the order granting its own request.[192] In an appeal filed by a party against an enforcement order which the appealing party had

---

[183] *See infra* paras. 1601 *et seq.*

[184] *See supra* paras. 1587 *et seq.*

[185] *See supra* paras. 1583 *et seq.*

[186] *See* Bellet and Mezger, *supra* note 5, at 651–52; G. Flécheux, note following CA Paris, Feb. 18, 1986, *Aïta*, *supra* note 100, at 587.

[187] *See, e.g.,* Cass. civ., Jan. 22, 1951, Russel v. Weiller, 1951 Bull. Civ. I, No. 21; 1951 REV. CRIT. DIP 167, and P. Francescakis' note; JCP, Ed. G., Pt. II, No. 6151 (1951), and Sarraute and Tager's note.

[188] Fouchard, *supra* note 7, ¶ 71 at 409. *See* the discussion of the issue by Loquin *supra* note 172, at 328 *et seq.*

[189] TGI Paris, Nov. 22, 1989, *Acteurs Auteurs Associés*, *supra* note 28. See, before the 1981 French reform, CA Toulouse, Jan. 29, 1957, Henri de Boussac v. Alfred G. Toepfer, 1957 REV. CRIT. DIP 699, and E. Mezger's note.

[190] *See* A.-D. Bousquet, note following CA Paris, Nov. 10, 1987, F.L. Smidth et Co. v. S.A. Sybetra, 1989 REV. ARB. 669, 682.

[191] Fouchard, *supra* note 7, ¶ 71 at 409.

[192] Mayer, *supra* note 5, at 92.

itself applied for, the Paris Court of Appeals held the appeal to be inadmissible for want of standing within the meaning of Article 546 of the New Code of Civil Procedure.[193]

SECTION II
THE EXTENT OF THE REVIEW BY THE COURTS

1601. — The extent of the review by the courts required under French law before an award is incorporated into the French legal order is the same whether the award was made outside France (Art. 1502 of the New Code of Civil Procedure) or in France in an international arbitration (Art. 1504 of the New Code of Civil Procedure). In both cases, the substantive review is performed by the Court of Appeals on the same grounds. The Court can refuse to recognize awards made outside France and it can set aside awards made in France in international arbitrations.[194]

Although on the whole it is based on the same philosophy, this system of court control is less restrictive than that which the courts of a host state are entitled to exercise under the 1958 New York Convention.[195] It is therefore in the interest of the beneficiary of an award made outside France to rely on the ordinary rules of French law rather than on the New York Convention when seeking enforcement of its award in France.[196] It is true that the French courts have recently emphasized the convergence of the New York Convention and the New Code of Civil Procedure, at least as regards the review of compliance with due process and with the international public policy of the jurisdiction in which the award is to be enforced.[197] The UNCITRAL Model Law's grounds for refusing recognition or enforcement are, however, identical to the rather outdated grounds set forth in Article V of the New York Convention.[198]

1602. — An analysis of all decisions of the Paris Court of Appeals between 1981 and 1990 shows that during that period eighty-eight awards made in international arbitration were reviewed by the Court of Appeals, and only fifteen were set aside or refused enforcement.[199]

---

[193] CA Paris, Nov. 10, 1987, F.L. Smidth et Co. v. S.A. Sybetra, 1989 REV. ARB. 669, and A.-D. Bousquet's note.

[194] On the summary review performed at first instance by the enforcement judge, see *supra* paras. 1575 *et seq.*

[195] See *infra* paras. 1694 *et seq.*

[196] On an example of the difficulties liable to arise from the reverse position, see *supra* para. 495.

[197] Cass. 1e civ., Mar. 24, 1998, Excelsior Film TV v. UGC-PH, Dalloz, IR 105 (1998); JCP, Ed. G., Pt. IV, No. 2128 (1998); 126 J.D.I. 155 (1999), and A.-E. Kahn's note; CA Paris, 1e Ch., Sec. C, Apr. 2, 1998, Compagnie Française d'Etudes et de Construction TECHNIP v. Entreprise Nationale des Engrais et des Produits Phytosanitaires dite ASMIDAL (Algérie), No. 97/6929, unpublished.

[198] Article 36 and, transposed into German law, Article 1059 of the ZPO, in force as of January 1, 1998.

[199] Sophie Crépin, *Le contrôle des sentences arbitrales par la Cour d'appel de Paris depuis les réformes de 1980 et de 1981*, 1991 REV. ARB. 521. *See also* SOPHIE CRÉPIN, LES SENTENCES ARBITRALES DEVANT LE JUGE FRANÇAIS – PRATIQUE DE L'EXÉCUTION ET DU CONTRÔLE JUDICIAIRE DEPUIS LES RÉFORMES DE 1980–1981,

(continued...)

1603. — The grounds listed in Article 1502 of the New Code of Civil Procedure for setting aside an award or refusing enforcement include the absence, nullity or expiration of the arbitration agreement, the irregular appointment of the arbitral tribunal, the incompatibility of decisions by the arbitrators with the terms of their brief, the failure to comply with the requirements of due process, and situations where recognition or enforcement of the award would be contrary to international public policy.

This list is exhaustive. Any alleged basis for review not listed in Article 1502 is inadmissible. This has been clearly confirmed by the courts. For example, the *Cour de cassation* held in a 1987 decision that "the role of the Court of Appeals, seized by virtue of Articles 1502 and 1504 of the New Code of Civil Procedure, is limited to the examination of the grounds listed in these provisions."[200] Clearly, therefore, in the context of an action to set aside an award or to obtain its enforcement, the Court of Appeals cannot review the merits of the dispute.[201] Errors of judgment, whether of fact or of law, are not in themselves grounds on which the award can be set aside or refused enforcement.[202] The same is true where the arbitral tribunal has distorted the meaning of documentary evidence.[203] Arguments

---

[199] (...continued)
at 156 (1995).

[200] Cass. 1e civ., Jan. 6, 1987, Southern Pacific Properties Ltd. v. République Arabe d'Egypte, 114 J.D.I. 638 (1987), and B. Goldman's note; 1987 REV. ARB. 469, and P. Leboulanger's note; 1988 RTD CIV. 126, and J. Mestre's note; for an English translation, see 26 I.L.M. 1004, 1006 (1987); XIII Y.B. COM. ARB. 152 (1988); 2 INT'L ARB. REP. 17 (Jan. 1987); *see also* CA Paris, Jan. 22, 1988, C.F.I.D. v. Ets. A. Arnaud, 1989 REV. ARB. 251, and Y. Derains' note; CA Paris, Dec. 17, 1991, Gatoil v. National Iranian Oil Company, which rejects a claim based on Article 1506 of the New Code of Civil Procedure (1993 REV. ARB. 281, and H. Synvet's note; for an English translation, see 7 INT'L ARB. REP. B1 (July 1992)).

[201] Cass. 1e civ., Feb. 23, 1994, André v. Multitrade, which approves the dismissal of an action to set aside which, while alleging breaches of international public policy, "seeks, in reality, to have the substance of the award revised, which is prohibited in international arbitration, the [losing party] considering, according to its own pleadings, the award to be wrong at law, contradictory, unfair, and thus contrary to international public policy" (1994 REV. ARB. 83, and the commentary by Pierre Mayer, *La sentence contraire à l'ordre public au fond, id.* at 615). See also, in Swiss law, Fed. Trib., Nov. 14, 1991, Main contractor v. Subcontractor, XVII Y.B. COM. ARB. 279, ¶ 10 at 284 (1992).

[202] CA Paris, May 20, 1994, SNC Danton Défense v. S.A. Cotelle, Bella et Delpha, 1994 REV. ARB. 397; *see also* Cass. 1e civ., Feb. 28, 1995, Société Générale pour l'Industrie v. Ewbank, 1995 REV. ARB. 597, and D. Bureau's note; 1996 RTD COM. 446, and observations by J.-C. Dubarry and E. Loquin; CA Paris, Mar. 5, 1998, Forasol v. CISTM, 1999 REV. ARB. 86, and E. Gaillard's note.

[203] See, before the May 12, 1981 Decree, Cass. 2e civ., Nov. 17, 1976, Dieffenbacher v. O.C.P., 1976 Bull. Civ. II, No. 306; Dalloz, Jur. 577 (1977), and J. Boré's note; 1977 REV. ARB. 281, and J. Robert's note; Cass. 2e civ., Apr. 28, 1980, Inex Film v. Universal Pictures, 1980 Bull. Civ. II, No. 88, at 64; Cass. 1e civ., Dec. 11, 1979, Elettronica v. Thomson-C.S.F., 1979 Bull. Civ. I, No. 313, at 255; Cass. 1e civ., Mar. 10, 1981, Arkhbaieff v. Entreprise roumaine d'Etat pour le commerce extérieur Arpimex, 1981 Bull. Civ. I, No. 82, at 69. See also, under the regime of the 1981 Decree, CA Paris, Mar. 12, 1985, Intrafor Cofor v. Gagnant, 1985 REV. ARB. 299, and the commentary by Eric Loquin, *Pouvoirs et devoirs de l'amiable compositeur. A propos de trois arrêts de la Cour d'appel de Paris, id.* at 199; Dalloz, IR 467 (1985), and observations by P. Julien; CA Paris, Nov. 5, 1985, Somax Inc. v. China Union Lines Ltd., 1987 REV. ARB. 81, and B. Moreau's note; CA Paris, Apr. 12, 1991, Fougerolle v. Butec Engineering, 1991 REV. ARB. 667, and observations by J. Pellerin, *aff'd*, Cass. 1e civ., Dec. 20, 1993, 1994 REV. ARB. 126, and P. Bellet's note; CA Paris, May 20, 1994, *SNC Danton Défense, supra* note 202. On this issue, generally, see Jean Robert, *La dénaturation par l'arbitre – Réalités et perspectives*, 1982 REV. ARB. 405.

based on the alleged distortion of the meaning of documentary evidence have sometimes been held to be so clearly inadmissible that the courts have awarded damages for wrongful suit against the party bringing the action.[204] Similarly, the allegation by a party that the arbitrators have distorted the meaning of its arguments "does not constitute one of the grounds on which an action can be brought to set aside an award under Article 1502 of the New Code of Civil Procedure."[205]

1604. — The first four grounds listed in Article 1502 are identical to those which apply in French domestic arbitration.[206] The fifth ground adapts the limited review of compliance with public policy so that awards made outside France or in international arbitration in France must comply with "international public policy."[207] However, the ground for setting aside or refusing enforcement of a domestic award based on non-compliance with various requirements of form does not apply in international arbitration.[208]

The difference in the extent of the review of awards is one of the most important aspects of the distinction between French domestic arbitration and international arbitration.[209] This is especially so as the statutory system organizing recourse against arbitral awards is mandatory,[210] and the parties therefore cannot agree to alter the applicable regime so as to have an international award governed by the regime found in Article 1484 of the New Code of Civil Procedure, for example.[211]

1605. — In hearing claims against an award in an action to set aside or an appeal against an enforcement order, should the competent court examine the factual and legal circumstances relating to the claims in question, or should it instead accept the various findings of fact made in the award submitted to it for review?

---

[204] CA Paris, Nov. 5, 1985, *Somax, supra* note 203.

[205] CA Paris, June 10, 1993, Compagnie Aeroflot v. AGF, 1995 REV. ARB. 448, 3d decision. But see Cass. 1e civ., June 29, 1994, which reversed a decision whereby the Court of Appeals had refused to exercise any control over an award despite the fact that it was hearing a claim based on the breach of international public policy (*Caisse régionale d'assurances, supra* note 28).

[206] *See* Art. 1484 of the New Code of Civil Procedure. This explains why an action to set aside an international award founded on Article 1484 1° was held admissible despite the fact that the applicant referred to the wrong provision for setting the award aside (CA Paris, June 15, 1989, Granomar v. Compagnie Interagra, 1992 REV. ARB. 80, and J.-J. Arnaldez' note). The court reviewing the award will generally rectify any such errors; *see* CA Paris, Nov. 14, 1996, Gefimex v. Transgrain, 1997 REV. ARB. 434, and observations by Y. Derains.

[207] On the controversy resulting from this restriction, see *infra* para. 1647. When the action is brought on the basis of Article 1484 but concerns international arbitration, the courts will hold it to be admissible "but have to understand it within the meaning of Article 1502 5° of the New Code of Civil Procedure" (CA Paris, Jan. 24, 1991, Salice v. Haas, 1992 REV. ARB. 158, and observations by D. Cohen).

[208] *See supra* para. 1406.

[209] *See supra* paras. 78 *et seq.*

[210] *See supra* para. 1596.

[211] Cass. 1e civ., Apr. 6, 1994, *Buzzichelli, supra* note 159. But see Article 176, paragraph 2 of the Swiss Private International Law Statute which allows the parties to agree to apply cantonal procedure, even in international arbitration. For the situation in the United States, see *supra* note 159.

The nature of the review performed by the courts implies that they should be entirely free to examine the circumstances of the case, both legal and factual. That is the necessary corollary of the liberalism of the courts as regards the arbitrability of the dispute in particular.[212] It therefore would seem appropriate for the trust placed by the courts in the arbitrators as a matter of principle to be accompanied by a subsequent review of the award which prevents the arbitrators from avoiding censure by the courts through careful reasoning based on the facts alone.

However, not all legal systems resolve this question in the same way. Some, such as French law, do allow the courts to consider both fact and law in carrying out their review.

Thus, in its 1987 decision in the *Southern Pacific Properties* case, the *Cour de cassation* held that:

> if the role of the Court of Appeals, seized by virtue of Articles 1502 and 1504 of the New Code of Civil Procedure, is limited to the examination of the grounds listed in these provisions, there is no restriction upon the power of the court to examine as a matter of law and in consideration of the circumstances of the case, elements pertinent to the grounds in question.[213]

The *Cour de cassation* has applied this principle in connection with Article 1502 1°, noting that:

> in particular, it is for the court to construe the contract in order to determine itself whether the arbitrator ruled in the absence of an arbitration clause.[214]

In its 1990 decision in the *Gas del Estado* case, the *Cour de cassation* applied that rule to Article 1502 2°, which concerns the constitution of the arbitral tribunal. The Court pointed out that:

> the Court of Appeals hearing the action under Article 1502 of the New Code of Civil Procedure is entitled to interpret the agreement and the arbitration rules referred to, in order to reach its own assessment of whether the arbitral tribunal was regularly constituted.

---

[212] *See supra* paras. 532 *et seq.*

[213] Cass. 1e civ., Jan. 6, 1987, *supra* note 200, 26 I.L.M. 1006 (1987).

[214] *Id. See also* CA Paris, June 16, 1988, Swiss Oil v. Petrogab, 1989 REV. ARB. 309, and C. Jarrosson's note; for an English translation, see XVI Y.B. COM. ARB. 133 (1991); CA Paris, Oct. 26, 1995, SNCFT v. Voith, 1997 REV. ARB. 553, and the commentary by Daniel Cohen, *Arbitrage et groupes de contrats, id.* at 471. On the control exercised over the Court of Appeals by the *Cour de cassation* in this area, see Cass. 1e civ., Mar. 8, 1988, Sofidif v. O.I.A.E.T.I., 1988 Bull. Civ. I, No. 64; 1989 REV. ARB. 481, and C. Jarrosson's note, and CA Paris, Dec. 19, 1986, O.I.A.E.T.I. v. SOFIDIF, 1987 REV. ARB. 359, and the commentary by Emmanuel Gaillard, *L'affaire SOFIDIF ou les difficultés de l'arbitrage multipartite (à propos de l'arrêt rendu par la Cour d'appel de Paris le 19 décembre 1986), id.* at 275.

Applying that principle, the Court upheld a decision in which the Court of Appeals, exercising its discretion, had properly interpreted the clauses of a contract whereby the parties had decided that they would each choose their own arbitrator and that, in the event of any difficulty, they would apply for assistance to the Argentine courts and not, as was wrongly held in the disputed arbitral award, to the ICC Court of Arbitration.[215]

The solution is substantially the same in the United States. There, the existence of an arbitration agreement (which the courts characterize—wrongly, in our view—as a question of "arbitrability")[216] is the subject of an independent review by the courts, except where the parties unequivocally agree that the question is to be resolved by the arbitrators.[217]

Swiss law resolves the question differently, providing as a matter of principle that the legislature's intention to limit the possible grounds of recourse against an award

> would be seriously compromised if the Federal Tribunal's full power to examine claims [which are liable to lead to the setting aside of the award] were to interpreted as entitling it freely to review the findings of fact made by the arbitral tribunal in the same way as an appeal court.

However, that principle has been qualified by the Federal Tribunal in two ways. First, when ruling on the jurisdiction of the arbitral tribunal,

> [the Federal Tribunal] is free to examine certain preliminary issues of substantive law, but only in so far as they need to be resolved in order to rule on the jurisdiction or lack of jurisdiction of the arbitral tribunal seized of the dispute.

Second, and perhaps more importantly, the Federal Tribunal

---

[215] Cass. 1e civ., Dec. 4, 1990, E.T.P.M. and Ecofisa v. Gas del Estado, 1991 REV. ARB. 81, 83, and P. Fouchard's note. Compare, regarding the non-existence of the arbitration agreement, the unsatisfactory position taken in CA Paris, Oct. 21, 1983, Isover-Saint-Gobain v. Dow Chemical France, which seems to leave the interpretation of the arbitration agreement entirely in the hands of the arbitrators (1984 REV. ARB. 98, and A. Chapelle's note), and, regarding the breach of international public policy, the awkward reasoning of CA Paris, Oct. 27, 1994, which also refers to "the discretionary interpretation of the contract" by the arbitrators (Lebanese Traders Distributors & Consultants LTDC v. Reynolds, 1994 REV. ARB. 709, 714; for an English translation, see 10 INT'L ARB. REP. E1 (Feb. 1995)).

[216] See supra para. 532.

[217] First Options of Chicago, Inc. v. Kaplan, 514 U.S. 938 (1995); 10 INT'L ARB. REP. 4 (June 1995); 6 WORLD ARB. & MED. REP. 128 (1995); XXII Y.B. COM. ARB. 278 (1997).

only reviews the findings on which the contested award is based—even in the case of an interim award concerning the jurisdiction of the arbitral authority—where one of the grounds mentioned in Article 190, paragraph 2, of the Swiss Private International Law Act has been raised in connection with those findings . . . .[218]

For example, if it is necessary to interpret the scope of the parties' agreement in order to examine the jurisdiction or constitution of the arbitral tribunal, the Federal Tribunal will do so itself and will disregard the disputed reasoning in the award on that aspect, as in French law. Likewise, in verifying that the award complies with international public policy, the Federal Tribunal may find that international public policy has been contravened because "an essential, duly established fact has been disregarded."[219] Thus, in practice, the extent of the review of an award performed by the Swiss courts will generally be comparable to that performed by the French courts in similar circumstances.

1606. — In order to be admissible before the French courts, a ground for setting the award aside must have been raised whenever possible before the arbitral tribunal itself.[220] Thus, for example, a party which fails to challenge the jurisdiction of the arbitral tribunal before the arbitrators themselves will be deemed to have ratified their jurisdiction, thereby precluding any subsequent challenge on that issue before the French courts.[221] The same applies where no objection is made to the composition of the arbitral tribunal,[222] the appointment of an arbitrator[223] or the expiration of the deadline within which the arbitral

---

[218] Fed. Trib., Sept. 2, 1993, National Power Corp. v. Westinghouse, 1994 BULL. ASA 244, 246; 1994 REV. SUISSE DR. INT. ET DR. EUR. 159, and observations by F. Knoepfler; Fed. Trib., Dec. 30, 1994, W. v. F. and V., 1995 BULL. ASA 217, 223. But see Fed. Trib., May 16, 1995, G. S.p.A. v. Z., which more clearly leaves it to the arbitrators to establish the true and mutual intention of the parties (1996 BULL. ASA 667; 1997 REV. SUISSE DR. INT. ET DR. EUR. 599, and observations by F. Knoepfler), and Fed. Trib., Sept. 6, 1996, X. v. Y., 1997 BULL. ASA 291, 303.

[219] Swiss Fed. Trib., Sept. 2, 1993, *National Power Corp.*, *supra* note 218, at 246.

[220] On the fact that silence will only constitute a waiver of an irregularity if the applicable procedural rules allow the arbitrators to cure the alleged irregularity, see CA Paris, Jan. 21, 1997, *Nu Swift*, *supra* note 176.

[221] This rule is widely accepted in comparative law. See, for example, in Australian law, Court of Appeal of New South Wales, May 18, 1993, Bulk Chartering & Consultants Australia Pty. Ltd. v. T&T Metal Trading Pty. Ltd., 8 INT'L ARB. REP. 9 (July 1993). The party submitting the request for arbitration cannot later validly claim that there is no arbitration agreement: see in French domestic arbitration law, Cass. 2e civ., Jan. 26, 1994, Ferruzzi France v. UCACEL, 1994 Bull. Civ. II, No. 38, at 21; 1995 REV. ARB. 443; in French international arbitration law, see CA Paris, June 24, 1997, Highlight Communications International AG v. Europex, 1997 REV. ARB. 588, and observations by D. Bureau. On this issue, generally, see Loïc Cadiet, *La renonciation à se prévaloir des irrégularités de la procédure arbitrale*, 1996 REV. ARB. 3. On the reverse scenario of the waiver of the arbitration agreement by the commencement of court proceedings, see *supra* para. 669.

[222] See, on this issue, CA Paris, 1e Ch., Sec. Supp., Sept. 27, 1985, Ets. Neu v. Improvair, No. N 8111, unpublished, cited by DE BOISSÉSON, *supra* note 71, at 835; CA Paris, June 24, 1997, *Highlight Communications*, *supra* note 221; CA Paris, Dec. 3, 1998, *Interpipe*, *supra* note 106. *Comp. with* CA Toulouse, Nov. 17, 1986, Robotique v. Filatures Pierre Mailhé et Fils, 1987 REV. ARB. 175, and L. Zollinger's note. On the application of this rule in the context of the New York Convention, see *infra* para. 1703, note 149.

[223] CA Paris, Apr. 2, 1998, *TECHNIP*, *supra* note 197.

tribunal must make its award.[224] Likewise, if a party considers that its opponent has breached the rules of due process by submitting a particular pleading or document, it must immediately protest to the arbitral tribunal, so that the tribunal will have an opportunity to remedy the breach. For example, the tribunal may allow the protesting party time to respond, or strike the disputed document from the record. If no objection is made, the party which considers itself to be the victim of a violation of due process will not be entitled to rely on that breach at a later stage as a ground on which to have the award set aside.[225] In addition, where the parties have initially agreed that the arbitrators are to make separate awards on jurisdiction and on the merits and the arbitral tribunal subsequently declares that it intends to proceed otherwise, a party which fails to protest immediately to the arbitral tribunal will not be entitled to base an action to set aside or challenging enforcement of an award on the arbitrators' failure to comply with the parties' initial agreement.[226]

As was rightly observed by the Swiss Federal Tribunal, such conduct would be contrary to the requirements of procedural good faith.[227] In its 1998 Rules, the ICC sets out the principle at Article 33 whereby a party who fails to raise an objection to a perceived failure to comply with the Rules, any other procedural rule, any direction of the tribunal or any provision of the arbitration agreement, will be deemed to have waived its right to object. Certain recent arbitration statutes, such as the new German law, contain the same rule (Art. 1027 of the ZPO).

A violation of international public policy is, by its nature, the only ground which cannot be ratified by the parties. Nevertheless, where the claim against the award could have provided the basis for a challenge of the arbitrators but no challenge was made, the French courts consider the action available under Article 1502 5° to be no longer admissible.[228]

However, a party will naturally not be penalized for having failed to raise an objection before the arbitral tribunal if it only became aware of the grounds for that objection after the award had been made. For example, if a party discovers on reading the award that the arbitral tribunal has based its decision on a document that it never received, it will of course

---

[224] CA Paris, 1e Ch., Sec. C, May 19, 1998, Torno SpA v. Kamugai Gumi Co. Ltd., No. 97/05722, unpublished, in a case where one party participated in the proceedings without any reservations by submitting two memorials after the expiration of the deadline before which, according to that party's later contention, the arbitrators should have made their award.

[225] *See infra* paras. 1643 and 1652. On the application of a similar rule in the context of the New York Convention, see *infra* para. 1699, and, in Swiss law, Fed. Trib., Aug. 17, 1994, Türkiye Elektrik Kurumu v. Osuuskuntat METEX Andelslag, 1995 BULL. ASA 198, and F.R. Ehrat's note; 1996 REV. SUISSE DR. INT. ET DR. EUR. 539, and observations by F. Knoepfler, Fed. Trib., Jan. 28, 1997, Thomson C.S.F. v. Frontier AG Bern, 1998 BULL. ASA 118. *But see* CA Paris, June 14, 1985, S.A.R.L. Anciens Ets. Harognan Comptoir Euro-Turc v. Turkish Airlines "Turk Hava Yollari A.O.", 1987 REV. ARB. 395, and observations by J. Pellerin.

[226] This is expressly provided for in Article 1065, paragraph 4 of the Netherlands Code of Civil Procedure. It is implicit in French law. *Comp.* Loquin, *supra* note 172, at 338.

[227] Swiss Fed. Trib., Sept. 7, 1993, F. SpA v. M., 1994 BULL. ASA 248, 249; 1994 REV. SUISSE DR. INT. ET DR. EUR. 162, and observations by P. Schweizer. On the precautionary measure of regularly inquiring of the parties throughout the proceeding as to any reservations they may have, see *supra* para. 1232.

[228] CA Paris, June 2, 1989, Gemanco v. S.A.E.P.A., 1991 REV. ARB. 87, 2d decision, and the commentary by Claude Reymond, *Des connaissances personnelles de l'arbitre à son information privilégiée – Réflexions sur quelques arrêts récents, id.* at 3.

be entitled to rely on that non-disclosure in bringing an action to set the award aside under Article 1502 4° of the New Code of Civil Procedure,[229] regardless of the fact that no objection was raised prior to bringing that action.

1607. — Under French law, it is not necessary to establish that the flaw affecting the award caused damage to the party relying on it for an award to be set aside or refused enforcement on the basis of Articles 1502 and 1504 of the New Code of Civil Procedure.

The issue arose in an action based on an arbitrator's failure to comply with the terms of his brief. The concern in French domestic law was that a broad interpretation of that ground for vacating an award might unduly extend the scope of recourse against awards[230] and, in particular, that it might lead to the possibility of setting aside an award on the basis of any procedural defect, however slight. This prompted the suggestion that in domestic law only serious procedural defects should lead an award to be set aside, and that there should at least be a requirement that the procedural breach in question actually cause damage to the party relying on it.[231] That view was supported by a decision in which the *Cour de cassation* appeared to be adopting that position, prior to the reform of French arbitration law.[232] In fact, as we shall see, the French courts have adopted a very conservative approach to actions based on claims that the arbitrators have exceeded the terms of their brief. They have used that ground to allow them to decide allegations that the arbitrators ruled *infra* or *ultra petita*, as well as claims that the arbitrators acted *ultra vires* (where, for example, they act as *amiables compositeurs* without having such powers conferred on them by the parties).[233] That being the case, the idea of creating a requirement that the "victim" prove that it suffered damage is of less relevance. It could even lead to excessive leniency with respect to certain awards. For example, how could one assess the damage allegedly caused by the fact that the arbitrators acted as *amiables compositeurs* where the parties had not authorized them to do so,[234] given that no action would lie against an award made by arbitrators not acting as *amiables compositeurs*, even if it were seriously flawed?[235] Above all, if the requirement of actual damage were to be extended to all of the cases listed in Article 1502, the review of arbitral awards would be considerably weakened. A good example is the review of compliance with the rules of due process. If a document which has not been disclosed to the other party is mentioned by the arbitrators in their award, should it be necessary to establish that, if the victim of that blatant violation of due process had been able to express its views on the undisclosed document, it would have succeeded in persuading the tribunal to rule

---

[229] *See infra* para. 1639.

[230] On this issue, see *infra* para. 1626.

[231] P. Fouchard, note following CA Paris, June 3, 1980, Belstar Productions v. Mercury Films, 1982 REV. ARB. 47, 52. *See also* Loquin, *supra* note 172, at 334 *et seq.*; Marie-Claire Rondeau-Rivier, *Arbitrage – La décision arbitrale*, J.-CL. PROC. CIV., Fasc. 1046, ¶ 43 (1986); CRÉPIN, *supra* note 199, ¶ 337.

[232] Cass. 2e civ., Oct. 15, 1980, Société des établissements Soulès et Cie. v. Saronis Shipping Co., 1982 REV. ARB. 40, and P. Courteault's note.

[233] *See infra* paras. 1626 *et seq.*

[234] *See infra* para. 1635.

[235] *See supra* para. 1603.

differently? A requirement of that kind would lead the reviewing judge to examine the substance of the dispute and, above all, it would tend towards defeating the necessary control of the conduct of the arbitrators and the parties which justifies the existence of the review exercised by the courts over awards. For that reason, we believe that it would be inappropriate to add to the grounds for review set out in Articles 1502 and 1504 of the New Code of Civil Procedure a condition of actual damage not already contained in such provisions.[236]

We shall now consider in turn each of the grounds of recourse provided for in Article 1502 of the New Code of Civil Procedure.

§ 1. – Where the Arbitrators Have Reached Their Decision in the Absence of an Arbitration Agreement or on the Basis of an Agreement Which Is Void or Has Expired

1608. — The purpose of this ground of recourse is to enable the courts to ensure that the arbitrators had jurisdiction over the dispute that they decided. If arbitrators reach their decision in the absence of an arbitration agreement or on the basis of an arbitration agreement which is void or has expired, they have no jurisdiction. It is essential that a court should ultimately be able to verify the existence of that jurisdiction.[237] As was rightly stated in one decision, although the arbitral tribunal must rule on its own jurisdiction if that jurisdiction is challenged, "[its] decision on [its] jurisdictional powers is not final and can be reviewed by the court hearing an action to set aside."[238] A number of recent arbitration statutes take the same position by requiring the courts to set aside awards where "the arbitral tribunal has wrongly declared itself to have or not to have jurisdiction."[239] This formulation is broader in scope than that used in Article 1502 1°, in that it also covers the situation where an arbitrator wrongly declines jurisdiction. Under French law, that situation is dealt with indirectly, by means of the review as to whether the arbitrator has complied with the terms of his or her brief.[240]

We shall examine the method used (A) when hearing an action to overturn an enforcement order or to set aside an award on this ground, before considering the substantive issues (B).

---

[236] See also, under the New York Convention, J. Linsmeau, note following CA Brussels, Jan. 24, 1997, Compagnie Inter-Arabe de Garantie des Investissments (CIAGI) v. Banque Arabe et Internationale d'Investissement (BAII), 1998 REV. ARB. 181, and J. Linsmeau's note, especially at 206. On this issue, in the context of the New York Convention, see *infra* para. 1699.

[237] On the meaning of the principle of "competence-competence," see *supra* paras. 650 *et seq.*

[238] CA Paris, June 16, 1988, *Swiss Oil, supra* note 214, XVI Y.B. COM. ARB. 136 (1991).

[239] *See, e.g.,* Art. 190, para. 2 of the Swiss Private International Law Statute.

[240] *See infra* para. 1629.

A. – METHOD

1609. — There is a question as to the method to be used in connection with Article 1502 1° because that provision does not specify which rules should be applied by the Court of Appeals when verifying the existence and validity of the arbitration agreement underlying the award. Should the Court apply a law selected under the traditional choice of law method, or should it apply instead French substantive rules adapted to the international nature of the situation, or simply the provisions of French domestic law?

1610. — There have not been many decisions by the French courts[241] determining the law governing the arbitration agreement through the application of choice of law rules regarding contracts (which designate either the law chosen by the parties or, in the absence of such a choice, the law most closely connected to the contract). The Paris Court of Appeals did hold in a 1985 decision that the existence and validity of the arbitration agreement should "be considered in the light of the law governing the disputed contract, in accordance with the French choice of law rule." The Court concluded that:

> what emerges . . . from the various aspects of the case, viewed as a whole, is that the parties intended to subject their obligations to the legislation of the place of performance, that is to say Hawaiian law, which is the main connecting factor in localizing the contractual relationship, [and] that, consequently, the conditions governing the formation of the contract, which will determine the disputed issue—namely, whether or not the parties agreed to the arbitration clause—are those provided for by the law in force in Hawaii.[242]

Similarly, the Paris Court of Appeals held in a 1987 decision that the arbitration agreement, like the main contract, is governed by the law chosen by the parties, which excludes any presumption of a connection with the *lex fori*.[243]

1611. —However, the courts now generally base their decisions as to the validity of the arbitration agreement on substantive rules of French international arbitration law. This

---

[241] In comparative law, see the references cited *supra* para. 442.

[242] CA Paris, 1e Ch., Sec. Supp., Sept. 27, 1985, O.P.A.T.I. v. Larsen Inc., No. L 8169, unpublished, cited by DE BOISSÉSON, *supra* note 71, at 825.

[243] CA Paris, Jan. 20, 1987, Bomar Oil N.V. v. Entreprise Tunisienne d'Activités Pétrolières (E.T.A.P.), 1987 REV. ARB. 482, and C. Kessedjian's note; 114 J.D.I. 934 (1987), and E. Loquin's note; for an English translation, see XIII Y.B. COM. ARB. 466 (1988). Compare Cass. 1e civ., Feb. 10, 1987, upholding the decision of a Court of Appeals which examined the validity of a submission agreement in the light of Italian law, its governing law (Penchienati v. S.A.I.M., Dalloz, Somm. 227 (1987), and observations by P. Julien). For a full discussion of this method, see the August 24, 1988 Partial Award by Messrs. Poudret, chairman, McGovern and Bonnasies, arbitrators, in ICC Case No. 5730, Société de lubrifiants Elf Aquitaine v. A.R. Orri, 1992 REV. ARB. 125, and D. Cohen, note following CA Paris, Jan. 11, 1990, Orri v. Société des lubrifiants Elf Aquitaine, *id.* at 95.

solution was first applied in the 1972 decision of the *Cour de cassation* in the *Hecht* case,[244] and was gradually derived from that of the autonomy of the arbitration agreement, with which it was confused for some time.[245] It was then developed by the Paris Court of Appeals in its numerous decisions declaring that "an arbitration clause in an international contract has a validity and effectiveness of its own,"[246] a principle to which the Court attached various consequences, particularly as regards the determination of which parties are bound by an arbitration agreement.[247] However, as discussed earlier, the principle that an arbitration agreement has "a validity and effectiveness of its own" should not be interpreted as a substantive rule pursuant to which the agreement is systematically valid. Such a rule would contradict Article 1502 1°, which acknowledges the existence, in international disputes, of arbitration agreements that are void. Instead, the principle of an arbitration agreement's validity and effectiveness is simply a substantive rule which is intended to reverse the principle applicable to domestic arbitration in Article 2061 of the Civil Code with respect to arbitrability,[248] and it provides the basis for various rules of interpretation concerning the scope of arbitration agreements.[249]

In practice, in most actions based on Articles 1502 1° and 1504 of the New Code of Civil Procedure, neither the parties nor the courts consider it necessary to specify which rules govern the examination of the continuing existence and validity of the arbitration agreement. This suggests that they are implicitly applying French substantive rules.[250]

In its 1993 *Dalico* decision, the *Cour de cassation* confirmed that French courts assessing the existence and validity of an arbitration agreement pursuant to Articles 1502 1° and 1504 of the New Code of Civil Procedure should only apply French substantive rules, which are described in that decision as "mandatory rules of French law and international public policy."[251] We consider that approach to be perfectly justified for the purposes of determining the conditions subject to which an award can be given effect in France.[252]

B. – SUBSTANCE

1612. —The substantive issues of whether an arbitration agreement is valid and in existence have been discussed in detail in the context of our examination of the arbitration

---

[244] Cass. 1e civ., July 4, 1972, Hecht v. Buisman's, 99 J.D.I. 843 (1972), and B. Oppetit's note; 1974 REV. CRIT. DIP 82, and P. Level's note.

[245] *See supra* para. 418.

[246] See the decisions cited *supra* para. 436 and, on the unsatisfactory nature of the principle, *supra* para. 440.

[247] On this issue, see *supra* paras. 498 *et seq.*

[248] Article 2061 states that an arbitration agreement is void unless otherwise specified by law; *see supra* para. 419.

[249] See, generally, *supra* para. 471.

[250] See, for example, regarding invalid consent, *supra* para. 527.

[251] Cass. 1e civ., Dec. 20, 1993, Comité populaire de la municipalité de Khoms El Mergeb v. Dalico Contractors, 121 J.D.I. 432 (1994), and E. Gaillard's note; 121 J.D.I. 690 (1994), and E. Loquin's note; 1994 REV. ARB. 116, and H. Gaudemet-Tallon's note; 1994 REV. CRIT. DIP 663, and P. Mayer's note.

[252] For a more detailed discussion of this method and its justification, see *supra* paras. 437 *et seq.*

agreement.[253] We will therefore restrict ourselves to a few remarks regarding cases where there is no arbitration agreement (1°), where the arbitration agreement is void (2°), and where the arbitration agreement has expired (3°).

1° Absence of an Arbitration Agreement

1613. — Allegations that there is no arbitration agreement rarely arise in isolation. They are usually encountered in two sets of circumstances: where the creation or survival of the arbitration agreement is disputed, and where doubts are raised as to the agreement's scope.

1614. — The creation or survival of an arbitration agreement has been the subject of several court decisions. For instance, where contractual negotiations have come to an end after the exchange by the parties of drafts containing arbitration clauses, is there an agreement between the parties, at least with regard to arbitration? The Paris Court of Appeals held that such an agreement did exist in a case where the word "draft" appeared in the margin beside some clauses of a contract, but not the arbitration clause.[254] On the other hand, it held there to be no such agreement where a contract containing an arbitration agreement had not been signed.[255]

The question arises in similar terms where, following a novation of or settlement relating to the contract containing the arbitration clause, one of the parties claims that the arbitration clause has become void. The novation or settlement affecting the main contract has no impact on the arbitration agreement because of the principle of the autonomy of the arbitration agreement. However, the Court of Appeals should examine whether at the time of the novation or settlement the parties intended to maintain the arbitration agreement in force.[256]

1615. — The determination of the scope of arbitration agreements where their existence is not disputed has also given rise to a great deal of litigation.

Sometimes the problem lies in determining exactly what subject-matter is covered by the arbitration agreement. This is often the case where an arbitration clause does not refer to all of the provisions of the contract containing it,[257] or where the clauses of several contracts must be interpreted in the light of each other,[258] or where a non-contractual dispute is

---

[253] *See supra* paras. 385 *et seq.*

[254] CA Paris, Sept. 27, 1985, *OPATI, supra* note 242.

[255] CA Paris, Feb. 26, 1988, Pia Investments Ltd. v. Cassia, 1990 REV. ARB. 851, 1st decision, and J.-H. Moitry and C. Vergne's note, *aff'd,* Cass. 1e civ., July 10, 1990, Cassia v. Pia Investments Ltd., 1990 REV. ARB. 851, 2d decision, and J.-H. Moitry and C. Vergne's note; 119 J.D.I. 168 (1992), and E. Loquin's note.

[256] On this issue, generally, see *supra* paras. 410 and 727 *et seq.*

[257] *See supra* paras. 513 *et seq.*

[258] *See supra* paras. 518 *et seq.*

submitted to arbitration on the basis of an arbitration clause contained in a contract.[259] Similar difficulties arise with contracts which are performed by parties other than those which actually signed them,[260] or where a contract containing an arbitration clause has been assigned or otherwise transferred to a party that did not initially sign the contract.[261]

More commonly, the dispute focuses on determining which parties agreed to be bound by the arbitration agreement. The courts have encountered this problem particularly with groups of companies (where a party seeks to initiate arbitral proceedings against a company other than the signatory of the arbitration agreement)[262] and with state contracts (where it is often unclear whether the arbitration agreement binds the state itself or only the state-owned entity that signed the agreement).[263]

2° Where the Arbitration Agreement Is Void

1616. — An arbitration agreement may be void for two reasons: first, where the dispute to which the arbitration agreement relates is non-arbitrable and, second, where the arbitration agreement itself is defective.

1617. —First, where public policy dictates either that a party is not entitled to refer disputes to arbitration, or that the subject-matter to which the arbitration agreement relates cannot be resolved by arbitration, the arbitration agreement is void and any award made on the basis of that agreement will also be void. The former case is known as subjective non-arbitrability,[264] the latter as objective non-arbitrability.[265]

In both such cases, the concept of arbitrability has broadened considerably over the past few years.[266] In practice, states and state-owned entities—as well as their co-contractors—cannot rely on provisions of their own law in order to avoid the application of an arbitration agreement to which they freely consented.[267] Further, the range of arbitrable disputes has continued to expand (to include, in particular, issues of antitrust, intellectual property, insolvency, and company law and, to a certain extent, consumer law).[268]

1618. — Second, an arbitration agreement may also be void if it is defective in some respect. One of the parties may lack the capacity or power to enter into an arbitration

---

[259] *See supra* para. 524.

[260] *See supra* para. 499.

[261] *See supra* paras. 704 *et seq.*

[262] *See supra* paras. 500 *et seq.*

[263] *See supra* paras. 507 *et seq.*

[264] *See supra* paras. 534 *et seq.*

[265] *See supra* paras. 559 *et seq.* On the relationship between arbitrability and public policy, see *infra* para. 1704.

[266] *See supra* para. 568.

[267] *See supra* paras. 514 *et seq.*

[268] *See supra* paras. 575 *et seq.*

agreement,[269] or its consent to the arbitration agreement may be invalid on the grounds of mistake, duress or misrepresentation.[270] An example of invalid consent is found in French law in instances where such consent is given together with a provision by which the parties agree to allow appeals to the courts, in violation of the mandatory system of judicial recourse.[271]

3° Where the Arbitration Agreement Has Expired

1619. — Articles 1502 1° and 1504 allow the Court of Appeals to set aside or refuse enforcement of an award which was made after the expiration of the arbitration agreement. The parties have considerable freedom on this issue, but where they have stipulated in the arbitration agreement—directly or by reference to a procedural law or to arbitration rules—that the arbitrators must make their award within a certain period of time, that deadline must be observed, failing which the award may be set aside or declared unenforceable.[272]

§ 2. – Irregular Composition of the Arbitral Tribunal

1620. — Under the regime established by the 1981 Decree, irregularities in the composition of the arbitral tribunal or the appointment of the sole arbitrator result primarily from the failure to comply with the procedures agreed by the parties in this respect. However, they may also result from non-compliance with the few principles in this area which are considered to be requirements of international public policy.

1621. — French international arbitration law contains no mandatory rules on this question other than that the intentions of the parties should be complied with. This will be so whether those intentions are set forth in the arbitration agreement itself or in any subsequent agreements, or whether they result from the conditions for the appointment of the arbitrators contained in a procedural law or arbitration rules chosen by the parties.[273]

By applying Articles 1502 2° and 1504, the courts can censure a failure to comply with the parties' intentions without making any judgment as to the appropriateness of the provisions agreed by the parties.[274] For example, where the parties have provided that the

---

[269] *See supra* paras. 435 *et seq.*

[270] On this issue, generally, see *supra* paras. 525 *et seq.*

[271] *See supra* para. 1597.

[272] On this issue, generally, see *supra* paras. 1379 *et seq.*

[273] *See supra* paras. 732 *et seq.*

[274] For an example of a decision overturning an order for enforcement of an award for the breach of rather unusual provisions contained in an arbitration agreement, see CA Paris, Feb. 11, 1988, Gas del Estado v. Ecofisa and E.T.P.M., 1989 REV. ARB. 683, and L. Zollinger's note, *aff'd*, Cass. 1e civ., Dec. 4, 1990, *E.T.P.M.*, *supra*

(continued...)

authority responsible for appointing the arbitrators shall be "the president of the Paris Commercial Court, in an emergency proceeding," a Court of Appeals hearing an action to set aside an award made by an arbitrator designated by the Commercial Court, rather than its president, will have no option but to set the award aside.[275]

When reviewing the arbitrators' compliance with the intentions of the parties as to the composition of the arbitral tribunal under Articles 1502 2° and 1504, the Court of Appeals must reach its own conclusions as to those intentions if they are expressed ambiguously, and in doing so the Court will not be bound by the findings of the arbitrators.[276]

The Court of Appeals must also examine whether the parties have expressly or tacitly waived the irregularity.[277] In one case the president of the Tribunal of First Instance reached a decision as to the independence of the arbitrators when hearing an action challenging an arbitrator under Article 1493, paragraph 2 of the New Code of Civil Procedure. It was held by the Court of Appeals that it could not hear any further claims concerning the legality of the constitution of the arbitral tribunal in an action to set aside or to resist enforcement of the award unless those claims were based on allegations of new irregularities which had subsequently come to light.[278]

1622. — The only other limits affecting the requirement of compliance with the intentions of the parties as to the composition of the arbitral tribunal are those that result from the principles of international public policy, including the equal treatment of the parties, the impartiality of the arbitral tribunal and the right to a fair hearing.[279]

In particular, the courts have held, with respect to multi-party arbitration, that the public policy requirement of equal treatment of the parties means that each party must have had equal rights in the appointment of the arbitrators.[280]

1623. — However, some authors suggest that there are two other situations in which an award can also be set aside or refused enforcement under Articles 1502 2° and 1504.

---

[274] (...continued)
note 215; CA Paris, July 1, 1997, Agence Transcongolaise des Communications-Chemins de fer Congo Océan (ATC-CFCO) v. Compagnie minière de l'Ogooué (Comilog), 1998 REV. ARB. 131, and D. Hascher's note.

[275] Cass. 1e civ., May 10, 1995, Laiguède v. Ahsen Inox, 1995 REV. ARB. 605, and A. Hory's note.

[276] Cass. 1e civ., Dec. 4, 1990, *E.T.P.M.*, *supra* note 215.

[277] *See supra* para. 1606.

[278] CA Paris, Apr. 6, 1990, Philipp Brothers v. Icco, 1990 REV. ARB. 880, and M. de Boisséson's note.

[279] *See supra* paras. 783 *et seq.* and 1019 *et seq.*

[280] *See* Cass. 1e civ., Jan. 7, 1992, B.K.M.I. v. Dutco, 1992 Bull. Civ. I, No. 2; 1992 REV. ARB. 470, and P. Bellet's note; 119 J.D.I. 707 (1992), 2d decision, and C. Jarrosson's note; 1992 RTD COM. 796, and observations by J.-C. Dubarry and E. Loquin; for an English translation, see 7 INT'L ARB. REP. B1 (Feb. 1992); XVIII Y.B. COM. ARB. 140 (1993), *overturning* CA Paris, May 5, 1989, B.K.M.I. Industrieanlagen GmbH v. Dutco Construction Co. Ltd., 1989 REV. ARB. 723, and P. Bellet's note; 119 J.D.I. 707 (1992), 1st decision, and C. Jarrosson's note; for an English translation, see XV Y.B. COM. ARB. 124 (1990); 4 INT'L ARB. REP. A1 (July 1989).

1624. — First, it has been argued that where an award is made outside France in a dispute which does not involve the interests of international trade, the Court of Appeals should ensure that there is compliance with both the intentions of the parties and the provisions of the law of the seat of the arbitration concerning the constitution of the arbitral tribunal.[281] However appropriate that may be, such an interpretation does not appear to reflect the philosophy of the 1981 Decree which, when defining the extent of the review performed by the Court of Appeals, chose not to distinguish between awards made outside France and those made in France in international arbitration.[282]

1625. — Second, it has been suggested that it might also be possible to set aside an award made by an arbitral tribunal where one of the members lacked the capacity to act as an arbitrator under his or her national law or under the procedural law chosen by the parties.[283] Although a breach of the procedural law chosen by the parties, like any failure to comply with their intentions, will fall within Article 1502 2°,[284] this is not the case of a failure to comply with the provisions of an arbitrator's national law. Even if one were to reason in choice of law terms,[285] the requirements as to the qualities of arbitrators are intended to protect not the arbitrators themselves—which is the case of genuine rules of capacity—but the parties to the arbitration. Because the choice of nationality as a connecting factor is generally based on the preoccupation that the party concerned should receive continuous protection, it has no place in these circumstances. As a result, the qualities required of arbitrators under French law, in the absence of which the award might be set aside or refused enforcement, depend solely upon the rules of law chosen by the parties, and on the considerations of the French conception of international public policy.[286]

§ 3. – Where the Arbitrators Have Failed to Comply with Their Brief

1626. — The third ground of recourse listed in Article 1502 of the New Code of Civil Procedure—the failure of the arbitrators to comply with the terms of their brief— seems very general in nature. Were it to be interpreted broadly, it would enable an award to be set aside where arbitrators fail to comply with absolutely any rule governing the conduct of the arbitral proceedings, or even any of the rules governing the merits of the case. Indeed, in a broad sense, the arbitrator's brief is to reach a fair decision in accordance with the rules

---

[281] Fouchard, *supra* note 7, ¶ 84.

[282] *See supra* para. 1560.

[283] DE BOISSÉSON, *supra* note 71, at 833–34.

[284] *See supra* para. 1620.

[285] *Comp. supra* para. 1611.

[286] On this issue, generally, see *supra* paras. 745 *et seq.*

governing the procedural and substantive aspects of the case.[287] This undoubtedly accounts for the fact that Article 1502 3° is often invoked by parties dissatisfied with the outcome of their case.[288]

However, the courts have rightly taken a much narrower view, and carefully remark that the purpose of this ground of recourse is not to enable the courts "to review the substantive aspects of the award," but simply "to verify, without having to rule on whether the arbitrators' decision was well-founded, that they complied with their brief with regard to the contested aspects of their award."[289] The courts are therefore able to set aside or refuse to enforce an award where the arbitrators have not observed the limits of the claims raised by the parties, or where the arbitrators have otherwise exceeded the powers that the parties conferred upon them.

A. – FAILURE TO OBSERVE THE LIMITS OF THE PARTIES' CLAIMS

1627. — The arbitrators fail to observe the limits of the parties' claims either when they do not decide all such claims, resulting in a decision *infra petita* (1°), or when they decide claims which were not made by the parties, thus ruling *ultra petita* (2°).

1° *Infra Petita*

1628. — The arbitrators fail to comply with their brief—which is to decide all the claims submitted to them—if they rule *infra petita*.

The consequences of such non-compliance have been disputed on the grounds that, in such situations, the party disadvantaged by that omission should "apply to the arbitrator again, or, in the absence of an agreement between the parties where the arbitration agreement was initially a submission agreement, the most diligent party should bring an action before the court."[290] However, except in the case of an interim award, the mandate of an arbitral tribunal ends when the award is made, thus terminating the tribunal's jurisdiction. Once the award has been made, it is, in principle, not possible to reapply to the tribunal seeking that it decide issues which it earlier failed to address, unless so provided by the applicable arbitration rules or the law chosen by the parties to govern the proceedings. To allow the reconstitution of the tribunal, an approach adopted in French domestic arbitration by virtue of Article 1475, paragraph 2, is nevertheless possible in international arbitration where the parties have chosen to have the proceedings governed by French law or by another law or

---

[287] *Comp.* Loquin, *supra* note 172, at 334.

[288] A claim before the French Court of Appeals was raised on this ground 166 times in international arbitration between 1981 and 1992, successfully so in 21 cases. *See* CRÉPIN, *supra* note 199, ¶ 371.

[289] CA Paris, Mar. 12, 1985, *Intrafor Cofor, supra* note 203.

[290] DE BOISSÉSON, *supra* note 71, at 837, citing CA Paris, 1e Ch., Sec. Supp., July 22, 1982, Campenon-Bernard v. S.A. Henry et Cie., No. II 8029, unpublished.

set of arbitration rules authorizing them to request the arbitrators to remedy their omission.[291] The French courts have also indicated their willingness to extend this option to international arbitration even where French law has not been expressly chosen to govern the arbitral proceedings.[292] Where this option is available, the party seeking to have the award set aside on the grounds of the omission cannot bring an action on that basis unless it has first unsuccessfully made such an application for rectification. This appears to be the position taken in legal systems which allow such a course of action while treating a failure by the arbitrators to comply with their brief as a ground on which an award can be set aside.[293]

Other laws are more explicit in allowing awards where the arbitrators have ruled *infra petita* to be set aside or refused enforcement. For example, the Swiss Private International Law Statute specifies that an award can be set aside if "the arbitral tribunal . . . failed to decide one of the claims."[294]

1629. — An award may be made *infra petita* as the result of an incorrect assessment by the arbitrators of the extent of their jurisdiction. Where the arbitrators go beyond the terms of the arbitration agreement, their award can be set aside or refused enforcement on the basis of Article 1502 1°. However, as Article 1502 1° only makes reference to the absence of an arbitration agreement, it does not cover the opposite case where the arbitrators consider the scope of the arbitration agreement to be less broad than it in fact is. This is in contrast with arbitration statutes which enable the courts to set aside an award "where the arbitral tribunal has wrongly retained or declined jurisdiction."[295] Under French law, such an error can therefore only be contested on the basis of Article 1502 3°. This was clearly stated by the Paris Court of Appeals in two decisions. In the first of those, the Court observed that:

> [t]his power of review, which is given to the court under Article 1502 1° of the New Code of Civil Procedure in the case where the arbitrators hold that they have jurisdiction over the case, cannot be denied to the court in a case like the present one, where the arbitrators have declined jurisdiction. To hold the contrary would mean granting different guarantees to the parties.[296]

In its second decision on this issue, the Court confirmed in more general terms that:

---

[291] On this issue, see Bellet and Mezger, *supra* note 5, at 647; Huet, *supra* note 32, at 19. For an example in French domestic arbitration, see CA Paris, Nov. 13, 1997, Lemeur v. SARL Les Cités Invisibles, 1998 REV. ARB. 709, and observations by Y. Derains; Cass. 2e civ., Jan. 7, 1999, Syseca v. Secta Autosur, No. R 97–10.292, unpublished. On the rules allowing the arbitral tribunal to be reconvened to rule on the omitted claim, see *supra* para. 1417.

[292] *See* CA Paris, 1e Ch., Sec. C, Mar. 25, 1997, Borgosesia S.p.A. v. Ardant, No. 95/80387, unpublished.

[293] *See, e.g.*, Art. 1065(1)(c) of the Netherlands Code of Civil Procedure; *see also* ALBERT JAN VAN DEN BERG, ROBERT VAN DELDEN, HENK J. SNIJDERS, NETHERLANDS ARBITRATION LAW 112 (1993).

[294] Art. 190, para. 2(c).

[295] Art. 190, para. 2 of the Swiss Private International Law Statute. *See supra* para. 1608.

[296] CA Paris, June 16, 1988, *Swiss Oil, supra* note 214, XVI Y.B. COM. ARB. 136 (1991). *See also* Loquin, *supra* note 172, at 339.

as the legal foundation of arbitration is the agreement between the parties, the arbitrators' decision as to their jurisdiction is necessarily subject to review by the Court in the context of an action to set the award aside, and in the case where the arbitrators have declined jurisdiction, that review will be of the compliance by the arbitrators with the terms of their brief (Article 1502 3° of the New Code of Civil Procedure).[297]

This solution was reiterated by the Paris Court of Appeals in its 1994 *Uzinexportimport* and 1995 *SNCFT v. Voith* decisions.[298]

1630. — Independently of any issue of jurisdiction, the arbitrators may also be held to have ruled *infra petita* on the grounds that they failed to reach a decision on any one of the parties' claims, whether by omission or by deliberate refusal to do so. However, the arbitrators are certainly not required to address every factual or legal allegation submitted by the parties, let alone every argument put forward. Thus, in one case, a party asserted that the arbitral tribunal had omitted to rule on certain issues raised in its brief concerning the limitation of liability, under the applicable law, in the event of a breach of a distribution contract. The Paris Court of Appeals considered that by basing its decision not on a breach of the distribution contract but on conduct prejudicial to the other party, the arbitral tribunal had "complied with its brief, which was to rule on the parties' claims." The Court added that the allegation concerning the arbitrators' failure to rule on certain issues raised in the party's brief did not fall within any of the grounds for the setting aside of the award under Article 1502 of the New Code of Civil Procedure.[299]

On the other hand, the arbitrators must decide all claims submitted by the parties. No doubt because it is expressed in vague terms,[300] this ground is often—and usually unsuccessfully—cited as the basis for actions against arbitral awards.[301]

---

[297] CA Paris, June 21, 1990, Compagnie Honeywell Bull S.A. v. Computacion Bull de Venezuela C.A., 1991 REV. ARB. 96, and J.-L. Delvolvé's note.

[298] CA Paris, July 7, 1994, Uzinexportimport Romanian Co. v. Attock Cement Co., 1995 REV. ARB. 107, and S. Jarvin's note; for an English translation, see 10 INT'L ARB. REP. D1 (Feb. 1995); CA Paris, Oct. 26, 1995, *SNCFT, supra* note 214.

[299] CA Paris, June 21, 1990, *Compagnie Honeywell Bull, supra* note 297.

[300] *See supra* para. 1626.

[301] *See, e.g.,* CA Paris, Feb. 14, 1989, Ofer Brothers v. The Tokyo Marine and Fire Insurance Co. Ltd., 1989 REV. ARB. 691, and P.-Y. Tschanz' note; CA Versailles, Oct. 2, 1989, Société des Grands Moulins de Strasbourg v. Compagnie Continentale France, 1990 REV. ARB. 115, and L. Idot's note; CA Paris, Mar. 8, 1990, Coumet et Ducler v. Polar-Rakennusos a Keythio, 1990 REV. ARB. 675, and P. Mayer's note; Cass. 1e civ., May 2, 1990, Alpha Transports v. V.O.F. Marleen, Cool Trans, 1991 REV. ARB. 285, and E. Loquin's note; CA Paris, May 25, 1990, Fougerolle v. Procofrance, 1990 REV. CRIT. DIP 753, and B. Oppetit's note; 1990 REV. ARB. 892, and M. de Boisséson's note; CA Paris, Nov. 29, 1990, Payart v. Morgan Crucible Co., 1991 REV. ARB. 659, 1st decision, and observations by J. Pellerin; 118 J.D.I. 414 (1991), and P. Kahn's note; CA Paris, May 10, 1994, Sheikh Mahfouz Salem Bin Mahfouz v. Al Tayar, 1996 REV. ARB. 66, and C.J.'s note.

2° *Ultra Petita*

1631. — The arbitrators will also fail to comply with their brief by ruling *ultra petita* or, in other terms, by ruling on claims not made by the parties.

This ground of recourse should not be confused with that of exceeding the terms of the arbitration agreement, which is covered by Article 1502 1°. The arbitration agreement may be very broad in scope, and the arbitrators may decide claims which were not raised by the parties while remaining within the terms of that agreement. If they do so, their award may be set aside solely on the basis of Article 1502 3°.[302]

The fact that arbitrators may have based their decision on allegations or arguments which were not put forward by the parties does not amount to a failure to comply with their brief.[303] They only fail to comply with their brief where they grant one of the parties more than it actually sought in its claims. For example, the Paris Court of Appeals set aside part of an award in which the starting-point for the accrual of interest was fixed at a date earlier than the date requested by the plaintiff.[304] In another example, it set aside an award where the arbitral tribunal reached a decision concerning the property rights of one of the parties, whereas that party's claim concerned only a company's by-laws.[305] Similarly, it has been held in a case concerning a French domestic arbitration that arbitrators went beyond the terms of their brief in ruling on damages not claimed by the parties.[306]

---

[302] Compare, on the interrelationship of these two provisions, DE BOISSÉSON, *supra* note 71, at 836.

[303] *See, e.g.,* Swiss Fed. Trib., Dec. 30, 1994, *supra* note 218. On the separate question of compliance with due process where arguments are raised by the court of its own motion, see *infra* para. 1639. On the fact that it is irrelevant whether or not a party was involved in the preparation of the terms of reference provided that the arbitrators remain within the limits of the arbitration agreement, see CA Paris, Mar. 11, 1993, Al-Kawthar Investment Co. v. BNP, 1994 REV. ARB. 735, and observations by D. Cohen; for an English translation, see 8 INT'L ARB. REP. F1 (Apr. 1993).

[304] CA Paris, June 28, 1988, Total Chine v. E.M.H., 1989 REV. ARB. 328, and J. Pellerin's note. *Comp.* CA Paris, Apr. 19, 1991, Parfums Stern France v. CFFD, 1991 REV. ARB. 673, and observations by J. Pellerin. See also, regarding the setting aside, on the grounds of a breach of due process, of an award which ordered a party to pay interest which had not been "formally demanded," CA Paris, Apr. 6, 1995, Thyssen Stahlunion v. Maaden, 1995 REV. ARB. 448, 5th decision, and the commentary by Catherine Kessedjian, *Principe de la contradiction et arbitrage, id.* at 381; 122 J.D.I. 971 (1995), and E. Loquin's note; 1996 RTD COM. 447, and observations by J.-C. Dubarry and E. Loquin.

[305] CA Paris, Jan. 19, 1990, Immoplan v. Mercure, 1991 REV. ARB. 125, and observations by J.-H. Moitry and C. Vergne. See also, in French domestic arbitration law, on the setting aside for breach of due process of an award which held a contract to be void although none of the parties sought to have the contract avoided, CA Paris, July 11, 1991, Saline d'Einville v. Compagnie des Salins du Midi, 1991 REV. ARB. 671, and observations by E. Loquin.

[306] Cass. 2e civ., Dec. 9, 1997, Hispano Suiza v. Hurel Dubois, 1998 REV. ARB. 417, and observations by L. Kiffer.

B. – WHERE THE ARBITRATORS HAVE FAILED TO ACT IN ACCORDANCE WITH THE POWERS CONFERRED ON THEM BY THE PARTIES

1632. — The arbitrators may fail to act in accordance with the powers conferred on them by the parties with regard to both the arbitral procedure (1°) and the merits of the dispute (2°).

1° Procedure

1633. — Under French international arbitration law, not all procedural irregularities constitute grounds on which to set an award aside. The only procedural irregularities which will have that effect are those which violate due process[307] and the requirements of international public policy.[308]

However, where arbitrators have not observed a procedural provision agreed by the parties, they may be considered to have failed to comply with their brief.[309] The Paris Court of Appeals took that view in its 1986 *O.I.A.E.T.I.* decision. Having found that the parties had agreed in the terms of reference that the arbitrators were to make a separate award on the jurisdiction of the tribunal and the admissibility of the dispute before reaching a decision on the merits, the Court set aside the award in which the arbitrators ruled on both jurisdiction and the merits.[310] However, that decision was overruled by the *Cour de cassation* on the grounds that in reaching that decision, "whereas the terms of reference contained no express, precise clause requiring the arbitrators to make two separate, successive awards on jurisdiction and on the merits, the Court of Appeals contravened" the provisions of Articles 1504 and 1502 3° of the New Code of Civil Procedure.[311] The requirement that the intention of the parties be expressed precisely in order to warrant a review of the compliance by the arbitrators with their brief is intended to limit the number of cases in which a breach of the procedural rules chosen by the parties will constitute grounds on which to set aside or refuse enforcement of an award.[312]

---

[307] *See infra* paras. 1638 *et seq.*

[308] *See infra* paras. 1645 *et seq.*

[309] See, for example, CA Paris, May 19, 1998, *Torno, supra* note 224, where the Court held that: "it is good law that where the parties agree on the applicable procedure, that agreement binds the arbitrators," but found allegations of the violation of the procedural calendar to be unfounded.

[310] CA Paris, Dec. 19, 1986, *O.I.A.E.T.I.*, and the commentary by Gaillard, *supra* note 214.

[311] Cass. 1e civ., Mar. 8, 1988, *Sofidif, supra* note 214. Compare the decision made on remand by CA Versailles, Mar. 7, 1990, O.I.A.E.T.I. v. COGEMA, 1991 REV. ARB. 326, and E. Loquin's note; for an English translation, see 5 INT'L ARB. REP. A1 (June 1990). See also CA Paris, Dec. 17, 1991, *Gatoil, supra* note 200, which held that "in the absence of an express and precise clause in the terms of reference obliging the arbitrators to rule in a separate decision on the incident of the postponement of their award, the arbitral tribunal had the power to rule on this incident in its decision on the merits" (1993 REV. ARB. 286; 7 INT'L ARB. REP. B4 (July 1992)). On the same question in the context of the New York Convention, see *infra* para. 1703.

[312] On terms of reference, see *supra* paras. 1235 *et seq.*

The *Cour de cassation* took a more conventional view of its role—which is limited to the review of legal issues—in a later decision. It held that a Court of Appeals had given a final interpretation as to the intentions of the parties, as evidenced by an agreement as to arbitral procedure, in deciding that an arbitral tribunal had not failed to comply with its brief by determining precisely the principles for evaluating loss when the parties had asked for an award "on the heads of liability and the principles on the basis of which any resulting awards of damages will be calculated."[313] The Court also rightly held that an award subject to review by the French courts need not follow any list of questions drawn up at the terms of reference stage. The Court considered the arbitrator's brief to be "principally limited by the subject of the dispute" as defined by the claims made by the parties, provided that those claims are within the scope of the arbitration clause on which the claims are based.[314] Similar caution is shown in decisions as to whether the arbitrators have complied with their brief in their examination of the merits of the dispute.

2° Merits

1634. — French arbitration law allows no control by the courts over the arbitrators' decision on the merits of a dispute, except with regard to compliance with the requirements of the French conception of international public policy.[315] An error of fact or law by the arbitral tribunal, however blatant, will not constitute a ground on which an award can be set aside or refused enforcement. This essential principle is not affected by the fact that the courts ensure that the arbitrators have complied with their brief. The caution shown by the courts in this respect is therefore perfectly justified.[316]

In practice, the issue of whether the arbitrators have complied with their brief as regards the merits of the dispute will arise in three situations: the first concerns *amiable composition*; the second concerns transnational rules or *lex mercatoria*; and the third concerns the conditions governing the application of a national law chosen by the parties.

1635. — With respect to *amiable composition*, two cases where the arbitrators can be held to have exceeded their powers should be distinguished. Arbitrators instructed to act as *amiables compositeurs* may sometimes consider that they are obliged to apply a particular law; conversely, arbitrators required to rule in law sometimes act as *amiables compositeurs* where the parties have not conferred such powers on them. These two situations are not comparable because the purpose of *amiable composition* is to give arbitrators greater freedom than would ordinarily be the case.

Thus, where arbitrators empowered to act as *amiables compositeurs* decide to rule in law, they only fail to comply with their brief if it is established that they considered themselves

---

[313] Cass. 1e civ., Feb. 28, 1995, *Société Générale pour l'Industrie*, *supra* note 202.

[314] Cass. 1e civ., Mar. 6, 1996, Farhat Trading Co. v. Daewoo, 1997 REV. ARB. 69, and J.-J. Arnaldez' note; 1997 REV. CRIT DIP 313, and D. Cohen's note.

[315] *See supra* para. 1603.

[316] On this issue, see CRÉPIN, *supra* note 199, ¶¶ 378 *et seq.*

to be required to rule solely in law. If, on the contrary, the arbitrators appear to have chosen to rule in law because they considered that to do so would be equitable, they comply with their brief. The courts do not take a restrictive position on this issue, and often infer from the fact that the arbitrators chose to apply a rule of law that they did so because the rule appeared to them to be equitable. For example, the Paris Court of Appeals has held that:

> although by empowering the arbitrators to act as *amiables compositeurs* the parties intended to exempt them from having to apply rules of law alone, the arbitral tribunal nevertheless had the option of referring to such rules in so far as it considered that they were apt to provide the most equitable outcome for the dispute.

The Court then refused to set the award aside, on the grounds that:

> in this case, the arbitrators never indicated that the award was founded exclusively on the rules [of Swedish law, the arbitrators having observed that the vendor, who was the defendant, had complied with those rules], which were mentioned in order to explain and justify the vendor's attitude at a particular point in time.[317]

The same is true where arbitrators required to act as *amiables compositeurs* apply transnational principles because such principles reflect their conception of fairness.[318]

Thus, in this context, the only situations where an award made by *amiables compositeurs* can be validly challenged on the basis of Article 1502 3° are the rare cases where the award shows either that the *amiables compositeurs* wrongly believed that they were required to refrain from exercising their equitable powers, or that they deliberately refused to exercise those powers.

On the other hand, where arbitrators required by the parties to rule in law have wrongly assumed the powers of *amiables compositeurs*, it is easier to establish that they have failed to comply with their brief.[319] Even in such cases, however, the French courts have adopted a very liberal approach. They have held that the fact that the arbitrators made reference to principles of equity is not sufficient to establish that they exceeded their powers. If the award is to be set aside or refused enforcement, it must also be established that the arbitrators actually used the powers of *amiables compositeurs* which they wrongly

---

[317] CA Paris, Mar. 15, 1984, Soubaigne v. Limmareds Skogar, 1985 REV. ARB. 285, and the commentary by Loquin, *supra* note 203. *See also* CA Paris, May 6, 1988, Unijet S.A. v. S.A.R.L. International Business Relations Ltd. (I.B.R.), 1989 REV. ARB. 83, and E. Loquin's note; in French domestic arbitration, see CA Paris, Jan. 20, 1989, Phocéenne de Dépôt v. Dépôts pétroliers de Fos, 1989 REV. ARB. 280, 2d decision, and L. Idot's note.

[318] CA Paris, Mar. 15, 1984, *Soubaigne, supra* note 317.

[319] *See, e.g.,* CA Paris, 1e Ch., Sec. Supp., Oct. 29, 1982, Raoul Duval v. General Cocoa Co., No. I 12239, unpublished.

assumed.[320] An exception will also be made where an equitable principle applies pursuant to the provisions of the governing law itself, as where that law confers on the courts the power to alter the consequences of the strict application of a given rule when they find the consequences to be too harsh. The exercise of such an option will not violate Article 1502 when provided for in the governing law.[321] Similarly, the fact that arbitrators required to rule in law have not identified the rules of law on the basis of which they reach their decision is not sufficient for their award to be set aside. In one such case, the Paris Court of Appeals satisfied itself that the arbitrators had carefully examined the disputed agreements and the conduct of the parties and reached their decision on the basis of trade usages and the general principle of good faith without any reference to equity.[322]

1636. — The second situation where arbitrators may conceivably go beyond the terms of their brief when applying rules governing the merits of the dispute is where, in the absence of any indication by the parties as to the applicable law, the arbitrators apply transnational rules rather than the law of a particular jurisdiction. It has often been argued that in doing so the arbitrators fail to comply with their brief, which is to rule in law and not in equity. That argument has been unequivocally rejected by the French courts. The *Cour de cassation* held in the *Compania Valenciana de Cementos Portland SA v. Primary Coal* case that:

> in referring to the group of rules of international commerce determined by practice and having received the sanction of national jurisprudence, the arbitrator ruled correctly as he was obliged to in accordance with the charter; thus, consequently, it was not for the Court of Appeals, instructed for violations

---

[320] CA Paris, Feb. 28, 1980, Compagnie financière Mocupia v. Inveko France, 1980 REV. ARB. 538, and E. Loquin's note, *aff'd*, Cass. 2e civ., Sept. 30, 1981, Inveko v. Mocupia, 1982 REV. ARB. 431, and E. Loquin's note; CA Versailles, July 13, 1994, Samu Auchan v. Boulogne Distribution, 1995 REV. ARB. 495, and C. Jarrosson's note.

[321] See, for example, on the assessment of damages, CA Paris, June 3, 1993, Echo v. Cogedep, 1995 REV. ARB. 468, 3d decision, and the commentary by Kessedjian, *supra* note 304. *See also* CA Paris, May 30, 1996, Arabian Construction v. Saipem, 1996 REV. ARB. 645, and D. Bureau's note. On this issue, generally, see *supra* paras. 1500 *et seq.*

[322] CA Paris, Dec. 11, 1997, Cubana v. Consavio International Ltd., 1999 REV. ARB. 124, and observations by D. Bureau.

covered by Articles 1504 and 1502 3° of the New Code of Civil Procedure, to examine the conditions of the arbitrator's determination and implementation of the selected rule of law.[323]

This decision, which carefully avoids taking a position on whether *lex mercatoria* constitutes a distinct legal order, is entirely justified, as the arbitrators' brief when the parties have not chosen the law governing the merits of their dispute is to rule on the basis of "rules of law"—and not necessarily rules of a national law—which they consider to be appropriate.[324]

1637. — The third situation where an award may be set aside or refused enforcement on the grounds that the arbitrators failed to comply with their brief with regard to the merits of the case is that where they do not apply the rules of law chosen by the parties. For this to be the case the rules of law (whether a national law or transnational rules) governing the merits of the dispute must have been clearly identified by the parties, and the arbitrators must have failed to comply with that choice.

For example, an award applying a national law other than that chosen by the parties could be set aside or refused enforcement under Articles 1502 3° and 1504. The same would be true were the arbitrators to apply transnational rules, rather than the national law chosen by the parties.[325]

That would also be the case, in theory, of an award which only applied a particular national law, despite the parties agreeing that transnational rules would govern their dispute. In such cases, however, the arbitrators have considerable freedom in determining the content of transnational rules. As a result, only particularly poorly drafted awards will be in violation, and not those which draw inspiration from a particular law in determining a transnational rule, for example.[326]

---

[323] Cass. 1e civ., Oct. 22, 1991, Compania Valenciana de Cementos Portland v. Primary Coal Inc., 1991 Bull. Civ. I, No. 275; 1992 REV. ARB. 457, and P. Lagarde's note; 1992 REV. CRIT. DIP 113, and B. Oppetit's note; 119 J.D.I. 177 (1992), and B. Goldman's note; 1992 RTD COM. 171, and observations by J.-C. Dubarry and E. Loquin; for an English translation, see 6 INT'L ARB. REP. B1 (Dec. 1991), *upholding* CA Paris, July 13, 1989, 1990 REV. ARB. 663, and P. Lagarde's note; 117 J.D.I. 430 (1990), and B. Goldman's note; 1990 REV. CRIT. DIP 305, and B. Oppetit's note; for an English translation, see XVI Y.B. COM. ARB. 142 (1991); 4 INT'L ARB. REP. B1 (Dec. 1989); *see also* CA Paris, June 12, 1980, Banque du Proche-Orient v. Fougerolle, 109 J.D.I. 931 (1982), 2d decision, and B. Oppetit's note; 1981 REV. ARB. 292, and G. Couchez' note, *aff'd*, Cass. 2e civ., Dec. 9, 1981, Fougerolle v. Banque du Proche-Orient; 1982 REV. ARB. 183, and G. Couchez' note; 109 J.D.I. 931 (1982), 3d decision, and observations by B. Oppetit; TGI Paris, Mar. 4, 1981, Norsolor v. Pabalk Ticaret Sirketi, 108 J.D.I. 836 (1981), and P. Kahn's note; 1983 REV. ARB. 466, 1st decision, *on appeal*, CA Paris, Nov. 19, 1982, 1983 REV. ARB. 465, and the commentary by Goldman, *supra* note 148, *aff'd*, Cass. 1e civ., Oct. 9, 1984, *Pabalk Ticaret Sirketi, supra* note 148.

[324] Art. 1496 of the New Code of Civil Procedure. On this issue, generally, see *supra* paras. 1443 *et seq.*

[325] On the unsatisfactory grounds for applying rules of law other than those chosen by the parties based on the theories of the incompleteness of the applicable law, trade usages understood as rules of law and international mandatory rules, see *supra* paras. 1511 *et seq.*

[326] Compare, on case law regarding compliance with the powers conferred upon *amiables compositeurs, supra* para. 1635.

Furthermore, if the national law chosen by the parties is itself inspired by other national laws, the arbitrators are perfectly entitled to refer to those national laws. Where the arbitrators examine the sources and content of the law which the parties have declared to be applicable, they do so in their entire discretion and their conclusions are not subject to review by the courts. The Paris Court of Appeals thus rejected an action to set aside an award where, in determining the content of the applicable Egyptian law, the arbitrators had referred to various provisions of French law on the grounds that those provisions had been of inspiration to Egyptian law. The action to set the award aside was based on Article 1502 3°, and the Court of Appeals rightly considered that the arbitrator had in fact applied Egyptian law to the dispute.[327]

§ 4. – Breach of Due Process

1638. — In both international and domestic arbitration, an arbitral award can be set aside or refused enforcement in France if the arbitrators have failed to comply with due process (Arts. 1502 4° and 1504). This principle, which applies to all forms of arbitration, including *amiable composition*,[328] is expressed in terms similar to those used in the New Code of Civil Procedure with respect to court proceedings (Arts. 14 *et seq.*). However, this does not mean that all of the rules of the New Code of Civil Procedure concerning compliance with the requirements of due process will automatically apply to international arbitration.[329]

When referring to those same requirements, the French courts refer in equal measure to *le principe de la contradiction* and to *les droits de la défense*, although the latter expression—frequently used prior to the reform of French arbitration law[330]—was abandoned in the 1980-81 legislation. As the Paris Court of Appeals held in one decision, the purpose of due process is to uphold the *droits de la défense*.[331]

Due process is related to the concept of international public policy in the sense that due process is embodied in the broader concept of procedural public policy. Thus, in a 1987 decision, the Paris Court of Appeals referred to "compliance with the fundamental notions of due process, within the French understanding of international public policy."[332] For that reason, in several arbitration statutes it was considered unnecessary to treat a breach of due

---

[327] CA Paris, Mar. 10, 1988, Crocodile Tourist Project Co. (Egypte) v. Aubert, 1989 REV. ARB. 269, and P. Fouchard's note.

[328] *See, e.g.*, CA Paris, July 11, 1991, *Saline d'Einville, supra* note 305. Although this concerned a domestic arbitration, the rule clearly applies in international arbitration. On this issue, generally, see Kessedjian, *supra* note 304.

[329] Mayer, *supra* note 5, at 80 *et seq.*, especially at 95.

[330] *See, e.g.*, PHILIPPE FOUCHARD, L'ARBITRAGE COMMERCIAL INTERNATIONAL ¶¶ 524 *et seq.* (1965).

[331] CA Paris, May 13, 1988, Diagrama v. Christian Dior, 1989 REV. ARB. 251, and Y. Derains' note.

[332] CA Paris, Nov. 27, 1987, C.C.M. Sulzer v. Somagec, 1989 REV. ARB. 62, and G. Couchez' note.

process as a separate ground for setting aside or refusing to enforce an award.[333] In contrast, French law considers the principle of due process—described by the *Cour de cassation* as a "superior principle" which is indispensable in providing a fair hearing[334]—to be sufficiently important to warrant separate treatment.

The principle of due process is also closely related to the principle of equal treatment of the parties. Due process implies that the parties should be given an equal opportunity to present their case. However, some laws on arbitration treat breaches of "the principle of equal treatment of the parties" and breaches of their "right to be heard in adversarial procedure" as separate violations.[335] The principle of equal treatment is capable of covering more than just an equal right to be heard. For example, it may apply to the constitution of the arbitral tribunal.[336] In any case, it is recognized in French law as a requirement of international public policy.[337]

The principle of due process also applies in some respects to the constitution of the arbitral tribunal. It is sometimes argued that if one arbitrator is a member of two arbitral tribunals set up in parallel to hear connected disputes, the requirements of due process may be contravened, because the arbitrator may have obtained information in the first arbitration which is relevant to the second arbitration but which is not raised in that second arbitration in argument. In ruling on a claim of that kind, the Paris Court of Appeals held that the principle of due process was not automatically breached solely because an arbitrator served in two parallel disputes, but that it could be breached where a decision made in one of the disputes might lead the common arbitrator to hold a preconceived opinion in the other dispute.[338]

Due process should not be confused with the requirement that arbitrators give reasons for their award. Parties sometimes seek to rely on Article 1502 4° of the New Code of Civil Procedure in support of a claim based on the failure to give reasons in the award, but the failure to give reasons is not in itself contrary to the principle of due process. It is true that where reasons have been given it is easier to assess whether there has been a breach of due process. However, an award can only be set aside or refused enforcement on the basis of Article 1502 4° if the parties were actually denied the opportunity to argue their respective claims adversarially. As the Paris Court of Appeals rightly observed in 1988, "contradiction in the reasons for the award is not to be confused with the violation of the principle of due process."[339]

---

[333] *See, e.g.*, Art. 1065 of the Netherlands Code of Civil Procedure, as amended by the Arbitration Act of July 2, 1986; Arts. 34 and 36 of the UNCITRAL Model Law.

[334] Cass. 1e civ., Feb. 5, 1991, Almira Films v. Pierrel, 1991 REV. ARB. 625, and L. Idot's note.

[335] *See, e.g.*, Art. 190, para. 2(d) of the Swiss Private International Law Statute.

[336] On this issue, generally, see *supra* paras. 792 *et seq.*

[337] *See infra* para. 1654.

[338] CA Paris, Oct. 14, 1993, Ben Nasser v. BNP, 1994 REV. ARB. 380, and P. Bellet's note; 121 J.D.I. 446 (1994), and E. Loquin's note; CA Paris, Apr. 2, 1998, *TECHNIP, supra* note 197. On this issue, generally, see *supra* paras. 982 *et seq.*

[339] CA Paris, May 13, 1988, *Diagrama, supra* note 331. *But see* CA Paris, Apr. 2, 1998, *TECHNIP, supra* note 197. On the fact that international public policy does not require reasons to be given, see *infra* para. 1658,

(continued...)

1639. — The principle of due process applies to all aspects of the arbitral proceedings. It requires that each party be given the opportunity to present its factual and legal argument, and to acquaint itself with and rebut that raised by its opponent.[340] Due process will therefore not be satisfied where an arbitral tribunal, having asked a party not to submit a large quantity of invoices, but to submit instead an accountant's report on the issue, subsequently found against that party for having failed to prove its claim by producing invoices.[341] Likewise, there will be a breach of due process allowing an award to be set aside where such award states that a defendant is in breach of contract, but that as the plaintiff submitted its evidence out of time, the issue cannot be addressed by the tribunal.[342] The principle of due process also implies that no written submission or other document can be communicated to the arbitral tribunal without also being communicated to the other party, and that the arbitral tribunal itself cannot raise any factual or legal argument without inviting the parties to comment. Contrary to a commonly-held view, the principle of due process applies to both arguments of fact and arguments of law. In particular, if the arbitral tribunal raises a legal argument, such as the application of a law other than that on which the parties have based their pleadings, it must invite the parties to present their observations adversarially.[343] In its 1995 decision in the *Thyssen* case, the Paris Court of Appeals set aside part of an award on the grounds that the arbitrators had decided on their own initiative that interest would accrue on the principal award of damages at the "one-year LIBOR rate," without having heard the parties on the issue. The Court rightly observed that "the principle of due process implies that the arbitral tribunal cannot introduce any new legal or factual issue without inviting the parties to comment on it."[344] The same court confirmed its position in its *VRV SpA* decision of November 25, 1997: "the arbitrators have the obligation to submit legal arguments they raise to the parties for their comment." Applying this principle, the court set aside an award

---

[339] (...continued)

and on this issue, generally, see *supra* para. 1392.

[340] *See, e.g.,* Cass. 1e civ., Jan. 7, 1992, Pakistan Atomic Energy Commission v. Société générale pour les techniques nouvelles, 1992 REV. ARB. 659, and observations by D. Bureau; CA Paris, Nov. 16, 1993, Ganz Mozdony v. SNCFT, 1995 REV. ARB. 477, and the commentary by Kessedjian, *supra* note 304; CA Paris, May 19, 1998, *Torno, supra* note 224; CA Paris, 1e Ch., Sec. C, Jan. 19, 1999, CIC International Ltd. v. Ministre de la Défense de la République Fédérale d'Allemagne, No. 1998/03375, unpublished.

[341] See the July 18, 1988 award of the Iran-U.S. Claims Tribunal in Avco Corp. v. Iran Aircraft Indus., Partial Award No. 377-261-3, 19 Iran-U.S. Cl. Trib. Rep. 200, recognition of which was refused by the United States Court of Appeals for the Second Circuit (Iran Aircraft Indus. v. Avco Corp., 980 F.2d 141 (2d Cir. 1992); XVIII Y.B. COM. ARB. 596 (1993)).

[342] CA Paris, Apr. 18, 1991, MORS v. Supermarket Systems, 1995 REV. ARB. 448, 2d decision, and the commentary by Kessedjian, *supra* note 304.

[343] *See supra* para. 1263. But see, where the arbitrators decided to apply transnational rules, the particularly evasive position of the court taken in response to a claim cleverly focused on this issue, in Cass. 2e civ., Dec. 9, 1981, *Fougerolle, supra* note 323. See also, in a case where the arbitral tribunal did not rely on earlier investigations carried out by one of the arbitrators on his own regarding the applicable law, and on which the parties were not invited to comment, Cass. 1e civ., Mar. 16, 1999, Etat du Qatar v. Creighton Ltd., No. Q 96-12.748, unpublished.

[344] CA Paris, Apr. 6, 1995, *Thyssen Stahlunion, supra* note 304, and the commentary by Kessedjian, *supra* note 304, at 403.

where there was found to be tortious liability without the parties being invited to state their position on that issue, both having argued on the basis of contractual liability.[345]

It is only where the rule relied on by the arbitrators is so general in nature that it must have been implicitly included in the pleadings that the arbitrators can dispense with the need to call for a specific discussion on that point. This will be the case, for example, of the principle of good faith in the performance of contracts, which will necessarily be among the elements taken into account—at least implicitly—by arbitrators who have been instructed to apply French law.[346] Likewise, the principle that contracts should be interpreted in accordance with their spirit, which simply reflects the need to establish the common intentions of the parties, is a "fundamental rule of interpretation of contracts under French law" which will always be applied by arbitrators, either implicitly or explicitly.[347]

1640. — Three observations should be made with regard to the implementation of the principle of due process.

1641. — First, it is sufficient for there to be compliance with the principle of due process that each party be given the opportunity to present its case, even though a party may in fact have decided not to do so. The Paris Court of Appeals held in its 1995 decision in the *Bin Saud Bin Abdel Aziz* case that if the defaulting party was informed of the existence of the proceedings, and if it was notified of the various procedural steps in accordance with the requirements of the arbitration rules chosen by the parties, the award made against it could not be refused enforcement on the basis of Article 1502 4° of the New Code of Civil Procedure.[348] This rule applies at all stages of the proceedings. For example, where the arbitral tribunal gives one party the opportunity to respond to a belated submission of witness evidence by a second party, the first party cannot subsequently claim that there has been a breach of due process where it fails to make any response.[349]

---

[345] CA Paris, Nov. 25, 1997, VRV v. Pharmachim, 1998 REV. ARB. 684, and G. Bolard's note. See also, in a case where due process was respected, CA Paris, Mar. 5, 1998, *Forasol*, *supra* note 202.

[346] CA Paris, Nov. 25, 1993, Paco Rabanne Parfums v. Les Maisons Paco Rabanne, 1994 REV. ARB. 730, and observations by D. Bureau. Compare, on the rejection of an argument based on an alleged violation of due process regarding the law governing the merits, where that law had been determined in the terms of reference, CA Paris, May 28, 1993, Société Générale pour l'Industrie v. Ewbank and Partners Ltd., 1993 REV. ARB. 664, and D. Bureau's note, *aff'd*, Cass. 1e civ., Feb. 28, 1995, *supra* note 202. On this issue, generally, see *supra* paras. 1261 *et seq.*

[347] CA Paris, May 28, 1993, Romak v. Philip Marine, 1995 REV. ARB. 468, 2d decision, and the commentary by Kessedjian, *supra* note 304. *See also* CA Paris, June 3, 1993, *Echo*, *supra* note 321.

[348] CA Paris, Mar. 24, 1995, Bin Saud Bin Abdel Aziz v. Crédit Industriel et Commercial de Paris, 1996 REV. ARB. 259, and J.-M. Talau's note. *See also* CA Paris, Mar. 25, 1983, Sorvia v. Weinstein International Disc Corp., 1984 REV. ARB. 363, 366, and J. Robert's note. On the requirement that the arbitrator be challenged as soon as the relevant facts are known by the challenging party, see Philippe Fouchard, *Le statut de l'arbitre dans la jurisprudence française*, 1996 REV. ARB. 326, 354.

[349] CA Paris, June 30, 1988, Industrie Pama v. Schultz Steel, 1991 REV. ARB. 351, and observations by J. H. Moitry and C. Vergne. See also, in a default situation, CA Paris, Mar. 11, 1993, *Al-Kawthar Investment*, *supra* note 303. On this issue, generally, see *supra* para. 1224.

1642. — Second, the parties are only given a satisfactory opportunity to present their case, submit their evidence and reply to the opponent's submissions if they are granted a reasonable period of time in which to do so. The court reviewing the award pursuant to Articles 1502 4° and 1504 of the New Code of Civil Procedure is responsible for determining whether the deadlines set by the arbitral tribunal for that purpose were reasonable. However, the French courts show considerable caution in performing that review. They will only set aside an award on that basis where the plaintiff clearly establishes that the allocated deadlines did not enable it to present its case appropriately.[350] The fact that due process does not mean that deadlines have to be continually extended is reflected in the 1998 ICC Rules, Article 15(2) of which requires the arbitrators to ensure that each party has a "reasonable opportunity" to present its case.

1643. — Third, and as mentioned earlier, a breach of due process will only justify an action to set aside or prevent enforcement of an award on condition that the party relying on the breach protested as soon as it became aware of it. Thus, for example, the Swiss Federal Tribunal held that a party that failed to seek an extension of time to comment on a new written submission and new evidence could not then contest the award on the grounds that it was denied the opportunity to present its observations on such documents.[351] Applying the same principle, the Paris Court of Appeals rejected a claim that due process had been violated as a result of the fact that the arbitral tribunal had taken into account documents submitted for the first time on the day of the hearing. The Court held that the party making that claim "had knowledge of the contested documents, and had the possibility, which it deliberately rejected by 'deeming' the session to be ended, to respond to these [documents] or to solicit an opportunity in which to do so from the arbitration tribunal, which did not deliver its ruling until a year later."[352]

In the same spirit of procedural fairness, the courts held there to be no breach of due process where an arbitral tribunal authorized the submission by one party of new evidence and a note in response to a late submission by its opponent, and then considered the proceedings closed.[353]

1644. — On the basis of these principles, the French courts have set aside or refused to recognize international awards in the following cases: where an expert's report requested by an arbitral tribunal was not communicated to the parties;[354] where an arbitral tribunal had

---

[350] *See, e.g.,* CA Paris, Jan. 12, 1996, Gouvernement de l'Etat du Qatar v. Creighton Ltd., 1996 REV. ARB. 428, 2d decision, and P. Fouchard's note, *aff'd,* Cass. 1e civ., Mar. 16, 1999, *supra* note 343, and on this issue, generally, see *supra* paras. 1246 and 1269 *et seq.*

[351] *See* Fed. Trib., Sept. 7, 1993, *supra* note 227.

[352] CA Paris, July 7, 1994, *Uzinexportimport, supra* note 298. On the decision rendered on the same day between the same parties, see *supra* paras. 736 and 1629, note 298. *See also* CA Paris, June 14, 1985, *Harognan, supra* note 225; CA Paris, Jan. 19, 1999, *CIC International, supra* note 340.

[353] CA Paris, Dec. 17, 1991, *Gatoil, supra* note 200; CA Paris, Feb. 21, 1984, S.A. Larco v. Wolfley, Train, de Meyer (Inconcoal Int.), 1987 REV. ARB. 395, and observations by J. Pellerin.

[354] CA Paris, Jan. 18, 1983, Sporprom Service B.V. v. Polyfrance Immo, 1984 REV. ARB. 87, and P. Mayer's note.

decided an issue on which neither the parties nor their counsels had been heard;[355] where an arbitral tribunal addressed an issue raised in a note which it had rejected on the grounds that it had been submitted out of time;[356] where the tribunal had relied on the personal knowledge of one of the arbitrators in determining the rental market for shop premises, and also referred to informal agreements which the parties had not discussed in their written submissions;[357] where the arbitrators raised a ground of tortious liability of their own motion and did not ask the parties to comment;[358] and where the tribunal based its decision on information from one of the arbitrators who was also sitting in an arbitral tribunal constituted in a parallel proceeding.[359]

It is important to note that where a breach of due process has occurred, it is not necessary to establish that it caused actual damage to one of the parties.[360]

In a large number of other cases, the French courts found allegations of the breach of due process to be unproven.[361]

---

[355] CA Paris, Jan. 19, 1990, *Immoplan, supra* note 305. Compare, in a case concerning a French domestic arbitration, the setting aside of an award where the arbitral tribunal conducted a site visit without the parties and without having notified the parties beforehand (CA Paris, Feb. 2, 1988, Marascalchi v. Donyo, 1989 REV. ARB. 62, and G. Couchez' note), and where the award was set aside because the arbitral tribunal decided to verify one party's accounts without allowing it to provide explanations regarding the figures used (Cass. 2e civ., June 21, 1995, France Pro v. Zirotti, 1995 REV. ARB. 448, 1st decision, and the commentary by Kessedjian, *supra* note 304).

[356] CA Paris, Apr. 18, 1991, *MORS, supra* note 342.

[357] CA Paris, June 10, 1993, *Compagnie Aeroflot, supra* note 205, and the commentary by Kessedjian, *supra* note 304. *See also* CA Paris, Mar. 6, 1986, Koch Shipping Inc. v. Petroci, 1987 REV. ARB. 390, and observations by J. Pellerin.

[358] CA Paris, Nov. 25, 1997, *VRV, supra* note 345.

[359] Cass. 1e civ., Mar. 24, 1998, *Excelsior Film TV, supra* note 197.

[360] *See supra* para. 1607. But see, in Swiss law, the requirement that, for an award based on several independent grounds to be set aside, a violation of due process must affect all of them (Fed. Trib., Apr. 7, 1993, ENS v. L., 1993 BULL. ASA 525, and the disapproving note by J.B.; 1994 REV. SUISSE DR. INT. ET DR. EUR. 154, and observations by P. Schweizer).

[361] *See, e.g.*, CA Paris, Nov. 18, 1983, Intercontinental Hotels NV v. Istanbul Turizm Ve Otelcilik, 1987 REV. ARB. 77, and observations by T. Bernard; CA Paris, Mar. 15, 1984, *Soubaigne, supra* note 317; CA Paris, Feb. 21, 1984, *Larco, supra* note 353; CA Paris, Apr. 26, 1985, Aranella v. Italo-Ecuadoriana, 1985 REV. ARB. 311, and E. Mezger's note; 113 J.D.I. 175 (1986), and J.-M. Jacquet's note; CA Paris, June 28, 1988, *Total Chine, supra* note 304; CA Paris, Feb. 14, 1989, *Ofer Brothers, supra* note 301; CA Paris, Feb. 16, 1989, Almira Films v. Pierrel, 1989 REV. ARB. 711, and L. Idot's note; CA Paris, June 2, 1989, T.A.I. v. S.I.A.P.E., and Gemanco v. S.A.E.P.A., 1991 REV. ARB. 87, and the commentary by Reymond, *supra* note 228; CA Paris, July 13, 1989, *Compania Valenciana, aff'd*, Cass. 1e civ., Oct. 22, 1991, *supra* note 323; CA Paris, Mar. 8, 1990, *Coumet et Ducler, supra* note 301; CA Paris, Apr. 6, 1990, *Philipp Brothers, supra* note 278; CA Paris, June 21, 1990, *Honeywell Bull, supra* note 297; CA Paris, Mar. 26, 1991, Comité populaire de la Municipalité d'El Mergeb v. Dalico Contractors, 1991 REV. ARB. 456, and H. Gaudemet-Tallon's note; for an English translation, see 6 INT'L ARB. REP. B1 (Sept. 1991); CA Paris, Apr. 4, 1991, Icart, v. Quillery, 1991 REV. ARB. 659, 2d decision, and observations by J. Pellerin; CA Paris, Feb. 12, 1993, *Unichips Finanziaria, supra* note 154; CA Paris, Nov. 25, 1993, *Paco Rabanne Parfums, supra* note 346; CA Paris, Sept. 11, 1997, *Alfalfas, supra* note 114, which rejected both the action to set aside and the application to compound the interest awarded; CA Paris, Dec. 11, 1997, *Cubana, supra* note 322. On this issue, generally, see CRÉPIN, *supra* note 199, ¶¶ 398 *et seq.*; Serge Guinchard, *L'arbitrage et le respect du principe du contradictoire (à propos de quelques décisions rendues en 1996)*, 1997 REV. ARB. 185.

§ 5. – Where Recognition or Enforcement Would Be Contrary to International Public Policy

1645. — Article 1502 5° of the New Code of Civil Procedure provides that "recognition or enforcement" of an award will be refused where that would be "contrary to international public policy." Article 1504 applies the grounds listed in Article 1502 to actions to set aside, and thus provides that an award made in France can be set aside if it is contrary to international public policy.[362]

We shall examine the method adopted by the Court of Appeals in determining whether an award is contrary to international public policy (A), before determining what is meant by the French conception of international public policy (B).

A. – METHOD

1646. — Three principles are applied by the courts when determining whether an award is contrary to public policy. The first concerns the international nature of public policy (1°), the second its application *in concreto* (2°), and the third its evolving character (3°). However, even for the purpose of determining whether an award made outside France can be recognized in France, the concept of the attenuated effect (*effet atténué*) of public policy—which amounts to being more liberal towards rights created abroad than towards the creation of the same rights in the territory of the forum—has no place in international arbitration.[363] This is because court control of compliance with international public policy is already carried out very sparingly, even where the award is made in France, leaving no room for further attenuation.

1° The International Nature of Public Policy

1647. — Unlike the first four grounds of recourse listed in Article 1502 of the New Code of Civil Procedure, which are borrowed word-for-word from the domestic arbitration provision at Article 1484 of the same Code, Article 1502 5° specifies that awards made outside France or in international arbitration in France must comply with "international public policy." Article 1484 simply refers to "public policy." The distinction between Articles 1484 and 1502 has been criticized on the grounds that Article 1502 is excessively lenient with respect to awards made outside France in cases which are either purely internal

---

[362] On this issue, generally, see Mayer, *supra* note 201; Ibrahim Fadlallah, *L'ordre public dans les sentences arbitrales, in* COLLECTED COURSES OF THE HAGUE ACADEMY OF INTERNATIONAL LAW, Vol. 249, Year 1994, Part V, at 369; JEAN-BAPTISTE RACINE, L'ARBITRAGE COMMERCIAL INTERNATIONAL ET L'ORDRE PUBLIC (1999).

[363] Cass. 1e civ., Nov. 19, 1991, Société des Grands Moulins de Strasbourg v. Compagnie Continentale France, 1992 REV. ARB. 76, and L. Idot's note. *See also* Fadlallah, *supra* note 362, ¶ 30. *But see Corte di Appello* of Milan, Dec. 4, 1992, Allsop Automatic Inc. v. Tecnoski snc, XXII Y.B. COM. ARB. 725 (1997).

to the country where they were made or are matters involving French interests alone.[364] It is argued that in those cases it would be more appropriate to apply, respectively, the public policy of the jurisdiction in question and French public policy. As discussed earlier in connection with the French legislature's decision to treat all awards made in international arbitration or outside France in the same way, this criticism only really concerns an extremely small number of disputes for which, in any event, alternative solutions can be found.[365] This has been confirmed in practice: there is no record of any award made outside France between 1981 and 1992 in an exclusively French dispute.[366]

The courts draw a clear distinction between domestic public policy and international public policy, pointing out that for the purposes of Article 1502 5° no account should be taken of the domestic public policy rules of a foreign jurisdiction,[367] or indeed of the rules of French domestic public policy (in other words, of the mandatory provisions of French domestic law). The Paris Court of Appeals has held that:

> a breach of domestic public policy—assuming that it has been established—does not provide the grounds on which to appeal against a ruling granting enforcement in France of a foreign arbitral award, because Article 1502 5° only refers to cases in which the recognition or enforcement of an award would be contrary to international public policy.[368]

Thus, the only relationship between international public policy under Article 1502 5° and French domestic public policy is purely negative: as international public policy is at the heart of domestic public policy, a rule which is not even a matter of domestic public policy could not be considered as belonging to international public policy.[369]

1648. — Conversely, it has sometimes been argued that the public policy to which Article 1502 5° refers should be taken to mean "truly international public policy," which can be defined as public policy derived from the comparison of the fundamental requirements of national laws and of public international law in particular.[370]

---

[364] See especially the authors cited *supra* para. 1561.

[365] *See supra* para. 1562.

[366] CRÉPIN, *supra* note 199, ¶ 458.

[367] CA Paris, Mar. 21, 1986, CTIP v. Ferich International, 1991 REV. ARB. 350, and observations by J.-H. Moitry and C. Vergne; CA Paris, Mar. 12, 1987, Z.O.P. v. F.T.P., Dalloz, IR 97 (1987). *See also* in Swiss law, Fed. Trib., Nov. 5, 1991, V. SA v. E.B.V., 1993 BULL. ASA 54; 1994 REV. SUISSE DR. INT. ET DR. EUR. 103, and observations by P. Schweizer.

[368] CA Paris, Mar. 12, 1985, *Intrafor Cofor*, *supra* note 203.

[369] CA Paris, Nov. 27, 1987, *C.C.M. Sulzer*, *supra* note 332; CA Paris, May 10, 1994, *Sheikh Mahfouz, supra* note 301. On the idea that international public policy is, in some respects, broader than domestic public policy, because certain rules apply only in an international context, see Mayer, *supra* note 362, at 641.

[370] *See* especially Pierre Lalive, *Transnational (or Truly International) Public Policy and International Arbitration, in* ICCA CONGRESS SERIES NO. 3, COMPARATIVE ARBITRATION PRACTICE AND PUBLIC POLICY IN ARBITRATION 257 (P. Sanders ed., 1987), and, for a French version, 1986 REV. ARB. 329; Lambert Matray, *Arbitrage et ordre public transnational, in* THE ART OF ARBITRATION – ESSAYS ON INTERNATIONAL
(continued...)

The concept of "truly international public policy" is perfectly legitimate when applied by arbitrators, who do not belong to any particular legal system, to exclude the law which would otherwise be applicable, for example.[371] However, it does not accurately reflect the requirements of Articles 1502 5° and 1504. The international public policy to which Article 1502 5° refers can only mean the French conception of international public policy or, in other words, the set of values a breach of which could not be tolerated by the French legal order, even in international cases. The goal of the review by the courts is to determine whether it would be appropriate to allow the enforceability of the award in the French legal order. It is therefore perfectly natural that its enforceability should be examined in the light of the fundamental considerations of French law. There is of course no reason why French law should not draw inspiration from concepts widely accepted outside France, and particularly from instruments adopted by international organizations, in defining what constitutes a fundamental consideration of French law. That is not, however, sufficient to justify applying "truly international public policy" when reviewing arbitral awards pursuant to Articles 1502 5° and 1504. It is therefore perfectly natural that the courts regard the expression with a degree of skepticism.[372]

2° The Application *In Concreto* of Public Policy

1649. — Where an arbitral award is reviewed in order to assess its compliance with the fundamental requirements of French law, public policy must be gauged from a practical standpoint, in the same way as for the review of a foreign court judgment for the same purpose.[373] Thus, in arbitration as in ordinary private international law thinking, it is not so much the abstract rule of law applied by the arbitrators which must be measured against the requirements of international public policy, as the actual result reached by the arbitrator or

---

[370] (...continued)
ARBITRATION – LIBER AMICORUM PIETER SANDERS 241 (J. Schultz and A.J. van den Berg eds., 1982); Jean-Hubert Moitry, *Arbitrage international et droit de la concurrence: vers un ordre public de la lex mercatoria?*, 1989 REV. ARB. 3.

[371] *See supra* paras. 1533 *et seq.*

[372] *See, e.g.,* CA Paris, May 25, 1990, *Fougerolle, supra* note 301. This decision holds that, by refusing to reconsider their decision in the light of facts subsequently revealed which showed that the position adopted by a party with regard to its subcontractors was the reverse of that it had expressed with regard to the owner, "the arbitrators did not reach a decision which infringes international public policy, as no principle of public policy—be it truly international and universally applied public policy—can authorize an arbitrator to allow a form of recourse prohibited by the procedural law governing the arbitration pursuant to the mutual intentions of the parties." *See also* Mayer, *supra* note 362, at 649. Compare with Swiss Fed. Trib., Apr. 19, 1994, which, after a long discussion of academic authority, refused to take a position on the point, preferring instead a "pragmatic approach " (Les Emirats Arabes Unis v. Westland Helicopters, 1994 BULL. ASA 404, 418–20). But see, in favor of the taking into account of a "universal conception of public policy, under which an award will be incompatible with public policy if it is contrary to the fundamental moral or legal principles recognized in all civilized countries," Swiss Fed. Trib., Dec. 30, 1994, *supra* note 218, at 224. On this issue, generally, see Homayoon Arfazadeh, *L'ordre public du fond et l'annulation des sentences arbitrales internationales en Suisse*, 1995 REV. SUISSE DR. INT. ET DR. EUR. 223.

[373] *See* HENRI BATIFFOL, PAUL LAGARDE, DROIT INTERNATIONAL PRIVÉ, Vol. I, ¶ 358 (8th ed. 1993).

the court.[374] In arbitration, that approach was endorsed by the Paris Court of Appeals in the *Reynolds* case. An action had been brought to set aside an award on the grounds that the arbitral tribunal had refused to take into account the Lebanese monopoly on tobacco imports in assessing the loss suffered by an exclusive distributor following the termination of its contract. This argument was rejected by the Court of Appeals on the grounds that:

> the scrutiny of the Court . . . must bear not upon the evaluation made by the arbitrators with regard to the cited requirements of public policy, but on the solution given to the dispute, annulment only being incurred if enforcement of that solution violates the aforementioned public policy.[375]

3° The Evolving Character of Public Policy

1650. — The understanding of international public policy in the light of which the award must be reviewed is that which is current at the time of that review. This rule is similar to that applied by the French courts to the review of foreign court judgments[376] and is known as the principle of the evolving character of public policy. Thus, an award which does not comply with the French conception of international public policy at the time it is made may be considered to be in conformity with public policy when its enforcement is sought. The reverse may also be true.

Such a situation clearly requires there to be a radical development of public policy and will therefore rarely arise in international commercial law. It is, however, conceivable in connection with economic public policy. The Versailles Court of Appeals, in a case concerning the fixing of margins for the importation and distribution of products under European Community rules, rightly held that:

---

[374] On this issue, see L. Idot, note following Cass. 1e civ., Mar. 15, 1988, Société des Grands Moulins de Strasbourg v. Compagnie Continentale France, 1990 REV. ARB. 115. The commentator considers that, in this case, the *Cour de cassation*, in contrast with the Court of Appeals, took an unsatisfactorily formalistic view of the violation of public policy (for an English translation, see XVI Y.B. COM. ARB. 129 (1991)). The Versailles Court of Appeals, ruling on remand, seems to have taken a more practical view of the assessment of public policy (Oct. 2, 1989, *supra* note 301). The same is true of the *Cour de cassation*'s decision rejecting the subsequent petition against the decision made on remand (Cass. 1e civ., Nov. 19, 1991, *supra* note 363).

[375] CA Paris, Oct. 27, 1994, *supra* note 215, 10 INT'L ARB. REP. E7 (Feb. 1995), and the commentary by Mayer, *supra* note 362, at 639. See also CA Paris, Mar. 30, 1995, Fabre v. Espitalier, 1996 REV. ARB. 131, and observations by J. Pellerin; CA Paris, Dec. 11, 1997, *Cubana*, *supra* note 322; Swiss Fed. Trib., Apr. 19, 1994, *Westland Helicopters*, *supra* note 372, at 418.

[376] BATIFFOL AND LAGARDE, *supra* note 373, ¶ 364; PIERRE MAYER, DROIT INTERNATIONAL PRIVÉ ¶ 204 (6th ed. 1998).

in accordance with Article 1502 5° of the New Code of Civil Procedure, international public policy should only be taken into account at the time when recognition or enforcement of the award is sought.[377]

However, that does not mean that facts arising after the making of the award should be taken into account in determining whether it complies with international public policy.[378]

B. – CONTENT

1651. — The requirements of international public policy concern both the arbitral procedure (1°) and the merits of the dispute (2°).

1° Public Policy Requirements Concerning the Arbitral Procedure

1652. — French law will not allow an arbitral award to be enforced if it was made in proceedings which did not satisfy the basic requirements of procedural justice.

However, if a party becomes aware of a procedural irregularity, it must object immediately. If it fails to do so, it will be deemed to have accepted the manner in which the proceedings were conducted.[379]

1653. — The first requirement of procedural public policy is compliance with due process. As French law treats the breach of due process as a separate ground on which an award can be set aside or refused enforcement,[380] we shall not examine it again here, although the courts do often treat due process as a matter of public policy.[381]

1654. — Unlike due process, the principle of equality of the parties is not considered separately in French law.[382] The courts have therefore had to recognize its existence under the umbrella of international public policy. The principle was established by the *Cour de cassation* in its *Dutco* decision.[383] The principle of equality should not be given a strictly mechanical meaning; it does not mean that each party should have precisely the same number of days in which to prepare its submissions, or exactly the same time to present its

---

[377] CA Versailles, Oct. 2, 1989, *Société des Grands Moulins de Strasbourg, supra* note 301. However, the court did not go on to apply that principle as the parties had only discussed the arbitrability of the subject matter. On this issue, see L. Idot's note following the decision.

[378] *Comp.* Cass. 1e civ., June 2, 1987, Vogeleer v. Guide de l'Automobiliste européen, 1987 Bull. Civ. I, No. 174; 1988 REV. ARB. 283, and P. Mayer's note.

[379] *See supra* para. 1606.

[380] *See supra* paras. 1638 *et seq.*

[381] *See supra* para. 1638.

[382] *But see* Art. 190, para. 2(d) of the Swiss Private International Law Statute.

[383] Cass. 1e civ., Jan. 7, 1992, *Dutco, supra* note 280 and para. 792.

oral pleadings, for example. What matters is that a general balance be maintained and that each party be given an equal opportunity to present its case in an appropriate manner.[384] However, the principle of equality does require that each party should have the same rights regarding the appointment of the arbitrators.[385]

Another situation which violates international public policy is that where a party has deceived the arbitrators—by submitting false documents, for example—even where the fraud is not discovered until after the award has been made.[386]

It was on the ground of a violation of international public policy that enforcement of an award was refused where one of the arbitrators, who was also sitting in a parallel arbitration, communicated erroneous information to the arbitral tribunal liable to have had an influence on the tribunal's decision. The *Cour de cassation* held that this "had created an imbalance between the parties in violation of the parties' rights to a fair hearing, so that the award made [outside France] in such conditions contravened French public policy" within the meaning of Articles 1502 5° of the New Code of Civil Procedure and V(2)(b) of the New York Convention.[387]

1655. — The rule that the claimant must prove its allegations of fact is sometimes also presented as a matter of international public policy.[388]

It has been argued that the dignity and impartiality of the judicial process is also a matter of public policy. When hearing an action to set an award aside on the basis of an alleged breach of such a principle, the Paris Court of Appeals carefully avoided taking a firm position on whether the principle in fact existed. The Court held that "although the general nature of the provisions of Article 1502 5° might enable [such a claim] to be examined on the basis of a principle of that kind," it had not been proven in that case that the award was made in an unfair or biased manner.[389] However, given that the concepts of dignity and impartiality are highly subjective, in our view they should not be treated as a public policy requirement distinct from the principles of due process and equality of the parties.

1656. — On the other hand, the *Cour de cassation* suggested in one case that the rule that "no one shall plead by proxy," according to which the name of the principal must be disclosed by an agent conducting proceedings in the principal's name, could be a requirement of international public policy. The petitioner argued that the decision it was challenging should have set aside, on the basis of Article 1502 5°, an award contravening that principle. The *Cour de cassation* held that the award which found a party liable towards

---

[384] On the relationship between equal treatment of the parties and due process, see *supra* para. 1638.

[385] On this issue, generally, see *supra* para. 792.

[386] *See* CA Paris, Sept. 30, 1993, *European Gas Turbines*, *supra* note 176.

[387] Cass. 1e civ., Mar. 24, 1998, *Excelsior Film TV*, *supra* note 197.

[388] *See* J. Pellerin, observations following CA Paris, Nov. 29, 1990, *Payart*, *supra* note 301. Compare, in French domestic arbitration, Cass. 2e civ., Feb. 28, 1990, which holds the rule to be applicable to arbitrators, even when acting as *amiable compositeurs* (Chantiers modernes v. Bétons chantiers, 1990 Bull. Civ. II, No. 43; 1991 REV. ARB. 649, and observations J. Pellerin).

[389] CA Paris, Dec. 20, 1984, G.P.L.A. v. The Canal Harbour Worms Co., 1987 REV. ARB. 49, and E. Mezger's note.

a third party, which was the beneficiary of a third party stipulation, was not contrary to the rule that "no one shall plead by proxy." It therefore upheld the Court of Appeals' finding that in those circumstances the arbitrators had not contravened a rule of public policy.[390] This might have led to the conclusion that the rule could therefore be considered to be a matter of international public policy. However, in a subsequent decision where a party's claim was in any case unfounded on the facts, the Paris Court of Appeals held that "as [the rule] is not a matter of domestic public policy, neither is it a matter of international public policy."[391]

1657. — The courts have likewise held that other procedural rules are not matters of international public policy.

1658. — This is the case of the requirement that the arbitrators should give reasons for their award. The *Cour de cassation* held in one case that the failure to give reasons is not "in itself contrary to the French understanding of international public policy."[392] It is only where the law applicable to the procedure or the arbitration rules stipulate that reasons must be given that non-compliance with such requirement would justify the award being set aside or refused enforcement, on the grounds that the arbitrators failed to comply with their brief.[393]

1659. — Another supposed principle that is not considered a matter of international public policy is that whereby an action to set an award aside will lead to a stay of proceedings. In one case, the Paris Court of Appeals was asked to set aside the arbitrators' decision not to stay proceedings pending the outcome of an action to set aside their interim award on jurisdiction. The Court held that "the suspensive effect of an action to set aside the award, which does not operate automatically, does not constitute a general principle of law a breach of which would be contrary to the French concept of international public policy."[394]

1659-1. — A further example of a principle held not to be a matter of international public policy is that whereby the bringing of a case before a court which has no jurisdiction suspends the statutory limitation period. A Court of Appeals considered this rule to be a matter of public policy and therefore refused to enforce an award made in Hamburg which held an action by two French companies against a Swiss company to be time-barred,

---

[390] Cass. 1e civ., May 10, 1988, Wasteels v. Ampafrance, 1989 REV. ARB. 51, and J.-L. Goutal's note.

[391] CA Paris, May 10, 1994, *Sheikh Mahfouz, supra* note 301. On this issue, generally, in French domestic law, see Pierre Julien and Natalie Fricéro, *Représentation en justice,* J.-CL. PROC. CIV., Fasc. 106, ¶¶ 23 *et seq.* (1999). In arbitral case law, see ICC Award No. 7539 (1995), French company v. Greek company, 123 J.D.I. 1030 (1996), and observations by Y. Derains.

[392] Cass. 1e civ., Nov. 22, 1966, Gerstlé v. Merry Hull, JCP, Ed. G., Pt. II, No. 15,318 (1968), and observations by H. Motulsky; 94 J.D.I. 631 (1967), and B. Goldman's note; 1967 REV. CRIT. DIP 372, and P. Francescakis' note. *See also supra* para. 1394.

[393] On the fact that the absence of reasons for an award does not constitute a breach of due process, see *supra* para. 1638. On this issue, generally, see *supra* paras. 1392 *et seq.*

[394] CA Paris, July 7, 1987, Pia Investments Ltd. v. Cassia, 1988 REV. ARB. 649, and E. Mezger's note. *See also* CA Paris, Dec. 17, 1991, *Gatoil, supra* note 200.

ignoring the fact that the claim had been made in time before a forum without jurisdiction. The *Cour de cassation* reversed this decision on the grounds that "the rule whereby a claim before a court which has no jurisdiction suspends a limitation period is not part of the French conception of international public policy."[395]

1660. — The French *Cour de cassation* has yet to decide whether the rule that civil proceedings are stayed pending the outcome of related criminal proceedings is a matter of international public policy. For it to be so would be very unhelpful in international arbitration as it would encourage parties to start criminal proceedings in the hope of disrupting the arbitral process.[396] However, the tendency of the courts seems to be moving towards having the rule apply in international arbitration, with the arbitrators nonetheless able to decide what impact, if any, the criminal proceedings should have on the arbitration.[397] The Swiss courts have held that the rule is not a matter of public policy.[398] That was also the position taken by the International Law Association in its resolution adopted in Helsinki on August 17, 1996, which provides that:

> [t]he fact that a pending or forthcoming court case, whether civil or criminal, is related to an arbitral proceeding should not, in itself, cause the discontinuation or suspension of the arbitral proceeding.[399]

2° Public Policy Requirements Concerning the Merits of a Dispute

1661. — Even more so than with procedural international public policy, the considerations of international public policy applicable to the merits of a dispute can only be described in general terms. For an award to be set aside or refused enforcement, its actual result[400] must be contrary to the fundamental convictions of French law applicable in an

---

[395] Cass. 1e civ., June 30, 1998, Mediterranean Shipping Co. v. URCOOPA, 1998 Bull. Civ. I, No. 227, at 157; 1999 REV. ARB. 80, and M.-L. Niboyet's note.

[396] *See* CA Paris, Jan. 24, 1991, *Salice, supra* note 207. Contrary to what is suggested by the commentator of the decision, the Paris Court of Appeals chose not to resolve this point, holding it to be irrelevant, and thus does not appear to us to have reached an implicit solution to the question.

[397] CA Paris, June 16, 1994, Bouyssou v. Gaillard, 1996 REV. ARB. 128, and observations by J. Pellerin; CA Paris, Feb. 10, 1995, Gruet v. Havet, 1996 REV. ARB. 135, and observations by J. Pellerin; CA Paris, Mar. 30, 1995, Fabre v. Espitalier, 1996 REV. ARB. 131, and observations by J. Pellerin; 1997 RTD COM. 231, and observations by J.-C. Dubarry and E. Loquin; TGI Paris, Feb. 12, 1996, Augier v. Hawker, 1996 REV. ARB. 135, and observations by J. Pellerin.

[398] Fed. Trib., Sept. 7, 1993, *supra* note 227. But see Art. 209(2) of the 1992 Act on Civil Procedure of the United Arab Emirates, which requires the arbitrator to stay the proceedings if "a criminal incident of any sort arises" (*see* Abdul Hamid El-Ahdab, *La nouvelle loi sur l'arbitrage de l'Etat des Emirats Arabes Unis*, 1993 REV. ARB. 229; Abdul Hamid El-Ahdab, *The New Arbitration Act of the State of the United Arab Emirates*, 11 INT'L ARB. REP. 32 (Aug. 1996)).

[399] THE INTERNATIONAL LAW ASSOCIATION, REPORT OF THE SIXTY-SEVENTH CONFERENCE – HELSINKI 32 (1996); 1996 REV. ARB. 563, and observations by E. Gaillard.

[400] *See supra* para. 1649.

international context as they stand at the time the court reaches its decision.[401] Examples of awards which would not be recognized in France would include decisions based on religious or racial discrimination, an award refusing to hold void a contract obtained by corruption,[402] or an award contravening a fundamental economic policy.

1662. — However, it is very rare for an award to be set aside or refused enforcement on such grounds. A claim based on the violation of substantive international public policy was raised forty-six times before the Paris Court of Appeals between 1981 and 1990, but only two awards were set aside on that basis, and only one enforcement order reversed.[403] In 1988, the *Cour de cassation* upheld a judgment in which the Paris Court of Appeals had set aside an award which contravened the principle of the stay of proceedings in insolvency cases.[404] After wavering briefly,[405] subsequent case law maintained that position.[406] Also in 1988, the *Cour de cassation* overruled a decision that upheld an enforcement order in respect of an award which had given effect to contractual provisions altering the statutory allocation of certain compensation payments to importers.[407] In a 1990 decision, the Paris Court of Appeals set aside an award which violated rules concerning the regulation of investments. Those rules "aim to maintain, in the general interest, a balance in economic and financial relations with foreign countries, by controlling movements of capital across national boundaries." They were therefore held to constitute requirements of international public policy.[408] In 1993, the Paris Court of Appeals recognized that:

---

[401] *See supra* para. 1650.

[402] On this issue, as it arises before arbitrators, see the references cited *supra* para. 1468. Compare, in England, with Westacre Investments Inc. v. Jugoimport-SDPR Holding Co. Ltd., [1998] 4 All E.R. 570; [1998] 3 W.L.R. 770; [1998] 2 Lloyd's Rep. 111 (High Ct., Q.B. (Com. Ct.) 1997).

[403] Crépin, *supra* note 199, at 580. *See also* CRÉPIN, *supra* note 199, ¶¶ 456 *et seq.*

[404] Cass. 1e civ., Mar. 8, 1988, Thinet v. Labrely, 1988 Bull. Civ. I, No. 65; 1989 REV. ARB. 473, and P. Ancel's note; Dalloz, Jur. 577 (1989), and J. Robert's note.

[405] CA Paris, Jan. 26, 1990, Société de Recherches et d'Etudes Techniques v. Société de Béton S.B.B.M., Dalloz, Jur. 201 (1991), and G. Cas' note; 1991 REV. ARB. 127, and observations by J.-H. Moitry and C. Vergne, *overturned by* Cass. com., Feb. 4, 1992, Saret v. SBBM, Dalloz, Jur. 181 (1992), and G. Cas' note; 1992 REV. ARB. 663, and observations by J.-H. Moitry.

[406] Cass. 1e civ., Feb. 5, 1991, *Almira Films, supra* note 334, *upholding* CA Paris, Feb. 16, 1989, *supra* note 361; Cass. com., Feb. 4, 1992, *Saret, supra* note 405; CA Paris, Feb. 27, 1992, Sohm v. Simex, 1992 REV. ARB. 590, and P. Ancel's note. *See also* CA Paris, Mar. 23, 1993, Ets. Marcel Sebin v. Irridelco International Corp., 1998 REV. ARB. 541, and P. Fouchard's note; TGI Paris, Feb. 2, 1996, Intertradex France v. Romanian Shipping Co., 1998 REV. ARB. 577, and the commentary by Philippe Fouchard, *Arbitrage et faillite, id.* at 471.

[407] Cass. 1e civ., Mar. 15, 1988, Société des Grands Moulins de Strasbourg v. Compagnie Continentale France, 1988 Bull. Civ. I, No. 72; Dalloz, Jur. 577 (1989), 2d decision, and J. Robert's note; 1990 REV. ARB. 115, and L. Idot's note.

[408] CA Paris, Apr. 5, 1990, Courrèges Design v. André Courrèges, 1991 REV. CRIT. DIP 580, and C. Kessedjian's note; 1992 REV. ARB. 110, and H. Synvet's note. The two commentators of this decision both criticized its severity.

a contract having influence-peddling or bribery as its motive or object is, therefore, contrary to French international public policy as well as to the ethics of international business as conceived by the majority of the international community.

However, the Court agreed with the arbitral tribunal that allegations of corruption had not been substantiated and therefore rejected the action to set aside the award.[409]

Also in 1993, the Paris Court of Appeals held that there is a "general principle of international public policy whereby contracts are to be performed in good faith."[410]

An award recognizing the validity of a usurious loan may be considered contrary to the French conception of international public policy if the applicable interest rate appeared to be extortionate in the light of criteria appropriate to the international nature of the agreement. That would only result in the award being set aside in part, because under French law a usurious interest rate is remedied not by avoiding the loan, but by reducing the rate to a legitimate level.[411]

In contrast, rules concerning the *res judicata* effect of court decisions,[412] the consequences of the termination of a contract,[413] and the possibility for an insurer to initiate arbitral proceedings by subrogation before arbitrators with jurisdiction over the insured[414] are not rules of international public policy.[415]

---

[409] CA Paris, Sept. 30, 1993, *European Gas Turbines, supra* note 176, 8 INT'L ARB. REP. B5 (Nov. 1993).

[410] CA Paris, Jan. 12, 1993, République de Côte d'Ivoire v. Norbert Beyrard, 1994 REV. ARB. 685, and the commentary by Mayer, *supra* note 201.

[411] See, on this last point, CA Paris, June 9, 1983, Iro-Holding v. Sétilex, 1983 REV. ARB. 497, and M. Vasseur's note. For a decision holding that compound interest is not contrary to international public policy, see Swiss Fed. Trib., Jan. 9, 1995, Inter Maritime Management S.A. v. Russin et Vecchi, 10 INT'L ARB. REP. D1, D6 (Sept. 1995); XXII Y.B. COM. ARB. 789 (1997).

[412] CA Paris, June 9, 1983, *Iro-Holding, supra* note 411.

[413] CA Paris, Apr. 6, 1990, *Philipp Brothers, supra* note 278.

[414] Cass. 1e civ., May 2, 1990, *Alpha Transports, supra* note 301.

[415] For a decision holding that statutes of limitations are not rules of international public policy, see, in Swiss law, Fed. Trib., Mar. 13, 1992, X. v. Y, 1992 BULL. ASA 365; 1994 REV. SUISSE DR. INT. ET DR. EUR. 106, and observations by P. Schweizer.

CHAPTER II
INTERNATIONAL CONVENTIONS

1663. — The recognition and enforcement of arbitral awards has been addressed in a number of international conventions.

The 1923 Geneva Protocol on Arbitration Clauses in Commercial Matters is primarily concerned with the recognition of the validity of arbitration agreements and the jurisdiction of national courts to rule on questions of arbitral procedure. However, it already envisaged that each contracting state should undertake to "ensure the execution by its authorities and in accordance with the provisions of its national laws of arbitral awards made in its own territory" pursuant to the Protocol's rules regarding arbitration agreements and arbitrators' jurisdiction.[1] In contrast, the 1927 Geneva Convention principally dealt with "the Execution of Foreign Arbitral Awards."[2] The principle was laid down for the first time in that Convention that the courts responsible for enforcing an award cannot review its merits. The Convention also set forth a number of substantive rules which have since become well established, including the requirements of compliance with due process and the limits of the arbitration agreement. Besides these rules, the Convention subjected the enforcement of awards to a number of rules framed in terms of jurisdiction and applicable law, and did not specify the limits of the review of awards which should be carried out by the courts in recognition and enforcement actions. The fact that the authors of the Convention failed to even harmonize the choice of law rules to be used by the courts of the place of enforcement underlines the inadequacy of this approach.[3]

Significant progress was made by the 1958 New York Convention, which still constitutes the main instrument used to enforce arbitral awards throughout the world.[4] Its continuing relevance was confirmed in 1985 by the UNCITRAL Model Law which, on the subject of the recognition and enforcement of foreign arbitral awards, simply adopted the provisions of the New York Convention.[5] Although too conservative,[6] this decision is nonetheless a tribute to the important role played over the past 40 years by the New York Convention.

The Geneva Convention of April 21, 1961, known as the European Convention owing to its regional character, addresses a number of different issues arising in international

---

[1] Art. 3. *See supra* para. 241.

[2] *See supra* para. 244.

[3] On this issue, see PHILIPPE FOUCHARD, L'ARBITRAGE COMMERCIAL INTERNATIONAL 107 (1965).

[4] On this Convention, see *supra* paras. 247 *et seq.*

[5] *See infra* paras. 1666 *et seq.* On the Model Law, see *supra* paras. 203 *et seq.*

[6] *See supra* para. 1594.

arbitration.[7] It only deals with the recognition and enforcement of awards indirectly, listing a limited number of grounds on which a decision to set aside an award at the seat of arbitration or in the country under the law of which the award was made will be recognized by the countries applying the Convention. In so doing it required the Contracting States—some 23 years prior to the *Norsolor-Hilmarton* case law [8]—to recognize awards set aside in the country of origin on grounds which are not found in the limitative list set forth in the Convention.[9]

Within its scope of application, the 1965 Washington Convention provides an extremely effective mechanism for the recognition and enforcement of ICSID awards. However, as ICSID arbitration is totally autonomous, awards are reviewed—sometimes in excessive detail—within the ICSID system by *ad hoc* committees.[10]

Other conventions, mostly regional, complement the existing mechanisms governing the recognition and enforcement of arbitral awards.

These include the Inter-American Convention on International Commercial Arbitration, signed in Panama on January 30, 1975, which is modeled on the New York Convention.[11] There is some debate as to its exact scope. It undoubtedly applies in relations between the countries which have ratified it and, as it contains no reciprocity condition, it may also apply to the enforcement of awards made in non-signatory countries.[12]

In addition, the 1987 Amman Arab Convention on Commercial Arbitration,[13] which established an Arab Centre for Commercial Arbitration based in Rabat, Morocco, provides that awards made under the auspices of the Centre can only be refused enforcement by the supreme courts of contracting states where the award is contrary to public policy.[14]

---

[7]   On this Convention, see *supra* paras. 274 *et seq.*

[8]   *See supra* para. 1595.

[9]   *See infra* para. 1715. On multilateral conventions regarding enforcement of arbitral awards, see Andrea Giardina, *The Practical Application of Multilateral Conventions, in* ICCA CONGRESS SERIES NO. 9, IMPROVING THE EFFICIENCY OF ARBITRATION AGREEMENTS AND AWARDS: 40 YEARS OF APPLICATION OF THE NEW YORK CONVENTION 440 (A.J. van den Berg ed., 1999).

[10] On this Convention, see *supra* paras. 301 *et seq.* On this issue, generally, see, for example, ARON BROCHES, SELECTED ESSAYS – WORLD BANK, ICSID, AND OTHER SUBJECTS OF PUBLIC AND PRIVATE INTERNATIONAL LAW (1995), and the references cited therein.

[11] *See supra* para. 294.

[12] On this issue, see Albert Jan van den Berg, *L'arbitrage commercial en Amérique Latine*, 1979 REV. ARB. 123, 194; Horacio Grigera Naon, *Latin America: Overcoming Traditional Hostility Towards Arbitration, in* PRACTISING LAW INSTITUTE, INTERNATIONAL COMMERCIAL ARBITRATION – RECENT DEVELOPMENTS, Vol. II, at 375, 412 (1988).

[13] See the text in 1989 REV. ARB. 743, and the commentary by Abdul Hamid El-Ahdab, *Le centre arabe d'arbitrage commercial à Rabat – Convention arabe d'Amman sur l'arbitrage commercial (1987)*, *id.* at 631; *see also* MATTHIEU DE BOISSÉSON, LE DROIT FRANÇAIS DE L'ARBITRAGE INTERNE ET INTERNATIONAL 982 (2d ed. 1990); Mahir Jalili, *Amman Arab Convention on Commercial Arbitration*, 7 J. INT'L ARB. 139 (Mar. 1990).

[14] Art. 35. On this Convention, see *supra* para. 297.

There are also a number of bilateral conventions concerning the recognition and enforcement in one country of arbitral awards made in the other contracting state.[15]

The existence of these bilateral conventions, and the fact that the benefit of some multilateral conventions such as the New York Convention may be subject to a reciprocity condition (Art. I(3)), make the application of these various instruments one of the important factors to be taken into account when selecting the seat of arbitration.[16]

1664. — The relationships between these various conventions are complex and sometimes raise awkward conflicts. Most authors consider that such conflicts should be resolved by applying the principle of maximum effectiveness, so that the convention most favorable to the recognition and enforcement of the award should prevail. In fact, conventions on enforcement often specify themselves that more favorable conventions should prevail.[17]

The relationships between conventions and national laws are subject to the same principles, and conventions usually stipulate that the conditions they impose simply represent the minimum level of recognition afforded to awards.[18]

1665. — The analysis of the main conventions on this subject—namely the 1958 New York Convention and the 1961 European Convention—is helpful in gaining an understanding of how awards made in contracting states are liable to be enforced in other contracting states.[19] However, it is of limited relevance for the enforcement of foreign awards in legal systems, such as that of France, where the national rules governing enforcement are more liberal than those of the conventions.

---

[15] *See supra* paras. 216 *et seq.* On this issue, see Franz Matscher, *Experience with Bilateral Treaties, in* ICCA CONGRESS SERIES NO. 9, IMPROVING THE EFFICIENCY OF ARBITRATION AGREEMENTS AND AWARDS: 40 YEARS OF APPLICATION OF THE NEW YORK CONVENTION 452 (A.J. van den Berg ed., 1999).

[16] On this issue, see *supra* paras. 1239 *et seq.* For example, prior to the ratification of the New York Convention by Turkey, Vienna was often selected as a situs in disputes concerning Turkey, so as to enable any award to be enforced in Turkey on the basis of the bilateral treaty between Turkey and Austria. Today, Paris is sometimes chosen by parties who may want to enforce an award in the United Arab Emirates, because the Emirates have not yet acceded to the New York Convention, but are party to a bilateral treaty with France.

[17] For an analysis of certain conflicts between conventions, see, for example, Albert Jan van den Berg, *The New York Convention 1958 and Panama Convention 1975: Redundancy or Compatibility?*, 5 ARB. INT'L 214 (1989); for the affirmation of the principle of maximum effectiveness in the context of a conflict between the 1869 Franco-Swiss Convention (today repealed) and the 1958 New York Convention, see Swiss Fed. Trib., Mar. 14, 1984, Denysiana v. Jassica, ATF 110 Ib 191; 1984 BULL. ASA 206; 1985 REV. CRIT. DIP 551, 1st decision, and B. Dutoit's note; for an English translation, see XI Y.B. COM. ARB. 536 (1986). On this issue, generally, see *supra* paras. 217 *et seq.*

[18] *See, e.g.*, Art. VII of the 1958 New York Convention and the case law cited *supra* paras. 267 *et seq. See also* Jacques Béguin, *Le droit français de l'arbitrage international et la Convention de New York du 10 juin 1958, in* PROCEEDINGS OF THE 1ST INTERNATIONAL COMMERCIAL ARBITRATION CONFERENCE 217 (N. Antaki and A. Prujiner eds., 1986).

[19] On the different forms of reciprocity that may affect the implementation of certain conventions, see *supra* paras. 261 and 276.

SECTION I
THE 1958 NEW YORK CONVENTION

1666. — The 1958 New York Convention on the Recognition and Enforcement of Foreign Arbitral Awards is one of the most extensively ratified international instruments in any domain.[20]

Its aim is to facilitate the recognition and enforcement[21] of awards in countries which have ratified it.[22]

1667. — Like the 1927 Geneva Convention, the New York Convention deals in parallel with recognition and enforcement.[23] In most cases, enforcement, not mere recognition, is sought. However, recognition may be requested where the party relying on an award merely wishes it to have a negative effect.[24] In such a case, it is not easy to distinguish between recognition and the *res judicata* effect of arbitral awards. The difficulties with this terminology might have been avoided if care had been taken to draw a clear distinction between *exequatur* (which integrates an award into a legal order or regardless of whether it will be enforced) and the actual enforcement of the award.[25]

1668. — The scope of the Convention does not depend on the nationality of the parties to the arbitration. It applies to all "foreign" awards, that is to say all awards made in a country other than that where enforcement is sought. The term "foreign" is also generally

---

[20] On the history of the Convention and its ratification, see *supra* paras. 247 *et seq.*

[21] The Convention does not, however, enable the courts to add to the award. See, for example, on the refusal to grant interest on an award for the period following its delivery, CA Brussels, Jan. 24, 1997, Compagnie Inter-Arabe de Garantie des Investissements (CIAGI) v. Banque Arabe et Internationale d'Investissement (BAII), 1998 REV. ARB. 181, and J. Linsmeau's note, especially at 198; 1997 BULL. ASA 334; XXII Y.B. COM. ARB. 643 (1997), *aff'd*, Belgian *Cour de cassation*, June 5, 1998, CIAGI v. BAII, 1998 REV. ARB. 715, and J. Linsmeau's note; 1998 BULL. ASA 719, with an introductory note by G. Block at 715; *see also* Bernard Hanotiau and Bruno Duquesne, *L'exécution en Belgique des sentences arbitrales belges et étrangères*, 1997 [BELG.] JOURN. TRIB. 305 (1997).

[22] For a commentary, see especially ALBERT JAN VAN DEN BERG, THE NEW YORK ARBITRATION CONVENTION OF 1958 (1981) and, for a consolidated presentation of court decisions on the application of the Convention in the various member states, see the Commentary in the YEARBOOK COMMERCIAL ARBITRATION by A.J. van den Berg, the latest of which is at XXI Y.B. COM. ARB. 394 (1996). On the desire for a uniform interpretation of the Convention and the necessity for counsel to consult the proper treatises and reference works, see Supreme Court of Hong Kong, High Court, Mar. 2, 1991, Shenzhen Nan Da Industrial and Trade United Co. Ltd. v. FM International Ltd., XVIII Y.B. COM. ARB. 377, 384 (1993).

[23] On the questionable application of the New York Convention to an action to set aside an award made in France, see CA Versailles, Jan. 23, 1991, Bomar Oil v. ETAP, 1991 REV. ARB. 291, and C. Kessedjian's disapproving note; for an English translation, see XVII Y.B. COM. ARB. 488 (1992); see also the discussion *supra* para. 495; the mistaken reference to the New York Convention in the reasoning as to which court had jurisdiction over an arbitral award, International Standard Electric Corp. v. Bridas Sociedad Anonima Petrolera, 745 F. Supp. 172 (S.D.N.Y. 1990); XVII Y.B. COM. ARB. 639 (1992); for a French translation, see 1994 REV. ARB. 739, and Y. Derains' note.

[24] On these notions, see VAN DEN BERG, *supra* note 22, at 243–45.

[25] On the similar ambiguities found, for example, in French law, see *supra* para. 1568.

interpreted as covering awards which are not considered "national" because of certain foreign aspects which characterize the dispute, even if such awards have been made in the country where the benefit of the Convention is sought.[26] The concept of an award is not defined by the Convention, which leaves the courts of each contracting state to define it according to their own law. The Convention also allows contracting states to restrict its territorial and substantive scope, by providing for a reciprocity reservation and a commercial reservation.[27]

1669. — The procedure (§ 1) and the substantive conditions (§ 2) governing the recognition and enforcement of foreign arbitral awards under the Convention will now be discussed in turn.

§ 1. – Procedure for Recognition and Enforcement of Foreign Arbitral Awards Under the New York Convention

1670. — The New York Convention contains a number of rules governing the procedure for recognition and enforcement of awards in the country where such recognition or enforcement is sought (the host country) (A). It also governs the relationship between proceedings in the host country and those liable to be initiated in the country where the seat of the arbitration is located or in the country the law of which governed the arbitral proceedings (the country of origin) (B).

A. – PROCEDURE IN THE HOST COUNTRY

1671. — The New York Convention does not determine the rules of jurisdiction and procedure under which an award must be recognized or enforced. It simply indicates, in its Article III, that "[e]ach Contracting State shall recognize arbitral awards as binding and enforce them in accordance with the rules of procedure of the territory where the award is relied upon" provided that such awards satisfy the conditions set forth in the Convention.[28]

However, the Convention prohibits states from imposing "substantially more onerous conditions or higher fees or charges on the recognition or enforcement of arbitral awards to which this Convention applies than are imposed on the recognition or enforcement of domestic arbitral awards" (Art. III *in fine*).

---

[26] On this issue, see V.S. Deshpande, *Jurisdiction Over 'Foreign' and 'Domestic' Awards in the New York Convention, 1958*, 7 ARB. INT'L 123 (1991); V.S. Deshpande, *'Foreign Award' in the 1958 New York Convention*, 9 J. INT'L ARB. 51 (Dec. 1992); Michael Pryles, *Foreign Awards and the New York Convention*, 9 ARB. INT'L 259 (1993).

[27] *See supra* paras. 261 *et seq.*

[28] *See infra* paras. 1693 *et seq.* In French law, the relevant procedures are those of Articles 1498 *et seq.* of the New Code of Civil Procedure. *See supra* paras. 1566 *et seq.*

This does not mean that the system for recognition and enforcement of foreign arbitral awards should necessarily be identical to the system applicable to domestic awards.[29] Nevertheless, where the host country has no specific procedure for the enforcement of foreign awards, the enforcement procedures for domestic awards will apply as a result of the Convention.[30] These local procedures should not be confused with the substantive conditions for recognition and enforcement determined by the Convention. Further, it is important to ensure that local procedures do not impair the objectives of the Convention by preventing rapid enforcement of awards through their complexity or ineffectiveness.

1672. — The Convention lays down two important rules concerning the burden of proof and the role of the courts. It also specifies which documents are to be submitted by the applicant for recognition or enforcement.

1673. — The first of these procedural rules concerns the burden of proving allegations which may prevent recognition and enforcement of the award. Under the 1927 Geneva Convention the party applying for enforcement was responsible for establishing that the award satisfied all conditions for recognition or enforcement, and hence that it contained none of the defects which might prevent such recognition or enforcement (Arts. 1 and 4). This principle is reversed in the New York Convention. The party applying for enforcement is only required to submit a certain number of documents to establish the authenticity and content of the award, and the existence of the arbitration agreement on which the award is based.[31] It is then "the party against whom the award is invoked" who must prove the existence of grounds for refusal of recognition and enforcement (Art. V).[32]

This represents enormous progress and reflects a radical change of attitude towards arbitral awards. The New York Convention recognizes that the award in itself constitutes a title capable of producing certain effects without the need for various extrinsic elements to be established.[33] This change of position went beyond the proposals of the ICC, which had suggested in 1953 that the 1927 Geneva Convention should be amended so as to reverse

---

[29] On the different ways of complying with the requirements of Article III, see VAN DEN BERG, *supra* note 22, at 236 *et seq.*

[30] See VAN DEN BERG, *supra* note 22, at 237, although the author cites a decision of the Tokyo Court of Appeals, Mar. 14, 1963, Hiroshi Nishi v. Casaregi, Compania di navigazione e commercio, 1964 REV. ARB. 102; I Y.B. COM. ARB. 194 (1976), which does not support this view because it was reached on the basis of ordinary Japanese law rules rather than the Convention.

[31] Art. IV. *See infra* para. 1675.

[32] For an example of the application of this rule to a party claiming not to have been informed of the arbitral proceedings against it, see Italian *Corte di Cassazione*, Aug. 8, 1990, Vento & C snc v. E.D. & F. Man (Coffee) Ltd., XVII Y.B. COM. ARB. 545, ¶ 8 at 548 (1992).

[33] On the importance of this development, see Jean-Denis Bredin, *La Convention de New-York du 10 juin 1958 pour la reconnaissance et l'exécution des sentences arbitrales étrangères/The New York Convention of June 10th 1958 for the Recognition and Enforcement of Foreign Arbitral Awards*, 88 J.D.I. 1002, 1020 (1960); Jean Robert, *La Convention de New York du 10 juin 1958 pour la reconnaissance et l'exécution des sentences arbitrales étrangères*, 1958 REV. ARB. 70, 77; Pieter Sanders, *A Twenty Years' Review of the Convention on the Recognition and Enforcement of Foreign Arbitral Awards*, 13 INT'L LAW. 269 (1979), and for a French version, 1979 DPCI 359, 360; FOUCHARD, *supra* note 3, at 516; VAN DEN BERG, *supra* note 22.

the burden of proof only in respect of certain grounds on which the enforcement of awards might be refused.[34] The New York Convention applied that suggestion to all such grounds. It also rightly distinguished between grounds which must be raised by the party seeking to prevent enforcement, and those which can be raised, on their own motion, by the courts of the jurisdiction where recognition or enforcement is sought.

1674. — The second important procedural rule contained in the Convention concerns the role of the courts of the host country. On this point, the Convention distinguishes two sets of grounds on which recognition or enforcement may be refused. Certain grounds, concerning the existence and validity of the arbitration agreement,[35] the conduct of the arbitral proceedings,[36] and the status of the arbitral award[37]—sometimes referred to as "irregularities internal to the arbitration"[38]—must be raised by the party against whom the award is invoked in order for them to be admissible. Other grounds, involving matters which are more important to the host country itself, can be raised by the courts of that country on their own motion. This is the case with the arbitrability of the dispute[39] and the non-compliance of the award with international public policy.[40] The distinction is appropriate, as non-arbitrability and non-compliance with international public policy are the only two issues which are liable to affect the fundamental values of the host country.

1675. — The Convention also specifies which documents are to be submitted by the party applying for recognition or enforcement. Article IV, paragraph 1 of the Convention states that:

> [t]o obtain the recognition and enforcement [of the award], the party applying for recognition and enforcement shall, at the time of the application, supply: (*a*) The duly authenticated original award or a duly certified copy thereof; (*b*) The original [arbitration] agreement . . . or a duly certified copy thereof.[41]

The Convention adds, in Article IV, paragraph 2, that:

---

[34] *See* ENFORCEMENT OF INTERNATIONAL AWARDS (ICC Publication No. 174, 1953) and the Preliminary Draft of the Convention, Articles III and IV, *reprinted in Enforcement of International Arbitral Awards – Report and Preliminary Draft Convention adopted by the Committee on International Commercial Arbitration at its meeting of 13 March 1953*, ICC BULLETIN, Vol. 9, No. 1, at 32 (1998).

[35] *See infra* paras. 1695 and 1700.

[36] *See infra* paras. 1696 and 1701.

[37] *See infra* para. 1677.

[38] FOUCHARD, *supra* note 3, at 517.

[39] *See infra* para. 1705.

[40] *See infra* para. 1710.

[41] For an example of a refusal to grant enforcement because of the failure to produce the arbitration agreement, see Italian *Corte di Cassazione*, Dec. 19, 1991, Israel Portland Cement Works (Nesher) Ltd. v. Moccia Irme SpA, XVIII Y.B. COM. ARB. 419 (1993).

> [i]f the said award or agreement is not made in an official language of the
> country in which the award is relied upon, the party applying for recognition
> and enforcement of the award shall produce a translation of these documents
> into such language. The translation shall be certified by an official or sworn
> translator or by a diplomatic or consular agent.

The purpose of authentication of the award is to enable the court hearing the application for recognition or enforcement to verify that the award is genuine and to establish the identity of its authors. Authentication therefore relates primarily to the content of the award and the identity and signature of the arbitrators. A copy will suffice, provided that it is duly certified.[42] The authors of the Convention chose not to specify which law should govern the authentication of the original or the certification of the copy.[43] Although one cannot go so far as to infer that the Convention thus established a principle in favor of the validity of the award—no such principle appears in the text of the Convention[44]—this voluntary omission allows the courts to apply either the requirements of form of the country of origin, or those of their own law.[45] The same desire for flexibility led the authors of the Convention to refrain from determining the authority responsible for accomplishing the necessary formalities. It is generally accepted that courts, notaries and diplomatic or consular agents of the country of origin may authenticate the original or certify the copy.[46]

Although the Convention provides that these documents are to be submitted by the party applying for enforcement "at the time of the application," the courts of several countries have held that the failure to produce the stipulated documents—usually the authentic copy—can subsequently be corrected.[47]

The requirement that the arbitration agreement should also be filed raises a question as to whether the existence and validity of the arbitration agreement should be verified by the court hearing the application for recognition or enforcement otherwise than in the manner and within the limits provided for in Article V. The answer is in the negative, because the

---

[42] On whether the original version from which a copy is made must also be authenticated, see VAN DEN BERG, *supra* note 22, at 256.

[43] But see Article 4, paragraph 1 of the 1927 Geneva Convention which requires the production of "the original award or copy thereof duly authenticated, according to the requirements of the law of the country in which it was made."

[44] *But see* VAN DEN BERG, *supra* note 22, at 253.

[45] For an illustration of courts using this discretion, see CA Brussels, Jan. 24, 1997, *CIAGI*, *aff'd*, Belgian *Cour de cassation*, June 5, 1998, *supra* note 21. *See also* Hanotiau and Duquesne, *supra* note 21.

[46] On this issue, generally, see VAN DEN BERG, *supra* note 22, at 255; GIORGIO GAJA, INTERNATIONAL COMMERCIAL ARBITRATION – NEW YORK CONVENTION, Vol. No. 1, at I.C.1 (1984).

[47] *See* Austrian *Oberster Gerichtshof*, Nov. 17, 1965, German party v. Austrian party, I Y.B. COM. ARB. 182 (1976); Imperial Ethiopian Gov't v. Baruch-Foster Corp., 535 F.2d 334 (5th Cir. 1976); II Y.B. COM. ARB. 252 (1977); Hong Kong Supreme Court, Aug. 23, 1991, Guangdong New Technology Import & Export Corp. Jiangmen Branch v. Chiu Shing trading as B.C. Property & Trading Co., XVIII Y.B. COM. ARB. 385, ¶ 4 at 387 (1993). See also, for a discussion of the liberalism of the courts in applying Article IV, VAN DEN BERG, *supra* note 22, at 248 *et seq.* The Italian courts seem, however, to have taken the opposing view: *Corte di Appello* of Bologna, Feb. 4, 1993, Subcontractor v. Contractor, XIX Y.B. COM. ARB. 700, ¶ 8 at 703 (1994), and the observations by A. J. van den Berg at 563.

intention of the authors of the Convention was clearly to confine the grounds on which recognition and enforcement can be refused to the grounds listed in Article V.[48]

The requirement for a translation into an official language of the country in which the award is relied upon is stipulated by the New York Convention as being mandatory (Art. IV(2)), whereas the 1927 Geneva Convention merely stated that translations "may be demanded" (Art. 4, para. 2). However, again in the interest of flexibility, the New York Convention does not determine to which country the authorities certifying the translation should belong.

B. – INTERACTION OF PROCEEDINGS IN THE HOST COUNTRY WITH PROCEEDINGS IN THE COUNTRY OF ORIGIN

1676. — Among the most difficult issues that arise under the New York Convention are those concerning the interaction of proceedings taking place in the country where recognition or enforcement is sought (the host country) with proceedings which may take place in the country where the seat of the arbitration is located, or in that under the law of which the award was made (the country of origin).

The essential principle laid down by the Convention is that the party applying for enforcement need not initiate any proceedings in the country of origin in order to obtain the benefit of the Convention in the host country (1°). However, the party resisting enforcement may enjoy the benefit in the host country of previous or pending proceedings in the country of origin (2°).

1° Optional Nature of Proceedings in the Country of Origin

1677. — In order to obtain the benefit of the New York Convention, a party applying for recognition or enforcement of an award is not required to initiate proceedings in the country of origin of the award. This is one of the main advances made by the Convention, which thus abolished the requirement of "double *exequatur*" contained in the 1927 Geneva Convention, whereby it was necessary to establish that "the award [had] become final in the State where it [had] been made" (Art. 1, para. 2(d)). The Geneva Convention also specified that an award would "not be considered as such if it is open to *opposition*, *appel* or *pourvoi en cassation* (in the countries where such forms of procedure exist) or if it is proved that any proceedings for the purpose of contesting the validity of the award are pending" (Art. 1, para. 2(d), *in fine*). In practice, this meant that the party seeking to rely on the award had to apply for *exequatur* in the country of origin in order to establish that the award was final. In order to remove this requirement of "double *exequatur*," the New York Convention merely refers to a "binding" award, rather than a "final" award (Art.V(1)(e)) and, as discussed earlier, the

---

[48] *See, e.g.*, VAN DEN BERG, *supra* note 22, at 250. For the position in French law, see *supra* para. 1576.

burden of proof is reversed.[49] The courts have sometimes had to remind parties of this rule in cases where it was claimed that the award in question should previously have been declared enforceable in the country of origin.[50]

1678. — However, problems still arise essentially because, unlike the word "final" used in the 1927 Geneva Convention, the word "binding" is not defined by the New York Convention.

This ambiguity has generated controversy as to whether the word "binding" should be given a specific meaning under the Convention or whether, on the contrary, an award can only be considered as being "binding" for the purposes of the Convention if it is binding under the law of the country of origin.

1679. — One group of authors favored the idea of a specific, autonomous meaning of the concept under the Convention. However, not all of them agreed as to the definition to be adopted, with three principal interpretations being proposed.

The first interpretation suggested that the expression "binding award" was simply another way of expressing the requirement that the award be "final." Under this interpretation, the New York Convention would thus simply reiterate, "in a more condensed and abstract form," the requirements of the 1927 Geneva Convention.[51] This interpretation was soon abandoned, on the basis that the purpose of the New York Convention was to make progress as compared to the Geneva Convention and that, in particular, the need to abolish "double exequatur"[52] precluded there being a requirement that an award be "final."[53]

The second interpretation of the word "binding," which is preferred by most authors who consider that it should be construed as an autonomous concept, is based on the distinction between ordinary and extraordinary recourse. A binding award would thus be an award which cannot be the subject of ordinary recourse proceedings (meaning those where the substance of the award is reviewed), even though it may still be the subject of extraordinary recourse (including actions to set aside).[54]

The third interpretation confines the cases where an award could be considered non-binding to a strict minimum. Under this interpretation, an award which is not enforceable in its country of origin can nevertheless be "binding" within the meaning of the Convention,

---

[49]   *See supra* para. 1673. *See also* Supreme Appeal Court of Kuwait, Cassation Circuit, Nov. 21, 1988, Contract party v. Contract party, XXII Y.B. COM. ARB. 748 (1997).

[50]   *See, e.g.,* Italian *Corte di Cassazione,* Apr. 15, 1980, S.a.s. Lanificio W. Banci v. Bobbie Brooks Inc., 110 J.D.I. 201 (1983). See also the French case law cited *infra* para. 1684.

[51]   Berthold Goldman, *Arbitrage (droit international privé), in* ENCYCLOPÉDIE DALLOZ – DROIT INTERNATIONAL 288 (1968).

[52]   *See infra* para. 1717.

[53]   For a discussion of this position, see P. Kahn, note following TGI Paris, réf., May 15, 1970, Compagnie de Saint Gobain – Pont-à-Mousson v. The Fertilizer Corporation of India, Ltd., 98 J.D.I. 312, 316 (1971).

[54]   *See, e.g.,* Sanders, *supra* note 33, 23 INT'L LAW. 275; 1979 DPCI 369; VAN DEN BERG, *supra* note 22, at 341 *et seq.* Compare with FOUCHARD, *supra* note 3, at 532 *et seq.* who, noting the ambiguity of the word "binding," observes that the authors of the Convention would have been better advised to follow the ICC draft, and thus to require only that the award not be set aside.

and the only grounds on which an award might be considered non-binding stem from the arbitral proceedings or from the award itself, irrespective of the position of the law of the country of origin of the award. An award would therefore only be considered non-binding within the meaning of the Convention if it could still be appealed before a second-tier arbitral tribunal, or if it were conditional on the occurrence of certain other events.[55]

1680. — In support of the idea that the word "binding" should have an autonomous meaning under the Convention, two main arguments have been put forward.

First, to resort to the concepts applied in the country of origin would amount to bringing back a form of double *exequatur*, a condition which the authors of the Convention intended to remove.[56] However, that argument is unconvincing. The application of the rules found in a given jurisdiction does not mean that court proceedings should be initiated in that jurisdiction.

The second argument is that, having debated at length whether the distinction between ordinary and extraordinary recourse should be used in the Convention, the authors of the Convention only rejected the distinction—despite the fact that it reflected the substance of the position on which they had agreed—because it was not common to all legal systems and, in those where it is present, it differs from one system to the next.[57] Once again, this argument is unsatisfactory. It is often the case that a proposal will be rejected because its content is unacceptable. This is of course the most natural interpretation of its rejection. However, it may also be rejected on the grounds that it is superfluous. In this case, the observation that not all legal systems share the same distinction tends to suggest that the authors of the Convention were, at the very least, reluctant to accept the idea. It is therefore not in keeping with the intention of the authors of the Convention to seek to reintroduce the distinction by way of interpretation. In fact, it must be acknowledged that the history of the Convention's negotiation sheds little light on this issue. As one author rightly commented, the debate on this question was "extremely confused."[58]

---

[55] RENÉ DAVID, ARBITRATION IN INTERNATIONAL TRADE ¶ 441 (1985). Compare with Henri Motulsky who defines "binding" as meaning "having an authority comparable to that of *res judicata*" (ECRITS – VOL. 2 – ETUDES ET NOTES SUR L'ARBITRAGE 396 (1974) ("L'exécution des sentences arbitrales étrangères")).

[56] Sanders, *supra* note 33, 23 INT'L LAW. 276; 1979 DPCI 370; VAN DEN BERG, *supra* note 22, at 341.

[57] VAN DEN BERG, *supra* note 22, at 342; Albert J. van den Berg, *New York Convention of 1958 – Consolidated Commentary – Cases Reported in Volumes XX (1995) – XXI (1996)*, XXI Y.B. COM. ARB. 394, 495 (1996).

[58] DAVID, *supra* note 55, at 399–400. For a more detailed description of the views expressed during the negotiations of the New York Convention, see Jacques El-Hakim, *Should the Key Terms Award, Commercial and Binding be Defined in the New York Convention?*, 3 J. INT'L ARB. 161, 168 (Mar. 1989): the Swiss expert considered it sufficient for the award not to have been set aside; the Dutch, Italian and Turkish representatives preferred the award to be not capable of appeal (as opposed to an action to set aside); the Guatemalan representative proposed that the award should not even be capable of being the subject of an action to set aside. Representatives of common law countries could not contribute in these terms, as they were not familiar with the distinction between ordinary and extraordinary forms of recourse. None of the alternative terms proposed ("enforceable," "ready for enforcement," "operative ") was retained.

1681. — The opposing view is that an award should only be considered binding if it is binding under the law of the country of origin.[59]

1682. — Regardless of the difficulties which may arise as a result of the absence of an autonomous definition of a concept of such importance to the operation of the Convention, the fact remains that the latter interpretation does appear to be closest to the intention of the authors of the Convention. Three arguments support this conclusion.

The first relates to the structure of Article V, paragraph 1(e) of the Convention. That provision states that recognition and enforcement can be refused where "[t]he award has not yet become binding on the parties, or has been set aside or suspended by a competent authority of the country in which, or under the law of which, that award was made." The setting aside or suspending of the award are thus expressly stated to be dependent on the procedures of the country of origin. It would be paradoxical if the same were not to be the case of the concept of an award being "binding on the parties," which appears in Article V, paragraph 1(e) alongside the reference to setting aside and suspending the award. Besides, even authors who favor an autonomous interpretation establish a relationship between the action to set aside an award and the award's binding character by opposing the two concepts.[60] If this premise is to be adopted, it is hard to imagine that the authors of the Convention would have taken different positions with respect to each of the two concepts.

The second argument is based on the idea that the binding nature of the award, or indeed of any legal instrument, cannot exist in isolation, but must stem from a legal system which recognizes that binding quality. It might be argued that the Convention itself constitutes the legal system from which the award derives its binding nature. However, it is difficult to accept that the Convention, which announces in its title that its purpose is to facilitate the enforcement of "foreign" arbitral awards, was intended to go that far. At a minimum, had it been intended to have effects as significant as the attribution of binding status to awards independently of the legal system of the seat of arbitration, the Convention would have contained more explicit provisions to that effect.

The third argument is based on ideas in favor at the time when the New York Convention was drafted, although the tendency to reduce the role of the seat of arbitration has gained ground since. When the Convention was drafted and signed, the role of the seat—or the role of the law under which the award was made—was still substantial. It would be hard to deny that fact by suggesting that the authors of the Convention envisaged that the binding nature

---

[59] In favor of this view, see especially GAJA, *supra* note 46, at I.C.3; J. GILLIS WETTER, THE INTERNATIONAL ARBITRAL PROCESS: PUBLIC AND PRIVATE, Vol. 2, at 404 (1979); JEAN ROBERT, L'ARBITRAGE – DROIT INTERNE – DROIT INTERNATIONAL PRIVÉ 408 (5th ed. 1983) (although this view is not found in the 6th edition published in 1993); H. Batiffol, note following Court of Appeals of The Hague, Sept. 8, 1972, Société Européenne d'Etudes et d'Entreprises v. République Socialiste Fédérative de Yougoslavie, 1974 REV. ARB. 311, 330; DE BOISSÉSON, *supra* note 13, at 454.

[60] *See supra* para. 1679.

of a "foreign" award could derive, in an entirely delocalized manner, from the Convention alone.[61]

1683. — The case law on this issue in countries which have ratified the Convention is sometimes described as being divided as to whether the concept of awards being binding is autonomous.[62]

Italian,[63] Swedish,[64] Dutch[65] and Belgian[66] decisions are cited as supporting an autonomous interpretation of the concept of binding awards. On the other hand, French, Swiss and, again, Italian case law is presented as taking the opposite view. The French courts clearly assess the binding nature of an award by reference to the law of the country of origin.[67] The Swiss Federal Tribunal has also decided in favor of examining the binding nature of awards in the light of the law of the country of origin, which it defines as the law governing the arbitral proceedings. In a 1982 decision, the Federal Tribunal stated that:

---

[61] See, e.g., Jan Paulsson, *Arbitre et juge en Suède – Exposé général et réflexions sur la délocalisation des sentences arbitrales*, 1980 REV. ARB. 441, 467–68. On other aspects of the importance of the seat under the Convention, see *supra* paras. 1687 and 1702.

[62] See, e.g., van den Berg, *supra* note 57, at 494. Compare, on the idea that the case law of different countries is moving towards an interpretation of the concept as being autonomous, El-Hakim, *supra* note 58, at 169.

[63] Tribunal of Naples, June 30, 1976, Società La Naviera Grancebaco S.A. v. Ditta Italgrani, IV Y.B. COM. ARB. 277 (1979), which, in fact, essentially concerns the burden of proof.

[64] Swedish Supreme Court, Aug. 13, 1979, AB Götaverken v. General National Maritime Transport Co. (GMTC), Libya, 1980 REV. ARB. 555, and the commentary by Paulsson, *supra* note 61; VI Y.B. COM. ARB. 237 (1981).

[65] Order of the President of the District Court of Amsterdam dated July 12, 1984, SPP (Middle East) Ltd. v. The Arab Republic of Egypt, X Y.B. COM. ARB. 487 (1985); 1986 REV. ARB. 101, and the commentary by Philippe Leboulanger, *Etat, politique et arbitrage – L'affaire du Plateau des Pyramides, id.* at 3; The decision (see *infra* para. 1691) in fact holds—rightly—that an award capable of being the subject of an action to set aside at the seat of arbitration cannot, as a result, be considered non-binding: "It results from both the legislative history of the Convention and the text of Arts. V, para. (1) under *e*, and VI that the mere initiation of an action for setting aside, to which the initiated *recours en annulation* must be deemed to belong, does not have as a consequence that the arbitral award must be considered as not binding. An arbitral award is not binding if it is open to appeal on the merits before a judge or an appeal tribunal. If this were otherwise, the words 'has been set aside or suspended' in Art. V, para. 1 under *e*, to which reference is made in Art. VI, would have no meaning. The drafters of the Convention chose the word 'binding' in order to abolish the requirement of double *exequatur* which was the result of the word 'final' in the Geneva Convention of 1927. Having regard to the system of Arts. 1504 and 1490 [of the] NCCP, the view expounded by the respondent would result in a reintroduction of double *exequatur*" (X Y.B. COM. ARB. 489 (1985)).

[66] CA Brussels, Jan. 24, 1997, *CIAGI*, *aff'd*, Belgian *Cour de cassation*, June 5, 1998, *supra* note 21.

[67] See, e.g., CA Paris, May 10, 1971, Compagnie de Saint-Gobain – Pont-à-Mousson v. The Fertilizer Corporation of India, Ltd., 1971 REV. ARB. 108, and the commentary by Bruno Oppetit, *Le refus d'exécution d'une sentence arbitrale étrangère dans le cadre de la Convention de New York, id.* at 97; CA Rouen, Nov. 13, 1984, Société Européenne d'Etudes et d'Entreprises (S.E.E.E.) v. République de Yougoslavie, 1985 REV. ARB. 115, and J.-L. Delvolvé's note, especially at 127; 112 J.D.I. 473 (1985), and B. Oppetit's note; for an English translation, see XI Y.B. COM. ARB. 491 (1986); 24 I.L.M. 345, 349 (1985). Having observed that the law of the place of arbitration is not necessarily that which governs the arbitral procedure, the court concluded that "according to the procedure applicable to the arbitration in question [which was not subject to any national law], the decision of the arbitrators is . . . binding on the parties within the meaning of the June 10, 1958 New York Convention."

[t]he question whether an arbitral award has become 'binding' . . . must first be determined under the law applicable to the arbitral procedure. The law applicable to the arbitral procedure can, within the framework of the autonomy of the parties, be freely chosen . . . . It follows . . . that the arbitral procedure is in the first place governed by the agreement of the parties and, failing such agreement, subsidiarily governed by the law of the country where the arbitration takes place."[68]

There are also a number of Italian decisions rejecting the autonomous interpretation of the binding effect of arbitral awards.[69]

1684. — In our opinion, the controversy as to whether the binding effect of an award is an autonomous concept is often expressed in terms which are too simplistic. A distinction should be drawn between certain principles which were clearly intended to apply under the Convention and the residual grounds found in the law of the country of origin which the party resisting enforcement is likely to invoke.

Two such principles are contained in the Convention. First, it is clear that the Convention requires no application for enforcement of the award to be made in the country where the award was made. The only documents that the applicant is required to submit are those identified in Article IV of the Convention.[70]

Second, the Convention makes it clear that the fact that an action to set aside the award still lies in the country of origin does not lead that award to be non-binding for the purposes of the Convention. This has been confirmed by the French courts[71] and by the Italian Supreme Court.[72]

These two principles, which clearly reflect the intentions of the authors of the Convention, does not mean that the law of the country of origin of the award has no bearing on the award's binding nature. Under the logic of the New York Convention, it is the law of the country of origin of the award which determines the conditions under which the award is binding. Thus, having observed that an action to set aside an award did not deprive the award of its binding status, a court did not contradict itself when it held that a party resisting

---

[68] Feb. 26, 1982, Joseph Müller A.G. v. Sigval Bergesen, ATF 108 Ib 85; 38 ANN. SUISSE DR. INTERN. 344 (1982); for an English translation, see IX Y.B. COM. ARB. 437, ¶ 5 at 439 (1984).

[69] *See, e.g., Corte di Appello* of Florence, Oct. 8, 1977, Bobbie Brooks Inc. v. Lanificio Walter Banci s.a.s., IV Y.B. COM. ARB. 289 (1979).

[70] This principle was confirmed in France by the Strasbourg Tribunal of First Instance in a judgment of October 9, 1970, Animalfeeds International Corp. v. Becker, 1970 REV. ARB. 166, and observations by B.M. *See also* Italian *Corte di Cassazione*, Apr. 15, 1980, *Lanificio W. Banci, supra* note 50.

[71] *See* TGI Paris, réf., May 15, 1970, Compagnie de Saint-Gobain – Pont-à-Mousson v. The Fertilizer Corporation of India, Ltd., 1971 REV. ARB. 108, and the commentary by Oppetit, *supra* note 67; 98 J.D.I. 312 (1971), and P. Kahn's note. Compare the terms of the Order of the President of the District Court of Amsterdam dated July 12, 1984 in *SPP, supra* note 65, or those used by the Hong Kong Supreme Court, High Court, June 2, 1992, Zhejiang Province Garment Import and Export Co. v. Siemssen & Co. (Hong Kong) Trading Ltd., XVIII Y.B. COM. ARB. 389 (1993).

[72] *Corte di Cassazione*, Nov. 3, 1992, Consolata Lucchetti v. Togna, XIX Y.B. COM. ARB. 685 (1994).

the enforcement of the award could, as the party bearing the burden of proof, establish that the award was not binding in the country where it was made.[73]

It is true that, in an important decision dated January 24, 1997 in the *CIAGI v. BAII* case, the Brussels Court of Appeals held that the binding character of the award was based on the intentions of the parties, who had provided in their arbitration agreement that any award would be binding. The Court went on to hold the law of Jordan, the country where the award was made, to be "irrelevant." This allowed the Court to reject the argument that, under Jordanian law, an award can only be binding after a judicial homologation procedure. The Court observed, obiter, that the homologation procedure relied upon was only necessary under Jordanian law, understood in the light of Belgian law, where enforcement was sought in Jordan.[74] The Belgian *Cour de cassation* followed the Court of Appeals: on June 5, 1998 it upheld the appeal court's decision on the grounds that "the question of whether the award can be subject to such recourse should be resolved by considering, in turn and alternatively, the arbitration agreement, the law selected by it for these purposes and, finally, the law of the country where the award was made." The Court could hardly have done more to confirm the primacy of the intentions of the parties over the law of the seat of the arbitration.[75] Although this decision is not in keeping with the initial philosophy of the New York Convention,[76] it has the merit of protecting the award from any idiosyncrasies of the law of the seat and of facilitating its enforcement while remaining within the confines of the Convention. In other legal systems, the courts would have instead applied the ordinary rules applicable to international arbitration, on the basis of Article VII of the Convention, which allows the application of those provisions most favorable to enforcement. This was in fact the approach taken by the French courts in the same matter.[77]

2° Possible Implications in the Host Country of Proceedings in the Country of Origin

1685. — Although the New York Convention does not make the recognition or enforcement of an award subject to any formalities in the country of origin, it does provide for certain consequences in the host country if proceedings are pending or have come to a close in the country of origin.

---

[73] TGI Paris, réf., May 15, 1970, *Compagnie de Saint-Gobain, supra* note 71.

[74] Decision cited *supra* note 21.

[75] Belgian *Cour de cassation*, June 5, 1998, *CIAGI, supra* note 21.

[76] *But see* G. Block and J. Linsmeau, notes following CA Brussels, Jan. 24, 1997, *supra* note 21.

[77] CA Paris, Oct. 23, 1997, Inter-Arab Investment Guarantee Corp. (IAIGC) v. Banque arabe et internationale d'investissement SA (BAII), 1998 REV. ARB. 143, and P. Fouchard's note. On the idea that the validity of the award does not exclusively depend on the law of the arbitration situs, also evidenced by the recognition of awards set aside in the country of origin, see *supra* para. 1595.

a) Effect in the Host Country of a Decision Setting Aside or Suspending an Award in the Country of Origin

1686. — Under Article V, paragraph 1(e) of the Convention, recognition and enforcement of an award may be refused if the party against whom it is invoked is able to establish that "the award . . . has been set aside or suspended by a competent authority of the country in which, or under the law of which, that award was made."[78]

1) Effect of a Decision to Set Aside

1687. — If an award is set aside in its country of origin, it loses the benefit of the New York Convention. In this respect, the Convention does not recognize the concept of a delocalized award, attributing considerable importance to the law of the country of origin. The Convention clarifies its perception of the connection of awards to legal systems by establishing a rule regarding jurisdiction over actions to set aside. Only the courts of the seat of the arbitration, or those of the country the law of which governed the arbitration (in other words, the law chosen by the parties to govern the arbitral procedure), are entitled to retain jurisdiction to set an award aside.[79] According to the Convention, all other jurisdictions must refuse to acknowledge the effects of a decision to set aside made elsewhere, and such a decision will have no effect on the Convention's operation.

The decision causing the award to lose the benefit of the Convention must be a genuine decision setting aside the award, and not simply a ruling overturning the award following a review of the merits of the dispute.[80]

Although an award which is set aside in its country of origin loses the benefit of the New York Convention, it can nevertheless be recognized by the legal system of another country under the law of that second country, even if that second country is a party to the Convention. The Convention clearly sets forth only the minimum conditions for the recognition and enforcement of awards, and it is not opposed to the idea that the law of a particular jurisdiction may be more liberal (Art. VII). This has been confirmed on a number of occasions by both the French courts, as French law has considerably relaxed its conditions governing enforcement as compared to the New York Convention and, more recently, by courts in the United States.[81]

---

[78] On the inconsistencies that may result from having two criteria (seat of the arbitration and applicable procedural law), see V.S. Deshpande, *Article V.1(e) of the 1958 New York Convention – A Plea for Harmonious and Purposive Interpretation*, 8 J. INT'L ARB. 77 (Sept. 1991).

[79] On the different conceptions of the jurisdictional rules on the setting aside of awards, see *supra* para. 1593.

[80] Compare, on the basis of Belgian law, Brussels Tribunal of First Instance, December 6, 1988, regarding an award made in Algeria and set aside by the local courts (Société Nationale pour la Recherche, le Transport et la Commercialisation des Hydrocarbures (Sonatrach) v. Ford, Bacon and Davis, Inc., XV Y.B. COM. ARB. 370, 376 (1990)), *aff'd*, CA Brussels, Jan. 9, 1990 (No. 726/89, unpublished, cited in Philippe Fouchard, *La portée internationale de l'annulation de la sentence arbitrale dans le pays d'origine*, 1997 REV. ARB. 329, 335 n.8).

[81] See the case law cited *supra* paras. 267 *et seq.*

1688. — The rule whereby the setting aside of an award in its country of origin causes it to lose the benefit of the New York Convention has prompted some authors to suggest that the absence of any possibility of an action to set aside the award in the country of origin would likewise lead the benefit of the Convention to be lost. This argument, which is in effect the denial of the idea that "a-national" awards can be considered as being "foreign" for the purposes of the Convention,[82] is based on a particular conception of the Convention's general philosophy. That conception assumes that the purpose of a convention on the recognition and enforcement of arbitral awards is to avoid having two different courts review the award and to determine where the primary review should be performed, so as to ensure that the importance of court control in other jurisdictions will be reduced accordingly. Against that background, it is argued that the drafters of the New York Convention chose to have the principal review carried out in the country of origin of the award, in order to lessen court intervention in the host country. Having attributed jurisdiction to the country of the seat or to the country the law of which was chosen by the parties to govern the procedure, the Convention places no restrictions on the extent of the review performed there. On the other hand, it does determine the maximum extent of the review in the host country. The temptation is to conclude that the necessary counterpart of limited court control in the host country is the existence of an action to set aside the award in the country of origin.[83]

That is the philosophy underlying conventions on the mutual recognition of judgments, as well as double taxation treaties, the object of which is essentially to allocate jurisdiction. The same philosophy had powerful advocates in the context of arbitration.[84]

It is that interpretation of the Convention which has prompted the question of whether awards made in countries which allow the parties to waive actions to set aside still retain the benefit of the Convention. The issue arose, between 1985 and 1998, with respect to awards made in Belgium in cases having no connection with Belgium other than the location of the seat of arbitration. Article 1717, paragraph 4 of the Belgian Judicial Code excluded, prior to its modification by the law of May 19, 1998, all actions to set awards aside in those circumstances. The question still arises today for awards made in Switzerland, Tunisia, Belgium and Sweden, where the parties have exercised their option to exclude all actions to set the award aside.[85]

---

[82] On this issue, see *infra* para. 1702.

[83] For reasoning in these terms, leading to the conclusion that there is room for a more radical streamlining of the review by the courts of the host country, see B. Oppetit, note following CA Rouen, Nov. 13, 1984, *S.E.E.E.*, *supra* note 67, 112 J.D.I. 473 (1985).

[84] *See, e.g.*, VAN DEN BERG, *supra* note 22, at 34 *et seq.* See also, on the idea that an "a-national" award, which is defined as one submitted to no national law, does not benefit from the application of the New York Convention, Albert Jan van den Berg, *Non-domestic arbitral awards under the 1958 New York Convention*, 2 ARB. INT'L 191 (1986), especially at 213 *et seq.* But see, more recently, Albert J. van den Berg, *The Application of the New York Convention by the Courts*, in ICCA CONGRESS SERIES NO. 9, IMPROVING THE EFFICIENCY OF ARBITRATION AGREEMENTS AND AWARDS: 40 YEARS OF APPLICATION OF THE NEW YORK CONVENTION 25 (A.J. van den Berg ed., 1999).

[85] On this legislation, see *supra* para. 1594. Compare with the French case law which, prior to its reversal by the Decree of May 12, 1981, also allowed the creation of a-national awards, *supra* para. 1589.

1689. — Commentators have been virtually unanimous in rejecting if not the conception of the New York Convention on which it is based, then at least the conclusion drawn from that conception whereby awards made in Belgium, Switzerland or Sweden in respect of which no recourse is available locally do not enjoy the benefit of the New York Convention.[86]

The rejection of that conclusion was inevitable, given that neither the text nor the structure of the New York Convention allow the exclusion from its scope of awards made in countries which choose to allow actions to set aside to be waived in certain circumstances or even to exclude such recourse altogether. As far as its text is concerned, the Convention states that it applies to binding foreign awards, subject to reciprocity. It would unquestionably be adding to this text to consider that it applies only to foreign awards which, though binding, may be the object of an action to set them aside in the country of origin. Admittedly, the Convention attributes jurisdiction to the courts of the country of origin to rule on actions to set awards aside. However, that is not accompanied by any requirement dictating how strict[87] or how lax such control should be. In addition, the analogy with conventions on the mutual recognition of judgments is misleading. Those conventions are based on reciprocal trust between the legal systems of the various state signatories, which is meaningless in arbitration, as no state can guarantee the quality of awards made on its territory.[88]

2) Effect of a Suspension

1690. — Under Article V, paragraph 1(e) of the Convention, recognition and enforcement may also be refused if the award has been suspended by a competent authority of the country in which, or under the law of which, the award was made.

---

[86]   On Belgian awards between 1985 and 1998, see Hans van Houtte, *La loi belge du 27 mars 1985 sur l'arbitrage international*, 1986 REV. ARB. 29, 36; Jan A.S. Paulsson, *Arbitration unbound in Belgium*, 2 ARB. INT'L 68, 72–73 (1986); on Swiss awards, see, for example, ANDREAS BUCHER, PIERRE-YVES TSCHANZ, INTERNATIONAL ARBITRATION IN SWITZERLAND ¶ 294 at 145 (1988); on Swedish awards, see Jan Paulsson, *Arbitrage international et voies de recours: La Cour suprême de Suède dans le sillage des solutions belge et helvétique*, 117 J.D.I. 589 (1990). *See also* Mauro Ferrante, *About the nature (national or a-national, contractual or jurisdictional) of ICC awards under the New York Convention*, in THE ART OF ARBITRATION – ESSAYS ON INTERNATIONAL ARBITRATION – LIBER AMICORUM PIETER SANDERS 129 (J. Schultz and A.J. van den Berg eds., 1982); on the applicability of the New York Convention to awards of the Iran-U.S. Claims Tribunal set up by the 1981 Algiers Accords, in spite of their delocalized character, see Aida B. Avanessian, *The New York Convention and Denationalised Awards (With Emphasis on the Iran–United States Claims Tribunal)*, 8 J. INT'L ARB. 5 (Mar. 1991). *See also* Iran v. Gould Marketing, Inc., 887 F.2d 1357 (9th Cir. 1989); XV Y.B. COM. ARB. 605 (1990). On this issue, generally, see ADAM SAMUEL, JURISDICTIONAL PROBLEMS IN INTERNATIONAL COMMERCIAL ARBITRATION: A STUDY OF BELGIAN, DUTCH, ENGLISH, FRENCH, SWEDISH, SWISS, U.S. AND WEST GERMAN LAW 293 *et seq.* (1989); Thilo Rensmann, *Anational Arbitral Awards – Legal Phenomenon or Academic Phantom?*, 15 J. INT'L ARB. 37, 53 (June 1998).

[87]   Compare with the system found in the 1961 Geneva Convention, which only gives effect in host countries to the setting aside of awards in the country of origin on certain grounds, *infra* para. 1715.

[88]   On the functioning of the Convention with respect to awards made in countries which enable the parties to exclude actions to set aside, see *infra* para. 1702.

The word "suspended" is not defined in the Convention. It is generally taken to refer to the case where a court suspects there to be a defect liable to affect the validity of the award and prevents enforcement of the award until the issue has been decided by the court with jurisdiction over an application to set the award aside.[89]

In a 1979 decision, the Swedish Supreme Court held that the suspension of enforcement proceedings which, in certain countries such as France,[90] results automatically from the commencement of an action to set an award aside, cannot be considered a suspension within the meaning of Article V, paragraph 1(e) of the New York Convention.[91] This decision is correct in our view, because the text of the Convention requires the award to be suspended "by a competent authority," which would appear to exclude a suspension operating automatically under the law of the country of origin. Furthermore, it would have been dangerous to have made the serious consequence of losing the benefit of the Convention contingent upon a procedural rule of the country of origin to which the Convention does not refer. Thus, both the terms used and the underlying purpose of the text lead to the conclusion that the authors of the Convention intended to refer to suspensions resulting from a court decision—even if only provisional—as only a court decision provides an indication of any doubts which the country of origin might harbor towards an award.[92]

b) Effect, in the Host Country, of Proceedings to Set Aside or Suspend the Award Pending in the Country of Origin

1691. — Article VI of the Convention states that:

> [i]f an application for the setting aside or suspension of the award has been made to a competent authority referred to in article V(1)(e), the authority before which the award is sought to be relied upon may, if it considers it proper, adjourn the decision on the enforcement of the award and may also, on the application of the party claiming enforcement of the award, order the other party to give suitable security.

This provision achieves a compromise between two equally legitimate concerns. The authors of the Convention wanted to ensure that a party wishing to frustrate the enforcement of an award could not prevent the operation of the Convention simply by initiating proceedings to set aside (or suspend) the award in the country of origin. However, they also wanted to ensure that the rule whereby an award loses the benefit of the Convention if it is set aside (or suspended) in its country of origin could not be defeated by the rapid

---

[89]   VAN DEN BERG, *supra* note 22, at 351.

[90]   On this issue, see *supra* para. 1591.

[91]   Aug. 13, 1979, *Götaverken*, *supra* note 64; see also, in the Netherlands, the July 12, 1984 Order of the President of the District Court of Amsterdam in *SPP*, *supra* note 65.

[92]   *See* van den Berg, *supra* note 57, at 500.

enforcement of the award in another jurisdiction while the issue was still pending in the country of origin.

Taking those two constraints into account, the Convention's authors decided to leave it to the courts of the host country to assess whether the grounds underpinning the action to set aside (or suspend) the award are sufficiently serious for there to be a genuine risk that the award will in fact be set aside.[93] If that is the case, they can refuse recognition or enforcement, or grant it on condition that security be given, so that in the event that the award is subsequently set aside (or suspended), the previously existing situation can be restored. The courts of the host country have full discretion in deciding on this question.[94]

1692. — This system clearly does not exclude all risk of diverging interpretations between the country of origin and the host country as to the seriousness of the grounds invoked.[95] However, that is a limitation inherent in the Convention once it allows court control in the country of origin to coexist with court control in the host country, without giving full precedence to either jurisdiction and without even limiting the grounds which can be used to justify an action in the country of origin.

This risk of diverging interpretations leads to a question as to the consequences, in the host country, of the setting aside of an award in the country of origin after it has been enforced in the host country. Some commentators consider that in such cases the courts which ordered enforcement could revoke their decision and retroactively apply Article V, paragraph 1(e) to deprive the award set aside of the benefit of the Convention.[96] However, given that the Convention is silent as to how to resolve this problem—which generally results from inadequate coordination between proceedings in the host country and those in the country of origin—the law of the host country must determine the finality of the enforcement order and, in particular, must decide whether certain events justify its withdrawal or variation. The French courts do not appear to exclude that possibility. In a 1970 decision, the Paris Tribunal of First Instance granted enforcement of an award made

---

[93] For an example of a negative assessment, see Swedish Supreme Court, Nov. 23, 1992, Datema Aktiebolag v. Forenede Cresco Finans AS, XIX Y.B. COM. ARB. 712 (1994); *see also* J. Gillis Wetter and Charl Priem, *Scandinavian Enforcement Drama*, 8 INT'L ARB. REP. 26 (Feb. 1993).

[94] For a discussion of court decisions reached on the basis of this provision, see W. Michael Tupman, *Staying Enforcement of Arbitral Awards under the New York Convention*, 3 ARB. INT'L 209 (1987); in French case law, see TGI Paris, May 15, 1970, *Compagnie de Saint Gobain, supra* note 71; CA Paris, Dec. 15, 1981, Norsolor v. Pabalk Ticaret Sirketi, 1983 REV. ARB. 465, 470, and the commentary by Berthold Goldman, *Une bataille judiciaire autour de la lex mercatoria – L'affaire Norsolor, id.* at 379; for an English translation, see VIII Y.B. COM. ARB. 362 (1983). Allowing the possibility of enforcement of an award in Italy despite the existence of a pending action to set aside in France (the seat of the arbitration), see Italian *Corte di Cassazione*, Nov. 3, 1992, *Consolata Lucchetti, supra* note 72. In Belgian case law, see CA Brussels, Jan. 24, 1997, *CIAGI, supra* note 21, *aff'd*, Belgian *Cour de cassation*, June 5, 1998, *supra* note 21. For an example of a decision to stay enforcement proceedings until the outcome of an action to set aside in the country of origin, see Europcar Italia, S.p.A. v. Maiellano Tours, Inc., 156 F.3d 310 (2d Cir. 1998); 13 INT'L ARB. REP. F1 (Sept. 1998).

[95] See, for example, the July 12, 1984 Order of the President of the District Court of Amsterdam in *SPP, supra* note 65, on the same day that the Paris Court of Appeals set the award aside (République Arabe d'Egypte v. Southern Pacific Properties Ltd., 112 J.D.I. 129 (1985), and B. Goldman's note; 1986 REV. ARB. 75; for an English translation, see 23 I.L.M. 1048 (1984)).

[96] *See* VAN DEN BERG, *supra* note 22, at 351.

in India, notwithstanding the existence of the possibility of recourse before the Indian courts in the future. However, the Tribunal carefully observed that any enforcement of the award by the winning party in the arbitration would be "at its own risks."[97] Of course, these risks are minimized by the case law according to which an award set aside in the country of origin can be nevertheless enforced in France if it meets the ordinary standards of enforcement of awards in that jurisdiction.[98]

§ 2. – Substantive Conditions Governing Recognition and Enforcement of Foreign Arbitral Awards Under the New York Convention

1693. — As discussed above,[99] the New York Convention makes a distinction between two types of grounds on which recognition and enforcement may be refused: those which must be raised by the party resisting recognition or enforcement and those which can be raised by the courts of the host country on their own motion. The list of grounds is exhaustive, and it of course excludes any revision of the merits of the award.[100]

A. – GROUNDS WHICH MUST BE RAISED BY THE PARTY RESISTING RECOGNITION OR ENFORCEMENT

1694. — In addition to the ground described in Article V, paragraph 1(e) concerning the setting aside or suspension of an award in the country of origin,[101] the grounds for refusing to grant recognition or enforcement of an award which must be raised by the party opposing recognition or enforcement are set forth in Article V, paragraph 1(a) to (d) of the Convention. These grounds are the existence of an invalid arbitration agreement (1°), a breach of due process (2°), an award which fails to comply with the terms of the arbitration agreement (3°) and irregularities affecting the composition of the arbitral tribunal or the arbitral proceedings (4°).

In the context of the controversy over whether awards set aside in the country of the seat can be enforced elsewhere,[102] certain authors have argued that if the courts of the host country find that one of the grounds listed in Article V of the Convention is satisfied, they may, but are not obliged to, refuse recognition or enforcement. The proponents of this interpretation find support in different official versions of the Convention which use neither

---

[97] May 15, 1970, *Compagnie de Saint-Gobain, supra* note 71, 1971 REV. ARB. 110.

[98] *See supra* para. 1595.

[99] *See supra* para. 1673.

[100] For a reminder of the principle, see Italian *Corte di Cassazione*, Feb. 22, 1992, Trans World Film SpA v. Film Polski Import and Export of Films, XVIII Y.B. COM. ARB. 433 (1993).

[101] *See supra* paras. 1685 *et seq.*

[102] *See supra* para. 1595.

the imperative nor the present tense, the meaning of which is more ambiguous.[103] In fact, even in the French version (which uses the future rather that the present tense), the Convention's objective is clear: it is to limit the conditions under which an award can be refused enforcement, with national laws remaining entitled, under Article VII, to take a more liberal stance.

1° Invalid Arbitration Agreements

1695. — Article V, paragraph 1(a) of the Convention provides that:

> [r]ecognition and enforcement of the award may be refused [only if the party against whom the award is invoked furnishes] proof that:
> (*a*) The parties to the [arbitration] agreement . . . were, under the law applicable to them, under some incapacity, or the said agreement is not valid under the law to which the parties have subjected it or, failing any indication thereon, under the law of the country where the award was made.[104]

Recognition and enforcement can thus be refused on the grounds that the arbitration agreement on which the award is based is invalid, whether as a result of the incapacity of a party or because circumstances such as mistake or duress vitiate the consent to arbitrate. Although in principle the concepts of capacity and power to contract should not be confused,[105] it is generally accepted that in the Convention the word "incapacity" also covers the absence of the power to contract. A strong indication to that effect is provided by the fact that during the negotiation of the Convention issues of "capacity" were discussed in connection with juridical persons, which suggests that the word "capacity" was not given its most accurate meaning. Issues of "capacity"—or the power to contract, strictly speaking—also arise in connection with arbitration agreements concluded by governments or public law entities. In such cases, the Convention allows the host country to verify whether the signatories of the arbitration agreement had the capacity (or, more accurately, the power) to bind the government or public entity in question.[106]

Article V, paragraph 1(a) addresses the question in choice of law terms, rather than using substantive rules. However, it does not specify the content of the applicable choice of law rules. With respect to capacity, it simply states that the issue is governed by the law applicable to the parties to the arbitration agreement. In fact, as it does not take a firm position on the determination of the law applicable to the issue of capacity, the Convention does not exclude the possibility of the legal system of the country where the review is

---

[103] *See* Jan Paulsson, *May or Must Under the New York Convention: An Exercise on Syntax and Linguistics*, 14 ARB. INT'L 227 (1998).

[104] This provision corresponds to provisions of national law such as Article 1502 1° of the French New Code of Civil Procedure. *See supra* paras. 1608 *et seq.*

[105] *See* EMMANUEL GAILLARD, LE POUVOIR EN DROIT PRIVÉ 48 *et seq.* (1985).

[106] On this issue, see VAN DEN BERG, *supra* note 22, at 277.

performed considering the question of capacity in the light of its own substantive rules, since the aim of such review is precisely to decide whether the award can be admitted into the legal order reviewing the award.[107] If, on the other hand, the choice of law approach is preferred in that jurisdiction, the terms of Article V, paragraph 1(a) appear to exclude the law governing the substance of the arbitration agreement and to favor the parties' personal law, as the Convention deals separately with the law applicable to capacity and the law applicable to the substance of the arbitration agreement.[108] However, it does not resolve the classic conflict between a party's national law and the law of its domicile, thus leaving the host country to determine the parties' personal law according to its own rules.

The law governing the substance of the arbitration agreement must be determined by applying a choice of law rule set forth in the Convention itself. The Convention opts in the first place for the law chosen by the parties, which is hardly surprising given the general acceptance of that principle in comparative law. The secondary choice of the law of the place where the award was made[109] is less satisfactory. The place where the award was made will not necessarily be selected by the parties, and in fact may well be chosen on the basis of considerations unrelated to the validity of the arbitration agreement.[110]

2° Breach of Due Process

1696. — Under Article V, paragraph 1(b), recognition and enforcement of the award may be refused if it is established that:

> the party against whom the award is invoked was not given proper notice of the appointment of the arbitrator or of the arbitration proceedings or was otherwise unable to present his case.[111]

Although it is undoubtedly one of the situations in which a party is "unable to present his case," a party's unawareness of the "appointment of the arbitrator or of the arbitration proceedings" is treated separately in the Convention.

This separate reference no doubt reflects the serious nature of such circumstances, but there is also a historic reason: the same ground was already provided for in the 1927 Geneva Convention (Art. 2(b)), and the authors of the New York Convention did not wish to appear to abandon it.

---

[107] On this reasoning, see *supra* paras. 463 *et seq.*

[108] But see VAN DEN BERG, *supra* note 22, at 277, who considers that the Convention does not prohibit a host country from determining the law "applicable to the parties" by reference to the law of the place where the contract was signed or the law which governs the substance of the contract.

[109] For an example of the application of the law of the seat, which is presented as having the closest connection with the arbitration agreement, see Court of Appeals of The Hague, Aug. 4, 1993, Owerri Commercial Inc. v. Dielle S.r.l., XIX Y.B. COM. ARB. 703 (1994).

[110] On this issue, see *supra* para. 1239. *See also* FOUCHARD, *supra* note 3, ¶ 18.

[111] This ground corresponds to provisions of national law such as Article 1502 4° of the French New Code of Civil Procedure. *See supra* paras. 1638 *et seq.*

Unlike the previous ground, Article V, paragraph 1(b) is expressed in terms of substantive rules, and not in choice of law terms. It is therefore wrong to suggest, as did an American decision, that this provision "essentially sanctions the application of the forum state's standards of due process."[112] In fact, the New York Convention creates an international substantive rule and considers a breach of that rule to be sufficient in itself to warrant the refusal of recognition or enforcement.[113]

1697. — As the principles of due process are usually considered to reflect the fundamental requirements of procedural justice, they may also form part of the public policy of the host country, which enables them to be raised by the courts of that jurisdiction on their own motion.[114]

1698. — The reference in Article V, paragraph 1(b) to a party's inability to present its case leaves no doubt as to the fact that the requirements of due process are satisfied where each party has been given the opportunity to present and explain its claims and evidence, regardless of whether that opportunity is actually used, or whether the parties elect instead to default. A party's "inability to present its case" cannot result from that party's own conduct. It can, however, be caused by a failure of the arbitral tribunal to grant adequate time limits, or by the other party concealing evidence, or by a *force majeure* event which the tribunal refuses to take into account in organizing the proceedings.

The judge in the host country must determine, under Article V, paragraph 1(b), whether a party was genuinely unable to present its case. Although this claim is often relied on in actions resisting enforcement, it is rarely accepted as justifying the refusal of recognition or enforcement in practice.[115] For example, a properly informed party that fails to appear before an arbitral tribunal cannot later rely on its own absence when claiming that recognition or enforcement should be refused.[116] Other allegations which do not constitute a breach of due process[117] include the fact that a request for arbitration is drafted in a foreign language,[118] a tribunal's refusal to re-open the proceedings after having raised an argument which did not

---

[112] Parsons & Whittemore Overseas Co. v. Société Générale de l'Industrie du Papier (RAKTA), 508 F.2d 969, 975 (2d Cir. 1974); I Y.B. COM. ARB. 205 (1976).

[113] On the nature of the rule, see FOUCHARD, *supra* note 3, at 343.

[114] *See infra* para. 1713.

[115] *Oberlandesgericht* of Cologne, June 10, 1976, Danish buyer v. German (F.R.) seller, IV Y.B. COM. ARB. 258 (1979).

[116] *See, e.g.,* Italian *Corte di Cassazione*, Aug. 8, 1990, *Vento & C snc, supra* note 32; Amsterdam Tribunal of First Instance, Apr. 24, 1991, V/O Tractorexport v. Dimpex Trading B.V., XVII Y.B. COM. ARB. 572, ¶¶ 3 *et seq.* at 574 (1992); *Corte di Appello* of Milan, Oct. 4, 1991, Black Sea Shipping Co. v. Italturist SpA, XVIII Y.B. COM. ARB. 415, ¶¶ 6 and 7 (1993). On this issue, generally, see *supra* paras. 1224 *et seq.*

[117] For an analysis of the case law on this ground, see VAN DEN BERG, *supra* note 22, at 302 *et seq.*

[118] *Appellationsgericht* of Basel, Feb. 27, 1989, N.Z. v. I., XVII Y.B. COM. ARB. 581, ¶ 5 at 583 (1992).

alter "the legal framework of the case,"[119] and the arbitrators' refusal to extend certain deadlines.[120]

In some rare cases, recognition or enforcement of an award has been refused on the grounds of a breach of due process. One example is the award made in a quality arbitration where the defendant was never informed of the identity of the arbitrators hearing the dispute.[121] It also occurred in a case where various documents were submitted by one party to the arbitral tribunal but not to the other party,[122] in another case where the defendant was not given the opportunity to comment on the report produced by the expert appointed by the tribunal,[123] and again where the arbitral tribunal criticized a party for having employed a method of presenting evidence which the tribunal itself had suggested.[124]

1699. — The Convention censures a breach of due process *per se*, without making the refusal of recognition or enforcement subject to proof by the party resisting enforcement of damage suffered as a result of the breach. In itself, a breach of due process is considered to be sufficiently important to justify such redress without the need for the party invoking it to establish actual damage. The opposite interpretation would add to the text of the Convention and would seriously detract from its intended dissuasive effect.[125]

3° Non-Compliance with the Terms of the Arbitration Agreement

1700. — Article V, paragraph 1(c) of the New York Convention allows recognition or enforcement to be refused if it is established that:

---

[119] TGI Paris, May 15, 1970, and CA Paris, May 10, 1971, *Compagnie de Saint-Gobain, supra* notes 71 and 67, and the commentary by Oppetit, *supra* note 67.

[120] *See, e.g., Obergericht* of Basel, June 3, 1971, Dutch seller v. Swiss buyer, IV Y.B. COM. ARB. 309 (1979); in the United States, Reasuransi Umum Indon. v. Evanston Ins. Co., No. 92 Civ. 4623 (MGC), 1992 WL 400733 (S.D.N.Y. Dec. 23, 1992); XIX Y.B. COM. ARB. 788, ¶ 9 at 791 (1994); 8 INT'L ARB. REP. B1 (Jan. 1993).

[121] *Oberlandesgericht* of Cologne, June 10, 1976, *supra* note 115.

[122] Amsterdam Court of Appeals, July 16, 1992, G.W.L. Kersten & Co. B.V. v. Société Commerciale Raoul Duval et Co., XIX Y.B. COM. ARB. 708 (1994).

[123] Supreme Court of Hong Kong, High Court, Jan. 15, 1993, Paklito Inv. Ltd. v. Klockner East Asia Ltd., XIX Y.B. COM. ARB. 664, ¶¶ 36 *et seq.* at 671 (1994).

[124] Iran Aircraft Indus. v. Avco Corp., 980 F.2d 141 (2d Cir. 1992); XVIII Y.B. COM. ARB. 596 (1993).

[125] But see, in favor of having to establish damage, ROBERT, *supra* note 59, ¶ 405 (but not in the 6th edition published in 1993). *See also* VAN DEN BERG, *supra* note 22, at 301, who bases his interpretation on the optional nature of the refusal of recognition and enforcement. Against having to establish damage, see *Oberlandesgericht* of Hamburg, Apr. 3, 1975, Firm P v. Firm F, II Y.B. COM. ARB. 241 (1977); Amsterdam Court of Appeals, July 16, 1992, *Kersten, supra* note 122; Brussels Tribunal of First Instance, Oct. 25, 1997, Denis v. Mercelis, 1997 [BELG.] JOURN. TRIB. 394; JACQUELINE LINSMEAU, L'ARBITRAGE VOLONTAIRE EN DROIT PRIVÉ BELGE ¶ 345 (1991), and note following CA Brussels, Jan. 24, 1997, *supra* note 21, 1998 REV. ARB. 181, especially ¶ 39. On the requirement that a party object to the alleged breach of due process in good time in order to be able to raise the defense at the time of recognition or enforcement, see *International Standard Electric, supra* note 23. On the requirements of French international arbitration law in this respect, see *supra* para. 1607.

[t]he award deals with a difference not contemplated by or not falling within the terms of the submission to arbitration, or it contains decisions on matters beyond the scope of the submission to arbitration, provided that, if the decisions on matters submitted to arbitration can be separated from those not so submitted, that part of the award which contains decisions on matters submitted to arbitration may be recognized and enforced.

This provision applies where the arbitrators have gone beyond the terms of the arbitration agreement. It complements Article V, paragraph 1(a), which concerns invalid arbitration agreements. The two grounds are similar in nature: in both cases, the arbitrator will have ruled in the absence of an arbitration agreement, either because the agreement is void (as in subsection (a)) or because it does not cover the subject-matter on which the arbitrator reached a decision (as in subsection (c)). For that reason, more recent arbitration statutes often either treat the two grounds as one, as in Article 1502 1° of the French New Code of Civil Procedure, or refer generally to the "absence of a valid arbitration agreement," as in Article 1065 of the Netherlands Code of Civil Procedure.

However, Article V, paragraph 1(c) does not cover all of the cases listed in Article 1502 3° of the French New Code of Civil Procedure, which provides that recognition or enforcement can be refused where "the arbitrator ruled without complying with the mission conferred upon him or her." That extends to decisions that are either *infra petita* and *ultra petita*, as well as to situations where the arbitrators have exceeded their powers in the examination of the merits of the case (for example, by acting as *amiable compositeurs* when that was not agreed by the parties, or by failing to apply the rules of law chosen by the parties).[126] Generally speaking, such situations cannot be said to be outside the terms of the arbitration agreement within the meaning of the New York Convention. In practice, it is only where the terms of reference—which, provided that they have been accepted by the parties, can constitute a form of arbitration agreement—set out the parties' claims in detail that arbitrators who have decided issues other than those raised in such claims can be said both to have ruled *ultra petita* and to have exceeded the terms of the arbitration agreement. If, on the other hand, the arbitration agreement is drafted in general terms and the claims are not presented in a way that contractually determines the issues to be resolved by the arbitrators, a decision that is rendered *ultra petita* would not contravene Article V, paragraph 1(c).[127]

It is important to note that the Convention provides that the refusal of recognition or enforcement can be confined to aspects of the award which fail to comply with the terms of the arbitration agreement, provided that those aspects can be separated from the rest of the award (Art. V(1)(c), *in fine*).

Once again, the courts have taken a very restrictive view of the application of this ground.[128]

---

[126] *See supra* para. 1626.

[127] *But see* Robert, *supra* note 33, at 78.

[128] See the cases described by van den Berg, *supra* note 57, at 490 *et seq.*

4° Irregularities Affecting the Composition of the Arbitral Tribunal or the Arbitral Proceedings

1701. — Article V, paragraph 1(d) of the New York Convention provides that recognition or enforcement of an arbitral award may be refused where

> [t]he composition of the arbitral authority or the arbitral procedure was not in accordance with the agreement of the parties, or, failing such agreement, was not in accordance with the law of the country where the arbitration took place.

Although it constitutes progress as compared to the 1927 Geneva Convention—which required compliance with both the agreement of the parties and the "law governing the arbitral procedure" (Art. 1, para. 2(c))—Article V, paragraph 1(d) of the New York Convention is more restrictive than the corresponding provisions in modern arbitration statutes.[129]

First, although French law, for instance, will also allow enforcement to be refused if the composition of a tribunal does not comply with the intentions of the parties under Article 1502 2° of the New Code of Civil Procedure, that is not the case where, in the absence of an agreement between the parties, the irregularity results solely from a violation of the law of the seat of the arbitration.[130] French law has significantly relaxed the control exercised by the French courts on this issue, as the requirements of the law of the seat are only relevant under French law if that law has been chosen by the parties to govern the arbitral procedure. Compliance with those requirements is thus only verified by the French courts where the parties have specified that French law will govern the procedure. That comparison again highlights the importance—which is excessive in our view—attributed by the New York Convention to the seat of the arbitration.[131]

Second, French law, again taken by way of illustration, will only allow the refusal of enforcement for violations of the rules governing the arbitral proceedings where it is possible to infer that by violating those rules the arbitrators did not "comply with the mission conferred upon them," within the meaning of Article 1502 3° of the New Code of Civil Procedure. The fact that the French courts have rightly adopted a restrictive interpretation of this ground, confining it to certain clear-cut situations (such as the arbitrators acting as *amiables compositeurs* without having been granted such powers, or their showing total disregard for the parties' choice of law[132]), also contrasts with the system adopted by the New York Convention. The Convention allows the courts to refuse enforcement where the arbitrators fail to comply not only with any of the procedural rules adopted by the parties, which is not the case in French law, but also, if the parties have not chosen procedural rules,

---

[129] *See, e.g.*, Art. 1502 of the French New Code of Civil Procedure; Art. 190 of the Swiss Private International Law Statute; Art. 1062 of the Netherlands Code of Civil Procedure; Secs. 66(3), 67 and 68 of the 1996 English Arbitration Act.

[130] *See supra* paras. 1620 *et seq.*

[131] *See supra* paras. 1682 and 1687.

[132] *See supra* paras. 1626 *et seq.*

where the arbitrators failed to comply with the procedural rules of the law of the seat of the arbitration. This is totally alien to French law and most other modern arbitration statutes. Here, the weakness of the New York Convention lies in the fact that it provides no criteria enabling the determination of which procedural rules are sufficiently important to justify the refusal of recognition or enforcement of an award in the event that the arbitrators fail to comply with them.

1702. — Both in respect of the composition of the arbitral tribunal and the arbitral procedure, Article V, paragraph 1(d) sets forth a dual jurisdictional standard based on the intention of the parties and the requirements of the law of the seat of the arbitration.

The intention of the parties may be reflected in a direct agreement as to the rules which are to govern the arbitration. It may also be expressed by reference to a law or to arbitration rules. However, under the Convention, the choice of a seat by the parties is not to be construed as the adoption of the procedural rules of that jurisdiction, as the Convention itself distinguishes between situations in which procedural rules apply as a result of the intentions of the parties and situations in which they apply, on a subsidiary basis, as a function of the seat of the arbitration.

The location of the seat of the arbitration may either result from the intention expressed by the parties, or from a choice made by any arbitral institution or by the arbitrators themselves. In each case, the rules of the law of the seat relating to the composition of the arbitral tribunal and to the arbitral procedure will only apply where no choice of procedural rule has been made, directly or indirectly, by the parties. The role of the seat of the arbitration is thus reduced as compared with the 1927 Geneva Convention, under which awards fully respecting the intentions of the parties could be refused enforcement if the arbitrators failed to comply with the rules of the seat of the arbitration.[133] The New York Convention treats the rules of the seat of arbitration as applicable on a purely subsidiary basis, even though they may not be perceived as such by the legal system to which they belong.[134]

However, this use of two competing criteria can lead to odd results because, as we have seen,[135] under the Convention a number of consequences follow the setting aside of an award at the seat of the arbitration. In the event of a conflict between the rules agreed by the parties and the mandatory provisions of the law of the seat, arbitrators whose goal it is to make an award that will be internationally enforceable may find themselves in a particularly delicate situation. If they do not comply with the mandatory provisions of the law of the seat, their award may be set aside in that jurisdiction, as a result of which the award may lose the benefit of the New York Convention.[136] If, on the other hand, they comply with those rules and thereby ignore the rules agreed by the parties, their award may be refused recognition or enforcement on the basis of Article V, paragraph 1(d). In order to avoid this inconsistency, one commentator has suggested that a failure to comply with the intentions

---

[133] *See supra* para. 1701.

[134] On the progress thus made by the New York Convention, see MOTULSKY, *supra* note 55, at 391.

[135] *See supra* para. 1687.

[136] *See supra* para. 1687.

of the parties as to the composition of the arbitral tribunal or the arbitral procedure should not constitute a ground on which to refuse recognition or enforcement where such failure is justified by the obligation to comply with the mandatory provisions of the law of the seat.[137] That interpretation is clearly contrary to the intention of the authors of the Convention. Their intention was undoubtedly to ensure that the parties' agreement should prevail over the provisions—mandatory or not—of the law of the seat.[138] The inconsistency of the Convention on this issue stems from its reluctance, even in 1958, to circumscribe the role of the seat, as more recent statutes—and case law[139]—now do.

However, contrary to what has sometimes been suggested, Article V, paragraph 1(d) of the Convention confirms that the operation of the Convention presents no difficulty in connection with "a-national" awards, that is to say awards against which no action to set aside is available at the seat of the arbitration.[140] This absence of recourse does not prevent the Convention from making recognition and enforcement conditional on compliance with the requirements of the law of the seat concerning the composition of the arbitral tribunal and the arbitral procedure, provided the parties are silent on such questions. Thus, if the parties are silent, an award made in Belgium which infringes the provisions of Belgian law regarding the composition of the arbitral tribunal[141] may conceivably be refused enforcement in another jurisdiction on the basis of Article V, paragraph 1(d), even though in the absence of any connection with Belgium other than the location of the seat the parties may waive any action to set the award aside, pursuant to Article 1717, paragraph 4 of the Belgian Judicial Code. The question may arise in the same terms with respect to awards made in Tunisia, Switzerland and in Sweden.[142]

It should be noted however that, since the reform of Belgian law on May 19, 1998, the exclusion of actions to set aside requires both the absence of any connection with the country in which the award was made other than the seat and the parties' waiver to that effect.[143] In these circumstances the parties should be considered as having expressed a particularly clear intention, albeit indirectly, as to the freedom of the arbitrators from the provisions of the law of the seat concerning the composition of the arbitral tribunal and the arbitral procedure. That intention should, as a result, be sufficient to exclude the subsidiary application of the provisions of the law of the seat under Article V, paragraph 1(d). In contrast, the waiver of all actions to set an award aside would certainly not prevent the refusal of recognition or enforcement on the basis of a breach of the parties' express agreement regarding the composition of the arbitral tribunal or the arbitral procedure, under the first scenario envisaged by Article V, paragraph 1(d). It could be argued that the exclusion of any recourse based on an irregularity in the composition of the arbitral tribunal or the arbitral procedure amounts to a departure from the mandatory nature of the rules on

---

[137] JÖRG GENTINETTA, DIE LEX FORI INTERNATIONALER HANDELSSCHIEDSGERICHTE 302 (1973).

[138] *See* VAN DEN BERG, *supra* note 22, at 330; MOTULSKY, *supra* note 55, at 391.

[139] *See, e.g.*, Belgian *Cour de cassation*, June 5, 1998, *CIAGI*, *supra* note 21.

[140] *See also Gould*, *supra* note 86.

[141] Arts. 1681 *et seq.* of the Belgian Judicial Code.

[142] *See supra* para. 1688.

[143] See also, on awards made in Switzerland and in Sweden, *supra* para. 1688.

this question chosen by the parties themselves, and that non-compliance with those rules could therefore not be censured under the New York Convention on the grounds that the parties' intentions have been disregarded. However, the issue must be resolved on a case-by-case basis by the court hearing the application for recognition or enforcement, according to its interpretation of the intentions of the parties. The court may consider that the parties genuinely intended to waive the mandatory nature of the rules which they had initially chosen, so that by virtue of the parties' own intentions the violation of such rules cannot be censured in any way. This will no doubt be the case where the rules violated were indirectly chosen by the parties, either as a result of a reference to a procedural law or to arbitration rules. A waiver of all recourse under Article 190, paragraph 2(a) of the Swiss Private International Law Statute referring specifically to the composition of the arbitral tribunal, may well provide a stronger indication of an intention to disregard the provisions of the law of the situs on this issue than a waiver expressed in general terms. On the other hand, the court may consider that the intention of the parties to comply with rules governing the composition of the arbitral tribunal or the arbitral procedure, particularly where those rules are the subject of precise terms agreed by the parties themselves, is not affected by the parties' agreement to waive all local recourse, especially if the latter provision is framed in general terms.

1703. — There are few decisions where a foreign award has been refused enforcement on the basis of Article V, paragraph 1(d). A 1968 decision of the Basel Court of Appeals is often cited: the Court refused to issue an enforcement order on the grounds that the arbitral tribunal had not complied with the express intention of the parties that their dispute be decided by a single award, following a two-stage arbitration (the first stage concerning the quality of the products, the second concerning damages).[144] This decision was inevitable given the totally unequivocal nature of the intention expressed by the parties.[145] Another illustration is a 1978 decision of the Florence Court of Appeals, where the Court refused enforcement of an award made in London by an arbitral tribunal comprising two arbitrators nominated by each of the parties, following the arbitrators' refusal, on the basis of the procedure then applicable in England,[146] to appoint a third arbitrator. The decision again blatantly disregarded the parties' agreement, which expressly stipulated that the arbitral tribunal was to comprise three members and designated the authority responsible for appointing the third arbitrator in the event of a disagreement between the first two.[147]

By contrast, there are a number of decisions rejecting claims brought on this ground, particularly where the party resisting enforcement relies on alleged breaches of minor

---

[144] Basel Court of Appeals, Sept. 6, 1968, Firm in Hamburg (buyer) v. Corporation (A.G.) in Basel (seller), I Y.B. COM. ARB. 200 (1976).

[145] Compare, in French law, *supra* para. 1633.

[146] Today, see the corresponding provisions in Section 17 of the 1996 Arbitration Act.

[147] *Corte di Appello* of Florence, Apr. 13, 1978, Rederi Aktiebolaget Sally v. S.r.l. Termarea, IV Y.B. COM. ARB. 294 (1979).

provisions of the arbitration rules chosen by the parties.[148] As was rightly observed in one United States decision,

> The Court does not believe that Art. V(1)(*d*) was intended . . . to permit reviewing courts to police every procedural ruling made by the arbitrator and to set aside the award if any violation of the . . . procedures is found.[149]

B. – GROUNDS WHICH CAN BE RAISED BY THE COURTS ON THEIR OWN MOTION

1704. — Under Article V, paragraph 2, of the New York Convention,

> [r]ecognition and enforcement of an arbitral award may also be refused if the competent authority in the country where recognition and enforcement is sought finds that:
> (*a*) The subject-matter of the difference is not capable of settlement by arbitration under the law of that country; or
> (*b*) The recognition or enforcement of the award would be contrary to the public policy of that country.

Most commentators consider that the review of the arbitrability of a dispute is just one aspect of the review of compliance with public policy.[150] That view—which would have led the authors of the Convention to provide for only one ground under Article V, paragraph 2—warrants further examination. We shall therefore consider in turn the case of non-arbitrability of the dispute, and the more general case of non-compliance with international public policy. As sensitive issues affecting the fundamental conceptions of the host country arise in both cases, the courts of that country are justified in being able to raise them on their own motion as grounds on which to refuse recognition or enforcement.

---

[148] *See, e.g., Reasuransi Umum Indon., supra* note 120; Supreme Court of Hong Kong, High Court, Mar. 2, 1991, *Shenzhen, supra* note 22, XVIII Y.B. COM. ARB. 377, ¶ 24 at 382 (1993).

[149] Compagnie des Bauxites de Guinée v. Hammermills, Inc., Civ. A. No. 90-0169 (JGP), 1992 WL 122712 (D.D.C. May 29, 1992); XVIII Y.B. COM. ARB. 566 (1993), especially ¶ 11 at 571. On the requirement that a party must object to the constitution of the arbitral tribunal before the arbitrators, see Supreme Court of Hong Kong, High Court, July 13, 1994, China Nanhai Oil Joint Serv. Corp. Shenzhen Branch v. Gee Tai Holdings Co. Ltd., 10 INT'L ARB. REP. 10 (Aug. 1995); XX Y.B. COM. ARB. 671 (1995); in the United States, AAOT Foreign Economic Ass'n (VO) Technostroyexport v. International Dev. and Trade Serv., Inc., 139 F.3d 980 (2d Cir. 1998); 13 INT'L ARB. REP. J1 (Mar. 1998); CA Paris, 1e Ch., Sec. C, Apr. 2, 1998, Compagnie Française d'Etudes et de Construction TECHNIP v. Entreprise Nationale des Engrais et des Produits Phytosanitaires dite ASMIDAL (Algérie), No. 97/6929, unpublished.

[150] *See, e.g.,* FOUCHARD, *supra* note 3, at 548; Sanders, *supra* note 33, 23 INT'L LAW. 270; 1979 DPCI 362; Pieter Sanders, *Commentary,* I Y.B. COM. ARB. 207, 216 (1976); Frédéric-Edouard Klein, *La Convention de New York sur la reconnaissance et l'exécution des sentences arbitrales étrangères,* REV. SUISSE DE JURISPRUDENCE 229, 249 (1961); VAN DEN BERG, *supra* note 22, at 360.

1° Non-Arbitrability of the Dispute

1705. — Article V, paragraph 2(a) of the New York Convention provides that recognition and enforcement of an arbitral award may be refused if the competent authority in the country where recognition and enforcement is sought finds that "the subject-matter of the difference is not capable of settlement by arbitration under the law of that country."

1706. — Certain commentators have argued that this provision goes too far, in that it allows the courts of the host country to refuse recognition or enforcement of the award on the basis of their own conception of disputes capable of resolution by arbitration.[151] However, certain rules regarding the arbitrability of the dispute do reflect fundamental policies of the country imposing them. This is the case in particular of the non-arbitrability of certain family law issues. For example, the recognition or enforcement of a foreign award granting a divorce is liable to contravene not only the principle that such matters are non-arbitrable in the host country, but also that country's understanding of international public policy. Other issues are considered to be non-arbitrable for less fundamental reasons. One example is the resolution of financial difficulties between spouses in divorce proceedings.[152] Some legal systems consider such a dispute to be non-arbitrable,[153] while others do allow its resolution by arbitration[154] without that seeming particularly offensive. Yet under the New York Convention, a country which does find it offensive can refuse to recognize or enforce an award resolving such a dispute made in a jurisdiction where the subject is perfectly arbitrable. In that respect, the ground of non-arbitrability set forth at Article V, paragraph 2(a) may not entirely coincide with the breach of public policy ground found in Article V, paragraph 2(b).[155]

It is no doubt in order to restrict the unsatisfactory consequences of reviewing arbitrability solely in the light of the views of the host country that many commentators consider arbitrability to be simply one aspect reviewed in the context of the examination of an award's compliance with international public policy.[156] That position amounts to suggesting that only cases of non-arbitrability founded on fundamental policies will suffice to justify the refusal to enforce an award under the New York Convention. In fact, that view does not reflect the intentions of the authors of the Convention, who rejected the French delegate's proposal that Article V, paragraph 2(a) be struck out on the grounds that it attributed an

---

[151] *See* MOTULSKY, *supra* note 55, at 396–97.

[152] *Id.*

[153] See, for example, the position in French international arbitration law, *infra* paras. 572 and 573.

[154] See, for example, Article 177, paragraph 1 of the Swiss Private International Law Statute, under which "[a]ny dispute involving property," i.e., any dispute which can be assessed in monetary terms, is arbitrable. *See supra* para. 568.

[155] On this issue, generally, see MOTULSKY, *supra* note 55, at 396–97.

[156] *See supra* para. 1704.

international impact to purely domestic rules and that compliance with international public policy would suffice.[157]

1707. — Another way of limiting court control of the arbitrability of a dispute, which is more in keeping with the letter of the Convention, entails distinguishing, as is generally the case with public policy, between non-arbitrability in domestic and international disputes. That distinction enables a dispute to be found non-arbitrable under a country's domestic law, without necessarily preventing the recognition in that country of a foreign award dealing with the same subject-matter. Using that approach, the United States federal courts, in particular, have recognized the arbitrability in international arbitration of disputes relating to securities transactions and antitrust law, despite the fact that those subjects have been held to be non-arbitrable under domestic law.[158]

Not all courts are so liberal. For example, the Belgian Supreme Court held, on the basis of a specific statute, that a dispute concerning the alleged breach of an exclusive automobile distribution contract could only be submitted to the Belgian courts.[159] The distinction between domestic and international disputes might have led to a different result but, however unsatisfactory that decision may be, it is contrary neither to the letter of the New York Convention nor to the intentions of the Convention's authors.[160]

1708. — On the whole, it would appear that the courts have rarely applied Article V, paragraph 2(a) in refusing to recognize or to enforce an award. Apart from the Belgian decision discussed above, there have only been a small number of decisions refusing enforcement on that basis. Among these are certain United States court rulings, not all of them satisfactory. For instance, the Federal Court for the Southern District of New York held, in a 1976 decision, that a dispute relating to the salvaging of an American warship was not arbitrable pursuant to the United States Public Vessels Act.[161] In a very questionable 1980 decision, the United States Court of Appeals for the District of Columbia held that the Libyan nationalizations of the 1970s constituted non-arbitrable acts of state and refused to grant enforcement of an award concerning those nationalizations on the basis of Article V, paragraph 2(a) of the Convention.[162] In that case, it was highly inappropriate to apply concepts specific to the United States which were relevant only to jurisdiction. As a settlement was reached when an appeal from that judgment was filed, the United States

---

[157] *United Nations Conference on International Commercial Arbitration – Summary Record of the Eleventh Meeting – Held at Headquarters, New York, on Tuesday, 27 May 1958*, UN Doc.E/Conf.26/SR.11, *reprinted in* GIORGIO GAJA, INTERNATIONAL COMMERCIAL ARBITRATION – NEW YORK CONVENTION – PART III – PREPARATORY WORKS III.C.83.

[158] See the references cited *supra* para. 568.

[159] Belgian *Cour de cassation*, June 28, 1979, Audi-NSU Auto Union A.G. v. S.A. Adelin Petit et Cie., V Y.B. COM. ARB. 257 (1980); *see also supra* para. 588.

[160] On the issue, generally, of the arbitrability of disputes relating to the rescission of exclusive concession agreements, see *supra* para. 588.

[161] B.V. Bureau Wijsmuller v. United States of America (S.D.N.Y. Dec. 21, 1976); III Y.B. COM. ARB. 290 (1978).

[162] Libyan American Oil Co. v. Libyan Arab Republic, 482 F. Supp. 1175 (D.D.C. 1980); VI Y.B. COM. ARB. 248 (1981).

Court of Appeals for the District of Columbia did not have the opportunity to examine the issue.

1709. — In order to avoid the unwelcome surprises liable to result from a subjective assessment of arbitrability by the courts, some commentators have suggested that a list of the subjects which each jurisdiction considers to be non-arbitrable should appear as an annex to the New York Convention when it comes to be revised.[163] To date, that proposal has not been implemented.

2° Awards Contravening International Public Policy

1710. — Although Article V, paragraph 2(b) is not explicit on this point, there is no doubt that the reference in that provision to public policy is in fact a reference to the international public policy of the host jurisdiction.[164]

1711. — The provision certainly refers to international public policy, and not domestic public policy. Not every breach of a mandatory rule of the host country could justify refusing recognition or enforcement of a foreign award. Such refusal is only justified where the award contravenes principles which are considered in the host country as reflecting its fundamental convictions, or as having an absolute, universal value.

The case law generated by the various courts which have applied Article V, paragraph 2 generally supports this view. In a 1975 decision, the Hamburg Court of Appeals stated that not all mandatory provisions of the host country were matters of public policy, as the latter only cover extreme cases.[165] In a 1974 decision, the United States Court of Appeals for the Second Circuit rightly defined the concept of public policy under the Convention as being limited to "the forum state's most basic notions of morality and justice."[166] That has been reiterated on a number of occasions by courts in the United States.[167] In the same spirit, the Court of Justice of the Canton of Geneva held, in a 1976 decision, that a violation of public

---

[163] VAN DEN BERG, *supra* note 22, at 375.

[164] *Comp. with* CA Paris, June 20, 1996, PARIS v. Razel, 1996 REV. ARB. 657, and observations by D. Bureau.

[165] *Oberlandesgericht* of Hamburg, Apr. 3, 1975, *supra* note 125. See also the decision of the German *Bundesgerichtshof* of May 15, 1986, which draws a distinction regarding the requirement of neutrality of the arbitrators between domestic and international public policy, thus recognizing an award made by an arbitrator appointed by the claimant where the defendant had defaulted (German (F.R.) charterer v. Romanian shipowner, XII Y.B. COM. ARB. 489 (1987)). *See also* Hans-Jochem Lüer, *German Court Decisions Interpreting and Implementing the New York Convention*, 7 J. INT'L ARB. 127 (Mar. 1990).

[166] *Parsons & Whittemore*, *supra* note 112, 508 F.2d 974 and the critical commentary of Joel R. Junker, *The Public Policy Defense to Recognition and Enforcement of Foreign Arbitral Awards*, 7 CAL. W. INT'L L.J. 228 (1977).

[167] *See, e.g.*, Fotochrome, Inc. v. Copal Co., 517 F.2d 512 (2d Cir. 1975); I Y.B. COM. ARB. 202 (1976).

policy implies "a violation of fundamental principles of the Swiss legal order, hurting intolerably the feeling of justice."[168]

1712. — It is equally clear that Article V, paragraph 2(b) refers to the host country's conception of international public policy, and not to a "genuinely international public policy" rooted in the law of the community of nations. The latter concept is only of relevance to international arbitrators who, having no forum, are required to apply only genuinely transnational concepts.[169] The logic of Article V, paragraph 2(b) of the New York Convention is entirely different: it is to enable the country where recognition or enforcement is sought to refuse to accept into its legal order an award which contravenes its fundamental convictions. The text of the Convention leaves no room for doubt on that point.[170] However, there is nothing to prevent each country from adopting, as part of its conception of international public policy, principles having some claim to universality, whether voluntarily or in order to honor its international commitments.

1713. — Although the Convention refers to the host country's conception of international public policy, that country must nevertheless exercise caution in applying it, as always with international public policy. This has been confirmed in a number of decisions of the United States Court of Appeals for the Second Circuit, which has held on several occasions that "the Convention's public policy defense should be construed narrowly."[171] However, courts in the United States have not always been as prudent in practice.[172]

In fact, although parties often base their actions resisting enforcement on Article V, paragraph 2(b) of the Convention, that ground is rarely accepted by the courts as justifying a refusal of recognition or enforcement. In an analysis covering the first twenty years of application of the Convention, of the one hundred and twelve decisions recorded as having applied the New York Convention, only three refused enforcement of an award on the grounds of a breach of public policy.[173] Of those three decisions, two are in fact based on the non-arbitrability of the subject-matter.[174] One decision, rendered by the Hamburg Court

---

[168] Sept. 17, 1976, Léopold Lazarus Ltd. v. Chrome Ressources S.A., IV Y.B. COM. ARB. 311, 312 (1979). See, similarly, Sanders, *supra* note 33, 23 INT'L LAW. 270; 1979 DPCI 362; VAN DEN BERG, *supra* note 22, at 360; MOTULSKY, *supra* note 55, at 396.

[169] On this issue, see *supra* para. 1553.

[170] *See also* FOUCHARD, *supra* note 3, at 518; VAN DEN BERG, *supra* note 22, at 361.

[171] *Parsons & Whittemore*, *supra* note 112, 508 F.2d 974, and *Fotochrome*, *supra* note 167, 517 F.2d 516.

[172] See, for example, the decision dated January 18, 1980 of the District Court of North Georgia which, after paying lip service to the principle laid down by the Court of Appeals for the Second Circuit, held the application by the arbitrators of French law provisions concerning the increase of the relevant interest rate by 5% two months after the date of the award was a penalty that was unacceptable in the United States, (Laminoirs-Trefileries-Cableries de Lens, S.A. v. Southwire Co., 484 F. Supp. 1063 (N.D. Ga. 1980); VI Y.B. COM. ARB. 247 (1981)).

[173] Sanders, *supra* note 33, 23 INT'L LAW. 271; 1979 DPCI 364 *et seq.*

[174] *Bureau Wijsmuller*, *supra* note 161 (non-arbitrability of a dispute concerning the salvage of a United States warship); CA Liège, May 12, 1977, Audi-NSU Auto Union A.G. v. S.A. Adelin Petit et Cie., IV Y.B. COM. ARB. 254 (1979) (non-arbitrability of the rescission of a contract for the exclusive distribution of motor
(continued...)

of Appeals on April 3, 1975, is genuinely based on Article V, paragraph 2(b) of the Convention. Furthermore, it could equally have been based on Article V, paragraph 1(b), as it censures a violation of the principles of due process:[175] the court refused enforcement of an award made under the auspices of the American Arbitration Association where the sole arbitrator relied on documents which had not been communicated to one of the parties.[176] Another decision refusing enforcement of an award under the New York Convention on the basis of a breach of international public policy was likewise based on a violation of the principles of due process: in a 1976 decision, the Cologne Court of Appeals refused enforcement of an award made after proceedings in which one of the parties did not know the names of the arbitrators.[177] The same ground served as the basis for a 1998 decision of the French *Cour de cassation* refusing to enforce an award made in reliance on information communicated to the arbitral tribunal by one of the arbitrators.[178] Similarly, the Hong Kong Supreme Court refused to give effect to an award made in a case in which a witness statement had allegedly been obtained through duress from a witness kidnapped by a party.[179]

SECTION II
THE 1961 EUROPEAN CONVENTION

1714. — The main focus of the 1961 European Convention is not the recognition and enforcement of arbitral awards.[180] The European Convention was intended instead to go beyond what was achieved by the New York Convention. It therefore addresses various aspects of arbitral procedure considered to be especially problematic. These include the capacity of public entities to submit disputes to arbitration, the capacity of foreign nationals to act as arbitrators, the organization of the arbitration, the jurisdiction of the courts and the applicable law. Unlike that of the New York Convention, the scope of the European Convention is defined not by reference to the seat of the arbitration but by reference to the parties' habitual residence or corporate headquarters: it is thus applicable where the parties are established in different contracting states.[181] As regards recognition and enforcement of awards, the European Convention merely seeks to supplement the New York Convention.

---

[174] (...continued)
vehicles). On these issues, see *infra* para. 1717.

[175] *See supra* para. 1697.

[176] *Oberlandesgericht* of Hamburg, Apr. 3, 1975, *supra* note 125.

[177] *Oberlandesgericht* of Cologne, June 10, 1976, *supra* note 115. See also *Southwire*, *supra* note 172.

[178] Cass. 1e civ., Mar. 24, 1998, Excelsior Film TV v. UGC-PH, Dalloz, IR 105 (1998); JCP, Ed. G., Pt. IV, No. 2128 (1998); 126 J.D.I. 155 (1999), and A.-E. Kahn's note.

[179] Supreme Court of Hong Kong, High Court, Aug. 12, 1992, J.J. Agro Industries (P) Ltd. v. Texuna Int'l Ltd., XVIII Y.B. COM. ARB. 396 (1993).

[180] On this Convention, see *supra* paras. 274 *et seq.*

[181] *See supra* paras. 278 *et seq.*

As noted in one decision,[182] it does not repeal the provisions of the New York Convention but, by virtue of its Article IX, simply restricts the grounds for refusal of enforcement of awards found in the New York Convention in disputes between parties from contracting states.[183]

1715. — Some of the negotiators of the European Convention would have preferred to restrict the grounds for refusal of recognition or enforcement under Article V of the New York Convention. However, as they failed to agree on that issue, they simply limited the consequences in the host country of a decision setting aside an award in the country of origin.[184]

As discussed earlier, under Article V, paragraph 1(e) of the New York Convention, recognition and enforcement can be refused by the courts of the host country if the award has been set aside or suspended by a competent authority of the country where, or under the law of which, the award was made.[185] That provision was considered as giving too much latitude to the courts of the country of origin. In particular, the authors of the European Convention were concerned that the setting aside of an award in the country of origin on the basis of the local understanding of international public policy would be recognized internationally. For that reason, Article IX of the European Convention provides that the benefit of the New York Convention will only be lost if the award was set aside in the country of origin on the basis of one of the four grounds which it lists in terms almost identical to those of the New York Convention. Those four grounds are as follows: the invalidity of the arbitration agreement for reasons other than the non-arbitrability of the dispute; a breach of due process; where the tribunal goes beyond the terms of the arbitration agreement; and where the tribunal disregards the intentions of the parties or, if the parties are silent, the law applicable to the constitution of the arbitral tribunal or the conduct of the arbitral proceedings. The German delegation suggested that the case of an award obtained by fraud should also be included, but that proposal was rejected on the grounds that it was already covered by the case of arbitral proceedings not complying with the intentions of the parties.[186] Thus, the fact that an award has been set aside on any other grounds, including the ground that the dispute is non-arbitrable, or that it contravenes international public policy, does not prevent its recognition or enforcement in another country which is a party to the Convention.[187]

---

[182] *Corte di Appello* of Florence, Oct. 22, 1976, S.A. Tradax Export v. S.p.a. Carapelli, III Y.B. COM. ARB. 279 (1978).

[183] *See infra* para. 1067.

[184] *See* Frédéric-Edouard Klein, *La Convention européenne sur l'arbitrage commercial international,* 1962 REV. CRIT. DIP 621, 632; Jean Robert, *La Convention européenne sur l'arbitrage commercial international signée à Genève le 21 avril 1961,* Dalloz, Chron. 173, 181 (1961); Dominique Hascher, *European Convention on International Commercial Arbitration of 1961 – Commentary,* XX Y.B. COM. ARB. 1006 (1995).

[185] On this issue, see *supra* paras. 1686 *et seq.*

[186] *See* DAVID, *supra* note 55, at 405–06.

[187] See, for example, Austrian *Oberster Gerichtshof,* Oct. 20, 1993, Radenska v. Kajo, which refuses to recognize an award set aside by the courts of Slovenia (for an English translation, see XX Y.B. COM. ARB. 1051 (1995);
(continued...)

That consequence is expressly provided for in relations between countries which are parties to the New York Convention by paragraph 2 of Article IX of the European Convention, and in more general terms by the first paragraph of that article. However, paragraph 2 of Article IX is now redundant, as all countries party to the European Convention are also party to the New York Convention.

1716. — In any event, the scope of the rule set forth in Article IX of the Convention is very limited, in two respects.

First, it only concerns the setting aside of awards. Contracting states remain free, as under the New York Convention, to refuse enforcement of an award on the grounds that it has not yet "become binding"[188] or that it has been "suspended by a competent authority of the country in which, or under the law of which, that award was made."[189] However, if that suspension has been ordered so as to enable the courts of the country of origin to hear, without prejudice, an action to set aside the award on a ground other than those listed in the European Convention, then neither the suspension, nor indeed the setting aside of the award to which it may lead, should prevent the recognition or enforcement of the award in the host country. Although the text of the Convention does not mention such a possibility, that result is the only one in keeping with its logic. The New York Convention, which only imposes the minimum conditions for the recognition and enforcement of awards,[190] does not oppose such a solution.

Second, Article IX of the European Convention only refers to the effects, in the host country, of the setting aside of an award in the country of origin. Contrary to what might be inferred from its title ("Setting aside of the arbitral award"), Article IX does not deal with the grounds on which the courts of contracting states may set aside an award made on their own territory. This restricts the scope of the Convention to such an extent that some commentators have sought to go beyond that limited perspective by suggesting, for example, that "the Convention sets forth which grounds justify the setting aside of an award, as opposed to the mere refusal of enforcement."[191] That argument is unconvincing. It is contradicted not only by the *travaux préparatoires* of the Convention, the authors of which failed to agree on the issue,[192] but also by the logic of the Convention. Article IX only includes the most objective grounds for setting aside an award, and omits breaches of international public policy and the issue of non-arbitrability (which, ideally, should itself be treated as an aspect of international public policy).[193] That is not to say that the Convention treats those grounds for setting an award aside as being illegitimate. It is inconceivable that

---

[187] (...continued)
for a French translation, see 1998 REV. ARB. 419, and P. Lastenouse and P. Senkovic's note; 125 J.D.I.1003 (1998)).

[188] *See* Art. V(1)(e) of the New York Convention and *supra* para. 1677.

[189] *See* Art. V(1)(e) of the New York Convention and *supra* para. 1690.

[190] *See* Art. VII.

[191] DAVID, *supra* note 55, at 405–06. *See also* Robert, *supra* note 184, at 182.

[192] *See supra* para. 1715.

[193] *See supra* para. 1704.

the Convention intended to prohibit the setting aside, at the seat of the arbitration, of an award granting a divorce or seriously contravening the fundamental convictions of the jurisdiction where it was made. The caution shown by the Convention simply reflects the variable and often unfortunately subjective nature of arbitrability and public policy grounds for setting aside an award. It also reflects the idea that there is no reason to have the conception of international public policy of the jurisdiction of the seat prevail over that of the host country by conferring on the former absolute international reach. The European Convention thus introduced an approach which subsequently led the French and United States courts to take no account of the setting aside of an award by the courts of the seat of the arbitration,[194] and which prompted the Swiss, Tunisian, Belgian, and Swedish legislatures to consider that certain awards can only be reviewed by the courts of the jurisdiction where they are to be enforced.[195]

---

[194] *See supra* para. 1595.

[195] *See supra* para. 1594.

TABLE OF ANNEXES

LEGISLATION

INTERNATIONAL CONVENTIONS

ARBITRATION RULES

FRANCE

NEW CODE OF CIVIL PROCEDURE[1]

BOOK IV[2]
ARBITRATION

TITLE I – ARBITRATION AGREEMENTS

CHAPTER I – THE ARBITRATION CLAUSE

Article 1442

An arbitration clause is an agreement by which the parties to a contract undertake to submit to arbitration the disputes which may arise in relation to that contract.

Article 1443

An arbitration clause is void unless it is set forth in writing in the main agreement or in a document to which that agreement refers.

Subject to the same penalty, the arbitration clause must either appoint the arbitrator or arbitrators or provide for a mechanism for their appointment.

Article 1444

If, after the dispute has arisen, a difficulty arises in the constitution of the arbitral tribunal as a result of the conduct of one of the parties or with respect to the implementation of the mechanism of appointment, the President of the *Tribunal de Grande Instance* shall appoint the arbitrator or arbitrators.

However, this appointment shall be made by the President of the *Tribunal de Commerce* if the agreement has expressly so provided.

If the arbitration clause is either manifestly void or inadequate for the purpose of constituting the arbitral tribunal, the President shall so state and declare that no appointment need be made.

---

[1] Translated by Emmanuel Gaillard and John Savage.

[2] Articles 1442 through 1491 are applicable to domestic arbitration. Articles 1492 through 1507 are applicable to international arbitration. Certain domestic law provisions are applicable to international arbitration where there is a cross-reference to that effect.

Article 1445

The dispute shall be submitted to the arbitral tribunal either jointly by the parties or by the most diligent party.

Article 1446

If void, the arbitration clause shall be deemed not written.

CHAPTER II – THE SUBMISSION AGREEMENT

Article 1447

A submission agreement is an agreement by which the parties to a dispute that has arisen submit such dispute to arbitration by one or more persons.

Article 1448

A submission agreement is void unless it sets forth the subject matter of the dispute.

Subject to the same penalty, it must either appoint the arbitrator or arbitrators or provide for a mechanism for their appointment.

A submission agreement shall lapse when an arbitrator whom it appoints does not accept the mission entrusted to him or her.

Article 1449

A submission agreement shall be evidenced in writing. It may take the form of minutes signed by the arbitrator and the parties.

Article 1450

The parties shall have the right to submit their disputes to arbitration even where proceedings are already pending before another jurisdiction.

CHAPTER III – COMMON RULES

Article 1451

The mission of arbitrator may only be entrusted to a natural person; such person must have full capacity to exercise his or her civil rights.

If the arbitration agreement appoints a juridical person, such person only has the power to organize the arbitration.

Article 1452

The constitution of the arbitral tribunal is complete only if the arbitrator or arbitrators accept the mission entrusted to them.

An arbitrator who is aware of a ground for challenge regarding his or her person shall so inform the parties. In such a case, he or she may accept his or her mission only with the agreement of the parties.

Article 1453

An arbitral tribunal shall be composed of a sole arbitrator or of several arbitrators in an uneven number.

Article 1454

When the parties appoint an even number of arbitrators, the arbitral tribunal shall be completed with an arbitrator chosen either in accordance with the mechanism envisaged by the parties or, in the absence of such mechanism, by the appointed arbitrators or, in the absence of agreement between the appointed arbitrators, by the President of the *Tribunal de Grande Instance.*

Article 1455

When a natural or juridical person is responsible for organizing the arbitration, the arbitral mission shall be entrusted to one or several arbitrators accepted by all the parties.

In the absence of such acceptance, the person responsible for organizing the arbitration shall invite each party to appoint an arbitrator and shall, if appropriate, proceed to appoint the arbitrator required to complete the arbitral tribunal. If the parties fail to appoint an arbitrator, such arbitrator shall be appointed by the person responsible for organizing the arbitration.

The arbitral tribunal may also be directly constituted in accordance with the procedures set forth in the preceding paragraph.

The person responsible for organizing the arbitration may provide that the arbitral tribunal make only a draft award and that if such draft is contested by one of the parties, the matter shall be submitted to a second arbitral tribunal. In such a case, the members of the second tribunal shall be appointed by the person responsible for organizing the arbitration, each of the parties having the right to have one of the arbitrators so appointed replaced.

Article 1456

If the arbitration agreement does not specify a time limit, the arbitrators' mission shall last only six months from the day the last arbitrator accepted his or her mission.

The statutory or contractual time limit may be extended either by agreement of the parties or, at the request of either of them or of the arbitral tribunal, by the President of the *Tribunal de Grande Instance* or, in the case provided for in Article 1444, paragraph 2, by the President of the *Tribunal de Commerce.*

Article 1457

In the cases provided for in Articles 1444, 1454, 1456, and 1463, the President of the *Tribunal*, seized as in expedited proceedings (*référé*) by a party or by the arbitral tribunal, shall rule by way of an order against which no recourse is available.

However, such order may be appealed when the President holds that no appointment shall be made for one of the reasons set forth in Article 1444 (paragraph 3). The appeal shall be brought, heard and decided as for recourse against jurisdictional decisions (*contredit de compétence*).

The President having jurisdiction is the President of the *Tribunal* designated by the arbitration agreement or, in the absence of such designation, the President of the *Tribunal* of the place where that agreement located the arbitral proceedings. If the agreement is silent, the President having jurisdiction is the President of the *Tribunal* of the place where the party or one of the parties opposing the application to the President resides or, if such party does not reside in France, the President of the *Tribunal* of the place where the party making the application resides.

Article 1458

When a dispute submitted to an arbitral tribunal by virtue of an arbitration agreement is brought before a national court, such court shall decline jurisdiction.

If the arbitral tribunal has not yet been seized of the matter, the court shall also decline jurisdiction unless the arbitration agreement is manifestly void.

In neither case may the court decline jurisdiction on its own motion.

Article 1459

Any provision or agreement contrary to the rules set forth in the present Chapter shall be deemed not written.

TITLE II – THE ARBITRAL PROCEEDINGS

Article 1460

The arbitrators shall determine the arbitral procedure without being bound to follow the rules established for the courts, unless the parties have provided otherwise in the arbitration agreement.

However, the fundamental principles of court proceedings set forth in Articles 4 to 10, 11 (paragraph 1) and 13 to 21[3] shall always apply to arbitral proceedings.

If a party is in possession of an item of evidence, the arbitrator may also order that party to produce it.

---

[3] These provisions contain a number of guiding procedural principles concerning the rights and obligations of the parties and the role of the judge:
- the subject matter of the dispute is determined by the claims of the parties;
- the judge shall rule on what is claimed and only what is claimed;
- the parties must base their claims on sufficient factual allegations;
- the judge may not base his or her decision on facts other than those alleged by the parties;
- the judge may request factual explanations from the parties;
- the judge may order any legally admissible investigatory measures;
- the parties must cooperate in all matters regarding evidence and the judge may draw any adverse inference from any refusal to cooperate;
- the judge may request legal explanations from the parties;
- no party may be judged without being heard or invited to be heard;
- the parties must inform one another in timely fashion of the facts, legal arguments and evidence on which they intend to base their case so as to allow the other party sufficient preparation of its rebuttal;
- the judge must ensure the respect of the principle of due process at all times;
- a party against whom a measure has been ordered without its knowledge may appeal that decision;
- the parties may defend themselves in person except for cases where legal representation is mandatory;
- the parties may freely choose their counsel;
- the judge may always hear the parties in person;
- conciliation of the parties is an integral part of the judge's role.

Article 1461

Procedural orders and minutes shall be made by all the arbitrators unless the arbitration agreement authorizes them to delegate this task to one of them.

Third parties shall be heard without being sworn.

Article 1462

Each arbitrator shall carry out his or her mission until it is completed.

An arbitrator may only be dismissed with the unanimous consent of the parties.

Article 1463

An arbitrator may only refuse to act or be challenged on a ground which is revealed or arises after his or her appointment.

Difficulties relating to the application of the present article shall be brought before the President of the competent court.

Article 1464

The arbitral proceedings shall come to an end, unless otherwise specifically agreed by the parties:

1°   On the dismissal, death, or incapability of an arbitrator or on the loss of his or her full capacity to exercise his or her civil rights;

2°   On an arbitrator refusing to act or being challenged;

3°   On the expiration of the time limit for arbitration.

Article 1465

The suspension of the arbitral proceedings is governed by the provisions of Articles 369 to 376.[4]

Article 1466

If, before the arbitrator, one of the parties challenges the principle or scope of the arbitrator's jurisdiction, the arbitrator shall rule on the validity or scope of his or her jurisdiction.

---

[4]   These provisions concern the suspension of judicial proceedings, which takes place automatically if certain events occur (if, for example, a minor is involved in the proceedings) or upon notification in other cases, provided that this event or notification takes place before the oral hearings have commenced. No decisions made or judgments issued after such suspension are valid unless affirmed by the party entitled to invoke that suspension.

Article 1467

Unless otherwise agreed, the arbitrator shall have the power to resolve an incidental claim for verification of a person's writing or forgery in accordance with Articles 287 to 294 and Article 299.[5]

In the case of an incidental claim for forgery of official documents, Article 313 is applicable before the arbitrator. The time limit for the arbitration shall continue to run from the day when the incidental claim has been decided.

Article 1468

The arbitrator shall fix the date upon which deliberations shall begin.

After this date, no claim may be made, nor any argument raised. No observation may be presented nor any evidence produced, except at the request of the arbitrator.

TITLE III – THE ARBITRAL AWARD

Article 1469

Arbitrators' deliberations shall be confidential.

Article 1470

The arbitral award shall be made by a majority vote.

Article 1471

The arbitral award shall succinctly state the respective claims and arguments of the parties.

Reasons shall be given for the decision.

Article 1472

The arbitral award shall indicate:
- the names of the arbitrators who made it;
- its date;
- the place where it was made;
- the last names, first names or denomination of the parties, as well as their domicile or corporate headquarters;
- if applicable, the names of the counsel or other persons who represented or assisted the parties.

Article 1473

The arbitral award shall be signed by all the arbitrators.

However, if a minority among them refuses to sign it, the others shall mention the fact and the award shall have the same effect as though it had been signed by all the arbitrators.

---

[5] These provisions grant the judge the right to verify the authenticity of contested or allegedly falsified writings. In the case of allegedly falsified writings, the proceedings shall be suspended pending a decision on that matter, unless the principal dispute may be decided without reference to the document at issue.

Article 1474

The arbitrator shall resolve the dispute in accordance with the rules of law, unless the parties, in the arbitration agreement, have empowered such arbitrator to rule as *amiable compositeur*.

Article 1475

The award brings an end to the arbitrator's jurisdiction over the dispute it resolves.

However, the arbitrator has the power to interpret the award, to rectify clerical errors and omissions affecting it, and to complete it when he or she has failed to rule on a claim. Articles 461 to 463[6] are applicable. If the arbitral tribunal cannot be reconvened, this power shall vest in the court which would have had jurisdiction in the absence of arbitration.

Article 1476

Once it is made, the arbitral award is *res judicata* in relation to the dispute it resolves.

Article 1477

The arbitral award may only be enforced by virtue of an enforcement order (*exequatur*) issued by the *Tribunal de Grande Instance* of the place where the award was made.

For this purpose, the original of the award, together with a copy of the arbitration agreement, shall be filed by one of the arbitrators or by the most diligent party with the secretariat of the court.

Article 1478

The enforcement order is affixed to the original of the arbitral award.

Reasons shall be given for any order refusing enforcement.

Article 1479

The rules on provisional enforcement of judgments are applicable to arbitral awards.

In the case of an appeal or an action to set aside, the First President or the magistrate conducting the procedure, once the matter is referred to him or her, may grant enforcement of the arbitral award and declare it provisionally enforceable. He or she may also order provisional enforcement pursuant to the procedure provided for in Articles 525 and 526;[7] his or her decision shall be the equivalent of an enforcement order.

Article 1480

An award shall be void unless it complies with the provisions of Articles 1471 (paragraph 2), 1472, with respect to the names of the arbitrators and the date of the award, and 1473.

---

[6] The judge may be requested by the parties to interpret, correct or supplement his or her judgment.

[7] Pursuant to these provisions, the refusal to allow the provisional enforcement of a judgment may be appealed. The provisional execution of judgments may also be ordered by a court of appeals when provisional enforcement was not requested of, or decided by, the first instance court.

TITLE IV – AVAILABLE RECOURSE

Article 1481

An arbitral award may not be the subject of opposition proceedings or of a petition to vacate before the *Cour de Cassation*.

It may be the subject of third party opposition proceedings before the court which would have had jurisdiction had there been no arbitration, subject to the provisions of Article 588 (paragraph 1).[8]

Article 1482

An arbitral award may be appealed unless the parties waived their right to appeal in the arbitration agreement. However, it may not be appealed where the arbitrator has been empowered to rule as *amiable compositeur*, unless the parties expressly reserved the right to do so in the arbitration agreement.

Article 1483

Where, in accordance with the distinctions made in Article 1482, the parties have not waived their right to appeal or have expressly provided for such right in the arbitration agreement, an appeal is the only form of recourse available, be it to obtain the revision or the setting aside of the arbitral award. The appellate judge shall rule as *amiable compositeur* where the arbitrator was empowered to do so.

Article 1484

Where, in accordance with the distinctions made in Article 1482, the parties have waived their right to appeal or have not expressly reserved such right in the arbitration agreement, an action to set aside what is characterized as an arbitral award may nonetheless be brought, notwithstanding any provision to the contrary.

It is available only in the following cases:

1° Where the arbitrator ruled in the absence of an arbitration agreement or on the basis of an agreement that was void or had expired;

2° Where the arbitral tribunal was irregularly constituted or the sole arbitrator irregularly appointed;

3° Where the arbitrator ruled without complying with the mission conferred upon him or her;

4° When due process has not been respected;

5° In all cases of nullity envisaged in Article 1480;

6° Where the arbitrator has violated a rule of public policy.

Article 1485

When a court seized of an action to set aside sets the arbitral award aside, it shall rule on the merits of the case within the limits of the arbitrator's mission, unless otherwise agreed by all the parties.

---

[8] This provision concerns the third-party opposition (*tierce opposition*) procedure.

Article 1486

Appeals and actions to set aside shall be brought before the Court of Appeals of the place where the arbitral award was made.

These forms of recourse are admissible immediately after the making of the award; they are no longer admissible if they have not been exercised within one month of the official notification of the award bearing an enforcement order.

Enforcement of the arbitral award shall be suspended for the period during which these forms of recourse may be exercised. The exercise of such recourse during that period shall also have a suspensive effect.

Article 1487

Appeals and actions to set aside shall be brought, heard and decided in accordance with the rules relating to procedure in litigation before the Court of Appeals.

The characterization of the form of recourse made by the parties at the time when the declaration is made may be modified or clarified at any time until the Court of Appeals is seized of the matter.

Article 1488

No form of recourse is available against an order granting enforcement of an award.

However, an appeal against or an action to set aside an award shall, within the limits of the court's jurisdiction, be deemed to constitute recourse against the decision of the judge who granted enforcement or to bring an end to that judge's jurisdiction.

Article 1489

An order refusing to grant enforcement may be appealed within one month of its official notification. In that case, the Court of Appeals shall, at the request of the parties, rule on the arguments which they could have raised against the arbitral award, whether on appeal or in an action to set aside.

Article 1490

Rejection of an appeal or of an action to set aside shall be deemed to be an enforcement order with respect to the arbitral award or those of its terms that have not been censured by the Court of Appeals.

Article 1491

An action to revise the arbitral award is available in the same cases and under the same conditions as those envisaged for court judgements.

It shall be brought before the Court of Appeals which would have had jurisdiction over other forms of recourse against the award.

TITLE V – INTERNATIONAL ARBITRATION

Article 1492

An arbitration is international when it involves the interests of international trade.

Article 1493

The arbitration agreement may, directly or by reference to arbitration rules, appoint the arbitrator or arbitrators or provide for a mechanism for their appointment.

If a difficulty arises in the constitution of the arbitral tribunal in an arbitration which takes place in France or which the parties have agreed shall be governed by French procedural law, the most diligent party may, in the absence of a clause to the contrary, apply to the President of the *Tribunal de Grande Instance* of Paris in accordance with the procedures of Article 1457.

Article 1494

The arbitration agreement may, directly or by reference to arbitration rules, determine the procedure to be followed in the arbitral proceedings; it may also submit the proceedings to a specified procedural law.

If the agreement is silent, the arbitrator shall determine the procedure, if need be, either directly or by reference to a law or to arbitration rules.

Article 1495

Where the international arbitration is governed by French law, the provisions of Titles I, II, and III of the present Book shall only apply in the absence of a specific agreement, and subject to Articles 1493 and 1494.

Article 1496

The arbitrator shall resolve the dispute in accordance with the rules of law chosen by the parties; in the absence of such a choice, in accordance with the rules of law he or she considers appropriate.

In all cases he or she shall take trade usages into account.

Article 1497

The arbitrator shall rule as *amiable compositeur* if the agreement of the parties conferred this mission upon him or her.

TITLE VI – RECOGNITION OF, ENFORCEMENT OF, AND RECOURSE AGAINST ARBITRAL AWARDS MADE ABROAD OR IN INTERNATIONAL ARBITRATION

CHAPTER I – RECOGNITION AND ENFORCEMENT OF ARBITRAL AWARDS MADE ABROAD OR IN INTERNATIONAL ARBITRATION

Article 1498

Arbitral awards shall be recognized in France if their existence is proven by the party relying on the award and if such recognition is not manifestly contrary to international public policy.

Such awards shall be declared enforceable in France by the enforcement judge under the same conditions.

Article 1499

The existence of an arbitral award is established by the production of the original of the award together with the arbitration agreement, or of copies of such documents which satisfy the conditions required for their authenticity.

If such documents are not in the French language, the party shall produce a translation certified by a translator registered on the list of experts.

Article 1500

The provisions of Articles 1476 to 1479 are applicable.

CHAPTER II – RECOURSE AGAINST ARBITRAL AWARDS MADE ABROAD OR IN INTERNATIONAL ARBITRATION

Article 1501

A decision which refuses recognition or enforcement of an award may be appealed.

Article 1502

An appeal against a decision which grants recognition or enforcement is available only in the following cases:

1°   Where the arbitrator ruled in the absence of an arbitration agreement or on the basis of an agreement that was void or had expired;

2°   Where the arbitral tribunal was irregularly constituted or the sole arbitrator irregularly appointed;

3°   Where the arbitrator ruled without complying with the mission conferred upon him or her;

4°   When due process has not been respected;

5°   Where the recognition or enforcement is contrary to international public policy.

Article 1503

The appeal provided for in Articles 1501 and 1502 shall be brought before the Court of Appeals having jurisdiction over the judge who made the decision. It may be brought within one month of the official notification of the judge's decision.

Article 1504

An arbitral award made in France in an international arbitration may be the subject of an action to set aside in the cases set forth in Article 1502.

No form of recourse is available against an order granting enforcement of such an award. However, an action to set aside shall, within the limits of the court's jurisdiction, be deemed to constitute recourse against the decision of the judge who granted enforcement or to bring an end to that judge's jurisdiction.

Article 1505

An action to set aside as provided for in Article 1504 shall be brought before the Court of Appeals of the place where the award was made. Such action is admissible immediately after the making of the award; it is no longer admissible if it has not been brought within one month of the official notification of the award bearing an enforcement order.

Article 1506
Enforcement of the arbitral award shall be suspended for the period during which recourse provided for in Articles 1501, 1502 and 1504 may be exercised. The exercise of such recourse during that period shall also have a suspensive effect.

Article 1507
The provisions of Title IV of the present Book, except those of the first paragraph of Article 1487 and of Article 1490, are not applicable to recourse proceedings.

REPORT OF THE KEEPER OF THE SEALS, MINISTER OF JUSTICE TO THE PRIME MINISTER ON THE DRAFT OF THE DECREE INSTITUTING THE PROVISIONS OF PARTS III AND IV OF THE NEW CODE OF CIVIL PROCEDURE AND MODIFYING CERTAIN PROVISIONS OF THIS CODE (EXTRACT)[9]

The New Code of Civil Procedure instituted by the Decree N° 75-1123 of 5 December 1975 only consists of two parts at the present moment. The first part contains those provisions which are common to all jurisdictions; the second contains those which are particular to each jurisdiction.

It is now proposed to complete the New Code by a part III which is devoted to special procedures in certain cases and by a part IV relating to arbitration. The institution of the provisions of these two new parts which complete the work of the Reform Commission on Civil Procedure presided by M. Jean Foyer, forms the first part of the present draft decree.

Furthermore, it appeared appropriate to make certain improvements which practice has shown to be advisable to the two parts of the New Code of Civil Procedure which have already been published. This is the object of the second part of the draft decree which also includes a third part concerning various transitory provisions.

(. . .)

Part IV – Arbitration – introduces into the New Code of Civil Procedure decree N° 80-354 of 14 May 1980, as completed by those provisions relating to international arbitrations (Title V) and to the recognition and enforcement of arbitral awards made abroad or in an international arbitration (Title VI).

The codification of the decree of 14 May 1980 invites comment on two points.

---

[9] Reproduced with kind permission from JEAN-LOUIS DELVOLVÉ, ARBITRATION IN FRANCE – THE FRENCH LAW OF NATIONAL AND INTERNATIONAL ARBITRATION 93 (1982).

Article 1475 which specifies the powers of the arbitrators as to the interpretation and rectification of the arbitral award no longer refers to article 464 of the New Code of Civil Procedure because this reference is not in accordance with the first sentence of paragraph 2 which does not cover the case of rectification provided for by article 464.

Article 1487 is completed by a paragraph which enables the description given by the parties at the time when the declaration is made of the remedy exercised against the arbitral award, to be modified or clarified until the matter has been listed in the court of appeal. In effect an appeal and an action for annulment are commenced by a declaration and it may be difficult in certain cases to specify at the moment of the declaration, the exact description of the remedy exercised.

The reform of the procedure in domestic arbitrations, without of course upsetting the principles laid down by the case-law of the Supreme Court as far as international arbitrations are concerned, nor those rules resulting in this domain from international conventions ratified by France, has raised a certain number of difficulties as far as the transposition of the new provisions to international arbitrations is involved.

On the one hand, in effect, the new regime of domestic arbitration contains some imperative provisions which could risk paralysing international arbitrations whereas the Supreme Court has clearly admitted the specificity and the validity of such an arbitration on our territory insofar as it involves the interests of international trade; on the other hand, and above all, since the decree of 14 May 1980, some uncertainty has been felt as to the existence of remedies against, in particular, awards made in France in an international arbitration and the jurisdiction in this field of the Courts of Appeal, in view of the centralization of the remedies before this jurisdiction in the domestic field.

These considerations explain the division of the field of international arbitration into two titles: the first title deals with an international arbitration as such (title V) in defining it and in marking in liberal terms its specificity as compared to a domestic arbitration; the second title (title VI) includes two chapters, one which is devoted to the recognition and enforcement of awards, the other to remedies.

The provisions of title V to a very large extent consecrate the solutions of the case-law of the Supreme Court, the terms of international conventions (in particular the convention of Geneva of 21 April 1961), as well as the practice of international trade as principally reflected by the most widely recognized rules of arbitration (the rules of arbitration of the United Nations Commission on International Trade Law – UNCITRAL – rules of the International Chamber of Commerce).

This is so as concerns the definition of an international arbitration (article 1492), the methods of appointment of arbitrators (article 1493), the choice of applicable rules to the arbitral proceedings by the parties or by the arbitrator (article 1494) and the powers of an arbitrator (article 1496 and 1497).

The new provisions on international arbitration only concern procedure and in no way affect the principles now well established by the case law of the Supreme Court as regards the legal regime of international arbitrations; such is the case in particular as regards the scope of an international arbitration agreement, where it has been judged that such an agreement is not affected because the main agreement is void, or because the arbitration agreement covers a dispute which has not yet arisen, or that such an agreement has been concluded by a State or by a public body or that the rules under which the dispute should be decided are of public policy.

In the field of the rules of procedure which are applicable to an international arbitration, the link with the provisions on domestic arbitrations (titles I, II and III) is ensured by article 1495 which provides that these provisions are to apply in the event where the international arbitration as defined in article 1492 shall have been made subject to French law by the intention of the parties or the arbitrator. But even in this case, the specificity and liberal approach which are particular to international arbitrations allow any particular agreement between the parties to prevail as well as the provisions of title V.

Chapter I of title VI which is devoted to recognition and enforcement covers both awards made abroad or in an international arbitration as defined in title V; the latter awards may have been made either in France or abroad.

Apart from the special provisions necessitated by the particular nature of these two types of awards (not contrary to French international public policy – article 1498 – proof of the existence of the award and the problem of translation into French – article 1499), this chapter (article 1500) refers one for the remainder to the relevant articles of title III relating to the authority of res judicata and the execution of awards made in a domestic arbitration.

Although it is not expressly indicated in this chapter, its provisions as well as those of chapter II obviously do not prevent the application of the applicable bilateral conventions or the convention of New York of 10 June 1958 on the recognition and enforcement of foreign arbitral awards, as concerns those awards made in the other contracting States, since France has made the declaration under article 1-3 of this latter convention.

Chapter II which relates to remedies is applicable both to awards made abroad, as well as to those awards made in France in an international arbitration. However, in this latter case, a special provision (article 1504) allows an action for annulment against such awards. In effect, if the possibility to bring before a French judge an action for annulment against an award made abroad is excluded, it is not on the other hand without importance for the French legal order to control the regularity of those awards made in France, even in an international arbitration. The provisions of article 1502 to which article 1504 refers, are therefore analogous to those of article 1484, the contrariety with public policy becoming here, it being an award made in an international arbitration, the contrariety with international public policy.

As far as an appeal is concerned, such a remedy was also excluded not only against awards made abroad but also those made in France in an international arbitration (in this latter case the action for annulment ensures, as indicated above, the necessary control). But the position is different as regards decisions which grant or refuse the recognition or enforcement of awards made abroad or in an international arbitration. Just as in the case of an action for annulment, the cases in which an appeal is open against the decision which grants recognition or enforcement (article 1502) are analogous to those which are mentioned in article 1484, with the same adaptation as regards the contrariety with public policy.

As in domestic arbitrations, the recourses set out in title VI are brought before a Court of Appeal (articles 1503 and 1505), whether it is an action for annulment against awards made in France in an international arbitration (the Court of Appeal in whose jurisdiction the award was made) or an appeal against the decision ruling on the recognition or enforcement (the Court of Appeal in whose jurisdiction the judge ruled).

The provisions concerning the time-limits are identical to those applicable in domestic arbitrations.

In order to emphasize the specificity of the remedies for awards made abroad or in an international arbitration, article 1507 excludes the application of the provisions of title IV, with the exception of those which are applicable in all events (procedure before a Court of Appeal and effects of the dismissal of an appeal or an action for annulment).

CIVIL CODE

Article 2059
All persons may submit to arbitration those rights which they are free to dispose of.

Article 2060[10]
One may not submit to arbitration questions of personal status and capacity, or those relating to divorce or to judicial separation or disputes concerning public collectivities and public establishments and more generally in all areas which concern public policy.

However, public establishments of a commercial or industrial nature may be authorized by decree to submit disputes to arbitration.

Article 2061[11]
An arbitration clause shall be void unless the law provides otherwise.

COMMERCIAL CODE

Article 631
The commercial courts shall have jurisdiction over:

1° disputes relating to commitments and transactions between traders, merchants and bankers;

2° disputes between shareholders of commercial companies;

3° those relating to commercial activities (*actes de commerce*) between all persons.

However, the parties may, at the time they enter into the contract, agree to submit to arbitration the disputes listed above, when they arise.

Article 631-1
Subject to the jurisdiction of disciplinary courts and notwithstanding any provision to the contrary, the civil courts have exclusive jurisdiction over lawsuits in which one of the parties is a company constituted in accordance with law n° 90-1258 of December 31, 1990 relating

---

[10] This Article does not apply in international arbitration.

[11] *Id.*

to the practice carried on by companies of liberal professions with a specific legislative or regulatory status or whose denomination is protected by law, as well as disputes between shareholders of such a company.

Nevertheless, the shareholders may agree, in the by-laws, to submit to arbitration disputes arising between them regarding their company.

CODE OF JUDICIAL ORGANIZATION

Article L. 311-11

The *Tribunal de Grande Instance*, sitting with a single judge, has jurisdiction over applications for recognition and enforcement of judicial decisions and foreign public acts, as well as of French and foreign arbitral awards.

SWITZERLAND

PRIVATE INTERNATIONAL LAW STATUTE (EXCERPTS RELATING TO INTERNATIONAL ARBITRATION)*

CHAPTER 1 – GENERAL PROVISIONS

I. SCOPE OF APPLICATION

Article 1

1. This Act governs in international matters:
    a. the jurisdiction of the Swiss courts or administrative authorities;
    b. the applicable law;
    c. the conditions for the recognition and enforcement of foreign decisions;
    d. bankruptcy and composition agreements;
    e. arbitration.
2. International treaties are reserved.

VI. ARBITRATION AGREEMENT

Article 7

If the parties have concluded an arbitration agreement covering an arbitrable dispute, a Swiss court seized of it shall decline jurisdiction unless
    a. the defendant has proceeded with its defense on the merits without raising any objection;
    b. the court finds that the arbitral agreement is null and void, inoperative or incapable of being performed; or
    c. the arbitral tribunal cannot be constituted for reasons manifestly attributable to the defendant.

---

* Translation reproduced with kind permission from ASSOCIATION SUISSE DE L'ARBITRAGE, THE NEW SWISS LAW ON INTERNATIONAL ARBITRATION (1990).

CHAPTER 12 – INTERNATIONAL ARBITRATION

I. SCOPE OF APPLICATION. SEAT OF THE ARBITRAL TRIBUNAL

Article 176

1. The provisions of this chapter shall apply to any arbitration if the seat of the arbitral tribunal is in Switzerland and if, at the time when the arbitration agreement was concluded, at least one of the parties had neither its domicile nor its habitual residence in Switzerland.
2. The provisions of this chapter shall not apply where the parties have in writing excluded its application and agreed to the exclusive application of the procedural provisions of cantonal law relating to arbitration.
3. The seat of the arbitral tribunal shall be determined by the parties, or the arbitration institution designated by them, or, failing both, by the arbitrators.

II. ARBITRABILITY

Article 177

1. Any dispute involving property may be the subject-matter of an arbitration.
2. If a party to the arbitration agreement is a state or an enterprise or organization controlled by it, it cannot rely on its own law in order to contest its capacity to be a party to an arbitration or the arbitrability of a dispute covered by the arbitration agreement.

III. ARBITRATION AGREEMENT

Article 178

1. As regards its form, an arbitration agreement shall be valid if made in writing, by telegram, telex, telecopier or any other means of communication which permits it to be evidenced by a text.
2. As regards its substance, an arbitration agreement shall be valid if it conforms either to the law chosen by the parties, or to the law governing the subject-matter of the dispute, in particular the law governing the main contract, or if it conforms to Swiss law.
3. The validity of an arbitration agreement cannot be contested on the ground that the main contract may not be valid or that the arbitration agreement concerns disputes which have not yet arisen.

IV. ARBITRAL TRIBUNAL

1. CONSTITUTION

Article 179

1. The arbitrators shall be appointed, removed or replaced in accordance with the agreement of the parties.

2. In the absence of such an agreement, the matter may be referred to the court where the arbitral tribunal has its seat; the court shall apply by analogy the provisions of cantonal law concerning the appointment, removal or replacement of arbitrators.

3. Where a court is called upon to appoint an arbitrator, it shall make the appointment, unless a summary examination shows that no arbitration agreement exists between the parties.

2. CHALLENGE OF ARBITRATORS

Article 180

1. An arbitrator may be challenged:
   a. if he does not meet the requirements agreed by the parties;
   b. if the arbitration rules agreed by the parties provide a ground for challenge; or
   c. if circumstances exist that give rise to justifiable doubts as to his independence.

2. A party may challenge an arbitrator whom it has appointed or in whose appointment it has participated only on grounds of which it became aware after such appointment. The ground for challenge must be notified to the arbitral tribunal and to the other party without delay.

3. In the event of a dispute and to the extent to which the parties have not determined the procedure for the challenge, the court of the seat of the arbitral tribunal shall decide; its decision is final.

V. LIS PENDENS

Article 181

The arbitral proceedings shall be pending from the time when one of the parties submits its request to the arbitrator or arbitrators designated in the arbitration agreement or, in the absence of such designation, from the time when one of the parties initiates the procedure for the constitution of the arbitral tribunal.

VI. PROCEDURE

1. PRINCIPLE

Article 182

1. The parties may, directly or by reference to arbitration rules, determine the arbitral procedure; they may also submit it to a procedural law of their choice.

2. Where the parties have not determined the procedure, the arbitral tribunal shall determine it to the extent necessary, either directly or by reference to a law or to arbitration rules.

3. Whatever procedure is chosen, the arbitral tribunal shall ensure equal treatment of the parties and the right of the parties to be heard in an adversarial procedure.

2. PROVISIONAL AND PROTECTIVE MEASURES

Article 183
1. Unless the parties have agreed otherwise, the arbitral tribunal may, at the request of a party, order provisional or protective measures.
2. If the party so ordered does not comply therewith voluntarily, the arbitral tribunal may request the assistance of the competent court. Such court shall apply its own law.
3. The arbitral tribunal or the court may make the granting of provisional or protective measures subject to the provision of appropriate security.

3. TAKING EVIDENCE

Article 184
1. The arbitral tribunal shall itself take the evidence.
2. Where the assistance of state authorities is needed for taking evidence, the arbitral tribunal or a party with the consent of the arbitral tribunal may request the assistance of the court of the seat of the arbitral tribunal. Such court shall apply its own law.

4. OTHER JUDICIAL ASSISTANCE

Article 185
For any further judicial assistance the court of the seat of the arbitral tribunal shall have jurisdiction.

VII. JURISDICTION

Article 186
1. The arbitral tribunal shall decide on its own jurisdiction.
2. Any objection to its jurisdiction must be raised prior to any defense on the merits.
3. The arbitral tribunal shall, in general, decide on its jurisdiction by a preliminary decision.

VIII. DECISION ON THE MERITS

1. APPLICABLE LAW

Article 187
1. The arbitral tribunal shall decide the dispute according to the rules of law chosen by the parties or, in the absence of such a choice, according to the rules of law with which the case has the closest connection.
2. The parties may authorize the arbitral tribunal to decide *ex aequo et bono*.

2. PARTIAL AWARD

Article 188

Unless the parties have agreed otherwise, the arbitral tribunal may make partial awards.

3. ARBITRAL AWARD

Article 189

1. The arbitral award shall be made in conformity with the rules of procedure and the form agreed by the parties.
2. In the absence of such agreement, the award shall be made by a majority decision, or, in the absence of a majority, by the presiding arbitrator alone. It shall be in writing, reasoned, dated and signed. The signature of the presiding arbitrator shall suffice.

IX. FINALITY. SETTING ASIDE

1. PRINCIPLE

Article 190

1. The award is final from the time when it is communicated.
2. Proceedings for setting aside the award may only be initiated:
   a. where the sole arbitrator has been incorrectly appointed or where the arbitral tribunal has been incorrectly constituted;
   b. where the arbitral tribunal has wrongly declared itself to have or not to have jurisdiction;
   c. where the award has gone beyond the claims submitted to the arbitral tribunal, or failed to decide one of the claims;
   d. where the principle of equal treatment of the parties or their right to be heard in adversarial procedure has not been observed;
   e. where the award is incompatible with public policy.
3. As regards preliminary decisions, setting aside proceedings can only be initiated on the grounds of the above paragraphs 2(a) and 2(b); the time-limit runs from the communication of the decision.

2. COMPETENT COURT

Article 191

1. Setting aside proceedings may only be brought before the Federal Supreme Court. The procedure is governed by the provisions of the Federal Judicial Organization Act relating to public law appeals.
2. However, the parties may agree that the court of the seat of the arbitral tribunal shall decide in lieu of the Federal Supreme Court; its decision is final. For this purpose the Cantons shall designate a sole Cantonal court.

X. EXCLUSION AGREEMENTS

Article 192

1. Where none of the parties has its domicile, its habitual residence, or a business establishment in Switzerland, they may, by an express statement in the arbitration agreement or by a subsequent agreement in writing, exclude all setting aside proceedings, or they may limit such proceedings to one or several of the grounds listed in Article 190, paragraph 2.
2. Where the parties have excluded all setting aside proceedings and where the awards are to be enforced in Switzerland, the New York Convention of 10 June, 1958 on the Recognition and Enforcement of Foreign Arbitral Awards shall apply by analogy.

XI. DEPOSIT AND CERTIFICATE OF ENFORCEABILITY

Article 193

1. Each party may at its own expense deposit a copy of the award with the Swiss court of the seat of the arbitral tribunal.
2. At the request of a party, that court shall certify the enforceability of the award.
3. At the request of a party, the arbitral tribunal shall certify that the award has been made in conformity with the provisions of this Act; such certificate has the same effect as the deposit of the award.

XII. FOREIGN ARBITRAL AWARDS

Article 194

The recognition and enforcement of a foreign arbitral award is governed by the New York Convention of 10 June, 1958 on the Recognition and Enforcement of Foreign Arbitral Awards.

UNCITRAL MODEL LAW ON INTERNATIONAL COMMERCIAL ARBITRATION
(As adopted by the United Nations Commission on International Trade Law on 21 June 1985)

CHAPTER I.   GENERAL PROVISIONS

Article 1 – Scope of application*

1. This Law applies to international commercial** arbitration, subject to any agreement in force between this State and any other State or States.
2. The provisions of this Law, except articles 8, 9, 35 and 36, apply only if the place of arbitration is in the territory of this State.
3. An arbitration is international if:
    (a) the parties to an arbitration agreement have, at the time of the conclusion of that agreement, their places of business in different States; or
    (b) one of the following places is situated outside the State in which the parties have their places of business:
        (i) the place of arbitration if determined in, or pursuant to, the arbitration agreement;
        (ii) any place where a substantial part of the obligations of the commercial relationship is to be performed or the place with which the subject-matter of the dispute is most closely connected; or
    (c) the parties have expressly agreed that the subject-matter of the arbitration agreement relates to more than one country.
4. For the purposes of paragraph (3) of this article:
    (a) if a party has more than one place of business, the place of business is that which has the closest relationship to the arbitration agreement;
    (b) if a party does not have a place of business, reference is to be made to his habitual residence.

---

* Article headings are for reference purposes only and are not to be used for purposes of interpretation.

** The term "commercial" should be given a wide interpretation so as to cover matters arising from all relationships of a commercial nature, whether contractual or not. Relationships of a commercial nature include, but are not limited to, the following transactions: any trade transaction for the supply or exchange of goods or services; distribution agreement; commercial representation or agency; factoring; leasing; construction of works; consulting; engineering; licensing; investment; financing; banking; insurance; exploitation agreement or concession; joint venture and other forms of industrial or business cooperation; carriage of goods or passengers by air, sea, rail or road.

5. This Law shall not affect any other law of this State by virtue of which certain disputes may not be submitted to arbitration or may be submitted to arbitration only according to provisions other than those of this Law.

Article 2 – Definitions and rules of interpretation

For the purposes of this Law:

(a) "arbitration" means any arbitration whether or not administered by a permanent arbitral institution;

(b) "arbitral tribunal" means a sole arbitrator or a panel of arbitrators;

(c) "court" means a body or organ of the judicial system of a State;

(d) where a provision of this Law, except article 28, leaves the parties free to determine a certain issue, such freedom includes the right of the parties to authorize a third party, including an institution, to make that determination;

(e) where a provision of this Law refers to the fact that the parties have agreed or that they may agree or in any other way refers to an agreement of the parties, such agreement includes any arbitration rules referred to in that agreement;

(f) where a provision of this Law, other than in articles 25*(a)* and 32(2)*(a)*, refers to a claim, it also applies to a counter-claim, and where it refers to a defence, it also applies to a defence to such counter-claim.

Article 3 – Receipt of written communications

1. Unless otherwise agreed by the parties:

(a) any written communication is deemed to have been received if it is delivered to the addressee personally or if it is delivered at his place of business, habitual residence or mailing address; if none of these can be found after making a reasonable inquiry, a written communication is deemed to have been received if it is sent to the addressee's last-known place of business, habitual residence or mailing address by registered letter or any other means which provides a record of the attempt to deliver it;

(b) the communication is deemed to have been received on the day it is so delivered.

2. The provisions of this article do not apply to communications in court proceedings.

Article 4 – Waiver of right to object

A party who knows that any provision of this Law from which the parties may derogate or any requirement under the arbitration agreement has not been complied with and yet proceeds with the arbitration without stating his objection to such non-compliance without undue delay or, if a time-limit is provided therefor, within such period of time, shall be deemed to have waived his right to object.

Article 5 – Extent of court intervention

In matters governed by this Law, no court shall intervene except where so provided in this Law.

Article 6 – Court or other authority for certain functions of arbitration assistance and supervision

The functions referred to in articles 11(3), 11(4), 13(3), 14, 16(3) and 34(2) shall be performed by . . . [Each State enacting this model law specifies the court, courts or, where referred to therein, other authority competent to perform these functions.]

CHAPTER II. ARBITRATION AGREEMENT

Article 7 – Definition and form of arbitration agreement

1. "Arbitration agreement" is an agreement by the parties to submit to arbitration all or certain disputes which have arisen or which may arise between them in respect of a defined legal relationship, whether contractual or not. An arbitration agreement may be in the form of an arbitration clause in a contract or in the form of a separate agreement.
2. The arbitration agreement shall be in writing. An agreement is in writing if it is contained in a document signed by the parties or in an exchange of letters, telex, telegrams or other means of telecommunication which provide a record of the agreement, or in an exchange of statements of claim and defence in which the existence of an agreement is alleged by one party and not denied by another. The reference in a contract to a document containing an arbitration clause constitutes an arbitration agreement provided that the contract is in writing and the reference is such as to make that clause part of the contract.

Article 8 – Arbitration agreement and substantive claim before court

1. A court before which an action is brought in a matter which is the subject of an arbitration agreement shall, if a party so requests not later than when submitting his first statement on the substance of the dispute, refer the parties to arbitration unless it finds that the agreement is null and void, inoperative or incapable of being performed.
2. Where an action referred to in paragraph (1) of this article has been brought, arbitral proceedings may nevertheless be commenced or continued, and an award may be made, while the issue is pending before the court.

Article 9 – Arbitration agreement and interim measures by court

It is not incompatible with an arbitration agreement for a party to request, before or during the arbitral proceedings, from a court an interim measure of protection and for a court to grant such measure.

CHAPTER III. COMPOSITION OF ARBITRAL TRIBUNAL

Article 10 – Number of arbitrators

1. The parties are free to determine the number of arbitrators.
2. Failing such determination, the number of arbitrators shall be three.

Article 11 – Appointment of arbitrators

1. No person shall be precluded by reason of his nationality from acting as an arbitrator, unless otherwise agreed by the parties.

2.   The parties are free to agree on a procedure of appointing the arbitrator or arbitrators, subject to the provisions of paragraphs (4) and (5) of this article.

3.   Failing such agreement,

    (a)   in an arbitration with three arbitrators, each party shall appoint one arbitrator, and the two arbitrators thus appointed shall appoint the third arbitrator; if a party fails to appoint the arbitrator within thirty days of receipt of a request to do so from the other party, or if the two arbitrators fail to agree on the third arbitrator within thirty days of their appointment, the appointment shall be made, upon request of a party, by the court or other authority specified in article 6;

    (b)   in an arbitration with a sole arbitrator, if the parties are unable to agree on the arbitrator, he shall be appointed, upon request of a party, by the court or other authority specified in article 6.

4.   Where, under an appointment procedure agreed upon by the parties,

    (a)   a party fails to act as required under such procedure, or

    (b)   the parties, or two arbitrators, are unable to reach an agreement expected of them under such procedure, or

    (c)   a third party, including an institution, fails to perform any function entrusted to it under such procedure,

any party may request the court or other authority specified in article 6 to take the necessary measure, unless the agreement on the appointment procedure provides other means for securing the appointment.

5.   A decision on a matter entrusted by paragraph (3) or (4) of this article to the court or other authority specified in article 6 shall be subject to no appeal. The court or other authority, in appointing an arbitrator, shall have due regard to any qualifications required of the arbitrator by the agreement of the parties and to such considerations as are likely to secure the appointment of an independent and impartial arbitrator and, in the case of a sole or third arbitrator, shall take into account as well the advisability of appointing an arbitrator of a nationality other than those of the parties.

Article 12 – Grounds for challenge

1.   When a person is approached in connection with his possible appointment as an arbitrator, he shall disclose any circumstances likely to give rise to justifiable doubts as to his impartiality or independence. An arbitrator, from the time of his appointment and throughout the arbitral proceedings, shall without delay disclose any such circumstances to the parties unless they have already been informed of them by him.

2.   An arbitrator may be challenged only if circumstances exist that give rise to justifiable doubts as to his impartiality or independence, or if he does not possess qualifications agreed to by the parties. A party may challenge an arbitrator appointed by him, or in whose appointment he has participated, only for reasons of which he becomes aware after the appointment has been made.

Article 13 – Challenge procedure

1.   The parties are free to agree on a procedure for challenging an arbitrator, subject to the provisions of paragraph (3) of this article.

2. Failing such agreement, a party who intends to challenge an arbitrator shall, within fifteen days after becoming aware of the constitution of the arbitral tribunal or after becoming aware of any circumstance referred to in article 12(2), send a written statement of the reasons for the challenge to the arbitral tribunal. Unless the challenged arbitrator withdraws from his office or the other party agrees to the challenge, the arbitral tribunal shall decide on the challenge.

3. If a challenge under any procedure agreed upon by the parties or under the procedure of paragraph (2) of this article is not successful, the challenging party may request, within thirty days after having received notice of the decision rejecting the challenge, the court or other authority specified in article 6 to decide on the challenge, which decision shall be subject to no appeal; while such a request is pending, the arbitral tribunal, including the challenged arbitrator, may continue the arbitral proceedings and make an award.

Article 14 – Failure or impossibility to act

1. If an arbitrator becomes *de jure* or *de facto* unable to perform his functions or for other reasons fails to act without undue delay, his mandate terminates if he withdraws from his office or if the parties agree on the termination. Otherwise, if a controversy remains concerning any of these grounds, any party may request the court or other authority specified in article 6 to decide on the termination of the mandate, which decision shall be subject to no appeal.

2. If, under this article or article 13(2), an arbitrator withdraws from his office or a party agrees to the termination of the mandate of an arbitrator, this does not imply acceptance of the validity of any ground referred to in this article or article 12(2).

Article 15 – Appointment of substitute arbitrator

Where the mandate of an arbitrator terminates under article 13 or 14 or because of his withdrawal from office for any other reason or because of the revocation of his mandate by agreement of the parties or in any other case of termination of his mandate, a substitute arbitrator shall be appointed according to the rules that were applicable to the appointment of the arbitrator being replaced.

CHAPTER IV. JURISDICTION OF ARBITRAL TRIBUNAL

Article 16 – Competence of arbitral tribunal to rule on its jurisdiction

1. The arbitral tribunal may rule on its own jurisdiction, including any objections with respect to the existence or validity of the arbitration agreement. For that purpose, an arbitration clause which forms part of a contract shall be treated as an agreement independent of the other terms of the contract. A decision by the arbitral tribunal that the contract is null and void shall not entail *ipso jure* the invalidity of the arbitration clause.

2. A plea that the arbitral tribunal does not have jurisdiction shall be raised not later than the submission of the statement of defence. A party is not precluded from raising such a plea by the fact that he has appointed, or participated in the appointment of, an arbitrator. A plea that the arbitral tribunal is exceeding the scope of its authority shall

be raised as soon as the matter alleged to be beyond the scope of its authority is raised during the arbitral proceedings. The arbitral tribunal may, in either case, admit a later plea if it considers the delay justified.

3. The arbitral tribunal may rule on a plea referred to in paragraph (2) of this article either as a preliminary question or in an award on the merits. If the arbitral tribunal rules as a preliminary question that it has jurisdiction, any party may request, within thirty days after having received notice of that ruling, the court specified in article 6 to decide the matter, which decision shall be subject to no appeal; while such a request is pending, the arbitral tribunal may continue the arbitral proceedings and make an award.

Article 17 – Power of arbitral tribunal to order interim measures

Unless otherwise agreed by the parties, the arbitral tribunal may, at the request of a party, order any party to take such interim measure of protection as the arbitral tribunal may consider necessary in respect of the subject-matter of the dispute. The arbitral tribunal may require any party to provide appropriate security in connection with such measure.

CHAPTER V. CONDUCT OF ARBITRAL PROCEEDINGS

Article 18 – Equal treatment of parties

The parties shall be treated with equality and each party shall be given a full opportunity of presenting his case.

Article 19 – Determination of rules of procedure

1. Subject to the provisions of this Law, the parties are free to agree on the procedure to be followed by the arbitral tribunal in conducting the proceedings.
2. Failing such agreement, the arbitral tribunal may, subject to the provisions of this Law, conduct the arbitration in such manner as it considers appropriate. The power conferred upon the arbitral tribunal includes the power to determine the admissibility, relevance, materiality and weight of any evidence.

Article 20 – Place of arbitration

1. The parties are free to agree on the place of arbitration. Failing such agreement, the place of arbitration shall be determined by the arbitral tribunal having regard to the circumstances of the case, including the convenience of the parties.
2. Notwithstanding the provisions of paragraph (1) of this article, the arbitral tribunal may, unless otherwise agreed by the parties, meet at any place it considers appropriate for consultation among its members, for hearing witnesses, experts or the parties, or for inspection of goods, other property or documents.

Article 21 – Commencement of arbitral proceedings

Unless otherwise agreed by the parties, the arbitral proceedings in respect of a particular dispute commence on the date on which a request for that dispute to be referred to arbitration is received by the respondent.

Article 22 – Language

1. The parties are free to agree on the language or languages to be used in the arbitral proceedings. Failing such agreement, the arbitral tribunal shall determine the language or languages to be used in the proceedings. This agreement or determination, unless otherwise specified therein, shall apply to any written statement by a party, any hearing and any award, decision or other communication by the arbitral tribunal.
2. The arbitral tribunal may order that any documentary evidence shall be accompanied by a translation into the language or languages agreed upon by the parties or determined by the arbitral tribunal.

Article 23 – Statements of claim and defence

1. Within the period of time agreed by the parties or determined by the arbitral tribunal, the claimant shall state the facts supporting his claim, the points at issue and the relief or remedy sought, and the respondent shall state his defence in respect of these particulars, unless the parties have otherwise agreed as to the required elements of such statements. The parties may submit with their statements all documents they consider to be relevant or may add a reference to the documents or other evidence they will submit.
2. Unless otherwise agreed by the parties, either party may amend or supplement his claim or defence during the course of the arbitral proceedings, unless the arbitral tribunal considers it inappropriate to allow such amendment having regard to the delay in making it.

Article 24 – Hearings and written proceedings

1. Subject to any contrary agreement by the parties, the arbitral tribunal shall decide whether to hold oral hearings for the presentation of evidence or for oral argument, or whether the proceedings shall be conducted on the basis of documents and other materials. However, unless the parties have agreed that no hearings shall be held, the arbitral tribunal shall hold such hearings at an appropriate stage of the proceedings, if so requested by a party.
2. The parties shall be given sufficient advance notice of any hearing and of any meeting of the arbitral tribunal for the purposes of inspection of goods, other property or documents.
3. All statements, documents or other information supplied to the arbitral tribunal by one party shall be communicated to the other party. Also any expert report or evidentiary document on which the arbitral tribunal may rely in making its decision shall be communicated to the parties.

Article 25 – Default of a party

Unless otherwise agreed by the parties, if, without showing sufficient cause,

    (a) the claimant fails to communicate his statement of claim in accordance with article 23(1), the arbitral tribunal shall terminate the proceedings;

    (b) the respondent fails to communicate his statement of defence in accordance with article 23(1), the arbitral tribunal shall continue the proceedings without treating such failure in itself as an admission of the claimant's allegations;

    (c) any party fails to appear at a hearing or to produce documentary evidence, the arbitral tribunal may continue the proceedings and make the award on the evidence before it.

Article 26 – Expert appointed by arbitral tribunal

1.   Unless otherwise agreed by the parties, the arbitral tribunal
    (a) may appoint one or more experts to report to it on specific issues to be determined by the arbitral tribunal;
    (b) may require a party to give the expert any relevant information or to produce, or to provide access to, any relevant documents, goods or other property for his inspection.
2.   Unless otherwise agreed by the parties, if a party so requests or if the arbitral tribunal considers it necessary, the expert shall, after delivery of his written or oral report, participate in a hearing where the parties have the opportunity to put questions to him and to present expert witnesses in order to testify on the points at issue.

Article 27 – Court assistance in taking evidence

The arbitral tribunal or a party with the approval of the arbitral tribunal may request from a competent court of this State assistance in taking evidence. The court may execute the request within its competence and according to its rules on taking evidence.

CHAPTER VI.   MAKING OF AWARD AND TERMINATION OF PROCEEDINGS

Article 28 – Rules applicable to substance of dispute

1.   The arbitral tribunal shall decide the dispute in accordance with such rules of law as are chosen by the parties as applicable to the substance of the dispute. Any designation of the law or legal system of a given State shall be construed, unless otherwise expressed, as directly referring to the substantive law of that State and not to its conflict of laws rules.
2.   Failing any designation by the parties, the arbitral tribunal shall apply the law determined by the conflict of laws rules which it considers applicable.
3.   The arbitral tribunal shall decide *ex aequo et bono* or as *amiable compositeur* only if the parties have expressly authorized it to do so.
4.   In all cases, the arbitral tribunal shall decide in accordance with the terms of the contract and shall take into account the usages of the trade applicable to the transaction.

Article 29 – Decision making by panel of arbitrators

In arbitral proceedings with more than one arbitrator, any decision of the arbitral tribunal shall be made, unless otherwise agreed by the parties, by a majority of all its members. However, questions of procedure may be decided by a presiding arbitrator, if so authorized by the parties or all members of the arbitral tribunal.

Article 30 – Settlement

1. If, during arbitral proceedings, the parties settle the dispute, the arbitral tribunal shall terminate the proceedings and, if requested by the parties and not objected to by the arbitral tribunal, record the settlement in the form of an arbitral award on agreed terms.
2. An award on agreed terms shall be made in accordance with the provisions of article 31 and shall state that it is an award. Such an award has the same status and effect as any other award on the merits of the case.

Article 31 – Form and contents of award

1. The award shall be made in writing and shall be signed by the arbitrator or arbitrators. In arbitral proceedings with more than one arbitrator, the signatures of the majority of all members of the arbitral tribunal shall suffice, provided that the reason for any omitted signature is stated.
2. The award shall state the reasons upon which it is based, unless the parties have agreed that no reasons are to be given or the award is an award on agreed terms under article 30.
3. The award shall state its date and the place of arbitration as determined in accordance with article 20(1). The award shall be deemed to have been made at that place.
4. After the award is made, a copy signed by the arbitrators in accordance with paragraph (1) of this article shall be delivered to each party.

Article 32 – Termination of proceedings

1. The arbitral proceedings are terminated by the final award or by an order of the arbitral tribunal in accordance with paragraph (2) of this article.
2. The arbitral tribunal shall issue an order for the termination of the arbitral proceedings when:
   (a) the claimant withdraws his claim, unless the respondent objects thereto and the arbitral tribunal recognizes a legitimate interest on his part in obtaining a final settlement of the dispute;
   (b) the parties agree on the termination of the proceedings;
   (c) the arbitral tribunal finds that the continuation of the proceedings has for any other reason become unnecessary or impossible.
3. The mandate of the arbitral tribunal terminates with the termination of the arbitral proceedings, subject to the provisions of articles 33 and 34(4).

Article 33 – Correction and interpretation of award; additional award

1. Within thirty days of receipt of the award, unless another period of time has been agreed upon by the parties:
   (a) a party, with notice to the other party, may request the arbitral tribunal to correct in the award any errors in computation, any clerical or typographical errors or any errors of similar nature;
   (b) if so agreed by the parties, a party, with notice to the other party, may request the arbitral tribunal to give an interpretation of a specific point or part of the award.

If the arbitral tribunal considers the request to be justified, it shall make the correction or give the interpretation within thirty days of receipt of the request. The interpretation shall form part of the award.

2. The arbitral tribunal may correct any error of the type referred to in paragraph (1)*(a)* of this article on its own initiative within thirty days of the date of the award.

3. Unless otherwise agreed by the parties, a party, with notice to the other party, may request, within thirty days of receipt of the award, the arbitral tribunal to make an additional award as to claims presented in the arbitral proceedings but omitted from the award. If the arbitral tribunal considers the request to be justified, it shall make the additional award within sixty days.

4. The arbitral tribunal may extend, if necessary, the period of time within which it shall make a correction, interpretation or an additional award under paragraph (1) or (3) of this article.

5. The provisions of article 31 shall apply to a correction or interpretation of the award or to an additional award.

CHAPTER VII.   RECOURSE AGAINST AWARD

Article 34 – Application for setting aside as exclusive recourse against arbitral award

1. Recourse to a court against an arbitral award may be made only by an application for setting aside in accordance with paragraphs (2) and (3) of this article.

2. An arbitral award may be set aside by the court specified in article 6 only if:
   (a) the party making the application furnishes proof that:
   (i) a party to the arbitration agreement referred to in article 7 was under some incapacity; or the said agreement is not valid under the law to which the parties have subjected it or, failing any indication thereon, under the law of this State; or
   (ii) the party making the application was not given proper notice of the appointment of an arbitrator or of the arbitral proceedings or was otherwise unable to present his case; or
   (iii) the award deals with a dispute not contemplated by or not falling within the terms of the submission to arbitration, or contains decisions on matters beyond the scope of the submission to arbitration, provided that, if the decisions on matters submitted to arbitration can be separated from those not so submitted, only that part of the award which contains decisions on matters not submitted to arbitration may be set aside; or
   (iv) the composition of the arbitral tribunal or the arbitral procedure was not in accordance with the agreement of the parties, unless such agreement was in conflict with a provision of this Law from which the parties cannot derogate, or, failing such agreement, was not in accordance with this Law; or
   (b) the court finds that:
   (i) the subject-matter of the dispute is not capable of settlement by arbitration under the law of this State; or
   (ii) the award is in conflict with the public policy of this State.

3. An application for setting aside may not be made after three months have elapsed from the date on which the party making that application had received the award or, if a request had been made under article 33, from the date on which that request had been disposed of by the arbitral tribunal.
4. The court, when asked to set aside an award, may, where appropriate and so requested by a party, suspend the setting aside proceedings for a period of time determined by it in order to give the arbitral tribunal an opportunity to resume the arbitral proceedings or to take such other action as in the arbitral tribunal's opinion will eliminate the grounds for setting aside.

CHAPTER VIII.   RECOGNITION AND ENFORCEMENT OF AWARDS

Article 35 – Recognition and enforcement
1. An arbitral award, irrespective of the country in which it was made, shall be recognized as binding and, upon application in writing to the competent court, shall be enforced subject to the provisions of this article and of article 36.
2. The party relying on an award or applying for its enforcement shall supply the duly authenticated original award or a duly certified copy thereof, and the original arbitration agreement referred to in article 7 or a duly certified copy thereof. If the award or agreement is not made in an official language of this State, the party shall supply a duly certified translation thereof into such language.***

Article 36 – Grounds for refusing recognition or enforcement
1. Recognition or enforcement of an arbitral award, irrespective of the country in which it was made, may be refused only:
    (a) at the request of the party against whom it is invoked, if that party furnishes to the competent court where recognition or enforcement is sought proof that:
    (i)   a party to the arbitration agreement referred to in article 7 was under some incapacity; or the said agreement is not valid under the law to which the parties have subjected it or, failing any indication thereon, under the law of the country where the award was made; or
    (ii) the party against whom the award is invoked was not given proper notice of the appointment of an arbitrator or of the arbitral proceedings or was otherwise unable to present his case; or
    (iii) the award deals with a dispute not contemplated by or not falling within the terms of the submission to arbitration, or it contains decisions on matters beyond the scope of the submission to arbitration, provided that, if the decisions on matters submitted to arbitration can be separated from those not

---

***   The conditions set forth in this paragraph are intended to set maximum standards. It would, thus, not be contrary to the harmonization to be achieved by the model law if a State retained even less onerous conditions.

so submitted, that part of the award which contains decisions on matters submitted to arbitration may be recognized and enforced; or

(iv) the composition of the arbitral tribunal or the arbitral procedure was not in accordance with the agreement of the parties or, failing such agreement, was not in accordance with the law of the country where the arbitration took place; or

(v) the award has not yet become binding on the parties or has been set aside or suspended by a court of the country in which, or under the law of which, that award was made; or

(b) if the court finds that:

(i) the subject-matter of the dispute is not capable of settlement by arbitration under the law of this State; or

(ii) the recognition or enforcement of the award would be contrary to the public policy of this State.

2. If an application for setting aside or suspension of an award has been made to a court referred to in paragraph (1)*(a)*(v) of this article, the court where recognition or enforcement is sought may, if it considers it proper, adjourn its decision and may also, on the application of the party claiming recognition or enforcement of the award, order the other party to provide appropriate security.

CONVENTION ON THE RECOGNITION AND ENFORCEMENT OF FOREIGN ARBITRAL AWARDS
(New York, June 10, 1958)

Article I

1. This Convention shall apply to the recognition and enforcement of arbitral awards made in the territory of a State other than the State where the recognition and enforcement of such awards are sought, and arising out of differences between persons, whether physical or legal. It shall also apply to arbitral awards not considered as domestic awards in the State where their recognition and enforcement are sought.
2. The term "arbitral awards" shall include not only awards made by arbitrators appointed for each case but also those made by permanent arbitral bodies to which the parties have submitted.
3. When signing, ratifying or acceding to this Convention, or notifying extension under article X hereof, any State may on the basis of reciprocity declare that it will apply the Convention to the recognition and enforcement of awards made only in the territory of another Contracting State. It may also declare that it will apply the Convention only to differences arising out of legal relationships, whether contractual or not, which are considered as commercial under the national law of the State making such declaration.

Article II

1. Each Contracting State shall recognize an agreement in writing under which the parties undertake to submit to arbitration all or any differences which have arisen or which may arise between them in respect of a defined legal relationship, whether contractual or not, concerning a subject matter capable of settlement by arbitration.
2. The term "agreement in writing" shall include an arbitral clause in a contract or an arbitration agreement, signed by the parties or contained in an exchange of letters or telegrams.
3. The court of a Contracting State, when seized of an action in a matter in respect of which the parties have made an agreement within the meaning of this article, shall, at the request of one of the parties, refer the parties to arbitration, unless it finds that the said agreement is null and void, inoperative or incapable of being performed.

Article III

Each Contracting State shall recognize arbitral awards as binding and enforce them in accordance with the rules of procedure of the territory where the award is relied upon, under the conditions laid down in the following articles. There shall not be imposed substantially more onerous conditions or higher fees or charges on the recognition or enforcement of arbitral awards to which this Convention applies than are imposed on the recognition or enforcement of domestic arbitral awards.

Article IV

1. To obtain the recognition and enforcement mentioned in the preceding article, the party applying for recognition and enforcement shall, at the time of the application, supply:
   (*a*) The duly authenticated original award or a duly certified copy thereof;
   (*b*) The original agreement referred to in article II or a duly certified copy thereof.
2. If the said award or agreement is not made in an official language of the country in which the award is relied upon, the party applying for recognition and enforcement of the award shall produce a translation of these documents into such language. The translation shall be certified by an official or sworn translator or by a diplomatic or consular agent.

Article V

1. Recognition and enforcement of the award may be refused, at the request of the party against whom it is invoked, only if that party furnishes to the competent authority where the recognition and enforcement is sought, proof that:
   (*a*) The parties to the agreement referred to in article II were, under the law applicable to them, under some incapacity, or the said agreement is not valid under the law to which the parties have subjected it or, failing any indication thereon, under the law of the country where the award was made; or
   (*b*) The party against whom the award is invoked was not given proper notice of the appointment of the arbitrator or of the arbitration proceedings or was otherwise unable to present his case; or
   (*c*) The award deals with a difference not contemplated by or not falling within the terms of the submission to arbitration, or it contains decisions on matters beyond the scope of the submission to arbitration, provided that, if the decisions on matters submitted to arbitration can be separated from those not so submitted, that part of the award which contains decisions on matters submitted to arbitration may be recognized and enforced; or
   (*d*) The composition of the arbitral authority or the arbitral procedure was not in accordance with the agreement of the parties, or, failing such agreement, was not in accordance with the law of the country where the arbitration took place; or
   (*e*) The award has not yet become binding on the parties, or has been set aside or suspended by a competent authority of the country in which, or under the law of which, that award was made.
2. Recognition and enforcement of an arbitral award may also be refused if the competent authority in the country where recognition and enforcement is sought finds that:
   (*a*) The subject matter of the difference is not capable of settlement by arbitration under the law of that country; or
   (*b*) The recognition or enforcement of the award would be contrary to the public policy of that country.

Article VI

If an application for the setting aside or suspension of the award has been made to a competent authority referred to in article V(1)(*e*), the authority before which the award is sought to be relied upon may, if it considers it proper, adjourn the decision on the enforcement of the award and may also, on the application of the party claiming enforcement of the award, order the other party to give suitable security.

Article VII

1. The provisions of the present Convention shall not affect the validity of multilateral or bilateral agreements concerning the recognition and enforcement of arbitral awards entered into by the Contracting States nor deprive any interested party of any right he may have to avail himself of an arbitral award in the manner and to the extent allowed by the law or the treaties of the country where such award is sought to be relied upon.
2. The Geneva Protocol on Arbitration Clauses of 1923 and the Geneva Convention on the Execution of Foreign Arbitral Awards of 1927 shall cease to have effect between Contracting States on their becoming bound and to the extent that they become bound, by this Convention.

Article VIII

1. This Convention shall be open until 31 December 1958 for signature on behalf of any Member of the United Nations and also on behalf of any other State which is or hereafter becomes a member of any specialized agency of the United Nations, or which is or hereafter becomes a party to the Statute of the International Court of Justice, or any other State to which an invitation has been addressed by the General Assembly of the United Nations.
2. This Convention shall be ratified and the instrument of ratification shall be deposited with the Secretary-General of the United Nations.

Article IX

1. This Convention shall be open for accession to all States referred to in article VIII.
2. Accession shall be effected by the deposit of an instrument of accession with the Secretary-General of the United Nations.

Article X

1. Any State may, at the time of signature, ratification or accession, declare that this Convention shall extend to all or any of the territories for the international relations of which it is responsible. Such a declaration shall take effect when the Convention enters into force for the State concerned.
2. At any time thereafter any such extension shall be made by notification addressed to the Secretary-General of the United Nations and shall take effect as from the ninetieth day after the day of receipt by the Secretary-General of the United Nations of this notification, or as from the date of entry into force of the Convention for the State concerned, whichever is the later.
3. With respect to those territories to which this Convention is not extended at the time of signature, ratification or accession, each State concerned shall consider the possibility

of taking the necessary steps in order to extend the application of this Convention to such territories, subject, where necessary for constitutional reasons, to the consent of the Governments of such territories.

Article XI

In the case of a federal or non-unitary State, the following provisions shall apply:

(a) With respect to those articles of this Convention that come within the legislative jurisdiction of the federal authority, the obligations of the federal Government shall to this extent be the same as those of Contracting States which are not federal States;

(b) With respect to those articles of this Convention that come within the legislative jurisdiction of constituent states or provinces which are not, under the constitutional system of the federation, bound to take legislative action, the federal Government shall bring such articles with a favourable recommendation to the notice of the appropriate authorities of constituent states or provinces at the earliest possible moment;

(c) A federal State Party to this Convention shall, at the request of any other Contracting State transmitted through the Secretary-General of the United Nations, supply a statement of the law and practice of the federation and its constituent units in regard to any particular provision of this Convention, showing the extent to which effect has been given to that provision by legislative or other action.

Article XII

1. This Convention shall come into force on the ninetieth day following the date of deposit of the third instrument of ratification or accession.
2. For each State ratifying or acceding to this Convention after the deposit of the third instrument of ratification or accession, this Convention shall enter into force on the ninetieth day after deposit by such State of its instrument of ratification or accession.

Article XIII

1. Any Contracting State may denounce this Convention by a written notification to the Secretary-General of the United Nations. Denunciation shall take effect one year after the date of receipt of the notification by the Secretary-General.
2. Any State which has made a declaration or notification under article X may, at any time thereafter, by notification to the Secretary-General of the United Nations, declare that this Convention shall cease to extend to the territory concerned one year after the date of the receipt of the notification by the Secretary-General.
3. This Convention shall continue to be applicable to arbitral awards in respect of which recognition or enforcement proceedings have been instituted before the denunciation takes effect.

Article XIV

A Contracting State shall not be entitled to avail itself of the present Convention against other Contracting States except to the extent that it is itself bound to apply the Convention.

Article XV

The Secretary-General of the United Nations shall notify the States contemplated in article VIII of the following:

   (*a*) Signatures and ratifications in accordance with article VIII;
   (*b*) Accessions in accordance with article IX;
   (*c*) Declarations and notifications under articles I, X and XI;
   (*d*) The date upon which this Convention enters into force in accordance with article XII;
   (*e*) Denunciations and notifications in accordance with article XIII.

Article XVI

1. This Convention, of which the Chinese, English, French, Russian and Spanish texts shall be equally authentic, shall be deposited in the archives of the United Nations.
2. The Secretary-General of the United Nations shall transmit a certified copy of this Convention to the States contemplated in article VIII.

LIST OF CONTRACTING STATES
(as of March 31, 1999)*

State	*Signature*	*Ratification Accession (a) Succession (s)*
Algeria (1-2)		February 7, 1989 (a)
Antigua and Barbuda (1-2)		February 2, 1989 (a)
Argentina (1-2)	August 26, 1958	March 14, 1989
Armenia (1-2)		December 29, 1997 (a)
Australia		March 26, 1975 (a)
Austria		May 2, 1961 (a)
Bahrain (1-2)		April 6, 1988 (a)
Bangladesh		May 6, 1992 (a)
Barbados (2)*		March 16, 1993 (a)
Belarus (1)	December 29, 1958	November 15, 1960
Belgium (1)	June 10, 1958	August 18, 1975
Belize (1)		February 24, 1981
Benin		May 16, 1974 (a)

---

*   For an updated list, see the UNCITRAL Web site, where the list is updated as soon as new information becomes available (<http://www.un.or.at/uncitral>).

State	Signature	Ratification Accession (a) Succession (s)
Bolivia		April 28, 1995 (a)
Bosnia and Herzegovina (1-2)		September 1, 1993 (s)
Botswana (1-2)		December 20, 1971 (a)
Brunei Darussalam (1)		July 25, 1996 (a)
Bulgaria (1)	December 17, 1958	October 10, 1961
Burkino Faso		March 23, 1987 (a)
Cambodia		January 5, 1960 (a)
Cameroon		February 19, 1988 (a)
Canada		May 12, 1986 (a)
Central African Republic (1-2)		October 15, 1962 (a)
Chile		September 4, 1975 (a)
China (1-2)		January 22, 1987 (a)
Colombia		September 25, 1979 (a)
Costa Rica	June 10, 1958	October 26, 1987
Côte d'Ivoire		February 1, 1991 (a)
Croatia (1-2)		July 26, 1993 (s)
Cuba (1-2)		December 30, 1974 (a)
Cyprus (1-2)		December 29, 1980 (a)
Czech Republic (a)		September 30, 1993 (s)
Denmark (1-2)		December 22, 1972 (a)
Djibouti		June 14, 1983 (s)
Dominica		October 28, 1988 (a)
Ecuador (1-2)	December 17, 1958	January 3, 1962
Egypt		March 9, 1959 (a)
El Salvador	June 10, 1958	February 26, 1998
Estonia		August 30, 1993 (a)*
Finland	December 29, 1958	January 19, 1962
France (1)	November 25, 1958	June 26, 1959
French Polynesia (1)		June 26, 1959
Georgia		June 2, 1994 (a)
Germany (b-1) (GDR: February 20, 1975 (a))	June 10, 1958	June 30, 1961
Ghana		April 9, 1968 (a)
Greece (1-2)		July 16, 1962 (a)
Guatemala (1-2)		March 21, 1984 (a)
Guinea		January 23, 1991(a)

State	Signature	Ratification Accession (a) Succession (s)
Haiti		December 5, 1983 (a)
Holy See (1-2)		May 14, 1975 (a)
Hungary (1-2)		March 5, 1962 (a)
India (1-2)	June 10, 1958	July 13, 1960
Indonesia (1-2)		October 7, 1981 (a)
Ireland (1)		May 12, 1981 (a)
Israel	June 10, 1958	January 5, 1959
Italy		January 31, 1969 (a)
Japan (1)		June 20, 1961 (a)
Jordan	June 10, 1958	November 15, 1979
Kazakstan		November 20, 1995
Kenya (1)		February 10, 1989 (a)
Kuwait (1)		April 28, 1978 (a)
Kyrgyzstan		December 18, 1996
Lao People's Democratic Republic		June 17, 1998 (a)
Latvia		April 14, 1992 (a)
Lebanon (1)		August 11, 1998 (a)
Lesotho		June 13, 1989 (a)
Lithuania		March 15, 1995 (a)*
Luxembourg (1)	November 11, 1958	September 9, 1983
Madagascar (1-2)		July 16, 1962 (a)
Malaysia (1-2)		November 5, 1985 (a)
Mali		September 8, 1994 (a)
Mauritania		January 30, 1997
Mauritius (1)		June 19, 1996
Mexico		April 14, 1971 (a)
Moldova (1)		September 18, 1998
Monaco (1-2)	December 31, 1958	June 2, 1982
Mongolia (1-2)		October 24, 1994 (a)
Morocco (1)		February 12, 1959 (a)
Mozambique (1)		June 11, 1998 (a)
Nepal (1-2)		March 4, 1998
Netherlands (1)	June 10, 1958	April 24, 1964
New Zealand (1)		January 6, 1983 (a)
Niger		October 14, 1964 (a)

State	Signature	Ratification Accession (a) Succession (s)
Nigeria (1-2)		March 17, 1970 (a)
Norway (1)		March 14, 1961 (a)
Oman		February 25, 1999 (a)
Pakistan	December 30, 1997	
Panama		October 10, 1984 (a)
Paraguay		October 8, 1997
Peru		July 7, 1988 (a)
Philippines (1-2)	June 10, 1958	July 6, 1967
Poland (1-2)	June 10, 1958	October 3, 1961
Portugal (1)		October 18, 1994 (a)
Romania (1-2)		September 13, 1961 (a)
Russian Federation (c-1)	December 29, 1958	August 24, 1960
San Marino		May 17, 1979 (a)
Saudi Arabia		April 19, 1994 (a)
Senegal		October 17, 1994 (a)
Singapore (1)		August 21, 1986 (a)
Slovakia (a)		May 28, 1993 (s)
Slovenia (1-2)		July 1, 1992 (s)
South Africa		May 3, 1976 (a)
Spain		May 12, 1977 (a)
Sri Lanka	December 30, 1958	April 9, 1962
Sweden	December 23, 1958	January 28, 1972
Switzerland	December 29, 1958	June 1, 1965
Syrian Arab Republic		March 9, 1959 (a)
Tanzania, United Republic of (1)		October 13, 1964 (a)
Thailand		December 21, 1959 (a)
The former Yugoslav Republic of Macedonia (1-2)		March 10, 1994 (s)
Trinidad and Tobago (1-2)		February 14, 1966 (a)
Tunisia (1-2)		July 17, 1967 (a)
Turkey (1-2)		July 2, 1992 (a)*
Uganda (1)		February 12, 1992 (a)
Ukraine (1)	December 29, 1958	October 10, 1960
United Kingdom of Great Britain and Northern Ireland (1)		September 24, 1975 (a)

State	Signature	Ratification Accession (a) Succession (s)
United States of America (1-2)		September 30, 1970 (a)
Uruguay		March 30, 1983 (a)
Uzbekistan		February 7, 1996
Venezuela (1-2)		February 8, 1995
Vietnam (1-2)		September 12, 1995
Yugoslavia (1-2)		February 26, 1982 (a)
Zimbabwe		September 26, 1994 (a)

Declarations and Reservations

(1) State will apply the Convention only to recognition and enforcement of awards made in the territory of another Contracting State.

(2) State will apply the Convention only to differences arising out of legal relationships whether contractual or not which are considered as commercial under national law.

EUROPEAN CONVENTION ON INTERNATIONAL COMMERCIAL ARBITRATION (Geneva, April 21, 1961)

The undersigned, duly authorized,

Convened under the auspices of the Economic Commission for Europe of the United Nations,

Having noted that on 10th June 1958 at the United Nations Conference on International Commercial Arbitration has been signed in New York a Convention on the Recognition and Enforcement of Foreign Arbitral Awards,

Desirous of promoting the development of European trade by, as far as possible, removing certain difficulties that may impede the organization and operation of international commercial arbitration in relations between physical or legal persons of different European countries,

Have agreed on the following provisions:

Article I – Scope of the Convention

1. This Convention shall apply:
   (a) to arbitration agreements concluded for the purpose of settling disputes arising from international trade between physical or legal persons having, when concluding the agreement, their habitual place of residence or their seat in different Contracting States;
   (b) to arbitral procedures and awards based on agreements referred to in paragraph 1 (a) above.
2. For the purpose of this Convention,
   (a) the term "arbitration agreement" shall mean either an arbitral clause in a contract or an arbitration agreement, the contract or arbitration agreement being signed by the parties, or contained in an exchange of letters, telegrams, or in a communication by teleprinter and, in relations between States whose laws do not require that an arbitration agreement be made in writing, any arbitration agreement concluded in the form authorized by these laws;
   (b) the term "arbitration" shall mean not only settlement by arbitrators appointed for each case (*ad hoc* arbitration) but also by permanent arbitral institutions;

(*c*) the term "seat" shall mean the place of the situation of the establishment that has made the arbitration agreement.

Article II – Right of legal persons of public law to resort to arbitration

1. In the cases referred to in Article I, paragraph 1, of this Convention, legal persons considered by the law which is applicable to them as "legal persons of public law" have the right to conclude valid arbitration agreements.
2. On signing, ratifying or acceding to this Convention any State shall be entitled to declare that it limits the above faculty to such conditions as may be stated in its declaration.

Article III – Right of foreign nationals to be designated as arbitrators

In arbitration covered by this Convention, foreign nationals may be designated as arbitrators.

Article IV – Organization of the arbitration

1. The parties to an arbitration agreement shall be free to submit their disputes:
    (*a*) to a permanent arbitral institution; in this case, the arbitration proceedings shall be held in conformity with the rules of the said institution;
    (*b*) to an *ad hoc* arbitral procedure; in this case, they shall be free *inter alia*
       (i)   to appoint arbitrators or to establish means for their appointment in the event of an actual dispute;
       (ii)   to determine the place of arbitration; and
       (iii)   to lay down the procedure to be followed by the arbitrators.
2. Where the parties have agreed to submit any disputes to an *ad hoc* arbitration, and where within thirty days of the notification of the request for arbitration to the respondent one of the parties fails to appoint his arbitrator, the latter shall, unless otherwise provided, be appointed at the request of the other party by the President of the competent Chamber of Commerce of the country of the defaulting party's habitual place of residence or seat at the time of the introduction of the request for arbitration. This paragraph shall also apply to the replacement of the arbitrator(s) appointed by one of the parties or by the President of the Chamber of Commerce above referred to.
3. Where the parties have agreed to submit any disputes to an *ad hoc* arbitration by one or more arbitrators and the arbitration agreement contains no indication regarding the organization of the arbitration, as mentioned in paragraph 1 of this article, the necessary steps shall be taken by the arbitrator(s) already appointed, unless the parties are able to agree thereon and without prejudice to the case referred to in paragraph 2 above. Where the parties cannot agree on the appointment of the sole arbitrator or where the arbitrators appointed cannot agree on the measures to be taken, the claimant shall apply for the necessary action, where the place of arbitration has been agreed upon by the parties, at his option to the President of the Chamber of Commerce of the place of arbitration agreed upon or to the President of the competent Chamber of Commerce of the respondent's habitual place of residence or seat at the time of the introduction of the request for arbitration. When such a place has not been agreed upon, the claimant shall be entitled at his option to apply for the necessary action either to the President of the competent Chamber of Commerce of the country of the respondent's habitual place of

residence or seat at the time of the introduction of the request for arbitration, or to the Special Committee whose composition and procedure are specified in the Annex to this Convention. Where the claimant fails to exercise the rights given to him under this paragraph the respondent or the arbitrator(s) shall be entitled to do so.

4. When seized of a request the President or the Special Committee shall be entitled as need be:

   (a) to appoint the sole arbitrator, presiding arbitrator, umpire, or referee;

   (b) to replace the arbitrator(s) appointed under any procedure other than that referred to in paragraph 2 above;

   (c) to determine the place of arbitration, provided that the arbitrator(s) may fix another place of arbitration;

   (d) to establish directly or by reference to the rules and statutes of a permanent arbitral institution the rules of procedure to be followed by the arbitrator(s), provided that the arbitrators have not established these rules themselves in the absence of any agreement thereon between the parties.

5. Where the parties have agreed to submit their disputes to a permanent arbitral institution without determining the institution in question and cannot agree thereon, the claimant may request the determination of such institution in conformity with the procedure referred to in paragraph 3 above.

6. Where the arbitration agreement does not specify the mode of arbitration (arbitration by a permanent arbitral institution or an *ad hoc* arbitration) to which the parties have agreed to submit their dispute, and where the parties cannot agree thereon, the claimant shall be entitled to have recourse in this case to the procedure referred to in paragraph 3 above to determine the question. The President of the competent Chamber of Commerce or the Special Committee, shall be entitled either to refer the parties to a permanent arbitral institution or to request the parties to appoint their arbitrators within such time-limits as the President of the competent Chamber of Commerce or the Special Committee may have fixed and to agree within such time-limits on the necessary measures for the functioning of the arbitration. In the latter case, the provisions of paragraphs 2, 3 and 4 of this Article shall apply.

7. Where within a period of sixty days from the moment when he was requested to fulfil one of the functions set out in paragraphs 2, 3, 4, 5 and 6 of this Article, the President of the Chamber of Commerce designated by virtue of these paragraphs has not fulfilled one of these functions, the party requesting shall be entitled to ask the Special Committee to do so.

Article V – Plea as to arbitral jurisdiction

1. The party which intends to raise a plea as to the arbitrator's jurisdiction based on the fact that the arbitration agreement was either non-existent or null and void or had lapsed shall do so during the arbitration proceedings, not later than the delivery of its statement of claim or defence relating to the substance of the dispute; those based on the fact that an arbitrator has exceeded his terms of reference shall be raised during the arbitration proceedings as soon as the question on which the arbitrator is alleged to have no jurisdiction is raised during the arbitral procedure. Where the delay in raising the plea

is due to a cause which the arbitrator deems justified, the arbitrator shall declare the plea admissible.

2. Pleas to the jurisdiction referred to in paragraph 1 above that have not been raised during the time-limits there referred to, may not be entered either during a subsequent stage of the arbitral proceedings where they are pleas left to the sole discretion of the parties under the law applicable by the arbitrator, or during subsequent court proceedings concerning the substance or the enforcement of the award where such pleas are left to the discretion of the parties under the rule of conflict of the court seized of the substance of the dispute or the enforcement of the award. The arbitrator's decision on the delay in raising the plea, will, however, be subject to judicial control.

3. Subject to any subsequent judicial control provided for under the *lex fori*, the arbitrator whose jurisdiction is called in question shall be entitled to proceed with the arbitration, to rule on his own jurisdiction and to decide upon the existence or the validity of the arbitration agreement or of the contract of which the agreement forms part.

Article VI – Jurisdiction of courts of law

1. A plea as to the jurisdiction of the court made before the court seized by either party to the arbitration agreement, on the basis of the fact that an arbitration agreement exists shall, under penalty of estoppel, be presented by the respondent before or at the same time as the presentation of his substantial defence, depending upon whether the law of the court seized regards this plea as one of procedure or of substance.

2. In taking a decision concerning the existence or the validity of an arbitration agreement, courts of Contracting States shall examine the validity of such agreement with reference to the capacity of the parties, under the law applicable to them, and with reference to other questions.
    (*a*) under the law to which the parties have subjected their arbitration agreement;
    (*b*) failing any indication thereon, under the law of the country in which the award is to be made;
    (*c*) failing any indication as to the law to which the parties have subjected the agreement, and where at the time when the question is raised in court the country in which the award is to be made cannot be determined, under the competent law by virtue of the rules of conflict of the court seized of the dispute.
    The courts may also refuse recognition of the arbitration agreement if under the law of their country the dispute is not capable of settlement by arbitration.

3. Where either party to an arbitration agreement has initiated arbitration proceedings before any resort is had to a court, courts of Contracting States subsequently asked to deal with the same subject-matter between the same parties or with the question whether the arbitration agreement was non-existent or null and void or had lapsed, shall stay their ruling on the arbitrator's jurisdiction until the arbitral award is made, unless they have good and substantial reasons to the contrary.

4. A request for interim measures or measures of conservation addressed to a judicial authority shall not be deemed incompatible with the arbitration agreement, or regarded as a submission of the substance of the case to the court.

Article VII – Applicable law

1. The parties shall be free to determine, by agreement, the law to be applied by the arbitrators to the substance of the dispute. Failing any indication by the parties as to the applicable law, the arbitrators shall apply the proper law under the rule of conflict that the arbitrators deem applicable. In both cases the arbitrators shall take account of the terms of the contract and trade usages.
2. The arbitrators shall act as *amiables compositeurs* if the parties so decide and if they may do so under the law applicable to the arbitration.

Article VIII – Reasons for the award

The parties shall be presumed to have agreed that reasons shall be given for the award unless they

(*a*) either expressly declare that reasons shall not be given; or

(*b*) have assented to an arbitral procedure under which it is not customary to give reasons for awards, provided that in this case neither party requests before the end of the hearing, or if there has not been a hearing then before the making of the award, that reasons be given.

Article IX – Setting aside of the arbitral award

1. The setting aside in a Contracting State of an arbitral award covered by this Convention shall only constitute a ground for the refusal of recognition or enforcement in another Contracting State where such setting aside took place in a State in which, or under the law of which, the award has been made and for one of the following reasons:

(*a*) the parties to the arbitration agreement were under the law applicable to them, under some incapacity or the said agreement is not valid under the law to which the parties have subjected it or, failing any indication thereon, under the law of the country where the award was made, or

(*b*) the party requesting the setting aside of the award was not given proper notice of the appointment of the arbitrator or of the arbitration proceedings or was otherwise unable to present his case; or

(*c*) the award deals with a difference not contemplated by or not falling within the terms of the submission to arbitration, or it contains decisions on matters beyond the scope of the submission to arbitration, provided that, if the decisions on matters submitted to arbitration can be separated from those not so submitted, that part of the award which contains decisions on matters submitted to arbitration need not be set aside;

(*d*) the composition of the arbitral authority or the arbitral procedure was not in accordance with the agreement of the parties, or failing such agreement, with the provisions of Article IV of this Convention.

2. In relations between Contracting States that are also parties to the New York Convention on the Recognition and Enforcement of Foreign Arbitral Awards of 10th June 1958, paragraph 1 of this Article limits the application of Article V (1) (*e*) of the New York Convention solely to the cases of setting aside set out under paragraph 1 above.

Article X – Final Clauses

1. This Convention is open for signature or accession by countries members of the Economic Commission for Europe and countries admitted to the Commission in a consultative capacity under paragraph 8 of the Commission's terms of reference.

2. Such countries as may participate in certain activities of the Economic Commission for Europe in accordance with paragraph 11 of the Commission's terms of reference may become Contracting Parties to this Convention by acceding thereto after its entry into force.

3. The Convention shall be open for signature until 31 December 1961 inclusive. Thereafter, it shall be open for accession.

4. This Convention shall be ratified.

5. Ratification or accession shall be effected by the deposit of an instrument with the Secretary-General of the United Nations.

6. When signing, ratifying or acceding to this Convention, the Contracting Parties shall communicate to the Secretary-General of the United Nations a list of the Chambers of Commerce or other institutions in their country who will exercise the functions conferred by virtue of Article IV of this Convention on Presidents of the competent Chambers of Commerce.

7. The provisions of the present Convention shall not affect the validity of multilateral or bilateral agreements concerning arbitration entered into by Contracting States.

8. This Convention shall come into force on the ninetieth day after five of the countries referred to in paragraph 1 above have deposited their instruments of ratification or accession. For any country ratifying or acceding to it later this Convention shall enter into force on the ninetieth day after the said country has deposited its instrument of ratification or accession.

9. Any Contracting Party may denounce this Convention by so notifying the Secretary-General of the United Nations. Denunciation shall take effect twelve months after the date of receipt by the Secretary-General of the notification of denunciation.

10. If, after the entry into force of this Convention, the number of Contracting Parties is reduced, as a result of denunciations, to less than five, the Convention shall cease to be in force from the date on which the last of such denunciations takes effect.

11. The Secretary-General of the United Nations shall notify the countries referred to in paragraph 1, and the countries which have become Contracting Parties under paragraph 2 above, of

    (*a*) declarations made under Article II, paragraph 2;

    (*b*) ratifications and accessions under paragraphs 1 and 2 above;

    (*c*) communications received in pursuance of paragraph 6 above;

    (*d*) the dates of entry into force of this Convention in accordance with paragraph 8 above;

    (*e*) denunciations under paragraph 9 above;

    (*f*) the termination of this Convention in accordance with paragraph 10 above.

12. After 31 December 1961, the original of this Convention shall be deposited with the Secretary-General of the United Nations, who shall transmit certified true copies to each of the countries mentioned in paragraphs 1 and 2 above.

IN WITNESS WHEREOF the undersigned, being duly authorized thereto, have signed this Convention.

DONE at Geneva, this twenty-first day of April, one thousand nine hundred and sixty-one, in a single copy in the English, French and Russian languages, each text being equally authentic.

ANNEX

COMPOSITION AND PROCEDURE OF THE SPECIAL COMMITTEE REFERRED TO IN ARTICLE IV OF THE CONVENTION

1. The Special Committee referred to in Article IV of the Convention shall consist of two regular members and a Chairman. One of the regular members shall be elected by the Chambers of Commerce or other institutions designated, under Article X, paragraph 6, of the Convention, by States in which at the time when the Convention is open to signature National Committees of the International Chamber of Commerce exist, and which at the time of the election are parties to the Convention. The other member shall be elected by the Chambers of Commerce or other institutions designated, under Article X, paragraph 6, of the Convention, by States in which at the time when the Convention is open to signature no National Committees of the International Chamber of Commerce exist and which at the time of the election are parties to the Convention.

2. The persons who are to act as Chairman of the Special Committee pursuant to paragraph 7 of this Annex shall also be elected in like manner by the Chambers of Commerce or other institutions referred to in paragraph 1 of this Annex.

3. The Chambers of Commerce or other institutions referred to in paragraph 1 of this Annex shall elect alternates at the same time and in the same manner as they elect the Chairman and other regular members, in case of the temporary inability of the Chairman or regular members to act. In the event of the permanent inability to act or of the resignation of a Chairman or of a regular member, then the alternate elected to replace him shall become, as the case may be, the Chairman or regular member, and the group of Chambers of Commerce or other institutions which had elected the alternate who has become Chairman or regular member shall elect another alternate.

4. The first elections to the Committee shall be held within ninety days from the date of the deposit of the fifth instrument of ratification or accession. Chambers of Commerce and other institutions designated by Signatory States who are not yet parties to the Convention shall also be entitled to take part in these elections. If however it should not be possible to hold elections within the prescribed period, the entry into force of paragraphs 3 to 7 of Article IV of the Convention shall be postponed until elections are held as provided for above.

5. Subject to the provisions of paragraph 7 below, the members of the Special Committee shall be elected for a term of four years. New elections shall be held within the first six months of the fourth year following the previous elections. Nevertheless, if a new procedure for the election of the members of the Special Committee has not produced results, the members previously elected shall continue to exercise their functions until the election of new members.

6. The results of the elections of the members of the Special Committee shall be communicated to the Secretary-General of the United Nations who shall notify the States referred to in Article X, paragraph 1, of this Convention and the States which have become Contracting Parties under Article X, paragraph 2. The Secretary-General shall likewise notify the said States of any postponement and of the entry into force of paragraphs 3 to 7 of Article IV of the Convention in pursuance of paragraph 4 of this Annex.

7. The persons elected to the office of Chairman shall exercise their functions in rotation, each during a period of two years. The question which of these two persons shall act as Chairman during the first two-year period after the entry into force of the Convention shall be decided by the drawing of lots. The office of Chairman shall thereafter be vested, for each successive two-year period, in the person elected Chairman by the group of countries other than that by which the Chairman exercising his functions during the immediately preceding two-year period was elected.

8. The reference to the Special Committee of one of the requests referred to in paragraphs 3 to 7 of the aforesaid Article IV shall be addressed to the Executive Secretary of the Economic Commission for Europe. The Executive Secretary shall in the first instance lay the request before the member of the Special Committee elected by the group of countries other than that by which the Chairman holding office at the time of the introduction of the request was elected. The proposal of the member applied to in the first instance shall be communicated by the Executive Secretary to the other member of the Committee and, if that other member agrees to this proposal, it shall be deemed to be the Committee's ruling and shall be communicated as such by the Executive Secretary to the person who made the request.

9. If the two members of the Special Committee applied to by the Executive Secretary are unable to agree on a ruling by correspondence, the Executive Secretary of the Economic Commission for Europe shall convene a meeting of the said Committee at Geneva in an attempt to secure a unanimous decision on the request. In the absence of unanimity, the Committee's decision shall be given by a majority vote and shall be communicated by the Executive Secretary to the person who made the request.

10. The expenses connected with the Special Committee's action shall be advanced by the person requesting such action but shall be considered as costs in the cause.

LIST OF CONTRACTING STATES AND SIGNATORIES
(as of June 1, 1999)

State	Signature	Ratification Accession (a), Succession (s)
Austria	April 21, 1961	March 6, 1964
Belarus	April 21, 1961	October 14, 1963
Belgium	April 21, 1961	October 9, 1975
Bosnia and Herzegovina		September 1, 1993 (s)
Bulgaria	April 21, 1961	May 13, 1964
Burkina Faso		January 26, 1965 (a)
Croatia		July 26, 1993 (s)
Cuba		September 1, 1965 (a)
Czech Republic		September 30, 1993 (s)
Denmark	April 21, 1961	December 22, 1972
Finland	December 21, 1961	
France	April 21, 1961	December 16, 1966
Germany, Federal Rep. of (GDR)	April 21, 1961	October 27, 1964 February 20, 1975 (a)
Hungary	April 21, 1961	October 9, 1963
Italy	April 21, 1961	August 3, 1970
Kazakhstan		November 20, 1995 (a)
Luxembourg		March 26, 1982 (a)
Moldova, Republic of		March 5, 1998 (a)
Poland	April 21, 1961	September 15, 1964
Romania	April 21, 1961	August 16, 1963
Russian Federation	April 21, 1961	June 27, 1962
Slovakia		May 28, 1993 (s)
Slovenia		July 6, 1992 (s)
Spain	December 14, 1961	May 12, 1975
The former Yugoslav Republic of Macedonia		March 10, 1994 (s)
Turkey	April 21, 1961	January 24, 1992
Ukraine	April 21, 1961	March 18, 1963
Yugoslavia	April 21, 1961	September 25, 1963

AGREEMENT RELATING TO APPLICATION OF THE EUROPEAN CONVENTION ON INTERNATIONAL COMMERCIAL ARBITRATION*

The signatory Governments of the member States of the Council of Europe,

Considering that a European Convention on International Commercial Arbitration was opened for signature at Geneva on 21st April 1961;

Considering, however, that certain measures relating to the organisation of the arbitration, provided for in Article IV of the Convention, are not to be recommended except in the case of disputes between physical or legal persons having, on the one hand, their habitual place of residence or seat in Contracting States where, according to the terms of the Annex to the Convention, there exist National Committees of the International Chamber of Commerce, and, on the other, in States where no such Committees exist;

Considering that under the terms of paragraph 7 of Article X of the said Convention the provisions of that Convention shall not affect the validity of multilateral or bilateral agreements concerning arbitration entered into by States which are Parties thereto;

Without prejudice to the intervention of a Convention relating to a uniform law on arbitration now being drawn up within the Council of Europe,

Have agreed as follows:

Article 1

In relations between physical or legal persons whose habitual residence or seat is in States Parties to the present Agreement, paragraphs 2 to 7 of Article IV of the European Convention on International Commercial Arbitration, opened for signature at Geneva on 21st April 1961, are replaced by the following provision:

"If the arbitral Agreement contains no indication regarding the measures referred to in paragraph 1 of Article IV of the European Convention on International Commercial Arbitration as a whole, or some of these measures, any difficulties arising with regard to the constitution or functioning of the arbitral tribunal shall be submitted to the decision of the competent authority at the request of the party instituting proceedings."

Article 2

1. This Agreement shall be open for signature by the member States of Council of Europe. It shall be ratified or accepted. Instruments of ratification or acceptance shall be deposited with the Secretary-General of the Council of Europe.
2. Subject to the provisions of Article 4, this Agreement shall come into force thirty days after the date of deposit of the second instrument of ratification or acceptance.
3. Subject to the provisions of Article 4, in respect of any signatory Government ratifying or accepting it subsequently, the Agreement shall come into force thirty days after the date of deposit of its instrument of ratification or acceptance.

---

* Done at Paris on December 17, 1962; entered into force on January 25, 1965.

Article 3

1. After the entry into force of this Agreement, the Committee of Ministers of the Council of Europe may invite any State which is not a member of the Council and in which there exists a National Committee of the International Chamber of Commerce to accede to this Agreement.
2. Accession shall be effected by the deposit with the Secretary-General of the Council of Europe of an instrument of accession, which shall take effect, subject to the provisions of Article 4, thirty days after the date of its deposit.

Article 4

The entry into force of this Agreement in respect of any State after ratification, acceptance or accession in accordance with the terms of Articles 2 and 3 shall be conditional upon the entry into force of the European Convention on International Commercial Arbitration in respect of that State.

Article 5

Any Contracting Party may, in so far as it is concerned, denounce this Agreement by giving notice to the Secretary-General of the Council of Europe. Denunciation shall take effect six months after the date of receipt by the Secretary-General of the Council of such notification.

Article 6

The Secretary-General of the Council of Europe shall notify member States, the Council and the Government of any State which has acceded to this Agreement of:

(a) any signature;
(b) the deposit of any instrument of ratification, acceptance or accession;
(c) any date of entry into force;
(d) any notification received in pursuance of the provisions of Article 5.

IN WITNESS WHEREOF, the undersigned, being duly authorised thereto, have signed this Agreement.

DONE at Paris, this 17th day of December 1962 in English and in French, both texts being equally authoritative, in a single copy which shall remain deposited in the archives of the Council of Europe. The Secretary-General shall transmit certified copies to each of the signatory and acceding Governments.

1962 PARIS AGREEMENT

LIST OF CONTRACTING STATES
(as of June 1, 1999)

State	Signature	Ratification Accession (a)
Austria	December 17, 1962	February 28, 1964
Belgium	February 11, 1963	October 9, 1975
Denmark	January 16, 1973	January 16, 1973
France	December 17, 1962	November 30, 1966
Germany, Republic of	December 17, 1962	October 19, 1964
Italy	December 17, 1962	May 10, 1976
Luxembourg	February 2, 1980	April 1, 1982
Moldova	February 4, 1998	February 4, 1998

INTER-AMERICAN CONVENTION ON INTERNATIONAL COMMERCIAL ARBITRATION
(Panama City, January 30, 1975)

The Governments of the Member States of the Organization of American States, desirous of concluding a convention on international commercial arbitration, have agreed as follows:

Article 1
An agreement in which the parties undertake to submit to arbitral decision any differences that may arise or have arisen between them with respect to a commercial transaction is valid. The agreement shall be set forth in an instrument signed by the parties, or in the form of an exchange of letters, telegrams, or telex communications.

Article 2
Arbitrators shall be appointed in the manner agreed upon by the parties. Their appointment may be delegated to a third party, whether a natural or juridical person.
Arbitrators may be nationals or foreigners.

Article 3
In the absence of an express agreement between the parties, the arbitration shall be conducted in accordance with the rules of procedure of the Inter-American Commercial Arbitration Commission.

Article 4
An arbitral decision or award that is not appealable under the applicable law or procedural rules shall have the force of a final judicial judgment. Its execution or recognition may be ordered in the same manner as that of decisions handed down by national or foreign ordinary courts, in accordance with the procedural laws of the country where it is to be executed and the provisions of international treaties.

Article 5
1. The recognition and execution of the decision may be refused, at the request of the party against which it is made, only if such party is able to prove to the competent authority of the State in which recognition and execution are requested:

a. That the parties to the agreement were subject to some incapacity under the applicable law or that the agreement is not valid under the law to which the parties have submitted it, or, if such law is not specified, under the law of the State in which the decision was made; or

b. That the party against which the arbitral decision has been made was not duly notified of the appointment of the arbitrator or of the arbitration procedure to be followed, or was unable, for any reason, to present his defense; or

c. That the decision concerns a dispute not envisaged in the agreement between the parties to submit to arbitration; nevertheless, if the provisions of the decision that refer to issues submitted to arbitration can be separated from those not submitted to arbitration, the former may be recognized and executed; or

d. That the constitution of the arbitral tribunal or the arbitration procedure has not been carried out in accordance with the terms of the agreement signed by the parties or, in the absence of such agreement, that the constitution of the arbitral tribunal or the arbitration procedure has not been carried out in accordance with the law of the State where the arbitration took place; or

e. That the decision is not yet binding on the parties or has been annulled or suspended by a competent authority of the State in which, or according to the law of which, the decision has been made.

2. The recognition and execution of an arbitral decision may also be refused if the competent authority of the State in which the recognition and execution is requested finds:

a. That the subject of the dispute cannot be settled by arbitration under the law of that State; or

b. That the recognition or execution of the decision would be contrary to the public policy ("ordre public") of that State.

Article 6

If the competent authority mentioned in Article 5.1.e. has been requested to annul or suspend the arbitral decision, the authority before which such decision is invoked may, if it deems it appropriate, postpone a decision on the execution of the arbitral decision and, at the request of the party requesting execution, may also instruct the other party to provide appropriate guaranties.

Article 7

This Convention shall be open for signature by the Member States of the Organization of American States.

Article 8

This Convention is subject to ratification. The instruments of ratification shall be deposited with the General Secretariat of the Organization of American States.

Article 9

This Convention shall remain open for accession by any other State. The instruments of accession shall be deposited with the General Secretariat of the Organization of American States.

Article 10

This Convention shall enter into force on the thirtieth day following the date of deposit of the second instrument of ratification.

For each State ratifying or acceding to the Convention after the deposit of the second instrument of ratification, the Convention shall enter into force on the thirtieth day after deposit by such State of its instrument of ratification or accession.

Article 11

If a State Party has two or more territorial units in which different systems of law apply in relation to the matters dealt with in this Convention, it may, at the time of signature, ratification or accession, declare that this Convention shall extend to all its territorial units or only to one or more of them.

Such declaration may be modified by subsequent declarations, which shall expressly indicate the territorial unit or units to which the Convention applies. Such subsequent declarations shall be transmitted to the General Secretariat of the Organization of American States, and shall become effective thirty days after the date of their receipt.

Article 12

This Convention shall remain in force indefinitely, but any of the States' Parties may denounce it. The instruments of denunciation shall be deposited with the General Secretariat of the Organization of American States. After one year from the date of deposit of the instrument of denunciation, the Convention shall no longer be in effect for the denouncing State, but shall remain in effect for the other States Parties.

Article 13

The original instrument of this Convention, the English, French, Portuguese and Spanish texts of which are equally authentic, shall be deposited with the General Secretariat of the Organization of American States. The Secretariat shall notify the Member States of the Organization of American States and the States that have acceded to the Convention of the signatures, deposits of instruments of ratification, accession, and denunciation as well as of reservations, if any. It shall also transmit the declarations referred to in Article 11 of this Convention.

IN WITNESS WHEREOF the undersigned Plenipotentiaries, being duly authorized thereto by their respective Governments, have signed this Convention.

DONE AT PANAMA CITY, Republic of Panama, this thirtieth day of January one thousand nine hundred and seventy-five.

LIST OF CONTRACTING STATES AND SIGNATORIES
(as of March 25, 1999)

State	Signature	Ratification	Deposit
Argentina	March 15, 1991	November 3, 1994	January 5, 1995
Bolivia	August 2, 1983		
Brazil	January 30, 1975	August 31, 1995	November 27, 1995
Chile	January 30, 1975	April 8, 1976	May 17, 1976
Colombia	January 30, 1975	November 18, 86	December 29, 1986
Costa Rica	January 30, 1975	January 2, 1978	January 20, 1978
Dominican Republic	April 18, 1977		
Ecuador	January 30, 1975	August 6, 1991	October 23, 1991
El Salvador	January 30, 1975	June 27, 1980	August 11, 1980
Guatemala	January 30, 1975	July 7, 1986	August 20, 1986
Honduras	January 30, 1975	January 8, 1979	March 22, 1979
Mexico	October 27, 1977 (1)	February 15, 1978	March 27, 1978
Nicaragua	January 30, 1975		
Panama	January 30, 1975	November 11, 1975	December 17, 1975
Paraguay	August 26, 1975 (1)	December 2, 1976	December 15, 1976
Peru	April 21, 1988	May 2, 1989	May 22, 1989
United States	June 9, 1978	November 10, 1986	September 27, 1990 (a)
Uruguay	January 30, 1975	March 29, 1977	April 25, 1977
Venezuela	January 30, 1975	February 22, 1985	May 16, 1985

1.   Mexico, Paraguay: signed ad referendum

a.   United States: reservations made at the time of ratification

1.   Unless there is an express agreement among the parties to an arbitration agreement to the contrary, where the requirements for application of both the Inter-American Convention on the Recognition and Enforcement of Foreign Arbitral Awards are met, if a majority of such parties are citizens of a state or states that have ratified or acceded to the Inter-American Convention and are Member States of the Organization of American States, the Inter-American Convention shall apply. In all other cases, the Convention on the Recognition and Enforcement of Foreign Arbitral Awards shall apply.

2.   The United States of America will apply the rules of procedure of the Inter-American Commercial Arbitration Commission which are in effect on the date that the United States

of America deposits its instrument of ratification, unless the United States of America makes a later official determination to adopt and apply subsequent amendments to such rules.

3.   The United States of America will apply the Convention, on the basis of reciprocity, to the recognition and enforcement of only those awards made in the territory of another Contracting State.

AMERICAN ARBITRATION ASSOCIATION INTERNATIONAL ARBITRATION RULES (Effective as of April 1, 1997)*

RECOMMENDED ARBITRATION CLAUSE

The clause recommended by the AAA is as follows: "Any controversy or claim arising out of or relating to this contract shall be determined by arbitration in accordance with the International Arbitration Rules of the American Arbitration Association." The parties may wish to consider adding:

    (a) "The number of arbitrators shall be (one or three)";

    (b) "The place of arbitration shall be (city and/or country)"; or

    (c) "The language(s) of the arbitration shall be _____ ."

AMERICAN ARBITRATION ASSOCIATION INTERNATIONAL ARBITRATION RULES

Article 1

1. Where parties have agreed in writing to arbitrate disputes under these International Arbitration Rules or have provided for arbitration of an international dispute by the American Arbitration Association without designating particular rules, the arbitration shall take place in accordance with these rules, as in effect at the date of commencement of the arbitration, subject to whatever modifications the parties may adopt in writing.

2. These rules govern the arbitration, except that, where any such rule is in conflict with any provision of the law applicable to the arbitration from which the parties cannot derogate, that provision shall prevail.

3. These rules specify the duties and responsibilities of the administrator, the American Arbitration Association. The administrator may provide services through its own facilities or through the facilities of arbitral institutions with which it has agreements of cooperation.

---

* Reproduced with kind permission of the American Arbitration Association. See also the AAA Web site <http://www.adr.org>.

I. COMMENCING THE ARBITRATION

NOTICE OF ARBITRATION AND STATEMENT OF CLAIM

Article 2
1. The party initiating arbitration ("claimant") shall give written notice of arbitration to the administrator and at the same time to the party against whom a claim is being made ("respondent").
2. Arbitral proceedings shall be deemed to commence on the date on which the administrator receives the notice of arbitration.
3. The notice of arbitration shall contain a statement of claim including the following:
    (a) a demand that the dispute be referred to arbitration;
    (b) the names and addresses of the parties;
    (c) a reference to the arbitration clause or agreement that is invoked;
    (d) a reference to any contract out of or in relation to which the dispute arises;
    (e) a description of the claim and an indication of the facts supporting it;
    (f) the relief or remedy sought and the amount claimed; and
    (g) may include proposals as to the means of designating and the number of arbitrators, the place of arbitration and the language(s) of the arbitration.
4. Upon receipt of the notice of arbitration, the administrator shall communicate with all parties with respect to the arbitration and shall acknowledge the commencement of the arbitration.

STATEMENT OF DEFENSE AND COUNTERCLAIM

Article 3
1. Within 30 days after the commencement of the arbitration, a respondent shall submit a written statement of defense, responding to the issues raised in the notice of arbitration, to the claimant and any other parties, and to the administrator.
2. At the time a respondent submits its statement of defense, a respondent may make counterclaims or assert setoffs as to any claim covered by the agreement to arbitrate, as to which the claimant shall within 30 days submit a written statement of defense to the respondent and any other parties and to the administrator.
3. A respondent shall respond to the administrator, the claimant and other parties within 30 days after the commencement of the arbitration as to any proposals the claimant may have made as to the number of arbitrators, the place of the arbitration or the language(s) of the arbitration, except to the extent that the parties have previously agreed as to these matters.
4. The arbitral tribunal, or the administrator if the arbitral tribunal has not yet been formed, may extend any of the time limits established in this article if it considers such an extension justified.

AMENDMENTS TO CLAIMS

Article 4

During the arbitral proceedings, any party may amend or supplement its claim, counterclaim or defense, unless the tribunal considers it inappropriate to allow such amendment or supplement because of the party's delay in making it, prejudice to the other parties or any other circumstances. A party may not amend or supplement a claim or counterclaim if the amendment or supplement would fall outside the scope of the agreement to arbitrate.

II. THE TRIBUNAL

NUMBER OF ARBITRATORS

Article 5

If the parties have not agreed on the number of arbitrators, one arbitrator shall be appointed unless the administrator determines in its discretion that three arbitrators are appropriate because of the large size, complexity or other circumstances of the case.

APPOINTMENT OF ARBITRATORS

Article 6

1. The parties may mutually agree upon any procedure for appointing arbitrators and shall inform the administrator as to such procedure.
2. The parties may mutually designate arbitrators, with or without the assistance of the administrator. When such designations are made, the parties shall notify the administrator so that notice of the appointment can be communicated to the arbitrators, together with a copy of these rules.
3. If within 45 days after the commencement of the arbitration, all of the parties have not mutually agreed on a procedure for appointing the arbitrator(s) or have not mutually agreed on the designation of the arbitrator(s), the administrator shall, at the written request of any party, appoint the arbitrator(s) and designate the presiding arbitrator. If all of the parties have mutually agreed upon a procedure for appointing the arbitrator(s), but all appointments have not been made within the time limits provided in that procedure, the administrator shall, at the written request of any party, perform all functions provided for in that procedure that remain to be performed.
4. In making such appointments, the administrator, after inviting consultation with the parties, shall endeavor to select suitable arbitrators. At the request of any party or on its own initiative, the administrator may appoint nationals of a country other than that of any of the parties.
5. Unless the parties have agreed otherwise no later than 45 days after the commencement of the arbitration, if the notice of arbitration names two or more claimants or two or more respondents, the administrator shall appoint all the arbitrators.

IMPARTIALITY AND INDEPENDENCE OF ARBITRATORS

Article 7

1. Arbitrators acting under these rules shall be impartial and independent. Prior to accepting appointment, a prospective arbitrator shall disclose to the administrator any circumstance likely to give rise to justifiable doubts as to the arbitrator's impartiality or independence. If, at any stage during the arbitration, new circumstances arise that may give rise to such doubts, an arbitrator shall promptly disclose such circumstances to the parties and to the administrator. Upon receipt of such information from an arbitrator or a party, the administrator shall communicate it to the other parties and to the tribunal.
2. No party or anyone acting on its behalf shall have any ex parte communication relating to the case with any arbitrator, or with any candidate for appointment as party-appointed arbitrator except to advise the candidate of the general nature of the controversy and of the anticipated proceedings and to discuss the candidate's qualifications, availability or independence in relation to the parties, or to discuss the suitability of candidates for selection as a third arbitrator where the parties or party-designated arbitrators are to participate in that selection. No party or anyone acting on its behalf shall have any ex parte communication relating to the case with any candidate for presiding arbitrator.

CHALLENGE OF ARBITRATORS

Article 8

1. A party may challenge any arbitrator whenever circumstances exist that give rise to justifiable doubts as to the arbitrator's impartiality or independence. A party wishing to challenge an arbitrator shall send notice of the challenge to the administrator within 15 days after being notified of the appointment of the arbitrator or within 15 days after the circumstances giving rise to the challenge become known to that party.
2. The challenge shall state in writing the reasons for the challenge.
3. Upon receipt of such a challenge, the administrator shall notify the other parties of the challenge. When an arbitrator has been challenged by one party, the other party or parties may agree to the acceptance of the challenge and, if there is agreement, the arbitrator shall withdraw. The challenged arbitrator may also withdraw from office in the absence of such agreement. In neither case does withdrawal imply acceptance of the validity of the grounds for the challenge.

Article 9

If the other party or parties do not agree to the challenge or the challenged arbitrator does not withdraw, the administrator in its sole discretion shall make the decision on the challenge.

REPLACEMENT OF AN ARBITRATOR

Article 10

If an arbitrator withdraws after a challenge, or the administrator sustains the challenge, or the administrator determines that there are sufficient reasons to accept the resignation of an arbitrator, or an arbitrator dies, a substitute arbitrator shall be appointed pursuant to the provisions of Article 6, unless the parties otherwise agree.

Article 11

1. If an arbitrator on a three-person tribunal fails to participate in the arbitration for reasons other than those identified in Article 10, the two other arbitrators shall have the power in their sole discretion to continue the arbitration and to make any decision, ruling or award, notwithstanding the failure of the third arbitrator to participate. In determining whether to continue the arbitration or to render any decision, ruling or award without the participation of an arbitrator, the two other arbitrators shall take into account the stage of the arbitration, the reason, if any, expressed by the third arbitrator for such nonparticipation, and such other matters as they consider appropriate in the circumstances of the case. In the event that the two other arbitrators determine not to continue the arbitration without the participation of the third arbitrator, the administrator on proof satisfactory to it shall declare the office vacant, and a substitute arbitrator shall be appointed pursuant to the provisions of Article 6, unless the parties otherwise agree.
2. If a substitute arbitrator is appointed under either Article 10 or Article 11, the tribunal shall determine at its sole discretion whether all or part of any prior hearings shall be repeated.

III. GENERAL CONDITIONS

REPRESENTATION

Article 12

Any party may be represented in the arbitration. The names, addresses and telephone numbers of representatives shall be communicated in writing to the other parties and to the administrator. Once the tribunal has been established, the parties or their representatives may communicate in writing directly with the tribunal.

PLACE OF ARBITRATION

Article 13

1. If the parties disagree as to the place of arbitration, the administrator may initially determine the place of arbitration, subject to the power of the tribunal to determine finally the place of arbitration within 60 days after its constitution. All such determinations shall be made having regard for the contentions of the parties and the circumstances of the arbitration.
2. The tribunal may hold conferences or hear witnesses or inspect property or documents at any place it deems appropriate. The parties shall be given sufficient written notice to enable them to be present at any such proceedings.

LANGUAGE

Article 14
If the parties have not agreed otherwise, the language(s) of the arbitration shall be that of the documents containing the arbitration agreement, subject to the power of the tribunal to determine otherwise based upon the contentions of the parties and the circumstances of the arbitration. The tribunal may order that any documents delivered in another language shall be accompanied by a translation into the language(s) of the arbitration.

PLEAS AS TO JURISDICTION

Article 15
1. The tribunal shall have the power to rule on its own jurisdiction, including any objections with respect to the existence, scope or validity of the arbitration agreement.
2. The tribunal shall have the power to determine the existence or validity of a contract of which an arbitration clause forms a part. Such an arbitration clause shall be treated as an agreement independent of the other terms of the contract. A decision by the tribunal that the contract is null and void shall not for that reason alone render invalid the arbitration clause.
3. A party must object to the jurisdiction of the tribunal or to the arbitrability of a claim or counterclaim no later than the filing of the statement of defense, as provided in Article 3, to the claim or counterclaim that gives rise to the objection. The tribunal may rule on such objections as a preliminary matter or as part of the final award.

CONDUCT OF THE ARBITRATION

Article 16
1. Subject to these rules, the tribunal may conduct the arbitration in whatever manner it considers appropriate, provided that the parties are treated with equality and that each party has the right to be heard and is given a fair opportunity to present its case.
2. The tribunal, exercising its discretion, shall conduct the proceedings with a view to expediting the resolution of the dispute. It may conduct a preparatory conference with the parties for the purpose of organizing, scheduling and agreeing to procedures to expedite the subsequent proceedings.
3. The tribunal may in its discretion direct the order of proof, bifurcate proceedings, exclude cumulative or irrelevant testimony or other evidence, and direct the parties to focus their presentations on issues the decision of which could dispose of all or part of the case.
4. Documents or information supplied to the tribunal by one party shall at the same time be communicated by that party to the other party or parties.

FURTHER WRITTEN STATEMENTS

Article 17
1. The tribunal may decide whether the parties shall present any written statements in addition to statements of claims and counterclaims and statements of defense, and it shall fix the periods of time for submitting any such statements.
2. The periods of time fixed by the tribunal for the communication of such written statements should not exceed 45 days. However, the tribunal may extend such time limits if it considers such an extension justified.

NOTICES

Article 18
1. Unless otherwise agreed by the parties or ordered by the tribunal, all notices, statements and written communications may be served on a party by air mail, air courier, facsimile transmission, telex, telegram, or other written forms of electronic communication addressed to the party or its representative at its last known address or by personal service.
2. For the purpose of calculating a period of time under these rules, such period shall begin to run on the day following the day when a notice, statement or written communication is received. If the last day of such period is an official holiday at the place received, the period is extended until the first business day which follows. Official holidays occurring during the running of the period of time are included in calculating the period.

EVIDENCE

Article 19
1. Each party shall have the burden of proving the facts relied on to support its claim or defense.
2. The tribunal may order a party to deliver to the tribunal and to the other parties a summary of the documents and other evidence which that party intends to present in support of its claim, counterclaim or defense.
3. At any time during the proceedings, the tribunal may order parties to produce other documents, exhibits or other evidence it deems necessary or appropriate.

HEARINGS

Article 20
1. The tribunal shall give the parties at least 30 days' advance notice of the date, time and place of the initial oral hearing. The tribunal shall give reasonable notice of subsequent hearings.
2. At least 15 days before the hearings, each party shall give the tribunal and the other parties the names and addresses of any witnesses it intends to present, the subject of their testimony and the languages in which such witnesses will give their testimony.

3. At the request of the tribunal or pursuant to mutual agreement of the parties, the administrator shall make arrangements for the interpretation of oral testimony or for a record of the hearing.

4. Hearings are private unless the parties agree otherwise or the law provides to the contrary. The tribunal may require any witness or witnesses to retire during the testimony of other witnesses. The tribunal may determine the manner in which witnesses are examined.

5. Evidence of witnesses may also be presented in the form of written statements signed by them.

6. The tribunal shall determine the admissibility, relevance, materiality and weight of the evidence offered by any party. The tribunal shall take into account applicable principles of legal privilege, such as those involving the confidentiality of communications between a lawyer and client.

INTERIM MEASURES OF PROTECTION

Article 21

1. At the request of any party, the tribunal may take whatever interim measures it deems necessary, including injunctive relief and measures for the protection or conservation of property.

2. Such interim measures may take the form of an interim award, and the tribunal may require security for the costs of such measures.

3. A request for interim measures addressed by a party to a judicial authority shall not be deemed incompatible with the agreement to arbitrate or a waiver of the right to arbitrate.

4. The tribunal may in its discretion apportion costs associated with applications for interim relief in any interim award or in the final award.

EXPERTS

Article 22

1. The tribunal may appoint one or more independent experts to report to it, in writing, on specific issues designated by the tribunal and communicated to the parties.

2. The parties shall provide such an expert with any relevant information or produce for inspection any relevant documents or goods that the expert may require. Any dispute between a party and the expert as to the relevance of the requested information or goods shall be referred to the tribunal for decision.

3. Upon receipt of an expert's report, the tribunal shall send a copy of the report to all parties and shall give the parties an opportunity to express, in writing, their opinion on the report. A party may examine any document on which the expert has relied in such a report.

4. At the request of any party, the tribunal shall give the parties an opportunity to question the expert at a hearing. At this hearing, parties may present expert witnesses to testify on the points at issue.

DEFAULT

Article 23

1. If a party fails to file a statement of defense within the time established by the tribunal without showing sufficient cause for such failure, as determined by the tribunal, the tribunal may proceed with the arbitration.
2. If a party, duly notified under these rules, fails to appear at a hearing without showing sufficient cause for such failure, as determined by the tribunal, the tribunal may proceed with the arbitration.
3. If a party, duly invited to produce evidence or take any other steps in the proceedings, fails to do so within the time established by the tribunal without showing sufficient cause for such failure, as determined by the tribunal, the tribunal may make the award on the evidence before it.

CLOSURE OF HEARING

Article 24

1. After asking the parties if they have any further testimony or evidentiary submissions and upon receiving negative replies or if satisfied that the record is complete, the tribunal may declare the hearings closed.
2. The tribunal in its discretion, on its own motion or upon application of a party, may reopen the hearings at any time before the award is made.

WAIVER OF RULES

Article 25

A party who knows that any provision of the rules or requirement under the rules has not been complied with, but proceeds with the arbitration without promptly stating an objection in writing thereto, shall be deemed to have waived the right to object.

AWARDS, DECISIONS AND RULINGS

Article 26

1. When there is more than one arbitrator, any award, decision or ruling of the arbitral tribunal shall be made by a majority of the arbitrators. If any arbitrator fails to sign the award, it shall be accompanied by a statement of the reason for the absence of such signature.
2. When the parties or the tribunal so authorize, the presiding arbitrator may make decisions or rulings on questions of procedure, subject to revision by the tribunal.

FORM AND EFFECT OF THE AWARD

Article 27

1. Awards shall be made in writing, promptly by the tribunal, and shall be final and binding on the parties. The parties undertake to carry out any such award without delay.

2. The tribunal shall state the reasons upon which the award is based, unless the parties have agreed that no reasons need be given.
3. The award shall contain the date and the place where the award was made, which shall be the place designated pursuant to Article 13.
4. An award may be made public only with the consent of all parties or as required by law.
5. Copies of the award shall be communicated to the parties by the administrator.
6. If the arbitration law of the country where the award is made requires the award to be filed or registered, the tribunal shall comply with such requirement.
7. In addition to making a final award, the tribunal may make interim, interlocutory, or partial orders and awards.

APPLICABLE LAWS AND REMEDIES

Article 28

1. The tribunal shall apply the substantive law(s) or rules of law designated by the parties as applicable to the dispute. Failing such a designation by the parties, the tribunal shall apply such law(s) or rules of law as it determines to be appropriate.
2. In arbitrations involving the application of contracts, the tribunal shall decide in accordance with the terms of the contract and shall take into account usages of the trade applicable to the contract.
3. The tribunal shall not decide as amiable compositeur or ex aequo et bono unless the parties have expressly authorized it to do so.
4. A monetary award shall be in the currency or currencies of the contract unless the tribunal considers another currency more appropriate, and the tribunal may award such pre-award and post-award interest, simple or compound, as it considers appropriate, taking into consideration the contract and applicable law.
5. Unless the parties agree otherwise, the parties expressly waive and forego any right to punitive, exemplary or similar damages unless a statute requires that compensatory damages be increased in a specified manner. This provision shall not apply to any award of arbitration costs to a party to compensate for dilatory or bad faith conduct in the arbitration.

SETTLEMENT OR OTHER REASONS FOR TERMINATION

Article 29

1. If the parties settle the dispute before an award is made, the tribunal shall terminate the arbitration and, if requested by all parties, may record the settlement in the form of an award on agreed terms. The tribunal is not obliged to give reasons for such an award.
2. If the continuation of the proceedings becomes unnecessary or impossible for any other reason, the tribunal shall inform the parties of its intention to terminate the proceedings. The tribunal shall thereafter issue an order terminating the arbitration, unless a party raises justifiable grounds for objection.

INTERPRETATION OR CORRECTION OF THE AWARD

Article 30

1. Within 30 days after the receipt of an award, any party, with notice to the other parties, may request the tribunal to interpret the award or correct any clerical, typographical or computation errors or make an additional award as to claims presented but omitted from the award.

2. If the tribunal considers such a request justified, after considering the contentions of the parties, it shall comply with such a request within 30 days after the request.

COSTS

Article 31

The tribunal shall fix the costs of arbitration in its award. The tribunal may apportion such costs among the parties if it determines that such apportionment is reasonable, taking into account the circumstances of the case.

Such costs may include:

    (a) the fees and expenses of the arbitrators;

    (b) the costs of assistance required by the tribunal, including its experts;

    (c) the fees and expenses of the administrator;

    (d) the reasonable costs for legal representation of a successful party; and

    (e) any such costs incurred in connection with an application for interim or emergency relief pursuant to Article 21.

COMPENSATION OF ARBITRATORS

Article 32

Arbitrators shall be compensated based upon their amount of service, taking into account their stated rate of compensation and the size and complexity of the case. The administrator shall arrange an appropriate daily or hourly rate, based on such considerations, with the parties and with each of the arbitrators as soon as practicable after the commencement of the arbitration. If the parties fail to agree on the terms of compensation, the administrator shall establish an appropriate rate and communicate it in writing to the parties.

DEPOSIT OF COSTS

Article 33

1. When a party files claims, the administrator may request the filing party to deposit appropriate amounts as an advance for the costs referred to in Article 31, paragraphs (a), (b) and (c).

2. During the course of the arbitral proceedings, the tribunal may request supplementary deposits from the parties.

3. If the deposits requested are not paid in full within 30 days after the receipt of the request, the administrator shall so inform the parties, in order that one or the other of

them may make the required payment. If such payments are not made, the tribunal may order the suspension or termination of the proceedings.

4. After the award has been made, the administrator shall render an accounting to the parties of the deposits received and return any unexpended balance to the parties.

CONFIDENTIALITY

Article 34
Confidential information disclosed during the proceedings by the parties or by witnesses shall not be divulged by an arbitrator or by the administrator. Unless otherwise agreed by the parties, or required by applicable law, the members of the tribunal and the administrator shall keep confidential all matters relating to the arbitration or the award.

EXCLUSION OF LIABILITY

Article 35
The members of the tribunal and the administrator shall not be liable to any party for any act or omission in connection with any arbitration conducted under these rules, except that they may be liable for the consequences of conscious and deliberate wrongdoing.

INTERPRETATION OF RULES

Article 36
The tribunal shall interpret and apply these rules insofar as they relate to its powers and duties. The administrator shall interpret and apply all other rules.

ADMINISTRATIVE FEES

The administrative fees of the AAA are based on the amount of the claim or counterclaim. Arbitrator compensation is not included in this schedule. Unless the parties agree otherwise, arbitrator compensation and administrative fees are subject to allocation by the arbitrator in the award.

Filing Fees

A nonrefundable filing fee is payable in full by a filing party when a claim, counterclaim or additional claim is filed, as provided below.

Amount of Claim	Filing Fee
Up to $10,000	$500
Above $10,000 to $50,000	$750
Above $50,000 to $100,000	$1,250
Above $100,000 to $250,000	$2,000
Above $250,000 to $500,000	$3,500
Above $500,000 to $1,000,000	$5,000
Above $1,000,000 to $5,000,000	$7,000

When no amount can be stated at the time of filing, the minimum filing fee is $2,000, subject to increase when the claim or counterclaim is disclosed.

When a claim or counterclaim is not for a monetary amount, an appropriate filing fee will be determined by the AAA.

The minimum filing fee for any case having three or more arbitrators is $2,000.

The administrative fee for claims in excess of $5,000,000 will be negotiated.

Hearing Fees

For each day of hearing held before a single arbitrator, an administrative fee of $150 is payable by each party.

For each day of hearing held before a multiarbitrator panel, an administrative fee of $250 is payable by each party.

There is no AAA hearing fee for the initial Procedural Hearing.

Postponement/Cancellation Fees

A fee of $150 is payable by a party causing a postponement of any hearing scheduled before a single arbitrator.

A fee of $250 is payable by a party causing a postponement of any hearing scheduled before a multiarbitrator panel.

Suspension for Nonpayment

If arbitrator compensation or administrative charges have not been paid in full, the administrator may so inform the parties in order that one of them may advance the required payment. If such payments are not made, the tribunal may order the suspension or termination of the proceedings. If no arbitrator has yet been appointed, the AAA may suspend the proceedings.

Hearing Room Rental

The Hearing Fees described above do not cover the rental of hearing rooms, which are available on a rental basis. Check with the administrator for availability and rates.

ICC RULES OF ARBITRATION
(Effective as of January 1, 1998)*

STANDARD ICC ARBITRATION CLAUSE

The ICC recommends that all parties wishing to make reference to ICC arbitration in their contracts use the following standard clause.

Parties are reminded that it may be desirable for them to stipulate in the arbitration clause itself the law governing the contract, the number of arbitrators and the place and language of the arbitration. The parties' free choice of the law governing the contract and of the place and language of the arbitration is not limited by the ICC Rules of Arbitration.

Attention is called to the fact that the laws of certain countries require that parties to contracts expressly accept arbitration clauses, sometimes in a precise and particular manner.

English
"All disputes arising out of or in connection with the present contract shall be finally settled under the Rules of Arbitration of the International Chamber of Commerce by one or more arbitrators appointed in accordance with the said Rules."

---

* Reproduced with kind permission of the International Chamber of Commerce from ICC RULES OF ARBITRATION (1998) – ICC RULES OF CONCILIATION (1998) (ICC Publication No. 581 – ISBN 92.842.1239.1(E)). Published in its official English version by the International Chamber of Commerce. Copyright © 1997 – International Chamber of Commerce (ICC), Paris. Available from the ICC International Court of Arbitration, 38 Cours Albert 1er, 75008 Paris, France. See also the ICC Web site <http:www.iccwbo.org>.

RULES OF ARBITRATION OF THE
INTERNATIONAL CHAMBER OF COMMERCE

INTRODUCTORY PROVISIONS

Article 1 – International Court of Arbitration

1. The International Court of Arbitration (the "Court") of the International Chamber of Commerce (the "ICC") is the arbitration body attached to the ICC. The statutes of the Court are set forth in Appendix I. Members of the Court are appointed by the Council of the ICC. The function of the Court is to provide for the settlement by arbitration of business disputes of an international character in accordance with the Rules of Arbitration of the International Chamber of Commerce (the "Rules"). If so empowered by an arbitration agreement, the Court shall also provide for the settlement by arbitration in accordance with these Rules of business disputes not of an international character.

2. The Court does not itself settle disputes. It has the function of ensuring the application of these Rules. It draws up its own Internal Rules (Appendix II).

3. The Chairman of the Court, or, in the Chairman's absence or otherwise at his request, one of its Vice-Chairmen shall have the power to take urgent decisions on behalf of the Court, provided that any such decision is reported to the Court at its next session.

4. As provided for in its Internal Rules, the Court may delegate to one or more committees composed of its members the power to take certain decisions, provided that any such decision is reported to the Court at its next session.

5. The Secretariat of the Court (the "Secretariat") under the direction of its Secretary General (the "Secretary General") shall have its seat at the headquarters of the ICC.

Article 2 – Definitions

In these Rules:

(i)   "Arbitral Tribunal" includes one or more arbitrators.

(ii) "Claimant" includes one or more claimants and "Respondent" includes one or more respondents.

(iii) "Award" includes, *inter alia*, an interim, partial or final Award.

Article 3 – Written Notifications or Communications; Time Limits

1. All pleadings and other written communications submitted by any party, as well as all documents annexed thereto, shall be supplied in a number of copies sufficient to provide one copy for each party, plus one for each arbitrator, and one for the Secretariat. A copy of any communication from the Arbitral Tribunal to the parties shall be sent to the Secretariat.

2. All notifications or communications from the Secretariat and the Arbitral Tribunal shall be made to the last address of the party or its representative for whom the same are intended, as notified either by the party in question or by the other party. Such notification or communication may be made by delivery against receipt, registered post, courier, facsimile transmission, telex, telegram or any other means of telecommunication that provides a record of the sending thereof.

3. A notification or communication shall be deemed to have been made on the day it was received by the party itself or by its representative, or would have been received if made in accordance with the preceding paragraph.

4. Periods of time specified in, or fixed under the present Rules, shall start to run on the day following the date a notification or communication is deemed to have been made in accordance with the preceding paragraph. When the day next following such date is an official holiday, or a non-business day in the country where the notification or communication is deemed to have been made, the period of time shall commence on the first following business day. Official holidays and non-business days are included in the calculation of the period of time. If the last day of the relevant period of time granted is an official holiday or a non-business day in the country where the notification or communication is deemed to have been made, the period of time shall expire at the end of the first following business day.

COMMENCING THE ARBITRATION

Article 4 – Request for Arbitration

1. A party wishing to have recourse to arbitration under these Rules shall submit its Request for Arbitration (the "Request") to the Secretariat, which shall notify the Claimant and Respondent of the receipt of the Request and the date of such receipt.

2. The date on which the Request is received by the Secretariat shall, for all purposes, be deemed to be the date of the commencement of the arbitral proceedings.

3. The Request shall, *inter alia*, contain the following information:
   a) the name in full, description and address of each of the parties;
   b) a description of the nature and circumstances of the dispute giving rise to the claims;
   c) a statement of the relief sought, including, to the extent possible, an indication of any amount(s) claimed;
   d) the relevant agreements and, in particular, the arbitration agreement;
   e) all relevant particulars concerning the number of arbitrators and their choice in accordance with the provisions of Articles 8, 9 and 10, and any nomination of an arbitrator required thereby; and
   f) any comments as to the place of arbitration, the applicable rules of law and the language of the arbitration.

4. Together with the Request, the Claimant shall submit the number of copies thereof required by Article 3(1) and shall make the advance payment on administrative expenses required by Appendix III ("Arbitration Costs and Fees") in force on the date the Request is submitted. In the event that the Claimant fails to comply with either of these requirements, the Secretariat may fix a time limit within which the Claimant must comply, failing which the file shall be closed without prejudice to the right of the Claimant to submit the same claims at a later date in another Request.

5. The Secretariat shall send a copy of the Request and the documents annexed thereto to the Respondent for its Answer to the Request once the Secretariat has sufficient copies of the Request and the required advance payment.

6. When a party submits a Request in connection with a legal relationship in respect of which arbitration proceedings between the same parties are already pending under these Rules, the Court may, at the request of a party, decide to include the claims contained in the Request in the pending proceedings provided that the Terms of Reference have not been signed or approved by the Court. Once the Terms of Reference have been signed or approved by the Court, claims may only be included in the pending proceedings subject to the provisions of Article 19.

Article 5 – Answer to the Request; Counterclaims

1. Within 30 days from the receipt of the Request from the Secretariat, the Respondent shall file an Answer (the "Answer") which shall, *inter alia*, contain the following information:
   a) its name in full, description and address;
   b) its comments as to the nature and circumstances of the dispute giving rise to the claim(s);
   c) its response to the relief sought;
   d) any comments concerning the number of arbitrators and their choice in light of the Claimant's proposals and in accordance with the provisions of Articles 8, 9 and 10, and any nomination of an arbitrator required thereby; and
   e) any comments as to the place of arbitration, the applicable rules of law and the language of the arbitration.
2. The Secretariat may grant the Respondent an extension of the time for filing the Answer, provided the application for such an extension contains the Respondent's comments concerning the number of arbitrators and their choice, and, where required by Articles 8, 9 and 10, the nomination of an arbitrator. If the Respondent fails to do so, the Court shall proceed in accordance with these Rules.
3. The Answer shall be supplied to the Secretariat in the number of copies specified by Article 3(1).
4. A copy of the Answer and the documents annexed thereto shall be communicated by the Secretariat to the Claimant.
5. Any counterclaim(s) made by the Respondent shall be filed with its Answer and shall provide:
   a) a description of the nature and circumstances of the dispute giving rise to the counterclaim(s); and
   b) a statement of the relief sought, including, to the extent possible, an indication of any amount(s) counterclaimed.
6. The Claimant shall file a Reply to any counterclaim within 30 days from the date of receipt of the counterclaim(s) communicated by the Secretariat. The Secretariat may grant the Claimant an extension of time for filing the Reply.

Article 6 – Effect of the Arbitration Agreement

1. Where the parties have agreed to submit to arbitration under the Rules, they shall be deemed to have submitted *ipso facto* to the Rules in effect on the date of commencement of the arbitration proceedings unless they have agreed to submit to the Rules in effect on the date of their arbitration agreement.

2. If the Respondent does not file an Answer, as provided by Article 5, or if any party raises one or more pleas concerning the existence, validity or scope of the arbitration agreement, the Court may decide, without prejudice to the admissibility or merits of the plea or pleas, that the arbitration shall proceed if it is *prima facie* satisfied that an arbitration agreement under the Rules may exist. In such a case, any decision as to the jurisdiction of the Arbitral Tribunal shall be taken by the Arbitral Tribunal itself. If the Court is not so satisfied, the parties shall be notified that the arbitration cannot proceed. In such a case, any party retains the right to ask any court having jurisdiction whether or not there is a binding arbitration agreement.

3. If any of the parties refuses or fails to take part in the arbitration or any stage thereof, the arbitration shall proceed notwithstanding such refusal or failure.

4. Unless otherwise agreed, the Arbitral Tribunal shall not cease to have jurisdiction by reason of any claim that the contract is null and void or allegation that it is non-existent provided that the Arbitral Tribunal upholds the validity of the arbitration agreement. The Arbitral Tribunal shall continue to have jurisdiction to determine the respective rights of the parties and to adjudicate their claims and pleas even though the contract itself may be non-existent or null and void.

THE ARBITRAL TRIBUNAL

Article 7 – General Provisions

1. Every arbitrator must be and remain independent of the parties involved in the arbitration.

2. Before appointment or confirmation, a prospective arbitrator shall sign a statement of independence and disclose in writing to the Secretariat any facts or circumstances which might be of such a nature as to call into question the arbitrator's independence in the eyes of the parties. The Secretariat shall provide such information to the parties in writing and fix a time limit for any comments from them.

3. An arbitrator shall immediately disclose in writing to the Secretariat and to the parties any facts or circumstances of a similar nature which may arise during the arbitration.

4. The decisions of the Court as to the appointment, confirmation, challenge or replacement of an arbitrator shall be final and the reasons for such decisions shall not be communicated.

5. By accepting to serve, every arbitrator undertakes to carry out his responsibilities in accordance with these Rules.

6. Insofar as the parties have not provided otherwise, the Arbitral Tribunal shall be constituted in accordance with the provisions of Articles 8, 9 and 10.

Article 8 – Number of Arbitrators

1. The disputes shall be decided by a sole arbitrator or by three arbitrators.

2. Where the parties have not agreed upon the number of arbitrators, the Court shall appoint a sole arbitrator, save where it appears to the Court that the dispute is such as to warrant the appointment of three arbitrators. In such case, the Claimant shall nominate an arbitrator within a period of 15 days from the receipt of the notification of the decision of the Court, and the Respondent shall nominate an arbitrator within a

period of 15 days from the receipt of the notification of the nomination made by the Claimant.

3. Where the parties have agreed that the dispute shall be settled by a sole arbitrator, they may, by agreement, nominate the sole arbitrator for confirmation. If the parties fail to nominate a sole arbitrator within 30 days from the date when the Claimant's Request for Arbitration has been received by the other party, or within such additional time as may be allowed by the Secretariat, the sole arbitrator shall be appointed by the Court.

4. Where the dispute is to be referred to three arbitrators, each party shall nominate in the Request and the Answer, respectively, one arbitrator for confirmation by the Court. If a party fails to nominate an arbitrator, the appointment shall be made by the Court. The third arbitrator, who will act as chairman of the Arbitral Tribunal, shall be appointed by the Court, unless the parties have agreed upon another procedure for such appointment, in which case the nomination will be subject to confirmation pursuant to Article 9. Should such procedure not result in a nomination within the time limit fixed by the parties or the Court, the third arbitrator shall be appointed by the Court.

Article 9 – Appointment and Confirmation of the Arbitrators

1. In confirming or appointing arbitrators, the Court shall consider the prospective arbitrator's nationality, residence and other relationships with the countries of which the parties or the other arbitrators are nationals and the prospective arbitrator's availability and ability to conduct the arbitration in accordance with these Rules. The same shall apply where the Secretary General confirms arbitrators pursuant to Article 9(2).

2. The Secretary General may confirm as co-arbitrators, sole arbitrators and chairmen of Arbitral Tribunals persons nominated by the parties or pursuant to their particular agreements, provided they have filed a statement of independence without qualification or a qualified statement of independence has not given rise to objections. Such confirmation shall be reported to the Court at its next session. If the Secretary General considers that a co-arbitrator, sole arbitrator or chairman of an Arbitral Tribunal should not be confirmed, the matter shall be submitted to the Court.

3. Where the Court is to appoint a sole arbitrator or the chairman of an Arbitral Tribunal, it shall make the appointment upon a proposal of a National Committee of the ICC that it considers to be appropriate. If the Court does not accept the proposal made, or if the National Committee fails to make the proposal requested within the time limit fixed by the Court, the Court may repeat its request or may request a proposal from another National Committee that it considers to be appropriate.

4. Where the Court considers that the circumstances so demand, it may choose the sole arbitrator or the chairman of the Arbitral Tribunal from a country where there is no National Committee, provided that neither of the parties objects within the time limit fixed by the Court.

5. The sole arbitrator or the chairman of the Arbitral Tribunal shall be of a nationality other than those of the parties. However, in suitable circumstances and provided that neither of the parties objects within the time limit fixed by the Court, the sole arbitrator or the chairman of the Arbitral Tribunal may be chosen from a country of which any of the parties is a national.

6. Where the Court is to appoint an arbitrator on behalf of a party which has failed to nominate one, it shall make the appointment upon a proposal of the National Committee of the country of which that party is a national. If the Court does not accept the proposal made, or if the National Committee fails to make the proposal requested within the time limit fixed by the Court, or if the country of which the said party is a national has no National Committee, the Court shall be at liberty to choose any person whom it regards as suitable. The Secretariat shall inform the National Committee, if one exists, of the country of which such person is a national.

Article 10 – Multiple Parties

1. Where there are multiple parties, whether as Claimant or as Respondent, and where the dispute is to be referred to three arbitrators, the multiple Claimants, jointly, and the multiple Respondents, jointly, shall nominate an arbitrator for confirmation pursuant to Article 9.
2. In the absence of such a joint nomination and where all parties are unable to agree to a method for the constitution of the Arbitral Tribunal, the Court may appoint each member of the Arbitral Tribunal and shall designate one of them to act as chairman. In such case, the Court shall be at liberty to choose any person it regards as suitable to act as arbitrator, applying Article 9 when it considers this appropriate.

Article 11 – Challenge of Arbitrators

1. A challenge of an arbitrator, whether for an alleged lack of independence or otherwise, shall be made by the submission to the Secretariat of a written statement specifying the facts and circumstances on which the challenge is based.
2. For a challenge to be admissible, it must be sent by a party either within 30 days from receipt by that party of the notification of the appointment or confirmation of the arbitrator, or within 30 days from the date when the party making the challenge was informed of the facts and circumstances on which the challenge is based if such date is subsequent to the receipt of such notification.
3. The Court shall decide on the admissibility, and, at the same time, if necessary, on the merits of a challenge after the Secretariat has afforded an opportunity for the arbitrator concerned, the other party or parties and any other members of the Arbitral Tribunal, to comment in writing within a suitable period of time. Such comments shall be communicated to the parties and to the arbitrators.

Article 12 – Replacement of Arbitrators

1. An arbitrator shall be replaced upon his death, upon the acceptance by the Court of the arbitrator's resignation, upon acceptance by the Court of a challenge or upon the request of all the parties.
2. An arbitrator shall also be replaced on the Court's own initiative when it decides that he is prevented *de jure* or *de facto* from fulfilling his functions, or that he is not fulfilling his functions in accordance with the Rules or within the prescribed time limits.
3. When, on the basis of information that has come to its attention, the Court considers applying Article 12(2), it shall decide on the matter after the arbitrator concerned, the parties and any other members of the Arbitral Tribunal have had an opportunity to

comment in writing within a suitable period of time. Such comments shall be communicated to the parties and to the arbitrators.

4. When an arbitrator is to be replaced, the Court has discretion to decide whether or not to follow the original nominating process. Once reconstituted, and after having invited the parties to comment, the Arbitral Tribunal shall determine if and to what extent prior proceedings shall be repeated before the reconstituted Arbitral Tribunal.

5. Subsequent to the closing of the proceedings, instead of replacing an arbitrator who has died or been removed by the Court pursuant to Articles 12(1) and 12(2), the Court may decide, when it considers it appropriate, that the remaining arbitrators shall continue the arbitration. In making such determination, the Court shall take into account the views of the remaining arbitrators and of the parties and such other matters that it considers appropriate in the circumstances.

THE ARBITRAL PROCEEDINGS

Article 13 – Transmission of the File to the Arbitral Tribunal
The Secretariat shall transmit the file to the Arbitral Tribunal as soon as it has been constituted, provided the advance on costs requested by the Secretariat at this stage has been paid.

Article 14 – Place of the Arbitration
1. The place of the arbitration shall be fixed by the Court unless agreed upon by the parties.
2. The Arbitral Tribunal may, after consultation with the parties, conduct hearings and meetings at any location it considers appropriate unless otherwise agreed by the parties.
3. The Arbitral Tribunal may deliberate at any location it considers appropriate.

Article 15 – Rules Governing the Proceedings
1. The proceedings before the Arbitral Tribunal shall be governed by these Rules, and, where these Rules are silent, by any rules which the parties or, failing them, the Arbitral Tribunal may settle on, whether or not reference is thereby made to the rules of procedure of a national law to be applied to the arbitration.
2. In all cases, the Arbitral Tribunal shall act fairly and impartially and ensure that each party has a reasonable opportunity to present its case.

Article 16 – Language of the Arbitration
In the absence of an agreement by the parties, the Arbitral Tribunal shall determine the language or languages of the arbitration, due regard being given to all relevant circumstances, including the language of the contract.

Article 17 – Applicable Rules of Law
1. The parties shall be free to agree upon the rules of law to be applied by the Arbitral Tribunal to the merits of the dispute. In the absence of any such agreement, the Arbitral Tribunal shall apply the rules of law which it determines to be appropriate.

2. In all cases the Arbitral Tribunal shall take account of the provisions of the contract and the relevant trade usages.

3. The Arbitral Tribunal shall assume the powers of an *amiable compositeur* or decide *ex aequo et bono* only if the parties have agreed to give it such powers.

Article 18 – Terms of Reference; Procedural Timetable

1. As soon as it has received the file from the Secretariat, the Arbitral Tribunal shall draw up, on the basis of documents or in the presence of the parties and in the light of their most recent submissions, a document defining its Terms of Reference. This document shall include the following particulars:
   a) the full names and descriptions of the parties;
   b) the addresses of the parties to which notifications and communications arising in the course of the arbitration may be made;
   c) a summary of the parties' respective claims and of the relief sought by each party, with an indication to the extent possible of the amounts claimed or counterclaimed;
   d) unless the Arbitral Tribunal considers it inappropriate, a list of issues to be determined;
   e) the full names, descriptions and addresses of the arbitrators;
   f) the place of the arbitration; and
   g) particulars of the applicable procedural rules and, if such is the case, reference to the power conferred upon the Arbitral Tribunal to act as *amiable compositeur* or to decide *ex aequo et bono*.

2. The Terms of Reference shall be signed by the parties and the Arbitral Tribunal. Within two months of the date on which the file has been transmitted to it, the Arbitral Tribunal shall transmit to the Court the Terms of Reference signed by it and by the parties. The Court may extend this time limit pursuant to a reasoned request from the Arbitral Tribunal or on its own initiative if it decides it is necessary to do so.

3. If any of the parties refuses to take part in the drawing up of the Terms of Reference or to sign the same, they shall be submitted to the Court for approval. When the Terms of Reference are signed in accordance with Article 18(2) or approved by the Court, the arbitration shall proceed.

4. When drawing up the Terms of Reference, or as soon as possible thereafter, the Arbitral Tribunal, after having consulted the parties, shall establish in a separate document a provisional timetable that it intends to follow for the conduct of the arbitration and shall communicate it to the Court and the parties. Any subsequent modifications of the provisional timetable shall be communicated to the Court and the parties.

Article 19 – New Claims

After the Terms of Reference have been signed or approved by the Court, no party shall make new claims or counterclaims which fall outside the limits of the Terms of Reference unless it has been authorized to do so by the Arbitral Tribunal, which shall consider the nature of such new claims or counterclaims, the stage of the arbitration and other relevant circumstances.

Article 20 – Establishing the Facts of the Case

1. The Arbitral Tribunal shall proceed within as short a time as possible to establish the facts of the case by all appropriate means.
2. After studying the written submissions of the parties and all documents relied upon, the Arbitral Tribunal shall hear the parties together in person if any of them so requests or, failing such a request, it may of its own motion decide to hear them.
3. The Arbitral Tribunal may decide to hear witnesses, experts appointed by the parties or any other person, in the presence of the parties, or in their absence provided they have been duly summoned.
4. The Arbitral Tribunal, after having consulted the parties, may appoint one or more experts, define their terms of reference and receive their reports. At the request of a party, the parties shall be given the opportunity to question at a hearing any such expert appointed by the Tribunal.
5. At any time during the proceedings, the Arbitral Tribunal may summon any party to provide additional evidence.
6. The Arbitral Tribunal may decide the case solely on the documents submitted by the parties unless any of the parties requests a hearing.
7. The Arbitral Tribunal may take measures for protecting trade secrets and confidential information.

Article 21 – Hearings

1. When a hearing is to be held, the Arbitral Tribunal, giving reasonable notice, shall summon the parties to appear before it on the day and at the place fixed by it.
2. If any of the parties, although duly summoned, fails to appear without valid excuse, the Arbitral Tribunal shall have the power to proceed with the hearing.
3. The Arbitral Tribunal shall be in full charge of the hearings, at which all the parties shall be entitled to be present. Save with the approval of the Arbitral Tribunal and the parties, persons not involved in the proceedings shall not be admitted.
4. The parties may appear in person or through duly authorized representatives. In addition, they may be assisted by advisers.

Article 22 – Closing of the Proceedings

1. When it is satisfied that the parties have had a reasonable opportunity to present their cases, the Arbitral Tribunal shall declare the proceedings closed. Thereafter, no further submission or argument may be made, or evidence produced, unless requested or authorized by the Arbitral Tribunal.
2. When the Arbitral Tribunal has declared the proceedings closed, it shall indicate to the Secretariat an approximate date by which the draft Award will be submitted to the Court for approval pursuant to Article 27. Any postponement of that date shall be communicated to the Secretariat by the Arbitral Tribunal.

Article 23 – Conservatory and Interim Measures

1. Unless the parties have otherwise agreed, as soon as the file has been transmitted to it, the Arbitral Tribunal may, at the request of a party, order any interim or conservatory measure it deems appropriate. The Arbitral Tribunal may make the granting of any such

measure subject to appropriate security being furnished by the requesting party. Any such measure shall take the form of an order, giving reasons, or of an Award, as the Arbitral Tribunal considers appropriate.

2. Before the file is transmitted to the Arbitral Tribunal, and in appropriate circumstances even thereafter, the parties may apply to any competent judicial authority for interim or conservatory measures. The application of a party to a judicial authority for such measures or for the implementation of any such measures ordered by an Arbitral Tribunal shall not be deemed to be an infringement or a waiver of the arbitration agreement and shall not affect the relevant powers reserved to the Arbitral Tribunal. Any such application and any measures taken by the judicial authority must be notified without delay to the Secretariat. The Secretariat shall inform the Arbitral Tribunal thereof.

AWARDS

Article 24 – Time Limit for the Award

1. The time limit within which the Arbitral Tribunal must render its final Award is six months. Such time limit shall start to run from the date of the last signature by the Arbitral Tribunal or of the Parties of the Terms of Reference, or, in the case of application of Article 18(3), the date of the notification to the Arbitral Tribunal by the Secretariat of the approval of the Terms of Reference by the Court.

2. The Court may extend this time limit pursuant to a reasoned request from the Arbitral Tribunal or on its own initiative if it decides it is necessary to do so.

Article 25 – Making of the Award

1. When the Arbitral Tribunal is composed of more than one arbitrator, an Award is given by a majority decision. If there be no majority, the Award shall be made by the chairman of the Arbitral Tribunal alone.

2. The Award shall state the reasons upon which it is based.

3. The Award shall be deemed to be made at the place of the arbitration and on the date stated therein.

Article 26 – Award by Consent

If the parties reach a settlement after the file has been transmitted to the Arbitral Tribunal in accordance with Article 13, the settlement shall be recorded in the form of an Award made by consent of the parties if so requested by the parties and if the Arbitral Tribunal agrees to do so.

Article 27 – Scrutiny of the Award by the Court

Before signing any Award, the Arbitral Tribunal shall submit it in draft form to the Court. The Court may lay down modifications as to the form of the Award and, without affecting the Arbitral Tribunal's liberty of decision, may also draw its attention to points of substance. No Award shall be rendered by the Arbitral Tribunal until it has been approved by the Court as to its form.

Article 28 – Notification, Deposit and Enforceability of the Award

1. Once an Award has been made, the Secretariat shall notify to the parties the text signed by the Arbitral Tribunal, provided always that the costs of the arbitration have been fully paid to the ICC by the parties or by one of them.
2. Additional copies certified true by the Secretary General shall be made available on request and at any time to the parties, but to no one else.
3. By virtue of the notification made in accordance with Paragraph 1 of this Article, the parties waive any other form of notification or deposit on the part of the Arbitral Tribunal.
4. An original of each Award made in accordance with the present Rules shall be deposited with the Secretariat.
5. The Arbitral Tribunal and the Secretariat shall assist the parties in complying with whatever further formalities may be necessary.
6. Every Award shall be binding on the parties. By submitting the dispute to arbitration under these Rules, the parties undertake to carry out any Award without delay and shall be deemed to have waived their right to any form of recourse insofar as such waiver can validly be made.

Article 29 – Correction and Interpretation of the Award

1. On its own initiative, the Arbitral Tribunal may correct a clerical, computational or typographical error, or any errors of similar nature contained in an Award, provided such correction is submitted for approval to the Court within 30 days of the date of such Award.
2. Any application of a party for the correction of an error of the kind referred to in Article 29(1), or for the interpretation of an Award, must be made to the Secretariat within 30 days of the receipt of the Award by such party, in a number of copies as stated in Article 3(1). After transmittal of the application to the Arbitral Tribunal, it shall grant the other party a short time limit, normally not exceeding 30 days, from the receipt of the application by that party to submit any comments thereon. If the Arbitral Tribunal decides to correct or interpret the Award, it shall submit its decision in draft form to the Court not later than 30 days following the expiration of the time limit for the receipt of any comments from the other party or within such other period as the Court may decide.
3. The decision to correct or to interpret the Award shall take the form of an addendum and shall constitute part of the Award. The provisions of Articles 25, 27 and 28 shall apply *mutatis mutandis*.

COSTS

Article 30 – Advance to Cover the Costs of the Arbitration

1. After receipt of the Request, the Secretary General may request the Claimant to pay a provisional advance in an amount intended to cover the costs of arbitration until the Terms of Reference have been drawn up.
2. As soon as practicable, the Court shall fix the advance on costs in an amount likely to cover the fees and expenses of the arbitrators and the ICC administrative costs for the

claims and counterclaims which have been referred to it by the parties. This amount may be subject to readjustment at any time during the arbitration. Where, apart from the claims, counterclaims are submitted, the Court may fix separate advances on costs for the claims and the counterclaims.

3. The advance on costs fixed by the Court shall be payable in equal shares by the Claimant and the Respondent. Any provisional advance paid on the basis of Article 30(1) will be considered as a partial payment thereof. However, any party shall be free to pay the whole of the advance on costs in respect of the principal claim or the counterclaim should the other party fail to pay its share. When the Court has set separate advances on costs in accordance with Article 30(2), each of the parties shall pay the advance on costs corresponding to its claims.

4. When a request for an advance on costs has not been complied with, and after consultation with the Arbitral Tribunal, the Secretary General may direct the Arbitral Tribunal to suspend its work and set a time limit, which must be not less than 15 days, on the expiry of which the relevant claims, or counterclaims, shall be considered as withdrawn. Should the party in question wish to object to this measure it must make a request within the aforementioned period for the matter to be decided by the Court. Such party shall not be prevented on the ground of such withdrawal from reintroducing the same claims or counterclaims at a later date in another proceeding.

5. If one of the parties claims a right to a set-off with regard to either claims or counterclaims, such set-off shall be taken into account in determining the advance to cover the costs of arbitration in the same way as a separate claim insofar as it may require the Arbitral Tribunal to consider additional matters.

Article 31 – Decision as to the Costs of the Arbitration

1. The costs of the arbitration shall include the fees and expenses of the arbitrators and the ICC administrative costs fixed by the Court, in accordance with the scale in force at the time of the commencement of the arbitral proceedings, as well as the fees and expenses of any experts appointed by the Arbitral Tribunal and the reasonable legal and other costs incurred by the parties for the arbitration.

2. The Court may fix the fees of the arbitrators at a figure higher or lower than that which would result from the application of the relevant scale should this be deemed necessary due to the exceptional circumstances of the case. Decisions on costs other than those fixed by the Court may be taken by the Arbitral Tribunal at any time during the proceedings.

3. The final Award shall fix the costs of the arbitration and decide which of the parties shall bear them or in what proportion they shall be borne by the parties.

MISCELLANEOUS

Article 32 – Modified Time Limits

1. The parties may agree to shorten the various time limits set out in these Rules. Any such agreement entered into subsequent to the constitution of an Arbitral Tribunal shall become effective only upon the approval of the Arbitral Tribunal.

2. The Court, on its own initiative, may extend any time limit which has been modified pursuant to Article 32(1) if it decides that it is necessary to do so in order that the Arbitral Tribunal or the Court may fulfil their responsibilities in accordance with these Rules.

Article 33 – Waiver
A party which proceeds with the arbitration without raising its objection to a failure to comply with any provision of these Rules, or of any other rules applicable to the proceedings, any direction given by the Arbitral Tribunal, or any requirement under the arbitration agreement relating to the constitution of the Arbitral Tribunal, or to the conduct of the proceedings, shall be deemed to have waived its right to object.

Article 34 – Exclusion of Liability
Neither the arbitrators, nor the Court and its members, nor the ICC and its employees, nor the ICC National Committees shall be liable to any person for any act or omission in connection with the arbitration.

Article 35 – General Rule
In all matters not expressly provided for in these Rules, the Court and the Arbitral Tribunal shall act in the spirit of these Rules and shall make every effort to make sure that the Award is enforceable at law.

APPENDIX I
STATUTES OF THE INTERNATIONAL
COURT OF ARBITRATION OF THE ICC

Article 1 – Function
1. The function of the International Court of Arbitration of the International Chamber of Commerce (the Court) is to ensure the application of the Rules of Arbitration and the Rules of Conciliation of the International Chamber of Commerce, and it has all the necessary powers for that purpose.
2. As an autonomous body, it carries out these functions in complete independence from the ICC and its organs.
3. Its members are independent from the ICC National Committees.

Article 2 – Composition of the Court
The Court shall consist of a Chairman, Vice-Chairmen, and members and alternate members (collectively designated as members). In its work it is assisted by its Secretariat (Secretariat of the Court).

Article 3 – Appointment
1. The Chairman is elected by the ICC Council upon recommendation of the Executive Board of the ICC.

2. The ICC Council appoints the Vice-Chairmen of the Court from among the members of the Court or otherwise.
3. Its members are appointed by the ICC Council on the proposal of National Committees, one member for each Committee.
4. On the proposal of the Chairman of the Court, the Council may appoint alternate members.
5. The term of office of all members is three years. If a member is no longer in a position to exercise his functions, his successor is appointed by the Council for the remainder of the term.

Article 4 – Plenary Session of the Court

The Plenary Sessions of the Court are presided over by the Chairman, or, in his absence, by one of the Vice-Chairmen designated by him. The deliberations shall be valid when at least six members are present. Decisions are taken by a majority vote, the Chairman having a casting vote in the event of a tie.

Article 5 – Committees

The Court may set up one or more Committees and establish the functions and organization of such Committees.

Article 6 – Confidentiality

The work of the Court is of a confidential nature and must be respected by everyone who participates in that work in whatever capacity. The Court lays down the rules regarding the persons who can attend the meetings of the Court and its Committees and who are entitled to have access to the materials submitted to the Court and its Secretariat.

Article 7 – Modification of the Rules of Arbitration

Any proposal of the Court for a modification of the Rules is laid before the Commission on International Arbitration before submission to the Executive Board and the Council of the ICC for approval.

APPENDIX II
INTERNAL RULES OF THE INTERNATIONAL
COURT OF ARBITRATION OF THE ICC

Article 1 – Confidential Character of the Work of the
International Court of Arbitration

1. The sessions of the Court, whether plenary or those of a Committee of the Court, are open only to its members and to the Secretariat.
2. However, in exceptional circumstances, the Chairman of the Court may invite other persons to attend. Such persons must respect the confidential nature of the work of the Court.

3. The documents submitted to the Court, or drawn up by it in the course of its proceedings, are communicated only to the members of the Court and to the Secretariat and to persons authorized by the Chairman to attend Court sessions.
4. The Chairman or the Secretary General of the Court may authorize researchers undertaking work of a scientific nature on international trade law to acquaint themselves with awards and other documents of general interest, with the exception of memoranda, notes, statements and documents remitted by the parties within the framework of arbitration proceedings.
5. Such authorization shall not be given unless the beneficiary has undertaken to respect the confidential character of the documents made available and to refrain from any publication in their respect without having previously submitted the text for approval to the Secretary General of the Court.
6. The Secretariat will in each case submitted to arbitration under the Rules retain in the archives of the Court all awards, terms of reference, and decisions of the Court as well as copies of the pertinent correspondence of the Secretariat.
7. Any documents, communications or correspondence submitted by the parties or the arbitrators may be destroyed unless a party or an arbitrator requests in writing within a period fixed by the Secretariat the return of such documents. All related costs and expenses for the return of those documents shall be paid by such party or arbitrator.

Article 2 – Participation of Members of the International Court of Arbitration in ICC Arbitration

1. The Chairman and the members of the Secretariat of the Court may not act as arbitrators or as counsel in cases submitted to ICC arbitration.
2. The Court shall not appoint Vice-Chairmen or members of the Court as arbitrators. They may, however, be proposed for such duties by one or more of the parties, or, pursuant to any other procedure agreed upon by the parties, subject to confirmation by the Court.
3. When the Chairman, a Vice-Chairman or a member of the Court or of the Secretariat is involved in any capacity whatsoever in proceedings pending before the Court, such person must inform the Secretary General of the Court upon becoming aware of such involvement.
4. Such person must refrain from participating in the discussions or in the decisions of the Court concerning the proceedings and must be absent from the courtroom whenever the matter is considered.
5. Such person will not receive any material documentation or information pertaining to such proceedings.

Article 3 – Relations between the Members of the Court and the ICC National Committees

1. By virtue of their capacity, the members of the Court are independent of the ICC National Committees which proposed them for appointment by the ICC Council.

2. Furthermore, they must regard as confidential, vis-à-vis the said National Committees, any information concerning individual cases with which they have become acquainted in their capacity as members of the Court, except when they have been requested by the Chairman of the Court or by its Secretary General to communicate specific information to their respective National Committee.

Article 4 – Committee of the Court

1. In accordance with the provisions of Article 1(4) of the Rules and Article 5 of its Statutes (Appendix I), the Court hereby establishes a Committee of the Court.
2. The members of the Committee consist of a Chairman and at least two other members. The Chairman of the Court acts as the Chairman of the Committee. If absent, the Chairman may designate a Vice-Chairman of the Court or, in exceptional circumstances, another member of the Court as Chairman of the Committee.
3. The other two members of the Committee are appointed by the Court from among the Vice-Chairmen or the other members of the Court. At each Plenary Session the Court appoints the members who are to attend the meetings of the Committee to be held before the next Plenary Session.
4. The Committee meets when convened by its Chairman. Two members constitute a quorum.
5. (a) The Court shall determine the decisions that may be taken by the Committee.
   (b) The decisions of the Committee are taken unanimously.
   (c) When the Committee cannot reach a decision or deems it preferable to abstain, it transfers the case to the next Plenary Session, making any suggestions it deems appropriate.
   (d) The Committee's decisions are brought to the notice of the Court at its next Plenary Session.

Article 5 – Court Secretariat

1. In case of absence, the Secretary General may delegate to the General Counsel and Deputy Secretary General the authority to confirm arbitrators, to certify true copies of awards and to request the payment of a provisional advance, respectively provided for in Articles 9(2), 28(2) and 30(1) of the Rules.
2. The Secretariat may, with the approval of the Court, issue notes and other documents for the information of the parties and the arbitrators, or as necessary for the proper conduct of the arbitral proceedings.

Article 6 – Scrutiny of Arbitral Awards

When the Court scrutinizes draft awards in accordance with Article 27 of the Rules, it considers, to the extent practicable, the requirements of mandatory law at the place of arbitration.

APPENDIX III
ARBITRATION COSTS AND FEES

Article 1 – Advance on Costs

1. Each request to commence an arbitration pursuant to the Rules must be accompanied by an advance payment of US $ 2 500 on the administrative expenses. Such payment is nonrefundable, and shall be credited to the Claimant's portion of the advance on costs.

2. The provisional advance on costs fixed by the Secretary General according to Article 30(1) of the Rules shall normally not exceed the amount obtained by adding together the administrative expenses, the minimum of the fees (as set out in the scale hereinafter) based upon the amount of the claim and the expected reimbursable expenses of the Arbitral Tribunal incurred with respect to the drafting of the Terms of Reference. If such amount is not quantified, the provisional advance shall be fixed at the discretion of the Secretary General. Payment by the Claimant shall be credited to its share of the advance on costs fixed by the Court.

3. In general, after the Terms of Reference have been signed or approved by the Court and the provisional timetable has been established, the Arbitral Tribunal shall, in accordance with Article 30(4) of the Rules, proceed only with respect to those claims or counterclaims in regard to which the whole of the advance on costs has been paid.

4. The advance on costs fixed by the Court according to Article 30(2) of the Rules comprises the fees of the arbitrator or arbitrators (hereinafter referred to as "arbitrator"), any arbitration-related expenses of the arbitrator and the administrative expenses.

5. Each party shall pay in cash its share of the total advance on costs. However, if its share exceeds an amount fixed from time to time by the Court, a party may post a bank guarantee for this additional amount.

6. A party that has already paid in full its share of the advance on costs fixed by the Court may, in accordance with Article 30(3) of the Rules, pay the unpaid portion of the advance owed by the defaulting party by posting a bank guarantee.

7. When the Court has fixed separate advances on costs pursuant to Article 30(2) of the Rules, the Secretariat shall invite each party to pay the amount of the advance corresponding to its respective claims.

8. When, as a result of the fixing of separate advances on costs, the separate advance fixed for the claim of either party exceeds one-half of such global advance as was previously fixed (in respect of the same claims and counterclaims that are the object of separate advances), a bank guarantee may be posted to cover any such excess amount. In the event that the amount of the separate advance is subsequently increased, at least one-half of the increase shall be paid in cash.

9. The Secretariat shall establish the terms governing all bank guarantees which the parties may post pursuant to the above provisions.

10. As provided in Article 30(2) of the Rules, the advance on costs may be subject to readjustment at any time during the arbitration, in particular to take into account fluctuations in the amount in dispute, changes in the amount of the estimated expenses of the arbitrator, or the evolving difficulty or complexity of arbitration proceedings.

11. Before any expertise ordered by the Arbitral Tribunal can be commenced, the parties, or one of them, shall pay an advance on costs fixed by the Arbitral Tribunal sufficient to cover the expected fees and expenses of the expert as determined by the Arbitral Tribunal. The Arbitral Tribunal shall be responsible for ensuring the payment by the parties of such fees and expenses.

Article 2 – Costs and Fees

1. Subject to Article 31(2) of the Rules, the Court shall fix the fees of the arbitrator in accordance with the scale hereinafter set out, or, where the sum in dispute is not stated, at its discretion.
2. In setting the arbitrator's fees, the Court shall take into consideration the diligence of the arbitrator, the time spent, the rapidity of the proceedings, and the complexity of the dispute so as to arrive at a figure within the limits specified, or, in exceptional circumstances (Article 31(2) of the Rules), at a figure higher or lower than those limits.
3. When a case is submitted to more than one arbitrator, the Court, at its discretion, shall have the right to increase the total fees up to a maximum which shall normally not exceed three times the fees of one arbitrator.
4. The arbitrator's fees and expenses shall be fixed exclusively by the Court as required by the Rules. Separate fee arrangements between the parties and the arbitrator are contrary to the Rules.
5. The Court shall fix the administrative expenses of each arbitration in accordance with the scale hereinafter set out, or, where the sum in dispute is not stated, at its discretion. In exceptional circumstances, the Court may fix the administrative expenses at a lower or higher figure than that which would result from the application of such scale, provided that such expenses shall normally not exceed the maximum amount of the scale. Further, the Court may require the payment of administrative expenses in addition to those provided in the scale of administrative expenses as a condition to holding an arbitration in abeyance at the request of the parties or of one of them with the acquiescence of the other.
6. If an arbitration terminates before the rendering of a final award, the Court shall fix the costs of the arbitration at its discretion, taking into account the stage attained by the arbitral proceedings and any other relevant circumstances.
7. In the case of an application under Article 29(2) of the Rules, the Court may fix an advance to cover additional fees and expenses of the Arbitral Tribunal and may subordinate the transmission of such application to the Arbitral Tribunal to the prior cash payment in full to the ICC of such advance. The Court shall fix at its discretion any possible fees of the arbitrator when approving the decision of the Arbitral Tribunal.
8. When an arbitration is preceded by attempted conciliation, one-half of the administrative expenses paid for such conciliation shall be credited to the administrative expenses of the arbitration.
9. Amounts paid to the arbitrator do not include any possible value-added taxes (VAT) or other taxes or charges and imposts applicable to the arbitrator's fees. Parties are expected to pay any such taxes or charges; however, the recovery of any such charges or taxes is a matter solely between the arbitrator and the parties.

Article 3 – Appointment of Arbitrators

1. A registration fee normally not exceeding US $ 2 500 is payable by the requesting party in respect of each request made to the ICC to appoint an arbitrator for any arbitration not conducted under the Rules. No request for appointment of an arbitrator will be considered unless accompanied by the said fee, which is not recoverable and becomes the property of the ICC.

2. The said fee shall cover any additional services rendered by the ICC regarding the appointment, such as decisions on a challenge of an arbitrator and the appointment of a substitute arbitrator.

Article 4 – Scales of Administrative Expenses and of Arbitrator's Fees

1. The Scales of Administrative Expenses and Arbitrator's Fees set forth below shall be effective as of January 1, 1998 in respect of all arbitrations commenced on or after such date, irrespective of the version of the Rules applying to such arbitrations.

2. To calculate the administrative expenses and the arbitrator's fees, the amounts calculated for each successive slice of the sum in dispute must be added together, except that where the sum in dispute is over US $ 80 million, a flat amount of US $ 75 800 shall constitute the entirety of the administrative expenses.

A. ADMINISTRATIVE EXPENSES

Sum in dispute (in US Dollars)			Administrative expenses[*]
up to	50 000		$ 2 500
from	50 001 to	100 000	3.50%
from	100 001 to	500 000	1.70%
from	500 001 to	1 000 000	1.15%
from	1 000 001 to	2 000 000	0.60%
from	2 000 001 to	5 000 000	0.20%
from	5 000 001 to	10 000 000	0.10%
from	10 000 001 to	50 000 000	0.06%
from	50 000 001 to	80 000 000	0.06%
over	80 000 000		$ 75 800

(*) For illustrative purposes only, the table on the following page indicates the resulting administrative expenses in US $ when the proper calculations have been made.

B. ARBITRATOR'S FEES

Sum in dispute (in US Dollars)			Fees [**]	
			minimum	maximum
up to	50 000		$ 2 500	17.00%
from	50 001 to	100 000	2.00%	11.00%
from	100 001 to	500 000	1.00%	5.50%
from	500 001 to	1 000 000	0.75%	3.50%
from	1 000 001 to	2 000 000	0.50%	2.50%
from	2 000 001 to	5 000 000	0.25%	1.00%
from	5 000 001 to	10 000 000	0.10%	0.55%
from	10 000 001 to	50 000 000	0.05%	0.17%
from	50 000 001 to	80 000 000	0.03%	0.12%
from	80 000 001 to	100 000 000	0.02%	0.10%
over	100 000 000		0.01%	0.05%

** For illustrative purposes only, the table on the following page indicates the resulting range of fees when the proper calculations have been made.

SUM IN DISPUTE (in US Dollars)	A. ADMINISTRATIVE EXPENSES(*) (in US Dollars)	B. ARBITRATOR'S FEES (**) (in US Dollars)	
		Minimum	Maximum
up to 50 000	2 500	2 500	17.00% of amount in dispute
from 50 001 to 100 000	2 500 + 3.50% of amt. over 50 000	2 500 + 2.00% of amt. over 50 000	8 500 + 11.00% of amt. over 50 000
from 100 001 to 500 000	4 250 + 1.70% of amt. over 100 000	3 500 + 1.00% of amt. over 100 000	14 000 + 5.50% of amt. over 100 000
from 500 001 to 1 000 000	11 050 + 1.15% of amt. over 500 000	7 500 + 0.75% of amt. over 500 000	36 000 + 3.50% of amt. over 500 000
from 1 000 001 to 2 000 000	16 800 + 0.60% of amt. over 1 000 000	11 250 + 0.50% of amt. over 1 000 000	53 500 + 2.50% of amt. over 1 000 000
from 2 000 001 to 5 000 000	22 800 + 0.20% of amt. over 2 000 000	16 250 + 0.25% of amt. over 2 000 000	78 500 + 1.00% of amt. over 2 000 000
from 5 000 001 to 10 000 000	28 800 + 0.10% of amt. over 5 000 000	23 750 + 0.10% of amt. over 5 000 000	108 500 + 0.55% of amt. over 5 000 000
from 10 000 001 to 50 000 000	33 800 + 0.06% of amt. over 10 000 000	28 750 + 0.05% of amt. over 10 000 000	136 000 + 0.17% of amt. over 10 000 000
from 50 000 001 to 80 000 000	57 800 + 0.06% of amt. over 50 000 000	48 750 + 0.03% of amt. over 50 000 000	204 000 + 0.12% of amt. over 50 000 000
from 80 000 001 to 100 000 000	75 800	57 750 + 0.02% of amt. over 80 000 000	240 000 + 0.10% of amt. over 80 000 000
over 100 000 000	75 800	61 750 + 0.01% of amt. over 100 000 000	260 000 + 0.05% of amt. over 100 000 000

ICC NATIONAL COMMITTEES
OR GROUPS

	founded		*founded*
Argentina	1947	Korea	1959
Australia	1927	Kuwait	1978
Austria	1921	Lebanon	1973
Bangladesh	1994	Lithuania	1994
Belgium	1920	Luxembourg	1921
Brazil	1939	Madagascar	1973
Burkina Faso	1976	Mexico	1945
Cameroon	1981	Morocco	1957
Canada	1945	Netherlands	1921
Chile	1993	Nigeria	1979
China	1994	Norway	1922
Colombia	1961	Pakistan	1955
Côte d'Ivoire	1975	Peru	1994
Cyprus	1980	Portugal	1934
Denmark	1920	Saudi Arabia	1975
Ecuador	1987	Senegal	1975
Egypt	1946	Singapore	1978
Finland	1927	South Africa	1958
France	1920	Spain	1922
Germany	1925	Sri Lanka	1955
Greece	1926	Sweden	1921
Hungary	1996	Switzerland	1922
Iceland	1983	Syria	1988
India	1929	Togo	1977
Indonesia	1955	Tunisia	1974
Iran	1963	Turkey	1934
Ireland	1979	United Kingdom	1920
Israel	1959	United States	1920
Italy	1920	Uruguay	1952
Japan	1923	Venezuela	1939
Jordan	1975	Yugoslavia	1927

Chinese Taipei Business Council of the ICC	1966

LCIA RULES
(Effective as of January 1, 1998)*

RECOMMENDED ARBITRATION CLAUSE

For contracting parties who wish to have future disputes referred to arbitration under the LCIA Rules, the following clause is recommended. Words/spaces in square brackets should be deleted/completed as appropriate.

> Any dispute arising out of or in connection with this contract, including any question regarding its existence, validity or termination, shall be referred to and finally resolved by arbitration under the LCIA Rules, which Rules are deemed to be incorporated by reference into this clause.
>
> The number of arbitrators shall be *[one / three]*.
>
> The place** of arbitration shall be *[City and / or Country]*.
>
> The language to be used in the arbitral proceedings shall be *[   ]*.
>
> The governing law of the contract shall be the substantive law of *[   ]*.

LCIA RULES

Where any agreement, submission or reference provides in writing and in whatsoever manner for arbitration under the rules of the LCIA or by the Court of the LCIA ("the LCIA Court"), the parties shall be taken to have agreed in writing that the arbitration shall be conducted in accordance with the following rules ("the Rules") or such amended rules as the

---

* Reproduced with kind permission of the London Court of International Arbitration. See also the LCIA Web site <http://www.lcia-arbitration.com/lcia>.

** The Arbitral Tribunal may hold hearings, meetings and deliberations at any convenient geographical place in its discretion; and if elsewhere than the seat of the arbitration, the arbitration shall be treated as an arbitration conducted at the seat of the arbitration and any award as an award made at the seat of the arbitration for all purposes.

LCIA may have adopted thereafter to take effect before the commencement of the arbitration. The Rules include the Schedule of Costs in effect at the commencement of the arbitration, as separately amended from time to time by the LCIA Court.

Article 1 – The Request for Arbitration

1.1 Any party wishing to commence an arbitration under these Rules ("the Claimant") shall send to the Registrar of the LCIA Court ("the Registrar") a written request for arbitration ("the Request"), containing or accompanied by:

(a) the names, addresses, telephone, facsimile, telex and e-mail numbers (if known) of the parties to the arbitration and of their legal representatives;

(b) a copy of the written arbitration clause or separate written arbitration agreement invoked by the Claimant ("the Arbitration Agreement"), together with a copy of the contractual documentation in which the arbitration clause is contained or in respect of which the arbitration arises;

(c) a brief statement describing the nature and circumstances of the dispute, and specifying the claims advanced by the Claimant against another party to the arbitration ("the Respondent");

(d) a statement of any matters (such as the seat or language(s) of the arbitration, or the number of arbitrators, or their qualifications or identities) on which the parties have already agreed in writing for the arbitration or in respect of which the Claimant wishes to make a proposal;

(e) if the Arbitration Agreement calls for party nomination of arbitrators, the name, address, telephone, facsimile, telex and e-mail numbers (if known) of the Claimant's nominee;

(f) the fee prescribed in the Schedule of Costs (without which the Request shall be treated as not having been received by the Registrar and the arbitration as not having been commenced); and

(g) confirmation to the Registrar that copies of the Request (including all accompanying documents) have been or are being served simultaneously on all other parties to the arbitration by one or more means of service to be identified in such confirmation.

1.2 The date of receipt by the Registrar of the Request shall be treated as the date on which the arbitration has commenced for all purposes. The Request (including all accompanying documents) should be submitted to the Registrar in two copies where a sole arbitrator should be appointed, or, if the parties have agreed or the Claimant considers that three arbitrators should be appointed, in four copies.

Article 2 – The Response

2.1 Within 30 days of service of the Request on the Respondent, (or such lesser period fixed by the LCIA Court), the Respondent shall send to the Registrar a written response to the Request ("the Response"), containing or accompanied by:

(a) confirmation or denial of all or part of the claims advanced by the Claimant in the Request;

(b) a brief statement describing the nature and circumstances of any counterclaims advanced by the Respondent against the Claimant;

(c) comment in response to any statements contained in the Request, as called for under Article 1.1(d), on matters relating to the conduct of the arbitration;

(d) if the Arbitration Agreement calls for party nomination of arbitrators, the name, address, telephone, facsimile, telex and e-mail numbers (if known) of the Respondent's nominee; and

(e) confirmation to the Registrar that copies of the Response (including all accompanying documents) have been or are being served simultaneously on all other parties to the arbitration by one or more means of service to be identified in such confirmation.

2.2 The Response (including all accompanying documents) should be submitted to the Registrar in two copies, or if the parties have agreed or the Respondent considers that three arbitrators should be appointed, in four copies.

2.3 Failure to send a Response shall not preclude the Respondent from denying any claim or from advancing a counterclaim in the arbitration. However, if the Arbitration Agreement calls for party nomination of arbitrators, failure to send a Response or to nominate an arbitrator within time or at all shall constitute an irrevocable waiver of that party's opportunity to nominate an arbitrator.

Article 3 – The LCIA Court and Registrar

3.1 The functions of the LCIA Court under these Rules shall be performed in its name by the President or a Vice-President of the LCIA Court or by a division of three or five members of the LCIA Court appointed by the President or a Vice-President of the LCIA Court, as determined by the President.

3.2 The functions of the Registrar under these Rules shall be performed by the Registrar or any deputy Registrar of the LCIA Court under the supervision of the LCIA Court.

3.3 All communications from any party or arbitrator to the LCIA Court shall be addressed to the Registrar.

Article 4 – Notices and Periods of Time

4.1 Any notice or other communication that may be or is required to be given by a party under these Rules shall be in writing and shall be delivered by registered postal or courier service or transmitted by facsimile, telex, e-mail or any other means of telecommunication that provide a record of its transmission.

4.2 A party's last-known residence or place of business during the arbitration shall be a valid address for the purpose of any notice or other communication in the absence of any notification of a change to such address by that party to the other parties, the Arbitral Tribunal and the Registrar.

4.3 For the purpose of determining the date of commencement of a time limit, a notice or other communication shall be treated as having been received on the day it is delivered or, in the case of telecommunications, transmitted in accordance with Articles 4.1 and 4.2.

4.4 For the purpose of determining compliance with a time limit, a notice or other communication shall be treated as having been sent, made or transmitted if it is dispatched in accordance with Articles 4.1 and 4.2 prior to or on the date of the expiration of the time-limit.

4.5   Notwithstanding the above, any notice or communication by one party may be addressed to another party in the manner agreed in writing between them or, failing such agreement, according to the practice followed in the course of their previous dealings or in whatever manner ordered by the Arbitral Tribunal.

4.6   For the purpose of calculating a period of time under these Rules, such period shall begin to run on the day following the day when a notice or other communication is received. If the last day of such period is an official holiday or a non-business day at the residence or place of business of the addressee, the period is extended until the first business day which follows. Official holidays or non-business days occurring during the running of the period of time are included in calculating that period.

4.7   The Arbitral Tribunal may at any time extend (even where the period of time has expired) or abridge any period of time prescribed under these Rules or under the Arbitration Agreement for the conduct of the arbitration, including any notice or communication to be served by one party on any other party.

Article 5 – Formation of the Arbitral Tribunal

5.1   The expression "the Arbitral Tribunal" in these Rules includes a sole arbitrator or all the arbitrators where more than one. All references to an arbitrator shall include the masculine and feminine. (References to the President, Vice-President and members of the LCIA Court, the Registrar or deputy Registrar, expert, witness, party and legal representative shall be similarly understood).

5.2   All arbitrators conducting an arbitration under these Rules shall be and remain at all times impartial and independent of the parties; and none shall act in the arbitration as advocates for any party. No arbitrator, whether before or after appointment, shall advise any party on the merits or outcome of the dispute.

5.3   Before appointment by the LCIA Court, each arbitrator shall furnish to the Registrar a written résumé of his past and present professional positions; he shall agree in writing upon fee rates conforming to the Schedule of Costs; and he shall sign a declaration to the effect that there are no circumstances known to him likely to give rise to any justified doubts as to his impartiality or independence, other than any circumstances disclosed by him in the declaration. Each arbitrator shall thereby also assume a continuing duty forthwith to disclose any such circumstances to the LCIA Court, to any other members of the Arbitral Tribunal and to all the parties if such circumstances should arise after the date of such declaration and before the arbitration is concluded.

5.4   The LCIA Court shall appoint the Arbitral Tribunal as soon as practicable after receipt by the Registrar of the Response or after the expiry of 30 days following service of the Request upon the Respondent if no Response is received by the Registrar (or such lesser period fixed by the LCIA Court). The LCIA Court may proceed with the formation of the Arbitral Tribunal notwithstanding that the Request is incomplete or the Response is missing, late or incomplete. A sole arbitrator shall be appointed unless the parties have agreed in writing otherwise, or unless the LCIA Court determines that in view of all the circumstances of the case a three-member tribunal is appropriate.

5.5   The LCIA Court alone is empowered to appoint arbitrators. The LCIA Court will appoint arbitrators with due regard for any particular method or criteria of selection agreed in writing by the parties. In selecting arbitrators consideration will be given to the nature of the transaction, the nature and circumstances of the dispute, the nationality, location and languages of the parties and (if more than two) the number of parties.

5.6 In the case of a three-member Arbitral Tribunal, the chairman (who will not be a party-nominated arbitrator) shall be appointed by the LCIA Court.

Article 6 – Nationality of Arbitrators

6.1 Where the parties are of different nationalities, a sole arbitrator or chairman of the Arbitral Tribunal shall not have the same nationality as any party unless the parties who are not of the same nationality as the proposed appointee all agree in writing otherwise.

6.2 The nationality of parties shall be understood to include that of controlling shareholders or interests.

6.3 For the purpose of this Article, a person who is a citizen of two or more states shall be treated as a national of each state; and citizens of the European Union shall be treated as nationals of its different Member States and shall not be treated as having the same nationality.

Article 7 – Party and Other Nominations

7.1 If the parties have agreed that any arbitrator is to be appointed by one or more of them or by any third person, that agreement shall be treated as an agreement to nominate an arbitrator for all purposes. Such nominee may only be appointed by the LCIA Court as arbitrator subject to his prior compliance with Article 5.3. The LCIA Court may refuse to appoint any such nominee if it determines that he is not suitable or independent or impartial.

7.2 Where the parties have howsoever agreed that the Respondent or any third person is to nominate an arbitrator and such nomination is not made within time or at all, the LCIA Court may appoint an arbitrator notwithstanding the absence of the nomination and without regard to any late nomination. Likewise, if the Request for Arbitration does not contain a nomination by the Claimant where the parties have howsoever agreed that the Claimant or a third person is to nominate an arbitrator, the LCIA Court may appoint an arbitrator notwithstanding the absence of the nomination and without regard to any late nomination.

Article 8 – Three or More Parties

8.1 Where the Arbitration Agreement entitles each party howsoever to nominate an arbitrator, the parties to the dispute number more than two and such parties have not all agreed in writing that the disputant parties represent two separate sides for the formation of the Arbitral Tribunal as Claimant and Respondent respectively, the LCIA Court shall appoint the Arbitral Tribunal without regard to any party's nomination.

8.2 In such circumstances, the Arbitration Agreement shall be treated for all purposes as a written agreement by the parties for the appointment of the Arbitral Tribunal by the LCIA Court.

Article 9 – Expedited Formation

9.1   In exceptional urgency, on or after the commencement of the arbitration, any party may apply to the LCIA Court for the expedited formation of the Arbitral Tribunal, including the appointment of any replacement arbitrator under Articles 10 and 11 of these Rules.

9.2   Such an application shall be made in writing to the LCIA Court, copied to all other parties to the arbitration; and it shall set out the specific grounds for exceptional urgency in the formation of the Arbitral Tribunal.

9.3   The LCIA Court may, in its complete discretion, abridge or curtail any time-limit under these Rules for the formation of the Arbitral Tribunal, including service of the Response and of any matters or documents adjudged to be missing from the Request. The LCIA Court shall not be entitled to abridge or curtail any other time-limit.

Article 10 – Revocation of Arbitrator's Appointment

10.1   If either (a) any arbitrator gives written notice of his desire to resign as arbitrator to the LCIA Court, to be copied to the parties and the other arbitrators (if any) or (b) any arbitrator dies, falls seriously ill, refuses, or becomes unable or unfit to act, either upon challenge by a party or at the request of the remaining arbitrators, the LCIA Court may revoke that arbitrator's appointment and appoint another arbitrator. The LCIA Court shall decide upon the amount of fees and expenses to be paid for the former arbitrator's services (if any) as it may consider appropriate in all the circumstances.

10.2   If any arbitrator acts in deliberate violation of the Arbitration Agreement (including these Rules) or does not act fairly and impartially as between the parties or does not conduct or participate in the arbitration proceedings with reasonable diligence, avoiding unnecessary delay or expense, that arbitrator may be considered unfit in the opinion of the LCIA Court.

10.3   An arbitrator may also be challenged by any party if circumstances exist that give rise to justifiable doubts as to his impartiality or independence. A party may challenge an arbitrator it has nominated, or in whose appointment it has participated, only for reasons of which it becomes aware after the appointment has been made.

10.4   A party who intends to challenge an arbitrator shall, within 15 days of the formation of the Arbitral Tribunal or (if later) after becoming aware of any circumstances referred to in Article 10.1, 10.2 or 10.3, send a written statement of the reasons for its challenge to the LCIA Court, the Arbitral Tribunal and all other parties. Unless the challenged arbitrator withdraws or all other parties agree to the challenge within 15 days of receipt of the written statement, the LCIA Court shall decide on the challenge.

Article 11 – Nomination and Replacement of Arbitrators

11.1   In the event that the LCIA Court determines that any nominee is not suitable or independent or impartial or if an appointed arbitrator is to be replaced for any reason, the LCIA Court shall have a complete discretion to decide whether or not to follow the original nominating process.

11.2   If the LCIA Court should so decide, any opportunity given to a party to make a re-nomination shall be waived if not exercised within 15 days (or such lesser time as the LCIA Court may fix), after which the LCIA Court shall appoint the replacement arbitrator.

Article 12 – Majority Power to Continue Proceedings

12.1 If any arbitrator on a three-member Arbitral Tribunal refuses or persistently fails to participate in its deliberations, the two other arbitrators shall have the power, upon their written notice of such refusal or failure to the LCIA Court, the parties and the third arbitrator, to continue the arbitration (including the making of any decision, ruling or award), notwithstanding the absence of the third arbitrator.

12.2 In determining whether to continue the arbitration, the two other arbitrators shall take into account the stage of the arbitration, any explanation made by the third arbitrator for his non-participation and such other matters as they consider appropriate in the circumstances of the case. The reasons for such determination shall be stated in any award, order or other decision made by the two arbitrators without the participation of the third arbitrator.

12.3 In the event that the two other arbitrators determine at any time not to continue the arbitration without the participation of the third arbitrator missing from their deliberations, the two arbitrators shall notify in writing the parties and the LCIA Court of such determination; and in that event, the two arbitrators or any party may refer the matter to the LCIA Court for the revocation of that third arbitrator's appointment and his replacement under Article 10.

Article 13 – Communications between Parties and the Arbitral Tribunal

13.1 Until the Arbitral Tribunal is formed, all communications between parties and arbitrators shall be made through the Registrar.

13.2 Thereafter, unless and until the Arbitral Tribunal directs that communications shall take place directly between the Arbitral Tribunal and the parties (with simultaneous copies to the Registrar), all written communications between the parties and the Arbitral Tribunal shall continue to be made through the Registrar.

13.3 Where the Registrar sends any written communication to one party on behalf of the Arbitral Tribunal, he shall send a copy to each of the other parties. Where any party sends to the Registrar any communication (including Written Statements and Documents under Article 15), it shall include a copy for each arbitrator; and it shall also send copies direct to all other parties and confirm to the Registrar in writing that it has done or is doing so.

Article 14 – Conduct of the Proceedings

14.1 The parties may agree on the conduct of their arbitral proceedings and they are encouraged to do so, consistent with the Arbitral Tribunal's general duties at all times:
(i) to act fairly and impartially as between all parties, giving each a reasonable opportunity of putting its case and dealing with that of its opponent; and
(ii) to adopt procedures suitable to the circumstances of the arbitration, avoiding unnecessary delay or expense, so as to provide a fair and efficient means for the final resolution of the parties' dispute.
Such agreements shall be made by the parties in writing or recorded in writing by the Arbitral Tribunal at the request of and with the authority of the parties.

14.2 Unless otherwise agreed by the parties under Article 14.1, the Arbitral Tribunal shall have the widest discretion to discharge its duties allowed under such law(s) or rules of law as the Arbitral Tribunal may determine to be applicable; and at all times the parties shall do everything necessary for the fair, efficient and expeditious conduct of the arbitration.

14.3 In the case of a three-member Arbitral Tribunal the chairman may, with the prior consent of the other two arbitrators, make procedural rulings alone.

Article 15 – Submission of Written Statements and Documents

15.1 Unless the parties have agreed otherwise under Article 14.1 or the Arbitral Tribunal should determine differently, the written stage of the proceedings shall be as set out below.

15.2 Within 30 days of receipt of written notification from the Registrar of the formation of the Arbitral Tribunal, the Claimant shall send to the Registrar a Statement of Case setting out in sufficient detail the facts and any contentions of law on which it relies, together with the relief claimed against all other parties, save and insofar as such matters have not been set out in its Request.

15.3 Within 30 days of receipt of the Statement of Case or written notice from the Claimant that it elects to treat the Request as its Statement of Case, the Respondent shall send to the Registrar a Statement of Defence setting out in sufficient detail which of the facts and contentions of law in the Statement of Case or Request (as the case may be) it admits or denies and on what grounds and on what other facts and contentions of law it relies. Any counterclaims shall be submitted with the Statement of Defence in the same manner as claims are to be set out in the Statement of Case.

15.4 Within 30 days of receipt of the Statement of Defence, the Claimant shall send to the Registrar a Statement of Reply which, where there are any counterclaims, shall include a Defence to Counterclaim in the same manner as a defence is to be set out in the Statement of Defence.

15.5 If the Statement of Reply contains a Defence to Counterclaim, within 30 days of its receipt the Respondent shall send to the Registrar a Statement of Reply to Counterclaim.

15.6 All Statements referred to in this Article shall be accompanied by copies (or, if they are especially voluminous, lists) of all essential documents on which the party concerned relies and which have not previously been submitted by any party, and (where appropriate) by any relevant samples and exhibits.

15.7 As soon as practicable following receipt of the Statements specified in this Article, the Arbitral Tribunal shall proceed in such manner as has been agreed in writing by the parties or pursuant to its authority under these Rules.

15.8 If the Respondent fails to submit a Statement of Defence or the Claimant a Statement of Defence to Counterclaim, or if at any point any party fails to avail itself of the opportunity to present its case in the manner determined by Article 15.2 to 15.6 or directed by the Arbitral Tribunal, the Arbitral Tribunal may nevertheless proceed with the arbitration and make an award.

Article 16 – Seat of Arbitration and Place of Hearings

16.1 The parties may agree in writing the seat (or legal place) of their arbitration. Failing such a choice, the seat of arbitration shall be London, unless and until the LCIA Court determines in view of all the circumstances, and after having given the parties an opportunity to make written comment, that another seat is more appropriate.

16.2 The Arbitral Tribunal may hold hearings, meetings and deliberations at any convenient geographical place in its discretion; and if elsewhere than the seat of the arbitration, the arbitration shall be treated as an arbitration conducted at the seat of the arbitration and any award as an award made at the seat of the arbitration for all purposes.

16.3 The law applicable to the arbitration (if any) shall be the arbitration law of the seat of arbitration, unless and to the extent that the parties have expressly agreed in writing on the application of another arbitration law and such agreement is not prohibited by the law of the arbitral seat.

Article 17 – Language of Arbitration

17.1 The initial language of the arbitration shall be the language of the Arbitration Agreement, unless the parties have agreed in writing otherwise and providing always that a non-participating or defaulting party shall have no cause for complaint if communications to and from the Registrar and the arbitration proceedings are conducted in English.

17.2 In the event that the Arbitration Agreement is written in more than one language, the LCIA Court may, unless the Arbitration Agreement provides that the arbitration proceedings shall be conducted in more than one language, decide which of those languages shall be the initial language of the arbitration.

17.3 Upon the formation of the Arbitral Tribunal and unless the parties have agreed upon the language or languages of the arbitration, the Arbitration Tribunal shall decide upon the language(s) of the arbitration, after giving the parties an opportunity to make written comment and taking into account the initial language of the arbitration and any other matter it may consider appropriate in all the circumstances of the case.

17.4 If any document is expressed in a language other than the language(s) of the arbitration and no translation of such document is submitted by the party relying upon the document, the Arbitral Tribunal or (if the Arbitral Tribunal has not been formed) the LCIA Court may order that party to submit a translation in a form to be determined by the Arbitral Tribunal or the LCIA Court, as the case may be.

Article 18 – Party Representation

18.1 Any party may be represented by legal practitioners or any other representatives.

18.2 At any time the Arbitral Tribunal may require from any party proof of authority granted to its representative(s) in such form as the Arbitral Tribunal may determine.

Article 19 – Hearings

19.1 Any party which expresses a desire to that effect has the right to be heard orally before the Arbitral Tribunal on the merits of the dispute, unless the parties have agreed in writing on documents-only arbitration.

19.2 The Arbitral Tribunal shall fix the date, time and physical place of any meetings and hearings in the arbitration, and shall give the parties reasonable notice thereof.

19.3 The Arbitral Tribunal may in advance of any hearing submit to the parties a list of questions which it wishes them to answer with special attention.

19.4 All meetings and hearings shall be in private unless the parties agree otherwise in writing or the Arbitral Tribunal directs otherwise.

19.5 The Arbitral Tribunal shall have the fullest authority to establish time-limits for meetings and hearings, or for any parts thereof.

Article 20 – Witnesses

20.1 Before any hearing, the Arbitral Tribunal may require any party to give notice of the identity of each witness that party wishes to call (including rebuttal witnesses), as well as the subject matter of that witness's testimony, its content and its relevance to the issues in the arbitration.

20.2 The Arbitral Tribunal may also determine the time, manner and form in which such materials should be exchanged between the parties and presented to the Arbitral Tribunal; and it has a discretion to allow, refuse, or limit the appearance of witnesses (whether witness of fact or expert witness).

20.3 Subject to any order otherwise by the Arbitral Tribunal, the testimony of a witness may be presented by a party in written form, either as a signed statement or as a sworn affidavit.

20.4 Subject to Article 14.1 and 14.2, any party may request that a witness, on whose testimony another party seeks to rely, should attend for oral questioning at a hearing before the Arbitral Tribunal. If the Arbitral Tribunal orders that other party to produce the witness and the witness fails to attend the oral hearing without good cause, the Arbitral Tribunal may place such weight on the written testimony (or exclude the same altogether) as it considers appropriate in the circumstances of the case.

20.5 Any witness who gives oral evidence at a hearing before the Arbitral Tribunal may be questioned by each of the parties under the control of the Arbitral Tribunal. The Arbitral Tribunal may put questions at any stage of his evidence.

20.6 Subject to the mandatory provisions of any applicable law, it shall not be improper for any party or its legal representatives to interview any witness or potential witness for the purpose of presenting his testimony in written form or producing him as an oral witness.

20.7 Any individual intending to testify to the Arbitral Tribunal on any issue of fact or expertise shall be treated as a witness under these Rules notwithstanding that the individual is a party to the arbitration or was or is an officer, employee or shareholder of any party.

Article 21 – Experts to the Arbitral Tribunal

21.1 Unless otherwise agreed by the parties in writing, the Arbitral Tribunal:

(a) may appoint one or more experts to report to the Arbitral Tribunal on specific issues, who shall be and remain impartial and independent of the parties throughout the arbitration proceedings; and

(b) may require a party to give any such expert any relevant information or to provide access to any relevant documents, goods, samples, property or site for inspection by the expert.

21.2 Unless otherwise agreed by the parties in writing, if a party so requests or if the Arbitral Tribunal considers it necessary, the expert shall, after delivery of his written or oral report to the Arbitral Tribunal and the parties, participate in one or more hearings at which the parties shall have the opportunity to question the expert on his report and to present expert witnesses in order to testify on the points at issue.

21.3 The fees and expenses of any expert appointed by the Arbitral Tribunal under this Article shall be paid out of the deposits payable by the parties under Article 24 and shall form part of the costs of the arbitration.

Article 22 – Additional Powers of the Arbitral Tribunal

22.1 Unless the parties at any time agree otherwise in writing, the Arbitral Tribunal shall have the power, on the application of any party or of its own motion, but in either case only after giving the parties a reasonable opportunity to state their views:

(a) to allow any party, upon such terms (as to costs and otherwise) as it shall determine, to amend any claim, counterclaim, defence and reply;

(b) to extend or abbreviate any time-limit provided by the Arbitration Agreement or these Rules for the conduct of the arbitration or by the Arbitral Tribunal's own orders;

(c) to conduct such enquiries as may appear to the Arbitral Tribunal to be necessary or expedient, including whether and to what extent the Arbitral Tribunal should itself take the initiative in identifying the issues and ascertaining the relevant facts and the law(s) or rules of law applicable to the arbitration, the merits of the parties' dispute and the Arbitration Agreement;

(d) to order any party to make any property, site or thing under its control and relating to the subject matter of the arbitration available for inspection by the Arbitral Tribunal, any other party, its expert or any expert to the Arbitral Tribunal;

(e) to order any party to produce to the Arbitral Tribunal, and to the other parties for inspection, and to supply copies of, any documents or classes of documents in their possession, custody or power which the Arbitral Tribunal determines to be relevant;

(f) to decide whether or not to apply any strict rules of evidence (or any other rules) as to the admissibility, relevance or weight of any material tendered by a party on any matter of fact or expert opinion; and to determine the time, manner and form in which such material should be exchanged between the parties and presented to the Arbitral Tribunal;

(g) to order the correction of any contract between the parties or the Arbitration Agreement, but only to the extent required to rectify any mistake which the Arbitral Tribunal determines to be common to the parties and then only if and to the extent to which the law(s) or rules of law applicable to the contract or Arbitration Agreement permit such correction; and

(h) to allow, only upon the application of a party, one or more third persons to be joined in the arbitration as a party, provided any such third person and the applicant party have consented thereto in writing, and thereafter to make a single final award, or separate awards, in respect of all parties so implicated in the arbitration;

22.2 By agreeing to arbitration under these Rules, the parties shall be treated as having agreed not to apply to any state court or other judicial authority for any order available from the Arbitral Tribunal under Article 22.1, except with the agreement in writing of all parties.

22.3 The Arbitral Tribunal shall decide the parties' dispute in accordance with the law(s) or rules of law chosen by the parties as applicable to the merits of their dispute. If and to the extent that the Arbitral Tribunal determines that the parties have made no such choice, the Arbitral Tribunal shall apply the law(s) or rules of law which it considers appropriate.

22.4 The Arbitral Tribunal shall only apply to the merits of the dispute principles deriving from "ex aequo et bono", "amiable composition" or "honourable engagement" where the parties have so agreed expressly in writing.

Article 23 – Jurisdiction of the Arbitral Tribunal

23.1 The Arbitral Tribunal shall have the power to rule on its own jurisdiction, including any objection to the initial or continuing existence, validity or effectiveness of the Arbitration Agreement. For that purpose, an arbitration clause which forms or was intended to form part of another agreement shall be treated as an arbitration agreement independent of that other agreement. A decision by the Arbitral Tribunal that such other agreement is non-existent, invalid or ineffective shall not entail ipso jure the non-existence, invalidity or ineffectiveness of the arbitration clause.

23.2 A plea by a Respondent that the Arbitral Tribunal does not have jurisdiction shall be treated as having been irrevocably waived unless it is raised not later than the Statement of Defence; and a like plea by a Respondent to Counterclaim shall be similarly treated unless it is raised no later than the Statement of Defence to Counterclaim. A plea that the Arbitral Tribunal is exceeding the scope of its authority shall be raised promptly after the Arbitral Tribunal has indicated its intention to decide on the matter alleged by any party to be beyond the scope of its authority, failing which such plea shall also be treated as having been waived irrevocably. In any case, the Arbitral Tribunal may nevertheless admit an untimely plea if it considers the delay justified in the particular circumstances.

23.3 The Arbitral Tribunal may determine the plea to its jurisdiction or authority in an award as to jurisdiction or later in an award on the merits, as it considers appropriate in the circumstances.

23.4 By agreeing to arbitration under these Rules, the parties shall be treated as having agreed not to apply to any state court or other judicial authority for any relief regarding the Arbitral Tribunal's jurisdiction or authority, except with the agreement in writing of all parties to the arbitration or the prior authorisation of the Arbitral Tribunal or following the latter's award ruling on the objection to its jurisdiction or authority.

Article 24 – Deposits

24.1 The LCIA Court may direct the parties, in such proportions as it thinks appropriate, to make one or several interim or final payments on account of the costs of the arbitration. Such deposits shall be made to and held by the LCIA and from time to time may be released by the LCIA Court to the arbitrator(s), any expert appointed by the Arbitral Tribunal and the LCIA itself as the arbitration progresses.

24.2 The Arbitral Tribunal shall not proceed with the arbitration without ascertaining at all times from the Registrar or any deputy Registrar that the LCIA is in requisite funds.

24.3 In the event that a party fails or refuses to provide any deposit as directed by the LCIA Court, the LCIA Court may direct the other party or parties to effect a substitute payment to allow the arbitration to proceed (subject to any award on costs). In such circumstances, the party paying the substitute payment shall be entitled to recover that amount as a debt immediately due from the defaulting party.

24.4 Failure by a claimant or counterclaiming party to provide promptly and in full the required deposit may be treated by the LCIA Court and the Arbitral Tribunal as a withdrawal of the claim or counterclaim respectively.

Article 25 – Interim and Conservatory Measures

25.1 The Arbitral Tribunal shall have the power, unless otherwise agreed by the parties in writing, on the application of any party:

(a) to order any respondent party to a claim or counterclaim to provide security for all or part of the amount in dispute, by way of deposit or bank guarantee or in any other manner and upon such terms as the Arbitral Tribunal considers appropriate. Such terms may include the provision by the claiming or counterclaiming party of a cross-indemnity, itself secured in such manner as the Arbitral Tribunal considers appropriate, for any costs or losses incurred by such respondent in providing security. The amount of any costs and losses payable under such cross-indemnity may be determined by the Arbitral Tribunal in one or more awards;

(b) to order the preservation, storage, sale or other disposal of any property or thing under the control of any party and relating to the subject matter of the arbitration; and

(c) to order on a provisional basis, subject to final determination in an award, any relief which the Arbitral Tribunal would have power to grant in an award, including a provisional order for the payment of money or the disposition of property as between any parties.

25.2 The Arbitral Tribunal shall have the power, upon the application of a party, to order any claiming or counterclaiming party to provide security for the legal or other costs of any other party by way of deposit or bank guarantee or in any other manner and upon such terms as the Arbitral Tribunal considers appropriate. Such terms may include the provision by that other party of a cross-indemnity, itself secured in such manner as the Arbitral Tribunal considers appropriate, for any costs and losses incurred by such claimant or counterclaimant in providing security. The amount of any costs and losses payable under such cross-indemnity may be determined by the Arbitral Tribunal in one or more awards. In the event that a claiming or counterclaiming party does not comply with any order to provide security, the Arbitral Tribunal may stay that party's claims or counterclaims or dismiss them in an award.

25.3 The power of the Arbitral Tribunal under Article 25.1 shall not prejudice howsoever any party's right to apply to any state court or other judicial authority for interim or conservatory measures before the formation of the Arbitral Tribunal and, in exceptional cases, thereafter. Any application and any order for such measures after the formation of the Arbitral Tribunal shall be promptly communicated by the applicant to the Arbitral Tribunal and all other parties. However, by agreeing to arbitration under these Rules, the parties shall be taken to have agreed not to apply to any state court or other judicial authority for any order for security for its legal or other costs available from the Arbitral Tribunal under Article 25.2.

Article 26 – The Award

26.1 The Arbitral Tribunal shall make its award in writing and, unless all parties agree in writing otherwise, shall state the reasons upon which its award is based. The award shall also state the date when the award is made and the seat of the arbitration; and it shall be signed by the Arbitral Tribunal or those of its members assenting to it.

26.2 If any arbitrator fails to comply with the mandatory provisions of any applicable law relating to the making of the award, having been given a reasonable opportunity to do so, the remaining arbitrators may proceed in his absence and state in their award the circumstances of the other arbitrator's failure to participate in the making of the award.

26.3 Where there are three arbitrators and the Arbitral Tribunal fails to agree on any issue, the arbitrators shall decide that issue by a majority. Failing a majority decision on any issue, the chairman of the Arbitral Tribunal shall decide that issue.

26.4 If any arbitrator refuses or fails to sign the award, the signatures of the majority or (failing a majority) of the chairman shall be sufficient, provided that the reason for the omitted signature is stated in the award by the majority or chairman.

26.5 The sole arbitrator or chairman shall be responsible for delivering the award to the LCIA Court, which shall transmit certified copies to the parties provided that the costs of arbitration have been paid to the LCIA in accordance with Article 28.

26.6 An award may be expressed in any currency. The Arbitral Tribunal may order that simple or compound interest shall be paid by any party on any sum awarded at such rates as the Arbitral Tribunal determines to be appropriate, without being bound by legal rates of interest imposed by any state court, in respect of any period which the Arbitral Tribunal determines to be appropriate ending not later than the date upon which the award is complied with.

26.7 The Arbitral Tribunal may make separate awards on different issues at different times. Such awards shall have the same status and effect as any other award made by the Arbitral Tribunal.

26.8 In the event of a settlement of the parties' dispute, the Arbitral Tribunal may render an award recording the settlement if the parties so request in writing ("a Consent Award"), provided always that such award contains an express statement that it is an award made by the parties' consent. A Consent Award need not contain reasons. If the parties do not require a Consent Award, then on written confirmation by the parties to the LCIA Court that a settlement has been reached, the Arbitral Tribunal shall be discharged and the arbitration proceedings concluded, subject to payment by the parties of any outstanding costs of the arbitration under Article 28.

26.9 All awards shall be final and binding on the parties. By agreeing to arbitration under these Rules, the parties undertake to carry out any award immediately and without any delay (subject only to Article 27); and the parties also waive irrevocably their right to any form of appeal, review or recourse to any state court or other judicial authority, insofar as such waiver may be validly made.

Article 27 – Correction of Awards and Additional Awards

27.1 Within 30 days of receipt of any award, or such lesser period as may be agreed in writing by the parties, a party may by written notice to the Registrar (copied to all other parties) request the Arbitral Tribunal to correct in the award any errors in computation, clerical or typographical errors or any errors of a similar nature. If the Arbitral Tribunal considers the request to be justified, it shall make the corrections within 30 days of receipt of the request. Any correction shall take the form of separate memorandum dated and signed by the Arbitral Tribunal or (if three arbitrators) those of its members assenting to it; and such memorandum shall become part of the award for all purposes.

27.2 The Arbitral Tribunal may likewise correct any error of the nature described in Article 27.1 on its own initiative within 30 days of the date of the award, to the same effect.

27.3 Within 30 days of receipt of the final award, a party may by written notice to the Registrar (copied to all other parties), request the Arbitral Tribunal to make an additional award as to claims or counterclaims presented in the arbitration but not determined in any award. If the Arbitral Tribunal considers the request to be justified, it shall make the additional award within 60 days of receipt of the request. The provisions of Article 26 shall apply to any additional award.

Article 28 – Arbitration and Legal Costs

28.1 The costs of the arbitration (other than the legal or other costs incurred by the parties themselves) shall be determined by the LCIA Court in accordance with the Schedule of Costs. The parties shall be jointly and severally liable to the Arbitral Tribunal and the LCIA for such arbitration costs.

28.2 The Arbitral Tribunal shall specify in the award the total amount of the costs of the arbitration as determined by the LCIA Court. Unless the parties agree otherwise in writing, the Arbitral Tribunal shall determine the proportions in which the parties shall bear all or part of such arbitration costs. If the Arbitral Tribunal has determined that all or any part of the arbitration costs shall be borne by a party other than a party which has already paid them to the LCIA, the latter party shall have the right to recover the appropriate amount from the former party.

28.3 The Arbitral Tribunal shall also have the power to order in its award that all or part of the legal or other costs incurred by a party be paid by another party, unless the parties agree otherwise in writing. The Arbitral Tribunal shall determine and fix the amount of each item comprising such costs on such reasonable basis as it thinks fit.

28.4 Unless the parties otherwise agree in writing, the Arbitral Tribunal shall make its orders on both arbitration and legal costs on the general principle that costs should reflect the parties' relative success and failure in the award or arbitration, except where it appears to the Arbitral Tribunal that in the particular circumstances this general approach is inappropriate. Any order for costs shall be made with reasons in the award containing such order.

28.5 If the arbitration is abandoned, suspended or concluded, by agreement or otherwise, before the final award is made, the parties shall remain jointly and severally liable to pay to the LCIA and the Arbitral Tribunal the costs of the arbitration as determined by the LCIA Court in accordance with the Schedule of Costs. In the event that such arbitration costs are less than the deposits made by the parties, there shall be a refund by the LCIA in such proportions as the parties may agree in writing, or failing such agreement, in the same proportions as the deposits were made by the parties to the LCIA.

Article 29 – Decisions by the LCIA Court

29.1 The decisions of the LCIA Court with respect to all matters relating to the arbitration shall be conclusive and binding upon the parties and the Arbitral Tribunal. Such decisions are to be treated as administrative in nature and the LCIA Court shall not be required to give any reasons.

29.2 To the extent permitted by the law of the seat of the arbitration, the parties shall be taken to have waived any right of appeal or review in respect of any such decisions of the LCIA Court to any state court or other judicial authority. If such appeals or review remain possible due to mandatory provisions of any applicable law, the LCIA Court shall, subject to the provisions of that applicable law, decide whether the arbitral proceedings are to continue, notwithstanding an appeal or review.

Article 30 – Confidentiality

30.1 Unless the parties expressly agree in writing to the contrary, the parties undertake as a general principle to keep confidential all awards in their arbitration, together with all materials in the proceedings created for the purpose of the arbitration and all other documents produced by another party in the proceedings not otherwise in the public domain - save and to the extent that disclosure may be required of a party by legal duty, to protect or pursue a legal right or to enforce or challenge an award in bona fide legal proceedings before a state court or other judicial authority.

30.2 The deliberations of the Arbitral Tribunal are likewise confidential to its members, save and to the extent that disclosure of an arbitrator's refusal to participate in the arbitration is required of the other members of the Arbitral Tribunal under Articles 10, 12 and 26.

30.3 The LCIA Court does not publish any award or any part of an award without the prior written consent of all parties and the Arbitral Tribunal.

Article 31 – Exclusion of Liability

31.1 None of the LCIA, the LCIA Court (including its President, Vice-Presidents and individual members), the Registrar, any deputy Registrar, any arbitrator and any expert to the Arbitral Tribunal shall be liable to any party howsoever for any act or omission in connection with any arbitration conducted by reference to these Rules, save where the act or omission is shown by that party to constitute conscious and deliberate wrongdoing committed by the body or person alleged to be liable to that party.

31.2 After the award has been made and the possibilities of correction and additional awards referred to in Article 27 have lapsed or been exhausted, neither the LCIA, the LCIA Court (including its President, Vice-Presidents and individual members), the Registrar, any deputy Registrar, any arbitrator or expert to the Arbitral Tribunal shall be under any legal obligation to make any statement to any person about any matter concerning the arbitration, nor shall any party seek to make any of these persons a witness in any legal or other proceedings arising out of the arbitration.

Article 32 – General Rules

32.1 A party who knows that any provision of the Arbitration Agreement (including these Rules) has not been complied with and yet proceeds with the arbitration without promptly stating its objection to such non-compliance, shall be treated as having irrevocably waived its right to object.

32.2 In all matters not expressly provided for in these Rules, the LCIA Court, the Arbitral Tribunal and the parties shall act in the spirit of these Rules and shall make every reasonable effort to ensure that an award is legally enforceable.

**THE LCIA
SCHEDULE OF FEES AND COSTS
(effective 1 January 1998)**

for arbitrations under the LCIA Rules; under UNCITRAL Rules when administered by the LCIA; when the LCIA acts as Appointing Authority only; and when the LCIA is appointed to decide challenges.

1.   Administrative Charges under LCIA and UNCITRAL Rules

1(a)   Registration Fee (payable in advance with
            Request for Arbitration
            non-refundable).   £1,500

1(b)   5% applied to the fees of the Tribunal
            (excluding expenses).*

1(c)   Time spent** by the Registrar and his/her deputy,
            and by the Secretariat of the LCIA in the
            administration of the arbitration.*

            Registrar and his/her deputy   £150
                                                                per hour

            Secretariat   £75
                                                                per hour

1(d)   Expenses incurred by the Secretariat in connection   at applic-
            with the arbitration (such as postage, telephone,   able hourly
            facsimile, travel etc.), and additional arbitration   rates or
            support services, whether provided by the Secretariat at cost
            from its own resources or otherwise.*

---

*   Items 1(b), 1(c), and 1(d) above, are payable on interim
    invoice; with the award, or as directed by the LCIA Court
    under Article 24.1 of the Rules.

** Minimum unit of time in all cases: 15 minutes.

2.   **Request to Act as Appointing Authority
            only**

2(a)   Appointment Fee (payable in advance with request -
            non-refundable)   £1,000

2(b)   As for 1(c) and 1(d), above.

3.   **Request to Act in Deciding Challenges
            to Arbitrators in non-LCIA
            arbitrations.**

3(a)   As for 2(a) and 2(b), above; plus

3(b)   Time spent by members of the LCIA Court in   At hourly rates
            carrying out their functions in deciding challenges.   advised by
                                                          members of the
                                                          LCIA Court

4.   **Fees and Expenses of the Tribunal**

4(a)   The Tribunal's fees will be calculated by reference
            to work done by its members in connection with the
            arbitration and will be charged at rates appropriate to
            the particular circumstances of the case, including its
            complexity and the special qualifications of the
            arbitrators. The Tribunal shall agree in writing upon
            fee rates conforming to this Schedule of Fees and
            Costs prior to its appointment by the LCIA Court.
            The rates will be advised by the Registrar to the
            parties at the time of the appointment of the
            Tribunal, but may be reviewed annually if the
            duration of the arbitration requires.

The fee rates shall be within the following bands:	£800 to £2,000 per normal working day
	and
	£100 to £250 per hour for periods less than or in addition to a normal working day

However, in exceptional cases, the rates may be higher or lower, provided that, in such cases, (a) the fees of the Tribunal shall be fixed by the LCIA Court on the recommendation of the Registrar, following consultations with the arbitrator(s), and (b) the fees shall be agreed expressly by all parties.

4(b)   The Tribunal's fees may include a charge for time spent travelling.

4(c)   The Tribunal's fees may also include a charge for time reserved but not used as a result of late postponement or cancellation, provided that the basis for such charge shall be advised in writing to, and approved by, the LCIA Court.

4(d)   Expenses incurred by the Tribunal in connection with the arbitration will be charged at cost.

4(e)   In the event of the revocation of the appointment of any arbitrator, pursuant to the provisions of Article 10 of the LCIA Rules, the LCIA Court shall decide upon the amount of fees and expenses to be paid for the former arbitrator's services (if any) as it may consider appropriate in all circumstances.

5.   **Deposits**

5(a)   The LCIA Court may direct the parties, in such proportions as it thinks appropriate, to make one or several interim or final payments on account of the costs of the arbitration. The LCIA Court may limit such payments to a sum sufficient to cover fees, expenses and costs for the next stage of the arbitration.

5(b)   The Tribunal shall not proceed with the arbitration without ascertaining at all times from the Registrar or any deputy Registrar that the LCIA is in requisite funds.

5(c)   In the event that a party fails or refuses to provide any deposit as directed by the LCIA Court, the LCIA Court may direct the other party or parties to effect a substitute payment to allow the arbitration to proceed (subject to any award on costs). In such circumstances, the party paying the substitute payment shall be entitled to recover that amount as a debt immediately due from the defaulting party.

5(d)   Failure by a claimant or counterclaiming party to provide promptly and in full the required deposit may be treated by the LCIA Court and the Arbitral Tribunal as a withdrawal of the claim or counterclaim respectively.

6.   **Interest on Deposits**

Interest on sums deposited shall be credited to the benefit of the parties depositing them, at a rate applicable to the amount of the deposit, as advised by the LCIA's bank from time to time.

7.   **Interim Payments**

7(a)   When interim payments are required to cover the
          LCIA's administrative costs or the Tribunal's fees or
          expenses, including the fees or expenses of any
          expert appointed by the Tribunal, such payments
          may be made out of deposits held, upon the approval
          of the LCIA Court.

7(b)   The LCIA may, in any event, submit interim invoices
          in respect of all current arbitrations, in March, June,
          September and December of each year, for payment
          direct by the parties or from funds held on deposit.

8.   **Notes**

8(a)   The costs of the arbitration (other than the legal or
          other costs incurred by the parties themselves) shall
          be determined by the LCIA Court in accordance with
          the Schedule of Fees and Costs.

8(b)   The parties shall be jointly and severally liable to the
          Arbitral Tribunal and the LCIA for such arbitration
          costs, until all such costs have been paid in full.

8(c)   The Tribunal's Award(s) shall not be transmitted to
          the parties unless and until the costs of the
          arbitration have been fully paid to date.

8(d)   Value Added Tax will be added to all charges at the
          appropriate rate.

8(e)   The LCIA's fees and expenses will be invoiced in
          sterling but may be paid in other convertible
          currencies at rates prevailing at the time of payment,
          provided that any transfer and/or currency exchange
          charges shall be borne by the payer.

8(f)   The Tribunal's fees may be invoiced either in the currency of account between the Tribunal and the parties or in sterling; the Tribunal's expenses may be invoiced in the currency in which they were incurred, or in sterling.

8(g)   The rates quoted in this Schedule may be reviewed from time to time.

8(h)   Any dispute regarding administration costs or the fees and expenses of the Tribunal shall be determined by the LCIA Court.

UNCITRAL ARBITRATION RULES

RESOLUTION 31/98 ADOPTED BY THE GENERAL ASSEMBLY ON 15 DECEMBER 1976

31/98. Arbitration Rules of the United Nations Commission on International Trade Law

The General Assembly,

Recognizing the value of arbitration as a method of settling disputes arising in the context of international commercial relations,

Being convinced that the establishment of rules for *ad hoc* arbitration that are acceptable in countries with different legal, social and economic systems would significantly contribute to the development of harmonious international economic relations,

Bearing in mind that the Arbitration Rules of the United Nations Commission on International Trade Law have been prepared after extensive consultation with arbitral institutions and centres of international commercial arbitration,

Noting that the Arbitration Rules were adopted by the United Nations Commission on International Trade Law at its ninth session* after due deliberation,

1. *Recommends* the use of the Arbitration Rules of the United Nations Commission on International Trade Law in the settlement of disputes arising in the context of international commercial relations, particularly by reference to the Arbitration Rules in commercial contracts;

2. *Requests* the Secretary-General to arrange for the widest possible distribution of the Arbitration Rules.

---

* *Official Records of the General Assembly, Thirty-first Session, Supplement No. 17* (A/31/17), chap. V, sect. C.

UNCITRAL ARBITRATION RULES

SECTION I. INTRODUCTORY RULES

SCOPE OF APPLICATION

Article 1

1. Where the parties to a contract have agreed in writing* that disputes in relation to that contract shall be referred to arbitration under the UNCITRAL Arbitration Rules, then such disputes shall be settled in accordance with these Rules subject to such modification as the parties may agree in writing.

2. These Rules shall govern the arbitration except that where any of these Rules is in conflict with a provision of the law applicable to the arbitration from which the parties cannot derogate, that provision shall prevail.

NOTICE, CALCULATION OF PERIODS OF TIME

Article 2

1. For the purposes of these Rules, any notice, including a notification, communication or proposal, is deemed to have been received if it is physically delivered to the addressee or if it is delivered at his habitual residence, place of business or mailing address, or, if none of these can be found after making reasonable inquiry, then at the addressee's last-known residence or place of business. Notice shall be deemed to have been received on the day it is so delivered.

2. For the purposes of calculating a period of time under these Rules, such period shall begin to run on the day following the day when a notice, notification, communication or proposal is received. If the last day of such period is an official holiday or a non-business day at the residence or place of business of the addressee, the period is extended until the first business day which follows. Official holidays or non-business days occurring during the running of the period of time are included in calculating the period.

---

* MODEL ARBITRATION CLAUSE
Any dispute, controversy or claim arising out of or relating to this contract, or the breach, termination or invalidity thereof, shall be settled by arbitration in accordance with the UNCITRAL Arbitration Rules as at present in force.
Note: Parties may wish to consider adding:
(a) The appointing authority shall be . . . (name of institution or person);
(b) The number of arbitrators shall be . . . (one or three);
(c) The place of arbitration shall be . . . (town or country);
(d) The language(s) to be used in the arbitral proceedings shall be . . .

NOTICE OF ARBITRATION

Article 3

1. The party initiating recourse to arbitration (hereinafter called the "claimant") shall give to the other party (hereinafter called the "respondent") a notice of arbitration.
2. Arbitral proceedings shall be deemed to commence on the date on which the notice of arbitration is received by the respondent.
3. The notice of arbitration shall include the following:
   (a) A demand that the dispute be referred to arbitration;
   (b) The names and addresses of the parties;
   (c) A reference to the arbitration clause or the separate arbitration agreement that is invoked;
   (d) A reference to the contract out of or in relation to which the dispute arises;
   (e) The general nature of the claim and an indication of the amount involved, if any;
   (f) The relief or remedy sought;
   (g) A proposal as to the number of arbitrators (i.e. one or three), if the parties have not previously agreed thereon.
4. The notice of arbitration may also include:
   (a) The proposals for the appointments of a sole arbitrator and an appointing authority referred to in article 6, paragraph 1;
   (b) The notification of the appointment of an arbitrator referred to in article 7;
   (c) The statement of claim referred to in article 18.

REPRESENTATION AND ASSISTANCE

Article 4

The parties may be represented or assisted by persons of their choice. The names and addresses of such persons must be communicated in writing to the other party; such communication must specify whether the appointment is being made for purposes of representation or assistance.

SECTION II. COMPOSITION OF THE ARBITRAL TRIBUNAL

NUMBER OF ARBITRATORS

Article 5

If the parties have not previously agreed on the number of arbitrators (i.e. one or three), and if within fifteen days after the receipt by the respondent of the notice of arbitration the parties have not agreed that there shall be only one arbitrator, three arbitrators shall be appointed.

APPOINTMENT OF ARBITRATORS (ARTICLES 6 TO 8)

Article 6

1. If a sole arbitrator is to be appointed, either party may propose to the other:
   - *(a)* The names of one or more persons, one of whom would serve as the sole arbitrator; and
   - *(b)* If no appointing authority has been agreed upon by the parties, the name or names of one or more institutions or persons, one of whom would serve as appointing authority.
2. If within thirty days after receipt by a party of a proposal made in accordance with paragraph 1 the parties have not reached agreement on the choice of a sole arbitrator, the sole arbitrator shall be appointed by the appointing authority agreed upon by the parties. If no appointing authority has been agreed upon by the parties, or if the appointing authority agreed upon refuses to act or fails to appoint the arbitrator within sixty days of the receipt of a party's request therefor, either party may request the Secretary-General of the Permanent Court of Arbitration at The Hague to designate an appointing authority.
3. The appointing authority shall, at the request of one of the parties, appoint the sole arbitrator as promptly as possible. In making the appointment the appointing authority shall use the following list-procedure, unless both parties agree that the list-procedure should not be used or unless the appointing authority determines in its discretion that the use of the list-procedure is not appropriate for the case:
   - *(a)* At the request of one of the parties the appointing authority shall communicate to both parties an identical list containing at least three names;
   - *(b)* Within fifteen days after the receipt of this list, each party may return the list to the appointing authority after having deleted the name or names to which he objects and numbered the remaining names on the list in the order of his preference;
   - *(c)* After the expiration of the above period of time the appointing authority shall appoint the sole arbitrator from among the names approved on the lists returned to it and in accordance with the order of preference indicated by the parties;
   - *(d)* If for any reason the appointment cannot be made according to this procedure, the appointing authority may exercise its discretion in appointing the sole arbitrator.
4. In making the appointment, the appointing authority shall have regard to such considerations as are likely to secure the appointment of an independent and impartial arbitrator and shall take into account as well the advisability of appointing an arbitrator of a nationality other than the nationalities of the parties.

Article 7

1. If three arbitrators are to be appointed, each party shall appoint one arbitrator. The two arbitrators thus appointed shall choose the third arbitrator who will act as the presiding arbitrator of the tribunal.
2. If within thirty days after the receipt of a party's notification of the appointment of an arbitrator the other party has not notified the first party of the arbitrator he has appointed:

(a) The first party may request the appointing authority previously designated by the parties to appoint the second arbitrator; or

(b) If no such authority has been previously designated by the parties, or if the appointing authority previously designated refuses to act or fails to appoint the arbitrator within thirty days after receipt of a party's request therefor, the first party may request the Secretary-General of the Permanent Court of Arbitration at The Hague to designate the appointing authority. The first party may then request the appointing authority so designated to appoint the second arbitrator. In either case, the appointing authority may exercise its discretion in appointing the arbitrator.

3. If within thirty days after the appointment of the second arbitrator the two arbitrators have not agreed on the choice of the presiding arbitrator, the presiding arbitrator shall be appointed by an appointing authority in the same way as a sole arbitrator would be appointed under article 6.

Article 8

1. When an appointing authority is requested to appoint an arbitrator pursuant to article 6 or article 7, the party which makes the request shall send to the appointing authority a copy of the notice of arbitration, a copy of the contract out of or in relation to which the dispute has arisen and a copy of the arbitration agreement if it is not contained in the contract. The appointing authority may require from either party such information as it deems necessary to fulfil its function.

2. Where the names of one or more persons are proposed for appointment as arbitrators, their full names, addresses and nationalities shall be indicated, together with a description of their qualifications.

CHALLENGE OF ARBITRATORS (ARTICLES 9 TO 12)

Article 9

A prospective arbitrator shall disclose to those who approach him in connexion with his possible appointment any circumstances likely to give rise to justifiable doubts as to his impartiality or independence. An arbitrator, once appointed or chosen, shall disclose such circumstances to the parties unless they have already been informed by him of these circumstances.

Article 10

1. Any arbitrator may be challenged if circumstances exist that give rise to justifiable doubts as to the arbitrator's impartiality or independence.

2. A party may challenge the arbitrator appointed by him only for reasons of which he becomes aware after the appointment has been made.

Article 11

1. A party who intends to challenge an arbitrator shall send notice of his challenge within fifteen days after the appointment of the challenged arbitrator has been notified to the challenging party or within fifteen days after the circumstances mentioned in articles 9 and 10 became known to that party.

2. The challenge shall be notified to the other party, to the arbitrator who is challenged and to the other members of the arbitral tribunal. The notification shall be in writing and shall state the reasons for the challenge.

3. When an arbitrator has been challenged by one party, the other party may agree to the challenge. The arbitrator may also, after the challenge, withdraw from his office. In neither case does this imply acceptance of the validity of the grounds for the challenge. In both cases the procedure provided in article 6 or 7 shall be used in full for the appointment of the substitute arbitrator, even if during the process of appointing the challenged arbitrator a party had failed to exercise his right to appoint or to participate in the appointment.

Article 12

1. If the other party does not agree to the challenge and the challenged arbitrator does not withdraw, the decision on the challenge will be made:
   (a) When the initial appointment was made by an appointing authority, by that authority;
   (b) When the initial appointment was not made by an appointing authority, but an appointing authority has been previously designated, by that authority;
   (c) In all other cases, by the appointing authority to be designated in accordance with the procedure for designating an appointing authority as provided for in article 6.

2. If the appointing authority sustains the challenge, a substitute arbitrator shall be appointed or chosen pursuant to the procedure applicable to the appointment or choice of an arbitrator as provided in articles 6 to 9 except that, when this procedure would call for the designation of an appointing authority, the appointment of the arbitrator shall be made by the appointing authority which decided on the challenge.

REPLACEMENT OF AN ARBITRATOR

Article 13

1. In the event of the death or resignation of an arbitrator during the course of the arbitral proceedings, a substitute arbitrator shall be appointed or chosen pursuant to the procedure provided for in articles 6 to 9 that was applicable to the appointment or choice of the arbitrator being replaced.

2. In the event that an arbitrator fails to act or in the event of the *de jure* or *de facto* impossibility of his performing his functions, the procedure in respect of the challenge and replacement of an arbitrator as provided in the preceding articles shall apply.

REPETITION OF HEARINGS IN THE EVENT OF THE REPLACEMENT OF AN ARBITRATOR

Article 14

If under articles 11 to 13 the sole or presiding arbitrator is replaced, any hearings held previously shall be repeated; if any other arbitrator is replaced, such prior hearings may be repeated at the discretion of the arbitral tribunal.

SECTION III. ARBITRAL PROCEEDINGS

GENERAL PROVISIONS

Article 15

1. Subject to these Rules, the arbitral tribunal may conduct the arbitration in such manner as it considers appropriate, provided that the parties are treated with equality and that at any stage of the proceedings each party is given a full opportunity of presenting his case.
2. If either party so requests at any stage of the proceedings, the arbitral tribunal shall hold hearings for the presentation of evidence by witnesses, including expert witnesses, or for oral argument. In the absence of such a request, the arbitral tribunal shall decide whether to hold such hearings or whether the proceedings shall be conducted on the basis of documents and other materials.
3. All documents or information supplied to the arbitral tribunal by one party shall at the same time be communicated by that party to the other party.

PLACE OF ARBITRATION

Article 16

1. Unless the parties have agreed upon the place where the arbitration is to be held, such place shall be determined by the arbitral tribunal, having regard to the circumstances of the arbitration.
2. The arbitral tribunal may determine the locale of the arbitration within the country agreed upon by the parties. It may hear witnesses and hold meetings for consultation among its members at any place it deems appropriate, having regard to the circumstances of the arbitration.
3. The arbitral tribunal may meet at any place it deems appropriate for the inspection of goods, other property or documents. The parties shall be given sufficient notice to enable them to be present at such inspection.
4. The award shall be made at the place of arbitration.

LANGUAGE

Article 17

1. Subject to an agreement by the parties, the arbitral tribunal shall, promptly after its appointment, determine the language or languages to be used in the proceedings. This determination shall apply to the statement of claim, the statement of defence, and any further written statements and, if oral hearings take place, to the language or languages to be used in such hearings.
2. The arbitral tribunal may order that any documents annexed to the statement of claim or statement of defence, and any supplementary documents or exhibits submitted in the course of the proceedings, delivered in their original language, shall be accompanied by a translation into the language or languages agreed upon by the parties or determined by the arbitral tribunal.

STATEMENT OF CLAIM

Article 18

1. Unless the statement of claim was contained in the notice of arbitration, within a period of time to be determined by the arbitral tribunal, the claimant shall communicate his statement of claim in writing to the respondent and to each of the arbitrators. A copy of the contract, and of the arbitration agreement if not contained in the contract, shall be annexed thereto.
2. The statement of claim shall include the following particulars:
   (a) The names and addresses of the parties;
   (b) A statement of the facts supporting the claim;
   (c) The points at issue;
   (d) The relief or remedy sought.
   The claimant may annex to his statement of claim all documents he deems relevant or may add a reference to the documents or other evidence he will submit.

STATEMENT OF DEFENCE

Article 19

1. Within a period of time to be determined by the arbitral tribunal, the respondent shall communicate his statement of defence in writing to the claimant and to each of the arbitrators.
2. The statement of defence shall reply to the particulars (b), (c) and (d) of the statement of claim (article 18, para. 2). The respondent may annex to his statement the documents on which he relies for his defence or may add a reference to the documents or other evidence he will submit.
3. In his statement of defence, or at a later stage in the arbitral proceedings if the arbitral tribunal decides that the delay was justified under the circumstances, the respondent may make a counter-claim arising out of the same contract or rely on a claim arising out of the same contract for the purpose of a set-off.
4. The provisions of article 18, paragraph 2, shall apply to a counter-claim and a claim relied on for the purpose of a set-off.

AMENDMENTS TO THE CLAIM OR DEFENCE

Article 20

During the course of the arbitral proceedings either party may amend or supplement his claim or defence unless the arbitral tribunal considers it inappropriate to allow such amendment having regard to the delay in making it or prejudice to the other party or any other circumstances. However, a claim may not be amended in such a manner that the amended claim falls outside the scope of the arbitration clause or separate arbitration agreement.

PLEAS AS TO THE JURISDICTION OF THE ARBITRAL TRIBUNAL

Article 21

1. The arbitral tribunal shall have the power to rule on objections that it has no jurisdiction, including any objections with respect to the existence or validity of the arbitration clause or of the separate arbitration agreement.
2. The arbitral tribunal shall have the power to determine the existence or the validity of the contract of which an arbitration clause forms a part. For the purposes of article 21, an arbitration clause which forms part of a contract and which provides for arbitration under these Rules shall be treated as an agreement independent of the other terms of the contract. A decision by the arbitral tribunal that the contract is null and void shall not entail *ipso jure* the invalidity of the arbitration clause.
3. A plea that the arbitral tribunal does not have jurisdiction shall be raised not later than in the statement of defence or, with respect to a counter-claim, in the reply to the counter-claim.
4. In general, the arbitral tribunal should rule on a plea concerning its jurisdiction as a preliminary question. However, the arbitral tribunal may proceed with the arbitration and rule on such a plea in their final award.

FURTHER WRITTEN STATEMENTS

Article 22

The arbitral tribunal shall decide which further written statements, in addition to the statement of claim and the statement of defence, shall be required from the parties or may be presented by them and shall fix the periods of time for communicating such statements.

PERIODS OF TIME

Article 23

The periods of time fixed by the arbitral tribunal for the communication of written statements (including the statement of claim and statement of defence) should not exceed forty-five days. However, the arbitral tribunal may extend the time-limits if it concludes that an extension is justified.

EVIDENCE AND HEARINGS (ARTICLES 24 AND 25)

Article 24

1. Each party shall have the burden of proving the facts relied on to support his claim or defence.
2. The arbitral tribunal may, if it considers it appropriate, require a party to deliver to the tribunal and to the other party, within such a period of time as the arbitral tribunal shall decide, a summary of the documents and other evidence which that party intends to present in support of the facts in issue set out in his statement of claim or statement of defence.

3. At any time during the arbitral proceedings the arbitral tribunal may require the parties to produce documents, exhibits or other evidence within such a period of time as the tribunal shall determine.

Article 25

1. In the event of an oral hearing, the arbitral tribunal shall give the parties adequate advance notice of the date, time and place thereof.
2. If witnesses are to be heard, at least fifteen days before the hearing each party shall communicate to the arbitral tribunal and to the other party the names and addresses of the witnesses he intends to present, the subject upon and the languages in which such witnesses will give their testimony.
3. The arbitral tribunal shall make arrangements for the translation of oral statements made at a hearing and for a record of the hearing if either is deemed necessary by the tribunal under the circumstances of the case, or if the parties have agreed thereto and have communicated such agreement to the tribunal at least fifteen days before the hearing.
4. Hearings shall be held *in camera* unless the parties agree otherwise. The arbitral tribunal may require the retirement of any witness or witnesses during the testimony of other witnesses. The arbitral tribunal is free to determine the manner in which witnesses are examined.
5. Evidence of witnesses may also be presented in the form of written statements signed by them.
6. The arbitral tribunal shall determine the admissibility, relevance, materiality and weight of the evidence offered.

INTERIM MEASURES OF PROTECTION

Article 26

1. At the request of either party, the arbitral tribunal may take any interim measures it deems necessary in respect of the subject-matter of the dispute, including measures for the conservation of the goods forming the subject-matter in dispute, such as ordering their deposit with a third person or the sale of perishable goods.
2. Such interim measures may be established in the form of an interim award. The arbitral tribunal shall be entitled to require security for the costs of such measures.
3. A request for interim measures addressed by any party to a judicial authority shall not be deemed incompatible with the agreement to arbitrate, or as a waiver of that agreement.

EXPERTS

Article 27

1. The arbitral tribunal may appoint one or more experts to report to it, in writing, on specific issues to be determined by the tribunal. A copy of the expert's terms of reference, established by the arbitral tribunal, shall be communicated to the parties.
2. The parties shall give the expert any relevant information or produce for his inspection any relevant documents or goods that he may require of them. Any dispute between a

party and such expert as to the relevance of the required information or production shall be referred to the arbitral tribunal for decision.

3. Upon receipt of the expert's report, the arbitral tribunal shall communicate a copy of the report to the parties who shall be given the opportunity to express, in writing, their opinion on the report. A party shall be entitled to examine any document on which the expert has relied in his report.

4. At the request of either party the expert, after delivery of the report, may be heard at a hearing where the parties shall have the opportunity to be present and to interrogate the expert. At this hearing either party may present expert witnesses in order to testify on the points at issue. The provisions of article 25 shall be applicable to such proceedings.

DEFAULT

Article 28

1. If, within the period of time fixed by the arbitral tribunal, the claimant has failed to communicate his claim without showing sufficient cause for such failure, the arbitral tribunal shall issue an order for the termination of the arbitral proceedings. If, within the period of time fixed by the arbitral tribunal, the respondent has failed to communicate his statement of defence without showing sufficient cause for such failure, the arbitral tribunal shall order that the proceedings continue.

2. If one of the parties, duly notified under these Rules, fails to appear at a hearing, without showing sufficient cause for such failure, the arbitral tribunal may proceed with the arbitration.

3. If one of the parties, duly invited to produce documentary evidence, fails to do so within the established period of time, without showing sufficient cause for such failure, the arbitral tribunal may make the award on the evidence before it.

CLOSURE OF HEARINGS

Article 29

1. The arbitral tribunal may inquire of the parties if they have any further proof to offer or witnesses to be heard or submissions to make and, if there are none, it may declare the hearings closed.

2. The arbitral tribunal may, if it considers it necessary owing to exceptional circumstances, decide, on its own motion or upon application of a party, to reopen the hearings at any time before the award is made.

WAIVER OF RULES

Article 30

A party who knows that any provision of, or requirement under, these Rules has not been complied with and yet proceeds with the arbitration without promptly stating his objection to such non-compliance, shall be deemed to have waived his right to object.

SECTION IV. THE AWARD

DECISIONS

Article 31

1. When there are three arbitrators, any award or other decision of the arbitral tribunal shall be made by a majority of the arbitrators.
2. In the case of questions of procedure, when there is no majority or when the arbitral tribunal so authorizes, the presiding arbitrator may decide on his own, subject to revision, if any, by the arbitral tribunal.

FORM AND EFFECT OF THE AWARD

Article 32

1. In addition to making a final award, the arbitral tribunal shall be entitled to make interim, interlocutory, or partial awards.
2. The award shall be made in writing and shall be final and binding on the parties. The parties undertake to carry out the award without delay.
3. The arbitral tribunal shall state the reasons upon which the award is based, unless the parties have agreed that no reasons are to be given.
4. An award shall be signed by the arbitrators and it shall contain the date on which and the place where the award was made. Where there are three arbitrators and one of them fails to sign, the award shall state the reason for the absence of the signature.
5. The award may be made public only with the consent of both parties.
6. Copies of the award signed by the arbitrators shall be communicated to the parties by the arbitral tribunal.
7. If the arbitration law of the country where the award is made requires that the award be filed or registered by the arbitral tribunal, the tribunal shall comply with this requirement within the period of time required by law.

APPLICABLE LAW, AMIABLE COMPOSITEUR

Article 33

1. The arbitral tribunal shall apply the law designated by the parties as applicable to the substance of the dispute. Failing such designation by the parties, the arbitral tribunal shall apply the law determined by the conflict of laws rules which it considers applicable.
2. The arbitral tribunal shall decide as *amiable compositeur* or *ex aequo et bono* only if the parties have expressly authorized the arbitral tribunal to do so and if the law applicable to the arbitral procedure permits such arbitration.
3. In all cases, the arbitral tribunal shall decide in accordance with the terms of the contract and shall take into account the usages of the trade applicable to the transaction.

SETTLEMENT OR OTHER GROUNDS FOR TERMINATION

Article 34
1. If, before the award is made, the parties agree on a settlement of the dispute, the arbitral tribunal shall either issue an order for the termination of the arbitral proceedings or, if requested by both parties and accepted by the tribunal, record the settlement in the form of an arbitral award on agreed terms. The arbitral tribunal is not obliged to give reasons for such an award.
2. If, before the award is made, the continuation of the arbitral proceedings becomes unnecessary or impossible for any reason not mentioned in paragraph 1, the arbitral tribunal shall inform the parties of its intention to issue an order for the termination of the proceedings. The arbitral tribunal shall have the power to issue such an order unless a party raises justifiable grounds for objection.
3. Copies of the order for termination of the arbitral proceedings or of the arbitral award on agreed terms, signed by the arbitrators, shall be communicated by the arbitral tribunal to the parties. Where an arbitral award on agreed terms is made, the provisions of article 32, paragraphs 2 and 4 to 7, shall apply.

INTERPRETATION OF THE AWARD

Article 35
1. Within thirty days after the receipt of the award, either party, with notice to the other party, may request that the arbitral tribunal give an interpretation of the award.
2. The interpretation shall be given in writing within forty-five days after the receipt of the request. The interpretation shall form part of the award and the provisions of article 32, paragraphs 2 to 7, shall apply.

CORRECTION OF THE AWARD

Article 36
1. Within thirty days after the receipt of the award, either party, with notice to the other party, may request the arbitral tribunal to correct in the award any errors in computation, any clerical or typographical errors, or any errors of similar nature. The arbitral tribunal may within thirty days after the communication of the award make such corrections on its own initiative.
2. Such corrections shall be in writing, and the provisions of article 32, paragraphs 2 to 7, shall apply.

ADDITIONAL AWARD

Article 37
1. Within thirty days after the receipt of the award, either party, with notice to the other party, may request the arbitral tribunal to make an additional award as to claims presented in the arbitral proceedings but omitted from the award.

2. If the arbitral tribunal considers the request for an additional award to be justified and considers that the omission can be rectified without any further hearings or evidence, it shall complete its award within sixty days after the receipt of the request.

3. When an additional award is made, the provisions of article 32, paragraphs 2 to 7, shall apply.

COSTS (ARTICLES 38 TO 40)

Article 38

The arbitral tribunal shall fix the costs of arbitration in its award. The term "costs" includes only:

(a) The fees of the arbitral tribunal to be stated separately as to each arbitrator and to be fixed by the tribunal itself in accordance with article 39;

(b) The travel and other expenses incurred by the arbitrators;

(c) The costs of expert advice and of other assistance required by the arbitral tribunal;

(d) The travel and other expenses of witnesses to the extent such expenses are approved by the arbitral tribunal;

(e) The costs for legal representation and assistance of the successful party if such costs were claimed during the arbitral proceedings, and only to the extent that the arbitral tribunal determines that the amount of such costs is reasonable;

(f) Any fees and expenses of the appointing authority as well as the expenses of the Secretary-General of the Permanent Court of Arbitration at The Hague.

Article 39

1. The fees of the arbitral tribunal shall be reasonable in amount, taking into account the amount in dispute, the complexity of the subject-matter, the time spent by the arbitrators and any other relevant circumstances of the case.

2. If an appointing authority has been agreed upon by the parties or designated by the Secretary-General of the Permanent Court of Arbitration at The Hague, and if that authority has issued a schedule of fees for arbitrators in international cases which it administers, the arbitral tribunal in fixing its fees shall take that schedule of fees into account to the extent that it considers appropriate in the circumstances of the case.

3. If such appointing authority has not issued a schedule of fees for arbitrators in international cases, any party may at any time request the appointing authority to furnish a statement setting forth the basis for establishing fees which is customarily followed in international cases in which the authority appoints arbitrators. If the appointing authority consents to provide such a statement, the arbitral tribunal in fixing its fees shall take such information into account to the extent that it considers appropriate in the circumstances of the case.

4. In cases referred to in paragraphs 2 and 3, when a party so requests and the appointing authority consents to perform the function, the arbitral tribunal shall fix its fees only after consultation with the appointing authority which may make any comment it deems appropriate to the arbitral tribunal concerning the fees.

Article 40

1. Except as provided in paragraph 2, the costs of arbitration shall in principle be borne by the unsuccessful party. However, the arbitral tribunal may apportion each of such costs between the parties if it determines that apportionment is reasonable, taking into account the circumstances of the case.
2. With respect to the costs of legal representation and assistance referred to in article 38, paragraph *(e)*, the arbitral tribunal, taking into account the circumstances of the case, shall be free to determine which party shall bear such costs or may apportion such costs between the parties if it determines that apportionment is reasonable.
3. When the arbitral tribunal issues an order for the termination of the arbitral proceedings or makes an award on agreed terms, it shall fix the costs of arbitration referred to in article 38 and article 39, paragraph 1, in the text of that order or award.
4. No additional fees may be charged by an arbitral tribunal for interpretation or correction or completion of its award under articles 35 to 37.

DEPOSIT OF COSTS

Article 41

1. The arbitral tribunal, on its establishment, may request each party to deposit an equal amount as an advance for the costs referred to in article 38, paragraphs *(a)*, *(b)* and *(c)*.
2. During the course of the arbitral proceedings the arbitral tribunal may request supplementary deposits from the parties.
3. If an appointing authority has been agreed upon by the parties or designated by the Secretary-General of the Permanent Court of Arbitration at The Hague, and when a party so requests and the appointing authority consents to perform the function, the arbitral tribunal shall fix the amounts of any deposits or supplementary deposits only after consultation with the appointing authority which may make any comments to the arbitral tribunal which it deems appropriate concerning the amount of such deposits and supplementary deposits.
4. If the required deposits are not paid in full within thirty days after the receipt of the request, the arbitral tribunal shall so inform the parties in order that one or another of them may make the required payment. If such payment is not made, the arbitral tribunal may order the suspension or termination of the arbitral proceedings.
5. After the award has been made, the arbitral tribunal shall render an accounting to the parties of the deposits received and return any unexpended balance to the parties.

BIBLIOGRAPHY

Only books primarily concerning arbitration are cited here. References to case notes and articles appear in the footnotes to the main body of text.

I. Treaties and Monographs

Aldrich, George H. *The Jurisprudence of the Iran-United States Claims Tribunal.* Oxford: Clarendon Press, 1996.

Amadio, Mario. *Le contentieux international de l'investissement privé et la Convention de la Banque Mondiale du 18 mars 1965.* Foreword by Lucien Siorat. Paris: LGDJ, 1967.

Amoussou-Guenou, Roland. *Le droit et la pratique de l'arbitrage commercial international en Afrique subsaharienne.* Thesis, University of Paris II (France), 1995.

Artuch Iriberri, Elena. *El convenio arbitral en el arbitraje comercial internacional.* Madrid: Eurolex, 1997.

Audit, Bernard. *Transnational Arbitration and State Contracts.* Center for Studies and Research in International Law and International Relations. Dordrecht: Martinus Nijhoff, 1987.

Baker, Stewart A., Davis, Mark David. *The UNCITRAL Arbitration Rules in Practice – The Experience of the Iran-United States Claims Tribunal.* Deventer: Kluwer, 1992.

Béguin, Jacques. *L'arbitrage commercial international.* Montreal: Université McGill, 1987.

Berger, Klaus Peter. *International Economic Arbitration.* The Hague: Kluwer, 1993.

Berger, Klaus Peter. *The Creeping Codification of the Lex Mercatoria.* The Hague: Kluwer, 1999.

Bernardini, Piero, Giardina, Andrea. *Codice dell'arbitrato.* 2 vols. Milan: Giuffrè, 1990 and 1994.

Bernardini, Piero. *Il diritto dell'arbitrato.* Bari and Rome: Laterza, 1998.

Bernini, Giorgio. *L'arbitrato – Diritto interno, convenzioni internazionali.* Bologna: CLUEB, 1993.

Bernstein, Ronald, Tackaberry, John, Marriott, Arthur, Wood, Derek. *Handbook of Arbitration Practice*. London: Sweet & Maxwell, 3d ed., 1998.

Besson, Sébastien. *Arbitrage international et mesures provisoires – Etude de droit comparé*. Zürich: Schulthess, 1998.

Blanchin, Claude. *L'autonomie de la clause compromissoire: un modèle pour la clause attributive de juridiction?* Foreword by Hélène Gaudemet-Tallon. Paris: LGDJ, 1995.

Böckstiegel, Karl-Heinz. *Arbitration and State Enterprises – A Survey on the national and international state of law and practice*. Deventer: Kluwer, 1984.

Boisséson, Matthieu de. *Le droit français de l'arbitrage interne et international*. Foreword by Pierre Bellet. Paris: GLN Joly, 2d ed., 1990.

Bonell, Michael Joachim. *An International Restatement of Contract Law – The UNIDROIT Principles of International Commercial Contracts*. Irvington: Transnational Juris Publications, 1994.

Born, Gary B. *International Commercial Arbitration in the United States*. Deventer: Kluwer, 1994.

Bourque, Jean-François. *Le règlement des litiges multipartites dans l'arbitrage commercial international*. Thesis, University of Poitiers (France), 1989.

Briguglio, A., Fazzalari, E., Marengo, R. *La nuova disciplina dell'arbitrato – Commentario*. Milan: Giuffrè, 1994.

Broches, Aron. *Selected Essays – World Bank, ICSID, and Other Subjects of Public and Private International Law*. Dordrecht: Martinus Nijhoff, 1995.

Broches, Aron. *Commentary on the UNCITRAL Model Law on International Commercial Arbitration*. The Hague: Kluwer, 1990.

Brower, Charles N., Brueschke, Jason D. *The Iran-United States Claims Tribunal*. The Hague: Martinus Nijhoff, 1998.

Bucher, Andreas, Tschanz, Pierre-Yves. *International Arbitration in Switzerland*. Basel: Helbing & Lichtenhahn, 1988.

Bucher, Andreas. *Le nouvel arbitrage international en Suisse*. Basel: Helbing & Lichtenhahn, 1988.

Budin, Roger P. *Les clauses arbitrales internationales bipartites, multipartites et spéciales de l'arbitrage "ad hoc" et institutionnel. Clauses modèles*. Lausanne: Payot, 1993.

Bühring-Uhle, Christian. *Arbitration and Mediation in International Business – Designing Procedures for Effective Conflict Management*. The Hague: Kluwer, 1996.

Bureau, Dominique. *Les sources informelles du droit dans les relations privées internationales*. Thesis, University of Paris II (France), 1992.

Carbonneau, Thomas E. *Alternative Dispute Resolution – Melting the Lances and Dismounting the Steeds.* Urbana and Chicago: University of Illinois Press, 1989.

Carbonneau, Tom. *Cases and Materials on Commercial Arbitration.* New York: Juris Publishing, Inc., Vol. 1, 1997.

Carbonneau, Tom. *Documentary Supplement for Cases and Materials on Commercial Arbitration.* New York: Juris Publishing, Inc., Vol. 1, 1997.

Cato, D. Mark. *Arbitration Practice and Procedure – Interlocutory and Hearings Problems.* Foreword by Lord Mustill. London: LLP, 2d ed., 1997.

Coe, Jack J. Jr. *International Commercial Arbitration – American Principles and Practice in a Global Context.* New York: Transnational Publishers, Inc., 1997.

Cohen, Daniel. *Arbitrage et société.* Foreword by Bruno Oppetit. Paris: LGDJ, 1993.

Coipel-Cordonnier, Nathalie. *Les conventions d'arbitrage et d'élection de for en droit international privé.* Paris: LGDJ, 1999.

Collins, Lawrence. *Provisional and Protective Measures in International Litigation.* Collected Courses of The Hague Academy of International Law, Vol. 234, Year 1992, Pt. III. Dordrecht: Martinus Nijhoff.

Coulson, Robert. *Business Arbitration – What you need to know.* New York: AAA, 3d ed., 1987.

Coussirat-Coustère, Vincent, Eisemann, Pierre-Michel. *Répertoire de la jurisprudence arbitrale internationale – Repertory of International Arbitral Jurisprudence.* Dordrecht: Martinus Nijhoff, Vol. 2 (1919-1945), 1989, Vol. 3 (1946-1988), 1991.

Craig, W. Laurence, Park, William W., Paulsson, Jan. *International Chamber of Commerce Arbitration.* Foreword by Michael Kerr and Pierre Bellet. Paris - New York: Oceana Publications/ICC Publishing, 2d ed., 1990.

Craig, W. Laurence, Park, William W., Paulsson, Jan. *Craig, Park, & Paulsson's Annotated Guide to the 1998 ICC Arbitration Rules with Commentary.* Paris - New York: Oceana Publications/ICC Publishing, 1998.

Crépin, Sophie. *Les sentences arbitrales devant le juge français – Pratique de l'exécution et du contrôle judiciaire depuis les réformes de 1980-1981.* Foreword by Philippe Fouchard. Paris: LGDJ, 1995.

Dasser, Felix. *Internationale Schiedsgerichte und Lex Mercatoria – Rechtsvergleichender Beitrag zur Diskussion über ein nicht-staatliches Handelsrecht.* Zürich: Schulthess, 1989.

David, René. *L'arbitrage dans le commerce international.* Paris: Economica, 1981.

David, René. *Arbitration in International Trade.* The Hague: Kluwer, 1985.

Delaume, Georges. *Transnational Contracts – Applicable Law and Settlement of Disputes (A Study on Conflict Avoidance).* New York: Oceana Publications, Inc., 1995.

De Ly, Filip. *International Business Law and Lex Mercatoria*. Amsterdam: North Holland, 1992.

Derains, Yves, Schwartz, Eric A. *A Guide to the New ICC Rules of Arbitration*. The Hague: Kluwer, 1998.

Dezalay, Yves, Garth, Bryant G. *Dealing in Virtue – International Commercial Arbitration and the Construction of a Transnational Legal Order*. Chicago: The University of Chicago Press, 1996.

Dolzer, Rudolf, Stevens, Margrete. *Bilateral Investment Treaties*. The Hague: Martinus Nijhoff, 1995.

Dore, Isaak I. *Theory and Practice of Multiparty Commercial Arbitration*. London: Graham & Trotman/Martinus Nijhoff, 1990.

Dutoit, Bernard, Knoepfler, François, Lalive, Pierre, Mercier, Pierre. *Répertoire du droit international privé suisse – Vol. 1 – L'arbitrage international*. Berne: Staempfli & Cie, 1982.

El-Ahdab, Abdul Hamid. *Arbitration with the Arab Countries*. The Hague: Kluwer, 2d ed, 1999.

Fouchard, Philippe. *L'arbitrage commercial international*. Foreword by Berthold Goldman. Paris: Dalloz, 1965.

Frutos-Peterson, Claudia. *L'émergence d'un droit effectif de l'arbitrage commercial international en Amérique Latine?* Thesis, University of Paris I (France), 1998.

Gaillard, Emmanuel, von Mehren, Robert. *International Commercial Arbitration – Recent Developments*. New York: Practising Law Institute, 1988 (2 vols.).

Gaja, Giorgio. *International Commercial Arbitration – New York Convention*. New York: Oceana Publications, Inc., 1984.

Glavinis, Panayotis. *Les litiges relatifs aux contrats passés entre organisations internationales et personnes privées*. Foreword by Philippe Fouchard. Paris: LGDJ, 1992.

Glossner, Ottoarndt. *Commercial Arbitration in the Federal Republic of Germany*. Deventer: Kluwer, 1984.

Goldman, Berthold. *Les conflits de lois dans l'arbitrage international de droit privé*. Collected Courses of The Hague Academy of International Law, Vol. 109, Year 1963, Pt. I. Dordrecht: Martinus Nijhoff.

Gouiffès, Laurent, Girard, Pascale, Taivalkoski, Petri, Mecarelli, Gabriele. *Recherche sur l'arbitrage en droit international et comparé*. Foreword by Bruno Oppetit, Hélène Gaudemet-Tallon and Philippe Fouchard. Paris: LGDJ, 1997.

Grigera-Naon, Horacio A. *Choice-of-law Problems in International Commercial Arbitration*. Tübingen: Mohr, 1992.

Hahn, Dominique. *L'arbitrage commercial international en Suisse face aux règles de concurrence de la CEE*. Geneva: Georg., 1983.

Hober, Kaj I. *Enforcing Foreign Arbitral Awards Against Russian Entities*. New York: Transnational Juris Publications, 1994.

Holtzmann, Howard M., Neuhaus, Joseph E. *A Guide To The UNCITRAL Model Law On International Commercial Arbitration – Legislative History And Commentary*. The Hague: Kluwer, 1989.

Hunter, Martin, Paulsson, Jan, Rawding, Nigel, Redfern, Alan. *The Freshfields Guide to Arbitration and ADR – Clauses in International Contracts*. The Hague: Kluwer, 1993.

Hunter, Martin, Landau, Toby. *The English Arbitration Act 1996 – Text and Notes*. The Hague: Kluwer, 1998.

Huys, Marcel, Keutgen, Guy. *L'arbitrage en droit belge et international*. Foreword by Ernest Krings. Brussels: Bruylant, 1981.

Jarrosson, Charles. *La notion d'arbitrage*. Foreword by Bruno Oppetit. Paris: LGDJ, 1987.

Jarvin, Sigvard (Lesguillons, Henry, ed.). *Lamy Contrats internationaux – Vol.7 – Prévention et règlement des litiges*. Paris: Lamy, 1994.

Johnson, Derek K. *International Commodity Arbitration*. London: LLP, 1991.

Jolidon, Pierre. *Commentaire du Concordat suisse sur l'arbitrage*. Berne: Staempfli, 1984.

Kassis, Antoine. *Problèmes de base de l'arbitrage en droit comparé et en droit international – Vol. I – Arbitrage juridictionnel et arbitrage contractuel*. Paris: LGDJ, 1987.

Kassis, Antoine. *Réflexions sur le Règlement d'arbitrage de la Chambre de Commerce Internationale – Les déviations de l'arbitrage institutionnel*. Paris: LGDJ, 1988.

Kazazi, Mojtaba. *Burden of Proof and Related Issues – A Study on Evidence before International Tribunals – Studies and Materials on the Settlement of International Disputes*. The Hague: Kluwer, Vol. 1, 1996.

Khan, Rahmatullah. *The Iran-United States Claims Tribunal – Controversies, Cases and Contribution*. Dordrecht: Martinus Nijhoff, 1990.

Klein, Frédéric-Edouard. *Considérations sur l'arbitrage en droit international privé*. Basel: Helbing & Lichtenhahn, 1955.

Lalive, Pierre, Poudret, Jean-François, Reymond, Claude. *Le droit de l'arbitrage interne et international en Suisse*. Lausanne: Payot, 1989.

Lalive, Jean-Flavien. *Contrats entre Etats ou entreprises étatiques et personnes privées – Développements récents*. Collected Courses of The Hague Academy of International Law, Vol. 181, Year 1984, Pt. III. Dordrecht: Martinus Nijhoff.

Lee, Eric. *Encyclopedia of Arbitration Law*. London: LLP, 1984.

Lee, Eric. *Encyclopedia of International Commercial Arbitration*. London: LLP, 1986.

Lew, Julian D.M. *Applicable Law in International Commercial Arbitration – A Study in Commercial Arbitration Awards*. Foreword by François Rigaux. New York: Oceana Publications/Sijthoff & Noordhoff International Publishers, 1978.

Li, Xiao-Ying. *La transmission et l'extension de la clause compromissoire dans l'arbitrage international*. Thesis, University of Dijon (France), 1993.

Linsmeau, Jacqueline. *L'arbitrage volontaire en droit privé belge*. Foreword by Guy Keutgen. Brussels: Bruylant, 1991.

Loquin, Eric. *L'amiable composition en droit comparé et international – Contribution à l'étude du non-droit dans l'arbitrage commercial*. Foreword by Philippe Fouchard. Paris: Litec, 1980.

Lörcher, Gino, Lörcher, Heike. *Das Schiedsverfahren – National – International – nach neuem Recht*. München: Jehle Rehm, 1998.

Mayer, Pierre. *L'autonomie de l'arbitre international dans l'appréciation de sa propre compétence*. Collected Courses of The Hague Academy of International Law, Vol. 217, Year 1989, Pt. V. Dordrecht: Martinus Nijhoff, 1989.

Mittal D.P. *New Law on Arbitration, ADR and Contract Law in India*. 1997.

Motulsky, Henri. *Ecrits – Vol. II – Etudes et notes sur l'arbitrage*. Foreword by Berthold Goldman and Philippe Fouchard. Paris: Dalloz, 1974.

Moura Vicente, Dário. *Da arbitragem comercial internacional – Direito aplicável ao mérito da causa*. Lisbon: Coimbra, 1990.

Mustill, Michael J., Boyd, Stewart C. *Commercial Arbitration*. London and Edinburgh: Butterworths, 2d ed., 1989.

Nygh, Peter. *Choice of Forum and Laws in International Commercial Arbitration*. The Hague: Kluwer, 1997.

Oehmke, Thomas. *International Arbitration*. New York: CBC, 1990.

Oppetit, Bruno. *Théorie de l'arbitrage*. Paris: PUF, 1998.

Ortscheidt, Jérôme. *La réparation du dommage dans l'arbitrage commercial international*. Thesis, University of Paris XII (France), 1999.

Osman, Filali. *Les principes généraux de la lex mercatoria – Contribution à l'étude d'un ordre juridique anational*. Foreword by Eric Loquin. Paris: LGDJ, 1992.

Park, William W. *International Forum Selection*. The Hague: Kluwer, 1995.

Patrikos, Apostolos. *L'arbitrage en matière administrative*. Foreword by Yves Gaudemet. Paris: LGDJ, 1997.

Peter, Wolfgang. *Arbitration and Renegotiation of International Investment Agreements*. The Hague: Kluwer, 2d ed., 1995.

Pham Liem, Chinh. *L'arbitrage commercial international au Vietnam*. Thesis, University of Paris II (France), 1999.

Racine, Jean-Baptiste. *L'arbitrage commercial international et l'ordre public*. Foreword by Philippe Fouchard. Paris: LGDJ, 1999.

Redfern, Alan, Hunter, Martin (with the assistance of Murray Smith). *Law and Practice of International Commercial Arbitration*. London: Sweet & Maxwell, 2d ed., 1991.

Regli, Jean-Pierre. *Contrats d'Etat et arbitrage entre Etats et personnes privées*. Geneva: Georg., 1983.

Robert, Jean (with the assistance of Bertrand Moreau). *L'arbitrage – Droit interne – Droit international privé*. Paris: Dalloz, 6th ed., 1993.

Robert, Jean. *Le phénomène transnational*. Paris: LGDJ, 1988.

Robert, Jean, Carbonneau, Thomas E. *The French Law of Arbitration*. New York: Matthew Bender, 1983.

Rubellin-Devichi, Jacqueline. *L'arbitrage – Nature juridique – Droit interne et droit international privé*. Foreword by Jean Vincent. Paris: LGDJ, 1965.

Rubino-Sammartano, Mauro. *International Arbitration Law*. Deventer: Kluwer, 1990.

Russell on Arbitration (Sutton, David St. John, Kendall, John, Gill, Judith, eds.). London: Sweet & Maxwell, 1997.

Samuel, Adam. *Jurisdictional Problems in International Commercial Arbitration: A Study of Belgian, Dutch, English, French, Swedish, U.S. and West German Law*. Zürich: Schulthess Polygraphischer Verlag, 1989.

Sanders, Pieter. *Quo Vadis Arbitration? – Sixty Years Of Arbitration Practice*. The Hague: Kluwer, 1999.

Sanders, Pieter. *Trends in the Field of International Commercial Arbitration*. Collected Courses of The Hague Academy of International Law, Year 1975, Pt. II. Dordrecht: Martinus Nijhoff.

Sanders, Pieter, van den Berg, Albert Jan. *The Netherlands Arbitration Act 1986*. Deventer: Kluwer, 1987.

Santos Belandro, R.B. *Arbitraje comercial international*. Montevideo: FCU, 1988.

Schlosser, Peter. *Das Recht der internationalen privaten Schiedsgerichtsbarkeit*. Tübingen: Mohr, 2d ed., 1989.

Schmitthoff, Clive M. *International Trade Usages*. Paris: ICC Publication No. 440/4, 1987.

Schwebel, Stephen M. *International Arbitration: Three Salient Problems*. University of Cambridge: Grotius, 1987.

Simmonds, Kenneth, Hill, Richard, Jarvin, Sigvard. *Commercial Arbitration Law in Asia and the Pacific*. Paris - New York: ICC Publishing and Oceana, 1987.

Sornarajah, M. *International Commercial Arbitration: the Problem of State Contracts*. Singapore: Longman, 1990.

Storme, Marcel, Demeulenaere, Bernadette. *International Commercial Arbitration in Belgium*. Deventer: Kluwer, 1989.

Toope, Stephen J. *Mixed international arbitration – Studies in arbitration between States and private persons*. Cambridge: Grotius, 1990.

van den Berg, Albert Jan. *The New York Arbitration Convention of 1958*. The Hague: Kluwer, 1981.

van den Berg, A.J., van Delden, R., Snijders, H.J. *Netherlands Arbitration Law*. The Hague: Kluwer, 1993.

Van Hof, Jacomijn J. *Commentary on the UNCITRAL Arbitration Rules – The Application by the Iran-U.S. Claims Tribunal*. The Hague: Kluwer, 1991.

Vulliemin, Jean-Marie. *Jugement et sentence arbitrale*. Zürich: Schulthess, 1990.

Westberg, John A. *International Transactions and Claims Involving Government Parties – Case Law of the Iran-United States Claims Tribunal*. Washington: ILI, 1991.

Wetter, Gillis J. *The International Arbitral Process: Public and Private, 4 vols*. New York: Oceana Publications, Inc., 1979.

Zahi, Amor. *L'Etat et l'arbitrage*. Alger: Office des Publications Universitaires, 1985.

II. Collective Works

Actes du séminaire sur l'arbitrage commercial. Alger: Chambre nationale de commerce, 1993.

Actes du 1er Colloque sur l'arbitrage commercial international/Proceedings of the 1st International commercial arbitration conference (Antaki, Nabil, Prujiner, Alain, eds.). Montreal: Wilson & Lafleur, 1986.

Acts of State and Arbitration (Böckstiegel, Karl-Heinz, ed.). München: Carl Heymanns Verlag KG, 1997.

Arbitrage international commercial – Manuel mondial/International Commercial Arbitration – A World Handbook, Union internationale des Avocats (Sanders, Pieter, ed.). Vols. 1 & 2, Paris: Dalloz, 1956 and 1960. Vol. 3, The Hague: Martinus Nijhoff, 1965.

Arbitrage et propriété intellectuelle, Institut Henri Desbois. Paris: Litec, 1994.

Arbitration and Expertise/Arbitrage et expertise. Paris: ICC Publication No. 480/7, 1996.

Arbitration Law in Europe. Paris: ICC Publication No. 353, 1981.

Arbitration in Spain (Cremades, Bernardo M., ed.). Butterworths, La Ley, Carl Heymanns Verlag KG, 1991.

Collection of ICC Arbitral Awards/Recueil des sentences arbitrales de la CCI 1974-1985 (Jarvin, Sigvard, Derains, Yves, eds.). Deventer: ICC Publishing/KLuwer, 1990.

Collection of ICC Arbitral Awards/Recueil des sentences arbitrales de la CCI 1986-1990 (Jarvin, Sigvard, Derains, Yves, Arnaldez, Jean-Jacques, eds.). Deventer: ICC Publishing/Kluwer, 1994.

Collection of ICC Arbitral Awards/Recueil des sentences arbitrales de la CCI 1991-1995 (Arnaldez, Jean-Jacques, Derains, Yves, Hascher, Dominique, eds.). Paris - New York: ICC Publishing/Kluwer, 1997.

Collection of Procedural Decisions in ICC Arbitration/Recueil des décisions de procédure dans l'arbitrage CCI 1993-1996 (Hascher, Dominique, ed.). Paris - New York: ICC Publishing/Kluwer, 1997.

Comentario breve a la ley de arbitraje (Montero, Aroca J., ed.). Madrid: Civitas, 1990.

Competition and Arbitration Law. Paris: ICC Publication No. 480/3, 1993.

Commercial Arbitration – Essays in memoriam Eugenio Minoli/Arbitrage commercial – Essais in memorian Eugenio Minoli. Association italienne pour l'arbitrage. Turin: UTEC, 1974.

Commercial Arbitration: an International Bibliography. Parker School of Foreign and Comparative Law, Columbia University (Smit, Hans, Pechota, Vratislav, eds.). New York: Sweet & Maxwell/Juris Publishing, 2d ed., 1998.

Conservatory and Provisional Measures in International Arbitration. Paris: ICC Publication No. 519, 1993.

Convention on the Settlement of Investment Disputes between States and Nationals of Other States – Analysis of Documents Concerning the Origin and the Formation of the Convention, 4 vols., 1969 (English, Spanish and French).

Dispute Resolution in Asia (Pryles, Michael, ed.). The Hague: Kluwer, 1997.

Droit et pratique de l'arbitrage international en France (Derains, Yves, ed.). Paris: FEDUCI, 1984.

Essays on International Commercial Arbitration (Šarčevič, Peter, ed.). London: Graham & Trotman/Martinus Nijhoff, 1989.

Etudes de droit international en l'honneur de Pierre Lalive. Basel and Frankfurt am Main, Helbing & Lichtenhahn, 1993.

Etudes de procédure et d'arbitrage en l'honneur de Jean-François Poudret. Lausanne: Payot, 1999.

Etudes offertes à Pierre Bellet. Paris: Litec, 1991.

Euro-Arab Arbitration – Arbitrage Euro-Arabe (Proceedings of the First Euro-Arab Arbitration Conference – Actes du premier colloque euro-arabe sur l'arbitrage) (Kemicha, Fathi, ed.). London: LLP, 1987.

Euro-Arab Arbitration II – Arbitrage Euro-Arabe II (Proceedings of the Second Euro-Arab Arbitration Congress, Bahrain) (Kemicha, Fathi, ed.). London: Graham & Trotman, 1989.

Euro-Arab Arbitration III – Arbitrage Euro-Arabe III (Proceedings of the Third Euro-Arab Arbitration Congress, Amman) (Kemicha, Fathi, ed.). London: Graham & Trotman, 1991.

Guide to ICC Arbitration. Paris: ICC Publication No. 448, 1994.

Hommage à Frédéric Eisemann, Liber amicorum. Paris: ICC Publication No. 321, 1978.

ICCA Congress Series No. 1 – New trends in the development of International Commercial Arbitration and the role of arbitral and other institutions (Hamburg 1982) (Sanders, Pieter, ed.). Deventer: Kluwer, 1983.

ICCA Congress Series No. 2 – UNCITRAL'S Project for a Model Law on International Commercial Arbitration (Lausanne 1984) (Sanders, Pieter, ed.). Deventer: Kluwer, 1984.

ICCA Congress Series No. 3 – Comparative arbitration practice and public policy in arbitration (New York 1986) (Sanders, Pieter, ed.). Deventer: Kluwer, 1987.

ICCA Congress Series No. 4 – Arbitration in settlement of international commercial disputes involving the Far East and arbitration in combined transportation (Tokyo 1988) (Sanders, Pieter, ed.). Deventer: Kluwer, 1989.

ICCA Congress Series No. 5 – I. Preventing delay and disruption of arbitration – II. Effective proceedings in construction cases (Stockholm 1990) (van den Berg, Albert Jan, ed.). Deventer: Kluwer, 1991.

ICCA Congress Series No. 6 – International Arbitration in a Changing World (Bahrain 1993) (van den Berg, Albert Jan, ed.). Deventer: Kluwer, 1994.

ICCA Congress Series No. 7 – Planning Efficient Arbitration Proceedings/The Law Applicable in International Arbitration (Vienna 1994) (van den Berg, Albert Jan, ed.). Deventer: Kluwer, 1996.

ICCA Congress Series No. 8 – International Dispute Resolution: Towards an International Arbitration Culture (Seoul 1996) (van den Berg, Albert Jan, ed.). Deventer: Kluwer, 1998.

ICCA Congress Series No. 9 – Improving the Efficiency of Arbitration Agreements and Awards: 40 Years of Application of the New York Convention (Paris 1998) (van den Berg, Albert Jan, ed.). Deventer: Kluwer, 1999.

ICCA International Handbook on Commercial Arbitration (Sanders, Pieter, ed.). 4 vols. Deventer: Kluwer.

ICSID Reports, Vol. 1. Cambridge: Grotius Publication Ltd., 1993.

ICSID Reports, Vol. 2. Cambridge: Grotius Publication Ltd., 1994.

ICSID Reports, Vol. 3. Cambridge: Grotius Publication Ltd., 1995.

International Arbitration in the 21st Century: Towards "Judicialization" and Uniformity? (Lillich, Richard B., Brower, Charles N., eds.). New York: Transnational Publishers, Inc., 1994.

International Arbitration – Liber Amicorum for Martin Domke (Sanders, Pieter, ed.). The Hague: Martinus Nijhoff, 1967.

International Arbitration – 60 Years of ICC Arbitration – A Look at the Future. Paris: ICC Publication No. 412, 1984.

International Commercial Arbitration and the Courts (Smit, Hans, ed.). New York: Transnational Juris Publications, 1990.

International Commercial Arbitration in New York (McClendon, J. Stewart, Everard Goodman Rosabel E., eds.). New York: Transnational Publishers, Inc., 1986.

International Dispute Resolution – The Regulation of Forum Selection (Goldsmith, Jack L., ed.). New York: Transnational Publishers, Inc., 1997.

Internationale Schiedsgerichtsbarkeit – Arbitrage International – International Arbitration (Gottwald, Peter, ed.). Band 9 der Veröffentlichungen der Wissenschaftlichen Vereinigung für Internationales Verfahrensrecht e. V. - Gieseking - Verlag - Bielefeld.

Investissements étrangers et arbitrage entre Etats et personnes privées – La Convention B.I.R.D. du 18 mars 1965. Paris: Pedone, 1969.

Ius Arbitrale Internationale – Essays in Honor of Hans Smit. The American Review of International Arbitration, Year 1992, Vol. 3, Nos. 1– 4.

L'apport de la jurisprudence arbitrale. Paris: ICC Publication No. 440/1, 1986.

L'arbitrage – Travaux offerts au Professeur Albert Fettweis. Brussels: E.Story-Scientia, 1989.

L'arbitrage et le droit européen – Arbitrage en Europees Recht – Arbitration and European Law. Brussels: Bruylant, 1997.

L'arbitrage international: choix du pays et des règles applicables. Cah. jur. fisc. exp., 1990, pp. 565–680.

L'arbitrage international dans le nouveau Code tunisien. Tunis: Centre d'études juridiques et judiciaires, 1995.

L'arbitrage international privé et la Suisse/Die internationale private Schiedsgerichtsbarkeit und die Schweiz (Wenger, W., Lalive, Pierre, eds.). Geneva: Georg, 1977.

L'arbitrage international à Paris. Cah. jur. fisc. exp., 1993, No. 5.

Le droit des relations économiques internationales – Etudes offertes à Berthold Goldman. Paris: Litec 1982.

Les commissions illicites – Définition, traitement juridique et fiscal. Paris: ICC Publication No. 480/2, 1992.

Les entreprises tunisiennes et l'arbitrage commercial international. Tunis: Imprimerie officielle, 1983

Le Tribunal des différends irano-américains (Stern, Brigitte, Labouz, Marie-Françoise, eds.). Cahiers du CEDIN. Paris: Université de Nanterre, 1985.

L'exécution des sentences arbitrales. Paris: ICC Publication No. 440/6, 1989.

Lex Mercatoria and Arbitration – A Discussion of the New Law Merchant (Carbonneau Thomas E., ed.). New York: Kluwer/Juris Publishing, Inc., 1998.

Liber Amicorum for the Rt. Hon. Lord. Wilberforce, PC, CMG, OBE, QC (Bos, Maarten, Brownlie, Ian, eds.). Oxford: Clarendon Press, 1987.

L'internationalité dans les institutions et le droit – Convergences et défis – Études offertes à Alain Plantey. Paris: Pedone, 1995.

L'internationalisation du droit – Mélanges en l'honneur de Yvon Loussouarn. Paris: Dalloz, 1994.

Litigation and Arbitration in Central and Eastern Europe (Rivkin W., David, Platto, Charles, eds.). The Hague: Kluwer/International Bar Association, 1998.

Objective Arbitrability – Antitrust Disputes – Intellectual Property Disputes (Blessing, Marc, ed.). ASA. Special Series, No. 6, March 1994.

Recueil de travaux suisses sur l'arbitrage international (Reymond, Claude, Bucher, Eugène, eds.). Zürich: Schulthess Polygraphischer Verlag, 1984.

Régler autrement les conflits: conciliation, transaction, arbitrage en matière administrative, Conseil d'État. Paris: La documentation française, 1993.

Répertoire pratique de l'arbitrage commercial international. Liège: Faculté de droit, 2d ed., 1997.

Resolution of International Disputes/Règlement de différends internationaux. Montreal: McGill Law Journal/Revue de droit de McGill, August, 1992.

Sixth Sokol Colloquium – Resolving Transnational Disputes Through International Arbitration (Carbonneau, Thomas E., ed.). Charlottesville: University Press of Virginia, 1984.

Stockholm Chamber of Commerce, Arbitration in Sweden. Stockholm: 2d ed., 1984.

Taking of Evidence in International Arbitral Proceedings/L'administration de la preuve dans les procédures arbitrales internationales. Paris: ICC Publication No. 440/8, 1990.

Transnational Rules in International Commercial Arbitration (Gaillard, Emmanuel, ed.). Paris : ICC Publication No. 480/4, 1993.

The Arbitral Process and the Independence of Arbitrators/La procédure arbitrale et l'indépendance des arbitres. Paris: ICC Publication No. 472, 1991.

The Arbitration Agreement – Its Multifold Critical Aspects, (Blessing, Marc, ed.). ASA, Special Series No. 8, Dec. 1994.

The Art of Arbitration – Essays on International Arbitration – Liber Amicorum Pieter Sanders (Schultz, Jan C., Van den Berg, Albert Jan, eds.). Deventer: Kluwer, 1982.

The Immunity of Arbitrators (Lew, Jordan D.M., ed.). Foreword by Michael Kerr. London: LLP, 1990.

The Internationalisation of Arbitration – The LCIA Centenary Conference (Hunter, Martin, Marriott, Arthur, Veeder, V.V., eds.). Dordrecht: Graham & Trotman/Martinus Nijhoff, 1995.

The Place of Arbitration (Storme, Marcel, De Ly, Filip, eds.). Gent: Mys & Breesch, 1992.

The 1989 Guide to International Arbitration and Arbitrators. New York: Transnational Juris Publications, 1989.

UNIDROIT. Principles of International Commercial Contracts. Rome: International Institute for the Unification of Private Law, 1994.

TABLE OF ARBITRAL AWARDS

A. – ICC AWARDS

TABLE OF ARBITRATION RULES

INTERNATIONAL CHAMBER OF COMMERCE (ICC)

---

[1] References in square brackets are to the corresponding provisions of the 1988 ICC Rules.

WORLD INTELLECTUAL PROPERTY ORGANIZATION (WIPO)

ZURICH CHAMBER OF COMMERCE

TABLE OF INTERNATIONAL INSTRUMENTS

TABLE OF JUDICIAL DECISIONS

Germany

Hong Kong

TABLE OF LEGISLATION

In addition to the references contained in the footnotes to this table, the English original, or a translation into English, of most of the laws referred to in this table can be found in the ICCA INTERNATIONAL HANDBOOK ON COMMERCIAL ARBITRATION or in the WORLD ARBITRATION REPORTER. The text in French, when available, can be found in the RÉPERTOIRE PRATIQUE DE L'ARBITRAGE COMMERCIAL INTERNATIONAL.

---

[1] For the official French translation (although the original Arabic text takes precedence), see 1993 REV. ARB. 478.

[2] For an English translation, see WERNER MELIS, A GUIDE TO COMMERCIAL ARBITRATION IN AUSTRIA 31 (1983).

---

[3] For a French translation, see 1994 REV. ARB. 782
and 790.

[4] For an English translation, see 1998 BULL. ASA
540.

[5] For an English translation, see 36 I.L.M. 1562
(1997); 13 INT'L ARB. REP. B1 (Sept. 1998); for a
French translation, see 1997 REV. ARB. 199.

---

[14] For an English translation, see 1995 BULL. ASA 443, 457.

[15] For a French translation, see 1984 REV. ARB. 533.

[16] For an English translation, see 7 WORLD TRADE & ARB. MATERIALS 157 (May 1995); for a French translation, see 1994 REV. ARB. 763.

[17] For a French translation, see 1997 REV. ARB. 311.

[18] For the original English text, see 8 WORLD TRADE & ARB. MATERIALS 47 (July 1996).

EUROPEAN UNION

FINLAND

FRANCE

---

[19] For a French translation, see RECHERCHE SUR L'ARBITRAGE EN DROIT INTERNATIONAL ET COMPARÉ 183 (1997).

---

[20] For an English translation, see 14 ARB. INT'L 1
(1998); for a French translation, see 1998 REV.
ARB. 441.

---

[21] For an English translation, see 11 ARB. INT'L 415 (1995).

[22] For an English translation, see 1995 BULL. ASA 417; for the Hungarian text as well as German and English translations, see 7 WORLD TRADE & ARB. MATERIALS 186 (May 1995).

[23] For an English translation, see 15 J. INT'L ARB. 42 (Sept. 1998).

[24] For a French translation, see 1983 REV. ARB. 131.

[25] For an English translation, see 1994 BULL ASA 82, and 1994 BULL ASA 285; 6 WORLD TRADE & ARB. MATERIALS 215 (Mar. 1994); for a French translation, see 1994 REV. ARB. 581.

---

[26] For an English translation, see ABDUL HAMID EL-AHDAB, ARBITRATION WITH THE ARAB COUNTRIES 1074 (1990)); 27 I.L.M. 1022 (1988); for the French translation, see 1993 REV. ARB. 750, 759.

[27] For an English translation, see 11 J. INT'L ARB. 30 (Dec. 1994); for a French translation, see 1994 REV. ARB. 405, 408.

[28] For English, French and German translations, see PIETER SANDERS AND ALBERT JAN VAN DEN BERG, THE NETHERLANDS ARBITRATION ACT 1986 (1987).

---

[29] For an English translation, see 10 WORLD TRADE AND ARB. MATERIALS 1 (Jan. 1998).

[30] For a French translation, see 1991 REV. ARB. 487.

[31] For a French translation, 1991 REV. ARB 498.

[32] For an English translation, see 10 J. INT'L ARB. 156 (June 1993).

[33] For a French translation, see 1994 REV. CRIT. DIP 172.

[34] For an English translation, see 8 INT'L ARB. REP. E1 (Sept. 1993).

[35] For a French translation of these decrees, see 1986 REV. ARB. 637, 642.

---

[36] For an English translation, see 7 WORLD TRADE & ARB. MATERIALS 2 (Mar. 1995).

[37] For a French translation, see 1989 REV. ARB 353.

[38] For an English translation, see STOCKHOLM CHAMBER OF COMMERCE, ARBITRATION IN SWEDEN (2d ed. 1984).

TAIWAN

THAILAND

TOGO

---

³⁹ For the original French, Dutch, and Italian texts,
as well as an English translation, see PIERRE
LALIVE, JEAN-FRANÇOIS POUDRET, CLAUDE
REYMOND, LE DROIT DE L'ARBITRAGE INTERNE ET
INTERNATIONAL EN SUISSE (1989).

---

⁴⁰ For an English translation, see 15 J. INT'L ARB.
116 (Dec. 1998).

---

[41] For the official French translation, see 1993 REV.
ARB. 721; for an English translation, see 5 ARB.
MATERIALS 376 (Sept. & Dec. 1993).

[42] For an English translation, see 6 WORLD TRADE &
ARB. MATERIALS 199 (July 1994).

[43] For a French translation, see 1993 REV. ARB. 343.

ALPHABETICAL INDEX

Index references refer to paragraph numbers.